ALL • IN • ONE

Lotus Notes and Domino R5

EXAM GUIDE

FIRST EDITION

Libby Ingrassia Schwarz

Ben Malekzadeh

Osborne / McGraw-Hill

New York • Chicago • San Francisco • Lisbon
London • Madrid • Mexico City • Milan • New Delhi
San Juan • Seoul • Singapore • Sydney • Toronto

Osborne/**McGraw-Hill**
2600 Tenth Street
Berkeley, California 94710
U.S.A.

To arrange bulk purchase discounts for sales promotions, premiums, or fund-raisers, please contact Osborne/**McGraw-Hill** at the above address. For information on translations or book distributors outside the U.S.A., please see the International Contact Information page immediately following the index of this book.

Lotus Notes and Domino R5 All-in-One Exam Guide, First Edition

1234567890 DOC DOC 01987654321

Book p/n 0-07-135091-8 and CD p/n 0-07-135092-6
parts of

ISBN 0-07-135090-X

Publisher
Brandon A. Nordin

Vice President & Associate Publisher
Scott Rogers

Acquisitions Editor
Michael Sprague

Project Editor
Mark Karmendy

Acquisitions Coordinator
Jessica Wilson

Technical Editor
Greg Neilson

Compositor and Indexer
MacAllister Publishing Services, LLC

Graphic Artists
Michael Mueller
Beth Young

Cover Design
Greg Scott

This book was composed with Quark XPress 3.32.

DEDICATION

First, last, and always, to Brian—there aren't enough words to tell you, but I hope you know anyway...

But, of course, this book also has many others that deserve appreciation for their help, support, and friendship...

First, thank you to everyone who helped on this book—Greg, Ben, Susan, and Marie, especially. What an effort!

To my wonderful family—my mom, my grandparents, my in-laws, and my Houston family, the Nichols/Newtons—who all knew when to ask about the work, and when to just cheer me along.

To all of my wonderful friends—there are too many of you to mention one at a time, but if you read the whole book and look at all the questions—you'll see yourselves—I may have been working, but I was thinking about you...

To all the colleagues and friends I've made at my various jobs, from IDI, BusinessWare, DRT/CGI, Total Seminars, Interliant, and, of course, Group Computing —you've taught me so much (especially you, Cinz, Rie, Daniel, Suz, Mike, Scott, Dale, Wayne, Chris, and Jim...)!

To all the cool folks I've met at all those conferences, some of whom have bugged me about this very book, others of whom I've learned from, and others I've just gotten to be friends with...

And last, to all my friends at Lotus—especially Mary, Martha, Gary, Roy, Joe, Greg, Glen, Barbara, and Michele...

—Libby Ingrassia Schwarz

This book is dedicated to all the people who have helped me along the way not only in my career, but also my life. While it is impossible to remember and to recognize each and everyone, there are some people that I can never be thankful enough to. There are also so many people behind the scenes that never get any recognition, as they just do their job without even being known. It is for that reason that I want to dedicate this book to all of them.

One can never forget about the people that brought them into this world, and helped raise them until they were able to survive on their own. You can never say enough about your parents and family, as they sacrificed everything to put me first, make sure I got the best education possible, and were always there to support me whenever needed.

Putting them aside, there is Mrs. Susan Spitzig, my sixth grade teacher from Moravian Academy in Bethlehem, PA., who to this day has made an impact on my life. Then the faculty members from Lake Forest Academy in Lake Forest, Illinois, especially Lynne Kulieke, Andy Reid, Ann Roberts, Karl Gedge, and Bill Bowler can never be thanked enough for preparing me for the second half of my first career as a college student. Then I was off to Lehigh University in Bethlehem, Pennsylvania, where the list will never end. Dr. James D. Jackson, Ron Ticho, Dr. Terry Curran, Scott Walter, Dr. Susan McGorry, Dean Therese Maskulka, Jennifer Volchko, Dale Falcinelli, Stephen Buell, Bob Roberts, Ernie Green, Craig Wood, and Dean Hobbs.

Then my real career started. I should first thank the Chicago Bulls for helping me make a decision to get into the IT field. I would then have to thank my sister, Nahid Jilovec, who not only helped point me into the right direction when it came to my career, but she also helped me find a job, and encouraged me to begin writing.

I would also need to thank Larry Rosenbaum, Carol Kazl, Greg Radcliff, Sean Keighron, Jay Dettling, Scott L. Thomas, Roland Lim, and Michael Butler all from Whittman-Hart; Cynthia Overby from Baxter Healthcare; Scott Brown, Eamon Galvin, Carolynn DiCostanzo, Ron Furmaniuk, Noreen Shilue, Donald McNeil, Bob McDonald, Tim Dempsey, Larry Mancini, and John Beck from Lotus Development Corporation; and Chris Miller, Dale Agger, and Jim Hoopes, from Duke Communications, for giving me first shot at writing; and to John Read, Scott L. Thomas, and Greg Neilson for getting me involved in this project.

—Ben Malekzadeh

To my darling wife Sue and our two boys, Timothy and Matthew: see, I really did need to get at the computers to do some work!

—Greg Neilson

For my husband, Ralph: thank you for always supporting me and giving me room to spread my wings.

—Susan Sann Mahon

ABOUT THE AUTHORS

Libby Ingrassia Schwarz, author of *Accelerated Lotus Notes Application Development Study Guide* and *Accelerated Lotus Notes System Administration Study Guide*, both from Osborne/McGraw-Hill, is the editor of *Group Computing* magazine and **group-computing.com**. Libby is also the chairperson for the Connections on Lotus Solutions conferences.

She has been in the computer industry doing technical writing, training, course development, and consulting in Lotus Notes, Windows NT, and other technologies since 1993.

Although she would rather be writing poetry for a living, little things like food and a roof over her head have turned her into a Jill of All Trades—and mistress of several—in the industry. She has planned and implemented installations, taught live, online, and video-based training classes, developed applications, and even slung cable through the bowels of major office buildings.

A frequent speaker at industry conferences, Libby has so many certifications that she needs a higher ceiling on her office walls. She is a Principle Certified Lotus Professional in both Application Development and System Administration for R4 and R5, a Certified Lotus Instructor, a Network+ and i-Net+ certified technician, a Microsoft Certified Trainer, a Microsoft Certified Systems Engineer, and a Certified Technical Trainer. You can email Libby at **libbys@groupcomputing.com** or get in touch with her alter ego at **libbys@notesgirl.com** for tales from the Domino trenches or a quick Domino haiku.

Ben Malekzadeh is the Vice President of Messaging and Migration Services at K-Plus Technology Solutions LLC, a Lotus/IBM Business Partner in Chicago specializing in Information Technology services to assist businesses in achieving competitive advantage.

He is also a Technical Editor for *Group Computing* magazine, and author of a weekly Notes/Domino Q&A column for *DominoWire*. He has also written numerous articles for international magazines that have been translated in many languages around the world. Mr. Malekzadeh was a contributing author for *Domino and the AS/400: Installation and Configuration*, from 29th Street Press.

He was previously the Manager of Architecture, Technology, and Planning for Baxter International. He managed a group that was responsible for defining the global architecture of all distributed Network and Desktop systems, as well as wireless device connectivity. While at Baxter, he was also the Project Manager and architect responsible for the 30,000-seat R5 global migration.

Previous to Baxter, Mr. Malekzadeh was a Senior Consultant at Whittman-Hart, where he was responsible for designing and deploying numerous R3, R4, and R5 global Lotus Notes infrastructures. Mr. Malekzadeh also designed numerous Lotus Notes Applications to help his customers leverage their investment into Notes. He was also a member of the Lotus Development Corporation R5 Beta Enablement Team. As part of the team, he was responsible for identifying, validating, documenting, and tracking software bugs before the product shipped, as well as creating training documentation for Lotus.

Mr. Malekzadeh is also a Principal at Thomas Consulting, Inc, where he develops Lotus Notes Administration tools and practice certification examinations. His exams are featured on the Lotus Education Web Site and used by people all around the globe to prepare and pass the certifications.

He has a Bachelor of Science degree in Business and Economics from Lehigh University, in Bethlehem, PA. He currently resides in Chicago, IL., and enjoys international traveling. He has visited over 30 different countries in 6 continents, just in the last 2 years.

Greg Neilson, PCLP, MCSE+I, MCNE, is a senior technical manager at a large IT services firm in Sydney, Australia. He is a Contributing Editor for *Microsoft Certified Professional Magazine*, a regular contributor to *Group Computing* magazine, and the author of *Lotus Domino Administration in a Nutshell* for O'Reilly and Associates. He is married with two young children and in his spare time he enjoys playing guitar in a covers band. He has 13 years IT experience and is currently completing his MBA from Edinburgh Business School by distance learning.

Susan Sann Mahon is an independent Certified Lotus Instructor and an R5 Principal Certified Lotus Professional for both Application Development and System Administration. She has worked with Notes for the past 6 years. She teaches, develops applications, and installs Notes and Domino for clients throughout the U.S. She has worked in the computer industry as a consultant, technical writer, courseware developer, and trainer since 1989 for various companies including IBM, Catapult, and Frito-Lay. Susan received a B.S. from Texas A&M University and an M.B.A. in Management Information Systems from the University of Dallas. In her "other" life, she worked as a professional singer and still enjoys performing when she's not busy with Notes! She has traveled extensively across North America, Europe, and the Caribbean. She can be reached at **smahon@tntrain.com**.

Marie Britton is a consultant and Domino CLP Principal Developer, working for North America's fifth largest IT services organization. Her experience includes years of Domino architecture and application design, as well as analysis and development with other messaging platforms and collaborative toolsets. In addition to her contribution to this book, Marie has also spoken at industry events and written for *DominoPro Developer* journal. Marie can be reached at **marie@mariebritton.com**.

John E. Hutton, PCLP, is a Senior Technical Consultant for Whittman-Hart in Chicago. John has a bachelor's degree in Management Information Systems and Accountancy from Miami University in Oxford, OH.

Khyle Keys, MCP, is the Windows 2000 Practice Manager for Infinet Resources of Chicago, IL. He has over 10 years experience in the IT industry and has designed Domino infrastructures for large companies.

Chris Noffke, PCLP, is a Consultant for Exacta Corporation in Brookfield, Wisconsin. He has a Masters of Science degree in Operations Management from the University of Wisconsin.

Scott L. Thomas, PCLP, is the author of *Lotus Notes Architecture and Design* and *R4 Lotus Notes Certification Exam Guide*, both published by Osborne/McGraw-Hill. He currently offers Lotus Notes certification advice and consulting from his Web site at **http://www.thomas-consulting.com**.

CONTENTS

INTRODUCTION

Introduction to Notes and Domino

As you begin studying for your Notes and Domino certifications, you may still (even after it's been on the market for over 10 years) be asked, "So what exactly is Notes, anyway? Some sort of mail client, right?" This is when you get to begin your sideline career of explaining Lotus Notes and Domino and the concepts of groupware and collaborative computing.

Lotus markets Notes and Domino as the premier groupware and collaborative computing products on the market, competing with Microsoft Exchange, Novell GroupWise, and others. Groupware is any software that enhances the ability of groups of people (departments, workgroups) to communicate and do business with each other. Groupware usually has multiple functions, including e-mail, knowledge management, and collaboration. Although Lotus Notes and Domino function quite well as strictly an e-mail engine, they can do much more. Notes and Domino perform a variety of other workgroup communication functions, including sharing documents, automating business processes using workflow applications, publishing Web sites and applications, creating Intranets, and more. The term "groupware" is starting to go out of fashion, lately, to be replaced by the newer collaborative computing. It may be new terminology, but it has essentially the same meaning.

With the release of Notes R4.5, Lotus introduced the term Domino to describe the server component of Notes, while reserving the term Notes to describe the workstation side of the software. Prior versions of Lotus Notes used Notes to describe both the server and workstation elements of the software. As of R5, two other software applications have been introduced, and are used throughout this book and the exams: the Domino Administrator and the Domino Designer. The Domino Administrator is the application (sometimes called a client) used to administer your entire Domino environment, from a single server to multiple Domino domains. The Domino Designer is the Integrated Development Environment (IDE) used to create and modify applications.

This book covers exams related to release 5 (R5) of Notes and Domino. Many of the technologies are the same among different versions of the software, so if you are familiar with or have been using R4.x, you have an advantage. There are, however, many changes as well.

Introduction to this Book

Certifications by software and hardware vendors are more than popular in the Information Technology industry; they have become necessary. These certifications allow companies to hire employees or consultants that have proven their knowledge of the products they will implement or support.

Like many other vendors, Lotus has implemented a set of vendor certifications for Lotus Notes. Lotus offers a Certified Lotus Specialist (CLS) certification and a Certified Lotus Professional (CLP) certification. The CLS designation can be obtained by taking either the Domino Designer Fundamentals (510) or Maintaining Domino Servers and Users (520) exams. You can get a CLP as an Application Developer by taking Domino Designer Fundamentals, Domino Application Security and Workflow (511), and Domino Application Architecture (512). You can get a CLP as a System Administrator by taking Maintaining Domino Servers and Users, Implementing a Domino Infrastructure (521), and Deploying Domino Applications (522). This book covers all of these exams.

In addition, there is a more advanced level of certification—the Principle level (PCLP)—in either System Administration or Application Development. This level of certification requires achieving the appropriate CLP and then taking an additional elective exam. The list of available elective exams can be found at the Lotus Certification Web site at **http://www.lotus.com/certification**. This book does not cover those elective exams.

Everyone has a different method of preparing for these certification exams. Some people take the official Lotus Education courses, offered by Lotus Authorized Education Centers (LAECs). Others attempt to study on their own or rely on their own knowledge of the software. Others look at the local bookstore for a guide to passing the exams. While there are many good books on the market to assist in designing and implementing a Notes and Domino application or environment, there are relatively few Lotus certification study guides on the market.

This book is a Lotus Notes and Domino Certification study guide. It is intended to be an in-depth reference to all six of the exams in the Certified Lotus Professional tracks. No matter what other types of studying you choose to do, this book will help you refine your study of the material actually covered on the exams.

The goal of this book therefore is to help you to pass the exams necessary to become certified in Application Development and/or System Administration. Specifically, the book is intended to prepare you to pass the six multiple-choice exams (listed previously) offered by Lotus through its independent testing vendors.

To that end, each part of the book covers a specific exam. Each part is separated into chapters that have objectives that relate to questions at the end of each chapter. These objectives are based on the lists of competencies published by Lotus Education in their Certification Exam guides. They are also based on personal experience with taking the Lotus Exams, teaching the official Lotus courses, and implementing Notes and Domino enterprise environments for a variety of companies. The chapters do build somewhat on each other throughout the book, in that if you do not have a great deal of experience in a particular area, you should review all of the chapters that relate to it throughout the book before testing on that topic. If you're taking the Maintaining Domino Servers and Users exam, for example, and you don't already have a great deal of experience with Domino servers, you may want to read not only the chapters that cover Domino servers in Part I, but also the chapters that cover Domino servers in Part II. An additional example of this relates to Parts III and VI—the areas of the book that cover Deploying Domino Applications and Domino Application Architecture. You should read both parts of the book before taking either exam. The competencies for the exams are closely related and covered completely between the parts.

To help you study, I recommend first reading each chapter, looking for the information required to understand the objectives as you read the text. Then you should answer the questions at the end of each section immediately after reading that particular section. Later in your studying, go through the chapters again. This time, read the bulleted lists and definitions. You will also want to look over the screen captures and graphics again. Then go over the questions again, to review the concepts and make sure you haven't forgotten anything. You will notice that certain concepts and details are covered more than once in the text of the book. This is not an insult to your intelligence! It is one way of ensuring that you have the opportunity to review important topics multiple times in the course of your studying. The topics that you see multiple times in the text are topics covered in depth in the courses and exam competencies (and on the exams themselves), and that you should expect to see covered thoroughly on the exams. In addition, because each test covers topics slightly differently or from a different perspective, different parts of the book may repeat similar information in a different way.

In addition to reading this book and answering the practice questions in each section, I would highly recommend that you work with Lotus Notes, the Domino Server,

Domino Designer, and Domino Administrator. This book assumes, that you have some experience with Lotus Notes, at least to have some familiarity with the uses and feel of the software.

For the System Administration track, you need access to a Notes client and a Domino server, as well as the Domino Administrator. You will need a user ID that has a regular Notes license. When you decide to set up a server to create your ID and to work through the server topics, keep in mind that you don't need any fancy hardware to set up a Notes server, and it can run on almost any operating system. If you do not already work with Domino, you can obtain a trial version from the Notes Net (**http://notes.net**). The exams assume that you have experience with all of the basic administration tasks, including planning and installing a Notes environment. The Notes environment should have more than one server, if possible. You will need to register users and servers and implement the basic Notes functions of mail, security, and replication.

For the Application Development track, you need all of the above, plus a Domino Designer. You need to be able to create applications, create and read code in various languages, provide different levels of security for the applications, and troubleshoot them.

You simply cannot get this type of experience from any source other than actually doing it. You should read each competency in the Lotus Exam guide and perform the tasks associated with it during your preparation.

Lotus Certification Paths and Resources

The certifications awarded by Lotus for R5 include the Certified Lotus Specialist (CLS), the Certified Lotus Professional (CLP), the Principal Certified Lotus Professional (Principal CLP), and the Certified Lotus Instructor (CLI). The exams covered in this book are required for CLP, Principal CLP, and CLI certifications.

The requirements for each certification were discussed above, but specifics can change without notice. To get specific and updated details about the exams, competencies, and other details of certification, refer to the Lotus Certification Web site at **http://www.lotus.com/certification**. If you obtain a CLS, CLP, or other Lotus certification, you can also access the private CLP Web site as part of your certification benefits. Details about Lotus courses and other education details can be found at **http://www.lotus.com/education**. In addition, you have access to the Lotus Education Help Line. If you have specific questions about taking the exams, taking official Lotus courses, or about the Lotus certifications, you can call the Lotus Education Helpline, at 1-800-346-6409 or 1-617-693-4436. The Helpline is open from 8:30 A.M. to 5:30 P.M.,

Eastern Time, Monday through Friday. (Note that this is the North America number—if you are an international reader, refer to the Web site for a number to call in your region.)

The Exams

After you have determined the path to take for your Lotus Notes certifications, it is time to choose and study for your first exam. If you have purchased this book, I will assume that you have made some of these decisions (such as which exams to take). As you begin studying, you may also want to think about the type of exam you'll take.

The multiple-choice tests require the tester to answer approximately 40 to 60 questions. These questions are presented multiple-choice format, with question types that can include true or false questions, questions with multiple answers, and questions that require users to interpret graphics or diagrams. Each test is computer-based and timed, with the time limit set specifically for each exam. The testing proctor will ensure that you know the time limit, and the test interface will show you how much time you have left at all times during the test. Each test is considered a closed-book exam. You will be given blank scratch paper (which must be returned to the testing proctor after the exam) and a pen or pencil if you need it. No other items may be brought into the testing center, including purses, pagers, notes, books, and calculators. At the beginning of the exam, the testing interface will display the exact number of questions on the exam and the passing percentage. When you have completed the test, the interface will display your percentage correct and the passing percentage. This will also be printed at the testing center for you to keep and will be forwarded to Lotus Education within 5 business days. If you do not pass one of the exams, you must register and pay the exam fee again through Sylvan Prometric or CATGlobal.

 NOTE The testing rules of each center are explained to the candidate both at registration time and at testing time. Be aware that Lotus and the testing centers both take these rules very seriously. If a candidate is accused and proven to have passed an exam through any inappropriate or questionable means, the candidate's scores will be dismissed and the candidate will have to retest after a 6-month waiting period. The candidate can take no Lotus certification exams within the 6-month waiting period.

The next step in pursuing your certification is to study for and take the exams you have selected. Obviously, everyone learns and studies differently. This book is an excellent study tool for all types of learning methods, in that we have tried to give you the opportunity both to read about the topics that you need to know and to work through some of the tasks that are required competencies. In addition to reading this book and working through suggested tasks and review questions, you may find that classes, Lotus' Learning Bytes, computer-based training, and a variety of practice exams will help you to pass the exams.

Many people find that hands-on experience is the best way to learn software and pass exams. One way to get this hands-on experience is to take classes. There are two sets of classes available to help you pass the Notes certification exams. First, there is the official Lotus Curriculum. These are hands-on, instructor-led courses that are usually 2 to 5 days in length for the technical courses. (The end user courses are recommended prerequisites, and each one takes a half-day.) You will find many of the same topics from this book covered in the courses. You will note, however, that Lotus' stated objective for students in the classes is learning the tasks related to their jobs—i.e., learning to be good system administrators and application developers. The courses are refined slightly differently than the exams, in my experience. The other instructor-led classes available include a variety of unofficial courses. In addition to the instructor-led classes, there are a variety of computer-based training (CBT) alternatives. After using all these methods to study, you may also want to buy some of the practice exams offered on the market. The practice exams not only give you the ability to test your knowledge, but also allow you to practice the act of taking an exam, including time limits and computerized testing. Mastering these skills can be a huge help in passing the exams. This book does contain a CD with some free practice exams, as well. Finally, as mentioned above, you can obtain a trial version of Lotus Notes and Domino from **http://notes.net**. This gives you the chance to practice all the skills and techniques necessary to pass the exams. Other study resources include the following:

- **IBM Redbooks** These books, produced by IBM, are in-depth resources covering various topics, such as security, development, and enterprise integration. You can obtain these Redbooks at **http://www.lotus.com/redbooks**.

- **Lotus Help Database/Yellow books** The Lotus documentation is available at **http://www.notes.net/notesua.nsf** and provides the best source of in-depth background information about specific commands, languages, tools, and tasks.

Additional information about Lotus technologies can be found at various magazines, journals, and Web sites. These may not map directly to certification issues, but provide good techniques and information in most cases:

- *Group Computing* magazine covers all Lotus technologies, including how-to articles, and is available to qualified subscribers in the U.S. for free (internationally available for US$39.95). The magazine also publishes a Web site, subscription-based print newsletter for developers (DominoPro Developer Journal), and free e-mail newsletters. Information is available at **http://www.groupcomputing.com**.

- *Iris Today* is a free, online magazine published by Iris—the developers of Notes and Domino. You can also download software, participate in forums, and get beta software at **http://www.notes.net**.

- *Lotus Advisor* magazine covers development topics in Lotus technologies and is available for US$79 in the U.S., more in other countries. The magazine also publishes two print newsletters and a Web site. Information is available at **http://www.advisor.com**.

- *The View* magazine is an in-depth journal covering Notes and Domino, and is available for US$347 in the U.S. and Canada, more internationally. Information about the magazine is available at **http://www.eview.com**.

- *DominoPower* magazine is a free, online magazine covering Notes and Domino technical topics. More information is available at **http://www.dominopower.com**.

How to Take the Tests

This section outlines some test-taking strategies that often make the multiple choice style exams easier.

- Use the time before you actually begin the test to jot down any memorized notes on the scratch paper provided.

- Go through the exam once, answering any questions you are certain of. Make notes of any questions that give you information that might help you answer another question you have seen.

- Mark any questions you are not sure of and return to them on your second pass.

- Answer **all** the questions. Blank questions are automatically considered wrong.

- Sometimes it helps to write or draw part of the information given in a question. This helps clarify scenario questions especially.

- Read each question slowly and carefully. Make sure you know what the question is asking before you answer. It is very easy to go too quickly and miss a key word.

- Visualize the Lotus Notes, Domino server, Domino Administrator, and/or Domino Designer interfaces as clearly as you can, including menus and dialog boxes. Draw diagrams to help you visualize, if that is necessary. Knowing where options are located and how to perform actions will be important.

Some of these strategies may work for you; others may not. I recommend using practice exams to try out these ideas to see which work for you. The more at ease you are with the testing format, the more you can concentrate on the questions. Good luck!

Registering for the Exams

After completing your studying, you can register for the exams by contacting one of Lotus' two Independent Testing Vendors.

- **Sylvan Prometric testing centers**   To contact Sylvan, use 1-800-74-Lotus (800-745-6887) or contact your local Lotus Education office for the location of the nearest Sylvan Prometric Regional Service Center. You may also register for exams online at Sylvan by going to Sylvan Prometric's Online Registration site at **http://www.2test.com**.

- **CATGlobal Testing Centers**   Complete your CATGlobal registration online at **http://www.catglobal.com**.

You will need the following information ready, either on the phone or online, when you register:

- Name
- Social Security Number or Testing ID
- Mailing address and phone number
- Company name
- Name and number of the exam you are registering to take
- When and where you wish to test
- Payment method (credit card, voucher, money order, or check—note that you cannot test until they receive payment, which can postpone testing if paying by money order or check)

PART I

Introduction
Maintaining Domino
Servers and Users

This section covers the first exam in the system administration track: Maintaining Domino Servers and Users (190–520). Passing this exam earns you a *Certified Lotus Specialist* (CLS) designation for system administration and is one of the required exams for the *Certified Lotus Professional* (CLP) designation in system administration. The competencies for this exam cover five basic areas:

- Monitoring, maintaining, and troubleshooting Domino applications

- Monitoring, maintaining, and troubleshooting Domino directories, users, and groups

- Monitoring, maintaining, and troubleshooting Domino messaging and replication

- Monitoring, maintaining, and troubleshooting Domino servers

- Monitoring, maintaining, and troubleshooting Domino systems

The competencies that are covered in each chapter are listed at the beginning of the chapter. Remember that Lotus reserves the right to change competencies at any time. You should download the most recent exam guide from Lotus Certification at **http://www.lotus.com/certification**. This exam assumes that your Domino environment has already been configured and that you have a basic understanding of the elements in the Domino system. If you are new to Domino administration or to any of the topics that are discussed, you might choose to begin with the related material in Section 2, "Implementing a Domino Infrastructure," because the chapters in that section will enable you to install and configure a Domino environment. Some of the information in the chapters in Section 1 is repeated in Section 2, because the exams cover some of the same material but from a slightly different perspective. In Section 1, the topics are covered by assuming that you need to monitor, maintain, and troubleshoot the element. In Section 2, the topics are covered by assuming that you are configuring the elements that are discussed.

Each chapter in this section is arranged according to the tasks that you would perform in a Domino environment, starting from the basics of maintaining the Domino servers and system to maintaining Domino applications and replication.

Domino Systems and Infrastructure

You should be able to answer questions based on the following objectives after reading this chapter:

- Monitoring, maintaining, and troubleshooting Domino applications
- Monitoring/maintaining agents
- Monitoring/maintaining log files
- Troubleshooting Agent Manager problems
- Monitoring, maintaining, and troubleshooting Domino servers
- Maintaining Domino server IDs
- Maintaining servers
- Monitoring server resources
- Monitoring server tasks
- Monitoring/maintaining servers
- Monitoring/maintaining/modifying server access control
- Running program documents
- Troubleshooting administration process problems
- Troubleshooting server access problems
- Troubleshooting server problems
- Monitoring, maintaining, and troubleshooting Domino systems
- Maintaining Domino certifier IDs
- Modifying/maintaining connectivity
- Monitoring/maintaining connectivity
- Monitoring/maintaining Domino access
- Monitoring/maintaining domains
- Monitoring/maintaining the Domino system
- Troubleshooting domain access problems
- Troubleshooting network/protocol problems
- Troubleshooting port (modem) problems

Your Domino environment rests on the Notes and Domino systems and infrastructure that you (or someone else) have built. One of your main tasks as an administrator is monitoring and maintaining the systems; the applications, mail, and other elements cannot function without this layer. Monitoring consists of using events, statistics, logs, and other tools to track how the system is performing. Maintenance consists of making changes as necessary in order to ensure that the system continues to perform correctly. Each of the chapters in Section 1 covers an aspect of monitoring and maintaining Domino servers and users. In this case, we start at the bottom layer of the Domino infrastructure, with the systems, server, and infrastructure.

Administration Tools

Much of the monitoring and maintenance that is described in this chapter, as well as in the next four chapters, revolves around using the tools that are provided in Domino and in the Administration client to perform the necessary tasks to keep the systems, servers, and clients running and connected. Many of these tools will be mentioned again in the rest of Section 1 and throughout this book. As you examine each of these tools, think about what is required to use them and how they can help with troubleshooting problems with the Domino system.

Domino Administrator

Domino Administrator gives an administrator access to a great deal of information about a server and domain. You also gain access to many of the tools that are required to administer the servers and systems.

People and Groups

To maintain users, groups, and mail-in databases or resources, use the People and Groups tab, as shown in Figure 1-1. In addition to editing users and groups, renaming and re-certifying users, and registering new users, the views in this tab give you access to user setup profiles and to the Move Mail File action. These options are discussed in greater detail in Chapter 3, "Domino Directories, Users, and Groups."

Files

The Files tab gives you the capability to open and view any database or template and to view any type of file in the data directory and subdirectories. The tools that are included on the Files tab include the Disk Space tools, as shown in Figure 1-2, which show the amount of used and free disk space on each drive in the selected machine.

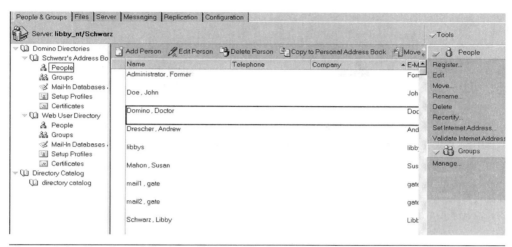

Figure 1-1   People and Groups tab

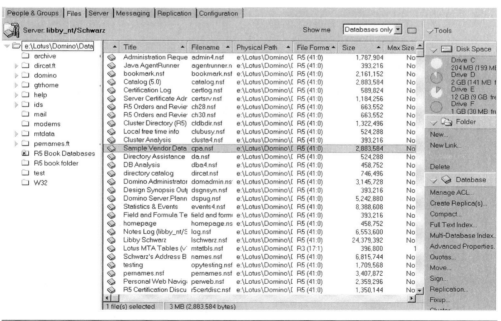

Figure 1-2   Disk Space tools

Use the Folder tools to create new folders in the data directory structure, to create and update directory links, and to delete folders. The Database tools, which are shown in Figure 1-3, enable you to perform the following tasks:

- Managing the *Access Control List* (ACL) of the database(s), if you have Manager access to the database

- Creating new replicas of a selected database(s), if your name is in the Create Replica Databases field of the server document

- Running the Compact task on a database(s), including modifiers such as maintaining the R4 structure of a database, or archiving a database

- Creating a full-text index for a database(s)

- Enabling or disabling multi-database indexing for a database(s)

- Enabling or disabling the advanced database properties for a database(s)

- Configuring quotas and warning thresholds on a database(s)

- Moving a database(s) to another server by using the *Administration Process* (AdminP)

- Signing design elements in a database(s) for design-element protection

Figure 1-3
Database tools

Database

Manage ACL...
Create Replica(s)...
Compact...
Full Text Index...
Multi-Database Index..
Advanced Properties.
Quotas...
Move...
Sign...
Replication...
Fixup...
Cluster...
Analyze...
Find Note...

- Enabling or disabling replication for a database(s)

- Running the Fixup task against a database(s), including modifiers such as running Fixup on transaction-logged databases, or running a Fixup that excludes views

- Maintaining databases in clusters (refer to Chapter 2, "Advanced Domino and Web Servers," for more information)

- Running a database analysis in order to monitor changes to the database design, data, access control, and replication settings

- Searching a database for a document note by either note ID or *Universal Note ID* (UNID)

Refer to Chapter 5, "Domino Applications and Replication," for more details concerning many of these Database tools.

Server

The Server tab is broken into four additional tabs: Status, Analysis, Monitoring, and Statistics.

Status Tab   Use the Status tab to monitor server tasks. (You could receive the same information by using the SHOW TASKS command at a server console.) The Tasks list, as shown in Figure 1-4, shows the ports and tasks that are running on the server and what those tasks are currently doing. You can also start and stop tasks and ports from this list,

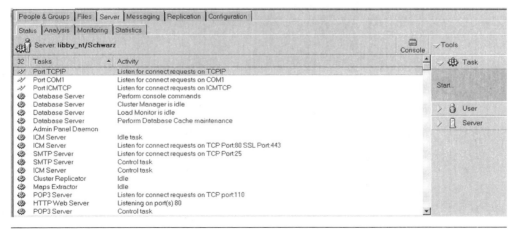

Figure 1-4   Tasks list in the Status tab

as well as run the TELL command against certain tasks. These features can be useful for obtaining information, such as telling the HTTP task to show file access information or all users with HTTP sessions, or telling the Agent Manager to show the scheduled agents. Use the Start and Stop port commands to stop and restart a port when troubleshooting the connectivity over a specific port or when making changes to the port configuration.

The bottom pane of the Status tab shows the users who are currently connected to the server and what databases they have open. (You could also obtain this information by using the SHOW USERS command at a server console.) You can drop users or send broadcast messages to them by right-clicking and using the Drop or Broadcast commands. These commands are also available from the User tools.

You also have access to the Server tools. Use these tools to accomplish the following tasks:

- Forcing a manual replication between the current server and another server, using any style and on all databases or a selected database. For more details about replication, refer to Chapter 5, "Domino Applications and Replication."

- Forcing mail to route manually between the current server and the selected server. For more information about mail routing, refer to Chapter 4, "Domino Messaging."

- Configuring ports by using the Setup Ports tool. Ports that are enabled on the server are listed in the Communication Ports list with a check mark. You can delete, rename, or move those ports in the list. Ports that are higher in the list will be used for communication first. When you select a port, the dialog box lists the driver, gives you the opportunity to enable or disable the port, and gives you the opportunity to encrypt all of the data that goes over that port. In addition, many of the ports have options that are available from a button on the dialog box. You can enable ports that are not currently enabled, although you will usually have to restart the server in order for new ports and other changes to take effect. Finally, you can create new ports, if necessary, by using the New button. Use the New Port dialog box to select a name and driver for any new ports.

- Use the Shutdown tool to stop the server remotely. This action shuts down the entire server.

Also available from the Status tab is the Console button, which displays the remote console as shown in Figure 1-5. Use the console to type commands that you want to run on the server. Your name (or a group that contains your name) must be in the

```
People & Groups | Files | Server | Messaging | Replication | Configuration |
Status | Analysis | Monitoring | Statistics |
Server: libby_nt/Schwarz                                    II      ■       ⟳
                                                          Pause   Stop    Tasks
COM2=XPC.2.15.0.,12288,
11/28/99 06:05:41 PM  Opened live remote console session for Libby
Schwarz/Schwarz
> 11/28/99 06:05:52 PM   ICM Server: 192.168.50.245 connected
11/28/99 06:05:52 PM   ICM Server: 192.168.50.245 disconnected
> 11/28/99 06:05:58 PM   Opened session for Gate/Schwarz (Release 5)
> 11/28/99 06:05:58 PM   Closed session for Gate/Schwarz
Databases accessed:     0    Documents read:     0    Documents written:      0
>
> Show Server

Lotus Domino « Server (Release 5.0.2 for Windows/32) 11/28/99 06:06:05 PM

Server name:              libby_nt/Schwarz
Server directory:         e:\Lotus\Domino\Data
Partition:                e.Lotus.Domino.Data
Elapsed time:             05:15:32
Transactions/minute:      Last minute: 37; Last hour: 17; Peak: 61
Peak # of sessions:       9 at 11/28/99 03:05:23 PM
Transactions:             5239
Availability Index:       100 (state: AVAILABLE)
Message Tracking:         Enabled
Shared mail:              Not Enabled
Number of Mailboxes:      2
Pending mail:  0          Dead mail:  0
Waiting Tasks:            0
Transactional Logging:    Not Enabled
> 11/28/99 06:06:24 PM   ICM Server: 192.168.50.245 connected
11/28/99 06:06:24 PM   ICM Server: 192.168.50.245 disconnected
>
Commands...  Show Server                                              ▼
```

Figure 1-5   Remote console

Administrators field on the Server document in order to administer the server from the remote console.

TIP   The Web Administrator tool has the same requirement: Your name (or a group that contains your name) must be in the Administrators field. In addition, your name (or a group that contains your name) must be in the Administer the Server from a Browser field on the Security tab.

If you use the live console, responses from the server should be shown as mixed with any other tasks or actions that are currently occurring on the server. With Live Console turned off, you only see the response from your commands. You can select commands to send to the server by using the Commands . . . button. When you select a command from this list, the command is pasted into the Commands area with the appropriate syntax. You merely need to complete the particular details (where necessary). After the command is complete, press Enter to send the command. After you have sent commands, you can click the drop-down arrow to retrieve commands that you have already sent and that you want to send again.

If you watch the server console when you send commands (when the console is *not* live), or when you display tabs that show you the same data as if you had typed a command, you can see the command and the output file to which the response is being directed, as shown in Figure 1-6. What you see is the command that you typed, followed by a greater-than symbol (>) and the name of the file to which the server sends the response. You can use this command to capture the server command output to a file at any time, simply by typing the command as described. To capture the output of a SHOW TASKS command, for example, type it this way:

```
SHOW TASKS > D:\OUTPUT.TXT
```

Similarly, you can run a set of commands from a batch file. In this case, you would create a text file that contained the commands that you wanted to run and place the file in the data directory. Each command should be on a separate line in the text file. If you want to place the text file somewhere other than the data directory, you will include the entire path when you run the file. To use the batch file, type the less-than symbol (<) at the console, followed by the name of the batch file (such as the following):

```
< MYBATCHCOMMANDS.TXT
```

Analysis Tab   The Analysis tab gives you access to the Notes Log, the Database Catalog, the Statistics Reports, and the Administration Requests databases. The Notes Log (LOG.NSF) records and stores information about all aspects of the Domino server and environment, including details about all output from commands, information about replication and routing, and database sizes and usage. You can manipulate the Notes Log to show more information by changing the logging level of specific elements. You can view the log by opening the documents that are displayed in the Notes Log. You can analyze or search the log file by using the Analyze . . . Log tool, as shown in Figure 1-7. Finally, you might want to minimize or control the growth and size of the Notes Log by using the NOTES.INI settings. For more information about how to accomplish these tasks, refer to the Notes Log section later in this chapter.

The Catalog, or Database Catalog, lists and displays all of the databases in the domain—with the exception of those that have the *List in Database Catalog* property

Figure 1-6
Capturing server command output in a file

```
> Show Cluster >D:\TEMP\24432127.TMP
```

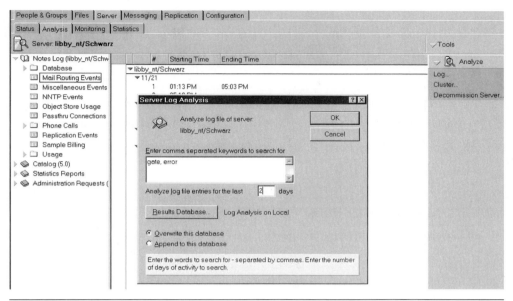

Figure 1-7   Analyze Log tool

disabled. Users and administrators can view documents concerning the databases that are organized in various views, such as by ACL levels or replica IDs. If you open one of the documents, as shown in Figure 1-8, you can add a bookmark for or open one of the databases, or you can obtain details about the design of the database (such as whether the database was based on a template).

The Statistics Reports database (STATREP.NSF) contains statistics about your Domino system. These statistics display information about the processes that are currently running on your server and are gathered from the server that is using the Collect task. If this task is not running, you can start it by using the Status tab and the Start Task tool, or you can type LOAD COLLECT at the server console. If you want Collect to run every time the server starts, you should add Collect to the ServerTasks= line in the NOTES.INI file. The Collect task gathers the statistics based on the Server Statistic Collection document, as shown in Figure 1-9, which is available under the Statistics and Events view on the Configuration tab.

You can edit or create the Server Statistic Collection document, which describes which server will collect the statistics and from which servers it should collect, including *All Servers in this domain*. The Options tab enables you to tell Collect to log the statistics to the STATREP.NSF database, as well as how often to gather the statistics.

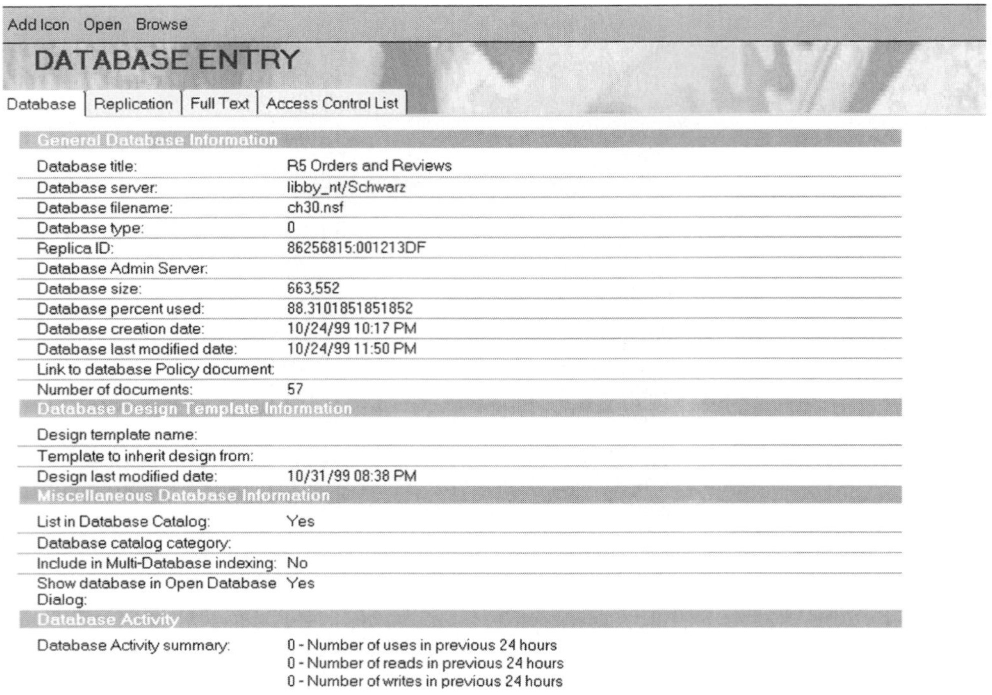

Add Icon   Open   Browse

DATABASE ENTRY

| Database | Replication | Full Text | Access Control List |

General Database Information

Database title:	R5 Orders and Reviews
Database server:	libby_nt/Schwarz
Database filename:	ch30.nsf
Database type:	0
Replica ID:	86256815:001213DF
Database Admin Server:	
Database size:	663,552
Database percent used:	88.3101851851852
Database creation date:	10/24/99 10:17 PM
Database last modified date:	10/24/99 11:50 PM
Link to database Policy document:	
Number of documents:	57

Database Design Template Information

Design template name:	
Template to inherit design from:	
Design last modified date:	10/31/99 08:38 PM

Miscellaneous Database Information

List in Database Catalog:	Yes
Database catalog category:	
Include in Multi-Database indexing:	No
Show database in Open Database Dialog:	Yes

Database Activity

Database Activity summary:	0 - Number of uses in previous 24 hours
	0 - Number of reads in previous 24 hours
	0 - Number of writes in previous 24 hours

Figure 1-8   Database Catalog document

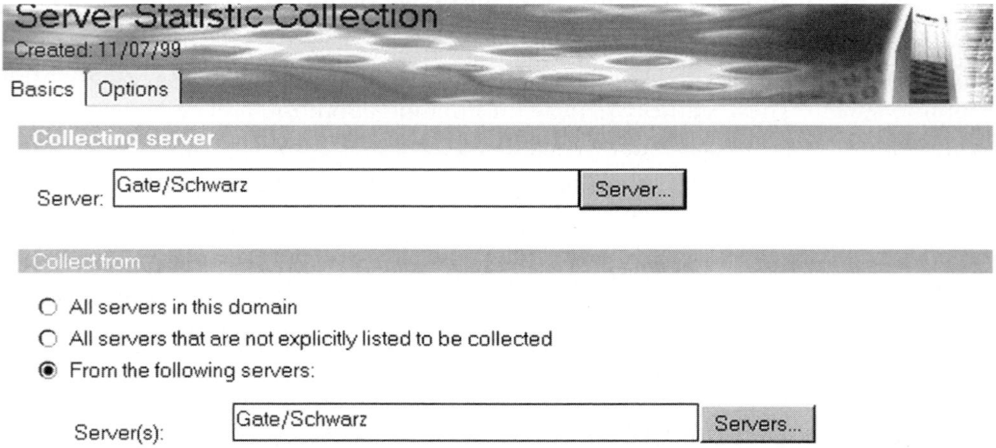

Server Statistic Collection
Created: 11/07/99

| Basics | Options |

Collecting server

Server: Gate/Schwarz   [Server...]

Collect from

○ All servers in this domain
○ All servers that are not explicitly listed to be collected
◉ From the following servers:

Server(s):   Gate/Schwarz   [Servers...]

Figure 1-9   Server Statistic Collection document

| People & Groups | Files | Server | Messaging | Replication | Configuration |

| Status | Analysis | Monitoring | Statistics |

Server: **libby_nt/Schwarz**

	Collection Time	Dead Mail	Mail Routed	Pend. Mail	Failed Replic
Notes Log (libby_nt/Schw					
Catalog (5.0)	* 11/27/99 07:11:47 AM	0	5,225	0	
Statistics Reports	* 11/27/99 06:11:46 AM	0	5,225	0	
1. Statistics Reports	* 11/27/99 05:11:48 AM	0	5,225	0	
Calendaring Sched	* 11/27/99 04:11:47 AM	0	5,225	0	
Clusters	* 11/27/99 03:11:47 AM	0	5,225	0	
Communications	* 11/27/99 02:11:47 AM	0	5,225	0	
Mail & Database	* 11/27/99 01:11:48 AM	0	5,225	0	
Network	* 11/27/99 12:11:46 AM	0	5,225	0	
Platform	* 11/26/99 11:11:48 PM	0	5,225	0	
System	* 11/26/99 10:11:46 PM	0	5,225	0	
Web Server & Retr	* 11/26/99 09:11:47 PM	0	5,225	0	
2. Alarms	* 11/26/99 08:11:47 PM	0	5,225	0	
3. Events	* 11/26/99 07:11:47 PM	0	5,225	0	
4. Spreadsheet Export	* 11/26/99 06:11:46 PM	0	5,225	0	
5. Graphs	* 11/26/99 05:11:46 PM	0	5,225	0	
6. Server Access	▼ libby_nt/Schwarz				
7. Single Copy Object	11/28/99 12:30:05 PM	0	N/A	0	
Administration Requests (	11/28/99 11:30:05 AM	0	N/A	0	
	* 11/28/99 10:30:05 AM	0	N/A	0	
	* 11/28/99 09:30:05 AM	0	N/A	0	
	* 11/28/99 08:30:03 AM	0	N/A	0	
	* 11/28/99 07:30:04 AM	0	N/A	0	

Figure 1-10   Statistics Reports view

After you configure statistic gathering, you can view statistics reports covering calendaring and scheduling, clusters, communications, mail and databases, network, platform, system, and Web server and retriever, as shown in Figure 1-10.

The other monitoring task that places data in STATREP.NSF is Event. This task gathers data based on events that occur on the server, such as replication or routing.

Finally, the Analysis tab contains the Administration Requests (ADMIN4.NSF) database. This database enables you to track requests that are being processed by the AdminP in order to see where they are in the process, to determine whether they need administrative attention, or to determine whether they need administrator approval. You can also use this database to determine whether a particular request has generated an error. If so, you can correct the problem that is causing the error and reset the request. Errors that you might have to fix include the following:

- Not having created a Certification Log (CERTLOG.NSF) as part of the AdminP configuration

- Not setting an administration server for the Domino Directory

- Not setting an administration server for other databases (every database should have an Administration server configured by using the ACL dialog box)
- Not having the proper access to perform a request

Use the views for the database to track requests, to determine when they will be (or were) performed, and to view any errors.

Monitoring The Monitoring tab provides another way to view the tasks on the servers, in order to see which tasks are running and which (if any) are stopped or are not running. In addition, you can see the results of some statistics according to the number of users who are accessing the server and according to the amount of dead or held mail, as shown in Figure 1-11. You can also organize the view according to the state of the tasks or based on a timeline.

Statistics Another way to view the statistics that are gathered by the Collect task (as described previously) is by using the Statistics tab, as shown in Figure 1-12. Each group of statistics can be expanded to show specific statistics, such as Mem.PhysicalRam or Mem.Allocated.

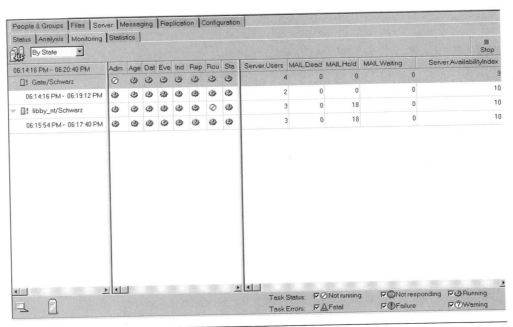

Figure 1-11   Monitoring tab, view by state

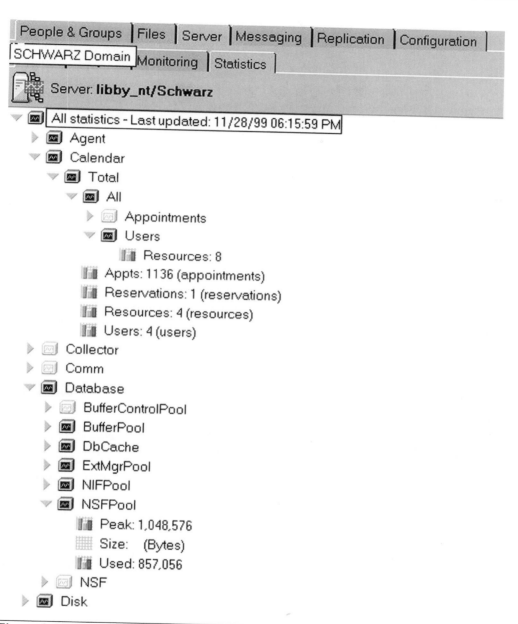

Figure 1-12   Statistics tab

Messaging

The Messaging tab is separated into the Mail tab and the Tracking Center tab. The Mail tab, shown in Figure 1-13, gives access to a list of mail users, a view of each MAIL.BOX on a server, the status of routed mail, and a graphical view of the mail-routing topology. Messaging tools include the capability to start and stop the Router, the capability to route mail manually, and a mail trace tool for troubleshooting.

The Tracking Center tab, which relies on the Mail Tracking Collector (MTC) task that is running on the server, enables you to track already-sent messages to determine where they are in their route. For more details about the tools that are provided in the Messaging tab, refer to Chapter 4, "Domino Messaging."

Replication

The Replication tab, shown in Figure 1-14, provides a graphical representation of the replication schedule (taken from the Connection documents), a way to view the Replication events (taken from the log), and the graphical Replication topology map (created by the MAPS task on the server and the Connection documents). Refer to Chapter 5, "Domino Applications and Replication," for more information about replication and replication topology.

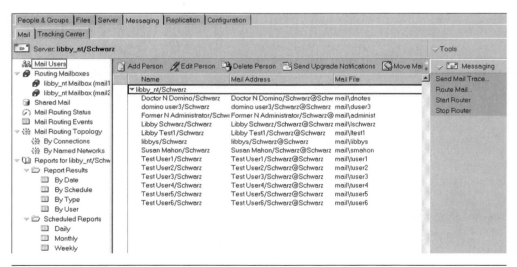

Figure 1-13 Messaging . . . Mail tab

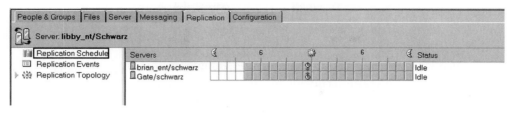

Figure 1-14   Replication tab

Configuration

The Configuration tab gives you access to a variety of configuration and monitoring tools, which are separated into views including Server, Messaging, Replication, Directory, Web, Statistics and Events, Cluster, and Miscellaneous.

Server   First, in the Server section, you can view the current Server document or all Server documents. Use the Server documents for security (Access Server and Not Access Server fields), to determine how the tasks running on the server should function (in the Server tasks tab), and for configuration of the network ports, including the Port name, protocol, *Domino Named Network* (DNN), and network address (such as an IP address).

The Server section also gives you access to the Configurations view. You can view or create Configuration Settings documents, such as the one shown in Figure 1-15. A Configuration Settings document can apply to one or more servers or to all servers in the

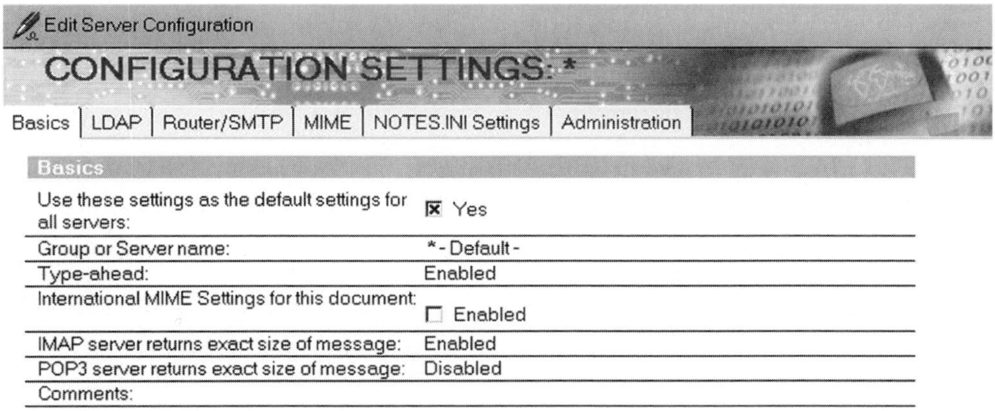

Figure 1-15   Configuration Settings document

domain. Use the Configuration Settings document to modify how the Router, SMTP, and MIME conversions are configured. You can also use the document to add settings to the NOTES.INI file.

You also have access to the Connections documents in this area, as shown in Figure 1-16. Use the Connections documents to specify how and when servers connect to each other for replication and mail routing. If servers are in the same DNN, they do not need a Connections document to perform mail routing; although, they will still need one for scheduled replication. Both Chapters 4 and 5 describe Connections documents in more detail, because they are used for mail routing and replication.

Use Program documents (listed next) to run specific programs at a scheduled time. An example of a use for a Program document would be to run the Compact task at a particular time, as shown in Figure 1-17.

The External Domain Network Information document enables a requesting server in your domain to obtain address information (not Notes addresses, but network addresses) from a server in a remote domain. This feature makes it easier for any server or client in your domain to access any server in the remote domain. A sample External Domain Network Information document is shown in Figure 1-18.

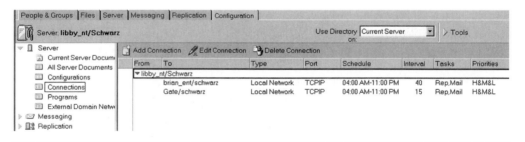

Figure 1-16　Connections document

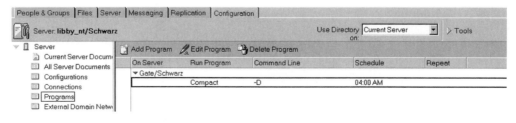

Figure 1-17　Program document

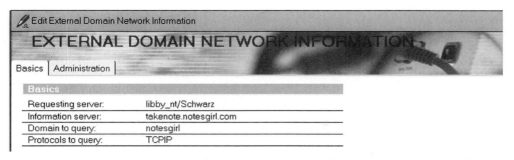

EXTERNAL DOMAIN NETWORK INFORMATION

Basics | Administration

Basics

Requesting server:	libby_nt/Schwarz
Information server:	takenote.notesgirl.com
Domain to query:	notesgirl
Protocols to query:	TCPIP

Figure 1-18   External Domain Network Information document

Messaging   Under the Messaging section, you will find more ways to configure connections and configurations. The documents that are found in this view are the same as the documents that are found in any connections or configurations views; they are organized under Messaging to make maintenance easier. In addition, in this section you will find Domain documents. You create Domain documents when you want to send mail to other domains; these can include adjacent domains and non-adjacent domains. Creating Domain documents determines how mail and calendaring will function among multiple domains. Other domain types include Foreign and Global domains. Use Foreign domains for non-Notes messaging. Use the Global Domain document to configure the use of R5 Internet mail. Refer to Chapter 4, "Domino Messaging," for more information about Domino messaging.

Replication   The Replication section provides access to the Connections documents again. These are still the same Connections documents that are available from any Connections view. Refer to Chapter 5 for more information about Replication.

Directory   The Directory section enables you to access the directory settings, including settings for the Directory Catalog and Directory Assistance documents. For more information about directories, refer to Chapter 3.

Web   Configuration information for a Domino Web server, such as Virtual Servers, Virtual Hosts, and File Protection documents (which are created from the Servers view) can be viewed in this section, as shown in Figure 1-19.

Statistics and Events   The Event Notification view shows all of the current event notifications. When an event occurs on a server, you can configure how you or other administrators should be notified. The Notification documents can be viewed or created here. In the Monitors section, you can create and view ACL Change, File, Replication,

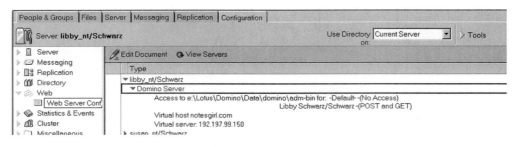

Figure 1-19   Web server Configurations view

and Statistic monitors. These monitors are set to watch a particular item on the server and to notify you or another administrator when a configured threshold is reached, as shown.

The Names and Messages view shows the documents that create the defaults for statistics thresholds, event messages, notification methods, and statistic names and descriptions. You can create probes for the Domino Server, mail, and TCP services. The probes check to see that the particular item is still responding. When a probe times out, it generates an event and notifies you (if you have created a notification profile in the Probe document). A sample of a TCP Probe document is shown in Figure 1-20.

Use the Server Statistic Collection view to create and view Server Statistic Collection documents for the servers in your domain, as described previously.

Cluster   Use the Cluster section to view the server documents of the servers in your domain and to add or remove them from clusters. You can also view which clusters already exist and which servers are in those clusters. Finally, this section gives you access to the Cluster directory (CLDBDIR.NSF). Chapter 2 has more details about clusters.

Miscellaneous   The Miscellaneous section contains the Certificates view, the Licenses view, and the Holidays view. The Certificates view contains the Internet, Notes

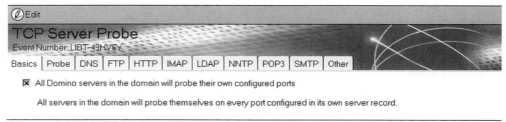

Figure 1-20   TCP Probe document

certificates, and Notes cross-certificates for this domain. The Licenses view shows the number of client and server licenses that are currently in use in your domain. The Holidays view shows the default and created holidays, organized by Holiday group (the default groups are Countries).

Tools   The tools in the Configuration tab are certification tools and registration tools. Using the certification tools, you can certify and cross-certify ID files. Certifying an ID file involves signing an ID file with a certifier and enables you to change its expiration date and password quality and add an alternate name and language (if an alternate language is in the Certifier ID). You can certify a Certifier ID with itself or its parent certifier in order to add an additional language, which enables servers and users who are certified with that certifier to use an alternate language and name, as well. To add an alternate language to a certifier, click the Certify tool. Choose the CERT.ID file as the certifier ID, then choose the same CERT.ID file as the file to be certified. In the Certify ID dialog box, click the Add button under the Subject Name list, as shown in Figure 1-21. In the Specify Alternate Organization Name dialog box, select an alternate language and type an alternate Organization name for the certifier.

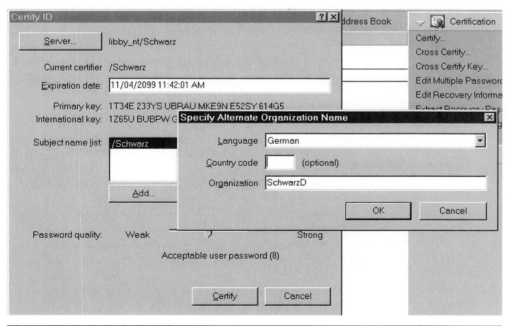

Figure 1-21   Adding an alternate language

Cross-certifying an ID enables IDs from two different hierarchical organizations to communicate. When there are two organizations, say, /Acme and /Zoom, users and servers from /Acme cannot use resources in /Zoom until they are cross-certified with /Zoom, because they cannot authenticate until they share a certificate in common. To issue a cross-certificate, choose the Cross Certify tool. Select the ID with which you want to create the cross-certification (it does not have to be the top-level certifier; you can cross-certify at lower levels of the Organization). Then, select the ID from the other Organization with which you want to cross-certify (not only does this certifier not have to be the top-level certifier, but it can even be a server or user ID if only one user or server needs to authenticate with your Organization). Use the Issue Cross Certificate dialog box, as shown in Figure 1-22, to add the cross-certificate to the Domino Directory.

You can also use the certification tools to add multiple passwords to an ID file, to add or extract recovery information, to examine ID files, and to open the Certification log. The Configuration tab also contains registration tools that enable you to register users, servers, Organizational Units, Organizations, or Internet certifiers.

Notes Log

As described previously, the Notes log displays information about the tasks and users on the server. In some situations, you might want to ensure that the log is capturing as much information as possible, such as while troubleshooting a particular problem. When you want to customize the data that the log stores, you can use the suggested

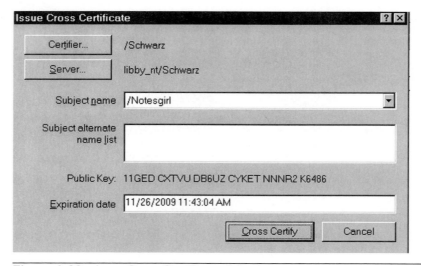

Figure 1-22   Issue Cross Certificate dialog box

NOTES.INI settings or preferences to enhance what is already being collected by default. Suggested settings and preferences are listed in Table 1-1.

Table 1-1   Customizing the Notes Log

Notes.INI Setting (or Preference, if noted)	Notes
Log_AgentManager	Set this option to 1 in order to log the execution of agents that are both partially and completely successful. Setting this option to 2 records only completely successful agent executions. If you set this option to 0, the execution of the agent will not be recorded.
Log_DirCat	This option records information about the DirCat task (builds and maintains the Directory Catalog). Set this option to 1 to record when DirCat starts and finishes, as well as to record the directories upon which it runs.
Log_Replication	This option records information about the Replica task and replication sessions. Use any of the following settings:
	0 (do not log replication events)
	1 (log server replication)
	2 (log replication at the database level)
	3 (log replication at the database element level)
	4 (log replication at the field level)
	5 (log summary information)
Log_Sessions	This option records information about the user sessions. Set this option to 1 to record each user session, and set this option to 0 if you do not want to log user sessions.
Log_Tasks	This option records information about the tasks that are running on the server. Set this option to 1 to record the status of server tasks.
Log_Update	This option records information about the Indexer task. Set this option to 1 to record startup and shut down of the Indexer task, as well as to record when the Indexer updates views and full-text indexes. If you set this option to 2, it will record all of this information plus the names of the views that Indexer updates.
Log_View_Events	This option records information about views being rebuilt when set to 1.

continued

Table 1-1   Customizing the Notes Log (*continued*)

Notes.INI Setting (or Preference, if noted)	Notes
Mail_Log_To_MiscEvents	When set to 1, this option displays mail events in the Miscellaneous view. When set to 0, mail events are only listed in the Mail Routing Events view.
Passthru_LogLevel	Use this option to determine how much network trace information is recorded in the log for any network connections. Use any of the following settings:
0 (records no information)	
1 (only records errors)	
2 (records summary progress information)	
3 (records detailed progress information)	
RTR_Logging	This option turns on (1) or off (0) logging for the Cluster replicator.
Log Modem I/0 (File...Preferences ...User Preferences...Ports)	When you select a COM port, you can select the Options button to enable Domino to log the input and output of any modems.
Log Script I/0 (File...Preferences ...User Preferences...Ports)	When you select a COM port, you can select the Options button to enable Domino to log the input and output of any modem scripts.

In general, you should add logging levels when you are troubleshooting a specific issue or problem, but you should scale back during normal operations in order to maintain the size of the log file. The LOG= setting in the NOTES.INI is an additional method of maintaining the size of the Log file. The syntax of the LOG= setting is as follows:

```
Log= logfilename, log_option, 0, days, size
```

If necessary, give the log file a name by using the first argument—but you will usually leave the default (LOG.NSF). In the log_option setting, use 1, 2, or 4 to log to the console, to force a database Fixup when you open the log, and to perform a full document scan. The days setting determines how many days worth of log entries to keep. The default is seven. The size setting determines the maximum number of words in the log file.

Agent Log and Agent Manager

Many databases contain agents, which are sets of automated tasks that can be run manually (from the menu or from a button in a database) or automatically (based on a schedule or an event). To monitor and maintain agents, you need to understand agent security and need to be able to check the Agent Log and use the Agent Manager.

Agent Security

When you run a manual agent, the agent uses your name for security access. The fields on the server document that relate to agent security, therefore, check for your name or for a group with your name. When you run a background agent (an agent that is run on a schedule or based on an event), the agent uses the name of the person who created, last saved, or signed the agent to pass the security in those fields. The fields in the Server document that determine how an agent can run are on the Security tab in the Agent Restrictions section and are listed as follows:

- Leave *Run Personal Agents* blank to enable anyone who can create a personal agent to run the agent on the server. You must have Reader access or higher and the *Create Personal Agents* right in the ACL in order to create a personal agent in a database. (To create shared agents, you must have at least Designer access to the database.)

- If you leave *Run Restricted LotusScript/Java agents* blank, only those who are listed in the field as follows can run agents that were created with this subset of LotusScript/Java features; the restricted features are those that do not affect the operating system or system time, for example.

- If you leave *Run Unrestricted LotusScript/Java agents* blank, no one can run these types of agents.

Agents are also affected by the ACLs of the databases in which they run. Whatever the agent is configured to do, such as delete, edit, or create a document, the user of the agent must also be allowed to do by the ACL of the database.

Agent Logging

You can check for logs that are related to how agents are working in two places. First, if you have added the Log_AgentManager setting to the NOTES.INI file, you can check the Miscellaneous Events view of the Notes Log for information about agents. In addition, you can use the Agent Log for each agent to see information about the last time the agent ran. To access the Agent Log, open the database and choose View . . . Agents. Select the agent that you are trying to troubleshoot, and choose Agent . . . Log from the

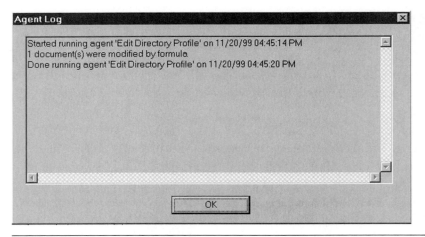

Figure 1-23 Agent Log dialog box

menus. The Agent Log dialog box, as shown in Figure 1-23, shows when the agent was last run and the result.

NOTE Do not be surprised that when you choose View . . . Agent, Notes automatically launches Domino Designer to show the agent's Design view.

Agent Manager

Agent Manager controls how agents run on the server. Look for the AMgr task on the server to make sure that it is running. You can use the TELL command with the Agent Manager task, as shown in Figure 1-24, to obtain information about the scheduled agents and the agent queue and status and to pause the scheduled agents. If you are trying to troubleshoot a particular agent, you might also use the Debug options.

The Show Me and Debug options are the equivalent of the following console commands:

- TELL AMGR SCHEDULE

- TELL AMGR STATUS

- TELL AMGR DEBUG

Sample output from these commands, as recorded in the Notes Log, is shown in Figure 1-25.

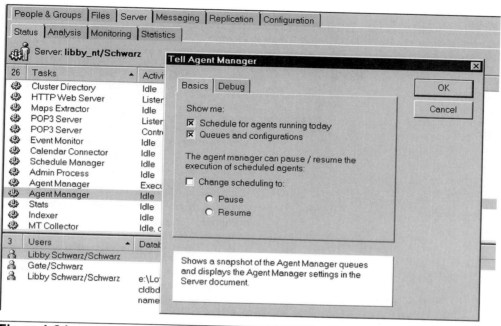

Figure 1-24 `Tell AMgr`

> Tell amgr schedule

> Tell amgr status
11/29/99 11:50:10 AM AMgr: Status report at '11/29/99 11:50:10 AM'
11/29/99 11:50:10 AM   Agent Manager has been running since '11/29/99 11:27:13 AM'
11/29/99 11:50:10 AM   There are currently '1' Agent Executives running
11/29/99 11:50:10 AM   There are currently '0' agents in the Scheduled Task Queue
11/29/99 11:50:10 AM   There are currently '0' agents in the Eligible Queue
11/29/99 11:50:10 AM   There are currently '0' databases containing agents triggered by new mail
11/29/99 11:50:11 AM   There are currently '0' agents in the New Mail Event Queue
11/29/99 11:50:11 AM   There are currently '0' databases containing agents triggered by document updates
11/29/99 11:50:11 AM   There are currently '0' agents in the Document Update Event Queue
11/29/99 11:50:11 AM AMgr: Current control parameters in effect:
11/29/99 11:50:11 AM   AMgr: Daily agent cache refresh is performed at '12:00:00 AM'
11/29/99 11:50:11 AM   AMgr: Currently in Daytime period
11/29/99 11:50:11 AM   AMgr: The maximum number of concurrently executing agents is '1'
11/29/99 11:50:11 AM   AMgr: The maximum number of minutes a LotusScript/Java agent is allowed to run is '10'
11/29/99 11:50:11 AM AMgr: Executive '1', total agent runs: 0
11/29/99 11:50:11 AM AMgr: Executive '1', total elapsed run time: 0

Figure 1-25 Sample output from `AMgr` commands

Table 1-2   NOTES.INI Settings for the Agent Manager

NOTES.INI Setting	Details
AMgr_DocUpdateAgentMinInterval	Use this setting to specify the minimum elapsed time between executions of the same document update-triggered agent. The default is 30 minutes. A longer interval causes the agent to run less frequently.
AMgr_DocUpdateEventDelay	Use this setting to specify the elapsed time between the document update and the execution of document update-triggered agents. The default is five minutes.
AMgr_NewMailAgentMinInterval	Use this setting to specify the minimum elapsed time between executions of the same new mail-triggered agent. The default is 0. A longer interval causes the agent to run less frequently.
AMgr_NewMailEventDelay	Use this setting to specify the elapsed time between the arrival of new mail and the execution of new mail-triggered agents. The default is one minute.
DominoAsynchronizeAgents	Use this setting to specify whether agents triggered by browser clients will run simultaneously (1) or one at a time (0).

You can control the Agent Manager by using a variety of NOTES.INI settings, as listed in Table 1-2.

Use the Server Tasks . . . Agent Manager tab to configure other Agent Manager settings that use the Server Document, as shown in Figure 1-26. Some of the fields are described in Table 1-3.

Administration Process (AdminP)

The Administration Process is a task that runs on the server (AdminP) and assists you with performing tasks such as user and server rename and recertification, moving mail files, and configuring clustering. To use AdminP, you must have a Certification Log on your server. If you do not have a Certification Log, create a new database called CERT-LOG.NSF and base it on the CERTLOG.NTF template. The Certification Log is shown in Figure 1-27. You must also have an Administration Requests database (ADMIN4.NSF), as shown in Figure 1-28. This database stores all of the requests and their results. The AdminP task should create this database the first time it is started. You must monitor the ADMIN4.NSF database to perform any necessary approvals and to resolve any

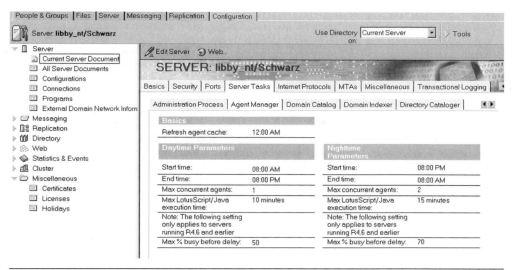

Figure 1-26   Agent Manager Settings in the Server Document

Table 1-3   Agent Manager Settings in the Server document

Field	Notes
Refresh Agent Cache	The Agent Cache lists the agents that can run during the current day, enabling the Agent Manager to access them quickly. The Agent Cache is refreshed by default at midnight.
Daytime Start time	Agents are run based on daytime and nighttime parameters, so agents that you schedule for the night period can take longer to execute or can have more agents that are running concurrently. This field determines when the daytime period begins and is set to 8 A.M. by default.
Daytime End time	This field determines when the daytime period ends and is set to 8 P.M. by default.
Daytime Max Concurrent Agents	Use this setting to limit the number of agents that can run simultaneously. The default is one for the daytime period.
Daytime Max LotusScript/Java execution time	Use this setting to limit the amount of time that an agent created with LotusScript or Java can take to run. The default is 10 minutes for the daytime period.
Nighttime Start time	This field determines when the nighttime period begins and is set to 8 P.M. by default.

continued

Table 1-3   Agent Manager Settings in the Server Document (*continued*)

Field	Notes
Nighttime End time	This field determines when the nighttime period ends and is set to 8 A.M. by default.
Nighttime Max Concurrent Agents	Use this setting to limit the number of agents that can run simultaneously. The default is two for the Nighttime period.
Nighttime Max LotusScript/Java execution time	Use this setting to limit the amount of time that an agent created with LotusScript or Java can take to run. The default is 15 minutes for the Nighttime period.

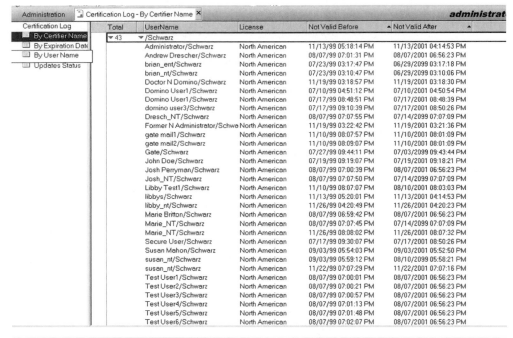

Figure 1-27   Certification Log

problems that are reported in error documents (and to rerun the requests that caused the errors).

To use AdminP, you must also have designated an Administration Server for the Domino Directory and for any database that you want AdminP to have the capacity to

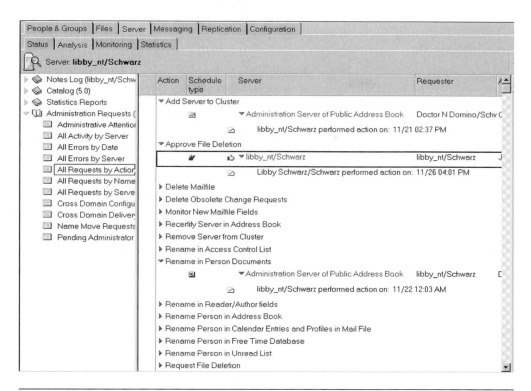

Figure 1-28   Administration Requests database

affect (such as when you rename a user or group and want that user's name updated in the ACL of a database).

The Server Tasks . . . Administration Process tab in the Server document sets the defaults regarding how the AdminP process will perform tasks. Each task runs based on an interval of some kind, such as immediate, daily, weekly, hourly, delayed, or interval. The default settings for these intervals are set in the Server document.

System Access

A user's ability to access and use the Domino servers (and therefore, Domino applications) is based on two main elements: the security settings for the servers and the environment, and the network or dial-up connectivity.

Security

Domino security is a multi-level process, starting with physical and network security and moving to server access and authentication, then narrowing in on database, form, view, and field security. In this section, we concentrate on the server security issues. One way that you can control access to your server is by using security settings in the Server document. On the Security tab of the Server document, you can determine which users can and cannot access the server, as shown in Figure 1-29. Some of the fields on the Security tab are described in Table 1-4.

Authentication with a server provides basic security for the server. Authentication, which is based on public keys, requires the user and server (or two servers) to share a common certificate—either one in the hierarchical Organization or a cross-certificate. If a user from another Organization needs to access your server, you must create a cross-certificate that enables this action. Remember that certificates can expire, so you have to recertify certifiers, servers, and users before their certificates expire.

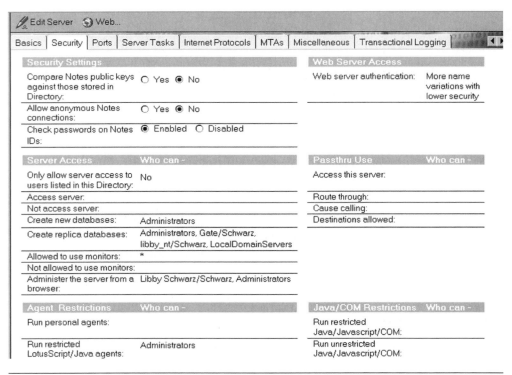

Figure 1-29 Server document security

Table 1-4 Security Settings on the Server document

Field	Notes
Compare Notes Public Keys against those stored in Directory	If you set this field to Yes, users who do not have public keys stored in this server's Domino Directory cannot authenticate with the server. The default is No.
Allow Anonymous Notes connections	If you set this field to Yes, Notes client users who do not have ID files that can authenticate with this server can access the server as Anonymous. This entry must be listed in the Access this server field and in database ACLs. The default is No.
Check passwords on Notes IDs	If you Enable this field, Notes will check a user's password against the password digest that is stored in the Person document in the Domino Directory during authentication. The default is Disabled.
Only allow server access to users listed in this Directory	If you set this field to No, users who do not have Person documents in this Domino Directory, and all servers, are denied access to the server. To enable access to servers, place the users' and servers' names in the Access this server field. This field enables you to deny access to users from other organizations and domains. The default is No.
Access Server	If you leave this field blank, all users except those who are listed in the Not Access Server field can access the server. You can place users, servers, groups, and hierarchical organizations with a wild card (such as */Remote/Acme) in this field.
Not Access Server	If you leave this field blank, all users can access the server. Use this field to deny access to users, servers, groups, and hierarchical organizations with a wild card (such as */Remote/Acme).
Create New Databases	If you leave this field blank, all users who can access the server can create new databases on the server. Add users, servers, groups, and hierarchical organizations with a wild card (such as */Remote/Acme) to limit access to those who are listed.
Create Replica databases	If you leave this field blank, no users can create replica databases on the server. Add users, servers, groups, and hierarchical organizations with a wild card (such as */Remote/Acme) to give access to those who are listed.

TIP You can view expiration dates for certificates by using the Certification Log (CERTLOG.NSF).

You can also enable and deny access to a server over a particular port by using the NOTES.INI settings *Allow_Access_port* and *Deny_Access_port*.

Connectivity

Another aspect of accessing a server is the connectivity to the server. Connectivity to a server is based on a physical network or dial-up connection, the appropriate protocols and name resolution, and server authentication and access (as described previously).

For either a network or dial-up connection, you must ensure that Notes has the proper ports and protocols configured. For network connections, you can use protocols such as NetBIOS, IPX/SPX, and *Transfer Control Protocol/Internet Protocol* (TCP/IP). TCP/IP is becoming increasingly common, because it is required for certain tasks such as HTTP and the *Internet Cluster Manager* (ICM) and enables servers and clients to communicate over the Internet. For a dial-up connection, Notes uses the X.PC protocol and a COM port.

Remember that you can configure ports by using the Server . . . Setup Ports tool from the Server . . . Status tab in Domino Administrator. You can trace connectivity by using the File . . . Preferences . . . User Preferences dialog box. Select the Ports panel and click Trace . . . , and use the Trace button on this dialog box (shown in Figure 1-30) to trace a connection to a server. Use the Notes Log options drop-down list to determine how much of the trace information is written to the Notes Log on that machine.

Use the Ports tab on the Server document to configure both Notes and Internet ports. On the Notes Network ports tab, shown in Figure 1-31, you can list the enabled ports and what protocols they are using, as well as a network address (such as an IP address) and a *Domino Named Network* (DNN).

On the Internet Ports tab, you can configure the *Secure Sockets Layer* (SSL) as well as ports for Web (HTTP), News (NNTP), Mail (POP3 and IMAP), and IIOP. Connection documents, described in detail in Chapters 4 and 5, are also important when connecting to other servers for replication or mail routing, because these documents provide port, addressing, and schedule information in order to make the connection.

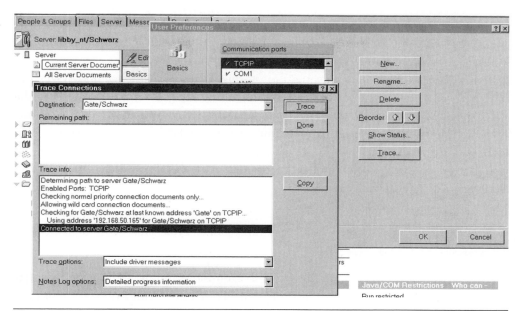

Figure 1-30   Tracing a connection

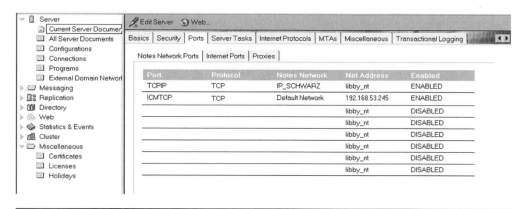

Figure 1-31   Notes Network ports tab

Summary

In this chapter, we discussed the tools that Domino provides for monitoring and maintaining your systems and servers. You learned about the log file and how to maintain it. You also learned about managing and monitoring agents by using Agent Manager and the Agent Logs. We discussed server tasks, including how to send commands to the tasks, monitor the tasks, and stop and start the tasks. This chapter also described some of the requirements for connectivity to Domino servers. Without the correct port/protocol configuration and the appropriate access, you will not be able to connect. Bear in mind that each of the requirements that are discussed in this chapter can be used as troubleshooting techniques.

Review Questions

1. Rachel wants to use the Folder tools in Domino Administrator to create a new replica of her application on Server1/Acme. Which of the following elements does she need in order to accomplish this task?
    A. Her name must be in the Access this Server field for Server1, or she will not be able to access the server at all.
    B. Her name must be in the Create New Databases field for Server1.
    C. Her name must be in the Create Replica Databases field for Server1.
    D. She must have Manager access to the application.

2. Jack wants to administer Server1 from a remote console session. Which of the following elements does he need in order to accomplish this task?
    A. His name must be in the Administrator field for Server1.
    B. His name must be in the Access this Server field for Server1, or he will not be able to access the server at all.
    C. His name must be in the Administer this Server from a Browser field for Server1.
    D. He must be listed as a manager of the Domino Directory.

3. Heidi wants to run a `Show Tasks` command and capture the output in a file for later use. Which of the following commands does she type?
    A. `Show Tasks >c:\files\showtasks.txt`
    B. `Show Tasks <c:\files\showtasks.txt`
    C. `Tell Show Tasks print c:\files\showtasks.txt`
    D. `c:\files\showtasks.txt`

4. Denise wants to run a `Show Tasks` command and other commands from a batch file. Which of the following commands does she type?
   A. `Show Tasks >c:\files\showtasks.txt`
   B. `Show Tasks <c:\files\showtasks.txt`
   C. `Tell Show Tasks print c:\files\showtasks.txt`
   D. `<c:\files\showtasks.txt`

5. Which task needs to be running on a server in order to gather statistics reports about that server?
   A. Event
   B. Report
   C. Collect
   D. Stats

6. Which of the following databases must exist on your server before you can rename users with AdminP?
   A. CERTLOG.NSF
   B. ADMIN5.NSF
   C. Administration Requests
   D. Administration Monitor

7. You have run AdminP in order to rename a user. That user used to have Designer access to DB1.NSF, but since the rename, the user only has the Default access: Reader. The user's name is changed in the Domino Directory and in the groups in the Domino Directory. What might be the problem?
   A. There is no Administration server for the Domino Directory.
   B. There is no Administration server for DB1.NSF.
   C. There is no CERTLOG.NSF.
   D. You have to approve a change of name in the ACL of databases request by using the Administration Requests database.

8. The Certifier ID for your Organization is about to expire. What do you do?
   A. Create a new Organization certifier. Use the new certifier to recertify the original CERT.ID.
   B. Create a new Organization certifier. Use the new certifier to recertify all of the users and servers in your Organization.
   C. Recertify the Organization certifier by using the C certifier.
   D. Recertify the Organization certifier by using itself.

9. In the following NOTES.INI setting, how many days are entries in the log file kept?

   `LOG=log.nsf,1,5,20000`

   A. 1
   B. 5
   C. 20,000
   D. 7, the default

10. Your Notes name is Joe Smith/Remote/Acme. You are trying to access the server Server2/Zoom. What do you need to do?
    A. Recertify Joe Smith with the /Zoom certifier.
    B. Enable Joe to access Server2/Zoom by using the Access this Server fielD.
    C. Create cross-certificates for /Zoom and /Acme.
    D. Create cross-certificates for /Zoom and /Remote/Acme.

Review Answers

1. **C is correct.** Rachel's name needs to be in the Create Replica Databases field on the server document.

2. **A is correct.** Jack's name must be in the Administrator's field in order for him to use the remote console.

3. **A is correct.** This command (`Show Tasks >c:\files\showtasks.txt`) will run Show Tasks and will place its results in the file listed.

4. **D is correct.** She can run the batch file by typing the name of the file after a less-than sign (<).

5. **C is correct.** In R5, you need the Collect task in order to gather statistics reports from a server.

6. **A and C are correct.** You need the Administration Requests database (`ADMIN4.NSF`) and the Certification Log (CERTLOG.NSF).

7. **B is correct.** If no administration server was listed for DB1.NSF, the database will not receive the name changes.

8. **D is correct.** You can recertify a certifier ID with itself in order to change the expiration date and the password-quality requirements (and to add an alternate language).

9. **B is correct.** The entries will be kept for 5 days.

10. **Either C or D** is a good answer, depending on how much access you want users of /Zoom to have in /Acme.

Advanced Domino and Web Servers

You should be able to answer questions based on the following objectives after reading this chapter:

- Monitoring, maintaining, and troubleshooting Domino servers
- Monitoring/maintaining Web services
- Troubleshooting clustering problems
- Troubleshooting partitioning problems

Domino Servers with an Enterprise, or Advanced, license might use clustering and/or partitioning. In addition, you might be using a Domino server as a Web server. This exam requires a knowledge of troubleshooting clustering and partitioning. You must also know how to monitor, maintain, and customize Web services in Domino. For more information about configuring the services that are described in this chapter, refer to Chapter 7.

Clustering

Clustering allows for failover and load balancing for Domino servers. In a cluster, two or more (up to six) servers contain replicas of the same databases and replicate those databases on a change-initiated (event) basis, rather than on a scheduled basis. Then, if one server goes out of service, another server in the cluster can provide service to the users for failover. For load balancing, databases that are highly used can be spread among clustered servers, which can be configured to send client connections to other servers in the cluster when they become too busy. Clusters have also been extended to the Web clients by using the *Internet Cluster Manager* (ICM). Using an ICM (which must be within the same domain as the cluster, although it can be inside or outside the cluster itself), Web clients can be failed over when a server that serves *Hypertext Transport Protocol* (HTTP) is out of service.

You configure a cluster by adding servers to the cluster using the Domino Directory. The servers in the cluster must communicate via the same protocol. In many cases, you might use a separate network for the intra-cluster communication, such as probes and cluster replication. Monitoring a cluster requires ensuring that the cluster members are functioning and that databases are available—and, in some cases, adding or removing servers from a cluster. You might also need to troubleshoot clustering problems.

Statistics and Logs

One way to monitor clusters is to use the statistics for clusters. You can see the cluster statistics in Domino Administrator's Server . . . Statistics tab, under Server . . . Clusters. In addition, you can type SHOW STAT SERVER.CLUSTER.* and SHOW STAT REPLICA.CLUSTER.* at the server console to see the statistics. You can also type SHOW CLUSTER at the server console to see the name of the cluster as well as cluster members and their availability, as shown in Figure 2-1.

You can also view log events that are related to cluster replication. By default, the cluster replicator creates replication log entries once per hour. You can view these entries in the Notes Log in the Replication Events view, as shown in Figure 2-2. You can also force the cluster replicator to generate a log entry at any time by typing TELL

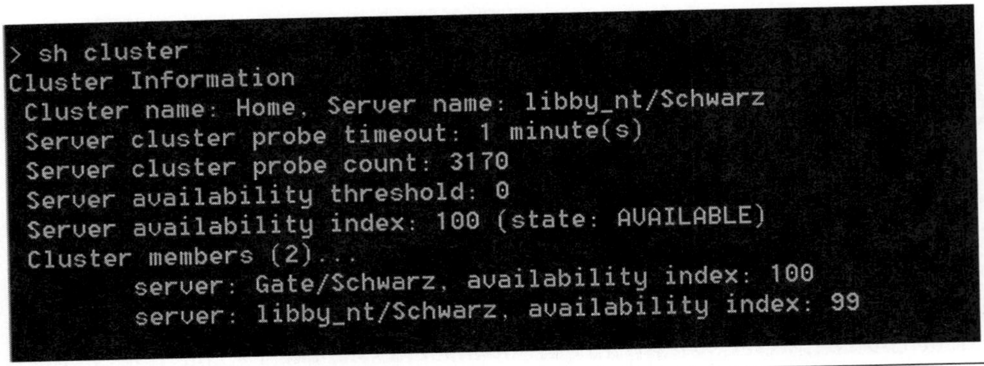

```
> sh cluster
Cluster Information
 Cluster name: Home, Server name: libby_nt/Schwarz
 Server cluster probe timeout: 1 minute(s)
 Server cluster probe count: 3170
 Server availability threshold: 0
 Server availability index: 100 (state: AVAILABLE)
 Cluster members (2)...
        server: Gate/Schwarz, availability index: 100
        server: libby_nt/Schwarz, availability index: 99
```

Figure 2-1   Server cluster statistics

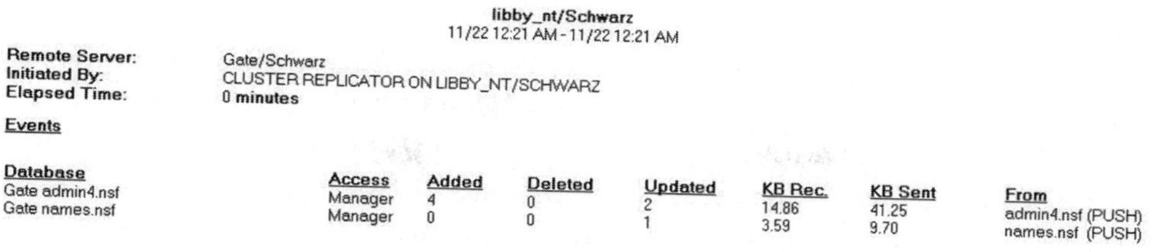

Figure 2-2   Cluster replication entries in the Notes Log

CLREPL LOG at the server console. This action generates a log entry that describes the events since the last cluster replication log.

Restricting the Server

Part of working with clusters involves configuring the server-availability threshold or the maximum users on the server to help with workload balancing. When you type the SHOW CLUSTER command, you see the server-availability index—a number from zero to 100 indicating how available a server is, with 100 being completely available. If a server becomes extremely busy, this number drops. If you want a user to be redirected to another server when this number becomes too low, you can set a server-availability threshold. By default, this number is zero. If you set the server-availability threshold to 60, for example, when the server's availability index reaches 60, the server will be marked BUSY and users will be redirected to other servers in the cluster (as long as they are available). If no other server in the cluster is available, the busy server will still service the request. To set a server-availability threshold, you can add the following line to the NOTES.INI file:

```
Server_availablility_threshold=number
```

If you set the availability threshold to 100, the server will automatically be in a BUSY state. You can also set a maximum number of active users on a server by using the SERVER_MAXUSERS= line in the NOTES.INI file. While replication will continue to occur even if a server has reached the maximum number of concurrent users, no new user requests will be serviced until some users disconnect.

Another way to force a server to redirect requests is to use the Server_ Restricted= setting in the NOTES.INI file. If you set this value to one, the server is restricted until it is restarted, and no new users can access the server. Users who are currently connected when you change the setting will not be disconnected. If you set this value to two, the server is restricted until you change the setting to zero.

Cluster Replication

Cluster replication is event driven, rather than schedule driven. Cluster replication is performed by the Cluster Replicator task, or CLREPL. You must have at least one CLREPL task in the `ServerTasks=` line in the NOTES.INI file in order for cluster replication to occur. You might decide to start more than one cluster replicator if databases are often waiting to be cluster replicated (look at the Replica.Cluster. WorkQueueDepth statistic).

For cluster replication to occur correctly, you must have a consistent ACL for the servers in the cluster. This goal can be accomplished by using the Enforce Consistent ACL setting for a database or by creating a group to contain the servers in the cluster. This group should be configured to have the ServerGroup type in the ACL, in order to ensure that private folders are replicated throughout the cluster. In addition, users should have consistent access to the databases and servers in the cluster, so that when failover or load balancing occurs, users have access to necessary data.

Next, databases in clusters should also be replicated via standard, scheduled replication. Occasionally, when the cluster replicator is busy or if a server is out of service for a time, changes might be missed by the cluster replicator. A scheduled replication can ensure that the databases stay synchronized.

Finally, you can enable or disable cluster replication for a specific database by using the Cluster Database Directory (CLDBDIR.NSF). This database exists in each member of a cluster and contains a list of all databases on the servers, which you can view by path name, replica ID, or server. The document that describes each database lists the server, file name, title, replica ID, and whether cluster replication is enabled or disabled, whether the database is in or out of service, and whether the database is marked for delete, as shown in Figure 2-3.

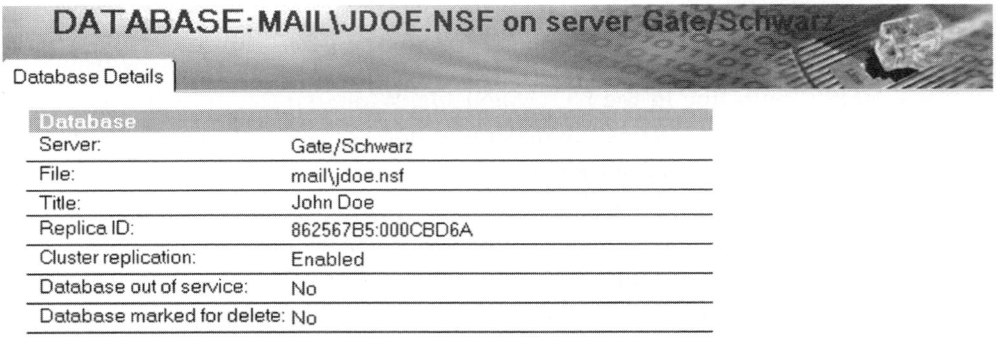

DATABASE: MAIL\JDOE.NSF on server Gate/Schwarz

Database Details

Database	
Server:	Gate/Schwarz
File:	mail\jdoe.nsf
Title:	John Doe
Replica ID:	862567B5:000CBD6A
Cluster replication:	Enabled
Database out of service:	No
Database marked for delete:	No

Figure 2-3   Database document in CLDBDIR.NSF

Cluster Directory (R5)	Tools... ▼					
Databases by Pa	Enable Cluster Replication on Selected Databases			Replica ID	Cluster Replication	▲ Out of Se
Databases by Re	Disable Cluster Replication on Selected Databases			C125650C:00636E18	Enabled	No
Databases by Se				C125650C:00636E18	Enabled	No
	★	mail50.ntf	libby_nt	85255B9E:0043AB03	Enabled	No
	★	mailbox.ntf	brian_ent	85255B9E:0043AB03	Enabled	No
	★	mailbox.ntf	Gate	85255B9E:0043AB03	Enabled	No
	★	mailbox.ntf	libby_nt		Enabled	No

Figure 2-4   Enabling or disabling cluster replication for a database

In any of the views, you can use the Tools action button to enable or disable cluster replication, as shown in Figure 2-4.

Database Availability

Earlier, we mentioned the availability of servers and how you can affect this availability by changing certain NOTES.INI settings. Similarly, you can configure the availability of specific databases to determine whether they are in service, out of service, or pending delete. To change these properties, use the Files tab of Domino Administrator. Select the database, and expand the Database tools. Select the Cluster tool.

When you mark a database out of service, users will be failed over to another replica when they make a request for this database. If a user is currently in the database, he or she continues to use the database until the database is closed. The user is then failed over the next time that he or she makes a request to open the database. If no other replicas of the database are available, users are denied access to the database. When you want to restore a database to service after marking it out of service, mark it In Service.

You might decide to delete a database from a cluster member. If you want to wait until all active users have completed their work in the database, you can mark the database as Pending Delete. Similar to marking a database out of service, this setting ensures that no new requests for the database are allowed, but it does *not* drop current users. After all users have closed their connections, a final replication of the database is completed—and the database is deleted.

Adding and Removing Servers
in a Cluster

You might need to add a server to or remove a server from a cluster. This task should be accomplished by using the Administration process. The easiest way to add a server to a cluster is to use the Add to Cluster action button, which is available in the All Server Documents view on the Configuration tab in Domino Administrator. Select the server to add to a cluster, and click the action button. After the request is verified, Domino

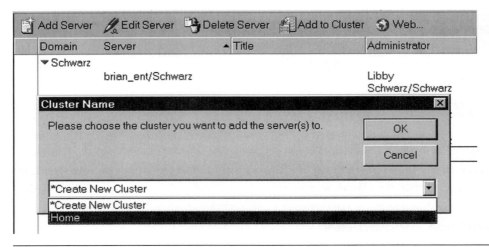

Figure 2-5 Deciding which cluster to join

prompts you to select an existing cluster or create a new cluster, as shown in Figure 2-5. After selecting a cluster, you are prompted to either process the request immediately or to wait for the Administration Process to process the request based on the default timings of the requests.

To remove a server from a cluster, use the Cluster view on the Configuration tab in Domino Administrator. Select the cluster and server and click the Remove from Cluster action button. You will have to confirm the request and decide whether to process the request immediately or to wait for the Administration Process to process the request based on the default timings of the requests.

Internet Cluster Manager (ICM)

ICM is new to R5 and enables Web clients to participate in clustering. Previously, only Notes clients could use the clustering features of Notes and Domino. The ICM (similar to clustering in general) requires the Enterprise Server license for the servers that are involved. The ICM server directs HTTP requests to the appropriate server in a cluster, based on availability. The ICM can run on a server in or out of the cluster, and you can also run multiple ICMs. Regardless, the ICM must be in the same Domino domain as the cluster, because the Domino Directory is necessary in order for the ICM to function.

If you run the ICM on a Web server (probably a member of the cluster), you will need either a separate IP address or a separate port for the ICM. The HTTP service and the ICM cannot both communicate over the default, which is port 80.

Partitioning

Partitioning enables you to run more than one Domino server on a single machine. All of the partitioned servers use the same program directory and files but have their own data directory (Domino Directory) and NOTES.INI file. You obtain the most benefit from running partitioned servers when you are running multiple domains.

Each partitioned server either needs its own IP address (you must use TCP/IP to use partitioned servers) or its own port number. If you elect to use a single IP address with multiple port numbers, you are *port mapping*. In this scenario, one of the partitioned servers responds to requests over port 1352 (the default Notes port) and forwards client requests to other servers based on port settings you add to that server's NOTES.INI file. The server that forwards these requests (the port-mapping server) should not be serving any other major functions. If you elect to give each server its own IP address, Notes and Web clients can access the individual servers directly. Note that if you use port mapping and the port-mapping server is unavailable, clients might not be able to connect to any of the partitioned servers.

Web Servers

Domino provides a Web server that can display, or serve, Domino databases as HTML. This action is performed via the HTTP task on the Domino server. Any Domino application (single database or multi-database) or HTML page can be served as HTML. The Domino Web server also supports Java applets, JavaScript, and CGI programs. In addition to making multiple Domino applications available on a single server, you can create virtual servers that enable you to use different host names on a single server.

The Domino Web server is configured by starting the HTTP task on the server. You can add the HTTP task to the `ServerTasks=` line in the NOTES.INI file, type LOAD HTTP at the server console, or start the task by using the Domino Administrator Server . . . Status tab. To start the HTTP task using Domino Administrator, open the Server . . . Status tab, expand the Task tools, and choose Start. Select the HTTP Web Server task from the Start New Task dialog box, and click the Start Task button.

Customizing HTTP

You will also need to configure and customize how the HTTP server communicates and works by using the Server document for this server. You can open the Server document by using the Configuration tab of Domino Administrator. First, determine the port and type of security by using the Ports . . . Internet Ports . . . Web tab, as shown in Figure 2-6.

	Web (HTTP/HTTPS)
TCP/IP port number:	80
TCP/IP port status:	Enabled
Authentication options:	
Name & password:	Yes
Anonymous:	Yes
SSL port number:	443
SSL port status:	Enabled
Authentication options:	
Client certificate:	No
Name & password:	Yes
Anonymous:	Yes

Figure 2-6 Web port

By default, HTTP communicates over port 80; HTTPS (which is HTTP that uses the Secure Sockets Layer) communicates over port 443. For normal connections, make sure that port 80 is enabled. To force connections to take place over the SSL port, disable or redirect port 80 and enable port 443. To force connections over a different port number (which will require users to know the port to communicate over), change port 80 to a different port number. You can also determine which client authentication options are allowed over this port—name and password or anonymous. Client certificate is also available for SSL connections over HTTPS. Name and password authentication requires a Person document with an Internet password in the Domino Directory or a secondary directory (refer to Chapter 3, "Domino Directories, Users, and Groups"). Anonymous connections will not require authentication to connect, but you must allow Anonymous access to databases as necessary.

Next, you can configure how HTTP works by using the Internet Protocols . . . HTTP tab, as shown in Figure 2-7.

The fields that are available for configuring and customizing the HTTP server via the HTTP tab are described in Tables 2-1, 2-2, 2-3, 2-4, and 2-5. Most of the time, when you make a change to one of the following fields, you must update the HTTP service by restarting it. You can use the command TELL HTTP RESTART at the server console or use the Tell Task tool on the Server . . . Status tab of Domino Administrator, as shown in Figure 2-8.

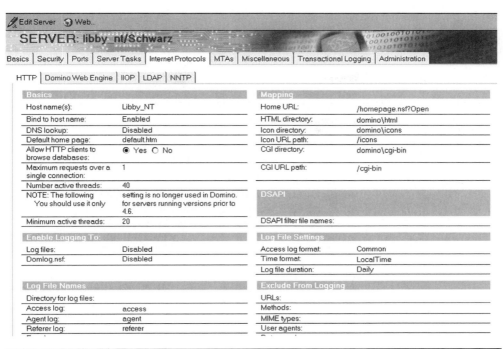

Figure 2-7 HTTP configuration

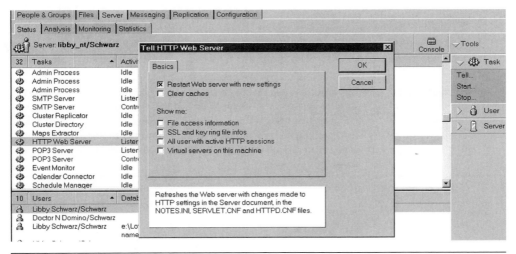

Figure 2-8 Telling the HTTP task to restart

Table 2-1 HTTP Tab Fields (Basics)

Field	Notes
Host name	Enter the host name of the Web server in this field. Entries can include any DNS host names that are registered for the server or the IP address(es) for the server. If you leave the field blank, the system looks up the host name in the TCP/IP settings and defaults to that name. You can have up to 32 entries.
Bind to host name	If you want to use an alias for the Domino Web server, enable this field. An alias enables a single Domino server to respond to multiple names.
DNS lookup	If you want the Domino server logs to list the DNS host names of connecting clients, enable this field. If this field is disabled, the logs only list the IP address of connecting browsers and clients. Enabling this field might affect server performance when looking up the DNS names.
Default home page	The default in this field is `default.htm`. If you create an HTML page called `default.htm` and place it in the \html directory, Web clients will see this page by default when they connect. You can also type a different name in order to use a different HTML page as the home page. You should clear the Home URL field if you want the contents of this field to be used, because the Home URL field takes precedence if both fields are completed.
Allow HTTP clients to browse databases	If this field is enabled, Web clients can use the OpenServer URL command (e.g., `www.notesgirl.com/?OpenServer`) to see a list of all of the databases on the server, as shown in Figure 2-9. If you are using virtual servers, and for greater security, this field should probably be disabled.
Maximum requests over a single connection	This field indicates the number of requests that a single browser connection can make to the Web server simultaneously. The default is one.
Number active threads	This field indicates the maximum number of active threads that the Web server will process at a time. A thread is usually equivalent to the number of clients that are accessing the server simultaneously. The default is 40. When the Web server reaches this number of threads, subsequent requests are placed in a queue and are processed when threads become available.

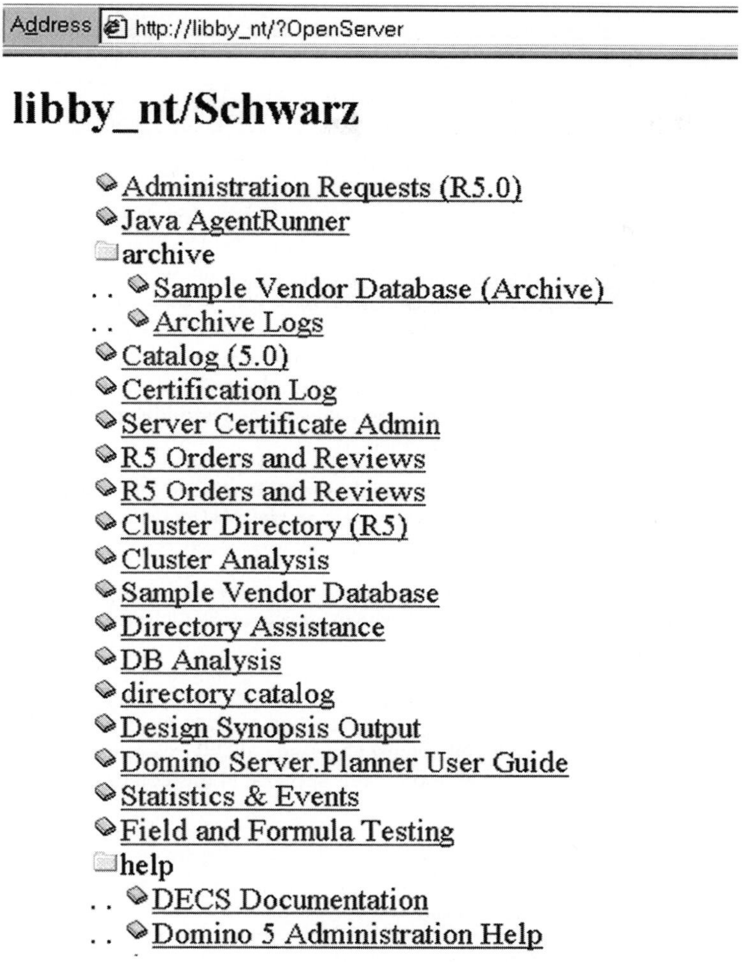

Address 🖉 http://libby_nt/?OpenServer

libby_nt/Schwarz

◈ Administration Requests (R5.0)
◈ Java AgentRunner
▭ archive
. . ◈ Sample Vendor Database (Archive)
. . ◈ Archive Logs
◈ Catalog (5.0)
◈ Certification Log
◈ Server Certificate Admin
◈ R5 Orders and Reviews
◈ R5 Orders and Reviews
◈ Cluster Directory (R5)
◈ Cluster Analysis
◈ Sample Vendor Database
◈ Directory Assistance
◈ DB Analysis
◈ directory catalog
◈ Design Synopsis Output
◈ Domino Server.Planner User Guide
◈ Statistics & Events
◈ Field and Formula Testing
▭ help
. . ◈ DECS Documentation
. . ◈ Domino 5 Administration Help

Figure 2-9   Browsing databases

Table 2-2 HTTP Tab Fields (Mapping)

Field	Notes
Home URL	By default, the Domino Web server runs the `/homepage.nsf/?Open-Database URL` command when browser clients contact the server. This action opens the `homepage.nsf` database but does not display the URL command to the browser—only the URL address appears (such as `http://www.notesgirl.com`). If you remove the leading slash (/), the URL command will be written to the browser address field. You can change the contents of this field to control which URL command occurs when clients contact the server. If you type an entire URL, such as `http://www.lotus.com`, the browser request is redirected to that URL. An example of a URL that you might type is `/mywebsite.nsf/$About?OpenAbout`, in order to open the About document of the `mywebsite.nsf` database without returning the URL command to the browser. If both this field and the Default Home Page field are completed, this field takes precedence.
HTML directory	The Domino Web server automatically looks for HTML files in this directory. The default is domino\html. If you do not want to store HTML files in this directory, change this field.
Icon directory	The Domino Web server automatically looks for icon files in this directory. The default is domino\icons. If you do not want to store icon files in this directory, change this field.
Icon URL path	This path is the URL path that takes you to the icons on the server. This path is especially useful if you change the directory location of icons and you have URL references to them in your HTML. Simply place the old URL reference in this field and move the files to the location that is specified in the icon directory field.
CGI directory	The Domino Web server automatically looks for CGI program files in this directory. The default is domino\cgi-bin. If you do not want to store CGI program files in this directory, change this field.
CGI URL path	This path is the URL path that takes you to the CGI program files on the server. This path is especially useful if you change the directory location of CGI program files and you have URL references to them in your HTML. Simply place the old URL reference in this field and move the files to the location that is specified in the CGI directory field.

This section describes the Web log files. You should periodically remove or archive old log files in order to save space on your server.

Table 2-3 HTTP Tab Fields (Logging, Log File Settings, Log File Names, and Exclude from Logging)

Field	Notes
Log files	Enable this field to configure the Web server to record log information in text files. Logs include access log, agent log, referrer log, error log, and CGI error log. This method is a faster way of logging than logging to the domlog.nsf.
Domlog.nsf	Enable this field to configure the Web server to record log information in a database called domlog.nsf.
Access log format	Choose Common in this field in order to log information into separate text files, using the common log file format (if the Log files field is enabled). Choose Extended Common to log using the extended log file format. The format for the log files is standardized, based on the specifications of the *World Wide Web Consortium* (W3C). You can find more information about the W3C and log files at `www.w3.org/tr/wd-logfile.html`.
Time format	Set this field to Local Time to record activity in the log files by using the local time zone that is currently set on the server. Set this field to GMT to use Greenwich Mean Time when recording activity.
Log file duration	Use this field to determine when a new log file should be created. Choices include daily, weekly, monthly, and never. Never creates one log file. Monthly creates a new log file each month; weekly creates a new log file each week; and daily creates a new log file each day (at midnight). The filenames use the numeric date information and the filename prefix (from the following fields) to create the filename. For example, a monthly file that is created for November 1999 for the access log would be called `access-log 111999.log`.
Directory for log files	You can use this field to specify a directory for the log files. By default, the field is blank—and the Web server stores the log files in the data directory.
Access log	By default, this field specifies that the Access Log will be named with the prefix access-log.
Agent log	By default, this field specifies that the Agent Log will be named with the prefix Agent-log.
Referer log	By default, this field specifies that the Referer Log will be named with the prefix Referer-log.
Error log	By default, Error specifies that the Error Log will be named with the prefix Error-log.
CGI error log	By default, CGI-error specifies that the CGI Error Log will be named with the prefix CGI-error-log.
URLs	Use this field to exclude certain URLs from logging, such as `/mydirectory/*`.
Methods	Use this field to exclude certain methods from logging, such as POST.

(continued)

Table 2-3 HTTP Tab Fields (Logging, Log File Settings, Log File Names, and Exclude from Logging) *(continued)*

Field	Notes
MIME types	Use this field to exclude certain MIME types from logging.
User agents	Use this field to exclude certain user agents from logging.
Return codes	Use this field to exclude certain return codes from logging, such as 403,300.
Hosts and domains	Use this field to exclude certain DNS host names or IP addresses from logging, such as .org or 192.199.*. To use DNS names, make sure to enable the DNS lookup option.

Table 2-4 HTTP Tab Fields (Timeouts)

Field	Notes
Input timeout	This setting, which is especially important when older browser versions are connecting to your server, closes a connection if the client does not send a request within a certain number of minutes after connecting to the server. The default is 2 minutes. If the client connects and then does not send a request within 2 minutes, the server drops the connection in order to enable other connections to be made.
Output timeout	This setting indicates the number of minutes that the Web server can take to send output (pages) in response to client requests. The default is 20 minutes. This field does not apply to CGI programs. If the server does not send the output in 20 minutes, the connection is dropped.
CGI timeout	This field indicates the number of minutes that are necessary for a CGI program (that is started by the Web server) to complete. When the limit is reached (5 minutes is the default), the server sends a warning message to the CGI program, waits 5 minutes, and then shuts down the program.

Table 2-5 HTTP Tab Fields (Web Agents)

Field	Notes
Run Web agents concurrently	This setting, which was previously set by a NOTES.INI variable called DomionAsynchronizeAgents=, determines whether agents that are triggered by browser clients run one at a time (also called serially) or concurrently (also called asynchronously). You should choose Enabled to run agents concurrently.
Web agent timeout (in seconds)	Sets the maximum number of seconds that an agent that is triggered by a browser client can take to run before the server shuts it down.

Other configuration options for the Domino Web server are contained in other fields of the Server document or in other documents. Some other options are described as follows:

- You can make Domino Web sites more accessible to being cataloged by Web site search crawlers by enabling the *Make this site accessible to web site search crawlers* option on the Internet Protocols . . . Domino Web engine tab of the Server document. This option changes what the Domino server uses when generating pages from a question mark (?), which is usually used in Domino URLs, to an exclamation point (!). Many Web crawlers that are used to create search engines do not accept the question mark, in that they ignore everything past the question mark in the URL.

- When Web clients download a file from a page or in a server directory, Domino includes the capability for clients that support this functionality to use byte-range serving. Byte-range serving (which is available as of HTTP 1.1) enables a client to download a file in sections (i.e., ranges of bytes), rather than as a single file. In other words, if something happens to stop the download, clients resume the download where they stopped, rather than having to start over. You do not have to enable byte-range serving; if you are using a client that supports this functionality, Domino automatically uses byte-range serving.

- You can improve the performance of Web clients by enabling Domino to cache some commands, designs, and users. On the Server document's Internet Protocols . . . Domino Web Engine tab, you can configure how many of each of these elements to cache and for how long. Loading, converting, looking up, and mapping each of these elements takes time—and this process is avoided when the element is cached.

- You can improve the performance of Web sites that use graphics on the pages (not referenced through pass-thru HTML) using progressive or interlaced rendering. You can use either .GIF or .JPG formats for graphics from the Domino Web Server. Select the format to which you want to convert your graphic by using the Conversion/Display section of the Internet Protocols . . . Domino Web Engine tab of the Server document. The default graphic type, .GIF, enables interlaced rendering, which displays each line of the image individually (therefore showing the page more quickly). When interlaced rendering is disabled, the entire image has to download before any part of the image is displayed. Similarly, the other supported graphic format, .JPG, supports progressive rendering, which displays the graphic in several passes (the image is added to and clarified at each pass). When progressive rendering is disabled, the entire image has to download before any part of the image is displayed.

- To determine how many lines will appear in a view on the Web, use the *Default Lines per view page* setting in the Internet Protocols . . . Domino Web Engine tab of the server document. By default, 30 lines are displayed. You can set this value from one to 1,000 (or whatever setting you place in the *Maximum lines per view page* field), based on what makes your view easiest to read and navigate.

- You can use the Domino Configuration database (DOMCFG.NSF) to configure customized Web message pages for the Domino server to display when a user fails to authenticate, is not authorized to use a database on the server, or deletes a page. In addition, if you are using session-based authentication, you can also configure a customized login page. To create these customized pages, create a database that is based on the DOMCFG.NTF template. This database tells the Domino Web server to use the customized pages for the specified errors.

Virtual Servers

You might want to host more than one Web site on the same Domino Web server. You can accomplish this goal by using virtual servers, which enable a single Domino Web server (not partitioned) to host multiple Web sites, such as **www.notesgirl.com** and **www.brightrock.com**. The data directory, program files, and Domino Directory are shared when using virtual servers. You can enable each site to have its own IP address, home page, and HTML, CGI, and icons directories.

To configure virtual servers, click the Web . . . action button in the Server Documents view and select the Create Virtual Server action.

You can choose between a virtual host and a virtual server. A virtual host is an alias for a Web site that enables a single IP address to respond to multiple DNS names.

In the Virtual Hostname document, type the host name to which you want the server to respond. You can set a default home page for the virtual host that is different from the default home page that is configured in the Server document. Similarly, you can configure different mapping settings and security requirements.

In the Virtual Server document, set an IP address, host name, and default home page. Note that a virtual server can have its own IP address or can share an IP address and have a unique host name. You can also configure a different default home page, mapping settings, and security requirements for each virtual server. When you configure a virtual host or a virtual server, you need to restart the HTTP task in order for the changes to take effect. You can also obtain information about virtual servers that are configured on your system by using the Tell Task tool, which is available from the Server . . . Status tab of Domino Administrator. In the Tell HTTP Web Server dialog box, you can ask the Web server to display all virtual servers that are configured on the machine, as shown in

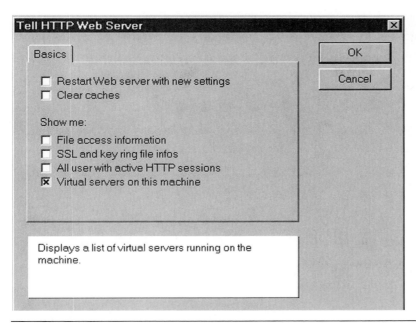

Figure 2-10   TELL HTTP WEB SERVER SHOW VIRTUAL SERVERS

Figure 2-10. This action is the equivalent of typing TELL HTTP SHOW VIRTUAL SERVERS at the server console.

Remapping and Redirecting

At times, you might need to move a Web site that is contained in a database from one server or host name to another. Obviously, you will want to be sure that you do not break all of the links; you also probably do not want to recreate all of the Virtual Server or Server documents. Remapping and redirecting enable you to move an application and to redirect users to the new location when they access the old location. Redirecting transfers users to the new location and displays the new URL in the browser. Remapping transfers users without displaying the new URL. To remap or redirect a URL or a directory, create a Mapping/Redirection document in the Domino Directory. While in the Server Documents view on the Configuration tab, select the Web action button and choose Create URL Mapping/Redirection, as shown in Figure 2-11.

The first choice in the Mapping/Redirection document indicates whether you want to map a URL to a directory, to a redirection URL, or to another URL. If you map a URL to a URL, you can create alias names for long, awkward filenames, and you can move or

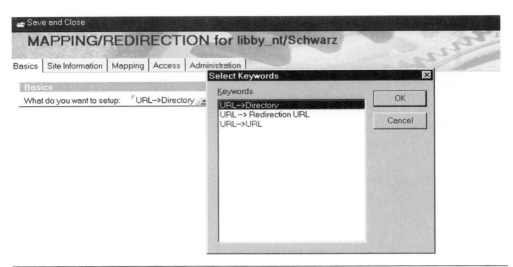

Figure 2-11 Create URL Mapping/Redirection

rename directories or files without breaking links or shortcuts that users might have for the files. The mapped URL is not displayed to the user. If you choose to map a URL to a different directory, you are renaming or moving directories without changing the URL that the user types or sees. If you choose to redirect a URL to another URL, you can map any incoming URL to another URL. Unlike remapping a URL, you can use this feature for elements inside a database, such as a page in a database. The new URL is displayed to the user.

After choosing the type of redirection/mapping, complete the IP address or host name for the site on the Site Information tab. If you leave this field blank, any virtual servers on the site will be affected. Use the mapping tab to indicate the incoming URL and the redirection/remapping that you want to occur.

For the URL to directory mapping, you can also choose which type of access that browser users should have to the directory. Set Execute access when directories contain CGI files or other programs that need to be run. Set Read access when directories contain HTML or graphics files that only users need to see. You must restart the HTTP task for redirection/remapping to take effect (you can use the `Tell HTTP Restart` command).

Web Authentication

Web users can be either anonymous or authenticated. When Web users are anonymous, you must first enable anonymous connections over the port, as shown in Figure 2-12,

(HTTP/HTTPS)	
TCP/IP port number:	80
TCP/IP port status:	Enabled
Authentication options:	
Name & password:	Yes
Anonymous:	Yes

Figure 2-12   TCP/IP port authentication options

in the Ports . . . Internet Ports . . . Web tab of the Server document. Here, you can also choose whether users can be authenticated by using Name and Password authentication.

Next, you can select various authentication options on the Server . . . Security tab. In the Web Server access section, decide whether Web authentication will have More name variations and less security or Fewer name variations and more security, as shown in Figure 2-13. When you choose less security, Domino can authenticate users based on last name, first name, common name, canonical name, hierarchical name (abbreviated), short name, or alias name. If the user types the name that is contained in any of these columns in the $Users view, with the correct Internet password, the user will be authenticated. When you choose more security, Domino requires the full hierarchical name, the common name, or an alias name. When using name and

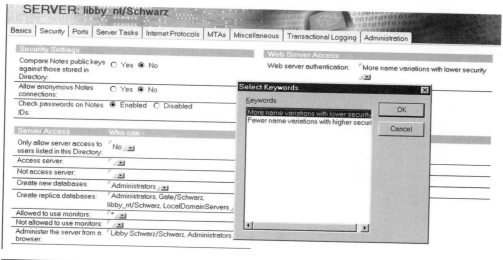

Figure 2-13   Determining the level of security for Web authentication

password authentication, each user must have a name and an Internet password specified in a Person document in the Domino Directory or in a secondary directory (Domino or LDAP) with Directory assistance configured.

With name and password authentication, you can apply normal options to the ACL for databases. With Anonymous authentication, you should ensure that you have an Anonymous entry in the ACL. Without this entry, users who have not been authenticated over the Web receive the ACL level that is given to the Default access. With this entry, Web users who have not authenticated will use the ACL level that is assigned to Anonymous. With the ACL, you can also set the *Maximum Internet name and password* field on the Advanced tab, as shown in Figure 2-14. This setting limits the access that any Web user can gain to the database. If Scott has Editor access in the ACL, for example, but the *Maximum Internet name and password* is set to Reader, Scott will only have Reader access when using the database over the Web.

Note that when you configure the name and password access, Domino will force users to authenticate when they try to do something that you have given restricted access to, when session-based authentication is enabled, or when Anonymous access is

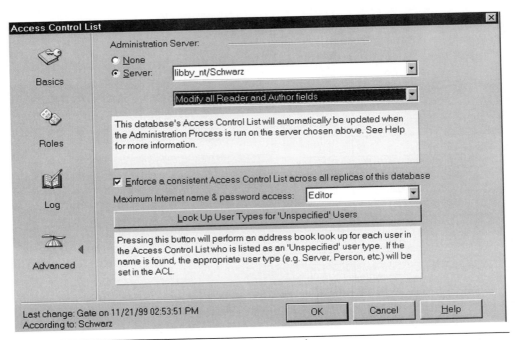

Figure 2-14 Maximum Internet name and password

not enabled on the server. If Anonymous access is enabled on the server, the user will not be forced to log in until he or she tries to access a database that is restricted (or until he or she tries to execute an action that is restricted). If Katie has Editor access to a database that also has an Anonymous entry that is given Reader access, for example, she will not be prompted to log in just to read the documents. She will have to log in when she tries to create a new document or edit a document that already exists in the database, because these actions are not permitted under Reader access.

Session-based authentication adds additional security to the basic name and password authentication. A *session* is defined as the period during which a browser client is logged in to the Domino server. To configure the additional security options that are available, use the Server document under the Internet Protocols . . . Domino Web Engine tab, as shown in Figure 2-15.

When the *Session Authentication* field is enabled, you can also specify the following items:

- You can log out idle users in a specified number of minutes by using the *Idle Session timeout* field. The default is 30 minutes.

- You can limit the maximum number of user sessions by using the *Maximum active sessions* field. The default is 1,000 sessions.

To use session authentication, the browsers that are used by the Web clients must permit cookies, which are used to track the user sessions.

NOTE Prior to R5.0.5. session-based authentication could only be usd for a single server. In R5.0.5 and newer, sessions can be tracked across multiple servers.

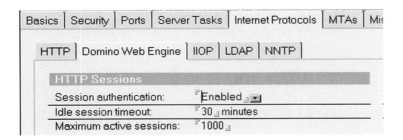

Figure 2-15 Session authentication field

Domino and IIS

Using Domino and Microsoft's *Internet Information Server* (IIS) concurrently is new to R5. IIS can process the browser-client requests for Domino applications. All URL requests that are directed toward the server go to the IIS server. The IIS server then passes requests for Domino applications (database files with .NSF extensions) to the Domino server. When you use this combination, do not run the HTTP task over port 80 on the Domino server, because a conflict will occur. To make this configuration work, you use the *Domino Internet Server Application Programming Interface* (DISAPI) extension, which is included with the Domino Server installation files. You will use the *Microsoft Management Console* (MMC), which is a management application that is used with IIS, to complete the configuration of the DISAPI.

An important aspect of the configuration is the security settings. You can use Anonymous access, basic authentication, Windows NT Challenge/Response, and SSL with IIS. When you use Anonymous access, the user can use Domino as either an anonymous user or can supply a name and password in order to use normal Domino security. In Basic Authentication and Windows NT Challenge/Response, IIS authenticates the user and password based on the NT user account. IIS then passes the username to Domino. Domino does not use the Internet password; rather, it assumes that IIS and NT have authenticated the user satisfactorily. Table 2-6 gives some details about the IIS security options and how they affect Domino.

Table 2-6   IIS Security

Option	Notes
Allow Anonymous Access	User does not need to be an NT user. If accessing secured Domino resources, needs a Domino user name and Internet password. This setting is closest to the default Domino security.
Basic Authentication	User must be a registered NT user. User must be a registered Domino user (same username as NT). No Anonymous access to the site; all access must be authenticated by NT/IIS. Does not use the Internet password field in the Person document.
Windows NT Challenge/Response (NTLM)	User must be a registered NT user. Only supported for Microsoft Internet Explorer users. User must be a registered Domino user (same username as NT). Does not use the Internet password field in the Person document.

To use Domino with IIS, you should also complete the related fields on the Internet Protocols . . . Domino Web Engine tab of the Server document. First, configure the server to use IIS by enabling the *Does this server use IIS?* field. Select HTTP or HTTPS as the protocol that IIS will generate to the Domino server. List the host name and port that IIS should use when generating URLs for this server.

Before using IIS with Domino, you should review the Domino Administration help to ensure that all of the features that you need are supported by IIS. Certain features, such as Domino's logging, the ICM, virtual servers, mapping and redirection, and the servlet manager are not supported.

Java Applets and Servlets

The Domino server supports the use of both Java applets and Java servlets. A Java applet is hosted on the Domino server. When the Web client needs the applet, the applet is downloaded from the server to the browser in which it will run. A Java servlet, on the other hand, runs on the server as requested by the Web clients.

To run Java applets on the Domino server, you need both the *Domino Internet Inter-Orb Protocol* (DIIOP) task and the IIOP protocol. These elements enable clients to access the Domino *Object Request Broker* (ORB) program, which processes the applet requests from the browsers. Figure 2-16 shows the Internet Ports . . . IIOP tab of the Server document. Use this tab to configure the IIOP port.

The Internet Protocols . . . IIOP tab, governs the number of threads that the IIOP protocol can use on the server (10 by default) and the timeout after which idle sessions will be disconnected (60 minutes by default).

You might need to configure access for the Java applets. Use the Security tab of the Server document to configure the users who can run restricted and unrestricted Java and JavaScript on the server. If the Restricted field is blank, only users in the Unrestricted field can run Java and JavaScript applets. If the Unrestricted field is also blank, no users can run Java and JavaScript applets. Note that if you plan to enable unauthenticated (i.e., Anonymous) access to the Java and JavaScript applets, include the Anonymous user in these fields.

The use of Java servlets on the Domino Server is configured by using the Internet Protocols . . . Domino Web Engine tab. To enable Java servlet support, choose a support option in the *Java Servlet Support* field. The default, None, does not load either the *Java Virtual Machine* (JVM) or the servlet manager with the HTTP task. Select Domino Servlet Manager in this field to load both the JVM and the servlet manager that comes with Domino. To use a third-party product, such as IBM WebSphere, as the servlet manager, use the Third Party Servlet Support option. You can also configure the servlet path, class path, servlet extensions, timeout threshold, and maximum active sessions.

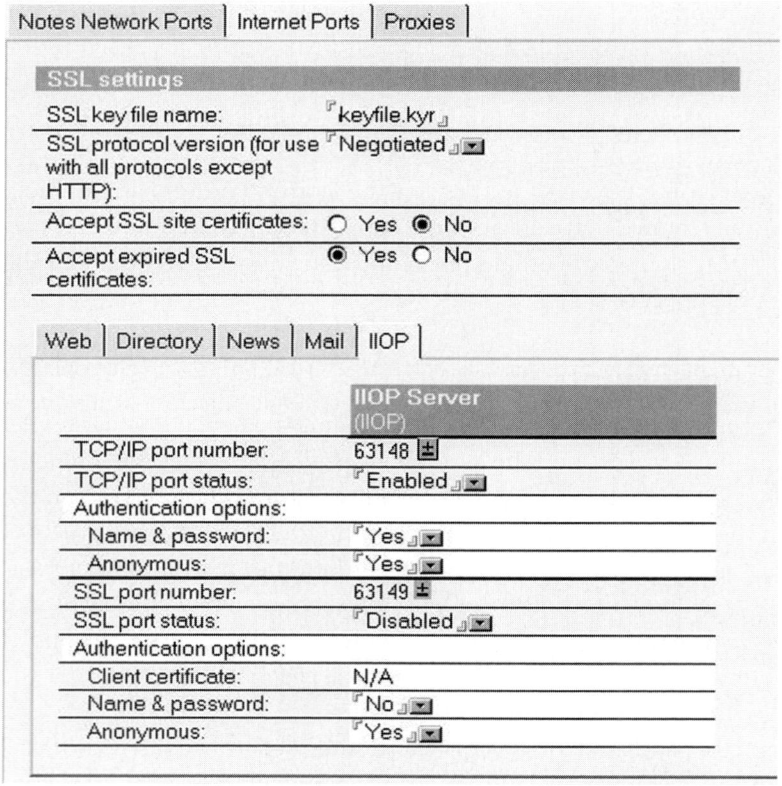

Notes Network Ports	Internet Ports	Proxies

SSL settings

SSL key file name:	"keyfile.kyr"
SSL protocol version (for use with all protocols except HTTP):	"Negotiated"
Accept SSL site certificates:	○ Yes ● No
Accept expired SSL certificates:	● Yes ○ No

Web	Directory	News	Mail	IIOP

	IIOP Server (IIOP)
TCP/IP port number:	63148
TCP/IP port status:	"Enabled"
Authentication options:	
Name & password:	"Yes"
Anonymous:	"Yes"
SSL port number:	63149
SSL port status:	"Disabled"
Authentication options:	
Client certificate:	N/A
Name & password:	"No"
Anonymous:	"Yes"

Figure 2-16 IIOP port

Summary

In this chapter, we covered some of the advanced server topics such as clustering, partitioning, and Web servers. You should know how to maintain servers that are clustered, including how to add and remove servers from a cluster, which tasks should be running in a cluster, and how to monitor the cluster by using the Cluster directory, SHOW CLUS-TER command, and the cluster statistics. You should know that only Enterprise server installations can be clustered or partitioned. Remember that partitioned servers share an executable directory, but each of the partitioned servers has its own data directory and Domino Directory. For Web servers, you should know how to monitor them, including the text logs, DOMLOG.NSF, and the filenames. You need to know how to implement security, virtual servers, and mapping and redirection.

Review Questions

1. Chris has set the Server Availability Threshold to 40. What will this setting do to his clustered server?
   A. No users will be able to connect once the server availability index reaches 40.
   B. No users will be able to connect once the server availability index reaches 60.
   C. All users will be dropped from the server once the server availability index reaches 40.
   D. All users will be dropped from the server once the server availability index reaches 60.

2. Michele has set up clustering between Server1 and Server2. DB1.NSF contains private folders that are not available on Server2 when Server1 fails. What might be the problem?
   A. Private folders do not replicate.
   B. Both servers must be given Manager access to DB1.NSF with the Unspecified type in order to replicate the private folders.
   C. Both servers must be given Manager access to DB1.NSF with the Server or ServerGroup type in order to replicate the private folders.
   D. Both servers must be given Manager access to DB1.NSF with the Person or PersonGroup type in order to replicate the private folders.

3. Mark has set up the ICM for his clustered servers. Where could he have placed the ICM(s)?
   A. On a single server inside the cluster
   B. On a single server outside the cluster
   C. On a single server inside the domain
   D. On a single server outside the domain

4. Mary installed three partitioned servers. Which of the following is/are not true?
   A. There are three Domino Directories on the physical machine.
   B. There are three sets of executables on the physical machine.
   C. There are three data directories on the physical machine.
   D. There are three NOTES.INI files on the physical machine.

5. Which of the following does Name and Password authentication require?
   A. Person document
   B. Notes USER.ID file
   C. HTTP password
   D. Internet password

6. Gary placed an entry in the Home URL field and in the Default Home page field. Which field determines what users will see?
   A. Home URL field
   B. Default Home page field

7. Kris wants to record the host names of the machines that access her Web server. Which of the following actions does she need to perform?
   A. Enable DNS lookup
   B. Disable DNS lookup
   C. Enable the Log files field
   D. Enable the DOMLOG.NSF field

8. What happened when Jim enabled the *Make this site accessible to Web site search crawlers* option in the Server document?
   A. All exclamation points (!) in the Domino URLs were replaced with question marks (?).
   B. All question marks (?) in the Domino URLs were replaced with exclamation points (!).
   C. The Domino URLs were kept to 32 characters.
   D. The Domino server ran an extra task called WebSearch.

9. You routinely enable users to download large files from your Web site. Which of the following enables those large files to be downloaded in sections and to be restarted where they left off if the download stops in the middle?
   A. Session-based download
   B. Session-based authentication
   C. Byte-range serving
   D. This functionality is not currently possible.

10. Which of the following do you configure by using DOMCFG.NSF?
    A. URL Redirection
    B. Virtual Hosts
    C. Custom error messages
    D. Virtual Servers

Review Answers

1. **A** is correct.   Once the availability index reaches the threshold, users can no longer connect—although current users can continue to use the server.

2. **C** is correct.   The servers need to be specified as Server or ServerGroup type in order to replicate the private folders.

3. **A, B,** and **C** are correct.   The only place where you could *not* place the ICM is outside the domain.

4. **B** is correct.   The partitioned servers use the same executable files, although they each have their own Domino Directories, NOTES.INI files, and data directories.

5. **A** and **D** are correct.   For name and password authentication, users must have a Person document and an Internet password in the Person document.

6. **A** is correct.   The Home URL field takes precedence.

7. **A** and **C** are correct.   She must enable DNS lookup to record host names instead of just IP addresses. She must enable the log files to record the information in the Access Log files.

8. **B** is correct.   The Domino URLs will use exclamation points (!) instead of question marks (?) with this option enabled.

9. **C** is correct.   Use Byte-range serving to enable users to resume downloads where they left off.

10. **C** is correct.   Use the DOMCFG.NSF to configure custom error messages.

Domino Directories, Users, and Groups

You should be able to answer questions based on the following objectives after reading this chapter:

- Monitoring, maintaining, and troubleshooting Domino Directories, users, and groups
- Localizing address books in multicultural settings
- Maintaining a directory configuration
- Maintaining groups
- Maintaining Notes user IDs (recertifying, moving, renaming, and recovering)
- Monitoring/maintaining Notes users (adding, removing, and upgrading)
- Troubleshooting directory problems
- Troubleshooting user problems

In this chapter, we examine the users and groups in your environment. They are obviously the purpose for having the Domino environment, so it is important to have the capability to monitor and maintain them. In addition, you must be able to monitor the directories in the Domino environment, which contain information about the users and groups as well as information about how your environment functions and communicates.

First, we will discuss the Domino Directory and the other directory services that are provided by Domino, including Directory Catalog, Directory Assistance, and LDAP. Next, we move on to discussing users. You should already know how to create users and groups (if not, refer to Chapter 6). In this chapter, however, we concentrate on the tasks that are necessary for maintaining your users and their user ID files, including renaming, recertifying, deleting, and recovering the users. Finally, we discuss groups, including group types, renaming and deleting groups, and maintaining group membership. You will notice that this chapter contains much of the same information as Chapter 7. The same types of information about directories are required for both sets of competencies; however, Chapter 7 contains more information about configuring the various directories than does this chapter.

Domino Directories

When you created the first server in your environment, Domino created a new Domino Directory (NAMES.NSF). This database was previously called the Public Name and Address Book (NAB). Domino Directory defines a domain, and all users and servers in the same Domino Directory are part of the same Notes domain. As you register users, servers, and certifiers or create groups, Person, Server, and Certifier documents are created in Domino Directory. You also use Domino Directory for administering the domain, by creating Connection, Configuration, Program, and other documents that are used for managing the Domino system and environment. You can also create additional Domino directories in order to store Web users (or other users) by creating a database that is based on the Domino Directory template (PUBNAMES.NTF). Any additional Domino directories on a server (either directories that you create, or replicas from other domains) are considered secondary Domino directories. The file NAMES.NSF is the primary Domino directory for your domain and should reside on each server in the domain.

In addition to Domino Directory itself, Domino provides the following three additional directory-service elements:

- Directory Catalog
- Directory Assistance
- LDAP service

Searches for users and groups always start with the primary Domino directory, then the Directory Catalog, and then Directory Assistance. This section discusses monitoring and maintaining each of these elements.

Domino Directory

As mentioned earlier, when you configure the first server in your domain, Notes creates a Domino directory with the filename NAMES.NSF. When you register and configure other servers, Notes places a replica of this Domino Directory on those servers. You must then create the appropriate Connection documents to ensure that changes to the documents are replicated correctly throughout your domain. Your Domino Directory should replicate with other servers in your domain multiple times during the day, depending on your domain configuration.

Domino Directory stores the following types of documents:

- Group documents define lists of users, servers, groups, and resources that can be used for mailing, access control, or server access and that contain the name of the group, the type of group, and the members of the group, as shown in Figure 3-1.

- Location documents contain user details with regards to how they use Notes in a specific place, including information about the mail server, mail file location, and type of connection, as shown in Figure 3-2. Location documents are primarily a workstation component; however, this information is useful to help administrators create documents for users or for administrators who use a client on the same machine as the server (not the recommended configuration).

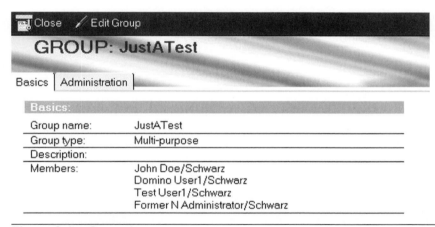

Figure 3-1   Group document

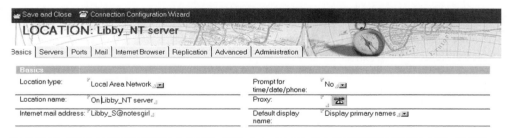

Figure 3-2   Location document

- Person documents contain information about the users in your domain, including the mail file, home server, Internet password, and public key, as shown in Figure 3-3. Person documents can also show information for non-Notes users that are added to the directory.

- Certificate documents contain information about Domino certificates and cross-certificates, including information about the certifier's public key as well as Internet certificates, as shown in Figure 3-4.

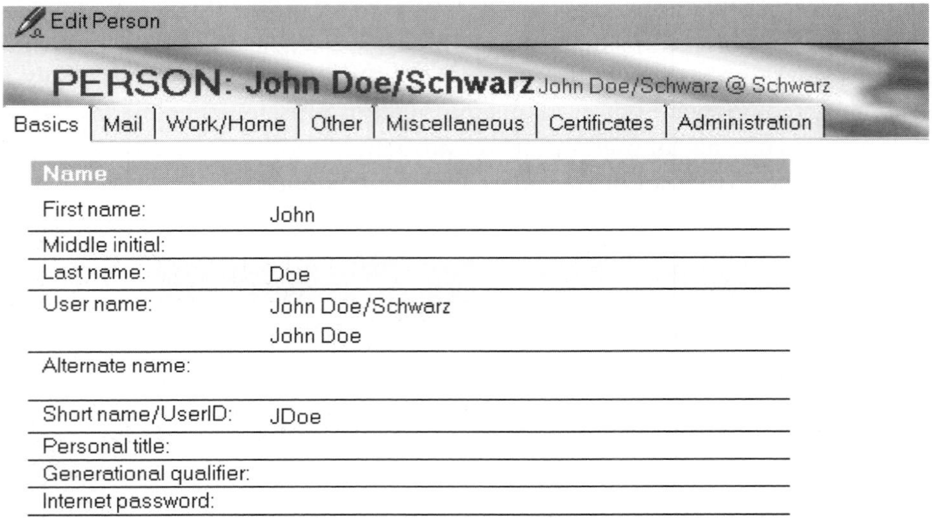

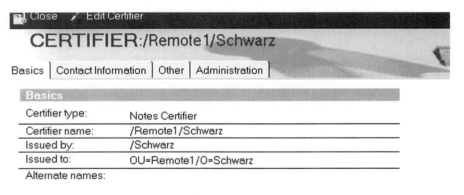

Figure 3-3 Person document

Figure 3-4 Certificate document

- Configuration Settings documents contain information about NOTES.INI, mail, and LDAP settings that you can change to determine how these features work, as shown in Figure 3-5.

- Connection documents enable replication and mail routing to occur on a schedule, as shown in Figure 3-6.

- Domain documents define external domains, including foreign domains, adjacent domains, global domains, and non-adjacent domains. The domains are used to configure mail routing. A Domain document is shown in Figure 3-7.

- External Domain Network Information documents enable your clients to connect to machines in other domains by providing the name and address of a server in this external domain, as shown in Figure 3-8.

- Mail-In Database documents enable the Router to find and route to mail-in databases that are not mail files, as shown in Figure 3-9.

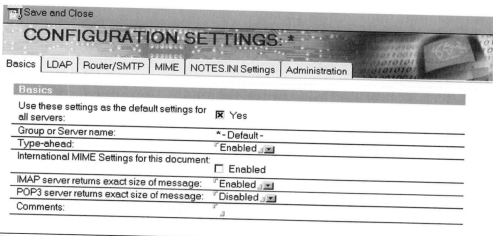

Figure 3-5   Configuration Settings document

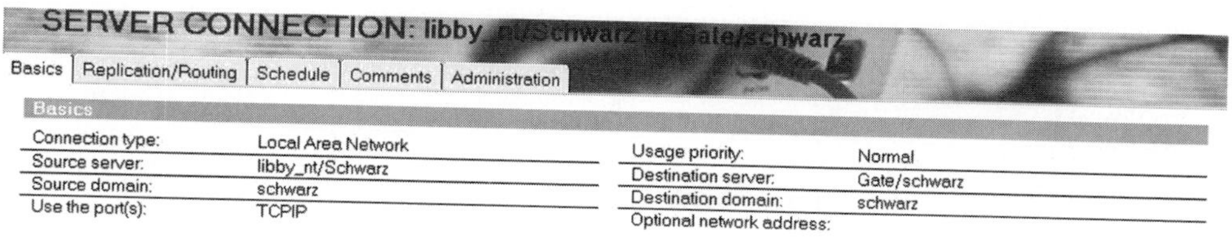

Figure 3-6   Connection document

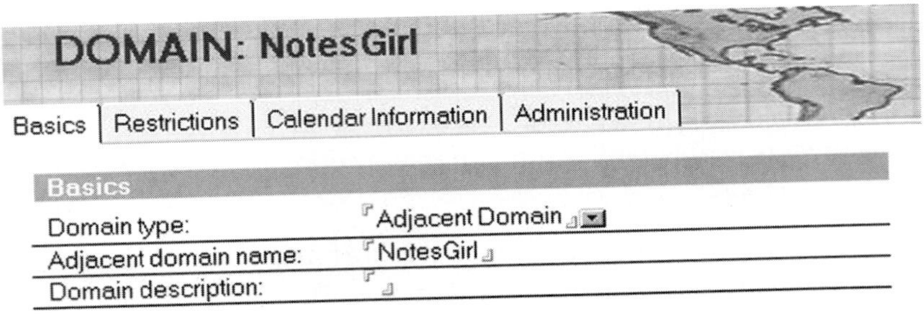

DOMAIN: NotesGirl

Basics | Restrictions | Calendar Information | Administration

Basics

Domain type:	Adjacent Domain
Adjacent domain name:	NotesGirl
Domain description:	

Figure 3-7   Domain document

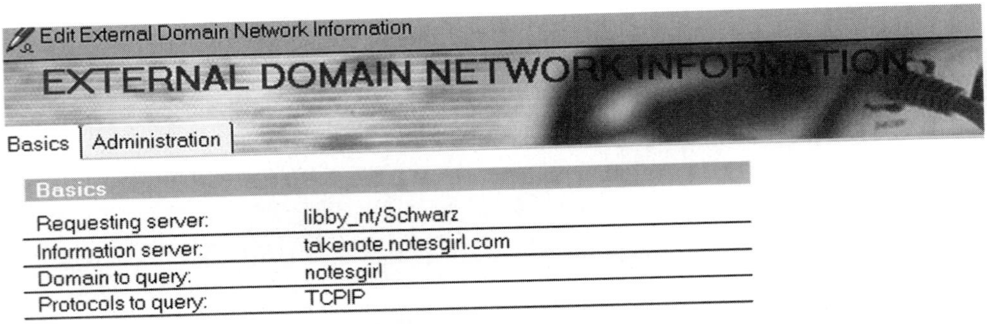

Edit External Domain Network Information

EXTERNAL DOMAIN NETWORK INFORMATION

Basics | Administration

Basics

Requesting server:	libby_nt/Schwarz
Information server:	takenote.notesgirl.com
Domain to query:	notesgirl
Protocols to query:	TCPIP

Figure 3-8   External Domain Network Information document

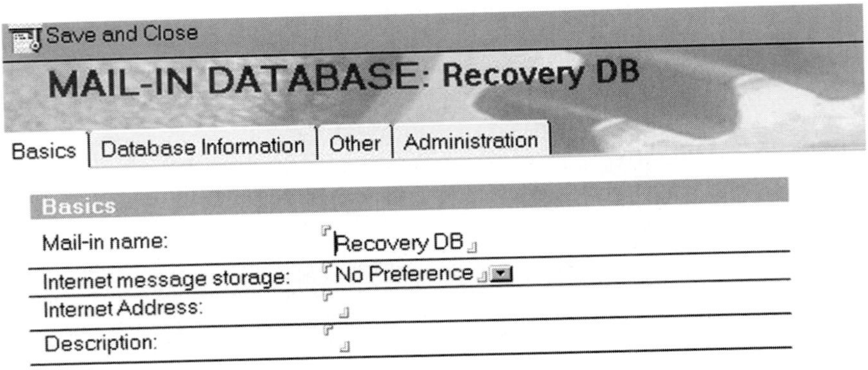

Save and Close

MAIL-IN DATABASE: Recovery DB

Basics | Database Information | Other | Administration

Basics

Mail-in name:	Recovery DB
Internet message storage:	No Preference
Internet Address:	
Description:	

Figure 3-9   Mail-In Database document

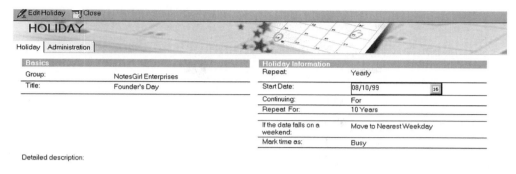

Figure 3-10   Holiday document

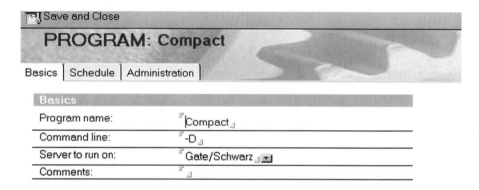

Figure 3-11   Program document

- Holiday documents define holidays for specific groups, which can then be downloaded into users' calendars in order to facilitate scheduling, as shown in Figure 3-10.

- Program documents enable you to schedule tasks or programs to run at specific times with command-line arguments, as shown in Figure 3-11.

- Resource documents are added to Domino Directory manually or from the Resource Reservation System to enable users to reserve and schedule these resources (such as rooms and using calendaring and scheduling), as shown in Figure 3-12.

- Server documents define settings in regards to server security, ports, clusters, tasks, protocols, networks, and other elements, as shown in Figure 3-13.

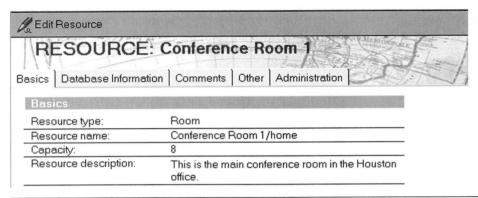

Figure 3-12   Resource documents

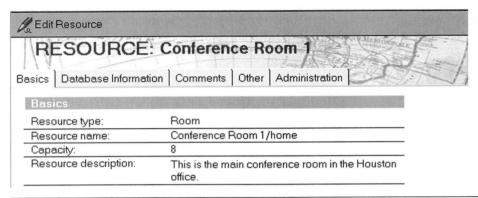

Figure 3-13   Server documents

- User Setup Profile documents enable administrators to give groups of users the same configuration options, such as connections, accounts, replicas, and bookmarks, as shown in Figure 3-14.

These documents are arranged into a variety of views in Domino Directory that give you the information necessary to administer your domain. You can also access the documents through the Domino Administrator interface. Use these documents to maintain your Domino environment, including configuring and routing mail, replicating, and running programs (such as Updall) on a schedule.

Save and Close

USER SETUP PROFILE: Home Users

| Basics | Databases | Dial-up Connections | Accounts | Name Servers | Applet Security | Proxies | MIME | Administration |

Basics

Profile name:	Home Users
Internet browser:	Microsoft Internet Explorer
Directory server:	libby_nt/schwarz
Catalog/Domain Search server:	libby_nt/Schwarz
Retrieve/open pages:	from Notes workstation
Sametime server:	

Figure 3-14   User Setup Profile documents

Domino Directory Profile Document

Use the Domino Directory Profile document to specify various settings for the Domino Directory. To access the Domino Directory Profile, open the Domino Administrator and choose Actions . . . Edit Directory Profile from the menus. The Domino Directory Profile document, shown in Figure 3-15, opens. This document stores the defaults for groups and Internet passwords, as well as the filename and path for the Directory Catalog for the domain.

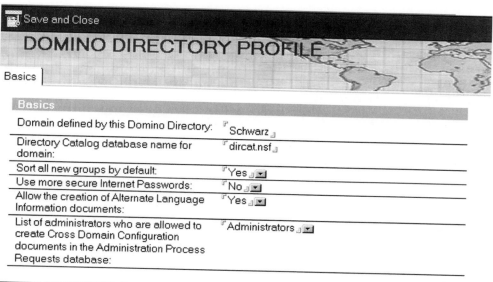

Save and Close

DOMINO DIRECTORY PROFILE

Basics

Basics

Domain defined by this Domino Directory:	Schwarz
Directory Catalog database name for domain:	dircat.nsf
Sort all new groups by default:	Yes
Use more secure Internet Passwords:	No
Allow the creation of Alternate Language Information documents:	Yes
List of administrators who are allowed to create Cross Domain Configuration documents in the Administration Process Requests database:	Administrators

Figure 3-15   Domino Directory Profile document

One important field in the Directory Profile document is the *Allow the creation of Alternate Language Information documents* field. This field enables you to open a Person document and choose Actions . . . Add Alternate Language Information in order to enable your Domino Directory to be functional in multi-cultural settings, as shown in Figure 3-16. You can create alternate language information for the first and last name, although the FullName (username) is inherited from the Person document and cannot be changed.

Domino Directory Security

Like all databases in Notes, the Domino Directory uses the ACL for security. In addition, however, there are eight predefined user roles that have been created and implemented for this database, as shown in Figure 3-17. These roles refine the rights that are given by the ACL by determining who can create and edit specific types of documents.

There are creator-type roles and modifier-type roles. The Creator roles apply to users at all levels of the ACL, including Managers. The Creator roles enable users with the Create Documents privilege to create documents using the Create Menu in the Domino Directory. Without this role, a user cannot create the specified document by using the Create Menu, although he or she might still be able to create the document programmatically. Do not consider the Creator roles a security feature.

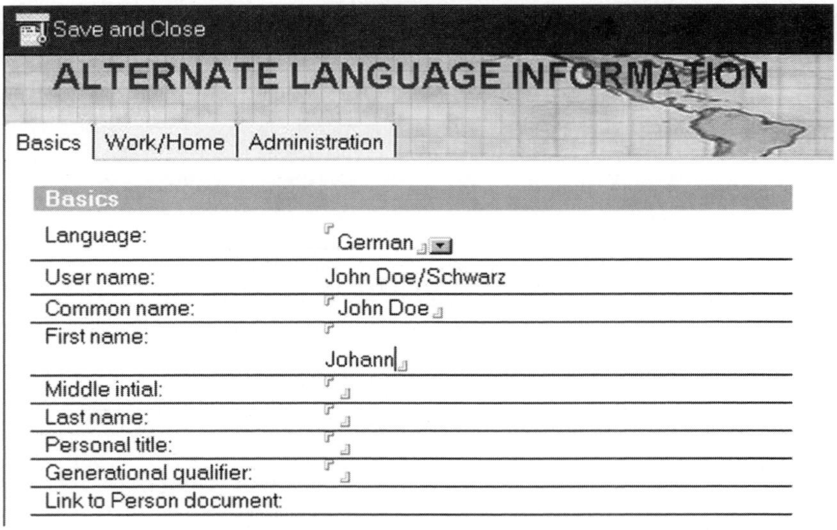

Figure 3-16 Adding Alternate Language Information

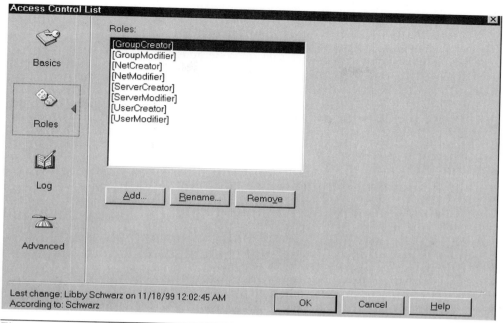

Figure 3-17 Roles in the Domino Directory

The Modifier roles apply to users who have Author access, in order to determine which documents they can edit. Users who have Editor access or higher can edit all of the documents in the database. Modifier roles are considered a security feature.

Remember that if a user has Reader access, he or she will not be able to create or modify documents even if you give the user Creator or Modifier roles. Roles refine the ACL, but they cannot expand it. When you assign the ACL for Domino Directory, be sure to include the following roles for the appropriate users, servers, and groups:

- **GroupCreator** The GroupCreator role must be added to a user who has both Author access or higher and the Create Documents privilege, in order to give them the capability to create new groups in Domino Directory.

- **GroupModifier** The GroupModifier role must be added to a user who has Author access, in order to give him or her the capability to modify Group documents in Domino Directory.

- **NetCreator** The NetCreator role must be added to a user who has both Author access or higher and the Create Documents privilege, in order to give him or her the capability to create any document in the Domino directory (other than Person,

Group, or Server documents). This privilege includes Connection, Configuration, and Program documents.

- **NetModifier**   The NetModifier role must be added to a user who has Author access, in order to give him or her the capability to modify any document in the Domino Directory (other than Person, Group, or Server documents).

- **ServerCreator**   The ServerCreator role must be added to a user who has both Author access or higher and the Create Documents privilege, in order to give him or her the capability to create new Server documents in the Domino Directory.

- **ServerModifier**   The ServerModifier role must be added to a user who has Author access, in order to give him or her the capability to modify Server documents in the Domino Directory.

- **UserCreator**   The UserCreator role must be added to a user who has both Author access or higher and the Create Documents privilege, in order to give him or her the capability to create new Person documents in the Domino Directory.

- **UserModifier**   The UserModifier role must be added to a user who has Author access, in order to give him or her the capability to modify Person documents in the Domino Directory.

You can also give users access to specific documents by placing their names in the Administrators field in a document. You can put a user's name in the Administrators field to give them access to a specific user, group, server, or other document without giving them a Modifier role. The user will be able to edit the document, even if he or she only has Author access to the database.

Database Performance

In order to improve database performance, the Domino Directory uses two of the advanced database properties that are new to R5. Because there are many small views in the database and the database is usually large (contains many documents), the *Document table bitmap optimization* property is enabled. In addition, because there is usually no significance to new documents in Domino Directory, the *Don't maintain unread marks* property is also enabled.

Directory Server

You can designate a server in your domain to serve as a directory server. This server can help the load on mail servers or other servers, because addressing and name lookups will be directed to the directory server. Your directory server should have replicas of all of the directories that are used in the domain, including secondary directories. All of the directory services, such as Directory Catalog, Directory Assistance, and LDAP, can use a directory server. Create the Directory Catalog on the directory server, for example, and make sure that the server contains a replica of all secondary directories so that updates can occur on the directory server. Other servers will then use the Directory Catalog for name lookup. Similarly, use the directory server as the repository for the secondary Domino Directories that are in use in Directory Assistance. The LDAP task can also run on the directory server.

To force Notes clients to use the directory server for name lookups, the name of the directory server should be in the user's Location documents, as shown in Figure 3-18. You can also add this information to a user's Location document by using a User Setup Profile document. Without a designated directory server, Notes clients use the server on which their mail server resides for address resolution.

Directory Catalog

The Directory Catalog is a file that you create—either on the server or for mobile users—in order to provide information about users from multiple directories in a small, lightweight database. Server directory catalogs provide the capability to combine multiple Domino Directories into a single database in order to streamline name lookups. Mobile directory catalogs provide remote users with a lightweight, portable Domino Directory and the capability to address users in multiple directories. The Server Directory Catalog provides the following capabilities:

- Mail addressing, using names in secondary Domino Directories for Notes users
- Mail addressing, using names in secondary Domino Directories for LDAP users
- Web client authentication, using credentials in secondary Domino Directories
- Type-ahead for addressing

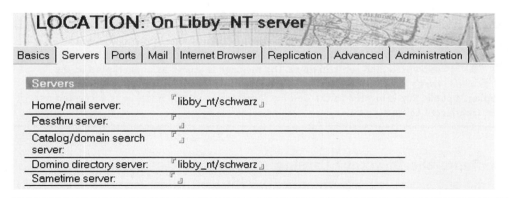

Figure 3-18   Location document specifying the directory server

The Mobile directory catalog provides the following capabilities:

- Mail addressing, using names in primary or secondary Domino Directories for Notes users
- Type-ahead for addressing

The purpose of a directory catalog is to concatenate the mailing information of users from many domains (or from many Domino Directories) while remaining small and lightweight. In other words, not all fields are contained in the catalog by default (although you can add other fields that are needed by your organization). The following list describes the fields that are contained in the Directory Catalog. Note that some fields are used by more than one type of entry (indicated next to the field listing), although most fields are only used by the Person document entry.

- FullName (also used by mail-in databases and resources)
- ListName (only used by groups)
- Type (also used by mail-in databases, resources, and groups)
- FirstName
- MiddleInitial
- LastName
- Location
- MailAddress
- ShortName
- MailDomain (also used by mail-in databases and resources)
- InternetAddress (also used by mail-in databases and resources)
- MessageStorage (also used by mail-in databases and resources)

 TIP Note that by default, the public key information is not stored in the directory catalog. Users who have a mobile directory catalog and want to send encrypted mail can still do so. The message is stored as unencrypted in the user's local mail file, but when the user connects in order to send mail, the recipient's public key is located in the Domino Directory—and the message is encrypted and then transferred to MAIL.BOX.

Configure the Directory Catalog

To use a directory catalog, create a new database based on the DIRCAT5.NTF template. Create the Directory Catalog Configuration document by clicking Create . . .

Configuration. If the catalog already exists, you can edit the Configuration document by opening the Configuration view. In the Configuration document, specify the directories to include in the directory catalog, the fields to include in the catalog, the terms by which to sort, whether to use Soundex, whether to enable or remove duplicate users, which group types to include, and other configuration settings.

You usually place replicas of all secondary Domino Directories that are included in the Directory Catalog on the same server, although this placement is not required. In addition, you must then run the DIRCAT task on the server in order to build the Catalog. If you type LOAD DIRCAT DIRCAT.NSF, the server starts the DIRCAT task and builds or synchronizes the Directory Catalog. The DIRCAT task should be run regularly to add any changes from the Domino Directories to the Directory Catalog. Use the Server Tasks . . . Directory Cataloger tab in the Server document to configure how DIRCAT will run.

Before the Directory Catalog is used, you must include the Catalog's name in the Directory Profile or in the Server document, as shown in Figure 3-19. An entry in the Server document takes precedence over the entry in the Directory Profile. You can create replicas of the Directory Catalog on other servers (inside and outside the current domain). Make sure that you replicate these frequently with the source Directory Catalog in order to keep the changes current. Do not run the DIRCAT task on these replicas, because replication conflicts will result. Only run the DIRCAT task in order to maintain the source Directory Catalog.

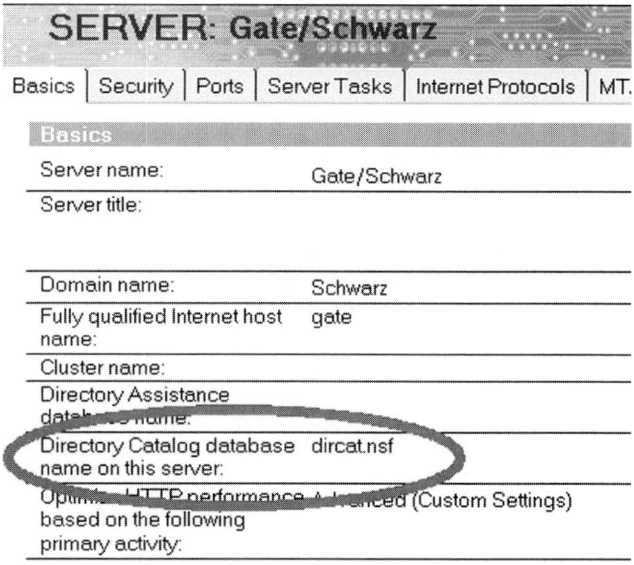

Figure 3-19   Directory Catalog field in the Server document

Users who are disconnected from the network can benefit from using a mobile Directory Catalog for quick mail addressing and type ahead, even when disconnected from the network. You should not use the same source Directory Catalog for server and mobile use; instead, create two separate Catalogs. To enable users to take advantage of the mobile Directory Catalog, they must have a replica on their Notes workstations. You can use a User Setup Profile to create a replica for them by adding a database link to the *Mobile Directory Catalogs* field, as shown in Figure 3-20. They also need to add the name of the Directory Catalog to their user mail preferences. If you use the User Setup Profile, the name will be added automatically. If not, users will have to create the replica and list the name in their preferences manually.

Customize and Maintain the Directory Catalog

If you want to customize the Directory Catalog, you might change the fields, how it performs name lookups, or other configuration details.

To change the fields that the Directory Catalog contains, edit the Configuration document in the Directory Catalog. You can add or remove field names in the *Additional Fields to Include* field. If you want to use the Directory Catalog on a server in order to authenticate Web users, for example, you would add the HTTPPassword field (the Internet Password field). You might also choose to add the Members field (from the Group document) to assist with free-time lookups. Note that any time you make a change to the fields, the Directory Catalog is rebuilt the next time the DIRCAT task runs.

The options you might change in order to determine how the directory catalog performs name lookups are the Sort By options, the Soundex option, the Duplicate Users option, and the Group types option:

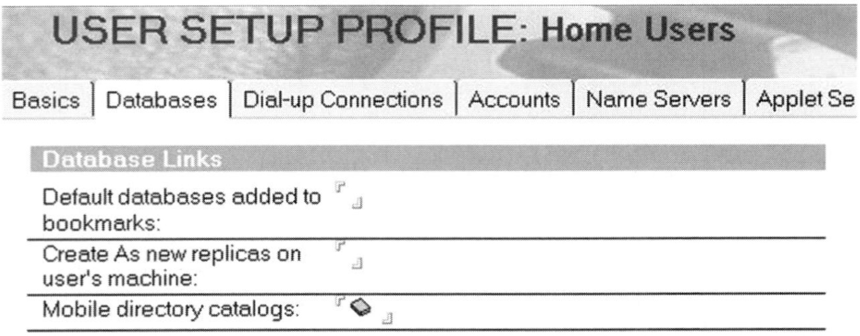

Figure 3-20 User Setup Profile to set up a mobile Directory Catalog

- Type-ahead only works if users enter the same element of a user's name that is selected in the Sort By options. If your users tend to search by typing in the last name of a user, for example, you should choose to Sort By Last Name. Other choices include Distinguished Name and Alternate Fullname. When users enter names in a different way, such as typing the first name, the lookup is only performed when the user sends or refreshes (by hitting the F9 key).

- Soundex is an option that enables users to type names phonetically (how they sound, rather than how they are spelled). Enabling Soundex makes the Directory Catalog much larger.

- You can choose to force the Directory Catalog to keep only the first occurrence of a name in the Domino Directories that it concatenates by enabling the Remove Duplicate Users option. If you choose No, users are given the opportunity to pick a name when duplicates are found.

- Although the Directory Catalog only uses Group Types for information (not for ACLs), you can choose to include types other than Mail and Multi-Purpose (if necessary).

Directory Assistance

Directory Assistance manages lookups in both multiple Domino Directories and in LDAP directories. Directory Assistance provides the following capabilities:

- Mail addressing using names in secondary Domino Directories for Notes users
- Mail addressing using names in secondary Domino Directories for LDAP users
- Mail addressing using names in Domino or in third-party LDAP Directories for Notes users
- Mail addressing using names in Domino or in third-party LDAP Directories for LDAP users
- Web client authentication using credentials in secondary Domino Directories
- Web client authentication using credentials in third-party LDAP Directories
- Type-ahead for addressing

To enable Directory Assistance, you create the Directory Assistance database, basing it on the DA50.NTF template. In this database, create Directory Assistance documents for each secondary Domino Directory. Use the Rules tab to set organizational hierarchies that are trusted for authentication. If a user does not match one of these rules, he or she cannot be authenticated via Directory Assistance.

LDAP

Lightweight Directory Access Protocol (LDAP) enables clients to access a directory, as well as a standard directory infrastructure for that directory. The LDAP directory has entries that are defined by attributes; they are similar to the attributes with which you are familiar in the Domino organizational hierarchy. Notes and Domino provide both LDAP server capabilities and LDAP client capabilities. To enable LDAP clients and applications (including Notes R5 clients or Microsoft Outlook Express clients) to search the Domino Directory via LDAP, enable the LDAP task on the server. The LDAP service provides the following capabilities in the Domino environment:

- Enabling LDAP searches on secondary Domino Directories, using Directory Catalog and Directory Assistance
- Referring LDAP clients to other LDAP directories by using Directory Assistance
- Enabling LDAP clients to add, edit, and delete entries in the directory
- Extending the LDAP schema (attributes)
- Searching based on alternate languages

You might want to customize the LDAP settings on the Domino server. On the Configuration tab in the Domino Administrator, expand the Directory section and choose the Directory Settings document. By default, Anonymous (non-authenticated) users can query the fields that are listed in the *Anonymous Users Can Query* field, as shown in Figure 3-21. You can add or remove fields from this list. Other fields in the LDAP settings are listed in Table 3-1.

You can also configure the LDAP ports by using the Server document. In the Server document, select the Ports . . . Internet Ports . . . Directory tab. The default port for LDAP is 389. To use LDAP over SSL, you must set port 636 as the default. You might disable port 389 to require LDAP clients to use port 636 and SSL. Use the fields on this tab to enable Anonymous connections or to require name and password authentication.

Notes users in your environment can access Domino and third-party LDAP directories by using an Account document in the personal name and address book on their workstations. You can add an account for a user by completing a User Setup Profile.

Domino Users

Domino users can be of two types. Some users have both Person documents and user ID files. These users can access the Domino server via a Notes client, because they have the capability to authenticate with the server via the public and private keys that are

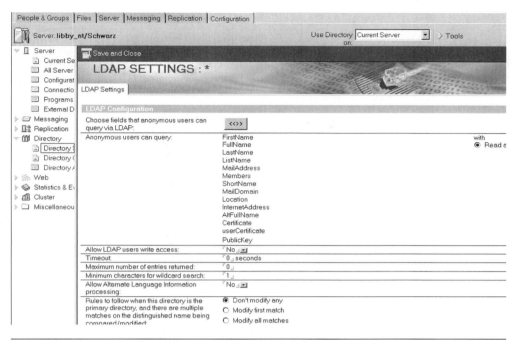

Figure 3-21   Anonymous LDAP users can query these fields.

contained in the ID files. Other users only have a Person document. These users can access the Domino server via browser (HTTP), SMTP, POP3, IMAP, LDAP, and NNTP clients. This section concentrates on the type of user who has both an ID file and a Person document. Renaming users who only have Person documents is accomplished manually.

Some of the tasks that you might need to perform for existing users include renaming, recertifying, and removing the users from the environment. In addition, you might need to recover a user by using the Password and ID Recovery tool that is new to R5.

TIP   Moving users really involves moving a user's mail file to a different server. This topic is covered in Chapter 4.

Most of these tasks use AdminP, which creates a series of request documents in the Administration Requests database (ADMIN4.NSF) to complete the renaming, recertifying, or deleting process. In other words, before you can use these tools, you must have AdminP configured correctly—including creating a CERTLOG.NSF database manually.

Table 3-1 LDAP Settings

Field	Notes
Allow LDAP users write access	Set this field to Yes in order to enable LDAP clients to add, edit, or delete documents in the Domino Directory. Note that the clients must also have the proper access in the ACL as well as the necessary roles or privileges. The LDAP clients should be authenticated before enabling this option.
Timeout	The number of seconds that an LDAP search can continue.
Maximum number of entries returned	A single LDAP search can only return this number of entries.
Minimum characters for wildcard search	You can specify the minimum number of characters that a user must provide before using a wild card to extend the search. If your LDAP server performance is slow, you might increase this number.
Allow Alternate Language Information Processing	Enable this option so that LDAP clients can complete transactions (search, read, edit, add, and delete) that specify alternate language information.
Rules to follow when this directory is the primary directory and there are multiple matches on the distinguished name being compared/modified	Choices include Don't modify any, Modify first match, and Modify all matches.

In addition, the renaming and recertifying processes require that you have access to the certifier ID and that the certifier document and the documents of its ancestors must be in the Domino Directory Certifiers view. Finally, the user's public key must be the same in the Domino directory as it is in the user's ID file. You will receive errors if the public key has been changed or is corrupted.

Renaming Users

Users need to be renamed if they change their name or if a mistake was made when registering them. To rename a user, open Domino Administrator's People and Groups tab, select the person to rename, and expand the People tools. To rename a user, you need the access levels listed in Table 3-2.

The Rename tool, shown in Figure 3-22, enables you to upgrade a flat user to a hierarchical status, to change the common name of the user, and to request a move to a new certifier.

To change a user's common name, select the *Change Common Name* button. Note that you can also select a number of days (from 14 to 60), during which the original name will still be honored. When prompted, select the correct certifier ID file and use

Table 3-2 Necessary Access to Rename a User

Database	Access Level
Domino Directory	Editor, with Create Document access and UserModifier role
Certification Log	Author, with Create Document access

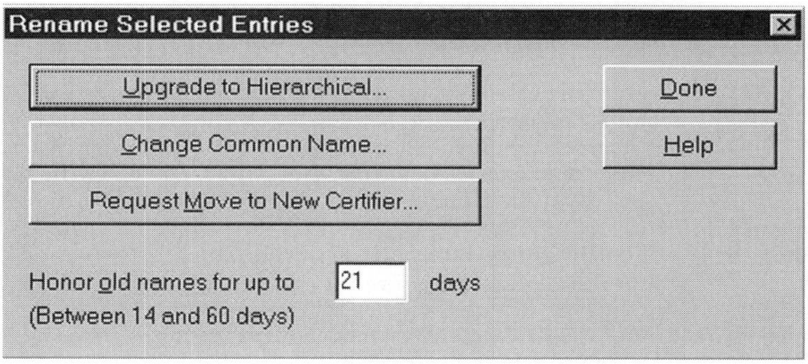

Figure 3-22 Rename tool

the Rename Selected User dialog box, to change the first, middle, or last name. You can also change the Qualifying Org Unit, also known as the User Unique Organizational Unit (UUOU). Then, select the *Rename* button.

The Domino Administrator processes the document and confirms the process. AdminP creates and performs the following requests to complete the rename process (Table 3-3). Each request is governed according to a time setting: immediate, interval, daily, or weekly. If you want AdminP to process a request more quickly, you can use the TELL ADMINP PROCESS command.

The Rename People tool also enables you to move a user to a different location in the hierarchical Organization or to a different Organization. To move a user to a different hierarchical Organization, the Domino Directory must contain the appropriate Cross-certificate documents. In addition, you need the access listed in Table 3-4 to complete this process.

To change a user's hierarchical unit, select the *Request Move to new certifier* button. Note that you can also select a number of days (from 14 to 60), during which the original name will still be honored. When prompted, select the original certifier ID file. When prompted by the Request Move for Selected Entries dialog box, type the name of the new certifier. If the certifier you type cannot be found in the Domino Directory Certifiers view, you cannot complete the request. After the Domino Administrator

Table 3-3   Rename Person Requests

Requests	Note
Initiate Rename in Address Book	Uses the Interval setting. The user is prompted to accept the new name the next time he or she authenticates with the server. If the user does not accept the new name, the process stops. If the user does not authenticate before the change request expires, the process stops.
Rename Person in Address Book	If the person accepts the new name, this request appears next. This request uses the Interval setting.
Rename in Access Control List	After the person is renamed in the Domino Directory, this interval request is created.
Rename in Person Documents	After the person is renamed in the Domino Directory, this daily request is created.
Rename Person in Free Time database	After the person is renamed in the Domino Directory, this immediate request is created.
Rename in Reader/Author fields	After the Rename in Person documents request is completed, this weekly request is created and executed.
Rename Person in Calendar Entries and Profiles in Mail File	After the Rename Person in Free Time database request is completed, this immediate request is created and executed.

Table 3-4   Necessary Access to Move a User in the Hierarchy

Database	Access Level
Domino Directory	Editor, with create document access and UserModifier role
Certification Log	Author, with create document access
Administration Requests	Editor

processes the request, AdminP takes over and adds and completes requests, as described previously. AdminP creates and processes the requests listed in Table 3-5 to complete this process.

Recertify Users

Use the Recertify People tool to recertify users whose certificates are about to expire. This process involves renewal, not moving. To recertify a user ID, you must have the access listed in Table 3-6.

Table 3-5   Moving a Person's Name in the Hierarchy

Requests	Note
Move Person's Name in Hierarchy	This request is completed immediately.
Initiate Rename in Address Book	Uses the Interval setting. The user is prompted to accept the new name the next time that he or she authenticates with the server. If the user does not accept the new name, the process stops. If the user does not authenticate before the change request expires, the process stops.
Rename Person in Address Book	If the person accepts the new name, this request is next. This request uses the Interval setting.
Rename in Access Control List	After the person is renamed in the Domino Directory, this interval request is created.
Rename in Person Documents	After the person is renamed in the Domino Directory, this daily request is created.
Rename Person in Free Time database	After the person is renamed in the Domino Directory, this immediate request is created.
Rename in Reader/Author fields	After the Rename in Person Documents request is completed, this weekly request is created and executed.
Rename Person in Calendar Entries and Profiles in Mail File	After the Rename Person in Free Time Database request is completed, this immediate request is created and executed.

Table 3-6   Necessary Access to Recertify a User

Database	Access Level
Domino Directory	Author, with Create Document access and UserModifier role
Certification Log	Author, with Create Document access

To recertify a user, select the user in the People and Groups view in Domino Administrator, and select the Recertify People tool. Select the appropriate certifier ID. In the Renew Certificates in Selected Entries dialog box, shown in Figure 3-23, type a new certificate expiration date. The default is to add two years to the current date. You can also enter a date in the *Only renew certificates that will expire before* field in order to renew only a subset of selected users.

AdminP performs the Recertify Person in Address Book request based on the default interval. The user's ID file is updated during the next authentication process.

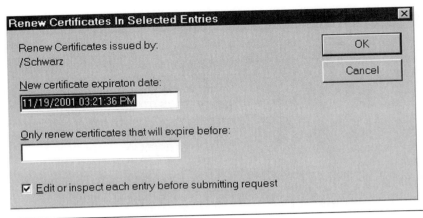

Figure 3-23   Renewing a certificate

Removing Users

Users may need to be deleted if they leave the company. To remove a user, open the Domino Administrator's People and Groups tab, select the person to remove, and expand the People tools. Select the Delete People tool. To delete a user, you need the access levels shown in Table 3-7.

After you select the Delete tool, you are prompted to confirm that you want to delete the selected user(s). After you confirm the deletion, the Domino Administrator gives additional choices that are related to the mail file and Windows NT account, as shown in Figure 3-24.

You have the following choices regarding the user's mail file:

- Choose *Don't delete mail file* to delete the Person document but leave the mail file on the server.

Table 3-7   Necessary Access in Order to Delete a User

Database	Access Level
Domino Directory	Author, with Delete Document access and UserModifier role or Editor access
Certification Log	Author, with Create Document access
If deleting the user's mail file . . .	
Domino Directory	Editor, with Delete Document access
Administration Requests	Editor, with Delete Document access

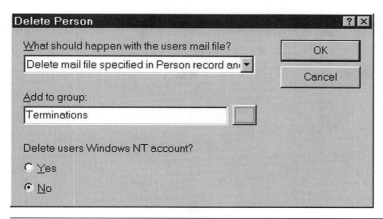

Figure 3-24 Delete Person dialog box

- Choose *Delete just the mail file specified in Person record* to delete the Person document and the mail file that is specified in the Person document.

- Choose *Delete mail file specified in Person record and all replicas* to delete the Person document and all replicas of the user's mail file.

If you choose to have AdminP delete the mail file, you will need to approve the file deletion in the Pending Administrator Approval view of the Administration Requests database before the file will be deleted. To approve the file deletion, place the document in Edit mode and use the appropriate action buttons.

Next, you might choose to add the user to a group as you process the deletion, as shown in Figure 3-25. You should have a Terminations (or similar) group in your Domino Directory. This group, which should be a Deny List Only type of group, should be in the Not Access Server field of the Server document. You can then place the terminated/deleted users in this group to ensure that they cannot access the server even if they retained a copy of their ID file. Using a group in the Not Access Server field prevents you from having to reboot the server in order for changes to take effect in that field.

Finally, you can choose to delete a user's Windows NT account as well, provided that the server is running Windows NT and that the user has a Windows NT account. When you click OK, Domino Administrator prompts you to decide how to process the request. Your choices are as follows:

- *Yes* forces AdminP to delete the user from the Domino Directory immediately. AdminP creates a Delete in Access Control List request in the Administration Requests database. Note that you might have to wait while all references to the user are removed from the Domino Directory.

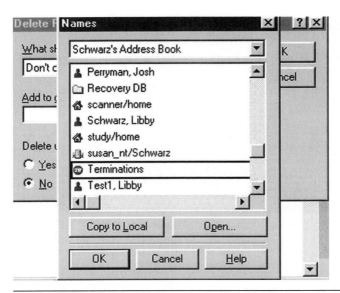

Figure 3-25   Adding the user to the Terminations group

- *No* forces AdminP to create a Delete in Address Book request in the Administration Requests database. Requests are processed based on the appropriate intervals.

- *Cancel* stops the deletion.

AdminP creates and processes the following requests in order to complete this process (see Table 3-8).

Users in Other Domains

You might want the ability to maintain users in other domains by using the Administration Process. You can use AdminP to perform the following user maintenance requests in other domains:

- Delete Person
- Rename Person

These requests are Cross-Domain Administration requests. They first perform an action in your domain's Domino Directory and then send a request to perform the same action in another domain's Domino Directory. To perform a Cross-Domain Administration request, the Administration Requests database needs to have Cross-Domain Configuration documents created for the tasks that you want to perform. The

Table 3-8 Delete User requests

Requests	Note
Delete from Domino Directory Immediately	You are answering this question when you choose Yes or No at this prompt. If you choose yes, move to the Delete in Access Control list request. If you choose No, move to the Delete in Address Book request.
Delete in Address Book	This interval request deletes all references to the user in the Domino Directory.
Delete in Access Control List	This daily request removes the user from all ACLs.
Delete in Person Documents	This daily request removes the user's name from other people's Person documents (if they are listed as an Administrator or Owner, for example). This action is only performed if the Delete in Address Book request is performed; otherwise, it occurs when all references are removed from the Domino Directory.
Delete in Reader/Author Fields	This delayed request is performed after deleting users in the ACLs of databases. Shared agents and other elements that are signed by the deleted person are reported in a Response document. Private design elements that are signed by the user create a Request to Delete Private Design elements, which must be approved by the administrator.
If you choose to delete the mail file . . .	
Get Information for Deletion	This request is carried out immediately and creates the Approve File Deletion request in the Pending Administrator Approval view of the Administration Requests database.
Approve File Deletion	Use the Pending Administrator Approval view of the Administration Requests database to edit and approve this request. The request is carried out when approved.
Request File Deletion	This option creates a Delete Mail File request immediately after you approve the File Deletion request.
Delete Mail File	This interval request is carried out on the person's home server. If the mail file uses shared mail, AdminP clears the links to the shared mail file and creates a Delete Unlinked Mail file request. The mail file is not yet deleted in this case.
Delete Unlinked Mail File	If the mail file uses shared mail, the mail file is not deleted until the Interval between purging mail file and deleting when using Object store setting is reached.

domain that originates the request needs an Outbound Cross Domain Configuration request, as shown in Figure 3-26. The domain that is receiving the request needs an Inbound Cross Domain Configuration request, as shown in Figure 3-27. If the domains are in different Organizations, appropriate cross-certificates need to exist in both Domino Directories.

Recover Users

New in R5 is the capability to recover user IDs and passwords. This feature requires configuration before use. To configure ID and password recovery, perform the following steps:

1. Create a mail-in database to hold the recovery information. Create a Mail-In Database document in the Domino directory, as shown in Figure 3-28.

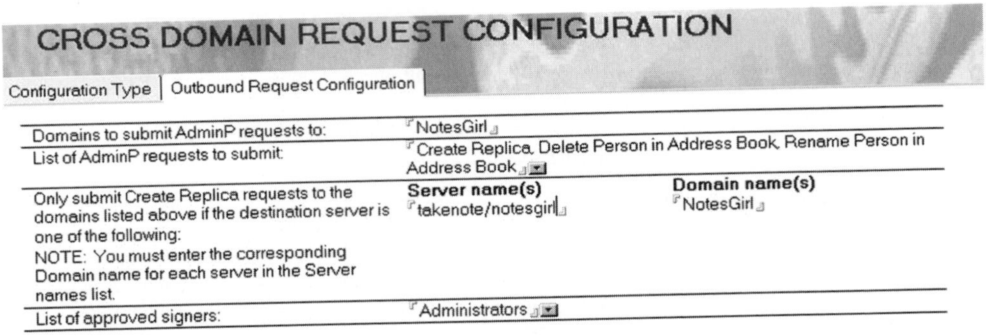

Figure 3-26   Outbound Cross-Domain Configuration request

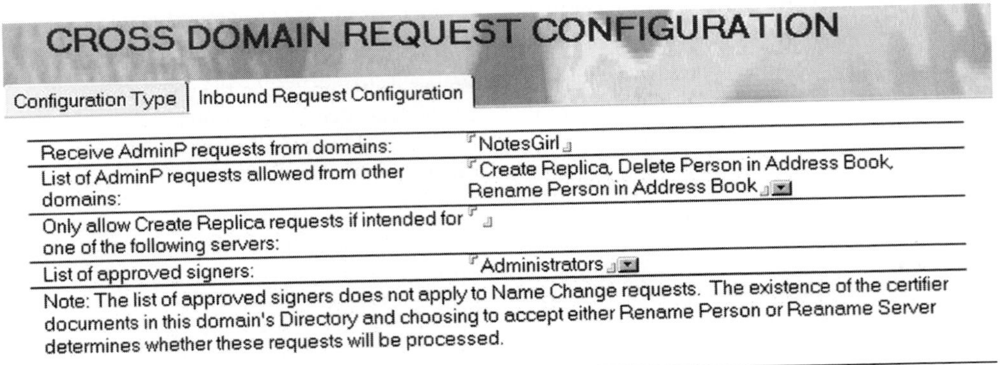

Figure 3-27   Inbound Cross-Domain Configuration request

MAIL-IN DATABASE: Recovery DB

Basics | Database Information | Other | Administration

Basics

Mail-in name:	Recovery DB
Internet message storage:	No Preference
Internet Address:	
Description:	

Figure 3-28   Mail-In Database document

2. In the Configuration tab of the Domino Administrator, open the Certification tools and choose Edit Recovery Information. Choose the certifier ID.

3. In the Edit Master Recovery Authority List dialog box, shown in Figure 3-29, place recovery information into the certifier ID. The recovery information (stored in the

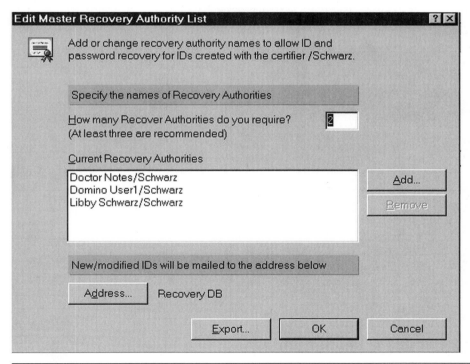

Edit Master Recovery Authority List

Add or change recovery authority names to allow ID and password recovery for IDs created with the certifier /Schwarz.

Specify the names of Recovery Authorities

How many Recover Authorities do you require? [2]
(At least three are recommended)

Current Recovery Authorities

Doctor Notes/Schwarz
Domino User1/Schwarz
Libby Schwarz/Schwarz

Add...
Remove

New/modified IDs will be mailed to the address below

Address...   Recovery DB

Export...   OK   Cancel

Figure 3-29   Edit Master Recovery Authority List dialog box

certifier ID) includes the names of the administrators who are permitted to recover IDs and passwords (called the recovery authorities), the number of recovery authorities that are required to recover a user's ID or password, and the address of the Recovery database. The Person documents of the users who are designated as recovery authorities must be available in the local (on the same machine as the Domino Administrator) address book or Domino Directory when you are making them recovery authorities. If necessary, copy the Person documents to your local address book. The Certifier document must also be available.

4. Any users who are registered with this certifier will now contain recovery information. The recovery information in the user's ID file takes the form of a recovery password that is randomly generated and encrypted with the public keys of the administrators (recovery authorities).

5. For users who were registered before you created the recovery information, you must select the Export button to add the recovery information to their ID files. In the Mail ID File Recovery Information dialog box, shown in Figure 3-30, add the names of the users who have already been registered and who need recovery information. You can use the Address button to select the users from the Domino directory. In the memo field, tell the users to open the document and select Actions . . . Accept Recovery Information.

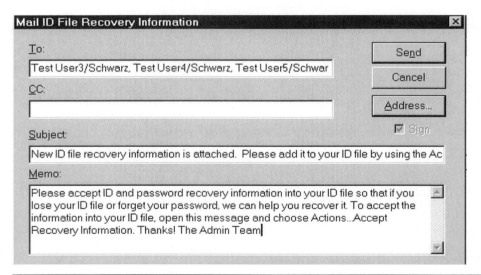

Figure 3-30   Mail ID File Recovery Information dialog box

6. Users must accept the recovery information as described. When they accept the recovery information, a copy of the ID file containing recovery data is sent to the mail-in database so that the information is available if the user's ID file becomes lost or corrupted.

When a user loses his or her ID file or forgets his or her password, you can use the recovery information to recover this information for them. If a user just forgets the password but still has the ID file, you do not need to send the user the ID file that is stored in the recovery database, but you will still use this file to obtain the recovery password for the user. To recover a user ID file or password, perform the following steps:

1. Open the mail-in database. Find the document that contains the user's ID file. Detach the ID file, as shown in Figure 3-31. Name the file with the user's name and the .ID extension (if necessary). Do not forget to delete this ID when you are finished with the recovery process.

2. In Domino Administrator, open the Configuration tab and select the Extract Recovery Password tool from the Certification tools. You will be prompted for your password. This password is used to decrypt the recovery password from the user's ID file.

3. As shown in Figure 3-32, you will be prompted to select the ID file to recover.

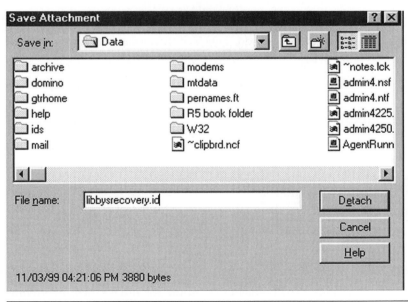

Figure 3-31   Detach the ID file

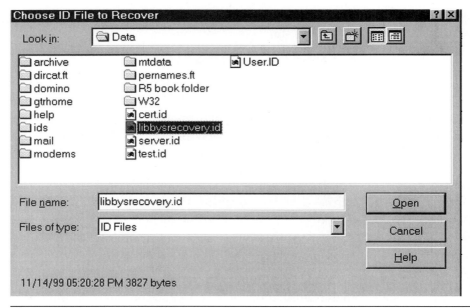

Figure 3-32   Choosing an ID to recover

4. Domino displays a dialog box with the recovery password. You will read this pass-word to the user (who should be at his or her workstation).

5. The user should select Tools . . . Recover ID from the Notes client. The user is prompted to enter a recovery password for each of the required recovery authori-ties, as shown in Figure 3-33.

6. After typing a recovery password from each of the required recovery authorities, the user is prompted to create a new password. The original password is never shown (as a security measure).

Domino Groups

Maintaining Domino groups requires three main tasks: editing the groups, deleting the groups, and managing the group membership.

Editing Groups

Editing a group includes changing any fields in the Group document, including name, type, description, members, owners, administrators, and foreign directory sync allowed. To edit a group, you need the access levels shown in Table 3-9.

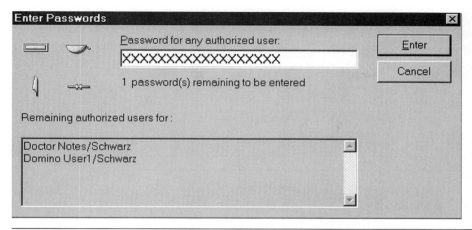

Figure 3-33   Typing a password from the required recovery authorities

Table 3-9   Necessary Access to Edit a Group

Database	Access Level
Domino Directory	Editor, with Create Document access or a GroupModifier role
Certification Log	Author, with Create Document access

To edit a group, select the People and Groups tab in the Domino Administrator, open the Groups view, and select the group that you want to edit. Expand the Groups tools and select Edit. The Domino Administrator displays the Group document, as shown in Figure 3-34.

If you choose to rename a group, you should be aware that no provision exists for enabling access to data by using the old name while the new name change is replicated across the domain. To work around this situation, either initiate the request during a weekend or during other off-hours, or force AdminP to complete the requests immediately by using the `Tell AdminP Process` command. Then force an immediate replication throughout the domain.

The available group types are as follows:

- Multi-purpose
- Access Control List only
- Mail only
- Servers only
- Deny List only

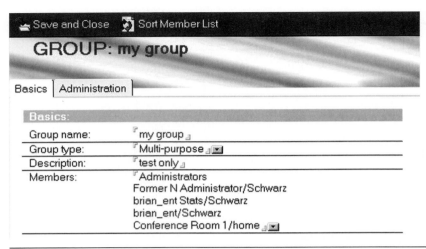

Figure 3-34 Group document

You can add and remove users, servers, and other groups in the Members field by typing or selecting the users or groups from the Domino Directory. You can nest Mail Only groups five deep; other group types can be nested six deep. The Owners and Administrators fields enable users who have Author access and do not have the GroupModifier role to edit the group.

An option that is available from the Actions menu while a group is selected is to rename the group. When you select this action, the Domino Administrator displays the dialog box in Figure 3-35 for you to give the group a new name. This action submits a Rename Group in Address Book request to the Administration Requests database. Although this request is an interval request by default, you can force AdminP to process the request immediately using the `Tell AdminP Process New` command. This action creates the following additional requests to process: Rename Group in

Figure 3-35
Renaming a group

Person Documents, Rename Group in Access Control List, and Rename Group in Reader/Author fields.

Deleting Groups

You might also need to delete groups, and to perform this task, you need the access levels shown in Table 3-10.

To delete the group, select the group name from the Groups view of the People and Groups tab. Expand the Groups tools, and choose Delete. Confirm that you want to delete the group, as shown in Figure 3-36. Domino prompts you to delete NT groups, as well.

Just as when deleting a user, Domino prompts you to decide whether to delete the group immediately or to send the request to the Administration Requests database, as shown in Figure 3-37. If you select Yes, the group is deleted immediately from the entire

Table 3-10   Necessary Access in Order to Delete a Group

Database	Access Level
Domino Directory	Author, with delete document access and a GroupModifier role, or Editor access

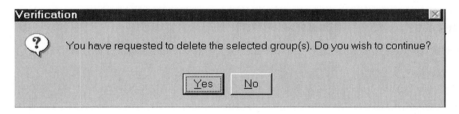

Figure 3-36   Deleting a group

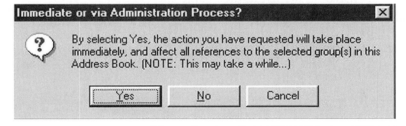

Figure 3-37   Immediate deletion or deletion via AdminP

Table 3-11 Requests to Delete a User

Requests	Note
Delete from Domino Directory Immediately	If you choose Yes, move to the Delete in Access Control List request. If you choose No, move to the Delete in Address Book request.
Delete in Address Book	This interval request deletes all references to the group in the Domino Directory.
Delete in Access Control List	This interval request removes the group from all ACLs.
Delete in Person Documents	This daily request removes the group's name from Person documents. This action is only performed if the Delete in Address Book request is performed; otherwise, it occurs when all references are removed from the Domino Directory.
Delete in Reader/Author Fields	This delayed request is performed after the deletion of groups in the ACLs of databases.

Domino Directory, and you wait while the request is completed. If you select No, a Delete in Address Book request is created in the Administration Requests database. Cancel stops the process.

AdminP creates and processes the requests shown in Table 3-11 to complete this process.

Maintaining Group Membership

In addition to managing group membership by editing the group, you can also use the Manage Groups tool. The benefit of this tool is that you can manage membership of multiple groups simultaneously as well as determine the group memberships of a user. The Manage Groups tool is shown in Figure 3-38.

On the left, select the Domino Directory whose users, servers, mail-in databases, resources, and groups you want to manage. All users, servers, mail-in databases, resources, and groups are listed on the left in the People and Groups list. These items can be listed alphabetically or by organization by using the drop-down list at the bottom. The right side shows the Group Hierarchies pane. First, select the Domino Directory whose groups you want to view. Then, select how you want to view the groups. Your choices are the following:

- All Group Hierarchies, to display all of the groups in the selected directory (see Figure 3-39)

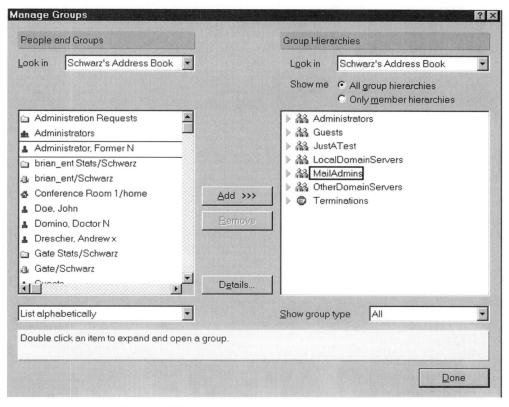

Figure 3-38 Manage Groups tool

- Only Member Hierarchies, to display only the groups to which the user, server, database, or group that is selected on the left belongs (see Figure 3-40)

You might choose to show all group types (or only a single type of group) from the drop-down list at the bottom-right. You can expand the group names in the Group Hierarchies pane to see the members of the group. Use the Add button to add users, servers, mail-in databases, resources, and groups from the People and Groups list to the groups in the Group Hierarchies pane. Use the Remove button to remove members from the groups in the Group Hierarchies pane. Use the Details button to view the Person, Server, Mail-in database, Resource, or Group documents for items in the People and Groups list.

Figure 3-39
All Group
Hierarchies

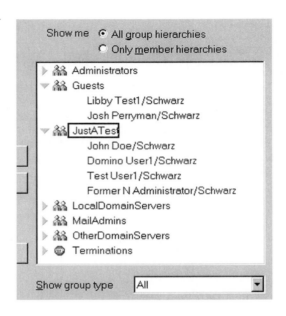

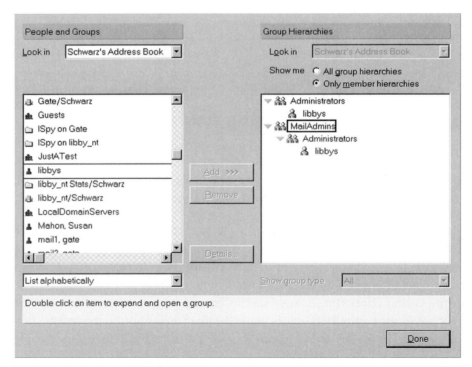

Figure 3-40 Only Member Hierarchies

Summary

In this chapter, we discussed the Domino Directory as well as the additional directory services that are provided with Domino, including Directory Catalog, Directory Assistance, and LDAP directory services. For the exam, you should know what each element of the directory services structure provides to the environment. Next, we discussed the maintenance of users and groups, including renaming, editing, and removing users and groups. For the exam, you should know how each of these steps is accomplished and what level of access you need to perform these tasks.

Review Questions

1. Simon has configured password and ID recovery in his organization. He needs to know what encrypts the recovery password. You tell him:
   A. Certifier ID public key
   B. Administrator's ID public key
   C. User ID public key
   D. Server ID public key

2. Simon has configured password and ID recovery in his organization. He needs to know where the recovery information is specified. You tell him:
   A. Certifier ID
   B. Administrator ID
   C. User ID
   D. Server ID

3. If Maggie needs to make sure that the Directory Catalog contains the newest changes from the secondary catalogs, what might she need to do?
   A. TELL DIRCAT RELOAD DIRCAT.NSF
   B. TELL DIRCAT REBUILD DIRCAT.NSF
   C. LOAD DIRCAT DIRCAT.NSF -RELOAD
   D. LOAD DIRCAT DIRCAT.NSF

4. Austin has Author access in the ACL of the Domino directory and needs to be able to modify the SoftballTeam group. What does the administrator in Austin's domain need to do to enable Austin to administer this group?
   A. Add him to the Administrator's field on the SoftballTeam group document
   B. Give him Editor access in the ACL
   C. Assign him the GroupModifier role
   D. Assign him the GroupCreator role

5. Emily created a mobile directory catalog for her remote users. A user calls and asks whether she can encrypt mail when using the mobile directory catalog, and if so, when the mail will be encrypted.
   A. No. To encrypt mail, you need to use a replica of the Domino directory.
   B. No. To encrypt mail, you need to copy the recipient's Person document into your local name and address book.
   C. Yes. The mail will be encrypted when you click send and store it in your outgoing mailbox on your local workstation.
   D. Yes. The mail will be encrypted when you connect in order to send and receive mail, just before the mail is transferred to the server's MAIL.BOX.

6. Which of the following functions can a server's Directory Catalog perform?
   A. Provide type ahead addressing to users
   B. Provide Web client authentication
   C. Provide mail addressing for LDAP users
   D. Provide mail addressing for Notes users

7. Which of the following functions can Directory Assistance perform?
   A. Provide type ahead addressing to users
   B. Provide Web client authentication using Domino or LDAP directories for credentials
   C. Provide mail addressing for LDAP users
   D. Provide mail addressing for Notes users

8. True or false: By default, LDAP users must authenticate in order to perform LDAP searches on a Domino directory.
   A. True
   B. False

9. Tyler wants to delete a user and ensure that the user cannot access the server without rebooting. Which steps does he *need* to take?
   A. Use AdminP to delete the user.
   B. Place the user's name in the Not Access this Server field in the Server document.
   C. Place the user's name in a group in the Not Access this Server field in the Server document.
   D. Approve the mail file deletion.

10. Morgan needs to move Doctor Notes/Schwarz to Doctor Notes/Remote1/ Schwarz. Which of the following actions should she perform?

    A. Use the Recertify Users tool.

    B. Use the Rename Users tool.

    C. She will have to recreate the user.

    D. Use the Edit Users tool.

Review Answers

1. **B** is correct. The recovery password is encrypted with the Administrator's public key.

2. **A** is correct. The recovery information is specified in the certifier ID. The recovery password is stored in the user ID.

3. **D** is correct. Loading the DIRCAT task will rebuild the directory catalog if necessary.

4. **A, B,** or **C** would accomplish this goal, but choice A is the best answer, because it only gives him access to the SoftballTeam group.

5. **D** is correct. The mail is encrypted before it is sent to the server.

6. **A, B,** and **D** are correct.

7. **All** are correct.

8. **B** is correct. Anonymous LDAP is enabled by default.

9. **A** and **C** are correct. He will need to approve the mail file deletion, but not in order to accomplish the immediate goals. If you list the name individually in the Server document, you will have to reboot the server. Putting the name in a group prevents this need.

10. **B** is correct. The Rename Users tool consists of a request to move the user to a different location in the hierarchy.

CHAPTER 4

Domino Messaging

You should be able to answer questions based on the following objectives after reading this chapter:

- Monitoring, maintaining, and troubleshooting Domino Messaging and replication
  - Forcing routing
  - Migrating to Domino from other mail systems
  - Monitoring/maintaining mail routing
  - Troubleshooting routing problems
- Monitoring, maintaining, and troubleshooting Domino applications
  - Monitoring/maintaining calendaring and scheduling
  - Troubleshooting calendaring and scheduling

Messaging is one of the prime tasks of your Domino environment. The Domino mail system supports mail using the following Internet standard mail protocols: Simple Mail Transfer Protocol (SMTP), Post-Office Protocol Version 3 (POP3), Internet Message Access Protocol (IMAP), and Multi-Purpose Internet Mail Extensions (MIME). In addition, Domino provides Notes mail (using Notes Remote Procedure Calls, or RPCs). Mail in your organization is likely to use Internet mail (using the standards-based systems that are supported by Domino and the MIME format) and Notes mail routing, which uses the Notes RPCs and a native rich-text format for messages. When users send mail between the systems, such as from Notes and Domino to the Internet, Domino performs the conversion from the Notes rich-text format to the necessary MIME format. You must be able to monitor and maintain the messaging environment, including both types of messaging (Internet and Notes-only).

To maintain the messaging in your Domino environment, you must understand a little bit about how routing works and how it is configured in your environment. Next, you must be able to use mail tracking, mail probes, mail usage reports, and other tracking mechanisms to determine the status of mail and messaging in your environment. If you determine that there are problems with messages after reviewing the monitoring tools, you must be able to fix the messaging. This solution can include working with mail Connection documents, forcing mail to route manually, and performing a mail trace or tracking an already-sent message. You might also need to verify that the Router task is running and what the inbound and outbound restrictions are on messaging in your environment (this task can also be considered customizing the messaging environment). Maintaining your messaging environment can also include migrating to Domino messaging from other messaging environments. In addition, you might need to enable your users to use POP3 and IMAP clients. Finally, you might also need to move mail files between multiple servers.

Most environments that use messaging also use calendaring and scheduling. For your users, messaging is closely related to calendaring and scheduling, so we will discuss the issues here. Calendaring and scheduling include the corporate calendar and holidays, resource reservations and profiles, and group scheduling using the Free Time database (BUSYTIME.NSF).

Mail Backgrounder

While this chapter does not describe configuring Domino messaging (this subject is covered in Chapter 11, "Implementing Domino Messaging"), you need to have some background in how the Domino mail system works. Before we discuss the server processes related to mail, it might be useful to refresh your memory about the front-end, or client, processes. These processes are not tested directly; however, to understand the routing process, you need to know how to use the client processes in Notes.

To begin a mail memo, the user opens his or her mail file and chooses the New Memo action button. This action displays the blank message form. The user either chooses the address button to place recipients in the TO: field or begins typing the user-name, waiting for Notes' type-ahead feature to complete the name. The user then types the body of the memo. Before sending, the user can choose the Delivery Options action button and request high or low priority or a return receipt. Other choices include the security options of signing, encrypting, and preventing copying. The user saves, saves and sends, sends, or discards the message.

During this mail process, the workstation-based mailer verifies the names in the TO:, CC:, or BCC: fields and then places the message in the server's mail-routing database, the MAIL.BOX. After the message has been delivered to the MAIL.BOX database, the Router determines where the message travels and how it gets to that destination. The Router decides where and how to route mail, taking into account the following factors:

- Is the mail going to a recipient on the same server and thus in the same Domino-Named Network (DNN)? If so, the message is delivered immediately.

- Is the mail going to a recipient on a different server in the same DNN? If so, the message is transferred and delivered immediately.

- Is the mail going to a recipient in another DNN, but still in the same domain? If so, the message is transferred based on the server Connection document.

- Is the mail going to a recipient in another domain altogether? If so, the message is transferred based on the server Connection document and the Domain documents.

Messaging is based on two main methods of routing. First, if two or more Domino servers are constantly connected and have the same protocol, they can be placed in the same DNN. Servers that are in the same DNN route mail to each other automatically and immediately. You can view the DNNs using the Messaging tab of Domino Administrator, in the Mail Routing Topology by Named Networks view, as shown in Figure 4-1. The MAPS Extractor task (or just MAPS) runs on the server to create this graphical map.

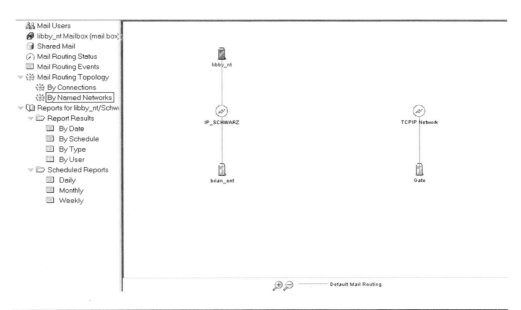

Figure 4-1   DNNs in the Domino Administrator

You can also check (and modify) which DNN a server is in via the Ports tab in the Server document, in the Notes Network field on the Notes Network Ports tab, as shown in Figure 4-2. Again, for servers to be placed in the same DNN, they must be constantly connected (i.e., servers that use dial-up connections should not be in the same DNN) and must use the same protocol.

The second method of routing (for servers that are not in the same DNN) is routing based on a schedule, which is created in a Connection document. Server Connection documents, which are created in the Messaging . . . Connections view in the Domino Administrator, determine the type of mail routing, the time of day that mail routes, the routing threshold, the default routing cost for that connection, and the router type. To route mail in both directions (i.e., to and from a particular server), two routing Connection documents are usually necessary. Figure 4-3 shows the Basics tab of the server Connection document. Table 4-1 describes the fields.

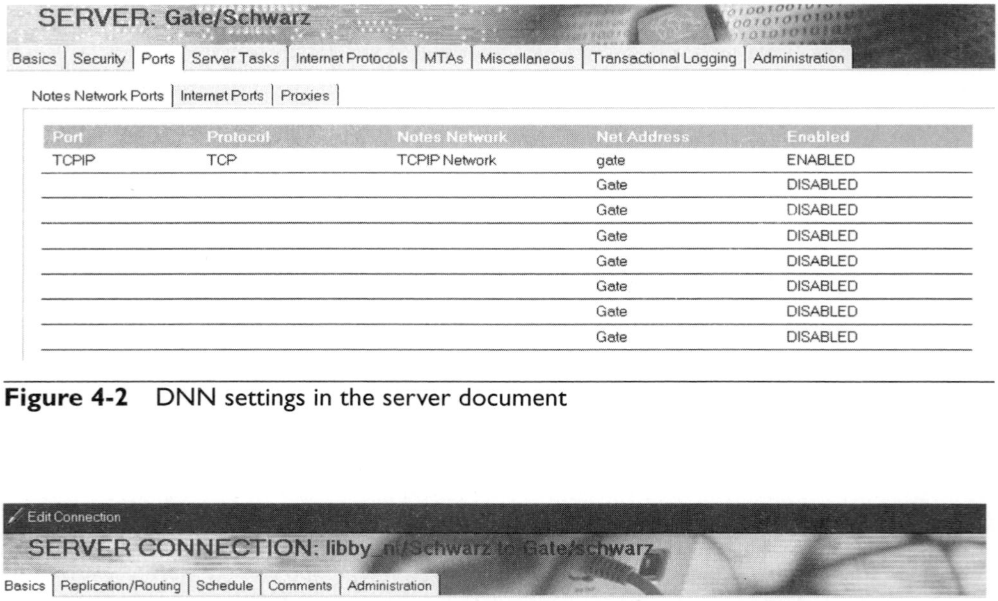

SERVER: Gate/Schwarz

Basics | Security | Ports | Server Tasks | Internet Protocols | MTAs | Miscellaneous | Transactional Logging | Administration

Notes Network Ports | Internet Ports | Proxies

Port	Protocol	Notes Network	Net Address	Enabled
TCPIP	TCP	TCPIP Network	gate	ENABLED
			Gate	DISABLED
			Gate	DISABLED
			Gate	DISABLED
			Gate	DISABLED
			Gate	DISABLED
			Gate	DISABLED
			Gate	DISABLED

Figure 4-2   DNN settings in the server document

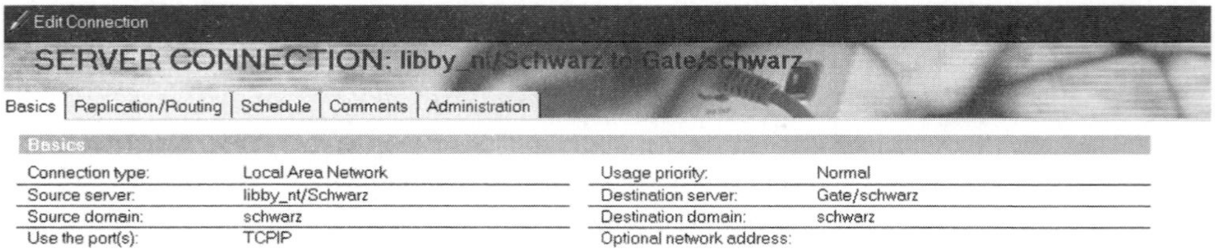

/ Edit Connection

SERVER CONNECTION: libby_nt/Schwarz to Gate/schwarz

Basics | Replication/Routing | Schedule | Comments | Administration

Basics

Connection type:	Local Area Network	Usage priority:	Normal
Source server:	libby_nt/Schwarz	Destination server:	Gate/schwarz
Source domain:	schwarz	Destination domain:	schwarz
Use the port(s):	TCPIP	Optional network address:	

Figure 4-3   The Basics tab of the connection document

Table 4-1   The Server Connection Basics Tab

Field	Description
Connection type	Choose the manner in which the servers connect to each other, such as Local Area Network, Notes Direct Dialup, or Network Dialup. Other fields on the tab are controlled by the type of connection. The fields described in this tab assume a Local Area Network connection.
Source Server	The source server is the one that initiates the connection.
Source Domain	The domain type of the source server
Use the port(s)	Determine which port the server should use to communicate.
Usage Priority	Choices are Normal and Low. If you want Domino to use some connections only as a last resort, set those to low priority.
Destination Server	The destination server is the one that receives the connection.
Destination Domain	The domain type of the destination server
Optional network address	Use this field if you are using TCP/IP or another protocol that requires a network address. If you are using TCP/IP, you can put the IP address of the server in this field.

These fields are usually part of creating a Connection document, which is covered in Chapter 11. For the purposes of maintaining and monitoring the connection, you might need to change the port or connection type.

The Replication/Routing tab, which is shown in Figure 4-4, enables you to configure the schedule for both replication (refer to Chapter 5, "Domino Applications and Replication") and mail routing. Refer to Table 4-2 for a description of the routing fields.

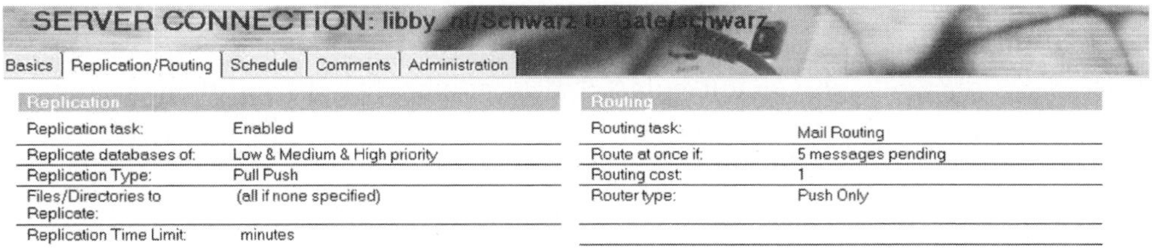

SERVER CONNECTION: libby_nf/Schwarz to Gate/schwarz

Basics | Replication/Routing | Schedule | Comments | Administration

Replication		Routing	
Replication task:	Enabled	Routing task:	Mail Routing
Replicate databases of:	Low & Medium & High priority	Route at once if:	5 messages pending
Replication Type:	Pull Push	Routing cost:	1
Files/Directories to Replicate:	(all if none specified)	Router type:	Push Only
Replication Time Limit:	minutes		

Figure 4-4   The Replication/Routing tab

Table 4-2 The Server Connection Replication/Routing Tab

Field	Description
Routing Task	The default in this field is Mail Routing, which refers to standard Notes RPC routing. Other choices include X.400 Mail routing and cc:Mail routing (which require additional configuration of an MTA, or Message Transfer Agent), SMTP routing, and None to disable mail routing.
Route at once if X messages pending	This threshold forces the Router to transfer and deliver messages when the threshold is reached. The default is five messages pending. If five messages are pending, the Router sends the messages regardless of the schedule.
Routing Cost	The routing cost determines the cost of the current connection. When multiple connections to a server are permitted, Domino chooses the connection with the lowest cost. By default, LAN connections have a low cost (1), and dial-up connections have a high cost (5). The cost of a connection is raised automatically if a connection fails, although the connection will be reset if you restart the Router or if inbound mail arrives from the failed server.
Router Type	Choices include Push Only (the default), Pull Only, Pull Push, and Push Wait. Usually, servers only push messages to the destination server; however, this field enables you to configure the Router to pull messages and to pull and push messages. The Push Wait option means that the server will not transfer mail to a remote Domino server until it receives a pull request from that Domino server.

NOTE Users can set messages as high or low priority in the mail client, but this setting can affect the routing. High-priority messages are always routed immediately, regardless of the schedule. Low-priority messages are always routed during the low-priority interval (midnight to 6 A.M. by default). Low-priority messages count toward the routing threshold but are not transferred when the threshold is reached. Messages to other users on the same server or within the same DNN are also delivered or transferred immediately, regardless of their priority.

The Schedule tab, as shown in Figure 4-5, determines when the specified options are valid (including times and days). Refer to Table 4-3 for a description of the fields.

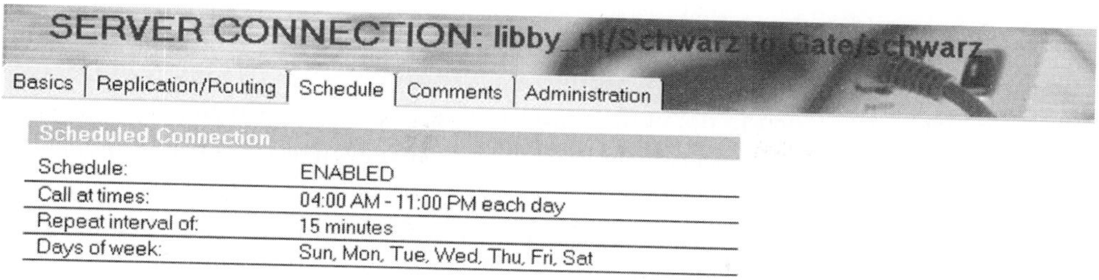

SERVER CONNECTION: libby_nt/Schwarz to Gate/schwarz

| Basics | Replication/Routing | Schedule | Comments | Administration |

Scheduled Connection

Schedule:	ENABLED
Call at times:	04:00 AM - 11:00 PM each day
Repeat interval of:	15 minutes
Days of week:	Sun, Mon, Tue, Wed, Thu, Fri, Sat

Figure 4-5   The Schedule tab

Table 4-3   The Server Connection Schedule Tab

Field	Description
Schedule	Choose whether the schedule is enabled or disabled. At times, you might need to disable a certain connection (for example, when a server is offline), but you might not want to delete the Connection document.
Call at Times	Times at which the server should make contact with the destination server. This field can be specific times or ranges of time. Be sure to include at least one Connection document that includes the low-priority mail interval, or these messages will never be transferred.
Repeat Interval	The value in this field describes how often the source server will attempt to contact the destination server. If only one time or one call is desired, this field can be left blank. If a call for routing starts at the first call on time (4 A.M. by default) and finishes at 4:15 A.M.—and the repeat interval is 60 minutes—the next call will be made at 5:15 A.M.
Days of Week	Choose the days of the week that this Connection document is valid. You can choose to have different connection times for the weekends, for example.

Monitoring Messaging

Now that you have an understanding of the basic functions of the Domino messaging environment, you need to be able to monitor messages. You monitor messages by using the following tools:

- Notes Log
- Mail routing statistics
- Mail status, which is visible in MAIL.BOX or the Mail Routing Status view
- Mail usage reports
- Mail probes

Notes Log

Use the Server . . . Analysis tab in the Domino Administrator to access the Notes Log, as shown in Figure 4-6. Documents in the Mail Routing Events view display both successful and unsuccessful routing messages. This view is also available from the Messaging tab, under the Mail Routing Events view.

Sometimes it can be difficult to find specific information in the Notes Log by scanning the log documents. If necessary, use the Analyze Log tool shown in Figure 4-7 to look for specific words in the log file.

When troubleshooting, you might feel that the Notes Log messages about routing do not give you enough information. To control the logging level, use the Configuration Settings document. In the Configuration Settings document, navigate to the Router/SMTP . . . Advanced . . . Controls tab. Use the *Logging Level* field to choose Minimal, Normal, Informational, or Verbose messages. Normal, which gives minimal

	#	Starting Time	Ending Time
▼ 11/06			
	1	03:43 PM	09:32 PM
▼ 11/07			
	1	01:45 PM	09:59 PM
▼ 11/08			
	1	04:06 PM	
▼ 11/10			
	1	06:38 PM	
▼ 11/11			
	1	05:28 PM	04:24 PM
▼ 11/12			
	1	04:24 PM	06:08 PM
	2	06:08 PM	08:11 PM
	3	08:11 PM	10:11 PM
	4	10:11 PM	10:57 PM
▼ 11/13			
	1	09:49 AM	

Figure 4-6   Mail routing events

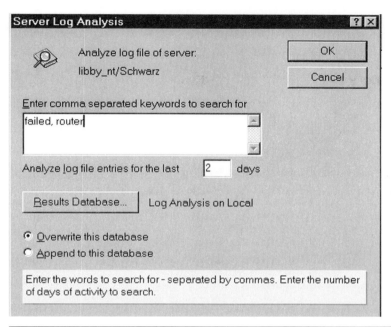

Figure 4-7 Analyzing the Notes Log

detail and warning messages, is the default. You should use Verbose only while you are troubleshooting (to maintain the Log file size).

Mail Routing Statistics

To view the mail routing statistics, use the Server . . . Statistics view in the Domino Administrator. Expand the Mail statistics, as shown in Figure 4-8. Useful statistics include the AverageDeliverTime, Dead, Hold, MaximumDeliverTime, Waiting, Total-Failures, and TransferFailures, for example. When you see high deliver times, dead or waiting messages, or failures, you need to determine whether there is a problem with a server, connection, or directory.

You can also obtain mail routing statistics by typing the following command at the console, if necessary (you can use the specific statistic if you know the name):

```
Show Stat Mail.*
```

or

```
Show Stat Mail.Waiting
```

Figure 4-8
Mail routing
statistics

Mail Status

The Mail Routing Status view under the Messaging tab is a graphical display of the number of dead or waiting messages on your server, as shown in Figure 4-9. Dead messages (which do not occur often) are messages that could not be delivered to the recipient—and neither could a Non-Delivery Report (NDR) be returned to the sender. This situation occurs when a Router is down, when network problems are occurring, or when a Person or Connection document has become corrupted, for example. Waiting,

Figure 4-9
Mail Routing Status
view

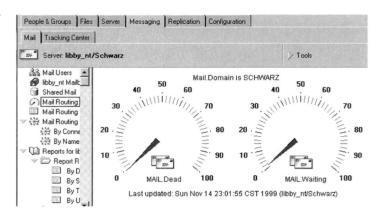

or pending, messages are messages that are in the message queue pending delivery. They might be waiting for a scheduled connection, for example, or they might be low-priority messages.

You can also view waiting or dead messages in the MAIL.BOX database on the server. In addition, you can view held messages, which are undeliverable messages that you have required the Router to leave in MAIL.BOX, rather than returning to the sender. You force this event to occur to determine why messages are not being delivered correctly. To view the contents of MAIL.BOX, open the Messaging tab in Domino Administrator and select the *Servername* mailbox (MAIL.BOX) view, where *Servername* is the name of the current server. In the Results pane, the Domino Administrator shows information about the held or dead messages, but does not show the message itself. We describe the options for resolving dead and held messages later in this chapter.

Mail Usage Reports

Mail usage reports are messaging reports that you define. They can be run once or can be based on a schedule. Before you can create mail usage reports, you must enable Message Tracking on the server. Message Tracking is run by the Message Tracking Collector (MTC) task on the server. To start Message Tracking, enable the MTC task on the server by typing LOAD MTC at the server console or by adding `MTC` to the `ServerTasks=` line in the NOTES.INI file. The MTC task creates the Mail Tracking Store database (MTSTORE.NSF) in the MTDATA directory. You can also start the MTC task using the Start Task tool on the Server tab. Select the Start Task tool, and in the Start New Task dialog box, select Message Tracking Collector (MTC).

 TIP If the MTDATA directory does not exist when you enable the MTC task for the first time, the task may fail to start. You might need to create the MTDATA directory manually.

After the MTC task has been running for a period, you can create the mail usage reports. To create a mail usage report, select any of the views under Report Results or Scheduled Reports in the Messaging tab. Select the Run Report action button to configure a report. The Report Request dialog box, shown in Figure 4-10, enables you to select a report type, time range, execution interval for the report, and other options. You can decide whether the report should be mailed or saved in the MTSTORE.NSF.

The reports might display data such as Top 25 Largest Messages or Top 25 Senders by Count. A sample report displaying the Message Volume is shown in Figure 4-11.

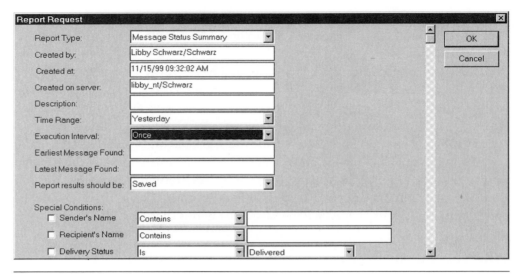

Figure 4-10   A mail usage report request

Mail Probes

Mail probes use a server task to determine how long it takes to deliver messages. The server task ISpy (or RunJava ISpy) must be running to probe the servers. In addition, the COLLECT task should be running in order to store the results of the mail probes in the Statistics database. Check to see whether the tasks are running by looking at the Task list on the Server Status tab. If the ISpy task is not running, you must start the task to use probes of any kind. To start the ISpy task, you can type LOAD ISpy at the server console, add ISpy to the ServerTasks= line in the NOTES.INI file, or use the Start Task tool in the Domino Administrator.

> **NOTE**   While most server tasks and other elements in Notes and Domino are not case-sensitive, the ISpy task is case-sensitive and should be typed as shown.

Create a mail probe on the Configuration tab of the Domino Administrator. Expand the Statistics and Events twistie and select Mail from the Probes choices. Click the New Mail Probe action button. In the Mail Probe document, as shown in Figure 4-12, use the Basics tab to determine which servers will send probes to which mail file. You can

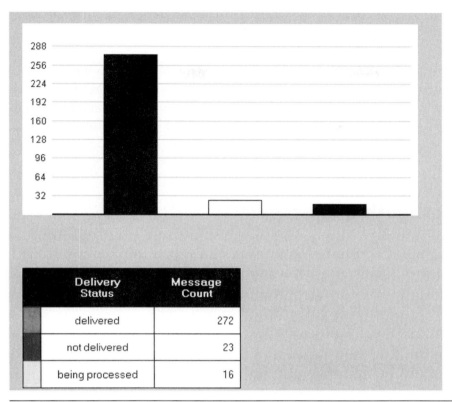

Figure 4-11   A sample message usage report

Delivery Status	Message Count
delivered	272
not delivered	23
being processed	16

Mail Probe
Event Number: LSCZ-4DNLAA
Basics | Probe | Other

☐ All Domino servers in the domain will probe themselves

Target mail address (destination)

Recipient: Administrator/Schwarz

Note: Only one mail address should be listed as the recipient. Do not use group names or multiple addresses as it will cause the probe to fail.

Probing servers (source)

Server(s): libby_nt/Schwarz   Servers...

Figure 4-12   Mail probe basics

also select *All Domino Servers in the domain will probe themselves* to force all servers to probe themselves using a local mail file. Otherwise, select a recipient and the servers that should try to reach that recipient.

On the Probe tab, select a send interval and a timeout interval. On the Other tab, determine what to do if the probe times out. You can generate an event for the Statistics and Events database. You can also use the *Create a new notification profile for this event* button to use the Profile Wizard to determine how you will be notified if the mail probe times out. You can also disable the probe on this tab.

Troubleshooting Messaging

When you monitor the messaging environment as described previously, you might discover messages that are not routing. When this situation occurs, you need to troubleshoot the messaging environment. Troubleshooting the messaging environment includes checking server Connection documents, checking the Router task, forcing routing manually, and using mail tracking and mail tracing. You will also use the MAIL.BOX to correct and release dead and held messages.

Server Connection Documents

As described previously, when servers are in different DNNs, they require a Connection document to schedule mail routing. If there is a large message queue or if messages are not being delivered to a particular destination, the problem might be a corrupt, deleted, or incorrect Connection document. Check to ensure that the appropriate Connection document exists and is enabled. Check the schedule in the Connection document to ensure that it provides a reasonable schedule. Check to ensure that a Connection document covers the low-priority interval so that low-priority messages are routed. You might need to recreate Connection documents in case of corruption or deletion.

Router Task

You can use the server console or the Domino Administrator to check the Router task. The router must be running for mail to be delivered or transferred. To check the Router using the Domino Administrator, you can use the Server . . . Monitoring tab to ensure that the Router task is running, as shown in Figure 4-13. Note that you also see information such as dead, held, and waiting mail in this view.

You can also use the Server . . . Status tab to determine the status of the Router task, as well as to start or stop the task if necessary. To start or stop the Router task, use the

Figure 4-13
The Server Monitoring tab

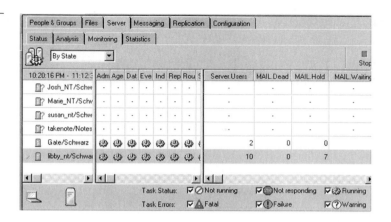

Start Task and Stop Task tools that are available on this tab. You can also type LOAD ROUTER or TELL ROUTER QUIT at the server console. You can also use the Messaging tools found on the Messaging tab (there is a Start Router tool and a Stop Router tool available).

Routing Mail Manually

Sometimes you might want to route mail to a particular server manually, so that you do not have to wait for the next connection time or for the routing threshold. This situation is especially true when you are troubleshooting routing problems. To route mail manually from the server console, type ROUTE servername. You can also use the Domino Administrator to force mail to route to a specified server. On the Messaging tab, expand the Messaging tools. Select the Route Mail tool to display the Route Mail dialog box, as shown in Figure 4-14. Select the server with which you want to route, and click the Route button.

Figure 4-14
The Route Mail dialog box

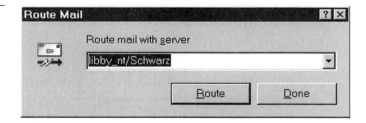

Mail Tracking and Tracing

When users have trouble sending messages, you might want to track or trace mail. Mail tracking traces the route of a message that a user has already sent, showing where the message is. A mail trace shows the path that the message itself takes, including where the message stops.

Mail Tracking

Mail tracking enables you to determine the location of a particular sent message. This procedure requires the MTC task described previously and the MTSTORE.NSF database. In addition, use a configuration settings document to enable and configure settings for Message Tracking. In Domino Administrator, select the Configurations tab. Then, select Configurations under the Messaging section. Add or edit a Configuration document. Figure 4-15 shows the Message Tracking tab, which is nested under the Router/SMTP tab. Table 4-4 describes the available fields.

After configuring Message Tracking, use the Tracking Center tab under the Messaging tab to track mail messages. Click the *New Tracking Request* button to start tracking a message. In the New Tracking Request dialog box, complete any of the fields that describe the message for which you are searching. The more fields you complete, the better your results.

After the tracking request runs, results are displayed in the Messages Found pane. To determine the delivery status and transfer details for that message, select the message and click the *Track Selected Message* button. The servers that the message hopped

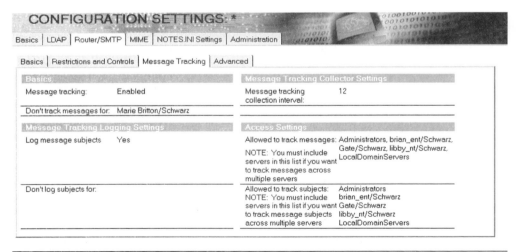

Figure 4-15   Message tracking settings

Table 4-4 Message Tracking Configurations

Field	Description
Message Tracking	Use this field to enable or disable message tracking. Even if the MTC task is running on the server, you cannot use message tracking if this setting is disabled.
Don't track messages for	Use this field to disable message tracking for selected users from the Domino Directory. This field applies to messages sent by selected users or groups.
Log message subjects	Use this field to choose to log message subjects. The default is to not log message subjects.
Don't log subjects for	Use this field to disable message subject logging for selected users from the Domino Directory. This field applies to messages sent by selected users or groups.
Message tracking collection interval	Enter how often the MTC should track messages, in minutes. The default interval is 15 minutes.
Allowed to track messages	Use this field to determine which users and servers can track messages. By default, only LocalDomainServers members are permitted to track messages.
Allowed to track subjects	Use this field to determine which users and servers can track message subjects. By default, only LocalDomainServers members are permitted to track message subjects. If a user or server is listed in this field, they are assumed to be permitted to track messages and do not have to be listed twice.

through are shown in the left pane, and the transfer details and status are shown in the right pane, as shown in Figure 4-16.

Mail Trace

You can send a mail trace to see which servers a message passes through on its way to its intended recipient. To send a mail trace, use the Send Mail Trace tool from the Messaging tools on the Messaging tab of the Domino Administrator. In the Send Mail Trace dialog box, select the user to whom you want to send the Mail Trace message. The user does not receive a message.

Either accept the default subject (Mail Trace Message) or type a new one and then decide whether you want to receive mail trace information from each server that the message hops to—or only from the last server the message crosses. You receive the results of the trace information in your mail file, as shown in Figure 4-17.

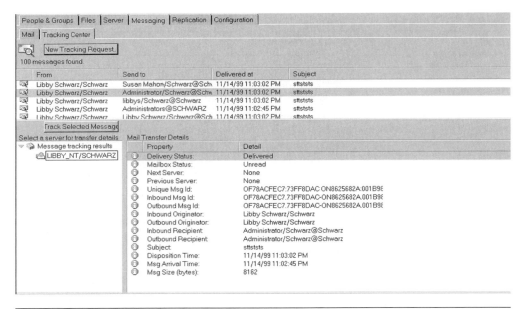

Figure 4-16   Message tracking details

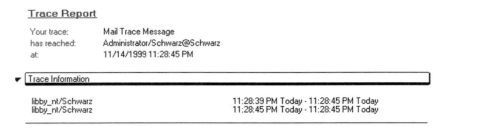

Figure 4-17   Viewing the results of a mail trace

MAIL.BOX

As described previously, when messages are pending, dead, or held, they are stored in the server's mailbox (MAIL.BOX). Pending messages are waiting to be transferred, and dead messages are both undeliverable and unreturnable to the sender. You can choose to have undeliverable messages held in the MAIL.BOX by using the Router/SMTP tab in the configuration settings document. Navigate to the Advanced . . . Controls tab, and set the *Hold undeliverable mail* option to Enabled, as shown in Figure 4-18.

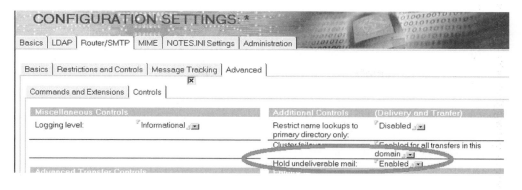

Figure 4-18 Choosing to Hold undeliverable mail

You can access MAIL.BOX via the Messaging tab in the Domino Administrator. Use the MMAIL.BOX action buttons to delete or release messages as needed. In addition, you can choose to correct an address via MAIL.BOX to make a message deliverable.

To delete a dead message, select the Delete Message action button while a dead message is selected in the view. To release messages, you have the following options:

- Release all dead messages, which forces the Router to attempt to resend all dead messages. If the Router is still unable to deliver the message or a non-delivery report, the Router re-marks the message as Dead.

- Release selected dead messages, which forces the Router to attempt to resend selected dead messages. If the Router is still unable to deliver the message or a non-delivery report, the Router re-marks the message as Dead.

- Release selected dead messages to recipients, which forces the Router to attempt to resend the Non-Delivery Notice (NDN) for the selected dead messages—the name you updated. If the Router is still unable to deliver the NDN, the Router re-marks the message as Dead.

- Release selected Held messages, which forces the Router to attempt to resend selected held messages. If the Router is still unable to deliver the message, the router re-marks the message as Held.

- Release selected Held messages for a final time, which forces the Router to attempt to resend selected held messages. If the Router is still unable to deliver the message, the Router delivers the NDN to the sender.

To correct an address using MAIL.BOX, open and edit the message. Correct the addresses in the Recipients field, and then save and close the message. The Router should attempt to deliver or transfer the message.

Customizing Mail Routing

You can improve and control the performance of messaging in your environment by customizing mail routing. You can improve performance by editing and customizing the Configuration documents for the servers.

The first element in mail routing that you can choose to customize is the number of MAIL.BOXes on your server. Because all mail is written to MAIL.BOX while in transit, there is sometimes a backlog when messaging is heavy or when large messages are written to the database. To improve performance by enabling the server to write to a different mail database when one is busy, use the Configuration settings document to create additional mailboxes. The *Number of mailboxes* setting, which can be from one to ten, is located on the Basics tab under Router/SMTP in the Configuration settings document.

Another option that might improve server performance is to disable type-ahead addressing from the Domino Directory. If you disable type-ahead addressing from the Domino Directory, users can use type-ahead from their personal address book or from the Directory catalog, select a name from the directory, or type a name manually. This setting is controlled in the Configuration settings document. Navigate to the Basics tab of the Configuration settings document and choose Disabled in the *Type Ahead* field.

You have the ability to place restrictions on both incoming and outgoing mail messages in Domino to improve the performance of the messaging environment. The restrictions, which you implement using the Router/SMTP . . . Restrictions and Controls tab in the Configuration settings document, enable you to prevent unwanted mail, to restrict for size, and to determine which users can send and receive mail through your servers. On the Router/SMTP . . . Restrictions and Controls . . . Restrictions tab, shown in Figure 4-19, you control the basic Notes routing. Refer to Table 4-5 for a list of the fields.

You can also control SMTP Inbound and Outbound routing by using those tabs. Figure 4-20 shows the SMTP Inbound Controls. Figure 4-21 shows the Outbound controls. Refer to Table 4-6 for some of the pertinent fields from both the Inbound and Outbound controls tabs.

The Delivery Controls tab places some limits on how the Router delivers mail to user mail files. Figure 4-22 shows the Delivery Controls tab. Table 4-7 describes the fields on the Delivery Controls tab. Remember that mail delivery occurs when a message is placed into a mail file.

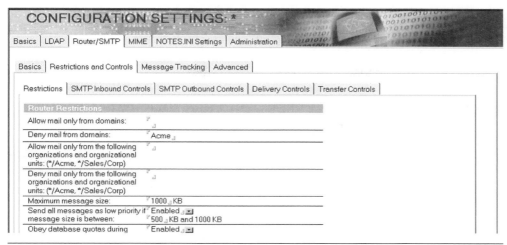

Figure 4-19   Router restrictions

Table 4-5   Router Restrictions

Field	Description
Allow mail only from domains	The server will accept mail from these domains. If you leave the field blank, all domains are permitted.
Deny mail from domains	The server will not accept mail from these domains. Leave this field blank to permit mail from all domains.
Allow mail only from the following organizations and organizational units	The server will accept mail from these Organizations and Organizational Units. If you leave the field blank, all Os and OUs are permitted. This setting applies only to users who have Notes-distinguished names.
Deny mail only from the following organizations and organizational units	The server will not accept mail from these Organizations and Organizational Units. If you leave the field blank, all Os and OUs are permitted. This setting applies only to users who have Notes-distinguished names.
Maximum message size	This field enables you to set a maximum size for messages (in kilobytes). If the message is larger than the specified size, a non-delivery notice is returned to the sender, and the message is not delivered or transferred.
Send all messages as low priority if message size is between	If you enable this setting, you can set a size range between which messages are only sent during the low-priority interval. If a message is between 500K and 1,000K, for example, you might force the message to be low priority.

(continued)

Table 4-5 Router Restrictions (*continued*)

Field	Description
Obey database quotas during delivery	Enable this setting to force the Router to obey the file size quota that you place on a mail database. If this setting is disabled, messages will be delivered even if the mail file exceeds its size quota.

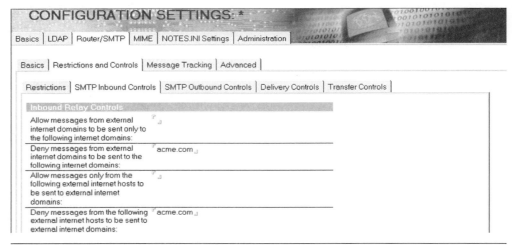

Figure 4-20   SMTP Inbound Controls

Figure 4-21   SMTP Outbound Controls

Table 4-6   SMTP Controls

Field	Description
(Inbound)	
Allow messages from external Internet domains to be sent only to the following Internet domains	Type domains to which this domain will send relay messages. Only domains listed here are permitted.
Deny messages from external Internet domains to be sent to the following Internet domains	Type domains to which this domain will not send relay messages. If you leave the field blank, all domains are permitted. You can use a wild card (*) to deny all.
Allow messages only from the following Internet hosts to be sent to external Internet domains	Type any host names that should be able to relay messages through this server. If you leave the field blank, all are permitted. You can also use IP addresses in this field.
Deny messages only from the following Internet hosts to be sent to external Internet domains	Type any host names that should not have the capacity to relay messages through this server. If you leave the field blank, all are permitted. You can use a wild card (*) to deny all. You can also use IP addresses in this field.
Verify connecting host name in DNS	Enable this option to force Domino to verify that the host name can be found in DNS before accepting messages. This function uses server resources.
Allow connections only from the following SMTP Internet host names/IP addresses	Type any domains/host names that should have the capability to connect to this domain. If you leave the field blank, all are permitted.
Deny connections from the following SMTP Internet host names/IP addresses	Type any domains/host names that should not have the capability to connect to this domain. If you leave the field blank, all are permitted. You can use a wild card (*) to deny all. Note that a domain will include all addresses, but actual addresses must match exactly.
Verify sender's domain in DNS	Enable this option to force Domino to verify that the sender's address can be found in DNS before accepting messages. This function uses server resources.
Allow messages only from the following external Internet addresses/domains	Type any Internet addresses that should have the capacity to send messages to this domain. If you leave the field blank, all are permitted.
Deny messages from the following Internet addresses/domains	Type any Internet addresses that should not have the capability to send messages to this domain. If you leave the field blank, all are permitted. You can use a wild card (*) to deny all.

(continued)

Table 4-6   SMTP Controls (*continued*)

Field	Description
Allow messages intended only for the following internet addresses	Type any Internet addresses that should receive messages via this server. If you leave the field blank, all are permitted.
Deny messages intended only for the following Internet addresses	Type any Internet addresses that should not receive messages via this server. If you leave the field blank, all are permitted.
(Outbound)	
Allow messages only from the following Internet addresses to be sent to the Internet	Type any Internet addresses that should be allowed to send Internet mail. If you leave the field blank, all are allowed to perform this function.
Deny messages from the following Internet addresses to be sent to the Internet	Type any Internet addresses that should not be allowed to send Internet mail. If you leave the field blank, all are allowed to perform this function. You can use a wild card (*) to deny all.
Allow messages from the following Notes addresses to be sent to the Internet	Type any Notes user addresses that should be allowed to send Internet mail. If you leave the field blank, all are allowed to perform this function.
Deny messages from the following Notes addresses to be sent to the Internet	Type any Notes user addresses that should not be allowed to send Internet mail. If you leave the field blank, all are allowed to perform this function. You can use a wild card (*) to deny all.

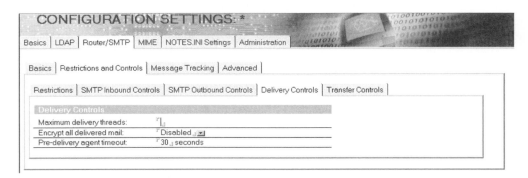

Figure 4-22   Delivery controls

Table 4-7   Delivery Controls

Field	Description
Maximum Delivery Threads	Use this number to limit the number of server threads used for mail delivery.
Encrypt all delivered mail	Enable this option to encrypt all mail as it is delivered.
Pre-delivery agent timeout	Use this field to set a limit on the number of seconds that an agent that uses the *Before mail arrives* trigger can take to execute. If the agent exceeds the limit, the agent is stopped.

Figure 4-23   Transfer controls

The Transfer Controls tab places some limits on how the Router transfers mail to the mailbox on other servers. Figure 4-23 shows the Transfer Controls tab. Table 4-8 describes the fields on the Transfer Controls tab. Remember that mail transfer occurs when the Router forwards a message to another server's MAIL.BOX.

Moving Mail Files

In Chapter 5, "Domino Applications and Replication," we describe how to move general files to different servers. Mail files are somewhat different from other mail files, however, and require some different options. You might need to move a mail file if a user transfers to another department or city, for example, or if you are taking a server out of use or are placing one in use.

Table 4-8   Transfer Controls

Field	Description
Maximum transfer threads	Use this number to limit the number of server threads that are used for mail transfer to all other servers. Usually, let Domino select this number based on the amount of memory in the server. Lotus recommends setting this number between one and 25 (based on load) if you set the field manually.
Maximum concurrent transfer threads	Use this number to limit the number of server threads used for mail transfer to a single other server. The default is half of the maximum transfer threads.
Maximum hop count	This number defines the number of hops a message can take before being determined undeliverable. A hop is counted each time a message hits a server's MAIL.BOX. The default is 25.
Low priority mail routing time range	The Router transfers mail that is marked as low priority during this time interval. Default is midnight to 6 A.M.
Initial transfer retry interval	If the Router fails at transferring a message to a remote server, it tries again after the number of minutes specified in this field. If the Router continues to fail, Domino raises the number. The default is 15 minutes.
Expired message purge interval	The Router checks for expired messages to purge often. The default is 15 minutes.

There are two ways to move a mail file: using the menus, or using the new R5 Admin tools. Both ways use the *Administration Process* (AdminP) to move the mail files. To move the mail file using AdminP, first ensure that you have AdminP running on the source and destination servers. In addition, you and the source server will need access to Create new replica databases on the destination server.

When moving using the menus in the Domino Administrator, open to the People and Groups tab and select the user(s) to move. Select Actions . . . Move Mail File from the menus. In the New Mail Server Name dialog box, shown in Figure 4-24, type the

Figure 4-24

Moving a mail file

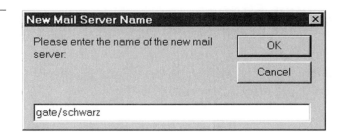

hierarchical name of the destination server. This action starts the process by submitting the requests to the Administration Requests database.

To move the mail files using the administration tools, open to the People and Groups tab and select the user(s) to move. In the people tools, select the Move tool from the tools list. In the Move Mail Files dialog box, shown in Figure 4-25, select the server to which you want to move the mail file(s).

Next, select a location on that server for the mail file—such as in the Mail directory or in another subdirectory, as shown in Figure 4-26. Again, this process submits a request to the Administration Requests database.

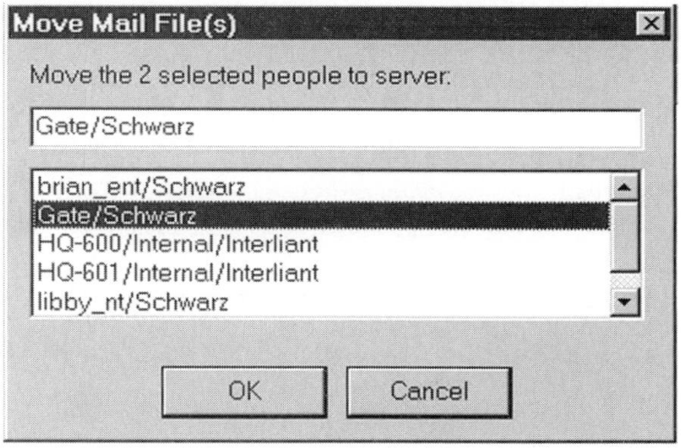

Figure 4-25
Moving mail files
using the tool

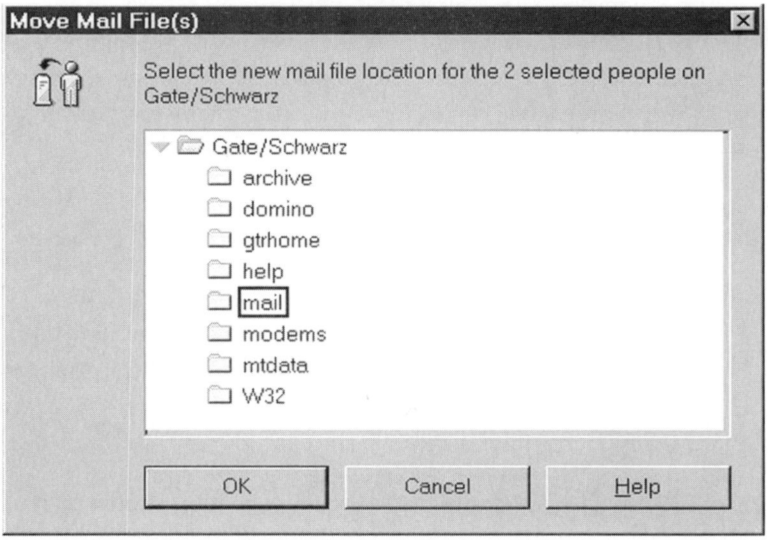

Figure 4-26 Where to place the mail file

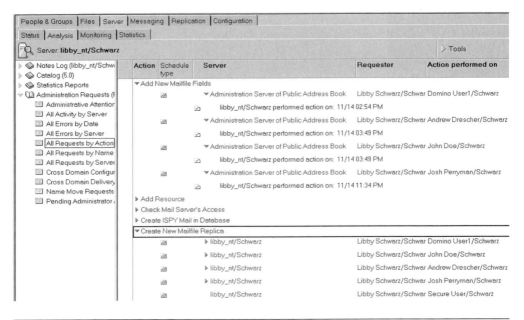

Figure 4-27 Requests in process for moving a mail file

As the first request completes and the Administration Requests database and the Domino Directory replicate between the source and destination servers (and the Administration server of the Domino Directory), the request is completed. Figure 4-27 shows some of the requests in process in the Administration Requests database (Admin4.NSF). Keep in mind that a Move Mail File request has many elements and waits for appropriate intervals to occur before completing each step.

Migrating to Domino

One important task in managing the Domino messaging environment is moving users from other messaging environments to Domino. The Domino Administrator provides tools that migrate both users and mail files from other messaging and directory environments. You should know three important aspects of migrating:

- Migrating imports data from a legacy or other messaging system and converts it to a format that the Domino Directory and Domino mail files understand.

- Importing moves data from an external mail source and makes the data available to be processed by the Domino mail system.
- Converting changes the imported data to Domino and Notes formats.

Domino contains tools for migrating from the following messaging or directory systems:

- LDAP Data Interchange Format (LDIF) files
  - Requires an LDIF export tool as well
  - Creates Person documents (no groups supported currently)
  - Has the option to create Notes IDs and mail files for migrated users
- Lotus cc:Mail and Organizer
  - Imports users and groups from the post office
  - Creates entries in the Domino Directory
  - Creates a Notes ID and mail file for imported users
  - Migrates contents of the cc:Mail mail boxes
  - Converts Organizer files to Notes database files
- Microsoft Exchange
  - Imports users and distribution lists (groups) from the Exchange server
  - Creates entries in the Domino Directory
  - Creates a Notes ID and mail file for imported users
  - Migrates the contents of mailboxes
- Microsoft Mail
  - Imports users and groups from the post office
  - Creates entries in the Domino Directory
  - Creates a Notes ID and mail file for imported users
  - Migrates the contents of mail boxes
- Microsoft Windows NT Server
  - Imports users and groups from the NT Domain Security Accounts Manager list
  - Creates entries in the Domino Directory
  - Creates a Notes ID and mail file for imported users

- Netscape Messaging Server
  - Imports users and groups from the Netscape Directory server (LDAP server)
  - Creates entries in the Domino Directory
  - Creates a Notes ID and mail file for imported users
  - Migrates IMAP4 mailboxes from the Netscape Messaging server
- Novell GroupWise 4.X and 5.X
  - Imports users and groups from the post office
  - Creates entries in the Domino Directory
  - Creates a Notes ID and mail file for imported users
  - Migrates the contents of mailboxes

NOTE   Note that the Migration tools are not installed by default when you install the Domino Administrator. Instead, you must complete a custom install and select the Migration tools, or they will not be available.

TIP   For more details about migrating from each of the supported directories or mail systems, refer to the Moving to Notes and Domino Release 5 book or to Domino Administrator help.

To begin the process of migrating users, open the People and Groups tab in the Domino Administrator and select Register from the People tools. Domino displays the Register Person dialog box, as shown in Figure 4-28. Click the Migrate People button to display the People and Groups migration dialog box.

First, select a foreign directory source from which to obtain the user and group information to migrate. Microsoft Mail and cc:Mail are post office-based directories. Selecting either of these options gives you the opportunity to indicate the path to the post office as well as to an administrator account and password. Exchange, GroupWise 5.x, and NT require access to the administration programs of those applications. In the case of migrating from an NT domain, you must be running Domino Administrator from an NT Domain Controller machine. Others such as GroupWise 4.x, LDIF, and Netscape import a file that contains the user information. Figure 4-29 shows the cc:Mail choices. Figure 4-30 shows migrating from a Netscape mail server. Figure 4-31 shows selecting a Windows NT domain.

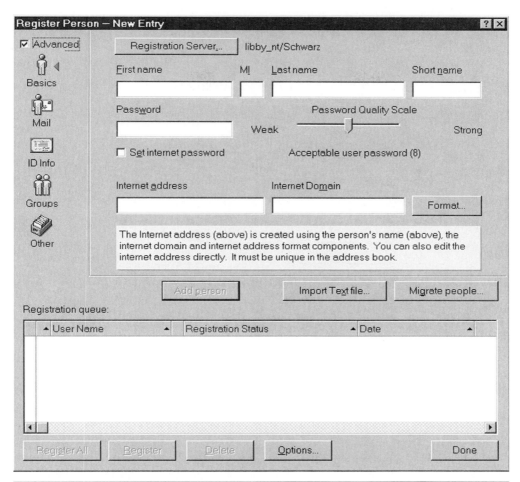

Figure 4-28   The Register Person dialog box

After selecting the directory source, select the people and groups to migrate from the *Available People/Groups* list, shown in Figure 4-32. Notice that each directory source has some specific migration options. When migrating from NT, for example, you have the following additional options:

- Generating random passwords
- Adding a full name provided to the Notes Person document
- Allowing the addition of empty groups to Notes

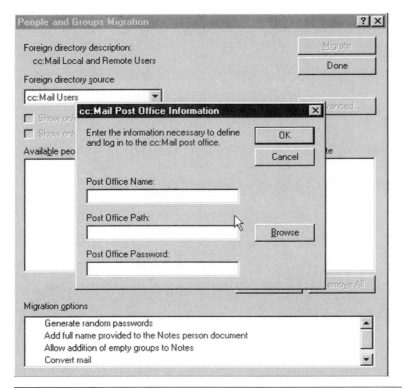

Figure 4-29   Accessing a cc:Mail post office

When you choose to add a group, you have some additional options, as shown in Figure 4-33. Options include creating a new group with specified settings—or if adding a group that already exists, you can choose to add members of the group to the existing Notes group, thereby merging the groups. Other options available for groups include adding the people in nested groups as Notes users and using the settings you just configured for all currently selected or nested groups.

When you select to add groups that already exist in the Domino Directory, the migration tool prompts you to determine how to handle the group, as shown in Figure 4-34. Choices include using the existing Notes group, creating a new group in the Domino Directory, and skipping the group. You are not prompted for issues regarding duplicate users until the users are actually being registered.

In addition, there are advanced options available for some migrations that you access by clicking the Advanced button. Figure 4-35 displays the Windows NT User Upgrade Options dialog box as an example.

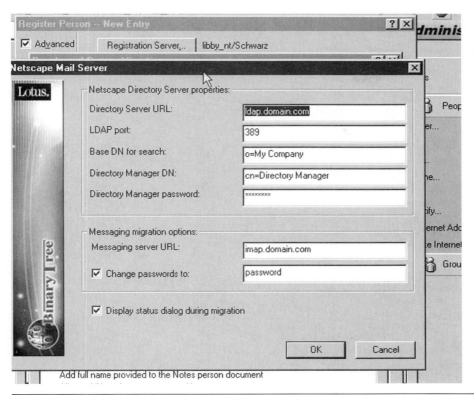

Figure 4-30   Exporting from a Netscape mail server

After selecting all of the users, groups, and options, click the Migrate button to add the users to the Registration queue, as shown in Figure 4-36. You can then migrate more users or click Done to create and register users. After you have added the users to the registration queue, you can examine and edit the settings for the users before registering them. This task includes viewing the randomly generated password in cases where that option is selected. You can then register the users.

 TIP   Note that NT, GroupWise, and Netscape will always use randomly generated passwords, because these applications do not migrate passwords. Other directory sources enable you to migrate the password if it matches the password-quality scale.

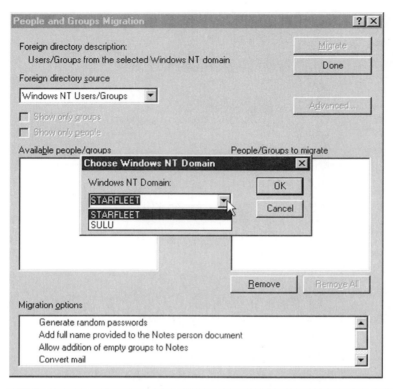

Figure 4-31   Selecting an NT domain

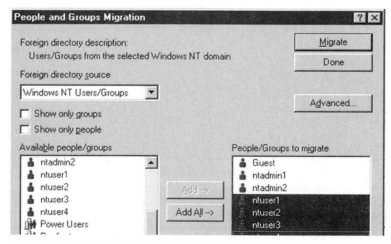

Figure 4-32   Selecting people and groups to migrate

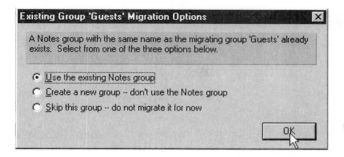

Figure 4-33   Group options

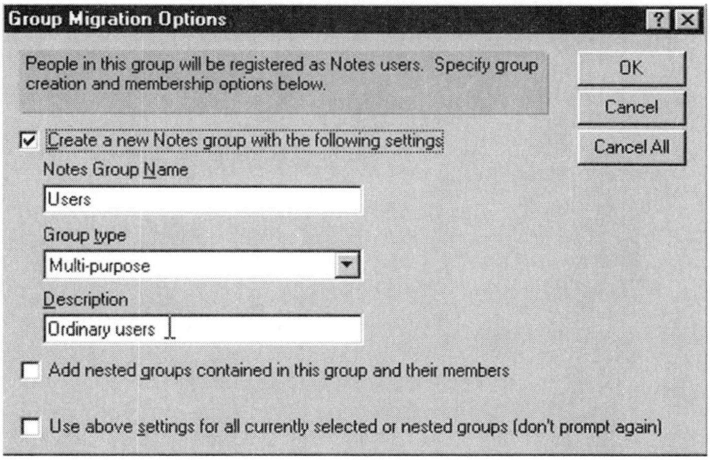

Figure 4-34   Adding a group with the same name

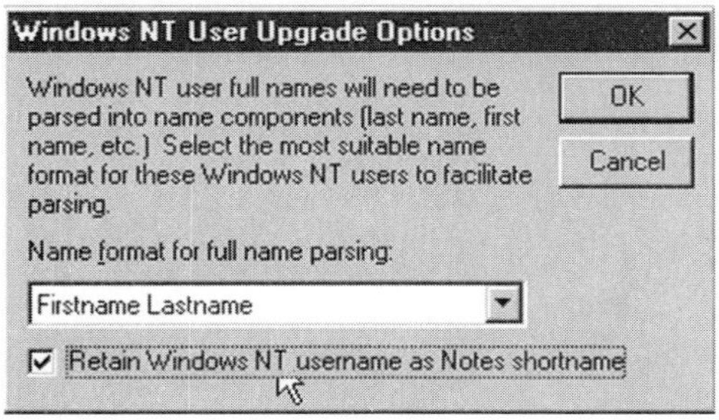

Figure 4-35   Advanced options for NT users

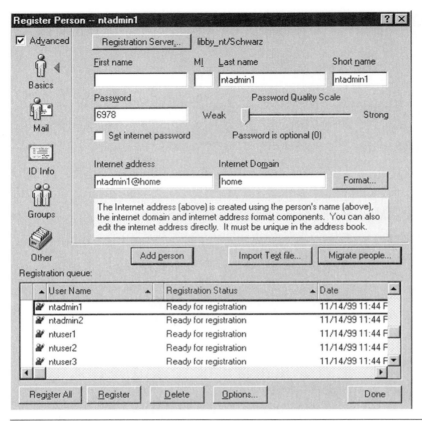

Figure 4-36 The Registration queue

POP3 and IMAP Clients

Domino provides POP3 and IMAP to enable clients who are using those protocols to receive their mail from the Domino Server.

POP3

POP3 is the Internet-standard Post-Office Protocol (Version 3). POP3 on the Domino server only enables the retrieval of messages from the Domino server to a POP3 client, such as Eudora and the Outlook Express component of Internet Explorer. Using a POP3 client requires SMTP to run on the server to transfer outgoing mail. In addition, note that POP3 clients cannot receive encrypted mail, because they do not log in to the

Domino server with a Notes ID file. The Domino POP3 server does support all of the following features, however:

- Basic name and password authentication

- SSL authentication

- SSL encryption

The following requirements and warnings apply to running POP3 on your server:

- Create a Person document and a mail file for all POP3 users. Users can access mail from both Notes and POP3 clients.

- Make sure the Person document contains an Internet password for the POP3 user.

- Start the POP3 task. To start the POP3 task, either type the command LOAD POP3 at the server console, add the POP3 task to the ServerTasks= line in the NOTES.INI file, or start the task by using the Start New Task tool in the Domino Administrator on the Server tab.

- Configure the POP3 port settings on the Server document of the POP3 server, as shown in Figure 4-37. In the Server document, select Ports . . . Internet Ports . . . Mail. By default, the POP3 port (110) is enabled. You can change the port number

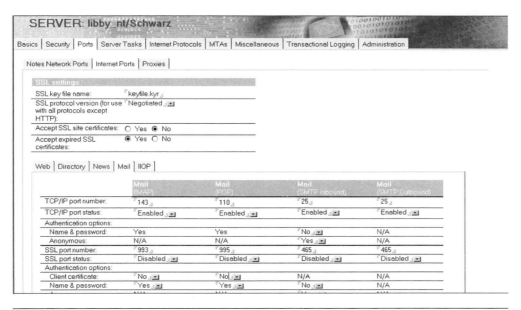

Figure 4-37   Configuring POP3 ports

or disable the port. You might disable the default POP3 port to require POP3 communication to travel over the SSL POP3 port (995). If so, make sure that this port is enabled. If you change the port number or status, you must restart the POP3 task.

IMAP

IMAP is the Internet-standard Internet Mail Access Protocol (usually Version 4). IMAP users can perform the following tasks from a Domino server:

- Get messages from the IMAP/Domino server and store them locally
- Access messages directly on the IMAP/Domino server
- Copy messages from the IMAP/Domino server to the local mail file, and then synchronize with the IMAP server

IMAP on the Domino server only enables the retrieval of messages from the Domino server to an IMAP client, such as the Outlook Express component of Internet Explorer. Using an IMAP client requires SMTP to run on the server in order to transfer outgoing mail. In addition, note that IMAP clients cannot receive encrypted mail because they do not log in to the Domino server with a Notes ID file. The Domino IMAP server does support all of the following features, however:

- Basic name and password authentication
- SSL authentication
- SSL encryption

The following requirements and warnings apply to running IMAP on your server:

- Create a Person document and a mail file for all IMAP users. Users can access mail from both Notes and IMAP clients. You do have to enable the mail file for IMAP access, however, by using the steps described as follows.
- Make sure that the Person document contains an Internet password for the IMAP user.
- Start the IMAP task by typing the command LOAD IMAP at the server console, by adding the IMAP task to the ServerTasks= line in the NOTES.INI file, or by starting the IMAP task using the Start New Task tool in the Domino Administrator on the Server tab.
- Configure the IMAP port settings on the Server document of the IMAP server, as shown in Figure 4-38. In the Server document, select Ports . . . Internet Ports . . .

Figure 4-38
IMAP port settings

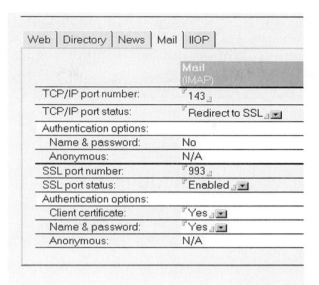

Mail. By default, the IMAP port (143) is enabled. You can change the port number or disable the port. You might disable the default IMAP port to require IMAP communication to travel over the SSL IMAP port (993). If so, make sure that this port is enabled. If you change the port number or status, you must restart the IMAP task.

Converting a Mail File for IMAP Use

Notes mail files must be converted to be used with IMAP clients. IMAP clients see public folders only in Notes mail files (these include Inbox and Trash, for example). They do not see views, such as Sent or Draft, nor do they see private views and folders. The IMAP conversion utility enables the folder references in the converted mail files. To convert the Notes mail file, use the console for the mail server. Type the following command:

```
LOAD CONVERT -M PATH\MAILFILE.NSF
```

The -M indicates that you are converting to IMAP. The path is relative to the Notes\Data directory, so if your users' mail files are stored in the standard mail directory, the path might be MAIL\USER1.NSF. You can leave out the name of the mail file and use *.NSF to convert all files in a specified directory. Figure 4-39 shows the results of the command at the console. As mentioned, even after the conversion, the user can still access the mail file through Notes.

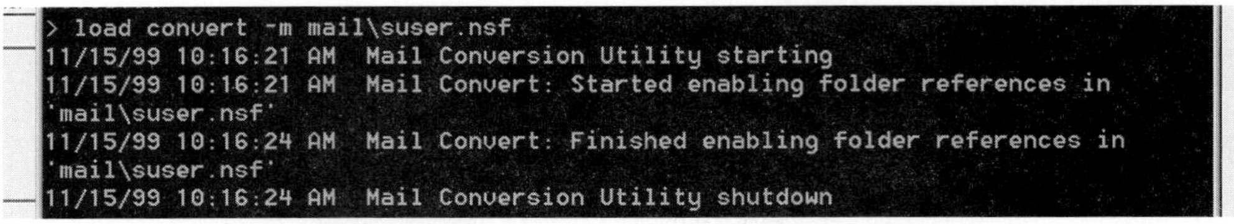

```
> load convert -m mail\suser.nsf
11/15/99 10:16:21 AM  Mail Conversion Utility starting
11/15/99 10:16:21 AM  Mail Convert: Started enabling folder references in
'mail\suser.nsf'
11/15/99 10:16:24 AM  Mail Convert: Finished enabling folder references in
'mail\suser.nsf'
11/15/99 10:16:24 AM  Mail Conversion Utility shutdown
```

Figure 4-39   Results of converting -M

Calendaring and Scheduling

Maintaining calendaring and scheduling includes maintaining group scheduling using the Free Time database (BUSYTIME.NSF), working with resource reservations and profiles, and maintaining the corporate calendar and adding holidays.

Group Scheduling

Users access calendaring and scheduling to check the free time of other users and to schedule meetings and appointments. The tasks that run on the servers to enable these functions are SCHED (the Schedule Manager) and CALCONN (the Calendar Connector). In addition, the process requires the Free Time database (BUSYTIME.NSF on mail servers; CLBUSY.NSF on clustered mail servers). All users who have a mail file on a server and have a calendar profile have an entry in the Free Time database. When the Schedule Manager task is started, it checks for BUSYTIME.NSF and creates this database if it does not already exist. The following list describes the basic process that group scheduling follows:

1. A user (Brian) creates a meeting invitation and searches for Libby's free time.

2. Domino sends a query for free time information to Brian's mail server.

3. If Brian and Libby are on the same mail server or are in the same mail cluster, the Free Time system (SCHED, CALCONN, and NNOTES) looks in BUSYTIME.NSF (or CLBUSY.NSF) and returns Libby's free time to Brian.

4. If Brian and Libby are not on the same server, Domino expands Libby's name to its hierarchical format and looks in her Person document for her mail server. CAL-CONN sends the request for free time to Libby's mail server. The Free Time system on Libby's mail server looks in the BUSYTIME.NSF and finds her free time, and CALCONN returns the information to Brian. If there is no free time information, the dialog box tells Brian that Libby's free time is unavailable.

The Schedule Manager task (SCHED) accepts `TELL` commands at the server console or via the Server Status tab in the Domino Administrator. These `TELL` commands can display the schedule for a user, validate the free time information in the database, and show all of the reservations and appointments in the free time database. To send `TELL` commands via the Domino Administrator, select Server . . . Status and select the Schedule Manager task from the task list. Select the Tell tool from the Task tools to display the Tell Schedule Manager dialog box, as shown in Figure 4-40. You will usually use these commands to troubleshoot the Free Time database. If you choose the last option, *Show all reservations and appointments in freetime database*, you will find this command similar to using the `TELL SCHED STATS` command at the console.

Resource Reservations

Resources can be rooms or equipment (such as overhead projectors) that are often used for meetings. To enable users to reserve rooms and other resources, create a Resource Reservations database. Choose File . . . Database . . . New to create the new database. Base the new database on the Resource Reservations template (RESRC50.NTF).

After you create the database, you must ensure that users who need to create resources have the necessary access and the appropriate role ([Create Resource]). You must also ensure that there is a site created. To create a site, choose Actions . . . New Site and complete the Site form, as shown in Figure 4-41.

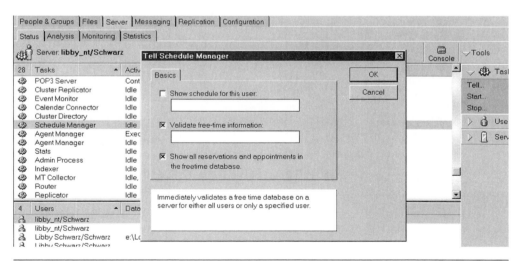

Figure 4-40 Sending `TELL` commands to SCHED

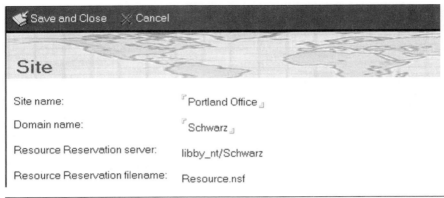

Figure 4-41   Creating a new site

After saving the site form, you can create resources in the database (if you have the [Create Resource] role) by using Actions . . . New Resource, as shown in Figure 4-42. The database must contain at least one resource before users can create reservations.

After creating resources in the database, Domino submits an Administration Process request to add the resource to the Domino Directory. Figure 4-43 shows a request to add a resource in the Administration Requests database.

After the resource is available in the Domino Directory, users can create reservations for the resource by using their mail file or by using the Reservations database. By default, all users can create reservations for resources, although you can limit this action by using the Owner Options tab in the Resource document. In addition, if you need to

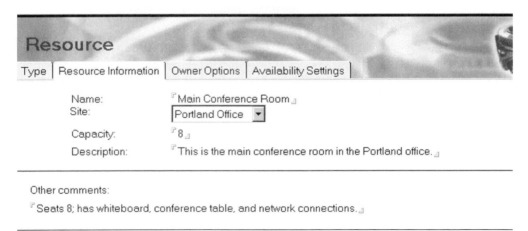

Figure 4-42   Creating a resource

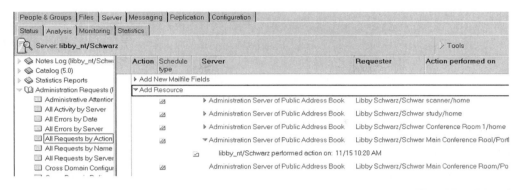

Figure 4-43 AdminP adds the resource to the Domino Directory.

prevent users from reserving a particular resource, you can choose to *Temporarily disable reservations*. Figure 4-44 shows a room that is reserved in the Resource Reservations database.

Holidays

The Domino Directory contains holidays for various nations or for other groups. These holidays can be imported into users' mail files. From within a user's mail file, choose Actions . . . Tools . . . Import Holidays. In the Import Holidays dialog box, select the group(s) whose holidays you want imported into your calendar. These holidays are then applied to the calendar based on the settings in the Holiday document. You can edit the holiday documents and add holidays. You might edit a Holiday document if your company gives a holiday as a day off that is not normally given as time off (or vice versa).

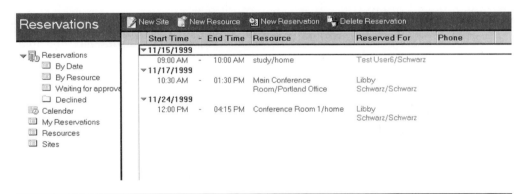

Figure 4-44 A reserved resource

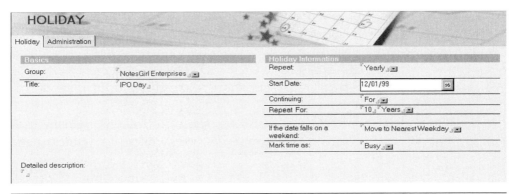

Figure 4-45 Adding a new holiday

You might create a new holiday if your company or area celebrates a day that is not already considered a holiday. To create a new holiday, select the Configuration tab in the Domino Administrator and expand the Miscellaneous section. In the Holidays view, select the Add Holiday action button. In the Holiday document, shown in Figure 4-45, choose the groups that will observe the holiday, type the title for the holiday, and select the repeat interval (such as yearly), the start date, and how long to continue observing the holiday. Decide what to do if the holiday falls on a weekend and whether to mark the time of the holiday as free or busy in the calendars of the users that import the holiday. When users import the holidays for groups that contain this holiday, it will be imported into their calendars. If you add, remove, or edit holidays after users have imported the holidays, they will have to run the Import Holidays action again to update the holidays.

Summary

In this chapter, we reviewed the basics of mail routing, including the fact that mail routes automatically among servers in the same Domino Named Network (DNN) without the need for a Connection document. To route to and from servers outside the same DNN, however, you create Connection documents. When monitoring and maintaining messaging, you should recognize whether mail requires a Connection document to route, as well as how to troubleshoot that Connection document if necessary. To troubleshoot a Connection document, you might need to change the routing schedule, the routing threshold, the routing interval, or the routing cost. We looked at the graphical view of DNNs and connections (created via the MAPS task on the server).

In addition, we looked at a variety of monitoring methods, including viewing and analyzing the Notes Log and looking at mail routing statistics and status in the Domino Administrator views. We enabled the MTC (Message Tracking Collector) so that we could look at mail usage reports and track sent messages. We also sent mail probes and mail trace messages. The MAIL.BOX database showed any pending, held, or dead messages. We used the built-in actions to release and resend the messages.

We used the Configuration settings document to customize mail routing in the environment, including adding mailboxes to improve performance and restricting the Router to help avoid unwanted messages or relaying. We looked at moving mail files using the Domino Administrator and examined the basics of migrating from other mail and directory systems to Domino. We configured Domino to enable IMAP and POP clients to access their mail on the Domino server, including converting mail files for IMAP use and configuring the necessary ports and tasks.

Finally, we looked at three aspects of *Calendaring and Scheduling* (C&S). First, we reviewed the C&S process, including the elements of the Free Time system (BUSY-TIME.NSF, SCHED, CALCONN, and NNOTES). Then, we looked at the steps Domino takes to verify a user's free time. Next, we looked at creating and using a resource reservations database, including the role necessary for creating new sites and resources. Finally, we explored the process of adding holidays to the Domino environment.

Review Questions

1. Jane looks at the pending mail in MAIL.BOX and notices that her mail is not routing to Server1, although it is routing to all other servers. Which of the following would not be the problem?

   A. There is no Connection document to Server1.

   B. The servers are in the same DNN.

   C. The servers are not in the same DNN.

   D. The Router task is not running on her current server.

2. Alan looks at his Notes Log and notices that mail is routing to Server2 regularly. He has the routing schedule set to only repeat every four hours, however. What is causing the mail to route more often?

   A. High-priority mail

   B. Low-priority mail

   C. Routing threshold

   D. Repeat interval

3. Kris looks at the Mail Routing by Named Network view in Domino Administrator, and she expects to see a graphical routing topology. When she does not see one, what task should she check for on the Server Status tab?

   A. MTC

   B. SCHED

   C. MAPS

   D. ROUTE MAP

4. David needs to run a mail usage report. What task needs to be running to enable him to perform this action?

   A. MTC

   B. SCHED

   C. MAPS

   D. ROUTE MAP

5. Susan wants to track a message that a user sent 2 days ago, because the user insists that the recipient has not received it. What does she do?

   A. Send a mail trace message

   B. Configure a mail probe

   C. Configure a new mail tracking request

   D. Look in the server's MAIL.BOX to see if the message is still pending

6. Scott is performing mail and directory migrations. Which of the following can he not migrate using the tools in the Domino Administrator?

   A. GroupWise 4.x

   B. Windows NT

   C. Netscape Mail Server

   D. Eudora Mail

7. When migrating users and groups from Windows NT to Domino, Katie notices that she has some duplicate groups. Which of the following is not an option?

   A. Do not migrate the group. Skip it and worry about it later.

   B. Add the NT group to an existing Domino group.

   C. Delete the existing Domino group and replace it.

   D. Add the NT users to the existing Domino group.

8. Which of the following tasks runs on the Domino server to enable users to read their mail with Outlook Express or Netscape Mail?
   A. SMTP
   B. MIME
   C. IMAP
   D. POP3

9. Which of the following requires that a mail file be converted before users can read mail using it?
   A. SMTP
   B. MIME
   C. IMAP
   D. POP3

10. You disabled port 110 and enabled port 995 in your server document. Why?
   A. You wanted to run IMAP instead of POP3.
   B. You wanted to run POP3 instead of IMAP.
   C. You wanted to run POP3 over SSL only.
   D. You wanted to run IMAP over SSL only.

Review Answers

1. **B** and **D** are both correct.   If the servers are in the same DNN, they do not need a Connection document, and mail should be routing. You know that the Router task is running on the server, because mail is routing to other servers.

2. **A** and **C** are both possible.   High-priority mail is routed automatically and immediately, without waiting for a scheduled connection time. In addition, when enough messages are pending that the routing threshold is reached, mail routes without waiting for the scheduled connection time.

3. **C** is correct.   The MAPS or MAPS Extractor task has to be running on the server in order to view the graphical topology maps.

4. **A** is correct.   The MTC task needs to run to view mail usage reports and to use mail tracking.

5. **C** is the best answer.   She should use a mail tracking request. Choice D is a possible answer, however, if the MTC task is not running on her server.

6. **D** is correct. He cannot migrate from Eudora mail.

7. **C** is not an option. The migration tool does not enable you to delete a Domino group while migrating.

8. **C** or **D** is correct. Both IMAP and POP3 enable users to read mail using the listed clients.

9. **C** is correct. You must convert a mail file before IIMAP users can access it to read their messages.

10. **C** is correct. You might disable the standard POP3 port to force all POP3 traffic to come in over SSL.

Domino Applications and Replication

You should be able to answer questions based on the following objectives after reading this chapter:

- Monitoring, maintaining, and troubleshooting Domino applications
  - Adding, moving, upgrading, and deleting databases
  - Backup/verify and restoring databases
  - Monitoring application size
  - Monitoring, maintaining, and repairing databases
  - Monitoring and modifying application access control
  - Troubleshooting data access control problems
- Monitoring, maintaining, and troubleshooting Domino messaging and replication
  - Forcing replication
  - Monitoring and maintaining replication
  - Replicating design changes
  - Resolving replication and save conflicts
  - Troubleshooting replication problems
- Monitoring, maintaining, and troubleshooting Domino servers
  - Reconfiguring and remapping directories and links
  - Running program documents

A Domino application requires monitoring and maintenance throughout its existence. This task is huge and ongoing. First, note that you can use a variety of tools to monitor your applications, including the Log file, the database analysis tool, and database statistics. Use these tools to determine what maintenance needs to be done on the application. To maintain an application, you must be able to manipulate the application.

You should also be able to work with the database properties and other elements of the application, such as agents, to ensure that users are getting the results they expect and need from the application—as well as to control database size and performance. Manipulating the application also includes adding databases to servers, as well as moving or deleting databases. After placing replicas on servers, you need to ensure that replication is configured correctly and is occurring on schedule. Next, maintaining an application and its replication requires ensuring that the proper users and servers have access to the database. You will also need to work with application backup and recovery. Ensuring that a database can be recovered is an essential element to making the database available to users. Finally, as things change in the organization, design changes can be made to databases. Part of maintaining a database is ensuring that these changes are reflected in the production database. These activities will also relate to troubleshooting the database. Some of the same actions that you perform to maintain the application are used to troubleshoot the application. You might also need to fix corruption or other database problems by using the appropriate tools. Remember that the point of this section of the exam is taking an application that has already been rolled out and configured and ensuring that it continues to function appropriately.

Monitoring Databases

You can monitor databases on a Domino server by using a variety of tools, including the Log, statistics, and database analysis. The Domino Administrator provides access to many of these monitoring tools.

Notes Log

One way to monitor the usage, size, and replication of applications is to use the Notes Log (LOG.NSF). Use the Server tab in the Domino Administrator to access the Log. Click the Analysis tab and expand the Notes Log twistie. The Database Sizes and Usage views show the information size and amount of usage for each database on the server, as shown in Figure 5-1. The documents in the Miscellaneous Events view can show warnings about corruption in databases, changes made by the `Design` or `Updall` tasks, information about the `Catalog` task (when it runs to include the database in the Database Catalog), and information about the agents that are run on the server. The documents in the Replication Events view display information about each replication that occurs and list any replication events (which might occur when there is a problem with replication). Review the Log daily to determine whether any maintenance tasks need to be performed on the server or databases.

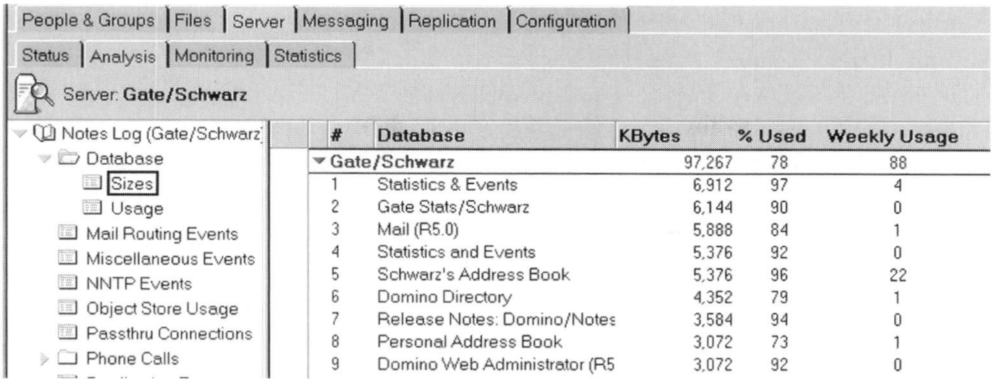

#	Database	KBytes	% Used	Weekly Usage
	▼ Gate/Schwarz	97,267	78	88
1	Statistics & Events	6,912	97	4
2	Gate Stats/Schwarz	6,144	90	0
3	Mail (R5.0)	5,888	84	1
4	Statistics and Events	5,376	92	0
5	Schwarz's Address Book	5,376	96	22
6	Domino Directory	4,352	79	1
7	Release Notes: Domino/Notes	3,584	94	0
8	Personal Address Book	3,072	73	1
9	Domino Web Administrator (R5	3,072	92	0

People & Groups | Files | Server | Messaging | Replication | Configuration

Status | Analysis | Monitoring | Statistics

Server: Gate/Schwarz

Notes Log (Gate/Schwarz)
- Database
  - Sizes
  - Usage
- Mail Routing Events
- Miscellaneous Events
- NNTP Events
- Object Store Usage
- Passthru Connections
- Phone Calls

Figure 5-1   Database Sizes view

Sometimes it is difficult to scan the Log manually. You can use the Analyze Log tool to run an analysis or to search the Notes Log for specific words in the file, as shown in Figure 5-2. From the Server . . . Analysis tab, expand the Analyze tools and select Log. Type the words to search for, determine how many days to search, and select the Results database.

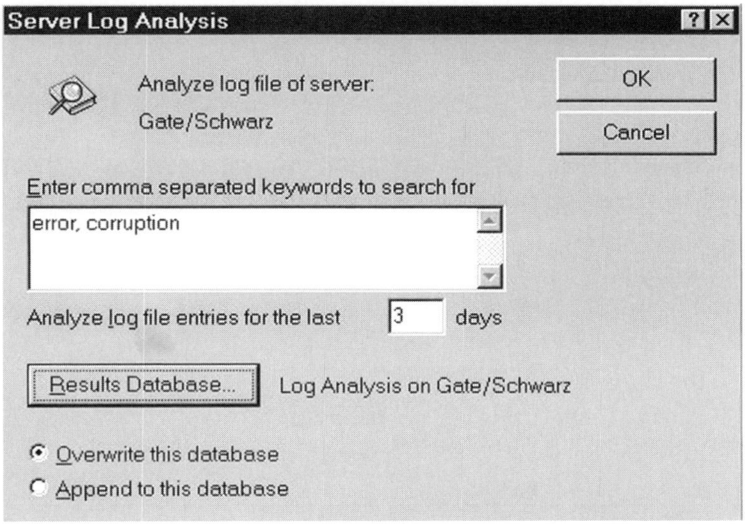

Server Log Analysis

Analyze log file of server:
Gate/Schwarz

OK   Cancel

Enter comma separated keywords to search for

error, corruption

Analyze log file entries for the last   3   days

Results Database...   Log Analysis on Gate/Schwarz

⦿ Overwrite this database
○ Append to this database

Figure 5-2   Analyzing the Notes Log

Statistics and Statistic Monitors

You might also want to review statistics to monitor the health of the applications on your server, as well as events such as low disk space, changes to the Access Control List (ACL), or replication activity. You can look at these statistics using the Server . . . Statistics tab or the Statistics Reports view under the Server . . . Analysis tab, but more often, you will create statistic monitors. With these monitors, you will be notified of a statistic that reaches a threshold, rather than having to look through all of the statistics to find ones that might be important. You can create the following types of monitors: ACL Change, File, Replication, and Statistic. To create a statistic monitor, select the Configuration tab in the Domino Administrator. Under the Statistics & Events twistie, expand the Monitors section and click Statistic. Use the New Statistic Monitor action button to create a new monitor. The Domino Administrator displays already-active monitors in the Results pane.

In the Statistic Monitor document, shown in Figure 5-3, use the Basics tab to select a server to monitor. You can also monitor all servers in the domain. Next, select a statistic to monitor, such as free space on a disk or the number of failed replications. Use the Threshold tab to set a threshold for the statistic—a number over or under which notification should take place. Use the Other tab to determine which severity-level warning to create when the threshold is reached. You can also choose to be notified by mail or pager or to have the event logged to an NT or Unix log by creating a notification profile for the event.

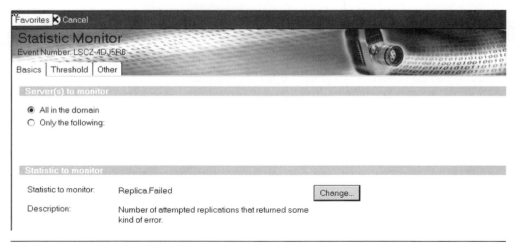

Figure 5-3   Creating a statistic monitor

Database Analysis

Sometimes it is useful to obtain a complete picture about a database in one location. Database analysis can give information about changes to the database, user activity, replication, and where the database is mentioned in the Notes Log. To create a database analysis for a database, go to the Files tab of the Domino Administrator. Select a database in the Results pane, and expand the database tools. Select the Analyze tool to display the Analyze Database dialog box, as shown in Figure 5-4. Select the items to analyze, how many days of activity to analyze, and select where the results should be written.

When the database has been processed, open the Database Analysis database to see the results. Results are organized by Date, Event Type, Source, and Source Database. Each document describes the date and time of the activity, the source of the information, and the event type, as well as a description of the event.

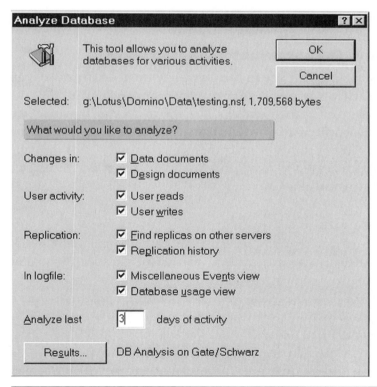

Figure 5-4   Analyzing a database

Manipulating Databases

The first step in manipulating databases is to work with the databases themselves— including the database properties and other elements of the database—to control database size and performance. In many cases, to keep a server running correctly or to change the purpose of a server, you might choose to add, move, or delete a database. You add databases when a new server comes into service in the organization or when you are creating a new database on an existing server. You might also be adding a server to make access easier for users. You move databases to make the application available on multiple servers or to distribute the workload more evenly. You can move a database manually or automatically by using the Administration Process. Regardless of whether you delete databases as part of the move process or delete them when a database is no longer in use, you might want to save space and other resources on the server. In any case, you might be working with clustered or non-clustered servers. As you read, look for some notes about working with adding, moving, and deleting databases in clustered environments. In addition, you might choose to use database or directory links when giving access to databases.

Database Size and Performance

You should monitor and maintain the size and performance of your databases. You can monitor the size of a database using the Domino Administrator, the LOG.NSF, the Database properties InfoBox, or database statistics. One way to decrease the size of the databases and increase their performance is to manipulate the database properties. The database cache also affects the performance of databases on the server. To maintain the size, you can compact the database, use quotas and thresholds, and archive documents using the database archiving tool or an agent.

Monitoring Database Size

You can monitor the size of databases on your servers using the Domino Administrator, the LOG.NSF, the Database properties InfoBox, or database statistics. To monitor the size of databases using the Domino Administrator, open the Administrator to the Files tab. To see the total size of databases and other files on a drive, open the disk space tool, as shown in Figure 5-5.

To view the size, maximum size, quota size, and warning threshold size for a database, scroll to the right in the Results pane of the Files tab, as shown in Figure 5-6. The size is the current database file size (in bytes). The maximum size, which only applies to R4.X databases, shows the maximum size to which the database can grow, as hard coded when the database was created. The quota size shows the size of the optional

Figure 5-5
Disk space tool

limit, which is set by the administrator at any time. The warning threshold, which should be lower than the quota, shows the size at which Domino writes to the LOG.NSF that the file has passed its threshold and is therefore approaching its quota.

You can also use the Notes Log (LOG.NSF) to monitor the database size. In Domino Administrator, go to the Server tab and then the Analysis tab. Expand the Notes Log twistie and the Database twistie, and then select Sizes. Each database is listed with its size in kilobytes and its percent used, as shown in Figure 5-7. For more detailed information, such as the size of each view in the database, open the document for a database. The Notes Log will also display warning messages about databases that have reached their threshold or quota.

To determine the size and percent used for a database from the database itself, open the Database properties InfoBox to the Info tab, as shown in Figure 5-8. The Size section displays the size of the database (in megabytes) and the number of documents in

	Title	Filename	Physical Path	File Forma	Size	Max Size	Quota	Warning	Created
	Administration Reque	admin4.nsf	g:\Lotus\Domino\[	R5 (41:0)	838,656	No limit	0	0	07/28/99 0!
	Java.AgentRunner	agentrunner.n	g:\Lotus\Domino\[	R5 (41:0)	393,216	No limit	0	0	03/06/99 1(
	bookmark.nsf	bookmark.nsf	g:\Lotus\Domino\[	R5 (41:0)	1,520,640	No limit	0	0	07/28/99 0!
	Local free time info	busytime.nsf	g:\Lotus\Domino\[	R5 (41:0)	327,680	No limit	0	0	07/28/99 0!
	Catalog (5.0)	catalog.nsf	g:\Lotus\Domino\[	R5 (41:0)	1,709,568	No limit	0	0	11/04/99 0!
	Server Certificate Adr	certsrv.nsf	g:\Lotus\Domino\[	R5 (41:0)	1,184,256	No limit	0	0	07/28/99 0!
	Copy Practice	copyprac.nsf	g:\Lotus\Domino\[	R5 (41:0)	458,752	No limit	0	0	11/03/99 0!
	Sample Vendor Data	cpa.nsf	g:\Lotus\Domino\[	R5 (41:0)	2,101,248	No limit	0	0	03/06/99 0!
	Statistics & Events	events4.nsf	g:\Lotus\Domino\[	R5 (41:0)	7,077,888	No limit	0	0	07/28/99 0!
	homepage	homepage.ns	g:\Lotus\Domino\[	R5 (41:0)	458,752	No limit	0	0	03/12/99 0!
	Notes Log (Gate/Sch	log.nsf	g:\Lotus\Domino\[	R5 (41:0)	1,350,144	No limit	0	0	07/28/99 0!
	Log Analysis	loga4.nsf	g:\Lotus\Domino\[	R5 (41:0)	262,144	No limit	0	0	11/09/99 1
	Lotus MTA Tables (v'	mtatbls.nsf	g:\Lotus\Domino\[	R3 (17:1)	382,976	1 GB	0	0	05/08/97 0!
	Schwarz's Address B	names.nsf	g:\Lotus\Domino\[	R5 (41:0)	5,505,024	No limit	0	0	07/28/99 0!
	New DB Library	new db library	g:\Lotus\Domino\[	R5 (41:0)	393,216	No limit	0	0	11/03/99 0:
	* 8625680D:007A2BE'	prac.nsf	g:\Lotus\Domino\[	R5 (41:0)	262,144	No limit	0	0	11/03/99 0!
	R5 Book	r5 book.nsf	g:\Lotus\Domino\[	R5 (41:0)	458,752	No limit	0	0	11/03/99 0!
	Libby Schwarz R5 Dis	r5 discussion.	g:\Lotus\Domino\[	R5 (41:0)	262,144	No limit	0	0	11/03/99 1:
	R5 Certification Discu	r5certdisc.nsf	g:\Lotus\Domino\[	R5 (41:0)	1,198,080	No limit	0	0	11/03/99 0!
	Reports for Gate/Sch	reports.nsf	g:\Lotus\Domino\[	R5 (41:0)	663,552	No limit	0	0	07/28/99 0!
	Gate Stats/Schwarz	statmail.nsf	g:\Lotus\Domino\[	R5 (41:0)	6,291,456	No limit	0	0	07/28/99 0!
	Statistics Reports	statrep.nsf	g:\Lotus\Domino\[	R5 (41:0)	1,350,144	No limit	0	0	07/28/99 0!
	testing	testing.nsf	g:\Lotus\Domino\[	R5 (41:0)	1,709,568	No limit	5 MB	4 MB	11/03/99 0!
	Domino Web Adminis	webadmin.nsf	g:\Lotus\Domino\[	R5 (41:0)	3,145,728	No limit	0	0	07/28/99 0!

Figure 5-6   Sizes in the Files tab

#	Database	KBytes	% Used	Weekly Usage
▼ Gate/Schwarz		97,267	78	88
1	Statistics & Events	6,912	97	4
2	Gate Stats/Schwarz	6,144	90	0
3	Mail (R5.0)	5,888	84	1
4	Statistics and Events	5,376	92	0
5	Schwarz's Address Book	5,376	96	22
6	Domino Directory	4,352	79	1
7	Release Notes: Domino/Notes	3,584	94	0
8	Personal Address Book	3,072	73	1
9	Domino Web Administrator (R5	3,072	92	0
10	Domino Administrator (R5)	2,816	83	0
11	Domino Web Administrator (R5	2,560	93	1
12	TeamRoom (5.0)	2,304	80	1
13	Sample Vendor Database	2,052	95	1
14	Domino R5 Certificate Authority	2,048	92	0
15	Server Web Navigator (R5.0)	2,048	71	1
16	Catalog (5.0)	1,670	93	15

Figure 5-7 Sizes in the log file

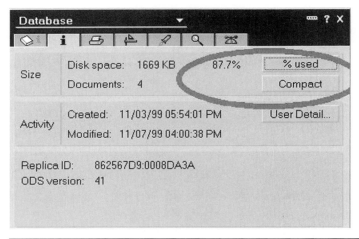

Figure 5-8 The Database Properties InfoBox Info tab

the database. Click the *%Used* button to calculate the percent of the database that is being used.

To view statistics related to database size and usage, you must configure a file monitor for the databases. The file monitor is useful to determine how much databases are being used and how much white space is in a database. When the white space (or unused space) in a database is high, you should compact the database to remove white space and reduce the size of the database. When you create a file monitor, you can have Compact run automatically when a database reaches a certain threshold of white space, such as 70 percent. To create a file monitor, open the Domino Administrator to the Configuration tab. Expand the Statistics & Events twistie and the Monitors twistie. Click to open the File view. In the File view, click the New File Monitor action button.

In the File Monitor document, type the name of the database to monitor (the filename, including the path relative to the data directory). Then, select which servers and whether to *Monitor unused space* and/or *Monitor for user inactivity*. The Unused Space tab sets the threshold for unused space in the database (70 percent by default) and provides the option to compact the database automatically when it reaches that threshold. On the User Inactivity tab, select a period to monitor (daily, weekly, or monthly) and the minimum number of user sessions during the period. Use the Other tab to determine which severity level the database event will maintain when written to the log and to configure a notification profile for the event. If you want Domino to notify you (by pager, broadcast, or via e-mail), to run a program, to write an event to an NT or Unix log, or to log the event to a database, click the *Create a new notification profile for this event* button to launch the Event Notification Wizard.

Database Properties

The properties of a database impact the way the database works for the users and how efficient the database is on the server. This statement is especially true for the new Advanced Database properties, so you should understand how to use these properties. To view the database properties, open the database and choose File . . . Database . . . Properties. Notes displays the Database properties InfoBox, as shown in Figure 5-9.

Setting database properties is a task best shared between a Domino administrator and a Domino application developer, because many of the properties require knowledge of the database elements. The following database properties are likely to improve database performance:

- If you disable the *Allow use of stored forms in this database* property, you will save memory and disk space in the database as well as improve database performance. When you disable this feature, the form that was used to create the document must be available in the database for Domino to display the document correctly. This option is on the Basics tab of the Database properties InfoBox.

- If you enable the Advanced database property of *Don't maintain unread marks*, you will improve database performance and reduce database size. In certain databases, it is important for users to be able to see which documents are unread; however, in

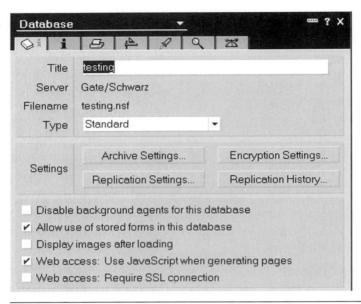

Figure 5-9   The Database properties InfoBox

reference databases, the Domino Directory, or the Log file, it is not useful to show unread marks. When you change this database property, compact the database to force the property to take effect.

- If you enable the Advanced database property of *Document table bitmap optimization*, you will improve view performance—especially for small views in large databases. When views are updated, Domino does a search to determine which documents to display in the view. In large databases, this process is extremely time-consuming. With this property enabled, however, Domino associates view tables with the forms of the documents stored in them. To make this procedure work correctly, use `Form=` as part of the selection formula. While maintaining the relationship between the form and the view table does require some database resources, the added efficiency is worth this cost in the smaller views in large databases. When you change this database property, compact the database to force the property to take effect.

- If you enable the Advanced database property of *Don't overwrite free space*, you can improve the performance of the database. By default, when users delete documents or other data from a database, Domino rewrites that space on the disk with a pattern. This action enhances security by ensuring that a disk utility will not have the capability to recover the data and also uses extra write and read (disk I/O) time on the disk. Enable this property if the data is secure or if the data does not need to be secured—or in databases such as MAIL.BOX or LOG.NSF, where the space in the database is quickly reallocated for new documents.

- If you disable the Advanced database property of *Maintain LastAccessed property*, you can improve database performance. This property controls whether Domino updates the *Access in this file* property each time a document is read. This property is useful when using the database-archiving tools based on inactivity in a document; however, this property also uses extra disk reads and writes (I/O) and affects database performance.

- If you enable the *Don't support specialized response hierarchy* property in the Advanced database properties, you will improve database performance and reduce database size. By default, documents store information that relates them to parent or response documents. The @AllChildren and @AllDescendants functions use this information—usually in view or agent-selection formulas. These functions do not work in databases that have this property enabled. When you change this database property, compact the database to force the property to take effect.

- If you enable the *Don't allow headline monitoring* property in the Advanced database properties, you will improve database performance. Headline monitoring enables users to have Domino automatically monitor databases for new documents or other pertinent information. This processing affects database performance, especially as more users enable monitoring on the database.

- Use the *Limit entries in $UpdatedBy fields* option to limit the number of entries stored in this field to improve database performance and reduce database size. By default, Domino stores the name of each user or server that edits a document. When the number of entries reaches the limit you set in this field, Domino begins removing the earliest entries to make room for the newest entries.

- Use the *Limit entries in $Revisions fields* option to improve database performance and reduce database size. By default, Domino stores the date and time each time a user edits a document—up to 500 editing sessions, using up to eight bytes of disk space. When the number of entries reaches the limit you set in this field, Domino begins removing the earliest entries to make room for the newest entries. Lotus suggests setting this field not lower than ten entries to avoid unnecessary replication or save conflicts. You can safely limit the entries in databases that do not replicate (or that replicate often) and in databases that are not edited often.

All but the first property are located in the Advanced Properties tab of the Database properties InfoBox, as shown in Figure 5-10.

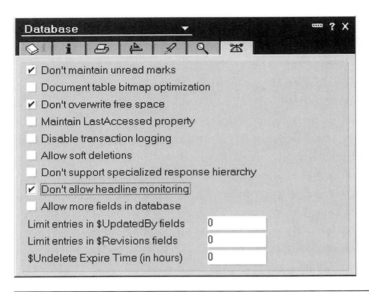

Figure 5-10 The Advanced Properties tab

Database Cache

The database cache is used to hold databases that have been recently closed in memory so that they can be opened again quickly. This feature speeds both the closing and opening processes for users and programs. A database remains in the cache for approximately 20 minutes or until it is opened again. During this time, the database can be opened quickly, because it is still in memory. The database cache stores either 25 databases or the value of the NSF_Buffer_Pool_Size setting (in the NOTES.INI file) divided by 300, by default. You can increase the NSF_DbCache_Maxentries setting to increase the number of databases that can be stored in the cache. You can also increase the amount of RAM (physical memory) in the server. Note that the actual, maximum number of databases stored in the cache is 1.5 times the permitted maximum. If the permitted maximum is 25, for example, the actual maximum is 37.5. You can determine information about the cache using statistics. To view the database cache statistics, use the following command:

```
Show Stat Database.DbCache.*
```

Domino will display all of the available database cache statistics. In addition, you can use the following commands to affect the database cache.

- Use the following command to display the names of the databases in the cache and how many entries the cache can hold:

```
Dbcache show
```

- Use the following command to close all the databases in the cache:

```
Dbcache flush
```

Compacting the Database

You compact a database to remove unused white space. In addition, although Domino always tries to reuse the space left by deleted documents, sometimes the database needs to be compacted before it can do this action. You also run Compact to enable or disable some of the advanced database properties. Compacting a database can also fix corrupted databases. When you run Compact in R5, Domino uses one of the following types:

- In-place compaction with space recovery
- In-place compaction with space recovery and file size
- Copy-style compacting

The first style of compacting, which is the fastest type, recovers white space in the database but does not reduce the file size. This style of compacting enables databases to retain their *Database Instance ID* (DBIID), which is used in transaction logging. This type of compacting enables users and servers to continue to read from and write to the database during compaction. This style is the default style of compacting that Domino runs when you do not specify an option and when the databases are enabled for transaction logging. You can force Domino to use this type of compacting by using the *-b* (case-sensitive option) argument.

The second style of compaction, which Lotus recommends that you run regularly (once a week or once a month), reduces file size and recovers white space. This type of compacting, which is slower than space recovery only, assigns new DBIIDs to databases. If you use this type of compacting with databases that use the transaction log, you should do a full backup of the databases as soon as you finish compacting them. As with the space recovery only style, users and servers can continue to read from and write to the database while this type of compaction is occurring. This style is the default style of compacting that Domino runs when you do not specify an option and when the databases are not enabled for transaction logging. You can force Domino to use this type of compacting by using the *-B* (case-sensitive option) argument.

The last style of compacting is copy-style compacting (-C argument). This type of compacting creates a new copy of the database during compaction and deletes the original after the compaction is complete. This style of compaction requires additional disk space to run. This type of compaction, which is the default for R4.X databases, creates a new database with a new DBIID. In other words, if you are using this style of compaction with databases that are using transaction logging, you should make a full backup after compacting completes. Unlike the other two types of compacting, users and servers cannot access the database for reading or editing while this type of compaction is occurring. To enable users to continue to read the database during copy-style compaction, you can use the -L argument. Copy-style compacting is necessary when you make structural changes to a database, such as some of the changes that are available in the Advanced Database properties (such as *Document table bitmap optimization* and *Don't support specialized response hierarchy*, both described previously).

If you compact an R4 database, the database will be converted to an R5 *On-Disk Structure* (ODS) and will no longer be available to local R4 clients. To prevent the conversion, use the -R argument with the Compact program or rename the database using a .NS4 extension.

You can run the Compact program from the server console, from the Domino Administrator, from a Program document, or from the Database properties InfoBox. To run Compact from the server console, type the command below. You could also run this command from the Server tab in Domino Administrator by selecting the Status tab and clicking the *Console* button.

```
Load compact databasename -argument
```

Another way to run the command from the Domino Administrator is to use the Task . . . Start tool. In the Administrator, go to the Server tab and to the Status tab. Expand the Task tools, and select the Start tool. In the Start New Task dialog box, shown in Figure 5-11, select Compactor and click the *Start Task* button. To use an advanced argument (listed as follows), enable the *Select advanced options* check box. In the Advanced Options dialog box, shown in Figure 5-12, select which database or databases that Compact should run on, and select any other options. You could also run the task from the Database tools on the Files tab.

You could create a Program document to run the Compact program based on a schedule. To create a Program document to run Compact, open the Configuration tab in Domino Administrator. Under the Servers section, select the Programs view and click the Add Program action button. On the Basics tab, type the program name (COMPACT), any command-line options and/or arguments, and the name of the server on which the program should run. Use the Schedule tab to enable and disable the Program document, as well as to set a schedule and a repeat interval.

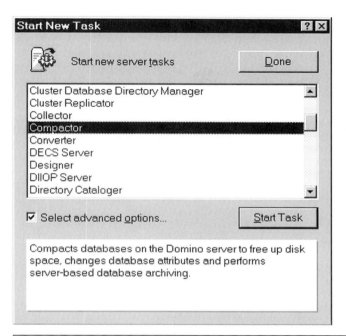

Figure 5-11 The Start New Task dialog box

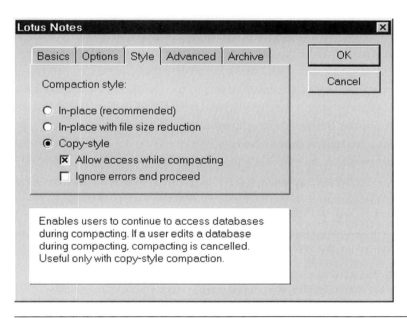

Figure 5-12 Advanced options available when starting Compact

Finally, you can run Compact from the Database properties InfoBox by using the Info tab. In the Info tab, click the *Compact* button. When the compaction is finished, Domino displays a message in the status bar.

A few of the many arguments that are permitted in the Compact program are listed as follows. For more details about the available options, refer to *Managing Domino Databases* or the Domino help databases. All options are case-sensitive.

- -A uses the Compact command to start the document archiving tool. The specified documents are archived, but the database is not compacted. To both archive and compact, use the *-a* option.

- -F and -f disable and enable the *Document table bitmap optimization* property. Domino performs a copy-style compaction.

- -D discards view indexes and performs a copy-style compact.

- -R compacts the database while retaining the current file format and ODS, using a copy-style compact.

Quotas and Thresholds

You can set a database quota to ensure that the database does not exceed a specified size. Set a warning threshold below this quota so that Domino will write a warning to the Log file. This action gives you time to increase the quota or to archive or delete some documents to reduce the database size. When the quota is reached, users will no longer have the capability to save documents in the database. Users see the following error message when opening or saving in the database: "Cannot allocate database object—database would exceed its disk quota." The same error message is written to the Notes Log. To set a quota, open the Domino Administrator to the Files tab. Select a database to which you want to apply a quota, and expand the Database tools. Select the Quotas tool to display the Set Quotas dialog box, as shown in Figure 5-13.

First, set the database quota (in megabytes). After you configure a quota, you can also set a warning threshold (in megabytes). Use the *More Info* button to determine whether the database has a current quota or threshold, as well as the current size of the database (in kilobytes).

 TIP   You can set quotas and thresholds for mail files in the same way as for any other database, but by default, documents delivered by the Router can continue to be added to the database. To force the Router to obey the quota, use the **Router/SMTP** tab in the **Messaging** section of the Configuration document.

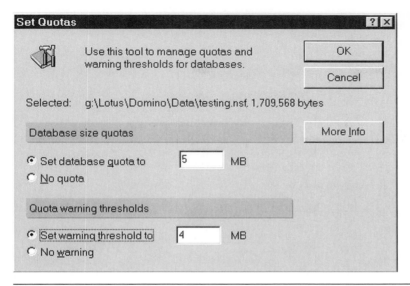

Figure 5-13   The Set Quotas dialog box

Archiving

To help prevent a database from becoming too large, you should archive unused documents regularly. When you archive documents, you copy the documents to an archive database that is usually based on the same design as the main database, and you then delete the documents from the active database. You can archive documents by using the archiving tool in the Database properties InfoBox or by using an archive agent. Note that the *Remove documents not modified in last X days* replication setting only deletes unused documents during replication and does not perform any archiving.

To use the archiving tool, open the Database properties InfoBox and click the *Archive Settings* button to display the Archive Settings dialog box (shown in Figure 5-14). In the Basics panel, select which documents to archive. You can archive documents that have not been read or accessed in a specified number of days, documents that have not been modified or updated in a specified number of days, or all documents that are marked as expired. Also, use this panel to choose an archive database. Archive databases are placed in an archive directory and are named with *a_databasename* by default.

On the Advanced panel, determine whether the archiving is manual or automatic on a server. If the archiving is manual, you can choose whether the archive is stored locally or is stored on a server. If you select manual, choose File . . . Database . . . Archive to archive the qualifying documents. Domino shows you a summary of the archiving

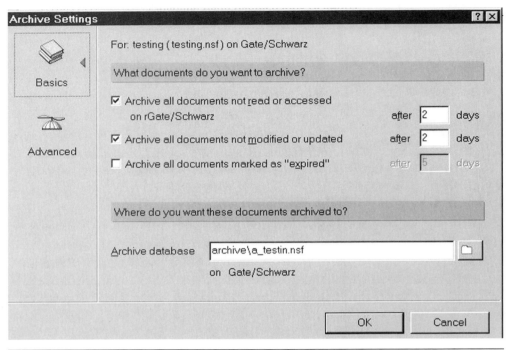

Figure 5-14   The Archive Settings dialog box

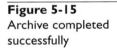
Figure 5-15
Archive completed
successfully

when complete, as shown in Figure 5-15. You can also choose the following additional options:

- You can choose whether to log the archiving, and if so, where to place the log.
- You can select not to delete documents that have responses, to avoid orphaning those documents and making them unavailable in a view.
- You can also choose to delete qualifying documents without archiving them.

You can also create your own archiving agent to perform similar tasks. To create an agent in the database, choose Create . . . Agent from the menus. You do not need

Domino Designer to create an agent. Give the agent a name, such as Archive and Delete, and make the agent Shared by using the check box. Choose how the agent should run from the *When should this agent run?* drop-down list. You can create an agent that runs manually, from a menu or button, automatically based on a schedule, or automatically based on a document event. If you choose a scheduled agent, create the specific schedule. You should have an archiving agent work on the database when other users or server processes (such as replication) are not using the database.

CAUTION   If you choose to have the agent run automatically, the agent is called a background agent. Ensure that the database property Disable background agents for this database is not enabled.

Next, select which documents the agent should run against. At this point, you will create a selection formula for the agent. You can choose to have the agent run against all documents, against selected documents, or against documents in a specific view. After a general selection, you can also add more specific selection criteria by using the *Add Search* button. Use this button to make a selection based on a date, field, form, author, or other criteria.

After selecting which documents and when, create an action for the agent to perform. You can add an action to an agent by using Simple actions, @Functions and @Commands, LotusScript, or Java. To create an archive agent using Simple actions, choose *Simple action(s)* from the drop-down list and click the *Add Action* button. In the Add Action dialog box, use the Copy to Database action.

TIP   Note that you should create a new database for the archive before creating this agent. An easy way to create this database is to make a new copy of the active database and then remove any unneeded fields, views, and other elements.

After selecting the database to which documents should be copied, you should add a second action to delete the documents from the current database.

Adding a Database to a Server

You can add a database to a server by creating a new replica or a new copy. A replica is a special type of copy that is linked to the original by a shared replica ID. Look for the replica ID on the Info tab of the Database properties InfoBox, as shown in Figure 5-16.

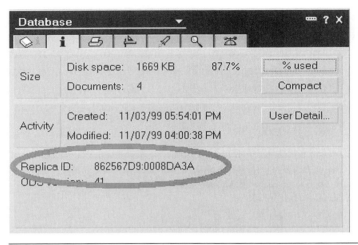

Figure 5-16   Replica ID

Two databases with the same replica ID can be synchronized via Notes replication. Two databases that are copies of each other and that do not have the same replica ID cannot be replicated. These databases begin with the same documents and design elements, but as users make changes, the two databases become different.

Creating a Replica

Create a new replica of a database on a server when you want to accomplish any of the following tasks:

- Making the database available locally to users of a particular server to limit network traffic

- Making databases more available in case a server goes down

- Making a replica available with a subset of the information contained in the database (this task requires a replication formula)

- Improving the performance of a database by making the database available in more locations

To create a new replica, you must have access to create replicas on the server with which you are working. The field on the Server document that enables this access is *Create Replica Databases* on the Security tab, as shown in Figure 5-17. If this field is blank, no one can create new replicas on the server.

Figure 5-17   Create Replica Databases

You have a variety of methods available for creating a new replica. First, you can create the new replica manually—from the Notes client or from anywhere you have the database open. Choose File . . . Replication . . . New Replica to display the New Replica dialog box.

In the New Replica dialog box, select the server on which you want the new replica placed from the *Server* drop-down list. If the server you want is not listed, type the fully distinguished name of the server. Next, type the filename if you need to change the name. You can also use the *Select Folder* button to select a specific folder in which to place the database. Otherwise, the database will be placed in the default data directory. You can select encryption and size limit settings (although remember that the size limit is not a factor for R5 databases).

To configure the new replica to contain only a subset of documents of the current database, use the *Replication Settings* button to access the Replication Settings dialog box, as shown in Figure 5-18. This feature enables you to create a replication formula.

Replication Settings   Replication settings, or a replication formula, might be intended to save disk space or to limit the items that users on a particular server see. The first panel is the Space Savers panel, which enables you to configure options such as

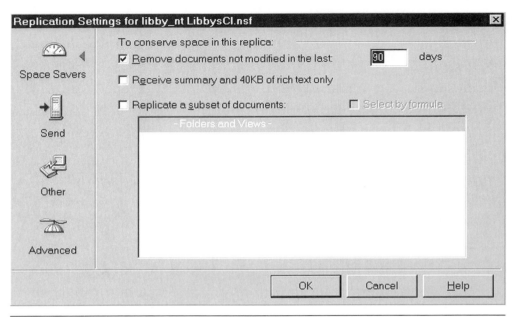

Figure 5-18 The Replication Settings dialog box

Remove documents not modified in the last X days, *Receive Summary and 40 KB of rich text only*, and *Replicate a subset of documents* to reduce the size of the current replica. Note that if you configure these settings, the documents are purged from the replica. They do not create deletion stubs, so other replicas are not affected.

TIP The Remove documents not modified in the last X days option is also what configures the purge interval for a database. The purge interval, which is one-third of the number in this field, occurs when Domino removes the deletion stubs of documents that you have deleted. When you delete a document, Domino leaves a deletion stub to indicate to other replicas that this document has been deleted and that it should be deleted in other replicas. This feature is what prevents replication from replacing the document, assuming that the document had not yet been created on the replica. Therefore, if the purge interval occurs before replication occurs, documents that you have deleted might reappear.

The Send panel governs which data this replica sends to other replicas of the database. You can configure the replica for the following options:

- Do not send deletions made in this replica to other replicas.

- Do not send changes in database title and catalog information to other replicas.

- Do not send changes in local security properties to other replicas.

You can use the Other panel to *Temporarily Disable Replication* for a database. Check this setting if your replicas are not synchronizing correctly. You can also set a replication priority (high, medium, or low) for the database. Then, when you create Connection documents, for example, you can choose to replicate high-priority databases. You can also set a publishing date if you are working with a CD-ROM—or a setting to only replicate incoming documents modified after a certain date.

Use the Advanced panel to configure what a server receives from other servers, including non-document elements. The Advanced panel is shown in Figure 5-19. You can also click the *Select by formula* check box to create an advanced replication formula.

TIP   If you choose to implement a replication formula or other replication settings using this dialog box, be aware that all documents in the database are affected by these settings. In other words, if you choose to replicate only documents in a particular view, the specified replica of the database will contain only those documents. Documents in other views will be removed from the database.

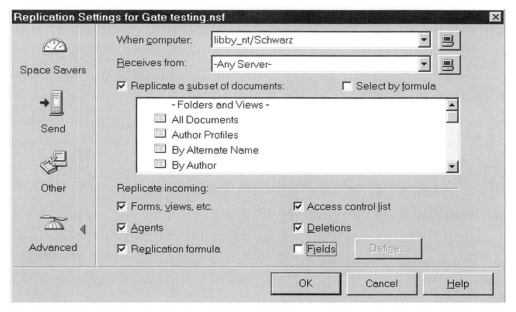

Figure 5-19   The Advanced panel

After you complete the replication settings, return to the New Replica dialog box by clicking OK. Next, determine whether the database should be created immediately or at the next scheduled replication. If you choose *Next Scheduled Replication,* ensure that you have a Connection document configured between the two servers. You can also select to copy the ACL and to create a full-text index as the new replica is created. When the options are all correct, choose OK to create the new replica.

You can also create a replica by using Domino Administrator and the Administration Process (AdminP). To use this method successfully, you need to make sure that the AdminP is running on both the destination and source servers. The source server must have *Create new replicas* access in the Server document of the destination server.

In the Domino Administrator, open the Files tab. Select the database from the list in the Results pane. If you have pinned open the Server list, as shown in Figure 5-20, you can drag the database to the server on which you need to create a new replica. The Domino Administrator displays the Select Destination Folder dialog box. Use this dialog box to tell Domino that you are either moving or adding the database to the server and where you want to locate the database on the destination server.

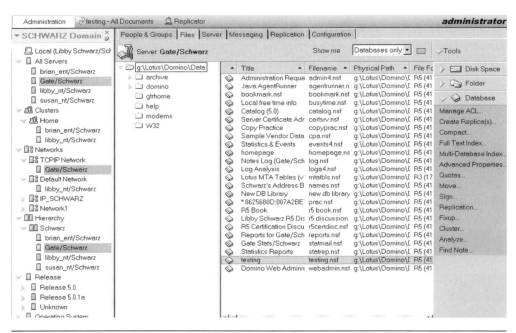

Figure 5-20   Server list in the Domino Administrator

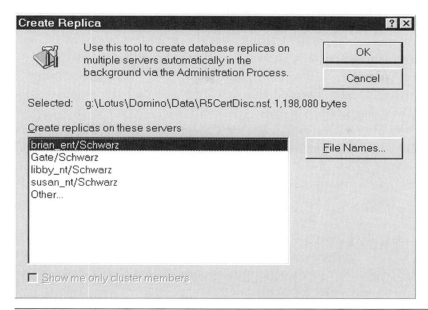

Figure 5-21   Create Replicas from the Domino Administrator

You can also select the Create Replicas tool from the Database tools or New . . . Replicas from the shortcut menu. Either of these options causes Domino to display the Create Replicas dialog box that is shown in Figure 5-21. Select one or more destination servers. To confirm or change the filename or path for any of the servers, click the *File Names* button, which displays the Edit Destination Path dialog box. When finished, click OK to have the Administration Process complete the request.

To verify that AdminP has processed the request to create a new replica successfully, open the Administration Requests (ADMIN4.NSF) database, as shown in Figure 5-22.

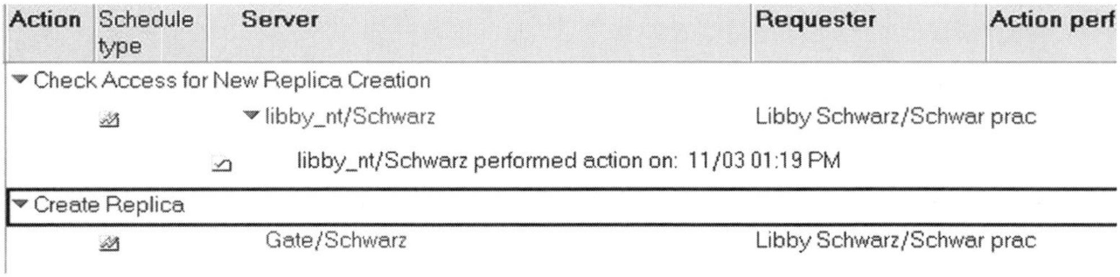

Action	Schedule type	Server	Requester	Action perf
▼ Check Access for New Replica Creation				
		▼ libby_nt/Schwarz	Libby Schwarz/Schwar prac	
		libby_nt/Schwarz performed action on: 11/03 01:19 PM		
▼ Create Replica				
		Gate/Schwarz	Libby Schwarz/Schwar prac	

Figure 5-22   Administration Requests performed

You will see that AdminP checked to verify that you and the server had the necessary access to perform the action and that the action was then performed. Note that the destination server creates the new replica, while the source server verifies access.

After you have created a new replica, you will want the replica to have the capability to replicate with the source database and with any other replicas of the database. In a clustered environment, the server will replicate automatically with other members of the cluster as soon as the database is added to the Cluster database directory. This task occurs automatically. In a non-clustered environment, you must create or edit a Connection document that includes this database and the appropriate servers to ensure that the database stays updated.

Creating a New Copy

If you want to create a new copy of a database instead of a replica, you will undertake a manual process only. You must have the *Create new databases* access on the Security tab of the destination Server document to perform this action. This field enables everyone to create new databases when the field is blank.

To create a new copy of a database, open the database. From the File menu, choose Database . . . New Copy. Domino displays the Copy Database dialog box.

As you would to create a new replica, select the destination server and the filename. You can also change the title of the database when creating a new copy. Choose whether to copy only the design of the database or both the design and the documents. Remember, this database will not have the capacity to replicate with the source database; however, if there is a template, the design might still be updated by the template. Domino makes the copy immediately.

Moving a Database

Move databases when you bring a new server online or when you change the purpose of a server. In some cases, you might be taking a server offline. You can move databases manually or using the Administration Process.

Moving the Database Manually

In many organizations, the Administration Process is not in use. Before beginning the process of moving a database, you must ensure that you have *Create new replica* access to the destination server. Use the steps detailed previously in Create a New Replica to create a new replica of the database on the destination server.

You will then need to delete the existing database on the source server. To delete a database, you need Manager access in the database ACL. Choose File . . . Database . . . Delete to remove the database permanently from the server.

Moving a Database Using the Administration Process

The details of AdminP itself are described in other areas of the book, but in this case, we discuss how to move a typical application using AdminP.

> **TIP** Note that a mail file is not considered a typical application; rather, it requires some additional steps. To understand moving mail files, refer to Chapter 4, "Domino Messaging."

Any time you use AdminP to move databases between servers, make sure that both the source and destination servers are running AdminP. You and the source server both need *Create new replica* access in the destination server's Server document. In addition, you need Manager access to the database for AdminP to accept the request.

You can move the database by dragging the database from the Files tab of the Domino Administrator to the destination server in the server list. As shown in Figure 5-23. Domino displays the Select Destination Folder dialog box. Indicate that you want to move the database by using the appropriate radio button. This action creates a request in the Administration Requests database, as shown in Figure 5-24.

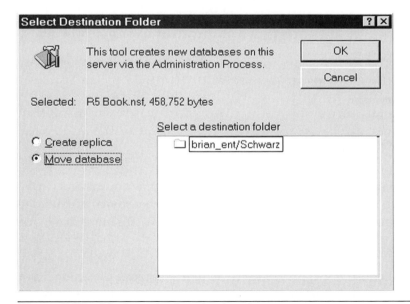

Figure 5-23 Moving a database by dragging

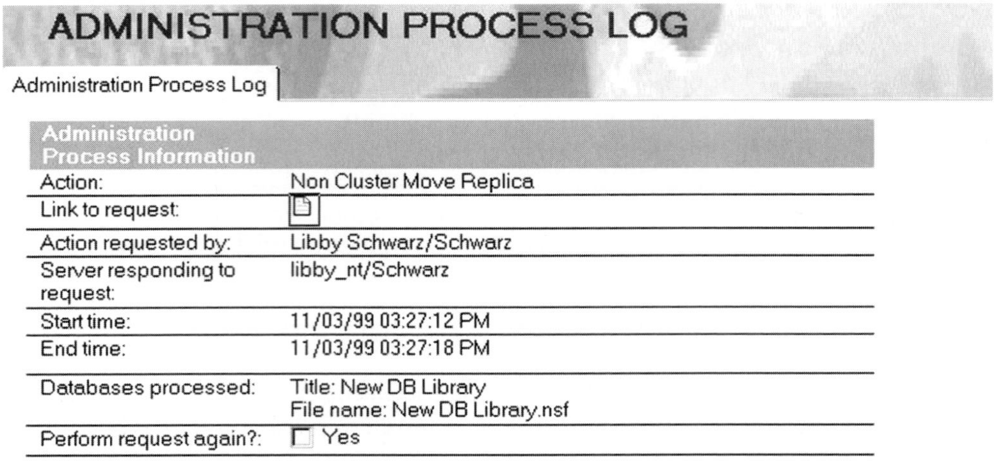

ADMINISTRATION PROCESS LOG

Administration Process Log

Administration Process Information	
Action:	Non Cluster Move Replica
Link to request:	[document icon]
Action requested by:	Libby Schwarz/Schwarz
Server responding to request:	libby_nt/Schwarz
Start time:	11/03/99 03:27:12 PM
End time:	11/03/99 03:27:18 PM
Databases processed:	Title: New DB Library File name: New DB Library.nsf
Perform request again?:	☐ Yes

Figure 5-24   A non-clustered database move request

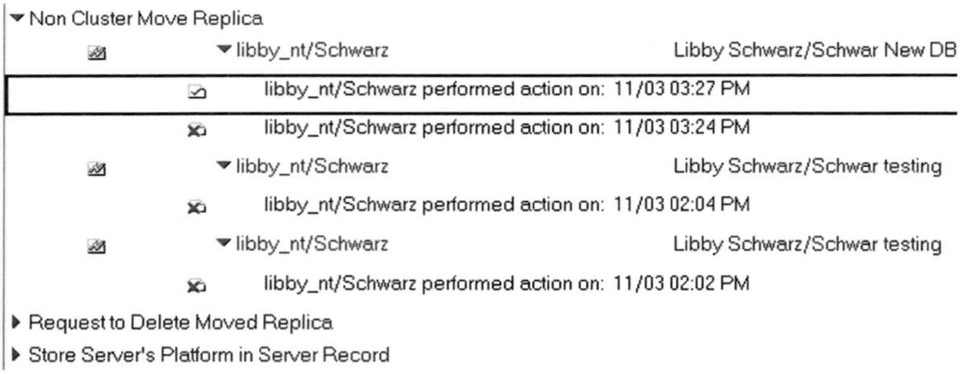

▼ Non Cluster Move Replica
    ▼ libby_nt/Schwarz   Libby Schwarz/Schwar New DB
        libby_nt/Schwarz performed action on: 11/03 03:27 PM
        libby_nt/Schwarz performed action on: 11/03 03:24 PM
    ▼ libby_nt/Schwarz   Libby Schwarz/Schwar testing
        libby_nt/Schwarz performed action on: 11/03 02:04 PM
    ▼ libby_nt/Schwarz   Libby Schwarz/Schwar testing
        libby_nt/Schwarz performed action on: 11/03 02:02 PM
▶ Request to Delete Moved Replica
▶ Store Server's Platform in Server Record

Figure 5-25   Requests in ADMIN4.NSF

As you can see in Figure 5-25, if you do not have the appropriate access to the database and to the server, the requests will fail. Also, remember that sometimes AdminP requests take time to process. If you need to force the request to occur immediately, use TELL ADMINP PROCESS ALL at the console.

To complete the move, AdminP needs to delete the database from the source server. This request needs administrator approval before AdminP completes the action, however. To approve the request, go to the Pending Administrator Approval view of the Administration Requests database, as shown in Figure 5-26.

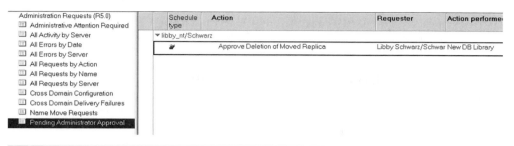

Figure 5-26   A request pending approval

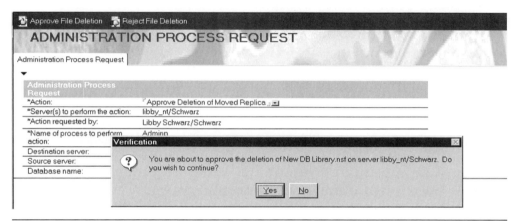

Figure 5-27   Approve the file deletion.

Put the document in Edit mode, and choose the Approve File Deletion action button to approve the deletion of the file, as shown in Figure 5-27.

Alternatively, you can select the database from the Files tab and select the Move tool from the Database tools. Domino displays the Move Database dialog box. You can move one or more databases using this tool. If you are working with a cluster, you can click the *Show me only cluster members* check box to limit the server options in the dialog box to cluster members. All other steps in the process are the same.

Adding and Moving Across Domains

The process of adding a new replica to a server across domains can be automated using the Administration Process, provided that you create the appropriate Cross Domain configuration documents.

The destination server will need an Inbound Cross Domain configuration document (in the Administration Requests database). In the Cross Domain Configuration view, choose the Add Configuration action button. On the Configuration Type tab, choose Inbound. On the Inbound Request Configuration tab, type the name of the domain from which to receive requests. If you want to receive requests from the Acme domain, for example, type *Acme* in this field. Next, choose the type of requests to receive from this domain. In this case, select Create Replica. Type the names of the servers for which to accept Create Replica requests. To accept Create Replica requests on the Gate/Schwarz server, for example, type the name of that server. Next, select approved signers for the request.

The source server (where the request is being initiated) needs an Outbound Cross Domain Configuration document. In the Cross Domain Configuration view, choose the Add Configuration action button. On the Configuration Type tab, choose Outbound. On the Outbound Request Configuration tab, type the names of the domains to which requests can be submitted. To submit requests to the Schwarz domain, for example, type that name in the field. Choose Create Replica as a type of AdminP request to submit to the other domain. Next, type in server and domain names for acceptable destination servers. Finally, include the names of approved signers.

In addition to the Inbound and Outbound configuration documents, to process these requests across domains, the following items are necessary:

- Mail Connection documents to enable the source server to send mail to the destination server's domain
- Cross-certification if the domains do not share a common certifier

While the AdminP can create replicas across domains, it cannot delete replicas across domains. That portion of the move process must be done manually when working across multiple domains.

Deleting Databases

You might choose to delete a database to reclaim space and other resources on a server. This action might also be part of moving the database to a different server. To delete a database, you need Manager access to the database in the ACL. If the database you are deleting is in a cluster, you will be able to use AdminP to delete the database. If the database is not on a server in a cluster, you will delete the database manually.

To delete a database that is in a cluster, first mark the database *Pending Delete* so that no new users will connect to the database. This action also ensures that the database is not deleted until all users have dropped their connections to the database. To mark a

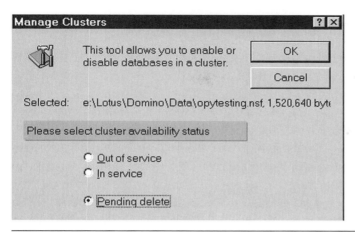

Figure 5-28   Marking a database for deletion

database for deletion, select the database in the Files tab of the Domino Administrator. Click the Cluster tool from the Tools list. In the Manage Clusters dialog box, shown in Figure 5-28, choose *Pending Delete*. Users who try to access the database receive an error stating that the database is in a restricted state until AdminP eventually deletes the database.

When the database is not in a cluster, simply select the database and choose File . . . Database . . . Delete. Before you delete a database, however, you might want to make an archive copy of the database. You can use the *Archive Settings* button on the Database properties InfoBox to create an archive of the database. You can also create an archive by making a replica or copy of the database and adding `Archive` to the filename and title. You can then create an agent in the original database to archive necessary documents and design elements.

Database and Directory Links

When you organize databases on your servers, you can put them in the default data directory, in a subdirectory under data, or outside the data directory. When you store them outside the data directory, you need to create either a database or a directory link to them so that they are seen as being on the server and can be accessed by users and server tasks. Creating database and directory links gives you two advantages:

1. You can take advantage of space on other servers, disks, or partitions without having to make any physical changes to your servers.

2. You can create added security.

When you create a database or directory link, users will see the name of the link in the Database Open dialog box as though the database or directory were located under the data directory. To create a link, open the Domino Administrator to the Files tab. In the Folder tools, click New Link. Domino displays the Create New Link dialog box.

In the New Link dialog box, type a name for the link. If you are using a link to move databases that are already in use, you should use the current name of the database or directory to make the transition easier for users. If you are creating a directory link, Domino uses a .DIR extension. For a database link, Domino appends the .NSF extension. To determine the object to which you are creating a link, Domino appends an extension when you select either the *Database* or *Folder* radio button. Then, in the *Path and Filename* field, type the physical location to which the link should point. If you want to place the databases in your e:\directorylinks folder, type this location in the field. You must create that directory and move databases to the directory manually. If you want to apply security to the directory link, add names in the *Who should be able to access this link?* field. If you do not want to restrict usage of the link, leave the field empty.

Replication

Now that there are applications on multiple servers, you must ensure that the applications stay synchronized by using Notes replication. As you know, replication is the process of exchanging data and synchronizing information between either two Domino servers or a Notes client and a Domino server. Replication can occur between any two databases that are the same on those multiple servers/clients. The word *same* is defined as sharing the same replica ID (as described previously).

How Replication Works

The task required for server replication is enabled automatically by the ServerTasks line in the NOTES.INI file. When the Domino server is installed and configured, the NOTES.INI file has the following line by default: `ServerTasks=Replica ...` This line ensures that the Replicator server task is running, and it will remain idle until needed. Replication requires more than the task running to occur, however. Replication must be initiated either manually at the server console or by Connection documents that have the replication schedule enabled within them. When you are maintaining an application, the replication schedule will already be configured by using Connection documents, but you might need to change the schedule or troubleshoot the replication. In addition, you might need to force replication to occur immediately.

With either method of initiating replication, there are four types of replication. These are pull-only, push-only, pull-push, and pull-pull. Be aware that although we will discuss compound replications, where the synchronization between the servers goes both ways, replication is a one-way process. The idea of two-way replication only indicates that a secondary replication is initiated immediately following another replication. The exam requires that you are familiar with these replication types.

Push Replication

In push-only replication, a one-way synchronization occurs. The initiating server calls or connects to the receiving server. The initiating server then pushes the changes in its databases to the receiving server. So, for example, if you have a server in your main office and a server in a satellite office, you might only permit administrators at the main office to make changes to the Domino Directory. When the administrators make these changes, however, the other replicas of the Domino Directory need to be updated. In this case, a push-only replication of the Domino Directory from the main office to the satellite office would be appropriate, as you can see in Figure 5-29.

Pull Replication

Pull-only replication is also a one-way synchronization. In this scenario, the initiating server calls the receiving server exactly as it would in push-only replication. Now, however, the initiating (or calling) server pulls the changes from the receiving (or remote) server's databases. So, in our previous example with a main office server and a satellite office server, the satellite office server might be controlling replication because of communications requirements. Therefore, we are still assuming that the changes to the Domino Directory will be made at the main office; however, now the satellite office server will call or connect to the main office server. The satellite office server will initiate a pull-only replication with the main office server and will pull all the Domino Directory changes down, as you can see in Figure 5-30.

Pull-Push Replication

Pull-push replication is the most common type of replication because it is the default —both when you create a replication Connection document and when you initiate a

Figure 5-29
Push-only
replication

Initiating   Receiving

Figure 5-30
Pull replication

Initiating   Receiving

replication at the server console. Pull-push replication is still one-way, as we discussed earlier; however, it is a compound replication. The initiating server makes the call to the remote server, initiates a pull replication with that remote server, and pulls the changes that exist in the remote server's databases to the server. Then, the initiating server immediately begins pushing its changes to the remote server. The initiating server controls both of the replications (i.e., it does all the work and makes all of the changes). In our scenario, we have the main office server and the satellite office server. In this case, we are assuming that there are administrators who are making changes to the Domino Directory at both locations. When changes are being made in both replicas, a full synchronization of the database is necessary. If you initiated a pull-push replication from the main office server, the server would call the satellite office and pull the satellite office's changes. The server would then initiate a push of the changes contained in its replica to the satellite office. At the end of the replication, the two databases would be completely synchronized. This process is described in Figure 5-31.

Pull-Pull Replication

Pull-pull replication is also a compound replication that uses two one-way replications to fully synchronize the databases. In this case, the initiating server makes the connection to the remote server and begins pulling the remote server's changes. When the first pull replication is completed, the Replicator task on the initiating server tells the remote server to begin a pull replication. The remote server then initiates a pull replication to complete the cycle. Each server's Replicator task does work in this type of replication. In our scenario of the main office server and the satellite office server, you might

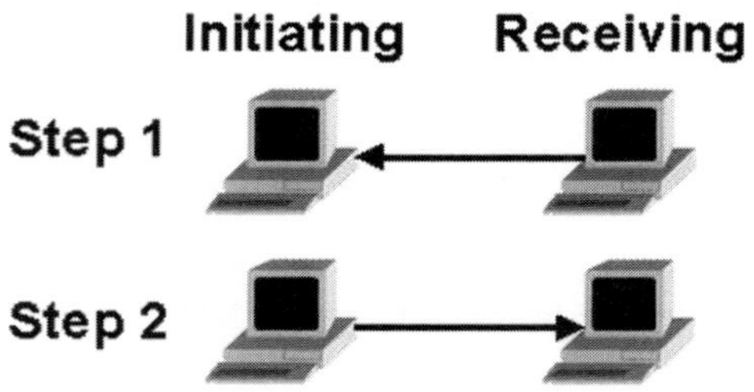

Figure 5-31
Pull-push replication

Initiating   Receiving

Step 1

Step 2

choose to use pull-pull replication if both Replicators or both servers are fairly busy. The pull-pull replication shares the work more equally between both servers. The main office server controls the replication, initiating a pull-pull replication with the satellite office and pulling the satellite office server's changes. When the changes have all been replicated up to the main office server, the main office server's Replicator will become idle. The satellite office server's Replicator task will then pull changes from the main office server, completing the replication (as shown in Figure 5-32).

The Replication Process

Understanding the process of replication will help when you need to troubleshoot problems. You will understand what occurs at each phase of replication. If the servers Home and Gate are on a pull-push replication schedule initiated by Home, the following steps will occur in the replication:

1. Home's Replicator task will see that it is supposed to initiate a replication with Gate. Home uses the Connection document to determine when and over which ports to initiate the replication.

2. Home initiates a replication with Gate. The two servers use authentication to verify each other's identities by using the public and private-key pairs. Completing authentication requires that the two servers have a certifier in common.

3. After authenticating, the servers compare a list of databases in the database cache. The servers compare replica IDs to see which databases they have in common that can be replicated.

4. After making a list of databases to replicate, the servers check the replication history of eachdatabase to determine the last successful replication. Any database with changes made after the last successful replication will be replicated.

Figure 5-32
Pull-pull replication

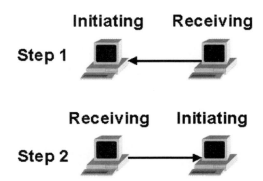

Initiating   Receiving

Step 1

Receiving   Initiating

Step 2

5. After determining which databases to replicate, the servers determine which elements (including ACL, design, and document changes) have changes and need to be replicated. The changes will be replicated based on the access permitted for each server in the database ACL. Home checks the ACLs on its databases to see which changes Gate can make in them. Similarly, Gate checks the ACLs on its databases to see which changes Home can make in them.

6. After determining which elements need to be replicated and which changes are permitted by the ACL, Home pulls the changes in Gate's databases to the local databases. ACL changes are made first, and then design and document changes (based on what the new ACL permits). When replicating, only changed fields on changed documents are replicated to save bandwidth and time during the replication.

7. After Home pulls the changes from Gate, Home's Replicator pushes the local changes to Gate.

8. When the replication is complete, Home uses Gate's server time to update the replication history with a new time stamp. If the replication was not successful, Home does not update the replication history but records an event in the Log instead.

Server Connection Documents and Replication Settings

Most of the time, replication is initiated automatically. To initiate replication automatically, there will be server Connection documents with replication schedule times enabled. You can use any of the four replication types in server Connection documents. In addition, you can use multiple Connection documents to create a complete schedule. For example, you might want to use pull-only replication from a central server to bring in changes from many other satellite offices. You might then want that central server to push out the collected changes to all of the satellite offices later in the day. To create this scenario, you would use two replication Connection documents per server: one that uses pull-only, and one that uses push-only.

In Figure 5-33, you can see a server Connection document with the fields pertinent to replication completed. When you are maintaining an environment that uses replication, you might need to change fields on the Connection document (to change the replication schedule, for example).

To edit a replication Connection document, open the Configuration tab in Domino Administrator. Click the Replication . . . Connections view. The Connection documents are available in the Results pane. To edit a connection, select the Connection document

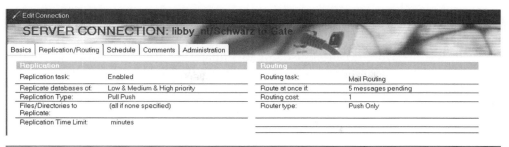

Figure 5-33   A server connection document with replication enabled

and click the Edit Connection action button. To change the replication schedule, open the Schedule tab. You can enable and disable the Connection document using the *Schedule* drop-down list. Next, complete the *Call at times* and *Repeat Interval of* fields. The *Call at times* are times or a range of times during which the originating server should contact the remote server. The *Repeat Interval* defines how many minutes should elapse before Domino starts the next replication. For example, assume that replication is scheduled to occur between 4 A.M. and 10 P.M., with a 60-minute repeat interval. If the first replication starts at 4 A.M. and completes at 4:45 A.M., the next replication will not begin until 5:45 A.M.—60 minutes after the replication completes.

Initiating Replication at the Server Console

If changes made to a database need to be replicated immediately, you might not want to wait for the scheduled replication to occur. In this case, you might want to initiate replication manually at the server console. You can use three commands at the server console to initiate replication: *PULL SERVERNAME DATABASENAME*, *PUSH SERVERNAME DATABASENAME*, and *REPLICATE SERVERNAME DATABASENAME*, where *servername* is the name of the server with which you wish to replicate, and *databasename* is either the name of the specific database you wish to replicate (relative to the data directory path) or a directory that you wish to replicate (again, relative to the data directory). You can also leave out the *databasename* if you wish to replicate all of the databases in the data directory.

The *pull* and *push* commands initiate pull-only or push-only replication, while the *replicate* command will initiate pull-push replication. You cannot initiate pull-pull replication from the server console.

Initiating Replication Using Domino Administrator

You can use the Domino Administrator to initiate replication. On the Server tab, expand the Server tools. Select the Replicate tool to display the Replicate From dialog box. Choose the server with which you want to replicate (the current server will be the initiating server), and then select the type of replication. You can choose pull, push, or push-pull replication from the drop-down list. Next, choose to replicate all databases in common, or select databases from the database list. Click the *Replicate* button to initiate replication.

Replication Topology

The Connection documents in your environment, which enable replication between multiple servers, create a replication topology. Sometimes you will find it useful to see this topology—to better understand which databases are replicating with other databases directly. The Domino Administrator provides a graphical representation of the replication topology by using the Replication tab, as shown in Figure 5-34.

In order for Domino Administrator to present this topology map, a server task called *MAPS Extractor* (MAPS) must be running on your server. This task looks at the Connection documents configured among the servers and creates the topology map. Double-clicking the lines in the topology map opens the specified Connection document. Use the map to understand which servers are connected for replication.

Multiple Replicators

Server Replicator tasks can only service one replication request at a time. While the Replicator is servicing that replication request, it can also keep track of up to five other replication requests. This feature is called the Replicator queue. When the Replicator queue is full, other replication requests will be dropped and will not occur. One way to avoid dropped replication requests on a busy server is to enable more than one Replicator task on the server. Obviously, multiple Replicators will require more server resources in terms of memory, server input/output, processor, and network bandwidth. For example, each Replicator uses a minimum of 3MB of RAM, even when idle.

To enable multiple Replicators, you will change the REPLICATORS line in the server's NOTES.INI file. You can do this task either directly in the NOTES.INI file by adding a line with REPLICATORS=2 (or however many Replicators you would like to enable). A better way of changing this parameter is by creating or updating a server Configuration document. Access Configuration documents in the Configuration tab of the Domino

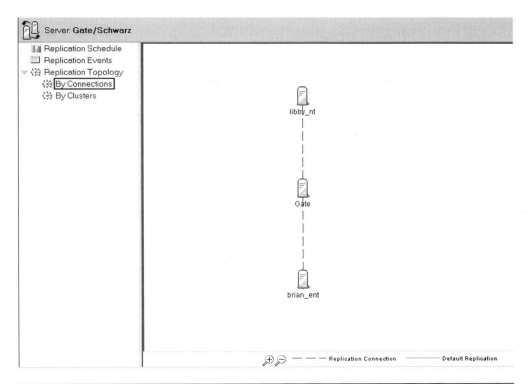

Figure 5-34   Replication topology

Administrator, under the Server twistie. To create a server Configuration document, click the Add Configuration action button. If possible, add the configuration parameter to an already-existing Configuration document by clicking the Edit Configuration button. This action opens the Configuration Settings form, as shown in Figure 5-35.

On the NOTES.INI tab, click the *Set/Modify Parameters* button. Domino displays the Server Configuration Parameters dialog box. Use the drop-down arrow next to the *Item* field to select the Replicators parameter. Type the number of Replicators to enable in the *Value* field. To enable the additional Replicators, click OK and then cycle the server.

 TIP   The maximum number of Replicators that you can enable is 10; however, you will usually enable no more than two or three Replicators.

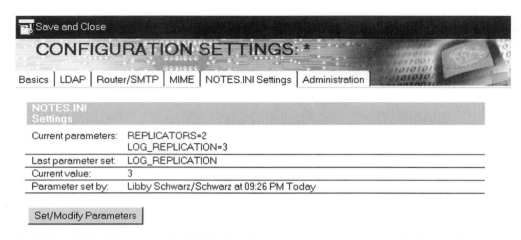

Figure 5-35   Configuration settings

Replication Problems

Many factors at all layers of the Notes and Domino environment can affect replication. These factors include the following:

- Server factors, such as authentication, server access lists, the server replication schedule, and the number of Replicators

- Database factors, such as the ACL, replica ID, replica ID cache, replication settings, replication history, and deleted documents

- Document factors, such as form access lists and merge replication conflicts

These factors can cause replication not to occur or to occur in an undesired manner. A good administrator will look at each of these factors when setting up replication, as well as when troubleshooting replication. We discuss each of the factors affecting replication here. To visualize the factors that affect replication, refer to Figure 5-36.

TIP **The exam will probably not ask questions about all of these factors, but you will be expected to know how to determine what will be replicated and why in any given scenario.**

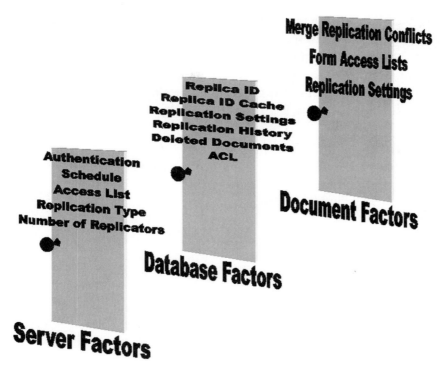

Figure 5-36   Factors affecting replication

Server Factors

The first layer of factors affecting replication is the server factors, such as the Replicator task being hung, the server being down, a disabled or deleted Connection document, replication being disabled on a database or server, or security issues. We can also add into the mix the replication type, as discussed previously. Finally, the capability to authenticate with and access the server are important server factors. If replication fails completely, make sure that the server is running and that the Replicator task is running. You can stop and restart the Replicator task using the Domino Administrator. Click the Server tab in Domino Administrator. Select the Replicator task from the Status list and right-click to access the shortcut menu. Click *Stop* on the short-cut menu to stop the task. To restart the task, expand the Task tools and click *Start.* From the Start New Task dialog box, select Replicator and click the *Start Task* button.

Also, check that the server attempting to request a replication can authenticate with the destination server. They must share some certificate in common that enables them to authenticate before replication can occur. In addition, the server access list in the Server document must enable the initiating servers to access the server. If the initiating server is not in the remote server's access list or is in the Not Access Server field, replication cannot occur.

Database Factors

The next factors that affect replication are at the database layer:

- Replica ID and the replica ID cache
- Database ACL
- Replication history
- Replication settings
- Deleted documents

As soon as another server is granted access for the purpose of replication (i.e., the servers have authenticated and the servers have passed the server access list), the servers check for databases that they have in common. The list of databases in common is stored in the replica ID cache. Each server maintains this list of databases that have matching replica IDs. Only the databases in the replica ID cache are replicated.

CAUTION Sometimes databases that are replicas of each other do not replicate. This situation can occur if the databases are not in the replica ID cache for some reason. Databases might not be in the replica ID cache if the cache has not been updated recently or if replication has been disabled for a database.

TIP To enable or disable replication for a database, go to the Files tab in Domino Administrator. Select the database, and choose Replication from the Database Tools. Choose Enable or Disable and click OK.

After the servers determine which databases can be replicated, the ACL of the database determines the level of replication that can occur. Table 5-1 describes what happens at each ACL level for the servers involved in replication.

Table 5-1 What Replicates at Each ACL Level

ACL Level	What Can Be Replicated?
No access	Nothing can be replicated. If either of the servers has No Access, replication does not continue. Use this option if you need to shut out a particular server at the database level.
Depositor	Do not use Depositor access for a server that needs to replicate. A server with Depositor access cannot replicate changes.
Reader	A server with Reader access to a database can receive changes, but it cannot distribute any changes. This level of access would only be appropriate in a situation where all changes made to a database are done at one source location and are then distributed.
Author	New documents could be created. Because a server does not author documents, however, this level is *not* recommended for an ACL setting for a server.
Editor	New and edited documents can be received and forwarded. This setting is common for any database that will be changed by multiple users at multiple locations.
Designer	In addition to receiving and forwarding new and edited documents, servers with Designer access will receive and forward new and edited design elements. Whichever server holds the replica of the database that is used by designers to update the design of the database must have Designer access.
Manager	Only one server should have Manager access to a database. Manager access enables the same changes as Designer access, with the additional capability to change the ACL and replication settings.

TIP A server must have the same or higher level of access to a database as the highest user on that server. If the manager of the NAMES.NSF database uses ServerA to open and modify the database, for example, ServerA must have at least Manager access to that database. Otherwise, the changes that user makes on the server cannot be replicated to other servers. Similarly, if users on ServerA have Author access to the Inventory database, ServerA should have at least Editor access to replicate both newly created and edited documents.

Another database-level factor that affects whether the database is replicated is the replication history for that database. The *replication history* is a list of dates, times, and servers that have completed replication with a particular database. To access the replication history, which is shown in Figure 5-37, open the Database properties InfoBox and click the *Replication History* button. When a successful replication is completed, the source server's time is used to time-and-date stamp the replication history. Replication

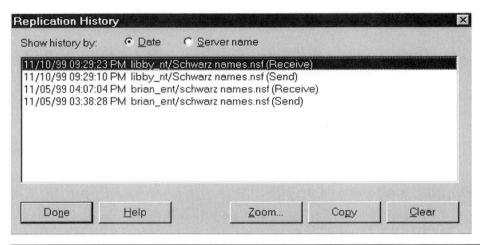

Figure 5-37   Replication history

history can be used to aid in troubleshooting replication. If replication has not been occurring as you expected, you could choose the Clear button to remove all replication history entries. This action will force a complete replication to occur at the next scheduled replication. Be aware that it will take a significantly longer time, because each element is being verified—not just being compared to the time stamp as usual. If you are only having replication problems with a particular server, you can select that server's replication history from the dialog box and click the Zoom . . . button. After you zoom in on a particular event, you can clear just that event.

> **NOTE**   Workstation replication does not update the replication history on a server-based database. Only server replication adds this time stamp.

Finally, replication settings for a database provide control over what can be sent and received during replication. Right-click the database icon to access the replication settings, as shown in Figure 5-38. The options in the Replication Settings dialog box are reviewed in Table 5-2.

One significant database-layer factor affecting replication is how replication deals with deleted documents. When you delete a document from one replica of a database, the document should be deleted from *all* replicas of the database. Some users wonder, however, why Notes does not just replace the deleted document with a copy of that document from

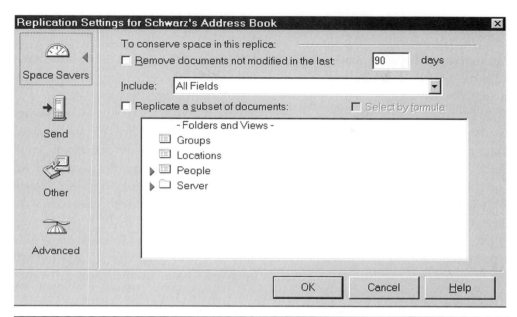

Figure 5-38   Replication settings

Table 5-2   Replication Settings

Panel	Option
Space Savers	This panel enables you to restrict the documents that you replicate based on folders, views, or formulas. Most often, laptop users edit these fields to minimize the size of a database. If you choose to restrict the documents you replicate in this dialog box, you are creating a replication formula. In addition, the R*emove documents not modified in the last ___ days* is an important field for all replicas. This field sets the purge interval for the deletion stubs in the database, as discussed later in the chapter. The purge interval is set to one-third of the value of this field. The default is 90 days; therefore, the default purge interval is 30 days.
Send	This panel enables you to limit the changes and deletions sent from this replica to other replicas.
Other	This panel enables you to disable replication temporarily if necessary. You also have the option to change the replication priority of the database, as discussed previously, and to limit incoming replications based on document modified dates.
Advanced	Advanced options enable you to limit incoming documents based on formulas and the specific server (or workstation) that is sending the document(s). This panel enables you to create a complex replication formula that enables the replicas of databases in different locations to contain a different subset of information.

another replica. When you delete a document from a database, Notes removes the document but leaves a deleted document identifier (called a deletion stub) in its place. This deletion stub is invisible to users but is used by Notes to indicate that the document has been deleted. If Notes does not see this deletion stub, Notes will assume that the document in the other replica is new and will add the document back into the database.

To save space in databases, Notes eventually deletes the deletion stubs. The amount of time that passes before Notes removes the deletion stubs is called the *purge interval*. You can set the purge interval for a database in the Space Savers panel of the Replication Settings dialog box, as discussed previously. The *Remove documents not modified in the last ___ day* field enables the administrator to set the purge interval. The purge interval is defined as one-third of the value of this field. The default value for this field is 90 days. The default purge interval, therefore, is 30 days.

In some cases, your users will complain that deleted documents are reappearing after replication occurs. If the users report this problem, it is likely that your purge interval occurs before your replication interval. To troubleshoot this problem, either increase the purge interval or replicate more often.

Document Factors

In addition to the server and database factors, document-layer settings also affect replication. Document-layer settings include the following items:

- Reader and Author fields in forms and documents
- Form and View access lists
- Merge replication conflicts

Most settings at the document layer are determined by and are the responsibility of the database designer. Anything that affects replication, however, needs to be a joint effort between the administrator and the designer.

The forms and views in databases have a Security tab on their Properties InfoBoxes. These security tabs enable the designer to refine the access given to users by removing them from the Form and View access lists. If you change the default Form and View access, you must include the servers that will be involved in replication.

Similarly, designers can place fields on forms in the database—called Reader and Author fields—which limit the users who can read and create documents with those forms. If these fields are on forms in databases that will be replicated, they can affect replication at the document layer. The servers that will be replicating the databases must be included in Reader and Author fields.

Finally, the designer has the capability to enable an option called Merge Replication Conflicts when creating forms in a database. Different users can edit the same document on different replicas of a database, which would cause a replication conflict when replication occurs between the databases.

There are two features to help prevent replication conflicts. First, Notes uses field-level replication rather than document-level replication. In other words, Notes only replicates the specific fields that have changed in the documents and databases, rather than replicating the entire document that has changes. Second, Notes enables design-ers to permit *Merge replication conflicts* for the forms in a database. If the *Merge replica-tion conflicts* property is enabled, as long as users do not change the same field, the changes will be made to the document when replication occurs—and there will be no replication conflict. If, however, the users both change the same field, a replication con-flict will occur. If the designer did not enable *Merge replication conflicts*, a replication conflict will occur even if the users edited different fields. To see whether the *Merge replication conflicts* option has been enabled, open the database to the Design . . . Forms view. Open the form and access the Form Properties InfoBox by right-clicking the form and choosing Form Properties. The *Merge Replication Conflicts* option is on the Basics tab, as shown in Figure 5-39.

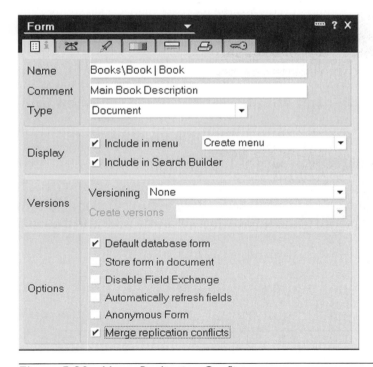

Figure 5-39   Merge Replication Conflicts

If the users are both editing documents in the same replica of a database and they edit the same document at the same time, a save conflict is created. Enabling *Merge replication conflicts* cannot prevent this result.

If a replication or save conflict is created, it is displayed in the view as a response document, as shown in Figure 5-40. Domino determines which document will be the main document and which document will be the conflict based on the following criteria:

- If one document has been edited or saved more times than the others, that document becomes the main document. All other documents become replication or save conflicts.

- If all documents have been saved and edited the same number of times, the last document to be saved becomes the main document. All other documents become replication or save conflicts.

- To determine which document wins when it has been edited in one replica and deleted in another, Domino looks at the number of changes and when they occurred. If the document was edited more than once, the document remains. If the document was edited more recently than the deletion, the document remains. Otherwise, Domino deletes the document from both replicas.

When replication or save conflicts occur, it is the database manager's responsibility to merge the data into a single document and remove the conflict document. This process is usually manual, although you can write advanced agents to assist with the process. You should check the $UpdatedBy field in the Document properties to determine which users last updated the documents. Obtain input from the users to edit the main document to include the correct data. Then, delete the conflict document.

Application Security

One element of an application that must be monitored and maintained at all times is the security of the application. Bear in mind that working with application security is complex, in that you will never do this task alone. You will always work with the appli-

Date	▲	Topic
11/10/1999		adfafda (Libby Schwarz)
11/07/1999		ldjfajfdo;afjdo;aijdolj (Libby Schwarz)
08/25/1999	1	▼ edited oneantoher (Libby Schwarz)
		[Replication or Save Conflict]

Figure 5-40   A replication or save conflict in a view

cation developer and with any database managers. In Notes, moreover, access to the application is also determined at multiple levels—i.e., network and server above the database level, and view, form, document, and field security below the database level. Only when a user passes the network level and the server level are the database level security methods applied.

Network and Server Security

These two security layers are described in more detail in other sections of this book, but you should recognize that they are a part of application security. A user or server that does not pass the network and server security layers cannot access an application. At the network layer, security relates to ports and protocols as well as to network encryption. Users and servers must communicate over the same protocols and ports. If a server is using TCP/IP, clients connecting to that server must also use this protocol. In addition, Notes uses a variety of ports over this protocol, including port 1352 for Notes communication, port 80 for HTTP communication, and port 443 for HTTP communication over a Secure Sockets Layer (SSL). Both servers and clients must have the capability to communicate over the same ports. In addition, these ports must be available through any firewalls or filtering in the environment.

After passing the network security layer, users must pass the server security layer. Server security consists of authentication and the security controls on the server document. *Authentication* is the process by which a user or server—using their ID file— verifies their identity within the Notes Organization. Each Notes Organization has a certifier (or multiple certifiers), and each ID file within the Notes Organization is stamped with this certifier. The authentication process compares the stamp on the user or server's ID file with the stamp that is part of the Notes Organization. Authentication is based on having this shared certifier stamp in common. The process is slightly different for Web users, because they do not necessarily have an ID file. For Web users, authentication is based on the username and password (from a Person document). If a user does not have a username and password, he or she might be able to log on as Anonymous (if permitted). Look for more information about Web users and security in Chapter 2, "Advanced Domino and Web Servers."

The second part of server access is based on what access is enabled in the Server document. To find the security information in the Server document, use the Configuration tab in the Domino Administrator. Select the Server document from the All Server Documents view in the Servers section. In the Server document, select the Security tab. The Server Access section determines which users, servers, and groups can access the specified server. If the *Access Server* field is blank, all users, servers, and groups can access the server. If a user is listed in the *Not Access Server* field, however, that user cannot access the server to access an application.

Database Security

Much of the security of an application comes from the database ACL, which is shown in Figure 5-41. The ACL determines who can access the database and which permissions he or she will have within the database. The ACL relies on the server's Domino Directory to identify people and groups to provide access to the database. One place to view and maintain the following security elements for a database is the ACL dialog box for an application:

- Access level
- Additional privileges
- User types
- Roles

There are seven available access levels for a database. These access levels can be further modified by using optional access-level privileges. These levels and the additional privileges are listed in Table 5-3.

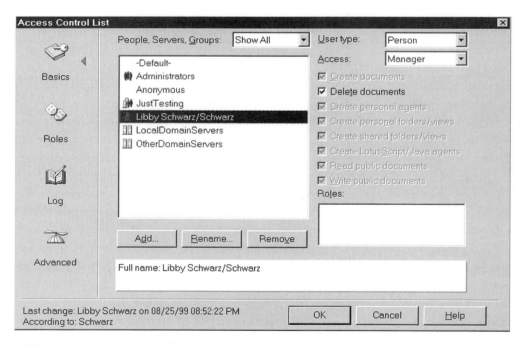

Figure 5-41 Access Control List

Table 5-3 Access Levels

Access Level	Access-Level Rights	Optional Access-Level Privileges
Manager	Modify ACL	Delete documents
	Delete database	
	Encrypt database	
	Modify replication settings	
Designer	Modify database design	Delete documents
	Create full-text index	Create LotusScript/Java agent
Editor	Create documents	Delete documents
	Edit any documents	Create personal agents
		Create personal folders/views
		Create shared folders/views
		Create LotusScript/Java agents
Author	Edit own documents (provided that they are listed in an Author field)	Create documents
		Delete documents (only own)
		Create personal agents
		Create personal folders/views
		Create LotusScript/Java agents
		Write public documents
Reader	Read documents	Create personal agents
		Create personal folders/views
		Create LotusScript/Java agents
	Write public documents	
Depositor	Can contribute documents but cannot read any, including their own	Write public documents
		Read public documents
No Access	No access at all	None

Table 5-4 Default ACL entries

Entry	Access Level	Notes
-Default-	Designer	This entry applies to any user who accesses the database without his or her name being listed individually in the ACL. In addition, this access level will be applied to Web users who do not authenticate with a name and password if there is no Anonymous entry in the ACL. To protect your data, you should change this access level immediately to Reader or No Access, depending on the application.
LocalDomainServers	Manager	You should add the servers in your local domain to the LocalDomainServers default group in the Domino Directory to ensure that those servers have the appropriate access level to the database.
OtherDomainServers	Manager	You should ensure that this group has lower access (usually) than LocalDomainServers.
Database Creator's name	Manager	Usually, this name will be removed after the database is placed on the production server and is replaced with the Administrators group (and perhaps with the Developers group).

When a database is first created, it has some default entries. Table 5-4 describes the default entries.

Depending on the function and intent of your database, a database ACL includes one or more of the ACL levels for your ACL entries. Every organization has different ACL standards, but here are some general guidelines for ACL levels:

- *Always have a manager.* Every database must contain at least one entry with Manager access to ensure that some person, server, or group member can adjust the ACL. Remember that managers can delete the database, though, so use this access level sparingly. As any long-time mail administrator is aware, it is indeed possible for users to accidentally delete databases.

- *Use groups whenever possible.* When setting a database ACL for the first time, you will find it tempting to simply enter the names of the people and/or servers that you know will need to access the database. You should always choose appropriate groups from the Domino Directory for ACL entries, however. This action makes the ACL flexible and improves forward maintenance.

- *Do not grant more access than necessary.* As with sparing the use of the Manager access level, it is generally appropriate to give users only the access level necessary for proper function of the database. You will find it easier to grant higher access levels when the business requirement exists than to try to undo any inappropriate actions that are taken by users who have higher-than-necessary access levels.

- *Select, and do not type, the user, server, and group names.* You should always select the names of users, servers, and groups that should have access to the database using the Domino Directory. A name that is not typed correctly will not give the correct security level.

TIP Be aware that when you first create a database, Notes gives the default ACL entry Designer access to the database. Few databases in an organization will have a business need for default users to have the capability to adjust the database design, full-text index, or replication settings. Most general-use applications should limit the default user to no more than Author or Editor access.

ACL Roles

In addition to specifying access levels, you can also assign ACL entries to be members of a larger designation called a role. ACL roles do not necessarily signify any particular security privileges; rather, they represent a convenient way to group ACL entries that might have different access levels.

You can create and maintain roles by using the Roles tab of the ACL dialog box (refer to Figure 5-42).

Add, rename, or remove roles by clicking the three buttons below the list of roles. Once you have added and named your roles, you can match ACL entries with the desired roles on the Basics tab. Each entry can belong to as many roles as you designate by selecting each desired role in the right-hand selection box while the ACL entry is highlighted (refer to Figure 5-43).

Now that you have seen how to create and assign roles—and have learned that they do not confer any particular security privileges—you might be wondering what function they have in your database(s). Because they can contain several different ACL entries, roles are a convenient, programmatic way to identify logical subsets of your users. Two primary @Functions will enable you to access a list of any given user's roles:

- **@UserRoles** @UserRoles enables you to directly access which roles a designated user has been assigned in the database ACL. This feature can help you build smart applications that automatically launch the Marketing frameset for users who have membership in the Marketing role, for instance.

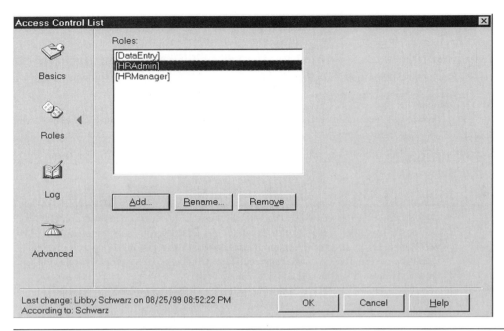

Figure 5-42   The ACL Role tab

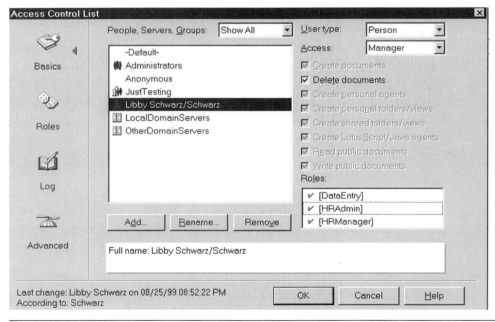

Figure 5-43   Assigning ACL entries to a role

- **@UserNamesList** @UserNamesList provides a text list of all applicable usernames, group memberships, and database role memberships.

 NOTE Be aware that many @Functions that rely on ACL settings or roles will not work on local database replicas unless "Enforce a consistent Access Control List across all replicas of this database" is selected in the Advanced tab of the ACL dialog box. For more information, see "Enforcing Consistent ACLs" later in this chapter.

ACL Log

Each ACL also has a log associated with it that tracks any changes. Access the ACL change log via the Log tab on the ACL dialog box (refer to Figure 5-44). The log enables you to view a rolling history of changes that you and other designers or administrators might make to the ACL. Use the ACL log when you need to troubleshoot issues that might arise from incorrect changes in the ACL.

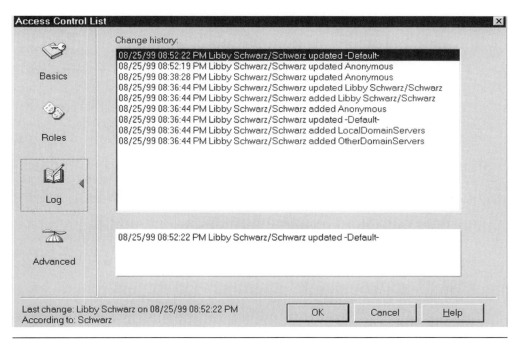

Figure 5-44 The ACL Log tab

Advanced ACL Settings

In addition to specifying ACL entries and creating and assigning roles, for proper ACL maintenance you need an awareness of the advanced ACL settings and their effects. Find the advanced ACL settings on the Advanced tab of the ACL dialog box (refer to Figure 5-45).

Administration Server As we have seen, the ACL is based on a large part from information pulled from the Domino Directory—Person names, Group names, and Server names. The ACL of a database is often set up initially and occasionally modified, but is not always updated on a daily or even monthly basis. By contrast, in large organizations the Domino Directory is constantly changing. Users change names or leave the company, and groups are added and deleted. In other words, ACL entries can become outdated when a person or group listed is no longer available in the Domino Directory.

To keep the ACL synchronized with the Domino Directory, designate an Administration server for the database at the top of the Advanced tab (refer to Figure 5-46). The Administration server should be a server that regularly runs the Aministration Process task (AdminP) and has Manager access to the database. For databases that have a des-

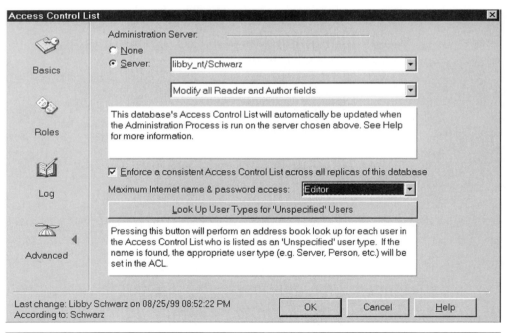

Figure 5-45 The ACL Advanced Settings tab

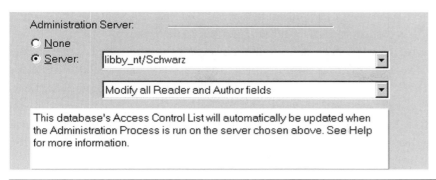

Figure 5-46   Administration server settings

ignated Administration server, the AdminP task updates any ACL entries that are out of synchronization with the Domino Directory. If administrators have removed any users from the Domino Directory, for example, the AdminP task on the Administration server removes the entries for those users from the ACL of the database.

In addition, you can also configure the Administration server to modify any Reader and Author fields contained in the database documents to reflect any changes in the Domino Directory (we will plunge further into the specifics of Reader and Author fields later in this chapter).

Enforcing Consistent ACLs Across All Replicas   Depending on the size and structure of your organization, your database might be replicated across several servers within your Notes domain. In addition, your organization might have many mobile users who replicate databases locally. Depending on the physical security of the other servers in your organization, you might choose to ensure that all replicas of the database throughout your organization enforce the same access rights, regardless of the server upon which they reside. You can do this task by selecting *Enforce a consistent Access Control List across all replicas of this database* in the middle of the Advanced ACL tab (refer to Figure 5-47).

Selecting this option ensures that if a server or person who is not a database manager makes a local ACL change on a replica, the replica does not replicate the ACL changes with other replicas of the database. The user or server that is attempting to initiate the

☑ Enforce a consistent Access Control List across all replicas of this database

Figure 5-47   Selecting to enforce consistent ACLs

replication receives an error message stating that the database will not replicate because a consistent access control cannot be maintained across databases.

Enforcing consistent ACLs throughout all replicas of a database also has some other ramifications. Keep in mind that without this setting, local replicas of a database (those replicas on a user's machine or on a server when accessed via the server's Notes client) do not enforce a database's ACL. Users who have Author access to a database can edit any document in a database, for instance. (In this example, however, the users' document edits will not replicate back to the server.) Enforcing a consistent ACL has the following effects:

- Local replicas of the database force user authentication for database access (i.e., the user will be forced to enter his or her password).

- Local replicas of the database enforce the user's given access level (not enabling authors to edit documents locally, for example).

- @Functions that are based on ACL settings such as @UserNamesList and @User-Roles will function as designed, even in local replicas.

NOTE Keep in mind that enforcing a consistent ACL is not designed to ensure that local data remains secure. To secure locally saved data, Lotus recommends utilizing database encryption.

Maximum Internet Name and Password Access In addition to specifying access levels for your users through ACL entries, you can also specify the maximum access level permitted via a Web browser. This setting is located in the middle of the Advanced ACL tab (refer to Figure 5-48). Notes and Domino enforce this maximum access level for any Web user, and this setting takes precedence over the access level assigned in the

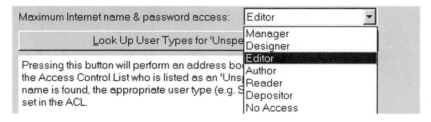

Figure 5-48 Maximum Internet name and password access

ACL. This setting is convenient if you require contributions or document edits to be made via the Notes client but also wish to enable Web users within your organization to browse the database for read-only purposes.

NOTE   Default maximum Internet name and password access for a database is Editor. Make sure that this access level is acceptable for your databases or that you adjust this setting accordingly. If you do not intend to enable Web access to the database, select No Access for this setting. Remember that if your database exists on any servers in your networked organization that enable anonymous HTTP access, many more users might be able to access your database than you originally intended.

Looking up Unspecified User Types   The fourth selection on the Advanced tab enables you to look up and define user types for any ACL entries with unspecified user types. The button to perform the lookup is located at the bottom of the Advanced tab. Using this method to verify user types can ensure that they are correctly assigned.

Maintaining the ACL from the Domino Administrator

You can modify the access levels given to users, servers, and groups by either using the ACL dialog box (as described previously) or by using the Domino Administrator. To change the ACL for one or more databases using the Domino Administrator, select the appropriate database(s) from the Files tab and expand the database tools. Select the Manage ACL tool to display the dialog box shown in Figure 5-49.

This Basics panel of the dialog box does not display the current settings for the database but does enable you to add, rename, or remove existing entries. You can only rename and remove an entry that you know exists. The tool does not display the current entries. You can use the Roles panel to add roles to all of the selected databases, but you cannot add users, servers, and groups to a role. That action must be done for each database individually. The Advanced panel enables you to modify the Administration server, the consistent ACL setting, and the Internet name and password setting for all of the selected databases.

NOTE   If a name or other element already exists in an ACL that you are trying to modify, Administrator gives you an error. To check the error, use the local Notes Log under the Miscellaneous view.

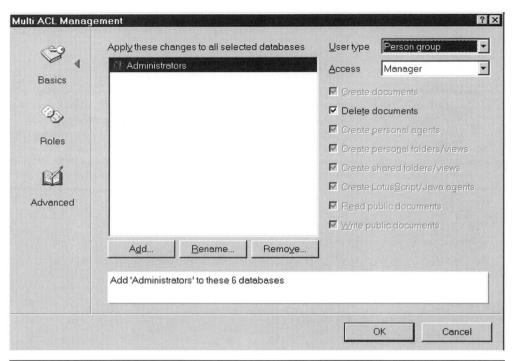

Figure 5-49 Multi-ACL management

TIP After R5.0.3, the Manage ACL tool gives the opportunity to view single ACLs via a button.

Document-Level Security

In addition to the database security that we have previously detailed, Notes also offers security at the document level. You can design a database that enables you or your users to specify particular readers and authors for given documents. This feature enables you to tightly control which pieces of data are available to which users—without building multiple databases.

Document-level security consists of the following items:

- **Author fields**   Author fields work in conjunction with the Author access level. As you recall from earlier in the chapter, the Author access level only enables users to edit their own documents. Document ownership is defined by the contents of any Author fields on the form. Author fields do not supersede the higher database-access levels, in that a database editor, designer, or manager can still edit any document (despite the presence of any Author fields).

- **Reader fields**   Reader fields define who can read any given document. They work independently of ACL settings, in that even database authors, editors, designers, and managers cannot read documents that do not specify them in a Reader field.

The database designer creates the Author and Reader fields, which rely on the field contents to include accurate Notes Names to work properly. (In other words, the names specified in a Reader or Author field have to match a common, abbreviated, or hierarchical name from the Domino Directory). Author and Reader fields can include person and server names, as well as valid groups from the Domino Directory. To define a Reader or Author field on a form, define a new field and set the field type to Reader or Author in the Field properties InfoBox.

NOTE   Author fields imply the capability to read as well as edit documents. Entries in a document's Author field do not need to be repeated in a Reader field in order for the document author to read the document.

Application Backup and Recovery

You should always have a tape backup of the important applications on your servers. In addition, many of the infrastructure databases (such as the Domino Directory) and the server and certifier ID files should be backed up. You can back up databases by using traditional backup utilities as well as transaction logging. Note that Lotus does not provide a backup utility; you need to obtain one from a third-party vendor. When you use the transaction log with a utility that is compliant with the log, you can do incremental backups (which take less time), rather than always doing full backups. If you use this combination of a backup utility with transaction logging, you should run incremental backups of the transaction log daily. You should also make sure to use the archiving style of transaction logging (instead of the circular style) and do a full backup of the databases at least weekly.

The transaction log is a file that stores the changes made to a database before Domino writes those changes to the database. When you open a document, edit a field, and then save the document, for example, the change is written to the transaction log. Later, when the server has extra processing time, it writes the changes to the actual database. In addition, transaction logging provides quicker recovery with fewer corruptions, because the data can be written from the log to the database in case of a crash.

Use the Server document to configure transaction logging. This process is described in Chapter 7, "Advanced Server Configuration." If a particular database should not be logged, use the advanced database property *Disable Transaction Logging*. After changing this property, you should flush the database cache (use the *dbcache flush* command) to ensure that all users and processes close the database. Then, reopen the database.

The best benefit of using transaction logging is how much easier it makes recovering from a system/power failure. When a system crashes or the power fails, transaction-logged databases that were open during the crash are automatically recovered and updated using the transaction log. Databases that are not transaction logged or are of an earlier format (R4, R3) must have the Fixup task run against them to perform this consistency check.

Updating Databases

Updating databases includes updating the views and full-text indexes, as well as updating the design of a database as changes are made to the template.

Updating Views and Full-Text Indexes

The view index is the internal system that Notes uses to determine which documents should appear in a particular view or folder. A full-text index is an index or list of all of the text in a database. As documents change in the database—or as documents are added and removed—these indexes need to be updated. There are two main server tasks that maintain these indexes: Update and Updall. In addition, you can update these indexes manually by using keyboard shortcuts and by using the Database properties InfoBox.

The Update task, which is listed in the `ServerTasks=` line of the NOTES.INI file, runs automatically on Domino servers to update indexes on views and folders in databases that have changed. The Update task constantly looks in its queue for changes to views or folders. Approximately 15 minutes after a change is recorded, Update works on all of the view indexes in the changed database. Update then updates full-text indexes that are configured for hourly or immediate updates. If Update finds a corrupted view or full-text index, it deletes and tries to recreate the index to fix the problem.

The Updall task runs at 2 A.M. (by default) to update the view and full-text indexes for all databases on a server. You can also run Updall manually when needed. When Updall runs, it updates both view and full-text indexes as well as purging deletion stubs and unused view indexes. When Updall runs automatically, it works on all view and full-text indexes; however, you can run this task with options to limit what it updates. The following list describes the ways to run the Updall task:

- Type the following command at the console. Both the databasepath and options arguments are optional. Options include -R to rebuild full-text indexes and all used views, -V to update all built views, and -T to specify a particular view to rebuild. For other options, refer to the Domino help database or the *Managing Domino Databases* book.

```
Load Updall databasepath options
```

- Use the Start Task tool in the Domino Administrator, as shown in Figure 5-50. In the task list, select Update All. To use options, enable the *Select advanced options* check box. Then click *Start Task*. Use the Basics tab in the Advanced Options dialog box to determine whether to index all databases, a particular database, or a particular view in the specified database. To select a specific database or view, you must

Figure 5-50
Starting Updall with
the Start Task tool

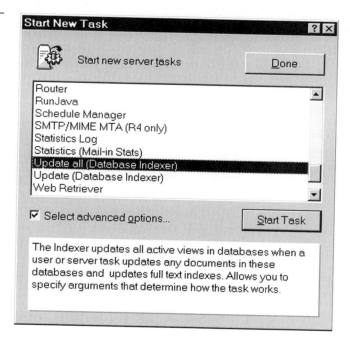

type the name of the database or view. Use the Update tab to decide whether to update all built view and/or full-text indexes. The Rebuild tab contains choices to rebuild full-text indexes only or full-text indexes and views.

- Run Updall from a Program document to run Updall at a scheduled time. While it does run at 2 A.M. by default from the NOTES.INI file, using a Program document enables you to include options and specific databases.

- You can use keyboard shortcuts to rebuild views. The F9 key updates the current view, SHIFT+F9 rebuilds the current view, and CTRL+SHIFT+F9 rebuilds or updates all views in a database. You can use these keyboard shortcuts inside the database or when the database is selected on the workspace.

- You can use the Full Text tab on the Database properties InfoBox to update the full-text index of a database.

Updating the Database Design

You should make design changes for databases in another database (usually a template) and use the Design task to make those changes in the production database. You

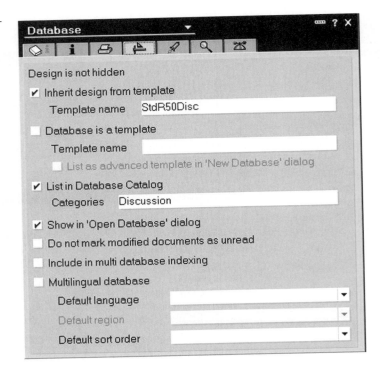

Figure 5-51
Does the database inherit from a template?

might also use a replica of the database and use replication to bring changes into the production database.

Use the Design tab of the Database properties InfoBox, as shown in Figure 5-51, to determine whether a database inherits its design from a template. If the database does inherit its design from a template, changes made to the template will be refreshed in the database when the Design task runs by default at 1 A.M. You might also run the Design task at the server console by typing the following command:

```
Load Design
```

Note that you cannot run Design against only a specific database; rather, it runs against all databases on the server when you run the task. You can also run Design from the Domino Administrator by using the Start Task tool. Select Designer from the task list and click Start Task.

You should note that the template that contains the design changes must be on the same server as the production database. Usually, a replica of the template lives on a development-only server. Designers make and test the design changes on this server, and then replicate the template to the production server. The design changes are applied to the production database when the Design task runs.

Fixing Databases

While R5 and transaction logging both limit database corruption, corruption still occurs occasionally. When a database or an element of a database becomes corrupted, you need to fix the element to enable users to continue to access the database. One way to know that an element of a database is corrupted is from the Notes Log. In the Miscellaneous Events view, you might see messages about corrupted documents or views. You can fix a database by using many of the tools discussed in this chapter—including Updall to fix corrupted views or full-text indexes and Compact to fix general corruption problems. You might also create a new replica of a database. You can also use the Fixup task to fix a corrupted database. Fixup runs automatically when a server starts to fix any problems that R4-format or non-transaction-logged databases might have had during shutdown. By default, Fixup does not run on transaction-logged databases, although each of the methods of running Fixup provides a way to do so. Use one of the following methods to run Fixup against a corrupted database:

- Use the Fixup tool from the Files tab in the Domino Administrator to run Fixup against one or multiple databases. When you select the databases, select Fixup to

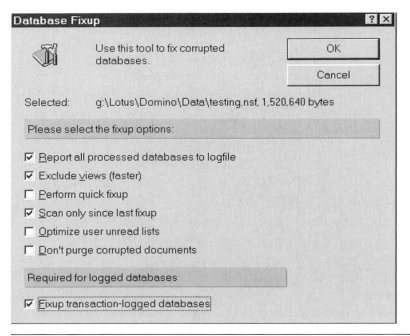

Figure 5-52 The Database Fixup dialog box

display the Database Fixup dialog box, as shown in Figure 5-52. Use the dialog box to select options for running Fixup, including excluding views, scanning only since the last Fixup, and to fix logged databases. Note that you cannot use the Domino Administrator until Fixup has completed, so this option is best for only one or two databases.

- Start Fixup from the Server tab in the Domino Administrator by using the Start Task tool. To start Fixup with options, enable the *Select advanced options* check box. This method enables you to run Fixup against any database or all databases, using any advanced options.

- You can run Fixup from the command line at a console (or from the remote console). In this case, you must know the command-line options, such as -Q to run a quick Fixup and -J to run Fixup against transaction-logged databases.

- To run Fixup on a scheduled basis, use a Program document.

Summary

In this chapter, you used various tools to monitor and maintain Domino applications and replication. The tools used to monitor the applications and replication included the Domino Administrator Files tab, the Notes Log, statistics and statistic monitors, and database analysis. Maintaining the databases started with moving databases, copying databases, creating new replicas of databases, and deleting databases. You also worked with the properties of the database to improve size and performance. Monitoring the size with quotas and thresholds helped you determine when to archive and compact the database. After a replica was placed on a new server, you monitored and verified replication for that database by using connection documents and manual replication. To verify the replication topology, you used the topology map produced by the MAPS task. We described the use of tasks such as Design, Compact, Fixup, Update, and Updall—which are all used for troubleshooting and maintaining the database. We also described security for databases, including how security affected replication.

Review Questions

1. Which of the following suggestions might you give to your developers to minimize replication conflicts?
   A. Enable the database property Merge Replication Conflicts.
   B. Enable the form property Merge Replication Conflicts.
   C. Disable the database property Document Bitmap Optimization.
   D. Enable the database property Don't Maintain Unread Marks.

2. Which command would you use to initiate a replication between Home and Gate if you are sitting at Gate and need the documents from Home to be replicated to Gate?
   A. Rep Gate
   B. Pull Gate
   C. Pull Home
   D. Rep Pull Home

3. During normal compaction, what can users and servers do to a database?
   A. Nothing
   B. Read only
   C. Write only
   D. Read and write

4. Which of the following events occur when a user creates a document that forces a database to exceed the warning threshold?

   A. The user receives an error dialog box saying that the database has reached the warning threshold.

   B. The user receives an error dialog box saying that he or she cannot add any more documents to the database.

   C. The warning message is written to the Notes Log.

   D. The user will not be able to create the document.

5. Brian enabled the *Don't support specialized response hierarchy* property on his discussion database to improve database performance. There is one view in the database that does not display as he expected, however. Which of the following possible causes can he rule out?

   A. He used @IsResponseDoc in a formula in the view.

   B. He used @AllChildren in a formula in the view.

   C. He used @AllDescendants in a formula in the view.

   D. He compacted the database after setting the property.

6. If the setting for the maximum number of databases in the database cache is 50, the actual maximum number of databases in the database cache is

   A. 50

   B. 37.5

   C. 150

   D. 75

7. If you use copy-style compaction with databases that use transaction logging, which of the following statements are true?

   A. Copy-style compacting cannot be done on databases that use transaction logging.

   B. Copy-style compacting does not create a new DBIID.

   C. Copy-style compacting does create a new DBIID.

   D. You should create a full backup after running a copy-style compaction on a transaction-logged database.

8. You are replicating the often-edited HR.NSF database between servers A, B, C, and D. You do not replicate often between A and D, although A replicates with B and C every day. Users on server D start complaining that they are deleting documents, but that those documents are reappearing. What might you suspect is the cause?
   A. Replication is occurring before the purge interval.
   B. The purge interval is occurring before replication.
   C. The deletion stubs are not being archived correctly.
   D. There is no purge interval set.

9. You are using AdminP to move a database from ServerA to ServerB. Which of the following statements are true?
   A. You need Create New Databases permission in the server document of the source server.
   B. You need Create New Replicas permission in the server document of the destination server.
   C. You need Manager access to the database.
   D. The Destination server needs Manager access to the database.

10. What is the name of the task that you need to enable on the server to see a graphical representation of the replication topology?
   A. COLLECT MAPS
   B. REPL MAPS
   C. MAPS
   D. REPL TOPOLOGY

Review Answers

1. **B is correct.** If you enable the Merge Replication property on the forms in your database, you will minimize the replication and save conflicts in the database.

2. **C is correct.** To force a replication with Home from Gate, where you want the documents from the Home server to be pulled to Gate, use the PULL command.

3. **D is correct.** With online, in-place compaction, users and servers can read from and write to databases while the databases are being compacted.

4. **C is correct.** A warning message is written to the Notes Log, and the user does not see an error message.

5. **A is correct.** The @IsResponseDoc function should still work as expected in this database.

6. **D is correct.** 75 is 1.5 times the maximum.

7. **C and D are both correct.** Because copy-style compacting does create a new DBIID for a database, it can no longer be recovered via the transaction log. Therefore, a new, full backup should be created.

8. **B is correct.** The database is not replicating before the purge interval, so the deletion stubs are being removed—and Domino replicates the documents back into the database.

9. **B and C are correct.** You need Manager access to be able to delete the database from the source server (part of moving it), and you need access to create new replicas on the destination server.

10. **B is correct.** Enable the MAPS task, which is also known as the MAPS Extractor.

PART II

Implementing a Domino R5 Infrastructure

The second exam in the System Administration track is the Implementing a Domino R5 Infrastructure exam (190-521). The audience for this exam is administrators with a basic knowledge of the Domino environment. It focuses on the implementation, creation, registration, configuration, and installation of the Domino server, systems, and users. The exam covers many of the same topics covered in the first part, *Maintaining Domino R5 Servers and Users*, but from the perspective of configuring the elements for the first time rather than maintaining them. You may want to read this part of the book first if you are less familiar with Domino or do not already have a production or lab environment configured.

The exam has 46 questions (6 of which are unscored) and requires a minimum score of 74 percent. The competencies for this exam are in six basic areas:

- Creating/Registering Systems Resources
- Installing
- Setting up Infrastructure, Servers, Workstations
- Setting up/Configuring Database Resources
- Setting up/Configuring Distribution and Monitoring
- Setting up/Configuring Domino Infrastructure Security

These general areas of competency are broken down further into specific tasks that you should be able to perform. To see a complete list, refer to the Lotus Domino R5 CLS Certification Exam Guide, available for download from **www.lotus.com/ education**. Each chapter in this section lists the specific competency areas that it covers. The section covers not only each of the competencies listed for the Implementing exam, but also allows you to create a functioning Domino environment.

Installing and Configuring Servers and Clients

You should be able to answer questions based on the following objectives after reading this chapter:

- Creating/registering systems resources
  - Creating/registering certificates (hierarchical)
  - Creating/registering groups
  - Creating/registering servers
  - Creating/registering users
- Installing
  - Installing clients of different license types
  - Installing servers of different license types
- Setting up infrastructure, servers, and workstations
  - Setting up infrastructure domains
  - Setting up infrastructure Domino Named Networks
  - Setting up infrastructure protocols
  - Setting up servers for different functions (mail, applications, mobile user connectivity: passthru, hub)
  - Setting up servers of different types (mail, applications, enterprise)
  - Setting up server protocols/ports
  - Setting up servers
  - Setting up workstations for different clients (Notes, Internet)
  - Setting up workstations for different locations (mobile, constantly connected)
- Setting up/configuring database resources
  - Setting up/configuring license tracking (Certlog)

In this chapter, we cover the basics of installing both servers and workstations (clients). Part of the installation process includes knowing what type of server or client you need to install to meet your needs. After you install a server or a client, you need to complete a setup, or configuration, process. You need to know how to set up domains, ports, protocols, and other elements as part of the configuration process. In addition, part of setting up the base of your infrastructure is registering certifiers, servers, and users. We will also add those servers and users to groups.

Before You Begin . . . Some Planning

Lotus Notes and Domino can be divided into two distinct types of software: the server and the workstation. The server software, as its name implies, is the serving component. The server software is character-based and runs on Windows NT, Linux (as of 5.0.2), UNIX, OS/2, and others. The server has a prompt and takes command-line input, similar to other text-based operating systems like DOS. The workstation is a graphical program and is the primary user interface to Notes. Even though the server can take commands directly from console prompts, 99 percent of all commands to the server can be and are handled through the Domino Administrator, one of the components of the workstation software. The other components of the workstation software are the Domino Designer, for application development work, and the Notes client, for mail, database use, and other functions. Installing Notes requires installing the server software on one or more systems, depending on the needs of the installation, followed by the installation of the workstation software on the client computers. You may install one or more of the workstation components. Note that the proper terms are as follows: the server is Domino; the client is the Notes client; the other tools are the Domino Administrator and the Domino Designer.

Planning the Notes Installation

Before installing a Domino server, you need to address three important organizational issues. First, you must design the Organization. An *Organization* is a hierarchical naming scheme applied to every server and user in a Notes environment. The Organization grants a unique identifying name to every server and user. Second, you must structure the domain. The *domain* defines pathways for email, a central repository for addresses and configurations, and other administrative features. The Domino Directory (formerly the Public Name and Address book) defines the domain for an environment. (The Domino Directory is discussed more fully in Chapter 8.) The third organizational issue to address is whether to create one or several Domino Named Networks (DNN). Organizations are never simple—there can be separate offices and different types of networks that prevent the smooth transport of email. These problems are handled by a sub-division of the Notes domain—the DNN. A domain can have many DNNs, each one handling a subgroup of the domain on a network that uses the same protocol and is constantly connected. If a user sends an email within the DNN, it is automatically and immediately sent to its recipient. If the email is going to a user outside the DNN, Domino checks for a Connection document within the Domino Directory to determine how it is to be sent. Mail is described in detail in Chapter 11. A plan of a sample Domino environment, including information about the Organization, domain, and DNNs is shown in Figure 6-1.

An important distinction between Organizations, domains, and DNNs occurs at installation time. Once a naming convention has been started, it cannot be changed easily without requiring the massive task of recreating all the names on the network. The same is also true for domains, as you must create a new first server in your organization to create a new domain. DNNs, however, can be created at any time.

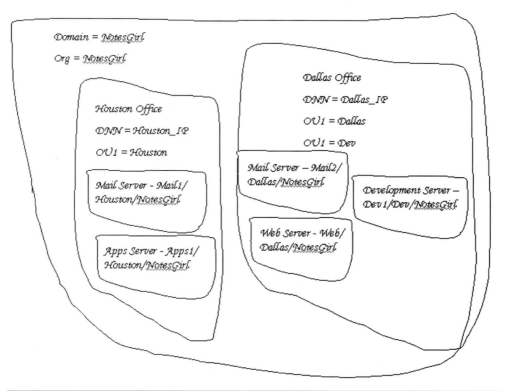

FIGURE 6-1   Sample Domino Environment Plan

In the next three sections, we will gain an understanding of Organizations, domains, and Domino Named Networks. We will then begin the installation of the Domino server with a better appreciation of the need for these items.

Planning an Organization

Each Organization needs a well-defined naming structure that applies unique names to each server and user in the environment. Naming is an integral part of verifying the rights of users and processes. When a user requests to look at a piece of email, a database, or a document, how does the system know that person has the right to perform the function they requested? Are they allowed to see a particular piece of information? Can they read a certain email? For that matter, where exactly are they located? The Organization addresses all of these issues. The discussion below covers four basic topics: authentication, flat versus hierarchical naming schemes, the levels in the hierarchical naming scheme, and some terminology specific to hierarchical naming in Notes.

Authentication is the process of verifying the identity of a user or a server as they request to access a server. Authentication is manifested via a series of encoded files with the .ID extension. The core identifier, the ID file from which all other ID files are created, is known as the CERT.ID. A new first Domino server installation usually creates the new CERT.ID file. Each level of an Organization adds its own unique stamp to a user or server ID, to describe where in the Organization they exist—not necessarily physically, but hierarchically. The essential part of every ID file for every server and user in the same Organization, however, will be the same CERT.ID. This allows authentication. Authentication is discussed more in Chapter 10.

Naming in Domino can be either flat or hierarchical. Flat names have a person or server known only by the given name, for example, Libby Schwarz or ServerA. No two names can be the same with flat names. Unfortunately, similarities in given names or functions can sometimes make it difficult to make unique names. There cannot be two persons with the name of "JohnS," for example, or two servers with the name of "ServerA." Furthermore, flat names are not very descriptive of the Organization. A server with the name of *Main* gives no information about the location or function of the machine. While Domino continues to support flat naming for backward compatibility, *hierarchical naming* has been the default naming convention since Notes v3 and is required for many of the tools and features that make R5 so useful.

Hierarchical naming adds other levels to the given name (or common name) to make names unique for security purposes. The extra levels are separated by a slash (/) to show the hierarchy. For example, a hierarchical name might look like these: Libby Schwarz/Authors/NotesGirl or ServerA/NotesGirl. These extra levels help define the function or location of the name and allow redundancy in parts of the names while keeping the complete name unique. It is perfectly acceptable to have Libby Schwarz/ Authors/NotesGirl and Libby Schwarz/Instructors/NotesGirl as part of the same organization.

> **NOTE**   Lotus recommends hierarchical naming for all Domino installations. R5 has some tools, such as the Administration process (AdminP), to assist in automating the process of converting from flat names to hierarchical names. Most organizations, for a variety of reasons, are in the process of converting from flat names to hierarchical names.

One significant difference between flat and hierarchical names is the number of certificates contained in an ID file. In flat naming, each ID file has multiple certificates included in it. These certificates give the user access to servers. In hierarchical naming, each ID file has only one hierarchical certificate, although it may also have multiple flat certificates for communicating with servers in companies that use flat naming.

> **NOTE**   A certificate is a stamp or code appended to an ID file in Notes by the process of registering (or certifying) the ID. The certificate contains an electronic signature that relates the ID to the certifier.

Hierarchical names use a tree structure to mimic the structure of your organization. Hierarchical naming is based on X.500 naming standards and is similar to the naming conventions used by Novell's NDS naming in NetWare Version 4 and 5, LDAP directory naming, and the naming structure used by Microsoft's Active Directory. An example of a hierarchical name for a user includes the common name, one to four optional Organizational Units, an Organization, and a Country Code. The Organization, or O, will usually be your company's name. (Note that Lotus uses the term *organization* to describe both the whole naming scheme and the highest level in a hierarchical name.) Organizational Units, or OUs, can be based on departments, geography, or other working units within your organization. The common name, or CN, will either be a user or server name. The Country Code is based on the International Standards Organization's (ISO) two-letter country codes. The paragraphs below discuss each of the levels of the hierarchical name. Figure 6-2 shows a graphical example of a hierarchical tree.

Country Code   The Country Code is an optional level of the hierarchical name. It contains a two-letter code specified by the International Standards Organization (ISO). The Country Code should only be used for organizations that have locations outside

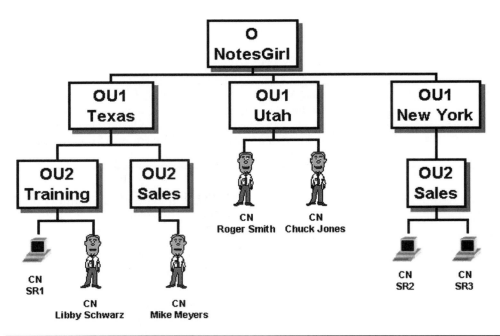

Figure 6-2 Hierarchical organizational tree

their country of origin. The Country Code, like all levels of the hierarchical name, will appear when a user's name is resolved, such as when sending email. If your organization needs to use multiple country codes, you will need to register different certifiers (Organizations) for each country code, such as NotesGirl/IT and NotesGirl/US. It is often easier to create an Organizational Unit for the country.

Organization   The Organization (O) is commonly the top level of a company's hierarchical naming scheme, as the Country code is not used often. Most often, companies will use their company name, or an abbreviation of it, for the Organization name, as it will be part of every name that is registered. The Organization is created during the setup of the first server, when the CERT.ID file is created. This CERT.ID file, which will be stored by default on the first server, will be used to register either the Organizational Units or users and servers. This file should be secured and backed up, as it is one of the most important files in your Domino environment. With it, another administrator could create users and servers in your Organization, if he or she has the necessary rights to the Domino Directory. During the registration process, the Organization is appended to each of the user and server's names, making it a required part of the hierarchical name.

There can be multiple Organizations in a single domain, if necessary, although this requires additional planning. Some reasons why this might be necessary would include a name change within a company or the need to connect to an external set of Domino servers. In a renaming situation, where a new Organization certifier was created, the administrator would need to recertify all the servers, users, and Organizational Units with the new Organization certifier.

Organizational Units   Organizational Units are optional levels in a hierarchical name that create further levels of uniqueness within your organization. OUs will appear beneath (or to the left of) the O name (or another OU) in the naming hierarchy.

Usually, OUs represent a division of your Organization based on geography, department, or workgroup. There can be up to four vertical levels of OU, with any number of OUs at any given level. For example, if your first level of OU within your Organization is based on geography, there can be any number of cities at that level.

Organizational Units can either help to ease the load on an administrator, or serve to increase it immensely. If the OUs are created without research into the patterns of movement in the company, every time a user transfers between departments, they might have to be re-certified. However, if OUs are used in a limited fashion, the users can make some movement without requiring re-certification. In addition, while four is the maximum vertical level, most Organizations will limit their use of OUs to one or two, to ensure that they do not become an administrative burden. On the other side of the coin, OUs can assist an administrator in decentralizing what he or she has to do. In many Organizations, and certainly in those that have only one certifier (the O), there would be only one or two administrators with access to this CERT.ID, and therefore only one or two administrators available to register new users or servers. However, if there are multiple certifiers (OUs) at lower levels, another administrator could take some of this burden. In our example company, NotesGirl, most of the administration is done in the central office in Houston. However, with geographically-based OUs, an administrator in Dallas could be given the rights to create users certified by the Dallas OU certifier, relieving some of the load on the central administrators.

In the Notes hierarchical naming, there is no functional difference between the name of a server and the name of a user. There is no relationship required for servers and users to be registered under the same OU. All the servers in the NotesGirl Organization might be certified by an OU called Servers, for example, that is directly under the O. This would result in a server called ServerA/Servers/NotesGirl. This would help to avoid the confusion of having a server called ServerA/Authors/Houston/NotesGirl that would need to be used by everyone in the Houston and Dallas offices. Another option would be to have the server certified directly under the O or under the Houston OU. The biggest restriction is to be consistent and clear for the benefit of your users and administrators.

Common Name   The Common Name (CN) is the actual name of the user or server. In the case of the user, you have fields for first name, middle initial, and last name. Only the last name field is required. In the case of a server, this is often the DNS host name or NetBIOS name of the server, although this is simply for ease of administration. The common name can use up to 80 characters. The Common Name would be the same name you would use as the complete name in a flat naming environment.

 NOTE   DNS stands for Domain Name Service. The DNS host name defines a server or workstation to the TCP/IP protocol and to TCP/IP applications. DNS host names require a DNS server or HOSTS file, which resolve the name into an IP address. NetBIOS names define servers and workstations to Microsoft applications.

Table 6-1, below, gives a quick review of the vital information to remember about the various levels of the hierarchical name.

Notes offers one further hierarchical level in a case where two people end up with the same hierarchical name, called the User Unique Organizational Unit (UUOU). The

Table 6-1   Hierarchical Name Info

Element	Description
• Country Code (C)	• Optional
	• Zero or two letters
	• Based on ISO standard two-letter codes available from the Notes Administrator's Guide. Before using the country code, clear your company's O name with your country's clearinghouse for x.500 names.
• Organization (O)	• Required for hierarchical naming
	• Three to 64 letters or numbers
• Organizational Unit (OU)	• Optional
	• Up to four vertical levels of OU allowed
	• Three to 32 letters or numbers per OU
• Common Name (CN)	• Required
	• Usually the person's first and last names, and middle initial for a user or a server name for a server
	• 80 maximum letters or numbers

UUOU adds a unique, descriptive comment to a name to differentiate it from another name. There are two engineers named Suzy Smith, for example, both in the Austin office of NotesGirl. Their names would be identical:

Suzy Smith/Austin/NotesGirl

An UUOU would allow their administrator to define them further in some way, such as "Redhead Suzy" and "Brunette Suzy." Now their names would be unique in the Organization:

Suzy Smith/Redhead/Austin/NotesGirl

Suzy Smith/Brunette/Austin/NotesGirl

Note that an UUOU does count as one of the four levels of OU allowed, but it gives the administrator the ability to create some level of distinction between users with the same names, in the same OUs.

Two more terms that you must know about hierarchical names are fully distinguished abbreviated hierarchical names versus fully distinguished canonicalized hierarchical names. Both contain exactly the same information but are written differently. A fully distinguished abbreviated name displays a name with the organizational levels separated by slashes. The levels are assumed by their place in the name. ServerA/Houston/NotesGirl, for example, describes the server machine named ServerA, which is in the Houston Organizational Unit in the NotesGirl Organization. When there are multiple levels of OUs, you start counting closest to the Organization, so the format looks like this: CN/OU4/OU3/OU2/OU1/O. A canonicalized name spells all this out in the description. That same server done canonically, for example, would look as follows:

CN=ServerA/OU=Houston/O=NotesGirl

Domino uses canonicalized names internally; humans generally use abbreviated names; the exam requires you to know both.

Domains

A *domain* defines pathways for email, the location of a central repository for addresses and configurations, and many other administrative functions. The Domino Directory, a database that holds much critical data, such as user and server names and configurations, defines domains.

Domains function in Notes as containers for many servers, databases, and users, all interconnected. Classically, there should only be one domain in an Organization for simplicity. Similarly, there is usually only one Organization in a domain, again, for simplicity. A domain is not limited by geography or connections.

TIP A Notes Domain is a completely separate issue from both Internet and Windows NT domains—although there are some tie-ins that make administration a little easier.

The Domino Directory holds all of the critical information about the users and servers in your Domino Domain. The Domino Directory contains configuration information about your Domino servers and the mail routing information needed to get mail from one user to another. The Domino Directory is created when the first Domino server is installed in an Organization. It is important to note that although the Domino Directory is one database, there should be replicas of the Domino Directory on all of the Domino servers within the domain. The Domino Directory contains many critical pieces of information including:

- **Connection documents** Contain information used when connecting to other servers.
- **Server documents** Define the configuration for all servers in the domain.
- **Certifier documents** Track all certifiers in the domain.
- **User (Person) documents** Contain information on all users in the domain.
- **Group documents** Create and define groups that can be used in mailing and security.

There is always one Domino Directory per domain and one domain per Domino Directory. The primary purpose of a domain is to organize and define mail routing paths. We will describe the Domino Directory more in Chapter 8.

NOTE It is important to understand the differences between a domain and an Organization in Notes. An Organization's primary purpose is naming and security. The primary purpose of a domain is mail routing.

Domino Named Network (DNN)

A Notes Domain is often spread among many far-flung geographical locations employing many different types of network topologies. Consider a company with two departments in differentoffices on the same floor of the same building. If one user sends mail to another user, they are in the same domain and probably on the same Ethernet network, so the mail is sent to the other user. There's a lot of traffic going on between those departments. Now take those two departments and separate them into different cities. The two networks might now be connected by a modem. How can the modem connection be controlled so that mail is only sent at certain intervals? What if the two departments are on the same network but are running different network protocols? These problems require a special subdivision of the domain into groups that share constant connections and common protocols. These subgroups of the domain are called Domino Named Networks (DNN) and are an important feature for handling network connections that are constantly connected and/or use different protocols. To see how a DNN provides this service, let's mentally sub-divide the domain into two separate DNNs called DeptA and DeptB. When an email is sent to a server, the mail server compares the DNN of the sender to the DNN of the recipient (Remember, all servers have a replica of the Domino Directory). If the DNNs match, the message is sent to the recipient immediately. If they are different, the server checks for a Connection document to tell it how to send the email to the other DNN. This gives the administrators control over the use of non-constant connections. Consider the two DNNs again. This time, they are all on the same "hard-wired" network, but the two servers use different protocols. There is another server that can handle both protocols. By checking the DNNs, and cross-referencing the proper Connection documents, the sending server knows to "route" the mail through the server that can handle both protocols.

DNNs are determined by two characteristics: the same protocol and constant connectivity. Servers that are in constant contact (i.e., same Local Area Network [LAN] or bridged/routed Wide Area Network [WAN]) and share the same protocol can be in the same DNN. For example, the two servers described in Figure 6-3 are both on the LAN, and both use the same protocol. They would probably be in the same DNN, because the servers fulfill both requirements. You can choose, however, to place the servers in different DNNs if this is more appropriate for your mail routing strategy.

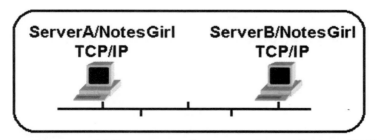

Same Protocol, Constant Connection - Same DNN

Figure 6-3 Servers A and B in the same DNN

If the two servers were connected via modem, however, regardless of whether they both used TCP/IP, they would be in different DNNs, as they are not constantly connected. Similarly, two servers connected via a LAN, using different protocols (TCP/IP and IPX/SPX) would be in different DNNs, as they do not meet the same protocol requirement. Servers that have multiple protocols will be in multiple DNNs. (See Figure 6-4.)

ServerA/NotesGirl, for example, uses the TCP/IP protocol. ServerB/NotesGirl uses the IPX/SPX protocol. They are connected to the same LAN. Because they use different protocols, they will not be in the same DNN. ServerC/NotesGirl uses TCP/IP but is connected only when dialed in using a modem. It will be in a third DNN. When ServerD/NotesGirl is installed, using the TCP/IP protocol, attached to the same LAN as ServerA/NotesGirl, it will probably share the same DNN as ServerA/NotesGirl.

DNNs are usually named for both their location and protocol to avoid confusion. ServerA/NotesGirl and ServerD/NotesGirl are both on a LAN in Houston using TCP/IP. An appropriate name for this DNN might be HOUSTON_IP or something similar.

To change a server's DNN, use the Ports . . . Notes Network Ports tab in the Server document. Each port should be configured with a protocol and a Notes Network. Note that if you do not configure a specific DNN, you may see Network 1, Default Network, or TCP/IP Network (for TCP/IP configurations). You should change this configuration, as you may not want all servers to think they are in the same DNN.

Server Role

Another planning item to consider before beginning the installation process is the role you intend each server to play. There are multiple installation types, or licenses, for servers, and these different installations lend themselves to different roles for the servers to play. The server installation types are mail, application, and enterprise. A mail server installation provides Domino mail, Internet mail, calendaring and scheduling,

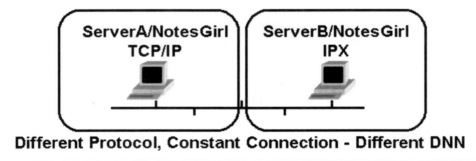

Different Protocol, Constant Connection - Different DNN

Figure 6-4 A different protocol calls for a different DNN

and access to Domino discussion databases. An Application server provides all the capabilities of the Domino mail server and serves access to custom databases for both Notes and browser (Web) clients, and the capability to use transaction logging on the databases on the server. An Enterprise server provides all the capabilities of an application server and adds the capability to cluster servers, the option to use the Internet Cluster Manager (ICM) for enabling Web clients to gain the benefits of clustered servers, and the capability to create partitioned servers.

The roles servers can play in an organization include a mail server, an application server, a hub server, a directory server, a Web server, and a passthru server. You will probably use an Enterprise server for hub servers. You can use Application servers for applications, Web, directory, and passthru. You can use a Mail server for mail and passthru. If you want to use clustering, you must install an Enterprise server. Clustering enables you to use multiple servers together for fail over and load balancing. If you want to use partitioning, where multiple servers run on the same physical machine, you must use an Enterprise server. If you want to use transaction logging for your databases, to enhance backup and recovery, you must use either an Application server or an Enterprise server. You will need this information when you install the servers.

Use the knowledge of domains, organization, DNNs, and the types and roles of servers to create a deployment plan for your organization before you begin installing servers.

Installing Servers

To install a server, first obtain a CD or other installation point that contains the installation files and the setup program. The Domino server is supported on Windows NT/2000, several types of Unix (including Sun Solaris, HP-UX, and IBM AIX), AS/400, OS/2, and Linux (as of version 5.0.2). You should read the Domino Release Notes for the version you are installing to ensure that you have correctly configured and patched your operating system.

 NOTE If you would like to install a trial version of the Domino server for practice, you can obtain one at www.lotus.com or at www.notes.net. The version of the software that you download will be a 90-day trial version of the software. You may also choose to apply the Quarterly Maintenance Releases (QMRs) and Upgrades (QMUs), which provide enhancements and bug fixes. These are available from www.notes.net. Be aware that some QMRs and QMUs change the appearance or function of the Domino Server or client—read the release notes for each update before applying the patch.

NOTE The examples here cover installing on Windows NT/2000. Installing to other operating systems may look different or require different options. Please consult the Release Notes or Domino help files for further information.

After your operating system and network are configured, begin the installation process by connecting to the installation media (either the CD or a installation drive). If necessary, unzip the installation files. If you have a CD from Lotus, the CD may launch automatically. If so, choose Install.

If you run from an official CD, you first choose whether to install clients or servers. When you choose servers, you further choose the type of server (mail, application, or enterprise), as shown in Figure 6-5. Bear in mind that to use clustering or partitioning, you must use the Enterprise installation. For normal Domino application use, including transaction logging, use the Application server installation. For mail only, you can use the Mail server.

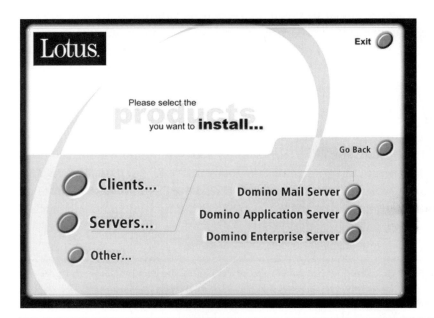

Figure 6-5 What type of server to install

After selecting a server type, decide whether to do a standard install or a custom install. You might choose to do a custom install to get the ability to run the Domino server as service under NT or to remove the Help files. After making this selection, the normal Installation Wizard starts, as described later.

If your CD does not launch automatically, or if you downloaded software from Lotus, you will then run the SETUP.EXE file.

The installation process uses the standard Installation wizard that most Windows programs use. You'll need to agree to the licensing and provide a name and organization. Note in Figure 6-6, where you provide the name and organization, you also choose whether to install a partitioned server.

Next, choose the installation location and location of the data directory, as shown in Figure 6-7. If you selected a partitioned server, you only choose the location of the program directory at this point. You will choose the names and locations of the data directories later in the install.

The next screen, shown in Figure 6-8, gives you the opportunity to choose between the Aplication, Mail, and Enterprise server installation. The differences among the installation options were described earlier in this chapter. Bear in mind that to use clustering or partitioning, you must use the Enterprise installation. For normal Domino application use, including transaction logging, use the Application server installation. For mail only, you can use the Mail server. In the bottom left corner, note the

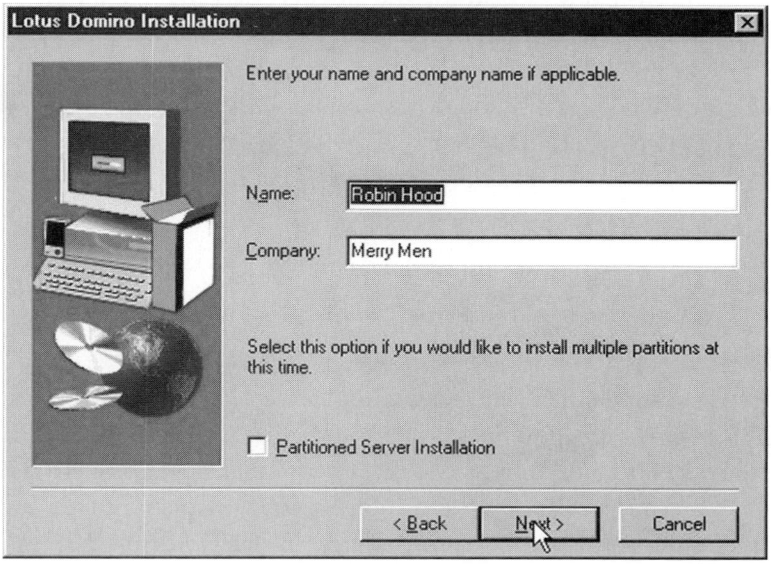

Figure 6-6 Partitioned server?

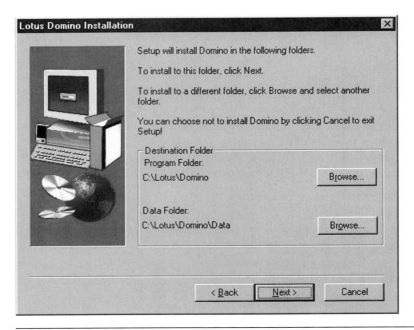

Figure 6-7   Installation location for non-partitioned server

Customize button. This button enables you to add the files necessary to run Domino as an NT service and to use the NT performance monitor to work with Domino-specific counters. In this case, the installation will be a Domino Application server installation.

After selecting the type of server and any additional options, choose where the installation should place the program icons and the program will begin copying files to your machine. When complete, you will be prompted to register your software and restart the machine.

Configuring the First Server

The installation process is only the first step. After you complete the installation, you need to configure the server. The setup program runs automatically when you start the server for the first time in an NT environment. In other environments, you need to run the setup program and then connect to the server using a browser. Instructions for these platforms can be found in the *Setting Up a Domino Server* book available from Lotus.

In the configuration process, you determine the name of the Domino domain, Organization, server, and administrator. ID files for the Organization, server, and adminis-

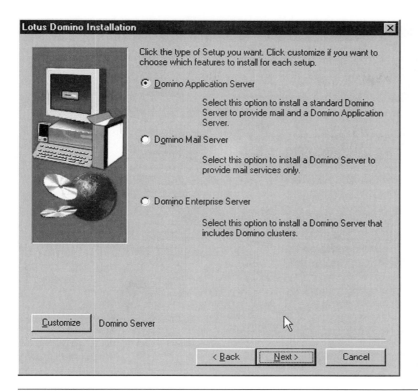

Figure 6-8   What type of server?

trator are created, as is the Domino Directory. The server ID and certifier ID are created and stored in the data directory of the server; Domino also creates Server and Certificate documents, and stores them in the Domino Directory. The administrator's user ID file is also created and stored in the Domino Directory, attached to the Person document created for that user.

In the first screen of the configuration, shown in Figure 6-9, decide whether the server is a first server in the domain (all the files above are created) or an additional server in the domain, where the server's ID file and Domino Directory would be available (having been registered and created by the other servers in the domain). This section will show the first server configuration. The additional server configuration is described later in this chapter.

Next, choose the Quick and Easy configuration or the Advanced configuration. If you choose Quick and Easy, Domino completes the configuration using default settings and information from your server. With Advanced configuration, you set the options. Figure 6-10 shows that for this exercise, we chose Advanced configuration. Note that just as

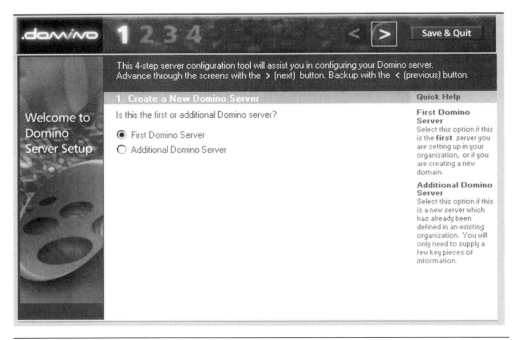

Figure 6-9 First or additional server

you use the right-facing arrow to move forward through the configuration screens, you can use the left-facing arrow to go back and change settings on a previous page.

Use the third screen of the configuration to determine what tasks the Domino server will run and what functions it will serve in your environment. The standard services that will be configured and started automatically include the Administration Process (AdminP), the Agent Manager, the Indexer, the Mail Router, and the Replicator. Table 6-2 describes the additional services that are available. These choices are shown in Figure 6-11.

The final page of the configuration program is used to determine the names of the domain, organization, server, and administrator, as well as to configure the ports and protocols in use on the server, as shown in Figures 6-12 and 6-13.

Use the Domain and Certifier name fields to give a name to your domain and organization. Choose whether Domino should create a new certifier ID or use one that you provide. Give the certifier a password. This is one of the most important files in your organization, so you should make it a secure password. Domino will create a CERT.ID (if you choose) and a Certificate document in the Domino Directory for the certifier. The Domain field will be appended to any mail you send outside your domain. The

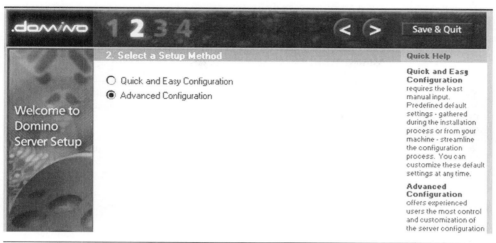

Figure 6-10 Easy or Advanced?

Table 6-2 Choose from the Following Services

Option	Notes
Additional Services	
Calendar Connector	Enabled by default, this runs the CalConn server task to enable Domino to look up free time for users on other servers using the Domino Directory.
Event Manager	Enabled by default, this starts the Event task on the server to enable Domino to monitor system events and activities.
Schedule Manager	Enabled by default, this creates the Schedule Manager server task, which builds the Free Time database on the server (BUSYTIME.NSF).
Statistics	Enabled by default, this starts the Statistics task to enable Domino to collect statistics about server tasks such as routing, replication, and disk space.
Web Browsers	
HTTP	This task enables Web clients (browsers such as Netscape Navigator and Internet Explorer) to access Domino applications. If you enable this task, you can also choose the primary activity (mail, applications, or both) or choose to customize the performance settings.
IIOP	This task enables the Domino server to install the Domino Object Request Broker (ORB) to allow objects in Domino to respond to IIOP requests.
Internet Mail Packages	
IMAP	Use the IMAP (Internet Message Access Protocol) task to enable IMAP clients to access their mail from a Domino server.

(continued)

Table 6-2 Choose from the Following Services (*continued*)

Option	Notes
POP3	Use the POP3 (Post Office Protocol version 3) task to enable POP3 clients to access their mail from a Domino server.
SMTP	Use the SMTP (Simple Mail Transfer Protocol) task to enable Notes, POP, and IMAP clients to send Internet mail from a Domino server.
Internet Directory Services	
LDAP	Use LDAP (Lightweight Directory Access Protocol) to allow LDAP clients to access directory information from a Domino server.
News Readers	
NNTP	Use NNTP (Network News Transfer Protocol) to allow NNTP clients to access news groups from a Domino server.
Enterprise Connection Services	
DECS	Use DECS to link Domino applications to data stored in a relational database or other data source.

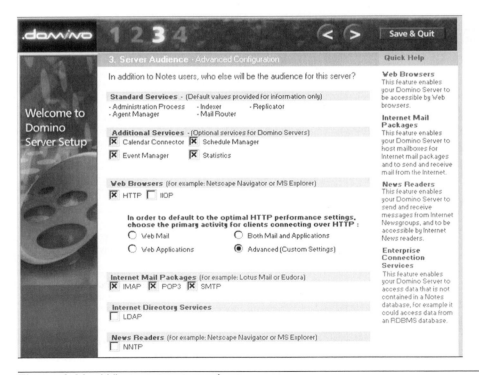

Figure 6-11 What services to run?

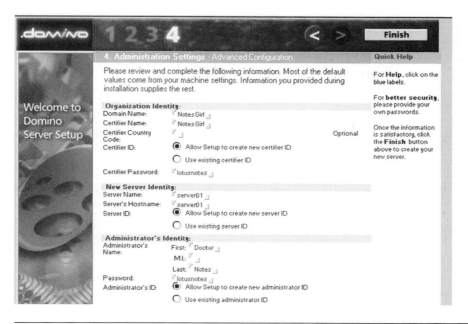

Figure 6-12   Identify the environment

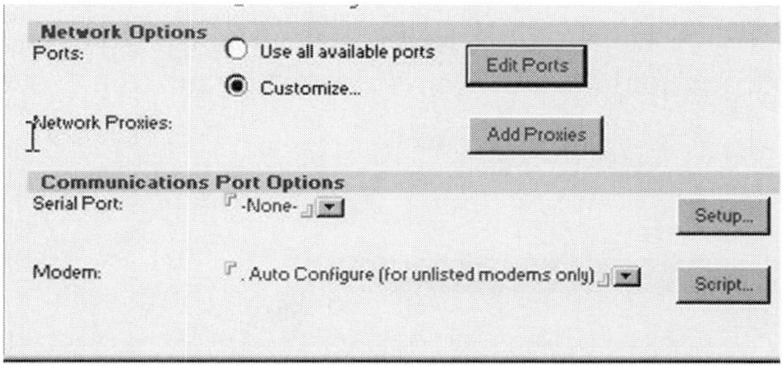

Figure 6-13   Ports and protocols

Domino Directory that Domino creates will be given the name of the domain you choose. You will also verify or complete the server name and the server's host name. Decide if the server should use an existing server ID or a new one. Domino will create a SERVER.ID and add a Server document to the Domino Directory. Add a name and password for the administrator. Domino will create a USER.ID and add a Person document to the Domino Directory.

Now we'll cover the opportunity to configure the ports and protocols for the server. If the server is connected to a network, you can use all the ports that are configured in the operating system or you can choose to customize the ports. You can also add ports later, using the Server document and Domino Administrator.

You may also have a modem that you want to connect to a serial port. You can choose the COM ports from the Serial Port drop-down list. If you add a COM port, you can complete the additional setup and configuration, such as logging the modem and script I/O, the port speed, and the dial timeout, as shown in Figure 6-14. You can select a modem type from the Modem drop-down list. You can also add a script. If you have chosen to allow users or servers to connect to the server remotely, you should either configure Notes Direct Dial-Up (where you will have a modem directly installed on the server and be using the X.PC protocol for dial-up access), or configure Network Dial-up (where the server connects using a network protocol instead of X.PC) or Passthru (where the server connects to an intermediary server).

After choosing all the configuration elements, click the Finish button. Domino creates a CERT.ID, Domino Directory, SERVER.ID, USER.ID, and the appropriate documents to go with each. When the configuration is complete, Domino displays the Congratulations page. Make a note of the passwords, server name, and domain name, if necessary. You can also take this opportunity to add an Administrators group to the ACL (Access Control List) of all databases and templates with Manager access, and to add the Anonymous entry to all ACLs with No Access, as shown in Figure 6-15. The name you set for the administrator will be added to the Administrators group that you create in this step. When this is complete, you can exit configuration and start the server.

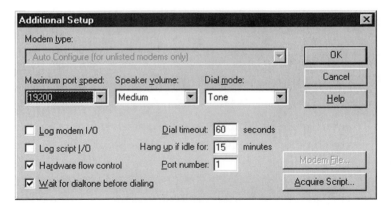

Figure 6-14   Configure the COM port and modem

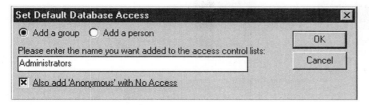

Figure 6-15   Setting the ACL

Installing Workstations

You will now need to install Notes clients to use mail and databases, Domino Designer to customize databases, and Domino Administrator to administer the users, servers, and systems. Similar to the server install, you need to obtain installation media (a CD, server installation point, or downloaded file) and begin with Setup.exe or by clicking Install if the CD launched automatically. The installation process is almost the same, in that you choose whether you are installing servers or clients (choose Clients this time). You then choose which clients you want to install: Notes, Domino Designer, and/or Domino Administrator. The Notes client is used for mail and accessing applications and databases for reading and editing of documents. The Domino Designer is used for creating applications or modifying existing applications (both for Notes and Web clients). The Domino Administrator is used to monitor and maintain the Domino environment. You will need the Domino Administrator if you need to register users and servers, for example. If you install the Designer or Administrator, the Notes client is also installed automatically. You can perform a standard install or a custom install. The custom install enables you to include Migration tools, single sign-on for NT, and other items, as shown in Figure 6-16.

You can choose to perform a shared installation, which allows Notes to use a file server for the program files and only requires a data directory locally. Select the directory for the program files and the data directory, and decide where to place the icon.

Configuring Workstations

After you restart your computer, you are ready to perform the configuration for the workstation. To configure your workstation, you must usually know the name of your server, your user name (or have your ID file), and your password. As you can see in Figure 6-17, though, you do have the option not to connect to a Domino server (you might use this if you are a remote user or only using the Notes client for POP3 mail).

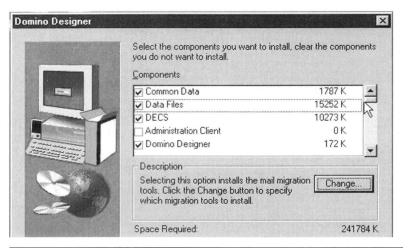

Figure 6-16   Custom Client Installation choices

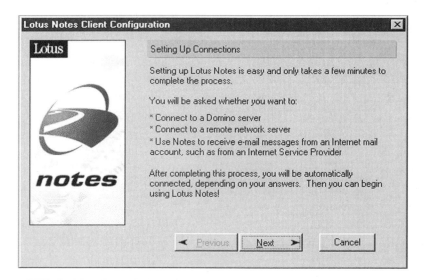

Figure 6-17   To connect or not to connect

If you choose not to connect to a Domino server, you need a copy of your ID file and your password.

If you choose to connect to a Domino server, you need to indicate how you plan to connect, such as over a local area network (LAN), over a phone connection, or both. If connecting over a LAN, you need to type the hierarchical name of your server. You must

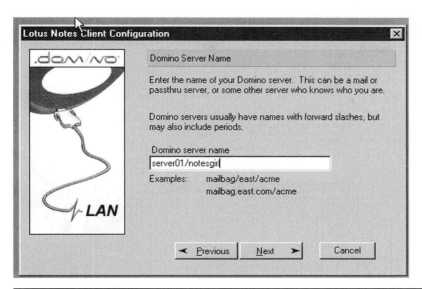

Figure 6-18 Server name

also have a protocol in common with the server (such as TCP/IP) configured in your operating system, and a working physical connection. You should test your physical and network connectivity before trying to complete the Domino configuration.

After you complete the server name, you have to tell Domino your name (see Figure 6-18). Either you can type your hierarchical name (and have Domino retrieve your ID file from the Domino Directory, if that is where it was stored), or you can point to your USER.ID file. When you are the administrator (created when the first server is created), your ID file is stored automatically in your Person document in the Domino Directory. You will use your name (and password) to complete your workstation configuration, as shown in Figure 6-19.

Notes prompts you to configure an Internet mail account, if you will be using the Notes client as a POP3 or IMAP client for another server, as shown in Figure 6-20. You can also create these accounts later. If you choose to create the account now, you are prompted for your Internet mail server, and the account and password.

You can also configure an NNTP account to use the Notes client to read newsgroups, and an LDAP account to use Notes to connect to an additional Directory server. If you choose to create any of these additional accounts, you are also prompted to configure how you want to connect to these accounts.

After the configuration wizard is complete, the setup process begins. The ID file is copied to the local data directory (this is when you're prompted for your password), a

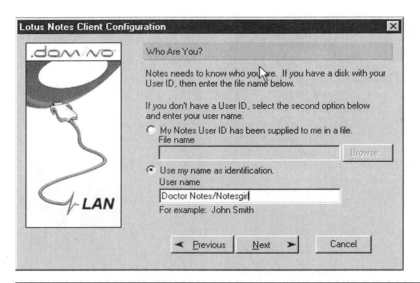

Figure 6-19   Use your name to complete the configuration

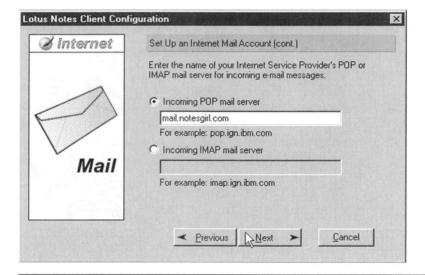

Figure 6-20   Internet Mail accounts

personal name and address book is created, and other files, such as bookmarks, are created. When this is complete, the client is started and you can begin working.

TIP You may be curious about installing the workstation software (Notes, Administrator, or Designer) on the same physical machine with the server. Let's start by saying that this is not recommended by Lotus. In fact, they have worked hard to make it difficult to do this, for both performance and security reasons. In most cases, I also recommend that you avoid putting the client software on the server machine. If you're in a lab environment, however, and don't have enough machines, or if you've lost network connectivity and need to troubleshoot, you may choose to install the Administrator, Notes, or the Designer on the same machine as your server. When you do so, however, there are some special steps you need to take into consideration, listed here:

---

1. Install the clients from the separate installers, as described earlier.

2. Do the install into separate directories (the defaults are usually fine).

3. Remove the NOTES.INI for the clients.

4. Add these lines to the server's NOTES.INI:
   ServerKeyFileName=server.id
   KeyFileName=youruser.id

5. Either create shortcuts on the desktop for the clients or modify the shortcuts in the Start . . . menu. Right-click on the shortcut and choose Properties. In the shortcut properties, select the Shortcut tab.

6. On the Shortcut tab, change the Target line to read c:\lotus\notes\notes.exe (or administrator.exe or designer.exe). Leave a single space following the file name and type =c:\lotus\domino\notes.ini.

Register Certifiers, Servers, and Users

After you have configured the administrator's workstation, you will need to register certifiers (such as Organizational Units), additional servers, and additional users to allow them to connect to the Domino server and environment.

Certification Log

Before you begin the process of registering these elements of your environment, you should create a Certification Log, which will track all the certificates you register, including when they expire. The Certification Log, which is not one of the files created automatically by Domino, is required to use the Administration Process (AdminP), which you use for renaming and re-certifying users, among other things. To create a Certification Log, choose File . . . Database . . . New from the menus. In the New Database dialog box, shown in Figure 6-21, choose to place the file on your newly configured server. In the *Title* field, give the database the name "Certification Log," and in the *File Name* field, use CERTLOG.NSF as the file name.

You will need to base the new database on the Certification Log template (CERTLOG.NTF). You may need to select your server (rather than the local workstation) as the template server to see the CERTLOG.NTF template. After you complete these fields, choose Ok to create the new database. Make sure that you give the Administrators group (or the administrators that will be doing registration) at least Author access with the Create Documents privilege in the Access Control List of the Certification Log, as shown in Figure 6-22. Other users (the -Default- entry) should have *No Access* or *Reader access* to the database.

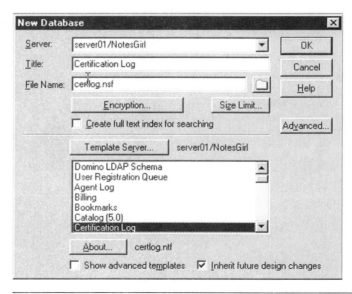

Figure 6-21   Create a new CERTLOG.NSF

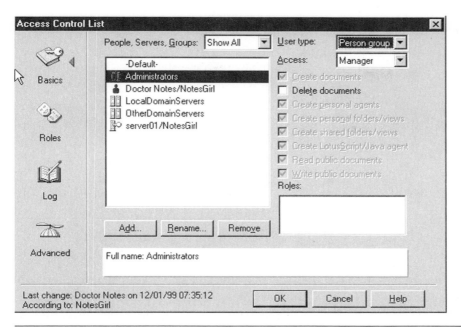

Figure 6-22 Certification Log ACL

Certifiers

As described earlier, a certifier is either an Organization (O) or an Organizational Unit (OU), which you use to register additional servers, users, and Organizational Units. When you look at a hierarchical name, it has the following format: CN/OU4/OU3/OU2/OU1/O. You can have up to four levels of OUs and one O.

NOTE When you are creating OUs, bear in mind that if you have created any UUOUs (User Unique Organizational Units), that these count toward the maximum of four levels deep.

All hierarchical names have an O element. Your domain will probably have only one O, although you may create additional Os in a domain if you are a widely spread-out company, want a completely separate development environment, or merge with other companies. When you need to share Domino resources with users and servers in different Os, you must have some kind of certifier in common, as this is basis for Domino communication and authentication. In this case, you will create a cross-certificate.

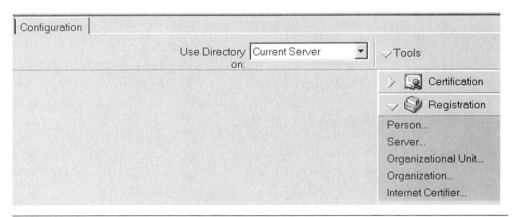

Figure 6-23   Where to go to register the OU

To create an Organizational Unit (OU), open the Domino Administrator to the Configuration tab and select the Registration . . . Organizational Unit tool, as shown in Figure 6-23. When you register an OU, you use either the O or another OU to certify the OU's ID file. In this case, you only have the O (the CERT.ID), so you will use that.

Select the certifier ID to use to register the OU, and type its password. Note that the two security requirements to create an OU are access to the CERT.ID (or other certifier) and its password, and access to create Certificate documents in the Domino Directory. Look for more information on password and ID backup and recovery later in this chapter.

Next, Administrator displays the Register Organizational Unit Certifier dialog box. If you have completed the Administration Preferences (File . . . Preferences . . . Administration Preferences), many of these fields may already be completed, although you can change them if you desire. Select a Registration Server—this should be the server that contains the Certification Log. If you want to certify the OU with a different OU, instead of the O, you can change the certifier in use by clicking the Certifier ID button. The Set ID File button enables you to determine where the new ID file will be stored. Next, choose a password. Note that it must match the password quality scale, which you can also change. Certifiers should have a password quality of ten or above for security. You can also select the security type (North American or International) and an administrator to send certification requests to. The dialog box is shown in Figure 6-24. You can create additional Organizational Units using the same procedure, certifying them either with the CERT.ID (the O), or with the OUs, up to four levels deep.

If you need to create a new Organization, use the Registration . . . Organization tool, also from the Configuration tab. The Register Organizational Certifier dialog box requires almost the same information, except you do not need a current certifier ID—

Figure 6-24
Register Organizational Unit dialog box

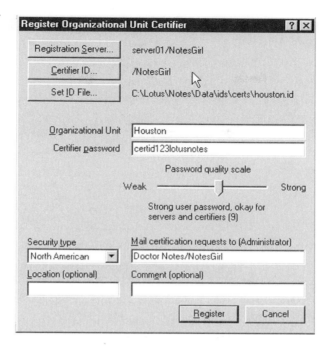

the new ID certifies itself and becomes the top level of a new organizational hierarchy —a new O. When you register Os or OUs, Domino creates a certifier ID and a Certificate document in the Domino Directory.

Servers

Most organizations have more than one server. Before you can configure additional servers in your organization, you must register those servers. You can choose to register servers with either the Organization certifier (CERT.ID) or with any OU certifier. To register servers, select the Configuration tab of the Domino Administrator. Expand the Registration tools and choose Server. You will select the certifier ID (or you may only be prompted for the password, if you have completed the Administration preferences and Domino can find the certifier ID). You will be prompted that the certifier ID has no recovery information (as described earlier) if you have not yet configured password and ID recovery.

In the Register Servers dialog box, shown in Figure 6-25, choose the Registration server (this should be the server with the CERTLOG.NSF; not local) and the correct certifier ID. Verify or change the Security type (North American or International) and the expiration date of the certificate.

Figure 6-25
Register Server

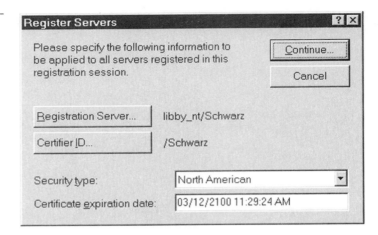

Figure 6-26
Basics panel

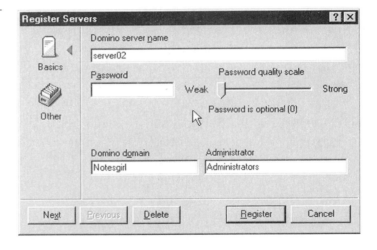

In the second dialog box (also called Register Servers), shown in Figure 6-26, type the common name for the server, and choose a password and the password quality scale. It is common to make the password optional and not create one for servers so that a server can be started without administrator intervention—especially if you plan to run the Domino server as an NT service, for example. Note that you cannot store the server ID in the Domino Directory if you give it a blank password, however. You should also complete the name of the Domino domain and type the name that should go in the Administrator's field in the Server document.

In the Other panel, in Figure 6-27, you can give the Domino server a title (this is a descriptive word or phrase to make it easier for users and administrators to identify the

PART II

Figure 6-27
Other panel

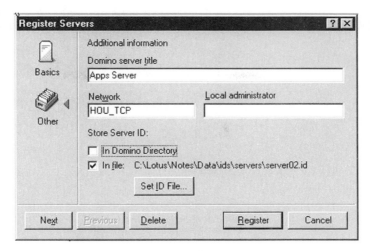

purpose of a server). You can also change the name of the Domino Named Network (DNN) in the Network field. This will need to be configured, either in this dialog box or in the Server document. Next, choose where the registered ID file should be stored: in the Domino Directory, in a file on the server or a diskette, or both. You can change the default location on the server or diskette by clicking the Set ID File button and navigating to the most secure location for the ID file.

When you register a server, the server ID file and a Server document are created in the Domino Directory. After you have registered additional servers, you can install and configure them. Additional servers are configured differently than first servers. This process is described later in this chapter.

Users

It is highly likely that you will have more users than just yourself in an Organization, so you will need to register users. You may also migrate users from other systems. You can register users using either the O certifier or any OU certifier. You can use the Register People tool from the People and Groups tab or the Registration . . . Person tool from the Configuration tab to register new users into your Organization. You can do a basic registration, where many options are set by default, as shown in Figure 6-28. When you use the basic registration, you give the user a name and password and add the user to groups—all other options are completed based on defaults configured in the Administration preferences.

You can also choose to click the Advanced option and complete all the configurations yourself. With Advanced registration, you can edit the password quality scale,

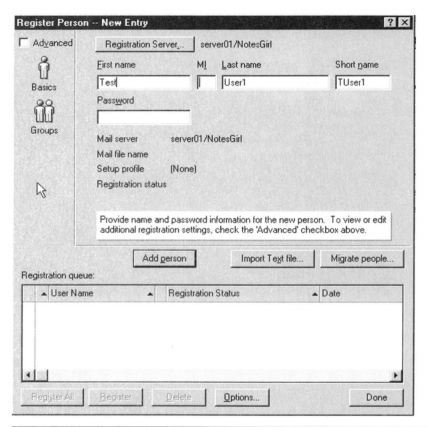

Figure 6-28 Basic registration dialog box

Internet domain and password, mail file name and location, mail server, and other items. Figure 6-29 shows the Basics panel of the Register Person dialog box.

You will complete the first name, last name, and middle initial. Only the last name field is required. As you complete the name, Domino automatically completes the short name field. You should enter a password next. If you want to store the user ID file in the Domino Directory, you must have a password in this field. Otherwise, you can choose to set the password quality to 0 (weak) and leave the password field blank, although this is not recommended. The password quality field will be set automatically based on the Administration Preferences, although you may change the quality requirements for each registration. Use the Set Internet Password checkbox to set the Internet Password field on the Person document to match the password for the ID file. This

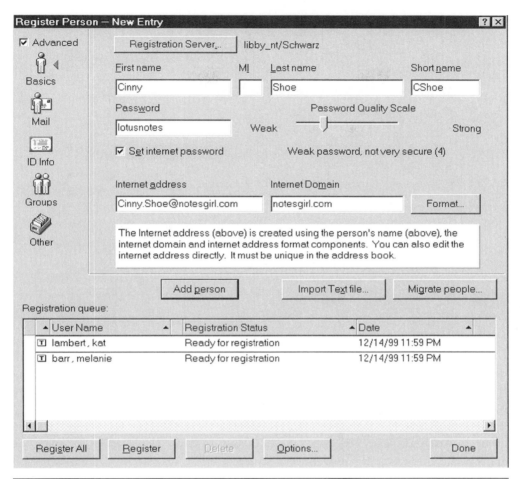

Figure 6-29 Register person basics

enables the user to access the server via HTTP if you are running that service. The Internet Address field is configured based on the settings for the Internet address format and the Internet domain. You can change the Internet Address format using the Format button, as shown in Figure 6-30.

On the Mail panel, shown in Figure 6-31, choose the mail server for this user, or accept the default set in the Administration preferences. Verify (or change) the mail file template, the mail system, and the mail file name. If the user will be using POP3, IMAP, or other mail protocols, you might choose to change the mail system. Some choices you make for the mail system will cause Domino not to create a mail file for the user.

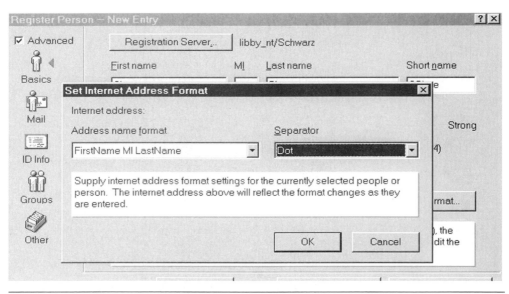

Figure 6-30 Change the Internet address format

Next, you can choose what level of access the user should have to his or her own mail file. By default, users have Manager access to their mail files. If you want to prevent them from deleting the mail file, changing design elements, or encrypting the file, you might choose to *limit their access*.

You can choose to create the mail file immediately or to create the file in the background (using AdminP). You can choose whether to create a full text index using the appropriate check box. If you want to set a quota and threshold on the mail file, you can also configure these settings on this panel. When you set a quota, if a user's file grows above that quota, he will not be able to add new messages or appointments until deleting some or having an administrator change the quota. Messages will continue to be delivered to the mail file even after the quota is reached, unless you use the *Obey database quotas during message delivery* setting on the Router/SMTP . . . Restrictions and Controls . . . Restriction tab of the Configuration document, which forces the Router to obey the quota. When a user reaches a threshold you have set, she is not prevented from adding new documents; however, an error message is written to the log. This gives you notice that the user is close to the quota.

The ID Info panel enables you to change the certifier for the current ID file. This is useful if you need to register a user under a different Organization or Organizational Unit. Next, you have the opportunity to change the security type—this should be either North American or International. This determines the type of ID file, the strength of the

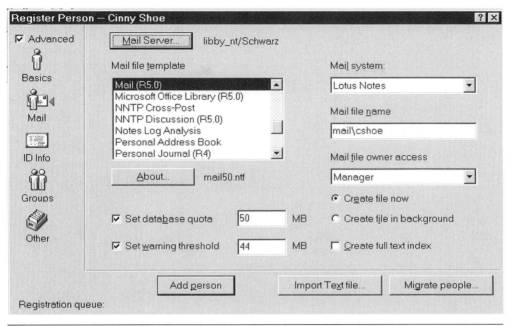

Figure 6-31 Mail panel

encryption keys used with mail and database encryption, and which type of Notes client the user can access. North American encryption keys are longer, and therefore more difficult to crack, than International encryption keys. Keep in mind that there are both North American and international ID files and software. This creates a mix-and-match puzzle that you may need to figure out. You *cannot* use a North American ID file with international software. You *can* use an international ID file with North American software. Further, international clients can access servers using North American software. You can also register international ID files from North American certifiers, by selecting the international security type when registering the user. Users can send encrypted mail between North American and international users, provided the recipient's public key is available, either in the Domino Directory or in the personal Name and Address book.

You can verify or change the certificate expiration date, which is two years from the current date, by default. In the location for storing the user ID file, select the Domino Directory or a file location and name. Remember that you must have a password on the ID file to store it in the Domino Directory. If you choose to store the ID file in a file, rather than in the Domino Directory (or in addition to the Domino Directory), you can

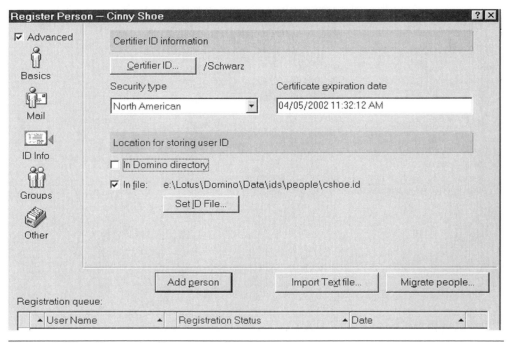

Figure 6-32 Change the file name or location

click the *Set ID File* button to change the file name or location, as shown in Figure 6-32. Remember that if you do choose to store the ID file in the Domino Directory, you must provide a password.

If you have created User Setup Profiles, you can assign one to this user on the Other tab, which is shown in Figure 6-33. Look for more information on User Setup Profiles later in this chapter. You can also assign a Unique Organizational Unit (UUOU). The UUOU is a word that you add to distinguish this user from another user with the same name and hierarchy. Note that you would not be able to register a user with a UUOU if you had already placed this user under the maximum of four organizational unit levels. Registering Joe Smith into CLP/Authors/Production/Houston/BrightRock, for example, would mean that you could not use a UUOU for this user. Next, if the certifier ID contains an alternate language, you can add an alternate language and an alternate name to the user you are certifying. The certifier ID must contain an alternate language before you can add an alternate language or name to a user ID. If you have the necessary rights in Windows NT, you can give a Windows NT account to the Notes user as you create the user. You can also add the Notes user to a specified NT group.

After you configure all of the settings for a user, click the *Add Person* button to add the person to the Registration Queue. You may add multiple users to the registration

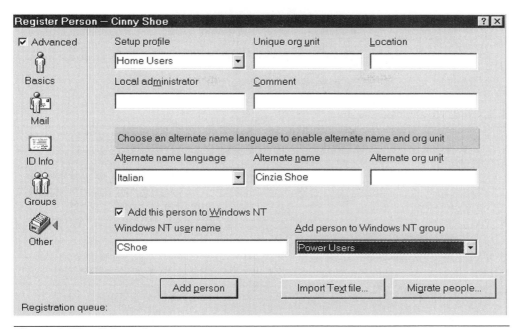

Figure 6-33   Other tab

queue before registering any users. When you are ready to register users, you may choose the Register All button to register all of the users in the registration queue. You may also select users (using the selection margin) and then register only the selected users by clicking the Register button. Before registering users, you may also want to select the Options button to configure the Registration Options, as shown in Figure 6-34. If you have users in the registration queue that you do not want to register at

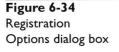

Figure 6-34
Registration
Options dialog box

all, you can select them and click the Delete button to remove the user from the registration queue. If you decide later that you want to register that user, you will have to recreate all the user settings. The registration options are described in Table 6-3.

Table 6-3   Registration Options

Option	Notes
Do not continue on registration errors	This option forces the registration process to stop when multiple users are selected to be registered, but the registration process encounters an error such as a user with too many OUs or a duplicate user. The default is to continue on registration errors.
Keep successfully registered people in the queue	This option maintains the list of users that have been successfully registered in the registration queue. The default is to remove successfully registered users from the queue.
Try to register queued people with error status	If the registration process encounters an error for a user, this option forces the process to try to register the person anyway. Some errors will force the process to fail regardless, but some errors will be passed over and the user will be registered. The default is not to register queued users who have error status.
Allow registration of previously registered people	This option enables Notes to re-register users that have already been registered in Notes. The default is not to register previously registered Notes users.
Don't prompt for a duplicate person	By default, Notes prompts the administrator for a solution when the registration process encounters a duplicate user. This option forces Notes to take one of the following options instead: • Skip the person registration • Update the existing address book entry
Don't prompt for a duplicate mail file	By default, Notes prompts the administrator for a solution when the registration process encounters a duplicate mail file. This option forces Notes to take one of the following options instead: • Skip the person registration • Generate a unique mail file name (Appends a number to the file name until a unique name is found.) • Replace the existing mail file (This option requires the user to have delete access to the mail file and that the mail file is being created now instead of in the background.)

When you register the users, Domino creates a user ID file (certified with the certificate of the certifier ID), a Person document in the Domino Directory, and a mail file. Elements in the user ID file include the following:

- User's name and up to one alternate name
- License (including a license number), indicating North American or International use
- The certificate from the certifier ID (associating the user ID with the certifier ID using the public and private keys of the certifier)
- The private key for the user (used for signing and decrypting messages)
- An Internet certificate for use with SSL connections and S/MIME mail messages (an Internet certificate comes from a Certification Authority [CA]) (Optional)
- Encryption keys, distributed by designers and other users for use in encrypting and decrypting data in documents (Optional)
- The password, which can be used to encrypt the private data on the ID (Optional)

You can also make the registration process easier in environments where you need to migrate or register many users at once. You can select the Migrate People button to display the People and Groups migration dialog box, as shown in Figure 6-35, if you need to migrate users and/or groups from the following mail and directory systems:

- LDIF (LDAP Data Interchange Format) files
- Lotus cc:Mail and Organizer® 2.x for cc:Mail
- Microsoft Exchange
- Microsoft Mail
- Microsoft Windows NT Server
- Netscape Messaging Server
- Novell GroupWise 4.x
- Novell GroupWise 5.x

For more information on registering users from an outside mail or directory system, please refer to Chapter 4, "Domino Messaging."

You can also register a large group of users from a text file. You can register users from a text file using the Register Person dialog box by clicking the Import Text file button. You can also register from a text file using the menus (People . . . People . . . Register from File). If you use the Register Person dialog box, you can change settings for each

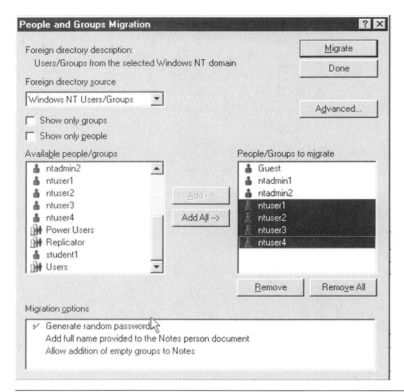

Figure 6-35   Migrating from another directory source

user individually after importing and before completing the registration. If you use the menus, you configure settings for all users in the group before importing the users. You cannot change these settings for individual users using this method. When creating a text file, use one line for each user, with each parameter (listed below) separated by a semicolon. If you choose not to set a parameter, you must still place a semicolon in its place in the list, unless it is the last item you are configuring. If you only want to set a name and password, for example, you could use the following:

```
Schwarz;Libby;N;;lotusnotes
```

If you want to apply a name, password, and short name, however, you would use the following:

```
Schwarz;Libby;N;;lotusnotes;;;;;;;;;;;lnschwarz
```

Items you should include in the text file are

- Last name (required)
- First name
- Middle initial
- UUOU
- Password (required)
- ID file directory (the directory must already exist and you must enable the directory option for storing the ID file)
- ID file name
- Mail server name (this will override any setting you configured during registration)
- Mail file directory
- Mail file name
- Location
- Comment
- Forwarding address
- Profile name (if you want to use a User Setup Profile)
- Local administrator
- Internet address (required for mail users)
- Short name
- Alternate name (certifier ID must contain an alternate language)
- Alternate Org unit (certifier ID must contain an alternate language)
- Mail template file

Groups

For ease of use in your Access Control Lists, Server documents, and for mailing use, you will want to have a variety of groups available in your Domino Directory. You create groups by opening the Groups view (People and Groups tab in Domino Administrator) and selecting the Add Group action button or using the Create Groups tool. When creating a group (shown in Figure 6-36), you must give the group a name, type, and members. You may also give the group a description and complete the Administration fields.

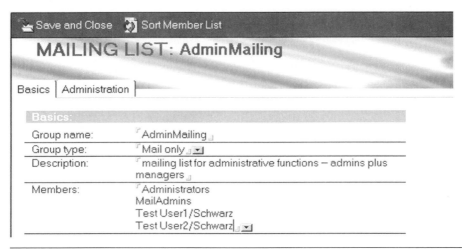

Figure 6-36   Creating a new group

The following are the available group types:

- Multi-Purpose
- Access Control List only
- Mail Only
- Servers only
- Deny List only

With the exception of the Deny List only group type, the groups are visible in the Groups view of the Domino Directory, shown in Figure 6-37. The Deny List only groups are only visible in the Deny Access Groups view of the Domino Directory. This group type is usually used in the Not Access Server field of the Server document so that terminated users can be restricted from accessing the server without having to reboot the server for a change to the Server document to take affect. Note that you cannot modify members of this group type using the Administration Process (AdminP). You should use different group types to make groups easier to manage.

Group members can be users, servers, or other groups. You can nest groups inside of other groups—for mail routing, groups can be nested up to five levels deep; for other purposes, groups can be nested up to six levels deep. By default, Domino creates a LocalDomainServers group and an OtherDomainServers group—these are added automatically to the ACL of databases. You must then add servers from within and outside your domain to these groups.

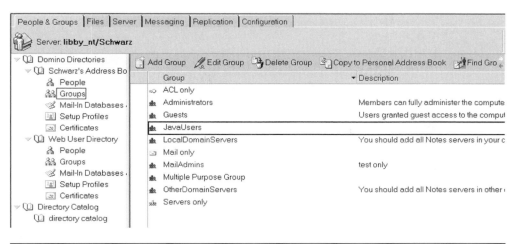

Figure 6-37   Groups in the Domino Directory

Configuring Additional Servers

After the first server in your domain, you may choose to add other servers to serve other functions for your environment. The process for configuring these additional servers is somewhat different than configuring the first server in the domain, although the installation process is the same. To begin, you must have registered an additional server (as described earlier), so that the server ID file is available during the configuration process. After installing, you will start the server, as you did when configuring the first server. When given the choice, select Additional Domino Server, as shown in Figure 6-38.

As with a first server configuration, you may now select a Quick and Easy configuration or the Advanced Configuration. In this case, we describe the Advanced Configuration. The third screen enables you to select the audience for the server. On this page, you are selecting the services to configure on the server, just as with a first server configuration. The final screen of the configuration enables you to indicate the name of the new server, where to obtain the server's ID file, where to connect to obtain a copy of the Domino Directory, and which ports the server should use. This screen in shown in Figure 6-39.

When the server connects to a server that contains a replica of the Domino Directory, it makes a new replica on the new server. The server ID file is copied to the server's data directory. When you are finished with the configuration and start the server, required files are created as services start.

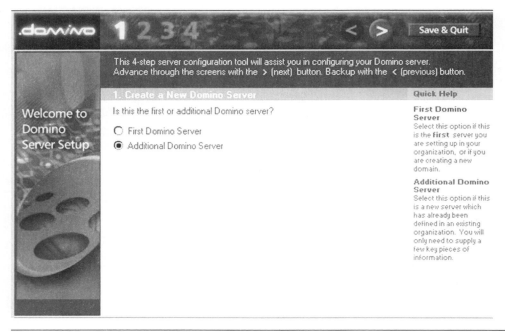

Figure 6-38 Configure an additional server

Additional Configuration

You may choose to do an additional configuration to make other setups easier. Two additional configuration steps you may take include configuring password and ID recovery, and creating and using User Setup Profiles.

Password and ID Recovery

A new feature in R5 is the capability to perform password and ID recovery on ID files. Before you can use the ID and password recovery feature, you must configure it. In addition, you must create a mail-in database to contain the recovery files. Finally, you must ensure that the users' ID files have the recovery information available to them. Use the following steps to configure password and ID recovery:

1. Create a Mail-In Database to hold the recovery information. The Administrators that will use the database for recovery require at least Reader access to the ACL. Create a Mail-In Database document for the database in the Domino Directory, as shown in Figure 6-40.

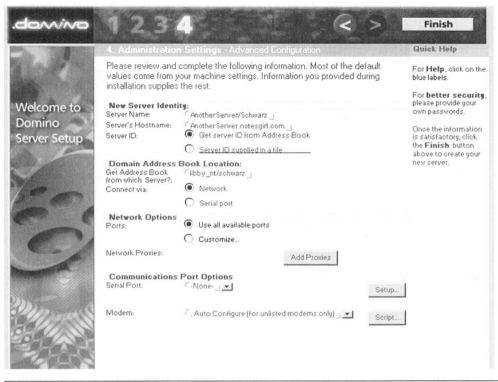

Figure 6-39 Get the name and NAMES.NSF for an additional server

Administration | □ Recovery DB ✕

▦ Save and Close

MAIL-IN DATABASE: Recovery DB

Basics | Database Information | Other | Administration

Basics

Mail-in name:	Recovery DB
Internet message storage:	No Preference ▾
Internet Address:	
Description:	

Figure 6-40 Mail-In Database document

2. In the Configuration tab of the Domino Administrator, open the Certification tools and choose Edit Recovery Information. Choose the Certifier ID that should contain the recovery information.

3. In the Edit Master Recovery Authority List dialog box, shown in Figure 6-41, place recovery information into the certifier ID. The recovery information (stored in the Certifier ID) includes the names of the administrators allowed to recover IDs and passwords (called the recovery authorities), the number of recovery authorities required to recover a user's ID or password, and the address of the Recovery database. The Person documents of the users you designate as recovery authorities must be available in the local (on the same machine as the Domino Administrator) address book or Domino Directory when you are making them recovery authorities. If necessary, copy the Person documents to your local address book. The Certifier document must also be available.

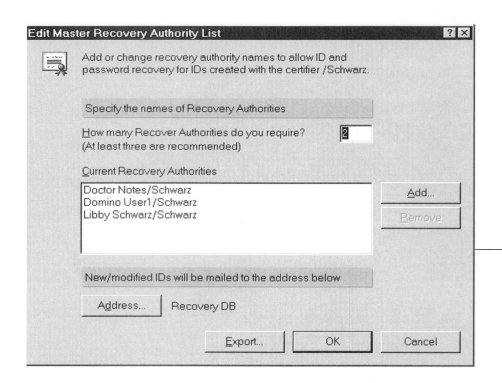

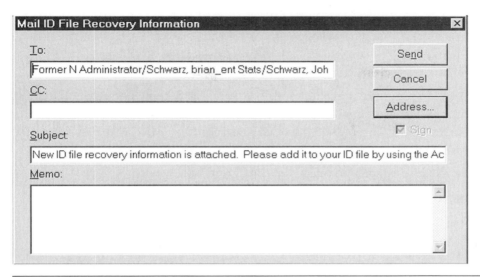

Figure 6-42 Mail ID File Recovery Information dialog box

4. Any users you register with this certifier will now contain recovery information. The recovery information in the user's ID file takes the form of a recovery password that is randomly generated and encrypted with the public keys of the administrators who are the recovery authorities.

5. For users registered before you created the recovery information, you must select the Export button to add the recovery information to their ID files. In the Mail ID File Recovery Information dialog box, shown in Figure 6-42, add the names of the users that have already been registered and need recovery information. You can use the Address button to select the users from the Domino Directory. In the memo field, tell the users to open the document and select Actions . . . Accept Recovery Information.

6. Users must accept the recovery information as described. When they accept the recovery information, a copy of the ID file is sent to the Mail-In Database, so that it is available if the user's ID file becomes lost or corrupted.

When a user loses his or her ID file or forgets his or her password, you can use the recovery information to recover it. If a user just forgets the password, but still has the ID file, you do not need to send them the ID file stored in the recovery database, but you will still use it to obtain the recovery password for the user. To recover a user ID file or password, use the following steps:

1. Open the Mail-In Database. Find the document that contains the user's ID file. Detach the ID file, as shown in Figure 6-43. Name it with the user's name and the .ID extension (if necessary). Don't forget to delete this ID when you are finished with the recovery process.

2. In the Domino Administrator, open the Configuration tab and select the Extract Recovery Password tool from the Certification tools. You will be prompted for your password. This password is used to decrypt the recovery password from the user's ID file.

3. You will be prompted to select the ID file to recover.

4. Domino displays a dialog box with the recovery password, as shown in Figure 6-44. You will read this password to the user (who should be at his or her workstation).

5. The user should select Tools . . . Recover ID from the Notes client. He or she is prompted to enter a recovery password for each of the required recovery authorities.

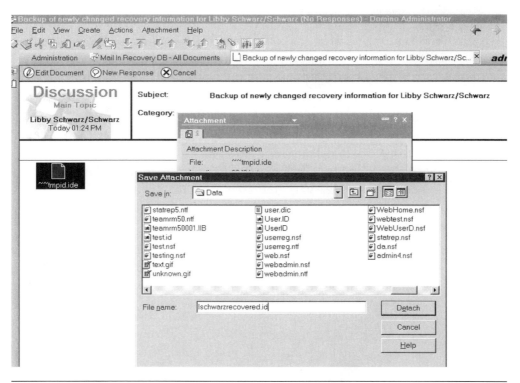

Figure 6-43   Detach the ID file

Figure 6-44
Recovery password

6. After typing in a recovery password from each of the required recovery authorities, the user is prompted to create a new password. His or her original password is never shown, as a security measure.

User Setup Profiles

Another tool you may use to aid in configuring users is the User Setup Profile. A user setup profile contains information such as settings to be used as defaults for the users in the workstation and in Location documents. Defaults that you can specify include passthru servers, connections to remote servers, Internet settings, and links to specific databases. You should create a user setup profile for each type of user before registering users. You can also modify a user setup profile and apply the changes to users after they are registered. To view, create, and edit user setup profiles, open the People and Groups tab of the Domino Administrator and select Setup Profiles. Use the Add Setup Profile action button to create a new profile (see Figure 6-45).

USER SETUP PROFILE: Remote users

| Basics | Databases | Dial-up Connections | Accounts | Name Servers | Applet Security | Pro› |

Basics

Profile name:	Remote users
Internet browser:	Microsoft Internet Explorer
Directory server:	libby_nt/schwarz
Catalog/Domain Search server:	libby_nt/Schwarz
Retrieve/open pages:	from Notes workstation
Sametime server:	

Figure 6-45   New User Setup Profile

In the User Setup Profile document, first give the profile a unique, descriptive name. Configure the Internet browser to be used by all workstations using this profile. Configure a Directory Server, Catalog/Domain Search server, and determine if users should retrieve Web pages from the Notes workstation, InterNotes server, or not at all.

In the Database tab, shown in Figure 6-46, you can include database links for each database you want automatically bookmarked in the client. When the client is configured, these databases will be added automatically to the bookmark list. You can also place database links for databases that should be created as new replicas on the local workstation—this is especially useful when configuring laptops or other remote clients. If you have configured a Directory Catalog for your environment, you can also add a database link to the Mobile Directory Catalogs field to have this database added to the users' workspaces.

Figure 6-46
Databases tab of the
User Setup Profile

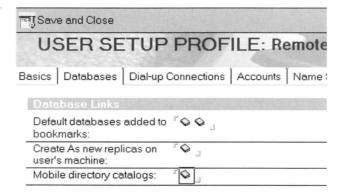

Use the Dial-up Connections tab (shown in Figure 6-47) to configure the connection to the default passthru server and to any other remote servers, including names and phone numbers of the servers.

Use the Accounts tab to add any POP3, IMAP, LDAP, or other accounts to Internet servers. Use the Name Servers tab to indicate any secondary TCP/IP or NDS name servers. The Applet Security tab gives you the opportunity to indicate trusted hosts for Java Applet security as well as what type of network security both trusted and untrusted hosts should be granted. Use the Proxies tab to configure default proxy server settings. Finally, use the MIME tab to indicate whether the clients should send mail in Notes Rich Text format or MIME format when sending to Internet addresses.

When you register users and apply the User Setup Profile, the users will have Account documents, Connection documents, and Location documents added and completed according to the settings. In addition, users will have the appropriate databases created

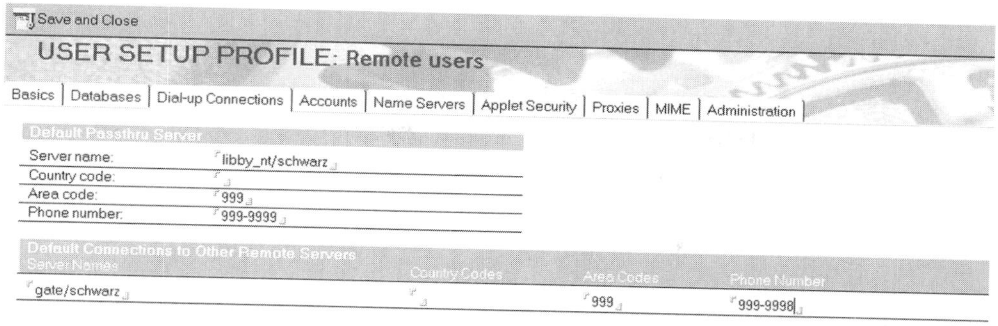

Figure 6-47 Dial-up connections

or bookmarked for them. You can edit the User Setup Profile to add more databases or change passthru settings at any time. When you save the information, the user will be updated.

Summary

In this chapter, you have configured your first server and additional servers. These servers can be of varying license types (Mail, Application, and Enterprise) and can be intended for a variety of purposes. It is usually a good idea to separate mail and application servers, as well as servers for hubs, passthru, or other purposes, as a redundancy feature. The more separated your server tasks are, the more stable each server will be and the more likely it will be that users can continue to perform at least some work in the event of a server failure.

In addition to configuring servers, you configured client workstations in this chapter. Again, you could choose between different client types, such as the Administrator, Designer, and Notes client. Bear in mind that in some environments, you might choose to use a Web client and non-Notes POP and SMTP clients, if necessary. This would require a different configuration. You might also choose to use the User Setup Profile to make configurations for users easier. Bear in mind the special configuration tasks you may face for mobile users, in terms of Connection and Location documents, as well as local replicas of their important databases.

Another element of configuring servers and users was the registration process. In this chapter, you registered certifiers, servers, and users, and created groups. It is always wise to create a Certification Log early in this process to have a record of the certified IDs in your organization and to allow AdminP to function.

Review Questions

1. Which of the following files is *not* created automatically for you when the first server is configured?
   A. CERTLOG.NSF
   B. NAMES.NSF
   C. SERVER.ID
   D. CERT.ID

2. Scott is trying to decide which server type to install on his new Domino server. If he wants to be able to use Transaction Logging, which of the following server installations could he select?
   A. Application
   B. Mail
   C. Enterprise
   D. Advanced

3. Phillip is registering a Joe Smith into the /Houston/Payables/Accounting/Finance/Acme hierarchy. He wants the user to have a UUOU (x1122) as well, as there is already a Joe Smith in that hierarchy. What happens when he registers Joe Smith into the listed hierarchy with a UUOU?
   A. He registers Joe with no problem, resulting in Joe Smith/ x1122/ Houston/ Payables/ Accounting/ Finance/ Acme.
   B. He registers Joe with no problem, but the OU4 was automatically dropped to make room for the UUOU, resulting in Joe Smith/ x1122/ Payables/ Accounting/ Finance/ Acme.
   C. He gets an error trying to register Joe, as there are one too many levels of OU when he adds the UUOU.
   D. He gets an error trying to register Joe, as he needs a Country code as well.

4. Josie is registering a User ID and has chosen to store the ID file in the Domino Directory. Which of the following is/are true?
   A. The ID file must be password-protected.
   B. The ID file will be attached to the Person document.
   C. This is the default location for the ID file.
   D. This is not possible—this ID file must be stored in a different physical location.

5. Elise is performing a client installation. She chooses to install the Domino Designer. Which of the following are installed?
   - A. Domino Designer
   - B. Domino Administrator
   - C. Notes Client
   - D. Mail Server

6. David is configuring Password and ID recovery for his Domino organization. When he creates the Mail-In Database, what is the lowest access level he can give to the administrators that will be performing the recovery?
   - A. No Access
   - B. Reader
   - C. Author
   - D. Manager

7. Which of the following contains the encrypted recovery password that is used in recovering User ID files?
   - A. CERT.ID
   - B. Administrator's USER.ID
   - C. Certifier document in the Domino Directory
   - D. Each user's USER.ID

8. What is used to encrypt the recovery password that is used in recovering USER ID files?
   - A. Administrator's private key
   - B. Administrator's public key
   - C. User's public key
   - D. Certifier ID's private key

9. During the first server configuration, Domino creates a variety of files and documents. Choose the line that correctly describes some of the files and documents that are created and where those files are stored.
   - A. User.ID (attached to the administrator's Person document in the Domino Directory); Server.ID (in the Data directory of the server); Cert.ID (attached to the certificate document in the Domino Directory).
   - B. User.ID (attached to the administrator's Person document in the Domino Directory); Server.ID (in the Data directory of the server); Cert.ID (in the Data directory of the server).

C. User.ID (in the Data directory of the server); Server.ID (in the Data directory of the server); Cert.ID (attached to the Certificate document in the Domino Directory).

D. User.ID (in the Data directory of the server); Server.ID (in the Data directory of the server); Cert.ID (in the Data directory of the server).

10. Suzy chooses to install North American versions of the Domino client and server software in the California office of her company. She has also registered the users in that office with the North American ID files. Another office in Japan has installed the International version and registered the users as International users. Which of the following statements are true?

A. When users from the California office travel to the Japan office, they can bring their ID files and use the Notes client software that is already installed there.

B. When users from the Japan office travel to the California office, they can bring their ID files and use the Notes client software that is already installed there.

C. Users from either office can send encrypted mail to all users in the organization because they all share a common Domino Directory.

D. Users in the California office can access and authenticate with servers in the Japan office.

Review Answers

1. **A** is correct.   Domino does not create CERTLOG.NSF automatically during the configuration process.

2. **A** or **C** are correct. Transaction logging is available with either Application or Enterprise servers. The Advanced server installation was only available previous to R4.6.

3. **C** is correct.   To use the UUOU, you must only have three other OU levels.

4. **A, B,** and **C** are correct.   When storing an ID file in the Domino Directory, which is its default location, you must give the ID file a password and it will be attached to the Person document.

5. **A** or **C** are correct. When you install either Domino Designer or Domino Administrator, the Notes client is installed as well.

6. **B is correct.** Reader access is sufficient for the administrators that will be performing the recovery, although you may choose to give some administrators Administrator or Designer access, to change the ACL and change the design of the database.

7. **D is correct.** Each user's ID file contains the encrypted recovery password.

8. **B is correct.** The recovery password is encrypted with the public key of the recovery administrator. The administrator's private key is used to decrypt the recovery password during the recovery process.

9. **B is correct.** Domino creates the User ID file, the Server ID file, and the Certifier ID file. The Server and Certifier are stored in the data directory of the server; the User's ID file is stored in the Person document in the Domino Directory.

10. **B and C are correct.** Users that have an international license can use the North American version of the software, so the Japanese users can use their international ID files with the North American software in the California office. Users from both offices can send encrypted mail, because the public keys are available in the Domino Directory. The international encryption will be used as the lowest common denominator when encrypted mail is sent between users with North American and International encryption.

CHAPTER 7

Advanced Server Configuration

You should be able to answer questions based on the following objectives after reading this chapter:

- Setting up servers for load balancing and failover (Clustering)
- Setting up servers for sharing resources (Partitioning, virtual servers)
- Setting up servers for Web/Internet connectivity
- Setting up/configuring transaction logging
- Setting up servers of different types (mail, applications, enterprise)

Some elements of server configuration are not required and are more advanced. These include configuring transaction logging, clustering, partitioned servers, and Web servers. Some of these, such as clustering and partitioning, require the Enterprise server to be installed. Transaction logging requires the Application or Enterprise server. In addition, you should configure the Administration Process (AdminP) to assist with administering the servers and environment.

Transaction Logging

Transaction logging, available on servers installed with either the Application or Enterprise license, logs the changes made to databases to a separate file (the transaction log). A change, or transaction, includes a series of changes, such as opening a database, creating and saving a document, and then closing the database. This series of changes is saved as a transaction. Before configuring transaction logging, it is recommended to have a separate disk device for the transaction log, both because it is large and because this will improve processing speed. It is recommended for this device to be mirrored.

Transactions are written linearly (sequentially) in the log as they occur. If these same transactions were being written directly to the databases, they would require skipping around to find the appropriate places for the data. Transaction logging, therefore, can improve the processing time, especially during high server activity. Note that transaction logging only works for R5 databases; databases using the R4 or earlier format will not participate in transaction logging.

When you decide to configure transaction logging in your environment, you should also get a third-party backup application that can support transaction logging, so that you can recover from media failures. When using a backup solution that supports transaction logging, you can do daily incremental backups, rather than full database backups.

To configure transaction logging, open the server document from the Configuration tab of the Domino Administrator. In the Server document, select the Transactional Logging tab, shown in Figure 7-1. Configure the settings as described in Table 7-1.

After you make changes to the Server document, you must restart the Domino server for the transaction logging to be started. When you restart the server, Domino assigns a DBIID (database instance ID) to all R5 databases and formats the transaction log (*.txn) and the control file.

When you first enable transaction logging, each R5 database is assigned a DBIID. This ID is recorded with the transactions included in the log. When you perform certain

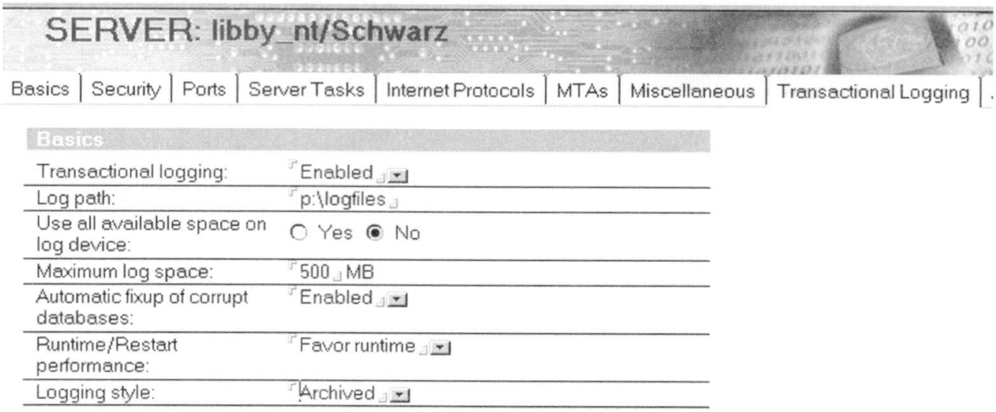

Figure 7-1   Transactional Logging tab in the Server document

Table 7-1 Transaction Logging Settings

Option	Notes
Transactional Logging	Use this field to enable or disable transactional logging for all databases on the server. You can disable transactional logging for a specific database using the database's advanced properties.
Log path	The default path for the transaction log file(s) is \logdir under the Domino\Data directory. Since Lotus recommends that you place the transaction log on a separate, mirrored disk device with a dedicated disk controller, you should usually change the path for the transaction log. You should make sure to include at least 1 GB of space for the transaction log.
Use all available space on device	If you have configured a separate disk for the transaction log, you should set this field to Yes.
Maximum log space	The maximum size for a transaction log is 4096 MB (4 GB). The default maximum is 192 MB. Domino creates between three and 64 log files, based on the maximum log size configured here. If you configured the log to use all available space on the device, you do not have to configure this setting.
Automatic fixup of corrupt databases	If you enable this setting (the default), Domino will run the FIXUP server task automatically if a database is corrupt and cannot be fixed via restoring data from the transaction log. If you disable this setting, you must run FIXUP -J manually to recover corrupt databases.
Runtime/Restart performance	You can configure how often Domino records a recovery checkpoint to the transaction log. The recovery checkpoint record in the transaction log shows each open database and where the starting point in the transaction log would be to recover the database. When Domino creates a recovery checkpoint record, it also forces changes to be saved to disk from memory.
	Your choices in this field include Standard (the default), Favor Runtime, and Favor Recovery. The Standard option forces Domino to store checkpoints on a regular basis. The Favor Runtime option records fewer checkpoints. This makes the server run more efficiently but may negatively impact restart recovery. Favor Restart Recovery Time records more checkpoints, which may slow normal processing a small amount, but requires fewer transactions to recover.
Logging style	You can use circular or archive logging. Circular (the default) reuses log files. You can only recover transactions that are stored in the log. The default, Archive, does not reuse the log file until it has been archived. The log file can only be archived when it is inactive, which means that it does not have any transactions necessary for current recovery. You should have backup software to archive the logs.

tasks, such as compacting the database with options, running Fixup, moving the database, or changing logging options, databases are assigned a new DBIID and old transactions cannot be restored to this database. When you perform any of these tasks, therefore, you should run a complete backup of the data first, so that you could restore from backup if data recovery is necessary.

Partitioned Servers

When installing servers with the Enterprise server license, you are given the option to install partitioned servers. Partitioned servers enable you to run multiple different servers on a single physical machine. The partitioned servers you install will share the Notes and Domino executable files, although each server will have its own NOTES.INI configuration file, its own data directory, and its own Domino Directory. The servers can be in different Domino domains, a configuration that takes best advantage of the resources of a partitioned server installation. If one partitioned server on a physical machine goes down or is stopped, the other partitioned servers on the machine can continue to run.

You must decide during the install process how many partitioned servers you will run on a machine. Make this decision based on how many servers you need and how many resources the server has. Ensure that you have the following hardware and software requirements:

- At least 128 MB of RAM for each partitioned server
- Best to use at least one processor for each partitioned server
- Add 100 MB of hard disk space for each partitioned server to the minimum requirements
- Use TCP/IP
- Sufficient IP addresses and NICs (or one server for port mapping)

After installing the partitioned servers (and giving each server/data directory a unique, easily distinguished name), you will need to configure the ports and protocols appropriately. When using partitioned servers, you can either use one IP address with port-mapping configured, or you can use a unique IP address for each partitioned server. Each option has advantages and disadvantages, described in Tables 7-2 and 7-3.

As described earlier, you can either use a single IP address and port mapping or use unique IP addresses when using partitioned servers. If you choose to use a single IP address and port mapping, be aware that you will designate one of the partitioned

Table 7-2   One IP Address

Advantages	Disadvantages
Only requires one IP address, especially useful in environments that do not have a large bank of available IP addresses	Servers are dependent on the port-mapping server; if the port-mapping server is down or unavailable, all the servers may be unavailable
	All servers must be in the same IP network
	I/O may be slow as all servers are sharing a single NIC

Table 7-3   Multiple IP Addresses

Advantages	Disadvantages
Not dependent on a port-mapping server	Recommended to use a NIC for each IP address to avoid negative impact on the computer's I/O
	Servers can be on different IP networks
	Faster I/O than one IP address method if you use separate NICs for each IP address

servers as the port-mapping server. This server will take all incoming requests and redirect them to the appropriate server. To understand port mapping, assume we have three partitioned serves on the same physical machine. These servers are called: Ophelia/Acme, Ariel/Acme, and Titania/AcmeWest. The shared IP address is 192.168.55.55. In the NOTES.INI file for the server that will be the port-mapping server (Ariel/Acme), you will include the following lines:

```
TCPIP_TcpIPAddress=0, 192.168.55.55:1352
TCPIP_PortMapping00=CN= Ophelia/O=Acme, 192.168.55.55:13520
TCPIP_PortMapping01=CN= Titania/O=AcmeWest, 192.168.55.55:13521
```

This enables the port-mapping server to answer all requests on port 1352 for the shared IP address and then map the requests to the other servers, based on the port numbers 13520 and 13521. If you had more servers, you could additionally use ports 13522–13524. These numbers must be used in ascending order, as must the numbers 00–04 in use before the common name of the port mapped servers. This is a common problem when port mapping does not work correctly.

In addition to the lines in the port-mapping server's NOTES.INI file, each additional server requires a line such as the one below in its NOTES.INI file. This line, for example, would be in Ophelia/Acme's NOTES.INI file:

```
TCPIP_TcpIpAddress=0, 192.168.55.55:13520
```

To configure the use of a separate IP address, with separate NICs, you may need any of the following lines added to the NOTES.INI file of each partitioned server.

- To allow Notes and Domino communication, use the following line:

```
TCPIP_TcipIPAddress=0, 192.168.55.55:1352
```

- To allow Web server communication, add the host name or IP address to the server document and then enable the *Bind to host name* field.

- To allow POP3 service communication, add the following line:

```
POP3Address=192.168.55.55 (or use hostname)
```

- To allow IMAP service communication, add the following line:

```
IMAPAddress=192.168.55.55 (or use hostname)
```

- To allow NNTP service communication, add the following line:

```
NNTPAddress=192.168.55.55 (or use hostname)
```

- To allow LDAP service communication, add the following line:

```
LDAPAddress=192.168.55.55 (or use hostname)
```

Additionally, you must be certain to configure the DNS (Domain Naming Service) or local HOSTS files to recognize each server's name and IP address. Finally, you must ensure that the Server document (on the Ports . . . Notes Network Ports tab) contains the IP address, host name, or common name of the server with the appropriate port and protocol enabled.

If you choose to use multiple IP addresses with a single NIC, you must add the IP addresses to the NIC in the appropriate manner for your operating system. In addition, only the first line listed above must be added to the NOTES.INI files.

Clustering

Enterprise servers can be clustered to provide load balancing and failover. Clusters are groups of two to six Domino R5, R4.5, or R4.6 servers that all contain replicas of important databases. The Domino cluster replicator keeps the data in these databases synchronized as changes are made (rather than based on a schedule as in normal replication). For load balancing, administrators can set maximum user loads. When the servers reach those loads, users are redirected to other cluster members. For failover, if a server is shut down intentionally or accidentally, users are redirected to other cluster members.

To configure a cluster, the servers that you want to make cluster members must have the following prerequisites:

- R5 or R4.6.2 Enterprise license/installation *or* R4.5 or R4.6 Advanced server license
- High-speed LAN (high-speed dedicated WANs are possible, although not recommended)
- TCP/IP
- Same DNN (and same set of protocols)
- Same Domino Domain and Domino Directory
- Hierarchical server IDs
- Domino Directory must have an administration server specified, and AdminP must be in use

To add a server to a cluster, go to the Configuration tab of the Domino Administrator and open the Server documents view. Select the Server document for the server you want to add to the cluster and click the Add to Cluster action button. After you verify that you really want to add the server to a cluster, specify the name of the existing cluster, or choose to create a new cluster, as shown in Figure 7-2. Bear in mind that a server can only be a member of one cluster at a time.

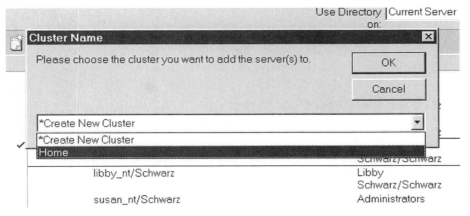

Figure 7-2   New or existing cluster

If you decide to create a new cluster, the next dialog box gives you the opportunity to give the cluster a name. Domino prompts you to decide if you want to perform the action immediately or if the Administration Process should perform the action. If you choose to have AdminP add the server to the cluster, you may need to force replication among the server that you are working on, the Administration Server of the Domino Directory, and the server you are adding to the cluster. If you chose to perform the action immediately, the cluster information is added to the Server document immediately. You should replicate with the server you have added to the cluster, if you are working on a server that is not part of the cluster. You can view the clusters in the Clusters view on the Configuration tab, shown in Figure 7-3.

After you add the server to the cluster, the following tasks should occur on the new cluster member:

- The Cluster Administrator (CLADMIN) task should start.

- The Cluster Manager task should start.

- CLADMIN adds the Cluster Database Directory task (CLDBDIR) and the Cluster Replicator task (CLREPL) to the ServerTasks= line in the NOTES.INI.

- CLADMIN starts the CLDBDIR and CLREPL tasks.

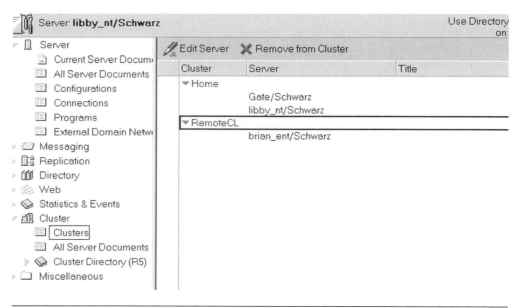

Figure 7-3   Clusters view

- CLDBDIR creates the Cluster Database Directory (CLDBDIR.NSF) and adds a document for each database to the directory.

If you have added multiple servers to the cluster, the Cluster Replicator replicates the Cluster Database Directory and the Domino Directory with other cluster members. To ensure that clustering works correctly, you should verify the following:

- You should have consistent protocols (including TCP/IP) among the cluster members.

- You should have a consistent ACL (Access Control List) among databases on different cluster members.

- You should make sure that all required cluster tasks (CLREPL, CLDBDIR) are running and are listed in the NOTES.INI file.

- You should make sure that the database replicas are distributed correctly on the appropriate cluster members.

- If you are using Calendaring and Scheduling over the cluster, ensure that CLBUSY.NSF exists.

- Verify that the CLDBDIR.NSF (the Cluster Database Directory) is created and that the databases on the cluster members have populated in the directory correctly.

Previously, only Notes clients could participate in clustering. In R5, the Internet Cluster Manager (ICM) allows Web clients (browsers) to participate in clustering as well. To use the ICM, run the ICM task on one or more servers inside or outside the cluster. The ICM server needs to be in the same Domino domain and share the same Domino Directory as the cluster members, but can be inside or outside the cluster. In addition, you can have one or more ICMs, either inside or outside the cluster. When you configure an ICM, the server(s) running the ICM is the middle-man between the Web clients and the cluster members—they take the connections from the Web clients, determine which cluster member should service the request, and generate a URL for the appropriate cluster member.

To configure the ICM, you will add the ICM information to the Server document for the ICM server. Open the Server document to the Server Tasks . . . Internet Cluster Manager tab, shown in Figure 7-4. Complete the necessary fields, as described in Table 7-4.

If you choose to have the ICM communicate over its own port and IP address to avoid conflict with the Web server, you need to complete the following steps. First, ensure that the IP address is available in the operating system. Then, use the Domino Administrator to create a new port. Open the Server tab in the Domino Administrator and expand the Server tools. Select the Setup Ports tool.

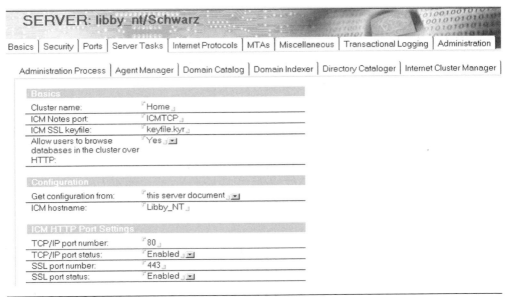

Figure 7-4 Internet Cluster Manager tab in the Server document

Table 7-4 Internet Cluster Manager Fields

Field	Notes
Cluster Name	Type the name of the cluster. If you leave this field blank (the default), Domino uses the cluster name of the Domino server from the Basics tab.
ICM Notes Port	Use this field to restrict the ICM's communication to occur only over the specified port. This is especially important if you need to limit the ICM's communication to a specific IP address to avoid conflict with HTTP. If you leave the field blank (the default), the ICM can communicate over any active Notes port.
ICM SSL Keyfile	Use this field to specify the SSL keyfile for the ICM to use. If this field is blank (the default), the ICM uses the keyfile specified in the Internet Ports tab.
Allow users to browse databases in the cluster over HTTP	Similarly to the *Allow HTTP clients to browse databases* field on the Internet Protocols . . . HTTP tab, this field gives you the opportunity to enable or disable browsing for ICM clients. This gives clients the ability to type **http://icmname/?OpenServer** to see a listing of databases.

(continued)

Table 7-4 Internet Cluster Manager Fields (continued)

Field	Notes
Get Configuration from	Choose whether the server should obtain its configuration from this Server document or another Server document. This field enables multiple servers to get the ICM information from the same location for consistency of configuration.
Obtain ICM configuration from	When the *Get Configuration from* field is set to Get ICM configuration from another Server document, this field is available. Type the name of the server to use to get the port and host-name configuration. When this field is available, the fields listed below are not available, as the information specified comes from the named server.
ICM hostname	Type the host name or IP address that clients should use to communicate with the ICM. This field is used by the Web server to create URLs that refer back to the ICM.
TCP/IP port number	Use this field to tell the ICM which port to use over TCP/IP. This is especially important if you are using the ICM on a server that is also responding to HTTP requests, as they cannot both communicate over port 80 (the default HTTP port). You must either give the ICM its own IP address or port number.
TCP/IP port status	Enable or disable the TCP/IP port.
SSL port number	Use this field to tell the ICM which port to use over SSL.
SSL port status	Enable or disable the SSL port.

Click New and give the new port a name (such as ICMPort). Use the TCP driver for the port. After you click OK, make sure the port is enabled. You may need to restart the server. You may also need to add the following line to the NOTES.INI file of the server:

```
ICMPort=TCP,0,15,0
```

In this case, ICMPort is the name of the port and TCP is the name of the driver. The numbers (0, 15, 0) are for the adapter or network number, the maximum number of sessions allowed over the port, and the data buffer size. You will need to add this line manually if you are not running the Domino Administrator on the ICM server. You may also need to add the name of the port to the Ports line of the NOTES.INI file, as shown in Figure 7-5.

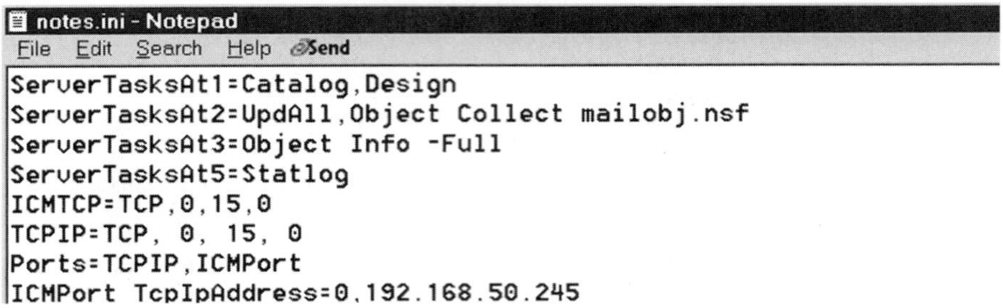

```
notes.ini - Notepad
File   Edit   Search   Help   Send
ServerTasksAt1=Catalog,Design
ServerTasksAt2=UpdAll,Object Collect mailobj.nsf
ServerTasksAt3=Object Info -Full
ServerTasksAt5=Statlog
ICMTCP=TCP,0,15,0
TCPIP=TCP, 0, 15, 0
Ports=TCPIP,ICMPort
ICMPort TcpIpAddress=0.192.168.50.245
```

Figure 7-5 Complete creating a new port using the TCP driver

After completing these steps, you need to add the port and IP address to the NOTES.INI file, as shown in the following line, where the port name is ICMPort and the IP address is 192.168.55.56:

```
ICMPort_TcpIPAddress=0, 192.168.55.56
```

Finally, when using this method, you must ensure that you complete the *ICM Notes Port* field on the Server document with the name of the port you have just configured.

Web Servers

One of the options available with a Domino server is the capability to run a Web application server. This option translates your Domino databases to HTML (Hypertext Markup Language—the language that Web browsers understand) on the fly and serves them up over the HTTP (Hypertext Transfer Protocol). This means that Web clients, such as Internet Explorer and Netscape Navigator, can use Domino Databases. Domino's Web server can also serve up static HTML pages, CGI programs, JavaScript, and Java applets. These elements can be embedded in Domino databases, or in the case of some elements, can be stored in a specific server directory and served up independently.

To configure a Web server in Domino, you run the HTTP task on the server. You can add the HTTP task to the ServerTasks= line in the NOTES.INI file, type LOAD HTTP at the server console, or start the task using the Domino Administrator Server . . . Status tab. To start the HTTP task using the Domino Administrator, open to the Server . . . Status tab, expand the Task tools, and choose Start. Select the HTTP Web Server task from the Start New Task dialog box, shown in Figure 7-6, and click the Start Task button.

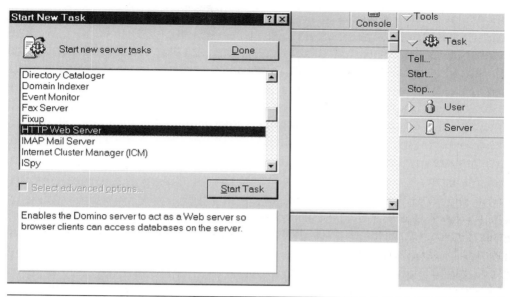

Figure 7-6   Start the Web server

In addition, you should enable either the TCP/IP port and/or the SSL port for client communications using the Server document for this server. You can open the Server document using the Configuration tab of the Domino Administrator. First, determine the port and type of security, using the Ports . . . Internet Ports . . . Web tab, as shown in Figure 7-7.

	Web (HTTP/HTTPS)
TCP/IP port number:	80
TCP/IP port status:	Enabled
Authentication options:	
Name & password:	Yes
Anonymous:	Yes
SSL port number:	443
SSL port status:	Enabled
Authentication options:	
Client certificate:	No
Name & password:	Yes
Anonymous:	Yes

Figure 7-7   Web port information on the Server document

By default, HTTP communicates over port 80; HTTPS (HTTP using Secure Sockets Layer) communicates over port 443. For normal connections, make sure port 80 is enabled. To force connections to go over the SSL port, disable or redirect port 80 and enable port 443. To force connections over a different port number (which will require users to know the port to communicate over), change port 80 to a different port number. You can also determine which client authentication options are allowed over this port—name and password or anonymous. Client certificate is added for SSL connections over HTTPS. Name and password authentication requires a Person document with an Internet password in the Domino Directory or a secondary directory (see Chapter 3). Anonymous connections will not require authentication to connect, but you must allow Anonymous access to databases as necessary.

The server's name should also be listed in the appropriate DNS (Domain Name Service) server, either with an Internet service provider or internally (if only for an intranet).

As described in Chapter 2, you can use a variety of additional fields when configuring the Web server. These are described in Tables 2-1 through 2-5, and should be reviewed while preparing for this exam. Other configuration options for the Domino Web server are contained in other fields of the Server document or on other documents. Some other options are described here:

- You can make Domino Web sites more accessible to being cataloged by Web site search crawlers by enabling the *Make this site accessible to web site search crawlers* option on the Internet Protocols . . . Domino Web engine tab of the Server document. This changes what the Domino server uses when generating pages from a question mark (?) usually used in Domino URLs to an exclamation point (!). Many Web crawlers used in creating search engines do not accept the question mark, in that they ignore everything past it in the URL.

- When Web clients download a file from a page or in a server directory, Domino includes the capability for clients that support it to use byte-range serving. A byte-range server (which is available as of HTTP 1.1) allows a client to download a file in sections (i.e., ranges of bytes), rather than as a single file. This means that if something happens to stop the download, clients resume the download where they were, rather than having to start over. You don't have to enable byte-range serving—if you're using a client that supports it, Domino automatically uses it.

Web Security

Much of the Web server security is based on the method of authentication to the server. As mentioned above, basic name and password authentication requires a Person document (in either the Domino Directory, or a secondary directory) and an entry in the

Internet password field of the Person document. When users authenticate using a secondary or LDAP directory, the authentication process begins in the primary Domino Directory. You would then configure Directory Assistance by listing the secondary directories and LDAP directories as trusted domains. Domino always searches the primary directory first; however, after that, other trusted domains will be searched in the order you specify in the Directory Assistance configuration.

If a user is allowed to use the Web server without authenticating, they are known as Anonymous, and this entry must be available in the ACLs of the databases on the servers. In addition to requiring name and password authentication, you can make that authentication session-based, a new R5 feature. As with typical name and password authentication, this requires a Person document with an Internet password. This type of authentication requires that users' workstations be enabled to accept cookies and is configured in the Server document. On the Internet Protocols . . . Domino Web Engine tab of the Server document, enable the Session authentication field. You may also choose to configure an Idle session timeout and the maximum number of active sessions. After you configure session-based authentication (sometimes also called cookie authentication), you should restart the HTTP task using the TELL HTTP RESTART command. If you configure this feature, you can use the TELL HTTP SHOW USERS command at the server console to view authenticated users, their IP address, and the time at which their session expires, as shown in Figure 7-8.

One of the benefits to session-based name and password authentication, in addition to being able to force users to timeout, is that users can log off without having to close their browser. To log out of a Web site, the user would append ?Logout to the end of a URL. In addition, because a login page, rather than a dialog box, is used with this type of authentication, you can configure customized login forms (using the DOMCFG.NSF). Figure 7-9 shows the default login page used with session-based name and password authentication.

You can also force users to use SSL (Secure Sockets Layer) on your server. SSL provides data encryption and both server and client certificates. To use SSL, ensure that the appropriate SSL ports are configured, using the Server document, on the Ports . . . Internet

```
> Tell http show users >D:\TEMP\79757626.TMP
04/05/2000 02:43:48 PM  There are 2 current HTTP user sessions
04/05/2000 02:43:48 PM  User Name                    IP Address      Expires
04/05/2000 02:43:48 PM  dnotes                       192.168.50.8    03:13:33
PM
04/05/2000 02:43:48 PM  Libby Schwarz                192.168.50.245  03:13:19
PM
>
```

Figure 7-8 Results of TELL HTTP SHOW USERS

Figure 7-9   Login page

Ports tabs, as shown in Figure 7-10. You may also configure database properties for particular databases to require SSL connections.

You will then need to configure the Server Certificate Admin database (CERT-SERV.NSF) (which should be created automatically during server setup). Use this database to request a server certificate (x.509 certificates) from a Certificate Authority and manage the certificates in the key ring file.

File Protection Documents

Another form of Web security that extends the normal ACL security to non-database files uses a File Protection document. The File Protection documents create system security for files such as HTML, JPEG, and GIF files, as well as CGI scripts, servlets, and agents. Note that while you can protect all of these items, you cannot protect documents that may be opened by CGI scripts, servlets, or agents.

To create a File Protection document for files or directories, you can start out in a Server document or with a Server document selected in the Server document view in the Domino Administrator (or Domino Directory). You can also start in a Virtual Server or Virtual Host document. Choose the Web . . . action button and select Create File Protection to open a new File Protection document. On the Basics tab, you can view the name of the server (and any virtual servers) the File Protection document should apply

Figure 7-10
Configure SSL Ports

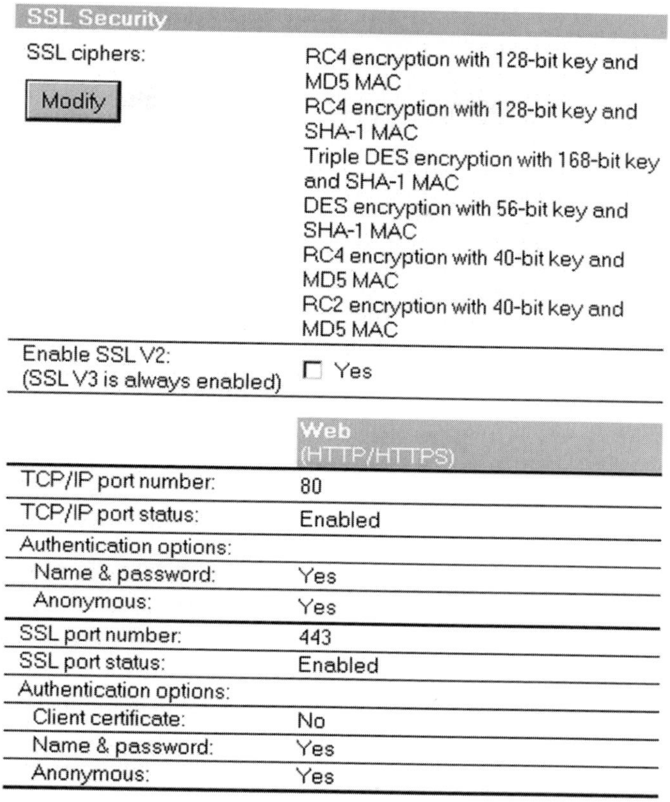

SSL Security	
SSL ciphers: Modify	RC4 encryption with 128-bit key and MD5 MAC RC4 encryption with 128-bit key and SHA-1 MAC Triple DES encryption with 168-bit key and SHA-1 MAC DES encryption with 56-bit key and SHA-1 MAC RC4 encryption with 40-bit key and MD5 MAC RC2 encryption with 40-bit key and MD5 MAC
Enable SSL V2: (SSL V3 is always enabled)	☐ Yes

Web (HTTP/HTTPS)	
TCP/IP port number:	80
TCP/IP port status:	Enabled
Authentication options:	
Name & password:	Yes
Anonymous:	Yes
SSL port number:	443
SSL port status:	Enabled
Authentication options:	
Client certificate:	No
Name & password:	Yes
Anonymous:	Yes

to. In addition, you can configure the drive, directory, or file to protect. The default path is the data directory. To configure a different path, use the full drive and path. You should create File Protection documents to protect any directories to which Web users might have access.

On the Access Control tab, you can view and edit the current Access Control List. Use the Set/Modify Access Control List to add users to the ACL and determine whether they should have Read/Execute access (GET), Write/Read/Execute access (POST and GET), or No Access. When users have GET access, they can open files and start programs. Users only need GET access to send information to CGI scripts and programs. If a user is not listed in the File Protection document, the user receives the default of No Access. By default, there should be one File Protection document, created at server startup for the \adm-bin directory, which gives access only to the user(s) listed in the Administrator's field when the server is configured. This document will not change automatically later.

If you change the Administrator's field and want to have this document changed too, you must do it manually.

After saving and closing the File Protection document, you must restart the HTTP task by using the TELL HTTP RESTART command.

Java Applets

When using the Domino Web server, you may want to take advantage of the options offered by programming Java applets. When you use the Java Notes classes, the Domino server can host the applet and provide it to the client to be downloaded when requested. If you want to run Java applets on a Domino Web server, you need to create the applets using Java Notes classes. You must also run the DIIOP (Domino Internet Inter-Orb Protocol) task on the server. In addition, you need to enable the IIOP (Internet Inter-Orb Protocol) port (default is port 63148) on the server. After you do this, the browser clients and Domino can use the Domino ORB (Object Request Broker). This server program processes the applet requests.

Note that you should complete the appropriate security fields on the Security tab of the Server document, shown in Figure 7-11. Complete the appropriate fields to allow restricted and unrestricted Java/JavaScript applets and applications to be run on the server. If you need to allow Anonymous users to run the applets or programs, add the entry Anonymous to the field.

Virtual Servers

You may want to host more than one Web site using the same Domino Web server. You can accomplish this by using virtual servers. This enables a single Domino Web server (not partitioned) to host multiple Web sites, such as **www.notesgirl.com** and www.brightrock.com. The data directory, program files, and Domino Directory are shared when using virtual servers. You can allow each site to have its own IP address, home page, and HTML, CGI, and icons directories.

To configure virtual servers, click the Web . . . action button in the Server Documents view and select the Create Virtual Server action. You can choose between a virtual host

Figure 7-11	Java/COM Restrictions	Who can -
Java applet security	Run restricted Java/Javascript/COM:	*, Anonymous
	Run unrestricted Java/Javascript/COM:	Libby Schwarz/Schwarz, JavaUsers, Administrators

and a virtual server. A virtual host is an alias for a Web site—this allows a single IP address to respond to multiple DNS names. Figure 7-12 shows a Virtual Hostname document.

In the Virtual Hostname document, type the hostname to which you want the server to respond. You can set a default home page for the virtual host that is different than the default home page configured in the server document. Similarly, you can configure different mapping settings and security requirements.

If you chose to create a virtual server, complete the Virtual Server document shown in Figure 7-13.

In the Virtual Server document, set an IP address, hostname, and default home page. Note that a virtual server can have its own IP address or can share an IP address and have a unique hostname. You can also configure a different default home page, mapping settings, and security requirements for each virtual server. When you configure a virtual host or a virtual server, you need to restart the HTTP task for the changes to take

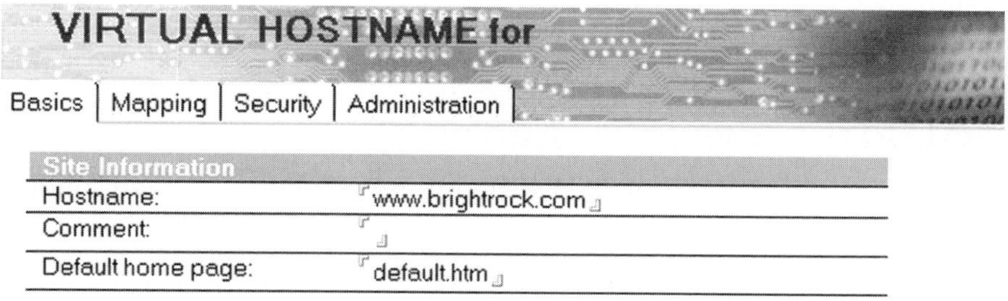

Figure 7-12   Create a virtual host

Figure 7-13   Create a virtual server

```
> Tell http show virtual servers >D:\TEMP\14593281.TMP
04/05/2000 02:54:29 PM  Virtual host: notesgirl.com based on base server
04/05/2000 02:54:29 PM  Virtual host: www.brightrock.com based on base server
04/05/2000 02:54:29 PM  Virtual host: www.brightrock.com based on base server
04/05/2000 02:54:29 PM  Virtual server: 192.197.99.150
04/05/2000 02:54:29 PM  Virtual host: www.bluecollartech.com based on
192.168.50.246
>
```

Figure 7-14   Results of Show Virtual Servers

effect. To restart the HTTP task, you should use TELL HTTP RESTART. This allows you to restart the HTTP task without restarting the entire server.

You can also get information about virtual servers configured on your system by using the Tell Task tool available from the Server . . . Status tab of the Domino Administrator. In the Tell HTTP Web Server dialog box, you can ask the Web server to display all virtual servers configured on the machine. This is the equivalent of typing TELL HTTP SHOW VIRTUAL SERVERS at the server console. Figure 7-14 shows the results of this command.

Administration Process (AdminP)

One task that runs on the server is intended to aid in your administration and configuration of the server, organization, domain, and users. This is the Administration Process, or AdminP. This task will start automatically when you start your servers and work with the Domino Directory, the Administration Requests database (ADMIN4.NSF), and the Certification Log (CERTLOG.NSF) to aid in adding, moving, deleting, and renaming users and groups, working with clusters, and moving mail and other files. Certain tasks in your Notes and Domino organization, in fact, require AdminP:

- Adding a server to and removing a server from a cluster
- Creating (multiple) replica stubs of a database using the Domino Administrator database tools
- Creating mail files during setup
- Populating the Server Build Number field in a Server document
- Password checking

As mentioned earlier, any time you start an R5 server, AdminP will start. You do have to perform some configuration to use the AdminP, however. First, you need to ensure that the Domino Directory has an Administration Server configured. By default, the first server in your domain will have this task. Having an Administration Server for the Domino Directory is vital for working with user and group names, the ACLs, and any moving or renaming. If there is no Administration Server for the Domino Directory, many of the Administration Requests will fail. To configure an Administration Server, you can use the Manage ACL Database tool from the Files tab in the Domino Administrator. The Administration Server field is on the Advanced tab, as shown in Figure 7-15.

In addition, any database that you want to be able to participate in AdminP, such as having group and user names changed in the ACL during a rename, should also have an Administration Server configured. If you do not configure an Administration Server for a database, it will not receive changes when you use AdminP for renames or deletions, for example.

Because AdminP works closely with the Administration Requests database and the Certification Log database, you must ensure that they exist before trying to use AdminP. When AdminP is first started on a server, it should create the Administration Requests

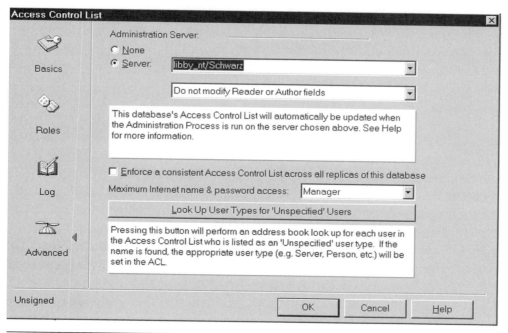

Figure 7-15 Administration server for the Domino Directory

database. All servers in the domain should have a replica of the Administration Requests database, so that requests can be replicated throughout the domain.

The Certification Log, on the other hand, is not created automatically by AdminP. To use AdminP for any certification or renaming tasks, you must configure this database. Create a new database on the Administration Server for the Domino Directory. Use the Certification Log (CERTLOG.NTF) template. It is important to use the Certification Log title and CERTLOG.NSF filename.

Other configuration steps you may need to take include ensuring that users who will perform AdminP requests have the appropriate level of access to the Administration Requests database (at least Author), the Certification Log database (at least Author), and the Domino Directory (at least Author with the necessary roles, depending on the requests).

Cross-Domain Requests

Finally, you may need to use the Administration Process to make requests in other domains or accept requests made in other domains. To do either, you must create Cross Domain Configuration documents in the Administration Requests database. These documents determine which types of requests can be sent between domains, as well as which administrators can make those requests. In addition to these documents, the following will also need to exist before cross-domain request will work:

- Cross-certificate documents if the domains are certified in different organizations
- A Connection document to enable the servers to connect to a server in the other domain

To create a Cross Domain Configuration document, open the Domino Administrator. Select the Server . . . Analysis tab and expand the Administration Requests database section. Select the Cross Domain Configuration view. Choose the Add Configuration action button to create a Cross Domain Configuration document.

First, select whether the document is for inbound requests (requests coming into this domain from an outside domain) or for outbound requests (requests initiated in this domain that will be processed in an external domain).

For Inbound Request Configurations, complete the fields described in Table 7-5. For Outbound Request Configurations, complete the fields described in Table 7-6.

Table 7-5 Inbound Request Configurations

Field	Notes
Receive AdminP requests from domains	List the domains from which your domain will accept requests for processing.
List of AdminP request allowed from other domains	Use the keyword list to select the type of requests that your domain will process from other domains. Possible requests include the following: Create Replica, Delete Person in Address Book, Delete Server in Address Book, Rename Person in Address Book, and Rename Server in Address Book.
List of Approved Signers	Use the Domino directory to select names of approved signers. These are users that are trusted signers for the request type for the destination domain. The following specific details apply:
	First, the user that signs a request has to be a manager for the Domino Directory. Second, the user that signs a request must be listed in the Directory Profile document as a user that has permission to create Cross Domain Configuration documents. See Chapter 8 for more information about the Directory Profile. Next, for any Create Replica requests, the user that signs the request and the source server for the request must both have Create Replica access to the destination server. Finally, any Delete requests must be signed by an administrator in the originating domain.

Summary

When configuring and installing servers, you must take some of the advanced features into consideration. When deciding what type of server installation to perform, remember that you need at least an Application server to allow databases to use transaction logging. In addition, you need an Enterprise server to use clustering or partitioning.

When you configure Transaction Logging, you should have a separate drive for the transaction log, if possible. After you have configured Transaction Logging, all R5 databases will participate in logging, unless specifically kept from it using the advanced database properties.

When using partitioning, you can use one IP address and a port-mapping server, or have multiple IP addresses and NICs for the partitions. You will probably have better performance with multiple IP addresses and NICs.

Table 7-6   Outbound Request Configurations

Field	Notes
Domains to submit AdminP requests to	List the domains to which your domain can forward requests for processing.
List of AdminP requests to submit	Use the keyword list to select the type of requests that your domain will process from other domains. Possible requests include the following: Create Replica, Delete Person in Address Book, Delete Server in Address Book, Rename Person in Address Book, and Rename Server in Address Book.
List of Approved Signers	Use the Domino directory to select names of approved signers. These are users that are trusted signers for the request type for the originating domain. The following specific details apply:
	First, the user that signs a request has to be a manager for the Domino Directory. Second, the user that signs a request must be listed in the Directory Profile document as a user that has permission to create Cross Domain Configuration documents. Chapter 8 has more information about the Directory Profile. Next, for any Create Replica requests, the user that signs the request and the source server for the request must both have Create Replica access to the destination server. Finally, any Delete requests must be signed by an administrator in the originating domain.
Only submit Create Replica requests to the domains listed above if the destination server is one of the following	This field is available if you select Create Replica as one of the requests that can be submitted to remote domains. The fields available are the server names and domain names.

When adding servers to clusters, bear in mind that the servers must be using TCP/IP and be in the same Domain and DNN. They must be in a high-speed LAN or WAN connection. A server can only be a member of a single cluster at a time.

You may also choose to configure your Domino server to be a Web server, using the HTTP task. When you configure the HTTP task, you should consider the port that the Web clients will use (80 by default), the authentication and other security you might want to configure, configuring virtual servers or hosts, and using Java applets.

Finally, to aid in configuring and administering other elements of your Domino environment, you will use the Administration Process (AdminP). This task starts automatically on all Domino servers, although you may need to do some additional configuration, such as setting Administration servers, creating the Certification Log, and configuring ACLs to ensure that users have the necessary access to perform their requested tasks.

Review Questions

1. Which level of R5 server license do you need to install to use transaction logging?
   A. Mail server
   B. Application server
   C. Enterprise server
   D. Advanced server

2. Which level of R5 server license do you need to install clustered servers?
   A. Mail server
   B. Application server
   C. Enterprise server
   D. Advanced server

3. When you configure transaction logging on a server, which of the following is true?
   A. Only databases specifically configured to do so participate in logging.
   B. The transaction log must reside on the same physical disk as the databases to be logged.
   C. All databases are logged by default.
   D. Archive-type logging is the default and recommended style of logging.

4. Which level of R5 server license do you need to install partitioned servers?
   A. Mail server
   B. Application server
   C. Enterprise server
   D. Advanced server

5. Partitioned servers share which of the following elements?
   A. NOTES.INI files
   B. Executable files
   C. Domino Directory
   D. Data directory

6. Which of the following shows the correct lines to include in the port mapping server's NOTES.INI file?
   A. TCPIP_TcpIpAddress=0,192.168.55.55:1352
      TCPIP_PortMapping01=CN=Server1/O=West,192.168.55.55:13521
      TCPIP_PortMapping02=CN=Server2/O=West,192.168.55.55:13522
      TCPIP_PortMapping03=CN=Server3/O=West,192.168.55.55:13523

B. TCPIP_TcpIpAddress=0,192.168.55.55:1352
   TCPIP_PortMapping00=CN=Server1/O=West,192.168.55.55:1352
   TCPIP_PortMapping01=CN=Server2/O=West,192.168.55.55:1352
   TCPIP_PortMapping02=CN=Server3/O=West,192.168.55.55:1352
C. TCPIP_TcpIpAddress=0,192.168.55.55:1352
   TCPIP_PortMapping00=CN=Server1/O=West,192.168.55.55:13520
   TCPIP_PortMapping01=CN=Server2/O=West,192.168.55.55:13521
   TCPIP_PortMapping02=CN=Server3/O=West,192.168.55.55:13522
D. TCPIP_TcpIpAddress=0,192.168.55.55:1352
   TCPIP_Port00=CN=Server1/O=West,192.168.55.55:13520
   TCPIP_Port01=CN=Server2/O=West,192.168.55.55:13521
   TCPIP_Port02=CN=Server3/O=West,192.168.55.55:13522

7. You routinely allow users to download large files from your Web site. Which of the following enables those large files to be downloaded in sections, and be restarted where they left off if the download stops in the middle?
   A. Byte-Range serving
   B. Session-based download
   C. Session-based authentication
   D. This is not currently possible.

8. You have configured name and password authentication for users on your server. When Jane has trouble logging in, which of the following might you try?
   A. Delete the cookie created by the Domino server and let the server recreate it.
   B. Enable Java on the workstation.
   C. Use the HTTP Password field to read the password to the user.
   D. Delete and recreate the password in the user's Internet Password field.

9. Which of the following is not necessary to host Java applets on the Domino server?
   A. DIIOP task
   B. IIOP port
   C. ORB task
   D. This is not currently possible.

10. There are graphics and HTML files on your server that you reference on your Domino Web site. Which of the following is true?

   A. You have to store those files in a database to use them in your Domino Web site.

   B. You can protect those files using File Protection documents.

   C. You cannot refer to these types of documents on a Domino Web site.

   D. Only an administrator can be given access to these files on the server.

Review Answers

1. **B** is correct.   For databases to use transaction logging, at least an Application server must be installed.

2. **C** is correct.   You need an Enterprise server to use clustering in R5. Prior to 4.6x, the Advanced server would have been correct.

3. **C** is correct.   By default, all databases participate in logging, unless excluded using an Advanced database property.

4. **C** is correct.   You need an Enterprise server to install partitioned servers in R5. Prior to 4.6x, the Advanced server would have been correct.

5. **B** is correct.   A set of partitioned servers on the same physical machine shares the Executable files, but each server has its own NOTES.INI file, Domino Directory, and Data Directory.

6. **C** is correct.   The important aspects in this case are the port mapping numbers (00–04 are possible) directly after the words port mapping — they must be in order from 00 without skipping; the port number in use at the end should start with 13520 and go in order without skipping to 13524.

7. **A** is correct.   When your users download large files, byte-range serving allows them to pick up where they left off in case of a crash.

8. **D** is correct.   You should reset the Internet password field on the Person document by deleting and recreating it.

9. **C** is correct.   You need the DIIOP task and the IIOP port/protocol to host Java applets on a Domino server.

10. **B** is correct.   You can protect HTML and graphics files on your Domino server using File Protection documents.

Directories

You should be able to answer questions based on the following objective after reading this chapter:

- Setting up/configuring directories (Domino, Catalog, Assistance)

One of the most important elements in your Domino environment is the Domino Directory. The Domino Directory defines a domain—all users and servers in the same Domino Directory are part of the same Notes domain. As you register users, servers, and certifiers, or create groups, Person, Server, and Certifier, and Group documents are created in the Domino Directory. You also use the Domino Directory for administering the domain, by creating Connection, Configuration, Program, and other documents used for managing the Domino system and environment.

In R5, in addition to the Domino Directory, you also use the Directory Catalog (mobile and server-based) and Directory Assistance, as well as LDAP, to provide directory functions. When you configure a Domino environment, you must be able to configure each of these elements.

Domino Directory

To discuss the Domino Directory, you need to recognize that in R5, you may be talking about a primary or secondary directory. The primary directory is the Domino Directory created when a new Domino domain is created. This file (NAMES.NSF) defines the domain and its members. You may also have secondary directories—usually the Domino Directories for other domains or for other purposes, such as Web users or non-domain common contacts. You may also hear the Domino Directory referred to as the domain directory, to clarify its function as the keeper of records about a single domain.

The Domino Directory serves the purpose (as described above) of containing information about all the domain members, servers, and certifiers. Additionally, you use the Domino Directory to contain configuration information to control your domain and servers. The Domino Directory stores the following types of documents:

- Group documents define lists of users, servers, groups, and resources that can be used for mailing, access control, or server access, and contain the name of the group, the type of group, and the members of the group, as shown in Figure 8-1.

- Location documents contain details for users about how they use Notes in a specific place, including information about mail server, mail file location, and type of connection, as shown in Figure 8-2. This is useful to help administrators create documents for users, or for administrators who use a client on the same machine as the server (not the recommended configuration).

- Person documents contain information about the users in your domain, including mail file, home server, Internet password, and Public key, as shown in Figure 8-3. Person documents can also show information for non-Notes users that you add to the Directory.

- Certificate documents contain information about Domino certificates and cross-certificates, including information about the certifier's Public Key, as well as Internet certificates, as shown in Figure 8-4.

- Configuration Settings documents contain information about NOTES.INI, mail, and LDAP settings that you can change to determine how these features work, as shown in Figure 8-5.

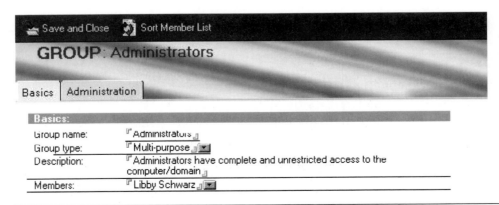

Figure 8-1   Group document

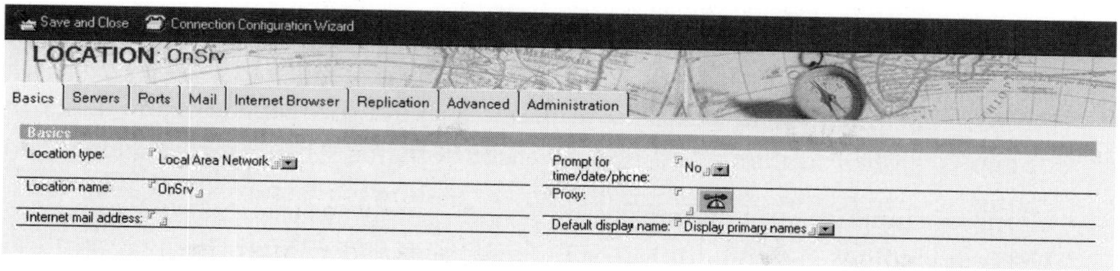

Figure 8-2 Location document

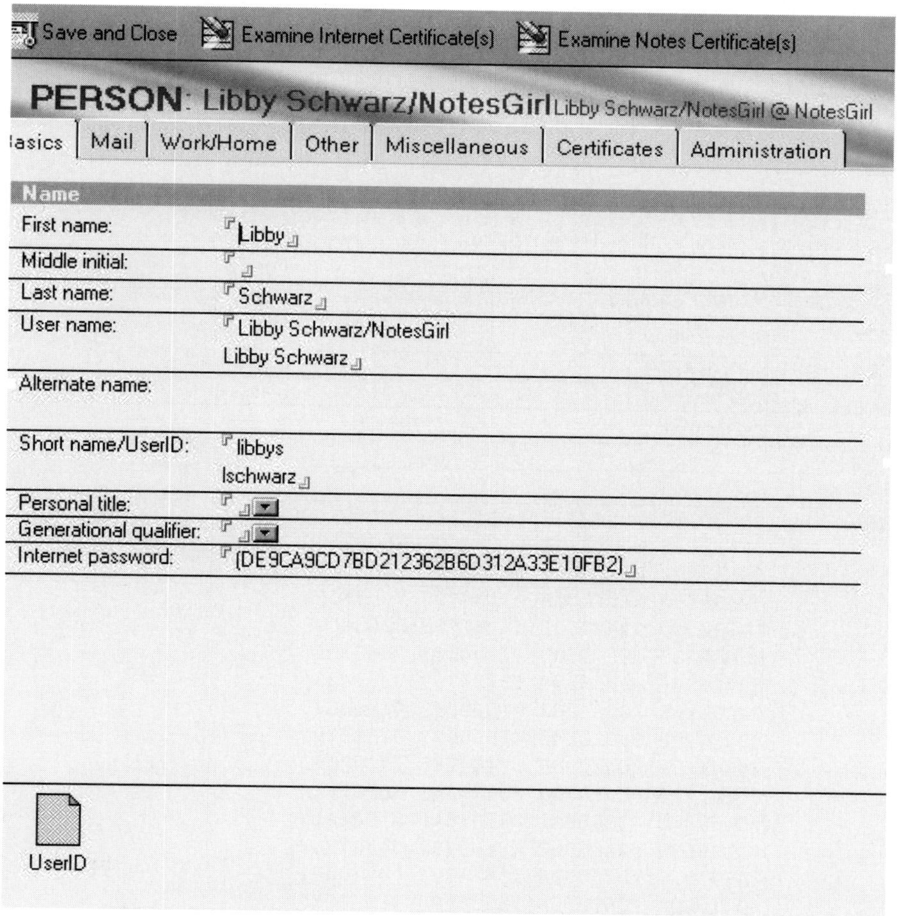

Figure 8-3 Person document

- Connection documents allow replication and mail routing to occur on a schedule, as shown in Figure 8-6.

- Domain documents define external domains, including foreign domains, adjacent domains, global domains, and non-adjacent domains. The domains are used to configure mail routing. A Domain document is shown in Figure 8-7.

- External Domain Network Information documents enable your clients to connect to machines in other domains by providing the name and address of a server or servers in this external domain, as shown in Figure 8-8.

- Holiday documents define holidays for specific groups, which can then be downloaded into users' calendars to facilitate scheduling, as shown in Figure 8-9.

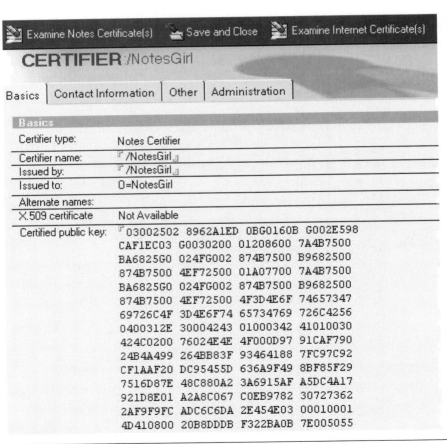

Figure 8-4 Certificate document

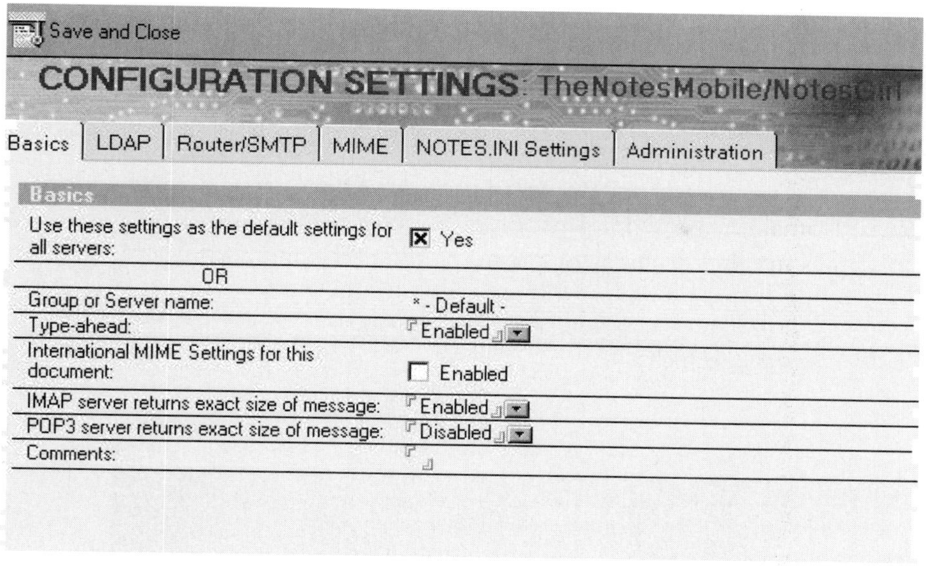

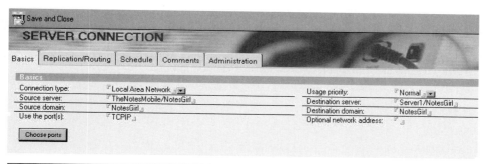

Figure 8-5 Configuration Settings document

Figure 8-6 Connection document

- Mail-in database documents enable the router to find, and place mail into, databases that are not mail files, as shown in Figure 8-10.

- Program documents enable you to schedule tasks or programs to run at specific times, with command-line arguments, as shown in Figure 8-11.

- Resource documents are added to the Domino Directory to enable users to reserve and schedule resources, such as rooms, using Calendaring and Scheduling, as shown in Figure 8-12.

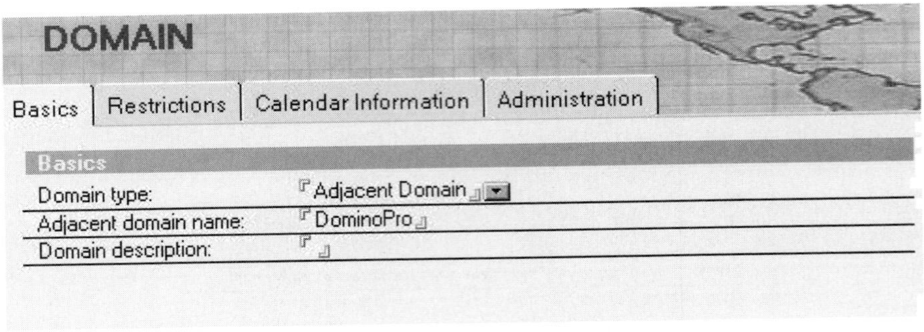

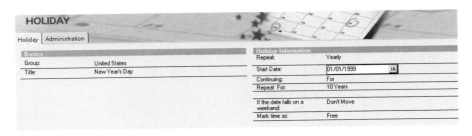

Figure 8-7 Domain document

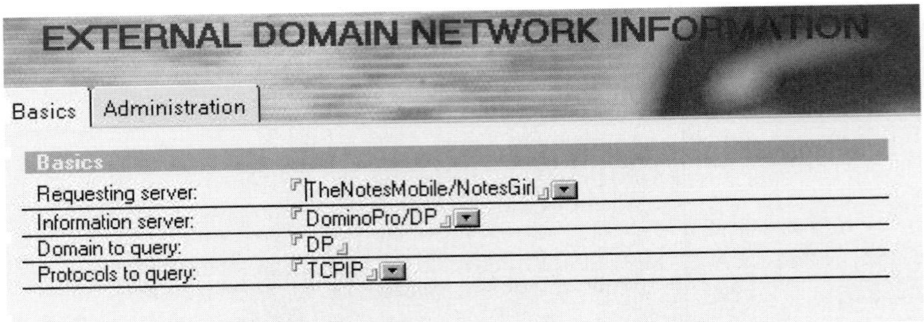

Figure 8-8 External Domain Network Information documents

Figure 8-9 Holiday documents

- Server documents define settings about server security, ports, clusters, tasks, protocols, networks, and other elements, as shown in Figure 8-13.

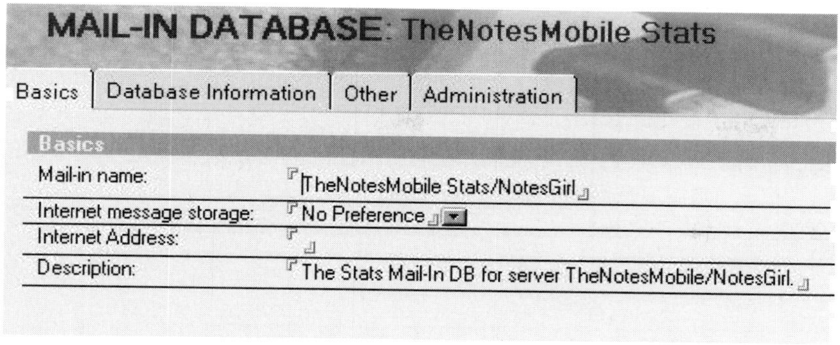

MAIL-IN DATABASE: TheNotesMobile Stats

| Basics | Database Information | Other | Administration |

Basics

Mail-in name:	TheNotesMobile Stats/NotesGirl
Internet message storage:	No Preference
Internet Address:	
Description:	The Stats Mail-In DB for server TheNotesMobile/NotesGirl.

Figure 8-10 Mail-in Database documents

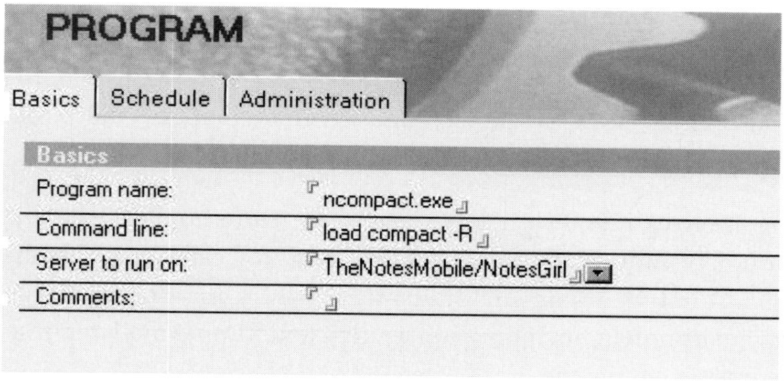

PROGRAM

| Basics | Schedule | Administration |

Basics

Program name:	ncompact.exe
Command line:	load compact -R
Server to run on:	TheNotesMobile/NotesGirl
Comments:	

Figure 8-11 Program documents

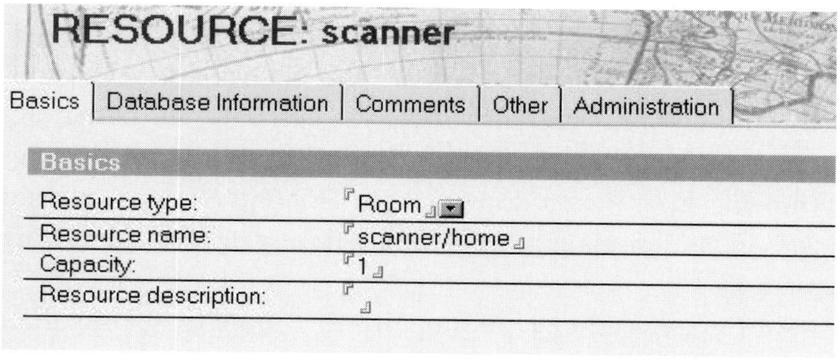

RESOURCE: scanner

| Basics | Database Information | Comments | Other | Administration |

Basics

Resource type:	Room
Resource name:	scanner/home
Capacity:	1
Resource description:	

Figure 8-12 Resource documents

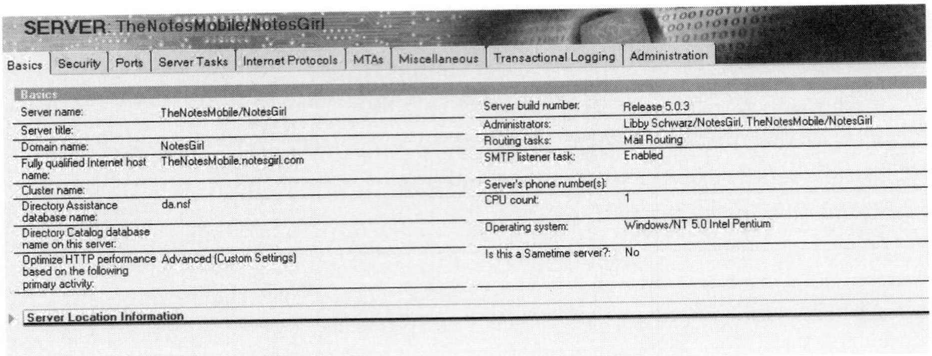

Figure 8-13   Server documents

- User Setup Profile documents enable administrators to give groups of users the same configuration options, such as connections, accounts, replicas, and book-marks, as shown in Figure 8-14.

These documents are arranged into a variety of views in the Domino Directory that give you the information necessary to administer your domain. You can also access the documents through the Domino Administrator interface. Use these documents to maintain your Domino environment, including configuring and routing mail, replicat-ing, and running programs on a schedule.

Configuring a Domino Directory is simple. The main tasks you should consider are replication of the directory, security, and configuring the directory profile.

Replicating the Domino Directory

When you configure the first server in your domain, Domino creates a Domino Direc-tory with the file name NAMES.NSF. When you register and configure other servers, Domino places a replica of this Domino Directory on those servers. You must then cre-ate the appropriate Connection documents to ensure that Domino can correctly repli-cate changes to the documents around your domain. Your Domino Directory should replicate with other servers in your domain multiple times during the day, depending on your domain configuration.

Note that you may want to replicate the Domino Directory more frequently than you replicate other databases on your servers. When you create Connection docu-ments, you might choose to create one specifically for the Domino Directories. This

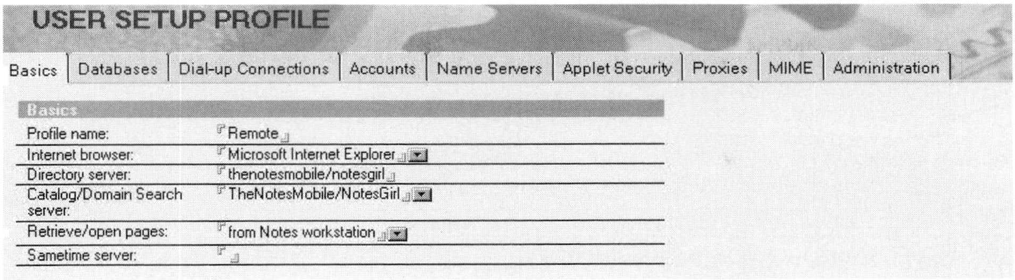

Figure 8-14 User Setup Profile documents

Connection document should replicate the Domino Directory often, such as every 30 minutes to an hour.

Domino Directory Security

When configuring security, you should limit editor and author access to the Domino directory as much as possible. As with all databases in Notes, the Domino Directory uses the Access Control List for security. By default, the Domino Directory template gives all users Author access to the directory; however, they are not given Creator and Modifier roles. They are also given ownership of their own records (look on the Administration tab of a Person document, as shown in Figure 8-15). Ownership in combination with Author access means that most users can edit their own records, but no others.

As you add other users and groups to the ACL for the Domino Directory, however, you need to consider the eight predefined user roles that have been created and implemented for this database, as shown in Figure 8-16. These roles refine the rights given by the ACL by determining who can create and edit specific types of documents.

There are Creator roles and Modifier roles. The Creator roles apply to users at all levels of the ACL, including Managers. The Creator roles allow users with the Create Documents privilege to create documents using the Create Menu in the Domino Directory. Without this role, a user cannot create the specified document using the Create Menu, although they may still be able to create a document programmatically. Do not consider the Creator roles a security feature.

The Modifier roles apply to users with Author access to determine which documents they can edit. Users with Editor access or above can edit all documents in the database. Modifier roles are considered a security feature.

Figure 8-15   Your own Person document

Remember that if a user has Reader access, they will not be able to create or modify documents even if you give them Creator or Modifier roles. Roles refine the ACL; they cannot expand it. When you assign the ACL for the Domino Directory, be sure to include these roles for the appropriate users, servers, and groups:

- **GroupCreator**   The GroupCreator role must be added to a user with Author access or above and the Create Documents privilege to give them the ability to create new Groups in the Domino Directory.

- **GroupModifier**   The GroupModifier role must be added to a user with Author access to give them the ability to modify Group documents in the Domino Directory.

- **NetCreator**   The NetCreator role must be added to a user with Author access or above and the Create Documents privilege to give them the ability to create any document in the Domino Directory other than Person, Group, or Server documents. This includes Connection, Configuration, and Program documents, for example.

- **NetModifier**   The NetModifier role must be added to a user with Author access to give them the ability to modify any document in the Domino Directory other than Person, Group, or Server documents.

- **ServerCreator**   The ServerCreator role must be added to a user with Author access or above and the Create Documents privilege to give them the ability to create new Server documents in the Domino Directory.

- **ServerModifier**   The GroupModifier role must be added to a user with Author access to give them the ability to modify Server documents in the Domino Directory.

- **UserCreator**   The UserCreator role must be added to a user with Author access or above and the Create Documents privilege to give them the ability to create new Person documents in the Domino Directory.

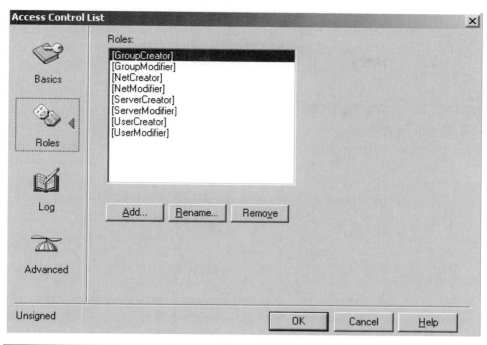

Figure 8-16 Roles in the Domino Directory

- **UserModifier** The UserModifier role must be added to a user with Author access to give them the ability to modify Person documents in the Domino Directory.

You should base the ACL and roles of the Domino Directory on the tasks an administrator needs to perform. If an administrator needs to add users, add groups, and add users to groups, she would need the UserCreator, GroupCreator, and GroupModifier roles. If she also needed to make changes to the users after they were registered, she should also have the UserModifier role. On the other hand, an administrator that dealt mostly with the server, doing tasks such as adding new servers, modifying server configurations, and adding or changing Connection document information would need the ServerCreator, ServerModifier, NetCreator, and NetModifier roles instead. You would not necessarily have to give the administrators that need to perform these tasks Manager access to the Domino Directory if these were the only tasks they needed to perform.

As mentioned above, you can also give users access to specific documents by placing their names in the Owners or Administrators field on a document. For example, users are listed as the owners of their own Person documents, by default, to allow them to modify those documents only. You can put a user's name in the Owner's field of a group they need to maintain, for example, to give them access to that specific group document, without giving them a Modifier role. The user will be able to edit the document, as long as they have Author access to the database.

Domino Directory Profile

Use the Domino Directory Profile document to specify various settings about the Domino Directory. To access the Domino Directory Profile, open the Domino Administrator and choose Actions . . . Edit Directory Profile from the menus. The Domino Directory Profile document, shown in Figure 8-17, is displayed. This document stores default settings for groups and Internet passwords, as well as the file name and path for the Directory Catalog for the domain.

Refer to Table 8-1 for a description of the fields in the Directory Profile document.

Directory Server

The Directory server is the Domino server that provides directory services for the organization. It is usually a dedicated server that does not serve other applications or mail. One benefit of designating a directory server is that it can take some of the work from other servers in the organization, such as mail servers. To use a server as a directory server, place replicas of all secondary directories on the server you want to use as a directory server. You should use the directory server as the repository for all replicas neces-

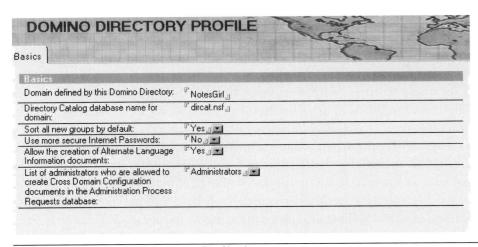

Figure 8-17 Domino Directory Profile document

Table 8-1   Directory Profile

Field	Note
Domain defined by this Domino Directory	Complete this field with the name of the Domino domain that this directory defines. This field should be completed automatically when the Domino server is configured.
Directory Catalog database name for domain	If you have configured a Directory Catalog (described below) for this domain, complete this field with the file name. Note that there should only be one server-based Directory Catalog for a domain and it should have the same file name on every server in the domain on which it resides.
Sort all new groups by default	If you choose Yes, all new groups will have their members sorted in alphabetical order by default. If you choose No, group members will be listed in the order in which they were added to the group.
Use more secure Internet Passwords	If you choose Yes, Domino uses stronger encryption when hashing the Internet Password field in the Person documents in the Domino Directory. This is recommended by Lotus in all environments where all the HTTP (Web) servers are R5.
Allow the creation of Alternate Language Information documents	Choose Yes to allow Alternate Language Information documents to be created in this Domino Directory. These documents allow LDAP clients to search on alternate names.
List of Administrators who are allowed to create Cross Domain Configuration documents in the Administration Process Requests database	As described in Chapter 7, you may need to use AdminP across domains. Use this field to select the names of users, servers, and groups that will be trusted as signers of AdminP requests. If blank, managers of the Domino Directory are assumed to be trusted.

sary to create and populate the Directory Catalog if you are using one in your organization (see "Directory Catalog" later in this chapter). Similarly, you should use the directory server for the replicas of secondary Domino Directories used by Directory Assistance. Finally, LDAP (if in use in your organization) should be configured on the directory server.

Other servers and users must then use the directory server for directory services to realize the benefits. To configure servers to use the directory server, make sure that it contains replicas of all the secondary directories. Then, when configuring Directory Catalog or Directory Assistance (as described later in this chapter), direct those services to look at the directory server for data. For Notes clients, you should configure them to look to the directory server to lookup mail addresses.

You can use the User Setup Profile document to configure Notes clients to refer to a specific directory server, as shown in Figure 8-18. You can also use a Location document to specify a directory server for a Notes workstation.

Note that Notes client will not use the directory server specified for type-ahead mail addressing if a mobile Directory Catalog is in use.

Using Multiple Directories

Earlier, we discussed the fact that you might have multiple directories on a server, including the primary Domino Directory, secondary Domino Directories, and LDAP directories. To use these additional directories for looking up or authenticating users you must use Directory Catalog or Directory Assistance. The main purpose of the Directory Catalog is to ensure that when users perform lookups in primary and secondary Domino Directories, that they are using the smallest, most efficient tool. Directory Assistance works with a Directory Catalog to extend this goal to LDAP directories. In addition, Directory Assistance provides the ability to allow Web authentication to be performed using LDAP and other directories. Bear in mind that the main purpose of the Directory Catalog is fast mail addressing and lookups. You want to ensure that you work with this goal by keeping the Directory Catalog as small and efficient as possible.

Another tool that Domino has provided for similar functions is Cascaded Address books. This is supported in R5 for backward compatibility, although Lotus recommends that you upgrade to the Directory Catalog and Directory Assistance. Cascaded address books require a replica of every address book on every server, with a NOTES.INI line to indicate the order of lookups in primary and secondary address books.

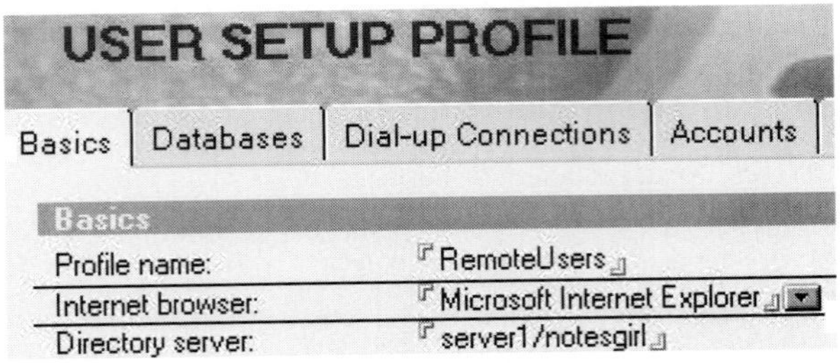

Figure 8-18 Directory Server from a User Setup Profile

Directory Catalog

The Directory Catalog is used to provide fast and efficient lookups by consolidating the users, groups, mail-in databases, and resources from Domino Directories into a single database. The Directory Catalog is a file you create, either on the server or for mobile users, to provide information about users from multiple directories in a small, lightweight database. Server Directory Catalogs provide the ability to combine multiple Domino Directories into a single database to streamline name lookups. Mobile Directory Catalogs provide remote users the ability to address users in multiple directories. A Server Directory Catalog provides these capabilities:

- Mail addressing using names in secondary Domino Directories for Notes users
- Mail addressing using names in secondary Domino Directories for LDAP users
- Web client authentication using credentials in secondary Domino Directories
- Type ahead for addressing

The Mobile Directory Catalog provides these capabilities:

- Mail addressing using names in secondary Domino Directories for Notes users
- Type ahead for addressing

The purpose of a Directory Catalog is to concatenate the mailing information of users from many domains (or contained in many Domino Directories), while remaining small and lightweight. This means that not all fields are contained in the catalog by default (although you can add others needed by your organization). The following list is the fields contained in the Directory Catalog. Note that some fields are used by more than one type of entry (noted next to the field listing), although most are only used by the Person document entry.

- FullName (also used by Mail-In Databases and Resources)
- ListName (only used by Groups)
- Type (also used by Mail-In Databases, Resources, and Groups)
- FirstName
- MiddleInitial
- LastName
- Location

- MailAddress

- ShortName

- MailDomain (also used by Mail-In Databases and Resources)

- InternetAddress (also used by Mail-In Databases and Resources)

- MessageStorage (also used by Mail-In Databases and Resources)

 TIP Note that by default, the Public Key information is not stored in the Directory Catalog. Users that have a mobile Directory Catalog that want to send encrypted mail can still do so—the message is stored in their local mail file unencrypted, but when the user connects to send mail, the recipient's public key is located in the Domino Directory, and the message is encrypted and then transferred to MAIL.BOX.

Configure the Directory Catalog

Before you implement a Directory Catalog, consider which server you should use. Lotus recommends that you create a single Directory Catalog and replicate it to other servers in the organization, rather than creating multiple Directory Catalogs for each domain. For this reason, you may want to use a hub server (if you're in a hub and spoke topology), so that replication to and from other servers is easy to implement. Next, if you plan to add more than one Domino Directory to the Directory Catalog, create local replicas of any additional directories that you want to include in the Directory Catalog. You could force the Directory Catalog to find information from the other Domino Directories, but this is not recommended by Lotus as it will take longer and use additional network bandwidth. If you do place local replicas on the directory server, you should remember to create Connection documents to ensure that the local replicas are updated regularly.

Next, after selecting and preparing the server, you're ready to implement a Directory Catalog. To implement a Directory Catalog in your environment, create a new database using the DIRCAT5.NTF template. Choose File . . . Database . . . New. Store the new Directory Catalog on the directory server. Give the file a title and filename, and base the file on the Directory Catalog template.

After you create the new Directory Catalog database, create the Directory Catalog Configuration document. Open the new Directory Catalog database and choose Create . . . Configuration. If the catalog already exists, you can edit the Configuration document by opening the Configuration view. In the Configuration document, specify the following information:

- **Directories to include in the Directory Catalog** These will all be Domino Directories but can be from different domains. This can be a local directory or a remote directory in either a mapped drive (such as y:\directories\directory.nsf) or over the network through Domino (such as portname !!! servername !!! filename).

- **Fields to include in the catalog** The fields described above are listed here automatically, but if you want to allow Web users to authenticate directly from the Directory Catalog, you should add the HTTPPassword field. You may also want to add the Members field to allow for group expansion on Directory Catalogs for use on servers. In addition, even if the servers don't use alternate languages, Lotus recommends that you add the AltFullName and AltFullNameLanguage fields.

- **What to sort on** You can choose to sort by *Distinguished Name, Last name*, or *Alternate Full Name*.

- **Whether to use Soundex** Soundex allows searching by phonetic spelling. The downside of allowing Soundex is that it increases the size of the Directory Catalog by 4 bytes for each entry. Since the purpose of the Directory Catalog is to be small and lightweight, this can be a bad choice.

- **Allow or remove duplicate users** If you suspect you may have duplicate user names among the directories being added to the Directory Catalog, you should choose whether users would be prompted to select the correct user or whether the DIRCAT task should remove duplicate entries.

- **Group types to include** Default in this field is Mail and Multipurpose (the recommended setting), although other choices include *All, All in First Directory Only*, and *None*.

- **Restrict Aggregation to this server** Use this field to restrict which server can update the Directory Catalog to the server or servers you select (the directory server). That server (or servers) must run the DIRCAT task.

- **Send Directory Catalog Reports to** Indicate a user that should receive Directory Catalog reports and information.

These fields are shown in Figure 8-19.

In addition, you may choose to customize the aggregation settings on the Advanced tab, shown in Figure 8-20. To understand these settings, you first need to understand that the Directory Catalog stores information from multiple documents in a single document and single field in the Directory Catalog. Each field in an aggregate document stores the field values from up to 255 entries from the source Domino Directories. That means, for example, that the FullName field in an aggregate document contains the

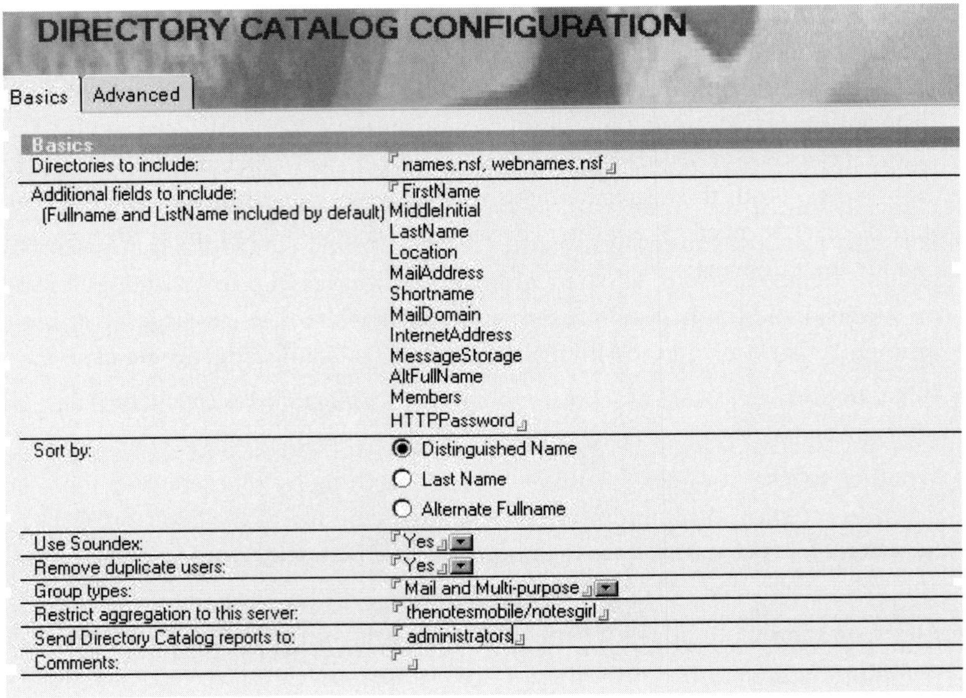

Figure 8-19 Directory Catalog Configuration

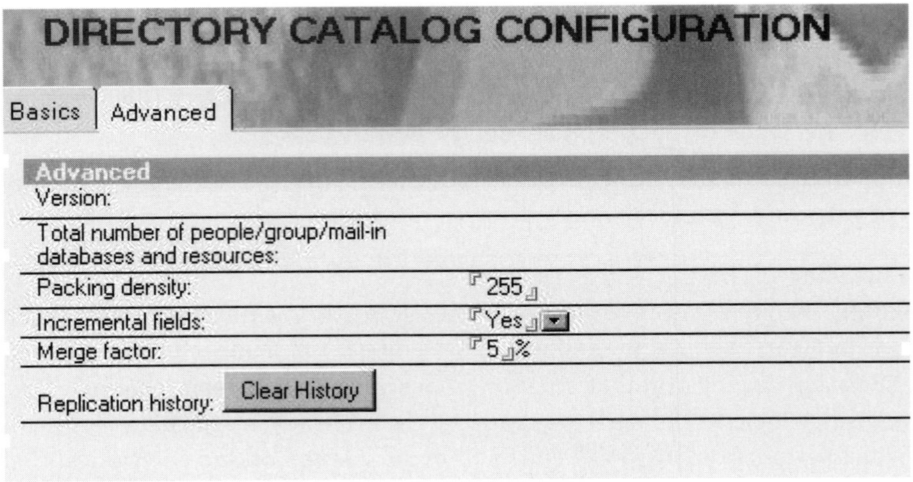

Figure 8-20 Directory Catalog Advanced Configuration

FullName data from up to 255 entries from the source Domino Directories. As changes are made in the source directories, the document changes, so the Directory Catalog has to replicate. That number (255) is the packing density. You can control this as part of the Advanced settings. In addition, to limit the replications, Domino stores the changes in temporary fields until 5 percent of the fields change. Then, the temporary fields are randomly merged with the aggregate fields so that at any one time, only a few of the aggregate documents need to replicate. The settings available to customize the aggregation include the following:

- **Packing Density**   The default is 255. If you decrease the packing density, the Directory Catalog grows in size.

- **Incremental Fields**   Choose *Yes* to store changes in temporary fields or choose No to make changes to aggregate fields immediately. Yes is the default.

- **Merge Factor**   This is 5 percent by default. Lotus recommends that you do not change this setting. This is the field that configures the number of fields that must have changed before the aggregate fields are updated.

- **Replication History**   This field shows the last time the aggregator pulled information from the source directories. You can click the *Clear History* button to force Domino to re-aggregate.

In addition, you must then run the DIRCAT task on the server to build the catalog. If you type **LOAD DIRCAT** *DIRCAT.NSF*, the server starts the DIRCAT task and builds or synchronizes the Directory Catalog. The DIRCAT task should run regularly to add any changes from the Domino Directories to the Directory Catalog. Use the Server Tasks . . . Directory Cataloger tab in the Server document to configure how DIRCAT will run, as shown in Figure 8-21. Use this tab to indicate the name of the Directory Catalog and the schedule on which the DIRCAT task will run.

Before the Directory Catalog will be used, you must include the catalog's name in the Directory Profile or in the Server document. An entry in the Server document (on the Basics tab) takes precedence over the entry in the Directory Profile. You can create replicas of the Directory Catalog on other servers (inside and outside the current domain). Make sure that you replicate these frequently with the source Directory Catalog to keep the changes current. Do not run the DIRCAT task on these replicas, as you will get replication conflicts. Only run the DIRCAT task to maintain the source Directory Catalog.

Users that are disconnected from the network benefit from using a Mobile Directory Catalog for quick mail addressing and type ahead even when disconnected from the network. You should not use the same source Directory Catalog for server and mobile use—create two separate catalogs. To allow users to take advantage of the Mobile

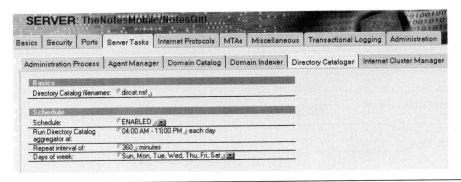

Figure 8-21   Directory Cataloger task in the Server document

Directory Catalog, they must have a replica on their Notes workstations. You can use a User Setup Profile to create a replica for them, by adding a database link to the *Mobile Directory Catalogs* field, as shown in Figure 8-22. They also need the name of the Directory Catalog added to their user mail preferences. If you use the User Setup Profile, it will be added automatically. If not, users will have to create the replica and list the name in their preferences manually.

Directory Assistance

Directory Assistance manages lookups in both multiple Domino Directories and in LDAP directories. Directory Assistance provides these capabilities:

- Mail addressing using names in secondary Domino Directories for Notes users
- Mail addressing using names in secondary Domino Directories for LDAP users
- Mail addressing using names in Domino or third-party LDAP directories for Notes users
- Mail addressing using names in Domino or third-party LDAP directories for LDAP users
- Web client authentication using credentials in secondary Domino Directories
- Web client authentication using credentials in third-party LDAP directories
- Type ahead for addressing

To enable Directory Assistance, you create the Directory Assistance database. Choose File . . . Database . . . New. Place the database on a server, preferably the directory server.

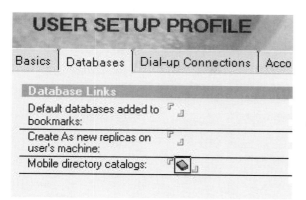

Figure 8-22   User Setup Profile to set up a Mobile Directory Catalog

Give the server a title and filename, and base it on the Directory Assistance (DA50.NTF) template. After you create the database, open the database to create Directory Assistance documents for each secondary Domino Directory, as shown in Figure 8-23.

You can use the Add Directory Assistance action button or choose Create . . . Directory Assistance from the menus. Use the Basics tab to choose whether you're configuring for a Notes or LDAP domain and then type in the domain name. In the Search Order field, you can add a number to determine the order this directory would be searched in relation to the directories represented by other documents in the Directory Assistance database. Finally, choose whether Directory Assistance is enabled for the directory represented by the document. Next, use the Rules tab to set organizational hierarchies that are trusted for authentication—if a user does not match one of these rules, they cannot be authenticated using the Directory Assistance. For each rule, indicate either an asterisk for each component or the name of the component, as shown in Figure 8-24. If you're creating Directory Assistance for a secondary Domino Directory, the third tab is the Replicas tab. On the Replicas tab, you can either add Database links to the secondary directories or indicate the server and filename to allow Domino to find the directory replicas. If you're creating Directory Assistance for an LDAP directory, the third tab is the LDAP tab. Complete the following fields on the LDAP tab:

- **Hostname**   Type the hostname for the LDAP host server.

- **Authentication credential**   Type the name and password necessary for authentication in the LDAP directory. Type the username in distinguished format, as it would be stored in the LDAP directory.

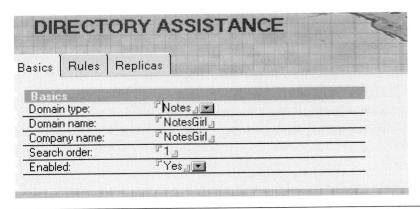

Figure 8-23   Create a Directory Assistance document

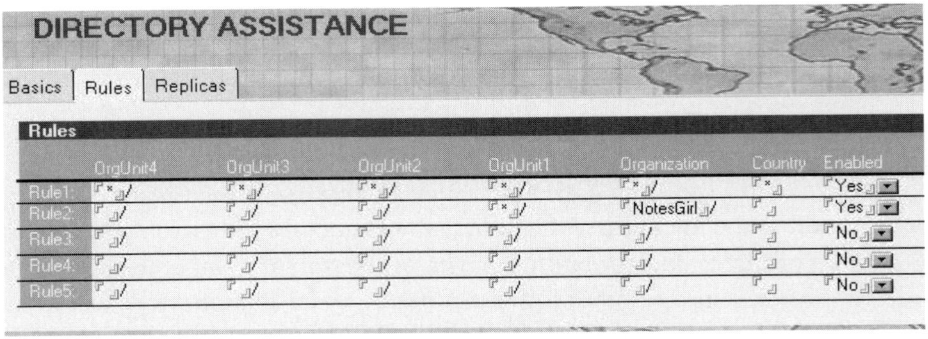

Figure 8-24   Directory Assistance Rules

- **Base DN for search**   Type the component or level that represents the search base.
- **Perform LDAP search for**   You can choose to perform LDAP searches for Notes Clients/Web Authentication and for LDAP clients.
- **Channel encryption**   You can choose SSL, to encrypt the connection between Domino and the LDAP server, or None.
- **Port**   If you chose SSL, the port should be 636; if you chose None, the port is 389.
- If you chose SSL, configure settings for SSL certificates and versions.
- **Timeout**   The default is 60 seconds until a search is terminated.
- **Maximum number of entries returned**   The default maximum number of entries is 100.

After you create the Directory Assistance database, you must identify the database to the servers that will use it. To identify the Directory Assistance database to the servers, select the Server documents for the servers in the Domino Administrator configuration tab. Then select Actions . . . Set Directory Assistance Information. Domino displays the Directory Assistance dialog box. Type the path and name of the Directory Assistance database. This creates an Administration Process (AdminP) request to Set Directory Assistance fields. Verify that the request is processed correctly by checking the Administration Requests database.

LDAP

LDAP stands for Lightweight Directory Access Protocol. This TCP/IP protocol allows clients to access a directory, as well as a standard directory infrastructure for that directory. The LDAP directory has entries that are defined by attributes; they are similar to the attributes you're familiar with in the Domino organizational hierarchy. Domino and Notes provide LDAP server and LDAP client capabilities. To allow LDAP clients and applications (including Notes R5 clients or MS Outlook Express clients) to search the Domino Directory, start the LDAP task on the server. You can choose to enable LDAP during server configuration or you can add the server task later. The LDAP service provides the following abilities to the Domino environment:

- Allow LDAP searches on secondary Domino Directories, using Directory Catalog and Directory Assistance
- Refer LDAP clients to other LDAP directories, using Directory Assistance
- Allow LDAP clients to add, edit, and delete entries in the directory
- Extend the LDAP schema (attributes)
- Search based on alternate languages

After starting the LDAP task, you must also ensure that the Domino Directory has a full-text index. To full-text index the Domino Directory, select the Domino Directory from the Files tab in the Domino Administrator. Right-click the file name and select Full Text Index from the shortcut menu. In the Full Text Index dialog box (shown in Figure 8-25), choose to create the full text index and how it should be updated.

If the organization uses multiple Global Domain documents, you must specify one of the documents to be the one that the LDAP service uses to put together and return Internet addresses to LDAP clients. In the Global Domain document, enable the Use as default Global domain field. Next, you may choose to use LDAP with Directory Assistance by configuring a Directory Assistance document that can search other LDAP servers. Finally, you must configure the LDAP clients to connect to the LDAP server on the Domino server.

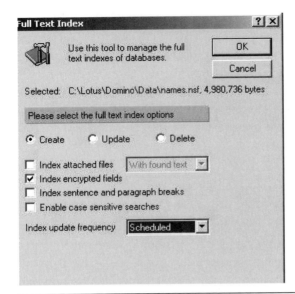

Figure 8-25 Create a Full Text Index

You may want to customize the LDAP settings on the Domino server. On the Configuration tab in Domino Administrator, expand the Directory section and choose the Directory Settings document. By default, Anonymous (non-authenticated) users can query the fields listed in the *Anonymous Users Can Query* field, shown in Figure 8-26. You can add or remove fields from this list.

Other fields in the LDAP settings are listed in Table 8-2.

Notes users in your environment can access Domino and third-party LDAP directories using an Account document in the personal name and address book on the their workstation. You can add an account for a user by completing a User Setup Profile, as shown in Figure 8-27.

Directory Summary

To compare the purposes of Directory Assistance and the Directory Catalog, refer to Table 8-3. The tasks that users and servers can perform using these tools are compared in this table.

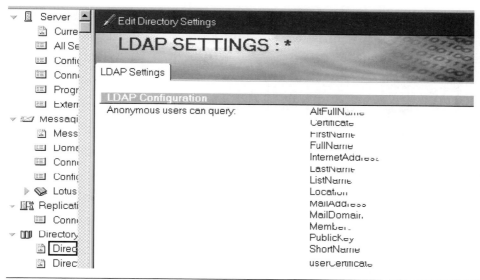

Figure 8-26 Anonymous LDAP users can query these fields

Table 8-2 LDAP Settings

Field	Notes
Allow LDAP users write access	Set this field to Yes to allow LDAP clients to add, edit, or delete documents in the Domino Directory. Note that the clients must also have the proper access in the ACL, as well as the necessary roles or privileges. The LDAP clients should be authenticated before enabling this option.
Timeout	This is the number of seconds an LDAP search can continue.
Maximum number of entries returned	A single LDAP search can only return this number of entries.
Minimum characters for wildcard search	You can specify the minimum number of characters a user must provide before using a wildcard to extend the search. If your LDAP server performance is slow, you might increase this number.
Allow Alternate Language Information Processing	Enable this field to allow LDAP clients to complete transactions (search, read, edit, add, delete) that specify Alternate Language information.
Rules to follow when this directory is the primary directory and there are multiple matches on the distinguished name being compared/modified.	Choices include Don't modify any, Modify first match, and Modify all matches.

Table 8-3 Directory Task Comparison

Task	Directory Assistance	Mobile Directory Catalog	Server Directory Catalog	Cascading Address Books
Perform address lookups in secondary Domino Directories for Notes mail users	Yes	Yes	Yes	Yes
Perform address lookups in LDAP directories for Notes mail users	Yes	No	No	No
Perform address lookups in secondary Domino Directories for LDAP clients	Yes	No	Yes	Yes
Refer LDAP queries to other LDAP directories	Yes	No	No	No
Allow Web clients to be authenticated in secondary Domino Directories	Yes	No	Yes	No
Allow Web clients to be authenticated in LDAP directories	Yes	No	No	No
Perform recipient type-ahead	Yes	Yes	Yes (unless clients have a mobile Directory Catalog)	Yes

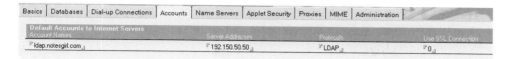

Figure 8-27   User Setup Profile to add an account

Summary

The first and most important database that Domino creates to define its domain is the Domino Directory. The first Domino Directory created in a domain is the primary Domino Directory and is called NAMES.NSF. As you register users, servers, and certifiers, Domino creates documents for these in the primary Domino Directory. You must configure replication for the Domino Directory carefully, to ensure that all the servers in the domain contain the same information. In addition, you must configure the additional security for the Domino Directory contained in the Roles.

In many cases, it is to your advantage to use multiple directories in the Domino environment. To use multiple directories, you can configure Directory Catalogs or Directory Assistance. Lotus recommends that you configure both. You can configure either a server or mobile Directory Catalog. The main purpose of the Directory Catalog is to provide fast and lightweight lookups in either the primary or secondary Domino Directories. You can also configure Directory Assistance. Directory Assistance provides additional lookups in LDAP directories as well as secondary Domino Directories. You may also choose to configure Domino to provide LDAP services to LDAP clients such as Notes clients and Outlook clients.

Review Questions

1. What is the default level of access of the users in your environment to the Domino Directory?
    A. Reader
    B. Author
    C. Editor
    D. No Access

2. What enables users to change their own Person documents in the Domino Directory by default?

 A. Editor access to the Domino Directory.

 B. Owner field in the Person document.

 C. UserModifierRole.

 D. Users do not have this ability by default.

3. Which of the following is considered a security feature of the Domino Directory?

 A. Creator roles

 B. Modifier roles

4. JP is trying to ensure that the Directory Catalog contains the newest changes from the secondary catalogs. What might he need to do?

 A. TELL DIRCAT RELOAD DIRCAT.NSF

 B. TELL DIRCAT REBUILD DIRCAT.NSF

 C. LOAD DIRCAT DIRCAT.NSF -RELOAD

 D. LOAD DIRCAT DIRCAT.NSF

5. Which of the following fields is not in the Directory Catalog by default?

 A. AltFullName

 B. FullName

 C. MailAddress

 D. HTTPPassword

6. Which of the following is true about groups in the Directory Catalog?

 A. The Members field is automatically included in the Directory Catalog to allow for group expansion.

 B. All group types are automatically included in the Directory Catalog.

 C. You can only include groups from the primary Domino Directory in the Directory Catalog.

 D. Mail and MultiPurpose groups are the default group types included in the Domino Directory.

7. Which of the following can a server Directory Catalog do?

 A. Provide type ahead addressing to users

 B. Provide Web client authentication

 C. Provide mail addressing for LDAP users

 D. Provide mail addressing for Notes users

8. Which of the following can Directory Assistance do?
    A. Provide type ahead addressing to users
    B. Provide Web client authentication using Domino or LDAP directories for cre-
        dentials
    C. Provide mail addressing for LDAP users
    D. Provide mail addressing for Notes users

9. True or False: By default, LDAP users must authenticate to perform LDAP searches
    on a Domino Directory.
    A. True
    B. False

10. Which of the following is true about Directory Catalog?
    A. You should run the DIRCAT task on every server you want to have a Directory
        Catalog on.
    B. You should use replication to update the Directory Catalog on other servers
        rather than the DIRCAT task.
    C. All users, including those with mobile Directory Catalogs, will use the Server
        Directory Catalog for type ahead.
    D. Only users without Mobile Directory Catalogs will use the Server Directory
        Catalog for type ahead.

Review Answers

1. **B is correct.**   Users have Author access to the Domino Directory by default.

2. **B is correct.**   With Author access and their names in the Owner field of the Per-
    son document, users have access to modify their own Person documents.

3. **B is correct.**   Modifier roles are considered a security feature, but Creator roles
    are not.

4. **D is correct.**   Simply load the DIRCAT task. Be sure to tell the DIRCAT task to
    quit if it's already running.

5. **A and D are correct.**   You may choose to add the AltFullName and HTTPPass-
    word fields to the Directory Catalog.

6. **D** is correct.   The Mail and Multipurpose group types are included automatically.

7. **A, B,** and **D** are correct.

8. **All** are correct.

9. **B** is correct.   Anonymous LDAP is enabled by default.

10. **B** and **D** are correct.

CHAPTER 9

Mobile and Remote

You should be able to answer questions based on the following objectives after reading this chapter:

- Setting up servers for different functions (mobile user connectivity: pass thru)
- Setting up workstations for different locations (mobile)
- Setting up/configuring server access (passthru)

When configuring servers and clients, you must consider the mobile and remote users. To provide for these types of users, you can configure servers to allow dial-in, remote access, and passthru services. When you configure these elements on a server, you must also configure the client machines for remote or disconnected use.

Remote Connections

A client (or workstation) can connect to a Domino server in various ways. If the client is local, it will connect via a local area network (LAN) or perhaps a wide area network (WAN). If the client is mobile or remote (there is no server at the same location as the client), the client can connect remotely using Notes direct dial-up, Network dial-up, or passthru. These same options are available for remote servers connecting when there is no LAN or WAN connection.

When a client connects using Notes direct dial-up, the modem responds directly to commands from the Notes client, rather than from an external program. This connection uses the X.PC protocol to make the modem connections. This type of connection is also useful for servers that do not have a LAN or WAN connection. With this connection, the Notes client and Domino server both need modems. This connection type uses Domino security, which is somewhat tighter than the security offered by most network dial-up connections.

A client can also connect via a Network dial-up connection. With this type of connection, the client and server use a remote access connection and a network protocol instead of the X.PC protocol. With this type of connection, clients can use not only Domino services, but also other network services. An example of this type of remote access or remote LAN connection is Microsoft Remote Access Service (RAS). RAS and some other remote access services also allow clients to use connections such as ISDN. Other remote access protocols that Domino supports include AppleTalk Remote Access and Microsoft Dial-up Networking (DUN).

When clients connect via passthru, they connect to their destination server using an intermediate server, known as the passthru server. Usually the client and the destination server do not share a common protocol. You can also use a hunt group with passthru. A hunt group allows one phone number to be answered by multiple modems.

Any of these connection types can connect servers to servers or clients to servers. In either case, you need to consider the server topology, ensure the communications ports are configured and functioning, and ensure that the appropriate protocols are configured and functioning. For more information on configuring ports and protocols, refer to Chapter 6. The most complicated type of remote access to configure is passthru access. This type of connection requires you to configure more documents for both the client and server.

Configuring Passthru

Passthru allows users to connect to multiple servers through a single dial-up or Internet connection. In the past, when users dialed in to their Domino servers, they had to make a separate phone call for each server that had databases that they needed. With passthru, however, the users can make one call and connect to any server that is set up to be accessed through the server they dial. It makes a single server available as a "gateway" to other Notes servers.

To understand the benefits of server passthru, imagine that you are on a business trip to a city in which your company has a remote office. When you get to the hotel in the evening, you want to check your mail. Instead of making the long-distance call to your home office, however, you want to call the local office, as shown in the diagram in Figure 9-1. This is an ideal use of remote passthru.

To use passthru in this example, the user would use dial-up to connect to the server at the local office. That server would act as a stepping-stone to the mail server and the database server in the home office. The connection between the local office server and your

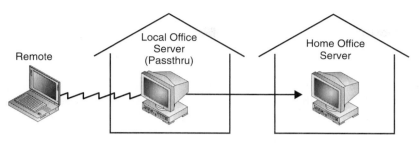

Figure 9-1 Passthru example

home office servers can be made in a variety of ways, including dial-up and LAN/WAN connection. Either way, the end-user only has to make one call or connection.

Another passthru example would be a situation where you only wanted to configure one server with modems. If you configured that server as a passthru server as well, users could dial in to the single server and then access the mail and application servers as necessary. Finally, you can configure passthru in a situation where the client machines do not share a protocol with the server they're trying to reach.

To configure passthru, you must create or edit some of a variety of documents, including Location, Connection, Server Connection, and passthru Server documents. The paragraphs below examine each of these documents in more detail.

You should create a Location document in the user's Personal Name and Address Book that specifies the default passthru server. The user's NAB has a set of Location documents that specify information about how the user works in that location. A typical Location document, for example, specifies information such as how the user connects to the Domino server (e.g., Local Area Network, Dial-Up Modem, or No Connection), how the user accesses and uses the Internet, where the user gets their mail, what the user's replication schedule is, and what the user's default passthru server is. If you used a User Setup Profile when creating this user, some of this information will be completed when the user is configured. If you did not use a User Setup Profile, the default Location documents (Home, Internet, Island, Office, and Travel) exist, but will need to be completed with the additional information necessary for passthru, as shown in Figure 9-2. You should configure the Servers tab with the name of the default Passthru server in this situation.

You can also use a User Setup Profile to configure the passthru information after the user is already configured. To configure the default passthru server using the User Setup Profile, complete the Default Passthru Server name and dialing information on the Dial-up Connections tab, as shown in Figure 9-3.

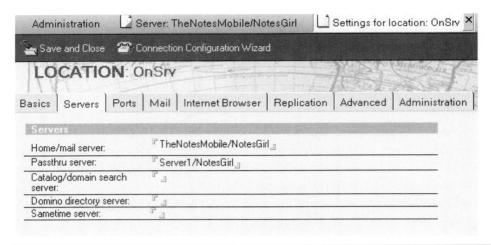

Figure 9-2 Location document with Passthru data

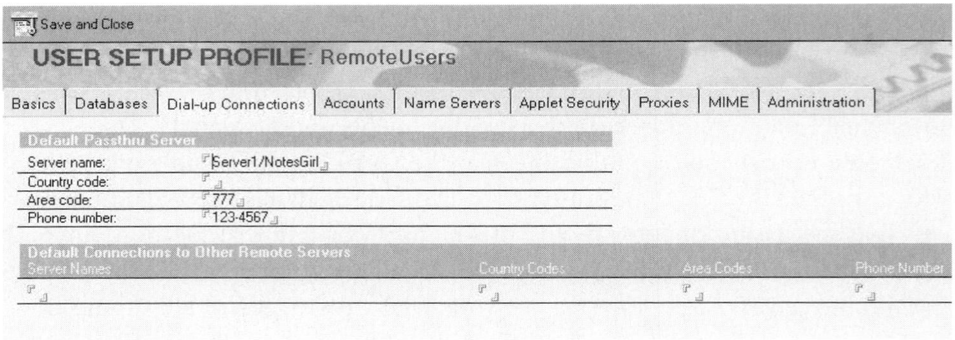

Figure 9-3 User Setup Profile Passthru information

If the user always contacts Server1/NotesGirl as the passthru server, for example, you could place this server name in the default passthru server field for all Locations. On the other hand, if the user contacts different passthru servers based on location, you can customize this information in each Location document.

You may need to create a Connection document in the user's Personal Name and Address Book that specifies the path to the passthru server. If you used the User Setup Profile to designate a default passthru server, Notes automatically creates a Dial-up Modem Connection document specifying the route to the passthru server. If you did not use a User Setup Profile, however, you must manually create a Connection document in the user's Personal NAB that designates a route to the passthru server.

This is not necessary if the user has a direct LAN connection to their passthru server. An example of a user's Connection document specifying the route to the passthru server is shown in Figure 9-4.

You may need to create a Connection document in the user's Personal Name and Address Book, specifying any other passthru server other than the default. If the user will access a passthru server that is different than the passthru server designated in their Location document, an additional Connection document is necessary in their Personal Name and Address book specifying the passthru server to use.

You also have the option to create additional Location documents in the user's Personal Name and Address Book, specifying alternative default passthru servers. As an alternative to creating additional Connection documents for different passthru servers, you can create additional Location documents that specify different passthru servers. This may be the best option if the alternate passthru servers are used with specific locations.

You will create Server Connection documents for the passthru server in the Public Name and Address Book, specifying the route from the passthru server to the destination servers. The passthru server must have a route to the destination server. This route should be specified in a Server Connection document, as shown in Figure 9-5.

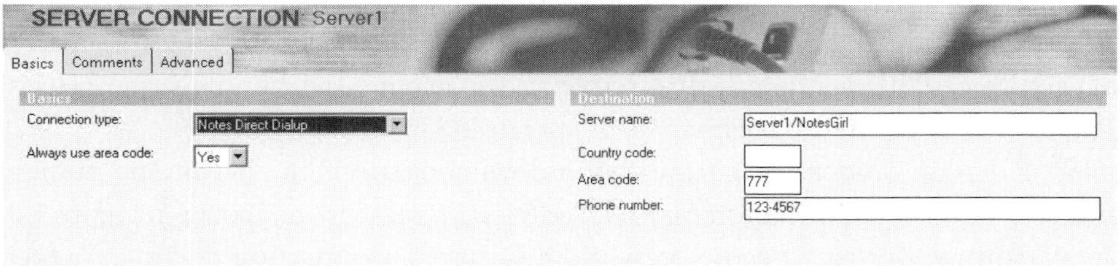

Figure 9-4   Connection document passthru information

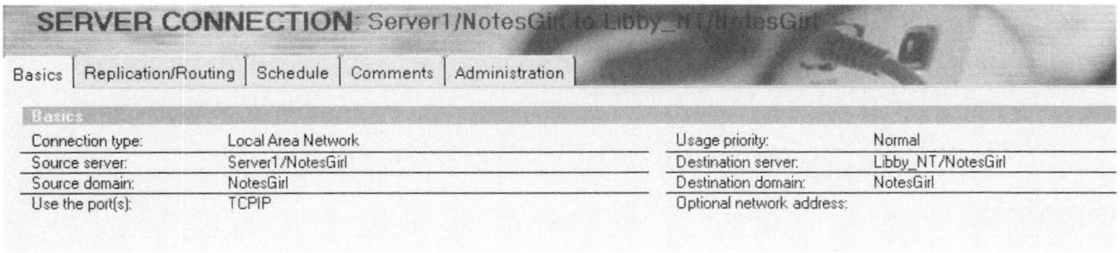

Figure 9-5   Connection document between the passthru and the destination server

To ensure the proper access, you must edit the Server document on the passthru server to allow passthru connections. Each server that will participate in passthru must allow passthru using the fields in the Passthru use section of the Security tab on the Server document, as shown in Figure 9-6.

For the restrictions in the Server document, the passthru server itself must list the users that can force it to call the destination servers in the Route through and Cause Calling fields. If a user is not listed in these fields, they cannot use this server for passthru. The *Destinations Allowed* field must also contain the names of all destination servers that this passthru server can be used to contact. If you leave this field blank, all destinations are allowed.

You will edit the Server documents for any destination servers to allow them to be accessed via passthru. Figure 9-6 shows a Server document for a server that is being accessed using passthru. In this case, the *Access this server field* is completed to show the users and servers that can access this server through passthru. If this field is blank, no users or server can access this server using passthru. Remember, this is the final destination server.

To use the passthru example described below, where a user on the road wanted to connect to his far away home server via a local office server, you would create the following documents (assuming that the user did not have the remote office's server as their default):

Create a passthru type Connection document specifying the remote server (SanDiego/NotesGirl) as the passthru server and specifying their home server (Houston/NotesGirl) as the destination server, as shown in Figure 9-7.

Create a dial-up modem type Connection document specifying the phone number and other connection information to reach SanDiego/NotesGirl, as shown in Figure 9-8.

The passthru server, SanDiego/NotesGirl, must have a Connection document specifying its route to Houston/NotesGirl, as shown in Figure 9-9.

SanDiego/NotesGirl must allow the user to use it for passthru, by adding the user (or group) to the fields in the Security tab of the Server document, as shown in Figure 9-10. In addition, Houston/NotesGirl must be an allowed destination.

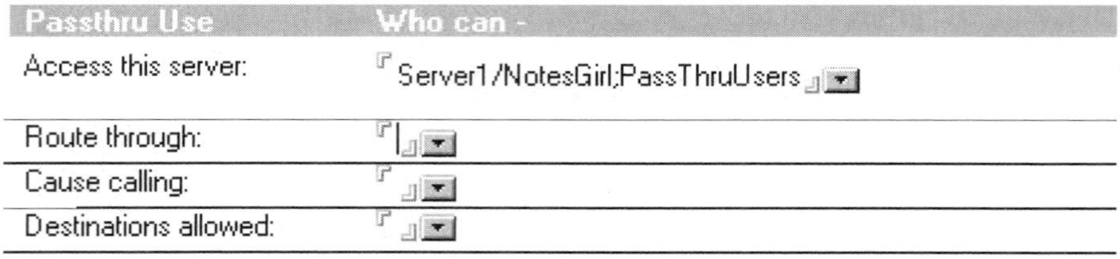

Passthru Use	Who can -
Access this server:	Server1/NotesGirl;PassThruUsers
Route through:	
Cause calling:	
Destinations allowed:	

Figure 9-6   Passthru restrictions in the server document

Figure 9-7   Passthru Connection document sample

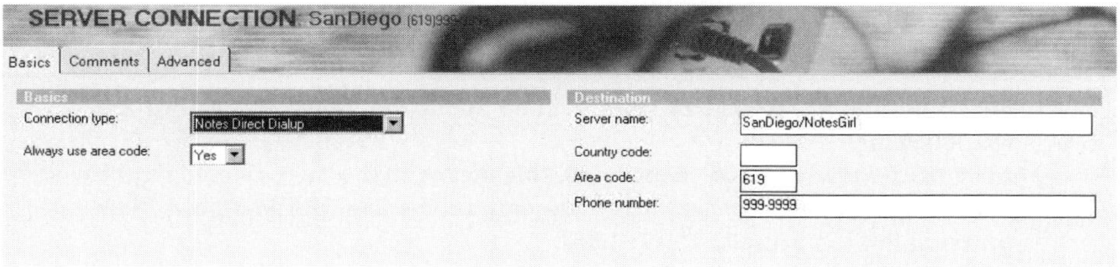

Figure 9-8   Connection document between client and remote server

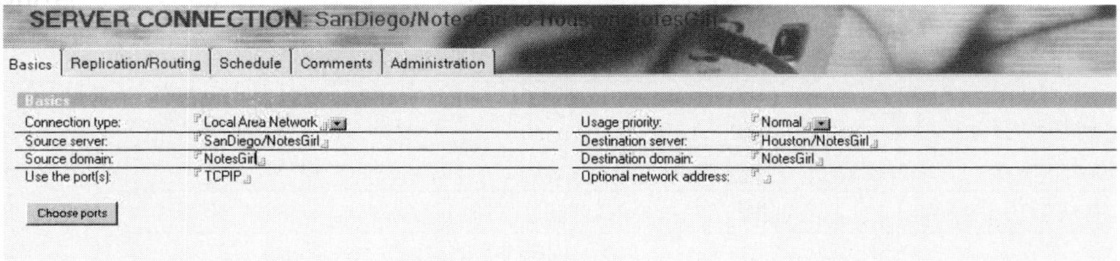

Figure 9-9   Connection document from passthru to destination

Figure 9-10
Passthru restrictions
on SanDiego/
NotesGirl

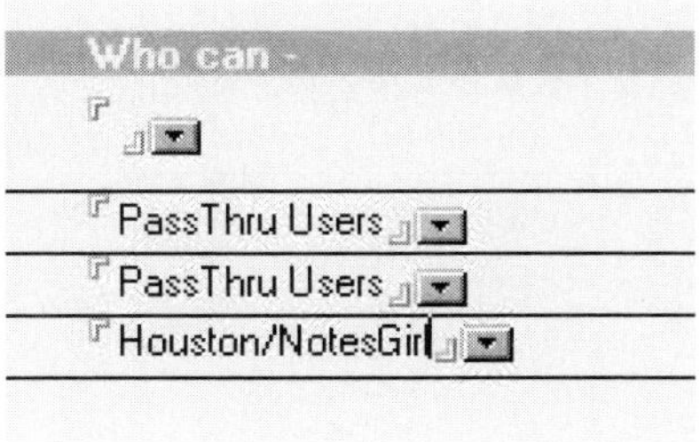

Finally, Houston/NotesGirl must allow access by the user and the passthru server (SanDiego/NotesGirl) in its Server document, as shown in Figure 9-11.

An additional use of passthru is in a scenario when servers have different protocols. If a user that uses TCP/IP needs to access a server that uses SPX, he cannot do so directly. If, however, another server in the organization that uses both TCP/IP and SPX is configured as his default passthru server, he can reach his destination server easily. One of the benefits of using passthru in this situation is that the database that the user is trying to access does not need to be on the passthru server. Since the passthru server is only acting as a "gateway" or stepping stone, the database only needs to reside on the ultimate destination, as shown in Figure 9-12.

TIP A few final warnings to keep in mind about the limits of passthru are the following:

The hard-coded limit for hops is 10. This means that a user cannot go through more than ten passthru servers on the way to the final destination. A more practical limit is actually 2 or 3 hops.

Passthru Use	Who can -
Access this server:	SanDiego/NotesGirl, PassThru Users
Route through:	
Cause calling:	
Destinations allowed:	

Figure 9-11 Destination server's passthru information

Figure 9-12
Using passthru for
protocol issues

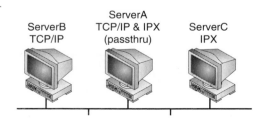

Summary

Users and servers can connect to remote Domino servers directly via modems, through other remote access services such as Microsoft RAS, or using intermediary servers called passthru servers. When you connect users or servers via modems, they use the X.PC protocol to connect directly from Notes client to Domino server or between two Domino servers. When you connect using other remote access services, called Network dialup, users or servers connect first using the remote service and then to the Domino server as though they were on the same LAN. This connection uses a network protocol to the Domino server rather than the X.PC protocol. When you connect to the destination server using passthru, a variety of documents must be created or edited, including Location, Connection, and Server documents.

Review Questions

1. Which of the following remote connection types uses X.PC?
   A. Notes Direct Dial up
   B. Hunt Group
   C. Passthru
   D. Network Dial up

2. With which type of connection does the Notes client and the Domino server both require modems physically attached?
   A. Notes Direct Dial up
   B. Hunt Group
   C. Passthru
   D. Network Dial up

3. Which of the following is not an example of a remote access connection type available in Domino?
   A. Microsoft RAS
   B. Microsoft DUN
   C. Microsoft ISDN
   D. AppleTalk Remote Access

4. Which of the following allows multiple modems to answer calls to a single phone number?

   A. ISDN
   B. Passthru
   C. Hunt groups
   D. RAS

5. Which of the following is not a reason to use a passthru server?

   A. The client machine and the destination server machine do not share a common protocol.
   B. The destination server machine does not have a modem connection to accept dial-up access.
   C. A remote user wants to dial-in to a single server to gain access to multiple Domino servers.
   D. A remote user wants to dial in using Microsoft RAS.

6. To provide for a user to access a default passthru server, which documents would you not need to edit or create?

   A. Location document defining the default passthru server
   B. Connection document between the passthru server and the destination server
   C. Connection document between the client and the destination server, defining the passthru server
   D. Connection document between the client and the passthru server

7. Joe Smith/SmithCo has a Location document that specifies Orange/SmithCo as his default passthru server. Orange/SmithCo has a Connection document to Yellow/SmithCo, Joe's mail server. Yellow/SmithCo allows Joe and Orange to access it via passthru. If Joe wants to read his mail by connecting to Orange, what else do you need to create or edit?

   A. Create a Connection document for Joe to access Yellow via Orange.
   B. Create a Connection document for Joe defining how he accesses Orange.
   C. Edit Orange's Server document to allow Joe to route through for passthru.
   D. Edit Yellow's Server document to allow Joe to route through for passthru.

8. Joe now needs to use Blue as his passthru server instead of Orange. What does he need to create?

   A. Connection document specifying how to access Blue.
   B. Connection document specifying Blue is the passthru server to access Yellow.
   C. Connection between Blue and Yellow.
   D. Edit Yellow's Server document to allow access by Blue.

Review Answers

1. **A is correct.**   Notes Direct Dial up uses the X.PC protocol.

2. **A is correct.**   Notes Direct Dial up requires that both the client and the server have modems directly attached.

3. **C is correct.**   You can use RAS, DUN, and AppleTalk Remote Access as remote access connection types available in Domino.

4. **C is correct.**   You can use a hunt group to allow multiple modems to answer a single phone number.

5. **D is correct.**   You would use a Network Dial-up connection to allow a user to dial-in via Microsoft RAS.

6. **C is correct.**   It is not necessary to define the connection between the client and the destination server if there is a default passthru server.

7. **B and C are both necessary.**   You do not need to define Joe's connection to Yellow, as he has a default Connection document. You do need to define how Joe will connect to Orange and you need to provide for Joe to access Yellow via Orange in Orange's Server document.

8. **A, B, C, and D are all correct.**

Configuring Domino Security

You should be able to answer questions based on the following objectives after reading this chapter:

- Setting up/configuring Domino Infrastructure Security
- Setting up authentication
- Setting up/configuring agent access
- Setting up/configuring database access (ACLs, user types, privileges, roles)
- Setting up/configuring file security
- Setting up/configuring server access (Server, domain)
- Setting up/configuring user access (administrator, Internet)

One of the most important elements in configuring your Notes environment is security. It will be important for administrators to understand the levels of security that are available, as well as how and when to implement those levels of security. In addition, certain elements of your Notes environment have additional security components, such as the ID files, the Domino Directory, and messaging. The key to unlocking the secured elements of a Domino and Notes environment is a user's name and identity, stored in the ID file, or in the Person document (for Web users). This chapter describes the user ID and how to use it to gain access to the Notes environment via authentication. In addition, we discuss the levels of security in Notes, from access to the server to access to the forms and views in databases. Finally, we describe the additional security elements that can be applied to certain facets of the Notes and Web environment.

Domino Server and User ID Files

The Domino Server and User ID files contain all the information that a server or user needs to access and pass through the various levels of Notes security. Without an ID, however, they cannot access Domino servers or databases. This clearly important file contains its own security elements. In Chapter 6, we discussed creating an ID for a new user or server with the registration process. Let's build on that knowledge by describing the elements that are contained in the ID file and how it is protected.

Components of the Notes ID

The Notes ID file for a user or server contains all the information necessary to identify a Notes user or server to the Notes environment. This includes not only the user's name, but also the following additional information, as shown in Figure 10-1:

- **User Name**   The common name of the Notes user is stored in the ID file.

- **User Notes License type**   When a user is created, the administrator assigns a type of license, either North American or International. The type of license cannot be changed after the ID is created.

- **Public and private keys**   The keys are randomly generated hexadecimal numbers that uniquely identify the user. The keys contain an element of the key of the certifier that was used to register the user. The keys are used in authentication, encryption, and signing. The public key is also stored in the user's Person document in the Domino Directory. The public key and private key are a mathematically-related pair.

- **Encryption keys**   Encryption keys are secret keys generated by you or another user that allow you to encrypt and decrypt fields on a form. This is an optional element of the Notes ID file.

- **Certificates**   The original certificate granted to a hierarchical ID is stored in the ID file. Any additional certificates are stored in the Domino Directory. If the ID file is flat, all certificates are stored in the ID file. Also, any flat certificates given to a hierarchical user are stored in the ID file.

- **Password**   Each ID file can contain a password for the protection of the ID file itself.

When the user or server ID is registered using the Domino Administrator client, you can choose where to store the ID file. You can store the ID file in the Domino Directory

Figure 10-1
Notes ID file

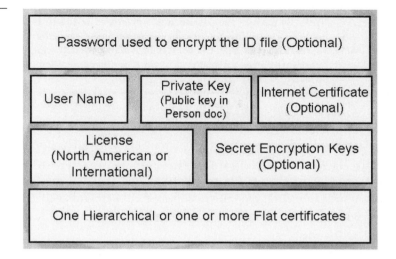

Password used to encrypt the ID file (Optional)

User Name

Private Key
(Public key in
Person doc)

Internet Certificate
(Optional)

License
(North American or
International)

Secret Encryption Keys
(Optional)

One Hierarchical or one or more Flat certificates

if the ID file has a password. You can also store the ID file separately in a directory that you configure. By default, Domino will create an IDs directory under the local data directory. Many users and administrators also maintain a backup copy of the ID files in case of loss or corruption. While an administrator could generate a new ID file for a user or server if necessary, this ID file would contain different public and private keys and none of the secret encryption keys. This would mean that if the user had encrypted any mail or other documents, no one could read them.

Security for the Notes User ID

Domino uses a password to protect the ID files. When you registered users, servers, and certifiers, you specified the minimum password security required for each ID that you created. While it is possible to choose not to password protect an ID file—by selecting zero as the minimum number of characters for the password—this opens your Domino environment up to security breaches. In addition, if you choose not to password protect an ID when you create it, you cannot store the ID file in the Domino Directory. The password, which can be up to 63 characters, is used to encrypt the ID file. When a user types in the password correctly, the ID file is decrypted and can be used to access the server or other object.

TIP By default, the password is only stored in the ID file and is only used to protect the ID file. You also have the option of checking the password at the server to verify that the correct ID is being used, forcing users to change their passwords after a set period of time, and keeping a log of the passwords to prevent re-use.

To change or set a password, the user examines the ID file by choosing File . . . Tools . . . User ID. On the Basics panel, click the Set Password button to change the password for the ID file. Notes prompts you to decrypt the ID using the current password before allowing you to change the password. When you see the Set Password dialog box shown in Figure 10-2, type the new password. Remember that passwords in Notes *are* case-sensitive. After you type and confirm the password, Domino resets the password in the User ID file.

If the user is a Web user, you must also configure an Internet password. You configure the Internet or HTTP password when you register the user by enabling the Set Internet Password checkbox. You can also set this password at any time by completing the Internet Password field (internally, this is the HTTPPassword field) on the user's Person

Figure 10-2
Set Password dialog

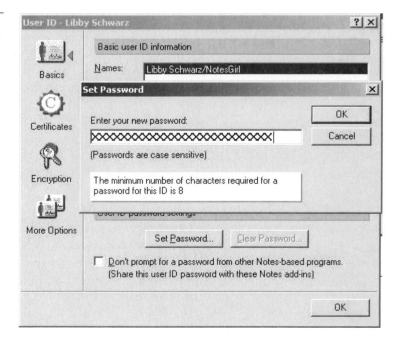

document. If the user will only access the Domino server via the Web, you do not necessarily need to register them and give them a Notes ID—they only need a Person document with an Internet password.

Notes provides the capability to set multiple passwords on a server or certifier ID file.
This enables you to require multiple administrators to be present to access a server or
certifier ID. To set multiple passwords on a server or certifier ID file, choose Edit Multiple Passwords in the Certification tools on the Configuration tab of the Domino
Administrator. After you select the ID file that needs multiple passwords, Domino displays the Edit Multiple Passwords dialog box, shown in Figure 10-3. Type the name of
an authorized administrator in the Authorized User field. Then type the password that
user will use to access the ID file. Finally, click *Add* to add that user to the list of authorized users. Finally, select the number of required authorized users required.

Notes passwords are protected from password-guessing and password-capturing programs by two additional security features. Password-capturing programs are deterred by
the anti-spoofing mechanism of Notes passwords. This anti-spoofing mechanism is the
hieroglyphics pattern displayed on the password dialog box as the users enter the passwords. It is very difficult for a password-capturing program to determine and copy the
icons that are used in this mechanism. The time-delay feature of Notes passwords
deters password-guessing programs. If a user types in an incorrect password to a Notes
ID file, Notes takes additional time to display the error message and give the user an

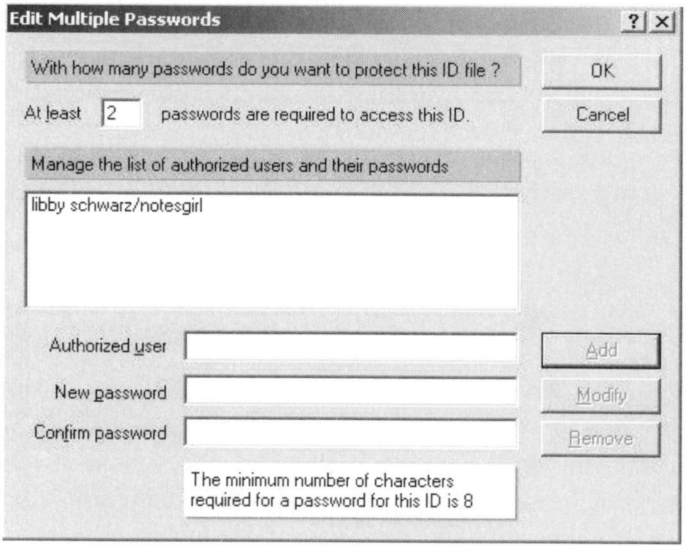

Figure 10-3
Edit Multiple
Passwords dialog

additional opportunity to type the password. The more times the user types the password incorrectly, the longer the interval becomes. Domino increases the interval exponentially, making it difficult for password-guessing programs to try a large number of passwords in an attempt to break into the ID file.

Physical and Network Security

Security in a Notes and Domino environment actually begins with security outside the Notes environment altogether. To secure your server, applications, and data, the security should begin at a hardware and network layer. First, place the servers and workstations in your environment in locked areas to prevent physical access. Second, fully implement the network operating system and the computer operating system security features to prevent access at the operating system level. These two levels of security are not necessarily the job of the Domino administrator, and will not be tested on the exam. They are, however, vital to the way in which you will begin implementing Domino security measures. If a user gains physical or network access to your servers, they may be able to circumvent many of the Domino security measures.

Next, bear in mind that network level security entails limiting access throughout your LAN and WAN, and to and from the Internet. Once you place your servers on the Internet to route mail or host a company Web site, they are vulnerable to passive and active attacks from Internet users. When opening your servers to the Internet, make sure that you aren't exposing your Domino network.

You can protect your company's network from Internet attacks by installing and configuring a firewall. A *firewall* is a system or group of systems designed to control access between a company's private network and the public Internet. A firewall can

- Limit access from the Internet to only those applications you choose to provide Internet users.
- Limit access to Internet services from within a company's private network.
- Act as a gateway for applications that store and forward data, such as mail.
- Provide encryption to data passing between the Internet and an internal network.

Chapter 36, "Web Security," goes into more detail about protecting your servers from Internet attacks. We touch on several types of firewalls, talk about the different TCP ports, and why you might want to allow users to connect to your Domino server using these specific ports. For now, understand that configuring a firewall basically comes down to what type of traffic do you want flowing in and out of your network and what type of traffic you might want to block.

Domino Security Overview

After a user or server gains ;securityaccess to his or her Notes ID file and to the necessary physical or network elements, the user or server has additional security layers to pass through before gaining access to the data in Domino. The next levels of security are Domino security measures. The list below outlines the basic options for securing the Domino environment, as also shown in Figure 10-4:

- Authentication in the Notes Organization
- Domino Server access lists
- Database Directory Links
- Database Access Control Lists
- User roles to refine user's access
- Form and/or View access lists
- Document access through Reader and Author fields
- Field and mail security through encryption
- Mail and data verification through signing

As with the physical and network security, not all of these security levels are the sole responsibility of the Domino administrator. The administrator has primary responsibility for server access, using IDs and access lists, and using ACLs for database access.

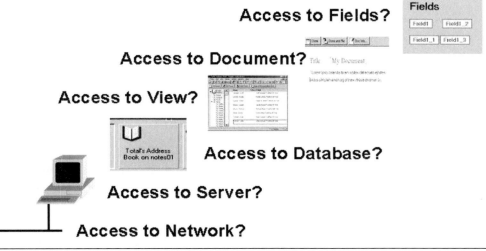

Figure 10-4   Notes and Domino security

Below this level of security, the administrator shares the security responsibility with the developer of the database. The lower levels of security are only discussed in this chapter lightly, as they are not tested for the administration exams. It is important, however, to understand how all the layers of security work in combination.

Notes Authentication

Authentication is the process by which a user or server, using their ID file, verifies their identity within the Domino organization. Each Domino organization has a certifier (or multiple certifiers). Each ID file within the Domino organization is stamped with this certifier. The authentication process compares the stamp on the user or server's ID file with the stamp that is part of the Domino organization. Authentication is based on having this shared certifier stamp in common. The following steps are used in the process of authentication, as shown in Figure 10-5:

1. The server or user requesting access generates a random number. The requesting server or user sends a package to the server containing this random number, its name, its public key, and its certificates.

2. The server takes the random number and signs it, using the signing methods that will be described later in this chapter. The server then sends this back to the requesting server or user.

3. When the requesting user or server receives the signed random number, it verifies that the signature is correct and that the random number matches the original random number. Because signing uses the public key for verification, only users with the correct public key can verify that the correct signature has been appended.

4. The server repeats the entire process in reverse to prove to the requesting server or user that the server is not an impostor.

Authentication between the Notes client and Domino server (or between two Domino servers) is always a two-way process of verifying the identity of both the requestor and the requested servers or users. Authentication is based on the trusted information (the common certificate) given to both parties by the certifier. Authentication is successful when the following tests are true:

- Hierarchical IDs must have a common certifier in their tree (common ancestor).
- Flat IDs must have some common certificate.
- Hierarchical IDs gaining access to flat resources must have some common certificate.
- If hierarchical IDs do not have a common ancestor, they must use the process of cross-certification to gain a common certificate.

Figure 10-5
Authentication

Cross-Certification

Sometimes users in different organizations need to share information and databases with each other. When they share databases that exist in different organizations, those users will need to be able to authenticate with the other's organization. When users need to authenticate outside their organization, the organizations must share certificates. The process of sharing certificates to allow authentication among users and servers that were not created with a common certificate is called *cross-certification*. Cross-certification requires each organization to obtain a certificate from the other organization, as they do not already share a hierarchical certificate to allow them to authenticate. When we described distinguished names earlier, we described a distinguished name as containing the certificates held by a user or server. We also described the registration process for users and servers, where the administrator chooses the hierarchical certificates from the appropriate certifier that should be included or inherited in the user or server's ID file. When users and servers are in different organizations, they are not registered using a common certifier ID. You can say that they have no ancestors or certificates in common. Authentication depends on having a certificate in common. Therefore, by default, users and servers in the same organization can authenticate. Users and servers in different organizations must be given a common certificate before they can authenticate.

Cross-certification begins when one company or organization, Company A, obtains an ID file from the other company, Company B. Company A then cross-certifies the ID file. The certificate that is created by the process of cross-certification is stored in Company A's Domino Directory. Company A then sends an ID to Company B. Company B performs the process of cross-certification. The certificate created by Company B is stored in Company B's Domino Directory. Both companies must have a certificate that relates to the other company in their Domino Directory before authentication can occur. The process of cross-certification creates a Cross-certificate document in the Domino Directory.

When two organizations have cross-certified with each other, the following are the results:

- Each organization completes the process of cross-certification on an ID that they obtain from the other organization.
- Each organization stores the Cross-certificate document that it creates in the Domino Directory.
- No user ID or server ID is altered.
- Individual users store Cross-certificate documents in their Personal Address Book. Servers store Cross-certificate documents in the Domino Directory.

Sometimes administrators also need to know the things that will not occur with cross-certification, including the following:

- Cross-certification will not work with flat certificates or organizations. Both organizations must use hierarchical naming to cross-certify.
- Cross-certification does not give the other organization the ability to pass on your certificate and give other organizations the ability to authenticate with you.
- Cross-certification does not alter your hierarchical name, your structure, or any user or server ID files in your organization.
- Cross-certification does not necessarily give access to all of your servers and databases to the cross-certified organization.

The process of cross-certification can occur between different levels of the two organizations. The reason that you choose to cross-certify at these different levels is related to the security that you wish to have between the organizations. If you cross-certify from organization ID to organization ID, for example, you open your entire organization and all your servers to the other organization. If you cross-certify from Server ID to User ID, however, you make a limited cross-certification that only allows limited access. This is more secure.

Cross-certification can occur at the following levels:

- **Certifier to Certifier**   Organization ID to Organization ID, Organization ID to Organizational Unit ID, or Organizational Unit ID to Organizational Unit ID

- **Certifier to server or user**   Organization ID or Organizational Unit ID to Server ID, or Organization ID or Organizational Unit ID to User ID

- **Server/User to Server/User**   Server ID to Server ID or Server ID to User ID

Certifier-to-Certifier Cross-Certification   When you cross-certify between two Organization certifiers, you are using very open security. If you cross-certify at the very top of your organization, from the Organization ID of Company A to the Organization ID of Company B, any user or server from either organization can authenticate with any user or server from the other organization, as shown in Figure 10-6.

If you cross-certify from the Organization ID of Company A to the Organizational Unit ID of Houston/Company B, anyone in Houston/Company B can authenticate with any user or server certified by the Company A Organization ID. Users or servers certified by Company A can authenticate with users or servers certified by Houston/Company B, as shown in Figure 10-7.

If you cross-certify from the Organizational Unit ID of Accounting/Company A to the Organizational Unit ID of Houston/Company B, the users and servers certified by Accounting/Company A can authenticate with the users and servers certified by Houston/Company B, as shown in Figure 10-8.

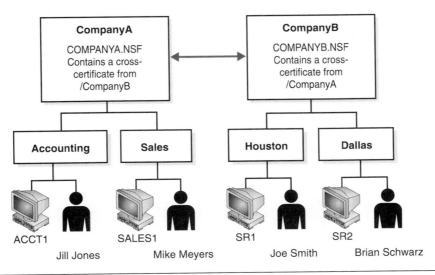

Figure 10-6   O-to-O cross-certification

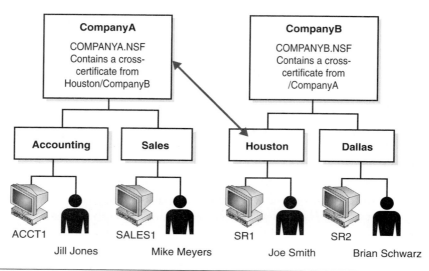

Figure 10-7   O to OU cross-certification

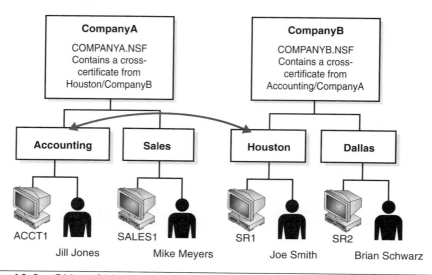

Figure 10-8   OU-to-OU cross-certification

Certifier-to-Server or User Cross-Certification   If you cross-certify the Organization ID of Company A to the Server ID of Srv1/Houston/Company B, Srv1/Houston/Company B can authenticate with all the users and servers in Company A. The users and servers in Company A, however, can only authenticate with Srv1/Houston/Company B. This example is shown in Figure 10-9.

If you cross-certify the Organizational Unit ID of Accounting/Company A to the Server ID of Srv1/Houston/Company B, Srv1/Houston/Company B can authenticate with the users and servers certified by Accounting/Company A. The users and servers certified by Accounting/Company A can authenticate with Srv1/Houston/Company B, as shown in Figure 10-10.

If you cross-certify the Organization ID of Company A to the User ID of Joe Smith/Houston/Company B, Joe Smith/Houston/Company B can authenticate with all of the users and servers certified by Company A. No users from Company A can authenticate with Company B. This option is displayed in Figure 10-11.

If you cross-certify the Organizational Unit ID of Accounting/Company A to the User ID of Joe Smith/Houston/Company B, Joe Smith/Houston/Company B can authenticate with all of the users and servers certified by Accounting/Company A. No users from Company A can authenticate with Company B. This option is displayed in Figure 10-12.

Server-to-Server and Server-to-User Cross-Certification   If you cross-certify the Server ID of Acct1/Accounting/Company A to the Server ID of Srv1/Houston/Company B, these two servers can authenticate with each other. No other users or servers in Company A can authenticate with any other user or server in Company B, as shown in Figure 10-13.

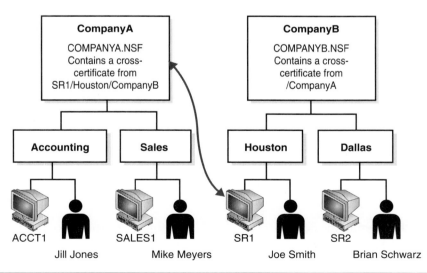

Figure 10-9   O-to-server cross-certification

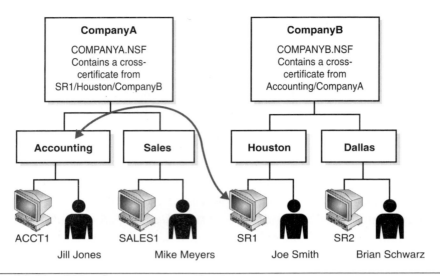

Figure 10-10   OU to Server cross-certification

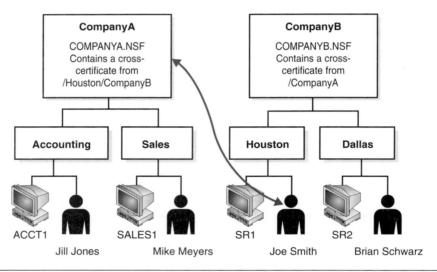

Figure 10-11   O-to-user cross-certification

If you cross-certify the Server ID of Acct1/Accounting/Company A to the User ID of Joe Smith/Houston/Company B, Joe Smith/Houston/Company B can authenticate to Acct1/Accounting/Company A, as shown in Figure 10-14. No other users from Company B can authenticate to Acct1/Accounting/Company A. No users from Company A can authenticate to Company B.

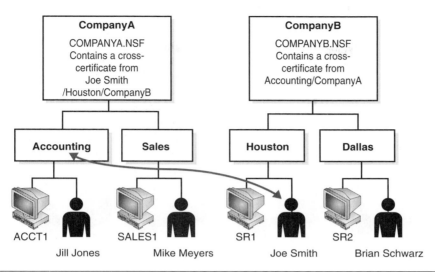

Figure 10-12   OU-to-user cross-certification

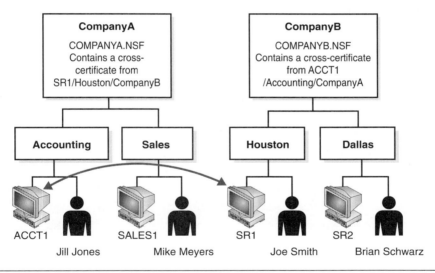

Figure 10-13   Server-to-server cross-certification

How to Cross-Certify with another Organization   To create a cross-certificate,
you should have a safe copy of the ID file to be cross-certified. You can create a safe copy
of an ID file by selecting ID Properties from the Certification tools on the Configuration tab. Select the ID you want to examine and type the password. In the ID dialog
box, select the More Options panel. Select the Create Safe Copy button.

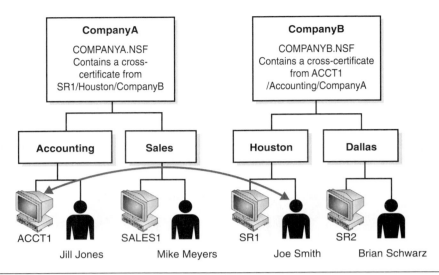

Figure 10-14 Server-to-user cross-certification

By default, Notes names all safe copies of ID files SAFE.ID. You may want to use a more specific name that includes the name of the original ID. Select a location to store the safe ID; by default, Notes tries to put it on a floppy diskette.

After creating the safe ID, send or give the ID file to the administrator at the other organization. When you receive a safe copy of an ID file that needs to be cross-certified, select Cross-Certify from the Certification tools on the Configuration tab. Domino prompts you to select an ID file to use to certify the safe ID. Then, Domino prompts you to select the ID to cross-certify. After you select the appropriate safe ID, Domino displays the Issue Cross Certificate dialog box, as shown in Figure 10-15. Cross-certification must be two-way for authentication to occur. Administrators in each organization must perform these steps.

You can also obtain a cross-certificate "on demand." Cross-certification on demand occurs when a user in one organization attempts to access a server in another organization and the user is not cross-certified. You may also use cross-certification on demand when you open mail that has been signed by a user in another organization and you are not cross-certified. Notes displays the following error message in this situation:

> Your local Address Book does not contain a cross-certificate for the organization named below. You therefore can't be sure that documents signed by its members are authentic or that you are actually communicating with its servers unless you

can verify that the key below is correct. Would you like to suppress this warning in the future by creating a cross-certificate for this organization?

If the warning message appears, either you are not cross-certified with the other organization, or you have a cross-certificate, but it is not stored in the Domino Directory. It may be stored in your Personal Address Book, for example, where other users cannot access it. If this is the case, paste a copy of the cross-certificate into the Domino Directory. Similarly, your organization may contain a cross-certificate in the Domino Directory that you may need to copy to your Personal NAB.

Notes displays the name of the organization and its public key, as well as *Yes*, *No*, and *Cancel* buttons that allow you to do one of the following actions:

- Choosing *Yes* allows you to cross-certify the O of the user or server. The cross-certificate will be placed in your personal NAB. Note that you can only access a server if that server has cross-certified you or your organization or if the server allows anonymous access.

- Choosing *No* does not create a cross-certificate with the other organization. Notes then offers you unauthenticated access to the server (if allowed) or the ability to read the signed message without verifying the signature. The original error message described previously appears each time you connect to a server in that organization or read a signed message from a user in that organization.

- Choosing *Advanced Options* allows you to create a cross-certificate for the server or sender of the message or any of its certifiers. If you cross-certify a certifier rather than a user or a server, and you place the cross-certificate in a Domino Directory, you can suppress the error message for all members of the organization. Note that you can only access a server if that server has cross-certified you or your organization or if the server allows anonymous access.

Finally, you may choose to cross-certify without having a safe copy of the certifier ID. When you need to cross-certify an ID verbally, you must contact the administrator at the other organization. Select the Cross Certify key option from the Certification tools on the Configuration tab of the Domino Administrator. Select the ID that you want to use as the certifier. In the Issue Cross Certificate dialog box, select (or confirm) the Certifier and the registration server. Next, type the subject name and public key, as shown in Figure 10-15.

In the Subject Name and Public Key fields, type the following information:

- The name of the ID to be certified, exactly as it appears on the Basics tab of the ID dialog box

- The public key of the ID to be certified, again exactly as it appears on the Basics tab of the ID dialog box

Figure 10-15
Issue Cross
Certificate
dialog box

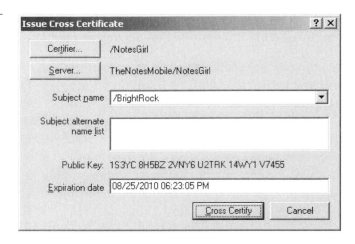

Again, remember that cross-certification must be two-way for authentication to occur. Administrators in each organization must perform these steps.

NOTE All of these methods require the person that issues the cross-certificates to have Editor or higher access to the Domino Directory and have the access and password necessary to open the certifier ID file that will be used in the cross-certification process.

Web Authentication

When users will access the server via a Web client (a browser), the user authenticates differently. With Web authentication, Domino does not require a Notes ID file for authentication. Instead, by default, Domino uses name and password authentication. Domino uses the user name and the Internet Password from the Person document in the Domino Directory for Web authentication. When users access an element of a Web site that is secured, Domino prompts for a user name and password.

If the user supplies a user name and password that Domino can verify in the Domino Directory (or in a secondary Domino or LDAP directory via Directory Assistance), the user is given the correct level of access to the secured item. The database may have a *Maximum Internet Name and Password* configured. If so, this overrides the level of access the user is granted in the ACL. If the user is granted Manager access in the ACL, for example, but the Maximum Internet Name and Password is set to Editor, the user will have Editor access. Note that the Maximum Internet Name and Password setting can only limit a user's access—a user with Reader access will not be raised to Editor access.

If the user is not required to authenticate, there are two options. First, the database may have an ACL entry for Anonymous. If so, any non-authenticated Web users have the level of access granted to Anonymous. Second, if there is no Anonymous entry, the user is granted the -Default- user's level of access. If you are placing a database in use on the Web, you should always include an entry for Anonymous. Figure 10-16 shows an ACL with an entry for Anonymous.

To verify that the HTTP port is accepting basic name and password authentication and anonymous authentication, open the Domino Administrator to the Configuration tab. Open the appropriate Server document to the Ports . . . Internet Ports . . . Web tab. Under Authentication options, verify that Name and Password is set to Yes. In addition, if you want Web users to be able to access any data on the server without authenticating, or by authenticating as Anonymous, you must also have the Anonymous option set to *Yes*.

TIP If you're using Virtual Servers, you may need to configure these settings for each virtual server. The default is to allow both Name and Password and Anonymous.

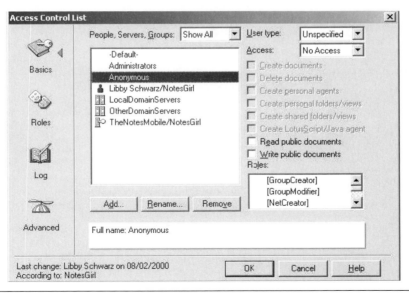

Figure 10-16 Anonymous entry in the ACL

By default, Domino uses the first column in a hidden view in the Domino Directory, called $Users, to verify a user's identity. The user has a variety of options for the user name they provide to Domino when this view is being used, as you can see in Figure 10-17. After Domino locates the user name, and verifies the password, the user's name is mapped to the Full Name, as shown in the third column.

If you want users to have fewer choices of the user name they must provide, use the Security tab on the Server Document. In the Web Server Authentication field, you may select either *More name variations with lower security* or *Fewer name variations with more security*, as shown in Figure 10-18. If you select *Fewer name variations with more security*, Domino uses the $LDAPCN view instead. This view has fewer options for the user name column.

Figure 10-17 $Users hidden view

Figure 10-18   Web Server Authentication options

Session-Based Authentication

In R5, this basic name and password authentication can be modified to avoid some of the issues that users find with the basic authentication. Some of these issues include multiple prompts to the user for credentials, sending credentials too often, and the inability to log out. Session-based authentication forces a user to establish a session on the server when they authenticate. This session is given a unique session ID number, which is stored in a cookie on the user's workstation. When the user tries to access the Web site, the cookie is included with the request for the secured resources. When the server receives the cookie, it verifies that the session ID is still valid and then allows access to the resources, without prompting the user.

If the user closes the browser, logs out, or is timed out, the cookie is destroyed and the session ID is invalidated. The user is prompted to log in again when accessing a secured resource.

To configure session-based authentication, open the server document to the Internet Protocols . . . Domino Web Engine tab. Under the HTTP Sessions section, choose Enabled for the Session authentication field. You can then select the Idle session timeout time and the maximum number of active sessions. After enabling session authentication, you need to restart the HTTP task. You can type Tell HTTP Restart at the Domino server console to restart the HTTP task without restarting the entire server. You can also select the HTTP task from the Server . . . Status tab. When you right-click on the task, you can select Tell Task . . . from the shortcut menu. Select Restart Web server with new settings from the Tell HTTP Web Server dialog box, as shown in Figure 10-19.

After you enable session authentication, Domino uses a login page, as shown in Figure 10-20, rather than the dialog box used with standard name and password authentication. You can control the appearance of this login page. Create the Domino Web Configuration database (DOMCFG.NSF), based on the template DOMCFG.NTF. You can either modify the existing $$LoginUserForm form in Domino Designer, or create a new form and use the Login Form Mapping document.

When you access a secured resource, Domino will prompt you using the new login form. You can append the ?logout command to the end of a URL. This destroys the cookie and logs the user out of the server. While the user is logged in, you can get information about the logged-in users by typing Tell HTTP Show Users at the Domino server console or by using the Server . . . Status tab in the Domino Administrator.

Domino Server Access

After using their ID or Person document and password to verify their identity and to gain access to the environment, the users or servers that are trying to access a database

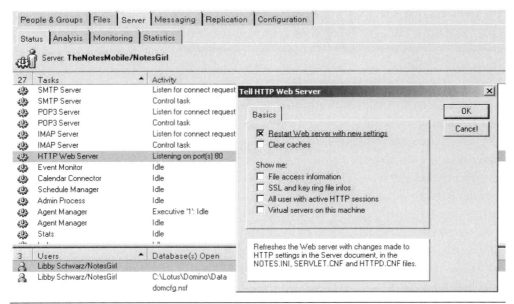

Figure 10-19 Restart the HTTP task

Figure 10-20 Login page

must also gain access to the server on which the database is stored. Each Server Document contains a *server access list*: a list of users (and servers) that are allowed (or not allowed) to access the server. The user must be allowed to gain access to the server based on the entries in this list. Most of the security settings that the user (or server) must pass are located on the Security tab, shown in Figure 10-21.

The Security Settings section sets a few of the security parameters for the server. In this section, you have the ability to determine whether the server will compare Notes public keys of users and servers that attempt to authenticate with the Notes public keys stored in the Domino Directory. This option is intended to prevent users from using fake user ID files. If an administrator chooses not to compare public keys, this authentication process is much more limited. This section also grants to the administrator the ability to allow Anonymous Notes connections. This allows any Notes ID to authenticate with the server, regardless of the certificates contained in the Notes ID. Finally, use this section to configure password checking, or verification, on Notes IDs. Password verification forces the Domino server to verify passwords during authentication, which is not the default configuration. If you enable password checking, Domino stores a copy of the current password in the Person document. In addition, Domino requires users to change their passwords on a regular basis.

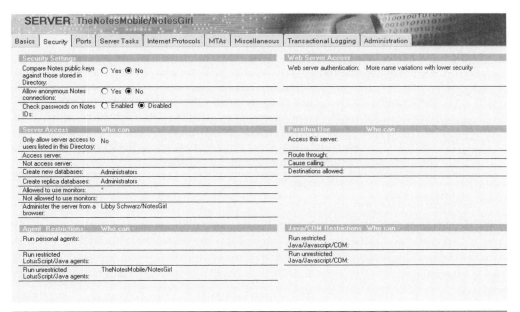

Figure 10-21   Security tab on the Server document

TIP If you allow anonymous connections, you must also provide for the anonymous users' access to databases. You can do this by creating an entry in the databases' ACLs called Anonymous. Users that do not authenticate will use the level of access determined by this entry. If you do not create an anonymous entry, anonymous users will be granted the default access to the database.

The Server Access section is where the administrator can restrict access to the server, for general use, for Passthru use, and for creating new and replica databases. In addition, the administrator can restrict access for use of monitors and for administering the server from a browser. You can choose to allow access to this server only to users that are listed in the Domino Directory, so that no users from other domains can gain access. If you enable this field, you must add any server that needs to access your server to the Access Server field, including servers that are listed in the local Domino Directory.

You can complete the Access Server field to select users and servers that should have access to this server. If you leave this field blank, all users, servers, and groups have access to the server. It is more secure, however, to place groups of servers and users in this field that should have explicit rights to access the server. This field is also called the server access list.

To deny access to the server to specific users, servers, and groups, place their names in the Not Access Server field. You might choose to populate this field with a Deny Access group, for example. This field overrides the server access list. If a user is in both the Access Server field and the Not Access Server field, the user will not be able to access the server.

TIP You should always use groups in these fields (or any field, in the Server document), rather than users' names. If you edit the field, such as to add or remove a user's name, you will have to restart the server to force the change to take effect. On the other hand, if you place a group in the field, you can edit the group and have the change take effect immediately.

Place any users that should have the ability to place or create new databases on the server in the Create new databases field. If this field is left blank, all users, servers, and groups can create new databases on the server. Place any users that should have the ability to create new replicas of databases on the server in the Create replica databases field. If this field is left blank, no users, servers, or groups can create new replicas on the server.

Place any users, servers, and groups that should be able to access the server via a Passthru server in the Access This Server field under the Passthru section. If this field is left blank, no users, servers, or groups may access this server using a Passthru server. In the

Route Through field, place the names of all users, servers, and groups that should be able to use this Notes server as a Passthru server to access other Notes servers. If this field is left blank, no users, servers, or groups can use this as a Passthru server. Use the Passthru Cause Calling field similarly. Again, if the field is blank, no one can use this server for Passthru. Finally, you can specify which destination servers the users who are using this server as their Passthru server may access. Passthru is discussed in more detail in Chapter 9.

The Security tab also contains Agent and Java/COM restrictions sections. Agent restrictions are described later in the chapter. The Java/JavaScript/COM restrictions apply to the users and groups that can execute Java applications and applets, Java servlets, JavaScript, and COM applications on the server. There are two categories—restricted and unrestricted. If the fields are blank (the default), no users or groups can run these types of applications, servlets, or applets.

Database Access

After gaining access to the server, users or other servers must then gain access to the databases that contain the data that they need. The security elements for database access include database and directory links and access control lists for the databases.

Directory Links

Databases can be stored in three places on Domino servers:

- Directly at the root of the default lotus\domino\data directory

- In a subdirectory of the lotus\domino\data directory, such as lotus\domino\data\mail

- In a directory elsewhere on the system, linked to the lotus\domino\data directory using a directory link or a database link

To use a directory link, you can create the link manually or automatically, via the Files tab in the Domino Administrator. Either way, first create a directory on the server that is not in the data directory. This will contain the database(s) that you want to link. To create the link manually, place a text file in the data directory that contains the path to the remote directory. The text file should be named with the name of the directory and a .DIR extension. When users look in the Open Database dialog box, they will see the name of the directory as though it was stored in the Notes data directory. If you place user or group names in the text file, only those users will be able to access the remote directory via the link. To create the link using the tools provided, open the Domino Administrator to the Files tab. Expand the Folder tools and select the New Link tool. Domino displays the Create New Link dialog box shown in Figure 10-22.

Figure 10-22
Create a new link

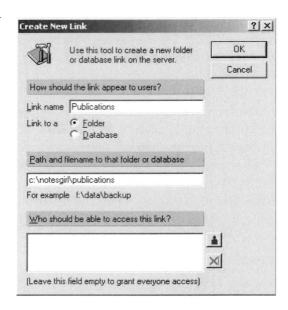

Create database links in a similar manner, but use the name of the database instead of the name of the directory when naming the text file. Users will see the database name in the Open Database dialog box.

To add security to the directory or database links, add the hierarchical names of users or the names of groups that should have access to the directory or database. If a user's name is not in the directory or database link file, he or she will be able to see the directory or database but will not be able to gain access to it.

Access Control Lists

One of the most important layers of security in Domino and Notes is the Access Control List (ACL). To determine who can gain access to a particular database and to determine what abilities the users or servers will have within that database, Domino provides an Access Control List for each database. The ACL determines the following three items of security:

- The users and servers that can access a database
- The functions that each user, server, or group can perform, based on privileges and user types
- Roles for the users, servers, and groups that refine the access to the database

To view the ACL and its privileges, right-click on the database icon and choose Access Control, or choose File . . . Database . . . Access Control from the menus for any particular database. This displays the ACL dialog box. You can also view the ACL by choosing File . . . Database . . . Access Control . . . while a database is selected. In the ACL dialog box, you have four panels, Basics, Roles, Log, and Advanced.

Using the Domino Administrator, you can manage the ACL of a single database by right-clicking on the database from the Files list. To manage the ACL of multiple databases, select the databases from the Files list using the Control or Shift keys. Then expand the Database tools and select Manage ACL. Domino displays the Multi ACL Management dialog box, as shown in Figure 10-23. Using this dialog box, you can add, change, or remove users, servers, and groups from the ACLs in multiple databases.

In the Basics panel, the center of the dialog box displays the levels of access for each user, server, and group, including the -Default- access level. The -Default- access applies for any users, servers, or groups that are not explicitly listed in the ACL. In most cases, for the tightest security, the -Default- ACL should be set to No Access. This prevents any user from inadvertently gaining access.

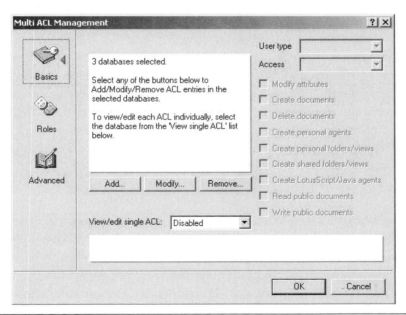

Figure 10-23 Multi ACL management

TIP If you are using the database with the Web, you should include the user Anonymous in the ACL. When non-authenticated Web users access the database, they are given the Anonymous user's level of access. If Anonymous is not available, Domino gives the user the -Default- level of access.

The two default groups, LocalDomainServers and OtherDomainServers, should always be listed in the ACL with an appropriate level of access. In addition, other users, groups, and servers should be listed as appropriate. Please note that in most cases it is desirable to use groups in the ACL rather than users, for ease of administration. If you have a group that contains user Joe Smith and Joe Smith is also listed individually in the ACL, the rights given to the individual listing take precedence.

On the right side of the first panel, you see the user type and level of access for the users, groups, and servers listed in the center. In addition, you see the additional privileges that can be given with each level of access. User types and privileges are described in the sections below.

The Roles panel allows the database manager to refine access to and use design elements inside the database by creating and applying user roles. User roles are described later in this chapter.

The Log panel shows all additions and modifications to the ACL of this database. The log shows the name of the user (or server) that made the ACL change, the time and date of the ACL change, and what change was made.

The Advanced panel allows an administrator to determine the administration server for the database. The database requires that an administration server is set to participate in many of the AdminP processes, such as renaming. After you assign an administration server, you can choose whether this server can modify Reader or Author fields.

The administrator can also use this panel to enforce a consistent level of security across all replicas of the database. This prevents users from making changes to local replicas that they would not be able to make to the server replica. This also helps to maintain data consistency and accuracy across different servers, such as in a clustering scenario.

If you will be using this database on the Web, you should verify the setting in the Maximum Internet Name and Password field. Regardless of what access level a user is granted via the ACL, this field overrides the access. If Joe Smith has Manager access in the ACL, for example, but the Maximum Internet Name and Password field is set to Editor, when Joe accesses the database via HTTP, he can only have Editor access. On the other hand, if Joe has Reader access and the Maximum Internet Name and Password field is set to Editor, when Joe accesses the database via HTTP, he still only has Reader access. The Advanced panel is shown in Figure 10-24.

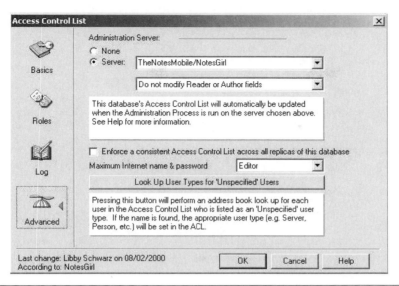

Figure 10-24   Advanced ACL

When using the Multi ACL management dialog box, there is no Log panel, and the Basics and Advanced panels look a bit different. Figure 10-25 shows the Basics panel on the Multi ACL management dialog box. The main difference is that the current ACL settings are not displayed by default. You can view the current ACL settings of the databases using the View/Edit Single ACL drop-down arrow.

ACL Levels

The ACL has seven basic levels of security, which you can then refine through assigning additional options: privileges and user types. These levels of security are all set on this panel of the dialog box. To assign a user or server to a level of the ACL, click the Add . . . button at the bottom of the Basics panel of the dialog box. You then have the option either to type in the name of the user, server, or group, or to choose a name from the Domino Directory. You may also remove or rename users, servers, and groups using the other buttons at the bottom of the dialog box.

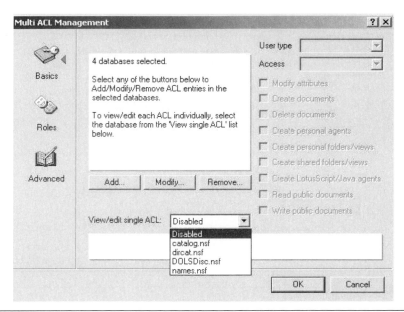

Figure 10-25   Multi ACL basics

If a user is not listed specifically in the ACL, either individually or within a group, he or she will be given the access level of the -Default- group. The -Default- group, which cannot be renamed or removed, is given Designer access by default when a new database is created. The user that creates the database is also added to the ACL automatically, with Manager access, when the database is created. Two other groups, LocalDomainServers and OtherDomainServers, are also in the ACL by default. These groups are standard Domino groups that are used in all Domino environments to determine the access level of the servers that house and replicate the databases. Both of these groups have Manager access when the database is created.

TIP   I generally recommend choosing a name rather than typing it in, to ensure that the hierarchical name is correct. I also recommend using groups in the ACL as often as possible. This allows an administrator to change access for users by changing group membership, rather than having to open each database and change the ACL manually.

After choosing a user, group, or server, choose the appropriate user type from the drop-down list. The available user types include Unspecified, Person, Server, Mixed Group, Person Group, or Server Group. These are used to refine the access given to any entry in the ACL.

Next, choose the Access level and privileges from the drop-down list and the check-boxes. The following paragraphs describe each level of security and the privileges that are available to refine them.

No Access   The lowest level of access to a database is *No Access*, which prevents a user or group from opening a database or from adding the database to their workspaces (if your organization still uses the R4-style workspace). This level of security is often recommended for the -Default- and Anonymous access to the database so that no one can gain access to data inadvertently. The only additional privileges available with No Access are the ability to Read public documents and to Write public documents, as shown in Figure 10-26. None of the other privileges are selected or available. With No Access, a server will not be able to replicate documents.

TIP   Public access allows users with limited access to create or view certain documents or forms. Public access to documents, forms, and folders can be granted on the Form, Document, or Folder properties InfoBoxes, on the Security tab. An example of Public Access in use in Domino is the user's ability to grant other users rights to their calendars or mail files. These rights are granted by giving users with No Access the ability to read and/or write public documents.

Depositor Access   The next level of access to a database is *Depositor access*. Depositor access allows a user to add the database to the workspace and open it. In addition, Depositors can create documents in the database. They cannot, however, read or edit

Figure 10-26
No Access

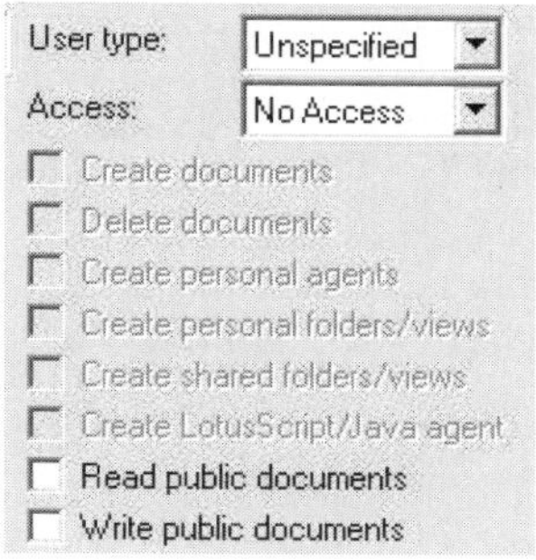

User type:	Unspecified ▼
Access:	No Access ▼
☐	Create documents
☐	Delete documents
☐	Create personal agents
☐	Create personal folders/views
☐	Create shared folders/views
☐	Create LotusScript/Java agent
☐	Read public documents
☐	Write public documents

any documents in the database, including their own. The views in the database will appear empty to a user with Depositor access. Depositor access is useful for mail-in databases, surveys, suggestion boxes, or evaluations. The users can create an evaluation for an instructor, for example, but will not be able to see or change any of the evaluations. The Create documents option is checked by default and cannot be changed. The read and write public documents options are also available and can be modified, as shown in Figure 10-27.

Reader Access   You can also assign *Reader access* to a database. Users with Reader access to a database can view documents in the database, but cannot create or edit documents in the database. This type of access is useful for informational databases, such as a corporate directory or a documentation database. The additional privileges for users with Reader access are Create personal agents, Create personal folders/views, and Create LotusScript/Java agents, as shown in Figure 10-28. The other privileges are all unchecked and unchangeable, with the exception of Read public documents, which is checked and unchangeable. With Reader access, a server will not be able to send documents during replication, but can receive them.

Figure 10-27
Depositor access

Figure 10-28
Reader access

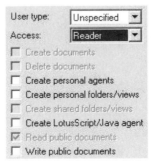

Author Access   The next level of access to a database is *Author access*. Users with Author access to a database have the ability to read documents in the database, create documents in the database, and edit the documents they create (if their name is listed in an Authors field included on the document). Author level access is the most common level of access to discussion and other databases (as opposed to Editor or above), as it helps to prevent Replication and Save Conflicts by limiting the number of users that can edit any given document. The additional privileges available for users with Author access are Create documents, Delete documents, Create personal agents, Create personal folders/views, and Create LotusScript/Java agents, as shown in Figure 10-29. The Read public documents option is checked and unavailable for change and the Write public documents option is available for change. With Author access, a server can replicate new documents only, although it is usually better to give servers Editor access.

Editor Access   Users with *Editor access* to a database start with the same level of access as users with Author access: read, create, and edit. Editor access also grants the ability to edit all documents in the database. It is usually recommended to give only one or two users this level of access to a database, to prevent Replication and Save conflicts. The Create documents option is checked by default, as shown in Figure 10-30, and is not available for change, as are both the Read and Write public documents privileges. All other privileges are available for modification for users with Editor access. This is the first level of access that can grant the ability to create Shared folders and views. Servers with Editor access can replicate new and changed documents.

Designer Access   *Designer access* gives a user all the rights allowed by Editor access, including reading, creating, and editing all documents in the database. Designers have the additional ability to create and modify all design elements in the database, including forms, views, navigators, and others. Designers have the ability to create and modify

Figure 10-29
Author access

Figure 10-30
Editor access

full text indexes, About and Using this database documents, and database icons. The Create documents, Create personal agents, Create personal folders/views, and Create shared folders/views privileges are granted to users with Designer access by default and cannot be changed, as are both the Read and Write public documents privileges. The privileges for Delete documents and Create LotusScript/Java agents are available to be modified, as shown in Figure 10-31. Servers with Designer access can replicate all new and changed documents and design elements.

Manager Access   Users with *Manager access* are granted all the abilities of users with Designer level access as a base. In addition, they are the only access level of users given the ability to change the ACL of the database. Managers can also encrypt a database, delete a database, and configure the replication settings for a database. Manager access is also necessary to add and configure roles. All privileges are granted by default to Managers and cannot be changed, with the exception of the Delete documents option, as shown in Figure 10-32. There should usually be only one user or group with Manager level access, and one server with Manager level access, to prevent problems with security and replication. Servers with Manager access can replicate all changes to the database, including new and edited documents, design elements, and the ACL.

The Domino system administrator and the application developer should work together to create and maintain the ACL for each database. Some aspects of security can affect how the application functions, which is the responsibility of the application developer or the database manager. On the other hand, some aspects of the ACL can affect the security of the Domino environment as a whole and can affect replication of the databases throughout the environment; both of which are the responsibility of the system administrator.

Figure 10-31
Designer access

Figure 10-32
Manager access

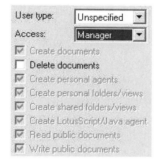

View and Form Access Lists

After a user is given access to a database through the ACL, the user then has to gain access to the forms and views in the database. This access can be granted or denied using View and Form access lists. View and Form access lists are primarily the responsibility of the application developer or designer of the database. The system administrator should understand this layer of security, however, to ensure that replication occurs correctly and to ensure that they understand the level of security necessary for the database.

To create Form and View access lists, use the Security tab on the Form and View properties InfoBoxes. These security tabs allow the designer to refine the access given to users.

In the View access list, the developer determines which users can use the view. All users with Reader access and above to a database are given access to the views by default, as shown in Figure 10-33. To refine this access, remove the check mark from the All readers and above option. You then have the option to add check marks next to the

Figure 10-33
View access list

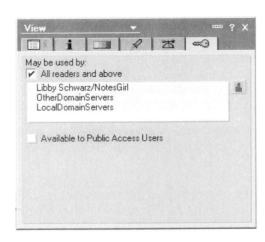

users, servers, and groups that should be able to gain access to the view. The users must, however, be given access to the database through the database ACL to use the view.

View access lists should not be considered true security measures for a database. A user with at least Reader access to the database could create a private view or folder to display the data. The View and Folder access lists should be used in combination with other security measures for the database.

The designer can refine access to forms using a similar method. To view the Form access list, open the Form properties InfoBox to the Security tab, as shown in Figure 10-34. The first option on this tab is the default read access for documents created with this form.

All users with Reader access and above are given this ability by default. You refine this access by removing this ability from all users with Reader access and giving it only to certain users. Note that a user must have access to the database through the database ACL to view documents in the database. If a Read access list exists, however, a user must be on that list to read documents created by the form, regardless of ACL level. The second option on the Form properties Security tab is the list of the users that can create documents with the form. By default, all users with Author access and above are given this ability. Remember that this access list is only able to refine the ACL, not change it. This means that a user with Reader access in the ACL will not be able to create a document with the form even if you have listed them in the form access create list. Similarly, if a user has Editor access or above and is able to read the documents created with this form (he or she is on the Read access list), that user will be able to create documents with this form regardless of the create access list.

Figure 10-34
Form access list

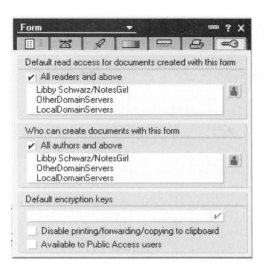

View and Form access lists not only must contain the users that should have access to the documents in the views or created by the forms but also must contain the names of the servers that will be replicating the databases.

Reader and Author Fields

Although default access to documents is granted through the settings set on the form and in the ACL, as described above, access in the database can be further limited through the use of Readers and Authors fields. Readers and Authors fields can be either editable or computed and must resolve to a list of names. As in the view and form access lists described previously, Readers and Authors fields refine and limit the abilities given in the ACL; they cannot override the ACL. Readers and Authors fields are the responsibility of the application developer. The important things to remember when discussing them with the designers is that they cannot override the database ACL and that servers that will be replicating the databases must be listed in these fields. In addition, users that are given Author access to a database must be listed in an Authors field on the documents they create to be allowed to edit those documents later.

Roles

Using and creating user roles can further refine the security for an application. User roles are created in the ACL dialog box (as opposed to groups, which are created in the Domino Directory) and allow the designer to group users, servers, and groups that should have similar rights and abilities within a specific database. Roles provide the following advantages to the designer or manager of a database:

- Roles help provide centralized security. Instead of changing user names in every Form or View access list, Readers or Authors field, and section within a database, designers and database managers change the users within a particular role or change the access of the role.

- Roles are listed in the ACL of a database, ensuring that when changes are made to the security of the database, the changes take effect in the design elements. If the security were all done at the level of the design elements, many database managers and designers might neglect to update the security correctly.

- Roles are in the databases, rather than in the Domino Directory. This enables the Administrator to limit the number of groups placed in the Domino Directory for special access within databases.

To create a role, open the database Access Control dialog box to the Roles panel, as shown in Figure 10-35. To add a new role to the database, click Add . . . and type in the name of the role that you want to add. The name can be up to 15 characters. You can

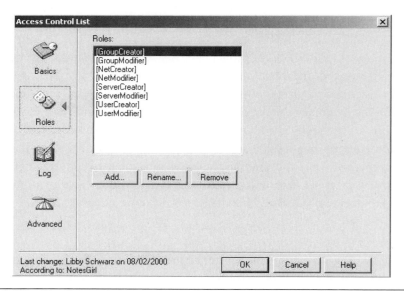

Figure 10-35   Database roles

also rename or remove user roles from the database's ACL from this panel on the dialog box. The database manager can add up to 75 roles to the database.

After creating the user roles, you must apply those roles to the users, servers, and groups listed in the database ACL. To apply a role to a user, open the Basics panel on the ACL dialog box, as shown in Figure 10-36. Select the user and choose the role or roles that the user should have from the Roles list on the right-hand side of the dialog box. This will associate this user role with the selected user, server, or group.

After creating and applying user roles, the user roles must be given function within the database. User roles can be used in the View and Form access lists, in Readers or Authors fields, and in section access lists. The system administrator will create and apply user roles in the access control list; however, the database designer will give the roles their function in the database. If you choose to implement this level of security, the system administrator and the database application developer should work together to plan the security.

Signing and Encryption

Signing and encryption are two additional security layers that can be applied to documents and databases. Signing has two meanings in Domino: databases and design elements can be signed by the developer that created them (or by another ID later); mail and documents can be signed to verify their authenticity. Encryption can be applied to various locations in Domino, including mail encryption, database encryption, document encryption, and port encryption.

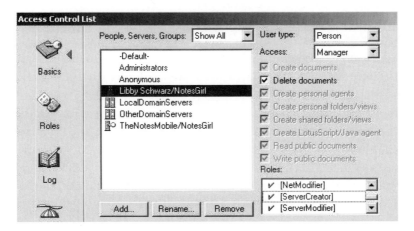

Figure 10-36   Assigning a Role

Signing

Signing is a process that places a verification stamp on a document or message that allows the reader to confirm that the signer was the last person to modify the document. A different type of signing can also be applied to documents and design elements using the Signtool in the Domino Administrator.

Mail and Document Signing   The signature is created using the user's private key (discussed previously) in combination with the data in the field. The signatures can be attached either to sections or to fields within documents or to an entire mail message. The following steps describe the process of signing a mail message:

1. The message is signed using the sender's private key, which is contained only in the sender's user ID file. The signature that is appended to the message contains the signature itself, the user's public key, and all of the sender's certificates.

2. The recipient then uses the certificates to verify the authenticity of the sender's public key. The public key is then used to verify the authenticity of the signature.

3. When the signature is verified, a message appears in the recipient's status bar to tell them that the message has been signed according to the appropriate certifier.

4. When the signature cannot be verified, a message appears in the recipient's status bar to tell them that the message may have been modified or corrupted since it was signed.

In addition to signing mail messages, any field on any form can be enabled for signing. This is the job of the database developer.

Sign a Database or Design Element   You can sign a database or design element using the Sign tool. This determines how the elements react with the Execution Control List (ECL) element of workstation security, as well as under what ID scheduled scripts and agents run.

Open the Domino Administrator to the Files tab while logged in with the appropriate ID file. Select the database(s) that you want to sign. Expand the Database tools and choose Sign. In the Sign Database dialog box, shown in Figure 10-37, select All Design documents, Documents of type, or This specific Note ID to sign. Click OK to replace the current signature with a signature for the current ID file. You can also choose to update rather than replace signatures, which is a faster process.

Figure 10-37
Signing databases

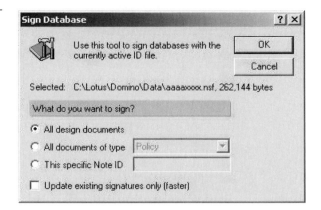

Encryption

Encryption is a security level that can be applied to databases, fields, mail messages, and network ports. *Encryption* means taking data and encoding it so that only a user that has the correct key can decode and read the data. Some encryption uses a combination of the public and private keys for encryption and decryption, while other encryption in Domino uses a single, secret key encryption method.

Field-level encryption and network port encryption are done using a single, secret encryption key. Field-level encryption allows an author or editor to apply one or more encryption keys to their document. These encryption keys are created using the Encryption panel on the User ID dialog box, as shown in Figure 10-38. When the encryption key(s) is applied, any data in encryption-enabled fields on the document is secured through encryption. All users that need access to data encrypted with this type of encryption key must have a copy of the encryption key in their user ID file.

Network port encryption uses a key that is generated for each new network session to encrypt all data that travels through a particular port. To enable Network port encryption, use the Encrypt network data option on the Ports panel of the User Preferences dialog box.

Other encryption, such as mail encryption, is done through a combination of the public and private keys stored in the Domino Directory and in the user ID file. The public key, which is created for each user when that user is registered, is stored in the user's Person document in the Domino Directory and in the User's ID file. Public keys are available to all users that have access to the Domino Directory. Part of a public key is shown in Figure 10-39. The private key is stored in the user ID file. It is only available to the

Figure 10-38
Field encryption

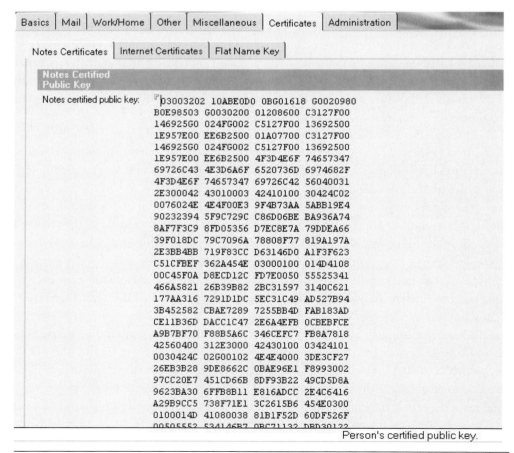

Figure 10-39 Public key

owner of that ID file. Either key can be used to encrypt or decrypt data. If data is encrypted using the public key, however, only the private key can decrypt the data.

Mail encryption is used on documents that are being sent to another user's mail database. Mail encryption can be accomplished in one of three ways:

- **Encrypt incoming mail**   When a user chooses to encrypt incoming mail, the messages are encrypted at the server. The mail messages cannot be read by administrators or by the server. This option can be set in the user's Person document in the Domino Directory.

- **Encrypt outgoing mail**   When a user chooses to encrypt outgoing mail, the messages are encrypted as you send them to other users. The message cannot be accessed by administrators or servers at any point in the transfer or delivery process.

- **Encrypt saved mail**   Encrypting saved mail prevents messages stored in your server or local mail database from being accessed by unauthorized users. Many laptop users, especially, use this type of encryption to protect their data in case of losing their laptop.

You also have the ability to encrypt an entire database. This is especially useful to laptop users that carry replicas of sensitive databases with them. To encrypt a local database, open the Database properties InfoBox and click the Encryption button. Choose to Locally encrypt the database and select a level of local encryption. The three levels are strong, medium, and simple. Strong and medium encryption cannot be used on systems that use disk compression. Simple encryption provides the fastest access to your data. Only the user with the appropriate ID file selected on this dialog box will be able to read the database. This type of encryption is created using the public and private keys stored in the ID file.

TIP   Note that only users with manager access to a database can encrypt the database.

Agent Security

Developers and administrators often create agents to automate tasks in a database. When agents run manually (that is, you click a button while in the database to activate the agent), they run under the ID currently in use—usually yours. When an agent runs automatically, based on a schedule or on a database event, it runs under the ID that signed the agent. This can either be the ID that last saved the agent, or the agent may have been signed using the Sign tool in the Domino Administrator.

Knowing the ID used to run an agent is important so that you can configure the proper agent access in the Domino Server document. On the Security tab of the Server document, shown in Figure 10-40, you can configure which users can run various types of agents, in the Agent Restrictions section.

In the Run Personal agents field, you would place users and groups that should be able to run personal agents. If the field is blank (the default), all users can run personal agents. In the Run restricted LotusScript/Java agents field, place the users that can run this type of agent. This type of agent uses a subset of LotusScript and Java features, especially excluding agents that access the file system or the system time. If the field is blank (the default), no users can run restricted LotusScript/Java agents, except the users that are listed in the Run Unrestricted LotusScript/Java agents. In the Run Unrestricted LotusScript/Java agents field, place the names of users that can run agents that include any LotusScript or Java features. If this field is blank (the default), no users can run this type of agent.

You can sign these agents (just as you can sign any design element in the database) with a special ID or the server's ID, so that you can limit the number of users that need to be listed in these fields. To sign an agent, you can open the agent while using the ID that you want to use to sign the agent. Save the agent and the signature will be replaced.

You can also sign the agent using the Sign tool. Open the Domino Administrator to the Files tab while logged in with the appropriate ID file. Select the database(s) that contains agents you want to sign. Expand the Database tools and choose Sign. In the Sign Database dialog box, select Agents under the All documents of type drop-down list. Click OK to replace the current signature with a signature for the current ID file.

Signing agents also affects how they run with workstation Execution Control Lists, or ECLs. ECLs restrict agents or scripts that run on a workstation (as opposed to the agents that run on the server, which is what the Agent security fields restrict). You can access

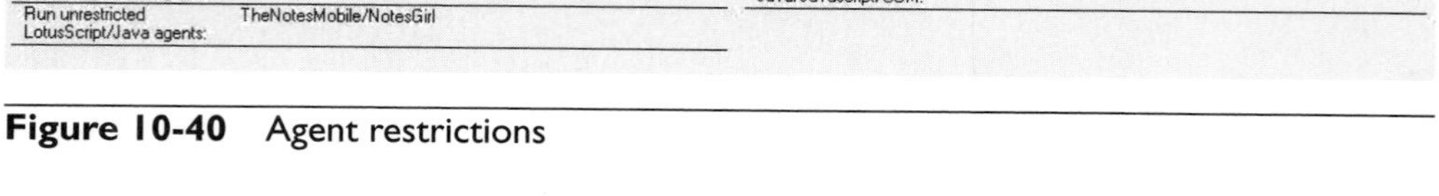

Agent Restrictions	Who can -	Java/COM Restrictions	Who can -
Run personal agents:		Run restricted Java/Javascript/COM:	
Run restricted LotusScript/Java agents:		Run unrestricted Java/Javascript/COM:	
Run unrestricted LotusScript/Java agents:	TheNotesMobile/NotesGirl		

Figure 10-40   Agent restrictions

and modify the ECL from the File . . . Preferences . . . User Preferences menu. On the Basics tab of the User Preferences dialog box, select the Security Options button to display the Workstation Security: Execution Control List dialog box. In the top right-hand side of the dialog box, select the workstation, Java applet, or JavaScript security radio buttons. In the When Signed By field, add or remove any names that should be able to run scripts, applets, or agents on your workstation. Using the checkboxes under the Allow section, select the specific types of scripts, applets, and agents that each user can run, based on what the script, applet, or agent will access or modify, as shown in Figure 10-41. You can also set execution levels for the Default (a script, applet, or agent with an unlisted signature would run under this level of access) and -No Signature- users.

File Security

In Domino R5, you can apply additional security to non-database files when they are accessed via HTTP. This security is applied to CGI files/scripts, HTML files, and JPG or

Figure 10-41
Workstation ECL

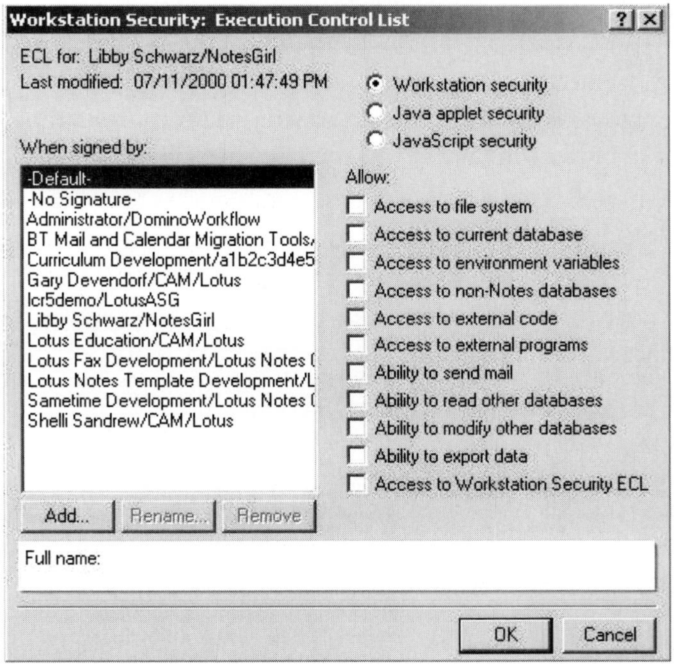

GIF graphics files. To apply access control security protection to these files, create File Protection documents.

To create a File Protection document, open the Server Document or Virtual Server document to which you want to apply the protection. Select the Web action button and choose to Create File Protection. Domino displays the File Protection document, shown in Figure 10-42.

On the Basics tab, define the files to protect in the Path field. The path is relative to the server's data directory, and can be a file, a directory, or a drive. If you're protecting files on a virtual server, you must also enter the IP address of the virtual server.

On the Access Control tab, click the Set/Modify Access Control List button. Use the drop-down arrow next to the name field to select users and groups from the Domino Directory. The -Default- user is given No Access automatically. Then select the level of access for each user from the following options:

- No Access
- Read/Execute (GET method)
- Read/Write/Execute (POST and GET method)

GET allows users to open files and start programs and is the most common access level granted. Use POST for directories that contain CGI scripts, as this method is used to send data to CGI programs.

After you save and close the document, you must restart the HTTP task for the protection document to take affect. You can type TELL HTTP RESTART as an easy way to restart the task.

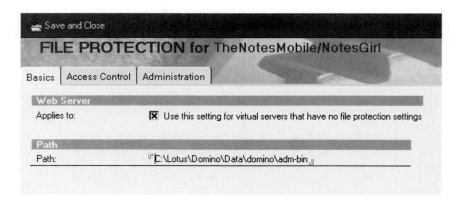

Figure 10-42 File protection

You can view the File Protection documents for your server(s) from the Configuration tab of the Domino Administrator. Expand the Web section and open the Web Server Configuration view. File Protection documents are listed under the servers to which they apply.

Securing the Domino Directory

The Domino Directory, as we have mentioned before, is the most important database in your Domino environment. The Domino Directory allows the system administrator to create users, servers, and groups, as well as to modify and refine those objects and others. Lotus implemented additional security in the Domino Directory to ensure that only the proper users, servers, and groups would have access to complete these tasks.

The Domino Directory, like all databases, uses the ACL levels as its first and primary layer of security. In addition, however, there are eight predefined user roles that have been created and implemented for this database. These roles refine the rights given by the ACL by determining who can create and edit specific types of documents. When you assign the ACL for the Domino Directory, be sure to include these roles for the appropriate users, servers, and groups:

- **GroupCreator** The GroupCreator role must be added to users with Author access or above to give them the ability to create new Groups in the Domino Directory.

- **GroupModifier** The GroupModifier role must be added to users with Author access to give them the ability to modify or delete Group documents in the Domino Directory. Users with Author access must also be in the Owners or Administrator's field for the Group documents they wish to edit.

- **NetCreator** The NetCreator role must be added to users with Author access or above to give them the ability to create any document in the Domino Directory other than Person, Group, or Server documents. This includes Connection, Configuration, and Program documents, for example.

- **NetModifier** The NetModifier role must be added to users with Author access to give them the ability to modify or delete any document in the Domino Directory other than Person, Group, or Server documents. Users with Author access must also be in the Owners or Administrator's field for the documents they wish to edit.

- **ServerCreator** The ServerCreator role must be added to users with Author access or above to give them the ability to create new Server documents in the Domino Directory.

- **ServerModifier**   The GroupModifier role must be added to users with Author access to give them the ability to modify or delete Server documents in the Domino Directory. Users with Author access must also be in the Owners or Administrator's field for the Server documents they wish to edit.

- **UserCreator**   The UserCreator role must be added to users with Author access or above to give them the ability to create new Person documents in the Domino Directory.

- **UserModifier**   The UserModifier role must be added to users with Author access to give them the ability to modify or delete Person documents in the Domino Directory. Users with Author access must also be in the Owners or Administrator's field for the Person documents they wish to edit.

The roles for the Domino Directory are shown in Figure 10-43.

Figure 10-43
Domino Directory
roles

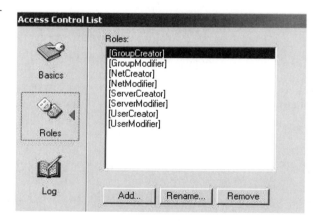

Review Questions

1. True or False. The public key is stored in a user's ID file and only they have access to it.
    A. True
    B. False

2. True or False. By default, a user's password is stored both in the ID file and in the Domino Directory.
    A. True
    B. False

3. Authentication will be successful in which situations?
   A. The same OU certifier created the user and server.
   B. The same O certifier created the user and server.
   C. The server was registered by Houston/NotesGirl and the user was registered by Accounting/Dallas/NotesGirl.
   D. The server was registered by Houston/ACME and the user was registered by Houston/NotesGirl.

4. True or False: Standard Domino authentication is a one-way process from the user to the server.
   A. True
   B. False

5. Aaron's server has run out of room on the drive that the lotus\domino\data directory is on. What can you suggest?
   A. Create a new \lotus\domino\data directory on a larger drive. Move all the data to the new drive.
   B. Create a new \lotus\domino\data directory on a larger drive. Create a directory link to this drive.
   C. Create a directory called anything but \lotus\domino\data on a larger drive. Create a directory link to this drive.
   D. Reinstall the Domino server on a larger drive.

6. Cindy tries to open a database listed in the Open Database dialog box called Accounting. She is denied access. When she asks the help desk to check, it shows that she is in the ACL of the database as an Editor. When the help desk calls you, what do you tell them to check?
   A. Tell them they looked at the wrong user in the ACL.
   B. Tell them to look for a database link file.
   C. Tell them to look for a directory link file.
   D. Tell them to look in the Server Access list.

7. Sylvia is the manager of the Domino environment and allows three other Database managers to help her with creating ACLs for databases. She notices that one database uses individual user names in the ACL instead of group names. Can she find out which database manager created the ACL for this database?
   A. Yes, she can look in the ACL dialog box, Basics panel for Log information.
   B. Yes, she can look in the ACL dialog box, Log panel for Log information.
   C. Yes, she can look in the Database Properties InfoBox, Log panel for Log information.
   D. No.

8. What is the lowest level of access a user needs in order to be able to edit the documents they create in a database?
   A. Editor
   B. Author
   C. Designer
   D. Manager

9. Dudley looks at the ACL for the Domino Directory and sees that he has Editor access. When he tries to create a new Group document in the Domino Directory, however, he cannot. Why not?
   A. The Domino Directory has additional security. To create a new group, he has to have Manager access.
   B. The Domino Directory has additional security. To create a new group, he has to be in the Administrators field of the server document.
   C. The Domino Directory has additional security. To create a new group, he needs the GroupCreator role.
   D. User error.

10. What level of access do you have to have to locally encrypt a database?
    A. Editor
    B. Manager
    C. Designer
    D. Author

Review Answers

1. **B is correct.** The public key is stored in both the user's ID file and the Domino Directory, and any user can access it. This statement describes the private key.

2. **B is correct.** By default, the password is stored only in the ID file. The password is only stored in the Domino Directory if Password checking is enabled.

3. **A, B,** and **C are correct.** In each of these cases, the user and server have a certificate in common. In D, they will have to cross-certify before they can authenticate.

4. **B is correct.** Standard Domino authentication is a two-way process that challenges both the user and server. Web (standard name and password) authentication is a one-way process.

5. **C** is the best answer.   Create a directory called anything but \lotus\domino\data on a larger drive. Create a directory link to this drive.

6. **B** or **C** is correct.   Tell them to look for a database link file or tell them to look for a directory link file. Either file can contain names that allow access only to those users, regardless of ACL.

7. **B** is correct.   Yes, she can look in the ACL dialog box, Log panel for Log information.

8. **B** is correct.   Users with Author access can edit documents they have created, as long as an Authors field with their name exists on the document.

9. **C** is correct.   The Domino Directory has additional security. To create a new group, he needs the GroupCreator role.

10. **B** is correct.   Manager access is needed to locally encrypt a database.

Implementing Domino Messaging

You should be able to answer questions based on the following objectives after reading this chapter:

- Setting up/configuring message distribution performance enhancements (multiple routers, multiple MAIL.BOXES)
- Setting up/configuring message distribution tracking
- Setting up/configuring message distribution using force
- Setting up/configuring message distribution using non-Notes/ Internet-based mail
- Setting up/configuring message distribution using Notes-based mail (shared, message-based)
- Setting up/configuring message distribution using schedules
- Setting up/configuring message distribution using a mixed messaging system

Many companies that implement Domino only do so for the messaging capabilities. While we know that Domino has much more to offer, messaging is an integral part of what we use it for. Domino provides internal messaging using Notes Remote Procedure Calls (NRPC), Notes Rich Text format, and Internet mail using standards-based messaging, including SMTP, IMAP, and POP with MIME format.

Messaging Primer

Before we discuss the server processes related to mail, it may be useful to refresh your memory about the front-end, or client, processes. To begin a mail memo, the user opens the mail file and chooses the New Memo action button. Notes displays the blank message form. The user either chooses the address button to place recipients in the To: field, or begins typing in the user name, waiting for Notes' type-ahead feature to complete the name for them. The user then types the body of the memo. Before sending, the user may choose the Delivery Options action button and request High or Low Priority, to sign or encrypt the memo, or a return receipt. The user saves, saves and sends, sends, or discards the message.

During the mail process, the mailer verifies the names in the To:, cc:, or bcc: fields and then places the message in the server's mail routing database, the MAIL.BOX. After the message has been delivered to the MAIL.BOX database, the router determines where it goes and how it gets there. The router task decides where and how to route mail, taking into account the following:

- Is the mail going to a recipient on the same server (and thus in the same DNN)?
- Is the mail going to a recipient on a different server in the same DNN?
- Is the mail going to a recipient in another DNN, but still in the same domain?
- Is the mail going to a recipient in another domain altogether?
- Is the mail going outside the Domino mail environment?
- Should the message be delivered using NRPC (native Notes routing) or SMTP?

As an introduction to messaging in Domino, refer to Table 11-1 for an overview of the Domino messaging terminology.

Mail Routing Within the Same DNN

NOTE The processes below refer to message-based, native Notes mail. While the basic process remains the same in shared mail, the placement of the mail messages is different. We will discuss these differences later in this section. The process changes somewhat if you select to have Domino route all messages using SMTP.

The mail routing process begins when the user composes a mail message in his or her mail database. Once the mail message is created and addressed, the mailer (a component of the Notes client/workstation) checks the recipients' names and addresses and places the message in the sender's server's MAIL.BOX. Once the message is in the MAIL.BOX, the router (a server task) takes over and determines the location of the

Table 11-1   Domino Messaging Terminology

Term	Definition
Domino Named Networks (DNN)	Servers that are in constant contact (the same LAN or WAN) and share the same protocol can be in the same DNN. When servers are in the same DNN, mail is routed immediately and automatically, regardless of Connection documents. We covered how to create Domino Named Networks (DNN) in the Installation and Configuration section of the book. However, in terms of mail, the main point is how mail is routed in a DNN —immediately and automatically. DNNs and Notes Named Networks (NNNs) are the same thing.
Message-based mail	Message-based mail is the most common form of mail in older mail products, and probably what you think of when you think of mail. In message-based mail, the entire mail message sent to a user—including both the body and the headers—is stored in the user's mail file.
Shared mail (pointer-based mail, single copy object store)	In shared mail, rather than storing the entire mail message sent to each user in that user's mail file, only the header of a message is stored in the user's mail file. The body of the message, including attachments, is stored in the single copy object store, or shared mail database. This can be a great space saver on servers, especially when the users tend to send a single message to multiple recipients.
Domains	All servers that share the same Domino Directory are in the same Domino domain. Often, an entire organization will stay within a single domain, although later in this book we will discuss situations in which this is not the case. In terms of mail, addressing of mail messages within a domain is based on that single Domino Directory, which simplifies addressing and type-ahead.

NOTE   Those of you who are familiar with TCP/IP or NT and other operating systems terminology, please note that domains in this book will always refer to Notes domains unless otherwise specified.

Router	The router is the server-based task that delivers and transfers mail. The router also searches the Domino Directory for recipients' home servers, as well as connections to other servers or domains, when necessary. Please note, if you are familiar with hardware and TCP/IP or NT and other operating systems, the term router may have a different meaning to you. In this book, the term router will always mean the server task used for mail delivery and transfer, unless otherwise specified.

continued

Table 11-1   Domino Messaging Terminology (*continued*)

Term	Definition
Mailer	The mailer is the workstation-based component that deposits a mail message on the sender's server's MAIL.BOX. The mailer touches the messages first, after the user composes the message. In addition, the mailer is responsible for looking up users in the Domino Directory to verify existence and spelling, as long as the users are in the same domain.
MAIL.BOX	The MAIL.BOX is a server database that temporarily holds messages as they are in the process of being delivered and transferred. It is often referred to as the server's outgoing mailbox. You may create multiple MAIL.BOXes in R5 to enhance mail performance.
Mail delivery	Mail delivery is the process of placing a message in the recipient's mail file. The router accomplishes delivery when mail is moved from the MAIL.BOX on the recipient's server to the recipient's mail file.
Mail transfer	Mail transfer is the process of moving mail between servers, from MAIL.BOX to MAIL.BOX. The Router takes messages bound for recipients on other servers from the MAIL.BOX of the sender's server and places it in the MAIL.BOX of the recipient's server, or an intermediate server on the way to the recipient's server.

recipient's mail file (whether on the same server or different server). This part of the process is the same in all server-based mail scenarios. The rest of the process is then defined by the location of the message recipient.

Mail Routing on the Same Server

When the router determines that the recipient's mail file is on the same server, the message is immediately delivered to the recipient's mail file. The router determines the location of the recipient's mail file from their Person document in the Domino Directory, as shown in Figure 11-1.

In a company called NotesGirl, for example, there is only one mail server, ServerA/NotesGirl. If Cindy Smith/NotesGirl sends Joe Jones/NotesGirl a message in this environment, the mailer on her workstation will first verify that Joe Jones/Notes-Girl is in the Domino Directory and that this is the correct spelling of his name, and then will deposit the message in the MAIL.BOX on ServerA/NotesGirl. The router task will then check to see whether ServerA/NotesGirl is Joe Jones' home server. When this is verified, the router will deliver the message to Joe Jones' mail file. Figure 11-2 shows a diagram of this example.

PERSON: User Test/NotesGirl User Test/NotesGirl @ NotesGirl

| Basics | Mail | Work/Home | Other | Miscellaneous | Certificates | Administration |

Mail

Mail system:	Notes
Domain:	NotesGirl
Mail server:	TheNotesMobile/NotesGirl
Mail file:	mail\utest
Forwarding address:	
Internet address:	
Format preference for incoming mail:	No Preference
Encrypt incoming mail:	No

Figure 11-1   Person document

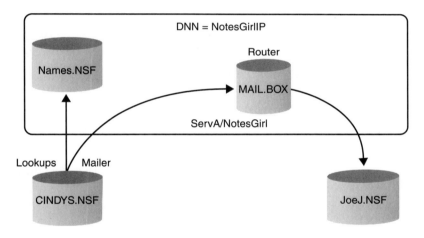

Figure 11-2   Mail routing on the same server

Mail Routing Between Different Servers

When the router determines from the recipient's Person document that the recipient resides on a different home server than the sender, the message is transferred from the MAIL.BOX on the sender's server to the MAIL.BOX on the recipient's server. The router uses the Server documents and Connection documents from the Domino Directory to determine a path to the other server. In the case where both servers have the same DNN, the router is able to transfer the mail to the remote MAIL.BOX automatically and immediately, without the need for a Connection document. The server can determine the DNN from the Ports . . . Notes Network Ports tab of the Server document, as shown in Figure 11-3. After the message is in the recipient's home server's MAIL.BOX, the router task for that server delivers the message to the recipient's mail file.

When NotesGirl expands, for example, they build a second mail server. This server—ServerB/NotesGirl—is on the same Local Area Network (providing a constant connection) as Server A and uses the same protocol, TCP/IP. The Notes administrator therefore places ServerB in the same DNN, NotesGirlIP.

When Cindy Smith/NotesGirl sends a message to Chloe Burns/NotesGirl, whose home server is ServerB/NotesGirl, the message is created in Cindy's mail file and the mailer verifies the spelling of Chloe's name and places the message in ServerA/Notes-Girl's MAIL.BOX. The router determines that Chloe's home server is ServerB/NotesGirl by looking at her Person document in the Domino Directory. Next, the router looks for a way to get to ServerB/NotesGirl. From the Server documents in the Domino Directory, the router determines that ServerA and ServerB are both in the NotesGirlIP DNN. The router can then immediately transfer the message to ServerB's MAIL.BOX. ServerB's router task then verifies that Chloe's mail file is on that server and delivers the message to her mail file. A diagram of this example is shown in Figure 11-4.

Mail Routing Between Different DNNs

When servers are not constantly connected and/or when they use different protocols, they must be placed in different DNNs, which changes the mail routing process. The process changes when the router determines from the Server documents that the home servers of the sender and the recipient are in different DNNs. At this point, the router needs to find a path to the remote server. This path is found in a server Connection document.

SERVER: TheNotesMobile/NotesGirl

| Basics | Security | Ports | Server Tasks | Internet Protocols | MTAs | Miscellaneous | Transactional Logging | Administration |

| Notes Network Ports | Internet Ports | Proxies |

Port	Protocol	Notes Network	Net Address	Enabled
TCPIP	TCP	NotesGirlIP	TheNotesMobile	ENABLED
test_ip	TCP	NG_IP	TheNotesMobile	DISABLED

Figure 11-3   Ports . . . Notes Network Ports

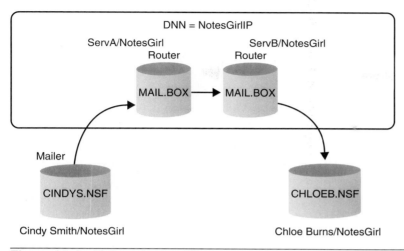

Figure 11-4   Mail routing on different servers

When servers are in different DNNs, mail routing requires a server Connection document for each direction of mail. To each server, mail routing is a one-way process. You send a message and it stops at its destination. When a reply is sent, this is another one-way process started by the other server. Because mail is one-way, all mail routing requires *two* Connection documents (one for each server). The Connection document also determines the schedule on which mail is transferred between the two servers.

After the router determines the path to the recipient's home server, and the mail routing schedule to follow, it transfers the mail message to the recipient's home server's MAIL.BOX. For example, when NotesGirl opens a second office in a different building, they connect the new server, ServerC, to the servers at the first location using modems. Because the servers are not constantly connected, the Domino administrator places them in separate DNNs and creates Connection documents for mail routing.

Cindy Smith/NotesGirl (whose home server is ServerA/NotesGirl) sends a mail message to Oscar Johnson/NotesGirl (whose home server is ServerC/NotesGirl). The router determines that Oscar is on a different mail server and that the mail server is in a different DNN. The router then uses the Connection document from ServerA to ServerC to find a path to ServerC. After finding the path, the router waits until the next scheduled mail routing time and transfers the mail to ServerC/NotesGirl's MAIL.BOX. ServerC's router then places the message in Oscar's mail file. A diagram of this example is shown in Figure 11-5.

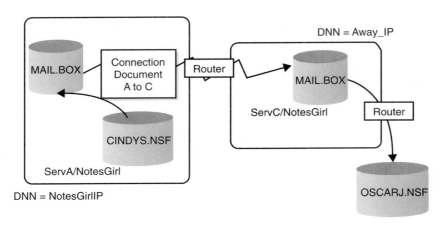

Figure 11-5   Mail routing to a different DNN

Another related scenario is that another user in the environment, on ServerB, tries to send a message to a user on ServerC. There is no Connection document between ServerB and ServerA. ServerB can, however, use the Connection document for another server in its DNN to route mail outside the DNN. In this case, when Joe, whose home server is ServerB, tries to send a message, the router uses ServerA's Connection document to find a path to ServerC, as shown in Figure 11-6.

Connecting to Different Servers

As described in our examples above, and in the requirements to route to servers outside your Domino Named Network, your servers must have a way to connect to each other. This path is determined by the Connection documents created in the server's Domino Directory. Let's take a moment to examine the server Connection document. Connection documents for mail are required any time the servers are not in the same DNN. Mail Connection documents define the path to the other server, the routing schedule, and any mail thresholds. As mentioned before, to create a complete mail route that allows users to send and receive, two mail Connection documents must be created for each connected server.

To create a Connection document, open the Domino Administrator to the Configuration tab. Expand the Server section and select the Connections view. Once in the

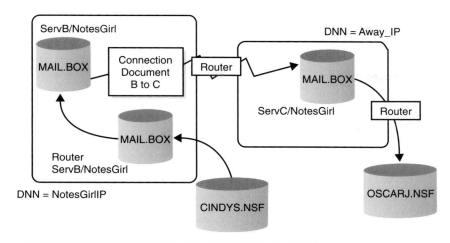

Figure 11-6 Mail routing to a different DNN using another connection

Connections view, click the New Connection action button to create a new server Connection document. You could also create the Connection document by opening the Domino Directory or by expanding the Messaging section.

On the Basics tab of the Connection document, first select the Connection type. This describes the way that the servers are connected, such as Local Area Network, Dialup Modem, and Passthru server. Choose the appropriate type for your servers. Please note that the value in this field changes other fields on the document. Also note that you can have multiple Connection documents between any two servers, using different connection types in case of WAN outages, and so on

Type the hierarchical name of both the source and destination servers. The source server is the server that originates the connection. Since mail is one way, to route mail between two servers, you will have a Connection document for each server, and each server will be a source server for one of the Connection documents. Also type the source and destination domains. This field refers to the Domino domain name, not to be confused with an NT Domain, DNS Domain, or any other usage of the word domain that you might be thinking about.

To complete the Use the Ports field, click the Choose Ports button and select the ports that you want to use for this connection. You may want to complete the Optional Network Address field with the IP address for the destination server.

You can complete the Usage Priority field if you want a certain connection only to be used as a last resort. For example, if two servers are connected over a bridged/routed WAN, this would probably be your first choice of methods to connect for mail routing. However, there are also modems on both servers as a backup scenario in case of the WAN link being down. You would make the Dialup Modem Connection document low-priority in this case.

On the Replication/Routing tab, you can disable the replication task, as this is a Routing Connection document. On the Routing section, select Mail Routing as the Routing task. The Route at Once If field is also known as the routing threshold. When the number of messages waiting in the MAIL.BOX for delivery to this server reaches the number in this field (the default is 5), the messages are routed without waiting for the next connection interval or connect at time. All waiting messages count toward the routing threshold; however, not all messages are sent. Messages can be low-, normal-, or high-priority, based on the sender's delivery options. If a message is high-priority, it will be routed immediately, without waiting for a connection time. If a message is normal priority, it will behave as normal—routed at the appropriate connection time, if mail is forced to route manually, or if the mail routing threshold is reached. If mail is low-priority, it counts toward the routing threshold but is only routed during the low-priority mail interval (this is between midnight and 6 A.M., by default, although you can configure it using a NOTES.INI setting).

The Routing Cost field is calculated automatically, based on the type of connection. A LAN connection type, for example, has a default routing cost of 1. A Dial-up connection type has a default routing cost of 5. In the case of two similar Connection documents, Domino will try to use the one with the lowest routing cost first.

The router type field can be set to push only, pull only, pull push, or push wait. This option is intended to help with dialing into remote or ISP servers.

On the Schedule tab, configure whether the schedule is enabled or disabled. At times you may need to disable a certain connection, such as when a server is offline, but you may not want to delete the Connection document. In the Connect at Times field, select the times at which the server should make contact with the destination server. This can be specific times or ranges of time, but should include the low-priority times, to ensure that low-priority mail can route. Complete the Repeat Interval field with how often the source server will attempt to contact the destination server. If only one time or one call is desired, this field can be left blank. The Connect At Times field and the Repeat Interval field work together based on previous routing times. If the first connection occurs at 4 A.M. and takes 15 minutes and the repeat interval is 30 minutes, the second connection occurs at 4:45 A.M. Finally, select the days of the week that this Connection document should apply.

CAUTION Here's a "gotcha" to be wary of when creating Connection documents. One of the end user mail options when sending mail is for Delivery Priority. The priority choices are low, normal, and high. By default, all mail is sent normal priority. Normal priority mail follows the mail settings in the Connection document—including schedule and mail threshold. High-priority mail is routed immediately. It causes the server to make an immediate connection to the remote server and sends all normal- and high-priority pending mail. Low-priority mail is routed by default from midnight to six in the morning. If there is no mail Connection document that covers the low-priority times, low-priority mail will not route.

Mail Routing Between Domains

When mail servers are in different domains, the addressing and delivery become more complex. When you see a Domino mail address that has been resolved, or checked, by the mailer, it looks something like this: Libby Schwarz/NotesGirl@NotesGirl. The last part of the email address, after the @ symbol, is the Domino (or Notes) domain.

When mail routes within the same domain, the domain portion of the address serves only to verify the domain for the router. This portion of the address is vital, however, if you intend to send messages outside your Notes domain. In most cases, sending mail outside your own domain will also mean sending outside your company. This may entail sending via SMTP (simple mail transfer protocol—the Internet standard messaging protocol), or you may be connected via Notes Net or other native Notes methods. You must have a Connection document describing a path and schedule to the other domain to be able to route mail to the other domain. In this respect, it is the same process as routing mail to a server on a different DNN. In addition, however, the router needs a Domain document, which shows the router the existence and definition of this other domain.

Adjacent Domains

Domains that are adjacent to your current domain have a direct physical connection to your current domain, such as through modems, bridges, routers, and public or private networks. To route mail to an adjacent domain, you must have a Connection document in your Domino Directory that describes a path from some server in your domain to some server in the adjacent domain. Mail can then be transferred between the two domains using the servers that are connected to each other.

To define an adjacent domain, create an adjacent Domain document in your Domino Directory, as shown in Figure 11-7.

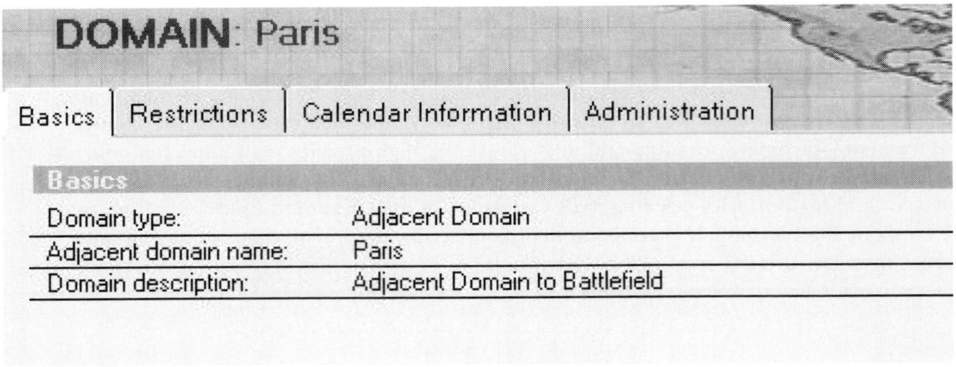

Figure 11-7 Adjacent Domain document

When user Christian in domain Battlefield needs to send a message to user Roxanne in domain Paris, for example, the router in domain Battlefield examines the address in the mail message, which looks like this: To: Roxanne @ Paris. It checks for a Domain document that defines the domain Paris. When it finds an Adjacent Domain document for domain Paris, it checks for a Connection document that specifies how and when to transfer mail to a server in domain Paris. Figure 11-8 shows that Christian's mail server, Server A, connects directly to Roxanne's mail server, Server B.

When routing mail among domains, however, mail can be routed using any server in either domain that has a Connection document to the other domain. Figure 11-9, for example, shows that Christian's mail server, Server A, does not have any Connection documents that allow it to connect to Roxanne's mail server, Server B. The router finds a Connection document, however, that shows a path from Server C, another mail router in domain Battlefield, to Server D, another mail router in domain Paris.

When you address messages to be sent to users in adjacent domains, you must use an explicit name to address the message. An explicit name includes not only a distinguished name, but also the domain. For example, you might address a message to Roxanne Smith/Executives/Paris @ Paris.

Non-Adjacent Domains

Domains that are non-adjacent to each other, however, do not have a physical connection. They cannot use modems or networks to connect directly to the other domain. There is no Connection document between the domains for mail routing, as there is no

Figure 11-8
Christian's server
connects to
Roxanne's server

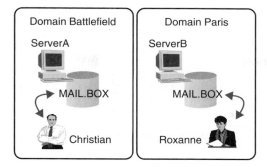

Figure 11-9
Routing via another
connection

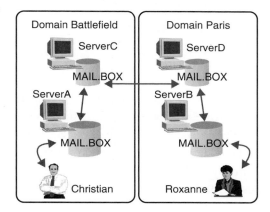

way to connect to that domain. In the case of a non-adjacent domain, an adjacent domain must be identified that can pass the mail messages between the two disconnected domains. Mail is transferred between two non-adjacent domains using a domain that is adjacent to both of them.

To define a non-adjacent domain, create a non-adjacent Domain document in the Domino Directory, as shown in Figure 11-10. An Adjacent Domain document and a Connection document will also have to exist for mail to route.

In our example above, when user Christian in domain Battlefield needs to send a message to user Roxanne in domain Paris, the router in domain Battlefield examines the address in the mail message, which looks like this: To: Roxanne @ Paris. It checks for a Domain document that defines the domain Paris. In this case, it finds a Non-Adjacent Domain document for domain Paris that specifies that any mail sent to

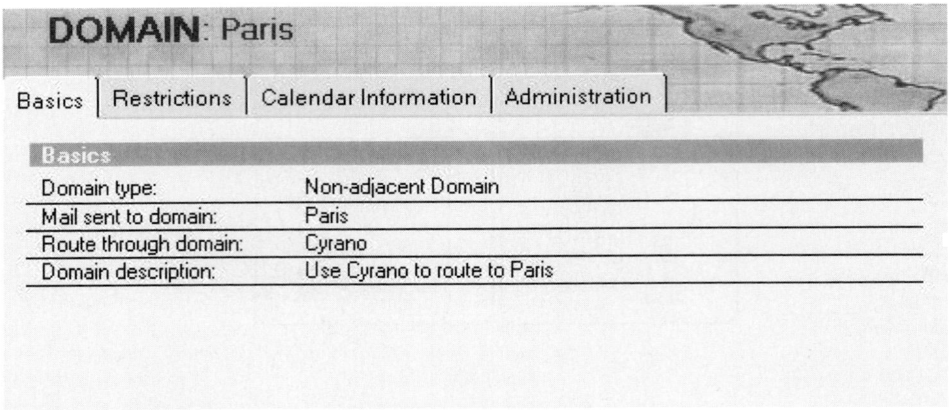

Figure II-I0 Non-adjacent Domain document

domain Paris should be routed through domain Cyrano. The router then searches for an Adjacent Domain document for domain Cyrano and a Connection document for a server in domain Cyrano. Figure 11-11 shows that Christian's mail server in domain Battlefield, Server A, connects to Server Horse in domain Cyrano. Server Horse in domain Cyrano then connects directly to Roxanne's mail server, Server B in domain Paris.

In the previous example, the following documents need to exist for mail routing to occur:

- The Domino Directory in domain Battlefield must have a Non-Adjacent Domain document for domain Paris that specifies that mail to Paris routes through Cyrano.

- The Domino Directory in domain Battlefield must have an Adjacent Domain document for domain Cyrano.

- The Domino Directory in domain Battlefield must have a Connection document that specifies a mail routing connection between Server A and Server Horse.

- The Domino Directory in domain Cyrano must have an Adjacent Domain document for domain Paris.

- The Domino Directory in domain Cyrano must have a Connection document that specifies a mail routing connection between Server Horse and Server B.

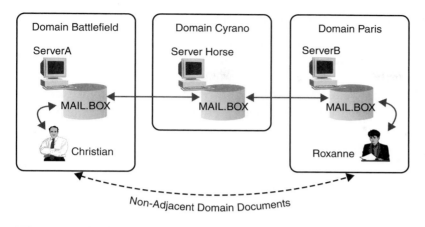

Figure 11-11 Connecting to Paris via Cyrano

> **TIP** In either the case of adjacent or non-adjacent domain routing, for Roxanne to respond to Christian, another set of documents must exist that specifies the route back to domain Battlefield, since mail routing is only one way. This includes Adjacent and/or Non-Adjacent Domain documents in the Domino Directory in domain Paris that specify either Battlefield or Cyrano and a mail-routing connection.

When you address a message to a user in an adjacent domain, you use an explicit name, such as Roxanne Smith/Executives/Paris @ Paris. When you address a message to a user in a non-adjacent domain, you can use the exact same address *if* you have a Non-Adjacent Domain document specified in the Domino Directory, as described above. If, however, you do not have a non-adjacent domain specified, you must use the explicit name to define both the adjacent and non-adjacent domains to use to route mail. If you do not have a Non-Adjacent Domain document for domain Paris, for example, you might address a message like the following example: Roxanne Smith/Executives/Paris @ Paris @ Cyrano. The router reads the domain names from right to left, in the order that it will transmit them. In this example, the message will first be sent to domain Cyrano and then from Cyrano it will be sent to domain Paris.

Controlling Mail Routing Among Domains

Administrators in each domain that participate in mail routing among domains have the ability to reject mail coming from a certain domain. You would probably do this to avoid overworking resources on your servers. Assume, for example, that you are the administrator of domain Cyrano, and you no longer want to route mail from domain Battlefield to domain Paris. You would place Battlefield in the Deny mail from Domains field of the adjacent Domain document that defines the relationship between Cyrano and Paris, as shown in Figure 11-12.

Non-Notes Mail

Sometimes when mail is going to another server or outside your Domino domain, it is also going outside your organization/company. In this case, it is likely that you want to send the message via the Internet. Domino can route mail directly to the Internet or it can route via a relay host or firewall. You can also send and receive mail directly from some other mail systems, such as cc:Mail and x.400, using MTAs (Message Transfer Agents). Note that you can send SMTP mail either inside or outside your local Domino domain.

SMTP Routing

SMTP mail routing is native to Domino in R5 and can be used both inside and outside your Domino environment. You may also use Notes routing to send mail to a server that runs SMTP and connects to the Internet. To route mail using the native SMTP routing, use a Configuration document, the Server document, and a Global Domain document to configure the routing.

Before you complete the Domino configuration necessary, you have some general configuration to complete. If you plan to send Internet mail, you must ensure that your

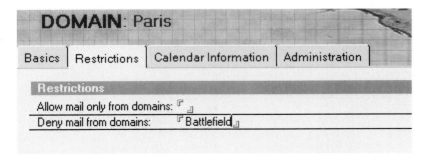

Figure 11-12 Routing Restrictions

server has some connection to an ISP or the Internet. If you connect via a relay host or through a firewall, you need to know the name and IP address. You should make sure that the server is successfully running TCP/IP and is listed in DNS (Domain Name Server) with an MX (mail exchanger) record. If your company will be known by multiple Internet Domain names, they should all be listed in DNS. These names will also be entered as aliases in a Global Domain document.

To configure your server to send SMTP mail outside of your local Internet domain (that is, to the Internet), you should create or edit a Configuration Settings document for your server. Open the Domino Administrator to the Configuration tab. Expand the Server section and select the Configurations view. Either open an existing Configuration document or use the Add Configuration action button to create a new one. On the Router/SMTP . . . Basics tab, you must enable the SMTP Used when sending messages outside of the local Internet domain option, as shown in Figure 11-13. When this option is disabled, this server will not be able to send SMTP mail.

To send mail within the local domain, you should configure it for All Messages to send both Notes and MIME format messages to other Domino servers in your Internet domain. Notes format messages will be converted to MIME format before being sent. This may cause poor performance. Set this field to MIME Messages Only to use SMTP

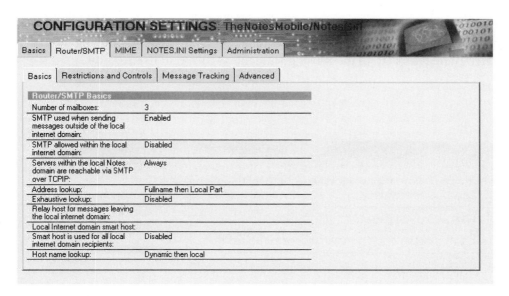

Figure 11-13   Send SMTP outside your Internet domain

routing only to send messages to other Domino servers that are configured to receive SMTP mail. When this field is set to the default (Disabled), no messages will be sent via SMTP in the local domain.

You also need to configure the Servers within the local Notes domain that are reachable via SMTP over TCP/IP field. The options in this field are Always and Only if in the same Notes Named Network. The Always option (which is the default) will cause Domino to send to all other Domino servers that are configured to receive SMTP mail. The other option (Only if in the same Notes Named Network) will only use SMTP to route to Domino servers within the local domain, even if servers outside the local network are configured to receive SMTP mail.

NOTE Domino Named Networks (DNNs) and Notes Named Networks (NNNs) are the same thing. Lotus implemented a terminology change, but the term is still somewhat inconsistent.

If you want to use a non-Domino SMTP server, you will need a Foreign SMTP Domain document and an SMTP Connection document. The Foreign SMTP Domain document defines real or virtual Notes/Domino domains to route mail outside the local domain to. The SMTP Connection document defines the route to a server that is connected to the Internet.

If you intend to use your servers for SMTP mail, they should be able to receive mail sent by SMTP routing. You enable a server to receive SMTP mail by enabling the SMTP listener in the Basics tab of the Server document, as shown in Figure 11-14.

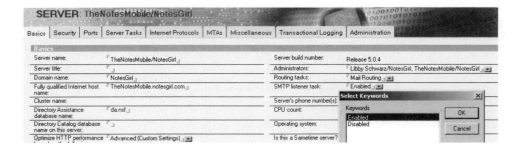

Figure 11-14   Enable SMTP Listener task

Local Internet Domain   To route SMTP mail, Domino must be able to determine the local Internet domain(s). Domino can look at the server's host name, but especially if there are multiple local domains, you should use a Global Domain document. To create a Global Domain document, create a new Domain document and select Global Domain as the type. Select R5 Internet Domains or R4.x SMTP MTA as the Global Domain role. You can also choose whether this is the default Global Domain for all Internet protocols. This is only necessary if you have more than one Global Domain document created. On the Restrictions tab, list all the Notes (Domino) domains and aliases that should be considered local Internet domains. On the Conversions tab, enter the local primary Internet domain and alternate Internet domain aliases.

Other Non-Notes Mail

Sometimes you want to connect to other non-Notes mail packages, such as cc:Mail, x.400 mail, or others. For some, Lotus provides an MTA (message transfer agent), such as the cc:Mail MTA. For others, you will need to use a gateway of some kind. If Lotus provides an MTA, you would use a Foreign x.400 or Foreign cc:Mail domain document, the appropriate Connection document type, and whatever other software (the MTA) that was necessary.

Mail Topology

First, what do we mean when we discuss topology? Topology in Domino, as in other computing areas, relates to where servers are located and how they are connected. We will discuss topology both for Domino mail routing and for replication.

The basic reason for a mail topology is so that you can control and predict how mail will be routed within your organization, especially when you have multiple DNNs or multiple domains. In many organizations, there are bandwidth and other communications reasons for controlling the topology as well. The main types of mail routing topologies are hub and spoke, end-to-end, ring, and mesh. You create your topology by enabling mail routing via Domino Named Networks and mail routing Connection documents.

Hub and spoke is probably the most common topology in enterprise environments, as it is the most efficient and organized. In hub and spoke, one server (the hub) schedules, initiates, and controls all mail routing. For example, you may have a corporate office in Houston and smaller offices all over the world. You might choose to have the hub server in Houston be the central Hub for your enterprise. In this case, the hub will call the other servers (or initiate the connection over a LAN or WAN) and initiate mail routing. All the other servers will be the spokes. They will only forward mail through (to and from) the hub when they are called by the hub. In addition, the spokes will only route mail to one another via the hub, never directly. The hub and spoke topology is shown in Figure 11-15. The hub and spoke can be expanded to have multiple levels, in which case it is called a binary tree topology.

End-to-end routing topology has each server connected in a line, as shown in Figure 11-16. Each server will talk to the server ahead of it in the line and the server after it in the line. In this chain, for example, the server in our Houston office would call the server in our Dallas office. The Dallas server would call to the Kansas City office. The chain would then reverse on itself, and Kansas would call Dallas, and so on.

A ring topology is very similar to the end-to-end topology, as shown in Figure 11-17. When the last server is reached in the line, however, it simply circles back around to the beginning. So, in our example, after Dallas calls Kansas City, Kansas City would turn around and call Houston.

In mesh topology, all servers connect directly to all other servers. This can be a difficult topology to administer, due to its complex and disorganized nature, and is not recommended. The mesh topology is shown in Figure 11-18.

Figure 11-15
Hub and spoke topology

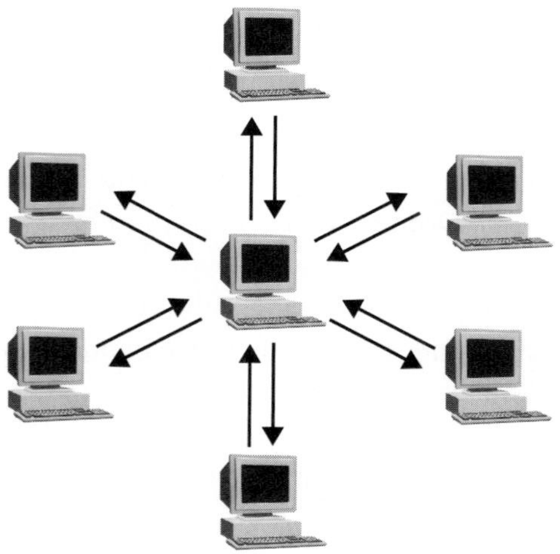

Figure 11-16
End-to-end topology

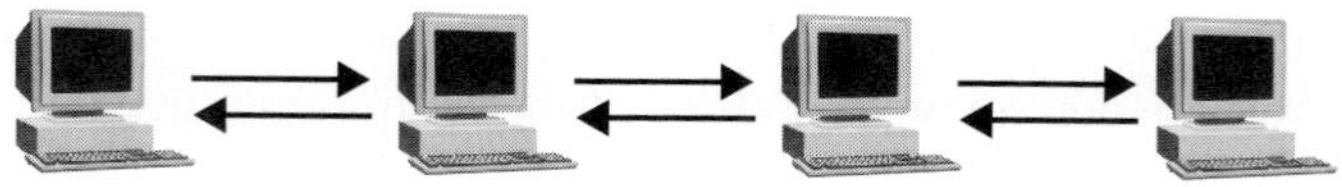

Figure 11-17
Ring topology

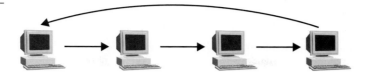

Figure 11-18
Mesh topology

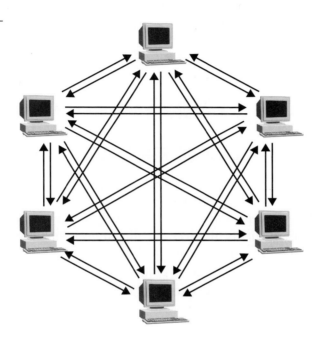

You will organize your mail routing Connection documents using one of these routing topologies or a combination of routing topologies. This will ensure that all the users in your organization can send and receive mail in a timely fashion. Bear in mind that you need two Connection documents for each mail routing connection.

After you create your mail routing Connection documents, you can view your organization's mail topology using the Domino Administrator Messaging tab. If you are running the MAPS task on your server, you can select the Messaging . . . Mail tab and expand the Mail Routing Topology section. You can view the mail routing topology based on Connection documents and/or Named Networks, as shown in Figure 11-19. If you double-click one of the connecting lines in the applet, Domino Administrator opens the specified Connection document for viewing.

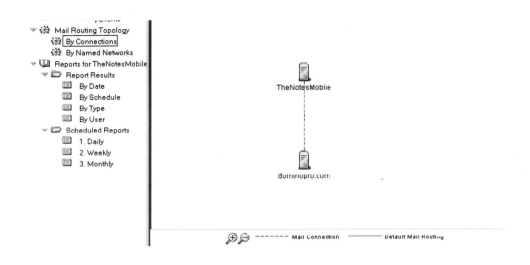

Figure 11-19 Viewing the routing topology using MAPS

Internet Mail Topology Issues

An additional part of planning a topology is dealing with Internet mail. This can include the types of clients that access mail and deciding how internal and external mail routes. Notes mail can be accessed by Notes clients and Web clients (using the HTTP task). If you enable it to, the Domino server can also provide POP3 and IMAP format for those client types. To allow POP3 clients to access mail, you would run the POP3 task on the server and configure a POP3 client to access it. To allow IMAP clients to access mail, you would run the IMAP task on the server and configure an IMAP client to access it. For IMAP access, the user's mail file would also need to be converted.

Users would need a Person document and Internet password to authenticate to use HTTP, POP3, or IMAP. A mail file would also need to exist for the user on the Domino server. A user has the option of accessing their mail using any of these clients. Note that for users receiving mail via IMAP and POP, you must provide SMTP for sending mail. Enable the SMTP listener task as described previously.

Determining how internal and external mail routes is a case of deciding when to use native Notes routing and when to use SMTP routing. This is discussed in more detail earlier in the chapter. Bear in mind that one of the issues is which servers will route mail to the Internet. You can choose to have all Domino servers route to the Internet, selected servers route to the Internet using SMTP, or have some send and some receive, based on what options you enable on each server. You might also use a dial-up connection to an ISP to route mail.

Shared Mail

Shared mail is sometimes also called pointer-based mail or object store mail. In message-based mail, discussed previously, each mail message is stored in its entirety in the user's mail file. In shared mail, messages are split between the user's mail file and another database called the single copy object store (SCOS).

The main purpose of shared mail is to save space on the mail server. When message-based mail is used, for example, any messages sent to multiple recipients get stored multiple times on the server. If I send a broadcast message to 15 users, that message is stored 15 times. In shared mail, however, the message itself would be stored only once. Each user would only have a pointer to the message, contained in a header. The body of the message is stored once, in the single copy object store. If we assume a simple text message of 10K, with message-based mail, the storage space required on the mail server is 150K. In shared mail, there would only be 10K for the message itself and another 15K (total) for the pointers in each user's mail file, for an overall savings of 115K. Then imagine the savings if the message included rich text with formatting or attachments, which can raise the size of the messages exponentially, as you can see in Figure 11-20.

TIP   The header, or pointer, portion of the message contains the following fields: To:, CC:, BCC:, Subject, and From fields. In addition, it contains a link, or pointer, to the content of the message that is stored in the shared mail database. The content is the message body, rich text components, and any attachments.

To the reader of the message, shared mail is transparent. There is no difference in the way a user sees or reads their messages when shared mail is enabled.

One thing to consider when deciding whether shared mail is a useful option is the pattern of use for mail in your environment. If users send messages to multiple recipients that have the same home server, you will have the greatest savings. If your users send many mail messages to only one or two recipients, you will still have some savings of space, but not as significant as in other scenarios. In addition, if your users are split among many mail servers and often send messages to users on those other servers, you will have a smaller amount of space savings. As we examine the shared mail configuration settings and processes, you will find other situations where shared mail would be more or less useful.

Figure 11-20
Shared mail
message size

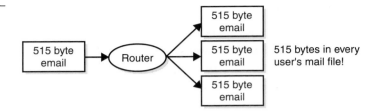

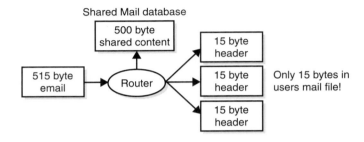

TIP In the real world, very few environments have implemented shared mail. While it is a good space saver, shared mail requires a large amount of ongoing maintenance. In addition, if the SCOS becomes corrupted, many users can lose messages or data. While shared mail can be a good option, you should be certain to perform regular, ongoing maintenance and backups if you decide to implement it.

Configuring Shared Mail

Shared mail can be enabled in multiple ways. The easiest, and most complete in terms of configuration is by typing the following command at the server console:

```
TELL ROUTER USE SHAREDMAIL.NSF
```

Insert the name of your shared mail database in place of SHAREDMAIL.NSF in the previous commands and in the following ones. The shared mail database can have any name other than MAILOBJ.NSF. This command creates the requisite files for shared mail and enables shared mail for all new messages.

When shared mail is enabled on a server, two files are created. These two files are MAILOBJ.NSF and *SHAREDMAIL.NSF*. By default, *SHAREDMAIL.NSF* is named MAILOBJ1.NSF. It can have any name, however, with the exception of MAILOBJ.NSF.

The file MAILOBJ.NSF is a pointer file. While it has a .NSF extension, it cannot be opened in Notes. It is a text file and can be opened either by using the Open With . . . option in Windows NT/2000 and 9x (available in Explorer or My Computer by holding down Shift while right-clicking on the file), or by opening NOTEPAD.EXE and then using File . . . Open to open the file. When you open this file, you will find a path to the other file, *SHAREDMAIL.NSF*. Whenever a new shared mail database is enabled, this path must change to reflect the active shared mail database.

The second file that is created by enabling shared mail is the *SHAREDMAIL.NSF*, again, by default MAILOBJ1.NSF. You can choose to name this file anything that makes sense in your environment, but be aware of two things. First, the exam most often uses the default name, which will increment by one if you choose to create another shared mail database. Second, the filename that you choose cannot be MAILOBJ.NSF and must have a .NSF extension. This database will be the repository for all the shared mail messages. It is called the object store, or single copy object store database (SCOS). As you might imagine, it can grow to be very large and requires careful backup and preventive maintenance. One aspect of preventive maintenance is setting a regular schedule by which you create a new shared mail database. You can use the

```
TELL ROUTER USE SHAREDMAIL.NSF
```

command again to create and enable an additional shared mail database.

There are three main configuration options for shared mail. In the NOTES.INI file, shared mail can be set to 0, 1, or 2. When the SHARED_MAIL setting is set equal to 0, shared mail is disabled, and message-based mail is used. This is the default setting until shared mail is enabled.

When SHARED_MAIL=1, the server console reports that shared mail will be used for mail delivery. This indicates two things. First, the shared mail database will be used for messages intended for two or more recipients only. If the mail message is only intended for one recipient, it is written in full to the user's mail file, as shown in Figure 11-21. If the message is intended for two or more recipients, the message is written to the first user's mail file until the router discovers the second recipient. When the router discovers the second recipient, it writes the message to the shared mail file and replaces the message in the first recipient's mail file with the header information only, as shown in Figure 11-22. The header information is then written to other recipients' mail files.

Figure 11-21
SHARED_MAIL=1,
Recipients=1

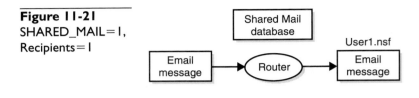

Figure 11-22
SHARED_MAIL=1,
Recipients=2

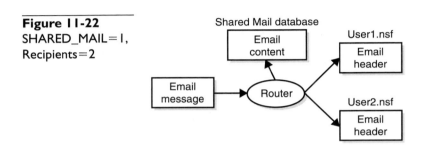

Setting SHARED_MAIL=1 also determines that shared mail will only be used when the recipients are on the local server as their home server. If the message has to be transferred to another server, it will reside in the MAIL.BOX until the router makes the transfer. Similarly, if the server is an intermediate step in reaching a recipient's final destination, the shared mail database will not be used.

By default, when you enable shared mail using the Tell Router Use command, SHARED_MAIL will be set equal to 2. When SHARED_MAIL=2, the console reports that shared mail is enabled for delivery and transfer. Again, this indicates multiple things to the server. First, all mail messages, regardless of the number of recipients, use the shared mail database. Therefore, messages that are created for just one user will use the shared mail database in the same way that messages for two or more recipients will.

In addition, because shared mail is enabled for both delivery *and* transfer, messages that are intended for recipients on other mail servers will use the shared mail database until the router transfers the message, as will messages stopping on the server as an intermediate step to another server. In many environments, this will not be desirable, if the server is often an intermediate step to other servers.

Creating a server Configuration document that changes the NOTES.INI SHARED_MAIL setting can also enable shared mail. To create a Configuration document, open the Domino Directory and expand the Servers view twistie on the navigation pane. Choose the Servers . . . Configurations view and click on the Add Configuration action button. This creates a blank Configuration document. Choose the appropriate server (or leave the asterisk for all servers maintained by this Domino Directory), and click the Set/Modify Parameters button. Under the Item keyword field, choose SHARED_MAIL, and set the value to 1 or 2, depending on the type of shared mail configuration that is appropriate for your environment. Save the Configuration document, as shown in Figure 11-23.

> **TIP** Be aware that the server will not implement the Configuration document immediately. The configuration change will not be implemented until you restart your server if you use the Configuration document.

You also have the option of changing or adding the SHARED_MAIL configuration directly in the NOTES.INI file itself. This leaves, however, more opportunities for mistakes and making errors in the server configuration that can affect other aspects of the server. You can also type the server console command

```
SET CONFIG SHARED_MAIL=1 [or 2]
```

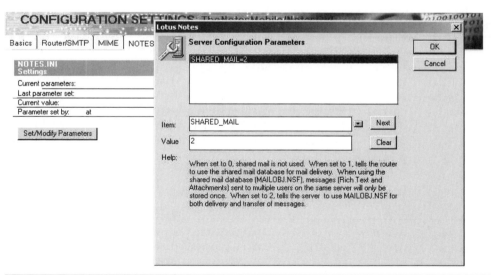

Figure 11-23   Set Shared_Mail=

Note that only the first method I mentioned will complete the entire shared mail configuration. If you use any of the other methods, you will need to create the shared mail database using the command

```
Load Object Create NEWSHAREDMAIL.NSF
```

By default, when you enable shared mail, all new mail messages sent on the server will use shared mail. You do not have to type any commands nor do anything to users' mail files. On the other hand, if mail has been routed on your mail server before shared mail was enabled, you must link these messages to the shared mail database for those messages to be stored in the shared mail file. The console commands used to link these messages to the shared mail file are discussed later in this chapter.

Mail Routing with Shared Mail

Mail routing when shared mail is enabled is very similar to message-based mail routing. When the user sends the message, the mailer makes the first check of the names in the Domino Directory, and transfers the message to the MAIL.BOX. Table 11-2 outlines the next steps taken by the router.

When SHARED_MAIL=1, messages that are being routed to other servers remain in the MAIL.BOX until routing takes place. When SHARED_MAIL=2, messages that are

Table 11-2   Shared Mail

Shared_mail =	Recipients =	Mail routing path
1	1	Router places entire message, header and content, in the user's mail file.
1	2 or more	Router places the entire message in the first user's mail file. The router then discovers the second and subsequent recipients in the To: or CC: field. The content of the message is written to the active shared mail database. The message in the first recipient's mail file is removed and replaced with the header information only. The header information is then written to the other recipients' mail files.
2	Any	The router receives the message and immediately splits it into header and content. The content is written to the shared mail database. The headers are written to the recipients' mail files.

being routed to recipients on other servers are stored in the shared mail database until they are transferred to other servers.

There are scenarios in which shared mail is not used by the mail messages, regardless of the SHARED_MAIL setting. When a user saves a message at compose time, for example, the saved copy of the message is stored completely in the sender's mail file. The router is the task that separates the messages in to header and body and places the mail messages in the shared mail database. If the message is saved at compose time, however, the router never touches it, as shown in Figure 11-24. A technique to avoid this issue is to suggest to your user to CC: themselves on messages they send out, rather than choosing the option of saving sent mail. This way, the router will touch the message and have the opportunity to place the body in the shared mail database and only the header will be placed in the user's mail file.

TIP   Shared mail is still used for the recipients' copies of the message in the scenarios above. It is the saved copy of the message that does not use shared mail.

Similarly, if a user edits a mail message that she has received, and then saves it, that mail message will be stored in her mail file in its entirety. Again, this makes sense, as the message is no longer the same as the message in the object store and the router has not had the opportunity to touch it after the changes were made.

In addition, when mail files are replicated, as in a situation where a user has a local replica of his mail file on his workstation or laptop, shared mail is not used. For a replica of a mail file to be useful, the entire message must be available in the replica. For

Figure 11-24
The router never sees the message

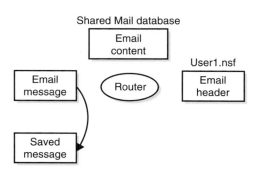

this reason, when a replica is created and when replication of a mail file occurs, all messages will be written to the mail file and shared mail will not be used for the messages in that mail file.

Finally, if a user uses Notes encryption to encrypt incoming messages, shared mail will not be used. This is a setting primarily used by laptop users to protect messages on their laptop from being read by a person who might obtain (and try to read) their local mail file without proper authorization. Encryption of outgoing messages does not affect shared mail, only encryption of incoming messages.

Shared Mail Security

Using shared mail is a security concern to some users. They worry that it would be easy for other users to have access to their mail messages. However, many security features built into the shared mail database should put these fears to rest. First, the icon for the shared mail database cannot be added to any workspace, opened or bookmarked. Second, the ACL of the shared mail database is set very rigidly. Only the server, as a server type, has access to the database. This means that even workstation software on the server machine cannot access the database, only the server software. Third, shared mail databases contain no views, and none can be added. Therefore, even if it were possible to open the database, no documents would be visible. Finally, the database is encrypted. Only the specific server ID that created the shared mail database can access it.

Other Shared Mail Configuration and Commands

There are a variety of shared mail commands that can be useful when you are configuring it or maintaining it. These commands are listed in Table 11-3.

Enhancing Mail Performance

Domino R5 provides a few techniques for enhancing mail routing performance. Two examples of elements that can improve messaging performance are increasing the number of MAIL.BOXES or mail routers.

When the MAIL.BOX is in use, by the router, for example, it requires exclusive access and is locked to other processes. That means that other data cannot be written to the MAIL.BOX during this time and must wait. Since this can be a long wait on a busy system, Lotus provides for the use of multiple MAIL.BOXES on R5 servers. This allows multiple tasks to be going on simultaneously between the router and the MAIL.BOX. To add an additional MAIL.BOX to a server, create or edit a Configuration Settings document

Table 11-3 Shared Mail Commands

Command	Usage and Info
TELL ROUTER USE *SHAREDMAIL.NSF*	The TELL ROUTER USE command can be used to enable shared mail. It will change the SHARED_MAIL setting in the NOTES.INI file to 2 automatically. It will also create the database link file, MAILOBJ.NSF, and the shared mail database itself, named MAILOBJ#.NSF, by default. You can also use the TELL ROUTER USE command to change the active shared mail database. While the router can only write to one shared mail database at a time (the active database), users can access multiple shared mail databases that may still be storing messages. For example, you have enabled shared mail on your server and your shared mail database, MAILOBJ1.NSF, is getting too large. This can cause corruption and slower response time. At this point, you may type **TELL ROUTER USE MAILOBJ2.NSF**. The new database, MAILOBJ2.NSF will be created and used as the active shared mail database, and the pointer file, MAILOBJ.NSF, will be updated with the new information.
LOAD OBJECT INFO *USER.NSF*, where *USER.NSF* is any user's mail file.	This will tell you if the specified mail file uses an object store (shared mail). If you have situations where there are many replicas being made, for example, this command may be useful to tell you if a a particular database is using shared mail.
LOAD OBJECT LINK *USER.NSF* *SHAREDMAIL.NSF*	The LOAD OBJECT LINK command links a particular mail file (*USER.NSF*) or a directory (use the directory name in place of the mail file name) to the specified shared mail database (*SHAREDMAIL.NSF*).
LOAD OBJECT LINK -RELINK *USER.NSF* *SHAREDMAIL.NSF*	When you use the LOAD OBJECT LINK command, all mail messages that have never used a shared mail database before are linked to the shared mail database. The -RELINK option allows all messages, including those that may have been previously linked, to be linked to the specified shared mail database.
LOAD OBJECT LINK UNLINK *USER.NSF*	Use this command when you want a particular mail file to stop using shared mail. If you need to move a user from one mail server to another, for example, first unlink the mail file from the shared mail database on the first server using the UNLINK command. You would then need to relink the user's mail file to the shared mail database on the new server.
LOAD OBJECT COLLECT *SHAREDMAIL.NSF* or *USER.NSF*	The LOAD OBJECT COLLECT command can be run either on the shared mail database or on a user's mail file. Run COLLECT when there are disconnected messages between the user's mail database and the shared mail file. When all the headers pointing to a particular message in the shared mail database have been deleted, for example, you have to run collect to remove the message content from the shared mail database.

 TIP The COLLECT task is scheduled for 2 A.M. by default in the **SERVERTASKSAT2** line of the **NOTES.INI**.

continued

Table 11-3   Shared Mail Commands (continued)

Command	Usage and Info
LOAD OBJECT COLLECT—FORCE *SHAREDMAIL.NSF*	Adding the -FORCE option to the LOAD OBJECT COLLECT will remove damaged messages, or any messages for which it cannot find a pointer. Run this option with caution, as messages can be deleted unintentionally if any mail files are unavailable or offline.
LOAD OBJECT SET -ALWAYS *USER.NSF*	We discussed situations above where shared mail is not used. If a mail file is replicated, for example, shared mail is not used. If you want to force these mail files to use shared mail, you can use the LOAD OBJECT SET -ALWAYS command. To disable shared mail for replica mail files, type LOAD OBJECT RESET -ALWAYS.
LOAD OBJECT SET -NEVER *USER.NSF*	You may occasionally want to have shared mail enabled on a specific server but exclude certain mail files. To exclude a particular mail file, use the LOAD OBJECT SET -NEVER command. To reverse this process and include a previously excluded mail file, type LOAD OBJECT RESET—NEVER *USER.NSF*.
LOAD OBJECT CREATE *SHAREDMAIL.NSF*	This command is another method of creating a new shared mail database. If you use this method rather than the TELL ROUTER USE *X.NSF* method, you must change the path in the MAILOBJ.NSF pointer file to tell the router that this is the new active shared mail database.

for that server. On the Router/SMTP . . . Basics tab, type the number of MAIL.BOXES you would like on that server in the Number of Mailboxes field. You must restart the server for Domino to create the additional MAIL.BOXES.

To use multiple routers, you have to use multiple servers. This is useful when routing with SMTP especially. Use one server for incoming SMTP and another server for outgoing SMTP. This may improve performance.

Troubleshooting and Tracking Mail

The MAIL.BOX database is the first tool for mail troubleshooting. It stores pending mail, mail awaiting transfer to users on other servers, and dead mail. When a message cannot be delivered to a recipient, it tries to send a Delivery Failure to the sender. This Delivery Failure report contains the original message as well as the failure message, as shown in Figure 11-25. When a delivery failure message is sent, the undeliverable message would not be considered dead, only undeliverable.

Sometimes, however, a Delivery Failure report (also known as a Non-delivery report, or NDR) also fails to reach the original sender of the message for some reason. A message in this state that can neither be delivered nor returned is considered dead, as shown in Figure 11-26.

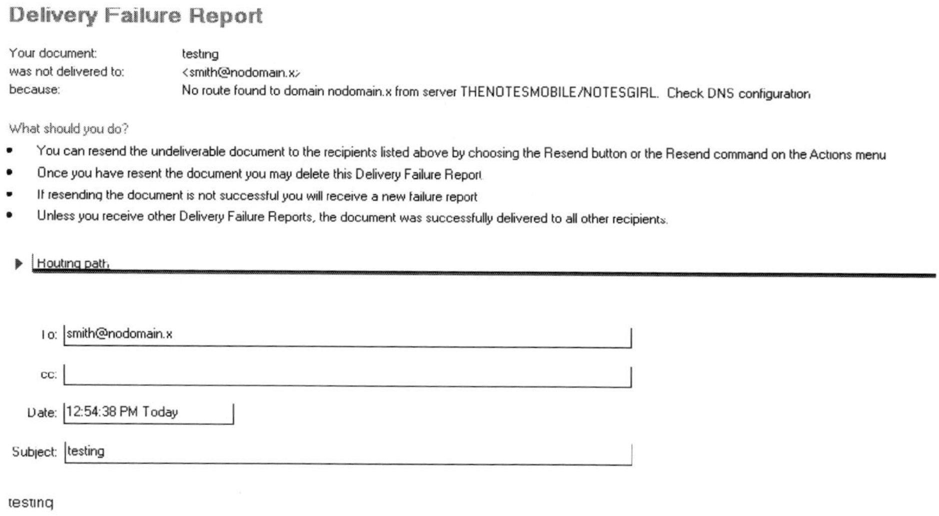

Delivery Failure Report

Your document: testing
was not delivered to: <smith@nodomain.x>
because: No route found to domain nodomain.x from server THENOTESMOBILE/NOTESGIRL. Check DNS configuration

What should you do?

- You can resend the undeliverable document to the recipients listed above by choosing the Resend button or the Resend command on the Actions menu
- Once you have resent the document you may delete this Delivery Failure Report
- If resending the document is not successful you will receive a new failure report
- Unless you receive other Delivery Failure Reports, the document was successfully delivered to all other recipients.

▶ Routing path:

To: smith@nodomain.x

cc:

Date: 12:54:38 PM Today

Subject: testing

testing

Figure 11-25   Delivery Failure message

| Mail | Tracking Center |

Server: **TheNotesMobile/NotesGirl**

Mail Users				
Routing Mailboxes	⊘ 🗑 Delete Message 🔁 Release...			
TheNotesMobile Mailbo	▼ Submit Time	From	Recipients	▲ Size
TheNotesMobile Mailbo:	📧 08/28 01:00 PM User Test/NotesGirl		User Test/NotesGirl	1,262
TheNotesMobile Mailbo:				
Shared Mail				

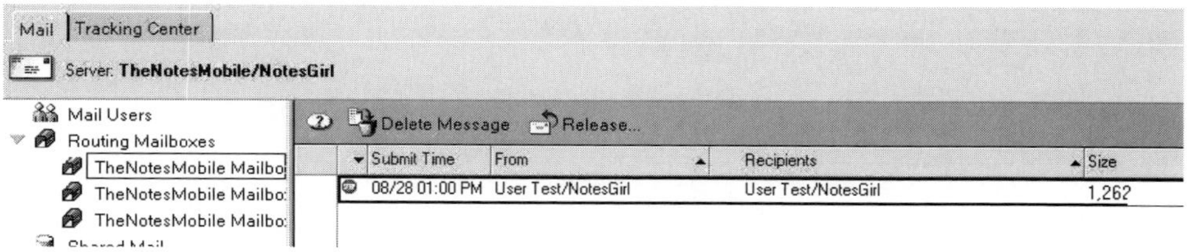

Figure 11-26   Dead mail

You should check the MAIL.BOX regularly for dead mail or mail that has been pending for an extended period. Both situations can mean that a remote server is unavailable for some reason. This can mean that a Connection document is wrong or has been disabled, or that a server or a user's mail file is unavailable for some reason. Note that while MAIL.BOX is a Domino database, it is not visible in the File . . . Open Database dialog box. Instead, to open the MAIL.BOX, choose File . . . Open Database and then type in the name MAIL.BOX on the filename line. Once you have the MAIL.BOX open, you will recognize dead mail by the red stop sign icon. After you have found the cause of the dead mail, you can choose the Release Dead Mail action button to deliver the message.

You can also use the Domino Administrator to view the contents of the MAIL.BOX(es). In the Domino Administrator, select the Messaging . . . Mail tab. Expand the Routing Mailboxes section. Each MAIL.BOX located on the server is listed in this section, as shown in Figure 11-27. If there is any pending or dead mail, you will see it in this view. You can also Delete or Release messages from this view.

You can also find out if you have dead or pending mail by typing either the SHOW SERVER or SHOW TASKS command at the server console. The SHOW SERVER command (shown in Figure 11-28) is better for this purpose than the SHOW TASKS command because of the number of items that SHOW TASKS will display.

Figure 11-27
Viewing the
MAIL.BOX

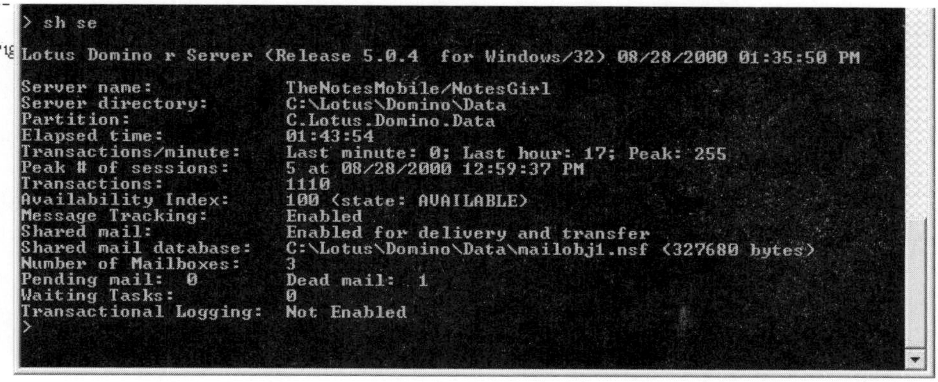

```
> sh se

Lotus Domino r Server (Release 5.0.4  for Windows/32) 08/28/2000 01:35:50 PM

Server name:              TheNotesMobile/NotesGirl
Server directory:         C:\Lotus\Domino\Data
Partition:                C.Lotus.Domino.Data
Elapsed time:             01:43:54
Transactions/minute:      Last minute: 0; Last hour: 17; Peak: 255
Peak # of sessions:       5 at 08/28/2000 12:59:37 PM
Transactions:             1110
Availability Index:       100 (state: AVAILABLE)
Message Tracking:         Enabled
Shared mail:              Enabled for delivery and transfer
Shared mail database:     C:\Lotus\Domino\Data\mailobj1.nsf (327680 bytes)
Number of Mailboxes:      3
Pending mail:    0        Dead mail:  1
Waiting Tasks:            0
Transactional Logging:    Not Enabled
>
```

Figure 11-28   Show Server command

To help you determine the cause of dead mail, you may want to send a Mail Trace message. To send a Mail Trace message, open the Domino Administrator to the Messaging tab. Expand the Messaging tools and choose Send Mail Trace. This displays the Send Mail Trace dialog box, as shown in Figure 11-29. At this point, you will either type in the user's mail address or choose it from the address book. The address that you are typing is any address to which you have not been able to send mail. You can choose to receive information in the form of a delivery report from either Each Router on the delivery path or only the Last Router on path. This choice determines how many separate messages you receive, although the data is the same.

The Mail Trace message is not delivered to the recipient's mail file. Instead, the message traces the entire path from your server to the server of the recipient and back. This is reported in a message (or messages, if you chose Each Router On Path) that you receive from the mail router. The message you receive, as shown in Figure 11-30, shows the path taken by the message and the amount of time the message took for each hop.

Sometimes when troubleshooting mail routing between servers, you may not want to wait for the scheduled mail routing times. You can create a Connection document that specifies a low mail routing threshold, such as forcing mail to route with one message pending. You can also force mail to route manually from the server console by typing in the following command:

```
ROUTE SERVERNAME
```

Use this command to force the messages waiting to be transferred to the specified server to transfer immediately, instead of waiting for the scheduled routing connection

Figure 11-29
Send Mail Trace

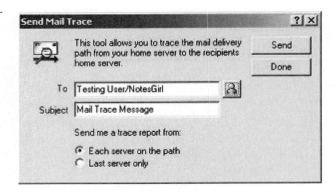

Trace Report

Your trace:	Mail Trace Message
has reached:	Testing User/NotesGirl@NotesGirl
at:	08/28/2000 01:39:42 PM

▸ Trace Information

TheNotesMobile/NotesGirl	01:39:37 PM Today - 01:39:42 PM Today
TheNotesMobile/NotesGirl	01:39:42 PM Today - 01:39:42 PM Today

Figure 11-30 Response from a Mail Trace

time. You can also force mail to route manually using the Domino Administrator. You can select the Route Mail option from the Messaging tools on the Messaging . . . Mail tab or from the Server tools on the Server . . . Status tab. Simply type or select the name of the server to which you want to route mail and choose Route, as shown in Figure 11-31.

Mail Tracking

One of the main elements of mail monitoring is mail tracking. Mail tracking allows you to view what happened to messages that your users have sent. To configure message tracking, create or edit a Configuration document. On the Router/SMTP . . . Message Tracking tab, choose Enabled in the Message Tracking field. You should also configure the Message Tracking Interval, any users that messages should not be tracked for, whether to log message subjects, and any users not to log message subjects for. You should also select users (and servers) allowed to track messages and message subjects, as shown in Figure 11-32.

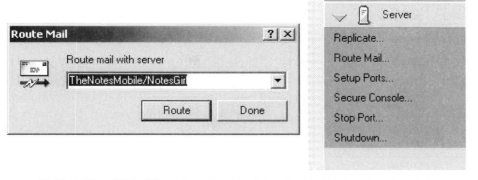

Figure 11-31   Route mail

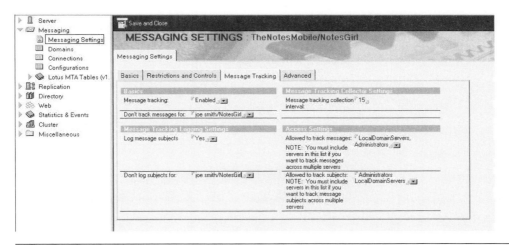

Figure 11-32   Configure Message Tracking.

After you save and close the document, you may need to restart the Domino server to start mail tracking. The router starts the MTC task (mail tracking collector) and creates the MTDATA directory.

    NOTE   You may need to create the MTDATA directory manually underneath the Domino data directory.

As messages are sent, information about the messages will be collected. You can then use the Messaging . . . Tracking Center tab to create a New Tracking Request (see Figure 11-33).

You can track based on sender, recipient, when the message was sent, subject, or message ID. If the MTC finds messages that meet the criteria, those messages are listed in the top pane of the tracking center. You can select the message that you are interested in and the transfer and delivery details of the message are displayed in the bottom pane, as shown in Figure 11-34.

Figure 11-33
Create a new tracking request.

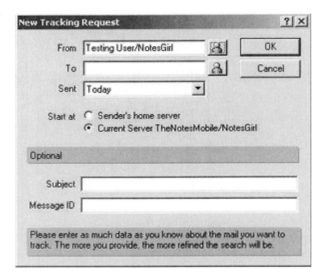

Review Questions

1. What does Emil need to do to enable message-based mail on his server?
    A. Set Message_BasedMail = 1 in the NOTES.INI.
    B. Type SET CONFIG Message_BasedMail = 1 at the console.
    C. Create a Configuration document in the Domino Directory.
    D. Nothing. Message-based mail is the default.

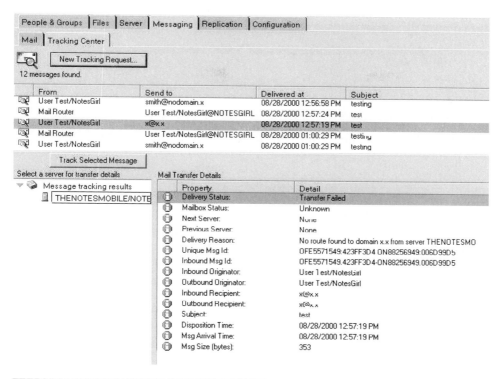

Figure 11-34   Message Tracking details

2. What does Fran need to do to enable shared mail on her server?
    A. Set Shared_Mail = 1 in the NOTES.INI.
    B. Type TELL ROUTER USE SHARED_MAIL at the console.
    C. Create a Configuration document in the Domino Directory.
    D. Nothing. Shared mail is the default.

3. Which element of Notes places newly created messages in the sender's server's MAIL.BOX?
    A. Mailer
    B. Router
    C. Deliverer
    D. Collector

4. Which element of Domino places messages in your mail file when they are being delivered?

   A. Mailer
   B. Router
   C. Deliverer
   D. Collector

5. Which element of Notes verifies the names of the recipients in the mail messages you send?

   A. Mailer
   B. Router
   C. Deliverer
   D. Collector

6. The router checks the Person documents of the sender and recipient of a message. The sender and recipient are on different servers. What happens to the mail message?

   A. The router looks at the Server document to see when it can deliver the mail messages.
   B. The router delivers the mail directly from the sender's mail file to the recipient's mail file.
   C. The router delivers the mail from the server's MAIL.BOX to the recipient's mail file.
   D. The router delivers the mail from the server's MAIL.BOX to the recipient's server's MAIL.BOX.

7. The router checks the Person documents of the sender and recipient of a message. The sender and recipient are on different servers. SHARED_MAIL is set equal to 1. Is shared mail used to transfer the message?

   A. Yes
   B. No

8. If the router finds the same DNN in the Server documents of the sender and the recipient, how is mail delivered?

   A. According to the schedule in the Server document
   B. According to the schedule in the Connection document
   C. According to the schedule in the Configuration document
   D. Immediately and automatically

9. If the router finds a different DNN in the Server documents of the sender and the recipient, how is mail delivered?
   A. According to the schedule in the Server document
   B. According to the schedule in the Connection document
   C. According to the schedule in the Configuration document
   D. Immediately and automatically

10. If shared mail is enabled for delivery, and you send a message to two people, when is the message body written to SHAREDMAIL.NSF?
    A. As soon as the router sees the first recipient
    B. As soon as the router sees the second recipient
    C. After the router writes the message to both users' mail files
    D. After the router writes the header to both users' mail files

Review Answers

1. **D is correct.** Message-based mail is the default.

2. **Either A or C.** You can enable shared mail by setting the SHARED_MAIL = line in the NOTES.INI to 1 or 2, by creating a Configuration document, or by using the TELL ROUTER USE SHAREDMAIL.NSF command at the server console.

3. **A is correct.** The Mailer places messages in the sender's server's MAIL.BOX.

4. **B is correct.** The Router delivers messages.

5. **A is correct.** The Mailer verifies recipients' names.

6. **D is correct.** The router delivers the mail from the server's MAIL.BOX to the recipient's server's MAIL.BOX.

7. **B is correct.** When SHARED_MAIL = 1, it is used for delivery only. To use SHARED_MAIL for delivery and transfer, set SHARED_MAIL = 2.

8. **D is correct.** Mail will route immediately and automatically in the same DNN.

9. **B is correct.** Mail in different DNNs will route according to the schedule in the Connection document.

10. **B is correct.** The message body is written to the SCOS as soon as the router sees the second recipient.

CHAPTER 12

Implementing Replication

You should be able to answer questions based on the following objectives after reading this chapter:

- Setting up/configuring replication distribution through force
- Setting up/configuring replication distribution through scheduling

Replication is the process of keeping data in multiple replica copies of a database synchronized. There is server-to-server replication as well as server-to-workstation replication. Replication requires several things in order to work. First, you must have a replica of a database on more than one Notes or Domino machine (workstation or server). Second, you must decide on the type of replication that you want to use, such as pull, push, pull-pull, and pull-push. Third, you must determine whether the replication will happen between server and server or server and workstation. Each requires specific settings and tweaks, but shares many common characteristics. Server-to-server replication requires resolution of the following issues: a Replicator task must be running on the server; replication must be initiated; a communication pathway between the servers must exist, including physical connectivity, shared network protocol, proper topology, (or if there is no shared protocol, a Passthru server must be used); and other factors must be resolved, like authentication, ACLs, database replica IDs, replication conflicts, and so on. Workstation-to-server replication necessitates almost the same things as server-to-server but requires different steps for initiation and scheduling.

Creating Replicas

Replication requires a replica, not a standard copy, of a database on more than one machine. A *replica* of a database is an exact duplicate of the original database, including an identical replica ID. A *copy* of a database, on the other hand, duplicates the original database but has a different replica ID. To create a copy, use File . . . Database . . . New Copy. To verify that the replica ID is different when you make a copy, right-click on the database icon or bookmark and choose Database Properties (or choose Database Properties from the File menu while in the database). In the Database Properties InfoBox, click on the Information tab to verify the replica ID, as shown in Figure 12-1.

You can create a replica of a database either through the operating system copy feature or internally in Notes. If you use Windows (2000, NT, or 9x), you can use Windows Explorer or My Computer to select the .NSF file and make a copy onto your workstation or server. Be aware that if you use this method, the database cannot be in use. If you are copying from a server, this may require you to shut down the Domino server program. An operating system copy, unlike an internal Notes copy, duplicates a database exactly, including the replica ID.

Using the Notes client, you can create a replica by selecting File . . . Replication . . . New Replica from the menus. If you have an icon for the database already added to your workspace (if you're still using the R4-style workspace), select the icon before choosing New Replica from the menu. If you have a bookmark, you can right-click and select Replication . . . New Replica from the short-cut menu. Notes displays the New Replica dialog box, as shown in Figure 12-2.

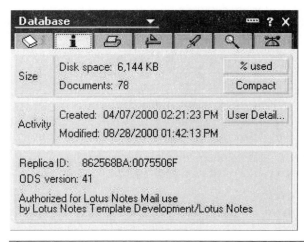

Figure 12-1   Replica ID

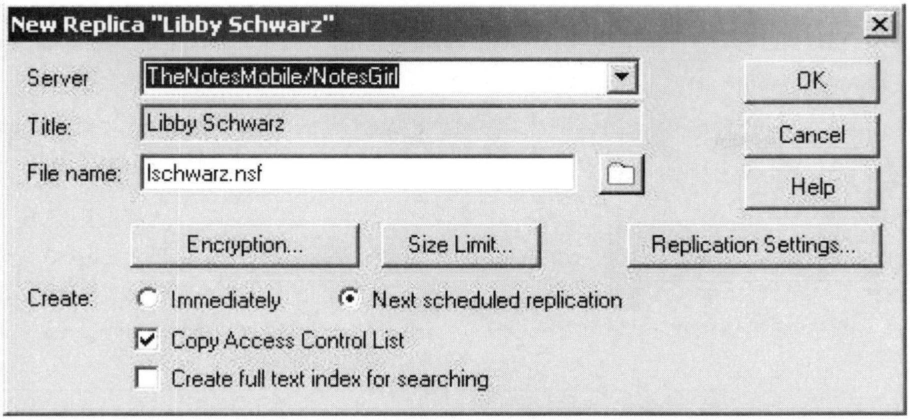

New Replica "Libby Schwarz"   [×]

Server   TheNotesMobile/NotesGirl   ▼   OK

Title: Libby Schwarz   Cancel

File name: lschwarz.nsf   📁   Help

            Encryption...   Size Limit...   Replication Settings...

Create: ○ Immediately   ⦿ Next scheduled replication
            ☑ Copy Access Control List
            ☐ Create full text index for searching

Figure 12-2   Partially completed New Replica dialog box

If you have a database selected or open when you choose to make a new replica, many of the fields will be completed, as you saw in Figure 12-2. If you do not have a database selected when you start to make a new replica, Notes displays the Choose Database dialog box first to enable you to select the database of which you want a replica. After you select a database, Notes displays the New Replica dialog box.

In the New Replica dialog box, type or select the name of the server on which you want to make a replica. If you are making a replica onto your workstation, leave Local as the name of the server (the default). The title of the database is completed for you, but you can edit the File Name field.

NOTE   **Your name must be in the Create Replica Databases field of the server document to create new replicas on a server.**

If you choose to create the replica immediately, the workstation's replicator immediately creates the replica and initializes the design and documents. This means that Notes copies the design and documents and makes the views ready for immediate use. If you choose to create the replica at the next scheduled replication, Notes creates a replica stub on the workspace. You will not be able to open a replica stub before it has been initialized through a complete replication, as it does not yet have any views. If you try to open a replica stub, you receive the error shown in Figure 12-3.

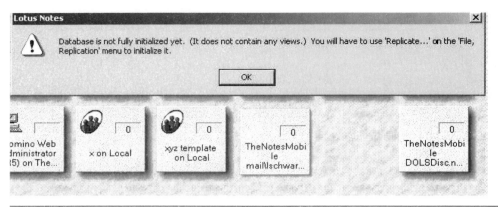

Figure 12-3   Replica stub error

Types of Replication

After you create replicas, you will need to replicate to keep the data synchronized. There are four types of replication: pull-only, push-only, pull-push, and pull-pull. Be aware that although we will discuss compound replications, where the synchronization between the servers goes both ways, replication itself is a one-way process. The idea of "two-way" replication only indicates that a secondary replication is initiated immediately following another replication.

Push Replication

Push-only replication causes a one-way synchronization of data. The initiating server calls or connects to the receiving server. The initiating server then pushes the changes in its databases to the receiving server. Another way to say this is that the source server—the server that initiated the call—writes its changes to the target, or receiving, server.

If you have a server in your main office and a server in a satellite office, for example, you may only allow administrators at the main office to make changes to the Domino Directory. When the administrators make these changes, however, the other replicas of the Domino Directory need to be updated. In this case, a push-only replication of the Domino Directory from the main office to the satellite office would be appropriate, as you can see in Figure 12-4.

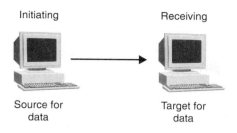

Figure 12-4 Push-only replication

Pull Replication

Pull-only replication is also a one-way synchronization. In this scenario, the initiating server calls the receiving server, exactly as it would in push-only replication. In this case, however, the initiating (or calling) server pulls the changes from the receiving (or remote) server's databases. In pull replication, the initiating server becomes the target server and the remote server becomes the source server.

In our example of a main office server and a satellite office server, the satellite office server may need to control replication because of a communications requirement, such as a dial-up modem. Continue to assume that the changes to the Domino Directory are made by administrators at the main office. The satellite office server, however, must call or connect to the main office server. It then initiates a pull-only replication with the main office server and pulls all the Domino Directory changes down, as you can see in Figure 12-5.

Pull-Push Replication

Pull-push replication is the most common type of replication because it is the default, both when you create a replication connection document, and when you initiate replication manually. While the name may suggest otherwise, pull-push replication is one-way replication, as we discussed earlier. It is, however, a compound replication. This means that two one-way replications occur in sequence. The initiating server makes the call to the remote server. The initiating server begins a pull replication with the remote

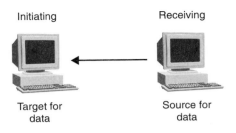

Figure 12-5 Pull-only replication

server and pulls to itself the changes that exist in the remote server's databases. Then the initiating server immediately begins pushing its changes to the remote server. The initiating server controls both of the replications; its replicator task does all the work and makes all the changes. The remote server's replicator task remains idle the entire time. The initiating server begins as the target of the changes from the remote or source server. When it begins to push changes, it becomes the source server and the remote server becomes the target.

In our scenario, we have the main office server and the satellite office server. In this case, we are assuming that there are administrators making changes to the Domino Directory at both locations. The remote administrators may be given the ability to register users, for example. When changes are being made in both replicas, a full synchronization of the database is necessary. If you initiated a pull-push replication from the main office server, it would call the satellite office and pull the changes from the Domino Directory at the satellite office. The main office server would then initiate a push of the changes contained in its replica to the satellite office. At the end of the replication, the two databases would be completely synchronized. This process is shown in Figure 12-6.

Pull-pull Replication

Pull-pull replication is also a compound replication that uses two one-way replications to synchronize the databases fully. In this case, the initiating server makes the connection to the remote server and begins pulling the remote server's changes. When the first pull replication is completed, the replicator task on the initiating server tells the remote server to begin a pull replication. The remote server then initiates a pull replication to complete the cycle. Each server's replicator task works in this type of replication.

In our scenario of the main office server and the satellite office server, you might choose to use pull-pull replication if both replicators or both servers are fairly busy. The

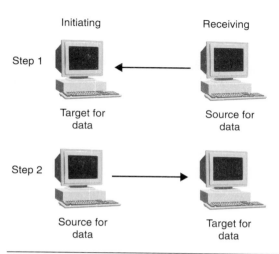

Step 1   Initiating   Receiving
         Target for   Source for
         data   data

Step 2   Source for   Target for
         data   data

Figure 12-6   Pull-push replication

pull-pull replication shares the work more equally between both servers. The main office server controls the replication, initiating a pull-pull replication with the satellite office and pulling the satellite office server's changes. When the changes have all been replicated up to the main office server, the main office server's replicator tags the satellite office server's replicator task and then becomes idle. The satellite office server's replicator task then pulls the changes from the main office server down, completing the replication, as shown in Figure 12-7.

Server-to-Server Replication

Replication of a database from one server to another server in a Domino environment requires resolution of several factors, including a replicator task, initiation, connectivity, and other factors. Servers run a replicator task automatically if they have the Server-Tasks=Replica . . . line in their NOTES.INI file. A server must run at least one replicator task in order to replicate a database. Domino places the replica task in the ServerTask line by default to ensure that the replicator task runs. For most servers, you will allow replication to run on a regularly scheduled basis. This requires you to leave the replica task in the NOTES.INI. You might remove the replica task if your server will not be replicating regularly and you need to free up server resources. Replicator tasks remain idle unless needed, but require 3MB of RAM even in that state.

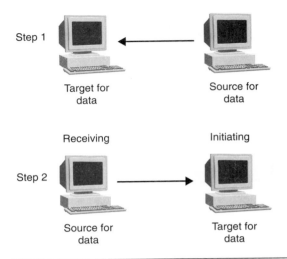

Step 1

Target for
data

Source for
data

Receiving

Initiating

Step 2

Source for
data

Target for
data

Figure 12-7   Pull-pull replication

Initiating Replication

Server-to-server replication is initiated in a few different ways, at the server console, via the Domino Administrator, or with a replication schedule. Server console initiation is less common because it requires an administrator to type the commands at the console. More often, you will start replication from the Domino Administrator or use a replication schedule to allow the server Connection documents to initiate replication automatically.

Initiating Replication at the Server Console

If changes made to a database need to be replicated immediately, an administrator may not want to wait for the scheduled replication to occur. In this case, you may choose to initiate replication manually at the server console. Three different commands initiate replication at the server console:

- PULL *servername databasename*
- PUSH *servername databasename*
- REPLICATE *servername databasename*

Servername is the name of the server with which you wish to replicate. *Databasename* is either the name of the specific database you wish to replicate (relative to the data directory path) or a directory you wish to replicate (again, relative to the data directory). You may also choose to leave out the *databasename* parameter, if you wish to replicate all the databases in the lotus\domino\data directory.

The PULL and PUSH commands initiate pull-only or push-only replication, while the REPLICATE command initiates pull-push replication. You cannot initiate pull-pull replication from the server console.

NOTE Another way to talk about replication is to use the words source database and target database. The target database is always the database that is receiving changes. The source database is always the database that contains the changes. This can be confusing when combined with remote servers and the concept of initiating. Pay close attention to the flow of information between servers in examples or questions. The source and target databases are always determined by the flow of information.

After you initiate replication, a series of factors affect whether the replication occurs. First, the initiating server must find a path to the indicated remote server. It finds a path to the remote server by locating a direct connection or by using a Connection document in the Domino Directory. After finding the remote server, the initiating server must verify that it is allowed to communicate with and use that remote server. The replicator must then verify that a replica database exists on the remote server. The initiating server must have the appropriate access to the remote database and all the documents in the remote database. These and other factors that affect replication are described more fully later in this chapter.

Initiate Replication from the Domino Administrator

You can initiate replication manually from the Domino Administrator. On the Server . . . Status tab, expand the Server tools. Select the Replicate tool. Select or type the server you want to replicate with in the Replicate from dialog box, as shown in Figure 12-8.

Choose the replication style and whether to replicate all databases in common or select a database to replicate. Click Replicate to start the replication. The dialog box remains up to allow you to select another server or database. When you're finished, click Done. You will not see any result from the replication without looking at the server console, remote console, or Notes log.

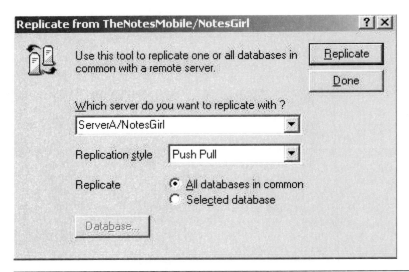

Figure 12-8 Replicate from dialog box

Server Connection Documents and Replication Settings

Most of the time, you will want replication to initiate automatically. To initiate replication automatically, you will create server Connection documents with replication schedule times enabled. You can use any of the four types of replication in server Connection documents. In addition, you can use multiple Connection documents to create a more complete replication schedule.

You may want to use pull-only replication from a central server to bring in changes from many other satellite offices, for example. You might then want that central server to push out the collected changes to all the satellite offices later in the day. To create this scenario, you would use two replication Connection documents per server, one that uses pull-only and one that uses push-only.

To create a server Connection document, open the Domino Administrator to the Configuration tab. Expand the Server section and open the Connections view. Choose the Add Connection action button or edit an existing connection. The Connection document is similar to the Connection document for a Mail Routing connection, discussed in Chapter 11.

On the Basics tab of the Connection document, specify the connection type, such as Local Area Network, Notes Direct Dialup, Passthru Server, or Network Dialup. This is the method that the source server will use to connect to the destination server. Type the hierarchical name of the source and destination servers. Also, type the name of the source and destination domains. Select the Choose Port button to determine which port or ports to use for the connection. You may also choose to type the IP address in the Optional Network Address field.

On the Replication/Routing tab, shown in Figure 12-9, make sure the replication task is enabled. In the next field, choose which databases should replicate based on priority. You can replicate Low, Medium, and High (the default), Medium and High, or High priority databases. Next, select the replication type (from those described above).

You can choose to replicate all the databases the two servers have in common by leaving the Files/Directories to Replicate field blank (the default). You can also type a file name or directory (in relation to the data directory) to limit the replication. Finally, enter a replication time limit. If you leave this field blank (the default), the server can take as much time as it needs to complete the replication. If the replication stops unexpectedly (a call is dropped, for example) or the replication isn't finished when the time runs out, and there is a value in this field, the replication picks up where it left off when it restarts.

On the Schedule tab, configure whether the schedule is enabled or disabled. At times you may need to disable a certain connection, such as when a server is offline, but you may not want to delete the Connection document. In the Connect at Times field, select the times at which the server should make contact with the destination server. This can be specific times or ranges of time but should include the low-priority times to ensure that low-priority mail can route. Complete the Repeat Interval field with how often the source server will attempt to contact the destination server. If only one time or one call is desired, this field can be left blank. The Connect At Times field and the Repeat Interval field work together based on previous routing times. If the first connection occurs at

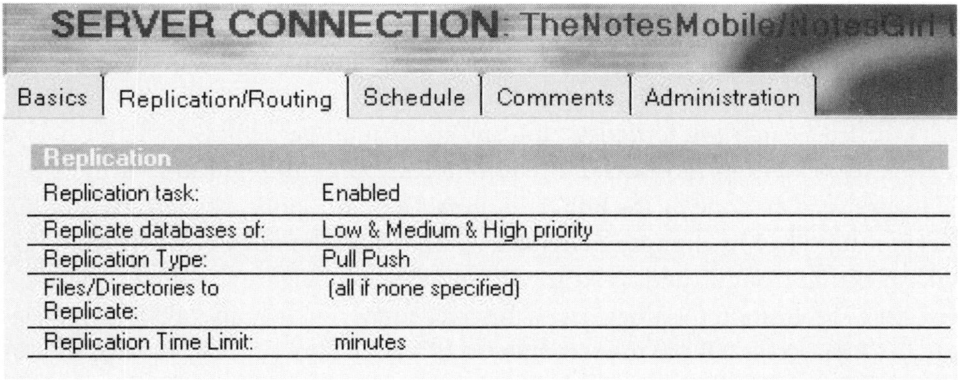

SERVER CONNECTION: TheNotesMobile/NotesGirl				
Basics	Replication/Routing	Schedule	Comments	Administration

Replication	
Replication task:	Enabled
Replicate databases of:	Low & Medium & High priority
Replication Type:	Pull Push
Files/Directories to Replicate:	(all if none specified)
Replication Time Limit:	minutes

Figure 12-9 Replication connection document

4 A.M. and takes 15 minutes and the repeat interval is 30 minutes, the second connection occurs at 4:45 A.M. Finally, select the days of the week that this Connection document should apply.

The connection documents that you create for replication should be determined by the replication topology that you have chosen to implement. The next section describes communications pathways, including the common replication topologies.

Communication Pathways

Once you have the replicator task running and replication initiated with the right type of replication, you must select the proper topology. In order to do this, you must have the proper physical connectivity, including network settings and protocols. If your servers do not share the same protocol, you must use a Passthru server to define the proper topology for the job. Topologies and Passthru servers are discussed below.

Replication Topologies

There are four basic replication topologies: hub and spoke, end-to-end, ring, and mesh. Topology relates to where servers are located and how they are connected. The basic reason for a replication topology is to control and predict how information is distributed within your organization.

In *hub and spoke* topology, one server (the hub) schedules, initiates, and controls all replication. This is the best way to control data and ensure that all data is accurate. You may have a corporate office in Houston, for example, and smaller offices all over the world. You might choose to have the hub server in Houston be the central hub for your enterprise. In this case, the hub calls the other servers (or initiates the connection over a LAN or WAN) and initiates replication. All the other servers are the spokes. They only pass information to other databases through (to and from) the hub when they are called by the hub. The hub and spoke can be expanded to have multiple levels, in which case it is called a *binary tree* topology. Hub and spoke topology will use pull, push, and pull-push replication in most cases. It will only use pull-pull replication if there is a need to reduce work done by the hub replicators. Hub and spoke is the most common replication topology in enterprise environments, as it is the most efficient and organized. An example of hub and spoke topology is shown in Figure 12-10.

End-to-end replication topology has each server connected in a line, as shown in Figure 12-11. Each server talks to the server ahead of it in the line and the server after it in the line. In this chain, for example, the server in our Houston office calls the server in

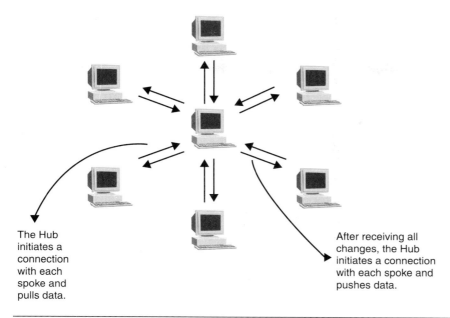

Figure 12-10   Hub and spoke topology

Figure 12-11   End-to-end topology

our Dallas office. The Dallas server calls the Kansas City office. The chain would then reverse on itself, and Kansas would call Dallas, and so on.

A *ring* topology is very similar to the end-to-end topology. However, when the last server is reached in the line, it simply circles back around to the beginning, as shown in Figure 12-12. So, in our example, after Dallas calls Kansas City, Kansas City would turn around and call Houston.

In *mesh* topology, all servers connect directly to all other servers, as shown in Figure 12-13. This can be a difficult topology to administer, due to its complex and disorganized nature, and is not recommended.

An organized replication topology must consider two basic issues of resource management: bandwidth and communication resources, and scheduling replications. Both

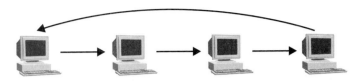

Figure 12-12 Ring topology

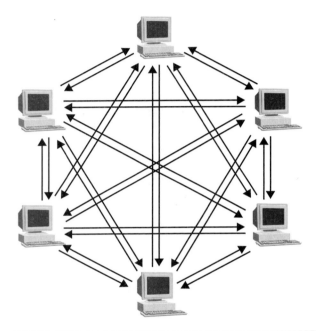

Figure 12-13 Mesh topology

issues influence the type of replication topology you will select for your Domino environment. Bandwidth and communication resources are not usually within the purview of Domino system administration but certainly must be considered. How fast are your links? Are they all 126K, or are some 126K and others 2126K?

To schedule replication properly, you must assure that information gets where it needs to go in a timely and error-free fashion. Users must not miss important information and servers need to be coordinated always with each other. Time zones and multiple schedules complicate these issues. If your servers are in different time zones, take into consideration their peak and low times as well as the peak and low times of your own servers. Also, plan your replication schedule so that your replicator is not over-worked and you do not lose changes in the replication. When creating your replication schedule, the Domino Directory is the most important database to consider. After determining the best replication topology and schedule for the Domino Directory, you should consider other databases that maintain the servers, such as the Administration Requests database and then any other databases that are used for your organization's business.

In your replication topology, your server Connection documents schedule one of the types of replication with another server, or set of servers. In the most popular type of topology, hub and spoke, the hub contacts all the servers and pulls the changes up to the hub from the spokes. After all of the scheduled pulls, the hub again contacts the spoke servers and then pushes the amassed changes out to the spokes.

For example, you may have a corporate office in Houston and smaller offices all over the world. You might choose to have the hub server in Houston be the central hub for your enterprise. In this case, the hub will call the other servers (or initiate the connection over a LAN or WAN), and initiate a pull only replication. The changes made in the databases that are being replicated—for example, NAMES.NSF, STATREP.NSF, and ADMIN4.NSF—are pulled up to the hub. The hub acts as the repository for all the changes. Later, the hub calls each of the spoke servers and pushes the combined changes out to the remote databases. This replication topology sample is shown in Figure 12-14.

Multiple Replicators

The server's replicator task only services one replication request at a time. While the replicator is servicing that replication request, it can also keep track of up to five other

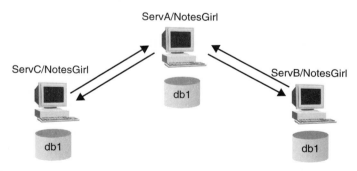

Figure 12-14   Sample topology

replication requests. This is called the *replicator queue*. When the replicator queue is full, other replication requests will be dropped and the requested replication will not occur. One way to avoid dropped replication requests on a busy server is to enable more than one replicator task on the server. Obviously, multiple replicators will require more server resources, in terms of memory, server input/output, processor, and network bandwidth. Each replicator uses a minimum of 3MB of RAM, even when idle.

To enable multiple replicators, change the REPLICATORS line in the server's NOTES.INI file. You can do this directly in the NOTES.INI file by adding a line with REPLICATORS=n (where n is the number of replicators you would like to enable). The recommended method of changing this parameter is by creating (or editing) a server Configuration document.

To create a server Configuration document, open the Domino Administrator to the Configuration tab. Expand the Server section and open the Configurations view. Click the Add Configuration action button. This opens a server Configuration document, as shown in Figure 12-15. You could also edit an existing Configuration document.

To add additional replicators, open the NOTES.INI settings tab and click the Set/Modify Parameters button. In the Server Configuration Parameters dialog box, fill in the Item field with the REPLICATORS parameter, as shown in Figure 12-16. In the value field, type in the number of replicators you want to enable.

You can verify that you have enabled multiple replicators by looking at the server console after a server restart. As the tasks start, you should see multiple instances of the replicator task. If you type in the command **Show Tasks** at the server console, you should see multiple replicator tasks in the server task list.

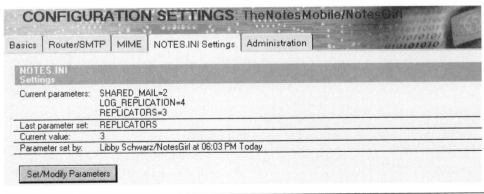

Figure 12-15 Configuration document

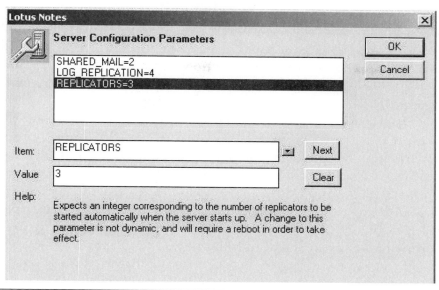

Figure 12-16 Enable multiple replicator tasks

NOTE You have the ability to enable a maximum of ten replicators. In most environments, however, you will enable no more than two or three replicators.

Replication Passthru

Sometimes servers in your environment are not directly connected. A common situation is when some servers use the TCP/IP protocol, for example, and other servers use IPX/SPX or the NetBEUI protocol. When you have servers that cannot communicate directly, you must create some type of communication path for these servers, or no data can be passed between them. Server Passthru can be used for replicating with a server to which you do not have direct connection or access. *Passthru* is an R4 and R5 feature that allows Notes workstations and Domino servers to use a designated server as a bridge to connect to another server that does not share a common protocol or direct connection with the workstation or server. This section describes how to configure and use Server Passthru for replication.

To understand the need for Server Passthru, consider the following example. There may be three servers in your environment. One server (MainServer) uses both TCP/IP and NetBEUI. The other servers are each running one of the two protocols, as shown in Figure 12-17. This means that the other servers, one (ServerA) running TCP/IP and one (ServerB) running NetBEUI, cannot communicate directly. If they are in the same domain, however, the Domino Directory and other databases will have to be updated. In this scenario, you could simply use hub and spoke topology and use the server with both protocols as the hub. You may have certain databases, however, that you do not wish to place on the hub. In that case, you would use the hub, MainServer, as a Passthru server for the other two servers.

Server Passthru requires you to create and edit two types of documents in the Domino Directory. First, you need to create a Connection document to schedule replication with a particular server, using a Passthru server. Second, you may need to create another Connection document specifying the connection to the server to use for Passthru. Finally, you need to edit your Server documents to allow Passthru.

The connection document that you create to schedule replication is the same as the replication connection document we created earlier. Fill in the source and destination servers, define it as a Passthru connection, and define the Passthru server or hunt group to connect through, as shown in Figure 12-18. This document also specifies which databases to replicate with which server and on what schedule.

You then need to create a Connection document to specify how to connect to the Passthru server. ServerB is trying to communicate with ServerC, but they do not share a protocol. Therefore, to communicate they will need to use ServerA as the Passthru. After you define this link, you also need to determine how to connect to the Passthru server, as shown in Figure 12-19.

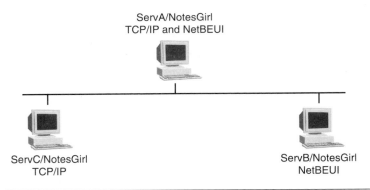

ServA/NotesGirl
TCP/IP and NetBEUI

ServC/NotesGirl
TCP/IP

ServB/NotesGirl
NetBEUI

Figure 12-17 Server passthru

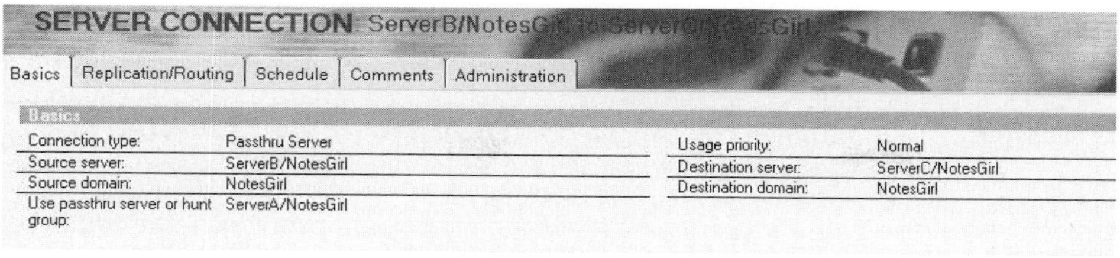

SERVER CONNECTION: ServerB/NotesGirl to ServerC/NotesGirl

Basics | Replication/Routing | Schedule | Comments | Administration

Basics

Connection type:	Passthru Server	Usage priority:	Normal
Source server:	ServerB/NotesGirl	Destination server:	ServerC/NotesGirl
Source domain:	NotesGirl	Destination domain:	NotesGirl
Use passthru server or hunt group:	ServerA/NotesGirl		

Figure 12-18   Passthru connection document

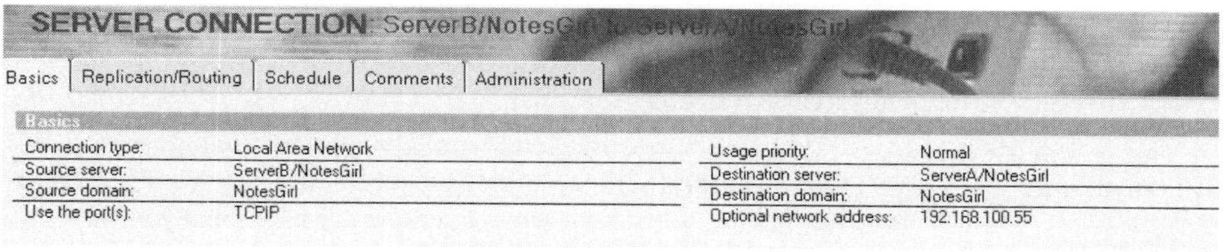

SERVER CONNECTION: ServerB/NotesGirl to ServerA/NotesGirl

Basics | Replication/Routing | Schedule | Comments | Administration

Basics

Connection type:	Local Area Network	Usage priority:	Normal
Source server:	ServerB/NotesGirl	Destination server:	ServerA/NotesGirl
Source domain:	NotesGirl	Destination domain:	NotesGirl
Use the port(s):	TCPIP	Optional network address:	192.168.100.55

Figure 12-19   Connection document to the Passthru server

Finally, you need to edit the Server documents for all the servers involved in the Passthru connection. By default, Passthru use is not allowed. Complete the Server document fields as described in Table 12-1.

NOTE   Only servers that use Domino Release 4 or 5 can initiate Passthru or be the Passthru server. Servers that use Notes V3.X can only be the destination of a Passthru connection.

A sample Server document with the necessary fields completed for Passthru is shown in Figure 12-20. After the Connection and Server documents are created and edited, Passthru will occur automatically and transparently, according to the replication schedule.

Factors Affecting Replication

There are many factors, at all layers of the Domino environment, that affect replication. These factors include the following:

Table 12-1   Passthru Server Fields

Field	Value and Info
Access this server	This field defines who can access this server using Passthru. You must include both servers and users. If it is blank, no one is allowed to access this server using a Passthru server.
Route through	This field defines who can use this server to route to another server. In our example, MainServer would have to allow both ServerA and ServerB to route through. If it is blank, no one is allowed.
Cause calling	This field is officially defined as who can cause this server to place a call to another server. However, any server seeking to use this server to replicate with another server must be in this list. In our example, MainServer must allow ServerA and ServerB in this list. If it is blank, no one is allowed.
Destinations allowed	This field defines remote servers that can be routed to use this server for Passthru. If it is blank, all remote servers are allowed. If you want to restrict which servers can be contacted using any particular Passthru server, you would complete this field.

Passthru Use	Who can -
Access this server:	PassThru Users,ServerB/NotesGirl,ServerC/NotesGirl
Route through:	PassThru Users,ServerB/NotesGirl,ServerC/NotesGirl
Cause calling:	ServerB/NotesGirl,ServerC/NotesGirl
Destinations allowed:	ServerB/NotesGirl,ServerC/NotesGirl

Figure 12-20   Sample passthru Server document

- Server factors, such as authentication, server access lists, server replication schedule, and number of replicators

- Database factors, such as the ACL, replica ID, replica ID cache, replication settings, replication history, and deleted documents

- Document factors, such as form access lists and merge replication conflicts

These factors can cause replication not to occur or to occur in an undesired manner. A good administrator will look at each of these factors when setting up replication as well as when troubleshooting replication. We discuss each of the factors affecting replication here. To visualize the factors that affect replication, refer to Figure 12-21.

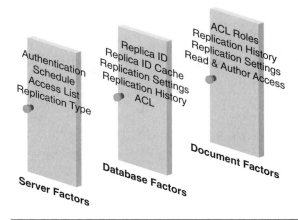

Figure 12-21   Factors affecting replication

EXAM TIP   The exam will probably not ask questions about all of these factors, but you will be expected to know how to determine what will be replicated and why in any given scenario.

Server Factors

The first layers of factors affecting replication are the server factors. We have already discussed the concepts of the replication schedule and the replicator task, both of which are clearly server factors. We can also add into the mix the replication type, as discussed earlier. Finally, the ability to authenticate with and access the server are important server factors. The server attempting to request a replication must be able to authenticate with the destination server. They must share some certificate in common that allows them to authenticate before replication can occur. In addition, the server access list in the Server document must allow the initiating servers to access the server. If the initiating server is not in the remote server's access list, or is in the Not Access Server field, replication cannot occur.

Database Factors

The next factors that affect replication are at the database layer. This includes the following factors:

- Replica ID and the Replica ID cache

- Database ACL

- Replication history

- Replication settings

- Deleted documents

As soon as another server is granted access for the purpose of replication (that is, the servers have authenticated and the servers have passed the server access list), the servers check for databases that they have in common. The list of databases in common is stored in the replica ID cache. Each server maintains this list of databases that have matching replica IDs. Only the databases in the replica ID cache are replicated.

 CAUTION Sometimes databases that are replicas of each other do not replicate. This can occur if the databases are not in the replica ID cache for some reason. Databases may not be in the replica ID cache if the cache has not been updated recently or if replication has been disabled for a database.

To enable or disable replication for a database, select the database from the Files tab of the Domino Administrator. Right-click and choose Replication from the short-cut menu, or select Replication from the list of Database tools. Choose Enable or Disable and click OK, as shown in Figure 12-22.

The replication for a database can also be disabled in the replication settings. To verify that replication is enabled, right-click on the database icon or bookmark and choose Replication settings. Select the Other panel. Verify that the option to Temporarily disable replication is not selected, as shown in Figure 12-23.

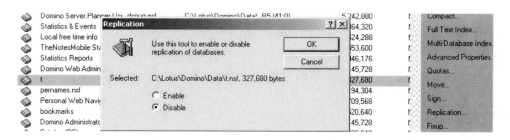

Figure 12-22 Enable or disable replication

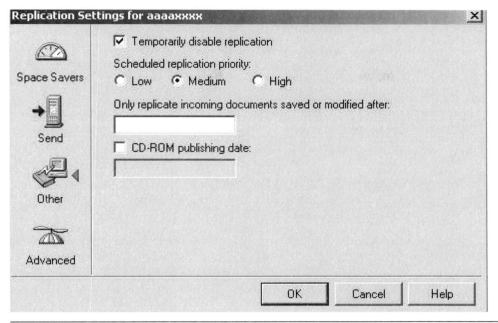

Figure 12-23 Temporarily disable replications

After the servers determine which databases can be replicated, the ACL of the database determines the level of replication that can occur. Table 12-2 describes what happens at each ACL level for the servers involved in replication.

> **NOTE** A server must have the same or higher level of access to a database as the highest user on that server. If the Manager of the NAMES.NSF database uses ServerA to open and modify the database, for example, ServerA must have at least Manager access to that database. Otherwise, the changes that that user makes on that server cannot be replicated to other servers. Similarly, if users on ServerA have Author access to the Inventory database, ServerA should have at least Editor access to replicate both newly created and edited documents.

Another database-level factor that affects whether the database is replicated is the replication history for that database. The *replication history* is a list of dates, times, and servers that have completed replication with a particular database. To access the replication history, shown in Figure 12-24, right-click on the database icon or bookmark. When a successful replication is completed, the source server's time is used to time and date stamp the replication history. Replication history can be used to aid in

Table 12-2   ACL and Replication

ACL level	What can be replicated
No access	Nothing can be replicated; if either of the servers has No Access, replication does not continue. Use this option if you need to shut out a particular server at the database level.
Depositor	Do not use Depositor access for a server that needs to replicate. A server with Depositor access could send new documents but would never receive documents.
Reader	A server with Reader access to a database can receive changes, but it cannot distribute any changes. This level of access would only be appropriate in a situation where all changes to a database are done at one source location and then distributed.
Author	New documents could be created. Since a server does not author documents, however, this is *not* recommended for an ACL setting for a server.
Editor	New and edited documents can be received and forwarded. This setting is common for any database that will be changed by multiple users at multiple locations.
Designer	In addition to receiving and forwarding new and edited documents, servers with Designer access will receive and forward new and edited design elements. Whichever server holds the replica of the database that is used by designers to update the design of the database must have Designer access.
Manager	Only one server should have Manager access to a database. Manager access allows the same changes as Designer access with the additional ability to change the ACL and the replication settings.

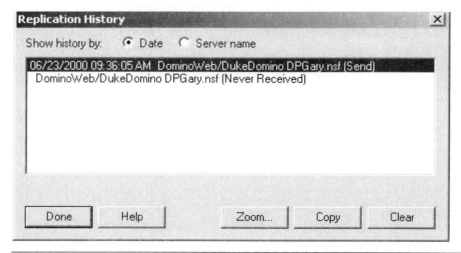

Figure 12-24   Replication History

troubleshooting replication. If replication has not been occurring as you expected, you can choose the Clear button to remove all replication history entries. This will force a complete replication to occur at the next scheduled replication. Be aware that it will take a significantly longer time, as each element is being verified, not just being compared to the time stamp as usually happens. If you are only having replication problems with a particular server, you can select that server's replication from the dialog box and click the Zoom . . . button. After you zoom in on a particular event, you can clear just that event.

NOTE   **Workstation replication does not update the replication history on a server replica of the database. Only server replication adds this time stamp. With workstation replication, the workstation updates its own replication history.**

Finally, Replication Settings for a database allow control of what can be sent and received during replication. Right-click on the database icon or choose Replication . . . Settings to access the replication settings, as shown in Figure 12-25. The options in the Replication Settings dialog box are described in Table 12-3.

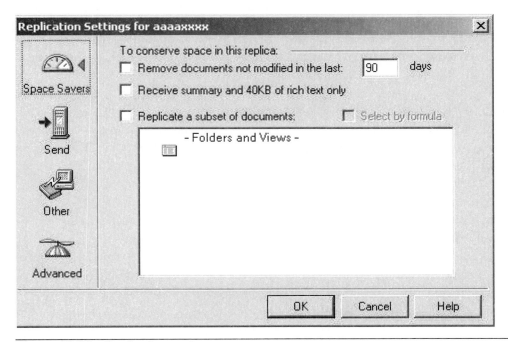

Figure 12-25   Replication settings

Table 12-3   Replication Settings

Panel	Option
Space Savers	This allows you to restrict the documents you replicate based on folders, views, or formulas. Most often, laptop users edit these fields to minimize the size of a database. If you choose to restrict the documents you replicate in this dialog box, you are creating a replication formula.
	In addition, the Remove documents not modified in the last ___ days is an important field for all replicas. This field sets the purge interval for the deletion stubs in the database, as discussed later in the chapter. The purge interval is set to 1/3 the value of this field. The default is 90 days; therefore, the default purge interval is 30 days.
Send	This panel allows you to limit the changes and deletions sent from this replica to other replicas.
Other	This panel allows you to disable replication temporarily if necessary. You also have the option to change the replication priority of the database, as discussed earlier, and to limit incoming replication based on document modified dates.
Advanced	Advanced options allow you to limit incoming documents based on formulas and the specific server (or workstation) sending. This panel allows you to create a complex replication formula that allows the replicas of databases in different locations to contain a different subset of information.

One significant database layer factor affecting replication is how replication deals with deleted documents. When you delete a document from one replica of a database, it should be deleted from *all* replicas of the database. Some users wonder, however, why Domino does not just replace the deleted document with a copy of that document from another replica.

When you delete a document from a database, Domino removes the document but leaves a deleted document identifier, called a deletion stub, in its place. This deletion stub is invisible to users but is used by Domino to know that the document has been deleted. If it does not see this deletion stub, Domino will assume that the document in the other replica is new and will add it back into the database.

To save space in databases, Domino eventually deletes the deletion stubs. The amount of time that passes before Domino removes the deletion stubs is called the *purge interval*. You can set the purge interval for a database in the Space Savers panel of the Replication Settings dialog box, as discussed earlier. The Remove documents not modified in the last ___ day field allows the administrator to set the purge interval. The purge interval is defined as one-third of the value of this field. The default value for this field is 90 days. The default purge interval therefore is 30 days.

In some cases, your users will complain that deleted documents are reappearing after replication occurs. If the users report this problem, it is likely that your purge interval occurs before your replication interval. To troubleshoot this problem, either increase the purge interval or replicate more often.

Document Factors

In addition to the server and database factors, document layer settings also affect replication. Document layer settings include the following:

- Reader and Author fields in forms and documents
- Form and View access lists
- Merge replication conflicts

Most settings at the document layer are determined by and are the responsibility of the database designer. Anything that affects replication, however, needs to be a joint effort between the administrator and the designer.

The forms and views in databases have a Security tab on their properties InfoBoxes. These security tabs allow the designer to refine the access given to users by removing them from the form and view access lists. If you change the default form and view access, you must include the servers that will be involved in replication.

Similarly, designers can place fields on forms in the database, called reader and author fields, which limit the users who can read and create documents with those forms. If these fields are on forms in databases that will be replicated, they can affect replication at the document layer. The servers that will be replicating the databases must be included in reader and author fields.

Finally, the designer has the ability to enable an option called Merge replication conflicts when creating forms in a database. Different users may edit the same document on different replicas of a database. This would cause a replication conflict when replication occurs between the databases.

Domino does provide a few methods of help to avoid replication conflicts. First, Domino uses field-level replication rather than document-level replication. What this means is that Domino only replicates the specific fields that have changed in the documents and databases rather than replicating the entire document that has changes on it. Second, Domino allows designers to enable Merge replication conflicts for the forms in a database. If the Merge replication conflicts option is enabled, as long as users do not change the same field, the changes will be made to the document when replication occurs and there will be no replication conflict. If, however, the users both change the same field, a replication conflict will occur. If the designer did not enable Merge replication conflicts option, a replication conflict will occur even if the users edited different fields. To see if the Merge replication conflicts option has been enabled, open the database to the Design . . . Forms view. Open the form and access Form properties InfoBox by right-clicking on the form and choosing Form Properties. The Merge Replication Conflicts option is on the Basics tab, as shown in Figure 12-26.

If the users are both editing documents in the same replica of a database, and they edit the same document at the same time, a Save conflict is created. This cannot be prevented by enabling the Merge replication conflicts option.

If a Replication or Save conflict is created, it is displayed in the view as a response document, as shown in Figure 12-27. To remove the Replication or Save conflict, open the Replication or Save conflict document. Use the information in the Replication or Save conflict document to determine which changes were not passed on to the main document. Open the main document and make those changes. Save and close the main document. Delete the Replication or Save conflict. This manual merging is the only way to clear a Replication or Save conflict, unless you create an agent that compares the documents for you.

Figure 12-26
Merge Replication
Conflicts

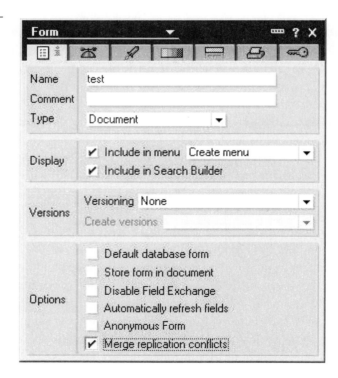

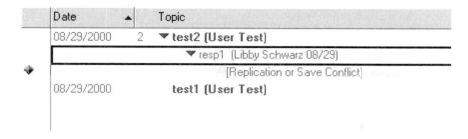

Figure 12-27 A replication conflict

Process of Replication

It is important to understand the process of replication. This gives you insight into creating a replication topology and into troubleshooting replication. First, we discuss the order in which replication occurs, as well as how this affects databases. Second, we look at how the replication actually occurs. The better your understanding of the process of replication, the easier replication questions will be on the exam.

Replication occurs in the following order:

1. ACL changes

2. Design changes

3. Document changes

When the ACL of a database has been changed, this element replicates first. After the ACL is replicated, the rest of the changes to the databases are made according to the newly updated ACL. The ACL also replicates completely. This means that if changes were made to the ACL on both databases, one set of changes is lost during replication. Let's use the NAMES.NSF database on ServerA and ServerB as an example. The ACL of NAMES.NSF on ServerA, changed 1/9/99 at 2 P.M., contains the following entries:

User	Access
ServerA	Manager
ServerB	Designer
John Doe	Reader

The ACL of NAMES.NSF on ServerB, changed 1/9/99 at 11 A.M., contains the following entries:

User	Access
ServerA	Manager
ServerB	Manager
John Doe	Author

When ServerA contacts ServerB for a pull-push replication, ServerA checks the time stamp and sees that it has the most recent ACL changes. It will not pull the ACL from ServerB. It will pull any other changes, such as design element and document changes from ServerB and write those changes to itself. When it begins the push part of the replication, ServerA sees that it has the most recently changed ACL. The ACL of ServerA completely overwrites the ACL of ServerB. When replication finishes, the ACL looks like the original ACL for ServerA.

Server-to-server replication always begins at the server level, with one server initiating the call to another server based on the Connection document schedule, as described earlier. Until replication is initiated, the server's replicator task is idle. After the call is made, the servers attempt to authenticate as discussed earlier. After authentication occurs, the called server verifies that the initiating server is allowed access by checking its own server document's server access list. Once authentication is complete and access is allowed, the server's replicator task compares the list of databases in the Replica ID cache to find the databases available for replication between the servers. After compiling this list, the servers use the replication history to determine the last successful replication. This date is then compared against the last date the database was modified. The database is only replicated if the modification date is more recent than the last replication date.

After determining which databases have been changed, the replicator task builds a list of changes to the database. This list includes ACL, design, and document changes that need to be replicated, based on the replication history, the document and field sequence numbers, and the replication settings. As long as all databases are version 4 or 5 databases, Domino only replicates the changed fields in the documents, rather than the entire documents.

When the replication completes successfully, the source server updates the replication history with a current time-date stamp.

Workstation-to-Server Replication

Most of the mechanics of workstation-to-server replication are the same as server-to-server replication. One of the main differences includes the fact that the workstation software does the work of the replication when replicating with a server; the server's replicator task does not become active. Another significant difference is the method of initiating and scheduling replication. We discussed earlier the methods of initiating server replication; here we discuss the methods of initiating workstation replication. The three main methods include the following:

- Initiating replication from the replicator page

- Initiating replication from a bookmark or database icon

- Using a Location document to schedule replication

Replicator Page on the Workspace

When you create a local replica of a database, an entry for it is automatically created on your workspace's replicator page. To examine your replicator page, as shown in Figure 12-28, click on the Replicator bookmark. On the replicator page, you see a list of databases that you have created from a replica on another Domino machine.

From the replicator page, you can click on the Start action button to initiate replication for all listed databases that are checked. The checkboxes allow you to select databases easily that should be replicated. As replication progresses, you will see a status bar at the bottom of the replicator page to let you know what database is currently being replicated and how far in to the replication it is. You will also have the ability to skip a database or stop replication, as shown in Figure 12-29.

You will also be able to obtain the following information from the replicator page:

- The last time that replication occurred for each database

- The server with which replication occurred for each database

- What was replicated at the last replication for each database

The Options button—the blue arrow, as shown in Figure 12-30—gives you the ability to specify the server to replicate with, and whether to send and/or receive changes.

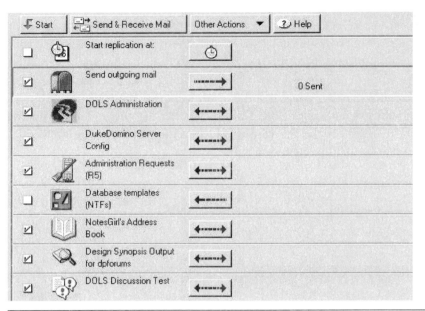

Figure 12-28   Replicator page

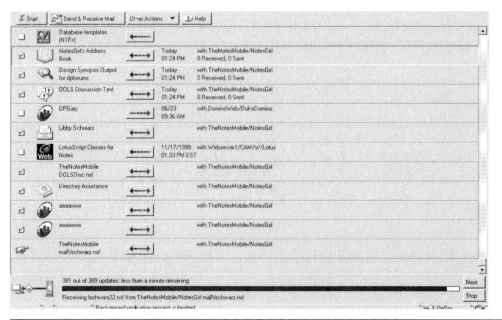

Figure 12-29   Initiate replication

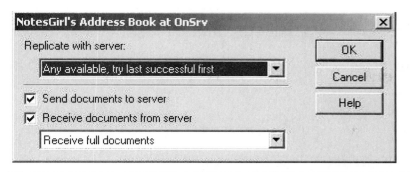

Figure 12-30   Replication options

Replicate from Bookmark or Workspace Icon

Another option for initiating workstation-to-server replication is to use the bookmark or replica icons. To use a bookmark, open the bookmarks window. Right-click on the bookmark and select Replication . . . Replicate from the short-cut menu, as shown in Figure 12-31.

If you are still using the R4-style workspace, you can initiate replication from the stacked icons on your workspace. Access the workspace from the Databases bookmark folder. Then stack your replica icons by choosing View . . . Stack Replica Icons. After the replica icons are stacked, you will see a drop-down arrow on the icons, as shown in Figure 12-32. When you click on the drop-down arrow, you can choose which replica to access and you can choose Replicate to initiate replication.

Scheduling Workstation-to-Server Replication

Similarly to the way that we scheduled server-to-server scheduled replication, you can schedule workstation-to-server replication. To schedule workstation-to-server replication, you will use the Location documents stored in your Personal Name and Address Book. Your Location documents can be found in one of two ways. First, you can open your Personal Address Book to the Advanced . . . Locations view and either open an existing Location document or create a new Location document. You can also click on the Current Location pop-up menu on the status bar in the workspace, as shown in Figure 12-33, and choose Edit Current to edit the current Location document.

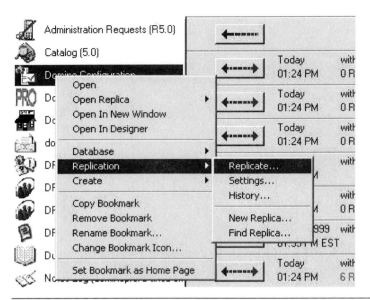

Figure 12-31 Replicate from a bookmark

Figure 12-32 Replicate from icon

Figure 12-33
Edit Location
document

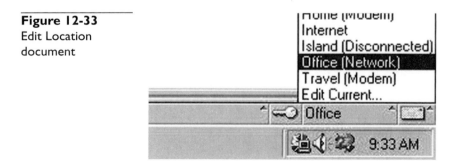

After you have the Location document open, select the Replication tab and choose enabled in the Replication Schedule field. Enabling this field causes Notes to display the fields for creating the schedule. You can then schedule the replications that are appropriate for that location. For example, for the Home (Modem) location, you may know that you will have your laptop connected every night from 9 P.M. to 11 P.M. You would schedule the replication of the databases you have in common with the server between those times. All databases that have replicas on the selected server will be replicated, based on the databases checked on the Replicator page. You can uncheck databases to disable replication temporarily. The scheduled replications will occur based on the location you have selected at any time. An example of a completed Location document is shown in Figure 12-34. You can also enable and schedule high-priority replication.

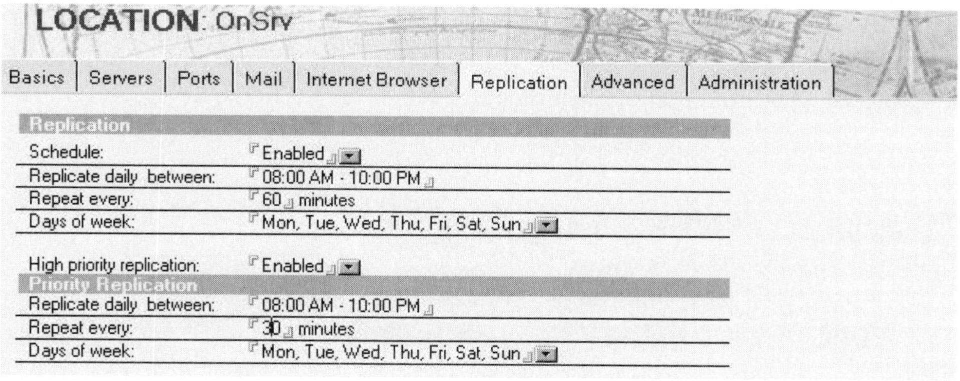

Figure 12-34   Schedule workstation replication

Troubleshooting Replication

Throughout the chapter, we have discussed the topic of replication. It should be clear by now that setting up and monitoring replication is one of the primary responsibilities of a Domino administrator. Troubleshooting replication is also an important task. As we discussed the replication topics, we mentioned some of the troubleshooting techniques for replication. The list below gives you some suggestions of where to look when you encounter replication problems.

- Are the server names spelled correctly in the server Connection documents?
- Are there too many replication connections occurring at the same time?
- Are the servers still connected? Is the network or modem not working?
- Is there a replication conflict for the Connection documents?
- Is one of the servers down?
- Does the ACL allow the servers to replicate?
- Can the servers authenticate?
- Is replication disabled on one of the databases?

When you are concerned about replication problems, you should look in your Notes log (LOG.NSF) for information. The Replication events and Miscellaneous events views are designed to give you information on when and how replication occurs as well as if and why it does not occur. In addition, you might change the NOTES.INI parameters for Log_Replication= to get more information about the replication issues. You can change this setting using a Configuration document for the server, as shown in Figure 12-35.

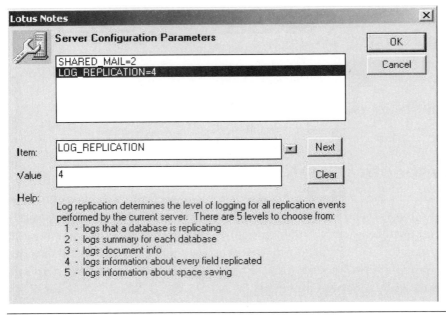

Figure 12-35 Log_Replication=

Review Questions

1. Amy created a copy of her Domino database on Server2 from its original home on Server1. When she tries to push the database, no errors are generated, but no changes are replicated. What is a possible way to determine the problem?
   A. Delete the copy and create a new one. The copy may have been corrupt.
   B. Open the database properties of both databases and check the Replica ID. They should be the same in order for replication to occur.
   C. Open the access control dialog box for the database and verify that the servers have the necessary rights to replicate changes.
   D. Verify that changes were actually made to the database.

2. Gary tells you the following things about Domino replication. Which ones are correct?
   A. You must manually start the Replica task on the server.
   B. The Replica task is automatically started on the server.
   C. If two databases on servers within the same DNN are replicas, they will automatically replicate.
   D. For two databases to replicate, you must force the replication manually.

3. The following is the correct way to create a new replica of a database:
   A. File . . . Database . . . New Copy
   B. File . . . Database . . . New Replica
   C. File . . . Replication . . . New Copy
   D. File . . . Replication . . . New Replica

4. Which server gets new data in a Push replication?
   A. The server that initiates the replication
   B. The server that is the destination of the replication

5. Which server gets new data in the PULL replication?
   A. The server that initiates the replication
   B. The server that is the destination of the replication

6. Which is the default type of replication?
   A. Pull-only
   B. Push-only
   C. Pull-push
   D. Pull-pull

7. Which command would force your server (Server1/NotesGirl) to call a remote server (Server2/NotesGirl) and initiate a replication that would fully synchronize the CERTBOOK.NSF database on both servers?

    A. PUSH Server1/NotesGirl CERTBOOK.NSF

    B. PULL Server1/NotesGirl Server2/NotesGirl CERTBOOK.NSF

    C. REPLICATE Server2/NotesGirl CERTBOOK.NSF

    D. REPLICATE Server1/NotesGirl CERTBOOK.NSF

8. Which databases are replicated if you do not specify databases in a replication Connection document?

    A. All databases that have replicas on the other server

    B. No databases are replicated

    C. NAMES.NSF only

    D. All .NTF files only are replicated

9. If you have a corporate office in Hong Kong where your administrators work, and hub offices in Tokyo, London, and New York that must all receive updates and send updates, what type of replication topology should you choose?

    A. Hierarchical topology

    B. Mesh topology

    C. Hub and spoke topology

    D. Wheel topology

10. What is the minimum level of the ACL to set servers that will be replicating a database that has users with Author access?

    A. Author

    B. Editor

    C. Manager

    D. Designer

Review Answers

1. **B, C,** and **D** are correct.   Open the database properties of both databases and check the Replica ID. They should be the same in order for replication to occur. Open the Access control dialog box for the database to verify that the servers have the necessary rights to replicate changes. Verify that changes were actually made to the database.

2. **B is correct.** The REPLICA task is automatically started on the server.

3. **D is correct.** Use File . . . Replication . . . New Replica to create a new replica.

4. **B is correct.** The server that is the destination of the replication get new data in a push replication.

5. **A is correct.** The server that initiates the replication gets new data in a pull replication.

6. **C is correct.** Pull-push is the default type of replication.

7. **C is correct.** REPLICATE Server2/NotesGirl CERTBOOK.NSF is the correct command.

8. **A is correct.** All databases that have replicas on the other server will be replicated if you do not specify a database.

9. **C is correct.** Hub and spoke topology is the best topology.

10. **B is correct.** Author access would enable the server to replicate any new documents, but not any documents that have been edited. Users with Author access can edit their own documents.

CHAPTER 13

Configuring Monitoring

You should be able to answer questions based on the following objectives after reading this chapter:

- Setting up/configuring monitoring administration tools (preferences, logs, Web-based, remote)
- Setting up/configuring monitoring monitors (ACL, file, STAT, probes)
- Setting up/configuring monitoring statistics (STATS)

As a Domino system administrator, you are expected to maintain the environment that you have created. In the previous chapters, we planned and configured your Domino environment, registered and installed users and servers, created replication and mail routing schedules, and implemented security. The main focus of this chapter is on monitoring the elements that you have already created. There is an implementation aspect to monitoring your environment, so that although the focus of this exam is implementing, you have to implement monitoring. First, you need to ensure that you're ready to administer and monitor your environment by configuring the Domino Administrator, Administration Preferences, and Web Administrator. Then, to ensure that the Notes Log, probes, statistics, and other monitoring tools will be ready to monitor your environment, you need to configure them.

Administration Tools

As a system administrator, you are expected to maintain and control activities on the server. You can do this type of activity in five main places:

- Domino Directory
- Server Console

- Domino Administrator
- Web Administrator
- Remote Console

We have already discussed and described the Domino Directory, and its uses, in Chapter 8. This section will focus on the uses of the Server Console, Domino Administrator, Web Administrator, and the Remote Console.

Server Console

The Server Console is a command-prompt based (DOS-like) interface that resides on the Domino server machine. It is also sometimes called the server shell. The server console must be running for the server to be considered "up." When you exit or close the server console, you are bringing down your Domino server. You can use the server console to type in commands that will return values either directly to the screen, to a text file, or to the Notes Log file. The commands can either perform an action or obtain information.

 EXAM TIP The console commands described in the following section are not all tested on the exam, but it is useful to know a variety of commands as they will be represented on the exam. In addition, these are not all of the available commands. You should know how to input the commands with the correct syntax as well as know what the command will do or return.

The commands listed here are some of the most common commands used at the Domino server console. Note that most commands also show an abbreviation. The commands in Domino can be abbreviated to the shortest length that still allows them to be unique.

- **SHOW SERVER or SH SE** Shows basic server information, including name and server directory. It can be used to view dead and pending mail, server uptime, transactions, and the shared mail status and database.

- **SHOW TASKS or SH TA** Shows the basic server information available with SHOW SERVER, plus a list of the tasks currently running on the server. This list includes some information about active users as well as all the idle and active tasks. The results of a **SHOW TASKS** command may be very long, and therefore **SH SE** may be more useful in many situations.

- **SHOW USERS** or **SH US**   Displays a list of active users. The list includes the name of the user or server, the databases they are using, and the number of minutes since they last used those databases.

- **BROADCAST "Message" "UserName"**   Allows an administrator to send a message to a user that is currently connected to the server. Use a **SHOW USER** to verify which users are connected, and then send them a message, using **BROADCAST**. The user name should be hierarchical and enclosed in quotes. An example of this command might be: **BROADCAST "Server going down in 5 min." "Doctor Notes/NotesGirl"**. If you do not specify a name, the message is sent to all currently connected users.

- **DROP ALL**   Allows you to disconnect all users; **DROP "UserName"** allows you to disconnect a currently connected user. This closes their connection to the server.

- **SHOW CONFIG Variable**   Allows the administrator to view the value of a variable that is set in the NOTES. INI. **SHOW CONFIG SHARED_MAIL**, for example, displays the value of the SHARED_MAIL variable. Another example would be **SHOW CONFIG REPLICATORS**, which would display the number of replicators enabled on the server. To see a complete list of available settings, refer to the Domino Administration Help database.

- **SET CONFIG Variable**   Allows the administrator to set the value of a variable that is stored in the NOTES. INI. **SET CONFIG SHARED_MAIL**=1, for example, changes the value of the SHARED_MAIL variable. Another example would be **SET CONFIG REPLICATORS**=2, which would enable two replicators on the server. To see a complete list of available settings, refer to the Domino Administration Help database.

- **TELL**   Allows the administrator to send a command to a specific Domino task, such as **TELL REPLICA QUIT** or **TELL ROUTER QUIT**. Many of the Domino server tasks accept Tell commands, such as HTTP, Router, Sched, AdminP, and AMgr.

- **LOAD**   Allows the administrator to start a specific Domino task, such as **LOAD REPLICA** or **LOAD ROUTER**.

- **ROUTE Servername**   Allows the administrator to force mail routing to the specified server immediately, rather than waiting for the schedule specified in the Connection document. For more information about mail routing, refer to Chapter 11.

- **REPLICATE** *Servername Databasename*   Allows the administrator to force a complete pull-push replication with the specified server. If the *databasename* parameter is also used, only the specified database will be replicated; otherwise, all databases

with replicas in the lotus\domino\data directory and subdirectories will be replicated. For more information about replication, refer to Chapter 12.

- **PUSH** *Servername Databasename*   Allows the administrator to force a push-only
replication with the specified server. If the *databasename* parameter is also used,
only the specified database will be replicated; otherwise, all databases with replicas in the lotus\domino\data directory and subdirectories will be replicated. For
more information about replication, refer to Chapter 12.

- **PULL** *Servername Databasename*   Allows the administrator to force a pull-only
replication with the specified server. If the *databasename* parameter is also used,
only the specified database will be replicated; otherwise, all databases with replicas in the lotus\domino\data directory and subdirectories will be replicated. For
more information about replication, refer to Chapter 12.

- **SET SECURE** *Password*   Allows the administrator to secure the console itself with
a password. Users or other administrators will not be able to type in console commands without the password if this has been set.

- **HELP**   Gives the administrator an overview of the available console commands,
including use and syntax.

- **QUIT** or **EXIT**   Allows the administrator to exit the server console. This command
shuts down all server tasks prior to shutting down the server.

Other examples of server commands include Show Directory, Show Diskspace, Show
Statistics, Show Memory, Show Performance, Show Schedule, and Show Port. For more
information about these and other server commands, refer to the Domino Administration Help database.

Domino Administrator

While you can control many of the Domino server tasks directly from the server console, it is not the recommended way of administering your server. Your server console
should be locked away—and therefore fairly inaccessible for regular administration.
Instead, you should use the Domino Administrator. This is the additional client software designed for the majority of your administration tasks.

The Domino Administrator is organized into three main sections—the server list, the
center pane containing tabs for the majority of your tasks, and the tools pane. Use the
server list, shown in Figure 13-1, to select the server to administer. You should have
access to all the servers that you administer, organized by Domain. If you have added
servers to the environment or think that the server list is not accurate (or if it is not visible), use the Administration . . . Refresh Server List option to rebuild the server book-

marks. You can also add a server to the favorites bookmark. Choose Administration . . . Add Server to Favorites. In the Add Server to Bookmarks dialog box, select or type the name of the server to add to the favorites bookmarks.

In the main window, or pane, of the Domino Administrator, you can select a tab to perform necessary administration tasks or view configuration information about your server. The tabs, shown in Figure 13-2, are as follows:

- People and groups
- Files
- Server
- Messaging
- Replication
- Configuration

Within most tabs, there are views available on the left; many tabs also have sub-tabs to further organize the data and tools available in each section. Each tab has context-sensitive tools available to the far right. You can expand or collapse the tools pane and each set of available tools. Figure 13-3 shows the tools available on the Files tab.

As you administer your environment, keep in mind that you can select which server to administer as well as which Domino Directory you want to modify. On the

Figure 13-1
Server list

Figure 13-2 Domino Administrator tabs

Figure 13-3
Files tab tools

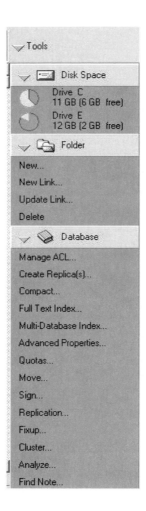

Configuration tab, you can select the Domino Directory to modify from the Use Directory On drop-down list.

The People and Groups Tab

The People and Groups tab allows you to register and manage users and groups. Use the tools associated with this tab to register new users, rename or recertify users, and move or delete users. In addition, you can access the Manage Groups tool from this tab, as shown in Figure 13-4. This tool allows you to view the membership of multiple groups while adding and removing users. You can sort the groups by their purpose. You can also select a user from the left-hand pane and choose the Only Member Hierarchies radio button to display only the groups to which the selected user belongs (do I hear a cheer?).

The Files Tab

The Files tab gives you access to all the files (including databases, templates, and flat files) in the Domino directories or linked directories. The tools available from this tab include a graphical representation of Disk Space, Folder tools that can be used to create new folders or directory links, and all the available Database tools. The Database tools include the Manage ACL tool that allows you to modify the ACL of multiple databases simultaneously, as shown in Figure 13-5.

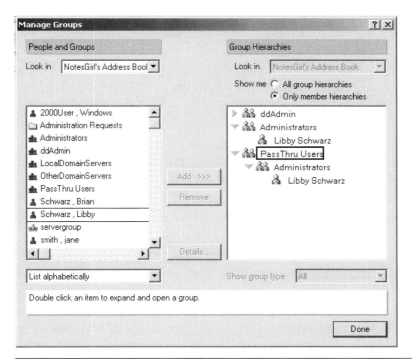

Figure 13-4 Manage Groups tool

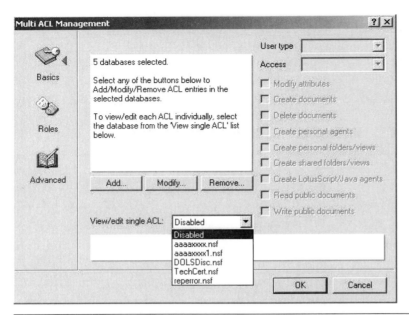

Figure 13-5 Manage ACL tool

Other tools available in the Database tools include Create Replicas, Advanced Properties, and a graphical interface for Fixup. Many, although not all, of the tools can be run against multiple databases. The Compact tool, another option from this tools list, allows not only compaction of selected databases (in-place, so that users can continue to access the database while it is being compacted), but is also the tool to kick off the archiving process. To kick off archiving from this tool, the database must have been configured for archiving using the Archive Settings button in the Database Properties InfoBox. It's worth noting that you can open database and template files directly from the file list in this tab.

The Server Tab

The Server tab is additionally broken down into Status, Analysis, Monitoring, and Statistics tabs. You can also run a remote server console by clicking the Console button. One useful tool here allows you to start or stop tasks on the selected server. The Statistics tab shows a list of available statistics and their most current values, as shown in Figure 13-6. In addition, you can easily monitor which tasks are running by looking at the server Status tab, shown in Figure 13-7.

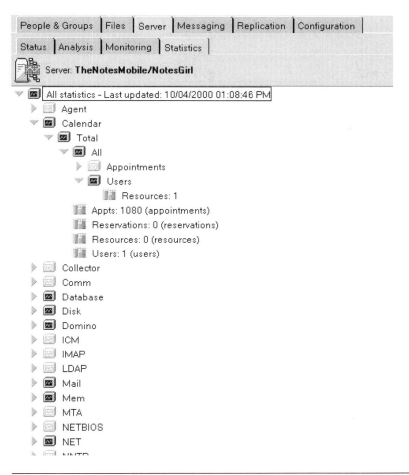

Figure 13-6   Server statistics

The Messaging Tab

The Messaging tab allows you to view and maintain the Domino messaging infrastructure. Available views include the mailbox view, which allows you to delete and release dead or stopped messages, a graphical mail-o-meter view for dead or waiting mail, and the Mail Routing topology views. To see the graphical Mail Routing topology views, either by Domino (Notes) Named Network or by connections, you must be running the Maps Extractor (MAPS) task on the server. The messaging tools allow you to configure message tracking, send mail traces, force mail to route, and stop-and-start the router on a given server.

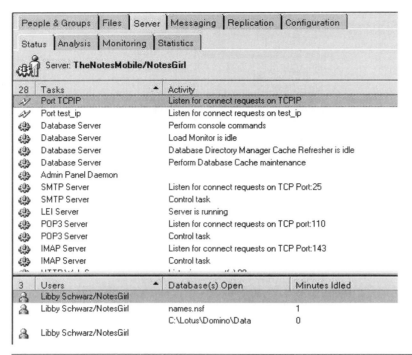

28	Tasks	▲	Activity
	Port TCPIP		Listen for connect requests on TCPIP
	Port test_ip		Listen for connect requests on test_ip
	Database Server		Perform console commands
	Database Server		Load Monitor is idle
	Database Server		Database Directory Manager Cache Refresher is idle
	Database Server		Perform Database Cache maintenance
	Admin Panel Daemon		
	SMTP Server		Listen for connect requests on TCP Port:25
	SMTP Server		Control task
	LEI Server		Server is running
	POP3 Server		Listen for connect requests on TCP port:110
	POP3 Server		Control task
	IMAP Server		Listen for connect requests on TCP Port:143
	IMAP Server		Control task

Figure 13-7 Server status

The Replication Tab

The Replication tab gives you many of the same tools that you found on the Messaging tab, including a graphical representation of your connections (Replication topology), a view from the Log of the Replication events, and an all-in-one glimpse at the current server's replication schedule, as shown in Figure 13-8. The Replication tab is the only tab that doesn't have any specific tools available.

The Configuration Tab

The Configuration tab is the catch-all that gives you all the abilities you're still wondering about. The view on the left-hand side gives you access to all the documents from the Domino Directory that you were worried you might still have to edit in by actually opening the Domino Directory itself. Instead, you can access Server, Connection, Configuration, Program, and External Domain Documents under the Server twistie, as shown in Figure 13-9. You also find additional documents, related to Messaging, Replication, Clustering, Statistics and Events, the Web server settings, and the Directory itself under the appropriate categories.

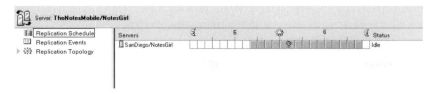

Figure 13-8   At-a-Glance Replication Schedule

Figure 13-9
Your portal to the
Server portion of
the Domino
Directory

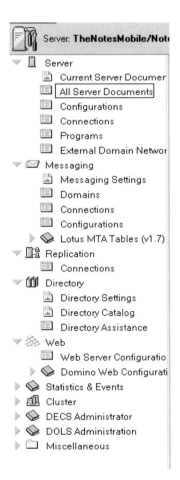

The tools available from the Configuration tab include Certification and Registration tools. Under the Certification tools, you will find the ability to Cross-Certify, Edit Multiple Passwords, and Edit and Extract Recovery Information. For those unfamiliar with the Recovery tool, this allows named Recovery Authorities to assist users with recovering lost or corrupted ID files and passwords. In addition, while you can register People from the People & Groups tab, you can register not only People, but also Servers, Organizations, and Organizational Units from the Registration tools here.

Administration Preferences

Mentioned previously, one of the tools provided to make administration smoother is the Administration Preferences. To access the Administration Preferences dialog box, shown in Figure 13-10, choose File . . . Preferences . . . Administration Preferences.

The Preferences dialog box is separated into the following four pages:

- **Basics** Allows you to indicate which Domains you administer from this client. In addition, you can choose to switch locations when you switch domains.

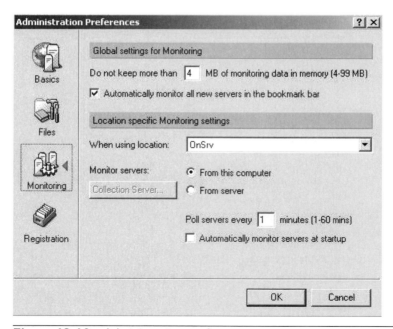

Figure 13-10 Administration preferences

- **Files**   Allows you to select which columns will be available when you're in the Files tab of the Administrator client.

- **Monitoring**   Allows you to configure the collection of monitoring data from the servers you administer, including how often and from which server or computer.

- **Registration**   Allows you to set the defaults for the registration process, including your registration server, where to store the ID files, mail options, and which certifier to use, as shown in Figure 13-11.

Web Administrator

Lotus provides not only the Domino Administrator client for remote administration, but also the Web administrator. When you run HTTP on a server for the first time, Domino creates the Web Administrator database (WEBADMIN.NSF). Domino gives the database a unique replica ID, so it does not replicate with other servers. To use the Web administrator, you must be listed in the Administer the Server from a browser field on the Server document. If the administrator's name appears in the Administrator's field of the Server document, you don't have any other security settings to configure.

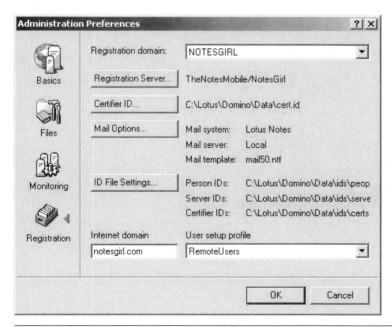

Figure 13-11   Registration preferences

If you have changed this field, however, you need to change or verify the following settings listed in Table 13-1.

After you configure the Web Administrator, you can do most of the typical administration tasks from this location. Figure 13-12 shows the Messaging . . . Mail Users view. One set of tasks you cannot perform in the Domino Administrator is certification (registration). To register users, servers, and certifiers, you need to use the Domino Administrator.

Table 13-1 Security for Web Administrator

Setting or Name	Level
Maximum Internet Name and Password	Manager
Names listed in the Administrators field of the Server document	Manager with ServerAdmin, ServerMonitor, DatabaseAdmin, FileRead, and FileModify roles
The server	Manager with no roles
-Default -	No access
Anonymous	No access
LocalDomainServers	Manager with ServerAdmin, ServerMonitor, DatabaseAdmin, FileRead, and FileModify roles
OtherDomainServers	No Access
Lotus Notes Template Development/Lotus Notes	Manager with ServerAdmin, ServerMonitor, DatabaseAdmin, FileRead, and FileModify roles

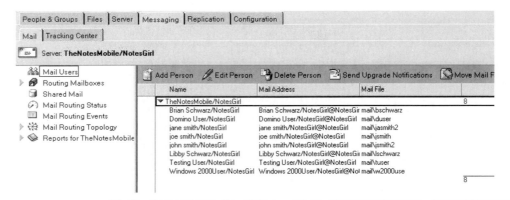

Figure 13-12 Messaging . . . Mail Users view

Remote Console

In the previous section, we discussed an administrator's ability to control the server using the server console. For administrators that do not have direct access to the server console for a machine, or for administrators that prefer to administer their servers remotely, Domino has included a console accessible in the Domino Administrator. The remote console is also available from the Web administrator. All of the console commands available at the server console are also available at the Remote console.

After opening the Domino Administrator, click the Server . . . Status tab. On the right side, click the Console button.

To see the commands act on the server immediately, including seeing other server activity as it occurs, choose the Live button. You can type a command in the Server Console command field. To select a command, click the Command button. This displays a list of available commands, including a description, as shown in Figure 13-13.

Figure 13-13 Select a command

After typing or selecting a command, press ENTER. This sends the command to the server console. If you can see the actual server console while using the Remote console, you will notice that the remote console commands are displayed on the server after you send them.

One of the benefits of the Remote console is that it gives you the opportunity to scroll back through your remote console session. This is especially useful when typing in a command that returns a long list of values, such as SHOW TASKS or SHOW USERS. In addition, you can scroll back through the list of commands that you have sent in a particular remote console session by clicking the drop-down arrow next to the Server console commands field.

 TIP To use the Remote Console, your name must be listed in the Administrator's field of the Server document in the Domino Directory.

Notes Log

When a warning or an error occurs in Domino, it displays on the Domino server console. If you are like most administrators, however, you will not be sitting by your server, waiting for errors. All activity that occurs on the server is therefore also written to the Notes Log database (LOG.NSF). You can view the Log by choosing File . . . Database . . . Open from the menus and accessing any server. From the server, select the Notes Log database for that server. You can also view the Log on the Server . . . Analysis tab of the Domino Administrator.

The Log shows all types of events that occur on the server, including replication events, mail routing events, and errors. This is one of the best ways to troubleshoot or verify the health of a server. An administrator should open and check the Log multiple times each day. The Miscellaneous Event view of the Log allows you to open Log documents that show all activity on the server, as shown in Figure 13-14.

The Notes Log can grow to be very large, which isn't always desirable. On the other hand, when you are troubleshooting something, you may want additional data. You have some control over the size of the log based on the type and amount of data that is stored in the file. You can change a variety of NOTES.INI settings to configure the Notes Log.

Table 13-2 shows the elements for which you can configure additional logging. Bear in mind that you should only choose to have additional logging when you are troubleshooting.

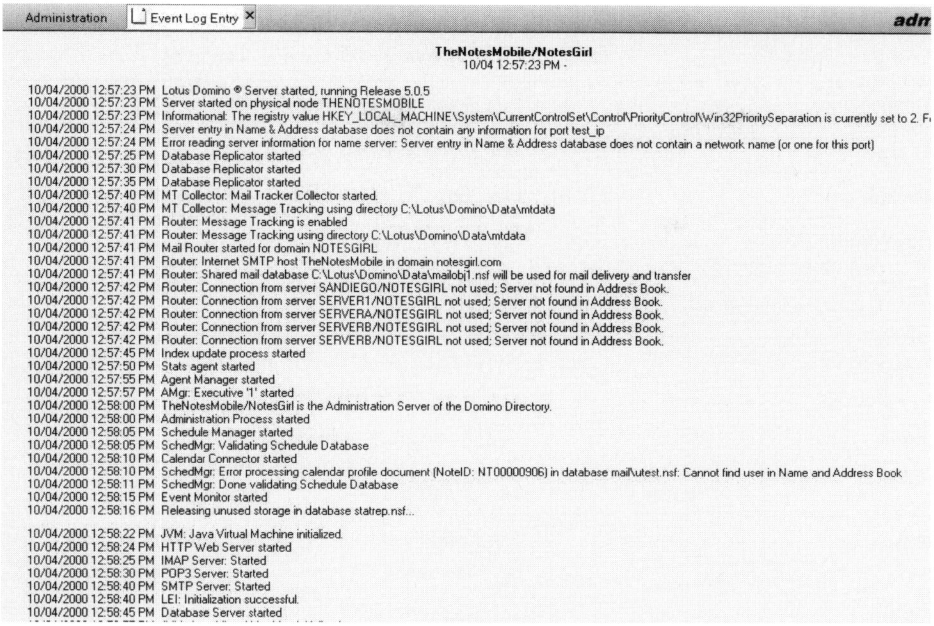

Figure 13-14 Miscellaneous Events in the Notes Log

You can also use the LOG= setting in the NOTES.INI to limit the number of days to keep data in the log or amount of information to store.

Monitors

Another option you have for monitoring your server is monitors you can configure to alert you when something occurs on the server. You can create ACL Change, File, Replication, and Statistic monitors. In the Domino Administrator, select the Configuration tab and expand the Statistics and Events section. There are views for each type of monitor under the Monitors section.

ACL Change

For many environments, there are multiple administrators. This can be confusing or can cause problems with access to databases if multiple changes are made to ACLs of important databases. You can have Domino warn you about changes made to the ACL of a database using an ACL Change Monitor. In the ACL Change monitors view, select the New ACL Change Monitor action button. Domino displays the ACL Change Monitor document shown in Figure 13-15.

Table 13-2 Additional Logging Elements

Task or Element	Configure Additional Logging
Agent manager	Log_AgentManager in NOTES.INI
Indexer activity	Log_Update in NOTES.INI
Mail routing	Mail_Log_To_MiscEvents in NOTES.INI
Messages generated when views are rebuilt	Log_View_Events in NOTES.INI
Modem I/O	File, Preferences, User Preferences, Ports, COMx Options
NNTP server	"NNTP log level" field in the NNTP Server section of the Server document
Replication	Log_Replication in NOTES.INI "Log all replication events" setting specified during server setup
Script I/O	File, Tools, Preferences, Notes Preferences, Ports, COMx, Options
Server tasks	Log_Tasks in NOTES.INI
Traced network connections	File, Preferences, Notes Preferences, Ports, Trace
User sessions	Log_Sessions in NOTES.INI
Web Navigator	"Retriever log level" field on the Server Tasks—Web Retriever tab of the Server document.
Web server	Web server information is recorded only in the Domino Web server log (DOMLOG.NSF)

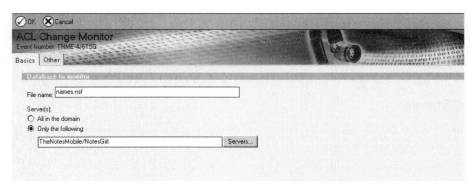

Figure 13-15 ACL Change Monitor

On the Basics tab, type the file name for the database to monitor. Then select whether to monitor all servers in the domain or the specified server or servers. On the Other tab, decide what type of event the monitor should generate when the ACL is changed. You can also create a Notification profile for the event. This lets you determine how you will be notified of the event's occurrence.

When you click the Create a new notification profile for this event button, Domino displays the Event notification wizard, as shown in Figure 13-16. On the first screen, choose the notification trigger: any event that matches the criteria, a specific built-in/add-in task or event, a custom monitor, or probe event. On the second screen, select a notification method, such as a broadcast, log, mail, or pager. Some of these will have additional notification options, such as an email address or database to log to.

When finished, close the wizard and then save and close the ACL Change Monitor.

File Monitor

Use a File Monitor to track unused space or user inactivity in a database. Knowing about unused space will let you compact the database as necessary. Knowing about user inactivity in a database can tell you if the database is not in use or if it is no longer accessible as it should be. In the File monitors view, select the New File Monitor action button. Domino displays the File Monitor document shown in Figure 13-17.

On the Basics tab, select the file to monitor and which server to monitor. Next, select what to monitor (unused space or user inactivity). Each item to monitor has an additional tab. On the Unused Space tab, decide how much unused space should trigger the

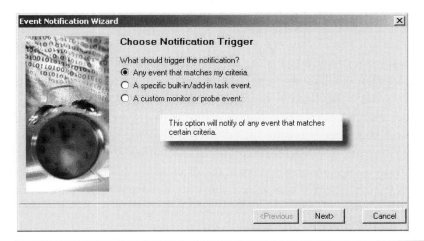

Figure 13-16   Notification wizard

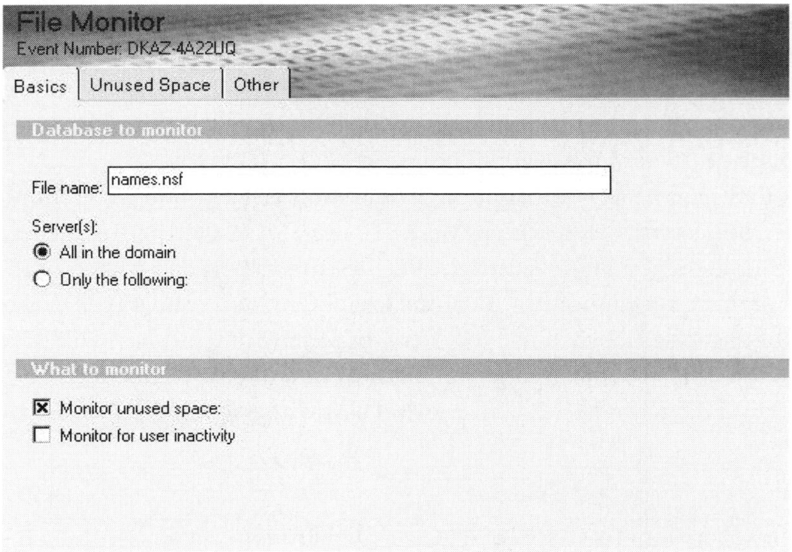

Figure 13-17   File Monitor

event and choose whether to compact the database automatically when the event is triggered. On the User Inactivity tab, decide what time periods to monitor and the minimum number of sessions. Use the Other tab to create a notification profile.

Replication Monitor

When databases replicate between servers, you need to know if a replication doesn't occur. This is especially true of databases such as the Domino Directory (NAMES.NSF). To be alerted if a particular database doesn't replicate with certain servers within a particular time period, create a Replication monitor. In the Replication monitors view, select the New Replication monitor action button. Domino displays a new Replication monitor document, as shown in Figure 13-18.

On the Basics tab, choose the file to monitor and the server on which it should be monitored. In addition, indicate which servers in the domain the file is configured to replicate with. Next, indicate the replication timeout—this is the maximum number of hours allowed to elapse between replications.

On the Other tab, create a notification profile.

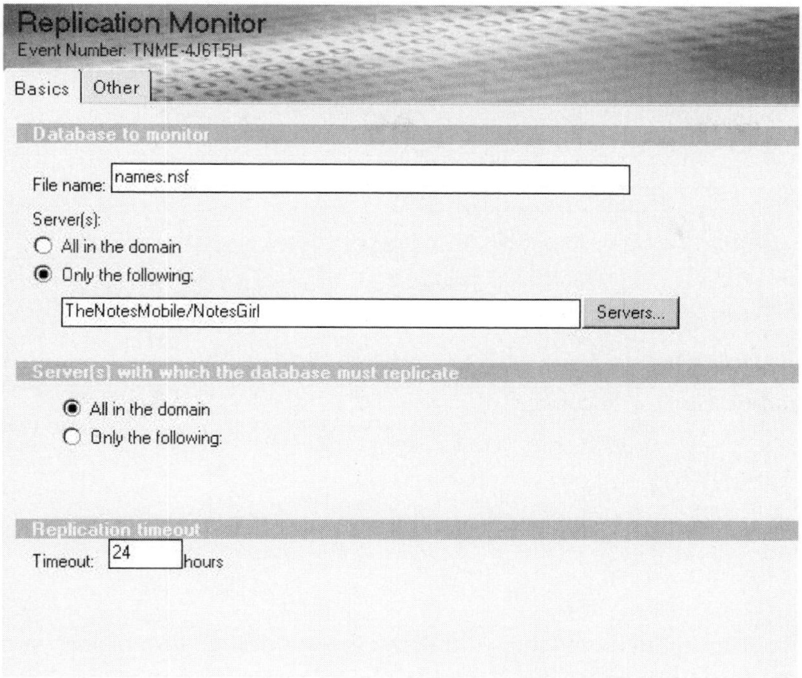

Replication Monitor
Event Number: TNME-4J6T5H

Basics | Other

Database to monitor

File name: names.nsf

Server(s):
○ All in the domain
◉ Only the following:

TheNotesMobile/NotesGirl   Servers...

Server(s) with which the database must replicate

◉ All in the domain
○ Only the following:

Replication timeout

Timeout: 24   hours

Figure 13-18   Replication monitor

Statistic Monitor

Domino tracks a variety of statistics for the operating system, hardware, and the Domino server. When these statistics reach certain thresholds, you may want to be notified. Statistic monitors can track any of the standard Domino statistics. In the Statistic monitor view, click the New Statistic Monitor action button. Note that some statistic monitors are already created by default, such as for free memory, free hard disk space, and the number of dead messages in mail.box.

In the New Statistic monitor document, shown in Figure 13-19, choose the server to monitor. Click the Change button to select the statistic to track. On the Threshold tab, choose when to generate the event, based on whether the statistic is less than, greater than, or a multiple of the threshold value you designate. Use the Other tab to create a notification profile.

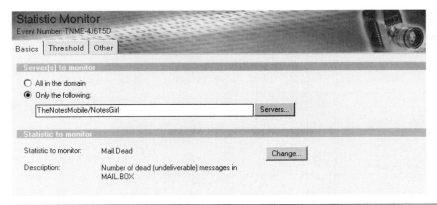

Figure 13-19 Statistic monitor document

Probes

You may want to constantly check whether your server is responding. With probes, you can check whether a server is accessible, whether you can open a certain database, whether mail can be sent to a certain recipient, and whether any configured TCPIP ports (such as HTTP, LDAP, and so on) can respond. Use Domino Server, Mail, and TCP server probes. Create Probes by opening the Domino Administrator to the Configuration tab. Expand the Statistics and Events section. Under the Probes section, each type of Probe has its own view.

Domino Server Probes

In the Domino Server probe view, click the New Domino Server Probe action button. Domino displays the new Domino Server Probe document, as shown in Figure 13-20. On the Basics tab, select the target server. This is the server that will be probed. You will also define the probing server (also called the source server). For the Domino Server probe, you can choose whether to check just the ability to access the destination server, or the ability to access the server and open a designated database.

On the Probe tab, choose either to probe using any available port, or select a specific port to probe over. Indicate the timeout threshold for the specified probe. On the Other tab, create a notification profile.

Mail Probe

In the Mail probe view, click the New Mail Probe action button. Domino displays the Mail Probe document, as shown in Figure 13-21 On the Basics tab, you can choose to

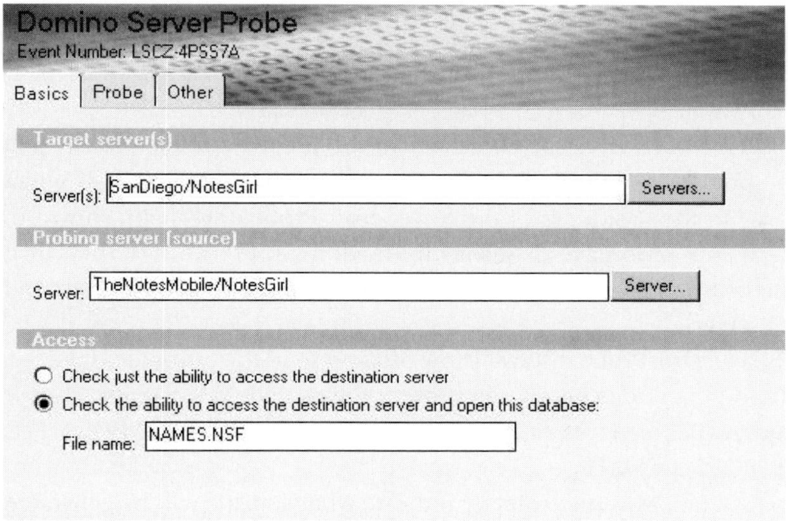

Figure 13-20   Domino Server probe

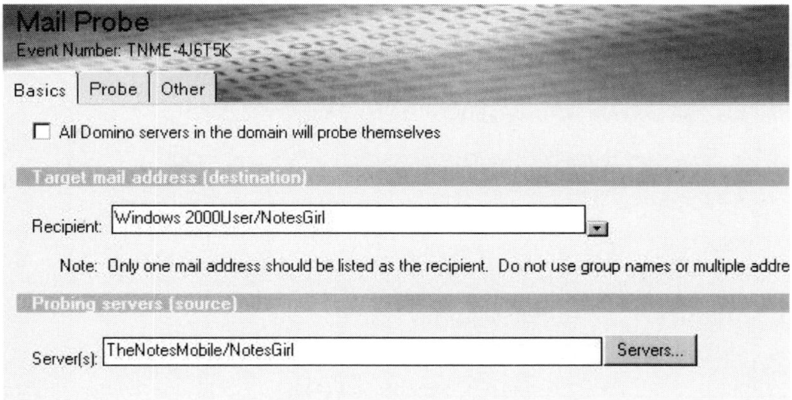

Figure 13-21   Mail probe

have all Domino servers in the domain probe themselves. If you enable this option, each server will probe a local mailbox. If all servers will not be probing themselves, place a single mail address to probe in the Recipient field. Do not use a group or multiple e-mail addresses, or the probe will fail. You will also select the probing (or source) server.

On the Probe tab, type the Send Interval and the Timeout threshold. The Send interval is how often the probe occurs. The timeout threshold is when an event will be generated for the probe. Use the Other tab to create a notification profile.

TCP Server Probe

If you are running TCPIP-based services, you can create a TCP server probe to verify that those services are responding. In the TCP Server Probe view, click the New TCP Server Probe action button. On the Basics tab of the New Server Probe document, shown in Figure 13-22, you can choose to have all servers in the domain probe all of their own configured ports (according to the server document). You could also select a target and probing (or source) server.

On the Probe tab, select the Probe interval (how often to send the probe) and the service timeout threshold (when to generate an event for the probe). You can also choose to probe all configured TCP services or specific services, including DNS, FTP, HTTP, IMAP, LDAP, NNTP, POP3, or SMTP.

Each port has its own tab. Most tabs merely indicate what statistic will be generated by the probe for that port. On the HTTP port tab, you can choose just to probe the port,

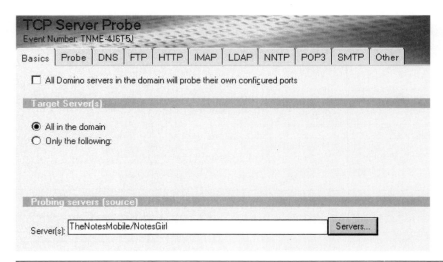

Figure 13-22 TCP Server probe

or you can choose to fetch a specific URL. Similarly, on the NNTP tab, you can choose to probe just the port or you can choose to send a specific command. Use the Other tab to create a notification profile.

Statistics

You can configure statistics and events to work with the Collect and Event tasks to gather data about your servers and inform you when certain thresholds or other events are reached. Statistics are continually updated and show the status of processes running on the system, such as the amount of free space or free memory. An Event is generated when a statistic hits a threshold or some other item occurs on the system. Statistics are collected by the Statistics Collector task (Collector) and placed in the database STA-TREP.NSF. You can create/edit the Statistics Collection document to collect statistics from a list of servers. Otherwise, the Collector task only collects statistics from the server on which it is running.

In the Statistics Collection document, choose a collection server and decide which server(s) to collect from. You can choose all servers in the domain, all servers that are not explicitly listed to be collected already, and any specified servers. Use the Options tab to log the statistics to a database. See Figure 13-23 for a Statistics Collection document.

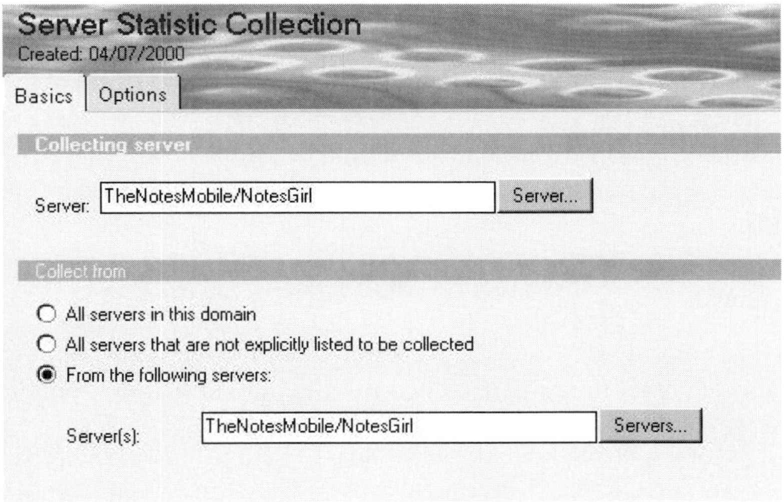

Figure 13-23 Statistics collection document

You can also choose to collect statistics on demand and have them mailed to yourself or someone else, using the STATS task. You need to run the STATS task on the server (type LOAD STATS) to create the server statistics mail-in database (STATMAIL.NSF).

Review Questions

1. Paul is a new Domino administrator. He wants to monitor the users on his server to understand how they are using it. What command can he type at the console to find out this information?

   A. SH TA

   B. TELL SERVER SHOW TASKS

   C. SH US

   D. TELL SERVER SHOW USERS

2. Which of the following commands would close the user sessions on Server1 so that Rick can shut it down?

   A. TELL SERVER DROP ALL

   B. TELL SERVER CLOSE CONN

   C. DROP USERS

   D. DROP ALL

3. Judy is listed as the manager of the Domino Directory and is in a group called Administrators. When she tries to type in a command at the remote console, however, she gets an error. What might be the problem?

   A. Neither Judy nor the Administrators group is in the RemoteAccess field of the Server document.

   B. The Administrators group is misnamed; it should be Admin.

   C. Neither Judy nor the Administrators groups has the NetModifier role in the Domino Directory.

   D. Neither Judy nor the Administrators group is in the Administrators field of the Server document.

4. John wants to see not only the results of the commands he types at the remote console, but also the other things that are occurring on the server. What option should he select?

   A. Pause output

   B. Echo on

   C. Live console

   D. Monitor on

5. Which of the following will let you see any new or changed servers in your bookmarks?
   A. Administration . . . Refresh Server List
   B. Administration . . . Show All Servers
   C. Administration . . . Show Server Changes
   D. Administration . . . Add Server to Favorites

6. Which tabs in the Domino Administrator can you use to register a new user?
   A. Configuration
   B. People and Groups
   C. Server
   D. Registration

7. Which of the following tasks is necessary to see the replication and routing topologies in the Domino Administrator?
   A. STATS
   B. ROUTER
   C. MAPS
   D. TOPS

8. Which task do you run to collect statistics and have them placed in STATREP.NSF?
   A. Event
   B. Report
   C. Collector
   D. Stats

9. Which task do you run to have the ability to mail statistics on demand?
   A. Event
   B. Report
   C. Collector
   D. Stats

10. Which of the following is true about the Web Administrator?
    A. You need to be listed in the Administrators field to use the Web administrator.
    B. You need to be listed in the "Administer this server from a browser" field to use the Web administrator.
    C. You need to run the WebAdmin task to use the Web administrator.
    D. You need to run the HTTP task to use the Web administrator.

Review Answers

1. **C** is correct. The SH US (Show Users) command tells Domino to list users who are currently connected and the databases they're using.

2. **D** is correct. To drop a single user, type DROP and the hierarchical name of the user inside quotes.

3. **D** is correct. Neither Judy nor the Administrators group is in the Administrators field of the Server document.

4. **C** is correct. By enabling the Live Console, Domino writes all activity on the server to the remote console as well.

5. **A** is correct. Use the Refresh Server List menu option to add any new or changed servers to your servers bookmark list.

6. **A** and **B** are both correct. Use either the Configuration or People and Groups tab to register a new user.

7. **C** is correct. You need to run the MAPS (or MAPS Extractor) task.

8. **C** is correct. Run the Collector task to place statistics in the STATREP.NSF database.

9. **D** is correct. Run the Stats task to mail statistics to users or databases on demand.

10. **B** and **D** are correct. You must be listed in the Administer the server from a browser field and you must be running HTTP.

PART III

Deploying Domino R5 Applications

The third exam in the System Administration track is the Deploying Domino R5 Applications exam (190-522). Passing this exam is the next (perhaps final, if you've taken the exams in order) step in gaining your Certified Lotus Professional (CLP) designation for System Administration, although it does not give you a certification by itself. The audience for this exam is administrators and architects with knowledge of Domino Administration, servers, clients, and architecture. This exam also requires some knowledge of Domino development and database design. You should already have passed at least the Maintaining Domino Servers and Users exam. The exam has 40 scored questions and 5 unscored questions, and requires a minimum score of 70 percent. The competencies for this exam cover two basic areas:

- Database Architecture

- Domino Infrastructure

These general areas of competency are broken down further into specific tasks that you should be able to perform. All tasks in this exam are geared toward being able to roll a Domino application or database out to production servers and users. To see a complete list, refer to the *Lotus Domino R5 CLP Certification Exam Guide*, available for download from **www.lotus.com/education**. Each chapter in this section lists the specific competency areas that it covers.

CHAPTER 14

Deploying Applications Based on Database Structure and Document Characteristics

You should be able to answer questions based on the following objectives after reading this chapter:

- Deploy applications based on the NSF structure: file attachments
- Deploy applications based on the NSF structure: loose objects
- Deploy applications based on the NSF structure: Note as the basic unit
- Deploy applications based on the NSF structure: NOTEID
- Deploy applications based on the NSF structure: NSF components
- Deploy applications based on the NSF structure: rich text structure
- Deploy applications based on the NSF structure: RRV
- Deploy applications based on the NSF structure: UNID
- Deploy applications based on document characteristics: archiving
- Deploy applications based on document characteristics: author access
- Deploy applications based on document characteristics: document size
- Deploy applications based on document characteristics: heterogenous data sources
- Deploy applications based on document characteristics: item data types
- Deploy applications based on document characteristics: item default values
- Deploy applications based on document characteristics: items
- Deploy applications based on document characteristics: reader access
- Deploy applications based on document characteristics: view hierarchies (response versus category)

In this chapter we'll look at the structure of Domino databases, and understand the main details that are important to us when deploying applications. We'll look at the implications of the new R5 database structure and what this means for mixed R4/R5 implementations. Then we'll learn what a NoteID and UNID (Universal Note ID) mean and then examine two common uses for these: for locating corrupt documents within a Domino database and also for the signing of design elements of an application before it is deployed.

Then we will look at the characteristics of documents and how these are related to application deployment. This includes the way that items are used within the NSF to hold document data, the power of reader and author fields, and archiving. Lastly, we will cover view hierarchies and their relevance to document content.

Deploying Based on NSF Structure

NSF is an acronym for Notes Storage Facility, which is the name of the file extension used for Domino databases and also the name of the internal subsystem that deals with database access for the Notes client and the Domino server.

R5 has introduced a new version of the NSF database format, which is known as ODS (On Disk Structure) version 41. If you have an R5 client, you can see the ODS version of a database in the Database Properties Info tab, as shown in Figure 14-1. This new ODS version provides the new R5 features, such as large database (> 4GB) sizes, transaction logging, and in-place compaction.

If you have an all-R5 environment with R5 Domino servers and R5 Notes clients, then the new version of ODS is transparent to you. However, if you have a mixed environment of R4 and R5, then you need to be careful how you work with this database version. Unless you have a small Notes/Domino implementation, then it is very likely

Figure 14-1
Database
Properties, Info tab

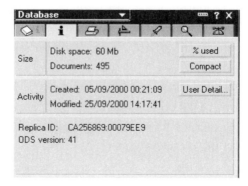

you need to understand the implications of the different ODS versions since your migration will not be instantaneous, and you will have a transition period where you have a mixed environment until the R5 migration is complete.

The main ODS versions you may come across are

- 17, for R3 databases
- 20, for R4 databases
- 41, for R5 databases

There are a couple of quick ways to check the ODS versions of all of the databases on your Domino server. The first is via the Files tab in Domino Administrator, as shown in Figure 14-2.

The File Format column lists the ODS version and for convenience lists the Notes version that this ODS version corresponds to. A couple of hints make this easier. First, if you click on the toggle button next to the Tools menu, rather than showing you all

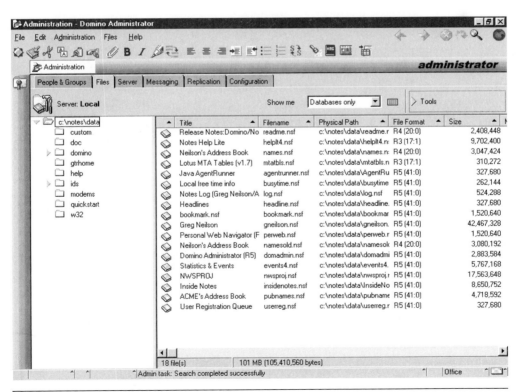

Figure 14-2 Domino Administrator, Files tab

database files within the current selected directory, it shows you all databases on the server. Secondly, this list is sortable by ODS version, by clicking on the column header.

Another way to list the ODS versions of all of the databases on the Domino server is via the SHOW DIRECTORY console command (which can be abbreviated as SH DIR). Figure 14-3 shows the output from this command.

Now that we've discussed ODS versions and how to determine the ODS versions of the databases on your Domino server, we need to discuss the implications of a mixed R4/R5 implementation:

- An R4 server or client is not able to directly read an R5 database that exists on its own filesystem. However, it is able to work with a Domino R5 server by sending network requests.

```
> sh dir
DbName                                 Version  Logged  ---Modified
Time----
D:\Lotus\Domino\Data\mail.box            V5      N/A    25/09/2000
04:00:02
D:\Lotus\Domino\Data\statrep5.ntf        V4      N/A    07/09/2000
01:03:54
D:\Lotus\Domino\Data\statrep.nsf         V5      N/A    25/09/2000
16:29:31
D:\Lotus\Domino\Data\statmail.nsf        V5      N/A    05/09/2000
03:50:05
D:\Lotus\Domino\Data\reports.nsf         V5      N/A    05/09/2000
03:50:04
D:\Lotus\Domino\Data\mailbox.ntf         V4      N/A    07/09/2000
01:03:52
D:\Lotus\Domino\Data\log.ntf             V4      N/A    07/09/2000
01:03:51
D:\Lotus\Domino\Data\events4.ntf         V4      N/A    07/09/2000
01:03:49
D:\Lotus\Domino\Data\events4.nsf         V5      N/A    14/09/2000
01:39:16
D:\Lotus\Domino\Data\cldbdir.nsf         V5      N/A    25/09/2000
07:27:17
D:\Lotus\Domino\Data\certlog.ntf         V4      N/A    07/09/2000
01:03:47
D:\Lotus\Domino\Data\admin4.nsf          V5      N/A    25/09/2000
00:02:51
D:\Lotus\Domino\Data\log.nsf             V5      N/A    25/09/2000
16:32:41
D:\Lotus\Domino\Data\names.nsf           V5      N/A    25/09/2000
09:31:29
```

Figure 14-3 Console command output from the SHOW DIRECTORY command

- When an R4 database is compacted on an R5 machine, it is automatically converted into the R5 format.

- If you rename an R4 database with an .NS4 extension on an R5 Domino server, it will not be automatically converted into R5 format.

- You can use COMPACT with the −R option to convert databases from R5 to R4 versions. This would be used if for any reason you needed to back out of an R4 to R5 server upgrade.

- This database format describes the internal database format only. It is totally different to the process of updating the design of databases to using templates that come with R5. These two events can happen at totally different times.

- Since ODS is an internal database structural issue, R4 and R5 clients and servers can replicate successfully between themselves. They will receive document changes, but the ODS changes are not replicated.

- New databases on an R5 server are created with the R5 format. This occurs even when using an R4 client. Similarly, when an R5 client creates a database on an R4 server, the resulting database will be in R4 format.

This brings us to discuss some basic architectural concepts within Domino databases. These help us to understand the internal operations of Notes and Domino and help us with our problem solving. A *note* is the basic building block record within a Domino database, hence the original product name of Lotus Notes. This database structure is optimized for "unstructured" data, which can be text, rich text, attachments, or OLE links. This is contrasted to structured data sources such as SQL Server, Oracle, and DB2 that have defined layouts for database records. Another way of describing this structure is to say that a Notes database is comprised of loose objects.

The *UNID* (Universal Note ID) is used to uniquely identify a given note across all replicas of a database. When replication occurs between replica copies of a database, it compares the UNIDs to ensure that the same element (which could a document or design element) is checked at each end for updates in each copy. The UNID is 16 bytes long.

The NoteID is a four-byte Note ID that it is assigned when the note is created within a database. It is unique within a replica copy of a Domino database but may not be unique across all replicas. It is used for programming convenience since it is much easier to use than the UNID. You can view the UNID and NoteID of a document by selecting a document within a database and then launching the InfoBox and selecting the last tab, Document IDs. Figure 14-4 shows an example of this. In a similar manner, you can obtain the IDs of a design element (a form, view, and so on) within Domino Designer by selecting the element and launching the Infobox. As before, the last tab shows the IDs.

Figure 14-4
Document IDs
tab within the
Document Info tab

Now let's explain what all of these numbers mean. The NoteID is the easiest to find, so we'll look at this first. It is on the last line and consists of all the numbers that follow the NT characters (for NoTeid). In the previous example, the NoteID is 00082252.

The UNID takes up the top two lines of output in the display. It comprises two parts: the Originator ID-File (OF for short) and the Originator ID-Note (ON for short). Both of these are randomly generated numbers that are created when the document is first created. Therefore, in this UNID for the document in Figure 14-5 is B7846541B4DEBFEB4A256960003BB4ED.

Now that we've covered some basic NSF concepts, we can look at why these can be useful in working with Domino databases. The first use is in dealing with database problems encountered by the server. When Domino finds a corruption within a database, it reports the database name together with the NoteID that has problems. Once you have this NoteID, you can use Domino Administrator to search for it. You open the Files tab, select the database to search, and launch the Find Note tool as shown in Figure 14-5. The tool can search by either the UNID or NoteID.

The other use for NoteID is signing design elements before application deployment. Workstation ECLs (these are discussed in Chapter 15) make use of ID the application signer, as do the server security sections for agents that run on servers (these are discussed further in Chapter 16). The Sign tool within Domino Administrator is used to sign databases. To use this, you open the Files tab, select the database to search, and launch the Sign tool as shown in Figure 14-6.

With this tool, you can elect to sign all elements, documents of a specific type, or a specific NoteID. Lastly, you have the option to update only signed database elements. Generally speaking, it doesn't take very long to sign all elements, so leaving this at the default will not take very long. The other options are available to reduce the time taken to sign the database before it is deployed. For example, if only one element has changed, you can check for the NoteID of the element within Domino Designer (remember, you can see this information in the Design InfoBox for the element), and specify it in the Sign tool. Alternatively, you can elect to sign all documents of a specific type (such as Forms or Views) and select these to be signed. Lastly, you can elect to only

Figure 14-5
Using the Domino
Administrator Find
Note tool

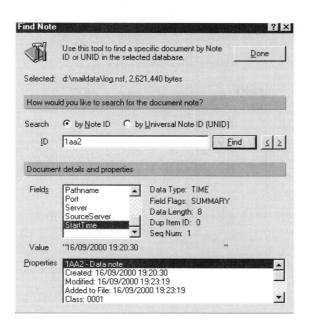

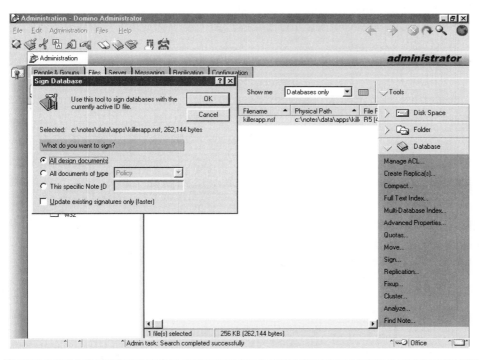

Figure 14-6   Using the Domino Administrator Sign tool

update the signatures of previously signed elements. This could be used if you have updated a number of existing design elements within the database and only want the signed elements to be updated rather than every database Note. The RRV, or record relocation vector, exists within a database to map the NoteID of each document within the database to its physical location.

Deploying Based on Document Characteristics

Reader and Author fields are special types of fields that can exist in a document and can control the access available to that document. These have been already extensively covered in this book, but let's quickly review them since the exam has a number of questions in this area. The rules you need to remember are

- Regardless of the access granted by a database ACL, if a Readers field exists in a document and a user or server is not listed in this Readers field, then it cannot be accessed. This has particular implications during replication, since if a server is not listed in the Readers field, it cannot read the document and thus cannot replicate it to any other servers.

- Author fields work with users who have Author access in the database ACL. If the user or server is listed in the Authors field, it has access to edit that document. This provides more granularity than simply providing Editor ACL access for all documents in the database.

- The Authors field has no meaning for users with Editor access or above in the database ACL.

- If a user is listed in the Authors field but not Readers field, it assumed that he is able to read the document and thus have Reader access by default.

- Most importantly, the Authors fields and Readers fields do not give people any more access than they already have in the database ACL, but they *can* modify and remove the access granted by the ACL.

Figure 14-7 shows the display of the values of a Readers field in a document. This is from the Properties InfoBox for the document, Fields tab.

Readers and Authors fields are also discussed again in detail in Chapter 18.

When deploying an application, the document size can help greatly in capacity planning. This size in bytes is shown on the first tab of the Document properties InfoBox.

Figure 14-7
Viewing the Readers
Field properties of a
document

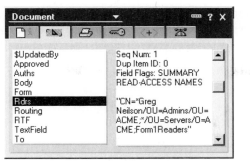

Once you know this size and the expected number of documents that will held in the database, you can start to get an estimate of the likely database size when deployed.

Typically, there is little you can do to reduce the size of documents since this is usually a function of the data contained within the document. However, one instance where you can save space is to not save the form design with each document. You should save the form with a documents in workflow applications that use multiple databases. In this case, the form design is not available, since it resides in a different database. Storing the design with the documents allows the documents to be displayed correctly—using the correct form (see Figure 14-8). However, this may be a waste of space if all documents are left in the same database in which they were created. This is a database property that can be viewed in Domino Designer by selecting the form and checking its Form properties InfoBox.

Figure 14-8
Database Property,
Store Form in a
document

Data within a document is stored as *items* in the Domino database. When the document is displayed, it is displayed in a form, and the fields in the form display the values of the items in the document, if the names of the item and the fields on the form are identical. There are a large range of possible types of items that can be stored in the database, which include all of the different field types (text, rich text, numbers, authors, readers, names, date/time, formula, and so on) as well as attachments, icons, notes, links, and HTML. In the internal database structure, each item record has an identifier that determines the item type, followed by the data contained in the item. When a document is created, it can contain default values in these items as determined by the values in the fields of the form used to create it.

Rich text fields within the Domino database are used to contain text, tables, bitmaps, OLE links, and document/view/database links. The Notes API documentation discusses rich text fields in detail and lists the main advantages of rich text fields versus regular fields as being

- Paragraphs in rich text can have mixed attributes
- Text can have mixed attributes (fonts, styles, and so on)
- A rich text field can hold megabytes of data

The rich text field is comprised of a number of CD records (which, the documentation suggests, stands for either Compound Document or Composite Data). In discussion of mail transfer from Domino to the Internet, you may have seen references to issues of the conversion of mail from the proprietary Notes CD format to MIME format; this is where the mention of CD comes from.

Deploying Based on Database Views

The hierarchies in which documents are displayed within views is very much dependant on the data values in these documents. The two main types of views are response views and categorized views. In the response views, each of the documents is displayed based on the form type it was created with. Each form or document has a type property, which can be either a document, response document, or a response to response document. Thus, in a response view the three levels displayed represent the types of forms used to create the documents within it.

Similarly, in a categorized view, shown in Figure 14-9, the column property of the first column in the view has a type of Categorized, rather than the usual Standard value. This categorized view allows the user to collapse and expand the list of documents within a category.

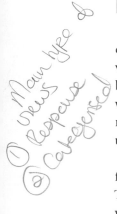

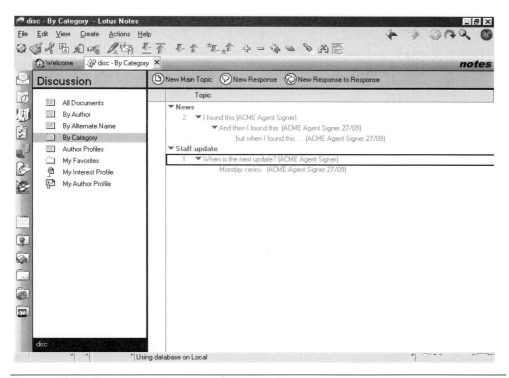

Figure 14-9 Sample view hierarchy, Category view

A view is a special type of note within the database that contains a hierarchy for parent and child documents for the response type of view. Also, categorized views contain the list of documents that share the same category.

Deploying Based on Archiving

Document archiving can be a useful tool to remove old and inactive documents from a database, and copy them to an archive database. In this way, these documents don't waste space within the primary application database, and at the same time the database views are smaller and require less maintenance by server tasks. Archiving can be done manually at a Notes client, or it can be configured to run automatically on a Domino server as the COMPACT task is run. Archiving is configured by selecting the Archive Settings on the Database Basics tab of the Database properties InfoBox as shown in Figure 14-10.

Figure 14-10
Archive Settings on
the Database
properties InfoBox

The Archive Settings Basics tab is shown in Figure 14-11. Here we set the criteria used to archive documents, which can be any length of time since the document was last accessed, the time since the document was last updated, or if the document is marked as expired. We can also specify the location of the archive database that the archived documents will be moved to.

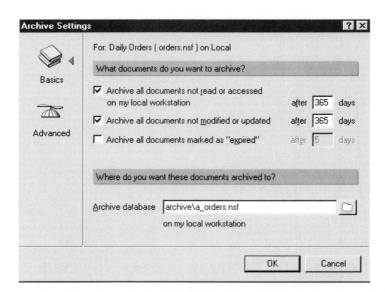

Figure 14-11 Archive Settings, Basics

The Archive Settings, Advanced tab is shown in Figure 14-12. Here we can specify whether the archival process will be done manually or automatically. Typically, a manual archive will be appropriate for databases that reside on Notes client machines, and an automatic archive will be appropriate for databases that reside on Domino servers. We can also elect to log all archival activity to a database, and lastly there are options to not delete documents that have response documents, and also to just delete documents instead of archiving them. Remember that when the archival process is done automatically, this is done when the COMPACT task on the Domino server is run against the database.

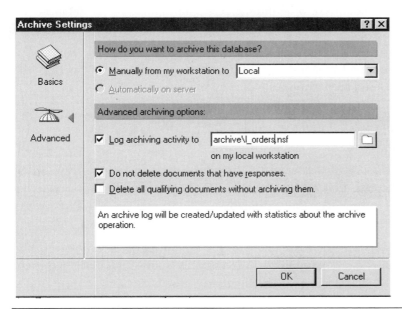

Figure 14-12   Archive Settings, Advanced

Summary

- The basic building block of the NSF database structure is the note. Domino databases are designed to handle unstructured data.

- R5 brings an updated database format from R4. This is also known as the ODS version. R5 is ODS version 41 and R4 was ODS version 30.

- The ODS version of a database can be viewed on the Info tab of the Database Properties InfoBox when using an R5 client.

- R4 clients cannot read R5 databases when they are accessed locally (using the local file system), but they can be accessed successfully when accessing a R5 Domino server across a network.

- The COMPACT utility in R5 automatically converts databases from R4 to R5 format. COMPACT −R can convert databases from R5 back to R4 format.

- Use the .NS4 file extension on an R5 Domino server to keep the database in R4 format.

- The NoteID and UNID are both identification numbers that can be used to identify notes within a database. The NoteID is unique within a given database replica, but the UNID is guaranteed to be unique across all replicas of the database. The NoteID is often used in programs since it is a much smaller number and easier to use.

- The Find Note tool within Domino Administrator can search a database by either NoteID or UNID and then display the document fields.

- If a Readers field exists in a document, then only those users and servers listed within it are able to read the document. This removes some access provided by entries in the database ACL.

- If an Authors field exists in a document, then those users and servers listed within it have access to edit that document. This is only relevant for those users and servers that have author access in the database ACL. Those whose access levels are higher (Editor, Designer, Manager) have their access levels unaffected.

- Document archiving can be a useful technique to remove old documents from a database. This can be run manually or automatically. When it is configured to run automatically, the COMPACT task actually does the archival work.

- The actual data values in a document are called items. These are displayed in forms when a field in the form has the same name as an item in the document selected for display.

Review Questions

1. Harry is mentoring a junior administrator about database deployment and has been asked the difference between a NoteID and UNID. Which answer best describes the difference between the two?

   A. A NoteID is guaranteed to be unique across all replicas of a database.

   B. A UNID is guaranteed to be unique across all replicas of a database.

   C. Both a NoteID and a UNID are guaranteed to be unique across all replicas of a database.

   D. Neither a NoteID nor a UNID are guaranteed to be unique across all replicas of a database.

2. Jacinta is investigating a document within a database that appears to be corrupted. She checks the document properties and sees the details NT00003B42. What does this number most likely refer to?

   A. Her serial number

   B. The document UNID

   C. The document NoteID

   D. The replica ID

3. Kevin is analyzing a Domino database corruption problem using the Find Note tool within Domino Administrator to find the source of the problem. Select all of the search options available within the Find Notes tool.

   A. NoteID

   B. Replica ID

   C. DBIID

   D. UNID

4. Lisa is deploying a Domino application within a mixed R4/R5 environment. Which of the following statements are true?

   A. All databases on the R5 Domino server should be in R4 format so that the R4 clients are able to access them.

   B. Replication between two replicas that are in R4 and R5 format automatically changes the R4 format database into R5 format.

   C. Running UPDALL on a R5 Domino server with R4 format databases automatically changes the format of these databases into R5 format.

   D. Running COMPACT –R against a database in R5 format converts it to R4 format.

5. Michael is deploying an application within a mixed R4/R5 environment. He gives the database an .NS4 extension. Why does he do this?

   A. To make the database not be visible within the Open Database dialog

   B. To make the database available as a template

   C. To ensure that the database stays in R4 format even after the COMPACT process runs against it

   D. To make the database accessible to R4 clients

6. Nicole is looking at the internals of a database that is to be deployed. When looking at NSF internals, what exactly is a *note*?

   A. An e-mail message

   B. A record within the database

   C. An electronic version of a post-it note

   D. A comment in the database made by a developer

7. Orville is deploying an application that has experienced problems with replication across servers. Only some of the documents in the Domino database are being replicated to other servers in the network. What could be the likely cause of this problem?

   A. The servers do not have ACL access to replicate changes in this database.

   B. There is no Connection document that schedules replication between the two servers.

   C. The documents have a Readers field and the server names are not listed within this field.

   D. The servers are located in different Domino Named Networks (DNN).

8. Patricia is listed as having Author access in a database ACL. In one of the documents in the database, she is listed in an Authors field but not in a Readers field. What level of access does she effectively have to this document?

   A. No access

   B. Read access

   C. Update access

   D. Not able to determine from the information given

9. Quentin has been asked to investigate an issue reported by a Domino application user. Apparently, some old documents within the database have disappeared and you have been asked to investigate the situation. What is the likely cause of this?
   A. Database Purge interval settings
   B. Archival settings
   C. Replication settings
   D. Database size quota settings

Review Answers

1. **B is correct.** The NoteID is unique within a given database but may not be unique to all replicas.

2. **C is the correct.** Recall that the beginning NT text stands for NoTeid.

3. **A and D are correct.** You can search on NoteID or UNID with the Find Note tool.

4. **D is correct.** R4 clients can access databases from a Domino server in R5 format, replication does not change the database format, and COMPACT is used to convert R4 format databases into R5.

5. **C is correct.** In order to make the database invisible to the Open Database dialog, there is a database property that needs to be set, and the same is the case that turns the database into a template. No special action is needed to allow R4 clients access R5 format databases from an R5 server.

6. **B is correct.** A note is a record within the database; it is the basic building block.

7. **C is correct.** A common problem with Readers fields is that if the servers are not listed within the Readers field, then they cannot read or replicate those documents.

8. **C is correct.** An entry in the Authors field gives the user with Author access update access to the document. One feature of the Authors field is that even if a Readers field exists and the user's name is not it, if the user's name is in the Authors field, then Domino assumes that they have access to read the document.

9. **B is correct.** It would appear that documents are being archived to another database.

Deploying Applications Based on Design Elements

You should be able to answer questions based on the following objectives after reading this chapter:

- Deploying applications based on design elements: actions versus shared actions
- Deploying applications based on design elements: fields
- Deploying applications based on design elements: forms, subforms, actions
- Deploying applications based on design elements: graphics
- Deploying applications based on design elements: OLE
- Deploying applications based on design elements: sections
- Deploying applications based on design elements: shared versus non-shared
- Deploying applications based on how attachments are handled
- Deploy applications based on why elements are in the NSF

In this chapter, we will look at some of the design elements within Domino application development, and look at ways that the code written by a developer can be easily reused within Domino Designer. Code reuse is a great boost for programmer productivity, but it does mean that the system administrators who are deploying the applications need to be aware of how Domino facilitates code sharing when solving problems that involve them.

Actions Versus Shared Actions

Actions are developer-provided shortcuts for an application that perform a task when a button is pressed. Figure 15-1 shows two actions *Print Me* and *Save Me*. Actions can also be configured to add themselves to the Action menu on the client. Actions can be added as part of a form or a view and can be built using simple actions, formula language, JavaScript, or LotusScript.

Shared actions are actions that can be used in multiple forms and views within the same database. We can see the available shared actions within a database by opening it in Domino Designer, selecting Resources, then Other, and then Shared Actions, as seen in Figure 15-2.

Then, when we wish to insert a shared action into a form or view, we open the form or view and select from the menus Create . . . Insert Shared Action. This launches a dialog box that allows us to select the shared action to use.

When viewing the action pane for a form (the list of actions is in the top right corner in Domino Designer), there is a visual cue as to which actions are defined within that form view, and which are shared actions. Figure 15-4 shows this. In this case, the details of the action, shown at the bottom right corner, are not editable.

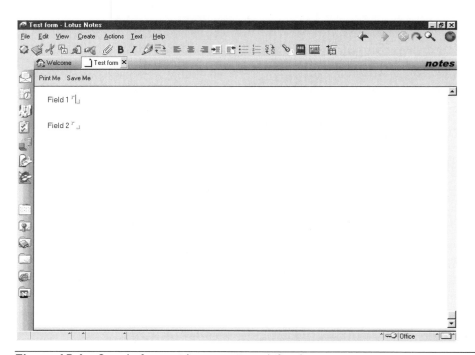

Figure 15-1 Sample form with two actions defined

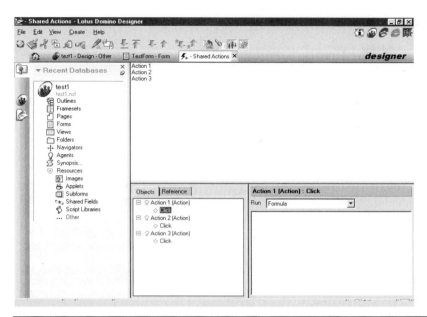

Figure 15-2   Viewing shared actions within a database

Figure 15-3
Selecting shared
actions to use
within a database

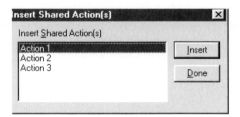

Fields and Shared Fields

A large number of available field types can be used within Domino applications. Many of these are straightforward, but others will require a little explanation. Here is a list:

- Text
- Date/time
- Number

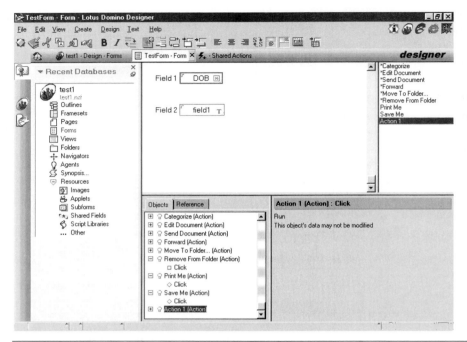

Figure 15-4   Viewing a shared action within a form

- **Dialog**   Users can select from a list of values. The list is displayed in a separate dialog box, which is launched when the user clicks on the small arrow that sits next to the field.

- **Checkbox**   Displays a list of values, and users can check all of the options they wish to select.

- **Radio button**   Provides a list of values, and users can select one.

- **Listbox**   Displays a list of values one at a time. Users can scroll through the list and select the choice they want.

- **Combobox**   Contains a list of choices in a drop-down listbox, and the user is able to select from the list.

- **Rich text**   Users can enter formatted text and attach files into this field.

- **Authors**   Used to hold the list of users and servers that have author access to this document. Refer to the discussion in Chapter 18 that describes author access.

- **Names**   Used to hold user names. Also provides an option to provide lookup of names from the Domino Directory.

- **Readers**   Used to hold the list of users and servers that have reader access to this document. Refer to the discussion in Chapter 18 that describes reader access

- **Password**   Doesn't display what the user is actually typing into the field, it only displays the '*' character (asterisk) instead.

- **Formula**   A new special type of field introduced in R5 for the processing of database subscriptions for the R5 Notes client.

Figure 15-5 shows the main types of field in action.

Now that we understand the main types of field available, we need to look at shared fields. These allow the programmer to define a field once within a database, and then use on multiple forms within the database without having to re-code the functionality in that field each time.

There are two ways to create a shared field. First, within Domino Designer, the programmer expands the Resources option in the Design pane (on the left-hand side) and then selects the Shared Fields option. This displays all of the shared fields that are currently defined within the database. By clicking on the New Shared field action button, you can create a shared field.

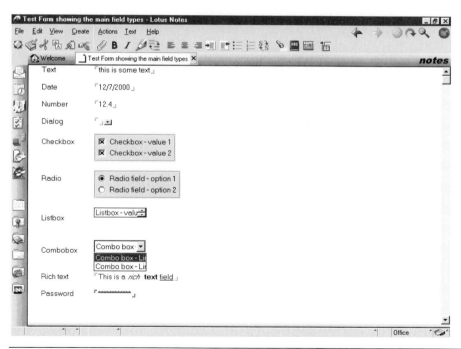

Figure 15-5   Sample form showing the main field types

The other way to create a shared field is by selecting an existing field within a form. Then from the menus, select Design, Share this field. This is shown in Figure 15-6. In this example, the selected field (called RichTextField) shows it is selected by displaying the name of the field with an underline.

Then, when a shared field is to be included in a form, the designer selects the menu option Create, Insert Shared Field, and selects from the available shared fields already shared within the database.

From Figure 15-7, we can see that within Domino Designer, we get a visual cue that a field is a shared field in the form because it has a darker border. The DOB shared field has a darker border around it compared to the regular fields in the form such as the inputtext field. This knowledge will be useful later when solving problems with that form.

One problem that you might come across is that the shared field definition may be missing from the database. This could be because the form was copied into another database but the shared field wasn't, or because the shared field has deleted or renamed. Either way, when you attempt to open a form that uses a shared field, you will receive the message *Cannot locate field definition for Field: <fieldname>*.

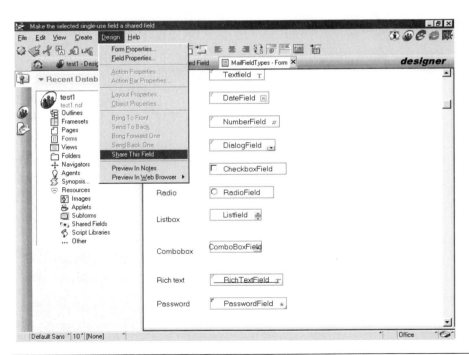

Figure 15-6   Sharing an existing field

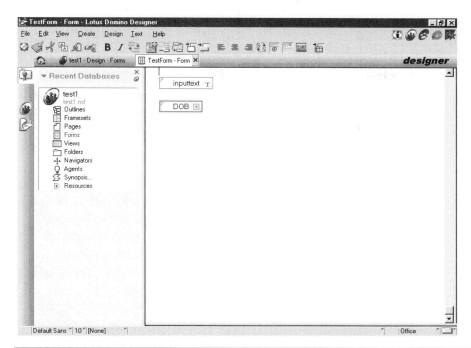

Figure 15-7   Form design showing a shared field

Forms Versus Subforms

By now, you are pretty familiar with forms, which we use within Notes to collect and display information to the user. We've seen how shared fields allow us to share field definitions within a database, and now we come to subforms. Subforms are groups of fields that we can share in forms within the same database. For example, if we have a group of fields such as name, address, zip code, and phone number that are used together in a number of forms, we can put these in a subform. We can then include this subform in the forms to use these shared definitions. As we shall soon see, one powerful use of subforms is that programmers can use a formula in the application to dynamically include a subform.

We can view the subforms already defined within a database, and also create more subforms, by viewing the database within Domino Designer, and selecting Resources and then Subforms from the list. This lists the defined subforms, as we see in Figure 15-8. Also, the way to create a subform is to select the New Subform action button on this screen.

The subform works very similarly to a regular form. When designing it, you add the necessary fields (which, of course, can include shared fields) and save it. Then, you can

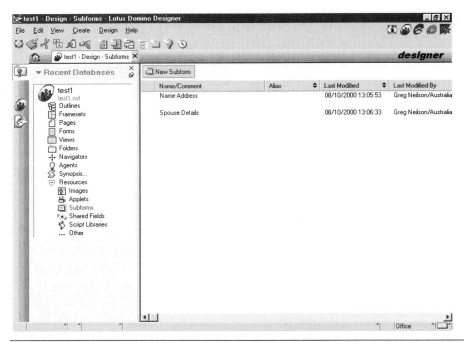

Figure 15-8   Subforms defined within a database

include this subform in another form, by selecting from the menus Create . . . Insert Subforms, which brings us a list of previously defined subforms in this database, as we see in Figure 15-9. Alternatively, we can select the form to insert here by using a formula that evaluates to the name of the subform to include.

The following field (called field1) is also in subform, but this is not highlighted visually until we click on it, as is shown in Figure 15-10.

One other thing we can see in Figure 15-14 is that we can optionally edit the included subform simply by double-clicking on it. When we use subforms in our forms, this is transparent to the user; they just encounter a form containing the fields within it.

One problem that may arise is that a subform may be missing from a database. It may have been inadvertantly deleted or may not have been copied when a form was copied. One important consequence of this is the error message that Notes displays when it attempts to load a subform that is not present within the current database. Notes will issue the error message *Subform: <subformname>* not loaded. To correct the problem, re-create or copy the subform.

Figure 15-9
Subforms defined
within a database

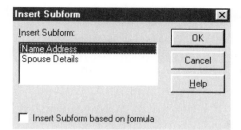

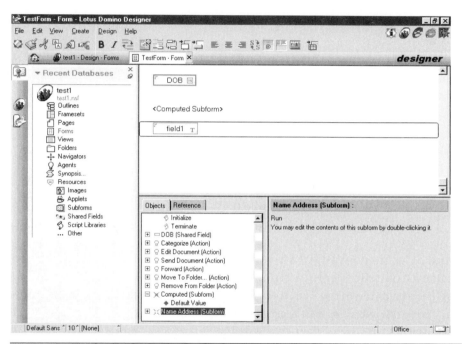

Figure 15-10   Selecting a field within a form that is part of a subform

Sections

Sections allow fields within a form to be grouped together and optionally collapsed or expanded. Figure 15-11 shows a couple of examples of Standard sections within a form. To create a standard section, you select the fields that will be part of the section; then from the menus, select Create . . . Section . . . Standard.

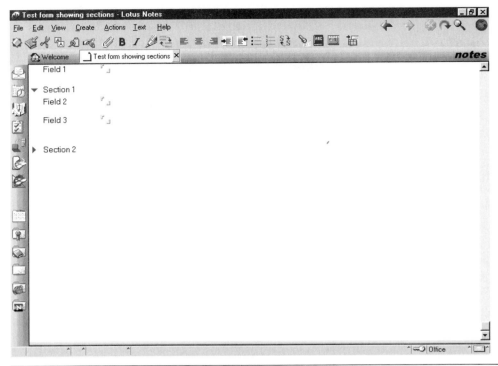

Figure 15-11   Example sections within a form

Controlled Access sections allow us to control who can edit the fields within that section. To create a Controlled Access section, you select the fields that will be part of the section and then from the menus select Create . . . Section . . . Controlled Access. Then, we need to determine who has edit access to this section. This is done by selecting the Section properties InfoBox and then choosing the Formula (middle) tab, as shown in Figure 15-12. This tab contains the formula used to determine who has edit access to this section of the form.

Attachments

One of the most powerful features within Notes/Domino is the capability to store file attachments within documents. The users of the database can then share these documents. Attachments can be stored within Rich Text Format (RTF) fields, and they are stored within the NSF file used for the database.

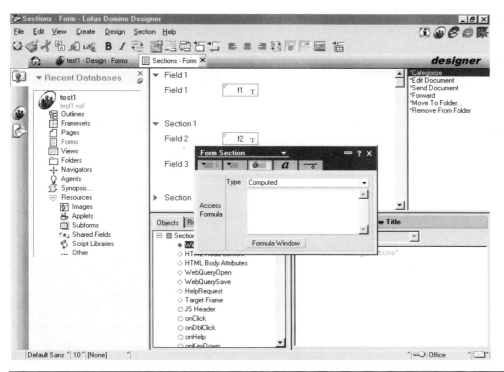

Figure 15-12   Section access properties

A special type of attachment that can be shared is an OLE link. OLE stands for Object Linking and Embedding and is a Microsoft technology that is used to create documents that use objects created by multiple programs. For example, an OLE document could consist of tables of figures created from a spreadsheet, surrounded by text, and created by a word processor. When you click on the OLE link, it activates the source object in edit mode, using the program actually used to create it, such as the word processor or spreadsheet program. So you might have some text within a Notes Rich Text Field that contains an OLE link back to the source document that it originated from. When you click on the link, the source document is launched as ready-to-edit by the program used to create it. Keep in mind that the only thing stored within the Notes document (and hence database) is the link itself, not the source document or the program used to create it. OLE technology only works on Windows platforms, so it will not work on Macintosh clients or (pre-R5) Unix clients.

Shared Graphic Images

We've covered shared database elements in this chapter, so it is probably no surprise that it is also possible to share graphic image files within a Domino database. These graphic images can be either in BMP, GIF, or JPEG formats. In a similar manner to what we have seen for the other shared database elements, we can view and create new shared images within Domino Designer when the opened database has the Resources tab opened and the Shared Images option is selected. Figure 15-13 shows an example of this.

To create a new image resource, click on the New Image Resource button. Domino Designer displays a standard Open File dialog to select the file to import into your database. Since graphics files tend to very large, this is a great way to reduce the space required for the Domino database. The graphic is only imported once and not every time it is used.

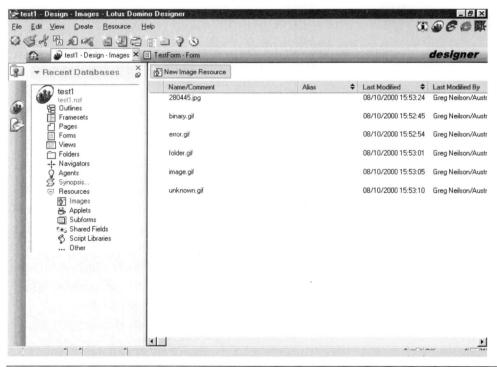

Figure 15-13   Shared images in a database

Then, to actually use the stored image, you select Create . . . Image Resource from the menus. This provides a dialog that allows you to select from the available images within the current database, as shown in Figure 15-14. To make this process as simple as possible, in this dialog you can actually see what the graphic is in the small display area in the right-hand side of the dialog.

Figure 15-14   Selecting a shared image resource to use

Summary

- The shared actions allow the same actions to be re-used in forms and views within the same database.

- Subforms are a collection of fields that can be included as a group in forms within the same database. We can also use a formula to determine at runtime which subform is displayed for the user.

- Shared Fields allow the same field definition to be used in forms in the same database.

- There are two types of sections. Standard sections allow groups of fields in a form to be collapsed and expanded as necessary. Controlled Access sections specify via a formula who can edit the fields within that section.

- File attachments are stored within rich text fields.

- When using OLE links within Notes, only the link is stored in the Notes document, not the entire original source document.

- Shared images of type BMP, GIF, and JPEG can be shared within a database.

Review Questions

1. Alison is deploying an application that uses shared actions. Which of the following statements about shared fields is correct?
   A. Shared actions can be used by forms and views in databases within the same server.
   B. Shared actions can be shared by forms and views in the same database.
   C. Shared actions can only be shared within the same form or view.
   D. Shared actions must be added to the Action menu of the Notes client.

2. Bob is deploying an application that uses shared fields. Which of the following statements about shared fields is correct?
   A. Shared fields can shared by forms in databases within the same server.
   B. Shared fields can be shared by forms in the same database.
   C. Shared fields can only be used within the same form.
   D. Only text fields can be shared fields.

3. Cindy is testing a new application for deployment. When opening a form, she receives the error message *Cannot locate field definition for Field: Address*. What is the likely cause of this problem?
   A. User error.
   B. The document is corrupted.
   C. The shared field definition is missing.
   D. The database is corrupted.

4. David is deploying an application that uses subforms. When opening a form, he receives the error message *Subform: Address not loaded*. What is the likely cause of this problem?
   A. User error.
   B. The document is corrupted.
   C. The subform definition is missing.
   D. The database is corrupted.

5. Elisa is troubleshooting an application that uses Controlled Access sections. Which statement best describes the function of a Controlled Access section?
   A. It determines who has read access to the fields within that section.
   B. It determines who has author access to the fields within that section.
   C. It determines who has editor access to the fields within that section.
   D. It determines who has manage access to the fields within that section.

6. Fred is coding an application that will use shared image resources. Which of the following graphic image types is not supported as a shared image resource?
   A. BMP
   B. TIFF
   C. JPEG
   D. GIF

7. Gillian is deploying a Domino application that frequently stores attachments within documents. Where are the attachments actually stored on the server?
   A. In a special database type on the server that supports attachments
   B. As separate distinct files on the server file system
   C. Within the application database NSF file in rich text fields
   D. Within the application database NSF file in an attachment field

Review Answers

1. **B is correct.**   Forms and views within the same database can use the shared action. The setting to add the action to the Actions menu is optional.

2. **B is correct.**   Forms within the same database can use shared fields.

3. **C is correct.**   The shared field definition is missing from the database.

4. **C is correct.** The subform definition is missing from the database.

5. **C is correct.** A Controlled Access section determines who has editor access to that section.

6. **B is correct.** Only BMP, GIF, and JPEGs are supported as shared image resources.

7. **C is correct.** Attachments are stored within the NSF file in a rich text field.

Deploying Applications Based on Coding

You should be able to answer questions based on the following objectives after reading this chapter:

- Deploying applications based on coding: C

- Deploying applications based on coding: Formula language

- Deploying applications based on coding: JavaScript

- Deploying applications based on coding: Java

- Deploying applications based on coding: LotusScript

Domino provides a wealth of alternatives for developers to code applications for Domino. Your job as a system administrator is to understand the various coding alternatives and what these mean when the application needs to be deployed.

This chapter explains the implications of deploying applications that use the differing options available for coding Domino applications. These options are introduced together with the important aspects of deploying applications that use them. If you would like to know more about these options, refer to the Chapter 40, which discusses these options for application developers. Of course, that level of knowledge is not examinable in the 522 exam, but it may provide useful background information about the differing coding alternatives.

Workstation ECLs (Execution Control Lists) are described in Chapter 18 and are relevant when implementing Formula language, Java, or JavaScript to a Notes client, since they can limit the actions that each of these can perform within Notes. Once you have read that chapter, make sure you understand their implication in deploying applications that use them.

Deploying Applications Written in C

Lotus provides a C language API (Application Programming Interface) that allows developers to write programs in the C programming language that can manipulate Notes and Domino resources. These completed programs can then run on the Domino server or Notes client. Typical uses for this are for server-based add-in tasks that can run on the Domino server or perhaps to delve deep into the internals of the Domino database structure. Programs that use the C API, of course, cannot run on a Web browser client.

The source code of the C program is kept in a text file. Before it can be run, it needs to be compiled, which converts the instructions within the program into a format the server operating system can execute. Therefore, the same program may be able to be coded to run on multiple platforms (say both Windows 2000 and Linux), but it must be compiled first by a C compiler on each of these of platforms before it can be run. This compiled C program is not part of a Domino database and must be distributed separately.

The documentation for the C API lists these as some possible purposes:

- Stand-alone applications
- Domino Server add-in tasks
- Notes client menu add-ins
- Notes client import and export libraries
- Database hook drivers
- Extension manager hook libraries
- Drivers for external (non-Notes) databases

A Notes C API program can work with Domino databases in the same way that the LotusScript and Java agents can. That is, they can create databases, create replicas, work with database ACLs, and scan every database on the server. Some of the things that can only be done with C API include working with performance statistics on the server, changing the server access lists, and reading and updating the free time information within the calendaring and scheduling database (BUSYTIME.NSF). Another reason why the C API may be used is if performance is a critical application issue.

The C API should be only used as a last resort when the task cannot be accomplished by other means. It requires much more coding than either Java or LotusScript agents that can perform the same task, and the finished product needs to be recompiled for each of the server and client platforms it is to run on.

Although it is not mentioned in the exam, be aware that there is also a Notes C++ API. This is an object-oriented version of the C API. The C++ language is an extension of the C programming language that provides capabilities for object-oriented programming. In this way, programmers can be more productive by achieving the same results with less program coding.

Deploying Applications Written in Formula Language

Formula language represents the oldest and simplest way to create or modify a custom application within the Notes/Domino environment. It comprises @Functions that can be used for input data validation and @Commands that can be used to manipulate the Notes graphical user interface. The formula language in Domino is closely related to the original macro language that was part of the Lotus 1-2-3 spreadsheet product.

There are often performance advantages in coding applications using the formula language, although it doesn't lend itself to complex programming requirements in the same way that LotusScript or Java does.

The formula language is most applicable when working with the current object that the user has open, which may be a view or a document, for example.

Applications that use formula language can run on the Notes client without any special configuration required, subject to the configuration of the Workstation ECL (refer to Chapter 18 for a description of the ECL). Given the large architectural differences between the Notes client and a browser client, it is probably not surprising that not all formula language components can run on a browser client. In fact, it is probably a little surprising that any of the formula language can be used with a browser client. Of course, the browser itself can't execute formula language, so as part of the Domino HTTP task, the formulas are executed on the server and the results evaluated and sent to the client. The @Commands are available to manipulate the Notes client menu functions and thus are not available for browser clients. The following is a list of @Functions that are not supported in Web applications:

- @Certificate
- @DbCommand (can only be used to move forward and backward within views)
- @DDEExecute, @DDEInitiate, @DDEPoke, @DDETerminate
- @DocMark, @DeleteDocument
- @DocChildren, @DocDescendants, @DocLevel, @DocNumber, @DocParentNumber, @DocSiblings (only available in column formulas)
- @IsCategory, @IsExpandable, @Responses

- @DialogBox, @PickList, @Prompt, @IsModalHelp
- @GetPortsList
- @Environment, @SetEnvironment (these can, however, be used to extract the values of CGI variables)
- @UserPrivileges
- @Platform

Deploying Applications Written in JavaScript

JavaScript is an interpreted scripting language that is imbedded in HTML and sent to a browser client. For example, if you check the HTML source you will see the JavaScript code within the <SCRIPT> and </SCRIPT> tags. The R5 Notes client now also understands JavaScript, but R4 clients do not have this ability. The initial purpose of JavaScript was for field validation of HTML form input at the client before it is submitted to the server. However, now there is a wide range of client-side functionality available using JavaScript. For example, it is now possible to create and manipulate new windows in the browser, work with cookies that store user information on the client machine, control the operation of multimedia elements, and also to interact with Java applets. JavaScript cannot run on the Domino server.

You need to be aware that there is a setting within the Notes client that optionally turns support for JavaScript on or off. If you select File. . . Preferences . . . User Preferences, on the Basics page under the Additional Options window is the option to Enable JavaScript, as shown in Figure 16-1. It is enabled by default.

Again, it is worth noting that the Workstation ECL can limit what operations JavaScript can perform on a Notes client. Refer to Chapter 18 for more details on this.

Recall that in order to serve browser clients, you need to have the HTTP task running on the Domino server.

Deploying Applications Written in Java

Java is an object-oriented programming language developed by Sun that is now very commonly used for application development, particularly within a networked environment. It is based on features of the C and C++ programming languages. One feature that makes it unique from regular programming languages is that the Java compiler does not produce an executable program directly. Instead, it creates an intermediate level of code known as bytecode. When the Java program is to be run, the Java Virtual Machine (JVM) then interprets and executes these bytecode instructions. In this way, Java can be "write once, run everywhere" since it is then platform-independent and can run on any operating system that has the JVM.

Java agents are similar to LotusScript agents in being able to access Domino "back-end" server objects via classes. Java has advantages in that there are far more programmers that know Java compared to those that know LotusScript. Other advantages of Java agents are that they can be multi-threaded and also that they can use the many standard language classes available that can greatly simplify programming effort required.

When deploying Java applets that will be run by the Notes client, you need to be aware that there is a setting that optionally turns support for Java on or off. If you select File . . . Preferences . . . User Preferences, you can choose to enable Java on the Basics page under the Additional Options window, as shown in Figure 16-1. It is enabled by default. Browser clients can also run Java applets. An "applet" is a special type of Java program that runs within a browser or Notes client. Java applets are specified within HTML using the <APPLET> tag. This specifies the Java applet to run and also its

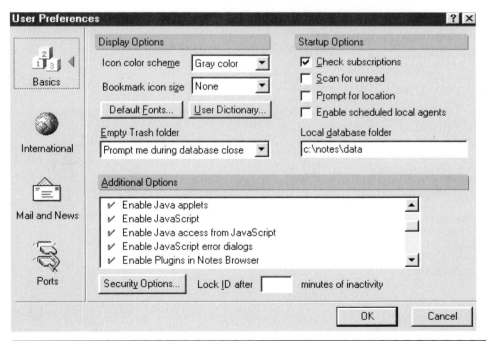

Figure 16-1   User Preferences: Enabling JavaScript

location, which can be on another server if required. The Domino server comes with a standard set of Java applets that are used to display views and to enable rich text editing in a browser. Applets are not part of a Domino database, and the files must be copied to the server in order to be deployed. Java applets typically have a .CLASS or .JAR file extension, and by default Domino expects to see these in the domino\html directory below the Domino data directory on the server.

Again, it is worth noting that the Workstation ECL can limit what operations Java can perform on a Notes client. Refer to Chapter 18 for more details on this.

When the Java agents are to be run on the Domino server, there are more configuration implications to consider. The Security tab of the Server document within the Domino Directory has a number of fields that may need to be configured, as we see in Figure 16-2. Note that the default entry, blank, for either of the Run restricted LotusScript/Java agents and Run unrestricted LotusScript/Java fields means that no one can run these types of agents. Values in these fields are cached within the server memory, so if specific entries that are added or deleted from these fields they will only take effect

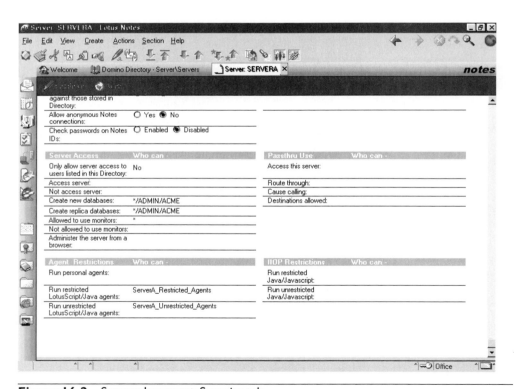

Figure 16-2　Server document: Security tab

the next time the server is started. One way around this is to create groups such as *<Servername> Unrestricted Agents* and *<Servername> Restricted Agents*, and add these groups to the appropriate field in the Server document. Users can then be added to these groups and their access to run these types of agents can take effect almost immediately.

You can see here that there are two types of server-based Java agents: restricted and unrestricted agents. This to be able to distinguish between agents that merely run on the server and work with Domino databases (restricted) against those that can change the server environment as well (unrestricted). Unrestricted agents are able to:

- Perform file input/output
- Set the system date and time
- Write to a server-based log file
- Read and update NOTES.INI environment variables
- Launch another application
- Call a C-language program routine
- Use encryption and signing
- Work with embedded objects

Unrestricted

As before, keep in mind that you need to have the HTTP task running on the Domino server in order to serve browser clients. There are special types of Java agents that can run on the browser and then directly communicate with the server in order to access Domino database objects. This requires the DIIOP task to be running on the server as well as HTTP, and it also requires the DIIOP protocol to be enabled and configured as we see in Figure 16-3. You may also see this technology referred to by the name CORBA (Common Object Request Broker Architecture), which allows distributed objects such as our browser client and Domino server to communicate.

Deploying Applications Written in LotusScript

LotusScript is a programming language used within Lotus products that is very similar to the Visual Basic language. It can be used when programming for a Notes client and also for agents that can be run on either the Notes client or the Domino server. It is not available on browser clients, although browsers can trigger LotusScript agents in Web applications that run on the Domino server.

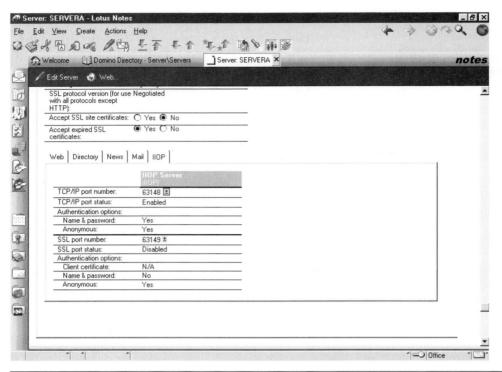

Figure 16-3 Server document: Internet Protocols, IIOP tab

The information about server-based LotusScript agents and server configuration is identical to that discussed earlier when discussing Java, so I will refer the reader to review that discussion. Of course, the DIIOP feature is only available for Java.

LotusScript agents can access both the "front-end" Domino classes (the current open Notes client session) and also "back-end" classes (any Domino database resource on the server), whereas Java agents can only access back-end classes. One other reason to choose LotusScript is that it enables code to be shared between LotusScript agents and LotusScript events.

So, in summary, when deploying server-based agents, the suggested process is to perform the following steps:

1. Create a group in the Domino Directory for each server that will run restricted agents and/or unrestricted agents. Typically, these might be called *<Servername> Restricted Agents* (see Figure 16-4).

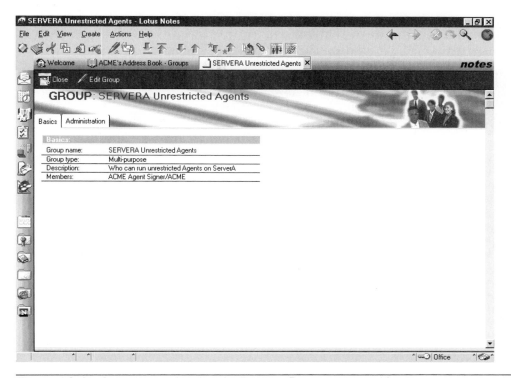

Figure 16-4   Group created within the Domino Directory to enable agent access

2. Add these groups to the *Run restricted agents* and *Run unrestricted agents* fields on the Security tab of the Server document for the server within the Domino Directory, as shown previously in Figure 16-2. The server will have to be restarted for these changes to take effect, since these values are cached in the server memory.

3. Create specific IDs that will be used to sign the database templates before they will be deployed. For example, one could be called *ACME Agent Signer/ACME*. You may need multiple IDs depending on your security and application requirements. As you have already learned, you create the IDs in Domino Administrator. There are two places that you can do this. In the People tab, select the People menu and choose Register . . . ; also, in the Configuration tab, select the Registration menu and choose the Person . . . Tab. Both will launch the Register Person dialog, as shown in Figure 16-5.

4. Add these created IDs to the groups created in step 1.

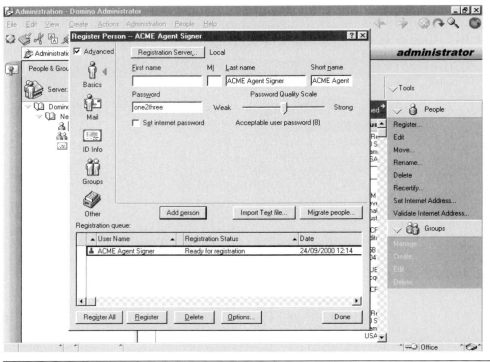

Figure 16-5 Creating the IDs in Domino Administrator for signing agents

5. Sign the database template with the appropriate ID created in step 3. This updates the design notes within the database with this ID. This is explained in detail in Chapter 14. First, you need to switch IDs to the ID that will sign that database, as shown in Figures 16-6 and 16-7 by selecting File . . . Tools . . . Switch ID. Select the ID file to open, and then enter the password.

6. To sign the database, in Domino Administrator by select the File tab. Then select the database(s) to be signed, and under the database tools is the option to the Sign the database, as we see in Figure 16-8. Database signing is covered in more detail in Chapter 14.

7. Deploy the application using this updated template. This is covered in detail in Chapter 21.

Figure 16-6 Switching IDs to sign in order to sign a database

Summary

- C API programs can be run on the Domino server or Notes client but not in a Web browser client. The application code is compiled into an executable for each type of destination platform (Windows NT, AIX, Linux, and so on) and is not part of a Domino database; it must be copied manually onto the destination server/client.

- Formula language code can be run on the Domino server or Notes client. For Web clients, there is some support for @Function formula processing by the Domino server HTTP task that evaluates formulas and includes the results in the created HTML sent to the client. @Commands are not supported at all by Web clients.

- JavaScript is supported by both Web and Notes clients. It cannot run on the Domino server.

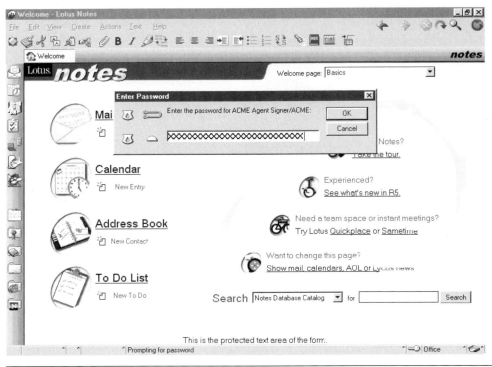

Figure 16-7   Switching IDs to sign in order to sign a database

- Java agents are supported by Notes clients and Domino servers. Java applets are supported by Web clients and Notes clients.

- LotusScript is supported by Notes clients and Domino servers. It is not supported by Web clients.

- Workstation ECLs are used on the Notes client to define what Java, JavaScript, and formula language code is able to change on the client. It is copied from the Domino Directory when the workstation is configured. The access levels in the ECLs are defined against the ID that is used to sign the database. For this reason, typically most companies will have a dedicated ID used to sign all custom Notes applications before deployment. (ECLs are described in detail in Chapter 18 but are mentioned here as a prompt when you are reviewing this material when preparing for the exam, since this is a closely-related topic for application deployment.)

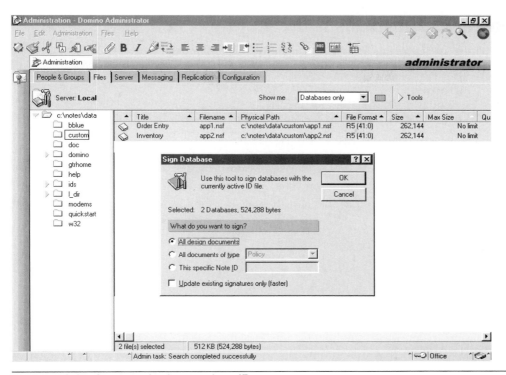

Figure 16-8   Signing a database with an ID

- For Java and LotusScript agents that will run on a Domino server, you need to ensure that the name of the ID used to sign the deployed agent has access to run restricted or unrestricted agents on the Security tab of the Server document in the Domino Directory. The default value for these fields (blank) means that no one can run these types of agents on the server. Unrestricted agents are able to modify the server environment, whereas restricted agents are only able to work with Domino databases.

- For any Web client to be supported, the HTTP task must be running and configured on the Domino server. The DIIOP Domino server task is also required to be configured and running to deploy Java applets that may directly communicate from the browser client to the backend Domino server to access Domino databases.

Review Questions

1. Abe is deploying a Domino database that includes a server-based Java agent. Which of the following activities would make this agent an unrestricted agent?
   A. Updating documents within the database
   B. Updating the database ACL
   C. Updating the system time
   D. Deleting documents within the database

2. Becky has been assigned a new application in her company. It was originally designed for Notes clients, and she is now to deploy it for Web clients. Which of the following application features may not operate as expected for the Web clients?
   A. Formula language @Commands
   B. JavaScript
   C. Java applets
   D. HTML

3. Chris has deployed a new application, which requires a server-based LotusScript agent to run on a schedule. He has just updated the Run restricted LotusScript/ Java agents field with his name, but the agent will not run. What might be the next thing he needs to do in order to have the application run?
   A. Update the run unrestricted LotusScript/Java agents field with his name.
   B. Do nothing. It might work later if he leaves it for another 15 minutes before trying again.
   C. Stop and restart the Domino server.
   D. Query the developer about why their application doesn't work.

4. Diana is deploying a Web application that will have browser clients. The clients are not able to access the application, and she suspects that the appropriate Domino server task may not be running. Which server task should Diana be looking for?
   A. Router
   B. HTTP
   C. SMTP
   D. NNTP

5. Eamon is assisting in the design of a Domino-based application that will have both Notes and browser clients. Which of the following Domino application development options are available for developers to use in the client?
   A. JavaScript
   B. Java applets
   C. None of the above
   D. All of the above

6. Francis is considering how to deploy a custom-developed application in her organization. It is currently designed for using Notes client only and includes a Notes C API program that runs on the Notes client. She has been asked by her manager to consider the possibility of rolling the application out to Web browser users. What best describes her response to her manager?
   A. Rollout the application to browser users as is. No further effort required.
   B. The Web browser can't work with Notes C API programs and those components will need to be rewritten for browser users.
   C. I don't know.
   D. I'll just try it and get back to you shortly.

7. George is part of a deployment team to implement a new Domino application that is intended for both Web browser and Notes clients. Which of the following Domino programming options may be used in this application?
   A. JavaScript
   B. Java applets
   C. HTML
   D. C API
   E. LotusScript

Review Answers

1. **C is correct.** Activities that update the server environment such as system time require access an unrestricted agent.

2. **A is correct.** @Commands configure the Notes client GUI and thus do not work within a browser.

3. **C** is correct. These fields from the Server document are cached within the server memory, so the server needs to be stopped and restarted for the updates to take effect.

4. **B** is correct. The HTTP server task is required to serve browser clients from Domino.

5. **D** is correct. Browsers have been able to use JavaScript and Java applets for quite some time now, and with R5 these can also be used in the Notes client.

6. **B** is correct. Programs that use the Notes C API must run on the Notes client or the Domino server; Web browsers can't use these.

7. **A**, **B**, and **C** are correct. LotusScript and the C API are only supported by the Notes client. HTML was a trick to remind you that both Notes and Web clients support it, and that the JavaScript and Java applets will be embedded within HTML code.

Deploying Based on Replication and Routing

CHAPTER 17

You should be able to answer questions based on the following objectives after reading this chapter:

- Deploying applications based on how to receive routed documents
- Deploying applications based on replication fundamentals
- Deploying applications based on routing fundamentals
- Deploying applications based on hops and document distribution
- Deploying applications based on how to send routed documents
- Deploying applications based on impact of replication on ACLs
- Deploying applications based on impact of routing on different client types
- Deploying applications based on impact of routing on remote users
- Deploying applications based on impact of routing on the database
- Deploying applications based on server's involvement in replication

When you deploy Domino applications, replication and routing should be part of your deployment plan. As you decide which servers to deploy your applications on, you will need to create and manage replicas, ensure that the replication schedule will be sufficient to keep the data updates, and predict how security and ACLs will affect the replication. You also need to configure and understand replication settings, if not all servers should receive all the data in the application. You should be able to predict what will replicate in a given scenario as well as troubleshoot replication problems. In addition, if you have configured clustering, you have some additional cluster replication deployment issues, such as scheduling standard replication in the cluster.

571

Many Domino applications (especially workflow applications) use mail routing as part of the application logic. If mail routing is part of the applications you're deploying, you need to ensure that the proper documents exist in the Domino Directory to ensure proper routing, such as Connection documents, Mail-in Database documents, and Person documents. You also need to know the routing topology of the server to ensure that messages will route appropriately.

Finally, you should take into consideration a few additional issues for replication and routing with end user workstations, especially with remote users.

In many cases, the material covered in this chapter has been covered in some way in other chapters in this book. The topics of replication and routing have been covered in depth in Chapters 4, 5, 10, and 11. Configuring for remote or mobile use was covered in Chapter 9. In some cases, we repeat material that is necessary for this exam, but if you are unfamiliar with any of the processes or documents, you may want to refer back to these chapters. Bear in mind that the goal of this chapter is to take into consideration replication and routing in terms of deploying your Domino applications.

Replication Deployment Issues

One of the first elements of deploying applications is creating replicas or copies of the applications on the appropriate servers. Then you have to ensure that you plan or confirm the replication topology for those applications, including creating Connection documents for the replication and reviewing or configuring replication settings and other replication factors, including security.

As you roll out the applications to various servers, one of your first tasks will be to create replicas. You shouldn't just create replicas on every server in your organization, as this can increase demand on the server and network resources. Keep in mind that each additional replica creates additional maintenance needs. You should only create a new replica of a database for the following purposes:

- Create a new replica of a database to improve performance of a heavily used database. You may combine this with creating and using a cluster.

- Create a new replica of a database to distribute the traffic in your network. Applications that are used frequently should be available on the same LAN segment as the majority of their users. You may also want to make sure a replica is available for users in remote locations.

- Create a new replica of a database to keep a test version of a database separate from a production version. You may want to implement a replication formula or disable replication to ensure that changes don't replicate to the production version until they have been tested. You might also choose to create a copy in this case, instead of a replica. Keep in mind that the copy will have a different replica ID. If the developer has hard-coded the replica ID in the design of the database, it must be modified if you make a copy instead of a replica. In addition, the copy version of the database cannot replicate with the replicas.

- Create a new replica of a database to provide better availability, such as in case a server becomes unavailable or goes down. You may want to combine this with creating and using a cluster.

- Create a new replica of a database to provide a replica that only contains a subset of data. You might use this technique for a workgroup that only needs a limited amount of the data.

- You will need to create replicas for the Domino environment administration databases, such as the Domino Directory (NAMES.NSF), the Administration Requests database (ADMIN4.NSF), and others.

- You may choose to create a replica to serve as a backup database. Note that this should never be your only backup of a database; there should always be a non-replicating backup of a database from which to restore in case of corruption. Corrupted data may replicate between databases. If this happens, a replica database will not be a clean backup to allow you to restore your data.

Create Replicas

After you plan which servers should have replicas, you need to create the replicas on the servers. You can create the replicas manually or use the Administration Process (AdminP). You will create the replicas manually if you do not have access to the Domino Administrator or if you want to implement any replication settings when you create the new replica. If you use AdminP, however, you can create multiple replicas simultaneously. Before you start the process of creating replicas, ensure that you have the necessary access to create them.

To create replicas on a server, you need to be listed in the Server document. On the Security tab, make sure administrators who will be creating replicas are listed in the Create Replica Databases field. The default for this field (blank) means that no one can create replicas on the server. Note that you should control the number of administrators and users to whom you give this right to control the number of replicas that get placed on the server. You will also need at least Reader access in the ACL of the source database to create a replica of the database.

You also need to consider the access for the servers that are the source and destination of the replicas. The source server (the server that the replica currently exists on) needs to be in the Create Replica Databases field of the destination server. The destination server should have at least Reader access in the ACL of the source database. If you have user or server names rather than group names in the Server document, you will have to restart the server if you make any changes.

If you plan to use the Administration Process to create the database, you should make sure that AdminP is configured correctly and running on both the source and destination servers.

To create a replica using AdminP, open the Domino Administrator to the Files tab. Select the database(s) from the file list. Drag the file(s) to the destination server on the server list. Domino displays the Select Destination folder dialog box, shown in Figure 17-1. You can choose to create a new replica or to move the database. You can also select the destination folder. If you want to organize your databases in subfolders, create these before you start creating the replica via AdminP.

If you want to create a new folder to organize your critical Domino applications, expand the Folder tools on the Files tab of the Domino Administrator. Select the folder under which you want to create the new folder. Click the New tool. In the Create New Folder dialog box, shown in Figure 17-2, type the name you want to give the new folder. You can only use this tool to create new folders under the lotus\domino\data directory or its subdirectories.

Figure 17-1
Select Destination
Folder dialog box.

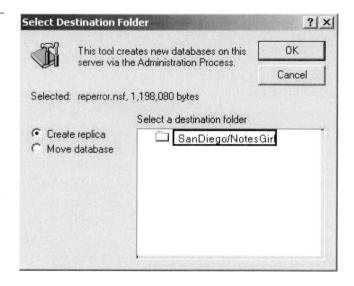

Figure 17-2
Create a new folder.

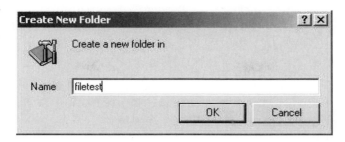

You can also create new replicas from the Files tab of the Domino Administrator by selecting the file or files and right-clicking. Select New . . . Replica(s) from the short-cut menu. In the Create Replica dialog box, shown in Figure 17-3, select the server or servers on which you want to create the new replicas. After you select the server(s), the File Names button becomes available. You can click this button to change the destination file name and path.

If you want to create the replica manually, open or select the database. You can do this from the Files tab in the Domino Administrator, from a bookmark, or by selecting File . . . Database . . . Open from the menus. While in the database, choose File . . . Replication . . . New Replica. In the New Replica dialog box, shown in Figure 17-4, you can select the server to create the new replica on.

You cannot change the database title, but you can change the file name and location, such as within a designated folder. The folder must already exist on the server. You can also edit the encryption settings or replication settings. If you click the Encryption button, Notes displays the Encryption for dialog box. You choose to locally encrypt the database using strong, medium, or simple encryption. This option is recommended for laptop users. You can also change replication settings by selecting the Replication Settings dialog box, shown in Figure 17-5.

Table 17-1 describes the options you can configure in the Replication Settings dialog box.

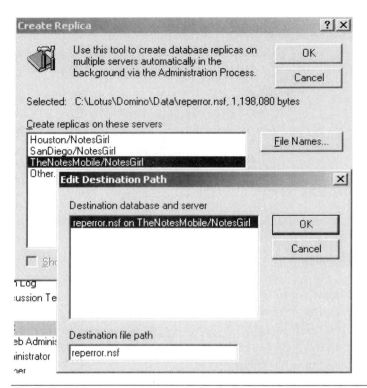

Figure 17-3   Create Replica.

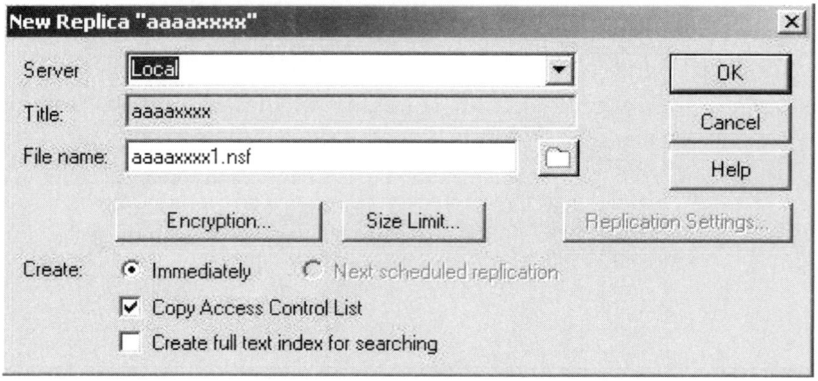

Figure 17-4   New Replica dialog box

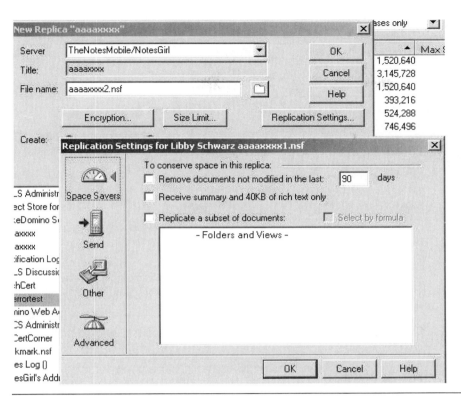

Figure 17-5   Replication Settings

Table 17-1   Replication Settings

Tab/Panel	Setting	Note
Space Savers	Remove documents not modified in the last x days.	The default in this field is 90 days. This setting determines when Domino purges deletion stubs and/or unmodified documents.
	Receive summary and 40KB of rich text only.	When you enable this field, you limit the size of the documents that this replica receives.
	Replicate a subset of documents.	When you enable this field, you can select by view, folder, or formula which documents this replica should receive.

continued

Table 17-1   Replication Settings *(continued)*

Tab/Panel	Setting	Note
Send	Do not send deletions made in this replica to other replicas.	This field indicates whether this replica can send deletions to other replicas.
	Do not send changes in database title and catalog info to other replicas.	This field indicates whether this replica can send changes to the database title or the Database Catalog categories to other replicas.
	Do not send changes in local security property to other replicas.	This field indicates whether this replica can send changes to the Encryption property to other replicas.
Other	Temporarily disable replication.	This field indicates whether this replica can replicate.
	Scheduled replication priority.	Use this field with Connection documents while scheduling replication. You can create replication connections based on high-, medium-, or low-priority databases.
	Only replicate incoming documents saved or modified after.	Use this field as the cutoff date so that this replica only receives documents saved and modified after this date.
	CD-ROM publishing date.	Use this field to specify the CD-ROM publishing date for this database. When you distribute a database via CD-ROM and then replicate with the server, setting this date will prevent the first replication from scanning the entire database for replication.
Advanced	Replicate options.	On the Advanced tab, you can decide what non-document elements this replica receives, such as forms, views, agents, replication formula, ACL, deletions, and fields. Usually, you will want this replica to receive all of the data from the hub, but in some cases, you may decide that not all agents or design elements should be available in a particular replica of the database. If you select the Fields checkbox, you can select the specific fields to replicate. This can be used to create a minimal Domino Directory replica, although in R5 it is better to do this by creating a Directory Catalog. You can also choose to receive a subset of documents from specific servers, based on view, folder, or formula using this tab.

NOTE The replication setting *Delete documents not modified in the last x days* sets not only the date to delete unmodified documents, but also the date to remove deletion stubs, also known as the purge interval. When documents are deleted from a database, Notes creates a deletion stub. This is the marker that remains in the database to indicate to Domino to delete the document in other replicas of the database. The purge interval is 1/3 of the number in this field, so if you leave the default of 90 days, the purge interval is 30 days. You must replicate more often than the purge interval or users may see the documents they deleted reappear in the database. If the purge interval is 30 days, for example, you must replicate more often, such as every 10 days, to ensure that the appropriate databases will be deleted from replicas of the database.

Choose whether to create the replica immediately or at the next scheduled replication. If you choose to wait until the next scheduled replication, you are only creating a replica stub. You have to populate the replica stub (using replication) before you can open it.

Replication Topology

After you have created the replicas on the appropriate servers, you need to create and view the replication topology. You create a replication topology by creating scheduled replication with Connection documents.

To create a server Connection document, open the Domino Administrator to the Configuration tab. Expand the Server section and open the Connections view. Choose the Add Connection action button or edit an existing connection. The connection document is similar to the connection document for a Mail Routing connection, discussed in Chapter 11.

On the Basics tab of the Connection document, specify the connection type, such as Local Area Network, Notes Direct Dialup, Passthru Server, or Network Dialup. This is the method that the source server will use to connect to the destination server. Type the hierarchical name of the source and destination servers. In general, you have to type the name of a server in these fields. One exception is if you create a group for servers in the Domino Directory. Make sure the group is a Servers Only group type. You can then use the name of this group as the destination of the replication.

Next, type the name of the source and destination domains. Select the Choose Port button to determine which port or ports to use for the connection. You may also choose to type the IP address in the Optional Network Address field.

On the Replication/Routing tab, shown in Figure 17-6, make sure the replication task is enabled. In the next field, choose which databases should replicate based on priority, as configured in the Replication Settings for the database. You can replicate Low, Medium, and High (the default), Medium and High, or High-priority databases. Next, select the replication type (from those described in Chapters 5 and 12).

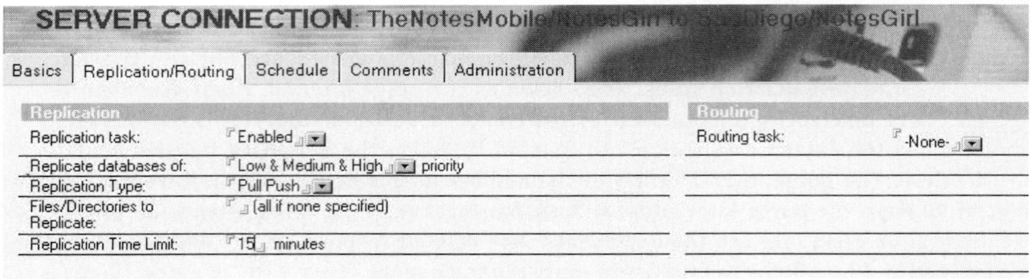

Figure 17-6 Replication Connection document

You can choose to replicate all the databases the two servers have in common by leaving the Files/Directories to Replicate field blank (the default). You can also type a file name or directory (in relation to the data directory) to limit the replication. If you have organized your critical applications into specific subdirectories on your servers, you can organize the replication Connection documents similarly. Finally, enter a replication time limit. If you leave this field blank (the default), the server can take as much time as it needs to complete the replication. If the replication stops unexpectedly (a call is dropped, for example) or the replication isn't finished when the time runs out, and there is a value in this field, the replication picks up where it left off when it restarts.

On the Schedule tab, configure whether the schedule is enabled or disabled. At times you may need to disable a certain connection, when a server is offline for example, but you may not want to delete the Connection document. In the Connect at Times field, select the times at which the server should make contact with the destination server. Complete the Repeat Interval field with how often the source server will attempt to contact the destination server. If only one time or one call is desired, this field can be left blank. The Connect At Times field and the Repeat Interval field work together based on previous routing times. If the first connection occurs at 4 A.M. and takes 15 minutes and the repeat interval is 30 minutes, the second connection occurs at 4:45 A.M. Finally, select the days of the week that this Connection document should apply.

The replication topologies you can create with the Connection documents include hub and spoke, end-to-end, ring, and mesh. In *hub and spoke* topology, one server (the hub) schedules, initiates, and controls all replication. This is the best way to control data and ensure that all data is up-to-date. You may have a corporate office in Houston, for example, and smaller offices all over the world. You might choose to have the hub server in Houston be the central hub for your enterprise. In this case, the hub calls the other servers (or initiates the connection over a LAN or WAN) and initiates replication.

All the other servers are the spokes. They only pass information to other databases through (to and from) the hub when they are called by the hub. The hub and spoke can be expanded to have multiple levels, in which case it is called a *binary tree* topology. Hub and spoke topology will use pull, push, and pull-push replication in most cases. It will only use pull-pull replication if there is a need to reduce work done by the hub replicators. Hub and spoke is the most common replication topology in enterprise environments, as it is the most efficient and organized. An example of hub and spoke topology is shown in Figure 17-7.

End-to-end replication topology has each server connected in a line. Each server talks to the server ahead of it in the line and the server after it in the line. In this chain, for example, the server in our Houston office calls the server in our Dallas office. The Dallas server calls the Kansas City office. The chain would then reverse on itself, and Kansas would call Dallas, and so on.

A *ring* topology is very similar to the end-to-end topology. However, when the last server is reached in the line, it simply circles back around to the beginning. So, in our example, after Dallas calls Kansas City, Kansas City would turn around and call Houston. In *Mesh* topology, all servers connect directly to all other servers. This can be a difficult topology to administer, due to its complex and disorganized nature, and is not recommended. For a review of the replication topologies, you can review Chapter 12.

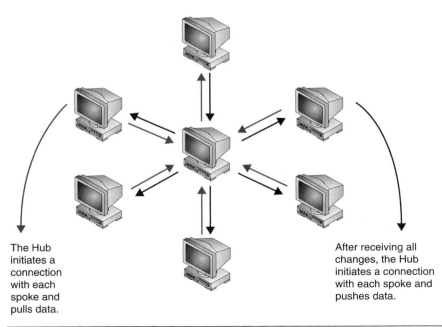

The Hub initiates a connection with each spoke and pulls data.

After receiving all changes, the Hub initiates a connection with each spoke and pushes data.

Figure 17-7   Hub and spoke topology

PART III

After you have created the replication topology, you may want to verify what it looks like. The Replication tab in the Domino Administrator provides a graphical replication topology view either By Connection (shown in Figure 17-8) or By Cluster. To view the graphic topology view, you must be running the MAPS extractor task on your server. If you are not already running this task, you can type LOAD MAPS at the server console to start it. You can also add it to the ServerTasks= line in the NOTES.INI or start it from the Server . . . Status tab in the Domino Administrator.

Replication Factors

There are many factors, at all layers of the Domino environment, that affect replication. These factors include the following:

- Server factors, such as authentication, server access lists, server replication schedule, and number of replicators

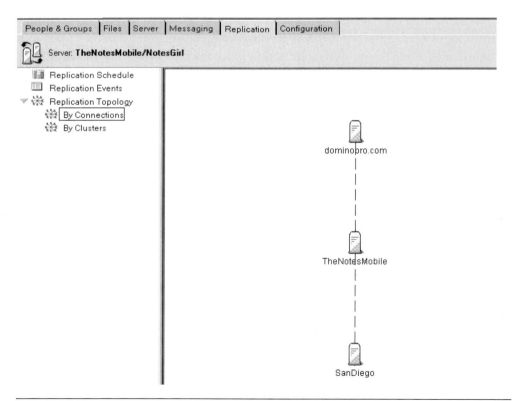

Figure 17-8   Graphical Replication Topology

- Database factors, such as the ACL, replica ID, replica ID cache, replication settings, replication history, and deleted documents
- Document factors, such as form access lists and merge replication conflicts

These factors can cause replication not to occur or to occur in an undesired manner. A good administrator will look at each of these factors when setting up replications as well as when troubleshooting replications.

The first layers of factors affecting replication are the server factors. The replication schedule and the replicator task running on the server (Replica) are server factors. In a clustering situation, the availability of the cluster and the cluster replicator task (CLRepl) are server factors. Replication types, such as pull, push, pull-push, and pull-pull are also server factors, as they are part of the initiation of replication. Finally, the abilities to authenticate with and access the server are important server factors. The server attempting to request a replication must be able to authenticate with the destination server. They must share some certificate in common that allows them to authenticate before replication can occur. In addition, the server access list in the Server document must allow the initiating servers to access the server. If the initiating server is not in the remote server's access list or is in the Not Access Server field, replication cannot occur.

The next factors that affect replication are at the database layer. This includes the following factors:

- Replica ID and the Replica ID cache
- Database ACL
- Replication history
- Replication settings
- Deleted documents

As soon as another server is granted access for the purpose of replication (the servers have authenticated and the servers have passed the server access list), the servers check for databases that they have in common. The list of databases in common is stored in the replica ID cache. Each server maintains this list of databases that have matching replica IDs. Only the databases in the Replica ID cache are replicated.

 NOTE Sometimes databases that are replicas of each other do not replicate. This can occur if the databases are not in the replica ID cache for some reason. Databases may not be in the replica ID cache if the cache has not been updated recently or if replication has been disabled for a database.

To enable or disable replication for a database, select the database from the Files tab of the Domino Administrator. Right-click and choose Replication from the short-cut menu, or select Replication from the list of Database tools. Choose Enable or Disable and click OK, as shown in Figure 17-9.

The replication for a database can also be disabled in the replication settings. To verify that replication is enabled, open the Replication settings. Select the Other panel. Verify that the option to Temporarily disable replication is not selected, as shown in Figure 17-10.

After the servers determine which databases can be replicated, the ACL of the database determines the level of replication that can occur. Table 17-2 describes what happens at each ACL level for the servers involved in replication.

As you plan the database's ACL, you want to consider enforcing a consistent ACL across all replicas of the database. This ensures that as replication occurs, the items you expect to replicate to and from a database aren't changed by altering the ACL. Be careful to audit the ACL and verify that it contains the proper entries before you enable Enforce a Consistent ACL. To enable this option, open the database ACL dialog box. On the Advanced tab, put a check mark in the Enforce a consistent ACL across all replicas of this database option, as shown in Figure 17-11.

TIP A server must have the same or higher level of Access to a database as the highest user on that server. If the Manager of the NAMES.NSF database uses ServerA to open and modify the database, for example, ServerA must have at least Manager access to that database. Otherwise, the changes that that user makes on that server cannot be replicated to other servers. Similarly, if users on ServerA have Author access to the Inventory database, ServerA should have at least Editor access to replicate both newly created and edited documents.

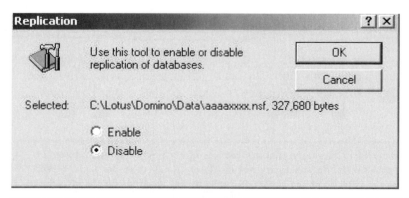

Figure 17-9 Enable or disable replication.

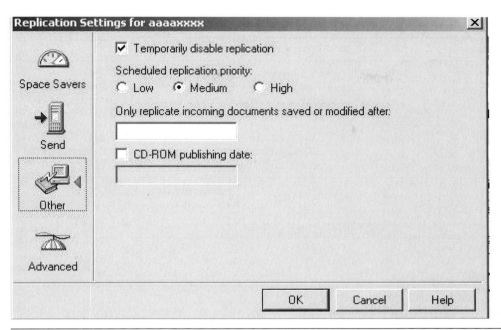

Figure 17-10 Temporarily disable replication.

Table 17-2 ACL and Replication

ACL Level	What Can Be Replicated
No access	Nothing can be replicated. If either of the servers has No Access, replication does not continue. Use this option if you need to shut out a particular server at the database level.
Depositor	Do not use Depositor access for a server that needs to replicate. A server with Depositor access does not replicate changes.
Reader	A server with Reader access to a database can receive changes, but it cannot distribute any changes. This level of access would only be appropriate in a situation where all changes to a database are done at one source location and then distributed.
Author	New documents could be created. Since a server does not author documents, however, this is NOT recommended for an ACL setting for a server.
Editor	New and edited documents can be received and sent. This setting is common for any database that will be changed by multiple users at multiple locations.

continued

Table 17-2 ACL and Replication *(continued)*

ACL Level	What Can Be Replicated
Designer	In addition to receiving and sending new and edited documents, servers with Designer access will receive and send new and edited design elements. Whichever server holds the replica of the database that is used by designers to update the design of the database must have Designer access.
Manager	Only one server should have Manager access to a database. Manager access allows the same changes as Designer access with the additional capability to change the ACL and the replication settings.

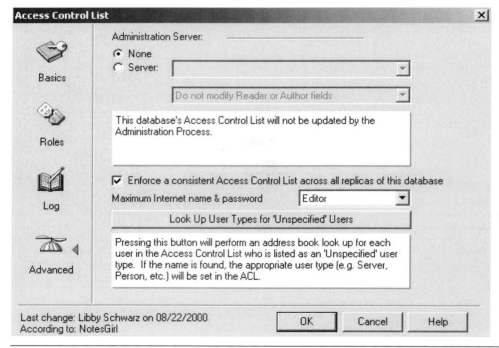

Figure 17-11 Enforce a consistent ACL.

As you assign ACL levels to servers in the ACLs of databases that will replicate, you should also consider the user types and privileges that you can assign. Servers should be placed in the database ACLs in groups (such as LocalDomainServers) of group type Server Group. This can help assure that security for the database is maintained.

If you have assigned an ACL level to a server or server group, you should also assign all the associated privileges with the level you have granted, to ensure that all appropriate changes can replicate.

Another database level factor that affects whether the database is replicated is the replication history for that database. The *replication history* is a list of dates, times, and servers that have completed replication with a particular database. To access the replication history, shown in Figure 17-12, choose File . . . Replication . . . History from the menu while in the database. When a successful replication is completed, the source server's time is used to time and date stamp the replication history. Replication history can be used to aid in troubleshooting replication. If replication has not been occurring as you expected, you could choose the Clear button to remove all replication history entries. This will force a complete replication to occur at the next scheduled replication. Be aware that it will take a significantly longer time, as each element is being verified, not just being compared to the time stamp as usually happens. If you are only having replication problems with a particular server, you can select that server's replication from the dialog box and click the Zoom . . . button. After you zoom in on a particular event, you can clear just that event.

 NOTE Workstation replication does not update the replication history on a server replica of the database. Only server replication adds this time stamp to server-based databases. Workstation-based databases update their own replication history.

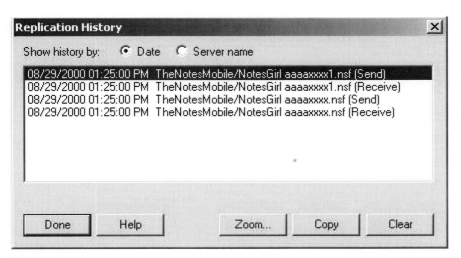

Figure 17-12   Replication history

Finally, Replication Settings for a database allow control of what can be sent and received during replication. Right-click on the database icon to access the replication settings, as described elsewhere in the chapter.

Order of Replication

One additional replication factor to consider is the order and process of replication. As you probably know, replication occurs in the following order:

1. ACL
2. Design
3. Data

When replication begins, after the servers authenticate with each other, gain access, and determine the replicas they have in common, the servers examine each other's ACLs to see what elements they can replicate. Then, based on the ACL and the type of replication, they replicate the appropriate elements. This is most important to understand how the ACL replicates. This is best understood through some scenarios.

Scenario 1

Server A and Server B are replicating with each other. They find Database 1 in common and check the ACLs to see what they can replicate. Server A's ACL looks like this:

- Server A = Designer
- Server B = Manager
- User Joe = Editor
- Changed 9/9/99

Server B's ACL looks like this:

- Server A = Manager
- Server B = Designer
- User Joe = Editor
- Changed 9/8/99

Server A initiates a pull-push replication with Server B. Server A evaluates the ACL on Server B and sees that it has the most recent ACL. Therefore, Server A will not attempt to pull the ACL from Server B.

During the pull replication, the ACLs remain unchanged. The rest of the replication, design, and data are replicated based on the current ACL. All data can replicate from B to A. All design documents can replicate from B to A.

During the push, Server A again sees that it has the most recent ACL and attempts to push its ACL to Server B. According to the ACL setting for Server A on Server B, Server A has the right to write to the ACL. The ACL overwrites completely, so after the replication the ACL on both databases is the same and looks like this:

- Server A = Designer
- Server B = Manager
- User Joe = Editor

Scenario 2

Server A and Server B are replicating with each other. They find Database 1 in common and check the ACLs to see what they can replicate. Server A's ACL looks like this:

- Server A = Designer
- Server B = Designer
- User Joe = Editor
- Changed 9/9/99

Server B's ACL looks like this:

- Server A = Manager
- Server B = Designer
- User Joe = Editor
- Changed 9/8/99

Server A initiates a pull-push replication with Server B. Server A evaluates the ACL on Server B and sees that it has the most recent ACL. Therefore, Server A will not attempt to pull the ACL from Server B.

During the pull replication, the ACLs remain unchanged. The rest of the replication, design, and data are replicated based on the current ACL. All data can replicate from B to A. All design documents can replicate from B to A.

During the push, Server A again sees that it has the most recent ACL and attempts to push its ACL to Server B. According to the ACL setting for Server A on Server B, Server A has the right to write to the ACL. The ACL overwrites completely, so after the replication the ACL on both databases is the same and looks like this:

- Server A = Designer
- Server B = Designer
- User Joe = Editor

In the future, neither A nor B can write ACL changes to each other, based on both having only Designer rights.

Clustering and Replication

When you decide to implement a cluster for high availability or failover, the Domino servers in the cluster run cluster replication. Cluster replication is event-driven, rather than schedule-driven like standard replication. This means that the replication occurs based on the event of a change being made to a database in the cluster. The cluster members run a cluster replicator task (CLRepl) to provide the cluster replication.

Servers in a cluster should also run standard, scheduled replication in addition to the cluster replication. If one cluster member is unavailable, the cluster changes are held in memory until it becomes available again. If the server holding the changes in memory restarts before the other cluster member comes back online, the cluster changes may not be written. To ensure that if a cluster member stops for a time it can synchronize completely when it comes back up, you should run the standard replication. Note that as with a server type group, you can use the name of a cluster as the destination for a replication connection document. If you need to restart a cluster or cluster member, you should run a manual (forced) replication from the Domino Administrator or server console.

One thing to note about cluster replication is that it does not enforce replication settings.

Routing Deployment Issues

As you roll out your applications that use Domino or SMTP mail routing as part of their application logic, you need to ensure that the proper mail routing documents have been created and that the necessary mail routing topology is in place.

Mail Documents

If your application will send mail to a user, you need to ensure that the user's Person document and mail file exist. If the application will send mail to a database that is not a user's mail file, you must create a Mail-In Database document for it.

When you register a new user in your environment, Domino creates a Person document and a mail file by default. To register a person to receive Notes mail, open the Domino Administrator and select the People and Groups tab. Expand the People tools and choose Register. In the Register Person dialog box, shown in Figure 17-13, enable the Advanced registration options. On the Basics panel, make sure to give the user a name and password. If you want the user to access applications via HTTP or to receive

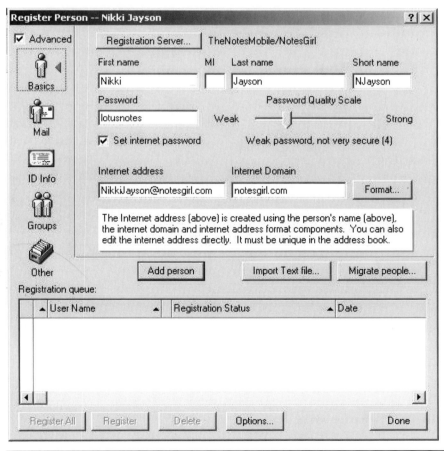

Figure 17-13   Basics tab of the Register Person dialog box

mail via POP3 or IMAP, check the Set Internet Password option. This sets the Internet Password (HTTPPassword field) to the same as the user's default password. You can change the Internet Password later in the Person document, if necessary.

On the Mail panel, you can select the user's Mail Server. This is configured based on the defaults set in the Administration preferences, but as shown in Figure 17-14, you can click the Mail Server button to change the setting. Make sure that the server you choose as the mail server is running the Router task and has connections or is in the same DNN as any other servers that the user needs to route to. Next, you can select the mail file template to base the user's mail file on. By default, Domino selects the standard Mail template, but if your organization has a customized template, you may want to select that. Under the Mail System drop-down, choose whether the user accesses

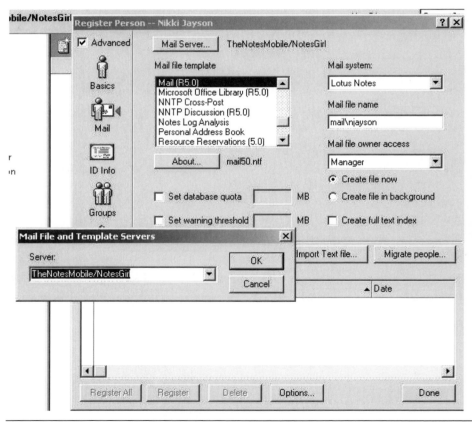

Figure 17-14 Mail Server options

their mail via Lotus Notes, IMAP, POP3, Other Internet, Other, or None. If you choose Other or Other Internet, Domino will not create a mail file for the user but will give you the opportunity to set a mail forwarding address. If you select None, Domino will neither create a mail file nor a forwarding address. Be aware that if you want the user to be able to use Lotus Notes, POP, or IMAP to access their mail, you can set this option to Lotus Notes. For IMAP use, you will also run a conversion process on the mail file.

The mail file will be placed in the \mail subdirectory automatically. You can change the directory or file name using the Mail File Name field. As you configure the mail options, you can also select the user's access to his or her own mail file, the database quota and threshold, when to create the file, and if Domino should create a full-text index of the file.

On the ID Info panel, you can select the location for the user's ID file, the certifier ID with which to certify the ID file, the security type (North American or International) for the ID file, and the ID file's expiration date. Use the Groups tab to assign the user to any appropriate groups. If you are using Mail-only groups for distribution lists, make sure to assign the user to the appropriate ones. For more details on registering users, refer to Chapters 3 and 6.

When you register the user, verify that Domino created the Person document by viewing the People view in the Domino Directory or from the People and Groups tab of the Domino Administrator. To ensure that Domino thinks the user is a Mail user, you can also use the Messaging tab's Mail Users view, which displays the name, mail address, and mail file name. You can also use this view to send upgrade notices to users or to move users' mail files. You can use the Files tab to expand the \mail subdirectory to ensure that the user's mail file has been created.

If you are sending mail to a database that is not a user's mail file, you must create a Mail-in Database document to allow the file to receive mail. To create a Mail-In Database document, open the Domino Administrator to the People and Groups tab. Select the Mail-In Databases and Resources view. Click the Add Mail-In Database action button to display the Mail-In Database document, as shown in Figure 17-15.

In the Mail-In name field, type the name that you want users to address mail to. This is the name users will type in the mail message, developers will use in mailing formulas, or users can select from the Domino Directory. Also select the type of Internet message storage (MIME or Notes Rich Text) and the Internet Address, if any, for the file. You can use the description field to ensure that users and administrators know the purpose for the database. On the Database Information tab, complete the Location information for the database. This includes the domain in which the database resides as well as the

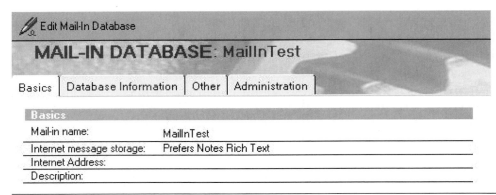

Figure 17-15   Mail-In Database document

hierarchical server name. If replicas of the file exist on more than one server, create a different mail-in database name for each server. Finally, type in the filename for the database. The file and path should be relative to the \lotus\domino\data directory. If you are in a mixed messaging environment where users and servers are listed in additional directories, you may want to enable the Foreign Directory Sync allowed option on the Administration tab. After you create and save the Mail-In Database document, the database should be able to receive messages.

Routing Fundamentals

As you deploy databases that require mail routing, you need to ensure that you have a firm grasp of the fundamentals of Domino mail routing so that you know if and when the messages generated as part of your applications will route. As you should already know, Domino servers are organized into domains and Domino Named Networks (DNNs). Domains are identified by the Domino Directory. Within a domain, all servers use the same Domino Directory that replicates among them. All documents needed to route mail within (and outside) of the domain should be available to the router via the Domino Directory, including Person documents, Mail-In Database documents, Server documents, Domain documents, and Connection documents. Within domains, Domino servers are further organized into Domino Named Networks, based on protocol and connection. If servers are in different DNNs, then the router relies on Connection documents to route mail.

DNNs

A Domino Named Network's main purpose is mail routing. Within a DNN, mail routes immediately and automatically. No other documents, such as Connection documents, are necessary. Servers in the same DNN must run the same protocol (have at least one protocol in common) and must be constantly connected. Servers that use dial-up to exchange mail cannot be in the same DNN. To verify or change a server's DNN, open the Server document to the Ports . . . Notes Network Ports tab, as shown in Figure 17-16.

For each port that is defined in the Server document, make sure that a protocol and Notes Network (the DNN) are defined. For different protocols, you should have different Notes Networks (DNNs).

Routing Connection Documents

For those servers that are not in the same DNN, mail cannot route immediately and automatically the way it does when they are in the same DNN. Instead, these servers require Connection documents to determine when and how mail routes. Mail connection documents define the path to the other server, the routing schedule, and any mail thresholds. To create a complete mail route that allows users to send and receive, two mail Connection documents must be created for each connected server.

To create a Connection document, open the Domino Administrator to the Configuration tab. Expand the Server section and select the Connections view. Once in the Connections view, click the New Connection action button to create a new server Connection document, as shown in Figure 17-17. You could also create the Connection document by opening the Domino Directory or by expanding the Messaging section.

SERVER: TheNotesMobile/NotesGirl

| Basics | Security | Ports | Server Tasks | Internet Protocols | MTAs | Miscellaneous | Transactional Logging | Administration |

| Notes Network Ports | Internet Ports | Proxies |

Port	Protocol	Notes Network	Net Address	Enabled
TCPIP	TCP	NotesGirlP	TheNotesMobile	ENABLED
test_ip	TCP	NG_IP	TheNotesMobile	DISABLED
			TheNotesMobile	DISABLED
			TheNotesMobile	DISABLED
			TheNotesMobile	DISABLED
			TheNotesMobile	DISABLED
			TheNotesMobile	DISABLED
			TheNotesMobile	DISABLED

Figure 17-16 Notes Network Ports on the Server document

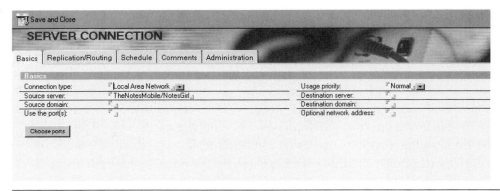

Figure 17-17   Create a Connection document.

On the Basics tab of the Connection document, first select the Connection type. This describes the way that the servers are connected, such as Local Area Network, Dialup Modem, and Passthru server. Choose the appropriate type for your servers. Please note that the value in this field changes other fields on the document. Also note that you can have multiple Connection documents between any two servers, using different connection types in case of WAN outages and so on.

Type the hierarchical name of both the source and destination servers. The source server is the server that originates the connection. Since mail is one way, to route mail between two servers, you will have a Connection document for each server. Each server will be a source server for one of the Connection documents. Also type the source and destination domains. This field refers to the Domino domain name, not to be confused with an NT Domain, DNS Domain, or any other usage of the word domain that you might be thinking about.

To complete the Use the Ports field, click the Choose Ports button and select the ports that you want to use for this connection. You may want to complete the Optional Network Address field with the IP address for the destination server.

You can complete the Usage Priority field if you want a certain connection only to be used as a last resort. For example, if two servers are connected over a bridged/routed WAN, this would probably be your first choice of methods to connect for mail routing. However, there are also modems on both servers as a backup scenario in case of the WAN link being down. You would make the Dialup Modem Connection document low-priority in this case.

On the Replication/Routing tab, you can disable the Replication task, as this is a routing Connection document. On the Routing section, select Mail Routing as the Routing task. The Route at Once If field is also known as the routing threshold. When the number of messages waiting in the mail.box for delivery to this server reaches the number in this field (the default is 5), the messages are routed without waiting for the next connection interval or connect at time. All waiting messages count toward the routing threshold; however, not all messages are sent. Messages can be low-, normal, or high-priority, based on the sender's delivery options. If a message is high-priority, it will be routed immediately, without waiting for a connection time. If a message is normal priority, it will behave as normal—routed at the appropriate connection time, if mail is forced to route manually, or if the mail routing threshold is reached. If mail is low-priority, it counts toward the routing threshold but is only routed during the low-priority mail interval (this is between midnight and 6 A.M., by default, although you can configure it using a NOTES.INI setting).

The Routing Cost field is calculated automatically, based on the type of connection. A LAN connection type, for example, has a default routing cost of 1. A dial-up connection type has a default routing cost of 5. In the case of two similar Connection documents, Domino will try to use the one with the lowest routing cost first.

The router type field can be set to push-only, pull-only, pull-push, or push wait. This option is intended to help with dialing into remote or ISP servers.

On the Schedule tab, configure whether the schedule is enabled or disabled. At times you may need to disable a certain connection, such as when a server is offline, but you may not want to delete the Connection document. In the Connect at Times field, select the times at which the server should make contact with the destination server. This can be specific times or ranges of time but should include the low-priority times to ensure that low-priority mail can route. Complete the Repeat Interval field with how often the source server will attempt to contact the destination server. If only one time or one call is desired, this field can be left blank. The Connect At Times field and the Repeat Interval field work together based on previous routing times. If the first connection occurs at 4 A.M. and takes 15 minutes and the repeat interval is 30 minutes, the second connection occurs at 4:45 A.M. Finally, select the days of the week that this Connection document should apply.

CAUTION Here's a "gotcha" to be wary of when creating Connection documents. One of the end user mail options when sending mail is for Delivery Priority. The priority choices are low, normal, and high. By default, all mail is sent normal priority. Normal priority mail follows the mail settings in the Connection document including schedule and mail threshold. High-priority mail is routed immediately. It causes the server to make an immediate connection to the remote server and sends all normal and high-priority pending mail. Low-priority mail is routed by default from midnight to 6 A.M. in the morning. If there is no mail Connection document that covers the low-priority times, low-priority mail will not route.

CAUTION When you route mail through other servers to get to a final recipient, be certain that you limit the router hops to fewer than 25. Twenty-five hops is the hard-coded limit of mail routing hops and messages will fail once this limit is reached. The hops are counted down from 25 each time the message passes through a server's **MAIL.BOX**.

As you create the Connection documents to ensure mail can route between the servers that contain your applications, make sure that you create two connections, so mail can route in both directions. In addition, remember that you do not need a mail connection for any servers that are in the same DNN.

For servers in different domains, you need a Domain document, defining what domain the server exists in, and a connection document to get to that server. Servers that are physically connected (or can connect, such as by dial-up), an Adjacent Domain document would be required. For servers that cannot connect directly, a Non-Adjacent Domain document is required to define an intermediary domain and server that can connect to both servers. Mail routing to a non-adjacent domain requires a server in an adjacent domain that can route mail to and physically connect to both servers. For more details on configuring mail routing and Connection documents, refer to Chapters 4 and 11.

End User Replication and Routing Issues

The applications you deploy will be used primarily by the end users in your environment. You may need to predict how the applications will be affected by replication and routing by users, both local and remote. Most of the application's replication and routing doesn't change very much, but there are some details to be aware of.

Deploy Using Setup Profiles

To roll out the application to the end user, you can create bookmarks or replicas with Setup Profiles. To create a Setup Profile, open the Domino Administrator to the People and Groups tab. Open the Setup Profiles view and click the Add Setup Profile action button to display the User Setup Profile document shown in Figure 17-18.

In the User Setup profile, give the profile a name, select the Internet browser the client should use, and indicate the Directory, Search, and Sametime servers, as necessary. On the Databases tab, you can indicate which databases should be added to the bookmarks and which ones should be created as new replicas. To add a database as a bookmark, open the database and choose Edit . . . Copy as Link . . . Database Link. In

```
Save and Close

USER SETUP PROFILE: RemoteUsers

Basics | Databases | Dial-up Connections | Accounts | Name Servers | Applet Security | Proxies | MIME | Administration

Basics
Profile name:                    RemoteUsers
Internet browser:                Microsoft Internet Explorer
Directory server:                TheNotesMobile/NotesGirl
Catalog/Domain Search
server:
Retrieve/open pages:             from Notes workstation
Sametime server:
```

Figure 17-18   User setup profile

Default databases added to bookmarks field, choose Edit . . . Paste. To add a new replica of a database, open the database and choose Edit . . . Copy as Link . . . Database Link. In the Create as new replicas on user's machine, choose Edit . . . Paste. You'll probably want to make a local replica of the user's mail file and the mobile Directory Catalog, if one is created in your environment. You can also create default connections on the Dial-up Connections tab.

NOTE   When you work remotely, you can choose to work with databases interactively, dialed in to the server, or you can choose to work offline and only dial in to replicate. When you work offline for the first time, Notes creates a local MAIL.BOX for outgoing mail.

As you register new users, you can assign a setup profile in the New User Registration dialog box. Any settings, including the bookmarks and new replicas, will be added to the user's workspace as you setup the user. If you make a change to the Setup Profile after you configure the user, the changes are pushed to the user's workstation when the user authenticates with the home server specified in their current Location document.

Location Documents

To ensure that local workstation replicas of database are synchronized with the server replicas and that mail routes correctly from local workstations, you should use Location documents.

You can run replication manually from the database, bookmark, or replicator, but you can also schedule replication using Location documents. In addition, while the

Person documents indicate the home/mail server and information on the mail file, you might want to have different information based on different locations.

Notes clients come with standard Location documents for sites such as Island (Disconnected) and Office (Network). You can access the Location documents either through the Personal Address Book or via the link at the bottom left of the workstation software. You can edit existing Location documents, or if in the Personal Address Book, create new ones.

On the Basics tab, shown in Figure 17-19, choose the type of location, such as Local Area Network or Notes Direct Dialup. Give the location a descriptive name. You can also include your Internet mail address, choose whether to be prompted for the time, date, and phone, the proxy server configuration, and whether to display the primary or alternate names.

Use the Servers tab to indicate the home/mail server for this location as well as the passthru, catalog, directory, and Sametime servers. The ports tab lets you enable specific ports for this location. Use the Mail tab to indicate where the mail file is located, on the server or locally. If you're at a dial-up location, you'll probably want to have a local replica of the mail file to work from, for example. If you indicate that the mail file is local, you have the opportunity to create a mail routing threshold—when the workstation should connect to the server to send mail automatically.

You should also indicate the path and file name for the mail file, the name of the Domain mail domain, and name of the Internet mail domain if you connect directly to the Internet with your client, rather than connecting to your Domino server to send. You can choose whether to send outgoing mail through the Domino server or directly to the Internet in the Send Outgoing Mail field.

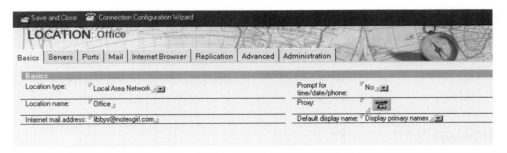

Figure 17-19   Location document basics

The Internet Browser tab enables you to select the browser to use when launching from mail or other links within Notes.

Use the Replication tab, shown in Figure 17-20, to enable a replication schedule. You can also enable a separate schedule for high-priority replication.

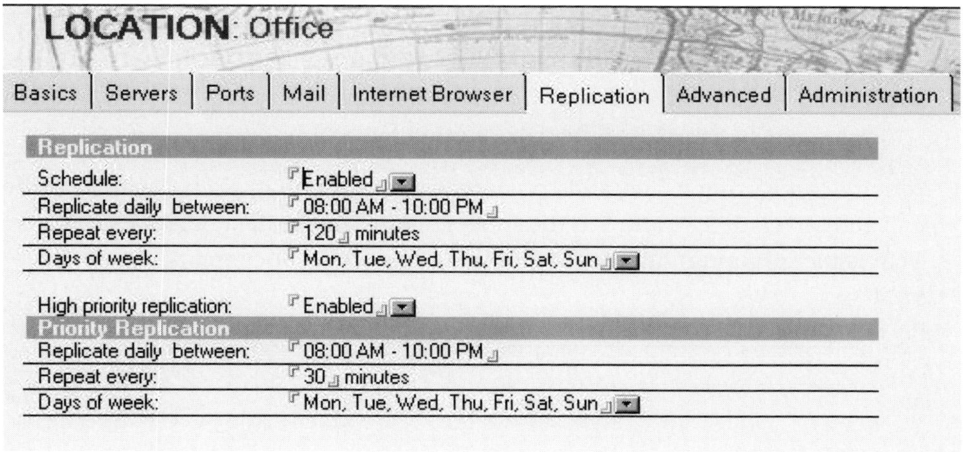

Figure 17-20   Location document replication schedule

Review Questions

1. Emily is rolling out Database 1 and she is trying to decide which servers to roll it out to. Her environment has five servers; Server 1 is the Hub. Servers 2 and 3 are the spokes at different locations. Server 4 is a cluster with Server 3. Server 5 is another spoke at a third location. The users serviced by Servers 3 and 5 use the application. It requires high availability. Which option describes the best deployment for the database?

   A. Place the database on Servers 3 and 5.

   B. Place the database on Servers 3, 4, and 5.

   C. Place the database on Servers 3 and 4.

   D. Place the database on Servers 1, 3, 4, and 5.

2. You want to create replicas of five important databases on Server 2, with Server 1 as the source. Which of the following describes the security requirements?

   A. Server 1 needs to be in Server 2's Access list. Server 2 must have at least Reader access in the ACL of the databases on Server 1.

   B. Server 2 needs to be in Server 1's Access list. Server 1 must have at least Reader access in the ACL of the databases on Server 2.

   C. Server 2 needs to be in Server 1's Access list. Server 2 must have at least Editor access in the ACL of the databases on Server 1.

   D. Server 1 needs to be in Server 2's Access list. Server 2 must have at least Manager access in the ACL of the databases on Server 1.

3. You are configuring a hub and spoke replication topology with Server 1 as the hub and servers 2, 3, 4, and 5 as the spokes. Assuming the default replication type, what is the minimum number of required Connection documents?

   A. 4

   B. 8

   C. 3

   D. 1

4. True or False: It's a good idea to perform backups of a database by creating a replica. As replication occurs, the database will be backed up sufficiently.

   A. True

   B. False

5. You want to create five replicas using the Domino Administrator. You are applying a replication formula. Which of the following methods of creating a replica should you use?

   A. Use drag-n-drop with AdminP.

   B. Create the replicas manually from the workstation.

   C. Use the New . . . Replica(s) tool on the Files tab of the Domino Administrator.

   D. Select all the files on the Files tab of the Domino Administrator. Right-click and choose New . . . Replica(s).

6. Which of the following can you edit when creating a new replica manually?

   A. Filename

   B. Path of the file (location)

   C. Create a new folder to store the database.

   D. Database title

7. You have configured Database 1 to replicate every 20 days to a remote site. Which of the following settings could cause deleted documents to reappear in the database after replication?

A. Do not send deletions made in this replica to other replicas.

B. Temporarily disable replication.

C. Do not receive deletions when this server replicates with any server.

D. Remove documents not modified in the last 45 days.

8. You want to view the mail and replication topology on your server to ensure that you have created the proper connection documents. Which of the following tasks is necessary to display the topology in the Domino Administrator?

A. TOPOLOGY

B. MAPS

C. ROUTER

D. REPLICA

9. Server A and Server B are replicating Database 1. In Server A's ACL, Server A has Editor access and Server B has Manager access. In Server B's ACL, Server A has Editor access and Server B has Designer access. If Server B has the more recent ACL change, what happens to the ACL after Server A initiates a standard pull-push replication?

A. ACL is not changed.

B. ACL is overwritten. Final ACL is Server A Editor and Server B Designer.

C. ACL is overwritten. Final ACL is Server A Editor and Server B Manager.

D. Replication cannot occur.

10. Server A and Server B start a pull-push replication. Server A has reader access. Server B has Editor access. There are changed documents in Server B's replica and changed Design elements in Server A's replica. What is the result of the replication?

A. Server A gets the new documents. Server B gets the new design elements.

B. Server A doesn't get anything. Server B gets the new design elements.

C. Server A gets the new documents. Server B doesn't get anything.

D. Server A doesn't get anything. Server B doesn't get anything.

Review Answers

1. **D** (1, 3, 4, and 5) is the best answer to ensure high availability, good bandwidth utilization, and organized replication.

2. **A** is correct. The source server (Server 1) needs to be listed in the destination server's (Server 2) access list. The destination server needs at least reader access in the ACL.

3. **D** is correct. You need one pull-push for each spoke. However, you could use a server group containing all of the spoke servers and only have one Connection document for these spoke servers.

4. **B** is correct. While having a replica can be one method of backup, corrupted documents can replicate and it is not a sufficient backup.

5. **B** is correct. You should create replicas manually from the workstation, as this is the only method that allows you to replicate settings.

6. **A** and **B** are correct. You can edit the filename and path when creating a new replica manually.

7. **D** is correct. If the purge interval (1/3 of 45 days) occurs before the replication interval, deletion stubs will be removed before replication takes place, and deleted documents may reappear in the database.

8. **B** is correct. You should run the MAPS (Maps Extractor) task

9. **B** is correct. When the pull portion of the replication takes place, B's ACL overwrites A's ACL. The final result is Server A Editor and Server B Designer.

10. **C** is correct. Server A can pull new documents. Server A cannot push and Server B cannot pull new design elements.

CHAPTER 18

Securing Applications

You should be able to answer questions based on the following objectives after reading this chapter:

- Securing applications based on ACL's impact on replication
- Securing applications: ACLs for replication
- Securing applications: Authors fields
- Securing applications: Authors
- Securing applications: Consistent ACLs
- Securing applications: Groups
- Securing applications: Notes users
- Securing applications: Read-only views
- Securing applications: Readers fields
- Securing applications: Roles
- Securing applications: Sections
- Securing applications: Security versus deterrence
- Securing applications: Web users
- Deploying Notes user authentication: Notes ID
- Deploying Web user authentication
- Designing a secure application
- Securing Domino applications based on Notes authentication
- Securing Domino applications based on password encryption
- Securing Domino applications based on the Domino Directory
- Securing Domino applications based on user ID
- Securing Domino applications based on Web authentication
- Securing Domino applications based on $Users
- Securing Domino applications
- Deploying server-based applications: Securing agents

As you deploy Domino applications for Notes and Web clients, one of your main goals is the security of the environment, application design, and data. Application security starts above the application level, at the server. Access to the servers requires authentication, whether the user accesses the server via a Notes client or via a Web browser. In addition, a user must be given access to the server via the server access list. Sometimes it isn't a specific user that needs access to a server, but rather an applet or agent. After a user gains access to the environment, he or she must gain access to the application itself, via ACLs, roles, and additional ACL privileges. After gaining access to the database itself, a user must also gain access to the design elements, documents, and data. Security options at this level include Reader and Author fields, view and form access lists, section security, and encryption. As users gain access to design elements especially, they may need to verify the signer or creator of the design element to verify its integrity. This is important so that it can pass Notes workstation security. The Execution Control List protects Notes client users from design elements that may contain dangerous code by only allowing elements signed appropriately to run or be accessible.

The job of the Domino Administrator lies mostly at the top of the security list—authentication, server access, and ACLs. It is also the job the administrator, however, to ensure that users have the proper access to the applications and that applications replicate correctly, which can be affected by security at lower levels. For this reason, it is important for administrators to have a good understanding of all Notes and Domino security layers.

In many cases, the material covered in this chapter has been covered in some way in other chapters in this book. The topic of Domino security has been covered in depth in Chapters 5, 10, 24, 34, 35, and 36. In some cases, we repeat material that is necessary for this exam, but if you are unfamiliar with any of the processes or elements, you may want to refer back to these chapters. Bear in mind that the goal of this chapter is to take Domino security into consideration in terms of deploying your Domino applications.

Authentication and Server Access

The first level of Domino security that users or other servers have to pass is at the server level. Users and servers must be able to authenticate with the Domino server. There is a different authentication process based on whether it is a Notes user (or other Domino server) or a Web user. The Notes user or Domino server bases authentication on the user ID or server ID file and a shared hierarchical or flat certificate. The Web user bases authentication on the user name and password in the Person document. Server access is further restricted based on the server access list.

Notes Authentication and ID Files

The Notes ID file for a user or server contains all the information necessary to identify a Notes user or Domino server to the Notes environment. This includes not only the user's name, but also the following additional information, as shown in Figure 18-1:

- **User Name**   The common name of the Notes user is stored in the ID file.

- **User Notes License type**   When a user is created, the administrator assigns a type of license, either North American or International. The type of license cannot be changed after the ID is created.

- **Public and Private keys**   The keys are randomly generated hexadecimal numbers that uniquely identify the user. The keys contain an element of the key of the certifier that was used to register the user. The keys are used in authentication, encryption, and signing. The Public key is also stored in the user's Person document in the Domino Directory. The Public key and Private key are a mathematically-related pair.

- **Encryption keys**   Encryption keys are secret keys generated by you or another user that allow you to encrypt and decrypt fields on a form. This is an optional element of the Notes ID file.

- **Certificates**   The original certificate granted to a hierarchical ID is stored in the ID file. Any additional certificates are stored in the Domino Directory. If the ID file is

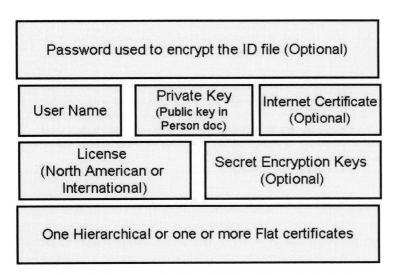

Figure 18-1   Notes ID file

PART III

flat, all certificates are stored in the ID file. Also, any flat certificates given to a hierarchical user are stored in the ID file.

- **Password** Each ID file can contain a password for the protection of the ID file itself.

When the user or server ID is registered using the Domino Administrator, you can choose where to store the ID file. You can store the ID file as an attachment in the Domino Directory if the ID file has a password. You can also store the ID file separately in a directory that you configure. By default, Domino will create an IDs directory under the local data directory. Many users and administrators also maintain a backup copy of the ID files in case of loss or corruption. While an administrator could generate a new ID file for a user or server if necessary, this ID file would contain different public and private keys and none of the secret encryption keys. This would mean that if the user had encrypted any mail or other documents, no one could read them.

Security for the Notes User ID

Domino uses a password to protect the ID files. When you registered users, servers, and certifiers, you specified the minimum password security required for each ID that you created. While it is possible to choose not to password-protect an ID file—by selecting zero as the minimum number of characters for the password—this opens your Domino environment up to security breaches. In addition, if you choose not to password-protect an ID when you create it, you cannot store the ID file in the Domino Directory. The password, which can be up to 63 characters, is used to encrypt the ID file. When a user types in the password correctly, the ID file is decrypted and can be used to access the server or other object.

> **TIP** By default, the password is only stored in the ID file and is only used to protect the ID file. You also have the option of checking the password at the server to verify that the correct ID is being used, forcing users to change their passwords after a set period of time, and keeping a log of the passwords to prevent reuse.

To change or set a password, the user examines the ID file by choosing File . . . Tools . . . User ID. On the Basics panel, click the Set Password button to change the password for the ID file. Notes prompts you to decrypt the ID using the current password before allowing the user to change the password. When you see the Set Password dialog box shown in Figure 18-2 displayed, type the new password. Remember that passwords in

Notes *are* case-sensitive. After you type and confirm the password, Domino resets the password in the User ID file.

If the user is a Web user, you must also configure an Internet password. You configure the Internet or HTTP password when you register the user by enabling the Set Internet Password checkbox. You can also set this password at any time by completing the Internet Password field (internally, this is the HTTPPassword field) on the user's Person document. If the user will only access the Domino server via the Web, you do not necessarily need to register them and give them a Notes ID—they only need a Person document with an Internet password.

Notes Authentication

Authentication is the process by which a user or server, using their ID file, verifies their identity within the Domino organization. Each Domino organization has a certifier (or multiple certifiers). Each ID file within the Domino organization is stamped with this certifier. The authentication process compares the stamp on the user or server's ID file with the stamp that is part of the Domino organization. Authentication is based on

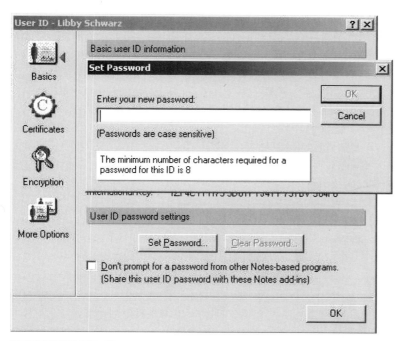

Figure 18-2 Set Password dialog.

having this shared certifier stamp in common. The following steps are used in the process of authentication, as shown in Figure 18-3:

1. The server or user requesting access generates a random number. The requesting server or user sends a package to the server containing this random number, his or her name, public key, and certificates.

2. The server takes the random number and signs it, using the signing methods that will be described later in this chapter. The server then sends this back to the requesting server or user.

3. When the requesting user or server receives the signed random number, it verifies that the signature is correct and that the random number matches the original random number. Because signing uses the public key for verification, only users with the correct public key can verify that the correct signature has been appended.

4. The server repeats the entire process in reverse to prove to the requesting server or user that the server is not an impostor.

Authentication between the Notes client and Domino server (or between two Domino servers) is always a two-way process of verifying the identity of both the requestor and the requested servers or users. Authentication is based on the trusted information (the common certificate) given to both parties by the certifier. Authentication is successful when the following tests are true:

Figure 18-3
Authentication

- Hierarchical IDs must have a common certifier in their tree (common ancestor).

- Flat IDs must have some common certificate.

- Hierarchical IDs gaining access to flat resources must have some common certificate.

- If hierarchical IDs do not have a common ancestor, they must use the process of cross-certification to gain a common certificate.

Web Authentication

When users will access the server via a Web client (a browser), the user authenticates differently. With Web authentication, Domino does not require a Notes ID file for authentication. Instead, by default, Domino uses name and password authentication. Domino uses the user name and the Internet password from the Person document in the Domino Directory for Web authentication. When users access an element of a Web site that is secured, Domino prompts for a user name and password, as shown in Figure 18-4.

If the user supplies a user name and password that Domino can verify in the Domino Directory (or in a secondary Domino or LDAP directory via Directory Assistance), the user is given the correct level of access to the secured item based on the ACL. The database may have a Maximum Internet Name and Password configured. If so, this overrides the level of access the user is granted in the ACL. If the user is granted Manager access in the ACL, for example, but the Maximum Internet Name and Password is set to Editor, the user will have Editor access. Note that the Maximum Internet Name and Password setting can only limit a user's access—a user with Reader access will not be raised to Editor access. Figure 18-5 shows the Maximum Internet Name and Password configuration on the Advanced panel of the ACL dialog box.

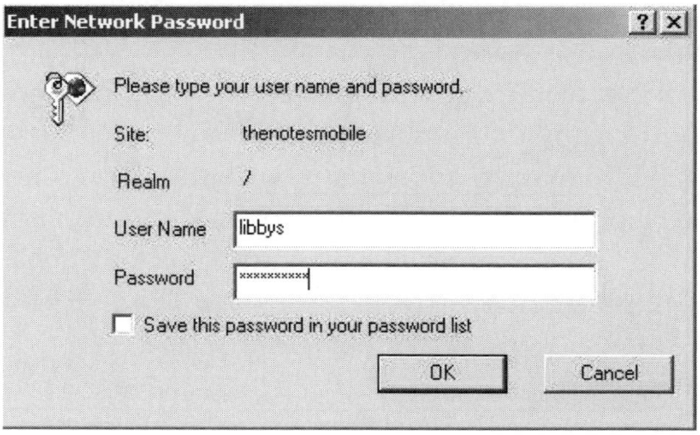

Figure 18-4
Prompting for a
Web user name and
password

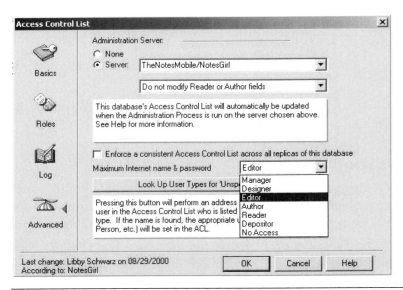

Figure 18-5   Configure the Maximum Internet Name and Password.

By default, Domino uses the first column in a hidden view in the Domino Directory, called $Users, to verify a user's identity. The user has a variety of options for the user name they provide to Domino when this view is being used, as you can see in Figure 18-6. After Domino locates the user name and verifies the password, the user's name is mapped to the Full Name, as shown in the third column.

If you want users to have fewer choices of the user name they must provide, use the Security tab on the Server document. In the Web Server Authentication field, you may select either *More name variations with lower security* or *Fewer name variations with more security*. If you select *Fewer name variations with more security*, Domino uses the $LDAPCN view instead. This view, shown in Figure 18-7, has fewer options for the user name column.

If the user is not required to authenticate, there are two options. First, the database may have an ACL entry for Anonymous. If so, any non-authenticated Web users have the level of access granted to Anonymous. Second, if there is no Anonymous entry, the user is granted the -Default- user's level of access. If you are placing a database in use on the Web, you should always include an entry for Anonymous. Figure 18-8 shows an ACL with an entry for Anonymous.

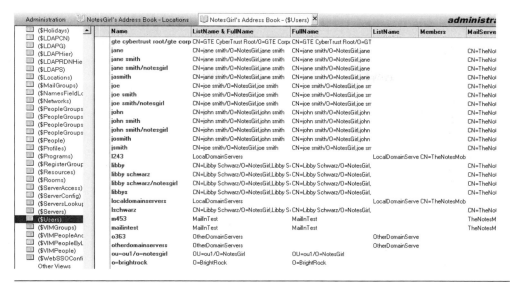

Figure 18-6 $Users hidden view

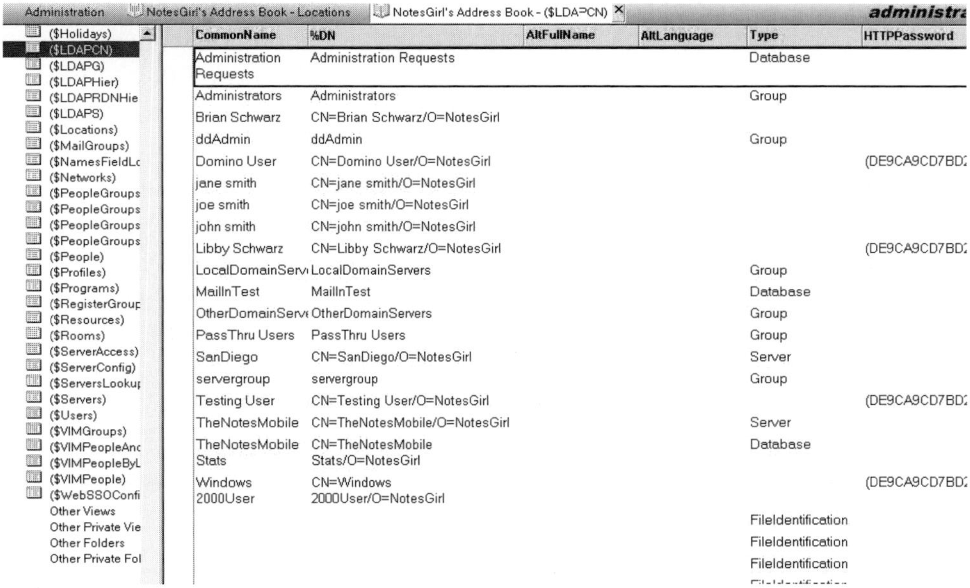

Figure 18-7 $LDAPCN hidden view

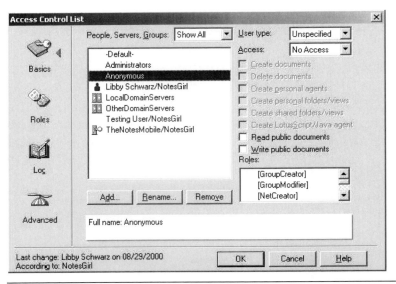

Figure 18-8 Anonymous entry in the ACL

To verify that the HTTP port is accepting basic name and password authentication and anonymous authentication, open the Domino Administrator to the Configuration tab. Open the appropriate Server document to the Ports . . . Internet Ports . . . Web tab. Under Authentication options, verify that Name and Password is set to Yes. In addition, if you want Web users to be able to access any data on the server without authenticating, or by authenticating as Anonymous, you must also have the Anonymous option set to Yes.

If your users need to authenticate over SSL, you need to enable the SSL port for the protocol. You should also choose whether to enable SSL authentication for client certificate authentication, name and password authentication, or anonymous authentication.

TIP If you're using virtual servers, you may need to configure these settings for each virtual server. The default is to allow both Name and Password and Anonymous over the HTTP port.

Session-Based Authentication

In R5, this basic Name and Password authentication can be modified to avoid some the issues that users find with the basic authentication. Some of these issues include multiple prompts to the user for credentials, sending credentials too often, and the inability to logout. Session-based authentication forces a user to establish a session on the server when they authenticate. This session is given a unique session ID number, which is stored in a cookie on the user's workstation. When the user tries to access the Web site, the cookie is included with the request for the secured resources. When the server receives the cookie, it verifies that the session ID is still valid and then allows access to the resources without prompting the user.

If the user closes the browser, logs out, or is timed out, the cookie is destroyed and the session ID is invalidated. The user is prompted to log in again when accessing a secured resource.

To configure session-based authentication, open the Server document to the Internet Protocols . . . Domino Web Engine tab. Under the HTTP Sessions section, choose Enabled for the Session authentication field. You can then select the Idle session timeout time and the maximum number of active sessions, as shown in Figure 18-9.

After enabling session authentication, you need to restart the HTTP task. You can type **Tell HTTP Restart** at the Domino server console to restart the HTTP task without restarting the entire server. You can also select the HTTP task from the Server . . . Status

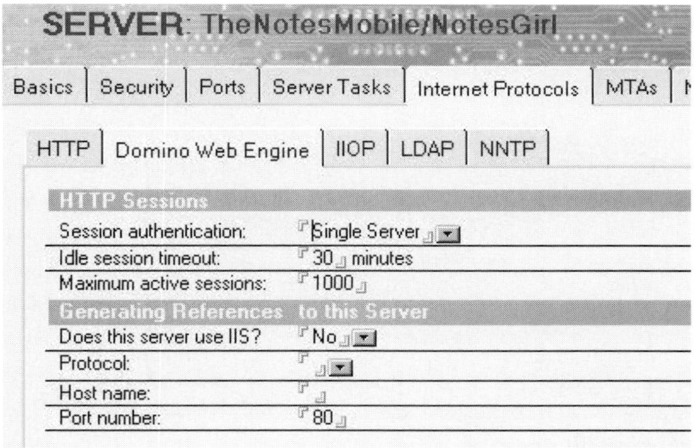

Figure 18-9 Enable session authentication.

tab. When you right-click on the task, you can select Tell Task . . . from the shortcut menu. Select Restart Web server with new settings from the Tell HTTP Web Server dialog box, as shown in Figure 18-10.

After you enable session authentication, Domino uses a login page, as shown in Figure 18-11, rather than the dialog box used with standard name and password authentication. You can control the appearance of this login page. Create the Domino Web Configuration database (DOMCFG.NSF) based on the template DOMCFG.NTF. You can either modify the existing $$LoginUserForm form in Domino Designer or create a new form and use the Login Form Mapping document.

When you access a secured resource, Domino will prompt you using the new login form. You can append the ?logout command to the end of a URL. This destroys the cookie and logs the user out of the server. While the user is logged in, you can get information about the logged-in Web users by typing **Tell HTTP Show Users** at the Domino server console or by using the Server . . . Status tab in the Domino Administrator. Log out also occurs when the user closes the browser (the cookie is destroyed and the unique session ID is invalidated) or when the user times out (the session ID is invalidated and the next time the user connects the cookie is destroyed and the user is prompted to login again).

Server Access

After using their ID or Person document and password to verify their identity and to gain access to the environment, the users or servers that are trying to access a database must also gain access to the server on which the database is stored. Each Server docu-

Figure 18-10
Restart the
HTTP task.

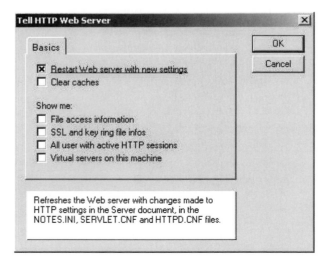

Welcome to the NotesGirl Intranet...

Please login using the username and password you were given.

Username
Password

Login

Figure 18-11 Login page

ment contains a *server access list*, a list of users (and servers) that are allowed (or not allowed) to access the server. The user must be allowed to gain access to the server based on the entries in this list. Most of the security settings that the user (or server) must pass are located on the Security tab, shown in Figure 18-12.

The Security Settings section sets a few of the security parameters for the server. In this section, you have the ability to determine whether the server will compare Notes public keys of users and servers that attempt to authenticate with the Notes public keys stored in the Domino Directory. This option is intended to prevent users from using fake user ID files. If an administrator chooses not to compare public keys, the authentication process described earlier is much more limited. This section also grants to the administrator the ability to allow Anonymous Notes connections. This allows any Notes ID to authenticate with the server, regardless of the certificates contained in the Notes ID. Finally, use this section to configure password checking, or verification, on Notes IDs. Password verification forces the Domino server to verify passwords during authentication, which is not the default configuration. If you enable password checking, Domino stores a copy of the current password in the Person document. In addition, Domino requires users to change their passwords on a regular basis.

TIP   If you allow anonymous connections, you must also provide for the anonymous users' access to databases. You can do this by creating an entry in the databases' ACLs called Anonymous. Users that do not authenticate will use the level of access determined by this entry. If you do not create an anonymous entry, anonymous users will be granted the default access to the database.

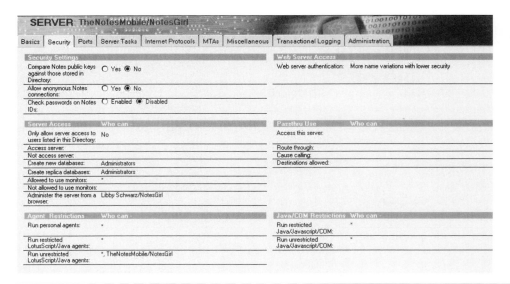

Figure 18-12   Security tab on the Server document

The Server Access section is where the administrator can restrict access to the server, for general use, for Passthru use, and for creating new and replica databases. In addition, the administrator can restrict access for the use of monitors and for administering the server from a browser. You can choose to allow access to this server only to users that are listed in the Domino Directory, so that no users from other domains can gain access. If you enable this field, you must add any server that needs to access your server to the Access Server field, including servers that are listed in the local Domino Directory.

You can complete the Access Server field to select users and servers that should have access to this server. If you leave this field blank, all users, servers, and groups have access to the server. It is more secure, however, to place groups of servers and users in this field that should have explicit rights to access the server. This field is also called the server access list.

To deny access to the server to specific users, servers, and groups, place their names in the Not access server field. You might choose to populate this field with a Deny Access group, for example. This field overrides the server access list. If a user is in both the Access server field and the Not access server field, the user will not be able to access the server.

 TIP   **You should always use groups in these fields (or any field in the Server document), rather than users' names. If you edit the field, such as to add or remove a user's name, you will have to restart the server to force the change to take affect. On the other hand, if you place a group in the field, you can edit the group and have the change take effect almost immediately.**

Place any users that should have the ability to place or create new databases on the server in the Create new databases field. If this field is left blank, all users, servers, and groups can create new databases on the server. Place any users that should have the ability to create new replicas of databases on the server in the Create replica databases field. If this field is left blank, no users, servers, or groups can create new replicas on the server.

Place any users, servers, and groups that should be able to access the server via a Passthru server in the Access this server field under the Passthru section. If this field is left blank, no users, servers, or groups may access this server using a Passthru server. In the Route through field, place the names of all users, servers, and groups that should be able to use this Domino server as a Passthru server to access other Notes servers. If this field is left blank, no users, servers, or groups can use this as a Passthru server. Use the Passthru Cause calling field similarly. Again, if the field is blank, no one can use this server for Passthru. Finally, you can specify which destination servers the users that are using this server as their Passthru server may access.

The Security tab also contains Agent and Java/COM restrictions sections. Agent restrictions are described later in the chapter. The Java/JavaScript/COM restrictions apply to the users and groups that can execute Java applications and applets, Java servlets, JavaScript, and COM applications on the server. There are two categories— restricted and unrestricted—based on the tasks that can be performed with the applications. If the fields are blank (the default), no users or groups can run these types of applications, servlets, or applets.

Database Security

One of the most important layers of security in Domino and Notes is the Access Control List (ACL). To determine who can gain access to a particular database and to determine what abilities the users or servers will have within that database, Domino provides an Access Control List for each database. The ACL determines the following three items of security:

- The users and servers that can access a database
- The functions that each user, server, or group can perform, based on privileges and user types
- Roles for the users, servers, and groups that refine the access to the database

To view the ACL and its privileges, right-click on the database icon and choose Access Control or choose File . . . Database . . . Access Control from the menus while in the database. This displays the ACL dialog box, as shown in Figure 18-13. You can also view the ACL by choosing File . . . Database . . . Access Control while a database is selected. In the ACL dialog box, you have four panels: Basics, Roles, Log, and Advanced. Figure 18-13 shows the dialog box with the Basics panel displayed.

Using the Domino Administrator, you can manage the ACL of a single database by right-clicking on the database from the Files list. To manage the ACL of multiple databases, select the databases from the Files list using the Control or Shift keys. Then expand the Database tools and select Manage ACL. Domino displays the Multi ACL Management dialog box, as shown in Figure 18-14. Using this dialog box, you can add, change, or remove users, servers, and groups from the ACLs in multiple databases.

In the Basics panel, the center of the dialog box displays the levels of access for each user, server, and group, including the -Default- access level. The -Default- access applies for any users, servers, or groups that are not explicitly listed in the ACL. In most cases, for the tightest security, the -Default- ACL should be set to No Access. This prevents any user from inadvertently gaining access.

TIP If you are using the database with the Web, you should include the user Anonymous in the ACL. When non-authenticated Web users access the database, they are given the Anonymous user's level of access. If Anonymous is not available, Domino gives the user the -Default- level of access.

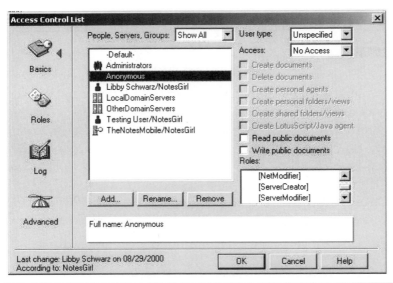

Figure 18-13   Database ACL

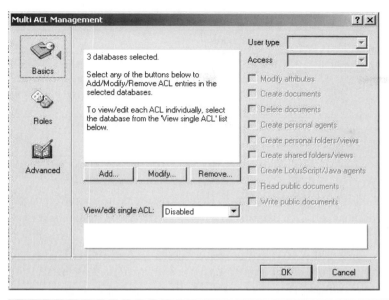

Figure 18-14 Multi ACL management

The two default groups, LocalDomainServers and OtherDomainServers, should always be listed in the ACL with an appropriate level of access. In addition, other users, groups, and servers should be listed as appropriate. Please note that in most cases it is desirable to use groups in the ACL rather than users, for ease of administration.

Often when creating an ACL, conflicts occur when users get placed in the ACL more than once. It is important to be able to know what will happen if an ACL conflict arises. For example, if you have a group that contains user Joe Smith and Joe Smith is also listed individually in the ACL, the rights given to the individual listing take precedence. Table 18-1 shows how to resolve ACL conflicts.

On the right side of the first panel, you see the User type and level of access for the users, groups, and servers listed in the center. In addition, you see the additional privileges that can be given with each level of access. User types and privileges are described in the following sections.

The Roles panel allows the database manager to refine access to and use design elements inside the database by creating and applying user roles. User roles are described later in this chapter.

The Log panel shows all additions and modifications to the ACL of this database. The log shows the name of the user (or server) that made the ACL change, the time and date of the ACL change, and what change was made.

Table 18-1   Resolving ACL Conflicts

Conflict	Resolution
A name is listed individually in an ACL and as a member of a group.	The access level assigned to the individual name takes precedence over the access level assigned to the group. This is true even if the individual access level is less than the group access level.
A name is found in two or more groups in an ACL.	The name receives the higher access level of the two groups.

The Advanced panel allows an administrator to determine the administration server for the database. The database requires that an administration server is set to participate in many of the AdminP processes, such as renaming. After you assign an administration server, you can choose whether this server can modify Reader or Author fields.

The administrator can also use this panel to enforce a consistent level of security across all replicas of the database. This prevents users from making changes to local replicas that they would not be able to make to the server replica. This also helps to maintain data consistency and accuracy across different servers, such as in a clustering scenario.

If you will be using this database on the Web, you should verify the setting in the Maximum Internet Name and Password field. Regardless of what access level a user is granted via the ACL, this field overrides the access. If Joe Smith has Manager access in the ACL, for example, but the Maximum Internet Name and Password field is set to Editor, when Joe accesses the database via HTTP, he can only have Editor access. On the other hand, if Joe has Reader access and the Maximum Internet Name and Password field is set to Editor, when Joe accesses the database via HTTP, he still only has Reader access. The Advanced panel is shown in Figure 18-15.

When using the Multi ACL management dialog box, there is no Log panel, and the Basics and Advanced panels look a bit different. Figure 18-16 shows the Basics panel on the Multi ACL management dialog box. The main difference is that the current ACL settings are not displayed by default. You can view the current ACL settings of the databases using the View/Edit Single ACL drop-down arrow.

The Advanced tab includes the same options, displayed differently, as shown in Figure 18-17.

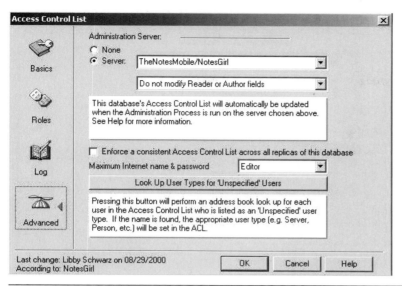

Figure 18-15 Advanced ACL

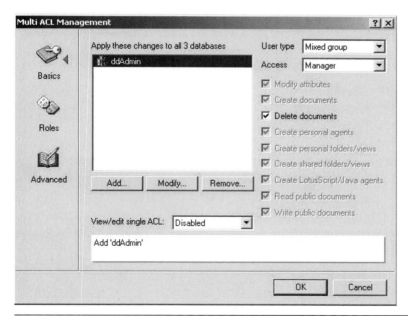

Figure 18-16 Multi ACL basics

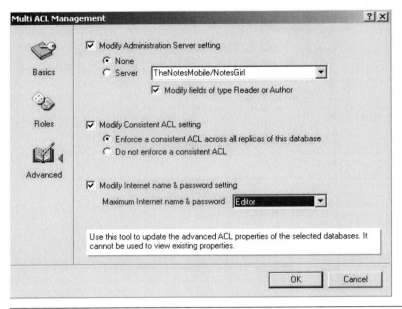

Figure 18-17   Multi ACL advanced

ACL Levels and Privileges

The ACL has seven basic levels of security, which you can then refine through assigning additional options: privileges and user types. These levels of security are all set on this panel of the dialog box. To assign a user or server to a level of the ACL, click the Add . . . button at the bottom of the Basics panel of the dialog box. You then have the option either to type in the name of the user, server, or group, or to choose a name from the Domino Directory. You may also remove or rename users, servers, and groups using the other buttons at the bottom of the dialog box.

Next, choose the Access level and privileges from the drop-down list and the check-boxes. The following paragraphs describe each level of security and the privileges that are available to refine them.

No Access

The lowest level of access to a database is No Access. *No Access* prevents a user or group from opening a database or from adding the database to their workspaces (if your organization still uses the R4-style workspace). This level of security is often recommended for the -Default- and Anonymous access to the database so that no one can gain access to data inadvertently. The only additional privileges available with No Access are the ability to read and write public documents. None of the other privileges are selected or available. With No Access, a server will not be able to replicate documents.

TIP   Public access allows users with limited access to create or view certain documents or forms. Public access to documents, forms, and folders can be granted on the Form, Document, or Folder properties InfoBoxes on the Security tab. An example of Public Access in use in Domino is the ability of users to grant other users rights to their calendars or mail files. These rights are granted by giving users with No Access the ability to read and/or write public documents.

Depositor Access

The next level of access to a database is Depositor access. *Depositor access* allows a user to add the database to the workspace and open it. In addition, Depositors can create documents in the database. They cannot, however, read or edit any documents in the database, including their own. The views in the database will appear empty to a user with Depositor access. Depositor access is useful for mail-in databases, surveys, suggestion boxes, or evaluations. The users can create an evaluation for an instructor, for example, but will not be able to see or change any of the evaluations. The Create documents option is checked by default and cannot be changed. The read and write public documents are also available and can be modified, as shown in Figure 18-18.

Reader Access

You can also assign Reader access to a database. Users with *Reader access* to a database can view documents in the database but cannot create or edit documents in the database. This type of access is useful for informational databases, such as a corporate directory or a documentation database. The additional privileges for users with Reader

Figure 18-18
Depositor access

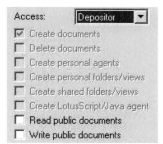

access are Create personal agents, Create personal folders/views, and Create Lotus-Script/Java agents, as shown in Figure 18-19. The other privileges are all unchecked and unchangeable, with the exception of Read public documents, which is checked and unchangeable. With Reader access, a server will not be able to send documents during replication but can receive them.

Author Access

The next level of access to a database is Author access. Users with *Author access* to a database have the ability to read documents in the database, create documents in the database, and edit the documents they create (if their name is listed in an Authors field included on the document). Author level access is the most common level of access to discussion and other databases (as opposed to Editor or above), as it helps to prevent Replication and Save Conflicts by limiting the number of users that can edit any given document. The additional privileges available for users with Author access are Create documents, Delete documents, Create personal agents, Create personal folders/views, and Create LotusScript/Java agents, as shown in Figure 18-20. The Read public docu-

Figure 18-19
Reader access

Figure 18-20
Author access

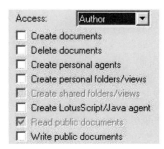

ments option is checked and unavailable for change and the Write public documents option is available for change. With Author access, a server can replicate new documents only, although it is usually better to give servers editor access.

Editor Access

Users with *Editor access* to a database start with the same level of access as users with Author access: read, create, and edit. Editor access also grants the ability to edit all documents in the database. It is usually recommended to give only one or two users this level of access to a database, to prevent Replication and Save conflicts. The Create documents option is checked by default, as shown in Figure 18-21, and is not available for change, as are both the Read and Write public documents privileges. All other privileges are available for modification for users with Editor access. This is the first level of access that can grant the ability to create shared folders and views. Servers with editor access can replicate new and changed documents.

Designer Access

Designer access gives a user all the rights allowed by Editor access, including reading, creating, and editing all documents in the database. Designers have the additional ability to create and modify all design elements in the database, including forms, views, navigators, and others. Designers have the ability to create and modify full-text indexes, About and Using this database documents, and database icons. The Create documents, Create personal agents, Create personal folders/views, and Create shared folders/views privileges are granted to users with Designer access by default and cannot be changed, as are both the Read and Write public documents privileges. The privileges for Delete documents and Create LotusScript/Java agents are available to be modified, as shown in Figure 18-22. Servers with Designer access can replicate all new and changed documents and design elements.

Figure 18-21
Editor access

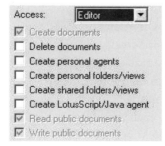

Figure 18-22
Designer access

Manager Access

Users with *Manager access* are granted all the abilities of users with Designer-level access as a base. In addition, they are the only access level of users given the ability to change the ACL of the database. Managers can also encrypt a database, delete a database, and configure the replication settings for a database. Manager access is also necessary to add and configure roles. All privileges are granted by default to managers and cannot be changed, with the exception of the Delete documents option, as shown in Figure 18-23. There should usually be only one user or group with Manager-level access, and one server with Manager-level access, to prevent problems with security and replication. Servers with Manager access can replicate all changes to the database, including new and edited documents, design elements, and the ACL.

> **NOTE** A user can check his or her access to a selected database by looking at the status bar. Click the icon to the left of the location to determine your access to the current database by displaying the Groups and Roles dialog box, shown in Figure 18-24.

If a user is not listed specifically in the ACL, either individually or within a group, they will be given the access level of the -Default- group. The -Default- group, which cannot be renamed or removed, is given Designer access by default when a new database is created. The user that creates the database is also added to the ACL automatically, with Manager access, when the database is created. Two other groups, LocalDomainServers and OtherDomainServers, are also in the ACL by default. These groups are standard Domino groups that are used in all Domino environments to determine the access level of the servers that house and replicate the databases. Both of these groups have Manager access when the database is created.

As described in the sections above, each ACL level has additional privileges. Sometimes it's easier to visualize these privileges using a table, as shown in Table 18-2.

Figure 18-23
Manager access

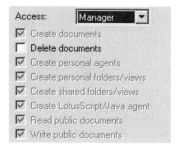

Figure 18-24
Groups and Roles
dialog box

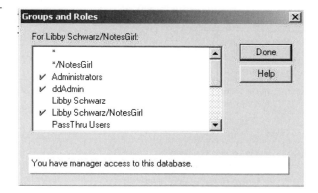

User Types

After choosing a user, group, or server, choose the appropriate user type from the drop-down list. The available user types include Unspecified, Person, Server, Mixed Group, Person Group, or Server Group. These are used to refine the access given to any entry in the ACL. Specifying the User Type ensures that, when an ID (person or server) tries to access a database, the server hosting the database matches not only the name or group membership of the ID in question, but also its User Type. The User Type is set at the top right of the ACL screen. You should specify a type for nearly every ACL entry (we'll discuss exceptions later). This is illustrated in Figure 18-25.

The User Types you can choose for your ACL entries are as follows:

- **Unspecified**   No User Type is assigned.

- **Person**   Corresponds to a single user ID and/or a Person document in the Domino Directory.

Table 18-2 Database ACL Privileges

Privilege	Purpose	Assigned by Default to
Create documents	Allows authors to create documents.	Managers, designers, editors, and depositors
Delete documents	Allows managers, designers, editors, and authors to delete documents. Authors can only delete documents they create.	No one
Create personal agents	Allows editors, authors, and readers to create personal agents in a database on a server.	Managers and designers
Create personal folders/views	Allows editors, authors, and readers to create personal folders and views in a database on a server.	Managers and designers
Create shared folders/views	Allows editors to create shared folders and views.	Managers and designers
Create LotusScript/Java agent	Allows designers, editors, authors, and readers to create LotusScript or Java agents in a database on a server.	Managers
Read public documents	Allows Depositor and No Access levels to see documents created from forms that have the property *Available to public access users* set.	Readers and above
Write public documents	Allows Depositor and No Access levels to create documents from forms that have the property *Available to public access users* set.	Editors and above

Figure 18-25
Access Control
List User Type

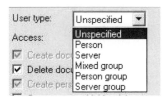

- **Server**   Corresponds to a single server ID and/or a Server document in the Domino Directory.
- **Mixed Group**   Corresponds to a group in the Domino Directory whose members include both Person and Server names.

- **Person Group**   Corresponds to a group in the Domino Directory whose members include only Person names.

- **Server Group**   Corresponds to a group in the Domino Directory whose members include only Server names.

For the most part, every ACL entry should have a User Type assigned. There are three primary exceptions to this rule:

- **Default ACL entry**   Every Access Control List must contain a Default entry that covers any user or server not explicitly or implicitly specified in the ACL (not listed by their name or as a member of a group). Because the Default entry covers any possible user or server who could access your database, it must have an Unspecified User Type.

- **Anonymous**   Databases that are available for Web access should include an ACL entry for Anonymous. Anonymous represents any Web user who accesses the database without authenticating using her user name and password as defined in the Domino Directory. The Anonymous ACL Entry must remain Unspecified, since it does not correspond to an ID or a Person, Server, or Group in the Domino Directory.

- **When using hierachical names**   For example, when using entries such as */CA/ NotesGirl in the database ACL.

Specifying User Types for your ACL entries is an added security measure that prevents possible security breaches in the Notes environment—it makes sure that the user(s) who have database access are the exact ones you intended. Let's use the following example to illustrate how neglecting to specify ACL User Types can cause problems.

You have created a Human Resources application that contains, among other things, sensitive salary information. The ACL includes the entries and access levels shown in Table 18-3, but no User Types are specified.

A user, Pat Jones/Acme, is not listed in the ACL and is not a member of the Human Resources group; he has no ability to open the database normally. However, Pat has the ability to create groups in the Domino Directory. He creates a group in the Domino

Table 18-3   Sample ACL

Default	No Access Rights
Hub01/Acme	Manager rights (read, write, and delete all documents)
John Smith/Acme	Author rights (can compose documents and edit own)
Human Resources	Editor rights (can edit any documents)

Directory called "John Smith/Acme" and puts the name Pat Jones/Acme as a member of this group. At this point, he is able to access the Human Resources database because the database ACL does not specify that "John Smith/Acme" is a single person and not a group. As you can see, this is a fairly serious breach of security, since a user who should be excluded from the application entirely is now able to access the database and view salary information.

The Domino system administrator and the application developer should work together to create and maintain the ACL for each database. Some aspects of security can affect how the application functions, which is the responsibility of the application developer or the database manager. On the other hand, some aspects of the ACL can affect the security of the Domino environment as a whole and can affect replication of the databases throughout the environment, both of which are the responsibility of the system administrator.

View and Form Access Lists

After a user is given access to a database through the ACL, the user then has to gain access to the forms and views in the database. This access can be granted or denied using View and Form access lists. View and Form access lists are primarily the responsibility of the application developer or designer of the database. The system administrator should understand this layer of security, however, to ensure that replication occurs correctly and to ensure that they understand the level of security necessary for the database.

To create form and view access lists, use the Security tab on the Form and View properties InfoBoxes. These security tabs allow the designer to refine the access given to users. In the view access list, the developer determines which users can use the view. All users with Reader access and above to a database are given access to the views by default, as shown in Figure 18-26. To refine this access, remove the check mark from the All readers and above option. You then have the option to add checkmarks next to the users, servers, and groups that should be able to gain access to the view. The users must, however, be given access to the database through the database ACL to use the view.

View access lists should not be considered true security measures for a database. A user with at least Reader access to the database could create a private view or folder to display the data. The view and folder access lists should be used in combination with other security measures for the database.

The designer can refine access to forms using a similar method. To view the form access list, open the Form properties InfoBox to the Security tab, as shown in Figure 18-27. The first option on this tab is the default read access for documents created with this form.

Figure 18-26
View access list

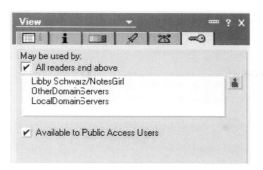

Figure 18-27
Form access list

All users with Reader access and above are given this ability by default. You refine this access by removing this ability from all users with Reader access and giving it only to certain users. Note that a user must have access to the database through the database ACL to view documents in the database. If a read access list exists, however, a user must be on that list to read documents created by the form, regardless of ACL level. The second option on the Form properties Security tab is the list of the users that can create documents with the form. By default, all users with Author access and above are given this ability. Remember that this access list is only able to refine the ACL, not change it. This means that a user with Reader access in the ACL will not be able to create a document with the form even if you have listed them in the form access create list. Similarly, if a user has Editor access or above and is able to read the documents created with this form (he is on the read access list), that user will be able to create documents with this form regardless of the create access list.

View and Form access lists not only must contain the users that should have access to the documents in the views or created by the forms, but also must contain the names of the servers that will be replicating the databases.

Document Level Security

In addition to the database security we've previously detailed, Notes also offers security at the document level. You can design a database that allows you or your users to specify particular readers and authors for given documents. This allows you to tightly control which pieces of data are available to which users, without building multiple databases.

Document-level security consists of the following:

- **Authors fields** Authors fields work in conjunction with the Author access level. As you recall from earlier in the chapter, the Author access level only allows users to edit their own documents. Document ownership is defined by the contents of any Author fields on the form. Authors fields do not supercede the higher database access levels, in that a database Editor, Designer, or Manager can still edit any document despite the presence of any Author fields.

- **Readers fields** Readers fields define who may read any given document. They work independently of ACL settings, in that even database Authors, Editors, Designers, and Managers cannot read documents that do not specify them in a Readers field.

The database designer creates the Authors and Readers fields, which rely on the field contents to include accurate Notes Names to work properly. (That is to say, the names specified in a Reader or Author field have to match to a common, abbreviated, or hierarchical name from the Domino Directory.) Authors and Readers fields can include Person and Server names, as well as valid groups from the Domino Directory. To define a Readers or Authors field on a form, define a new text field and set the field type to Readers or Authors in the Field properties InfoBox. Although you can learn more about form design in Chapter 25, "Creating Pages and Forms," Figure 18-28 illustrates how to define a Readers or Authors field on a form.

Figure 18-28
Field Type Selection
for Authors and
Readers field types

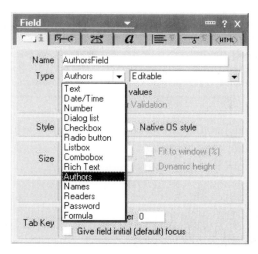

 NOTE Authors fields imply the ability to read as well as edit documents—
entries in a document's Authors field do not need to be repeated in a Readers
field in order for the document author to read the document.

Readers Field

A Readers field on a document restricts who can see the document in a database. To create a Readers field on a document, we create a field of the Readers data type on a form (see Figure 18-29). If the field is editable, the author or editors of the document can specify the users that have access to the document.

Figure 18-29
Readers Field
Properties InfoBox

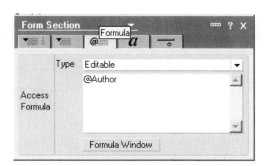

CAUTION   When you make the Readers field editable, you may want to add an additional hidden, computed Readers field that includes the names of replicating servers and administrator or database manager names. Without it, if the document author leaves your name out of the editable Readers field, you can't see the document regardless of your access to the database!

When using Readers fields, it is important to recognize that they interact with other security features of a database. Assuming a user has at least Readers access to a database, the following rules determine who can read documents:

- If a document contains a blank Readers field, all users with Readers access or above in the ACL can read the document.

- If a document contains multiple Readers fields, all users listed in all Readers fields can read the document.

- If a document uses a Form Read Access list, described earlier, all users listed in the Form Read Access list and in any of the Readers fields can read the document.

- If a document contains a Readers field and an Authors field, users that are in the Authors field can read the document, even if they are not listed in the Readers field. Authors fields are discussed in the next section.

Readers fields as well as Form Read Access lists contribute to a problem with categorized views. If a view is designed with the view property *Unread marks: Standard (compute in hierarchy)* enabled, users see unread marks next to categories that have been updated with newly created documents. Users who are unable to read some of the documents in the view may still see unread marks next to categories that when expanded contain no documents. Be aware of this potential problem when taking the exam.

Authors Field

An Authors field on a document is used to limit the users that can edit the document. This field can give users with Author access the ability to edit documents, regardless of whether they created the documents. Essentially, this type of field gives Editor access to a document without giving Editor access to the database. Keep in mind that an Authors field does not override a database's ACL and it only affects users who have Author access to a database.

To create an Authors field on a document, we create a field of the Authors data type on a form (see Figure 18-30). If the field is editable, the Author or Editor of the document can specify the users that can edit the document.

Figure 18-30
Authors Field
Properties InfoBox

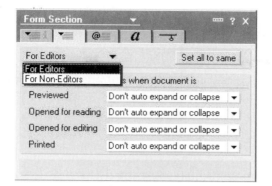

When using Authors fields, like Readers fields, it is important to recognize that they interact with other security aspects of a database. The following rules determine who can edit documents when the documents contain Authors fields:

- An Authors field does not pertain to users with Reader access or below in the database ACL. They *will not* be able to edit documents in the database.

- An Authors field does not affect users with Editor access and above in the database ACL. They *will* be able to edit documents in the database. To keep users with Editor access from editing a document, do not include them in the document's Readers field. They will be unable to see the document in the database and therefore cannot edit the document.

- In a document with multiple Authors fields, a user listed in any one of the fields can edit the document.

- In a document with an Authors field, if the field is blank, only users with Editor access or above in the database ACL will be able to edit the document. If a user has Author access to a database and wants to edit a document they create, their name *must* be in an Authors field on the document. To ensure the creator of a document can edit the documents they create, place a *computed when composed* field on the form with the formula @UserName.

When to Use Readers and Authors Fields

Readers and Authors fields allow you and your database users to tune information access finely within a single database. Sensitive documents can be stored in a publicly accessed database but remain available for view only by appropriate persons. Work groups can share edit capabilities on departmental documents but protect their documents from editing by others. Readers and Authors fields can extend and enhance the functionality of your databases in many ways:

- For the employee review application mentioned at the beginning of the chapter, Readers fields would be used to ensure that employees couldn't read each other's review documents. Authors fields would ensure that managers might edit their team members' forms in order to complete the review process.

- In databases used for the storage of common information sets (such as a Document Library database), editable Authors fields allow users to specify exactly who may edit their documents.

- In workflow databases, dynamic Authors fields ensure that at each stage in the approval routing process, only the designated person may approve the document.

 NOTE Readers fields are the only secure way to prevent access to documents within a database. While database designers can simulate this functionality by using limited-access views or forms, these methods do not ensure the privacy of the information contained in the documents. Users can build private views that circumvent form-level or view-level security measures.

Common Pitfalls with Document Level Security

Although Readers and Authors fields offer much functionality, there are a few points to be aware of when using them in your database design.

- Users *cannot see* a document that contains a Readers field that does not include their names. This applies to servers as well as end users. This means that if server names (or groups containing server names) are not included in a document's Readers field, the server will not be able to see that document to replicate it or run agents on it. This can cause unexpected results and unusual replication behavior. To prevent this, it is a good design practice to add an additional, hidden Readers field containing *LocalDomainServers*, *NotesAdministrators*, and/or other groups as appropriate, in order to ensure proper replication and the ability to troubleshoot the application.

- Categorized views may exhibit unusual behavior when accessed by users who do not have access to read some of the documents in the view. Because the view is indexed at the server, the view categories are built from the documents the server may read. The end-user still sees these categories in the view, even though the documents in the categories do not appear underneath the categories (see Figure 18-31). For more information on categorized views, refer to Chapter 29, "Creating Navigation."

Figure 18-31
Categorized view
behavior when user
cannot see all
documents

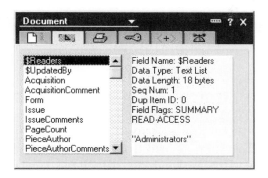

- Readers and Authors fields must contain valid Lotus Notes names to function properly. This means that if your users are allowed to choose their own document authors or readerss, they should use the Address Dialog helper in order to properly specify the users they intend.

- Readers and Authors fields can contain Notes names that are common or abbreviated. This means that a Readers or Authors field containing a common name (John E. Smith) will not distinguish between John E. Smith/Exec/Acme and John E. Smith/Marketing/Acme. This also means that unless a database specifies an administration server with the correct options (see earlier in the chapter), users who go through a name or OU change may lose access to documents they created before the change.

If a document is created from a form with a Form Read Access list, a $Readers field is added to the document. The value of the $Readers field is the form's read access list. In other words, only users, groups, and servers contained in a document's $Readers field can read the document or see the document in the database. We can see the contents of a $Readers field from the Fields tab of the Document properties InfoBox (see Figure 18-32).

We can also see a list of authorized Readers of a document by looking at the Security tab of the Document properties InfoBox. Later in the chapter, we'll see how to use the InfoBox to modify the list of Readers for a particular document.

Figure 18-32
$Readers Field
on Document
properties InfoBox

We can also see actual editors, as opposed to allowable editors, of a document if the document contains an Authors field. The $UpdatedBy field on a document automatically stores the names of users who have edited the document. View the contents of the $UpdatedBy field from the Fields tab of the Document properties InfoBox (see Figure 18-33). If the document contains an Authors field, users can hold their mouse pointer on the Authors field to view a text pop-up displaying the contents of the $UpdatedBy field.

Figure 18-33
$UpdatedBy Field
on Document
properties InfoBox

Changing Document Security

Now that we know how to check the security of a document, let's find out how to modify the security. In the next few sections, we will discuss each of the four methods of controlling document access mentioned earlier. Almost all of these security methods refine the ACL, not override it. For example, including someone with Depositor access in a Form Read Access list does not allow that person to view documents in the database. Keep this simple fact in mind for the exam.

Form Read Access

By default, anyone with at least Readers access can read documents in a database. The Form Read Access list determines which users or group of users can read documents created by a specific form. This method applies to every document created with the form. A user not in the list, regardless of ACL level, will not be able to see these documents in the database. Remember to include your replicating servers in the list. Otherwise, the documents will not be replicated because the servers can't "see" them.

To modify the Form Read Access list, click the Security tab in the Form properties InfoBox (see Figure 18-34). Remove the checkmark from the *All Readers and above* option below *Default read access for documents created with this form*. Click the *Add read access* icon to select each user, group, server, and role you want to include in the read access list. As we mentioned earlier, all documents created with this form will contain a $Readers field that contains a list of allowable readers.

Figure 18-34
Form Read
Access list

We should point out that the Author or Editor of a document can also determine who can read the document. On the Security tab of the Document properties InfoBox, read access to a document can be modified with the *Who can read this document* option. It works like the form property in that you can select the users, groups, servers, and roles to whom you want to give Read ability to the document.

Form Create Access

By default, anyone with at least Author access can create documents in a database. The Form Create Access list determines which users or group of users can create documents using a specific form. A user not in the list, regardless of ACL level, will not be able to see the form from the Create menu. A database designed with an action button that creates a document using the restricted form will display an error message to a user not listed in the Form Create Access list (see Figure 18-35) when they click the action. Remember that the Form Create Access list only refines the ACL; it doesn't override it. This means that a user with Readers access in the ACL included in the Form Create Access list will not be able to create a document with the form.

To modify the Form Create Access list, click the Security tab in the Form properties InfoBox. Remove the checkmark from the *All authors and above* option below *Who can create documents with this form*. Click the *Add create access* icon to select each user, group, server, and role you want to include in the Form Create Access list.

Figure 18-35
Form Create Access
error message

Secured Sections

Another element that can be considered part of document security is access-controlled sections. Sections in general are used to organize pages and forms. A section groups text, graphics, and fields (on forms only) into an area that can collapse into a single line. In addition, sections provide a way for the designer to collapse information that is not necessary or interesting to all users. There are two types of sections: Standard sections and Controlled Access. Pages can only have Standard sections; however, forms can accommodate both types of sections.

Standard Sections

To create a section, select the elements to be placed in the section and choose Create . . . Section from the menus. On a form, where you have a choice of section types, you choose Create . . . Section . . . Standard. After you create a section, the first line of text appears as the section title automatically, and the section will be collapsed and displayed with a small triangle to the left of the section called a *twistie*. To expand or collapse the section, click the blue twistie (it looks like a sideways triangle) to the left of the section title. Sections, like everything else, have properties that govern the way they act and appear.

Controlled Access Sections

A controlled access section functions much like a standard section, in that it organizes the text and other elements on a form and limits the length of the form. It has the additional function of limiting the users that can edit the fields in a section. Note that you may only use Controlled Access sections on forms. The tabs in the InfoBox for Controlled Access sections are displayed in Figure 18-36. Note that this InfoBox may be called the form Section InfoBox in Designer. The Standard section InfoBox will just be called Section.

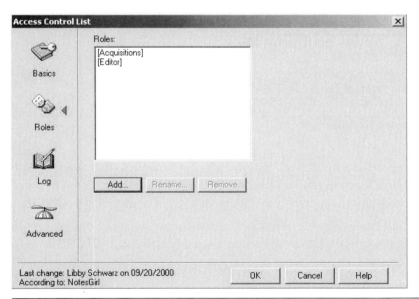

Figure 18-36 Controlled Access Section properties

- The *Section Title and Border* tab has similar elements to the same tab for the Standard section, including *Title Text*, *Border Style*, and *Border Color* fields. Note that there is also a field for a *Section Field Name*. Use this field only if the application will be used with v3 as well as R4 and R5 clients.

- The *Expand/Collapse* tab determines how the section appears by default when opened, edited, previewed, or printed. You can also set the auto expand or collapse differently for Editors and Non-Editors, using the drop-down selection at the top right, as shown in Figure 18-37. Use the *Set All to Same* button to set all the view options at once.

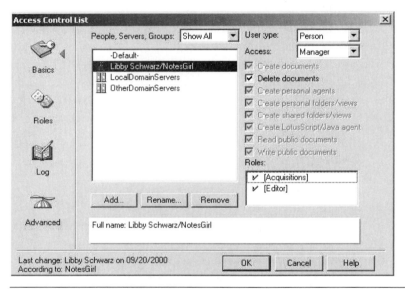

Figure 18-37   Expand/Collapse

- The *Formula* tab defines the Access formula, which determines who Notes considers an Editor. The formula can be Editable, Computed for Display, or Computed when Composed, and must resolve to a name or a list of names.

- The *Font* tab and *Paragraph Hide When* tab offer the same basic options as they do on the Standard section InfoBox. There are a few options, such as Preview only, removed in Controlled Access Sections.

Note that anyone with Reader access to the database can read the information in a Controlled Access section unless prevented by Hide-When options. In addition, the Controlled Access formula will not override the Access Control List for the database.

User Roles

Using and creating user roles can further refine the security for an application. User roles are created in the ACL dialog box (as opposed to groups, which are created in the Domino Directory) and allow the designer to group users, servers, and groups that should have similar rights and abilities within a specific database. Roles provide the following advantages to the designer or manager of a database:

- Roles help provide centralized security. Instead of changing user names in every form or view access list, Readers or Authors field, and section within a database, designers and database managers change the users within a particular role or change the access of the role.

- Roles are listed in the ACL of a database, ensuring that when changes are made to the security of the database, the changes take effect in the design elements. If the security were all done at the level of the design elements, many database managers and designers might neglect to update the security correctly.

- Roles are in the databases, rather than in the Domino Directory. This enables the administrator to limit the number of groups placed in the Domino Directory for special access within databases. In addition, most developers do not have access to the Domino Directory. Roles let developers do many of the same things without this additional access.

To create a role, open the database Access Control dialog box to the Roles panel, as shown in Figure 18-38. To add a new role to the database, click Add . . . and type in the name of the role that you want to add. The name can be up to 15 characters. You can also rename or remove user roles from the database's ACL from this panel on the dialog box. The database manager can add up to 75 roles to the database.

After creating the user roles, you must apply those roles to the users, servers, and groups listed in the database ACL. To apply a role to a user, open the Basics panel on the ACL dialog box, as shown in Figure 18-39. Select the user and choose the role or roles that the user should have from the Roles list on the right-hand side of the dialog box. This will associate this user role with the selected user, server, or group.

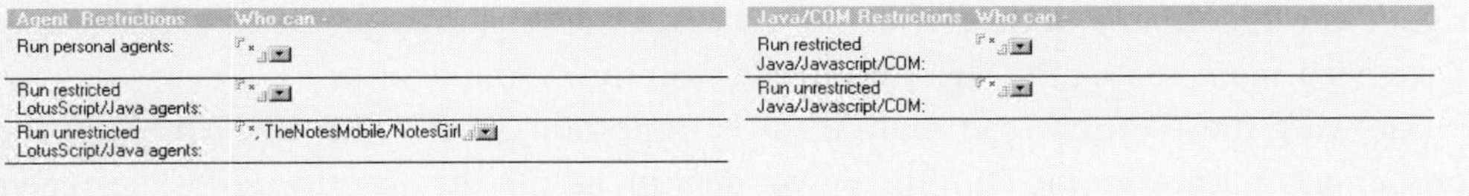

Figure 18-38 Database roles

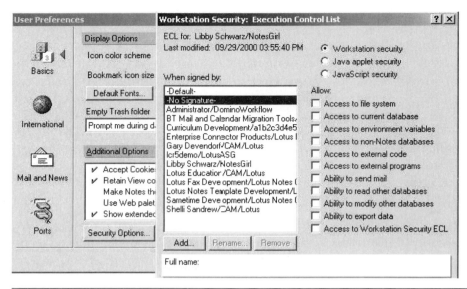

Figure 18-39   Assigning a role

After creating and applying user roles, the user roles must be given functions within the database. User roles can be used in the view and form access lists, in Readers or Authors fields, and in section access lists. The system administrator or Manager of the database will create and apply user roles in the access control list; however, the database designer will give the roles their function in the database. If you choose to implement this level of security, the system administrator and the database application developer should work together to plan the security.

Agent Security

Developers and administrators often create agents to automate tasks in a database. When agents run manually (that is, you click a button while in the database to activate the agent), they run under the ID currently in use—usually yours. When an agent runs automatically, based on a schedule or on a database event, it runs under the ID that signed the agent. This can either be the ID that last saved the agent, or the agent may have been signed using the Sign tool in the Domino Administrator.

Knowing the ID used to run an agent is important so that you can configure the proper agent access in the Domino Server document. On the Security tab of the Server document, shown in Figure 18-40, you can configure which users can run various types of agents, in the Agent Restrictions section.

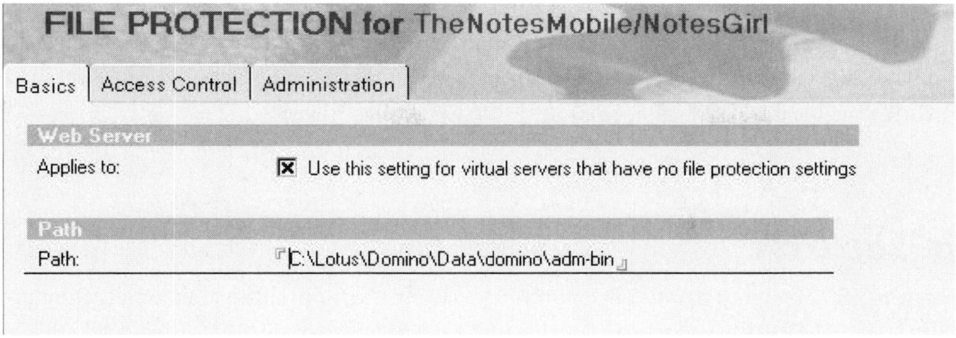

Figure 18-40 Agent restrictions

In the Run Personal Agents field, you would place users and groups that should be able to run personal agents. If the field is blank (the default), all users can run personal agents. In the Run Restricted LotusScript/Java Agents field, place the users that can run this type of agent. This type of agent uses a subset of LotusScript and Java features, especially excluding agents that access the file system or the system time. If the field is blank (the default), no users can run restricted LotusScript/Java agents, except the users that are listed in the Run Unrestricted LotusScript/Java agents. In the Run Unrestricted LotusScript/Java agents field, place the names of users that can run agents that include any LotusScript or Java features. If this field is blank (the default), no users can run this type of agent.

You can sign these agents (just as you can sign any design element in the database) with a special ID or the server's ID, so that you can limit the number of users that need to be listed in these fields. To sign an agent, you can open the agent while using the ID that you want to use to sign the agent. Save the agent and the signature will be replaced.

You can also sign the agent using the Sign tool. Open the Domino Administrator to the Files tab while logged in with the appropriate ID file. Select the database(s) that contains agents you want to sign. Expand the Database tools and choose Sign. In the Sign Database dialog box, select Agents under the All documents of type drop-down list. Click OK to replace the current signature with a signature for the current ID file.

Signing agents also affects how they run with workstation Execution Control Lists, or ECLs. ECLs restrict agents or scripts that run on a workstation (as opposed to the agents that run on the server, which is what the Agent security fields restrict). You can access and modify the ECL from the File . . . Preferences . . . User Preferences menu. On the Basics tab of the User Preferences dialog box, select the Security Options button to display the Workstation Security: Execution Control List dialog box. In the top right-hand side of the dialog box, select the workstation, Java applet, or JavaScript security radio buttons. In the When Signed By field, add or remove any names that should be able to run scripts, applets, or agents on your workstation. Using the checkboxes under the

Allow section, select the specific types of scripts, applets, and agents that each user can run, based on what the script, applet, or agent will access or modify. You can also set execution levels for the Default (a script, applet, or agent with an unlisted signature would run under this level of access) and -No Signature- users.

File Security

In Domino R5, you can apply additional security to non-database files when they are accessed via HTTP. This security is applied to CGI files/scripts, HTML files, and JPG or GIF graphics files. To apply access control security protection to these files, create File Protection documents.

To create a File Protection document, open the Server document or Virtual Server document to which you want to apply the protection. Select the Web action button and choose to Create File Protection. Domino displays the File Protection document.

On the Basics tab, define the files to protect in the Path field. The path is relative to the server's data directory and can be a file, a directory, or a drive. If you're protecting files on a virtual server, you must also enter the IP address of the virtual server.

On the Access Control tab, click the Set/Modify Access Control List button. Use the drop-down arrow next to the Name field to select users and groups from the Domino Directory. The -Default- user is given No Access automatically. Then select the level of access for each user from the following options:

- No Access
- Read/Execute (GET method)
- Read/Write/Execute (POST and GET method)

GET allows users to open files and start programs and is the most common access level granted. Use POST for directories that contain CGI scripts, as this method is used to send data to CGI programs.

After you save and close the document, you must restart the HTTP task for the protection document to take effect. You can type **TELL HTTP RESTART** as an easy way to restart the task.

You can view the File Protection documents for your server(s) from the Configuration tab of the Domino Administrator. Expand the Web section and open the Web Server Configuration view. File Protection documents are listed under the servers to which they apply.

Review Questions

1. Authentication will be successful in which situations?
   A. The same OU certifier created the user and server.
   B. The same O certifier created the user and server.
   C. The server was registered by Houston/NotesGirl and the user was registered by Accounting/Dallas/NotesGirl.
   D. The server was registered by Houston/ACME and the user was registered by Houston/NotesGirl.

2. Which of the following users could edit documents they had created in the database?
   A. Joe has Editor access. His name is not listed in the Authors field.
   B. Susie has Author access. Her name is not listed in the Authors field
   C. Lizzy has Author access. Her name is listed in the Authors field.
   D. George has Reader access. His name is listed in the Authors field.

3. Jane is rolling out a database to Server 1. It has five scheduled agents. Only the AgentUser group (which contains a default user name—Company AgentUser—and the servers' names) can run agents on the server. What does Jane need to do before deploying the database?
   A. Add her name to the Run agents fields in the Server document.
   B. Add her name to the AgentUser Group.
   C. Sign the agents in the database with the Company AgentUser ID.
   D. Nothing. Just roll out the database.

4. Which of the following is required for Lydia to authenticate with Server 1 using a Web client?
   A. User name and Web password
   B. User name and Internet password
   C. User ID file and Web password
   D. User ID file and Internet password

5. Which of the following is required for Mary to authenticate with Server 1 using a Notes client?
   A. User ID file and password
   B. User name and password
   C. User ID file signed with the same certifier as the server
   D. User name

6. Kitty has tried to access the Domino Web server using her short name KittyB. She knows that she is using the right password but is not being authenticated. What might be the problem?

   A. She does not have an ID file.

   B. The server is using the $LDAPCN view for authentication.

   C. The server is using the $Users view for authentication.

   D. She can never authenticate with the short name.

7. The ACL for DB1.NSF has -Default- as Author, Fitz as Designer, and Anonymous as Reader. The Maximum Internet Name and Password is Editor. When Fitz accesses the database using Internet Explorer and authenticates, what access does he have?

   A. Author

   B. Designer

   C. Reader

   D. Editor

8. The ACL for DB1.NSF has -Default- as Author, Georgiana as Designer, and Anonymous as Reader. The Maximum Internet Name and Password is Editor. When Georgiana accesses the database using Internet Explorer but does not authenticate, what access does she have?

   A. Author

   B. Designer

   C. Reader

   D. Editor

9. Which of the following is true about session-based authentication?

   A. You have to restart the Domino server after you enable it.

   B. You have to restart the HTTP task after you enable it.

   C. It alters the hidden view that Domino uses for authentication.

   D. You can configure the timeout interval in a Configuration document.

10. Meg is in the ACL of DB1 with Author access. She is also a member of the Administrators group, which has Manager access. Finally, she is also a member of the Sales Associates group, with Reader access. What access does she end up with?

    A. Author

    B. Manager

    C. Reader

    D. Editor

Review Answers

1. All except **D** are correct.   Choices **A**, **B**, and **C** all provide scenarios in which the user and server share a certificate in common.

2. **A** and **C** are correct.   A user with Editor access does not need to be listed in an Authors field. Users with Author access can edit their own documents if they are listed in an Authors field in that document. Users with Reader access cannot edit documents.

3. **C** is correct.   She should sign the agents with the ID of a user listed in the group that is listed in the agent access list.

4. **B** is correct.   It requires her user name and the Internet password field.

5. **C** is correct.   She needs an ID file that has a certificate in common with the server.

6. **B** is correct.   By default, Domino uses the $Users view. For more security, you can configure it to use the $LDAPCN view, but when you do, you can no longer use the short name.

7. **D** is correct.   Fitz's access is overridden by the Maximum Internet name and password field.

8. **C** is correct.   If she does not authenticate, and accesses via a Web client, she gets the access assigned to Anonymous.

9. **B** is correct.   You must restart the HTTP task to enable it.

10. **A** is correct.   If a user is listed in a group and individually, the user gets the rights assigned to them individually.

Integrating with Host Data

You should be able to answer questions based on the following objectives after reading this chapter:

- Integrate with host data
- Integrate with host data: batch versus live
- Integrate with host data: ODBC
- Integrate with host data: reading and writing
- Integrate with host data: SQL
- Maintain data integrity
- Maintain data integrity: adding items to a database
- Maintain data integrity: changing items in a database
- Maintain data integrity: data duplication
- Maintain data integrity: data percolation
- Maintain data integrity: deleting items from a database

One of the most common issues that you face as you roll out applications is making sure that you plan for any connections outside of Notes and Domino that are coded into the application. It is common to use the enterprise connectors provided with Domino, including DECS and LEI to create connectivity between your Domino Application and an external data source. Note that there are other options, such as Lotus-Script Extensions for Lotus Connectors and ESB, but these are not covered on the exam. Each of these solutions uses Domino (Lotus) Connectors as a base, to determine the platforms that are possible on the back end. DECS provides the real-time or live connection to host data. LEI provides batch, or scheduled, connections to the back-end data. This chapter concentrate on DECS, as it is provided with Domino R5, although we will also note the other integration options. In addition, keep in mind that the purpose here is to plan your deployment based on how these elements are integrated into your applications, not to learn how to integrate them. There are other exams and books that cover that topic in greater detail.

Domino Connectors

Also known as Lotus Connectors, these are the tools that work with DECS, LEI, and the LotusScript Extensions to provide the connection to the back-end data. The three elements provided by the connector are

- Connection
- Authentication
- Translation

Lotus has connectors for a variety of systems, some of which are included with Domino and some of which you can obtain separately. Examples of systems you can connect to include the following:

- DB2, Oracle, Sybase, files, EDA/SQL, and ODBC connectors are included with Domino/Notes.
- PeopleSoft (7.0 and 7.5), SAP R/3 1.5, JD Edwards, Oracle Applications, and OLE DB (MS SQL Server 7) connectors can be obtained separately from Lotus or Lotus's business partners.

Each type of connector has some requirements to ensure that the connectivity is successful. These requirements include software installed on the physical machine with the Domino, DECS, or LEI server, software installed on the physical machine with the source server, user name, password, and others. Some additional requirement examples for the built-in connectors are described in the following section.

ODBC

The following are the requirements for ODBC connectivity to function:

- You must have installed an appropriate ODBC driver for the operating system. Note that the driver must be 32-bit on NT and OS/2.

- The ODBC driver must be thread-safe.
- The ODBC Administrator must be present.
- There must be ODBC data sources defined in the ODBC Administrator.
- You must have already installed client software. For example, if you want to connect to DB2 through ODBC, you must have installed both ODBC and the DB2 client.

EDA/SQL

The following are the requirements for EDA/SQL connectivity to function:

- The connection requires EDA/Client software for the host operating system. The EDA/Client version must be Release 3.2 or later and must be 32-bit on Windows NT and OS/2.
- An EDA server on the platform where the EDA supported database resides.
- Connectivity to the EDA server.

Oracle

The following are the requirements for Oracle connectivity to function:

- If installing on an OS/2-based server, you need Oracle SQL*Net version 2.
- If installing on a Windows NT-based server, you need Oracle SQL*Net version 1 or 2.
  - In either case, SQL*Net must be the same version as SQL*Net installed on the Oracle data server.
  - A network connection must exist between the server machine and the Oracle data server machine via SQL*Net.

DB2

When making a connection to DB2, the connectivity software needed depends on the operating system platform. You will need the following:

- IBM eNetwork Communications Server for your operating system platform (see **www.software.ibm.com/enetwork/commserver** for more information).
- DB2 Enterprise Edition or DB2 CAE (Client Application Enabler) version 2.1.2 or later.

- To connect to DB2 on an AS/400 or mainframe, a DDCS gateway must be installed. No additional software is required on the AS/400. DB2/400 is part of the base operating system on the AS/400 and can be both the target of DB2 connection requests from other platforms (NT, OS/2, UNIX), and a source of requests for DB2 connections to other DB2 databases in the network.

LCTEST

Before you begin to configure DECS or LEI, you will want to be certain that your connection to the remote data source is working. LCTEST is a tool that tests system connectivity to the following data sources:

- DB2
- EDA/SQL
- ODBC (Open Database Connectivity)
- Oracle
- Sybase

To run LCTEST, first find the LCTEST.EXE program for you operating system platform. The file should be located in the Domino program directory. The following are the program file names for the associated operating systems:

- Windows 95/NT on Win32 uses NLCTEST.EXE
- OS/2 uses ILCTEST.EXE
- Windows NT/Alpha uses ALCTEST.EXE

After you locate the application, double-click to launch the tester. The tester lets you select the back-end you want to connect to. You may then be prompted for more information, depending on the source.

DECS

Domino Enterprise Connection Services (DECS) is a new service. It is included with Domino R5 and available for Domino 4.6.3 and later. DECS provides real-time connectivity to relational databases on the back-end. DECS uses two main elements to provide this link:

- DECS server add-in task

- DECS administrator database (DECSADMIN.NSF)

One of the benefits of DECS is that the DECS Administrator database allows easy forms-based connections and links between the Domino application and the back-end source. The connectivity can be provided to both Notes clients and Web clients.

First, the developer will create an application that requires connectivity to the source data. Then you install the DECS components and create a connection and an activity. With the activity, you create mappings that define where back-end data needs to be linked to the application.

When you install a Domino server, the DECS components are selected for installation by default. You can verify that the component is selected by doing a customized installation. If you do not install the DECS component when you install the server, you must install the DECS components from the installation media to use DECS.

When you are ready to start the DECS task, you can type LOAD DECS at the server console. You can also add DECS to the ServerTasks= line in the NOTES.INI file.

To verify that the DECS task is running on the server, you can use the SH TA command at the server console. When you first start the DECS server task, you can see the task load and any automatically-starting tasks begin, as shown in Figure 19-1.

When the DECS server task is first loaded, it creates the DECS Administrator database. This database defines the forms and fields in your Domino applications that you want to complete with external data. You also use this database to define when to intercept Notes/Domino document events, such as an open, delete, or update. You can open the database from the Domino Administrator or Notes client. To access the database from Domino Administrator, choose the Configuration tab. You should be able to expand the DECS Administrator views on the left side, as shown in Figure 19-2.

You can also open the DECS Administrator database directly from the Notes client by choosing DECSADM.NSF from the File . . . Database . . . Open dialog box.

```
> load decs
10/03/2000 06:02:57 PM  DECS Server started
10/03/2000 06:03:11 PM  DECS: Activity started: test
>
```

Figure 19-1   DECS server task running on the server

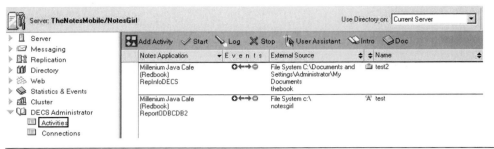

Figure 19-2   Open DECS Administrator from the Domino Administrator

DECS Administrator

Within the DECS Administrator database, you complete two types of documents: connections and activities. Connection documents define the following elements:

- The type of source to connect to.
- The name of the data source, such as the remote server or database.
- The user name and password necessary to connect to the remote resource.
- Selection type, such as whether to connect to a view, table, or procedure on the remote system.
- Additional details about the view, table, or procedure selected. You need to define the connectivity information before you try to complete this data, as DECS tries to make the connection to allow you to select specific details.

NOTE The Connection document described here is different than the routing or replication connection described in other chapters.

These details are defined slightly differently for each connection type. A Sybase connection, for example, has you define both a SQL Server and database name. Figure 19-3 shows an example of a DB2 Connection document. Domino names the connection automatically, following internal conventions. If a user name was supplied, it is indicated in the Connections view in parentheses.

You can create connections to the following back-end systems by default:

- DB2
- EDA/SQL

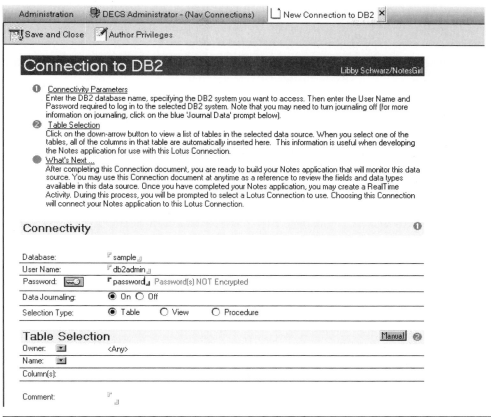

Figure 19-3 Create a DB2 Connection document

- File system
- ODBC
- Oracle
- Sybase

To create connections to other systems, you may need to obtain a separate Domino Connector tool to work with the DECS system. In addition, you may need to install specific software on your Domino server to ensure that there is connectivity between the two systems.

After you create a connection to a specific back-end source, you can create an Activity. Use the Activity document to determine the mapping between your Domino application and the back-end source, via the connection you already created. Note that before you create an Activity document, you should have created and tested the connection to the data source as well as an appropriate Domino application to contain the data.

To create an Activity, use the Activities view of the DECS Administrator database. Choose the Add Activity action button. The DECS Administrator displays the RealTime Activity document, as shown in Figure 19-4.

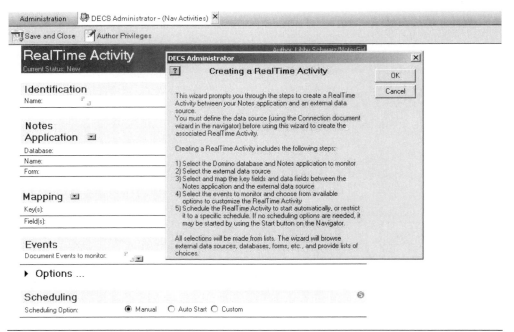

Figure 19-4   RealTime Activity document

First, give the Activity a name that you will be able to use to identify it later. Next, click the drop-down arrow next to the Notes Application section to choose the Domino application that should receive the data. After you select a Domino application, DECS displays the forms available in the application. Select the form that you want to use to obtain the data.

Next, select a Connection to use. You can select the drop-down arrow in the Lotus Connection section to choose a connection that already exists, from the Connections view. You can also click the New button in the same section to create a new Connection document. Even if you choose to create a new connection, you will still have to select the connection to use, as shown in Figure 19-5.

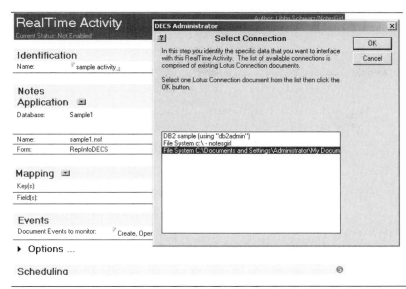

Figure 19-5 Select a connection to use.

Next, complete the Mapping section. The drop-down arrow next to the Mapping section title displays the Key and Data Field mapping dialog box. In the Key section, select fields from the Domino database and the external source to serve as the keys. The key is the field (or fields) used to identify the data uniquely. It should be an element that is unique to the item, such as an ID number or First and Last name fields. The number of key fields must be the same for both the Domino application and the external data source.

After selecting the key or keys, you can select the data fields to map to each other. Any field not used as a key is available to be selected in this section. As with keys, you must select the same number of data fields on the Domino application and the external data source. Selecting the keys and data fields is shown in Figure 19-6.

The next section to complete in the Activity document is the Events section. In this section, select the Domino document events to monitor, including Create, Open, Update, and Delete, as shown in Figure 19-7. After selecting the events to monitor, you can also choose specific details or options. There are general options, which apply to all events, as well as specific options for each event.

To edit the options, expand the Options . . . section, as shown in Figure 19-8. While you can often leave the defaults in these fields, you may choose to complete some of the fields that especially deal with data integrity. Table 19-1 lists these fields and their options.

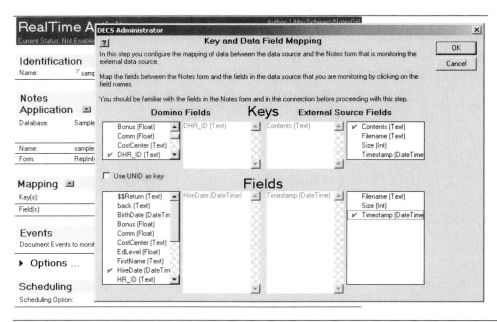

Figure 19-6   Select key and data field mappings.

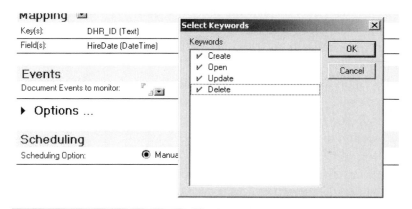

Figure 19-7   Choose the event to monitor.

▼ Options ...

Figure 19-8 RealTime Activity Options section

Table 19-1 RealTime Activity Options

Field Name	Field Data
Monitor Order	Use this field if you're using more than one RealTime activity for a single Notes form in an application.
Max. Connections	Use this field to determine how many connections can be made to a database simultaneously.
Form Override	By default, only the specified form is monitored for events. Use this field to indicate that you want all fields to be monitored.
Filter Formula	You can use this field to insert a formula to limit the documents that will be processed by the RealTime Activity document.
Multi-value data	Use this field to specify that non-key fields are to be considered multi-value fields.

continued

Table 19-1   RealTime Activity Options (*continued*)

Field Name	Field Data
Data integrity	Options in the data-integrity field are to prevent both precision and data loss, allow precision loss, and allow precision loss and truncation of text (excluding key fields). This specifies what should be done for losses during conversion. The first option specifies to write an error to the log for any conversion that will result in loss. The second option does not write errors in numerical or date-time fields. The final option allows not only data loss, but also truncating of data to fit in application fields.
Trim-trailing spaces	Options in this field include the following: Trim spaces on all fields, Trim spaces on all non-key fields, and Do not trim spaces on any fields.
Data Storage	Options in this field include the following: Remove all real-time fields from documents, Leave all real-time fields in documents, and Leave selected real-time fields in documents. This field determines which real-time fields that are created by the process are stored in the database when it is saved to disk.
Caching	You will probably want to check the Disable option for this field for Real-Time activities. This determines whether the HTTP task will cache documents effected by the RealTime activity documents after requests by Web clients.
Pre-create formula	Use this field to add a formula to be evaluated before document data is stored in the connection.
Stored procedure	Use this option to execute a stored procedure in the connection; it is used to store data that has been entered into the document.
Pre-open formula	Use this field to add a formula to be evaluated before document data is retrieved from the connection.
Post-open formula	Use this field to add a formula to be evaluated after document data is retrieved from the connection.
Stored procedure	Use this option to execute a stored procedure in the connection; it is used to determine the data retrieved into the document.
Missing External Records	If no matching record is found in the connection when opening a document, use this field to determine what Domino should do. Options include the following: Create Record, Generate Error, or Ignore.
Pre-update formula	Use this field to add a formula to be evaluated before document data is saved to the connection.
Stored procedure	Use this option to execute a stored procedure in the connection; it is used to store the changed data in the document.

continued

Table 19-1   RealTime Activity Options (*continued*)

Field Name	Field Data
Conflict Detection	Option ensures that connection data hasn't changed. If it has, the update to the connection fails.
Field Level Updates	This option ensures that only fields that correspond to changed fields in the Domino application are updated.
Key Field Updates	The options in this field are Block, Delete/Insert, or Ignore. This option determines what happens if data in key fields changes.
Pre-delete formula	Use this field to add a formula to be evaluated before document data is removed from the connection.
Stored Procedure	Use this option to execute a stored procedure in the connection; it is used to remove the data from the document.

The final option in the RealTime activity document is the Scheduling section, as shown in Figure 19-9. Options include a manual start, AutoStart, and Custom. Manual activities can be started and stopped using the action buttons in the navigator or on the action button bar. AutoStart activities start and stop with the Domino server. If you select Custom, the form displays additional options for Run Time and days.

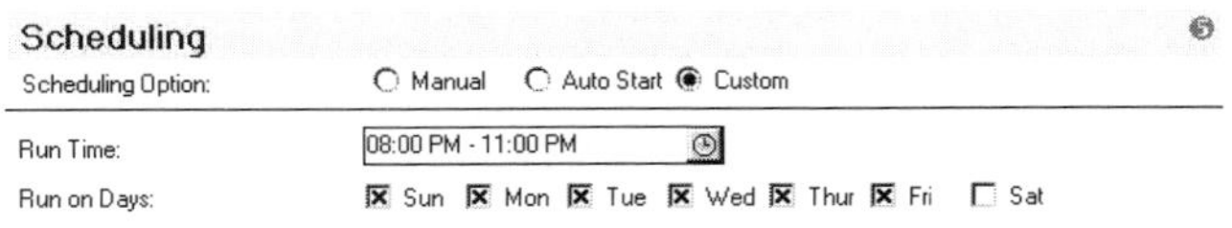

Figure 19-9
Scheduling section

Note that we described the manual method of creating the required documents. You can also enable the User Assistant, which runs a wizard to help you create the necessary connections and activities. Figure 19-10 shows the User Assistant option in the database navigator.

After you have created both Connection and Activity documents, you need to initialize the keys and populate the Domino application with the data from the external data source. To do this, you may need to first sign the DECS Administrator database, or at least the Agents, so that the Initialize Keys agent can run on the server. To run the agent against a particular activity, open the Activities view. Select the activity you want to initialize and select Actions . . . Initialize Keys from the menus. This creates a document for each unique key found in the external data source.

Figure 19-10
User Assistant
option enabled

DECS with Domino Infrastructure

There are some Domino infrastructure elements that you may choose to install that can affect DECS. DECS operates on all server platforms, although you should verify that as new platforms are released or supported by Domino. For example, the Linux platform was not supported for DECS in its original release. DECS can be used by both Web and Notes clients, based on how the Domino application is created. You can choose to run DECS on a single server and replicate data to the application on other servers if you choose to store the data in the application. Otherwise, you will need to run DECS on any server that needs access to the data.

DECS allows the real-time queries with both Notes and Web clients. You may need to allow the user to type in the key-field value manually in the application and then perform a real-time query to the back-end source.

LEI

Lotus Enterprise Integrator (LEI) was formerly known as NotesPump. It provides the same types of connectivity to enterprise sources as DECS, but on a scheduled or event-driven basis rather than the real-time activity that DECS provides. Note, however, that LEI does contain a RealTime Notes Activity option that does provide real-time connectivity and is the equivalent to DECS.

LEI uses the following components:

- LEI server

- LEI Development Client

- LEI databases (including the LEI Administrator database, LEI Log database, Script Vault, and the LEI documentation)

Installing LEI

LEI is installed separately from the Domino server, unlike DECS. In addition, you do not have to install LEI on the same physical machine as the Domino server. If you do choose to install on the same machine as the server, however, make sure the Domino server is not running when you do the install. On the other hand, if you are installing them on separate machines, the Domino server must be running while you install LEI.

When you perform the installation, choose whether this is the first LEI server, whether you want to only install the development client, or whether to install an additional LEI server into an existing cluster. In LEI, a cluster refers to LEI servers that are controlled from the same administration application.

Next, type the name of the LEI server and the name of the Domino server where the LEI Administrator database resides, either on the same physical machine or a different machine. The LEI installation program will prompt you to indicate whether you are installing LEI on the same machine with the Domino server or not.

Other choices you must make during server installation include name and location of the LEI databases, ACL options for the LEI databases, and whether you are upgrading from NotesPump. In addition, you can choose whether your LEI servers are monitored by Simple Network Monitoring Protocol (SNMP). Finally, if you've installed LEI on the same machine as your Domino server, you can choose to install it as a server add-in task. You can also choose to run it as a stand-alone server.

Running LEI

If you choose to run LEI on the Domino server, you can add it to your ServerTasks= line in the NOTES.INI file. If you choose to install LEI as an add-in task, it should be listed here automatically. If you review the tasks listed in the Domino Administrator's Server tab, you can verify that LEI is running, as shown in Figure 19-11. When you run LEI as an add-in task, any LEI server messages will display on the Domino server console.

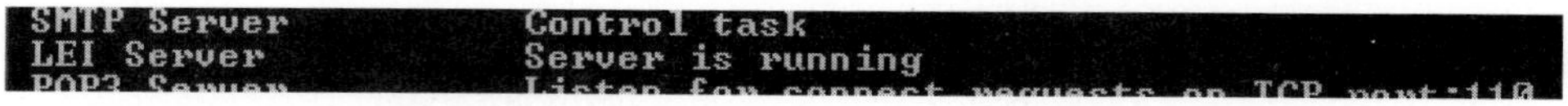

Figure 19-11 Is LEI running?

You can also run LEI as a separate server. You will run the application from the Domino executable directory, with the appropriate prefix based on the operating system. To run the LEI server on Windows NT, for example, type the following in the Start . . . Run dialog box:

```
C:\domino>nlei
```

After the LEI server is running, you will configure LEI. Configuring LEI is similar to configuring DECS, in that you need to create a connection and an activity.

For this exam, this is all the detail you need to know for LEI. For more information about LEI and Enterprise Integration in general, you should refer to the Lotus Enterprise Integration Web site at **www.lotus.com/dominoei**. You may also choose to refer to the *Domino Enterprise Integration Guide*, official documentation available from Lotus, or *Lotus Domino R5.0 Enterprise Integration: Architecture and Products*, an IBM Redbook available from **www.redbooks.ibm.com**.

Review Questions

1. Which application should you use to test your Domino connectivity to a back-end source?
   A. LEITEST
   B. DCTEST
   C. LCTEST
   D. DEITEST

2. Which tool should you use for the easiest real-time connectivity to enterprise data sources?

   A. LCTEST

   B. DECS

   C. LEI

   D. DEI

3. What needs to be done first in creating a DECS connection to a back-end source?

   A. Create an Activity document.

   B. Create a Connection document.

   C. Initialize the keys.

   D. Ensure connectivity exists to the enterprise source.

4. If there are two key-data fields on the enterprise source side, how many must there be on the Domino side?

   A. 1

   B. 2

   C. 3

   D. 4

5. Which events are available for monitoring?

   A. Create

   B. Open

   C. Update

   D. Delete

6. By default, all forms in the database are monitored for the specified events.

   A. True.

   B. False, and you cannot change this behavior.

   C. False, and you can change the behavior by using the Form Override option.

   D. False, and you can change the behavior by using the Form Filter option.

Review Answers

1. **C is correct.**   You use the LCTEST tool to test connectivity to your enterprise-source application.

2. **B is correct.**   Both B and C can be used for real-time connectivity, but B, DECS, provides easier configuration.

3. **D** is correct. Before you create a connection, create an activity, and initialize the keys, you need to ensure that connectivity to the enterprise source exists.

4. **B** is correct. There should be the same number of key fields on both sides of the mapping.

5. **A, B, C,** and **D** are all correct.

6. **C** is correct. Only one form is monitored by default, although you can use the form override option to monitor other forms.

CHAPTER 20

Planning the Domino Infrastructure

You should be able to answer questions based on the following objectives after reading this chapter:

- Capacity plan based on application size

- Capacity plan based on application views

- Capacity plan based on bandwidth

- Capacity plan based on indexes

- Capacity plan based on performance

- Capacity plan based on server size

- Capacity plan based on sorting and categorizing

- Deploy applications based on access (remote, connected, and so on)

- Deploy applications based on connectivity (connected, disconnected, and so on)

- Deploy based on application capacity planning

- Deploy based on license types

In this chapter, we'll discuss a number of areas that can influence the capacity planning for your infrastructure. These include the views, full-text indexing, size of applications, and types of user access. Then we'll look at the special considerations you need to examine when planning to implement access via either Notes or Web browser access. Lastly, we'll examine the important area of client and server licensing and a tool you can use to help you estimate the number of licenses you need for your implementation.

Planning for Size and Performance

Capacity planning in a Domino environment will involve the optimization of a number of factors. We'll look at these in turn to better understand how these factors affect our implementation and what steps we can take to improve the capacity and performance.

The first factor we will look at is application size. Typically, once an application is written and ready for deployment, you will have some idea of the likely number of documents that will be in the database. With this information, and some information about the database, you can start estimating the likely database size of the application. The Show Database server console command (which can be abbreviated as SH DA) tells us a lot of information about the contents of a database. Figure 20-1 shows the output of this command run against a Domino Directory.

Of particular interest is the view sizes, which we will be covering later. The first step is to estimate how large each document will be, which you can view from the first tab in the Document properties Infobox, as shown in Figure 20-2.

Therefore, to produce an estimate of likely database size, you need to sum the product of the estimated number of each type of document by its size. Then, for view size information, you can sum the size of each view in the test database multiplied by the ratio of the estimated number of documents that will be in that view to the number of documents in that view in the test database. Lastly, since the design will be unchanged, we add to this the size of the database template. This would appear to involve a lot of mathematics to arrive at an estimated size, but using a spreadsheet will greatly simplify the task in producing the estimated size.

As you might have seen with that last example, the size of views in a database is not insignificant. And if we then add the server CPU cycles used in keeping the views updated as documents that are added, deleted, or modified, then we can realize how important it is that each view created is really needed. There are some view properties as shown in Figure 20-3 that can be useful in ensuring that the updating of views is only done as necessary. These properties can be viewed and updated in Domino Designer by opening the view, selecting the View Infobox, and then choosing the Advanced (the second last) tab.

The Refresh index and Discard index are the relevant fields here for configuration of these views. The Refresh index field controls how the UPDATE server task maintains the view index and has these options available:

- **Auto, after first use** The view is updated automatically each time the view is opened after the view is used for the first time. This means that the first time a user attempts to open this view, it has to first be created before it can be displayed.

```
> sh da names
ACME's Address Book
Document Type                              Live           Deleted
     Documents                             4,719          1,167
     Info                                  1              0
     Form                                  75             0
     View                                  74             3
     Icon                                  1              0
     Design                                1              0
     ACL                                   1              0
     Help Index                            0              0
     Help                                  1              0
     Macro                                 20             8
     Shared Field                          6              0
     Repl. Formula                         3              0
     Private Design                        0              0
     Unknown                               3              0
View sizes                                 Bytes
     Server\Mail-In Databases and Resources   10,448
     Server\Clusters                       12,496
     Server\Programs                       37,072
     Server\Licenses                       0
     Server\Connections                    46,888
     Server\Setup Profiles                 9,424
     Server\Ser_vers                       62,248
     Server\Configurations                 10,448
     Server\Domains                        10,448
     Server\Deny Access Groups             9,424
     Server\Mail Users                     1,063,896
     ($Clusters)                           10,448
     ($Profiles)                           9,424
     ($Programs)                           42,792
     ($ServerConfig)                       9,424
     ($Domains)                            10,448
     ($Networks)                           54,056
     ($Servers)                            45,864
     Server\Networks                       12,496
     Server\V3 Stats and Events            10,448
     ($ServersLookup)                      18,640
     ($Resources)                          10,448
     ($Rooms)                              10,448
     People                                1,392,176
     Groups                                113,448
     Server\Certificates                   86,824
     Locations                             9,424
     Server\External Domain Network Information   10,448
     ($ExternalDomainNetworkAddresses)     9,424
     ($ExternalDomainNetworkConfigurations)   9,424
     ($RegisterGroups)                     121,640
     People\Alternate Language Information   10,448
```

Figure 20-1   Show Database command sample output

```
($NamesFieldLookup)              4,698,352
Server\Holidays                  69,416
($Holidays)                      119,592
Server\Web Configurations        19,664
($LDAPCN)                        1,194,968
($LDAPS)                         655,744
($LDAPG)                         688,512
($LDAPHier)                      942,040
Server\File Identifications      39,120
($FileIdentifications)           39,120
($Connections)                   84,776
($People)                        1,234,904
($Groups)                        72,488
($CrossCertByName)               9,424
($CrossCertByRoot)               9,424
($Certifiers)                    86,824
($PeopleGroupsHier)              0
($Locations)                     17,616
($Users)                         7,217,920
($VIMGroups)                     564,608
($VIMPeopleAndGroups)            1,621,552
($VIMPeopleByLastName)           0
($ServerAccess)                  89,684,504
($VIMPeople)                     1,063,896
($PeopleGroupsFlat)              2,132,104
($Adminp)                        405,288
($PeopleGroupsCorpHier)          0
($PeopleGroupsByLang)            1,230,808
($MailGroups)                    10,448
$$ViewTemplateDefault            0
($LDAPRDNHier)                   0
(LoginPeopleView)                0
People\People by Certifier       0
People\People by Certifier       0
People\Certified People          684,416
People\Internet Registered       826,752
People\Certified (no PUB Key)    37,072
(LoginPeopleView2)               618,880
(VIMSelect_Backup)               669,056
(VIMSelect1)                     1,096,664
(VIMSelect2)                     304,936
(People's Groups)                6,077,432
```

Figure 20-1   Show Database command sample output (*continued*)

- **Automatic**   Views are kept updated regardless of them being actually used. This means that the views will be faster to open, but more CPU cycles are used to keep the views updated even if some of them are never used. Unless you have a special

Figure 20-2
Document size
information

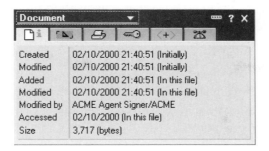

Figure 20-3
View properties
Infobox, Advanced
tab

requirement to select this option, you would be advised to use the Auto, after first use option. In that way, views that are not used are not updated.

- **Manual** Views are updated only when the user presses F9 to update the open view.

- **Auto, at most every *n* hours** Views are automatically updated only every *n* hours. Users have the option to press the F9 key to force the views to be updated. This option might be suitable for large databases that have frequent changes. In this way, you are limiting the amount of view update activity at the expense of the view not always being up-to-date.

The Discard index option is used by the UPDALL server task to determine if and when a view index can be deleted. This means that before the view can be used again, it must be re-created. By default, UPDALL is scheduled to run on the daily server at 2 A.M. The Discard index field can be one of these values available:

- **After each use**   The view index is ready for deletion after the database is closed. It is actually deleted the next time the UPDALL task runs. This option would save disk space for holding the index but would mean that the index has to be recreated again before it can be used. This would be suitable for large databases that have views that are infrequently accessed.

- **If inactive for *n* days**   The view index is ready for deletion if it has not been used for the *n* days. Again, it is actually deleted the next time the UPDALL task runs. Disk space to hold the index is saved and the index must be recreated before it can be used. This again would be suitable for large databases that may have views that are infrequently accessed. An advantage of this setting over the *After each use* is that this is factor of actual view usage (or rather non-usage), as opposed to the expected usage of the view when the application was designed.

- **Never**   The view index is never deleted. This option is used when the view is frequently used and users cannot wait for the view to be built before it can be accessed. This also means that the view index is maintained, and using disk space, even if it is never used.

There is one last subject we need to look in the subject of views. When using categorized and sorted fields in a view, this can have a vast impact on the amount of view indexing that is required. When using multiple columns in a view that can be sorted, each of the available sort options needs to be indexed so that it can be displayed upon demand. For example, a single-sorted column is a one-view index, but if we have four columns that have the option to be user sorted, then we have five indexes of the same view that have to be updated: the view as it is opened, plus a sorted view for each of the four columns that can be selected. Similarly, columns that can be categorized use sorting to maintain their index. Figure 20-4 shows the view Column InfoBox, Sorting tab. So the lesson here is to include user sorting of views only when absolutely necessary, since it means that more view indexing is required.

On a closely-related subject, we have the subject of full-text indexing. This keeps an index of all the database contents so that documents can be quickly and easily located given a word or phrase. The full-text indexing properties of a database are part of the Database Properties, Full-Text tab, as shown in Figure 20-5.

The use of a full-text index can make for fast searches, but at the cost of disk space—which can be, at worst, up to 20 percent of the size of the source database. View indexes are included in the database NSF structure, but full-text indexes are created in a subdirectory called <*databasename*>.FT underneath the location of the source database.

Figure 20-4
Column InfoBox,
Sorting tab

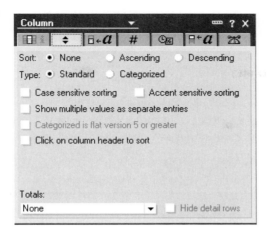

Figure 20-5
Database
Properties,
Full-text tab

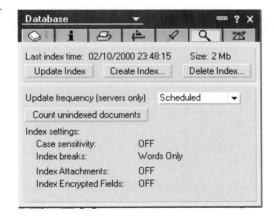

As we can see from Figure 20-5, here we have the option to create, delete, or update the full-text index for the database. We can also configure the full-text update frequency, which can be Daily, Scheduled, Hourly, or Immediate. If Daily is selected, it occurs when the UPDALL task runs daily at 2 A.M. The scheduled option only works if you also have a Program document in the Domino Directory that runs UPDALL. Then the full-text index is updated when this scheduled execution of UPDALL is run. The immediate task updates as soon as the database is closed. The hourly option uses the Chronos server task to update the full-text indexes. Again, we have yet another trade-off. First, we have to decide whether or not to create a full-text index at all to speed up searches within the database. Then we have to decide how often this full-text index is to be maintained—the more often, the better data currency in the full-text index, but the more server cycles are used to keep maintaining these full-text indexes.

The index settings for the full-text index should generally be left as is unless you have a application-specific reason why you need to include these, since these add to the size of the full-text index. In particular, large attachments within documents can require significant server work in being indexed, so you would need to ensure that these attachments really do need to be indexed at all.

> **TIP**   The NOTES.INI setting **UPDATE_NO_FULLTEXT**=**1** tells the **UPDATE** task on the Domino server task not to create or maintain full-indexes on the server. This can be useful for servers designated as mail database servers since it stops users from creating full-text indexes of their mail database on your server.

Bandwidth usage is another concern when planning our Domino implementation. Together with the LAN/WAN capacity, this can help determine where servers should and could be located. Like any design being considered, this can often involve trade-offs. For example, a decision to centrally locate servers in a given city for a multi-national enterprise can reduce the administration costs, but at the same time this increases the WAN link size and costs to the other locations. Whether this makes sense economically depends on the cost of network bandwidth—in Northern America, bandwidth is plentiful and very cheap, whereas in Asia the costs of the WAN network links will be a large part of the total Domino implementation cost. At the same time, centralizing the servers into a single location means that the number of servers can be reduced, and a small central-support team created that manages them. Contrast this with many smaller servers all over the world. Then there is the cost of the local administration of these servers since despite our efforts to manage and control everything centrally, there are still times when someone needs to physically be at the server to perform a task.

In the book *Lotus Notes and Domino 5 Scalable Network Design* by John Lamb and Peter Lew (McGraw-Hill, ISBN 0-07-913792-X), there is a bandwidth figure quoted for each active user of 3.7Kbps, which is derived from research carried out by IBM Global Services and IBM Research. Similarly, they have estimated that typically 1/3 of all users will be active at a given time. Combining these figures and allowing for 60 percent utilization of the WAN link by Notes traffic, the book suggests a conservative rule of thumb that approximately $x/2$ users can be supported by a WAN link of x Kbps. For example, a 128Kbps link can support around 62 users. Of course, your environment may be very different to here and you need to validate these figures yourself, but this is a useful starting point when looking at networking and server placement options.

Domino server-sizing and performance used to be a black art. One way that this used to be done is from reading the results of a NotesBench report from **www.notesbench.org**, which was a Lotus-approved method of measuring server performance against a set of pre-defined workloads. Unfortunately, the numbers from these simulations were not always directly applicable to "real world" use.

Now the latest way to predict server performance is via the Server.Load tool—this is the set of database template files that come with Domino R5. Then a set of data provided by the server vendor has to be downloaded and added to complete the application. Once you have all of these databases, you can model your desired server setup —the server function, the types of users to support, and so on to gain an indication of how many users that server platform can support.

When we deploy applications, we need to consider our user base and how they will access the applications we deploy. For example, in many organizations much of the staff are equipped with laptop computers and spend much of their time out of the office. These users will typically connect to your Domino servers via a dialup link, so unless you are forcing them to only use your Domino applications when dialed up, you will need to have these users make a local replica of the database, and when necessary, have them dial-in as needed so that their updates can be replicated to and from the server. This local replica may need to be considered carefully, since it is very likely that the replica creation and initial replication will occur over a slow dialup connection. We may think nothing of deploying a 20MB database on a server, but our users will curse us if we force them to stay connected while this database is replicated over the dialup link. One way to handle this may be with selective replication formulas that have the user only replicate the documents relevant to them. Selective replication settings are shown in Figure 20-6. These are available after the database is selected and then by choosing File, Replication, Replication Settings from the menus.

In this figure, we see that only documents with the value of the user's name in the Owner field will be replicated. Of course, the application needs to be designed to function this way in the first place, since a replication formula such as this can have drastic unintended consequences if implemented without consulting the designer of the application.

Closely related to this is the decision whether users will directly access the database on the server or via a local replica. This can work for applications, but can also work well for mail. For example, in *Lotus Notes and Domino 5 Scalable Network Design* as mentioned earlier, the authors discuss a scenario within IBM where users access their mail via a local replica rather than to the server copy directly. This reduces the server load in that the mail data is only sent across the network once. This is not much of a savings for regular mail documents, which are typically only read once and deleted or filed. But it does save bandwidth for calendar items since they are usually accessed multiple times as the user needs to refer to them. In this type of scenario, the LAN-connected users are replicating with their home server every 10 minutes, which replicates mail and sends outgoing mail from their local MAIL.BOX to the server.

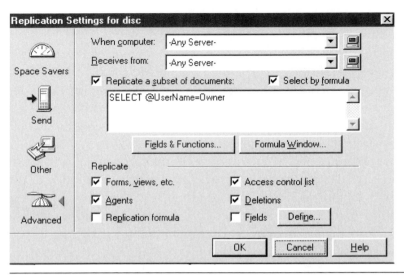

Figure 20-6 Selective Replication settings

This same option can also be used for applications that need to be deployed. However, the use of this needs to be considered closely and it may not be suitable for all applications. For example, applications that have many updates by different people may suffer from replication conflicts if they are deployed in this matter.

Transaction logging, a new R5 feature, is often talked about in terms of improved database integrity, but at the same time it can greatly improve server performance. This is because the server is writing instead to a sequential transaction log file rather than multiple NSF files. After the log entries have been completed, the server continues on and writes the database changes back to the database as a non-critical background task. Typically, the best option is to use a dedicated disk for transaction logging—if the disk was used for anything else, the disk heads would be continually moving backwards and forwards to do the two tasks, which would slow down the write performance for the Domino server. Since these transaction logs are now very important for the health of your Domino server, it is typical to implement these on a RAID disk array. If you do use RAID, use RAID-1, mirroring, which duplicates writes on both disks, rather than RAID-5, which can be slower than regular disk activity. Figure 20-7 shows the transaction logging page of the Server document within the Domino Directory.

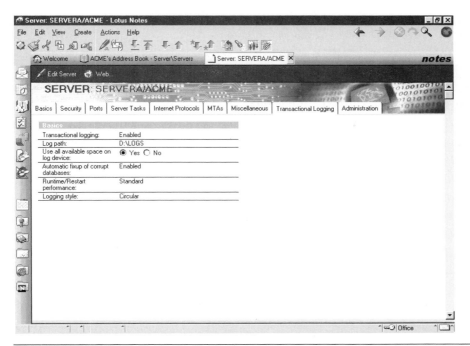

Figure 20-7   Server document, transaction logging settings

There are a couple of fields here that have important implications to how transaction logging works on your Domino server. The last field, the Logging field, is important— it determines whether you can do point-in-time recoveries of your Domino databases, or whether you can only restore your databases to the last backup. In circular mode, the log files are reused as necessary and are only intended as performance improvement. Domino is only concerned that the last committed database changes in the log have been written to disk. In archival mode, all log files since the last full backup are retained, so that these can be used as needed to perform a restore and then replay the log transactions over them to achieve a point-in-time recovery.

Another important field on this document is the Runtime/Restart performance field. This controls how much of the database changes are held within memory. There are three options available:

- **Favor runtime**   Uses more memory and improves performance. When the server is restarted after a failure, that are a lot of committed transactions in the logs that need to be replayed against the server databases.

- **Standard**   A compromise between the other two options.

- **Favor restart recovery time**   Uses less memory and improves data integrity. When the server is restarted after failure, there are fewer committed transactions to process against the server databases.

Regardless of what option is selected, transaction logging also improves server restart time after a server failure. Instead of having to check for open databases at the time of failure and running FIXUP against each of them, it only needs to replay the committed transactions from the logs to the server databases and the server is ready to start serving client requests.

The application-level clustering functionality from the Domino Advanced Server product can be used to provide both failover and load balancing for better reliability and availability of your servers. Notes clients have the functionality built-in to be able to failover to another replica in the cluster when an open database request fails. Web clients need the ICM (Internet Cluster Manager) functionality implemented in order to failover to other replicas of the database. The ICM builds upon the technology of clustering and requires that a cluster already exist. Clustering was discussed in detail in Chapter 2, but is mentioned again as a useful technology to balance workload across Domino servers.

Web Versus Notes—Special Considerations

Although we spend a lot of time discussing the different application elements supported by Web and/or Notes clients, as an administrator there are other considerations when considering to deploy each of the user types.

Firstly, there are the different security models of the two client types. As you are aware, when using a Notes client, the password is stored within the user's ID file, which is usually stored locally on the user machine. When the user changes his or her password, the new password is stored within this ID file. This is in contrast to when a Web user is authenticated. He or she is authenticated against the Internet password field in the Person document within the Domino Directory. This means that this Internet password field must be entered in within this Person record, and that whenever this password is to be changed it needs to be done by an administrator who can update the record.

We also need to consider the differing load on the server of Web users compared to Notes users. This is because of the different functionality supplied by the Notes client versus a Web browser. IT managers commonly want to consider using Web browsers rather than the Notes client, since this appears to save them the cost of the client plus the deployment of the client. However, when a Notes client is used, both the client and the server share the work, and a client-server data exchange takes place as needed. In contract, with a Web browser client, nearly all of the work is done at the server. Once this is complete, an HTML page is sent to the client, which the client renders and displays to the user. A useful rule of thumb when comparing the server load of these two types of users is that Web users require four times the amount of work as the Notes client. In this way, if your standard server implementation was to support 1,000 users per user, then this same server setup could support approximately 250 Web-browser users. Of course, this is an approximation and you would need to validate this in your own conditions, but this is a useful starting point.

When using Domino as a Web server, this also implies that Domino will probably be running behind network security devices such as firewalls, which act to protect it from malicious attacks from hackers while allowing enough access for it to perform its work. This is commonly done via TCP/IP port filtering, so you as the Domino Administrator need to know which ports are needed for specific functionality. These ports can be changed from the standard defaults by updating the port numbers used in the Ports . . . Internet Ports section of the Server document within the Domino Directory. Figure 20-8 shows a sample entry for LDAP. However, the clients for these services will be expecting

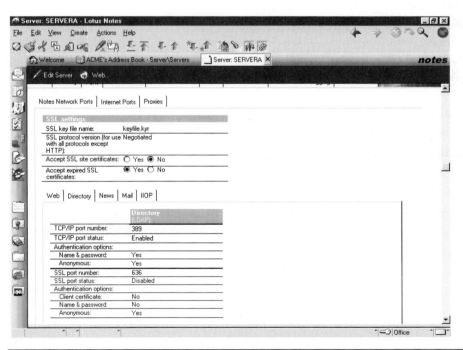

Figure 20-8   Setting up ports for Internet services in the Server document

these standard ports to be used, so if these are changed, then every client will need to be configured to use the updated port numbers.

The TCP/IP ports used by Web services by Domino are follows:

- **SMTP** Port 25 (465 for SSL)
- **HTTP** Port 80 (443 for SSL)
- **POP4** Port 110 (995 for SSL)
- **NNTP** Port 119 (563 for SSL)
- **IMAP** Port 143 (993 for SSL)
- **LDAP** Port 389 (636 for SSL)
- **IIOP** Port 63148 (63149 for SSL)

Also, port 1352 is used by Notes clients, so if you also need to use Notes clients via the Internet, you need to ensure that this port is enabled for use.

License Types

Although we commonly refer to the Domino server as if there were only type of Domino server, as far as licensing goes, there are actually four types of Domino server licenses. These are

- **Domino Mail Server** Supports only mail, calendaring, and discussion databases only.
- **Domino Application Server** Adds support for custom applications.
- **Domino Enterprise Server** Adds clustering and partitioning support, multi-processor systems with five to eight processors.
- **Domino Advanced Enterprise Server** A special version of the Enterprise Server that supports multi-processor systems with nine or more processors.

The Domino Mail Server only supports applications built from templates signed by the ID Lotus Notes Template Development/Lotus Notes, so you need to keep this in mind if you are intending to modify the standard mail template MAIL50.NTF or the standard discussion database template DISCW50.NTF. So it follows that if you want to modify these templates, you can't use databases based on these on a Domino Mail Server; you must use a Domino Application Server.

Typically in a medium-to-large implementation of Domino, each Domino server is designated for a specific purpose. In this case, the specific server types can use the different license types as needed within the enterprise, which can considerably reduce the licensing costs. For example, your dedicated mail servers and mail routing hubs can use the Domino Mail Server license, and those hosting applications and replication hubs can use the Domino Application Server. Those servers that host applications or mail databases that are deemed mission-critical can then use the Domino Enterprise Server.

There are two main types of Notes client licensing. As is common within the IT industry, each client license is known as a CAL (Client Access License). There is a Notes for Collaboration license, which is a set fee per user, and a Notes for Messaging license. The Messaging client license allows the user to use Lotus Notes to send and receive mail only. The Collaboration client license then also allows usage of Notes applications as well.

Web users only need to be licensed if they are authenticated (that is, they have a Person record in the Domino Directory). For authenticated users that all belong to the same company, there is a license called the iNotes w/Domino Per User CAL. For authenticated users that do not belong to the same company, there is a license called the iNotes w/Domino Per Server CAL.

There is some functionality within the Domino Directory that can assist you with your licensing. In the Servers\Licenses view within this Directory, it contains a count of the required number of server and client licenses to support your current implementation. If you have multiple domains within your enterprise, it follows that you would then need to sum the totals from each Domain to determine your total number of licenses required. Figure 20-9 shows an example of this view.

Lastly, you should be reminded the importance of obtaining sufficient licenses for the products that are installed in your enterprise. There can sometimes be pressure from ignorant business managers who would prefer not to pay for licenses for all installed server and client software. In many countries, there are industry consortiums supported by the major software vendors that are actively working to stamp out software piracy. Not only do you expose your firm to large fines, but this can also lead to a significant loss of business reputation, which can be even more costly. As an IT professional you should not support piracy of software.

Summary

- There are three main types of server license: Domino Mail Server, Domino Application Server, and Domino Enterprise Server. There is also a Domino Advanced

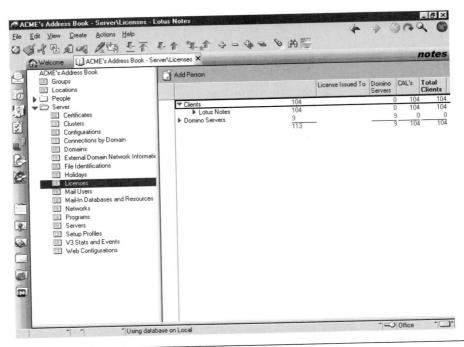

Figure 20-9 Server\Licensing view in the Domino Directory

Enterprise server for systems with nine or more CPUs. The Domino Mail server only supports mail, calendaring, and discussion databases. Domino Application Server is the regular Domino server we commonly refer to as Domino. Domino Enterprise Server then adds support for partitioning and clustering, plus systems with five to eight CPUs.

- There are two types of Notes client license: one for messaging alone, and another for application use. Only authenticated Web users need to be licensed.

- Web-browser clients have a different authentication method than Notes clients. Notes clients have an ID file, which contains information about the user including the password. Web clients use the Internet password field in their Person record in the Domino Directory.

- When Domino functions as an Internet server, there are a number of standard TCP/IP ports used to serve clients. These include port 80 for HTTP, port 110 for POP3, port 119 for NNTP, port 143 for IMAP, and port 389 for LDAP. Regular Notes clients use port 1352 for Notes RPC access.

- View refresh and discard index options can be used to minimize the disk space used and server CPU cycles consumed for views that are infrequently used. Views indexes are only deleted by the UPDALL server task.

- When views contain columns that can be user-sortable, each available sort option is indexed within the database. This can lead to many indexes needed for a given view.

- A full-text index can speed up searches within a database, but can take up to 20 percent of database size in disk space for the index.

- When deploying applications that reside on the user workstation, selective replication can be used to ensure that only documents relevant to that user are replicated locally.

- Transaction logging can be a useful option to improve server disk write performance, since it writes to a sequential log file rather than the database files. The actual database files can then be updated as a background non-critical task. It also improves server restart time after a failure, since the server no longer needs to check each database first. It replays transactions against the server databases and is ready to start processing.

Review Questions

1. Shaun is implementing new Domino servers that will be used for clustering mail databases for important executives in his firm. What type of Domino server license would be most appropriate in this situation?
   A. Domino application server
   B. Domino mail server
   C. Domino enterprise server
   D. All of the above

2. Tina is configuring a Domino server to serve Web clients over the Internet. What TCP/IP ports will need to open in the firewalls in order for her to serve HTTP requests?
   A. Port 110
   B. Port 80
   C. Port 119
   D. Port 25

3. William is deploying an application that will contain publicly available information about the company for their corporate Web site. Users will access this content from a browser and will not need to login because the Anonymous entry in database ACL has Reader access. What type of client license is required in this circumstance?

A. None

B. Notes for Colloboration License

C. Notes for Messaging License

D. The iNotes w/Domino Per Server CAL

4. Abbie is setting up a Domino server that will allow connections by Notes clients from the Internet to connect to other servers via passthru. This server will use which TCP/IP port to service Notes clients?

A. 80

B. 1253

C. 1352

D. 1523

5. Brad is configuring the discard index options for a view in a new database application. The view will be used by a single user who will open the view once a month to check for status information. What would be the best option for the Discard index setting?

A. After each use

B. If inactive for n days

C. Never

D. Unable to say with the information specified

6. Cindy is considering implementing a full-text index for a server-based database application she is about to deploy. What is a good reason for implementing a full-text index?

A. Saves disk space

B. Saves time when searching

C. Saves network traffic between the server and client

D. Saves replication time between servers

7. David is configuring selective replication for an application being deployed. What is not a reason to implement selective replication?

A. Increased application security

B. Reduced replication traffic between server and client

C. Faster server backup times

D. Reduced replication traffic between servers

8. Erica is configuring the settings for view refresh time on a new application. Which server task controls the updating of view indexes?
   A. REPLICA
   B. UPDATE
   C. AMGR
   D. DOMIDX

9. Fred is planning the server configuration for a server he is about to deploy. Which NOTES.INI setting stops the creation and maintenance of full-text indexes on the server?
   A. NO_FULL_TEXT=1
   B. FULL_TEXT=0
   C. UPDATE_NO_FULLTEXT=0
   D. UPDATE_NO_FULLTEXT=1

10. Gertrude is considering implementing transaction logging on her Domino server. Which is not a reason to implement transaction logging?
    A. Faster server restart performance
    B. Faster disk write performance
    C. Faster disk read performance
    D. Improved data integrity

Review Answers

1. **C is correct.** Although the server will only be serving mail databases, in order to obtain clustering, the Domino Enterprise license is required.

2. **B is correct.** HTTP uses TCP/IP port 80.

3. **A is correct.** Since the Web users will not need to be authenticated, they will not need to be licensed.

4. **C is correct.** Port 80 is used for HTTP. The other answers are there simply to ensure that you really do know that 1352 is used for Notes clients.

5. **A is correct.** Since the view is only used infrequently by a single user, it is feasible to have it rebuilt as required.

6. **B is correct.** A full-text index will actually use more disk space, and the network traffic between the server and client should be unaffected. Replication activity would not make use of a full-text index.

7. **C is correct.**   Backup times will be unaffected by selective replication. The other options are reasons to implement selective replication.

8. **B is correct.**   UPDATE controls the updating of view indexes.

9. **D is correct.**   Use UPDATE_NO_FULLTEXT=1 to prevent the creation and maintenance of full-text indexes on a server.

10. **C is correct.**   Transaction logging doesn't affect database read performance.

Distributing Application Design

You should be able to answer questions based on the following objectives after reading this chapter:

- Distribute application design changes based on design
- Distribute application design changes based on the impact on ACL
- Distribute application design changes based on replication
- Distribute application design changes

After you deploy applications, your designers may need to make design changes to them. If the databases are based on templates, they can be updated using the Design task, or design refreshes or replacements from the menus. You can also distribute database design using replication if you configure replication formulas. One of the items you have to plan for your deployment is how application changes should be distributed. Plan for the tasks that support design updates as well, such as Design and Updall. In addition, you need to plan for other methods of distributing design changes, such as via replication.

Design Templates

When developers create applications, they often create templates to ensure a consistent design for the application. It also enables developers to update the design of the database manually or automatically. Usually, templates have the file extension .NTF, although it is a database property that really makes the file a master design template.

Figure 21-1

Design tab in Database properties

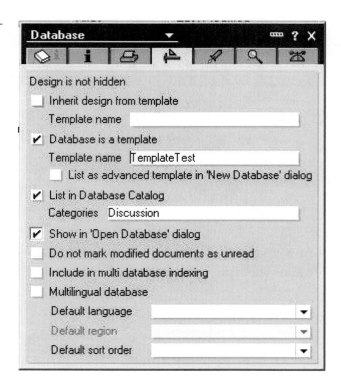

To define a file as a template, open the .NSF or .NTF file. Open the Database properties InfoBox and open the Design tab, as shown in Figure 21-1.

To indicate that the database is a template, enable the *Database is a template* checkbox. Then type a name in the Template name field. This is the name that will appear in the Template list in the New Database dialog box. The name should not have spaces. After you give the template a name, you can also choose to have it appear as an Advanced template in the New Database dialog box. This means it will not be available until you choose to show advanced templates.

Link to the Template

You can link databases to the design template in three ways. First, you can link the entire database to the template when you create the new database. In the New Database dialog box, you can choose a template on which to base the new database. You can also choose whether the database should inherit future design changes or only inherit the design once. If you enable the *Inherit future design changes* option, as shown in

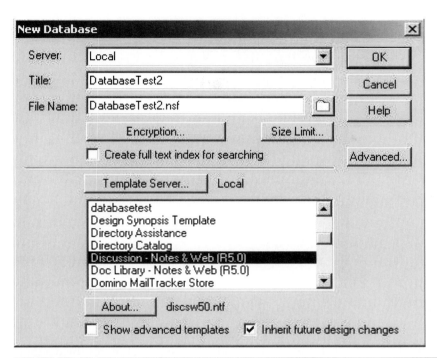

Figure 21-2 Create a new database based on a template.

Figure 21-2, you can make changes to the template later and either refresh the design or allow the Design task to push the changes automatically. Note that if you do not give the template an .NTF file extension, it will not be visible in the New Database dialog box.

If you have already created a database but want it to link to a template later, you can access the Design tab on the Database properties InfoBox. In this case, enable the *Inherit Design from Template* option, and type the name of the template to attach the file to. This is the template name, not the file name.

Specific Database Elements

You can also link or unlink specific design elements from the template. To do this, open the Domino Designer to the design view for the element you want to link or unlink. Right-click and access the design tab of the Design Document properties, as shown in Figure 21-3.

On the Design tab, you can set the specified element to inherit from a different design template than the rest of the database. Just type the template name in the *Inherit*

Figure 21-3
Design Document
properties

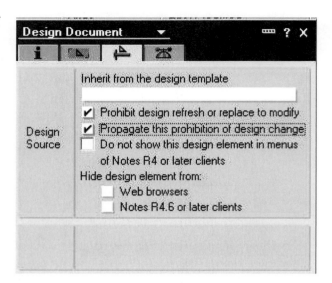

from the design template field. This field will override the template link for the database as a whole.

You can also choose for the element not to inherit from a template by enabling the *Prohibit design refresh or replace to modify* option. This ensures that the design element will not be updated when the Design task runs or if you choose to refresh or replace the design. You can force this prohibition into other replicas of the database by enabling the *Propagate this prohibition of design change* field.

If you're trying to link or unlink an agent's design from a template, choose the Agent properties and follow the same steps described earlier.

Some design elements are unlinked by default, such as the icon, and the About Database and Using Database documents. If you want these to be linked, you need to disable the *Do not allow design refresh/replace to modify* checkbox from the Design tab of the Design Document properties InfoBox, as shown in Figure 21-4.

Applying the Changes

As developers make changes to the design of templates, these changes must be pushed out to the production databases based on the templates. Obviously, it is possible to make design changes directly to the production database; however, this is not the

Figure 21-4
Icon Design document

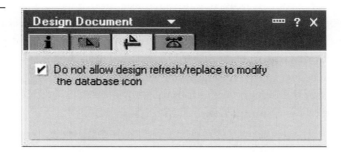

recommended procedure in most cases. It doesn't allow for easy and thorough testing while preserving the environment you know is working.

It makes more sense therefore to make changes via a template. The developer makes changes directly to the template, tests those changes, and then pushes the changes to the production database or databases. The changes can be implemented using one of the following methods:

- Refresh design
- Replace design
- Replication

Refresh the Design

You can refresh the design elements of a database. This updates the elements of a database that are linked to a template with any changes made to the template. In addition, it overwrites any changes that were made to the design of the database locally. The database design can be refreshed automatically using the Designer task on the server or manually using the Refresh Design menu option.

Design Task

A task called Design runs on the Domino servers by default. When the design of a template changes, the Designer task updates all databases that inherit design from the template. By default, the Designer task runs daily by default at 1 A.M. A related task, Updall, runs by default at 2 A.M. and is responsible for updating the view indexes of those databases updated by the Design task. In addition, after updating database designs, the Designer task also reloads the LDAP schema if the server that runs the LDAP service.

The Design task can only update databases that have a master template available locally. For each server that you want to update database design automatically, ensure that you create local replicas of the design templates. Note that you cannot run the Design task only against a specific folder or database. The task will run against all databases on the server linked to a template available locally.

You can run the Design task automatically via the NOTES.INI file, or manually from the console or the Domino Administrator.

Running the Design Task from the Console

To run the Design task from either the server console or from the remote console, type in Load Design.

Running the Design Task from the Domino Administrator   You can also run the Design task from the Start . . . Tasks tool in the Domino Administrator. Open the Server . . . Status tab in the Domino Administrator. Expand the Task tools and choose Start. In the Start New Task dialog box, choose Designer . . . Start Task, as shown in Figure 21-5. The Design task will run against all databases and their related templates on the server.

Figure 21-5
Run the Design task.

Refresh Design

In addition to using the Designer task, either manually or automatically, an administrator, developer, or end user can choose to refresh the design of a database from the menus while in the database. This process updates a database whose design is linked to a template. Please note that any design elements that are configured to prohibit Design Replace or Refresh are not updated.

To access the Refresh Design option, choose File . . . Database . . . Refresh Design from the menus while in the database you want to refresh. This command lets you manually perform the same process that the Designer task performs automatically. At this point, you have the ability to refresh the design from a different server, rather than only the locally available server, as shown in Figure 21-6.

After you select a server to refresh the design from, you are prompted with a warning, shown in Figure 21-7, that Domino will refresh any forms, views, and other elements. The important thing to note with this warning is that any changes you may have made locally to a form, view, or other element will be overwritten by the Design Refresh from the template. This is true in any form of refreshing or replacing the design of a database that is based on a template. Any changes you've made to an element linked to a template will be lost.

Figure 21-6
Refresh the design
from any server.

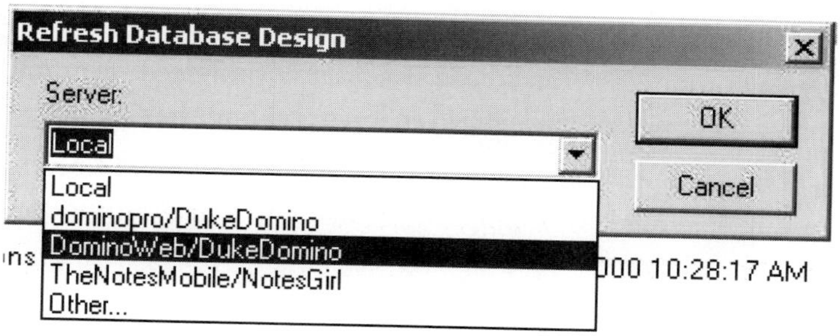

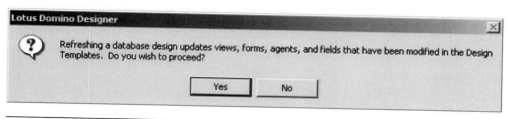

Figure 21-7 Refresh design warning

You might choose to refresh the design of a database manually in the following situations:

- If a database is stored locally (not on a server), the Design task won't automatically update the design.
- You've changed the template and want to apply the changes immediately, rather than waiting for the scheduled run of the Design task.

What Isn't Refreshed?

Some database elements are not refreshed during either an automatic or manual design refresh. Some of the items are based on having the *Prohibit design refresh or replace to modify* option enabled:

- The database icon is not refreshed unless you disable the default *Prohibit design refresh* or *replace to modify* option.
- The database title and category are not refreshed.
- The template property *List as advanced template in New Database* is not refreshed.
- The Database ACL and Encrypt Database settings will not be refreshed.
- Using This Database and About This Database documents are not refreshed unless you disable the *Prohibit design refresh or replace to modify* option.
- Any other elements whose design you protected from updates (if *Prohibit design refresh or replace to modify* is enabled) will not be updated.
- Private views, agents, and folders are not refreshed from templates. These should not be added to templates, as they will cause errors during the design refresh/ replace process.

What Is Refreshed?

Most elements in the database are updated or refreshed during either the manual or automatic procedure. This assumes that the design element has been changed in the template that the refresh occurs from. The following is a list of the elements that are refreshed:

- Forms, fields, form actions, and event scripts
- Views, folders, and view actions
- Agents

- Pages

- Framesets

- Navigators

- Shared fields

- All of the File, . . . Database Properties selections, with the exception of the previously indicated properties

Replace Design

As another alternative, you can also choose to replace the design of a database. The Replace Design command makes a database identical to a template—including one it is not currently associated with. It is the only way to distribute design changes if the database doesn't already inherit changes from a template. You need at least Designer access in the ACL to replace the design of a database with the design from a template.

To replace the design of a database, open the database. From the menus, choose File . . . Database . . . Replace Design. In the Replace Database Design dialog box, shown in Figure 21-8, choose the template you want to use. You can choose this from any template server or from the local machine. You can also choose to link the template to the database for any future design changes.

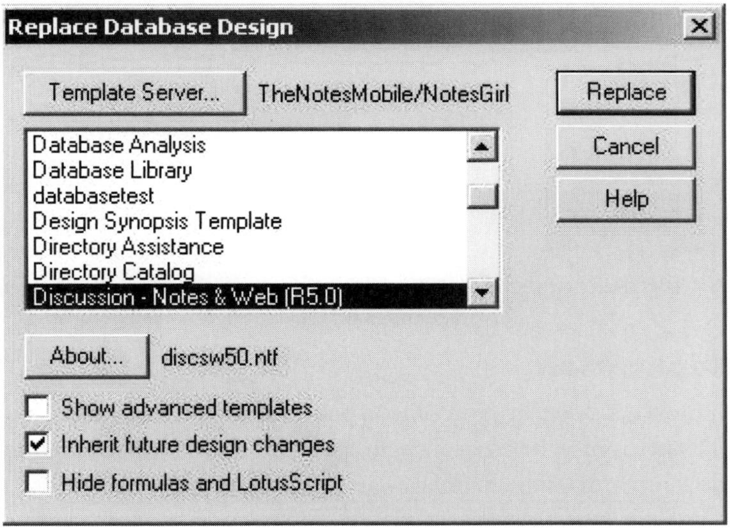

Figure 21-8
Replace design

What Isn't Replaced?

As with the Design Refresh, when you replace a design, not all elements are changed. Some of the items are based on having the *Prohibit design refresh or replace to modify* option enabled.

- The database icon is not replaced unless you disable the default *Prohibit design refresh or replace to modify* option.
- The database title and category are not replaced.
- The template property *List as advanced template in New Database* is not replaced.
- The Database ACL and Encrypt Database settings will not be replaced.
- Using This Database and About This Database documents are not replaced unless you disable the *Prohibit design refresh or replace to modify* option.
- Any other elements whose design you protected from updates (that is, if *Prohibit design refresh or replace to modify* is enabled) will not be replaced.
- Private views, folders, and agents will not be replaced with the Design Replace.

What Is Replaced?

The following elements are changed during a Design Replace.

- Forms, fields, form actions, and event scripts
- Views, folders, and view actions
- Agents
- Pages
- Framesets
- Navigators
- Shared fields
- All of the File . . . Database Properties selections, with the exception of the properties indicated earlier

Replication

In most cases, replication plays a part in distributing design changes. If you have multiple servers in your environment, you will need to distribute design changes, either to the templates or the databases, using replication.

If you decide to place all your templates on a single server, these templates will be used to refresh or replace the design of the databases located on that server. These databases are probably in production on other servers, however, which need to be updated with the new design elements as well. After the design is updated on the template server, scheduled or manual replication can push out the design changes to the others servers. The other servers do not need to run the Designer task in this case.

You may also choose to store a replica of the design template on each server and have the design changes to the template be distributed by replication. In this case, you must run the Designer task on each server to which you replicate the templates to ensure that the design changes are applied.

For details on Replication, please refer to Chapters 5, 12, and 17.

To distribute design changes, a server must have at least Designer access in the ACL of the template or database.

After the Redesign

Any time you redesign a form, you need to note what happens to documents that were created with the existing form. Some form changes, such as formatting, automatically show in their updated manner when users open an existing document. Other changes, such as new fields, do not automatically appear in existing documents. You have to update the existing documents by editing and resaving them. You can do this manually or by using an agent. If the database replicates, redesign the form on only one database and let the changes replicate to other replicas.

Many changes made to a form do not require that the form be resaved. However, if the *Store Form in Document* option is configured, all changes will require resaving. Otherwise, the following changes made to a form will display automatically in the already created documents:

- Computed field formula
- Static text (including text properties or formatting) or graphics on the form
- Pop-ups
- Form actions and buttons
- Form name (as long as you leave the original name as a synonym to the right of the pipe or vertical bar [|] symbol)

The following changes will always require that you resave the documents created with the form:

- New field
- Different field data type
- New field name
- Deleting a field
- Changing the form name if you don't leave the original name as a synonym
- Different form type, such as from Main to Response
- Any changes to a form with the *Store form in document* option enabled

One of the best ways to update the documents in a database that are affected by changes to the forms is to create an agent. The agent may need to edit and resave a document, applying the changes, or add, rename, or remove a field. You may also want to force a document to be viewed with another form. The following are the formulas you would use for these agents. The agents should be manual agents.

Use the following formula to edit and resave a document automatically:

```
@Command([ToolsRefreshAllDocs])
```

Use the following formula to insert a new field into existing documents:

```
FIELD New field name := value;
```

In this case, *New field name* is the name of the field, and *value* is the value you want the field to have. The value can be the field default value, a formula that calculates the value, or a null value (""").

When you delete fields from forms, documents that already contain the fields continue to store the field and values. This agent can remove the field. You should compact the database after running the agent to reduce the database size.

Use the following formula to remove the field:

```
FIELD Field name := @DeleteField;
```

Use the following formula in an agent to rename a field on a document after you've renamed it in a form:

```
FIELD New field name := Old field name;
FIELD Old field name := @DeleteField;
```

In this formula, *New field name* is the new name for the field, and *Old field name* is the original name for the field.

If you delete a form and then a user tries to open a document created with that form, the user will get an error. Instead you should create an agent using the following options. In the Agent design, do the following:

1. Choose All documents in database in the *Which documents should it act on* field. Then click Add Search.

2. In the Add Condition dialog box, choose the *By Form Used* option. Then select the name of the obsolete form, and click OK.

3. Use the following formula for the agent:

```
FIELD Form := "Reassigned form name";
```

In this formula, *Reassigned form name* is the name of the form that the documents should use.

If you're creating a workflow-type application, you might have chosen to store the form with the documents created. This enables users that don't have the original form in their mail files to receive and view documents from a database. You can remove the stored form from the document by removing the internal Notes fields that link the document to the form. Use the following formula in the agent:

```
SELECT $TITLE="Old form name";
FIELD $TITLE:=@DeleteField;
FIELD $INFO:=@DeleteField;
FIELD $WINDOWTITLE:=@DeleteField;
FIELD $BODY:=@DeleteField;
FIELD $ACTIONS:=@DeleteField;
FIELD FORM:="New form name";
```

In this formula, *Old form name* is the name of the form used to create the documents, and *New form name* is the form that will display the documents in the future.

Review Questions

1. Which task is responsible for distributing design changes from templates to databases?
    A. Updall
    B. Update
    C. Template
    D. Design

2. Which of the following does a master design template have, assuming you can find it in the Templates field in the New Database dialog box?
    A. .NSF extension
    B. .NTF extension
    C. Complete the *Database is a template* field in the Database properties.
    D. Give the file a template name in the Database properties.

3. True or False: If you create a new database based on a template, it will always contain a link to the template no matter what.
    A. True
    B. False

4. True or False: After you have created a database, you cannot link it to a template. That must be done at create time.
    A. True
    B. False

5. Which of the following elements will not inherit design changes by default?
    A. About Database document
    B. Views
    C. Database Icon
    D. Shared Agents

6. The following items will be updated by default during a Design Refresh process:
    A. Database ACL
    B. Database title
    C. Navigators
    D. Database Encryption properties

7. The following items are not replaced during a Replace Design process:
    A. Forms
    B. Views
    C. Pages
    D. Using Database document

8. Which level of access does a server need to push Design changes to other servers during replication?
    A. Manager
    B. Editor
    C. Designer
    D. Author

9. Which of the following changes to a form require that an already created document be edited and resaved to display the change?
   A. Static text or graphics on the form
   B. Form actions
   C. Buttons on a form
   D. New fields

10. These changes to a form do not require you to edit and resave documents created before the changes were made:
    A. Changes to a field name
    B. Changes to form name (when you have left the original name as a synonym)
    C. Changes to a form name (when you have not left the original name as a synonym)
    D. Deleted field

Review Answers

1. **D is correct.** The Design task is the server task used to distribute design changes automatically.

2. **B, C, and D are correct.** You must name the template with an .NTF extension, indicate that the database is a template, and give the database a template name.

3. **B is correct.** You must tell it to link the template when you create the database; you can always remove the link either for the entire database or for certain elements.

4. **B is correct.** You can link a database to a template at any time.

5. **A and C are correct.** About Database document and database icon will not inherit changes by replace or refresh by default, although you can enable the *Allow design refresh/replace to modify* options.

6. **C is correct.** Navigators are the only item in this list that are updated by default in a design replace or refresh.

7. **D is correct.** Using Database document will not be replaced or refreshed by default.

8. **C is correct.** Designer access is required to distribute design changes via replication.

9. **D is correct.** New Fields would require a document to be edited and resaved to display.

10. **B is correct.** Changes to form name when you have left the original name as a synonym would not require you to edit and resave documents created before you made the change.

PART IV

Domino R5 Designer Fundamentals

The first exam in the Application Development track is the Designer Fundamentals exam (190-510). Passing this exam gains you a Certified Lotus Specialist (CLS) designation for Application Development. The audience for this exam is developers with a basic knowledge of the Domino Designer client and the ability to create multiple Notes databases for any of the available clients. The exam has 40 questions and requires a minimum score of 70 percent. The competencies for this exam cover four basic areas:

- **Client**   Relates to the ability to create, modify, or troubleshoot applications or databases for web clients and notes clients.

- **Database**   Relates to the ability to create a database, set database properties, and implement basic security features.

- **Design Elements**   Includes developing forms, fields, pages, views, outlines, framesets, actions, and agents for use in databases.

- **Formulas**   Includes creating and troubleshooting formulas.

These general areas of competency are broken down further into specific tasks that you should be able to perform. To see a complete list, refer to the *Lotus Domino R5 CLS Certification Exam Guide*, available for download from **www.lotus.com/education**. Each chapter in this section lists the specific competency areas that it covers. The section covers not only each of the competencies listed for the Designer Fundamentals exam, but also allows you to create a functioning application.

CHAPTER 22

Know Thy Client

You should be able to answer questions based on the following objectives after reading this chapter:

- Creating, modifying, and troubleshooting for Web clients
- Creating, modifying, and troubleshooting for any client
- Creating, modifying, and troubleshooting for Notes clients

Before you use your mouse to create a Notes/Domino application, you must first determine which clients exist in your environment. Clients who might access an application include both Notes and Web clients. While one of the goals of R5 is to enable developers to program once for both Notes and Web clients, it is still necessary to choose the appropriate design elements or formula components based on the audience of your application. In addition, there are differences between various Notes clients (different versions) and between various Web clients (different browsers). This chapter discusses planning, creating, testing, and modifying applications that are appropriate for Notes or Web clients.

Note that many specific details related to these competencies are also covered in other chapters in this section.

Which Clients?

The most important aspect of developing applications in an arena in which multiple clients can access your handiwork is to determine before you start which clients will actually access your applications. Unfortunately, this step is not always possible, because decisions are made that do not consider the application development process; however, you should create applications based on which clients you know (or suspect) will access your applications. Obviously, the only way to determine which clients will access your applications is to know your environment. If you create and test (of course) an application for Notes R5 clients, only to realize that Internet Explorer clients are the new standard at your customer's remote sites, you will have to redesign and retest a large amount of your development. Some of your application might even have to be restructured completely. In addition, if you only tested for Internet Explorer when creating an application that will be placed on an Internet server, you might have many support calls from Netscape Navigator users. The moral of this story is to know your users and what clients they expect to use. Also, test your application with all possible clients.

Test Your Application

As you develop your applications, you should test each element in each of the clients with which the application will be used. Designer makes this process easy to do with the Preview buttons, as shown in Figure 22-1.

The Default buttons enable you to preview your application in Notes and Domino. There will also be buttons for other browsers, based on what is installed on your workstation. In this case, there is a button to test Internet Explorer (the installed browser). As you develop each portion of your application, use these buttons to test each element. You can also access the previews from the shortcut menus of most elements. Keep in mind that the F9 key does not work in most browser areas (unless you are using the View applet), so in order to see changes that you have made to your design elements, you should refresh or reload the element in the browser.

What to Avoid

Another important aspect of developing for multiple clients is knowing what to avoid in your applications. While most design elements in Notes are applicable to both Notes and Web clients, some elements are not supported in one area or the other. While you will learn more about each of these elements in later chapters, Table 22-1 displays elements that are not fully supported on the Web. Note that this list is not comprehensive. The elements that are listed here are ones that are important for the Domino Designer

Figure 22-1
Preview buttons

Fundamentals exam and knowledge level. For a comprehensive list of elements that are not supported on the Web, refer to Appendix D of *Application Development with Domino Designer,* or the Domino Designer Help database.

Table 22-1   Features that are not supported for Web clients

Element	Notes
@Functions and @Commands	
@DBCommand	Only supported with *ViewNextPage* and *ViewPreviousPage* to move forward and backward in view pages.
@DeleteDocument	
@DialogBox	
@PickList	
@Prompt	
@Environment, @SetEnvironment, ENVIRONMENT	Use CGI variables to obtain information about a Web user's environment.
@Command([FileCloseWindow])	This command is available if you choose the database property *Use JavaScript when generating pages.*
@Command([FileSave])	This command is available if you choose the database property *Use JavaScript when generating pages.*
@Command([ViewRefreshFields])	This command is available if you choose the database property *Use JavaScript when generating pages.*
Action and Agent elements	
Simple actions	
Default view and form actions	
LotusScript for forms, actions, or buttons	Use LotusScript only for agents on the Web.
Using Agents *Manually from Actions menu*	
Field properties	
Native OS style—including text and date type fields	
Use Address dialog for choices, Use Access Control List for choices, and Use View dialog for choices in Names type fields	

continued

[handwritten notes:] In Pages (and forms?) graphics that has the page prop of do not hed, set, are ignored by the web and displayed as tiles. Headers n/a web. Info displays on top (that news in it and is seperately scrollable)

Field help desc. cannot be displayed on the web

Table 22-1 Features that are not supported for Web clients (*continued*)

Form properties and elements
Versioning
Anonymous forms
Merge replication conflicts
Automatically refresh fields
On Open: Show Context pane
Layout regions
Popup hotspots
Other elements
Private views and folders

date pickers does not work on the web.
file upload only available on the web.

When you think you might need to use one of these features (or other features that are not supported on Web clients), you might use hide-when options to hide the elements from Web clients. Hide-when is available for most elements in the Properties InfoBox for that element. Use the *Hide* "element" from *Web browsers* to create elements that users can see on Notes clients but not on Web browsers, as shown in Figure 22-2.

Figure 22-2
Hiding from Web browsers

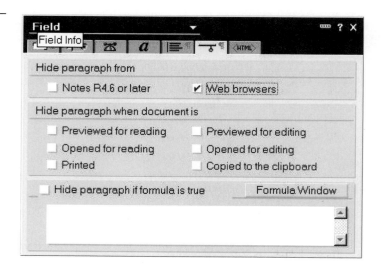

What to Use

Some Notes design elements are specifically intended for use with Web clients. When designing for Web clients, take advantage of some of the following options:

- Java applets, such as the Editor applet for rich-text fields, the View applet, the Outline applet, and the Action bar applet, which provide a more Notes-like interface and additional element functions for Web users. Figure 22-3 shows the Editor applet.

- The database property *Web access: Use JavaScript when generating pages,* which enables you to have more than the default Submit button on forms. Figure 22-4 shows this option.

- The database launch property *When Opened in a browser,* to select the element that Domino displays first to Web users of a database (shown in Figure 22-5). Options include a frameset, page, or navigator, among others. *Generate HTML for all fields → hidden*

- The form property *Generate HTML for all fields,* in order to ensure that hidden fields *fields are* are calculated, as shown in Figure 22-6. *calculated*

- An *Anonymous* entry in the ACL for the database. This entry governs the access level for non-authenticated Web users.

- A maximum access for Web users on the ACL, as shown in Figure 22-7.

- Action buttons that mimic options that are usually found on menus. Web users do not have a Create, View, or Action menu. You should therefore create action buttons to enable users to create documents, edit documents, save documents, open views, and navigate the database.

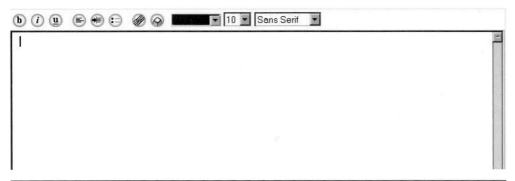

Figure 22-3   Editor applet

Figure 22-4
Setting the database
property

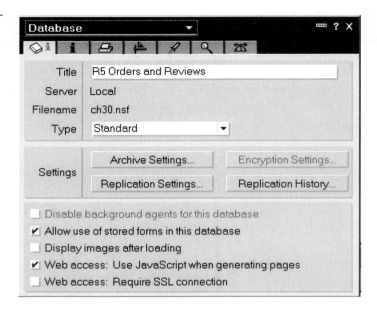

Figure 22-5
Database launch
property for Web
users

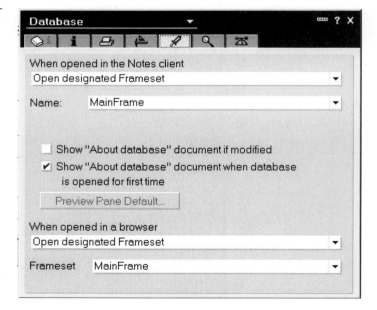

Figure 22-6
Generate HTML for all fields.

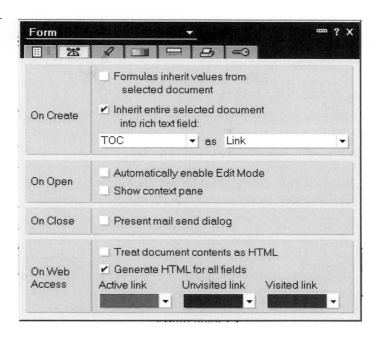

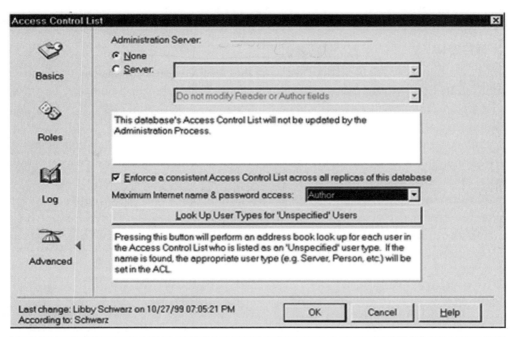

Figure 22-7 Maximum access for Web users

- Embedded views and folders. These items enable you to create views that contain the appearance of views and folders in Notes clients, especially when you use the View applet.

Functions to Use

Specific functions are included in R5 to help make Web programming easier. While the syntax and other details of these functions are described in more detail later in this section, pay special attention to using these functions:

- @BrowserInfo enables you to test the browser for certain characteristics, such as whether JavaScript is enabled or whether frames are supported. If you are using an element that depends on a certain level of support from a browser, use this function to check the browser.

- @UserRoles checks the ACL of a database and lists the roles for the current user. When used with Web clients, this function also appends the $$WebClient role.

Both of these functions can be used with the conditional (@If) to select which elements to show to a user, based on how they view the application.

@ UserNamesList — { current user name / any group names / any roles

Summary

One of the goals of R5 Designer is to enable developers to create a single application that can be used with both Web and Notes clients. There are some elements, however, that are not supported for Web clients or Notes clients. You should optimize your application for the client who will be using it, and you should ensure that you have not included elements that cannot be used with a particular client. Test your applications in the clients that will access them. Verify which elements enhance a Web user's experience, and use them appropriately.

The elements in this chapter are repeated in the appropriate following chapters, so there are no practice questions or answers in this chapter. Pay close attention to which elements can be used with which clients as you go through the rest of the chapters in this section.

Creating a Database

You should be able to answer questions based on the following objectives after reading this chapter:

- Creating a database
- Setting properties for a database

To begin your Domino development journey, you must create one or more Notes databases. These databases serve as containers for your other design elements (such as forms and views), as well as for the data that your users want to store. A Notes database is a single container that is used as the repository for both design elements and documents. Items such as forms, views, pages, outlines, framesets, and navigators are examples of design elements in databases. In addition to design elements, you will also find documents in databases. Documents contain the data that is entered by users. Usually, Notes databases will contain many documents about related topics. These documents can contain rich text, graphics, tables, buttons, fields, formulas, and many other types of information.

A database might or might not have the capacity to stand completely alone to solve a business process need. An application is one or more Notes databases that can be combined with other elements (such as ODBC data sources) and that are designed to store and share information in a manner that solves a particular business function. Figure 23-1 shows some of the distinctions between Domino databases and applications.

To understand Notes applications, start by imagining a business process or function that happens in your office. A familiar example might be a discussion database that enables a department in your office to keep in touch. If the employees in your help desk department want to improve their ability to answer questions, they might create a discussion database to post and comment on problems that they encounter in the organization. This database would have forms enabling the help desk employees to describe the

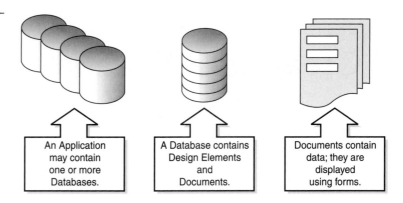

Figure 23-1
Domino application elements

| An Application may contain one or more Databases. | A Database contains Design Elements and Documents. | Documents contain data; they are displayed using forms. |

problem they are working on or to ask a question—or perhaps to post some interesting fact that they just learned. There would be a second form to enable other team members to comment on the posts. When the forms are filled out by users and are saved, documents are created in the database. The database would contain one or more views to display the documents. At least one of the views would probably enable you to see the thread of the conversation. This database type is similar to the forums or newsgroups typically found on the Internet or Usenet. This simple example of a Notes application might use one or more databases and could be used either with a Notes client or over the Web.

The first item we discuss in this chapter is what Notes applications are best used for —and therefore, what types of Notes applications you might create. Then, you will create a Notes database similar to the one just discussed, using one of three methods. Next, we will discuss the database properties that you can manipulate for your databases. Finally, watch for troubleshooting tips throughout the chapter. Certain options or properties that you might set are often the cause or solution for a particular symptom.

Notes Databases and Applications

A Notes database is a single container for many types of objects. These objects include design elements and documents. Some of the design elements found in Notes databases include the following:

- **Pages**   Used for display.
- **Forms**   Used for capturing information (creating documents) and displaying gathered data.

- **Views**   Used to display a list of the documents in the database.

- **Navigators**   Used to move through a database using a graphical format.

- **Outlines**   Used to move through a database using a list format.

These elements and others enable a developer to display and gather information in a Notes database. After a user completes a form, which is one of the main design elements, Notes stores the data that the user inputs as a document. The documents, which are listed in views, can be selected, read, deleted, or otherwise manipulated. Notes databases can stand alone, connect to each other, or connect to outside data sources such as an Oracle or Access database. Notes databases and applications can serve a variety of business functions, including the following:

- Workflow applications automatically forward information to the appropriate people. These types of applications can include mailed forms, mailed links, or a combination of the two. These types of applications usually replace or revise paper-based business processes.

- Tracking applications monitor tasks, projects, other applications, or processes. Tracking applications use agents that are automated using formulas, LotusScript, or JavaScript.

- Collaboration applications enable groups to discuss and work together on projects.

- Data integration applications use OLE, ODBC connectors, and other types of connections to integrate a Notes/Domino application and a transactional or relational database system such as Oracle, SQL, or Access.

Within each of these types of applications, as well as within other types of Notes applications, Domino has tools that enable the following procedures:

- **Personalization**   Occurs in many types of applications by providing content that is linked to you, based on username, access rights, roles, or other current information. Subscriptions to databases, which bring the latest information in that database to your start page, are one example of personalization.

- **Globalization**   Occurs in many types of applications by providing content that is appropriate in language, date format, and currency format to the current locale. The Global Workbench application is included with Domino Designer to provide this functionality.

Creating a Database

Now that you are bursting with excitement over what you can do with Notes databases, you need to start creating them. There are three main methods of creating Notes databases:

- Create a blank database from scratch
- Use a predefined Notes template
- Copy an existing database

Creating a Database from Scratch

Before you can create a database, you must first install and open the Domino Designer as described in Chapter 6, "Installing and Configuring Servers and Clients." Note that you can also create databases in the Notes client by using the same techniques. When you create a database from scratch, the database initially has no design elements (remember that design elements are forms, views, navigators, etc.), with the exception of a default view. Use this method when none of the templates or current databases closely match the needs for the new database. To create a new database from scratch, start in either the Notes client or the Designer client. Choose File . . . Database . . . New to display the New Database dialog box, shown in Figure 23-2.

 Default view (handwritten annotation)

Figure 23-2
New Database
dialog box

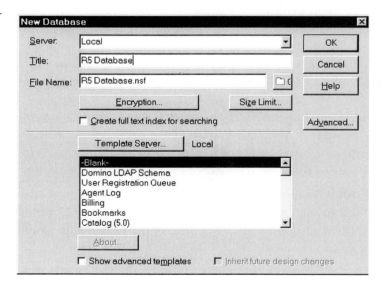

In the New Database dialog box, complete the Server field with the name of the server on which you want to create the new database. You can either type the name of the server or select it by clicking the drop-down arrow. This field defaults to Local, which indicates that the database will be created in your current \NOTES\DATA directory.

NOTE In most cases, you should create the database locally (i.e., on your local hard drive) first. Develop your database, add security, and only then add the database to the server, when you are ready to test the database. Keeping your database local prevents users from accessing the database before you have completed development.

After deciding where the database should reside, give the database a title. The title, which can be a maximum of 32 characters, will appear in the Open Database dialog box and on the Bookmarks list in Notes clients. The filename field fills in automatically as you give the database a title. Be careful. While Notes can handle filenames with spaces and is not case sensitive for filenames, not every operating system is so tolerant. Many developers adhere to a file-naming convention within their environment that enables easy administration of the database files from within Notes or within the operating system.

By default, Notes database files have an .NSF extension. They might also have an .NS4 or .NS3 extension when you are developing databases for older versions of Notes. When completing the filename, remember that by default, the new database stores itself in the \NOTES\DATA folder of whichever server (machine) you choose to host the database. If you want the file in another folder, type the folder and filename (relative to the \DATA directory), or select the location using the Folder button to the right of the filename field. Note that if you are not storing the database locally, the folder in which you place the database must be accessible as a mapped drive on your current machine.

Encrypting the Database   Another option in the New Database dialog box enables you to encrypt the new database. When you encrypt a database, you encode it so that only the user(s) listed in the dialog box can open and use the database. This user possesses the necessary encryption key in his or her user ID file to decrypt, or decode, the database. Laptop users find local encryption especially handy as a security measure for their local databases. To encrypt a database at creation time, choose the Encryption button to display the Encryption dialog box, as shown in Figure 23-3. Note the username listed on the dialog box, which indicates the user(s) who will be able to open the database after encryption is applied. When you select the Encryption

[handwritten margin note: Title max of 32 characters]

[vertical text: PART IV]

button, Notes assumes that the process will encrypt the database for the user who is currently logged in, based on the active USER.ID file. You can choose from Simple, Medium, or Strong Encryption. Table 23-1 provides an overview of the different levels of encryption.

Bear in mind that local encryption prevents users who are not listed in the Encryption dialog box from opening the local replica, but does not prevent access to the database when it resides on a server. Security (when a database is on a server) should be implemented using *Access Control Lists* (ACLs). (For more information about security,

Figure 23-3
Encryption dialog box

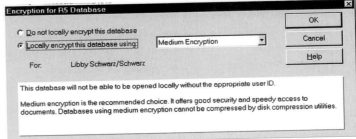

Table 23-1 Encryption levels

Level of Encryption	Description
Simple	As with all levels of encryption, the database requires the specified USER.ID to be opened locally. Simple encryption enables disk compression on the database and provides the fastest access to documents. Simple encryption only provides a limited level of security.
Medium	Medium encryption requires the USER.ID to open the database locally. This level of encryption does not enable the database to be compressed using disk-compression utilities. While still offering relatively quick access to documents, medium encryption also offers more security. In most cases where you require encryption, use medium encryption.
Strong	Strong encryption requires the USER.ID to open the database locally. This level of encryption does not enable the database to be compressed using disk-compression utilities and provides a high degree of security, although access to documents is somewhat slower than with other levels of encryption.

refer to Chapter 10, "Configuring Domino Security," and Chapter 26, "Creating Fields and Formulas.")

Database Size   The Size Limit button on the New Database dialog box does not apply to R5 databases. R5 databases have a theoretically unlimited size. (Lotus has tested and certified up to 64GB.) When placing the database on an R4.X server, however, you might want to implement a size limit by using this button. By default, databases placed on an R4 server will have a hard-coded size limit of 1GB, although you can use the Size Limit button to raise this limit to 4GB. Again, when placing the database on an R5 server, this button and the size limit do not apply.

Advanced Options   Designer offers a number of advanced options while creating a database. First, you have the capability to create a full-text index while creating the database by enabling the Create Full Text Index for Searching checkbox. Look for more details about indexing in Part VI, "Domino R5 Application Architecture." The other advanced options available while creating a database reside in the Advanced Database Options dialog box, which is available by clicking the Advanced button. The options on this dialog box are all new to R5 and are enabled by the new file structure of the databases, known as the *On Disk Structure* (ODS). This version of the ODS, updated since R4.X, is Version 41. Advanced Database options, shown in Figure 23-4, are geared primarily toward better performance and/or reduced database size.

UNREAD MARKS : COMPACT

Do Not Maintain Unread Marks   Notes databases keep unread marks internally to enable users to see which documents they have not read in a database. The maintaining of the unread marks, however, takes up system resources and slows database performance. Use this property when you do not want to maintain unread marks in databases where it is unnecessary, such as the Domino Directory, the Notes Log, or MAIL.BOX, which do not require this property. Note that if you change this property, you must run the COMPACT task on the database for the change to take effect. This option improves database performance and decreases database size.

Document Table Bitmap Optimization   Domino uses internal document information tables to determine where documents should appear in a view. When updating or rebuilding views, Domino searches each table for the documents that should appear in the particular view that is being updated or rebuilt. With the Document Table Bitmap Optimization property enabled, Domino associates the forms used by documents shown in the table with that table. During an update or a rebuild, therefore, Domino only has to search the tables associated with the forms used by the documents in the view. While the association does create a small performance cost, the benefit of the

PART IV

Figure 23-4
Advanced Database
options

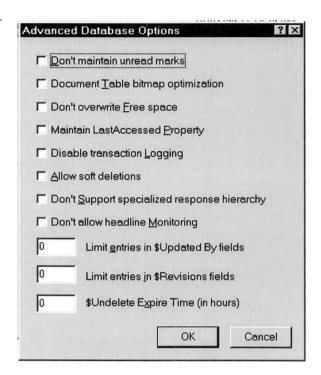

more efficient update or rebuild of views usually compensates for the cost. This situation is especially true for small views in large databases, where the search for the necessary document information in the internal tables would take a long time because of the size of the database. Note that this property only works on views that use Form = in the selection formula for the view. For more information about views and selection formulas, refer to Chapter 27, "Creating Views, Columns, and Folders." Also note that if you change this property, you must run the COMPACT task on the database for the change to take effect. This option improves database performance.

Do Not Overwrite Free Space When you delete anything in a Notes database, Notes immediately overwrites that location with a pattern. This security feature ensures that the data cannot be retrieved by using an undelete program from the operating system. This feature uses extra disk *Input/Output* (I/O); however, there is a great deal of moving back and forth along the disk to write over the deleted areas. On some systems—or for certain databases—this security feature is unnecessary. In locations where the server is physically secure—or for databases where this level of security is not necessary, such as for a help database—you can use this property to improve database performance. The next COMPACT task that you run against the database will remove the free space.

Maintain LastAccessed Property   The LastAccessed property forces Domino to store the date when a document was last modified or read. Naturally, this property requires extra resources in the database. With this option disabled, the database only stores information that is related to the most recent changes to a document, rather than also tracking reads to the document. Only enable this advanced property when you need to take an action (such as archiving or deleting) based on the most recent use (including reading) of a document. Leaving this database property deselected improves database performance.

Disable Transaction Logging   Transaction logging enables quick recovery of information if a server goes down unexpectedly. Notes first writes each change to a database to the transaction log. Then, Notes takes the changes from the transaction log and commits them to the database. If the server crashes, the server recreates any transactions that have not been written to the database by reviewing the transaction log. When transaction logging is enabled on a server, all databases on the server participate in this feature by default. To disable transaction logging for a specific database, enable this property. For more information about transaction logging, refer to Chapter 8, "Directories."

Allow Soft Deletions   Soft deletions are a new feature in R5; they enable documents that have been deleted from a database to be recovered for a certain period of time. Allowing soft deletions and creating a special view that displays the deleted items can enable deleted documents to be recovered without having to restore the database from a backup. This option works in coordination with the $Undelete Expire Time field, discussed next. Look for more information about recovering deleted documents in Chapter 27, "Creating Views, Columns, and Folders."

Do Not Support Specialized Response Hierarchy   Many views in Notes databases display a relationship, or thread, between documents—creating a response hierarchy of parent, children, and grandchildren documents. An example of a view with a response hierarchy is shown in Figure 23-5. The specialized response hierarchy is established using the @AllChildren and @AllDescendants functions. These functions maintain information relating a response document to its parents. (For more information about views and these @Functions, refer to Chapter 27, "Creating Views, Columns, and Folders.") Maintaining this information requires extra space in the database and extra resources. In databases that do not require this format in views, enable this option to improve database performance and reduce database size. When you change this property, you must run the COMPACT task on the database for the change to take effect.

Figure 23-5
Hierarchical view
sample

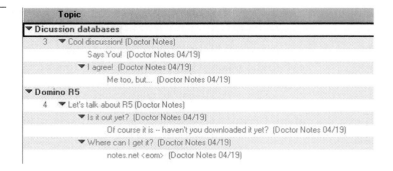

Do Not Allow Headline Monitoring   Headlines, which are a new feature for Notes clients in R5, enable users to create a subscription to databases that are of special interest to them. When those databases change, Notes alerts the user based on a profile they created for their subscriptions. To enable a particular database to participate in headline monitoring, this option must be disabled. (Note that this option is not the only requirement for configuring headlines. Headlines also require a particular type of form, called a profile form. If many users subscribe to a database, however, Notes uses a significant amount of database resources to complete the monitoring. Enabling this option, which disables headline monitoring on the database, improves database performance.)

Limit Entries in the $UpdatedBy Field   Notes reserves the $UpdatedBy field for storing the names of the users or servers that made each change to a document, creating a complete-edit history for each document in the database. Maintaining this complete history of updates requires both space and resources in the database. In addition, updates and rebuilds of views and replications are slowed by having to look at this complete history. For databases that do not require a complete record of all changes, limit the number of entries stored in this field by entering a number in this property. When the number of changes exceeds the number placed in this property, the oldest change-history item will be removed. Enabling this property improves database performance and decreases database size.

Limit Entries in the $Revisions Field   By default, the $Revisions field stores up to 500 entries that record the dates and times of changes that are made to the documents in the database. According to Lotus, each of these entries can use up to 8 bytes of space in the database. As the database grows and more changes are made, the $Revisions field can grow large and unwieldy, slowing database access and eating space on the hard drive. To improve database performance and limit database size for databases that do not need all 500 entries, limit the number of entries in the $Revisions field. Lotus recommends 10 entries as a place to start when tweaking this variable. Because the $Revisions field is used in preventing replication conflicts, maintaining fewer than 10 entries might cause more replication conflicts in the database. (For more information about replication and replication conflicts, refer to Chapter 5, "Domino Applications and Replication.") When the $Revisions field reaches the number specified in this property, Notes deletes the oldest revision entry.

+ Soft deletions.

$Undelete Expire Time (in Hours)   As mentioned previously, the capability to provide soft deletions is a new R5 feature. This feature enables Notes to recover documents that users have mistakenly deleted—without requiring restoration of the database from a backup. In coordination with the Allow Soft Deletions option, this field specifies the amount of time that a deleted document can be recovered. Specify the amount of time in hours.

Creating a Database Using a Template

The next method for creating a new database—using a predefined Notes template—enables a developer to spend little time creating individual design elements while still developing a complete and useful database. A template file is similar to a Notes database and usually has an .NTF extension rather than the .NSF extension used by databases. The template contains all of the necessary design elements to create a functioning database; however, the template usually does not contain any data (documents). The file also has a database property that defines the database as a template (discussed later in this chapter). Designers can use these templates to create new databases without having to develop all of the design elements. Lotus provides a variety of templates with Designer, most of which map to the most common types of applications created, including document or database libraries, mail and address book databases, discussion databases, and resource reservation databases. You can also obtain database templates from **http://www.notes.net**. Databases based on these templates can be used as is or can be customized to meet specific needs. When deciding whether to use a template or develop a database from scratch, consider how closely the template resembles your actual need. If the template requires significant customization, it might be faster to create the database from scratch. Bear in mind that even if you decide not to base the entire database on a template, you can copy elements (such as a form, view, or formula) from a template into your database.

To create a new database based on a template, choose File . . . Database . . . New to display the New Database dialog box. The top half of this dialog box was discussed previously in this chapter. For now, when basing the new database on a template, focus on, the bottom half of this dialog box. Begin by choosing a template server. The template server is the machine on which all of the available templates reside. By default, all machines contain most of the available templates. In many enterprise environments, however, administrators remove template servers and place them only on a dedicated development server. Also remember that client machines and server machines contain different templates by default. Next, select the template on which to base your database. Table 23-2 contains a list of some of the templates that are available by default in R5 Designer. Figure 23-6 shows the process of creating a new database based on the Document Library template.

Table 23-2 Available R5 templates

Database Title	Design Template Name	Filename	Purpose/ Description
Discussion— Notes and Web (R5)	StdR50Disc	DISCW50.NTF	Databases created with this template can be used for either a Notes client or a Web client. The template provides hierarchical views that enable topics to exist in a threaded discussion.
Document Library—Notes and Web (R5)	StdR50WebDocLib	DOCLBW50.NTF	Databases created with this template provide storage for other documents. This template provides review and workflow features.
Personal Journal (R4)	StdR4Journal	JOURNAL4.NTF	Databases created with this template provide an open set of forms for storing notes and documents.
Team Room (R5)	Std50TeamRoom	TEAMRM50.NTF	This template enables designers to create databases that can be used for collaboration, including discussions, to-do items, archiving, newsletters, and reviews.

Figure 23-6
Selecting a template
to create a new
database

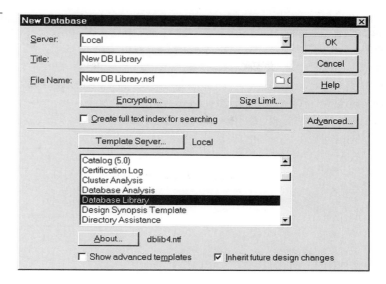

When uncertain about the appropriate uses for a particular template, you can click the About . . . button (as shown in Figure 23-7) to view the About this Database document for the selected template. The two other options that relate to creating a database from a template are Show Advanced Templates and Inherit Future Design Changes. The Show Advanced Templates option displays any templates that have been marked as Advanced Templates. Mark a template as an Advanced Template by using one of the database properties for files indicated as templates. The Inherit Future Design Changes option enables Designer to link the template to the new database, even after the database exists. By default, when you create a new database from a template, the database is linked only once at design time. The newly created database essentially copies all of the design elements from the template and then becomes a unique file with no link to the template. Selecting this option, however, makes the database maintain a link to its template. If design elements such as forms or views are edited, deleted, or added in the template, Domino pushes those changes into the database when a task called Design is run at the server. This method of creating a database can be quick and efficient if the templates closely match your needs for the new database. In addition, you benefit from permanently linking the new database to the design elements in the template, enabling you to make changes in the template that will be shared with the databases based on the template.

Figure 23-7
About this Database
document for the
Document Library
template

Creating a Database from Another Database

Another method of creating a new database that also minimizes the required development work is to copy an existing database. If there is a database in your environment that has the same design elements as the database you need to create, why reinvent the wheel? After copying the database, delete all of the documents and make any customizations. For an existing database, first open either the Notes client or the Designer client. Open the database you want to copy (in the Notes client), or select the bookmark for that database (in the Designer client). Choose File . . . Database . . . New Copy to display the Copy Database dialog box, as shown in Figure 23-8.

Select a server to host the new copy of the database. When initially creating a database, this server will usually be local (your local \NOTES\DATA directory). Change the filename of the new copy if you are storing the new database in the same location as the original database. You might also choose to change the title of the database, although this action is not required. For database copies, you have the option of copying only the design elements or the design elements and documents. In cases where you are creating a new database based on an existing database, you will likely want to copy only the database design. You can also enable the ACL checkbox to copy the ACL from the existing database. Keep in mind that you might not want to copy the ACL if you need Designer access to the new database but do not already have this access for the existing database. Look for more discussion of ACLs and security in Chapter 24, "Understanding and Implementing Basic Security." Be certain to verify that the design of the database you are copying is not hidden. To verify that the design is available, open the

Figure 23-8
Copy Database
dialog box

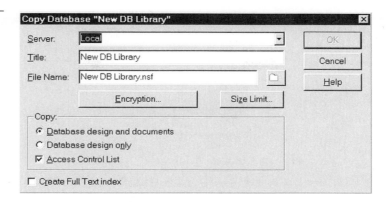

database properties for the existing database by choosing File . . . Database . . . Properties. In the Database Properties dialog box, click the Design tab. If you see *No design
information is available* at the top of this tab, you can still copy the design of the database, but you will not be able to modify the design.

> **NOTE**   To hide the design of a database that was created from a template (as
> described previously), choose File . . . Database . . . Replace Design. In the
> Replace Design dialog box, shown in Figure 23-9, select the name of the tem-
> plate upon which the database was originally based. After selecting the tem-
> plate, enable both (check-mark visible) the Inherit Future Design Changes, and Hide Formulas
> and LotusScript. When you choose OK, the design will be replaced, and the formulas will no
> longer be available in the Domino Designer. Open the Database properties InfoBox to verify
> that the design is hidden. On the Design tab, Notes displays No Design Information Available.
> You retain access to the layout of the forms, views, and other design elements, however. To
> make the design visible again when hidden using this method, simply replace the design
> again. This time, ensure that the Hide Formulas and LotusScript option is disabled.

Creating a database by copying an existing database can also be effective when creating a new database that is similar to an existing database. Examples of good uses for this
option include when you are creating an Archive database for an existing database, or
when you are creating similar databases for multiple departments.

Creating a Database Using
Combined Methods

Although creating a database is described as using three distinct methods, you should
realize that in the real world, you would probably use a combination of these methods,

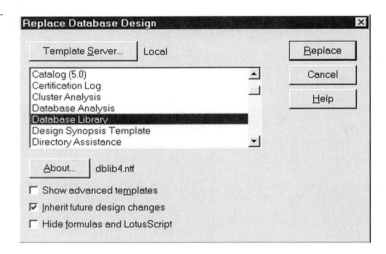

Figure 23-9
Replace Design
dialog box

especially while you are in the learning process. Any time you create or develop a database, you can use elements from other databases to enhance your creation. This action can be done either by copying the element and then modifying it to fit your needs, or by copying an element and linking just that element to a design template, so that it will be updated by changes to the template.

To copy a design element from an already-existing database or from a provided template, simply open the database or template in the Designer client. Select the design element, such as a view, field, form, page, or other element from the current database, and copy the element. Then, open your new database and paste the element in the appropriate location. Then, modify the element as necessary to fit your needs in the new application.

To copy a design element and link just that element to a design template, follow these steps. First, in the Designer client, open the template or database that contains the design element that you want to copy. In most cases, you will be copying from a design template, such as those listed earlier. After copying the design element, open your database and paste the design element in the appropriate view. You should be prompted with the dialog box shown in Figure 23-10, which asks whether you want to link that element with the element in the design template. If you say yes, this element will be updated automatically when the element in the design template is updated. This procedure overwrites any changes to the design element that you make in the new database, however, unless you change a design element property.

Figure 23-10

Linking a design
element to a
template

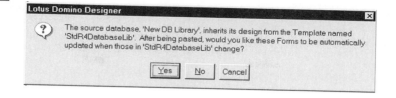

To verify that this design element is linked to a template, open the Design Document for that element. To access the Design Document, go to the appropriate design view, such as the Forms view or the Views view in the Designer client. Click the design element in the view and choose Design . . . Design Properties. (This Design properties InfoBox is also available by clicking the Properties smarticon.) On the Design tab of this dialog box, you can use the Inherit from the Design template field to ensure that this element continues to be linked to the specified design template.

NOTE   You can also force a particular element not to inherit a design. If you are creating a database based on a template—but you want to modify certain elements and prevent those elements from being overwritten—you can use the Prohibit Design Refresh or Replace to Modify option. If you enable this option, the database itself can obtain design information from a template while a particular design element is separated from the link.

Summary of Steps to Create a New Database   To create a new database, follow these steps:

1. If you are copying a previously existing database, select the database. Open the database properties to verify that the design is not hidden.

2. Choose File . . . Database . . . New Copy.

3. Choose to copy only the database design. Choose a database title, filename, and location for the new database.

4. Determine whether you need encryption or a size limit (for databases residing on R4.X only). Also, decide whether or not to copy the ACL. Choose OK to make the copy.

5. Open the copied database in Designer to make any needed design changes.

6. If you are creating a database from scratch or from a template, choose File . . . Database . . . New.

7. Choose a database title, filename, and location for the new database.

8. Decide whether you will use a template. If so, select a template server.

9. Select the correct template. If the template you need is not listed, you might need to enable the Show Advanced Templates option.

10. If the database should inherit changes made to design elements in the template (such as changes to views, forms, navigators, and formulas), enable the Inherit Future Design Changes option.

11. In either case, determine whether you need encryption or a size limit (for databases residing on R4.X only). Also, choose whether you should create a Full Text Index.

12. Set any Advanced Options, and click OK to create the new database.

13. Open the new database in Designer to create any necessary design elements.

Database Properties

After creating a database, you might want to set or view the database properties. Some of the properties might have been set at create time (using the New Database dialog box), or you might choose to set other properties after the database is created. To access the database properties, choose File . . . Database . . . Properties. The Information button (shown in Figure 23-11) is available at the top-right corner of the Designer window (with the preview buttons) and also opens the Properties InfoBox. The Database properties InfoBox, shown in Figure 23-12, enables the developer to view or set options for the entire database. The Database properties InfoBox is organized into tabbed pages, as are all properties InfoBoxes. The options available to change or view are described as follows.

The Basics Tab   The first tab of the Database properties InfoBox is the Basics tab, which is shown in Figure 23-12. This tab gives general information about the database.

Figure 23-11
The Information
button

Figure 23-12
The Database
properties InfoBox

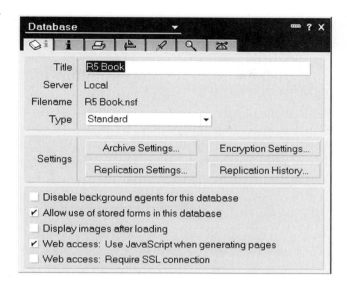

The first field is the Database Title field. Edit this field to change the title that you gave the database. This tab also displays the server name and filename. Neither of these fields can be edited in this dialog box. You can also view or change the Database Type. The template used to create the database usually determines the database type. Databases created without a template are standard-type databases by default.

Other options available on this tab include both the Archive and the Encryption settings. The Archive Settings button displays the Archive Settings dialog box, shown in Figure 23-13. To keep documents that are no longer currently important but might be necessary at some point, create an archive database. Use the Archive button to force Notes to copy documents to an archive database automatically (if the database resides on a server), based on the amount of time a document has been unused, unchanged, or expired. You can also archive documents manually, on a local workstation, based on the same characteristics. Archiving enables you to store copies of documents in a new database. Complete the following options to configure archiving for a database:

- Archive all documents not read or accessed on my local workstation

- Archive all documents not modified or updated

- Archive all documents marked as expired

- Archive database

- Manually from my workstation to

- Automatically on server

- Log archiving activity to

- Do not delete documents that have responses

- Delete all qualifying documents without archiving them

The Encryption settings, which are available from the Encryption Settings button, are the same as described previously, with one addition. This Encryption dialog box, shown in Figure 23-14, enables you to encrypt the database for someone other than the current user. You can click the For button on the Encryption dialog box to select another user from the Domino Directory or from your Personal Address Book. This feature enables you to encrypt the database locally for that user. Be aware, however, that you will not be able to access the database if you encrypt it for another user. Only the user who is listed on the Encryption dialog box can access an encrypted database. When trying to access a database that has local encryption for someone other than your current USER.ID, you will receive the error shown in Figure 23-15.

The Basics tab also enables you to set replication settings and view and clear your Replication History. Look for more information about the replication options in Chapter 5, "Domino Applications and Replication," and Chapter 39, ""Designing and Planning for Replication and Routing." This tab contains five additional check boxes:

Figure 23-13
Archive Settings
dialog box

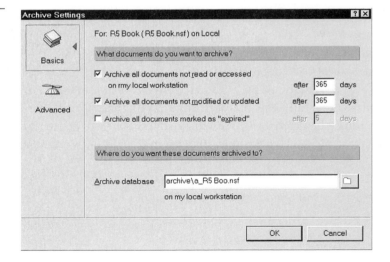

Figure 23-14
Encryption dialog
box

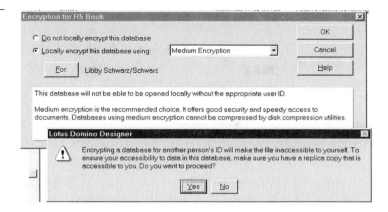

Figure 23-15
Local encryption
error

- *Disable background agents for this database.* Ensures that no agents run in the background on this database. Agents are said to be running in the background (as opposed to the foreground) when the agent has been scheduled based on time or has been triggered by an event, such as new mail arriving. For more information about agents, refer to Chapter 28 "Creating Actions, Agents, and Hotspots."

- *Allow use of stored forms in this database.* Enables a form in the database to be stored with the document created by the form. By default, forms and data are stored separately. The form collects data and then displays that data, but they remain separate elements. In some cases, however, such as when a document is going to be mailed to a database where the form will not be available, storing the form and the data together makes sense. Checking this option enables Notes to display the data properly. Disabling this option enhances performance in the database and reduces the size of the database, because storing the form with the data consumes extra space and resources.

- *Display images after loading.* Forces all of the text of the document to be displayed before any images. In a document where this option is not enabled, the text and images will be displayed in the order in which they appear. In some cases, it is preferable for users to be able to see the text immediately, especially if there are large graphics or slow connections. Selecting this option can improve database performance and is most useful for Web clients or remote clients.

- *Web Access: Use JavaScript when generating pages.* Is a new option R5 that grants more flexibility when displaying forms and documents for Web clients. This option improves the behavior of the database for some Web clients, because documents and navigators display more quickly. When using JavaScript to render the pages, the client does not evaluate the formulas in hotspots display time—only when the user clicks the hotspot. This feature speeds up the display time for Web clients. In addition, this option enables additional @Commands and more than one button on a form. Some of the additional @Commands that are only available when this option is in use include @Command(FileSave) and @Command(FileCloseWindow). For the uses of these and other @Commands, refer to Chapter 26, "Creating Fields and Formulas." Finally, this option enables you to place more than a single button on a form being used with Web clients. By default, with this option disabled, all Web forms have a single button (added automatically—you do not have to create this button) called Submit. Any other buttons would be ignored and would not be displayed to the browser. With this option enabled, however, the Domino server and Web client do not create and display a Submit button; rather, you must do this task manually. You can also create additional buttons, which the Web client (via the Domino server) displays as created.

- *Web Access: Require SSL connection.* Forces users who are logging in to the database using a Web client to use a *Secure Sockets Layer* (SSL) when accessing this database. SSL provides an additional layer of security for those who are using the database over the Internet. Using a type of encryption, SSL ensures the security of data transferred between the server and the client. Be aware that enabling SSL for a database inflicts a performance hit in return for the added security.

The Basics tab covers a wide range of details about the database. Some of these options, such as enabling stored forms and displaying images after loading, affect both the size and performance of the database.

The Info Tab   The Info tab displays basic information about the database, as shown in Figure 23-16. First, you can see the size of the database in kilobytes. Second, you can see the number of documents created in the database. The Percent (%) Used button

Figure 23-16
The Info tab

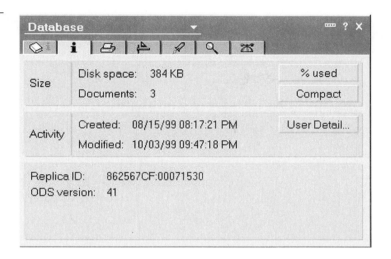

enables Notes to calculate the amount of space in the database that is being used by documents or design elements, rather than white space. To reduce the amount of white space in the database, you can click the Compact button. Compacting the database reduces the amount of unused white space.

 NOTE   Be aware that compacting the database has other effects, such as enabling some of the advanced database properties and updating the ODS of an R4 database residing on an R5 server to the new R5 ODS. To prevent these side effects (if unwanted), do not run COMPACT from the button available in this infobox. Instead, run the COMPACT task from the Domino Server console with the appropriate argument, such as —R, to prevent updating to the newer ODS version.

[handwritten margin note: Seve task Compact prevents update to new ODS]

The Activity section of the Info tab enables you to view the activity that has occurred in this database. The created and last modified dates are listed. You can also click the User Detail button. The User Activity dialog box can also display uses, reads, and writes in the database, as shown in Figure 23-17. If you select the Record Activity option, Notes lists the users who are working in the database and their actions, which can help you audit the database.

At the bottom of the Info tab, note the Replica ID of the database, which is a unique number assigned to the database. When you make a copy of the database (File . . . Database . . . New Copy), this number is changed. This number is different from the

Figure 23-17
The User Activity
dialog box

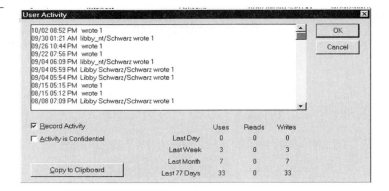

original copy of the database, and the databases are not linked to each other. If you make a replica of the database, however (File . . . Replication . . . New Replica), the databases have the same Replica ID and are permanently linked. They can be synchronized at any time using the process of replication. For more information about replication, refer to Chapter 12, "Implementing Replication."

The Printing Tab   The Printing tab, shown in Figure 23-18, configures the printing defaults for the database. First, you can set text for the headers and/or footers of the documents in the database. You can use the buttons to add page numbers, dates, times, tabs, or the title of the database to either the header or the footer. You can also set the font, size, and style for the header and/or footer. Finally, you can choose whether the header and footer should be placed on the first page of any printed topic. The Printing tab sets the defaults for all pages printed from the current database, but be aware that you can set printing properties from other properties infoboxes, as well.

The Design Tab   The Design tab, shown in Figure 23-19, displays and enables you to edit information about the database's design, assuming that the design of the database is not hidden. In our example, the first line of the tab indicates that the design is not hidden. If the design had been hidden, the tab would indicate only that the design is not available. The second option on the tab indicates whether the selected database should inherit its design from a design template. When you created the database from a template, you had the option to maintain a link to the template. If you chose to do so, or if you select to link the database to a template here, the design of the template might overwrite any design changes made to the database itself. In addition, Domino will push any design changes made in the template to the database. These changes will

Figure 23-18
The Printing tab

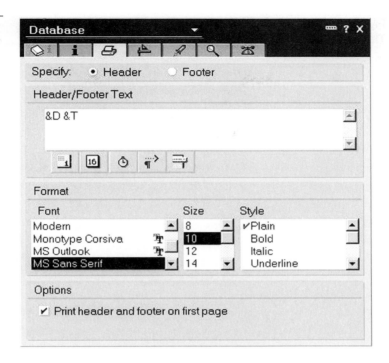

occur based on the schedule of the DESIGN server task or based on when you choose to refresh the design. To link the database to a design template, indicate the template from which the database should inherit its design. Also, use the tab to indicate that the specified database (regardless of its .NSF or .NTF extension) is a design template by enabling the Database is a template option. If you choose to make a database a template, you can give it a template name here. Enabling this option makes this database available in the New Database dialog box as a template option. After making the database a template and giving it a name, you could also specify that it should appear as an advanced template by enabling the List as Advanced Template in New Database dialog option.

Next, determine whether to list the database in the Database Catalog. The Database Catalog, which is created when an administrator runs the CATALOG server task, lists all databases in an organization. By default, Notes enables the List in Database Catalog option. One view in the Database Catalog enables you to view databases based on category. To place the database in a particular category, type the name of an existing or new category in the Categories field.

Figure 23-19
The Design tab

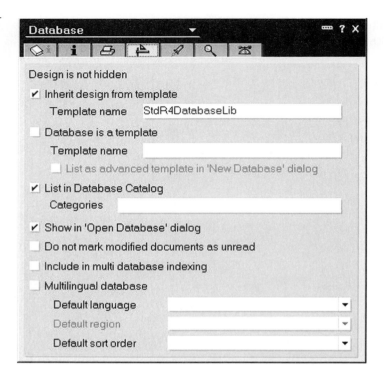

The Show in Open Database dialog option determines whether the database is visible to users when they select File . . . Database . . . Open. In some cases, you might not want the database to be visible in this dialog box, but be aware that it is not a security measure. Users can type the name of the database (if they know the name) to access the database regardless of whether the database is listed.

The next option is Do Not Mark Modified Documents as Unread. This option lists only the newly created documents as unread in all the views in the database. Only implement this option if the unread status of modified documents does not matter to your users, although it saves some space in the database and speeds the updating or rebuilding of effected views.

The Include in Multi-Database Indexing option enables Notes to list this database in a Search Site database. A Search Site database enables you to create a single index for multiple databases, which makes searching your Notes environment (or Web site) easier for users. To include a database in this index, enable this option.

The final options on the Design tab relate to multi-language databases. In R5, Domino Designer contains many features that are intended to make it easier for developers to create applications that will be used in many countries, regions, or languages. If your users or company need to use your application this way, select the Multilingual Database option. Then, specify a default language, region, and sort order based on language.

The options on the Design tab help you configure the overall design of your database, from specifying a template from which to inherit design changes to determining where the database will be available for users.

The Launch Tab   The Launch tab, shown in Figure 23-20, enables the manager or designer of a database to specify what happens when the users open the database. There are separate options for opening the database in a Notes client or in a Web client. The first option, called On Database Open, enables you to specify what happens when a user opens the database in a Notes client. The available options are described as follows.

Figure 23-20
The Launch tab

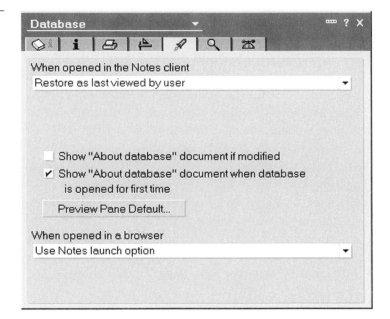

- *Restore as last viewed by user* is the default option. This option displays the database as it was when it was last opened. For example, if a user was in the default view the last time the database was open, then Notes displays the default view. This option also enables you to select two additional options: Show About Database document if modified and Show About Database document when database is opened for first time. These two options appear in addition to the basic option. The About Database document is a predefined document that enables the designer to add help information to the database. By default, this option is shown the first time that you open any database.

- The *Open About Database document* option opens an informational document created by the designer as help for the database. To access the About Database document in the Designer client, open Designer and click the Resources . . . Other design view. The About Database Document is available in the right-hand pane. Double-click to open and edit the document.

- The *Open Designated Frameset* option displays a multi-pane interface to the user. This interface, which is a new option in R5, can contain views, forms, pages, outlines, and other elements in each pane. When selecting this option using the drop-down list, choose a specific frameset for Notes to display to the user. For more details about creating and naming framesets, refer to Chapter 32, "Creating a Workflow Application." When choosing to have a frameset opened automatically, you can also use the About document options that were previously described in the first option.

- The *Open Designated Navigator* option displays a graphical interface that can contain buttons, text, and links. The navigator enables users to move around in the database, create documents, review documents, and perform other specified actions. When you choose to display a navigator, you must select which type of navigator to display: Folders, Standard Navigator, or Page. The Folders navigator is the default navigator that includes links to all of the views and folders in a database. The Standard Navigator enables you to select a specific navigator to be displayed to the user by using the drop-down list. For more details about creating and naming navigators, refer to Chapter 31, "Planning and Designing Workflow Applications." You can also choose to have Notes display a Page, which is a new design element for R5 that can contain text, graphics, links, buttons, and embedded elements. The Page option enables you to select a specific page (by using the drop-down list) for Notes to display to the user. For more details about creating and naming pages, refer to Chapter 25, "Creating Pages and Forms." When you choosing to have a navigator opened automatically, you also have the About document options.

- The *Open Designated Navigator in its own Window* option is similar to the previous option. In this case, however, the navigator opens in a separate window from the window in which the database appears. You must still select the type of navigator (folders, standard navigator, or page) and the specific navigator that you want to open. The About document options are not available with this option.

- The *Launch First Attachment in About Database* option checks the About Database document for its first listed attachment. This attachment is then launched using the application in which it was created (if available).

- The *Launch First Doclink in About Database* option checks the About Database document for its first listed doclink. Doclinks are links created in Notes to other Notes documents, views, or databases. This link is then launched inside Notes.

These options govern what happens when a user opens the database within the Notes client. The next option governs the Preview pane behavior in Notes. The Preview pane enables you to view the parent or doclink of a current document in another pane in the same window. The Preview Pane default button enables you to select from three default options which determine how Notes will arrange the Preview pane within the window. You can also select to have the Preview pane maximized when the database is opened.

The final option on the tab governs what a Web client, or browser, displays when a user opens the database. The options are as follows:

- *Use Notes Option* (the default option). This option enables the designer to display the same element to a Notes client and to a Web client.

- The *Open About Database document* option is the same as for the Notes client.

- The *Open Designated Frameset* option is the same as for the Notes client.

- The *Open Designated Page* option enables the designer to display a specified page to the Web client. For more information about pages, refer to Chapter 25, "Creating Pages and Forms."

- The *Open Designated Navigator in its own Window* option is the same as for the Notes client.

- The *Open first doclink in About database document* option is the same as for the Notes client.

- The *Open Designated Doclink* option enables you to select a particular doclink to open when a Web client opens the database. To specify a doclink, open the document, view, or database that you want to link to and choose Edit . . . Copy as Link. In the properties InfoBox, click the Paste Doclink button. After pasting the link, you can test the link to ensure that it works by clicking the Go To Doclink button. When a user opens the database, the Web client displays the document, view, or database referred to by this link.

- The *Launch first document in view* option displays a document from the selected view when the user first opens the database. Use the drop-down list to select the view from which the document should be displayed. The Web client displays whichever document is listed first in this view.

The Launch Options tab enables you to determine what a user will see first when opening a database. Test to ensure that whichever option you select has no errors and contains directions or buttons for navigating to other locations in the database.

The Full Text Tab In many cases, users need to be able to search for specific information in an application. To prepare your applications for this task, create a full-text index. A full-text index is a list that is stored in a separate file and that contains all of the words in the database. The Full Text tab enables you to create a full-text index and determine how often Notes or Domino updates the index. The Full Text tab, shown in Figure 23-21, enables you to create or delete a full-text index. After you create an index, the tab also enables you to update the index, determine the number of unindexed documents, and review the index settings. You will also see the size of the index and the last time it was indexed.

Figure 23-21
The Full Text tab

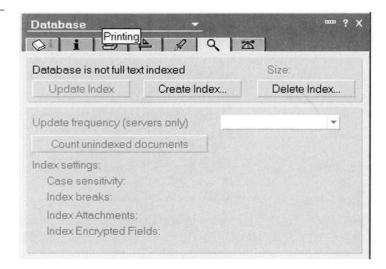

When you click the Create Index button to begin the full-text indexing process, you have a number of index options, as shown in Figure 23-22. You can choose to index attached files, for example. If you choose to index files that are attached to documents in the database, you can also decide whether to use the raw text-only method (which is faster) or the binary attachment method (which is more accurate). Choosing to index attachments in the database makes the index itself larger. The Index Encrypted Fields option ensures that all fields are indexed, including those that are encrypted. Encrypted fields are those that have been encoded for security purposes. (For more information about encryption, refer to Chapter 24, "Understanding and Implementing Basic Security.") Indexing encrypted fields increases the size of the full-text index. By default, the full-text indexer uses word breaks for indexing, which means that you can search for individual words. If you select the Index Sentence and Paragraph Breaks option, you can also search for words as they appear in the same sentence or paragraph. This option increases the size of the index but enables more context-sensitive searches. The option to enable case-sensitive searches indicates that Notes will complete searches exactly as typed. If you enable this option, for example, a search for "domino" will not find "Domino". Enabling case-sensitive searches increases the size of the index. Finally, if the database and full-text index reside on a server, you can determine how often the index should be updated. The choices are Daily, Scheduled, Hourly, and Immediate. Note that this option does nothing if the database and index are on your workstation. You must update the index manually by clicking the Update Index button if the database and index only reside on a workstation.

Figure 23-22
Creating a full-text
index

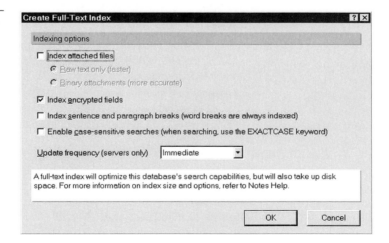

Creating a full-text index helps your users use databases and applications, but at a cost. The index takes up a significant amount of space on the hard disk of the server— up to 20 percent of the size of the database, according to Lotus. Be certain that there is sufficient space for the index before creating the index. Many of the options that make the index more searchable also make it larger, as described previously. Note that you must have Designer access to create a full-text index (more information about access levels and security will appear in Chapter 24, "Understanding and Implementing Basic Security").

The Advanced Tab   When you created the database earlier in this chapter, you reviewed and examined the advanced options. The options under the Advanced tab of the Database properties InfoBox, shown in Figure 23-23, are the same as those described previously.

Synopsis

When creating a database in Notes, you have the capability to set some defaults for the database. These defaults include the advanced options that might make the database smaller or more efficient. You can change or review these options, as well as some additional options that are not available at create time, using the Database properties InfoBox. In addition, other options such as the Launch and Printing options can be set

Figure 23-23
The Advanced tab

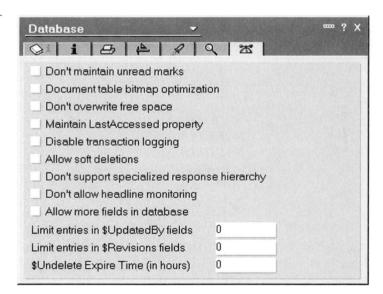

using this InfoBox. For the exam, concentrate on knowing which options can be enabled or disabled to improve database size and performance, as well as knowing the Launch options for the database.

Practice

As discussed in the introduction, each chapter contains a practice section that is devoted to applying the skills that you learned in the chapter. Lotus Education gears its exams and questions towards job tasks. You cannot simply understand the concepts behind Notes development; rather, you must also have hands-on experience. This practice section gives you the opportunity to create and set properties for a Notes database.

First, create a database using a template. This database can be used to discuss your certification issues and questions with any other certification-seekers in your organization. Refer to the included CD-ROM for a sample copy of this database.

1. Open the Domino Designer client.

2. Select File . . . Database . . . New.

3. The Server field should remain local. You will create the database on your local hard drive.

4. The Title field should be R5 Certification Discussion.

5. Remove the spaces from the filename and abbreviate it so that the filename is R5CertDsc.NSF.

6. Under the Template Selection field, choose Discussion—Notes & Web (R5) (discw50.ntf).

7. Click OK to create the new database.

The New Database dialog box for this database should look similar to Figure 23-1. After creating the database, open the database and look at the Database Properties infobox and the types of design elements that are included in this database. Use this exercise to become familiar with the design elements available.

Next, create a new Notes database for use in some of the later chapters. Take the following steps and refer to the included CD-ROM for a sample copy of this database, if necessary. Because many of the chapters in this book build upon this database, be sure to create the database according to the specifications, and keep a copy available for each practice. This database will be used for ordering books from Notes and Web clients (eventually). This database will also contain reviews and discussions.

Figure 23-24
New database for
R5 certification
discussion

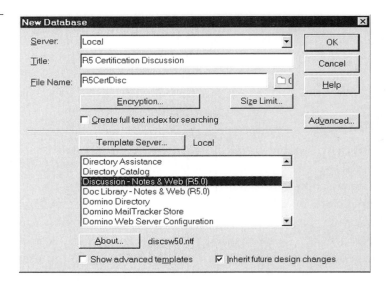

1. Open the Domino Designer client.

2. Select File . . . Database . . . New.

3. The Server field should remain local. You will create the database on your local hard drive.

4. The Title field should be R5 Orders and Reviews.

5. Remove the spaces from the filename and abbreviate it so that the filename is R5ORDREV.NSF.

6. You will be creating the database from scratch, so you can leave the Template field blank.

7. Do not encrypt the database locally or give the database a size limit.

8. You will apply advanced properties later.

9. Click OK to enable Notes to create the Database.

10. The database should open in your Designer client in Design mode.

Figure 23-25 shows the New Database dialog box for this database. Note that on the CD-ROM, each chapter's practice database uses the chapter number as the filename (for example, CH23.NSF).

Figure 23-25
The R5 Orders and
Reviews database

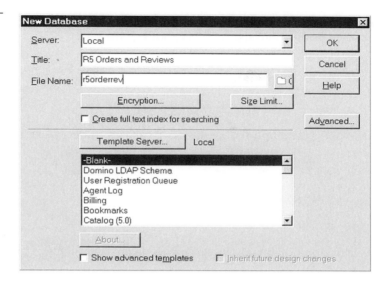

Review Questions

1. Barry is creating a new database for his company. When he looks through the templates and other databases that are available, he does not find any that have the same design elements that he wants. What method would probably be the most efficient way to create the new database?

   a. Create the database using a template. Then, use the Designer client to modify all of the existing design elements.

   b. Create the database by copying another database. Then, use the Designer client to modify all of the existing design elements.

   c. Create the database from scratch. Then, copy the design elements from other templates and databases.

   d. Create the database from scratch. Then, create the design elements necessary from scratch.

2. When Denise creates a new database, she completes the Server field with the name of her home server. Where is the best place for her to create new databases?

   a. Ask the administrator which server is the default server for new databases.

   b. Create the database locally and move it to a server when it is ready for testing.

   c. Create the database locally, and move it to a server as soon as it is created.

   d. She did the right thing—creating the database on the same server on which her mail file resides.

3. Which level of local encryption enables the database to be compressed using disk encryption while also providing some security?
   a. Simple
   b. Medium
   c. Strong
   d. User

4. What is the size limit on new R5 databases, as determined by the Size Limit button?
   a. 1GB
   b. 4GB
   c. 16GB
   d. none

5. The Don't Maintain Unread marks database property is best applied where and why?
   a. Apply this database property to files such as the Domino Directory and the Notes Log. These files do not need to display unread marks, and changing this property will improve performance and decrease database size.
   b. Apply this database property to users' mail files. They will notice when they get new mail, and it will improve performance.
   c. Apply this database property to headline-monitored databases. The headlines will show the new documents, and it will improve performance.
   d. To improve database performance, do not apply this property.

6. Melanie applied the Document Table Bitmap Optimization advanced property to her new database to help improve the performance of her large database. Unfortunately, nothing seems to have changed. What did she forget to do? Choose all answers that apply.
   a. She has to refresh the design of the database after making this change.
   b. She has to COMPACT the database after making this change.
   c. She has to make sure that the view is designed to take advantage of this setting.
   d. She has to enable the index process to run before the database will use the new property.

7. Sean created a new database and applied the Allow Soft Deletions property so that his users could recover deleted documents. After applying the property, he tries to test the recovery of a document but cannot figure out how to do this task. What did he probably forget to do?

a. He forgot to run the COMPACT task.

b. He forgot to create a view to display the deleted items.

c. He forgot to set the $Undelete Expire Time value to a reasonable amount.

d. He forgot to apply the correct template to the database to take advantage of the property.

8. To ensure that the new database she is creating takes the correct design, Katherine uses the DISCW50.NTF template. She wants to make some design changes, however, and does not want those changes to be overwritten. What can she do?

a. Instead of using the template to create the new database, just copy the database elements into a blank database.

b. Uncheck the Inherit Design from Template check box in the Database properties.

c. Uncheck the Inherit future design changes in the New Database dialog box.

d. Nothing. Changes will always be inherited if you use design elements that have been used in a template.

9. Joe's database exists on his workstation. When he sets the Full Text Index Update settings to Immediate, he expects the full-text index to update each time a change is made to the database. Will the index update as such?

a. Yes. The Immediate setting causes the full-text index to be updated to reflect any changes to the database.

b. No. The Immediate setting only works on server-based databases.

c. No. The Immediate setting only kicks off the first full-text indexing.

d. No. There is no Immediate setting—only Daily, Scheduled, and Hourly.

10. Enabling which of the following does NOT improve database performance?

a. *Disable Transaction Logging*

b. *Do Not Support Specialized Response Hierarchy*

c. *Maintain LastAccessed Property*

d. *Allow Soft Deletions*

Review Answers

1. **D is correct.** Create the database and the design elements. If you can find design elements in other databases that match your needs, that method is more efficient; however, it was determined in the question that this procedure was not possible.

2. **B is correct.** Always create your databases locally and conduct your development there, until you are ready for your users to see and test the database. If it is necessary to create the database on a server, always ask the administrator where to place the database.

3. **A is correct.** Medium and Strong encryption both have more security but do not enable disk compression.

4. **D is correct.** There is no hard-coded size limit on R5 databases. R4.X databases have a default 1GB size limit that can be raised to 4GB.

5. **A is correct.** You should apply the Do Not Maintain Unread Marks database property to databases that are either seldom read or where new documents are not the most important aspect of the database.

6. **B and C are correct.** Both are required to take advantage of this setting. She must run the COMPACT task against the database to force the change to take effect. In addition, the view must be designed to take advantage of the setting in order to notice a difference. Specifically, you must use FORM= as part of the selection formula for the view.

7. **B is correct.** The database must be designed with a view that can display deleted items for the users to be able to restore accidentally deleted documents.

8. **B and C are correct.** A is a possible answer, although she would also have to check that the design element itself is not set to receive design changes.

9. **B is correct.** The automated index updates are only available if the database resides on a server.

10. Both **C** and **D** do not specifically improve performance of the database. The LastAccessed property actually degrades performance when enabled.

CHAPTER 24

Understanding and Implementing Basic Security

You should be able to answer questions based on the following objectives after reading this chapter:

- Reading ACLs
- Troubleshooting

Nearly every Notes application within an organization requires some security measures in order to function properly. Security concerns for a Notes database encompass decisions such as which users will have access to the application, which processes might be initiated by certain users, and which saved data is available to which subsets of users. Application security should help accomplish the business purpose of the application. Let's use an example of a Notes application to facilitate the employee review process. We can identify several areas in which application security will come into play:

1. **Composing review forms** The review process might begin by requiring an employee to list his or her accomplishments from the prior year. For this application, employees must have the appropriate security rights in order to compose and submit their review forms.

2. **Reading submitted review forms** After an employee has submitted his or her required review form, he or she should not be able to read other employees' review forms. You might choose to design the application so that employees might not even read or adjust their own review forms after they have submitted them.

3. **Editing submitted review forms** To continue the review process, an employee's manager needs to read and add the employee's comments to the saved review form before sending the form along for human resources approval. Managers, however, should not necessarily be able to read or edit saved reviews for employees who are not within their department.

4. **Reading and editing completed review forms** After a review form has been initiated and edited by an employee's manager, human resources personnel might need access to read all completed review forms across all departments. They might also need the capability to edit completed review forms in order to update salary information.

In this example, security is an integral part of the function and purpose of the application, because part of the function relies on who can see what information. This situation is not always the case, however. Many applications will only need the most basic security measures to accomplish a business purpose. A department discussion database, for example, will more than likely permit anyone within a department to read or compose documents. Or, an employee announcement database will permit anyone to read the information—with a select group permitted to compose and save documents in the database.

Database-Level Security

Notes offers granular security to database designers in the sense that controls can be put in place throughout the application. At the most basic application level, however, security is implemented at the database level with the ACL, which determines who can access the database and what permissions they will have within the database. The ACL relies on the server's Domino Directory to identify people and groups in order to provide them with access to the database. To access a database's ACL dialog box, choose File . . . Database . . . Access Control from the pull-down menu (see Figure 24-1).

The ACL dialog box indicates which users and user groups have access to the database. The Basics tab of the dialog box (we will address the other tabs later) enables you to view each ACL entry, its user type, and its access level. You can also add and remove ACL entries.

ACL Entries

Now that you have learned that the purpose of an ACL is to enable the database owner to control who can access the application, the next step is actually adding entries to

Figure 24-1
Database Access
Control List dialog
box

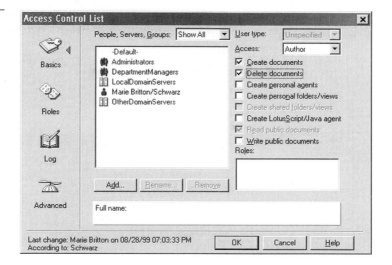

your database ACL. While in the ACL dialog box, you can click the Add button to access
the Add User dialog box, as seen in Figure 24-2.

Using the Person button, you can pull ACL entries directly from the server's Domino
Directory. You can also type a name directly into the entry box. If you choose to obtain
your ACL entry names from the Domino Directory (which is always a good idea, in
order to get the spelling exactly right), Notes presents you with yet a third dialog box
that enables you to specify multiple entries at once (see Figure 24-3).

As you can see from Figure 24-3, you can add entries by selecting the name of a person, server, or group within the Domino Directory. In addition to these types of entries,
you can also use a wild card character (*) in place of the common name or organizational component of a hierarchical name to grant access to a group of users who have
those hierarchical elements in their names. The ACL entry */Marketing/Acme, for
example, grants access to John Smith/Marketing/Acme and Bob Jones/Marketing/Acme
but not to Jane Johnson/Systems/Acme.

 NOTE ACL entries that represent a person in the Domino Directory do not
necessarily correspond to a valid Notes ID. They can represent Web users who
are individually authenticated to the application but are not Notes users. If you
choose to add a person(s) to the ACL who is only a Web user, make sure to use
the first name listed in the UserName field of the Person document in order to guarantee
the user correct access via the Web.

Figure 24-2
Add User dialog box

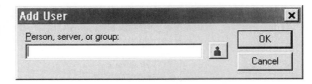

Figure 24-3
Names dialog box

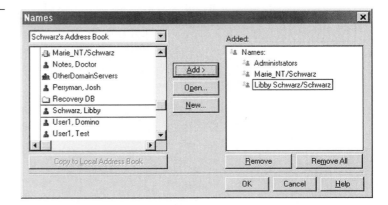

ACL User Types

Once you have added all of your desired ACL entries, you should make sure to specify a User Type for each appropriate entry. Specifying the User Type ensures that when an ID (i.e., Person or Server) tries to access a database, the server hosting the database matches not only the name or group membership of the ID in question, but also its User Type. The User Type is set at the top-right of the ACL screen. You should specify a type for nearly every ACL entry (we will discuss exceptions later). This concept is illustrated in Figure 24-4.

The varied User Types you can choose for your ACL entries are as follows:

- **Unspecified**   No User Type is assigned.
- **Person**   Corresponds to a single user ID and/or a Person document in the Domino Directory.
- **Server**   Corresponds to a single server ID and/or a Server document in the Domino Directory.
- **Mixed Group**   Corresponds to a group in the Domino Directory whose members include both user and server names.

Figure 24-4
ACL User Type

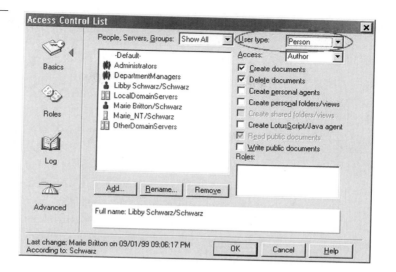

- **Person Group**   Corresponds to a group in the Domino Directory whose members include only user names.

- **Server Group**   Corresponds to a group in the Domino Directory whose members include only server names.

For the most part, every ACL entry should have a User Type assigned. There are two primary exceptions to this rule:

- **Default ACL entry**   Every ACL must contain a Default entry that covers any user or server that is not explicitly or implicitly specified in the ACL (is not listed by its name or as a member of a group). Because the Default entry covers any possible user or server that could access your database, it must have an unspecified User Type.

- **Anonymous**   Databases that are available for Web access should include an ACL entry for Anonymous. Anonymous represents any Web user who accesses the database without authenticating using his or her username and password as defined in the Domino Directory. The Anonymous ACL entry must remain unspecified, because it does not correspond to an ID or a Person, Server, or Group in the Domino Directory.

Specifying User Types for your ACL entries is an added security measure that prevents possible security breaches in the Notes environment. This precaution makes sure that the users who have database access are the exact users you intended. Let's use the following example to illustrate how neglecting to specify ACL User Types can cause problems:

You have created a human resources application that contains, among other items, sensitive salary information. The ACL includes the entries and access levels shown in Table 24-1, but no User Types are specified.

A user, Pat Jones/Acme, is not listed in the ACL and is not a member of the human resources group; therefore, he has no ability to open the database normally. Pat has the ability to create groups in the Domino Directory, however. He creates a group in the Domino Directory called John Smith/Acme and puts the name Pat Jones/Acme as a member of this group. At this point, he can access the human resources database because the database ACL does not specify that John Smith/Acme is a single person and not a group. As you can see, this situation represents a fairly serious breach of security, because a user who should be excluded from the application entirely is now able to access the database and view salary information.

ACL Levels and Rights

Now that we have successfully put the fear of unspecified User Types into you, let's actually look at which type of access you can grant to each of your ACL entries. In addition to requiring a User Type, each ACL entry needs an access level associated with it in order to specify which rights that user or group should have. After all, that is the whole point of an ACL: specifying who has which rights within a database.

The Seven ACL Levels

There are seven ACL levels you can assign to grant the desired access level. In addition to the primary seven levels, you can also grant specific access-level privileges (such as the capability to delete documents) separately for each ACL entry. We discuss the details of these privileges later, but first we should survey the seven main ACL levels.

Table 24-1   Sample ACL

Default	No Access Rights
Hub01/Acme	Manager rights (read, write, and delete all documents)
John Smith/Acme	Author rights (can compose documents and edit own)
Human Resources	Editor rights (can edit any documents)

Keep in mind that the list of access levels is hierarchical. Each access level automatically includes all rights available for the levels below it (refer to Table 24-2).

Table 24-2   ACL levels

Access Level	Access-Level Rights	Optional Access-Level Privileges
Manager	Modify ACL	Delete documents
	Delete database	
	Encrypt database	
	Modify replication settings	
Designer	Modify database design	Delete documents
	Create full text index	Create LotusScript/Java agent
Editor	Create documents	Delete documents
	Edit any documents	Create personal agents
		Create personal folders/views
		Create shared folders/views
		Create LotusScript/Java agent
Author	Edit own documents	Create documents
		Delete documents (only own)
		Create personal agents
		Create personal folders/views
		Create LotusScript/Java agent
		Write Public Documents
Reader	Read documents	Create personal agents
		Create personal folders/views
		Create LotusScript/Java agent
		Write Public Documents
Depositor	Can contribute documents but not read any, including their own	Write Public Documents
		Read Public Documents
No Access	No access at all	None

One point to keep in mind with the aforementioned access levels is that they assume no presence of view, form, or document-level security. Document-level security (which we will discuss later in this chapter) and view and form security (discussed in Chapter 34, "Domino Security Architecture"), can sometimes take precedence over database-level security, depending on the exact settings.

Depending on the function and intent of your database, a database ACL includes one or more of the ACL levels for your ACL entries. Every organization has different ACL standards, but here are some general guidelines for ACL levels:

- *Always have a manager.* Every database must contain at least one entry with Manager access, to ensure that some person, server, or group member can adjust the ACL. Remember that managers can delete the database, however, so use this access level sparingly. As any long-time mail administrator is aware, it is indeed possible for users to accidentally delete databases.

- *Use groups whenever possible.* When setting a database ACL for the first time, it is always tempting to simply enter the names of the people and/or servers that you know will need to access the database. You should always choose appropriate groups from the Domino Directory for ACL entries, however, which makes the ACL flexible and improves forward maintenance.

- *Do not grant more access than necessary.* As with sparing use of the Manager access level, it is generally appropriate to give users only the access level necessary for proper function of the database. You will always find it easier to grant higher access levels when the business requirement exists, rather than to try undoing any inappropriate actions taken by users with higher-than-necessary access levels.

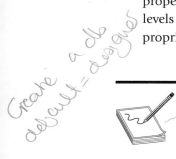

Create a db
default = designer

> **NOTE** Be aware that when you first create a database, Notes gives the Default ACL entry Designer access to the database. Few databases in an organization will have a business need for default users to have the capability to adjust the database design, full-text index, or replication settings. Most general-use applications should limit the Default user to no more than Author or Editor access.

Access-Level Security Privileges

In addition to the seven ACL levels, various other privileges can be set for each ACL entry. These options appear to the right-hand side of the ACL dialog box and are available depending on the access level selected (refer to Figure 24-5).

Figure 24-5
Access-level
privileges

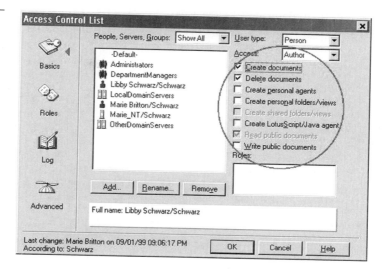

These privileges enable you to fine-tune your ACL entries to achieve exactly the desired permissions for each person, server, or group. Each privilege is automatically included in the ACL rights for some access levels but is optional for other levels. We describe these various privileges in Table 24-3.

Private view = desktop.dsk.

> **TIP** With R5, you can easily tell at a glance whether a view is private and where it is stored (on the server or in the DESKTOP.DSK file). As you can see in Figures 24-6 and 24-7, private views stored on the server are indicated with a dashed line underneath the view icon, while private views stored on a user's desktop are indicated with a dashed line and a small CPU icon.

ACL Roles

In addition to specifying access levels, you can also assign ACL entries to be members of a larger designation called a role. ACL roles do not necessarily signify any particular security privileges; rather, they represent a convenient way to group ACL entries that might have different access levels.

You can create and maintain roles by using the Roles tab of the ACL dialog box (refer to Figure 24-8).

Table 24-3 Additional ACL privileges

Setting	Significance	Associated ACL Levels	Notes
Create documents	The ability to compose and save new documents	Manager (automatic)	
		Designer (automatic)	
		Editor (automatic)	
		Author	
Delete documents	The ability to permanently remove documents from a database	Manager	
		Editor	
		Author	
Create personal agents	The ability to create personal (non-shared) agents within the database	Manager (automatic)	
		Designer (automatic)	
		Editor	
		Author	
		Reader	
Create personal folders/views	The ability to create personal folders or views that are stored on the server	Designer (automatic)	Deselecting this option will still enable users to create personal folders or views, but the views will be stored in the user's DESKTOP.DSK rather than on the server copy of the database.
		Editor	
		Author	
		Reader	

continued

Table 24-3   Additional ACL privileges (*continued*)

Setting	Significance	Associated ACL Levels	Notes
Create shared folders/views	The ability to create shared folders or views in the database	Manager (automatic)	Give this privilege sparingly, because shared folders and views are available to all users. Having too many users with this capability can clutter your database.
		Designer (automatic)	
		Editor	
Create LotusScript/ Java agent	The ability to use LotusScript or Java when creating an agent	Manager (automatic)	Enabling this setting has no effect unless you also enable the Create personal agents setting. In addition, users who have the capability to create personal agents but not LotusScript/Java agents do not receive an error message until they attempt to save a LotusScript agent that they have already created.
		Designer	
		Editor	
		Author	
		Reader	
Read public documents	Ability to view documents, views, or folders marked as *available to public access users*	Manager (automatic)	Public documents and views/folders are intended to enable access to certain users who might not have the capacity to access other design elements in a database.

continued

Table 24-3 Additional ACL privileges (*continued*)

Setting	Significance	Associated ACL Levels	Notes
		Designer (automatic)	
		Editor (automatic)	
		Author (automatic)	
		Reader (automatic)	
		Depositor	
		No Access	
Write public documents	Ability to create and save documents, views, or folders marked as available to public access users	Manager (automatic)	
		Designer (automatic)	
		Editor (automatic)	
		Author (automatic)	
		Reader	
		Depositor	
		No Access	

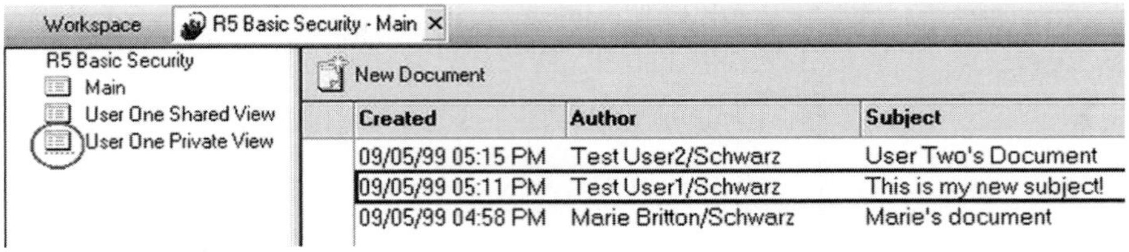

Figure 24-6 A private view stored on the server

Add, rename, or remove roles by clicking the three buttons below the list of roles. Once you have added and named your roles, you can match ACL entries with the desired roles on the Basics tab. Each entry can belong to as many roles as you designate,

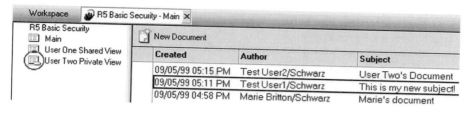

Figure 24-7   A private view stored on the desktop

Figure 24-8
The ACL Role tab

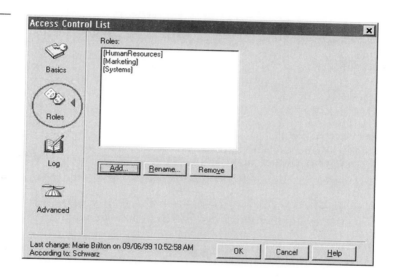

by selecting each desired role in the right-hand selection box while the ACL entry is highlighted (refer to Figure 24-9).

Now that you have seen how to create and assign roles—and now that you have learned that they do not confer any particular security privileges—you might be wondering what function they actually have in your database. Roles are a convenient, programmatic way to identify logical subsets of your users, because they can contain several different ACL entries. Two primary @Functions will enable you to access a list of any given user's roles:

- **@UserRoles**   @UserRoles enables you to directly access which roles a designated user has been assigned in the database ACL. This knowledge can help you build

Figure 24-9
Assigning ACL
entries to a role

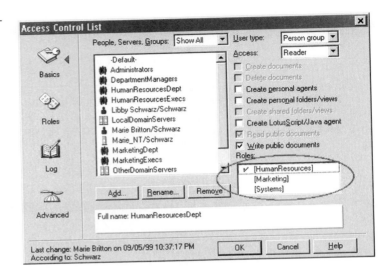

smart applications that automatically launch the Marketing frameset for users with membership in the Marketing role, for instance.

- **@UserNamesList** @UserNamesList provides a text list of all applicable usernames, group memberships, and database role memberships.

> **NOTE** Be aware that many @Functions that rely on ACL settings or roles will not work on local database replicas unless Enforce a consistent Access Control List across all replicas of this database is selected in the Advanced tab of the ACL dialog box. For more information, see "Enforcing Consistent ACLs" later in this chapter.

ACL Log

Each ACL also has a log associated with it that tracks any changes. Access the ACL change log via the Log tab on the ACL dialog box (refer to Figure 24-10). The log enables you to view a rolling history of changes that you, other designers, or administrators might make to the ACL. Use the ACL log when you need to troubleshoot problems that might arise from incorrect changes in the ACL.

Figure 24-10
The ACL Log tab

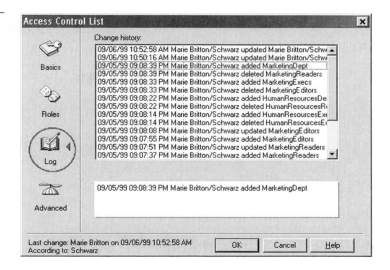

Advanced ACL Settings

In addition to specifying ACL entries and creating and assigning roles, for proper ACL maintenance you need an awareness of the advanced ACL settings and their effects. Find the advanced ACL settings on the Advanced tab of the ACL dialog box (refer to Figure 24-11).

The Advanced tab has many items that can be important for the proper function and maintenance of your database. We will explore these elements individually at a later time.

Administration Server

As we have seen, the ACL is based largely on information pulled from the Domino Directory: Person names, Group names, and Server names. The ACL of a database is often set up initially and occasionally modified, but not always updated on a daily or even monthly basis. By contrast, in large organizations the Domino Directory is constantly changing. Users change names or leave the company, and groups are added and deleted. For this reason, ACL entries can become outdated when a person or group listed is no longer available in the Domino Directory.

To keep the ACL synchronized with the Domino Directory, designate an administration server for the database at the top of the Advanced tab (refer to Figure 24-12). The

Figure 24-11
The ACL Advanced
tab

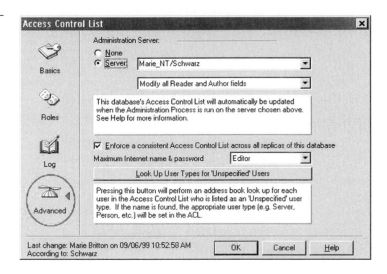

Figure 24-12
Administration
server settings

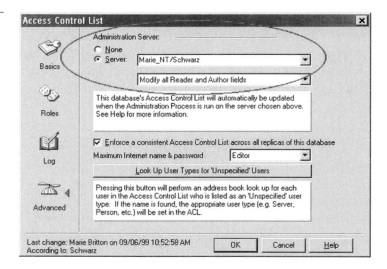

administration server should be a server that regularly runs the *Administration Process* task (ADMINP) and has manager access to the database. For databases that have a designated administration server, the ADMINP task updates any ACL entries that are out of synchronization with the Domino Directory. If administrators have removed any users from the Domino Directory, for example, the ADMINP task on the administration server removes the entries for those users from the ACL of the database.

In addition, you can also configure the administration server to modify any Reader and Author fields contained in the database documents to reflect any changes in the Domino Directory (we will further explore the specifics of Reader and Author fields later in this chapter).

Enforcing Consistent Access Control Lists Across All Replicas

Depending on the size and structure of your organization, your database might be replicated across several servers within your Notes domain. In addition, your organization might have many mobile users who replicate databases locally. Depending on the physical security of the other servers in your organization, you might choose to ensure that all replicas of the database throughout your organization enforce the same access rights, regardless of the server on which they reside. You can do this task by selecting Enforce a consistent Access Control List across all replicas of this database in the middle of the Advanced ACL tab (refer to Figure 24-13).

Selecting this option ensures that if a server or person who is not a database manager makes a local ACL change on a replica, the replica does not replicate the ACL changes with other replicas of the database. The user or server that is attempting to initiate the replication receives an error message stating that the database will not replicate because a consistent access control cannot be maintained across databases.

Enforcing consistent ACLs throughout all replicas of a database also has some other ramifications. Keep in mind that without this setting, local replicas of a database (those

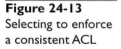

Figure 24-13
Selecting to enforce a consistent ACL

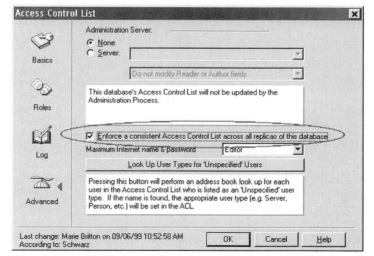

replicas on a user's machine or on a server when accessed via the server's Notes client) do not enforce a database's ACL. Users who have author access to a database can edit any document in a database, for instance. (In this example, however, the user's document edits will not replicate back to the server.) Enforcing a consistent ACL has the following effects:

- Local replicas of the database force user authentication for database access (i.e., the user will be forced to enter his or her password).

- Local replicas of the database enforce the user's given access level (not permitting authors to edit documents locally, for example).

- @Functions that are based on ACL settings, such as @UserNamesList and @User-Roles, function as designed—even in local replicas.

> **NOTE** Keep in mind that enforcing a consistent ACL does not necessarily ensure that local data remains secure. To secure locally saved data, Lotus recommends using database encryption.

Maximum Internet Name and Password Access

In addition to specifying access levels for your users through ACL entries, you can also specify the maximum access level permitted via a Web browser. This setting is located in the middle of the Advanced ACL tab (refer to Figure 24-14). Notes and Domino enforce this maximum access level for any Web user, and this level takes precedence over the access level assigned in the ACL. This setting is convenient if you require contributions or document edits to be made via the Notes client, but you wish to permit Web users within your organization to browse the database for read-only purposes.

> **NOTE** The default maximum Internet name and password for a database is Editor. Make sure that Editor is acceptable for your databases or that you adjust this setting accordingly. If you do not intend to permit Web access to the database, select No Access for this setting. Remember that if your database exists on any servers in your networked organization that enable anonymous HTTP access, many more users might be able to access your database than originally intended.

Figure 24-14
Maximum Internet
name and password
access

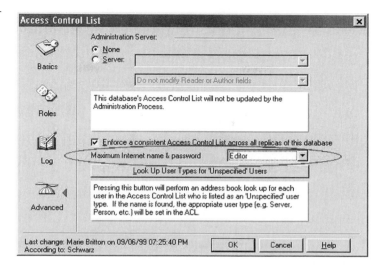

Access Control List

Administration Server:
○ None
○ Server:

Do not modify Reader or Author fields

This database's Access Control List will not be updated by the
Administration Process.

☑ Enforce a consistent Access Control List across all replicas of this database
Maximum Internet name & password   Editor

Look Up User Types for 'Unspecified' Users

Pressing this button will perform an address book look up for each
user in the Access Control List who is listed as an 'Unspecified' user
type. If the name is found, the appropriate user type (e.g. Server,
Person, etc.) will be set in the ACL.

Last change: Marie Britton on 09/06/99 07:25:40 PM
According to: Schwarz   OK   Cancel   Help

Looking Up Unspecified User Types

The fourth selection on the Advanced tab enables you to look up and define User Types
for any ACL entries with unspecified User Types. The button to perform the lookup is
located at the bottom of the Advanced tab (refer to Figure 24-15). Using this method to
verify User Types can ensure that they are correctly assigned.

Document-Level Security

In addition to the database security that we have previously detailed, Notes also offers
security at the document level. You can design a database that enables you or your users
to specify particular readers and authors for given documents. This feature enables you
to tightly control which pieces of data are available to which users—without building
multiple databases.

Document-level security consists of the following two elements:

- **Authors fields** Authors fields work in conjunction with the Author access level.
  As you will recall from earlier in the chapter, the Author access level only enables
  users to edit their own documents. Document ownership is defined by the contents of any Authors fields on the form. Authors fields do not supercede the higher

Figure 24-15
Looking up
unspecified
User Types

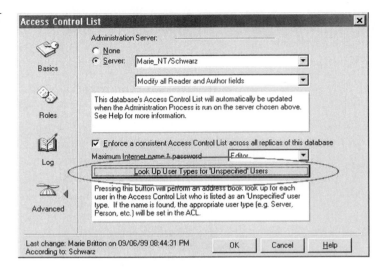

database access levels, in that a database Editor, Designer, or Manager can still edit any document despite the presence of any author fields.

- **Readers fields** Readers fields define who can read any given document. They work independently of ACL settings in that even database Authors, Editors, Designers, and Managers cannot read documents that do not specify them in a Readers field.

The database designer creates the Authors and Readers fields, which rely on the field contents to include accurate Notes names to work properly. (In other words, the names specified in a Readers or Authors field have to match to a common, abbreviated, or hierarchical name from the Domino Directory). Authors and Readers fields can include person and server names as well as valid groups from the Domino Directory. To define a Readers or Authors field on a form, define a new text field and set the field type to Readers or Authors in the Field Properties InfoBox. Although you will learn more about form design in Chapter 25, "Creating Pages and Forms," Figure 24-16 illustrates how to define a Readers or Authors field on a form.

NOTE Authors fields imply the capability to read as well as edit documents. Entries in a document's Authors field do not need to be repeated in a Readers field in order for the document Author to read the document.

Figure 24-16
Field type selection for Authors and Readers field types

When to Use Readers and Authors Fields

Readers and Authors fields enable you and your database users to finely tune information access within a single database. Sensitive documents can be stored in a publicly accessed database but remain available for view only by appropriate persons. Work groups can share editing capabilities for departmental documents but can protect their documents from editing by others. Readers and Authors fields can extend and enhance the functionality of your databases in many ways:

- For the employee review application mentioned at the beginning of this chapter, Readers fields would be used to ensure that employees could not read each other's review documents. Authors fields would ensure that managers might edit their team members' forms in order to complete the review process.

- In databases used for storage of common information sets (such as a Document Library database), editable Authors fields enable users to specify exactly who can edit their documents.

- In workflow databases, dynamic Authors fields ensure that at each stage in the approval routing process, only the designated person can approve the document.

NOTE Readers fields are the only secure way to prevent access to documents within a database. While database designers can simulate this functionality by using limited-access views or forms, these methods do not ensure the privacy of the information contained in the documents. Users can build private views that circumvent form-level or view-level security measures.

Common Pitfalls with Document-Level Security

Although Readers and Authors fields offer much functionality, there are a few points to be aware of when using them in your database design:

- Users *cannot see* a document that contains a Readers field that does not include their names. This situation applies to servers as well as end users. In other words, if server names (or groups containing server names) are not included in a document's Readers field, the server will not have the capability to see that document to replicate it or run agents on it. This situation can cause unexpected results and unusual replication behavior. To prevent this result, it is a good design practice to add an additional, hidden Readers field containing LocalDomainServers, NotesAdministrators, and/or other groups as necessary in order to ensure proper replication and the capacity to troubleshoot the application.

- Categorized views might exhibit unusual behavior when accessed by users who do not have access to read some of the documents in the view. Because the view is indexed at the server, the view categories are built from the documents that the server might read. The end user still sees these categories in the view, although the documents in the categories do not appear underneath the categories (refer to Figure 24-17). For more information about categorized views, refer to Chapter 27, "Creating Views, Columns, and Folders."

- Readers and Authors fields must contain valid Lotus Notes names to function properly. In other words, if your users are allowed to choose their own document authors or readers, they should use the Address Dialog helper in order to properly specify the users they want.

Created	Author	Subject
▼ Executive		
▼ General		
09/05/99 05:15 PM	Test User2/Schwarz	User Two's Document
09/05/99 04:58 PM	Marie Britton/Schwarz	Marie's first document
▼ Marketing		
09/06/99 10:40 AM	Test User1/Schwarz	User One Test
09/05/99 05:11 PM	Test User1/Schwarz	This is my new subject!

Figure 24-17   Categorized view behavior when the user cannot see all documents

Security issue.

- Readers and Authors fields can contain Notes names that are common or abbreviated. In other words, a Readers or Authors field containing a common name (such as John E. Smith) will not distinguish between John E. Smith/Exec/Acme and John E. Smith/Marketing/Acme. This idea also means that unless a database specifies an administration server with the correct options (see the sections earlier in this chapter), users who go through a name or OU change might lose access to documents that they created before the change.

Synopsis

When designing security for a database, you set the basic access rights by editing the ACL. The ACL consists of server, person, and group names corresponding to users in the Domino Directory. Most ACL entries will require a User Type to indicate whether they represent a single ID or a group. There are seven main access levels for users: Manager, Designer, Editor, Author, Reader, Depositor, and No Access. In addition to specifying access levels, database designers can also designate ACL roles to group users into logical subsets. There are also several advanced ACL options, including the capability to specify an administration server to maintain database ACL, the capability to limit access rights of Web users, and the capability to look up unspecified user types in the ACL List. Beyond database security, documents can include security by the use of Readers and Authors fields. For the exam, you should focus on understanding the seven access levels and how database roles work and can be accessed by the designer, as well as which options are available on the Advanced tab. Focus also on the basic functionality of Readers and Authors fields, as well as their uses in database design.

Practice

First, if you created the second database in the previous chapter (R5ORDREV.NSF), open that database. If you did not create the database, you can open CH24.NSF, which is available on the accompanying CD-ROM. Let's consider what the security needs of this database might be. Because the purpose of the database is to enable Notes and Web users to order books, the security and user considerations for this database might be as follows:

- Any server within the immediate corporate network should have the capacity to replicate the database and/or alter its design and access rights.

- Any server in an external domain should not have the capability to view the database contents.

- Members of the NotesAdmin group need the capability to fully control the database (i.e., granting access rights, altering the replication settings, or encrypting the database).

- The NotesDesigners group members need the capability to alter the database design when necessary.

- Any unauthenticated Web user should have the capacity to view the information in the database but not create any documents.

- The BookOrderers group members need the capability to edit any document in the database.

- Members of the MarketingDept, SalesDept, HRDept, and ITDept groups each need the capacity to contribute and edit their own documents.

Now that we know how the users should interact with this database, let's alter the ACL appropriately:

1. Access the database ACL by choosing File . . . Database . . . Access Control. This action should present you with the Access Control dialog box, as illustrated in Figure 24-1.

2. Click to add new members to the ACL.

3. Click the person-shaped button to choose the appropriate group from the ACL list, or simply type the name in the input box provided. (Your first name should be LocalDomainServers.)

4. Click OK after you have chosen the appropriate group name.

5. Change the User Type to server group.

6. Change the access level to Manager.

7. Click to select Delete Documents.

8. Click Add to add additional entries. The additional entries should be as follows, based on the previous listing:

   a. OtherDomainServers should be set to No Access with no privileges. The User Type should be Server Group.

   b. NotesAdmin should be set to Manager with the privilege to delete documents. The User Type should be Mixed Group.

   c. NotesDesigners should be set to Designer with all privileges granted. The User Type should be Person Group.

   d. Anonymous should be set to Reader access. The User Type should be set to Unspecified.

   e. BookOrderers should be set to Editor with all privileges granted. The User Type should be set to Person Group.

   f. MarketingDept, SalesDept, HRDept, and ITDept groups should be set to Author with all privileges granted except Create Personal Folders/Views. The User Type should be Person Group in each case.

 NOTE   Your Domino Directory might or might not have these or similar groups, depending on whether you are working in a lab environment or in a production environment. If you are working in a production environment, it is likely that you will not have access to add these groups to the Domino Directory. If the groups are not in your Domino Directory, simply type the names in the Add User dialog box.

---

9. After all of the entries have been completed, click OK in the ACL dialog box to save all of your ACL changes.

Review Questions

1. Bill has just created a database on a development server. He wants to give members of the NotesAdmin group the capability to encrypt his database. What access level must he grant to the NotesAdmin group?
   a. Author
   b. Designer
   c. Manager
   d. Depositor

2. MaryAnn is responsible for maintaining a production application with many Readers and Authors fields used to control document access. She wants to make sure that if a user's name changes, the Readers and Authors fields in this database are updated in this database with the user's new name. How can she achieve this goal?
   a. Specify an administration server and turn on the setting to Modify Readers/Authors Fields.
   b. Make sure that all users are listed individually in the database ACL.
   c. Make sure that the users are included in at least one database role.
   d. Enable the Track Name Change setting in the ACL Log.

3. Leigh maintains a Notes application where the application users might author their own documents. The users are all contained in the group SalesAuthors. Leigh wants to provide Web access to this application, but she only wants to allow people to read the database over the Web. How can she accomplish this task?
   a. Exclude the Anonymous entry from the ACL.
   b. Create a Group called SalesAuthorsWeb in the Domino Directory, listing all the same users and setting that group's access to Reader.
   c. Create an ACL role called [NoWeb] and place the SalesAuthors group in that role.
   d. Specify the Maximum Internet Name and Password setting to Reader.

4. Sherry finds a database in production with many ACL entries, but she cannot tell which entries are for users, which are for servers, and which groups represent servers or users. What is a quick way she can find out what type of user(s) each ACL entry represents?
   a. Open the ACL and the Domino Directory at the same time.
   b. There is no quick way. She will have to look up each entry individually.
   c. Click Look up Unspecified User Types on the Advanced ACL tab.
   d. Run AdminP on the server that hosts the database.

5. Stephanie wants to create a database where one particular form is available to users who are not otherwise permitted to access the database. How can she accomplish this task?

   a. There is no way to enable users who cannot access a database to view forms within the database.

   b. Designate the form as Available to Public Access Users and grant the appropriate ACL entry the capability to Read Public Documents.

   c. Create an ACL entry called Anonymous and give it Reader access, then place it in an ACL role corresponding to the form name.

   d. Create a $NoAccessReader field on the form in question.

6. Chad has a database where users fall into one of three ACL roles: Marketing, Sales, or Systems. He wants to make his forms dynamic, so that they appear differently to different users (depending on the role to which they belong). How can he do this task?

   a. Use the @UserRoles function in his form formula.

   b. Use the @IsRoleMember function in his form formula.

   c. Grant access using wild card characters, such as */Marketing/Acme.

   d. Select Enforce consistent ACL across all replicas.

7. Scott has created a database that will enable access for Web users. He would like unauthenticated Web users to have a different set of access rights to the database than default Notes users. How does he accomplish this task?

   a. Alter the Maximum Internet Name and Password setting on the Advanced ACL tab.

   b. Create an ACL role called [Anonymous].

   c. Create an ACL entry called Anonymous with the access rights desired for unauthenticated Web users.

   d. Create an ACL entry called */* with the access rights desired for unauthenticated Web users.

8. Terry is working on a local replica of a database that he has been designing. Although the database was working when he was testing on the server replica, his @UserRoles functions do not seem to be working as expected when he is designing locally. What can he do to improve this situation?

   a. Full text index the database.

   b. Remove all the groups listed in the ACL.

   c. Make sure to specify an administration server.

   d. Enforce a consistent ACL on his local replica.

9. Ravyn has created a database, and she would like to make sure that members of a certain group can create personal views for their use. She wants to make sure that the users' private views are stored in their local DESKTOP.DSK file, however. How can she perform this task?

   a. Design all views in the database as Shared—Personal on First Use.

   b. There is no way to ensure that this result will occur.

   c. Select the ACL option to Create Personal Views/Folders.

   d. Deselect the ACL option to Create Personal Views/Folders.

10. Michele needs to check the last time the LocalDomainServers ACL entry was changed. How can she perform this action?

    a. Right-click the ACL entry for LocalDomainServers and choose Edit History from the pop-up menu.

    b. Open the Miscellaneous Events view in the server log on the server that hosts the database.

    c. Click the Log tab of the ACL dialog box.

    d. Click View Log from the Advanced tab of the ACL dialog box.

Review Answers

1. *C*
   D is correct.   Only database managers can encrypt a database.

2. A is correct.   Specify an administration server and enable Modify Readers/ Authors Fields. This method is the only native way that Notes will automatically propagate directory changes (such as name changes to the values in Readers or Authors fields) in a database.

3. D is correct.   This way is the only easy method to give the same users different access levels on the Web than they have in Notes.

4. C is correct.   Clicking Look up unspecified user types will accomplish this task.

5. B is correct.   A way to enable a form to be seen by users who are otherwise excluded from a database is to designate the form as Available to Public Access Users and to grant the appropriate ACL entry the capability to Read Public Documents. Calendar entries work in this manner in a standard Notes mail database.

6. A is correct.   @UserRoles is the @Function that helps him determine a user's role membership.

7. **B is correct.**   The Anonymous ACL entry is reserved for users who access a database via the Web but who are not authenticated to the server with a username and password.

8. **D is correct.**   To have @UserRoles function as expected when working locally, consistent ACLs must be forced across all replicas.

9. **D is correct.**   The ACL option to Create Private View/Folders actually refers to a user's capability to create a private view *on the server*. Deselecting this option forces private views to be stored on the desktop.

10. **C is correct.**   The ACL log provides a rolling edit history of ACL changes and would provide her with the information she needed.

Creating Pages and Forms

You should be able to answer questions based on the following objectives after reading this chapter:

- Create, modify, and troubleshoot pages
- Create, modify, and troubleshoot forms

Pages and forms represent two key building blocks of all Notes applications. Both of these design elements can be used to display data. Forms, however, can also collect data. Both pages and forms are used with both Notes clients and Web clients. Most likely, however, you will find pages in use with Web clients because they offer a convenient way to display text, graphics, links, or other embedded elements such as outlines or navigators (described in Chapter 29, "Creating Navigation"). Use forms to obtain data and then to display that data (this process is sometimes accomplished using a single form; however, other databases use one form to get the data and a different form to display the data). When used to display data, the form and the data combine to make a document. This chapter describes how to create pages and forms, which elements can be placed on pages and forms, and how to display pages and forms to your database users.

Creating a Page

The *page*, as described earlier, is a database design element used to display graphics, data, and other objects to users of a database. Expect to see a number of questions about this new R5 design element. One goal of the page is to make Web-site creation easier with Notes and Domino. A page gives users a starting point into the database, application, or Web site. Use pages to let your users know what to expect from the application, how to navigate through the application, and where elements of the application are located. This statement holds true whether you use the page in an application designed for Notes clients or for an application designed for the Web. To understand the use of a page, simply imagine the front page (or home page) of most of the Web sites that you know (use **http://www.lotus.com** as an example). What do you find on that page? You find text, graphics, some navigational tools, and links to other parts of the Web site or to other sites. Place all of these elements (and more) on a page.

To create a page, open the Domino Designer client, and then open a database in which to create the page. If you select the Pages Design view, you can create the new page by clicking the New Page action button. To create the page from any design view, choose Create . . . Design . . . Page. Designer automatically creates a new page and displays it in the Designer Client Work pane, as shown in Figure 25-1.

Pages differ from forms in that you do not use pages to create documents. You cannot view a page in the same way that you can view or display a form or document. Pages, for example, cannot be displayed in views; rather, you use views to display and view documents. Pages can, on the other hand, be displayed to users by placing the page inside a frameset, making the page an entry on an outline, or by linking to the page from somewhere else (such as on a form, document, or other page). You might

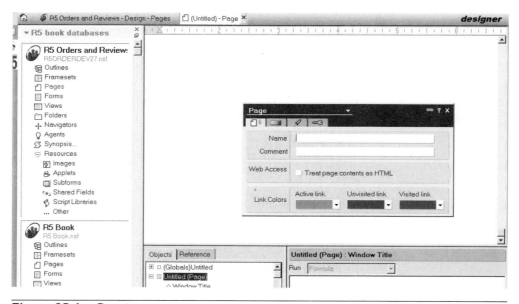

Figure 25-1   Creating a new page

also display a page by making an action or button that displays the page when used. Finally, you can use the database launch properties (described in Chapter 23, "Creating a Database") to launch the page automatically when the user opens the database. Each of these options requires that you create and save the page and then reference the page in another location.

Page Properties

Properties govern the appearance and action of each element in Notes. Properties determine the name of the element as well as how the element will act or will be displayed by Notes. You can view and change the Page properties by right-clicking the Work pane and choosing Page properties, or by clicking the Display InfoBox button (top right-hand corner of the Designer client). The Page properties InfoBox, which you can see in Figure 25-1, enables you to determine how the page will appear and act for the Notes and Web clients.

Page Info Tab

The first tab, the Page Info tab, contains fields that enable you to name the page, create comments about the page, and perform other options (described as follows). The name, specified here, can contain spaces if necessary. You can also create an alias for the page. An alias makes it easier to create a multilingual database. In any language, use the alias (not the name) in formulas. That way, you can change the name of the page as needed for the appropriate language—without needing to change any of your formulas. To create the alias (which will be displayed next to the name in the Pages Design view), use the vertical bar symbol (|) found above the backslash (/) on your keyboard. Place the name, then the vertical bar, and then the alias, as shown in Figure 25-2. The alias

Figure 25-2
The Page properties
InfoBox

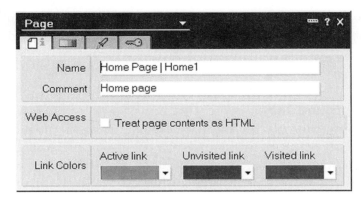

should be a shortened, easy-to-remember version of the name, to make the alias easy to use in formulas.

After creating the name and alias, you might choose to add a comment to the page. This comment, a text field, enables you to document the design element. The Pages Design view displays the comment under the name and alias, as shown next. If you remember to document your design elements, you and other developers will find your application easier to modify later.

The next option on the Page Info tab affects access by Web clients. This option, *Treat Page contents as HTML*, configures Notes to pass the contents of the page directly as HTML. Normally, the Domino server creates the HTML from what you place on a page. When you use this option, however, the Domino server just passes the HTML to the browser. In cases where you have an existing Web page that you want to use as a starting point, you could copy and paste the HTML onto the page, set this option, and then the page would appear in text format with HTML tags in Domino Designer. In the browser, however, the page would appear as rendered HTML. Note that you can also use File . . . Import to bring HTML content into your page. In this case, however, you will not need to enable this option, and the contents are displayed as already-rendered HTML in the Designer client. Figure 25-3 shows a page in Designer with pasted HTML.

Finally, on the bottom of the Page Info tab, you can select colors for active links, unvisited links, and visited links. Active links are red (unless you change their color) and are those links that the user has currently selected. Unvisited links, which are blue by default, are those links that the user has not yet clicked. Visited links, which are purple by default, are those links that the user has clicked. Be careful when changing the color associated with links. Most users who are familiar with the default colors used for links will make assumptions about what links mean based on their colors. Only change the link colors when you have a specific reason for doing so.

Background Tab

The Background tab enables you to determine the background color or graphics for the page. Choose either a background color or a graphic background. The first field, Color, enables you to choose your colored background. Use the Web palette as you design to ensure that what you design reflects what your Web users will see.

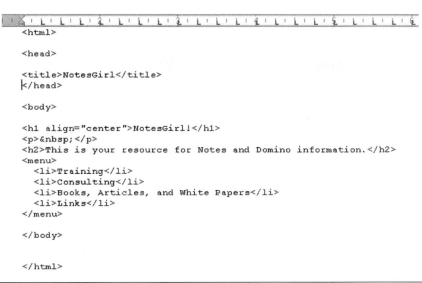

```
<html>

<head>

<title>NotesGirl</title>
</head>

<body>

<h1 align="center">NotesGirl!</h1>
<p> </p>
<h2>This is your resource for Notes and Domino information.</h2>
<menu>
  <li>Training</li>
  <li>Consulting</li>
  <li>Books, Articles, and White Papers</li>
  <li>Links</li>
</menu>

</body>

</html>
```

Figure 25-3   Using previously written HTML

 NOTE   To ensure that Designer uses the Web palette for colors, choose File . . . Preferences . . . User Preferences. In the Basics panel of the User Preferences dialog box, choose Use Web Palette under the Additional Options list.

You might also use this tab to add a background graphic to your page. Be aware that a background graphic can slow the loading of the page into the Notes or Web client, so balance your graphic use for both appearance and display times. You can either paste or import a graphic in one of the following formats:

- **.BMP**   Bit-mapped graphic
- **.JPG**   Also known as JPEG; Joint Photographic Experts Group graphic
- **.GIF**   Graphics Interchange Format
- **.PCX**   PC Exchange format
- **.TIFF**   5.0; Tagged Image File Format

Although you might use any of these file formats, be aware that Domino translates graphics in other formats to .GIF or .JPG when displaying them to a Web client. To prevent discrepancies between how a graphic looks when you create it and when the users view it, use a .GIF or a .JPG when possible. To paste a graphic, you must first copy the graphic from your graphics program onto the clipboard. Then, on the Page properties InfoBox, choose Paste. If the graphic is already the same size as the page, the graphic will be pasted once. If the graphic is already smaller, Designer tiles the graphic to cover the page. Choose the *Do Not Tile Graphic* option if you want to display the graphic only once.

If you prefer to import the graphic, click the Import button. Then choose the file to import from the file types listed. Again, Designer tiles the images by default. To remove a graphic background from the page, either add a new graphic using the paste or import method or click the Remove button to have no graphic background.

Alternatively, place a graphic background into the page using a shared image resource. A s*hared image resource* (a new R5 feature) enables a graphic image to be stored only once in the database but to be displayed as many times as necessary. This feature makes the database smaller and makes design easier, because the graphic exists as part of the database and will be replicated or moved with the database. Other elements, such as Java applets and subforms, can also be considered shared resources because they can be used multiple times in your database while needing to be stored only once. Before you can insert a shared image resource into your page, you must have added it to your database.

Create a shared resource by opening your database in Designer and clicking the Resources twistie to expand those items. Next, choose the Images view, as shown in Figure 25-4. Any image resources already stored in the database exist in this view. To add a new image resource, click the New Image Resource action button. Designer displays the Open File dialog box, enabling you to choose a file to insert (in either .GIF, .JPG, or .BMP format). Designer automatically converts the image to .GIF or .JPG format. Use the Image Resource properties InfoBox to change the name, alias, comment, or size of the image. The Design tab of the Image Resource properties InfoBox enables you to hide this design element from either Notes clients or Web browsers.

Once you create a shared image resource, you can use this resource as the background image for your page. In the Background tab of the Page properties InfoBox, click the Browse Images button next to the Resource field. The Insert Image Resource dialog box displays all of the shared image resources stored in this database, as shown next. The dialog box also displays the name and a preview of the image. Select an image, and click OK to choose that image for your background. You can also insert a background image based on a formula by clicking the Formula button. For more information about formulas, refer to Chapter 26, "Creating Fields and Formulas."

Figure 25-4
Shared Resource
Images view

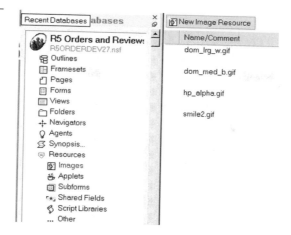

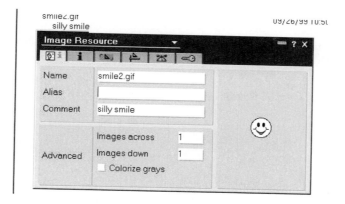

You can also select the *Hide graphic in design mode* option, which is intended to add speed to your design time. You can also choose *Hide Graphic on 16 color displays,* which enables users who have low-end graphics displays to see the data without having to suffer through the painful psychedelic experience that can come from displaying 32-bit color on a 16-bit display. Finally, this tab enables you to choose not to tile the background graphic. If you enable this option, Designer adds a single image of the background graphic to the page. The image is aligned in the top-left corner of the page. Web clients ignore this option (they display the background graphic in tiled format).

Launch Tab

Each page has launch options, just as each database has launch options (as discussed in Chapter 23, "Creating a Database"). In the case of pages, these launch options refer to the items on the page that can be automatically launched for viewing by the user when the page is accessed. Set these options on the Launch tab, which is shown in Figure 25-5. The Auto Launch drop-down box offers you the following options:

- **First attachment**   Launches the first document or graphic attached to the page.
- **First document link**   Launches the first Notes document link on the page.
- **First OLE object**   Launches the first linked or embedded OLE object on the page.

Another launch option links the page to a frameset and launches the page in a particular frame of the frameset. A *frameset* is a navigational tool used in both Notes and on the Web that breaks the interface into sections (called frames), each of which contain different documents, pages, or views. For more information about framesets and frames, refer to Chapter 30, "Creating Framesets." When linking a page to a particular frame of a frameset for launch purposes, select a frameset from the drop-down box in the Auto Frame section. Only framesets in the current database are available. After

Figure 25-5
The Launch tab

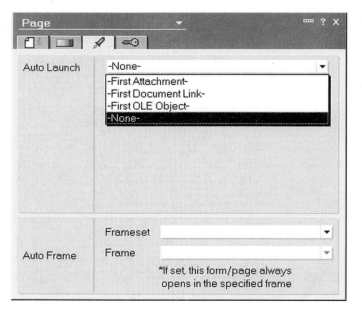

Takes precedence over frameset settings

selecting a frameset, choose a named frame from that frameset from the Frame drop-down box. The page will then always open in the specified frame. To implement this element, the database must contain a named and saved frameset with named frames.

Security Tab

The final setting available in the Page properties InfoBox is located on the Security tab, which offers the option of making the page available to public-access users. A public-access user is a user who has no access to the database but has been given the privilege to read and/or write public documents via the ACL of the database. For more information about the ACL and other security concerns, refer to Chapter 24, "Understanding and Implementing Basic Security."

Creating a Form

Although a page only displays information to users of your database, application, or site, a form obtains and displays information. A form contains many of the same elements as pages, such as text, graphics, sections, and embedded elements, but a form also contains fields. Use fields to request input or calculate data. The form is similar to a stencil for the data that you want to gather. The form gives structure to the data, helping users input and view the data. First, create the forms for your database. Then place the necessary elements on the form to create a structure for the data. When users place data on a form and save the form, Notes creates a document. The documents might or might not be displayed using the same form that was used to create them. Rarely is the form actually stored with the document, because this action makes the database much larger.

To create a new form, open the database and choose Create . . . Design . . . Form. You can also go to the Design . . . Forms view from the Navigation pane and click the Create form smart icon or action button.

> **NOTE** Designer displays different smart icons and action buttons, depending on the context. The Create form SmartIcon and action button are only available in the correct view. This statement holds true for all of the elements in Notes and Designer.

The Design view opens the new form, displaying the work area at the top and the Programmer's pane at the bottom, as shown in Figure 25-6. The work area enables you to add static text, graphics, fields, and so on, while the Programmer's pane enables you to create formulas for the form. You can hide the Programmer's pane by toggling it on

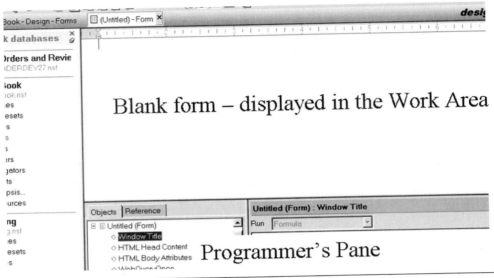

Figure 25-6 The work area and Programmer's pane

and off, using View . . . Programmer's pane. (Note that the smart icon still calls this pane the Design pane, which is a holdover from R4.x.) You might also want to show the ruler to aid in layout by choosing View . . . Ruler or by clicking the View Ruler smart icon.

Form Properties

After creating the form, set the properties for the form by using the Form Properties InfoBox. To open the Form properties InfoBox, which is shown in Figure 25-7, perform one of the following actions:

- Right-click the form and choose Form Properties from the shortcut menu.
- Choose File . . . Document Properties while you are in Design mode on a form. This action displays the form properties in this context.
- Click the Display InfoBox button while you are in Design mode on a form.

Domino Designer opens the Form properties InfoBox. Look for a number of questions covering the options in this InfoBox on the exam. Let's examine the options on each tabbed page.

Figure 25-7
The Form
properties
InfoBox

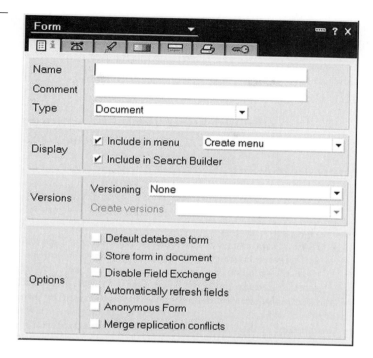

Form Info Tab

The first tab on the Form properties InfoBox is the Form Info tab, which is displayed in Figure 25-7. This tab enables you to set some basic details, such as the name and type of the form. The following paragraphs describe each of the options that are available:

- **Name**   The form name should be a descriptive name for the form, including information about the purpose of the form or the type of data contained in the form. The form name can be up to 256 bytes, including alphanumeric characters, spaces, and punctuation; however, Notes only displays the first 64 characters of a form name. The form name is case-sensitive. Form names can also use synonyms, which are also known as *aliases*. Aliases, if used, will be the name that is stored and used internally by Notes. Aliases can be useful in situations where long names make using them in formulas cumbersome or when you want the form to have multiple names, such as when translating the application into another language. To create a synonym for a form name, type the form name first (this name will be used in the Create menu and in the view), then use the pipe or vertical bar (|)

symbol. Next, type the alias (this alias will be used internally in the Form field and in formulas). Other Notes design elements also use aliases, including views and keyword choices. For example, the Book Review form with the alias name Review is shown next. After typing the form name and the synonym, click the check mark to have Designer check the syntax.

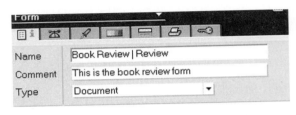

NOTE Form names can also be cascaded off the Create menu. In some cases, you might want to group a set of forms together under a menu choice. To cascade a form name, first type the name of the menu choice under which you want to cascade the name. Then, type a / (backslash) and the name of the form. Be aware that the menu choice portion of the form name must be precisely the same on all the forms that you want cascaded (including capitalization). You will usually find it easiest to copy the first portion of the name from an already-created form when you are placing multiple forms under the same cascaded menu choice. To enable forms to be selected using the keyboard, place an underscore (_) in the form name before the letter to be used as the accelerator key. To use the letter s in test as the keyboard shortcut, you would type the name as Te_st.

- **Comment** This text field enables the designer to document the form's purpose or other information.

- **Type** Three types of forms are available in Notes: *Document, Response,* and *Response-to-Response.*

  - Use the *Document (or Main Topic)* form, which is the default document type, unless the application requires a hierarchical relationship between documents. When using a Document form type, the documents created by that form are Main (or Parent) documents.

  - Notes always associates a *Response* document with a Main document. The Response document becomes a child document to a Main document and usually inherits some information or data from this parent document. When Cassandra creates a new Question document in the Technical Support database, for example, Mike wants to respond to the question. When he creates a Response document, he wants some of the information from Cassandra's document, such as the date and subject, to be included in his response. This feature, called inheritance, is discussed more thoroughly later.

- A *Response-to-Response* document can be associated with either a Main document or a Response document. This feature enables a third hierarchical response level in the database. In the previous scenario, for example, Scott, the database moderator, needs a third type of document in order to comment on either the questions or the answers. This document would need to be a Response-to-Response type.

 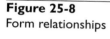

NOTE   When discussing Response and Response-to-Response documents, you also need to understand the difference between the children and descendants. Think of a Main document as a parent. A Response document that is directly responding to that Main document would be that Main document's child. Next, a Response-to-Response document that responds to the Main document can be a child as well. Finally, there can also be a Response-to-Response document responding to a Response document, and this document is a descendant, not a child. You need to understand these relationships when selecting documents for a view or in an agent. Figure 25-8 graphically shows the possible relationships between forms.

Children Descendents

- **Include In Menu**   The form can be included in the Create menu, the Create . . . Other dialog box, or neither. If you choose to place the form in the Other . . . dialog box, a separate option on the Create menu called Other . . . is displayed. This

Figure 25-8
Form relationships

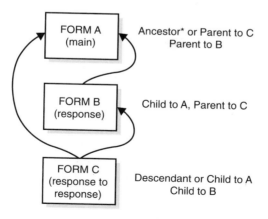

* Ancestor is not a common Notes term

option then opens a separate dialog box from which to select these forms, enabling you to keep the Create menu less cluttered. The form name, not the synonym, appears in the menu options or the Other . . . dialog box. By default, Notes includes the form in the search builder for the purposes of enabling users to search for information by form. When securing or hiding the form, exclude the form from the search builder by removing the check mark from the *Include In Search Builder* option. The search builder helps designers choose documents for views and agents.

- **Versioning**   Version tracking enables users to save both an original document and any edited versions of the document. The version tracking helps in situations where each change to a document must be maintained and must be visible. Designer offers four version tracking options:

  - **None**   In the default option, there is no version tracking. When a user edits and saves a document, Designer replaces the original document.

  - **New versions become responses**   In this option, when a user edits and saves a document, the document becomes a response to the original document. This feature helps prevent replication and save conflicts. When replication occurs, if users on multiple servers have edited the document, there will merely be multiple Response documents. Select this option if the original information is more important than the changes. If multiple people work on the chairman's major speech, for example, the basic text remains intact while each writer puts his or her spin on the text. The chairman and the writers can view the different versions and compare them against the original.

  - **Prior versions become responses**   When you enable this option, Notes makes the most recently saved version of a document the Main document. Notes makes all predecessors Response documents to the main document. The original document becomes the first Response document. Use this option when the changes are more important than the original.

  - **New versions become siblings**   When using this setting, all new versions of a document become new documents at the same level as additional Main documents. Use this option if the time stamp of the revisions is not important. This option makes visualizing the relationships between documents difficult, because all documents exist in the same generation.

  When version tracking is enabled, a *Create Versions* option is also available. *Create Versions* includes the following features:

- **Automatic—File Save**   When a user edits and saves a document, Notes automatically uses the version tracking setting to create a new document.

- **Manual—File, New Version**   In this option, the edited document replaces the original version unless the user chooses File . . . Save as New Version at save time.

- **Default Database form**   This setting makes the selected form the default form for the database. If Notes cannot find the form that is associated with a particular document, this form is used to display the document. There can be only one default form per database, distinguished in the Design . . . Forms view with an asterisk (*).

- **Store form in Document**   By default, Notes stores the form and data separately. Selecting this option, however, causes Notes to store the data and form together. Use this option for documents or forms that will be mailed to users or to mail-in databases. The documents (and the database) will be larger, however, and already-created documents will not reflect design changes made to the form.

When Notes tries to determine which form to use to display a document, it follows a set of rules. These rules are described in Table 25-1.

NOTE   The Allow the Use of Stored forms in this database option on the Database properties InfoBox must be enabled to use this option.

Table 25-1   Document Display Rules

What Is the Situation?	Which Form Displays the Document?
A form is stored with the document.	The form stored with the document is used to display the document.
The form used to create the document is available. There is no form stored with the document.	The form used to create the document is used to display the document.
The view has a form formula.	The formula determines the form used to display the document.
The form used to create the document is not available.	The default form for the database is used to display the document.

- **Disable Field Exchange**   Field exchange (Notes/FX) enables Lotus Notes applications and OLE server applications to share or exchange field information. This option causes Field Exchange to be disabled. The fields, however, can remain on the form. The Lotus Notes Help database is available to give you more information about Notes/FX.

- **Automatically Refresh Fields**   Any time it might be necessary for users to see updated information on a form as they complete it—such as when they perform calculations on an order form—you should enable this option. Notes will be forced to recalculate every field on the form each time the user moves to a different field. Be aware, however, that this option slows movement through the form, especially on forms with multiple calculated fields.

- **Anonymous form**   Notes enables users to create documents anonymously, which is a handy feature for surveys or for ballot box-types of applications. When using this feature, Notes replaces the default internal field $UpdatedBy with an $Anonymous field with a value of one. To create a form that enables users to respond without being identified (even by developers or administrators), make the form anonymous.

- **Merge Replication Conflicts**   Choosing this option can, in some cases, prevent the replication conflicts that occur when the same document is edited at the same time on two different servers. When the servers replicate a document that has been edited on both servers, the documents could create a replication conflict. In Notes, however, replication works at the field level rather than at the document level. When Domino detects changes on a document, the servers replicate only the changed fields, rather than the entire document. If you enable *Merge Replication conflicts*, and users have edited two different fields, Domino does not create replication conflicts. For example, say that Mike and Brian are both working on the same set of documentation. The documentation exists in two replicas of a Notes database on two servers. They both have Editor-level access to a set of documents, and they both edit those documents to add to the documentation. They both edit the same document, but Mike edits the Topic field and Brian edits the Body field. If *Merge Replication conflicts* is enabled, when replication occurs, the two fields on the document will be updated, and no replication conflict will occur. If both Mike and Brian update the Topic field, however, a replication conflict will occur.

NOTE   A save conflict occurs when the same document is opened and edited simultaneously by two users on the same server. In the previous example, if Mike and Brian were both working on the same database on the same server, any time they both edited the same document at the same time, a save conflict would occur.

Defaults Tab

The next tab on the Form properties InfoBox, called Defaults, determines the default settings. Figure 25-9 shows the settings available on this tab.

- **On Create**   There are two options for the form at creation time, and both options relate to inheritance. *Inheritance* is the capability of a form to pull some information for its fields from another form. This capability only exists when composing documents. After the document has been created and saved, it can only access information on another document programmatically (through formulas or LotusScript), not via inheritance. Additionally, for inheritance to work correctly, the user must have a document selected in a view when he or she begins to create the new document that needs to inherit information. This document can be any form type (Main document, Response, or Response-to-Response). The two *On Create: Inheritance* options are discussed in the following paragraphs.

  - **Formulas inherit values from selected document**   When this option is selected, fields can inherit their values from fields on the selected document. This option helps avoid unnecessary typing and mistakes when transferring information from one form to another. To configure inheritance, set the default value for the field to the name of the field from which it should inherit its value. For example, the designer of a Call Tracking database wants the call response to

on create

doc selected.

Figure 25-9
The Defaults tab

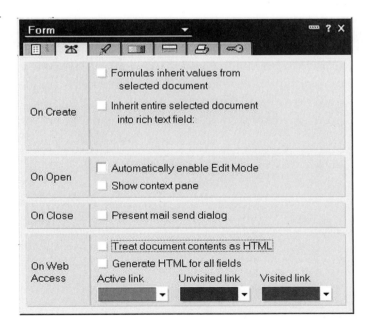

include the question that the user asks. The question is typed into a field called Question. In the Call Response form therefore, there should be a field for which the default value is Question, and the inheritance option should be enabled.

- **Inherit entire selected document into rich text field**   Choose this option to copy an entire document into the Rich Text field on the new document. The document can be copied into the Rich Text field as a link, as collapsible rich text, or simply as rich text. Note that a Rich Text field must exist on the form you are designing to choose this option. The link option will create a doclink to the selected document. The Collapsible Rich Text option will create a collapsible section that contains the contents of the selected document. The rich text option copies the contents into the indicated Rich Text field. An example is forwarding mail or sending replies to mail that include the message history.

  To enable inheritance, you must use fields whose values are defined by the fields on the selected documents. This portion of inheritance will be described in Chapter 26, "Creating Fields and Formulas."

- **On Open**   There are two options for opening documents created with this form. These options are described in the following paragraphs:

- **Automatically Enable Edit Mode**   When users open documents that were created with forms with this option enabled, the documents are automatically opened for editing. The default for opening a document would ordinarily be Read mode. A user would then have to click an action button or use a menu choice to use Edit mode. This option can save time for data entry when documents will be edited each time they are opened.

- **Show Context Pane**   A Context pane is another partition in the open window that displays additional information to the user. In this option, shown next, you can open a Context pane to display either the Parent document of the current document or a doclink included in the document. This option is especially useful when combined with the inheritance options for Response documents.

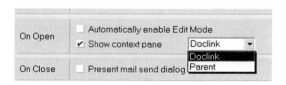

NOTE   The phrases On Create and On Open can be confusing, but the distinction is important. On Create refers to the time when the user is completing a form, before the form has been saved. On Open refers to any time the document (created by completing and saving a form) is opened after it has been saved. Therefore, when a user begins to create a question in the database by choosing Create . . . Question from the menu, the document goes into Create mode. After the user saves the question, the help desk person then opens the Question document.

- **On Close**   The designer can specify that the Mail Send dialog box will open when a user closes a document. This feature enables the user to send the document to a mail user, save the document, or discard changes to the document. The form must have the required addressing and mail fields to mail the document. See Part V, "Application Security and Workflow," for more detail.

- **On Web Access**   These options specifically address access by Web clients. The first option, *Treat document contents as HTML*, enables Notes to pass the contents of the form and/or document directly as HTML. When you want to use an existing Web page as a starting point, copy and paste the HTML onto the form and set this option. In Designer, the form appears as text with HTML tags but is translated into HTML for Web clients. You can also use File . . . Import to bring HTML content into your form. In this case, however, you do not need to enable this option, and the contents are displayed as already-rendered HTML in the Designer client. Figure 25-10 shows a form that has HTML copied and pasted.

Figure 25-10
You can paste HTML directly into forms.

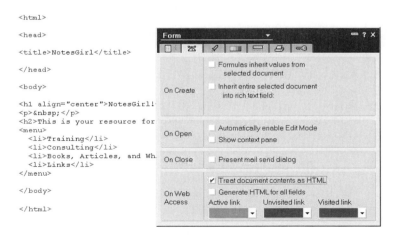

NB

Generate HTML for all fields = calculation and availability of hidden fields.

Next, set the *Generate HTML for all fields* option. This feature is especially useful when you have hidden fields on your forms. Without this option enabled, the data from those fields would not be available on the Web. By forcing Domino to generate HTML for these fields, however, you ensure that the form behaves as expected. In addition, setting this property makes data from hidden fields available to JavaScript in Web applications.

Finally, on the bottom of the Form Info tab, you can select colors for active links, unvisited links, and visited links. Active links are red (unless you change their color) and are those links that you have currently selected. Unvisited links, which are blue by default, are those links that you have not yet clicked. Visited links, which are purple by default, are those links that you have clicked.

> **CAUTION** Be careful when changing the color associated with links. Most users have become familiar with the default colors used for links and will make assumptions about what the link means based on its color. Only change the link colors when you have a specific reason for doing so.

Launch Tab

The Launch tab on the Form properties InfoBox, as shown in Figure 25-11, enables a doclink, attachment, or other object on a form to be launched automatically. This option enables the designer to place information from other documents, databases, or applications on the forms they create. The default setting for the *AutoLaunch* option (-None-) ensures that nothing launches automatically (users can still launch links or objects manually). The drop-down list contains options to launch other objects automatically, including the following:

- First attachment
- First document link
- First OLE object
- URL
- Any object from the OLE-enabled applications installed on the workstation

> **TIP** The users see different lists for every workstation, because each workstation has different applications. Notes lists all OLE-enabled applications in this option, because these applications can launch any objects or attachments that are created with them.

Figure 25-11
The Launch tab

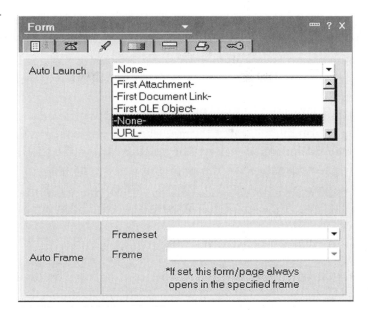

If the designer chooses to launch the first attachment, document link, or URL, the object launches immediately when the user selects Create . . . *Formname*. If the designer chooses any of the OLE options, the following additional options become available, as shown in Figure 25-12:

- **Launch in place**   OLE objects can be launched either in place or out of place. When objects are launched out of place (the default setting), the new application launches separately and becomes the active window. When an OLE object launches in place, the application opens within a Notes window.

- **Create object in field**   When creating a new OLE object, the designer chooses whether to create the object in the first Rich Text field or in any other Rich Text field on the form (if one already exists on the form, it will be listed here). If the object should not be displayed as part of the form, the designer can also select None.

- **Launch When**   This option enables the designer to toggle on and off the three options of Creating, Editing, and Reading, all of which are toggled on by default. Keep the purpose of both the object and the form in mind when you set the *Launch When* option. For example, if the object should be created when the document is created, select *Launch When Creating*. If the document automatically launches in Edit mode (an option on the Defaults tab), select *Launch When Editing*.

- **Hide When**   This option enables the designer to hide the Notes document automatically upon certain events. In other words, the user only sees the application that launches the external object and never sees the Notes document. The Notes document can remain hidden during the following events: Opening Create, Opening Edit, Opening Read, Closing Create, Closing Edit, and Closing Read. All of the Opening options are selected by default. Each of the Closing options is available for selection only when the corresponding Opening option is already selected.

- **Present document as modal dialog**   This option enables the designer to launch the document or object into a dialog box without enabling the end user to access the Notes menus while the object is active.

Another launch option on this tab is the *AutoFrame* option, which is used to relate the form/document to a frameset and to cause the form and/or document to launch in a particular frame of the frameset. A *frameset* is a navigational tool used in Notes and on the Web that breaks the interface into sections (called frames) that contain different information. This information can be related so that when you select a link or click a

Figure 25-12
OLE launch options

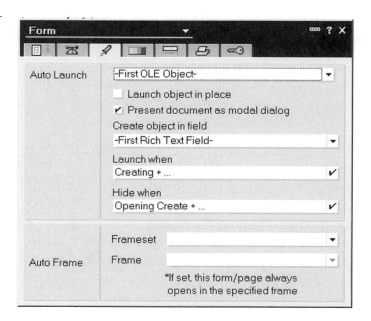

document in one frame of the frameset, it opens into another, or they can be unrelated so that links clicked in a frame open in the same frame. For more information about framesets and frames, refer to Chapter 30, "Creating Framesets."

In the case of linking a form to a particular frame of a frameset for launch purposes, you first select a frameset from the drop-down box in the Auto Frame section. Only framesets in the current database are available. After selecting a frameset, choose a named frame from that frameset from the Frame drop-down box. Then the form (and any documents created with the form) will always open in the specified frame. To implement this element, the database must contain a named and saved frameset with named frames.

Form Background Tab

The Form Background tab sets the background color and any background graphics you want displayed on the form, as shown next. The fields on the Form Background tab are discussed in the following paragraphs.

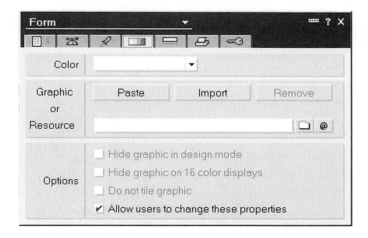

The Form Background tab determines the background color or graphic for the form (just as for a page, as described earlier). Choose either a background color or a graphic background. The first field, *Color*, enables you to choose your colored background. To ensure that what you design is closest to what your Web users see, use the Web palette as you design.

You can also use this tab to add a background graphic to your form. To paste a graphic, copy the graphic from your graphics program onto the clipboard. Then, on the Form properties InfoBox, choose Paste. If the graphic is already the same size as the form, Designer will paste the graphic once. If the graphic is smaller, Designer will tile the graphic to cover the form. Choose the *Do Not Tile Graphic* option to display the graphic once. If you prefer to import the graphic, click the Import button. To remove a graphic background from the form, either add a new graphic using the paste or import method or click the Remove button to have no graphic background. Another way to place a graphic background into the form is to use a shared image resource, as described previously. Other options you can enable on the Background tab are described as follows:

- **Hide Graphic in Design Mode**   Sometimes it is easier for the developer to design the fields and formulas on a form without viewing the graphics. This option hides graphics during design time.

- **Hide graphic on 16 color displays**   This option hides the graphic from users who have lower-quality displays.

- **Do not tile graphics**   This option places a single image of the background graphic to the form. Web clients ignore this option; instead, they still display the tiled background graphic.

- **Allow users to change these properties**   This option enables the users to change these properties for ease of viewing as they use the form or documents created with the form.

Header Tab

This tab provides a new R5 feature for your form that is called a header. The header is a portion of the form that does not scroll when the rest of the form scrolls. This feature keeps some text, graphics, or other elements available for the users of the form at all times. Any element that you can place on a form can be placed in the form header; however, a table cannot be the first element in a form header. If you choose to place a table in the form header, place text or some other element in the header first. This option only affects Notes clients. If you view a form that has a header on it in a Web client, the information usually stored in the header portion of the form will be at the top of the form but will scroll with the rest of the form. To create a header on your form, place your cursor on the form directly below all of the elements that should appear in the header. Open the Form properties InfoBox, click the Header tab, and select the *Add Header to form* checkbox. Then set the following properties for the header, as shown here:

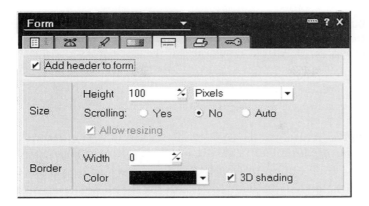

- **Size**   In the *Size* section of the tab, choose the *Height* for the header. The height can be set in pixels, based on a percentage of the form size, or can be set to fit to the content of the information in the header. You can also set a *Scrolling* property for the header, which determines whether the header itself scrolls. You can also choose to enable the header to be resized by users.

- **Border**   In the Border section of the tab, choose the *Width* and *Color* of the border between the header and the rest of the form. Setting the width to zero removes the border. You can also determine whether the border is flat or has *3D Shading*.

NOTE   Note that if you have a graphic background on a form for which you configure a header, the graphic background only appears in the header. Do not forget, though, that because Web clients do not display headers, this form looks different between the two clients. The Memo form in the mail template has an example of a header. The address and subject information at the top of the form does not scroll as a user reads the mail message.

Printing Tab

The Printing tab is similar in most of the Properties InfoBoxes available in Notes, including the Database properties InfoBox and the Document properties InfoBox. The Printing tab defines the settings used for printing the documents created with this form and enables you to create headers and footers for the pages in the database as well as specify the font, font size, and font style. Headers and footers can contain automatic elements such as the time, date, and page number. By default, the headers and footers will print on every page except the first. You can force them to print on the first page as well, however, by using the checkbox at the bottom of the InfoBox.

NOTE The options set here become the default settings for any documents created with this form. Users can override them with the Document properties InfoBox for the specific document that the user prints.

Security Tab

Most security settings for the form are discussed elsewhere in this book. For now, however, take note of the option to *Disable Printing/Forwarding/Copying to Clipboard*. This option enables the designer to enforce any security they have placed on the form, even outside the Notes application. This tab is shown in Figure 25-13.

What Else to Put on a Page or Form

As you might imagine, there is a lot more to a page or form than just its properties. Although the properties define basic details about the page or form, what you put on the page or form is what matters to your users. All of the elements that can be placed on a page can also be used on form. The following is a list of the elements that can be used on pages or forms:

Figure 25-13
The Security tab

- Text and HTML
- Horizontal rules
- Graphics and imagemaps
- Sections
- Tables
- Hotspots, links, and attachments
- Embedded elements, such as views, folder panes, navigators, outlines, or date pickers
- Actions
- Applets
- OLE objects

Other items that can be used on both pages and forms include Hide-When attributes for elements and window titles. In addition to those elements, you can use the following elements on forms only:

- **Fields**   Gather or compute data
- **Subforms**   A mini-form, which can be reused
- **Access-controlled sections**   Add some security to the standard sections
- **Layout regions**   Used for flexibility of design
- **Advanced embedded elements**   Upload controls or group schedulers

The thread common to elements that can be placed on forms but not pages is that elements on forms can require input or programming. Items on a page can neither require nor accept input from users. In addition, elements on pages usually do not have a great deal of programming associated with them. The items that can be placed only on forms either are designed for or require input. The following sections describe the elements that can be placed on pages and forms.

Text and HTML

The first element that a developer places on a page or form is static text. The static text gives the page or form its shape and style. Static text can be placed anywhere on the page or form, simply by clicking and typing. Use the normal formatting tools available to format this text, including the Text properties InfoBox and the Text menu choices. Your automatic reaction at this point is probably that text is a fairly obvious element and does not really deserve its own section. To a certain extent, you are correct. The topic of text will not be a significant aspect of your exam, and you probably already know what text is and how to create it. The one trick that you might like to know, however, is how text reacts when users view your application using a Web client rather than a Notes client.

When viewed over the Web, the HTTP task in the Domino server converts the text in your applications to HTML. For those of you who are familiar with HTML, you know that HTML limits the sizes, fonts, and styles that users can see when viewing your application in a Web client. First, many Web clients are limited in HTML to Default Sans Serif fonts (no feet on the letters) and a Default Serif font (feet on the letters), based on the fonts available on the client system. You never know exactly how your text will appear to your users unless you design your text using these fonts. Similarly, font sizes in HTML do not map exactly to the 10, 12, or 14 points that Notes uses. Instead, the seven HTML sizes map approximately to the point sizes. Although you can create any text that you feel is necessary and format it using the Text properties InfoBox or the choices from the Text menu, test your choices on all of the clients in which you expect your database to be viewed. This exam should include a variety of browsers (Web clients), because not all browsers understand HTML tags in the same way. Other HTML tips include avoiding tabs, indents, and line spacing, because HTML does not support these elements. Tables or spaces created in a monospaced font such as Courier can help you avoid the tab and indent problems.

NOTE To preview your forms, pages, and other elements in Notes clients and browsers, use the preview buttons in the upper-left corner of Domino Designer. Designer always has a button for a Notes preview and a Domino preview. Designer displays other preview buttons based on the browsers installed on your system. One of the best ways to figure out what will happen to your text when you display the text through Web clients is to become familiar with HTML. So, create some test pages. A ton of HTML tutorials and how-to pages can be found on the Web, so use your favorite search engine and look for HTML.

Regardless of whether you design for Notes clients, Web clients, or both, be aware that your monitor, video card, and screen resolution are probably better and higher than what the users have available when they view your page or form. Be sensitive to this factor, and test your page or form with a variety of clients and at a variety of settings so that you can gauge what your users will see.

You can also add HTML directly to a page or form. As mentioned earlier, you can use pages and sites that you have already created in HTML in your Notes application. In cases where you have an existing Web page that you want to use as a starting point, you could copy and paste the HTML onto the page or form. Then, set the *Treat page contents as HTML* (or *Treat Document Contents as HTML* for forms) option, and the page or form contents appear as tagged text in the Designer client but are translated into HTML for Web clients. Finally, you can place HTML on the page or form and mark it as HTML by selecting Text . . . Pass-Thru HTML from the menu.

Although you cannot add fields to pages (only to forms), you can add computed text to either element. Computed text is text that is evaluated and rendered at display time using a formula. To create computed text, place your cursor where you want the text and choose Create . . . Computed Text from the menus. The Domino Designer displays the placeholder <Computed Value> on the page and shifts the focus to the Programmer's pane, giving you the opportunity to add a formula that determines the text. In the Info List (the left-hand pane) on the Objects tab, select the Computed Text . . . Value object. In the Script area of the Programmer's pane, type the formula for the computed text.

Horizontal Rules

Use a horizontal rule, or line, for separating areas of the page or form or for otherwise organizing the appearance of the data on the page or form. Creating a horizontal rule is equivalent to drawing a horizontal line in a graphics program or using the <HR> HTML tag. To create a horizontal rule on your page or form, place the cursor where you want the horizontal rule and choose Create . . . Horizontal Rule from the menus. After creating the horizontal rule (as shown next), change its properties by double-clicking the horizontal rule to display the Properties InfoBox.

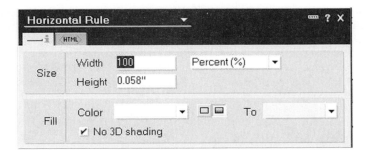

The Horizontal Rule Info tab enables you to change the size and color of the line. First, you can change the width (you might also think of this measurement as length) of the line. This measurement can be made in either absolute inches or in relative percentage of the page that it will cover. To change whether the line uses relative or absolute measurement, click the drop-down arrow on the right side of the InfoBox. By default, the line measures 100 percent of the width of the page or form. You can also change the height of the line, which is always measured in absolute inches.

The options on the HTML tab of the properties InfoBox incorporate additional HTML attributes into the horizontal rule. Domino adds the specified attributes to the HTML that it creates automatically.

Graphics and Imagemaps

Similar to creating background graphics for your pages or forms, you can also add graphics to the page or form itself. The big difference is that these graphics will be inline with the text and other elements on your page or form, rather than behind these elements as another layer. When adding graphics for visual appeal, remember that these fun and funky items also slow the loading of the page or form and/or document. Graphics on the page or form can take the form of background graphics, as discussed previously, or they can be stand-alone, inline, or imagemaps. Stand-alone graphics usually make the page or form more visually interesting, while imagemaps contain links and are used for navigation (similar to graphical navigators, which are described in Chapter 29, "Creating Navigation").

Designer provides a variety of methods that you can use to add graphics to your pages or forms. First, you can copy and paste graphics from other applications. Next, you can use the File . . . Import to bring in graphics in supported formats. Supported formats include .BMP, .JPG or .JPEG, .GIF, .PCX, and .TIFF 5.0. Similarly, use the Create . . . Picture menu choices to import graphics in the same formats, in addition to .CGM and .PIC formats. Lastly, you can use the shared image resources described previously to store graphics with the database and insert them wherever necessary without adding to the size of the database. To insert shared image resources, choose Create . . . Image Resource.

After inserting or pasting the graphic, use the Picture properties InfoBox to change the size and scaling of the picture or to determine how text wraps around the picture. Open the Picture properties InfoBox by right-clicking the graphic. The Picture Info tab displays the source of the picture, such as the inline image described here. You can also choose to scale the image larger or smaller, based on percentages. Note that some browsers do not support scaling. In this case, the browser displays the image in its original size, regardless of the sizing and scaling applied in Designer.

Use the Alternate Text option to make your page or form more accessible to people with disabilities or to describe the image to users who choose not to have graphics displayed in their Web clients. Alternate text can be used with a screen-reader device and a speech synthesizer. Together these devices use the alternate text to describe the image orally. Alternate text is also visible as a pop-up when users hold the mouse pointer over the image. You can also add a caption to the graphic image, which is centered on or below the image.

Created with
Domino!

[handwritten note:] Imagemap: any graphic that has hotspots / links. Navigator : many graphs.

The Hotspots section of the InfoBox enables you to use a graphic to create an imagemap. An imagemap is any graphic that has hotspots or links. These hotspots or links either perform an action or take the user to a different page, site, or application when clicked. You can use imagemaps to assist with navigation. Some users confuse imagemaps and navigators. An imagemap, which is a single graphic with many hotspots, is stored on a page or on a form. A navigator is an independent design element and often uses multiple graphics, rather than a single graphic.

To make a graphic into an imagemap, click one of the three *Add Hotspot* buttons to create polygon-shaped, circular, or rectangular hotspots on the graphic. After clicking a button, use the mouse to draw a hotspot over a portion of the graphic. You can also add hotspots by right-clicking the graphic or using the Picture menu. After creating the hotspot, add an action or link to the hotspot using the Hotspot properties InfoBox shown next. You can add a URL link, a link to other databases, views, or documents, or a link to a named element, such as another page, form, view, or frameset. One benefit of using an imagemap is that you can switch the picture in the imagemap without redoing the hotspots. To replace the graphic, click the graphic to select it and then choose Picture . . . Replace Picture from the menus. If you switch the picture, do not forget to change the caption and alternate text.

The other tabs in the Picture properties InfoBox determine which type of border the graphic will have, the alignment of the graphic, and other formatting defaults.

Sections

Users often complain about being forced to scroll down repeatedly to get to the information they want to see in pages and forms. You can respond to this complaint by organizing your pages and forms with sections. A section groups text, graphics, and fields (on forms only) into an area that can collapse into a single line. In addition, sections provide a way for the designer to collapse information that is not necessary or interesting to all users. Two types of sections exist: standard sections and controlled access sections. Pages can only have standard sections; however, forms can accommodate both types of sections.

Standard Sections   To create a section, select the elements to be placed in the section and choose Create . . . Section from the menus. On a form, where you have a choice of section types, you would choose Create . . . Section . . . Standard. After you create a section, the first line of text automatically appears as the section title, and the section will be collapsed and displayed with a small triangle to the left of the section (called a *twistie*). To expand or collapse the section, click the blue twistie (which looks like a sideways triangle) to the left of the section title. Sections, much like everything else, have properties that govern the way they act and appear. To customize the section, right-click the section and choose Section Properties to display the Section Properties InfoBox. Use the Section Title and Border tab to set the text for the section title and the formatting for the section's border. The properties for the section are discussed as follows.

Title

On the Title tab, type the title to be displayed at the top of the section when you have selected the Text radio button. By choosing the Formula radio button instead, you can use a formula to create the section title. When you choose the Formula radio button, the client also displays the Formula Window button. This button causes Designer to display a larger window for creating more complex formulas (again, formulas will be discussed in Chapter 26, "Creating Fields and Formulas"). The drop-down boxes at the bottom of the Title tab enable you to create a border around the section. This border is set to None by default.

Expand/Collapse Tab

The Expand/Collapse tab, shown next, sets defaults for the display settings of the section. By default, each of the rules on the Expand/Collapse tab is set to *Don't auto expand or collapse*. The section remains in the state it was in when last viewed. The other options are *Auto-Expand* or *Auto-Collapse*. You have the ability to set the Expand/Collapse options when the document is previewed, opened for reading, opened for editing, and/or printed. In other words, you can select for a particular section to expand automatically when printing or for a section to collapse automatically when reading. This feature enables you to use the sections most effectively for organizational and form-length purposes. The other options on this tab enable the title to be hidden when the section is expanded and for the section itself to be visible only when the document is in Preview mode (otherwise, the elements simply appear without being contained in the section).

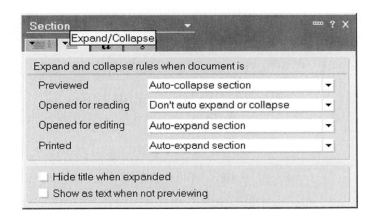

Font
The Font tab sets the font, size, style, and color of the section title.

Hide-When
This tab sets options for hiding the section by formula, based on the client in use or based on the state of the document. Hide-When options are discussed in depth later in this chapter.

Controlled-Access Sections

all can read except when using hide-when options.

A controlled-access section functions much like a standard section in that it organizes the text and other elements on a form and limits the length of the form. This section has the additional function of limiting the users who can edit the fields in a section. Note that you can only use controlled-access sections on forms. The tabs in the InfoBox for controlled-access sections are displayed in Figure 25-14. Note that this InfoBox can be called the Form Section InfoBox in Designer. The Standard Section InfoBox will just be called Section.

Figure 25-14
Controlled-access
section properties

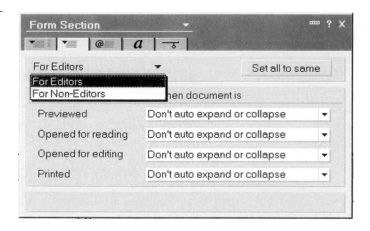

- The *Section Title and Border* tab has similar elements to the same tab for the Standard section, including *Title text, Border Style,* and *Border Color* fields. Note that there is also a field for a *Section Field Name.* Use this field only if the application will be used with version 3 as well as version R4 and R5 clients.

- The *Expand/Collapse* tab determines how the section will appear by default when opened, edited, previewed, or printed. You can also set the Auto Expand or Collapse differently for users who have Editor and Non-Editor access by using the drop-down selection at the top right. Use the *Set All to Same* button to set all the view options at once.

- The *Formula* tab defines the Access formula, which determines who Notes considers an Editor. The formula can be *Editable, Computed for Display,* or *Computed when Composed* and must resolve to a name or list of names.

- The *Font* tab and *Paragraph Hide When* tab offer the same basic options as they do on the Standard Section InfoBox. There are a few options, such as *Preview only,* that are removed in controlled-access sections.

Note that anyone with Reader access to the database can read the information in a controlled-access section unless prevented by Hide-When options. In addition, the Controlled Access formula will not override the ACL for the database.

Tables

The next element used to organize information on your pages and forms is tables. Tables have undergone a huge improvement in R5, because R5 offers more types of tables and more flexible table formatting for both Web and Notes clients. Choose from the following table types:

- Standard
- Nested (or Recursive)
- Tabbed
- Rolling
- Programmatic

These table types provide flexibility in organizing your data. R5 also introduces a new Table Wizard (displayed when you choose Create . . . Table) that walks you through the steps required to create these new table types.

To add a new table, open the page or form and select Create . . . Table. Designer displays the Create Table dialog box, shown in Figure 25-15. This dialog box enables you to create a standard table, a tabbed table, a timed animated table, and a programmatic table. Each of these table types can also be created from a standard table by manipulating the Table properties InfoBox.

Figure 25-15
Create Table
dialog box

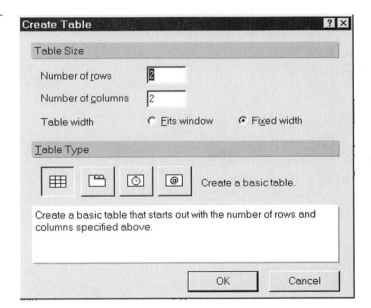

Standard Tables

The standard table is similar to the table that has been available in Notes for some time. After creating a standard table, right-click and choose Table Properties to display the InfoBox, as shown next. The Table Layout tab gives you three options for the width of the table on the page: *Fit to Window*, *Fit with Margins*, and *Fixed Width*. With the *Fixed Width* option, you can also choose how the table is aligned: *left*, *right*, or *center*. The next portion of the tab enables you to size individual cells based on width or all cells based on height, row spacing, and column spacing. You can also choose the *Auto-size* button to size the cells based on their contents. Use the *Vertically Align* drop-down menu to determine whether the text in a particular cell will be aligned at the top, center, or bottom.

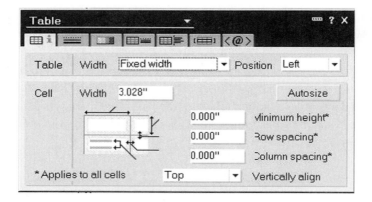

The Cell Borders tab determines the style, color, and thickness of the cell borders. For Web clients, the top left-hand cell governs the appearance of the table. If the cell has borders, all cells will have borders. In addition, colors and styles of the cell borders do not apply to Web clients.

The Table/Cell Background tab sets the background for the cells in the table, similar to the way you set the background for the page. First, set the background for the entire table. This colored background can either be solid (the same for all cells), or you can choose to highlight certain rows and columns with a different color by using the choices from the *Style* drop-down list. Next, you can change the color for individual cells. This color can be solid or gradient by clicking the *Style* buttons to the right of the cell color choice. Use the *Apply to all* button to choose this color for all the cells in the table. The cell color sits on top of the table color. Finally, you can add an image as a background to cells. Use a shared image resource or a formula to determine the image. As with cell colors, once you apply an image to a cell, you have the option of applying that image to all cells. The Table Borders tab determines the outside border of the table.

Note that if you have also applied cell borders, you can get a double-border effect where the cell border meets the table border.

The Table Margins tab, shown next, sets margins for the table on the page—in either absolute inches or relative percentages. This tab also determines how text wraps, both around the outside of the table and inside the table. Finally, if you need the table to be compatible with R4 clients, you can choose the R4 spacing checkbox. R5 tables are displayed slightly smaller than their R4 counterparts.

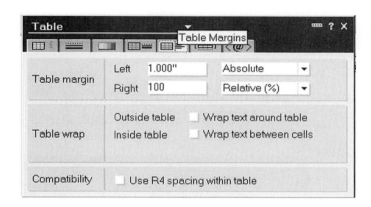

The Table Rows tab, shown in Figure 25-16, contains options for special display methods for tables. These options enable you to turn a standard table into other table types, as discussed next. The biggest difference between the standard table and the other table types is how many rows the client displays simultaneously and what factor determines which rows the client displays. To change from a standard table to another type, use the *Show only one row at a time* radio button, turning the standard table into a tabbed, animated, or programmatic table based on the other selections made. The other options available on this tab are discussed next.

Use the Table Programming tab to add HTML code to the tables. As with the HTML tab for pages, this option adds to the code that the Domino server creates for the table. You will also use some of the fields on this tab for creating programmatic tables, as discussed next. This tab is shown in Figure 25-17.

Tabbed Tables

Create a tabbed table using the second button on the Create Table dialog box. This type of table displays each of its rows as a different tab, each of which can be named, can have colors or other formatting, and can contain other elements (such as another table, text, fields, or any embedded element). Shown next is a tabbed table that also contains a standard table. This table is recursive—one table stored within another. (A recursive

Figure 25-16
The Table Rows tab

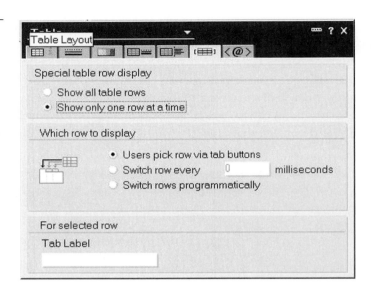

Figure 25-17
The Table
Programming tab

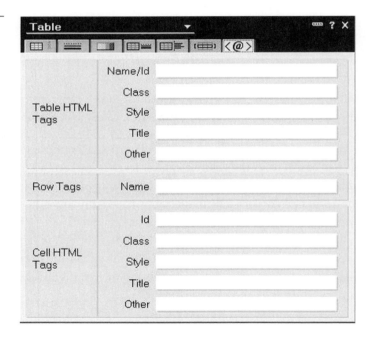

8 levels of table

table is a fancy name for a table nested within another table.) You can nest up to eight levels of tables deep. To create a recursive table, simply put your cursor inside a cell of an existing table and use the same methods to create another table. A recursive table (a table within a tabbed table) is shown next.

Each of the other table types (programmatic and animated) is based on the tabbed table format, showing only one row at a time. With the tabbed table, users choose the row to view based on the tab that they select. The other types of tables automate this process.

In the Table properties InfoBox (refer to Figure 25-16), you can create this type of table from a standard table by selecting the *Show only one row at a time* radio button on the Table Rows tab. In the *Which Row to Display* section, leave the selection called *Users Pick row via Tab Buttons* enabled to maintain a simple tabbed table. Use the last field on this tab, Tab Label, to give each row's tab a label (refer to Figure 25-16).

Animated Tables

The third button in the Create Table dialog box creates an animated, or rolling, table. Notes displays the table one row at a time to the user. By default, the row switches every 2 seconds, although you can change the amount of time using the Properties InfoBox. In addition, you can select a specific transition to use when switching rows. These transitions are similar to those used in PowerPoint or Freelance to switch slides, such as sliding in from the left or right or dissolving in and out. Note, however, that you can only create transition effects when the cells have a background color. Finally, you can also control how the rows roll: *continually*, *upon click*, or *when opened*. To change the options for the rolling tables, use the Table Rows tab of the Table properties InfoBox in Figure 25-18.

Programmatic Tables

The last type of table is a programmatic table. Programmatic tables are the only table types that cannot be created in a standard Rich Text field. These tables require either a field (when creating the table on a form) or an action hotspot (when creating the table on a page) to function correctly. The programmatic table displays a different row either based on the value of a field or based on clicking a particular hotspot. To create this type of table, first choose Create . . . Table from the menus. Choose the last button for a programmatic table.

Figure 25-18
Rolling tables

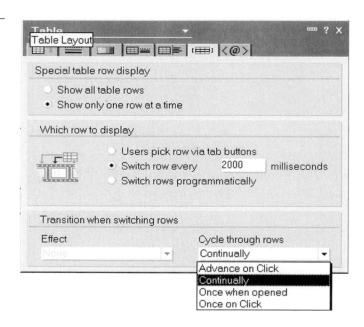

After creating the table, give the table and each of the rows a name using the Table Programming tab of the Table properties InfoBox. In the *Name/ID* field of the *Table HTML Tags* section, give the table a name, as shown next. When referring to the table later, use this name preceded by a dollar sign ($). Do not use the dollar sign when naming the table here. To name each row, click the row and then type a name in the *Row Tags* section in the *Name* field. Add a name for each row of the table. Use these names to refer to the table and its rows either in a hotspot action (on pages) or in a formula (on forms). To match the example and test this table, name the table Payment and name the rows Credit, Check, and Choose, as shown here.

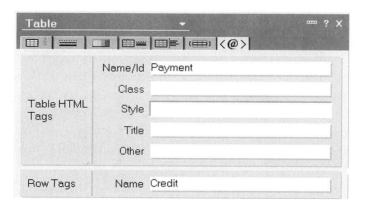

On a form, you would now create a couple of fields to enable the user to determine which row to view. Although we will not discuss fields in detail until the next chapter, you can follow the instructions here to get a feel for how to insert and use fields to create programmatic tables on forms. After creating the table according to the previous instructions, create a field called $TableName, where the *TableName* is the same name you gave the table in the Table properties InfoBox earlier. To create a field, choose Create . . . Field from the menus. When Designer displays the Field properties InfoBox, type the table name (with the dollar sign) in the Name field. From the example we started previously, the field name would be $Payment. (Note: Table names are case-sensitive. $payment is not the same name as $Payment.) In the Type fields, choose Number and Computed, as shown in Figure 25-19. The field will have a formula (created as follows) that will tell the table which row to display. This field should be a hidden field. To hide a field, use the Paragraph Hide When tab on the Field properties InfoBox. Enable all of the hide options so that the field is never visible.

Now we have to create a way for our users to choose a row to view. Create a field (by choosing Create . . . Field as shown previously). Give the field a name. In this case, use Pay to be consistent with the example. This field enables the users to make a choice. For now, select Radio button and Editable as the type for this field. On the Control tab in the Field properties InfoBox, you can type a list of choices. Your users will choose from these selections, so make them clear and descriptive. Type Credit Card | 0 and Check | 1 as the selections in the Choices field, as shown in Figure 25-20.

Figure 25-19
$TableName field
with properties

Figure 25-20
Pay field—used
to choose

The choices in this example also have numbers next to them, which are aliases (or synonyms). When we created forms, we gave them both form names and aliases. The form name was used for the users, and the alias is used for programming and coding. The same principle applies here: Your users will select options based on what you type to the left of the vertical bar (|), but you will write formulas based on the alias or the text to the left of the bar. Notice that the aliases are numbers and that they start with zero. Designer internally references the rows in the table starting at zero as well. Using numbers just makes things less confusing (it is not required). On this tab, you must also enable the Refresh fields on keyword change option. This option forces the table to be recalculated as your users select a different option.

After you have created the method for choosing which row to view, create a simple formula in the $Payment field. For now, because we discuss formulas in Chapter 26, simply type this formula into the Script area of the Programmer's pane, as shown below:

```
@If(Pay="0";0;@If(Pay="1";1;2))
```

When you type the formula, the Value object for the $Payment field should be highlighted in the Objects list. This formula states that if a user selects 0 (which is the alias for Credit) in the Pay field, the table should display 0, which is the first row. Otherwise, if the user selects 1 (which is the alias for Check) in the Pay field, the table should display the second row. Otherwise, if neither row is selected in the Pay field, the formula tells Notes to display a third row added to the table that instructs users to make a choice.

After typing the formula, save the form and use the Notes or Web Preview buttons to test your programmatic table. When testing programmatic tables, it is useful to apply cell colors (which you can add using the Table properties InfoBox) to ensure that you know which row Notes is displaying.

You cannot use fields on a page, so you will create an action hotspot. To create an action hotspot, type some text below the table. Each line of text should refer to a different row of the table. Users will click this text to select which data they want to display (which translates into which row to display). Make sure that the references for each row are on a separate line, as shown in Figure 25-21.

After typing the text, select the text and make it an action hotspot by choosing Create . . . Hotspot . . . Action Hotspot. After you create the hotspot, look for the hotspot object in the Programmer's pane, as shown next. In the *Click action* for the hotspot, create a formula. Because we have not really discussed formulas yet, use the sample formula shown here until you learn more about formulas in general in Chapter 26.

```
FIELD $Sample:= "row1";
@Command ([RefreshHideFormulas])
```

The formula first creates a temporary field called $Sample, taken from the name of the table, and then assigns the field value to the name of one of the rows. The second line of the formula refreshes the table when you click that hotspot. For each hotspot, use the row name for the row you want to display when the user clicks that location. You will learn much more about how to create formulas for programmatic tables in the next chapters when we discuss fields and formulas.

Figure 25-21
Programmatic table
on a page

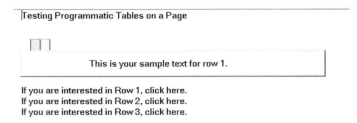

Testing Programmatic Tables on a Page

This is your sample text for row 1.

If you are interested in Row 1, click here.
If you are interested in Row 2, click here.
If you are interested in Row 3, click here.

Hotspots, Links, and Attachments

Some common items placed on pages and forms are hotspots, links, and attachments. Hotspots are a method of creating an action on a page or form. Buttons and links are common hotspots. A link can be to another Web site (a URL link), a link to a document or other item on this site (usually a doclink, database link, or view link), or it can be a link to a named element (such as a different page, view, or navigator). Links are used primarily for navigation. Links (or some form of navigation) are particularly necessary on pages. You have to provide some way to get from your page to the rest of your database or site. You might also place an attachment on a page. When you insert an attachment, users can open, view, or save (download) the attached document. If something important to your application has been created in another application, you will find it easy for users to gain access to that element through attachments. Avoid excessive use of attachments, however, because they can make the database large and unwieldy.

Hotspots   A hotspot is a button, text spot, or graphic that performs an action. Hotspots perform actions such as linking to another document or a URL, performing an action or running a formula, and creating pop-up text. Hotspots can exist on forms or on any document in a Rich Text field. To create a hotspot, select the text or graphic that you want to make the hotspot (except for button hotspots)and then choose Create . . . Hotspot. Then choose the type of hotspot that you want to create. The hotspot types are described in the following paragraphs:

- **Link Hotspot**   A link hotspot jumps a user to a document, view, or database when the user clicks the hotspot or graphic. Similar to a doclink, the link hotspot enables a more descriptive link than the doclink icon. To create a link hotspot, you must first select the document, view, or database that you want to link to and choose Copy as Link. Once the link is on the clipboard, select the text or graphic that you want to make into the hotspot and choose Create . . . Hotspot . . . Link Hotspot. Link hotspots are especially useful for cross-referencing to other views, documents, or databases. See "Links" for more details.

- **URL Link**   This type of link enables the designer to type any URL for the jump location of the hotspot. See "Links" for more details.

- **Text Pop-Up**   A text pop-up enables a small amount of text to be displayed in a Pop-up dialog box when the user clicks the text and holds down the mouse button. Only use this feature for small amounts of text, because there is no scrolling available. Use text pop-ups for definitions or footnotes, as shown in Figure 25-22.

- **Button**   A hotspot button enables the user to perform an action, formula, or script from a button in a form or in any Rich Text field. To create a button hotspot, place your cursor where you want to place the button and either choose Create . . . Hotspot . . . Button from the menus or click the Create Hotspot button smart icon. The Hotspot Button properties InfoBox enables you to label the button and determine its width. The width by default is two inches. If the button label will be long, you might also want to enable the option to wrap the text of the label. Then give the button hotspot an action to perform using an @Function, @Command, simple action, or LotusScript. Creating these actions will be discussed in Chapter 28, "Creating Actions, Agents, and Hotspots." A button hotspot and its properties are shown in here:

Figure 25-22
Creating a text
pop-up

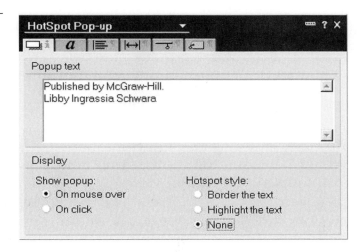

- **Formula Pop-up** A formula pop-up is similar to a text pop-up, except that instead of typing static text for the pop-up, the designer can create an action, formula, or script that resolves to the text to be displayed.

- **Action Hotspot** An action hotspot is similar to a button, except that the action hotspot will be any text or graphic that can perform the indicated action, formula, or script.

Links A link is a method of directing users to another item, element, or location within your application or site (or elsewhere). First, decide which type of link you want to create and to which area you want to link. Most pages have links that enable users to navigate the current database, site, or application. You can also add links to other databases, sites, and applications.

First, create a URL link. This type of link enables users to go from your page (or site) to a URL. One way to create a URL link for pages viewed by Web clients is to select a URL from a Web site and paste it onto your page. This procedure does not work for pages viewed in Notes clients, however. To create a URL link for either client, type some text or insert a graphic. Then select this text or graphic and choose Create . . . Hotspot . . . Link Hotspot. In the Hotspot Resource Link InfoBox, shown next, select URL as the type of link. In the value field, type or paste the URL to which you want the hotspot to take the users. Remember to include the full URL, including the protocol (for example, **http://www.dominopro.com**), as shown here:

Another type of link—to an object in this database or in another database—can be created in a similar manner. The first step to creating this type of link is to open the element to which you want to link. To link directly to a document, a view, or even to another database, select that element. With the element selected, choose Edit . . . Copy as Link from the menus. Choose the type of link to copy (such as a document link, view link, or database link). Then go back to the page and paste this link into the page. This type of link is shown here:

This is a doclink --> 🗋 ₌

You can create a similar type of link, but with text or a graphic of your choosing—rather than the standard Notes link graphics—by choosing the Create . . . Hotspot . . . Link Hotspot while you have the element in the Clipboard, as shown here:

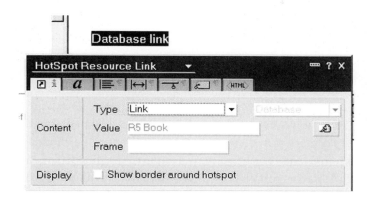

To create a link to a named element, such as a page, view, navigator, folder, frameset, or form, follow the steps to create a hotspot link (as described previously). In the HotSpot Resource Link InfoBox, however, choose *Named Element* as the Link Type. Then select the type of named element from the drop-down list. Next, choose the specific named element. The *Browse* button (which looks similar to a folder), the *Formula* button (which looks similar to the @ symbol), and the *Paste* button (which looks similar to a glue jar) give you three methods of selecting the named element. When you click the *Browse* button, you can select the type of object, the database from which to select the object, and the specific named elements from that database, as shown here:

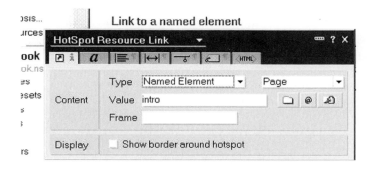

Attachments   When the element that you want your users to access is not already a Notes element or a Web page, you can choose to insert the element as an attachment. Attachments in general are part of the end-user curricula. To refresh your memory, however, if you want to attach a file to a page (or to a form or document), choose Create . . . Attachment. When Notes displays the Create Attachment(s) dialog box, select the file or files that you would like to insert and click *Create*. When a Notes user clicks the attachment in your page, he or she can view, launch, or detach the attachment. For Web users, the browser might display the attachment, open the attachment in its native application, or enable the attachment to be saved, based on the settings of the user's machine and browser.

Embedded Elements   Embedded elements, which are another common item on pages or forms, enable you to place other design elements on a page or form. When designing for both Notes and Web clients, embedding elements makes them appear similar for both clients. If you do not embed the elements, they look and function differently in different clients. The other reasons to use embedded elements on a page (or on a form) include having more of the functions of the element that would be available in the Notes client but that might not be available to the Web client. You will also have the ability to combine multiple design elements to create a useful interface for your users. The elements that can be embedded on a page or form include the following:

- Views
- Folders
- Outlines
- Navigators
- Date pickers

To embed an element into a page or form, place the cursor in the desired location and choose Create . . . Embedded Element from the menus. Then select the item you want to embed from the submenu. To embed a view in a page or form, choose Create . . . Embedded Element . . . View. When Designer displays the Insert Embedded View dialog box, select a view from the current database to insert. Note that you can only embed one view and one folder in a page or form. In addition, remember that date pickers do not work for Web clients (we will talk about date pickers later). Some of the elements that you can embed, such as views and outlines, will give you additional options (properties) that you can set to control the appearance and function of the elements.

On forms, you can add additional embedded elements, such as a file upload control or a group scheduler. You can add these elements to forms but not pages, because they require additional programming that you cannot place on a page.

The file upload control enables users on the Web to attach documents to your form. This element, which is only supported for Web clients, enables users to either type in a path and filename or browse for a file to attach to the document that they are creating or editing. This element also requires server-side support from an administrator, who must define a \TEMP directory on the server. Without this directory, the attachment cannot be saved with the document.

To add a file upload control to a form, open the form and place your cursor where the control should appear. Choose Create . . . Embedded element . . . File Upload Control. You should access the properties InfoBox for the control. Most of the properties enable you to set visual properties, such as spacing, alignment, and margins, which are similar to properties for any text. Because the file upload control is not supported for Notes clients, you should set the Hide-When Paragraph option to *Hide Paragraph from Notes R4.6 or later*.

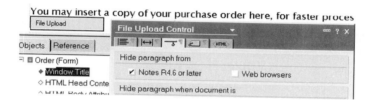

The group scheduler displays the schedule of a group or team, enabling users to schedule appointments or meetings around a team's schedule. Add the group scheduler to a form by choosing Create . . . Embedded element . . . Group Scheduler. The group scheduler requires additional programming to define the members of the group and to associate information about those members with the attributes of the scheduler. Refer to the Domino Designer help for more information about programming for a group scheduler.

Actions   An *action* automates a specific task in Notes, such as moving a document to a folder or choosing an item from a Notes menu. Actions can be associated with views, forms, or pages. You can select or access an action through the Actions menu, using an action button or via a hotspot. Notes includes many built-in actions that are usually visible on the Actions menu. We will discuss actions in more detail later in Chapter 28.

To add an action to a page, choose Create . . . Action. Designer displays the Action pane, as shown in Figure 25-23. You can then add a formula or a predefined simple

Figure 25-23
Creating a new
action

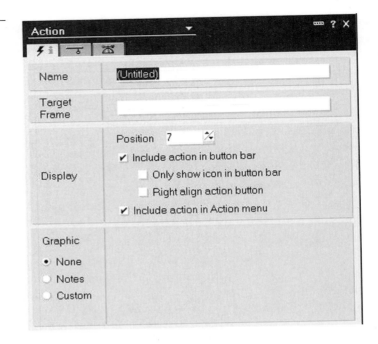

action to the action. You can also use the Action properties InfoBox to determine whether the action will be available from the Actions menu or as a button.

Applets   An applet in this context refers to a Java applet inserted to add functions to the page. You can either create your own applets or obtain prebuilt applets. Designer includes the capability to display outlines, views, rich-text fields, and action bars as applets. This feature provides a better interface when using these elements from Web clients. To insert your own applet onto a page or form, choose Create . . . Java Applet from the menu. Designer displays the Create Java Applet dialog box, shown in Figure 25-24. Choose the files required for the Java applet from the operating system, the shared resources, or from a Web server.

OLE Objects   Object Linking and Embedding (OLE) enables Notes to share data with other applications, such as spreadsheet and graphics applications like Excel or Freelance. OLE objects on pages can appear as graphics, text, icons, or rich text. These objects can be opened and edited by double-clicking, or they can be launched automatically via the launch options described previously. To insert an OLE object into a page, choose Create . . . Object from the menus. Designer displays the Create Object dialog box, as shown in Figure 25-25. Choose whether you want to insert a link to a

Figure 25-24
Inserting a Java
applet

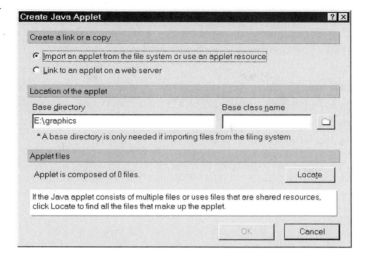

Figure 25-25
Creating an OLE
object

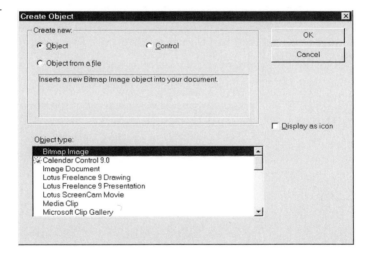

new object, to an object that you create from a file that already exists, or to a control element. Then select the specific application, file, or control object to embed. You might also choose to display the object only as an icon by using the checkbox. After you insert them, most OLE objects require further programming to achieve their full function.

Hide-When   Hide-when formulas and options enable text, graphics, fields, sections, and other design elements to be hidden based on a formula or event. For example, the Hide tab of the Text properties InfoBox, shown in Figure 25-26, shows how the developer can select events or write a formula to hide the selected design element. Document events include the following: *Previewed for reading, Previewed for editing, Opened for reading, Opened for editing, Printed,* and *Copied to the Clipboard.* In addition, a formula based on the current user or other event can be added to further customize the form. Hide-when is available for text, fields, sections, and other design elements. Use hide-when to make the form look one way in Edit mode, for example, and to look another way in Read mode. For example, a data entry person might need instructions on the fields that someone just reading the data would not need to see. Hide-when options can be used for the following purposes:

- Displaying one field to enter or edit a value and one field to display the value

- Showing actions at some times and not others

- Displaying particular sections or views to certain users only

- Hiding fields on the form for use in a view or other computation

- Displaying one element to Notes clients and another element to Web clients

Figure 25-26
Hiding text from
Notes 4.6 and later

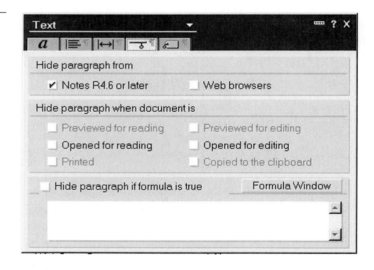

NOTE   Hide-when is paragraph-level formatting. If you use hide-when on some text on some part of a line, everything on that line will use hide-when. Place separate elements that require different hide-when settings in different paragraphs by pressing Enter to move to the next line.

Window Title   The window title appears in the Title bar of a Notes or Web client for a form, page, or document—and in the tabbed window interface of the Notes client. If you do not set a window title, the word (Untitled) appears. This message can confuse users, so you should usually set a window title. To set a window title, you will use the Script area of the Programmer's pane of the form or page, as shown next. While you are in Design mode on the page or form, click the background. On the Objects tab of the Info List, select the Window Title object. Type the formula or text to use for the window title into the Script area, using proper syntax. Note that the Window title either can be static text or can change dynamically based on a formula. Enclose the text in quotation marks (such as "Book Order") to make the window title static text.

Forms Only

In the previous paragraphs, we discussed elements that can be placed on pages or forms. In some cases, the basic element—such as a standard section—can be placed on a page, while the more advanced element, the controlled-access section, can be placed on a form. In the following sections, we describe the remaining elements that can only be placed on forms. These elements include fields, subforms, and layout regions. The other elements that you can only use on forms—controlled access sections and advanced embedded elements—were described previously.

Fields   Fields, which are described in excruciating detail in Chapter 26, "Creating Fields and Formulas," are the key element for obtaining and displaying data in your applications. Place fields on forms. When fields are completed (either by users or by a formula), the data is then saved, and Notes creates a document.

Subforms   A subform is similar to any other form in that it can contain all of the same design elements. The subform assists with consistency in applications by enabling multiple forms to share a group of the same design elements. If a company wants every form created in a database to share the company's logo, for example, a subform with this logo could be an easy way to insert this item on all of the forms. If you make a change to a subform, Designer automatically updates all forms using that subform. Use subforms to create forms in any of the following ways:

- **Include subforms in the Insert . . . Subform dialog box**   This option enables the designer to add the subform at any point to the form that he or she is creating. This option is available on the Subform properties InfoBox.

- **Include the subform in the New Form . . . dialog box**   This option includes the subform in the dialog box displayed to designers when they first create a new form. They then have the option to base the new form on the existing subform. The subform appears immediately at create time if this option is selected. This option is available on the Subform properties InfoBox.

- **Add the subform based on the result of a formula**   This procedure is called a *Computed Subform*. The designer can add a computed subform by checking the Insert Subform based on the formula option on the Insert . . . Subform dialog box. This option enables the subform to be displayed based on values in the parent form, user roles or names, or other form events.

To create a subform, choose Create . . . Design . . . Subforms. To view the subforms, expand the Resources item in the Design view of the database. The options on the Subform properties InfoBox are described in the following paragraphs. The Subform properties InfoBox is shown here:

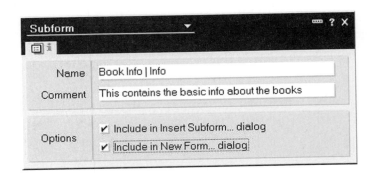

- **Name**   As always, you should give this design element a descriptive, unique name.

- **Comment**   As with most R5 design elements, use the Comment field to document the element.

- **Include in Insert Subform . . . dialog**   This option, which is selected by default, enables the subform to be added to a form at design time. If this option is not selected, the subform can only be inserted programmatically (through a function or formula) into a form.

- **Include in New form . . . dialog**   When you select this option, Designer automatically displays the Insert Subform dialog box when you are creating a new form, with this subform listed as an option.

To use a computed subform, create the subform and choose the option to include the subform in the Insert Subform dialog box. Then when you create or edit the form in which you want to use the subform, choose Create . . . Insert Subform on the Insert Subform dialog box. Instead of choosing a subform and clicking OK, choose Insert Subform based on formula option. This option displays a computed subform placeholder in the form and enables the designer to create a computed subform formula. The computed subform formula can use field values from the parent document, user roles, or other characteristics that are available at compose time.

Layout Regions   A layout region is a design area that designers can place on forms or subforms. A layout region gives the designer more control over the placement and layering of text and other design elements. In a layout region, the designer can place items more precisely. In a form, the designer normally relies on paragraph alignment and spacing to place design elements in a particular location. In a layout region, however, the designer can drag elements around a grid to place them at a precise location in the region. Previously, designers relied on layout regions to enable them to control tab order on fields in a form. In R5, this action can be done natively in forms and subforms.

Layout regions do not support all of the design elements that forms and subforms support. Table 25-2 compares the supported and unsupported elements in a layout region.

To create a layout region on a form or subform, place the cursor on the form and choose Create . . . Layout Region . . . New Layout Region from the menus. This action

Table 25-2   Layout Region Elements

Unsupported Elements	Supported Elements
Sections	Static Text
Links, including DocLinks, Database Links, and View Links	Graphics
Rich-text fields	Graphic buttons
DialogList type fields	Buttons
Hotspots, including pop-ups (except for buttons and graphic buttons)	Fields (except rich-text fields and DialogList type fields)
Attachments	Layering
Tables	DialogList type fields
Horizontal rules	
Java applets	
Page breaks	
Shared actions	
Shared fields	
Subforms	

inserts a layout region box that can then be sized. To change the size or other characteristics of the layout region, right-click and select Layout properties to display the Layout properties InfoBox, as shown here:

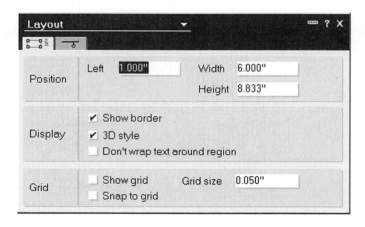

The Basics tab on the InfoBox enables the designer to determine the size and position of the layout region, using the Left, Width, and Height fields. In addition, the layout region can have a border or a three-dimensional style gray background using the Show border option and the 3D-style option. The other options on the Basics tab enable the designer to display a grid, which enables the designer to line up elements in the layout region with each other more easily. There are also grid size options and snap-to-grid options. The other tab on the Layout Region properties InfoBox is a hide-when tab. Layout regions can be hidden using the same document events and formulas that are used to hide other design elements.

After creating a layout region, the designer can place other design elements in this region, based on the supported elements described previously. To place static text in a layout region, either click the Create Textbox smart icon or choose Create . . . Layout Region . . . Text. Notes displays an untitled text box in the layout region. Double-click the text box to display the Control InfoBox. In layout regions, instead of text and other elements having properties, they have controls. These controls are defined by the designer for each element using the Control InfoBox in a similar manner to a properties InfoBox. A static text Control InfoBox is shown in Figure 25-27.

The first tab enables the designer to set the alignment of the text (left, right, or center) as well as whether or not the text should be vertically aligned. The text itself is defined in the *Text* field on this tab. Type any text that you want to appear in this text box in the layout region. Finally, you can use the *Left, Top, Width*, and *Height* options to set the size and position of the text box. The size and position can also be set by clicking and dragging the control boxes at the edges of the text box itself.

Figure 25-27
Text controls on a
layout region

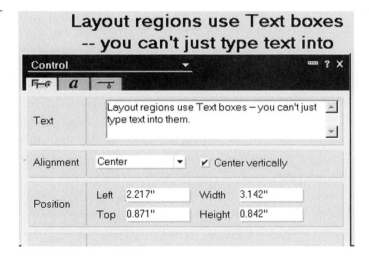

The Text tab, which is next in the Control InfoBox, enables the designer to set the text properties for the text in the text box, including font, size, color, and style. Finally, the last tab in the Control InfoBox is a hide-when tab. Hide-when in layout regions is different than hide-when in a form or subform, and one of its defining characteristics is that it is paragraph-level formatting. In other words, if you enable a hide-when formula or option for any part of a paragraph (up until you press Enter), those same hide-when options are enforced for everything in that paragraph or on that line. In layout regions, however, each element can be hidden independently. You can place a graphic, a button, and some text on a single line, for example, and have three different hide-when formulas for the three elements.

NOTE You cannot type text in a layout region the way you would when creating a form or subform, nor can you copy and paste text directly into a layout region. You must use text boxes instead.

Another element that you might want to add to a layout region is a field. Fields are created in layout regions in the same way that they are created on forms or subforms. In layout regions, however, fields have some additional characteristics defined by their controls. When you add a field to a layout region, the field is displayed as an Untitled Edit Control. All field types (except rich-text fields and dialog-list keyword fields) can be used in layout regions. For all field types except for dialog lists, the following additional options are available and are accessed on the Control tab of the Field properties InfoBox:

- Edit Control Options, including multi-line, scroll bar, and border
- Layout options, including left, top, and width

These options enable the designer to determine the size, appearance, and position of the text, time, number, authors, readers, and names types of fields when these fields are placed within a layout region. These controls enable a designer, for example, to require a text field to have multiple lines. You should use the multi-line and scroll bar options together to give the cleanest look to the user. The field type options that are available in a layout region are shown in Figure 25-28.

One important use for layout regions is creating dialog boxes. You can combine the @DialogBox function with a form created with a layout region, which creates an attractive, user-friendly dialog box.

Figure 25-28
Field types in a
layout region

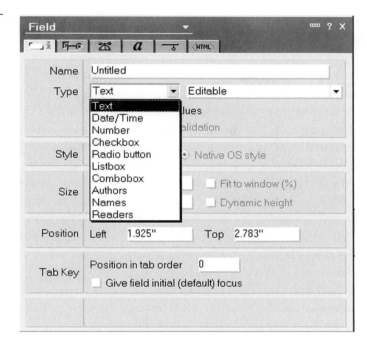

Summary

In this chapter, you learned to create pages and forms as well as most of the elements
that can be used on your pages and forms. Most of the interaction your users have with
your applications will force them to use your forms to input or view data or view data
on your pages. Remember that pages are used to display static information and forms
are used to collect information. Make sure that you take good design rules and ease of
usability into consideration when you create the text, graphics, and other elements on
your forms and pages. For testing purposes, ensure that you have created pages and
forms and have tested how they function for both Notes and Web clients. Know how
the various elements that can be placed on pages and forms appear, as well as which
ones cannot work on pages.

Practice

Use this practice to create pages and forms for your practice database. If you created the
R5 Orders and Reviews database in Chapter 23, "Creating a Database," open that database to get started. If you did not create the database, use the CH25.NSF file that is

provided on the CD-ROM. Copy the database to your local data directory. You also need to remove the Read Only file property by opening Windows Explorer and navigating to the file. Right-click the file, and choose Properties from the shortcut menu. On the General tab, look for the Read Only attribute. Remove the check mark. You can now access the database from Notes or Designer.

First, create a new page in the database. This page will be the home page when the database is used on the Web. To create the page, choose the *New Page* action button while in the Pages Design view. When Designer displays the page in the Work area, add text, a horizontal rule, and graphics for the users, as shown in Figure 25-29. Did you insert the graphic, or did you use a shared-image resource? Remember that a shared-image resource saves space in your database and enables you to reuse elements more easily. Call the page Main, and give it a light-gray background. Later, you will want to create hotspots to link the text to other locations in your database. Do not forget to create a window title for your page, which will make it easier for users to navigate your application.

To ensure that this page launches first (on the Web, especially), change the database launch properties. You can also have this page launch first in a Notes client if desired. You must save the page before it is available for selection in the Database Launch tab. Figure 25-30 shows the page previewed in Internet Explorer. Feel free to add more elements for practice.

Figure 25-29
New page for
practice

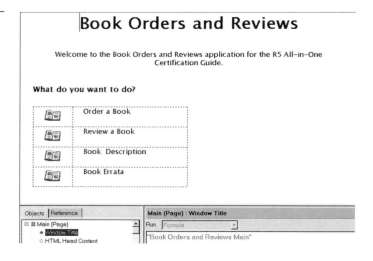

Figure 25-30
Preview of the page

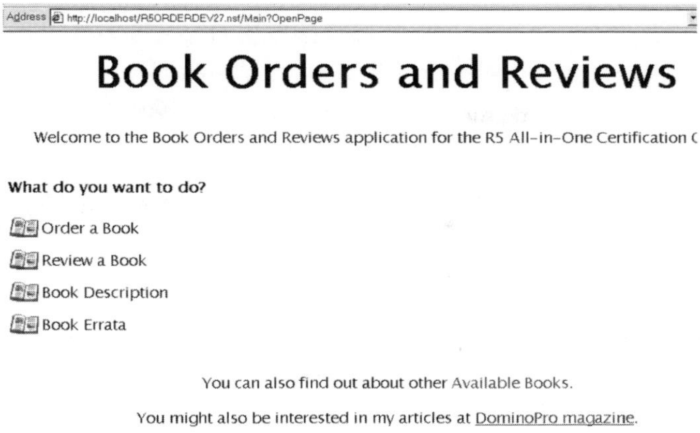

Address ⓔ http://localhost/R5ORDERDEV27.nsf/Main?OpenPage

Book Orders and Reviews

Welcome to the Book Orders and Reviews application for the R5 All-in-One Certification (

What do you want to do?

Order a Book

Review a Book

Book Description

Book Errata

You can also find out about other Available Books.

You might also be interested in my articles at DominoPro magazine.

Next, create the default form for the Orders and Reviews database. The default form will be a Book form, which will enable users to see descriptions of the books and to decide which books to review and which books to order. Use the same shade of gray as the background for the main form (this color gives users some continuity). Add some static text as a frame for the fields that will eventually be placed on the form. In addition, move some of the text into sections so that when the data is viewed, readers do not have to view information that they might not want. To make sure the information is completed, though, those sections expand automatically when the form is in Edit mode. Figure 25-31 shows the form in Designer. Again, these exercises will just give you a start; we will add other elements, including fields and hotspots, as we progress.

You will also need to create two response forms. The first response form will enable users to create reviews of the books. The second response form should enable a user to order a book. Use Figures 25-32 and 25-33 to get started on these forms. Do not forget that these are response-type forms. Note the header, which is used to keep some information on the form visible at all times. Remember that this element will not be visible when this form is used on the Web, however.

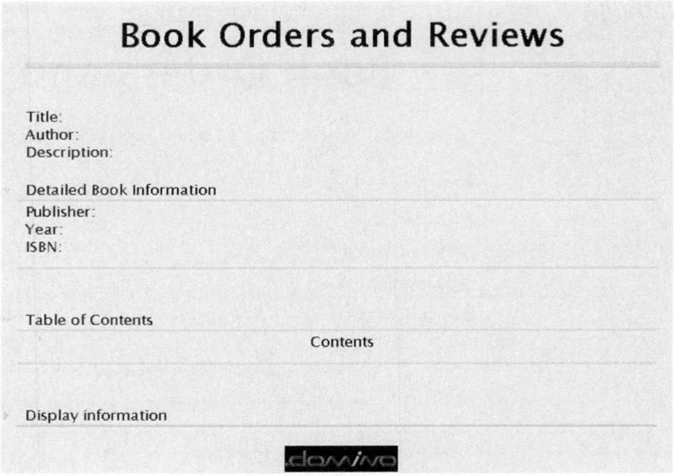

Figure 25-31
Book form

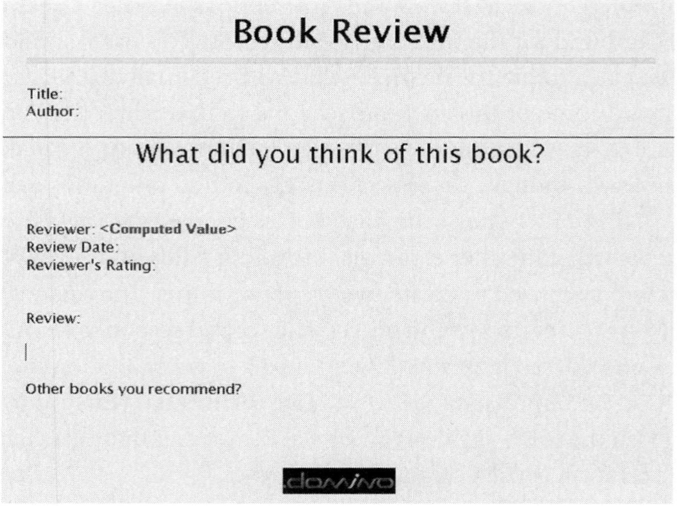

Figure 25-32
Review form

For the Order form in Figure 25-33, use a programmatic table with another table nested inside one of the cells. The fields on this form should be familiar; they are similar to the ones used in the Programmatic table section in this chapter. Figure 25-34 shows the value for the $Payment field. This field is hidden; therefore, on the Form properties you have to make sure to choose Generate HTML for all fields.

Figure 25-33
Order form

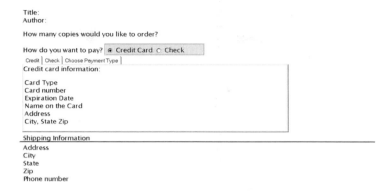

Figure 25-34
$Payment field

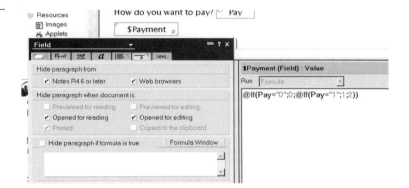

Review Questions

1. Brian creates a page and inserts a programmatic table. When he tries to create the $TableName field, however, he receives an error. What is the problem?
   a. Pages cannot have programmatic tables.
   b. $TableName is a reserved field that can only be used by Designer.
   c. Pages cannot have fields.
   d. Pages cannot have tables.

2. Susan imported HTML onto a page from an existing Web page. Which option(s) does she need to enable to ensure that Domino displays the page correctly?
   a. Generate HTML for page.
   b. Treat page contents as HTML.
   c. Nothing; the page will automatically appear in correct form.
   d. She cannot import HTML; rather, she must copy and paste the HTML.

3. Graphics are stored in Notes and Domino in which native-file formats?
   a. .PCX
   b. .TIF
   c. .JPG
   d. .GIF

4. Mike uses the following element to ensure that he only has to make changes to his graphics one time and that those changes will be distributed throughout his database:
   a. subforms
   b. shared-image resources
   c. linked images
   d. OLE

5. Katie knows that the News form she is creating will be sent to her users' mail files. She wants the data to look the same in her application as when the data is viewed in the users' mail files. What does she do?
   a. She enables versioning.
   b. She marks that form as the Default form for the database.
   c. Nothing; by default, the form and data are stored together.
   d. She stores the form with the document.

6. Scott does not know why his formula (which depends on a hidden field) is not working when he uses the Application Review form on the Web. What can you tell him to help him?
   a. Enable Treat Document Contents as HTML.
   b. Enable Generate HTML for all fields.
   c. Enable the Automatically Enable Edit Mode option.
   d. Nothing; hidden fields do not work with Web clients.

7. Alison has placed a background graphic on her new form, but it only repeats across the top quarter of the form, rather than throughout the form. Why?
   a. She created a header on the form.
   b. She disabled Tile Graphic.
   c. She forgot to use an image resource.
   d. This appearance is the default appearance.

8. The following is/are true about a header on a form:
   a. A header does not appear in Web clients.
   b. A header does not appear in Notes clients.
   c. You cannot have a table in the header.
   d. You cannot make a header scroll.

9. Which of the following embedded elements can be used on a page?
   a. File upload controls
   b. Group schedulers
   c. Views
   d. Date pickers

10. Because a file upload control is not supported for Notes clients, what is the best way for Janelle to ensure that her form looks correct to both types of clients—Notes and Web?
    a. She creates two different forms: one for Notes and one for the Web.
    b. She creates two subforms: one that is used for Notes clients and one that is used for Web clients.
    c. She uses hide-when to hide the file upload control from Web clients.
    d. File upload controls are supported for both Notes and Web clients.

PART IV

Review Answers

1. **C is correct.** You cannot place fields on pages. You should use hotspots to control the programmatic tables on pages.

2. **C is correct.** When you import HTML onto a page or form, it appears correctly in both Designer and to the Web/Notes clients. If she had copied and pasted, then she would have had to enable the Treat page Contents as HTML option.

3. **C and D are correct.** JPG and GIF file formats are supported natively in R5.

4. **B is correct.** Shared-image resources are the best choice. Subforms might be another way to accomplish this task; however, subforms are less efficient and slower to load.

5. **D** is correct.   If you are mailing documents to a database that does not contain the form used to create the documents, you should consider storing the form with the document. Do not forget that this action significantly increases the size of your database.

6. **B** is correct.   He needs to generate HTML for all fields to use hidden fields with Web clients.

7. **A** is correct.   If a graphic background is used on a form that also has a header, the background graphic only appears in the header portion of the form.

8. **A** is correct.   Headers are not visible to Web clients. You can have a table in a header—it just cannot be the first element.

9. **C** and **D** are correct.   You can only use file upload controls and group schedulers on forms.

10. **C** is correct.   Using hide-when does not negatively impact the speed of the form. Either choices A or B, however, might also solve this problem.

CHAPTER 26

Creating Fields and Formulas

You should be able to answer questions based on the following objectives after reading this chapter:

- Create, modify, and troubleshoot fields
- Code formulas

As discussed in the previous chapter, the big difference between a page and a form is the element's purpose. Pages are intended to display information (often in a static format), whereas forms are intended to gather information. The element placed on a form to gather the information is a field. The field holds a single type of information, such as text, names, numbers, or lists. You can create fields for use either on a single form or on multiple forms. Then choose whether the users will complete the field or whether the result of a formula will provide the value for the field. In this chapter, we define the characteristics of a field and the available field types by using the Field properties InfoBox. Next, we cover formulas, including @Functions, @Commands, and their appropriate syntaxes.

Creating a Field

The major defining characteristics for a field include its name, its data type, whether it is computed or editable, how Notes or the Web displays the field to users, and whether the field contains formulas. Use the options in the Field properties InfoBox, shown in Figure 26-1, to define the majority of these characteristics. As discussed in the last chapter, it is useful to build the static text and other design elements of the form first to give the form some shape and to remind yourself of the organization of the form. In addition, it is a good idea to draw all of your forms, including static text, design elements, and fields, before beginning to create your form in Designer. This prevents you from forgetting the name or function of fields as you add more of them to your form.

To insert a field onto a form, place your cursor in the form where you would like to insert the field. Choose either the Create Field smart icon or Create . . . Field from the menus. Either choice inserts the field and displays the Field properties InfoBox automatically. When you first insert the field, the field has the name Untitled and is of a text type, indicated by the T in the corner of the field:

Change the field name, because you need a unique, descriptive name for each field on a form. You might also choose to change the field type. Make these changes by using the Basics tab of the Field properties InfoBox.

The Basics and Control Tabs

The Basics tab on the Field properties InfoBox sets the defining information about the field, such as field name and data type. The Basics tab changes dynamically based on

Figure 26-1
The Field properties
InfoBox

the field's data type. The selections you make on the Basics tab determine the fields that will be available on the Control tab. The options on the Control tab are described throughout this section.

- **Name** Give each field a descriptive, unique name. No two fields can have the same name on the same form, although you can repeat field names on different forms or subforms within a database. The length of the field name is limited to 32 characters. When naming a field, do not use spaces (use dashes, underscoring, or capitalization instead). In addition, field names cannot begin with numbers and should not (in general) begin with dollar signs ($) or at-symbols (@), because these symbols have specific, reserved meanings in Notes (unless, of course, you are creating one of these reserved fields). Finally, certain field names are reserved for use by Notes, such as SendTo, CopyTo, Sign, and Form. These names should never be used for purposes other than those defined by Notes.

- **Type** The following choices are available for data type: text, date/time, number, dialog list, checkbox, radio button, listbox, combobox, rich text, authors, names, readers, password, and formula. In addition, for each type of field, make the choice as to whether the field is editable, computed, computed for display, or computed when composed. In addition, remember that the data type changes the rest of the options that are available in the dialog box.

- **Allow Multiple values** This option, which is available for most field types, enables Notes to recognize multiple values in a particular field. The user can create lists in the field, for example. In addition, multi-value options on the Options tab will be available for editing. Although a field with this option enabled can permit multiple values, Notes restricts each field to a single type of value. If a field is a text type, for example, numeric values must be converted to text (using a function such as @Text) for use in the field. The following field types do not enable multiple values to be selected here:

  - Check box
  - Radio button
  - Combobox
  - Rich text
  - Password
  - Formula

- **Compute after validation**   This option is available if you select *Computed* or *Computed for Display* options for the field. This option ensures that the field will not be computed until after Notes or Domino executes any field-validation formulas (to be discussed later in this chapter).

- **Style**   The two choices here are Notes style and Native OS style. When you select the Native OS style (which is new to R5), Notes displays fields differently. Text fields, for example, appear fixed in width and height with an outlined box. In Notes style, the same field appears with brackets and grows in width, then height, as you type. Similarly, date/time fields appear as a graphical calendar control (shown in Figure 26-2) when in Native OS style. (Note that the option name changes for Date/Time fields to Calendar/Time control.) When you select the Native OS style, you have four additional choices:

  - **Width**   A fixed width for the field, in inches

  - **Height**   A fixed height for the field, in inches

  - **Fit to window (%)**   Changes the width to a percentage of the window size

  - **Dynamic Height**   Enables the height of the window to grow dynamically (up to three lines)

- Native OS style does not affect display on the Web, and this option is not available for the following field types:

  - Dialog list

  - Check box

  - Radio button

  - Listbox

  - Combobox

  - Rich text

- **Tab Key**   The tab key options set a tab order for the fields on a form. This option ensures that as users complete the form, they can move through the fields in a logical fashion. By default, users tab through fields left to right and top to bottom. To change this option, set a numeric value for the default tab order. You can also give one field initial or default focus by using that checkbox.

Field Types

One of the most important defining characteristics of a field is its data type. Although Notes can display most information in a text or rich-text field, other field types enhance the capabilities of the application.

- **Text field type**   This field type, which is common for simple user input, has the fewest options. Users can type letters, punctuation, spaces, and numbers (unless used mathematically or derived from a formula) into the field. They cannot use the field for graphics, attachments, or other objects, however. Note that numbers will be understood as text strings when placed in text fields. The user cannot change the formatting of a text field type; rather, the developer sets the formatting for the field as he or she designs the field. Options on the Control tab for text fields in the Native OS style include *Display: Allow multiple lines* and *Input: Pressing tab key moves to next field*. If you choose not to enable multiple lines, users will only be able to type a single line in the field. When the text field is in the Notes style, the option on the Control tab enables you to determine whether Notes should display the field delimiters. If you enable this option, Notes will not display the brackets that are usually used to denote the field. Figure 26-2 shows a text field in Notes style and the same field in Native OS style. These are shown as previewed in a Notes client, because the Web client does not use the Native OS style.

- **Date/Time field type**   The Date/Time field includes both time and date data, which Notes can display in a variety of formats. When you select a date/time field, you can choose to display it as a Notes field, which appears as a text-style field, or you can choose to display it in Native OS style. The Native OS style, mentioned previously, causes Notes to display a calendar or date graphical control, also

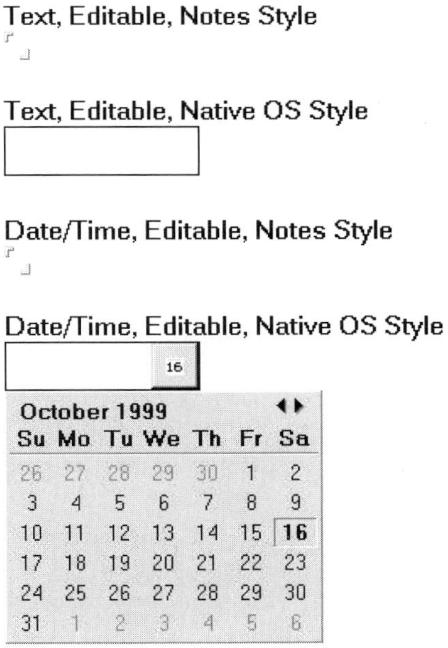

Figure 26-2
Native OS versus
Notes style fields

Text, Editable, Notes Style

Text, Editable, Native OS Style

Date/Time, Editable, Notes Style

Date/Time, Editable, Native OS Style

known as a date picker. Remember that the Native OS styles (and the graphical date picker) are only supported in Notes clients. Internally, Notes stores times and dates in the format MM/DD/YYYY HH:MM:SS. If users enter a two-digit year between zero and 49, Notes assumes that the year refers to the years 2000–2049. If users enter a two-digit year between 50 and 99, Notes assumes the years 1950–1999. To force users to use four-digit years instead of two-digit years, enable the *Require User enter four digit years* option on the Control tab. This option forces all Date fields that use years to require all four digits of the year. When you select a Date/Time field, you can customize the field with the following additional options from the Control tab:

- **On Display: Use Preferences From**   Use this option to determine whether the Date/Time display options should be determined by the user's preferences or by the designer's customization. Choices are User's settings and Custom. To help you determine how the field appears to users, the Sample field shows the current display settings, as shown in Figure 26-3.

- **Display Date**   Enable the Display Date checkbox to use the Date/Time field to display a date to users. After choosing to display the date, you have additional options. First, choose which part of the date to display by using the Show drop-down list. Choices include the following: All (which displays weekday, day, month, and year); Only month, day, and year; Only weekday, month, and day; Only month and year; Only month and day; Only year; Only month; Only day;

Figure 26-3
Sample of the
Date/Time display

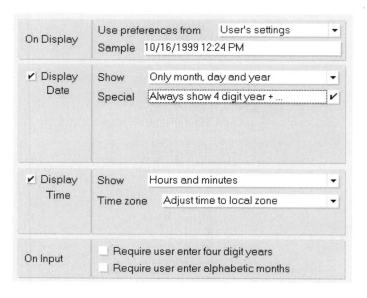

and Only weekday. Next, address the set of Special options: Show "today" when appropriate; Always show four-digit year; Show four-digit year for 21st Century; and Show year only when not this year. Next, if using a custom display, you should determine the format, including the choices YMDW, WMDY, and WDMY (where Y is year, M is month, D is date, and W is weekday). Next, select your separators. A slash (/) is the default. Note that if you choose a comma (,) as the date separator, use a semicolon (;) when placing multiple date values in a list. Similarly, if you use a semicolon as the date separator, use a comma to place multiple date values in a list. Finally, choose how many characters to display for each element of the date: one or two for date; one, two, three, or four for month; two or four for year; and one or two for weekday. You can also choose to have the weekday displayed inside parentheses.

- **Display time** Use this checkbox to choose to display the time portion of a date/time field. You can use this checkbox with Display Date or without it. Use the Show field to determine which element of the time to show. Choices include All; Hours, Minute, and Seconds; Hours and Minutes; and Hours only. You should also configure the Time Zone option. Choices include Adjust time to local zone, Always show time zone, and Show only if zone not local. Adjusting the time to the local zone causes Domino to display the time on a document as though it had been created/set in the local time zone. If a user in Texas creates a document at noon, for example, a user in Boston would see the document as being created at 11:00 A.M. Choosing Always show time zone, on the other hand, displays the time where the document was created. In the previous example, the reader in Boston would still see that the document had been created at 12 P.M. Central Standard Time (noon). These choices are valid only when both the date and time are included in the field. If you selected to create a custom display, you might also set a format and separator for the time. Choose either 12-hour or 24-hour clocks for the time format. The default separator is a colon (:).

- **On Input: Require user enter four digit years** This option forces users to enter all four digits of a year, such as 1999 rather than 99, which removes any ambiguity from date fields. As mentioned previously, by default Notes and Domino R5 assume the 1900s if a two-digit year is between 50 and 99, and Notes assumes the 2000s if the two-digit year is between 00 and 49.

- **On Input: Require user enter alphabetic months** This option forces users to enter months alphabetically, rather than numerically. This action can remove confusion about European date formats (where the day comes first) versus the American format (where the month comes first).

The following illustration shows some of the Date/Time options that are available on the Control tab:

> **Time and Date formats**
>
> ⌈Oct/16/1999 12:29 PM⌋
>
> ⌈(Saturday) 16/Oct/1999 12:29:57 PM⌋
>
> ⌈16 Oct 12 PM CDT⌋
>
> ⌈12:29:57:57 PM CDT⌋
>
> ⌈Saturday 10/16/99⌋

- **Number field type**   Use the Number field type for numeric values that will be used in calculations. The Control tab determines the format, preferences, and decimal places of a number. Choose decimal, percent, scientific, or currency for the number format. If you select custom preferences for formatting the display, you can determine the decimal symbol (a period by default) and the thousands separator (a comma by default). You can also choose to set those formats based on the user's preferences. Decimal places can be fixed or varying. Other formatting choices include adding parentheses when the number is negative and adding punctuation when the number is in the thousands. If number is formatted as currency, you can select a currency symbol, insert a custom symbol, determine whether the symbol should follow the number, and decide whether there will be a space next to the number. Figure 26-4 displays the number formatting options on the Control tab.

  One warning about Number fields used in calculations is that they must have a default value. If a Number field used in a calculation does not have a default value and the user does not enter a value, Notes interprets the value as a null text string. This situation would result in the calculation failing with the message, *Incorrect data type for operator or @Function: Number expected*. To avoid this result, use a zero as a default value when using a Number field in a calculation.

- **Rich Text field type**   A rich-text field is similar to a text field, but it gives a user the capability to insert formatted text, doclinks, attachments, hotspots, graphics, OLE objects, and other objects. You can use a rich-text field to launch an OLE object

Figure 26-4
Number formatting options on the Control tab

automatically by using the form-launch options described previously. Use rich-text fields anywhere on a form, except in a layout region. Note that you cannot display the value of a rich-text field in a view or use it in a formula. When using the rich-text field with Web clients, specify how the browser accesses and displays the field. In R5, the choices are Using HTML or Using Java applet. If you choose to display using HTML, documents can be displayed with formatted text; however, if they are edited and resubmitted over the Web, the text will lose all of its formatting. In addition, users cannot add formatting to the text while in the Web client. If you choose to display using a Java applet, the browser client uses the Editor applet when users edit the rich-text field. The Editor applet, shown in Figure 26-5, enables users to add some formatting to the rich text, including font color, a few font choices, font size, bold, italics, underline, bulleted and numbered lists, paragraph alignment and indenting, international characters, and links. Users can also cut, copy, and paste within the field. When you insert a rich-text field, the options on the Control tab include *Display: Show field delimiters; Input: Pressing tab key moves to next field;* and *Storage: Store contents as HTML and MIME.*

This is the rich text field using HTML.

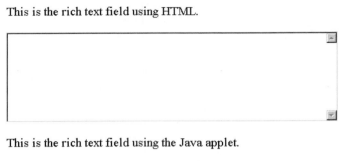

This is the rich text field using the Java applet.

Figure 26-5   The Editor applet

- **Authors field type**   Use an Authors field in coordination with the ACL for the database to determine who can edit documents. Users who have Author access in the ACL can create documents. To give these users the capability to edit the documents they create, add an Authors field to the form that captures the name of the user who created the document. The Authors field cannot override the ACL; rather, it is just a refinement to the access granted at that location. In other words, if a user has Reader access in the ACL, placing that user's name in the Authors field will not enable him or her to edit the document. Authors fields do not affect users who are listed as Editor or higher in the ACL. For editable Authors fields, the Control tab contains an option for how users can choose the names to place in the field. The options in the Choices field include *None, Use Address dialog for choices, Use Access Control List for choices*, and *Use View dialog for choices*. The Address dialog is the same dialog box that is available when addressing a mail message—enabling users to select from the Domino Directory and from any other available directory. If you choose to enable the user to select names using the View dialog, you can also choose the database, view, and column from which to pick those names. Other options on the Control tab include *Allow values not in list, Look up names as each character is entered, Display entry helper button* (without which users have to know to press CTRL+Enter to access the lists), *Refresh fields on keyword change*, and *Refresh choices on document refresh*. None of the lookup options (the options available in the Choices) is available from Web clients. Refer to Chapter 24, "Understanding and Implementing Basic Security," for more details about database security.

- **Names field type** The Names field type displays user or server names as they would appear in a Notes ID file and displays a hierarchical name in a distinguished name format, rather than in the canonical format stored internally. When using the @UserName function in a computed Names field, for example, instead of displaying CN=Libby Schwarz/OU=Authors/O=Schwarz, this field would display Libby Schwarz/Authors/Schwarz. This type of field, unlike Readers and Authors fields, does not affect security. This field has the same options on the Control tab as the Authors field type. The following illustration compares @UserName in a text field and @UserName in a Names field:

@UserName in a Text field

⌜CN=Libby Schwarz/O=Schwarz⌟

@UserName in a Names field
Libby Schwarz/Schwarz

NOTE A fully distinguished name is one that contains all of the elements of a Notes hierarchical name, including the common name, Organizational Units (OU), if any, organization, and country code (if any). An example of a fully distinguished name is Libby Schwarz/Authors/Schwarz. When Notes stores this name internally or displays it in canonicalized format, Notes adds the labels for each portion of the name, as shown previously. This format is awkward for users to read, however, so Names fields display usernames in hierarchical format without the labels. In other field types, you can achieve the same result by using the [Abbreviate] keyword with the @Name function. This @Function is described in detail later in this chapter.

- **Readers field type** Adding a Readers field to a form enables you to add tighter restrictions to a document created with the form. If you place a Readers field on a form, you must list users in the field or in a Read Access list to enable them to view the document. The field has the same lookup and other options on the Control tab as the Authors field. For more information about Readers fields and security, refer to Chapter 24.

- **Password field type**   This field type, which is new to R5, enables a designer to request a password from a user while still maintaining the user's privacy. As the user types the password, the field displays only asterisks. Note, however, that Domino does not secure or encrypt the contents of the field by default. A user could look at the properties for the document to see the value of the field. Lotus suggests that after using the data from this field, a designer should either erase the contents of the field or encrypt them. Refer to the Domino Designer help for more information. Here's an example of how a password field displays text:

Please type your password...
⌐******** ⌐ (password field)

Please type your password...
⌐ password⌐ (text field)

- **Formula field type**   Designers use this field type, which is new to R5, in conjunction with HEADLINES.NSF to enable and populate subscriptions. When a database is enabled for subscriptions, users can be informed of new or changed documents that match their subscription. This field type populates the subscription list. For more information about Formula fields and subscriptions, refer to the Domino Designer help. You might also want to use the HEADLINES.NTF to see the default subscription form and the formula field.

- **Keywords field types**   In R4 and earlier, Notes had three keyword field types, all of which resided under the name *keyword* in the Field Types dialog box. In R5, Notes independently lists five formats for keyword fields in the Field Types list box. Keyword fields provide the user with a list of choices to complete the field. This feature enables the designer to enforce consistency and to limit the responses to a question to the types of answers that he or she wants. The keyword list can be generated programmatically or by typing the list. Expect to see these fields referred to both independently by name and as a category—keyword fields. You might also see these field types referred to as Choice List fields. The keyword field types are described as follows:

- Dialog lists, which are not available in layout regions, present the user with a list of choices. You can choose *Allow Values Not In The List* and *Allow Multiple Values with this field type*. Users can access the items in a dialog list by pressing Enter to see the list, by clicking the Entry Helper button to see the list, by pressing the space bar to cycle through the entries in the list, or by typing a letter (Domino displays entries that begin with that letter). An example of a dialog list is shown in Figure 26-6.

- Checkboxes enable users to select one or more options by clicking the checkbox or by pressing the spacebar while they are on a particular item. Checkboxes automatically enable multiple values, but you cannot enable users to add values not in the list. When selecting a checkbox field type, also select a border style and a number of columns. An example of a checkbox is shown here:

Checkbox	Where would you like to purchase your book?	☐ Barnes and Noble ☐ Amazon ☐ Fatbrain ☐ Other

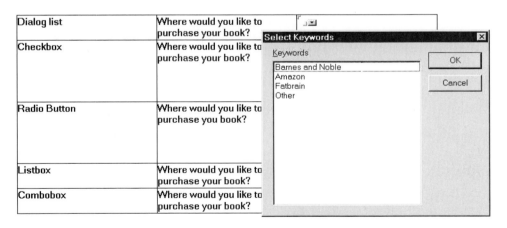

Figure 26-6   Dialog list

- Radio buttons enable users to select only one option by clicking the button. Because Radio buttons are assumed to permit only one value, you cannot choose to Allow multiple values. You also cannot enable users to add values that are not in the list. As with the checkbox, select a border style and number of columns. An example of a radio button is shown here:

Radio Button	Where would you like to purchase you book?	○ Barnes and Noble ○ Amazon ○ Fatbrain ○ Other

- Listboxes display the list of choices in a scrollable box. To change the size of the list box, use the width and height options for the field. You can choose to enable multiple values in this field, although users cannot add values that are not included in the list. A sample listbox is shown here:

Listbox	Where would you like to purchase your book?	Fatbrain

- Comboboxes display a list of items in a drop-down box when users click the Entry Helper button. You can change the width of the combobox and enable values that are not already in the list. A sample combobox is shown here:

Combobox	Where would you like to purchase your book?	
		Barnes and Nob Amazon Fatbrain Other

After selecting how the keyword field appears to the users, determine how to generate the choices for the keyword lists.

- **Enter choices (one per line)**   This option enables the developer to enter the choices manually. These static-text choices are always the same when presented to the user. Update the design of the form to add or delete a choice. To enable the user to add a choice other than the listed keywords, however, select the option to Allow values not in list (when available), giving the user the option to add an item to the keyword list. If the list of choices changes little or remains static, use this option. If the list changes frequently, however, it might be easier to use one of the other options.

> **NOTE** Any items that a user adds to the keyword list using this option would not remain in the list permanently. You must add a formula to add items to the list using user input.

To enter keyword choices, type the choices in the window, pressing Enter after each choice. You have the option of using synonyms (aliases) in the keyword lists, which are similar to the synonyms discussed for form names. Shown next is a keyword list that uses synonyms. To use a synonym in the keyword list, type the keyword option that you want displayed to the user, type a pipe (or vertical bar) character (|), and then type the alias that you want to use internally. In keyword lists, the most common alias is numeric. Keyword aliases offer the capability to change the name of the option presented to the user without having to change any formulas that use the keyword.

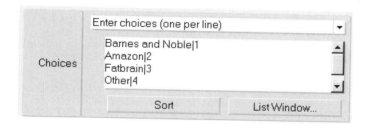

> **NOTE** When using keyword fields in column formulas in views, Domino displays the alias by default, rather than the keyword that the user sees when making a choice. To avoid this situation, use a formula to display the full name, rather than the alias. If, for example, you want to display the name of the store/vendor instead of the numbers, you might use the following formula: @If(Dialog= "1"; "Barnes and Noble"; Dialog ="2"; "Amazon"; Dialog ="3"; "Fatbrain"; Dialog ="4"; "Other"; "No vendor selected")

- **Use Formula for choices** When using a formula to determine keyword choices, you can enable the choices to change dynamically. Use this option to base the choices you present to the user on the user, other input, or data from outside Notes and Domino. After typing the formula, click the green check mark to check the syntax and insert the formula.

- **Use Address Dialog for choices** Using the Address dialog presents the user with a Names dialog box that enables the user to choose from the personal address book or the Domino Directory. To speed lookups, you might choose to enable the *Look up names as each character is entered* option. This option emulates the lookup in Mail Memo documents, as shown in Figure 26-7.

- **Use Access Control List for choices** This option presents the user with a dialog box that pulls groups, users, servers, and roles from the ACL for the database. Use this option when users, servers, or groups with access to the database provide the best choices for the field, as shown in Figure 26-8.

- **Use View Dialog for choices** This option enables the designer to specify a view (described by database, view, and column) for selecting the entries. See Figure 26-9 for an example.

After you select the data type, interface, and method of placing choices in the field, the field is almost ready for use. The following paragraphs describe the additional options that are available on the Control tab:

- If Allow Values Not in List is enabled, the user can type new keywords at the bottom of a dialog list or combobox.

Figure 26-7
Using Address
Dialog for choices

Pick a user:

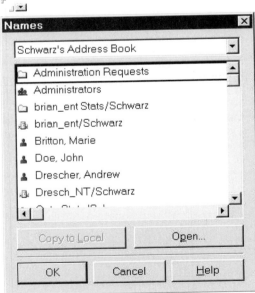

Figure 26-8
Using Access
Control List for
choices

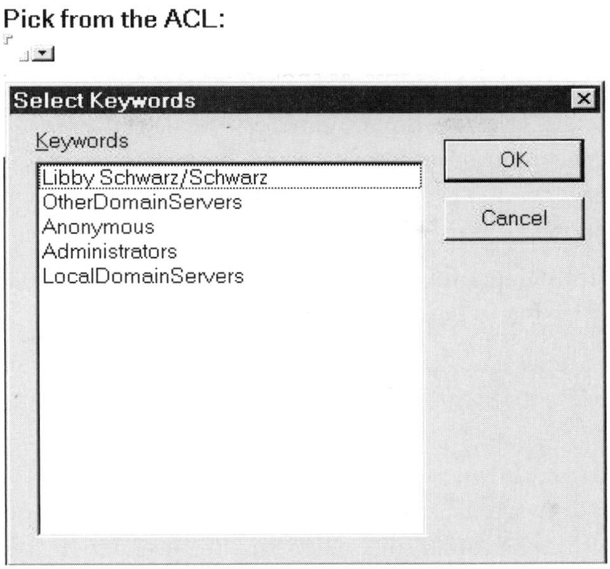

Pick from the ACL:

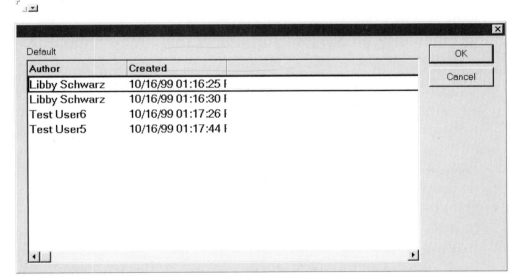

Figure 26-9   Use View Dialog for choices

- Look up names as each character is entered speeds the selection process when using an Address Dialog for choices.

- Don't display entry helper button. This choice, which is available for dialog lists, removes the list button automatically displayed next to the field and forces the user to type the correct option or choose CRTL+ENTER to see the list.

- Refresh fields on keyword change should be used if other formulas in the form depend on the field's value. To hide paragraphs or fields depending on the value of a keyword field, for example, you would need to have this option enabled.

- Refresh choices on document refresh. This option updates the keyword list each time the user refreshes the document. Use this option when the keyword list is not a statically typed list, because the keywords might change.

Editable Versus Computed Fields

Another option you must choose as you create a field is how the field will obtain a value. Fields can be editable, in which case, the user adds the data when creating a document, or computed, in which case the designer adds a formula to determine the value when creating the form.

- **Editable** The user manually enters information into an editable field. Editable fields also have up to three formulas: the default value formula, the input translation formula, and the input validation formula. The default value formula serves as a starting point for the user. He or she can choose to overwrite the default value or leave the value. The input translation formula changes or manipulates the value of the field after the user completes the field. Typical input translation formulas provide for correct capitalization or spacing. Input validation formulas test the value of a field. Use them to ensure that users put a value in a field or that users put the correct type of data in a field. Each of these three events is described in more detail later in the chapter.

- **Computed** When users create, refresh, or save documents, Notes recalculates the calculated value of a computed field. The designer creates a formula to give the field a value. The end user cannot change a computed field.

- **Computed for display** In a Computed for display field, the value is recalculated every time the document is opened for reading or editing—or any time the document is refreshed. Notes does not store the value of the field when the user saves the document. Because this data is not stored when the document is closed, the data in this field cannot be displayed in a view. This type of data will only be displayed for viewing in an open document. You can use Computed for display fields to save space in databases if it is not necessary to store the value of the field.

(handwritten: ueue) • **Computed when composed** Notes only calculates the value of a Computed when composed field—when the user creates the document. The field is never recalculated. This field type is useful for a date stamp on a document, for example, or for a field showing the original creator of the document.

The Advanced Tab

The Advanced tab offers choices related to field-level help, multi-value options, and security, as shown in Figure 26-10.

- **Help description** Use this field for a brief description of how the user should use the field. Notes displays this text in the status bar at the bottom of the workspace if the user has turned on Field Help (by using View . . . Show . . . Field Help). You can use up to 70 characters in this field. Bear in mind, however, that Web users cannot see the field help. *(handwritten: HELP CANNOT BE VIEWED ON THE WEB.)* *(handwritten right margin: 70 characters in Help field)*

- **Multi-value options** These options are grayed unless you have enabled the Allow multiple values option on the Basics tab. The two choices in this section are *Separate values when user enters* and *Display separate values with.* The choices for both options are the same and include the following: space, comma, semicolon, new line, and blank line. Note that when the field is a keyword field, these options are not available. *(handwritten: → except dialog list)*

Figure 26-10
The Advanced tab

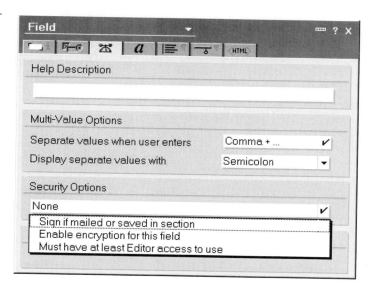

(handwritten right margin: PART IV)

• Security options   These options enable the designer to secure the field with signing, encryption, and an ACL. The Sign if mailed or saved in section option is used mostly with workflow or controlled-access sections. The Enable encryption for this field option enables this field's data to be encrypted with either a secret encryption key or a public encryption key that you add to the form. Finally, set the *Must have at least Editor access to use* option to restrict the field to users who have Editor access or above in the ACL for the database. For more information about security, refer to Chapters 10, 18, and 24.

The Font Tab

The Font tab, shown next, is similar to the Font tab shown in other InfoBoxes. In general, this tab enables the designer to set the font for anything that is affected by font, including static text, section titles, and fields. The Field Properties Font tab sets the default font for the field display. This tab defines the font typed into fields, unless it is a rich-text field. A rich-text field retains the default font, but the user has the capability to change the font information.

The Paragraph Alignment Tab

The Paragraph Alignment tab, shown next, is similar to the Paragraph Alignment tab shown in other InfoBoxes. This tab enables the designer to set spacing, alignment, and list defaults for the paragraph. Note the options available for lists, which now include bullets, circles, squares, check marks, numbers, upper and lower-case letters, and upper and lower-case Roman numerals.

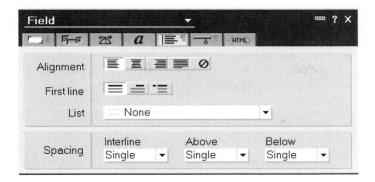

The Paragraph Hide-When Tab

The Hide-When tab, shown next, enables you to hide a field. Remember that when you choose to hide a field, you are hiding everything on the same line as the field. If you are trying to use one field for capturing data, therefore, and another field to display the data, you need to repeat the static text next to both fields.

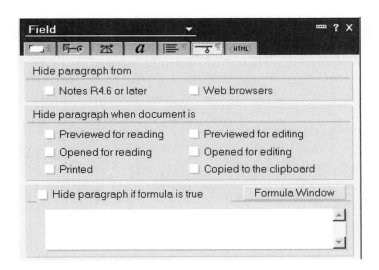

PART IV

The HTML Tab

The last tab of the Field properties InfoBox enables designers to add extra options in HTML for a field, as shown next. The HTML tag attributes are primarily for use with Web applications using HTML, JavaScript, and Cascading Style Sheets.

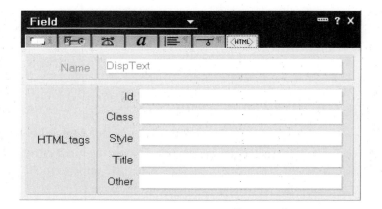

Shared Fields

In many cases, you might want to use a particular field more than one time in a Domino database. To create fields that you can reuse, create shared fields. Shared fields, like Subforms, enable a design element to be reused on multiple forms within a database. The main difference between the two is that a subform enables a group of design elements, including text, graphics, and fields, to be reused. A shared field enables a particular field to be reused from form to form. Shared fields can be created using the following methods:

- Create a new shared field by choosing Create . . . Design . . . Shared Field from the menus. This action displays the Shared Field properties InfoBox. The options on this InfoBox are the same as those for any other field.

- Share an existing single-use field by choosing Design . . . Share this field. This option automatically shares the field and makes it available in the Insert Shared Field dialog box. There is no option to stop sharing a field. To turn a shared field into a single-use field, cut the field and paste it back onto the form.

- Copy shared fields from another database by using the Resources . . . Shared Fields view. Copy the shared fields you want to use in the new database, and then paste them into the Shared Fields view in the new database.

To insert an already-created shared field onto a form, choose Create . . . Insert Shared Field. This action will bring up the Insert Shared Fields dialog box, shown next. Choose the shared field you want to insert, and click OK.

You should remember that any change made to a shared field affects that field on every form in the database on which it was used. If you rename a shared field, for example, you need to edit all the forms that use the field. Remove the old field, and insert the new field. For already-created documents, you should create an agent that assigns the data from the old field to the new field. If you delete a shared field from a form, it is only removed from that form. To remove the field completely, clear it from the Shared Fields view. If a shared field is removed after documents have been created using it, users might receive an error that says, *Cannot locate field definition for Field: <field name>*. When users click OK on the error, however, they see the contents of the shared field as non-editable text. Using shared fields, like using subforms, saves development time and helps ensure consistency between forms in the database.

Fields for Inheritance

Earlier, we discussed the idea that you might want to inherit information from one document onto a second document. If you are creating a response to a review of a book, for example, you might want to inherit some of the information about the book so that the person creating the response does not have to retype the response. You might also want to have a field inherit information from another field on the same form. If you have had a user enter some information about himself or herself, such as a birth date or ID number, for example, you might want to display that again later in another field.

For the first type of inheritance, the inheriting field must use the value of the original field as its default value (if editable) or value (if computed). The fields do not have to use the same name, but they can. In addition, you must enable the form property *Formulas inherit values from selected documents*. Do not forget that inheritance only occurs when the document is created. If a change is made to the original document, it will not be reflected in the document that inherited its information unless you create an agent to update the fields. Finally, for inheritance to work correctly, the user must have the original document opened or selected. This statement is true for both Notes and Web clients. Web clients can also have a reference in the URL to the parent document.

For inheritance among fields on the same form, the form property enabling inheritance does not have to be selected. The inheriting field must merely be below or to the right of the field from which it is inheriting data. Again, use the original, or parent, field as the formula for the inheriting field.

Categories Fields

In many Notes views, the documents will be organized by category, as shown next. Although a field called Categories is not required to create a categorized view, a Categories field enables the user to use the Action . . . Categorize menu option if the designer has created a view that uses the categories.

```
▼Active
   Libby Schwarz      10/16/99 01:27:17 |
▼Archived
   Libby Schwarz      10/16/99 01:27:11 |
   Libby Schwarz      10/16/99 01:27:21 |
```

Often, the Categories field will be a keyword field that enables the designer to specify a list of categories. The value of the Categories field will then be used to group documents that have the same purpose or content, based on the selected category.

Formulas in Fields

In all fields, whether editable or computed, the designer has the option to define the value using a formula. The designer creates a formula with one of the available programming languages. There are now a variety of programming languages available in Notes: the formula language discussed in this chapter, LotusScript, and JavaScript. LotusScript is an object-oriented programming language that is similar to C++ or Visual Basic. You do not have to know LotusScript or JavaScript for the Domino Designer Fundamentals exam.

The formula language uses elements such as constants, variables, keywords, and @Functions. Formulas are one of the basic elements of creating applications, and they appear in everything from Hide-When elements to columns to fields. This chapter describes how to create and use formulas, including syntax. For this exam, you must be able to read and evaluate a formula in the same way that Notes will. This section is not intended to be a complete reference for using formulas or any of their elements, however. For more information about formulas, especially if you have never written formulas in Notes before, use the Domino Designer help documentation to supplement this guide.

Formula Components

Writing a formula is a little bit like baking a cake. You have a set of ingredients from which you can choose to put a cake together. As long as you choose the sugar and not the salt, the cake should turn out right. The first things to know about a formula are what the ingredients, or elements, of a formula are and how to put them together. To put formulas together correctly, you have to use the correct syntax and the correct formula elements. The correct syntax includes elements such as separators, case, parentheses, and quotation marks. The different elements of a formula that you will be joining together using this correct syntax are called components. The following are the components of formulas in Notes: constants, variables, operators, keywords, @Functions, and @Commands. Each of these components is discussed in the following sections.

Syntax

Syntax is one of the most important elements of application development. You should know how to apply the following basic syntax rules when developing formulas:

- *Use separators correctly.* The colon (:) is used to separate list items. A semicolon (;) is used to separate multiple statements or arguments. Both colons and semicolons are also used to end lines. Spaces are ignored in most cases, with the following exceptions. First, all keyword formula components must be followed by at least one space. In addition, in text constants, include spaces where appropriate.

- *Use case correctly.* Most elements of Notes are not case-sensitive. Keyword formula components, however, should be used in upper case. In addition, most field names, @Functions, and @Commands are used in mixed case. Using case correctly makes it easier for developers to read and understand formulas written by other developers—something you will be glad of when you want to pass off your early applications to some other newbie.

- *Use parentheses when necessary to control the order of evaluation and to enclose @Function arguments.* Remember to use the same number of open and closed parentheses in complex formulas.

- *Use quotation marks to enclose text strings in formulas.* If you enclose a field name in quotation marks, it will be treated as a text string. To use a single quote in a text string, place an escape character (\) before it, as in "Libby\'s."

- *Use a single data type in all formulas.* To combine data types in formulas, use conversion @Functions such as @Text and @TextToNumber.

- *When using logical operators, ensure that each expression can be evaluated individually.* Each expression must produce a true or false result without elements from the other side of the expression. The expression Select Form = "Question" | "Answer" is incorrect, for example, because only the first half of the expression can be evaluated. Use the expression Select Form = "Question" | Form = "Answer" instead.

- *To use time values as text, enclose them in quotation marks.* To use time values as time constants, enclose them in square brackets.

Constants

Constants can be any piece of static text, including numbers, times, and words. These elements cannot change. Surround text constants by quotation marks to use them in formulas (such as "Constant"). When you use times and dates as constants, enclose them in square brackets (such as [4:52 P.M.]). For a mathematical comparison, in the equation $2x-y$, the 2 is a constant.

Variables

Variables in Notes are most often field names, but they can also be temporary variables. Field names used in formulas can be used alone or as part of an @Function formula to create a new result. When using field names as variables, most often they will be used without quotes. When you are creating a formula, Designer makes the field names available on the Reference tab. You can click a field name and choose Paste, as shown next. This action is highly recommended, because most of the mistakes made in formulas are syntax and typographical errors. Temporary variables are set only inside a formula and are used to store information only while the formula is being evaluated. In our mathematical comparison of $2x-y$, both x and y are variables.

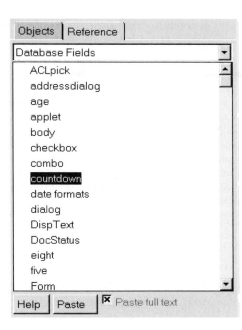

The following are some specific issues to keep in mind when using fields as variables:

- The data types of all fields in a formula must be correct. Some functions require text fields; others require number or time fields. Use functions such as @Text, @TextToNumber, and @TextToTime when necessary.

- If you want to modify a field in a formula, you must clearly define that you are manipulating an existing field by using the FIELD keyword. If you do not use this keyword, Domino assumes that you are using a temporary variable and does not modify the existing field any time you use a field name to the left side of a formula. Author:="Libby" would set a temporary variable called Author with the value "Libby." If you had intended to set the value of the field Author equal to Libby, you would need to say, FIELD Author := "Libby."

- A field with no value, or a null field, is evaluated as a text constant " ". To avoid errors, do not permit numbers or other non-text fields to resolve to a null value. Instead, ensure that you have a correct default value specified.

Operators

Operators perform the actions on the constants and variables in a formula. In our mathematical comparison of $2x-y$, the minus sign $(-)$ is the operator. The operators available in Notes are listed as follows in the order in which Notes evaluates them (see Table 26-1).

NOTE Concatenation is used with text strings, while addition is used with numbers. Also, the operators | (or) and & (and) sometimes confuse new developers. Using & (and) between logical expressions means that both expressions must be true for the whole expression to be true. Using | (or) between two expressions means that the whole expression is true if either part is true. Or is less limiting and will return more true values. And is more limiting; it will be true less often. The equals sign (=) is used in Notes for comparison. MyName = (is equal to) UserName and does not set something to have the value of something else. That is an assignment function carried out by the symbol := (a colon plus the equals sign).

This order of evaluation is subject to the normal mathematical order of evaluation: parentheses, exponents, multiplication, division, addition, and subtraction. For example, in the mathematical formula $2+(5-3)$, you would evaluate the $5-3$ first and then add the result to the 2. Formulas in Notes will be evaluated the same way—for example, @UpperCase is @Left ("Libby and Brian"; 5). Notes evaluates the @Left function first and then evaluates the @UpperCase function.

Table 26-1 Operators

Operation	Operator	Example
Assignment	:= (Colon, equal)	UserName := "Libby" (assigns value of Libby to the temporary variable UserName)
Concatenation	: (Colon used for lists); + (Plus used for text)	"Apples" :"Cherries" :"Strawberries"; UserName + "developed this database." Returns Libby developed this database.
Arithmetic	* (Multiplication); / (Division); + (Addition); - (Subtraction)	TotalPrice*8.25; NumberOfBooks/Price; TotalPrice + Tax + Shipping; NumberOf Books—DiscountedBooks
Comparison	= (Equal to); < (Less than); > (Greater than); !=, =!, <>, >< (Not equal to)	SELECT Form = "Questions"; SELECT NumberOfBooks < 50; SELECT NumberOfBooks > 100; SELECT UserName != "Libby" Logical & (And);	(Or); ! (Not)

SELECT Form = "Questions" & Form =;"Answers"

Keywords

The Formula keywords described as follows perform special functions within Notes formulas. You will notice that they are capitalized here. The capitalization is a convention for ease of reading the formulas, not a requirement. If you do not capitalize them in formulas, however, Designer capitalizes them automatically.

- **SELECT** This keyword is used to choose a value or form for an action. Most often, you will see the SELECT keyword used in selection formulas. If a SELECT keyword *Select @All* is needed in a formula but has been left out by the designer, SELECT @ALL will be appended to the formula automatically. For example, SELECT Form = "Answer" in a formula would choose all documents created with the form Answer. SELECT is also used often to evaluate keyword values for hide-when formulas.

- **DEFAULT** The DEFAULT keyword is used to set a value in a field. If a field does not exist in a document, Notes will evaluate the document as though it does exist, with the specified value. For example, DEFAULT MyName := Author sets the field MyName equal to the field Author in the document.

- **FIELD** This keyword is similar to DEFAULT in that it sets a field value. If the field does exist, its value will be replaced with the indicated value. If the field does not exist, it will be created with the assigned value. For example, FIELD CarColor := "Blue." assigns the value Blue to the field CarColor. You should remember that if you are trying to manipulate the value of an existing field, you must use this keyword.

- **REM** As in many programming languages, the REM statement enables the designer to make remarks about the formula. Anything immediately after the REM keyword will be ignored and will not be evaluated as part of the formula. REM is usually used to document the purpose of a formula or program.

- **ENVIRONMENT** Its basic purpose is to enable the developer to assign an environment variable in either the NOTES.INI file (Windows) or the Preferences file (Macintosh).

@Functions

An @Function (pronounced "at" function) is a predefined Notes formula that is used to perform specified actions. These functions enable the developers to add functionality to the applications without a complete object-oriented programming language (although this language is provided in LotusScript). The exam focuses on some of the @Functions that are new to Release 5 as well as some of the commonly used building

PART IV

blocks. This section describes some of the @Functions that are tested on the exam, including their use, syntax, and examples. For more information about @Functions, there is a list in the appendix to help you study. Additionally, the Notes User Help database has a complete listing that includes examples of all available @Functions. Ensure that you know how to use the @Functions listed, including where they can be placed, what their arguments are, and which functions can or cannot be used with Web clients. @Functions are one of the focus points of the Domino Designer Fundamentals exam, because they can be involved with all aspects of an application—from the window title of its forms to the buttons and agents that make things happen.

Working with Text

Many @Functions work with the text that users have entered. These @Functions convert the text (or convert to text), compare elements, extract elements, and correct the text. Some examples are listed as follows:

- @Text (value) is used to convert a number, date, or other type of value to a text string. Remember that only one type of data can be in a field, so to show that a particular user created a document on a particular day, for example, you need to convert the date to text:

```
"This document was created at " + @Text(@Created) + " by " +
@Name([CN]; @UserName)
```

Note that @Text has additional time-date and number components that you can use to format the item further. Time-date components include S0, which would return only the date; D2, which would return only the month and day; and Z2, which would force Domino to display the time zone at all times. For more details about the time-date and number components, refer to the Domino Designer Help database or to the Formula language programming guide.

- @Length (string) counts the number of characters in the string, returning a number:

```
@Length ("How many characters is this?")
```

This function might also count the characters from the value of a field (One):

```
@Length (One)
```

- @Contains (string; substring) determines whether the contents of the substring are contained in the string. The following formula, for example, searches the field One for the string "Libby." If it finds the string, the formula returns a value of true (1):

```
@Contains(One;"Libby")
```

You might use this function with @If to test for a particular value and then return another item based on that value:

```
@If(@Contains(One; "Libby");"Libby is the author of this docu-
ment"; "You're not Libby, are you?")
```

- @Left (string; n) returns the specified number (n) of left-most characters from a string, searching left to right. The following formula, for example, returns the five left-most characters from the string:

```
@Left("Libby Ingrassia Schwarz";5)
```

Similar @Functions include @Right and @Middle. To concatenate a first initial and the first seven characters of the last name, for example, you might use this formula:

```
@Left(@Name([CN];@UserName)1)+@Right(@Name([CN];@UserName;7)
```

- @ProperCase(string), @UpperCase(string), and @LowerCase(string) convert the characters in a string to the specified case. These are often used in input translation event formulas:

```
@ProperCase("pass that test!")+ @UpperCase("pass that
test")+@LowerCase("PASS THAT TEST!")
```

- @Trim(string) removes extraneous spaces from text strings. This function is also often used in input translation formulas:

```
@Trim("    there    are    too    many    spaces here, don't you
think?")
```

See Figure 26-11 for a sample of the text @Functions described previously.

Time, Date, and Number Functions

The following functions manipulate dates, times, or numbers. In some cases, they use the system clock or other means to return the values.

- @Created returns the time and date that a document was created, and this value does not change. The display format of @Created depends on the formatting of the date/time field, as described previously. Similar functions include @Accessed, which shows the date and time that the document was last accessed, and @Modified, which returns the date and time that the document was last saved.

- @Now returns the current date and time. This function updates unless the function is in a Computed when Composed event. Similar functions include @Today, @Tomorrow, and @Yesterday. _Returns any date_

```
"This document was created at " + @Text(@Created) +" by " + @Name([CN]; @UserName)
This document was created at 10/16/99 01:35:26 PM by Libby Schwarz

@Length("How many characters is this?")
28

@Length(One)
66

@Contains(One; "Libby")
1

@If(@Contains(One; "Libby");"Libby is the author of this document"; "You're not Libby, are you?")
Libby is the author of this document

@Left("Libby Ingrassia Schwarz"; 5)
Libby

@Left(@Name([CN];@UserName);1)+@Right(@Name([CN];@UserName);7)
LSchwarz

@ProperCase("pass that test! ")+ @UpperCase("pass that test ")+@LowerCase("PASS THAT TEST! ")
Pass That Test! PASS THAT TEST pass that test!

@Trim(" there  are   too   many   spaces here, don't you think?")
there are too many spaces here, don't you think?
```

Figure 26-11   Text @Function sample

- @Adjust(time-date;y;m;d;h;m;s) changes a given date and time value by the amount specified in each argument. The arguments can be positive or negative. For example, the following formula adds 2 days and 12 hours to the creation time of a document:

  ```
  @Adjust(@Created;0;0;2;12;0;0)
  ```

- @Sum(number, number, ...) calculates the value of the numbers or number lists. For example, the following formula returns 15 as the value:

  ```
  @Sum(1:2:3:4:5)
  ```

Here's a sample of the number and time functions described previously:

```
@Created
 10/16/99

@Nuw
 10/16/99 01:37:09 PM

@Adjust(@Created;0;0;2;12;0;0)
 10/19/99 01:37 AM

@Sum(1:2:3:4:5)
 15

@Sum ((1+2)-(3+4)-(5+6))
 -15
```

Username and Environment Functions

The following functions access the user's environment, usually through the USER.ID file currently in use or through the current NOTES.INI file. For some formula types, such as replication formulas, selection formulas, and some triggered agents, the environment is the server or workstation that contains the database.

- @UserName returns the current user or server name. Note that when you test this function in a Web browser, you will most often return a value of Anonymous unless you force a login. By default, values returned by @UserName are fully distinguished names, including the hierarchical components. If @UserName is placed in an Authors, Readers, or Names field, however, Domino displays the name in abbreviated format. Domino continues to store the name in canonicalized format. In R5, you can also use @UserName to return the alternate user or server name by using an argument of 1. @UserName(1) returns the alternate user or server name. @UserName(0) returns the primary name. If the argument is eliminated, Domino returns the primary name by default.

- @Name ([action]; name) manipulates names as specified by the action. Some of the available action keywords are shown in the following table. Some of the actions are intended to be used with names from other systems, such as e-mail systems that use the RFC821 or RFC822 format and therefore have additional name components that a Notes name does not have. Note also that while @Name is not new to R5, it has been enhanced for R5. This function is therefore an excellent potential source of questions.

- @UserRoles requires that the database should either be on a server or should have the *Enforce a Consistent Access Control List* across all replicas of this database property set via the ACL dialog box. When those conditions are met, it returns the roles that the current user has for the database. User roles must be defined in the ACL to return anything for this function. When the function is used with a Web client, it returns $$WebClient as one of the roles.

- @UserNamesList is similar to (and a superset of) @UserRoles. This function displays not only the roles for the user, but also the current user's name and the groups to which the user belongs. Similar to @UserRoles, this function requires that the database should either be on a server or should have the *Enforce a Consistent Access Control List across all replicas of this database* property set. Both @Functions can be useful for determining the outcome of a hide-when formula or when deciding which subform Domino should display to a user.

Table 26-2 Available Name Actions

Action Keyword	What it Does
[Abbreviate]	Removes the component labels from a hierarchical name.
[Address821]	New to R5; shows an RFC821 address syntax—translates from an RFC822 syntax if necessary.
[C]	Displays the country code component of the name.
[Canonicalize]	Using the Notes ID, adds the hierarchical components to a name.
[CN]	Displays the common name component of the name.
[G]	Displays the given name component of the name (does not work with Notes names).
[HierarchyOnly]	Removes the common name component and displays the hierarchical components of the name.
[LP]	New to R5; returns the local part (the part to the left of the @ symbol) for an Internet e-mail address.
[O]	Displays the Organization component of the name.
[Oun]	Displays the indicated Organizational Unit (OU) component of the name. If a number is used (n), assume that the OUs are counted from right to left (closest to the Organization is OU1).

- @Platform displays the platform on which the current user is running. Similarly, @Version displays the current version of Notes or Domino that is running (displayed by build number). @ClientType returns whether the user is on a Web client or a Notes client. This value returns either "Notes" or "Web" text strings.

- @ValidateInternetAddress ([keyword]; address) determines whether a given Internet address is valid, based on either the RFC821 or RFC822 addressing scheme. Use the keywords [Address821] and [Address822]. RFC821 addresses are as follows: libbys@notesgirl.com. RFC822 addresses also have a phrase, such as "Schwarz, Libby" <libbys@notesgirl.com>. You would usually place the function in an Input Validation event for a field that requested an e-mail address. The function returns a null value if the address is correct. Otherwise, the function returns a specific error describing what is wrong with the address.

[handwritten annotation: returns (0) if correct]

Refer to Figure 26-12 for a sample of the functions described previously.

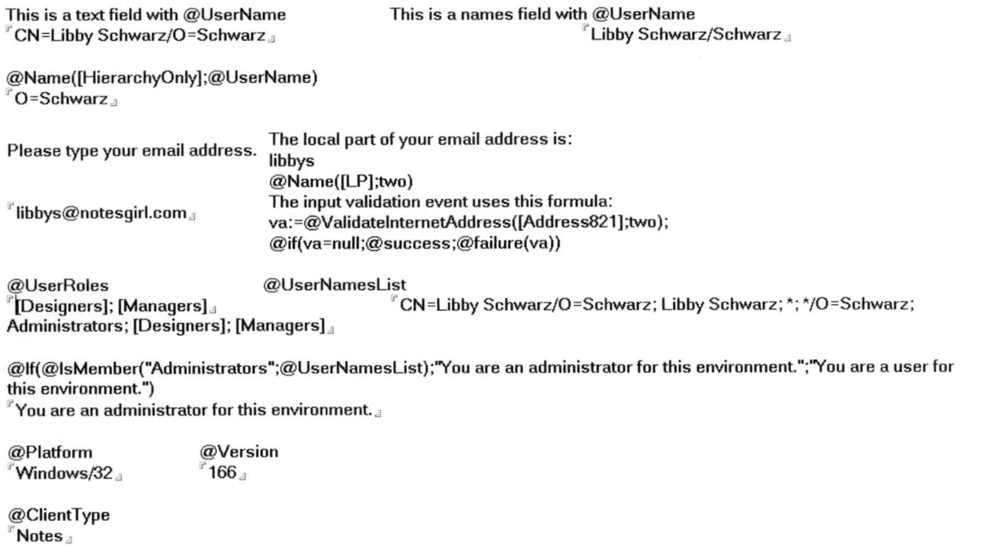

This is a text field with @UserName
  ⌐CN=Libby Schwarz/O=Schwarz⌐

This is a names field with @UserName
  ⌐Libby Schwarz/Schwarz⌐

@Name([HierarchyOnly];@UserName)
  ⌐O=Schwarz⌐

Please type your email address.

  ⌐libbys@notesgirl.com⌐

The local part of your email address is:
libbys
@Name([LP];two)
The input validation event uses this formula:
va:=@ValidateInternetAddress([Address821];two);
@if(va=null;@success;@failure(va))

@UserRoles
  ⌐[Designers]; [Managers]⌐
Administrators; [Designers]; [Managers]⌐

@UserNamesList
  ⌐CN=Libby Schwarz/O=Schwarz; Libby Schwarz; *; */O=Schwarz;

@If(@IsMember("Administrators";@UserNamesList);"You are an administrator for this environment.";"You are a user for this environment.")
  ⌐You are an administrator for this environment.⌐

@Platform   @Version
  ⌐Windows/32⌐   ⌐166⌐

@ClientType
  ⌐Notes⌐

Figure 26-12   Name and environment functions

Other @Functions

The following are some additional @Functions that you must know:

99 arguments

- @If is used for conditional statements and enables you to determine what to do based on another field, a user name, or other condition. The @If statement evaluates the given conditions and then returns the specified action. If none of the statements apply, then the negative (else) action is returned. @If statements will always have an odd number of arguments (with a minimum of three) to enable the negative statement. @If statements can be nested. You can use up to 99 arguments in an @If statement. The syntax for the @If is as follows:

```
@If (condition1; action1; condition2; action2; else action)
```

You might use the following example to display the words "New Form" the first time a document is created with this form and the Author's name any other time. This formula would be placed in the Window Title event:

```
@If (@IsNewDoc; "New Form" ;@Author)
```

Cannot use @deletedoc on web.

- @DeleteDocument works on selected documents, permanently removes a document, can only be used in an agent, and cannot be used on the Web. If you place this formula in an agent, for example, it will delete documents that have a DocStatus field set to Archived:

```
@If (DocStatus != "Active"; @If(DocStatus = "Archived"; @Delete-
Document;"");"");SELECT @All
```

- @BrowserInfo("property") enables you to determine certain characteristics of the browser in use by a client. This function enables you to tailor the user's experience to his or her browser. If the user is using an older browser that does not support frames, for example, you could redirect the user to a different version of your application or at least warn him or her that unexpected results will occur. @BrowserInfo works in coordination with the BROWSER.CNF file stored in the Notes\Data directory. This file, which is editable, compares the specified property to the stored values for browsers such as *Microsoft Internet Explorer* (MSIE) and Netscape Navigator. If you want to know, for example, whether the user is viewing your application in a frames-compatible browser, use the following formula:

```
@BrowserInfo("Frames")
```

Refer to Figure 26-13 for a sample of the @BrowserInfo function as viewed on a MSIE Version 5 browser.

@BrowserInfo("frames")	this browser supports frames	1
@BrowserInfo("cookies")	this browser supports frames	1
@BrowserInfo("Robot")	this browser is not a robot.	0
@BrowserInfo("Tables")	this browser supports tables	1
@BrowserInfo("Version")		5
@BrowserInfo("JavaScript")	this browser supports javascript	1
@BrowserInfo ("BrowserType")		Microsoft

Figure 26-13 @BrowserInfo

- @UserNameLanguage (argument) is useful for determining the language tag for the alternate name of a user. To determine the language tag for the alternate name, use @UserNameLanguage (1). Note that the primary name (0) returns a null value. If the language associated with the alternate name were Italian, for example, the function would return it.

- @PickList displays a dialog box showing either a view or the Address dialog box. One syntax example for @PickList is as follows:

```
@PickList([Custom];[Single];server:file;view;title;prompt;col-
umn;categoryname)
```

Keywords other than [Custom] and [Single] include [Name] (to display the Address dialog box instead of a view), [Folders], and [Room]. The server and title arguments can either be null, can use the current database, can specify the server and filename, or can use the database's replica ID.

This list of examples is short and is intended to help you understand some of the syntax rules and uses of some of the @Functions you are expected to know for the exams. This list is not comprehensive or exhaustive, however. To obtain a list of all @Functions that are available in Notes, refer to the Domino Designer Help database. In addition, when choosing an @Function from the lists that are available in the formula windows or Reference List, click Help or press F1 while any @Function is selected to receive help on that @Function.

@Commands

@Commands are a special type of @Function that automates the standard Notes menu choices as well as some special Notes commands. They are often used in formulas for buttons, actions, smart icons, and agents. For example, @Command ([FileSave]) saves the current document in the same way that choosing File . . . Save or pressing CTRL+S would. There are two types of @Commands: @Command and @PostedCommand. The only difference between the two types of @Commands is the order in which they are evaluated. @Commands are evaluated as they are reached in the document, in sequence from top to bottom and left to right.

NOTE   There are a few exceptions. Certain @Commands are always run last, and some examples include the following: [FileCloseWindow], [FileExit], [Tool-sRunMacro], and the navigation commands.

@PostedCommands are evaluated in order after all other @Functions or @Commands have been evaluated. This statement is true regardless of their location in the form. In Lotus Notes v3, @Commands are run at the end after all other @Functions, similar to the way that @PostedCommands are run in Notes Releases 4 and 5. Forms converted from v3 therefore have their v3 @Commands automatically converted to @PostedCommands to preserve the order of evaluation.

The basic syntax for an @Command is as follows: @Command([CommandName]; parameter). Not each @Command has an additional parameter, although some have multiple parameters. Separate any parameters that are included with a semicolon. @PostedCommands use the same commands and have the same syntax such as @PostedCommand ([CommandName]; parameters).

NOTE   There is a complete reference to @Commands in the Domino Designer Help database and in the official Lotus publication, *Domino Designer Programming Guide, Volume 1: Formula Language*. For more information, please refer to this database or documentation.

An example of a good use for an @Command might be a button that automatically creates a new document or saves the current one. To create a button that automatically creates a new answer to a question in a database, the button would have the following formula: @Command ([Compose]; "Answers"). When the user clicked the button, a new document would be created using the form "Answers." Some sample

@Commands are described in Table 26-3. One important aspect of understanding @Commands is knowing where and when to use them. Each @Command has some usage rules, such as only using them in Notes or in a view.

Table 26-3 Examples of @Commands

@Command	Function	Example	Usage
[Compose]	Creates a new document with the specified form. You can specify a different server and database with the appropriate arguments.	@Command ([Compose]; "Main Topic")	Web or Notes. When composing a response or response-to-response-type document, a document must be selected in the view.
[FileCloseWindow]	Closes the active Notes window.	@Command ([FileClose Window])	Web or Notes. For the Web, apply Use JavaScript . . . This command always executes last.
[FileExit]	Closes all open Notes windows and exits Notes.	@Command ([FileExit])	Notes only; do not use in dialog boxes; always executes last.
[FilePrint]	Prints the current document or view.	@Command ([FilePrint]) [ViewRefresh Fields], @Command ([ViewRefresh Fields])	Refreshes the fields on the current document or the documents in the current view recalculates all fields on a document without closing it. You need to have the Use JavaScript database property enabled; also for use with the Web View applet.
[OpenNavigator]	Opens the specified Navigator in the current database.	@Command ([Open Navigator]; "Main Navigator")	Web or Notes
[CalendarFormat]	Changes an open calendar view as specified in the argument. Sample arguments include 1, 2, 7, 14, and 30. The arguments define the number of days the calendar view displays. An additional option of 365 exists on the Web only. If there is no argument, it cycles to the next view.	@Command ([Calendar Format]; 1)	Web or Notes, in a calendar view.

continued

Table 26-3 Examples of @Commands (*continued*)

@Command	Function	Example	Usage
[OpenFrameset]	Opens the designated frameset in the current database.	@Command ([OpenFrameset]; "Main Frames")	Web or Notes, in Action formulas.
[OpenPage]	Opens the designated page in the current database.	@Command ([OpenPage]; "Home Page")	Web or Notes, in Action formulas.

Field Event Formulas

When we created fields earlier, we discussed the idea that in an editable field, a designer could create a default value by using the Default Value event. Similarly, when you created a window title for your form, you used a Window Title event. These events, and the other field and form events, are good examples of when formulas can be used. The three main field events that are available for placing formula language in editable fields are Default Value, Input Translation, and Input Validation, as shown in Figure 26-14. If the symbol next to the event is filled in, there is a formula in that event. Other field events, such as onBlur and onClick, are used for JavaScript, and field events such as Entering and Exiting are used for LotusScript.

A Default Value formula, as we have discussed already, places a value in an editable field that the user can accept or change. An Input Translation formula evaluates the data that the user has typed into the field and then edits that data. For example, the @Trim and @ProperCase functions described previously would be placed in the Input Translation event to have the desired effect. These formulas are evaluated when the document is refreshed, recalculated, or saved. One option that we discussed earlier was the capability to refresh fields automatically as the user moved to the next field. If this situation is true, the user will see the results of an Input Translation formula as he or she tabs to the next field. Input Validation formulas are used to require data to be entered into certain fields or to require a certain type of data to be entered into a field. This type of formula makes a particular field, such as a Name or Categories field, required before the document can be saved. Domino evaluates this type of formula—similarly to the Input Translation formula—when the document is refreshed, recalculated, or saved, or if the designer is using the Automatically Refresh Fields option (as discussed), the formula will be evaluated as soon as the user moves to another field.

Figure 26-14
Field events

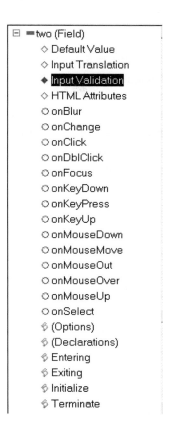

Input Validation formulas are written using an @If function in combination with the @Success and @Failure functions. For example, the following formula requires the user to complete the Name field before moving on in the document: @If(Name=""; @Failure("You must type your name before continuing.");@Success). If the user exits without completing this field, he or she will receive an error similar to the one shown here:

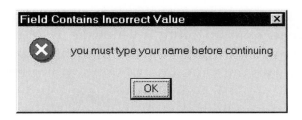

Summary

This chapter introduced you to the wonders of fields and formulas. These elements enable an application to accept and calculate data. There are many field types, each of which displays data differently and treats data differently. You should know when it is necessary or advisable to use different kinds of fields. Within fields, as well as in other objects, you can add formulas to calculate values or to perform actions. Know the elements of a formula, how to use @Functions and @Commands, and how to evaluate a formula in the same way that Notes and Domino evaluate the formula.

Practice

Use this practice to understand and create fields and formulas for your database. This practice is in two parts. First, using the Field and Formula Testing database (FFTEST.NSF), you can review and preview the fields and formulas described throughout this chapter. Copy the database to your local data directory and remove the Read Only file property.

Next, if you created the R5 Orders and Reviews database with the appropriate forms in Chapter 25, you can open that database to get started. If you did not create the database or create the forms, use the CH25.NSF that is provided on the CD-ROM. As always, you will need to copy the database to your local data directory and remove the Read-Only file property.

Each of the three forms that you created in the previous chapter has many opportunities for fields and formulas. There is no single answer for which fields and formulas are appropriate, but some suggestions are listed as follows. The following images are the design synopsis for the forms and fields in the database. To create or view a design synopsis, choose File . . . Database . . . Design Synopsis. In the Design Synopsis dialog box, shown in Figure 26-15, first select the design elements to include on the synopsis. Next, you can select Database Information, as shown in Figure 26-16. On the Content tab, shown in Figure 26-17, choose the specific details you want to display for the selected elements. If you want to see the field details (as shown), be sure to enable the Include Subcomponents option. Finally, in the Output tab (Figure 26-18), choose how to display the results of the Design Synopsis. If you choose to write the output to a database, you can also select where that database should be stored and its title and filename.

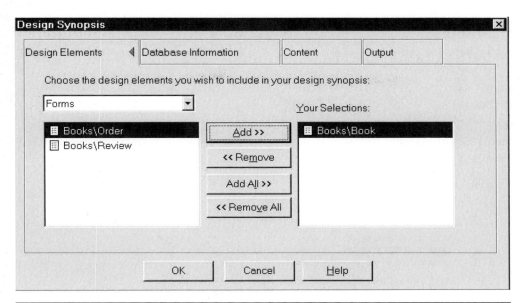

Figure 26-15   Design Synopsis dialog box

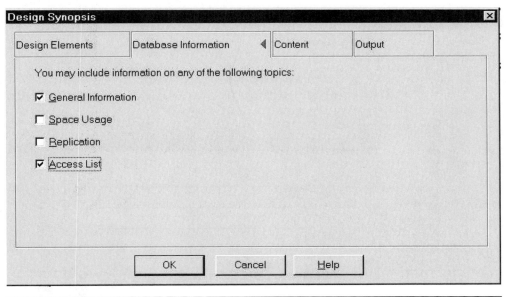

Figure 26-16   Database Information tab

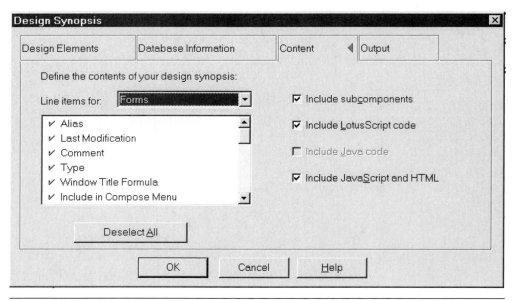

Figure 26-17 Content tab

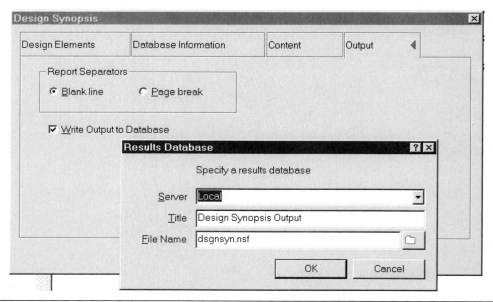

Figure 26-18 Output tab

The following tables were exported directly from the design synopsis created by Domino Designer. Each field in the three forms is shown in the table. Information available about the fields includes the name, data type, and field type (editable, computed, and so on). Any formulas are also included. Table 26-4 shows the field information for the Book form, and Table 26-5 shows the field information for the Order form. Table 26-6 shows the field information for the Review form, and Table 26-7 describes the database's shared fields. Note that some information, such as hide-when, is not included in the design synopsis. Refer to the forms included on the CD-ROM for those details.

Table 26-4   Book Form Fields

Field:	BookTitle
Datatype:	Text
Help Description:	[Not Assigned]
Field Type:	Editable
Sign When Mailing/In Section:	No
Encryption:	Disabled
Update Requires Editor Access:	No
Is Scripted:	No
Field:	**BAuthor**
Datatype:	Text
Help Description:	[Not Assigned]
Field Type:	Editable
Sign When Mailing/In Section:	No
Encryption:	Disabled
Update Requires Editor Access:	No
Is Scripted:	No
Field:	**BDescr**
Datatype:	Text
Help Description:	[Not Assigned]

continued

PART IV

Table 26-4   Book Form Fields (*continued*)

Field Type:	Editable
Sign When Mailing/In Section:	No
Encryption:	Disabled
Update Requires Editor Access:	No
Is Scripted:	No
Field:	**BPub**
Datatype:	Keywords
Help Description:	[Not Assigned]
Field Type:	Editable
Keyword User Interface:	Standard
Allow Values Not In List:	Yes
Allowable Keywords:	McGraw-Hill
	Duke Communications
	IDG
Sign When Mailing/In Section:	No
Encryption:	Disabled
Update Requires Editor Access:	No
Is Scripted:	No
Field:	**Date**
Datatype:	Time
Time Format:	10/1999
Input Multi-Value Separator(s):	Semicolon
Display Multi-Value Separator:	Semicolon
Help Description:	[Not Assigned]
Field Type:	Editable
Sign When Mailing/In Section:	No
Encryption:	Disabled
Update Requires Editor Access:	No

continued

Table 26-4   Book Form Fields (*continued*)

Default Value Formula:	"Month, Year"
Is Scripted:	No
Field:	**ISBN**
Datatype:	Text
Help Description:	[Not Assigned]
Field Type:	Editable
Sign When Mailing/In Section:	No
Encryption:	Disabled
Update Requires Editor Access:	No
Is Scripted:	No
Field:	**TOC**
Datatype:	Rich Text
Help Description:	[Not Assigned]
Field Type:	Editable
Sign When Mailing/In Section:	No
Encryption:	Disabled
Update Requires Editor Access:	No
Is Scripted:	No

Table 26-5   Order Form Fields

Shared Field Reference:	**dispBkTitle**
Shared Field Reference:	**dispBkAuthor**
Field:	**OrderNo**
Datatype:	Number
Number Format:	General
Percentage (value * 100)%:	No
Parentheses on Negative Numbers:	No

continued

Table 26-5   Order Form Fields (*continued*)

Punctuated at Thousands:	No
Help Description:	[Not Assigned]
Field Type:	Editable
Sign When Mailing/In Section:	No
Encryption:	Disabled
Update Requires Editor Access:	No
Default Value Formula:	I
Is Scripted:	No
Field:	**Pay**
Datatype:	Keywords
Help Description:	[Not Assigned]
Field Type:	Editable
Keyword User Interface:	Radio Buttons
Allowable Keywords:	Credit Card|0
	Check|I
Sign When Mailing/In Section:	No
Encryption:	Disabled
Update Requires Editor Access:	No
Is Scripted:	No
Field:	**$Payment**
Datatype:	Number
Number Format:	General
Percentage (value * 100)%:	No
Parentheses on Negative Numbers:	No
Punctuated at Thousands:	No
Help Description:	[Not Assigned]
Field Type:	Computed
Sign When Mailing/In Section:	No

continued

Table 26-5 Order Form Fields (*continued*)

Encryption:	Disabled
Update Requires Editor Access:	No
Formula:	@If(Pay = "0"; 0; @If(Pay = "1"; 1; 2));
Is Scripted:	No
Field:	**CardType**
Datatype:	Keywords
Help Description:	[Not Assigned]
Field Type:	Editable
Keyword User Interface:	Standard
Allow Values Not In List:	No
Allowable Keywords:	Amex|1
	Visa/MC|2
	Discover|3
Sign When Mailing/In Section:	No
Encryption:	Disabled
Update Requires Editor Access:	No
Is Scripted:	No
Field:	**CardNo**
Datatype:	Text
Help Description:	[Not Assigned]
Field Type:	Editable
Sign When Mailing/In Section:	No
Encryption:	Disabled
Update Requires Editor Access:	No
Is Scripted:	No
Field:	**ExpireDate**
Datatype:	Time
Time Format:	10/1999

continued

PART IV

Table 26-5   Order Form Fields (*continued*)

Help Description:	[Not Assigned]
Field Type:	Editable
Sign When Mailing/In Section:	No
Encryption:	Disabled
Update Requires Editor Access:	No
Is Scripted:	No
Field:	**CardName**
Datatype:	Text
Help Description:	[Not Assigned]
Field Type:	Editable
Sign When Mailing/In Section:	No
Encryption:	Disabled
Update Requires Editor Access:	No
Is Scripted:	No
Field:	**CardAddress**
Datatype:	Text
Help Description:	[Not Assigned]
Field Type:	Editable
Sign When Mailing/In Section:	No
Encryption:	Disabled
Update Requires Editor Access:	No
Is Scripted:	No
Field:	**CardCity**
Datatype:	Text
Help Description:	[Not Assigned]
Field Type:	Editable
Sign When Mailing/In Section:	No
Encryption:	Disabled

continued

Table 26-5   Order Form Fields (*continued*)

Update Requires Editor Access:	No
Is Scripted:	No
Field:	**CardState**
Datatype:	Keywords
Help Description:	[Not Assigned]
Field Type:	Editable
Keyword User Interface:	Standard
Allow Values Not In List:	No
Sign When Mailing/In Section:	No
Encryption:	Disabled
Update Requires Editor Access:	No
Is Scripted:	No
Field:	**CardZip**
Datatype:	Text
Help Description:	[Not Assigned]
Field Type:	Editable
Sign When Mailing/In Section:	No
Encryption:	Disabled
Update Requires Editor Access:	No
Is Scripted:	No
Field:	**ShipToCard**
Datatype:	Keywords
Help Description:	[Not Assigned]
Field Type:	Editable
Keyword User Interface:	Radio Buttons
Allowable Keywords:	No|0
	Yes|1
Sign When Mailing/In Section:	No

continued

Table 26-5   Order Form Fields (*continued*)

Encryption:	Disabled
Update Requires Editor Access:	No
Is Scripted:	No
Field:	**ShipName**
Datatype:	Text
Help Description:	[Not Assigned]
Field Type:	Editable
Sign When Mailing/In Section:	No
Encryption:	Disabled
Update Requires Editor Access:	No
Is Scripted:	No
Field:	**ShipAddr**
Datatype:	Text
Help Description:	[Not Assigned]
Field Type:	Editable
Sign When Mailing/In Section:	No
Encryption:	Disabled
Update Requires Editor Access:	No
Is Scripted:	No
Field:	**ShipCity**
Datatype:	Text
Help Description:	[Not Assigned]
Field Type:	Editable
Sign When Mailing/In Section:	No
Encryption:	Disabled
Update Requires Editor Access:	No
Is Scripted:	No
Field:	**ShipState**

continued

Table 26-5   Order Form Fields (*continued*)

Datatype:	Text
Help Description:	[Not Assigned]
Field Type:	Editable
Sign When Mailing/In Section:	No
Encryption:	Disabled
Update Requires Editor Access:	No
Is Scripted:	No
Field:	**ShipZip**
Datatype:	Text
Help Description:	[Not Assigned]
Field Type:	Editable
Sign When Mailing/In Section:	No
Encryption:	Disabled
Update Requires Editor Access:	No
Is Scripted:	No
Field:	**ShipPhone**
Datatype:	Text
Help Description:	[Not Assigned]
Field Type:	Editable
Sign When Mailing/In Section:	No
Encryption:	Disabled
Update Requires Editor Access:	No
Is Scripted:	No
Field:	**ShipEMail**
Datatype:	Text
Help Description:	[Not Assigned]
Field Type:	Editable
Sign When Mailing/In Section:	No

continued

Table 26-5 Order Form Fields (*continued*)

Encryption:	Disabled
Update Requires Editor Access:	No
Input Validation Formula:	va :=
	@ValidateInternetAddress([Address821];
	ShipEMail);@If(va = null; @Success;
	@Failure(va));
Is Scripted:	No

Table 26-6 Review Form Fields

Shared Field Reference:	**dispBkTitle**
Shared Field Reference:	**dispBkAuthor**
Field:	**Reviewer**
Datatype:	Author Names
Help Description:	[Not Assigned]
Field Type:	Editable
Sign When Mailing/In Section:	No
Encryption:	Disabled
Update Requires Editor Access:	No
Default Value Formula:	@Name([CN]; @UserName);
Is Scripted:	No
Field:	**ReviewedOn**
Datatype:	Time
Time Format:	10/17/1999
Input Multi-Value Separator(s):	Semicolon
Display Multi-Value Separator:	Semicolon
Help Description:	[Not Assigned]
Field Type:	Editable

continued

Table 26-6   Review Form Fields (*continued*)

Sign When Mailing/In Section:	No
Encryption:	Disabled
Update Requires Editor Access:	No
Default Value Formula:	@Created
Is Scripted:	No
Field:	**Rating**
Datatype:	Keywords
Help Description:	[Not Assigned]
Field Type:	Editable
Keyword User Interface:	Radio Buttons
Allowable Keywords:	*
	**
	***
	****
Sign When Mailing/In Section:	No
Encryption:	Disabled
Update Requires Editor Access:	No
Is Scripted:	No
Field:	Review
Datatype:	Rich Text
Help Description:	[Not Assigned]
Field Type:	Editable
Sign When Mailing/In Section:	No
Encryption:	Disabled
Update Requires Editor Access:	No
Is Scripted:	No
Field:	**Otherbooks**
Datatype:	Text

continued

PART IV

Table 26-6 Review Form Fields (*continued*)

Input Multi-Value Separator(s):	Comma, Semicolon
Display Multi-Value Separator:	Semicolon
Help Description:	[Not Assigned]
Field Type:	Editable
Sign When Mailing/In Section:	No
Encryption:	Disabled
Update Requires Editor Access:	No
Is Scripted:	No

Table 26-7 Shared Fields

Field:	dispBkAuthor
Datatype:	Text
Help Description:	[Not Assigned]
Field Type:	Computed when Composed
Sign When Mailing/In Section:	No
Encryption:	Disabled
Update Requires Editor Access:	No
Formula:	Bauthor
Is Scripted:	No
Last Modification:	10/17/99 02:38:59 PM
Field:	**dispBkTitle**
Datatype:	Text
Help Description:	[Not Assigned]
Field Type:	Computed when Composed
Sign When Mailing/In Section:	No
Encryption:	Disabled
Update Requires Editor Access:	No
Formula:	BookTitle
Is Scripted:	No
Last Modification:	10/17/99 02:38:55 PM

Figure 26-19 shows the Order form and Figure 26-20 shows the Review form. You can also access these forms and their fields in the CH26.NSF database, which is included on the CD-ROM.

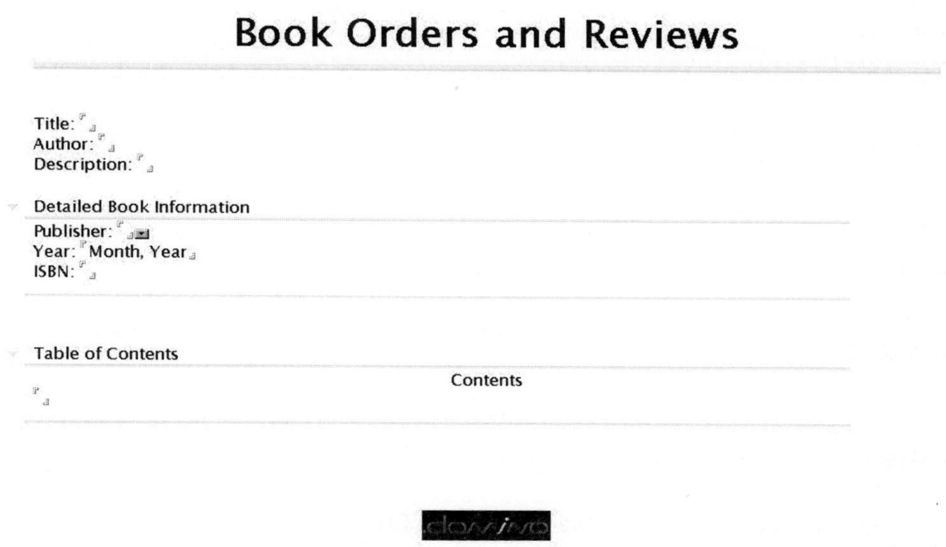

Book Orders and Reviews

Title: *⌐
Author: *⌐
Description: *⌐

~ Detailed Book Information
   Publisher: *⌐
   Year: *Month, Year⌐
   ISBN: *⌐

~ Table of Contents

                                    Contents
      *
      ⌐

domino

Figure 26-19   Order form

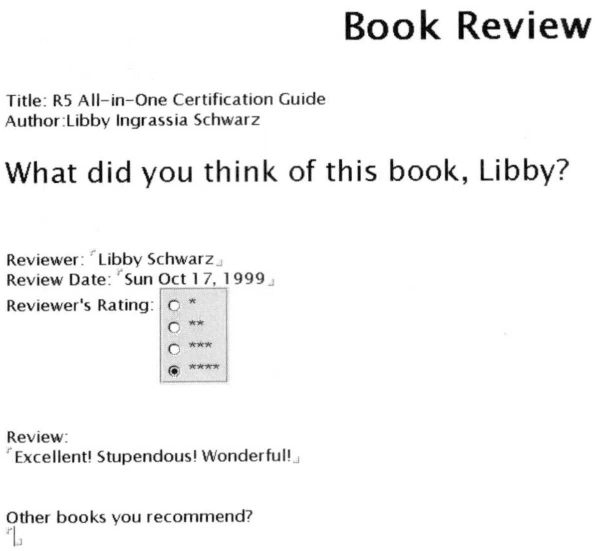

Book Review

Title: R5 All-in-One Certification Guide
Author:Libby Ingrassia Schwarz

What did you think of this book, Libby?

Reviewer: ⌜Libby Schwarz⌟
Review Date: ⌜Sun Oct 17, 1999⌟
Reviewer's Rating:
- ○ *
- ○ **
- ○ ***
- ◉ ****

Review:
⌜Excellent! Stupendous! Wonderful!⌟

Other books you recommend?
⌜ ⌟

Figure 26-20 Review form

Review Questions

1. Eric has decided that he wants to display the first and last name of the current user in the WrittenBy field. He uses a Computed when Composed Names type field. Which formula should he place in the value event for this field?
    a. @UserName
    b. @Name([CN];@UserName)
    c. @Name
    d. @Name([LP];@UserName)

2. Nandita wants to create a field that enables Web users to format text as the text is typed. What type of field does she create?
    a. Rich Text field, with Display Using HTML on Web access selected
    b. Rich Text field, with Display Using Java applet on Web access selected
    c. Text field, with Display using HTML on Web access selected
    d. Text field, with Display Using Java applet on Web access selected

3. Andy wants to capture the employee's department, which is contained in the OU of the hierarchical ID, on the two main forms in his Employee Suggestions database. He wants to minimize the number of fields in his database and work as efficiently as possible. What is the best way for him to capture that information and reuse the definition of the field he creates?

    a. Use a single-use text field on the first form. Use the formula @Name([OU]; @UserName). Enable inheritance on the second form, and create a computed field that uses the field name from the first form as its value.

    b. Use a single-use text field on the first form. Use the formula @Name([HierarchyOnly]; @UserName). Enable inheritance on the second form, and create a computed field that uses the field name from the first form as its value.

    c. Create a shared field. Use the formula @Name([OU];@UserName). Insert the shared field on both forms.

    d. Create a shared field. Use the formula @Name([HierarchyOnly]; @UserName). Insert the shared field on both forms.

4. Cynthia wants to force a document to expire one month after its creation—if its status is completed—and after 45 days otherwise. She is creating an ExpireOn field based on the creation date. Which of the formulas does she use?

    a. `@If (Status= "Completed"; @Adjust (@Created; 0;1;0;0;0; 0); @Adjust (@Created; 0;0;45;0;0;0))`

    b. `@If (Status= Completed; @Adjust (@Created; 0;1;0;0;0;0); @Adjust (@Created; 0;0;45;0;0;0))`

    c. `@If (Status= "Completed"; @Adjust (@Created; 1); @Adjust (@Created; 45))`

    d. `@If (Status= "Completed"; @Adjust (@Created; 1;0;0;0;0; 0); @Adjust (@Created; 0;45;0;0;0;0))`

5. Urvish is creating an application that will be used in multiple countries. He wants to be sure that he captures the user's alternate name and alternate language. What formulas does he use?

    a. `@Name(0) and @UserNameLanguage(0)`

    b. `@Name([1];@UserName) and @UserNameLanguage(1)`

    c. `@UserName(1) and @UserNameLanguage(1)`

    d. `@AlternateName(1) and @AlternateLanguage(1)`

6. Gretchen wants to use proper case on the BookTitle field, even if her users forget to enter the value that way. What formula should she use, and where should she put the formula?

   a. Use @ProperCase(BookTitle) in the Default Value event of the BookTitle field.

   b. Use @ProperCase(BookTitle) in the Input Translation event of the BookTitle field.

   c. Use @ProperCase(BookTitle) in the Input Validation event of the BookTitle field.

   d. Use @ProperCase(BookTitle) in the onBlur event of the BookTitle field.

7. Cary has created a formula that has the correct syntax but causes an error at run time. Which of the following pieces of information does the Designer Error dialog box give him when he previews the form?

   a. The name of the field with the error

   b. The name of the form with the error

   c. The code number of the error

   d. The description of the problem

8. Which of the following would you use in an editable field to show the date the document was created?

   a. @Today

   b. @Now

   c. @Created

   d. @Date

9. For which of the following field types can you use Native OS style?

   a. Dialog List

   b. Text

   c. Rich Text

   d. Date/Time

10. What does the following formula return when the assignment is completed? What does it return when the assignment is not completed? Assume that Caroline Smith/East/Acme creates the document on January 1, 2000 at 2:30 P.M.

```
@If(Status="Completed"; "Thank You, "+ @Left(@Name([CN]; @User-
Name); " ")+". You have completed the assignment."; "Please com-
plete the assignment by " +
@Text(@Adjust(@Created;0;0;1;12;0;0)))
```

a. Returns the text string, *Thank You, Caroline Smith/East/Acme. You have completed the assignment.* when the assignment is complete. Otherwise, it returns the text string, *Please complete the assignment by January 3, 2000 2:30 AM.*

b. Returns the text string, *Thank You, Caroline Smith. You have completed the assignment.* when the assignment is complete. Otherwise, it returns the text string, *Please complete the assignment by January 2, 2000 2:30 AM.*

c. Returns the text string, *Thank You, Caroline. You have completed the assignment.* when the assignment is complete. Otherwise, it returns the text string, *Please complete the assignment by January 3, 2000 2:30 AM.*

d. Returns the text string *Thank You, Caroline Smith/East/Acme. You have completed the assignment.* when the assignment is complete. Otherwise, it returns an error.

Review Answers

1. **B is correct.** @UserName would show the fully distinguished name, although it would not show the labels for the hierarchical elements.

2. **B is correct.** She needs to create a rich-text field that uses the Java Editor applet when accessed by Web browsers.

3. **C is correct.** He wants to capture the field definition, not the field value, so he needs to use a Shared field. He also wants only the Organizational Unit (OU).

4. **A is correct.** Choice B forgets the quotation marks around the value of the Status field. Choice C does not remember to use all of the arguments in the @Adjust function. Choice D places the 1 and the 45 in the wrong positions.

5. **C is correct.** @UserName and @UserNameLanguage both use the argument (1) to work with the alternate name or language.

6. **B is correct.** Use the Input Translation event for editing the values placed in the field by users.

7. **A and D are correct.** When Designer describes logic errors at run time, such as when previewing a form, it indicates the name of the field with the error and a description of the problem.

8. **C is correct.** @Today and @Now will change to match the current information as shown by the system clock. @Date is used to translate numbers to a date value.

9. **B and D are correct.** You cannot use Native OS style for Dialog lists (or any keyword type fields) or for rich-text fields.

10. **C is correct.** If the Status field is set to Completed, the formula takes the username from the current ID, pulls the common name, and then takes the portion of the common name that is to the left of a space—the first name—and places the name between the other text strings. If the Status is anything but completed, the formula takes the date and time the document was created and adds one day and 12 hours. The formula then turns that value to text and displays it with the rest of the text string.

CHAPTER 27

Creating Views, Columns, and Folders

You should be able to answer questions based on the following objectives after reading this chapter:

- Create, modify, and troubleshoot views
- Create, modify, and troubleshoot columns

You have spent the last two chapters creating and enhancing forms, fields, and formulas—all for the purpose of obtaining and displaying information. Users will create documents using these forms. You can bet that after they create those documents, they will want to be able to access them. Users can access the documents in the database via lists. In Notes, a view is a list of the documents in the database. Without a view, you cannot access the data that users have added to the database. Views can show all documents in a database or specific documents based on a selection formula. Views in Notes databases compare somewhat to queries in relational databases. In Notes databases, however, views are predefined queries rather than ad-hoc queries. The designer of a database creates the views, designs the format of the views, determines how the views will be organized, and chooses the documents that will be displayed. Another Notes design element that displays lists of documents is a *folder*. In this chapter, we discuss how to create and modify views and folders, how to understand the different types of views and folders, and how to use these elements within Notes.

View Basics

Views list the documents in a database and organize them by two main elements: rows and columns. Each row represents one of the documents in the database. A column represents a field, a combination of fields, or another type of information. You will find one or more views in each database. A view index—an internal system maintained by Domino—actually determines the order of documents in the views.

Folders are similar to views in design and purpose. The main difference between the two is the manner in which documents are selected for them. For a view, designers select the documents by using a selection formula. In a folder, users choose the documents that will be available there by dragging or copying them. When a document appears in a folder, Notes does not remove the document from the view from which it was copied. If a user deletes a document from a folder, however, Notes deletes the document from the entire database. Both views and folders are displayed in the Navigation pane on the left side of a Notes database. Shown here are views and folders in the Navigation pane of a test database:

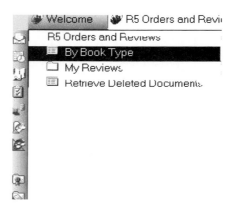

A designer must understand what is important about the documents in a database, to know what to show in a view. Decide on the purpose for the view before creating the view. Knowing the purpose of the view helps you to decide which type of view to create, to determine which properties to give the view, and to understand how to design and define the columns in the view. The following sections describe these elements of creating a view.

Creating a View

Similar to when you created a form, you have a variety of methods available for creating a view (or a folder). You can copy a view from the current database or from another database, and alternatively, you can create a view from scratch. To copy a view from the current database, you can create a new view and inherit the design features of the original view. The steps for creating a new view are listed as follows:

1. Choose Create . . . View . . . from the menus, or click the New View action button.

2. This action displays the Create View dialog box, which is displayed in Figure 27-1.

3. Give the view a descriptive name. You should also give the view an alias (similar to a form name's synonym) to make changing the name or using the view name in formulas easier. The view's name can be up to 64 characters, including the alias. The name is case-sensitive and can include any characters, including letters, numbers, and spaces. The view names, similar to form names, can also be cascaded to organize the View menu for users. To create an alias (synonym) in this dialog box, use the pipe or vertical bar symbol (|) between the name you want displayed to the users and the name to use internally (alias). To cascade names from the View menu, use the backslash symbol (\) between the name you want to group views under and the view name.

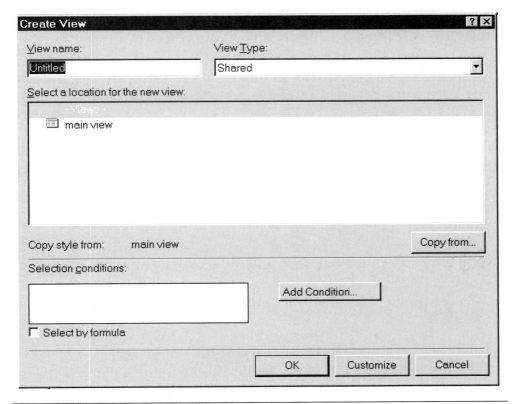

Figure 27-1   The Create View dialog box

4. In the View Type drop-down list, select the view type. The following are the types of views that are available in Notes:

handwritten margin note: 3 not in "create folders option"

- Shared

- Shared, contains documents not in any folder

- Shared, contains deleted documents

- Shared, private on first use

- Shared, desktop private on first use

- Private

For more information about these view types, refer to the View Types section. Bear in mind that this is the only opportunity to choose the view type (it cannot be changed later).

5. Select a location for the view by clicking the folder or view where you want to store this view. To store the view at the top level, just leave the word Views selected. To store the view under another view, select a view in the *Select a location for the new view* field.

6. To copy the design for the new view from another view, choose the Copy From button. When Designer displays the Copy From dialog box, select the view to copy.

7. To select which documents will be displayed in this view, use a selection formula. This formula can be created in this dialog box, either by using simple selection conditions created in the Search Builder window or by creating a custom selection formula. To open the Search Builder window, shown in Figure 27-2, click the Add Condition . . . button. Then add the appropriate condition, based on author, field, form, form used, or date. You could select all documents based on the author, for example, for a shared, personal, or first-use view. Alternatively, you could select a view based on the form used. Custom selection formulas are described later in this chapter.

8. Click OK to create the view. If you did not choose to copy the view appearance from another view, click the Customize button to go directly to Design mode. If not, you will be able to open the view from the Design . . . Views view to begin editing the view.

Creating folders is essentially the same as creating views. Choose Create . . . Folder. Give the folder a name, and choose whether the folder is Shared, Private, Shared, Private on first use, or Shared, Desktop private on first use. Click the Copy From button to

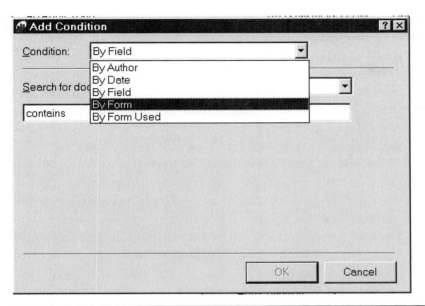

Figure 27-2   Add Condition dialog box

inherit the design of a particular view or folder. Click the Customize button to design the folder. No selection options are available on a Create Folder dialog box.

View Types: Shared Views

A designer creates a shared view for the use of many users—in general, any user who has reader access in the ACL. Most often, the shared view is available in the Navigation pane and in the View menu for easy access. Views can also be hidden, however, by placing the name in parentheses. The shared view will be stored in the database. Users must have Editor (with the Create Shared Folders/Views right), Designer, or Manager access to the database to create shared views. Two special shared views are Shared, contains documents not in any folders and Shared, contains deleted documents. These two view types do not require an additional selection formula, because the selection formula is predefined by the type. Use the Shared, contains documents not in any folders to recover lost documents—especially as you create complicated selection formulas. Use the Shared, contains deleted documents formula in combination with the Allow soft deletions database property. You will also need to set the $Undelete Expire time (in hours) on the Database properties InfoBox. This feature enables you to create a view from which mistakenly deleted documents can be recovered. After enabling soft deletions, setting the Undelete time period, and creating a view that contains the soft-deleted documents, create a view action that enables those documents to be recovered by using the @UndeleteDocument function.

Two other special Shared views are the Shared, private on first use and Shared, desktop private on first use. Create these types of views (usually with the @UserName function) to give personal views to users without forcing them to create the views themselves. The view starts as a shared view that is stored in the database. When a user opens the view, the view becomes private. If the view is the Shared, private on first use, it will be stored in the database if the user has the Create Personal Folders/Views right in the ACL. If the user does not have this right, the private view is stored in the user's DESKTOP.DSK. Notes also stores all Shared, desktop private on first use views in the DESKTOP.DSK. One item to note for the exam is that the view is no longer updated with changes made by the developer after the view has become private. To see any changes after opening the view, the user will have to delete the private version of the view and open the Shared version again.

 NOTE Note that Shared, private on first use views are not security measures. Even if you use a selection formula to omit certain documents from the view, a user can create a private view that shows all documents in the database.

View Types: Private Views

Private views are created and used by only one user. Users who have reader access or higher can create private views. The storage for a private view is determined by the Create Personal Folders/Views option on the ACL dialog box. Although this type of view is usually stored in the workstation's DESKTOP.DSK file, if this checkbox is enabled, the view will be stored in the database.

Similarly, there are Shared, Private, Shared, private on first use, and Shared, desktop private on first use folders. These folders have the same elements and characteristics of the views. Again, the main difference between views and folders is the manner in which documents are selected for them. Views use selection formulas. Users move or copy documents into folders.

Calendar = View

View Properties InfoBox

After you create the view, you should define it further by using the View properties InfoBox. This dialog box sets the default options for the Views you create.

The View Info Tab

Use the View Info tab to name (or rename) the view. Although you might have already given the view a name when you created it, this tab, shown next, enables you to rename the view, to create an alias (synonym) for the view, and to create a comment about the view.

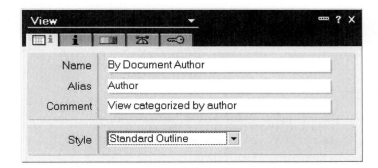

- **Name**   Use this field to give the field a new name if necessary. The name is case-sensitive and can include any characters, including letters, numbers, and spaces. To display cascading names from the View menu, use the backslash (/) symbol in the same way that cascading form names were created previously.

- **Alias**   Use the Alias field to create an alias for the view, although an alias can also be created by using the pipe or vertical bar (|) symbol in the Name field. The view alias, like a form alias, enables the name of the view to be translated or changed without changing any formulas that might use the view name.

- **Comment**   Use this field to comment on the view or purpose of the view.

- **Style** Use this option to choose between a standard outline-view style and a Calendar-Style design. When you choose to create a Calendar-Style view, Designer changes options on some of the other tabs as well, as shown here:

The Options Tab

Use the Options tab on the View properties InfoBox, shown here, to set some of the default attributes for the view:

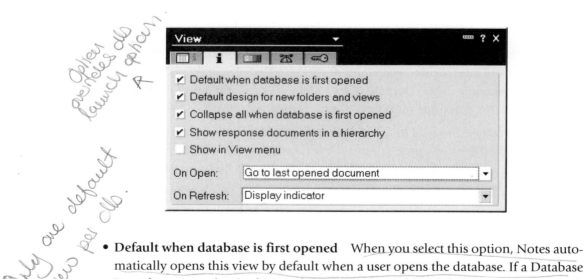

- **Default when database is first opened** When you select this option, Notes automatically opens this view by default when a user opens the database. If a Database Launch property (set in the Database properties InfoBox) defines a navigator with a particular view or another automatic launch option, Notes ignores this option. Only one default view is permitted per database. Notes indicates the default view with an asterisk (*).

- **Default design for new folders and views**   Select this option to make the current view the default design for any new views or folders that are created in this database. In other words, new views and folders will automatically inherit design elements from this view. The designer can choose another view from which to inherit by clicking the Options button when creating a new view.

- **Collapse all when database is first opened**   If documents are grouped by using categories in the view, this option forces all of the categories to be collapsed—hiding the documents—when the database is first opened. Categories are discussed in greater depth later in this chapter. This option is not available for Calendar-Style views.

- **Show response documents in a hierarchy**   This option is one of the requirements necessary to show the response type and response-to-response type documents in the view, indented under their Parent documents. This option is not available for Calendar-Style views.

- **Show in view menu**   This option determines whether the view is listed in the View menu. In R5, the Navigator pane is often used instead of the View menu.

- **On open**   The On Open options determine what is automatically displayed when the view opens. This setting can affect how quickly the view is opened when selected by a user, especially in the case of databases that have a large number of documents. These options include the following:

  - **Go to last opened document**   When the view is opened, the last document that the user had opened is displayed in the view. This setting is the default.

  - **Go to top row**   This option displays the first document in the view each time that the view is opened.

  - **Go to bottom row**   This option displays the last document in the view each time that the view is opened.

- **On Refresh**   Each view displays the results of an internal view index. This index is an internal list that tracks the order and number of documents that should appear in this view. As documents are changed, deleted, and added, the view index changes. The view index must be refreshed to display the changes in the view. The speed of using the view can be affected by this setting. This option sets the view to refresh in one of the following ways:

  - **Display indicator**   With this option, a blue circular arrow refresh indicator is displayed in the upper left-hand corner of the view when the view needs to be refreshed. When the indicator is displayed, the user can either click the indicator or press F9 to update the view.

- **Refresh display** This option forces the view to refresh itself automatically when changes are made.

- **Refresh display from top row** This option forces the view to refresh automatically, beginning with the first (top) document in the view.

- **Refresh display from bottom row** This option forces the view to refresh automatically, beginning with the last (bottom) document in the view.

The options to open the view and to refresh the display from the top row and bottom row should be chosen based on how the view is organized. If the view is sorted based on a date column, for example, documents will be added either to the top or to the bottom of the view when they are created. If the newest documents appear at the top first, open from the top of the view and then refresh from the top of the view (and vice-versa).

The Style Tab

The Style tab, shown next, enables the developer to create the visual presentation of the view, including the background, columns and rows, and titles:

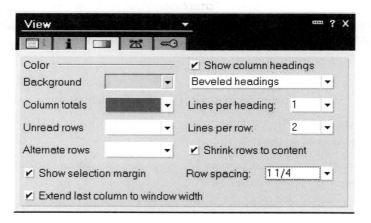

- **Background** Choose a color for the background of the view. By default, the view background is white.

- **Column Totals** Create a separate color for the background of the columns that have the Total option set. The Total option adds the values in a column and creates a total. By default, this option is displayed in dark gray.

- **Unread rows** If the designer chooses to display unread marks by using the Advanced tab, this option enables those documents that are unread to be displayed in a different color. The color is black by default.

- **Alternate Rows**   Use this option to display every other document (row) in the view in a different background color. This option is disabled by default.

- **Show Selection Margin**   The margin to the left of the documents that enables the user to select multiple documents is the selection margin. Use this option to determine whether multiple documents are displayed in the view. If this option is disabled, a user can still select multiple documents by using SHIFT+Click. When a user selects more than one document, Notes displays the selection margin automatically. This option is enabled by default.

- **Extend last column to window width**   This option forces the last column in the view to extend to the far right of the window, regardless of column or view widths.

- **Show column headings**   Use this option to determine whether the column headings will be displayed in the view. By default, the column headings are displayed.

- **Heading Display Type**   When the Show column headings option is selected, use this option to determine whether Notes displays the headings as simple headings or beveled headings. Simple headings use the background color of the view to display the column headings, whereas beveled headings use a gray three-dimensional effect to display the headings.

- **Lines per heading**   When the Show column headings option is enabled, use this option to determine the number of lines that will be available for the column heading. If the column headings are longer or consist of multiple words, this setting enables them to use more than one line. This feature lets more columns fit in the view. This setting can be from 1 to 5.

- **Lines per row**   Use this option to enable each row to spread over multiple lines. In a case where an address or a large amount of text will be displayed in the view, this feature enables the lines to take more than one line to display each document. This setting can be from 1 to 9.

- **Shrink Rows to content**   When the Lines per Row option is set to more than one, use this option to shrink rows to fit the content. This feature enables those rows that do not need more than one line to display the data in a smaller format, saving space on the screen. This option ensures that only the necessary lines, up to the number specified in the Lines per Row option, are used for display.

- **Row spacing**   This option enables additional space to be inserted between rows for clarity. Especially in cases where long lines of text are being displayed in a view, having some extra space between the lines makes reading the view easier for users. The settings for this option can be Single, 1-1/4, 1-1/2, 1-3/4, and Double spaced.

When the view is in the Calendar Style instead of the default outline style, Designer presents different options on this tab. Options for Calendar-Style views include a date background color, busy rows color, colors for non-month views, and showing conflict marks.

The Font Tab

Designer displays the Font tab, shown next, only when the view is in the calendar style. The options on the Font tab set the font face, style, color, and size for the time slots, headers, and day and date information in the Calendar-Style view.

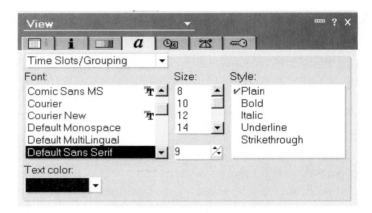

The Date and Time Format Tab

Designer only displays the Date and Time Format tab, shown here, for Calendar-Style views. Use this tab to enable time slots and time grouping and to determine the initial and allowed formats of the Calendar view.

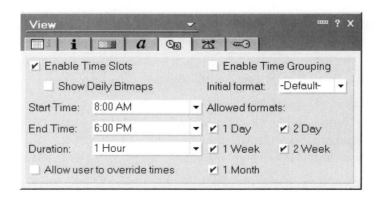

The Advanced Tab

The Advanced tab sets additional options for the view, as displayed in Figure 27-3, related to indexing, unread marks, and how the view should be displayed to Web browsers.

- **Refresh index** The view index, as described previously, is the internal list that enables Notes to determine internally which documents should be in each view. This option enables the designer to determine the refresh rate of the View index. The options for the index refresh rate are described as follows:

  - **Auto, after first use** This option forces the index to refresh every time the view is opened after the first time the view is opened. This option is the default. Changes are added to the view index incrementally, as they are made—which is easy for the users, because they never have to be concerned about the accuracy of the view. The views can take longer to open, however, as changes are written to the view index. *[handwritten: accuracy not crucial.]*

  - **Automatic** This option is similar to the default option in that the index is refreshed automatically. The user does not have to open the view for the index to update, however, as in the default. This feature ensures that changes are reflected in the views and that views open more quickly. *[handwritten: changes reflected]*

Figure 27-3
The Advanced tab

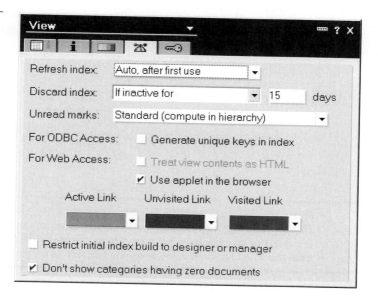

- **Manual**   This option forces the user to be responsible for updating the view. In the case of a large database that does not change regularly, this option might be a good choice, because it will enable the database to open more quickly.

- **Auto, at most every x hours**   This option is the compromise that enables the view index to refresh automatically, based on a schedule. If a large database changes often, this option enables the database to open quickly and to be updated on a regular basis. If the database has changed since the last update, the refresh icon will be displayed for the user to update the view manually.

- **Discard index**   This option determines when the view index for this view will be deleted. Whenever the index is deleted, the user will have to wait while a new index is generated, which can take several minutes. The Updall task on the server deletes the view index based on the Discard Index settings. When Updall runs (at 2 A.M. by default), it deletes the indexes. The reason for deleting a view index is usually related to disk-space savings. The options for discarding the view index are described in the following paragraphs:

  - **Never**   If the designer selects this option, the view index is never deleted. Changes to the view index are made to the existing index, which ensures that the users do not have to wait for the view index to be created when they open the view. This option, however, uses more disk space than the other options. This option should be selected for frequently used views.

  - **After each use**   This option deletes the view index each time the database is closed, which forces the user to wait for the view to rebuild each time the view is opened. While this option might save some disk space, it should only be used for infrequently used views.

  - **If inactive for x days**   This option enables the designer to compromise between the speed and disk savings and enables the designer to set a number of days of inactivity, after which the view index will be deleted. If the view index has been deleted, the user will have to wait while the index is recreated when the view is opened.

NOTE   Users always have the capability to refresh the view by pressing F9 or by clicking the refresh indicator. The refresh indicator will appear any time changes are made to the database but have not been updated in the view. The refresh indicator is a blue curved arrow on the left side of the column headings.

- **Unread marks**   On the Style tab, the designer chooses whether unread rows are displayed in a different color. Use these options to determine how unread marks will be tracked in the database:

  - **None**   This option, which is the default, does not show a special indicator for unread documents in the database. This option uses the least processor overhead and therefore opens the view the fastest. Use this option if the read or unread status is not significant for the documents in this database. Although Unread documents will not be visually marked, the Navigate Next or Previous Unread SmartIcons will enable the user to find unread documents in the database.

  - **Unread Documents only**   This option displays unread documents with an asterisk as well as any color options chosen by the designer on the Style tab. If the view is categorized, however, the unread marks will only appear when the category is expanded enough to display the unread documents in the view. This option is the compromise, because the unread documents open faster than in the standard option but open slower than when unread documents are not marked at all.

  - **Standard (compute in hierarchy)**   This option always displays a special indicator to notify the user about unread documents. If the documents are in a collapsed category, the asterisk and color options are displayed on the category until the category is expanded. This option uses the most processor overhead and is therefore slower to open—but gives the users the most information about the documents. This option is especially useful in categorized views that have time-sensitive material or wherever the new documents are important to the users.

- **For ODBC access: Generate Unique Keys in index**   This option assigns special, unique keys for files that obtain their data from a source external to Notes, via the Open Database Connectivity (ODBC) standard.

- **For Web access: Treat view contents as HTML** and **For Web Access: Use applet in the browser**   These two options determine how the view will be treated for Web clients. With neither option selected, Domino uses the default Web display for browser clients. By default, Web views that use the standard display have 30 lines per page (governed by the HTTP section of the server document), no selection margin, and a default navigation bar. To select a document, the user clicks the first non-categorized column, which is a link to the document. When displayed using HTML, views use show text only, with none of the Notes/Domino default links, headers, and so on. To see a more Notes-like interface, use the Java applet for Web access. The applet, shown in Figure 27-4, provides more control over expanding and collapsing categories without regenerating the page each time, resizable columns, the document selection margin, and the capability to use F9 to refresh the view. In addition, the View applet is programmable using the following @Commands:

- @Command([ViewCollapse])
- @Command([ViewExpand])
- @Command([ViewCollapseAll])
- @Command([ViewExpandAll])
- @Command([ViewRefreshFields])
- @Command([MoveToTrash])
- @Command([EmptyTrash])
- @Command([Folder])
- @Command([RemoveFromFolder])

The main benefit of the View applet is the flexibility it gives to Web users and the fact that it makes a Web user's experience more like the Notes user's experience.

Other options on this tab include the colors for the links when used on the Web. As discussed previously, it is often easiest for the user if the application's links are in the standard colors. In addition, you can Restrict initial index build to Designer or Manager. The final option on this tab is Don't show categories having zero documents.

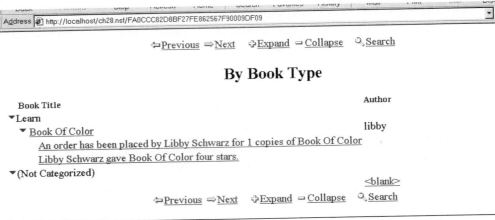

Figure 27-4   Web view using the Java applet

The Security Tab

The Security tab determines which users and groups can use this view. For more details about security, refer to Chapter 24, "Understanding and Implementing Basic Security."

Selecting Documents for the View

When designing a view, a developer must determine which documents should appear in that view. When you create the view, you can choose the documents by using the Search Builder (accessible from the Add Condition button). Additionally, either when creating the view or at any time, you can create a Selection formula to determine which documents to display in the view. The use of the Search Builder window to select documents for the view was discussed previously in this chapter. Now, let us discuss the use of custom selection formulas to select documents for the view.

To add a selection formula to a view, click the View Selection event in the Objects tab of the Info List. In the Script area, choose either Easy or Formula from the drop-down list. If you choose Easy, access the Search Builder window by clicking the Add Condition button. If you choose Formula, create the selection formula in the following formula window. By default, the selection formula is SELECT @All, which will display all documents in the database. Another option for a selection formula includes selecting by the form or forms used, for example:

```
SELECT Form = "Book" | Form = "Review"
```

This selection formula would display any documents that were created with either the form Book or the form Review (see Figure 27-5). If these forms were cascaded, you would need to include the cascaded portion of the name, unless you used an alias. When there is an alias, use the alias to create any formulas.

Another example is as follows:

```
SELECT Form = "Book" & Publisher = "McGraw-Hill"
```

Figure 27-5
Selection formula example

This selection formula displays all documents that were created with the Book form and that have the value McGraw-Hill in the Publisher field.

Also see the following example:

```
SELECT Form = "Book" | @IsResponseDoc
```

This selection formula displays all documents created with the Book form as well as all documents that are response documents. This formula would be useful when there are multiple main documents in a database.

A few @Functions are used primarily for selection formulas (or selective replication formulas). Some of these @Functions are discussed in the following paragraphs.

The @AllChildren function refers to all documents that are response documents to a particular main document. @AllChildren only refers to immediate responses of a document, not to any response-to-response documents, which are different from the @IsResponseDoc selection formula mentioned previously because the @IsResponse-Doc includes any documents created with a response or response-to-response type of form. The @AllChildren function will only return documents that respond to other documents already selected. An example of this function is as follows:

```
SELECT Form = "Main Topic" | @AllChildren
```

This selection formula displays the documents that were created with the Main Topic form and any documents that are immediate responses (or children) to those documents.

The @AllDescendants function is similar to the @AllChildren function but includes in a view the response-to-response documents that are the grandchildren to a main document. For example, look at the following formula:

```
SELECT Form = "Main Topic" | @AllDescendants
```

This selection formula includes the documents that were created with the Main Topic form, the documents that are responses to those documents, and the documents that are the responses-to-responses.

Figure 27-6 displays the differences between @IsResponseDoc, @AllChildren, and @AllDescendants.

Adding Columns to the View

After the view has been created, the appropriate documents have been selected, and the default attributes have been set, you should create and define columns for the view. The

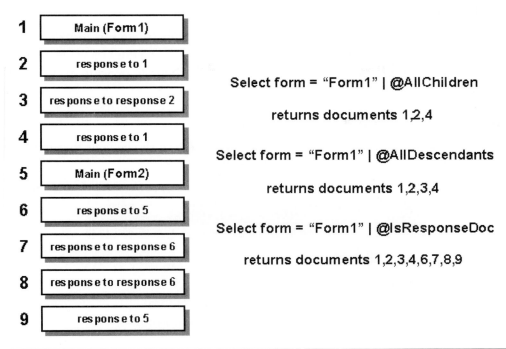

1 Main (Form1)

2 response to 1

3 response to response 2

4 response to 1

5 Main (Form2)

6 response to 5

7 response to response 6

8 response to response 6

9 response to 5

Select form = "Form1" | @AllChildren

returns documents 1,2,4

Select form = "Form1" | @AllDescendants

returns documents 1,2,3,4

Select form = "Form1" | @IsResponseDoc

returns documents 1,2,3,4,6,7,8,9

Figure 27-6   Children, responses, and descendants

columns in the view determine what information the user sees about the documents displayed in the views. Columns can be defined by a simple action, a field, or a formula. (Folder columns are created in the same way as View columns.)

To create a column in the view, there are multiple options. First, you can double-click the gray area where the column headers are displayed, which automatically creates a column and displays the Column properties InfoBox. Second, you can right-click the column header area and choose either to insert or to append a new column. You can also use the Create menu or the appropriate smart icon to add a new column.

NOTE   Inserting a column places it to the left of the current column. Appending a column places it to the right of the current column. Double-clicking to add a column appends the column. Using the Create Insert New Column Smart-Icon inserts the column.

Column Properties InfoBox

After you add the column to the view, define the column attributes by using the Column properties InfoBox and determine the contents of the column by using either a function, field, or formula. First, we will discuss the attributes to be set in the Column properties InfoBox.

The Column Info Tab

Use the Column Info tab of the Column properties InfoBox, shown here, to determine name, width, and other general style attributes of the column:

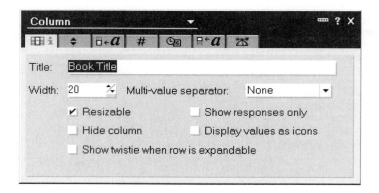

- **Title**   Use the title field to give the column a descriptive title. Keep the title to a reasonable length, because it will be cut off if the column width is not wide enough to display it all. Column titles are not required.

- **Width**   Use this option to set the default width of the column. By default, the width is set to 10. Change the width by dragging the column header or by changing this number.

- **Resizable**   Choose this option to give the user the power to change the width of the column as he or she uses the view. This setting is checked by default.

- **Hide Column**   This option hides the column from the view. Use this type of column for sorting documents.

- **Show twistie when row is expandable**   If you choose to categorize columns in the view, the categorized columns can be expanded or collapsed. This option shows the user when the category is collapsed and when it can be expanded, as well as giving the user a way to perform this action (clicking the twistie) other than using the Expand and Collapse smart icons.

- **Multi-value separator**   When a column contains multiple values per document, such as when displaying keyword choices or names, use this option to determine how the multiple values are displayed to the user. The default choice is None, which displays the data as it is stored internally. The designer can also choose to separate the multiple values with commas, spaces, semicolons, or new lines.

- **Show responses only**   This option is required to show only a response or a response-to-response type of document in a column. For example, most databases that include a discussion element will want to display the hierarchy of the main document with its children and descendants indented underneath. An example of this type of view is available in the Discussion Thread view of a database created with the discussion template, shown next. You must also select the related option of Show Response Hierarchy (in the View properties InfoBox) to create this view effect.

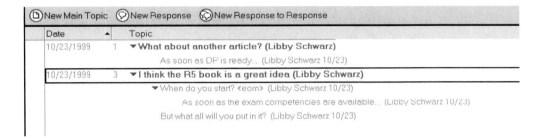

- **Display values as icons**   Notes provides 170 icons, which are available in the *Notes Application Developer's Guide*, to be displayed in a column instead of text or numbers. Use this option to indicate the type of document and the presence of attachments, for example, as in the Mail template. To display an icon, the column requires a formula that results in a number between zero and 170. The available icons are shown in Figure 27-7.

The Sorting Tab

The Sorting tab, shown in Figure 27-8, determines the order in which Notes displays the documents in the view and how Notes organizes those documents.

- **Sort**   Use the Sort option to sort documents in ascending order, descending order, or not at all. By default, columns are not sorted. Notes sorts in the following order: numbers, letters, accented letters, and punctuation or special characters.
- **Type**   If the column is sorted, this option determines whether the sort type will be Standard or Categorized. The Categorized option, which is discussed in more detail later in this chapter, enables the designer to group documents based on the values in a predefined field.

Figure 27-7
View icons

Figure 27-8
Sorting tab

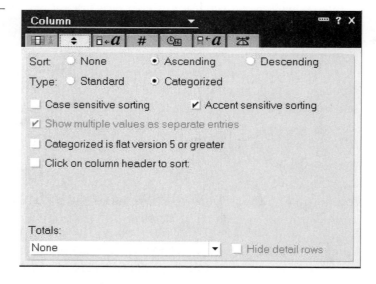

- **Case Sensitive Sorting** By default, sorting is case-insensitive. This option gives the designer the capability to enable sorting based on case.

- **Accent Sensitive Sorting**   Use this option to sort based on accented letters.

- **Show multiple values as separate entries**   Most fields in Notes (except rich text and a few keyword fields) can display multiple values in a single field. This option gives each of the multiple values its own entry in a sort.

- **Categorized is flat version 5 or greater**

- **Click on Column Header to Sort**   Use this option to enable the users to sort the data in the view at any time. The options enable the user to sort ascending, descending, or both. These options will add arrows to the column header that the user can click to sort the column. The list also contains a Change to view option, which enables the designer to designate a view to be switched to when the user clicks the column header. This option can confuse users, so it is usually a good idea to describe what will happen in the column header (for example, *click here for the By Date view*).

- **Secondary Sort Column**   If the *Click on column header to sort* option has been enabled, this option gives the user an additional sorting column and refines the sorting order without requiring any user action.

- **Totals**   This option enables the values in a column to be totaled. Options in this drop-down list include the following: *Total, Average per document, Average per subcategory, Percent of parent category*, and *Percent of all documents*.

The Text Tab

Use the Text tab, shown next, to determine how the text in the columns will be formatted. After selecting the font, size, style, color, and justification, the designer can also click the Apply to All button to apply the formatting to all columns in the view.

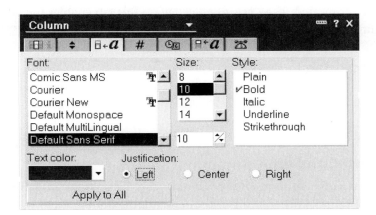

The Numbers Tab

Use the Numbers tab to select the style and formatting of numbers used in the columns. This setting can include the currency style for columns that display dollar amounts as well as parentheses for negative numbers and punctuation for larger numbers. The Numbers tab options are shown here:

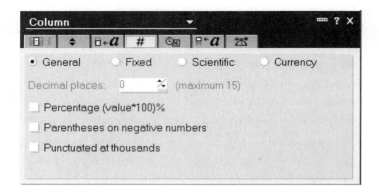

The Date and Time Format Tab

The Time/Date tab enables the designer to format any date or time elements that might be included in the column. The options on this tab are similar to those already discussed for Time fields.

The Title Tab

Use the Title tab, which is similar to the Text tab, to change the formatting of the column headers. Remember that if the column header is too long for the column, the header will be truncated. The *Apply to All button* on this tab enables the designer to set all the column titles in the view to the same formatting.

The Advanced Tab

Use the Advanced tab to determine how to refer to the column programmatically. Also, if you want this column to be the link column in the view, enable the *For Web Access: Show values in this column as links* option.

Define the Column

Once you have set the attributes for the column, use the Column properties InfoBox to determine the value of the column. You can determine the value of a column in three ways: a simple function, a field, or a formula.

Using a Function

Using a simple function to determine the value of a column enables the designer to use values such as the Author's simple name, the Author's distinguished name, the creation or modification date, the size, or information about the document's attachments for the column value. To use a simple function for the column value, click the Simple Function radio button in the Script pane for any column. Designer displays the list of available simple functions in the script window, as shown in Figure 27-9. Choose the appropriate function. To preview the values of the columns, click the Refresh button. If there are any documents in the database that Notes would display in this view, they will be used to preview the values of the columns. The simple function Number in View is the default value for all new columns.

Using a Field

Another common way of determining the value displayed in a column is to use a field value from a form in the database. This method takes the value of a field on the documents displayed in the view and displays it directly in the column. To use a field value to determine the display value of the column, click the Field radio button. Then choose the field that you want to use from the list presented in the Script pane.

NOTE   When you change the definition of a column from a simple function to a field (and then to a formula), the previously existing value is lost. If you are unsure about losing a formula or function, copy the column before changing the value.

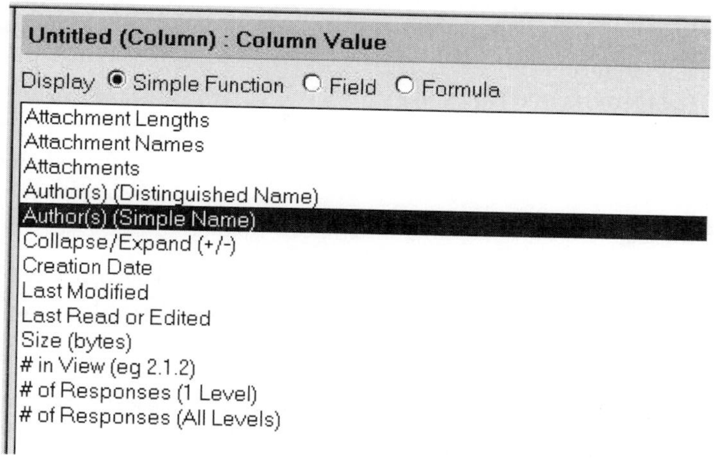

Figure 27-9
Create a column using a simple function.

> **Untitled (Column) : Column Value**
>
> Display ● Simple Function   ○ Field   ○ Formula
>
> Attachment Lengths
> Attachment Names
> Attachments
> Author(s) (Distinguished Name)
> **Author(s) (Simple Name)**
> Collapse/Expand (+/-)
> Creation Date
> Last Modified
> Last Read or Edited
> Size (bytes)
> # in View (eg 2.1.2)
> # of Responses (1 Level)
> # of Responses (All Levels)

> **NOTE** Certain field types cannot be used in column formulas: rich-text fields, computed-for-display fields, and any encrypted fields.

Using a Formula to Determine Column Values

Finally, the value of a column can be determined by using a formula. A formula will also enable you to combine field values or to add text to a column entry. To use a formula to determine a column display value, click the *Formula radio* button. For example, examine the following formula:

```
@If(Form= "Book"; BookTitle; @If(Form= "Review"; "Review of: " +
dispBkTitle; @If(Form= "Order"; "Order for: "+ dispBkTitle; "")))
```

If the document was created with the Book form, this formula displays contents of the BookTitle field. If the formula was created with the Order or Review form, the formula displays the book title combined with some static text.

Here is another example. Examine the following formula:

```
@If(Rating="1";151;@If(Rating="2";152;@If(Rating=4>3";153;@If(Rat-
ing="4";154;162))))
```

This formula displays an icon based on the value of the keyword selected in the Rating field. In addition to the formula, you must select the *Display values as icons* option in the Column properties InfoBox.

The following formula shows one way to add static text to a column:

```
"The customer is " + CustomerName + "with" + CompanyName + "."
```

This formula combines the values of the CustomerName and CompanyName fields with accompanying static text, spaces, and punctuation.

To show the date that an order was created, you might use the following formula:

```
"Order created on " + @Text(@Created)
```

If the developer wants to display the values of a keyword field in a column but wants to use synonyms when defining the keywords, a formula similar to the one as follows might be necessary:

```
@If (Software ="1"; "Lotus Notes"; Software = "2"; "MS Office";
Software = "3"; "Visio"; Software = "4"; "Netscape"; "No Software
package selected")
```

In this example, the column would display the word (Microsoft Office and so on) relating to the choice that the user made in the document. If the user chose Lotus Notes as the value of the Keyword field when he or she was completing the document, for example, the column would display Lotus Notes. Without this formula, however, the column would display the number 1, because that is the value stored internally for the keyword Lotus Notes.

 TIP   Remember that only one data type can be used in a single column; therefore, the @Text or other translation functions can be used to ensure that all elements of a column are the same data type.

Categorizing the View

Documents in a view can be organized or grouped according to a field on the form from which they were created, as discussed previously and in the chapter dealing with forms. This type of organization can make views easier to understand and documents easier to locate. A designer can categorize a view by creating a column that uses sorting and categorized options. The value of the column should be a field that results in an easily sortable value, such as an Author or Keyword field. The designer can enable the user to use the Categorize action to categorize a view by using a Categories field on the form being used to create the documents. This field must result in a list of words or names on which you want to base the categories.

To create a categorized view, first make sure that you have included a field on the forms that can be organized by category. Then create a column (probably far to the left) that refers to this field. Next, in the Column properties InfoBox, choose Categorized on the Sorting tab. You might also want to choose to *Show twistie when row is expandable* on the Column Info tab. More than one column can be categorized if necessary.

Embedding the View

As described in Chapter 25, "Creating Pages and Forms," you can embed a view (or the Folder pane) into a page or a form. One of the benefits of embedding a view is that you can add other elements to make a clear and useful design. In addition, embedded views give you more control over how the view looks and performs on the Web.

To embed a view or view applet (the view is displayed by using the applet in the browser), open the form or page and choose Create . . . Embedded Element . . . View. After you embed the view, you can customize the embedded view by using the Embedded View properties InfoBox, shown next. The *Web Access: Display* option determines whether Domino displays the embedded view using HTML, the Java applet, or whatever was selected in the View properties. On the Display tab, select width and height. Also, select whether Notes should display scroll bars with the embedded view. Finally, decide whether Notes should display the contents of the view only or if it should continue to display the column headers as well.

One additional option with embedded views is the capability to show only a single category in the embedded view. If you have embedded a categorized view, you can program two events in the Programmer's pane. First, you can program which view to display in the Embedded Selection event. Next, you can program the Show Single Category event. Place a formula or category name in the Script pane for this event to restrict the view to only one category. Single category views must be categorized. In addition, Notes or Domino will not display the category name in the view, as shown here:

This is an embedded view.

The categories available in the view include a variety of book types, but only the certification type is shown here...

Book Title	Author
Accelerated R4	Libby Schwarz
Network+	Brian Schwarz

Summary

Create views and folders in Domino applications to enable users to see document lists. The designer selects the documents for a view, based on a selection formula. Users select documents for a folder by clicking and dragging or by using a button or action. In the view, columns display data from the displayed documents. Data in a column can be of only one type and can include fields, @Functions, and formulas. Views can be flat or categorized. On the Web, Notes views can be displayed using HTML or a Java applet. The applet makes the view seem more Notes-like and provides extra features. Views can also be embedded in pages or forms.

Practice

Next, if you created the R5 Orders and Reviews database with the appropriate forms and fields in Chapter 26, you can open that database to get started.

Create a view in the database so that users can see the books that have been added, along with their responses. The design synopsis of this view is shown in Table 27-1.

Table 27-1   View Design

Name:	By Book Type
Last Modification:	10/23/99 04:43:11 PM
Comment:	[Not Assigned]
Default Database View:	Yes
No Response Hierarchy:	Disabled
Categories Initially:	Expanded
Unread Marks:	None
Refresh Frequency:	Automatic
Discard Index:	Never
View May Be Used By:	All Users
Time Relative Formulas:	No
Selection Formula:	SELECT @All
Subcomponents:	
Column Number:	1

continued

Table 27-1 View Design (*continued*)

Name:	By Book Type
Column Title:	[Not Assigned]
Column Formula:	Categories
Column Width:	1 Characters
List Separator:	
Hidden:	No
Responses Only:	No
Icon:	No
Number Format:	General
Percentage (value * 100)%:	No
Parentheses on Negative Numbers:	No
Punctuated at Thousands:	No
Time Format:	10/23/99 04:47:54 PM
Sorting:	Ascending, Categorized
Justification:	Left
Totals:	None
Hide Detail Values:	No
Column Number:	**2**
Column Title:	[Not Assigned]
Column Formula:	@If(Form = "Order"; "An order has been placed by " + @Name([CN]; @UserName) + " for " + @Text(OrderNo) + " copies of " + dispBkTitle; @Name([CN]; @UserName) + " gave " + dispBkTitle + @If(Rating = "1"; " one star."; @If(Rating = "2"; " two stars."; @If(Rating = "3"; " three stars."; @If(Rating = "4"; " four stars."; ""))))));
Column Width:	1 Characters
List Separator:	
Hidden:	No

continued

Table 27-1 View Design (*continued*)

Name:	By Book Type
Responses Only:	Yes
Icon:	No
Number Format:	General
Percentage (value * 100)%:	No
Parentheses on Negative Numbers:	No
Punctuated at Thousands:	No
Time Format:	10/23/99 04:47:54 PM
Sorting:	No
Justification:	Left
Totals:	None
Hide Detail Values:	No
Column Number:	**3**
Column Title:	Book Title
Column Formula:	`@If(Form = "Book"; BookTitle; @If(Form = "Review"; "Review of:" + dispBkTitle; @If(Form = "Order"; "Order for: " + disp-BkTitle; "")));`
Column Width:	20 Characters
List Separator:	
Hidden:	No
Responses Only:	No
Icon:	No
Number Format:	General
Percentage (value * 100)%:	No
Parentheses on Negative Numbers:	No
Punctuated at Thousands:	No
Time Format:	10/23/99 04:47:54 PM
Sorting:	No

continued

PART IV

Table 27-1   View Design (*continued*)

Name:	By Book Type
Justification:	Left
Totals:	None
Hide Detail Values:	No
Column Number:	**4**
Column Title:	Author
Column Formula:	BAuthor
Column Width:	10 Characters
List Separator:	
Hidden:	No
Responses Only:	No
Icon:	No
Number Format:	General
Percentage (value * 100)%:	No
Parentheses on Negative Numbers:	No
Punctuated at Thousands:	No
Time Format:	10/23/99 04:47:54 PM
Sorting:	No
Justification:	Left
Totals:	None
Hide Detail Values:	No

This view looks like the one shown in Figure 27-10 in Notes.

You might also want to create a view that enables users to retrieve accidentally deleted documents. Remember that to use this type of view, the database must also have two database properties set.

1. Open the Database properties InfoBox. On the Advanced tab, enable the *Allow soft deletions* property.

Book Title	Author
▼ Certification	
Accelerated R4	Libby Schwarz
Network+	Brian Schwarz
▼ Learn	
Book Of Color	libby
An order has been placed by Libby Schwarz for 1 copies of Book Of Color	
Libby Schwarz gave Book Of Color four stars.	

Figure 27-10   View previewed in Notes

2. You also have to set the $Undelete Expire Time so that Notes knows how long documents can be recovered. In this case, set this property to 48 hours.

3. Next, create a new view called Retrieve Deleted Documents. When creating the view, make the type Shared, contains deleted documents. Remember that you can only choose the view type when you are creating it.

4. You can inherit the design of the main view of the database, created previously. The most important item to remember is that the view must have the capability to display something descriptive about any document in the database.

5. To make the view useful, you will also need a view action that uses the @UndeleteDocument function. We discuss more about view actions in Chapter 28, "Creating Actions, Agents, and Hotspots," but just to make the view useful, we will create one here. While in the view, choose Create . . . Action from the menus.

6. In the Action InfoBox, give the action a name such as Undelete Selected Document. Choose to include the action in the button bar, and select a Notes icon to display with the action.

7. In the Click event for the action (in the Programmer's pane), use @UndeleteDocument as the formula.

8. Test the view and the view action in the Notes client. You cannot use the Refresh button to test this type of view. This view and action do not work on the Web.

Review Questions

1. Elizabeth's users have told her that they need to be able to retrieve deleted documents. What can she do to help them?
   a. She can use a SELECT @All as the selection formula for a view.
   b. She can create a Shared, contains documents not in any folder view.
   c. She can create a Shared, contains deleted documents view.
   d. She can recreate the view index.

2. Doug is creating a view that needs to show both main documents (created with the Main form and their responses (created with the Response form). Which selection formula should he use?
   a. SELECT Form = "Main" & Form = "Response"
   b. SELECT Form = "Main" | @IsResponseDoc
   c. SELECT Form = "Main" | Form = "Response"
   d. SELECT Form = "Main" & @AllChildren

3. Ashley is troubleshooting a view that should show both Main documents and Response documents. The Response documents should be indented under their parent documents. Which of the following actions might help?
   a. Enable the database property Show response documents in hierarchy.
   b. Enable the view property Show response documents in hierarchy.
   c. Enable the column property Show response documents in hierarchy.
   d. Create a column with the Show responses only property enabled.

4. The Discard Index property is set to *If inactive for 1 day*. The view was last used at 2 P.M. on Tuesday. When will the View index actually be discarded?
   a. At 2 P.M. on Wednesday
   b. At 2 A.M. on Wednesday, when Updall runs
   c. At 2 P.M. on Thursday
   d. At 2 A.M. on Thursday, when Updall runs

5. Which of the following is a good reason to display a view on the Web by using the Java applet?
   a. You want users to be able to select multiple documents from the view.
   b. You want users to have the default navigation bar available.
   c. You want users to be able to expand and collapse categories in the view without having Domino regenerate the page.
   d. You want users to be able to click the column header to sort.

6. Cara wants to create a view that will display all documents that were created with the form Student Profile and all the responses to these documents at any level. What formula would she use for the selection formula?
   a. SELECT form = "Student Profile" & @AllDescendants
   b. SELECT form = "Student Profile" | @AllDescendants
   c. SELECT form = "Student Profile" | @IsResponseDoc
   d. SELECT form = "Student Profile" & @AllChildren

7. To make a Single Category view, which of the following actions does Walter have to perform?
   a. Use the View applet.
   b. Embed the view on a page or form.
   c. Enable the Show single category option on the View properties InfoBox.
   d. Create a formula for the Single Category event that evaluates to a category name.

8. When Krickett uses a Single Category view, which of the following statements are true?
   a. The view is embedded on a page or form.
   b. The view displays the category title.
   c. The view cannot be used on the Web.
   d. The view must be displayed using HTML when used on the Web.

9. Which of the following is true about the Embedded view that Samantha created?
   a. She can embed up to three views on a page or a form.
   b. The Embedded view will only use the same Web display option as the Normal view.
   c. She can choose which view to embed based on a formula.
   d. Embedded views only work on forms, not pages.

10. C.J. is creating a view for use on the Web and wants the date column to be the one that links users to the documents. How does he accomplish this task?
    a. He has no control over which column is displayed as a link.
    b. He can use the View applet.
    c. For the date column, he can select the column property *Show values in this column as links*.
    d. He can make the date column the first column in the view.

Review Answers

1. **C** is correct. She will also need to enable the *Allow soft deletions* database property.

2. **C** is correct. This will display documents created with either the form Main or the form Response. Choice **B** would show not only responses to Main, but also any other responses in the database.

3. **B** and **D** are correct. She needs to enable the view to show Response documents in a hierarchy. She will also need to create a column that displays the Response documents only.

4. **D** is correct. The View index can be discarded after it has been unused for 24 hours, which would occur at 2 P.M. on Wednesday. The index is only actually discarded the next time after that (when Updall runs), however, so choice **D** is correct.

5. **A, C,** and **D** are all correct. Users do not have the default navigation bar available, however, so you might want to create some view actions for them.

6. **B** is correct. It displays all documents that were created with the Student Profile form or all descendants of those documents.

7. **B** and **D** are correct. A single category view must be embedded on a page or form and must have a formula in the Single Category event that evaluates to the name of a category. It does not have to use the View applet.

8. **A** is correct. The view must be embedded.

9. **C** is correct. The embedded view can be chosen based on a formula.

10. **C** or **D** is correct. Although selecting the Column property gives him more flexibility in the view design, he can also simply make that column first in the view.

CHAPTER 28

Creating Actions, Agents, and Hotspots

You should be able to answer questions based on the following objectives after reading this chapter:

- Create, modify, and troubleshoot actions
- Create, modify, and troubleshoot agents

As you think about your application and how users will work with it, you will probably begin to imagine some tasks that you would like to automate for them. This situation is especially true for your Web users, because they will not have the Notes menus available. Actions, agents, and hotspots are three methods of adding automation to your applications. An *action* can be associated with a form or a view. Either it is displayed as a button at the top of the form or view, or it is available from the Actions menu. An *agent* enables a user action to be automated and accessed from anywhere in the application. *Hotspots*, which were described in Chapter 25, "Creating Pages and Forms," are placed on pages, documents, forms, and navigators to add links or other actions.

Actions

Actions can be associated with pages, forms, or views. Users can access actions either from the Actions menu or from a button on the Action bar. You can create a single-use action, which you will use with a specific page, form, or view. You can also create shared actions, which you can reuse with many elements in a database. Designers often add actions to enable Web users to perform actions in applications that are usually performed using Notes menus or smart icons. Actions also automate standard tasks that might ordinarily require a few steps or make selections from a few menus. Creating an action makes it easier for your users to perform certain tasks.

Notes also provides default page, form, and view actions. You cannot change what these actions do, but you can change how they appear to users. To view the default actions provided with Notes, choose View . . . Action Pane from the menus while in a page, form, or view. Designer displays the Action pane, as shown in Figure 28-1, showing the default actions, including Categorize, Forward, and Edit Document. Users can access these default actions from the Actions menu, or they can add them to the Action button bar. To include the default action on the button bar, double-click the action to display the Action InfoBox, as shown in Figure 28-2.

Enable the *Include action in button bar* property. You can also select the position for the action on the bar. Other options include the following:

- **Only show icon in button bar** Only displays the icon you select (and not the name of the action) in the button bar.

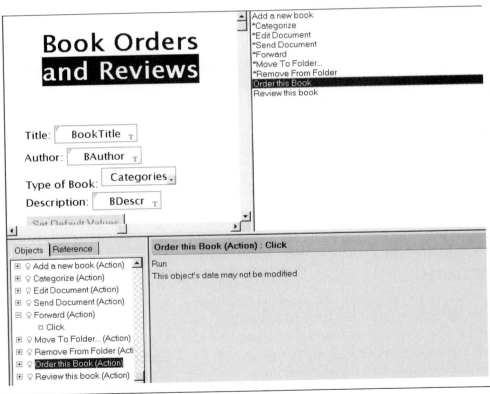

Figure 28-1   Action pane in a form

Figure 28-2
Action InfoBox

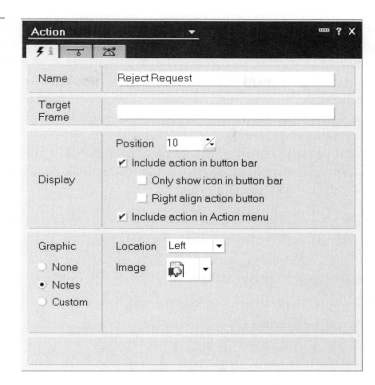

• **Right align action button**   Display the button to the far right of the page, form, or view, rather than at the left (the default).

Next, choose a graphic icon for the action button. By default, Designer has the *None* radio button selected. The action button displays only the name of the action with no icon. You can select a Notes icon or a custom icon. You can select custom icons from the operating system or from shared-image resources that are already stored with the database.

Creating Single-Use Actions

To create a custom action (single-use) instead, choose Create . . . Action from the menus. In the Action InfoBox, choose a name and other display options for the action. These options are the same for default actions and for custom actions. When you give an action a name, you can cascade it, which is similar to the cascading for views and forms. Type a name under which to cascade the actions, such as Tools or Create. Then type a backslash (/) and the name for the action. In a Notes client, the actions are grouped under the cascade name, as shown in Figure 28-3. To use cascaded actions on the Web, use the Java applet for the action bar, as described later in this chapter.

After creating the action and selecting how users can access the action, you must create an action for it to perform. You can program actions with simple actions, @Functions, @Commands, LotusScript, and JavaScript.

Simple actions are predefined formulas that make it easy for newer programmers to add actions their applications. You cannot use simple actions with Web clients. The simple actions include the following:

- **Copy to database**   Copies the selected document to a database you specify. The database must be on the same server.

- **Copy to folder**   Copies the selected document to a folder you specify. The folder must be in the current database.

- **Delete from database**   Deletes the current document.

- **Mark document read**   Marks the selected document read. Use this action if you change a field value programmatically but do not want users to have to reread the document.

- **Mark document unread**   Marks the selected document read.

- **Modify field**   Replaces or appends the value you specify in the field you specify. This action only works with text values.

- **Modify fields by form**   Replaces the text value of several fields on a specified form with the values you specify. Again, this action only works with text values.

- **Move to folder**   Which moves the selected document to a folder you specify. This action removes the document from the current folder, unlike the *Copy to Folder* action, which places a new copy of the document in the new folder without removing it from the current folder.

- **Remove from folder**   Removes the document from a folder but does not delete it from the database.

Figure 28-3
Cascaded actions
in Notes

- **Reply to sender**   Sends an automatic reply to the sender (or all recipients) of a message. This action will not reply to a message that was originated by an agent. You can include text and the body of the message to which you are replying.

- **Run agent**   Runs an agent from the current database.

- **Send document**   Works with a SendTo field on the current document to mail the document. Refer to Part V (on workflow applications) for more information about sending documents automatically.

- **Send mail message**   Sends the selected document or a link to the selected document—to the specified recipients.

- **Send newsletter summary**   Sends summaries of documents that match specified characteristics to specified users.

- **@Function formula**   Adds an @Function formula that updates an existing document or creates a new document when run.

Instead of simple actions, you might choose to use a formula by using @Functions and @Commands. Add the formula to the Click event for the action by using the Script pane. Some commonly used actions are described as follows. Note that although you might see these actions available in a Web client, only the @Functions and @Commands that are supported on the Web will work. Others will appear but will do nothing. Always verify the usage of an @Function or @Command before using it. Some cannot be used in actions, such as @DeleteDocument; others cannot be used with Web clients, such as @Command([FileSave]) (unless the Database property Use JavaScript when generating pages is enabled).

- In a view or form, create a response to the currently selected document by using the following formula:

  ```
  @Command([Compose]; "ResponseFormName")
  ```

- Save and close the current document by using this formula:

  ```
  @Command([FileSave]);
  @Command([FileCloseWindow])
  ```

- In a view, use this formula to return soft-deleted documents to their original views:

  ```
  @UndeleteDocument
  ```

- Provide the ability for a Web user to delete a document by using a form action with the following command:

  ```
  @Command([EditClear])
  ```

Note that in a Notes client, this command only marks the document for deletion without actually deleting the document.

- Go to a view from a page, form, or other view by using the following command:

```
@Command([OpenView]; "ViewName")
```

You can also create actions by using LotusScript or JavaScript. One note is that LotusScript actions will not be available on the Web. LotusScript is only available on the Web using agents. To use an action that calls LotusScript on the Web, create an action that runs an agent that contains the LotusScript. To run an agent from an action, use the following:

```
@Command([ToolsRunMacro]; "AgentName")
```

After programming the action, you can also select other properties for the action, including hide-when options and Action publishing options. Use hide-when actions to show only the appropriate buttons, using either document events or a hide-when formula. For example, an action to place a document in Edit mode would only be necessary when the document was opened for reading or previewing. Similarly, a common action in forms is saving and closing the current document. This action would only be necessary when the document was in Edit mode. In addition, you might want to hide actions from Web users when they use functions or commands that are not supported on the Web.

The Advanced tab for the action contains options that are related to NotesFlow publishing. These options enable the actions you create to be available in other applications that you may launch using OLE automation.

Creating Shared Actions

You can also create actions that you can reuse in more than one place in the application. These are shared actions. Shared actions are stored in the Resources Design view. Choose Resources . . . Other . . . Shared Actions, which creates a form that stores the shared actions. If necessary, choose Create . . . Shared Action while in this view to create the next shared action. The steps for creating an action are the same as mentioned previously: name the action, select where it will be available to users and what its icon looks like, and create a formula for the action to run. Shared actions in a database are shown in Figure 28-4.

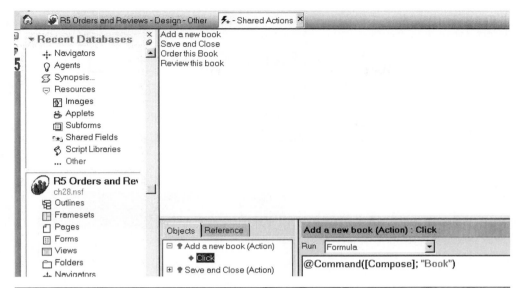

Figure 28-4   Shared actions in a database

After you create and save the shared action, place it with a page, form, or view for use. To insert a shared action, open the Action pane for a page, form, or view by selecting View . . . Action Pane from the menus. Click the Action pane and choose Create . . . Insert Shared Action. Designer displays the Insert Shared Action(s) dialog box, as shown in Figure 28-5. Select the action to insert, and click the Insert button. When finished, click Done. Designer inserts the actions into the current page, form, or view. The only item relating to the shared action that you can change in the page, form, or view is its position. All other properties are defined in the Shared Action view.

Formatting the Action Bar

When you choose to display actions using the Action bar, Notes displays the actions at the top of the pages, forms, and views in a gray bar. You can change the properties of this bar using the Action Bar properties InfoBox. To open the Action bar properties, select an action in the Action pane of a page, form, or view. Select Design . . . Action Bar properties. Designer displays the Action Bar properties InfoBox, as shown in Figure 28-6.

Figure 28-5
Insert a shared
action

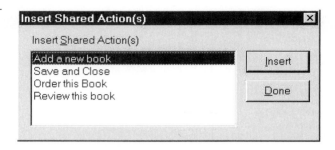

Figure 28-6
Action Bar
properties

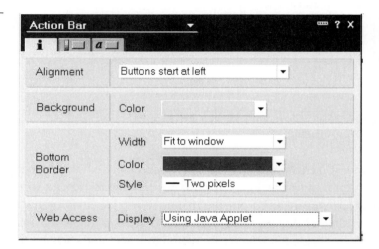

On the Action Info tab, select the alignment of the buttons. They can start at either the left or right. Select the background color for the Action bar (the default is gray). Next, select the width, color, and style of the bottom border for the action bar. Finally, choose whether to use HTML or the Java applet to display the Action bar to Web clients. The Action bar applet enables cascaded actions and a more Notes-like appearance for the actions. The applet also enables users to scroll across the Action bar when necessary.

The Button Background tab determines the height, width, and margin of the buttons. You can also determine when the button border is visible and the color or image for the button background. The Button Font tab determines the font face, size, style, and color of the text on the buttons.

Agents

An agent is similar to an action in that it automates a normally manual action. Users can access an agent via the Actions menu or through another action. Unlike actions, which designers create, either designers or end users can create agents. In addition, agents are not associated specifically with particular design elements, such as pages, forms, or views. Agents are accessible from anywhere in the application. An agent is similar to a macro in other applications, because it automates a set of manual tasks. Unlike macros, agents are not recorded by doing the actions but by using the Agent Design window, as shown in Figure 28-7. Some examples of good uses for agents might include the following:

- Automating repeatable processes

- Automating processes that are complex for the average user

- Automating processes that occur on schedule or after a repeated event

Agents are defined by the following elements: what triggers the agent to run, whether the agent is personal or public, and how documents are selected for the agent to run on them.

Figure 28-7   Agent Design window

To create an agent, choose Create . . . Agent from the menus or go to the Agents Design view and choose the New Agent action button. Designer displays the Agent Design window. From the Agent Design window, name the agent, and then decide whether the agent is personal or shared. The default, which is a personal agent, can be created by anyone who has been given the Create Personal Agents capability on the Access Control List dialog box. A shared agent can be created by someone who has Designer-level access or higher. A shared agent can be used by other users of the database, whereas a personal agent can only be used by the person who created the agent.

 NOTE At this point, you only have one opportunity to decide whether an agent is shared or personal. Once you save the agent, you cannot change it from one type to another. To do so, you would have to recreate the agent.

You can also set other properties of the agent by clicking the Options button, which displays the Options dialog box (as shown in Figure 28-8). In this dialog box, you can make the following choices:

- **Show search in search bar menu** This option enables a user to view the agent's search formula when he or she uses the Search bar in this database. As a result, a user could preview the documents on which the agent would act.

Figure 28-8
Agent options

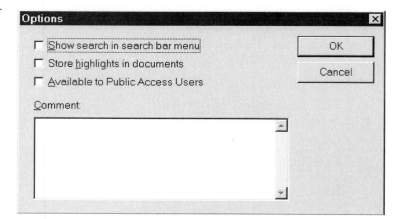

- **Store highlights in documents**   This option enables the user to see a red highlight around the search words in each document after the agent has run.

- **Available to Public Access Users**   This option enables the agent to be available for users who have Public access to the database.

- **Comments**   This field enables the designer to add a description of the agent's purpose and function. The first few words of the description can be viewed in the Agents view.

The next option in the Agent Design window is *When should this agent run?*. Use this option to choose the trigger for the agent. Agents can be triggered either manually or automatically. The options available from the drop-down list include the following:

- Manually from Actions list

- Manually from Agents list

- Before New Mail arrives

- After New Mail has arrived

- If Documents have been created or modified

- If Documents have been pasted

- On Schedule More than Once a Day, Hourly, Daily, Weekly, or Monthly

- On Schedule Never

The first two choices are manual triggers, which means that a user has to activate the agent by clicking a button or selecting the agent from the Actions menu. These options are not available to Web users. The other choices are triggered either by an event or on a schedule. When an application event occurs—such as before or after mail is received or when documents are saved, created, or pasted—the agents that use the *Before New Mail arrives, After New Mail has arrived, If Documents have been created or modified,* and *If Documents have been pasted triggers* activate. The other selections activate on schedule, based on days, weeks, hours, or months. If you choose to activate an agent based on a schedule, in addition to choosing *On Schedule Hourly, Daily, Weekly, Monthly,* or *Never,* click the Schedule button to create the schedule.

If you choose to schedule an agent on a scheduled basis, Designer enables you to select the interval and the server on which the agent should run by using the Schedule button, as shown in Figure 28-9. By default, this field contains the current server. If the agent will need to be run on a different server, this field must be updated. If you select the *Choose when agent is enabled button,* you can select the server when the agent is

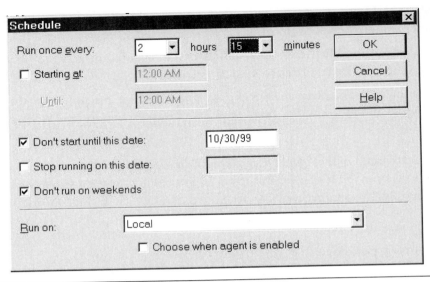

Figure 28-9 The Schedule dialog box

enabled. You might choose to use the *On Schedule Never* option if the agent will only be triggered by an action or by another button and not by schedule event or from the menus. If an automatic trigger is selected, the designer can further designate the schedule of the agent by using the Schedule . . . button. Agents can also be run from Action buttons in forms and views.

The next option in the Agent Design window determines the documents on which the agent will act. This option is automatically specified for certain triggers. If the trigger is *Before New Mail arrives*, for example, Notes automatically selects all new mail messages. The *Which document(s) should it act on* drop-down list has the following options for choosing documents:

- All documents in database
- All new and modified documents since last run
- All unread documents in view
- All documents in view
- Selected documents
- Run once

In addition, a search query using forms, keywords, or other settings can be created by using the Add Search . . . button.

Finally, define the action that the agent will perform. Agent actions can be defined by any of the following:

- Formula
- Simple Action
- LotusScript
- Imported Java
- Java

The following list describes some of the simple actions that are available by clicking the Add Action button in this dialog box:

- Copy to database or folder
- Delete from database
- Mark documents read or unread
- Modify field or fields
- Move to or remove from folder
- Reply to sender
- Send document, message, or newsletter summary

An example of an agent that can be created with a simple action is one that modifies a field value. To create an agent to modify a field value, select Create . . . Agent from the menus. Type a name for the agent, and choose Shared. Set the agent to run manually from the Actions menu on selected documents. By clicking Selected documents, you require users to run the agent from a view or from within a document. Click the Add Action button and choose the Modify field action from the drop-down list. Select a field from the drop-down list as well. The field drop-down list displays all of the available fields in the current database. Place a value in the Value field and decide whether the value should replace the current value or should be appended to it. If you modify a keyword field that uses synonyms, use the synonym as the value. You might have an approval field with the keywords yes and no, for example, with 0 and 1 as the synonyms. If you created an agent called Approve, it would replace the value of the Approve field with 0 for *yes*.

You can also use an @Function formula to create an action for an agent to run. If you use an @Function formula, you can choose what the agent does to the documents from the following selections, as shown in Figure 28-10.

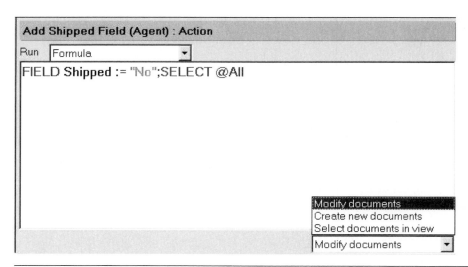

Figure 28-10   Creating an agent with a formula

- Modify documents
- Create new documents
- Select the documents

By default, Notes modifies the documents. There might be times, however, when a new document needs to be created with the changes without altering the existing document—or when no changes should be made, such as when testing the selection criteria. An example of an agent you might create using a formula would be to add a field to already-created documents in a database after you add a new field to a form. The agent formula could be as follows:

```
FIELD NewField := "This is a new field"
```

Note that you would not see the value of this field on the documents unless you also add the field to the form. The value is available, however, but in a programmatical manner. To view the field and its value, add the field to the form or use the Document properties InfoBox. Another common agent created with a formula would be an agent to place documents in a folder, such as the following:

```
@AddToFolder("Mine";"My Reviews")
```

In this formula, the agent removes the selected documents from the folder My Reviews and places them in the folder Mine instead. If you do not include the second argument, the document is not removed from a folder.

Testing and Troubleshooting Agents

After creating agents using the previous information, you might need to test or troubleshoot the agents. Two ways to test the agent before running it against live documents include the following:

- Running the agent in Test mode after saving the agent. After you have created and saved the agent, open the Agents view. Select the agent you want to test, and choose Actions . . . Test from the menus. The agent will be tested, and the Test Run Agent Log dialog box will be displayed, as shown in Figure 28-11. The dialog box lists the number of documents that the agent found to run on and what the agent would have done. This option enables you to verify that the agent acted as you intended and found the correct number of documents.

- You can also choose to make a copy of the database in which to run the agent, which enables you to run the agent in Real mode without affecting production data. After you run the agent in this copy of the database, you can verify that it acted correctly on the documents in the copy.

- One way to verify that an agent is running correctly, or to troubleshoot the agent when it is not running properly, is to use the Agent Log. The Agent Log shows data for the last time the agent was run. To view the Agent Log, select the agent from the Agents view and choose Agent . . . Log from the menus. Designer displays the

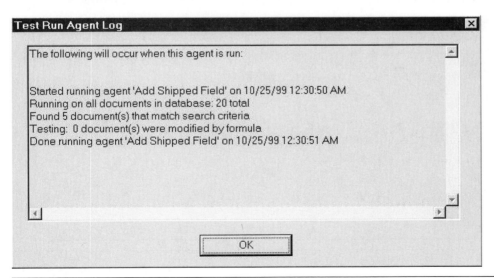

Figure 28-11   Testing an agent

Agent Log dialog box, as shown in Figure 28-12. Note that the Agent Log is similar to the dialog box displayed during the testing of an agent and contains the same information.

The following are two of the issues that are likely to cause problems with an agent:

- Access
- Agent Manager settings in the server document (the Agent Manager is the server task that runs agents on the server and is controlled by the server document settings)

An agent either runs under the Access level of the user who created or modified the agent (for scheduled or event-triggered agents) or under the Access level of the person running the agent (for agents that are triggered manually). If the person who runs or creates the agent, for example, only has Author access to the database, only documents they created would be affected by the agent—regardless of the selection formula for the agent. Similarly, in the Agent Manager settings of the server document, the Notes Administrator has the ability to define which users can run agents on the server. If the user who creates or runs the agent does not have the right to run agents on the server, the agent cannot run on that server. The Notes Administrator can also limit the times

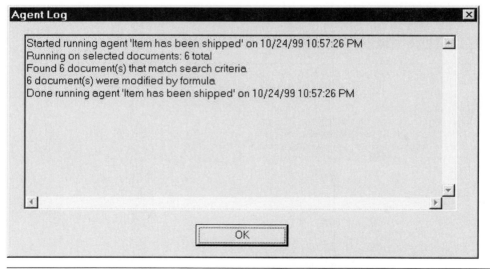

Figure 28-12　Agent Log dialog box

that agents can be run on the server and the number of agents that can run on the server at a time. Verify these settings with the Notes Administrator if the agent is not running as expected.

Hotspots

Hotspots such as buttons, links, and pop-up text provide a method of adding actions to Notes design elements such as pages, views, framesets, forms, folders, or navigators. The following are the available hotspot types:

- Link
- Text pop-up
- Button
- Formula pop-up
- Action hotspot

A common use for buttons is to provide Web users with an interface for performing common actions (similar to a common use for actions, which we described previously). Web clients can access more than one button on a form or other design element only if the following conditions are met:

- If the browser supports JavaScript
- If the database property *On Web Access: Use JavaScript when generating pages* is enabled

If this option is not enabled, Domino places a single button on every form—a Submit button. If you place any buttons on a form, only the first one is recognized, and Domino assumes the button is a Submit button. Therefore, to use multiple buttons on a form or other design element, use the JavaScript option. Note that Domino does not place a Submit button on the forms when you use this option, so you should create one. To create a Submit button for your forms, perform the following actions:

1. Open the form and place your cursor where you want to place the Submit button.
2. Choose Create . . . Hotspot . . . Button.
3. In the Button properties InfoBox, type **Submit** as the name of the button.
4. In the Click event, use the following formula:

```
@Command([FileSave]);
@Command([FileCloseWindow])
```

You might also want to set field values for the current document. If, for example, you had some default values that you wanted a user to be able to insert into certain fields, you might place the following formula into a button on a form:

```
FIELD BPub := "McGraw-Hill";
FIELD Date :=  [09/09/99];
@All
```

This formula sets the field BPub to McGraw-Hill and the date to September 9, 1999 when the button is clicked. Refer to Chapter 25, "Creating Pages and Forms," for more details about creating hotspots.

Summary

Actions, agents, and hotspots provide a method for automating actions in applications. These items can automate repetitive tasks and tasks that are too complicated for most users to work through. You can also use them to create an interface for Web users. Actions are associated with pages, forms, or views, and they are always stored with those elements. You can also create shared actions, which are stored with the database. Actions can be accessed from the Actions menu (in Notes clients) or from the Action bar. The Action bar can be displayed by using a Java applet to make the action more flexible for Web users.

Agents are not associated with a particular design element and can be run throughout a database. Agents can be triggered manually or based on an event or schedule. Both actions and agents run simple actions or formulas. The formulas can be created with @Functions, @Commands, and other languages, as specified. Hotspots are placed on design elements such as pages, forms, and navigators. To use multiple button hotspots on a form, use the database property *Use JavaScript when generating pages*.

Practice

Next, if you created the R5 Orders and Reviews database with the appropriate forms, fields, and views in Chapter 27, you can open that database to get started.

First, create some shared actions to use in the forms and views of the database. The design synopsis for the shared actions is shown in Table 28-1.

Place the *Order this book* and *Review this book* actions in the views of your database. You might also want to make the Order and Review actions available in the Book form. Use the Save and Close action in all of the forms.

Table 28-1   Shared Actions

Action:	**Add a new book**
Formula:	@Command([Compose]; "Book");
Action:	**Save and close**
Formula:	@Command([FileSave]); @Command([FileCloseWindow]);
Action:	**Order this book**
Formula:	@Command([FileSave]); @Command([Compose]; "Order");
Action:	**Review this book**
Formula:	@Command([FileSave]); @Command([Compose]; "Review");

We would like to add a field to the Order form to specify whether the order has been shipped (think about creating a view based on the value in this field). You can go to the Order form and add the field; however, the documents you have already created do not have this field. You can create an agent to add the field and set its value to "No." You can create another agent to enable users to indicate when Orders have been shipped, as shown in Table 28-2.

Two factors are not apparent in the design synopsis:

- The Add Shipped Field agent also has an additional Search—By Form Used: Order, which ensures that it only adds the field to the Order form.

- You should create a Shipped field on the Order form manually as well, which makes the field available for new documents created with the form and displays the value on the already-created documents. The design for this field is shown in Table 28-3.

Table 28-2   Agents

Name:	**Add Shipped Field**
Last Modification:	10/24/99 10:50:11 PM
Comment:	[Not Assigned]
Shared Agent:	Yes
Type:	Java

continued

Table 28-2   Agents (*continued*)

Name:	Add Shipped Field
State:	Enabled
Trigger:	Manually From Actions Menu
Acts On:	All documents in database
Formula:	FIELD Shipped := "No";@All;
Name:	**Item has been shipped**
Last Modification:	10/24/99 10:50:48 PM
Comment:	[Not Assigned]
Shared Agent:	Yes
Type:	Formula
State:	Enabled
Trigger:	Manually From Actions Menu
Acts On:	Selected documents
Formula:	FIELD Shipped := "Yes";@All;

Table 28-3   Shipped Field

Field:	Shipped
Datatype:	Keywords
Help Description:	[Not Assigned]
Field Type:	Editable
Keyword User Interface:	Radio Buttons
Allowable Keywords:	Yes
	No
Sign When Mailing/In Section:	No
Encryption:	Disabled
Update Requires Editor Access:	No
Default Value Formula:	"No"
Is Scripted:	No

Review Questions

1. Joe creates two actions. He wants both actions to be available from an action button called Tools. How can he accomplish this task?
   a. In the Action properties InfoBox, select Cascade and type **Tools** as the cascade name.
   b. Use the Action bar applet. Enable the Cascade property on the Action Bar properties InfoBox.
   c. Type **Tools\ActionName** as the name of the actions.
   d. Create the actions as shared actions. When they are inserted on a form, they will be cascaded automatically.

2. Actions can be associated with which design elements?
   a. Pages
   b. Forms
   c. Views
   d. Documents

3. True or false: You can use the default actions with Web clients.
   a. True
   b. False

4. Amy creates an action using the Modify Field simple action. When her Web clients use the action, the field does not change. What should she do?
   a. Enable the *Display using Java Applet Action* property for the action.
   b. Enable the *Display using Java Applet Action bar* property.
   c. You cannot use simple actions for Web clients.
   d. Add the Simple Action Run @Function formula with a value of @Command([ReloadWindow]).

5. Laura created a shared action that creates a new main topic in the discussion database. Where can she insert the shared action?
   a. Form
   b. View
   c. Page
   d. Agent

6. Randy wants to create a new field called BatWeight to his Softball Bats form. He wants to set a default value of 28 oz. Which of the following formulas can he put in his agent?

   a. `SET FIELD BatWeight := "28 oz"`

   b. `BatWeight := "28 oz"`

   c. `NewField BatWeight := "28 oz"`

   d. `FIELD BatWeight := "28 oz"`

7. Jody tests a new form in a Web browser but notices that there is not a Submit button to save and close the form. What is causing this result to occur?

   a. He forgot to enable the form property *Use JavaScript when generating pages*.

   b. He forgot to disable the form property *Use JavaScript when generating pages*.

   c. He forgot to enable the database property *Use JavaScript when generating pages*.

   d. He forgot to disable the database property *Use JavaScript when generating pages*.

8. Heather created three buttons to set some of the fields automatically on her NewEmployee form. When she uses the form in a Notes client, the buttons are available. When she uses the form in Netscape Navigator, the buttons are not available. How can you help her troubleshoot this problem?

   a. Tell her she forgot to disable the form property *Use JavaScript when generating pages*.

   b. Tell her she forgot to enable the database property *Use JavaScript when generating pages*.

   c. Tell her that only one button is supported on the Web and that she should use actions instead.

   d. Tell her that only one button is supported by Netscape Navigator. She should use the @BrowserInfo function to check for Netscape.

9. Marie creates an agent with this formula @AddToFolder("New Employees"; "In Process"). What does the agent do?

   a. Removes the selected document from the In Process folder and places it in the New Employees folder.

   b. Removes the selected document from the New Employees folder and places it in the In Process folder.

   c. Places the selected document in both the New Employees folder and in the In Process folder.

   d. Nothing. This @Function is not supported in Agents.

Review Answers

1. **C** is correct. To cascade actions, use the name to cascade from followed by a backslash and the name of the action. If you want to use cascaded actions with Web clients, use the Display Using Java Applet property for the Action bar.

2. **A, B,** and **C** are correct. Although an action might be available in a document, it is stored with the form that is displaying the document, not with the document.

3. **B** is correct. None of the default actions are available with Web clients. You must create actions that mimic the functions of the default actions, using @Functions and @Commands, to make them available on the Web.

4. **C** is correct. You cannot use simple actions on the Web. She should create an action that uses FIELD fieldname := fieldvalue; @Command([ReloadWindow]).

5. **A, B,** and **C** are correct. Shared actions can be inserted anywhere you can create a single-use action. You cannot refer to an action from an agent.

6. **D** is correct. To create and set a field, use the FIELD keyword. Without the keyword, such as in choice **B**, the field is set as a temporary variable only.

7. **D** is correct. When the database property *Use JavaScript when generating pages* is enabled, you must create a Submit button. Domino will not generate one for you.

8. **B** is correct. When the database property *Use JavaScript when generating pages* is disabled, Domino generates a default Submit button for the forms and only recognizes a Submit button, even if you create other buttons for the form.

9. **A** is correct. The @Function is supported in Agents but not in actions.

PART IV

CHAPTER 29

Creating Navigation

You should be able to answer questions based on the following objective after reading this chapter:

- Creating, modifying, and troubleshooting outlines

In Chapter 27, "Creating Views, Columns, and Folders," you created views and folders to enable users to access the documents in your application. The navigation that is provided by views and folders in the default Navigation pane, however, is limited. Notes provides additional navigation functions in the outlines, imagemaps, and navigators. The outline is a customized version of the folders and views that are offered in the default Navigation pane. An imagemap is a graphic or set of graphics that is stored on a page or form, on which you can create navigation links or other actions. A navigator is another graphical element that can provide navigation in your application.

Outlines

Outlines (and imagemaps and navigators) create alternate methods of navigation for your applications. Outlines can contain links to the views and folders in the application (similar to the Folder pane), but they can also contain links to other elements, such as pages and actions. In the outline, each of these is represented by an outline entry. An outline can also help you plan your application. You can create outline entries for the pages, forms, views, and other elements that will appear in your database before you actually create those elements. This outline can serve as your planning phase for your applications.

Creating an Outline

To create an outline, go to the Outlines design view. Click the New Outline action button, or Create . . . Design . . . Outline from the menus. Designer displays a blank outline, as shown in Figure 29-1. To set the properties for the outline, open the Outline properties InfoBox, as shown in Figure 29-2.

In the Outline properties InfoBox, give the outline a name, an alias, and a comment. You can also determine whether the outline should be available for public-access users (those users who have No Access to the database but are given the Read Public documents and Write Public documents rights in the ACL).

Generating a Default Outline

An easy way to get started with outlines is to enable Designer to generate a default outline. The default outline contains links to each of the views and folders that are in the database. In addition, the outline contains placeholders for the other shared and private views and folders, called *Other views, Other Private views, Other folders,* and *Other Private folders.* Figure 29-3 shows a default outline.

Figure 29-1   New Outline action button

Figure 29-2
Outline properties
InfoBox

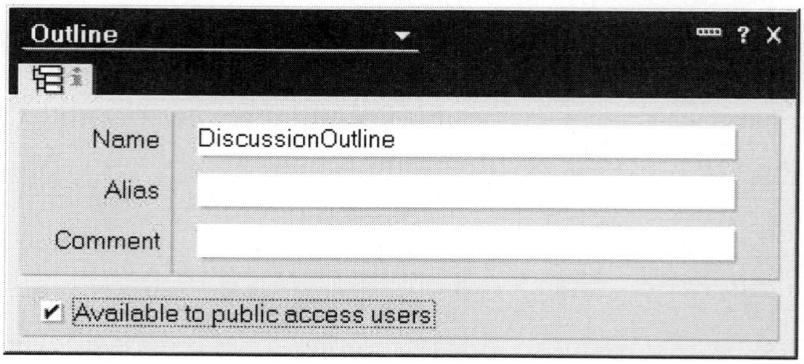

Figure 29-3   Default outline

Creating Outline Entries

After you create the outline (whether blank or with the default entries), you will want to create new entries or customize the default entries. To create a new outline entry, click the New Entry action button or choose Create . . . Outline Entry from the menus.

Designer places the new outline entry into the outline below the currently selected entry (if there are any) and displays the Outline Entry properties InfoBox, as shown in Figure 29-4. On the Outline Entry Info tab, give the outline entry a label. This text is what the user sees when he or she uses the outline. You can also give the outline entry an alias that you can use when programming with the outline entry. Another way to label the outline entry is programmatically. Use the *Label* event in the Programmer's pane to add a computed label.

Next, determine the content to which the outline entry will link. The outline entry can have the following content types:

- **None**   Use this content type when creating a top-level entry.
- **Action**   Creates an outline entry associated with an action.

Figure 29-4
Outline Entry prop-
erties

- **Link** Creates an outline entry that provides a link.

- **Named Element** Includes a page, form, frame set, view, folder, or navigator.

- **URL** Creates an outline entry that contains a URL link.

When you create an action outline entry, create an action for the entry to perform by clicking the Formulas button (@). Designer displays the Edit Formula dialog box, as shown in Figure 29-5. Use the Fields & Functions button, or the @Commands button, to insert the elements of an action, as described in Chapter 28, "Creating Actions, Agents, and Hotspots." This action creates a computed value for the outline entry.

When you create a link for the outline entry, you should have a link on the clipboard. Go to any document, view, or database and choose Edit . . . Copy as Link. Then, click the Paste button in the Outline Entry InfoBox. Designer pastes the link.

To insert a named element outline entry, choose the named element type from the drop-down list. You can click the Browse button to display the Locate Object dialog box, as shown in Figure 29-6. This feature makes it easy to select the named element from the current database or another database. If you are using the outline as a planning tool and the named element does not yet exist, simply type what you intend to name the element and create that element later. You can also choose to insert the named element based on a formula (click the formula button), or you can paste the named element.

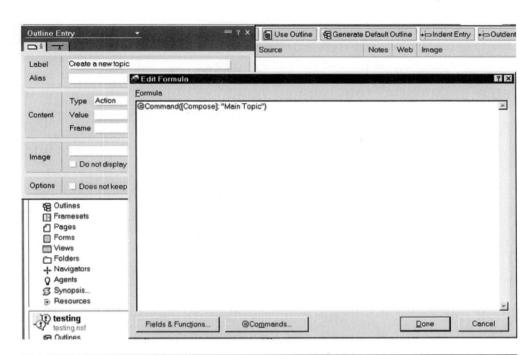

Figure 29-5   Editing the formula for an outline entry action

When you choose to make an outline entry a URL, you can type the URL, paste the URL, or select the URL based on a formula. Be sure to include the protocol when using a URL, such as **http://www.lotus.com,** as shown in Figure 29-7.

For any of the content types, you can also select the frame in which Notes should display the content. Chapter 30 describes frame sets and frames in more detail. To select the frame for the content, type the name or alias of the frame. In addition, on the Outline Entry Info tab, you can choose to display an image with the outline entry. Click the *Browse images* button to select a shared image resource from the database, or click the *Formula* button to choose an image based on a formula. By default, Notes displays views and folders with the icons that are usually associated with them. To force Notes not to display an image, select the *Do not display an image* property. Use the Entry Hide When tab to choose hide-when options for the outline entry. You can hide the entry from Notes 4.6 or later, for Web clients, or based on a formula.

As you create additional outline entries, you might want to create a hierarchy for those entries. Use the *Indent Entry* and *Outdent Entry* action buttons to create the hierarchical structure of the outline. You might also need to reorder the outline elements.

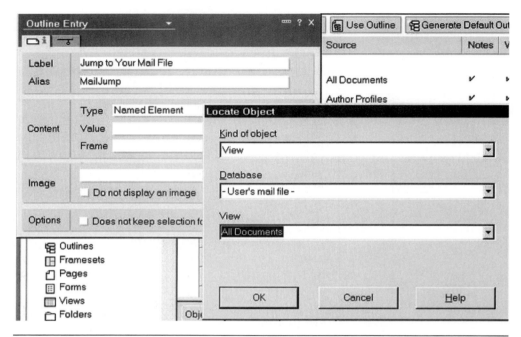

Figure 29-6 Locate Object dialog box

Figure 29-7
Using a URL in an
outline entry

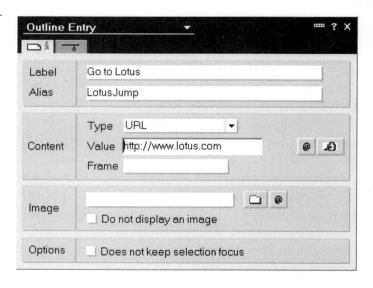

You can click and drag outline entries in the outline. Finally, to remove an outline entry, you can select the entry and press Delete or choose Edit . . . Clear from the menus.

Using the Outline

Outlines are not independent design elements. In order for Notes to display them, they must be embedded on another element, such as a page, form, or in the rich-text field of a document. To embed an outline on a new, blank page, you can click the Use Outline action button. Designer embeds the outline on a new page, as shown in Figure 29-8. You can then add other elements to the page, give it a name, and choose to display it as described in Chapter 25, "Creating Pages and Forms."

You can also embed the outline on a page or form by using the Create . . . Embedded Element menu option from within an existing page or form. Place your cursor where you want to embed the outline, and choose Create . . . Embedded Element. Designer places the outline in the page or form. You can then set the properties for the embedded outline by using the Embedded Outline properties InfoBox, as shown in Figure 29-9.

Use the Embedded Outline properties InfoBox to determine how the page or form will display the outline. First, select either the tree style or the flat style. The tree style displays the hierarchy that you created with the outline, showing the entries that have entries indented under them as expandable sections—similar to the way you see categorized views. Use the *Show Twisties* property to decide whether Notes should display the twisties for expanding and collapsing the hierarchy. Figure 29-10 shows a sample outline in the tree style.

If you chose the flat style, Notes displays only one level of the outline at a time. When a user clicks an entry that has entries indented underneath, Notes displays those entries

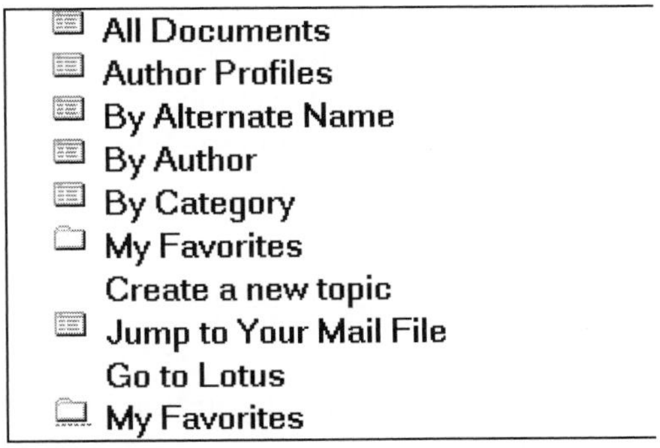

Figure 29-8
Embedding an out-
line on a page

- All Documents
- Author Profiles
- By Alternate Name
- By Author
- By Category
- My Favorites
  Create a new topic
- Jump to Your Mail File
  Go to Lotus
- My Favorites

Embedded Outline
Name
Type
Tree style
Show twisties
Title style
Hide
Target frame
Root entry
Display as saved
Width
6.325"
Fit to content
Outline size
Height
1.750"
Fit to content
Show scroll bar
Web access
Using HTML

Figure 29-9 Embedded outline properties

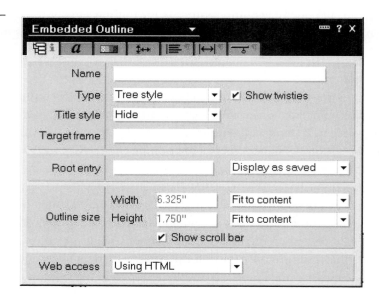

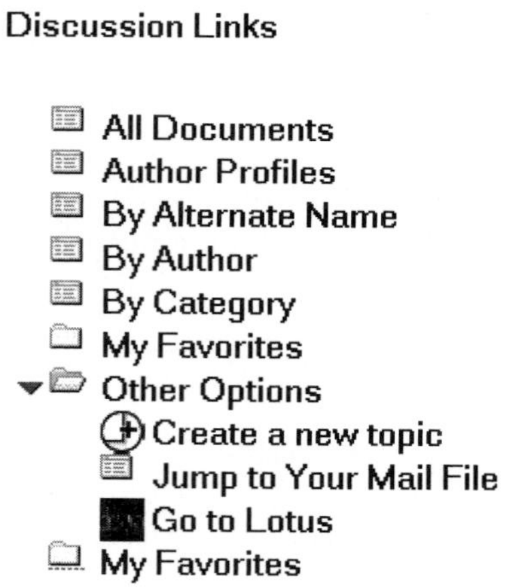
Discussion Links
All Documents
Author Profiles
By Alternate Name
By Author
By Category
My Favorites
Other Options
Create a new topic
Jump to Your Mail File
Go to Lotus
My Favorites

Figure 29-10 An embedded outline in the tree style

as a new outline. Figure 29-11 shows a sample outline in the flat style. The flat style embedded outline can be either vertical or horizontal. Use the horizontal format if you want the outline to be displayed left-to-right across the top of the page or form. When you use a flat style embedded outline, you might want to include the Simple title style. Users can click the title to navigate back up to the previous outline level.

Figure 29-11
A flat style embed-
ded outline

Discussion Links

R5 Certification Discussion
🖫 All Documents
🖫 Author Profiles
🖫 By Alternate Name
🖫 By Author
🖫 By Category
🗀 My Favorites
🗁 Other Options
🗀 My Favorites

Another option that is useful with the flat style is the *Root Entry* option. If you type the name or alias of an outline entry in this field, Notes only displays that entry and its subentries, if any, when the outline is first displayed. If you have defined the Simple title style, users can click the title to navigate back up to the higher levels of the outline. If you hide the title, users need a link, button, or other mechanism to enable them to navigate to the higher levels of the outline.

Use the *Outline Size* options to select the height and width of the embedded outline. Choose *Fixed width, Fit to Window,* or *Fit to Content* for the width, and *Fixed height* or *Fit to Content* for the height. Enable the *Show scroll bar* option to display a scroll bar with the embedded outline when needed.

The *Web Access* options determine whether Domino will display the outline using HTML or using the Java applet. Use the outline applet to enable Web users to take advantage of some of the functions that are usually reserved for Notes. For example, they will be able to see mouse-over options (such as color changes), and they will see background images. Figure 29-12 shows the outline being previewed by using HTML (the default). Figure 29-13 shows the outline being previewed by using the Outline Java applet.

The next tab in the Embedded Outline properties InfoBox is the Font tab. Use this tab to set the font face, size, style, and color for the title font, top-level font, and sub-level font. You might want to select different colors for normal, for when the text is selected, and for when the text is moused over. This feature helps the user know where he or she is on the outline.

Use the Background tab to set background colors for the control, title, top-level, and sublevels of the embedded outline. You can set the background color to change when the area is moused over. In addition, you can set a background image. Select the background image from the shared image resources that are stored with the database, or insert the image based on a formula.

PART IV

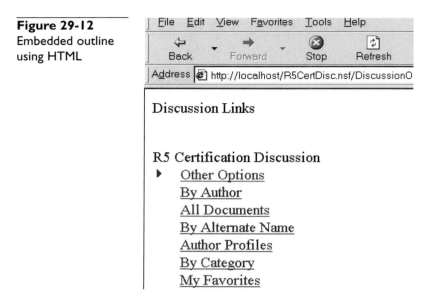

Figure 29-12
Embedded outline
using HTML

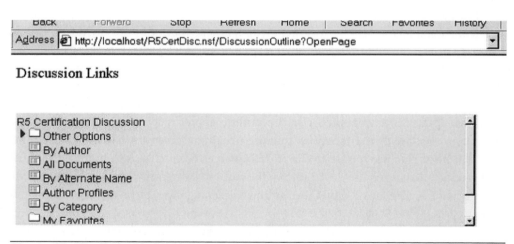

Figure 29-13   Embedded outline using the Outline applet

Use the Layout tab to configure the layout for the entries and the entry labels. You can configure different layout options for the title, top level, and sublevels. The other tabs in the Embedded Outline InfoBox include Paragraph Alignment, Paragraph Margins, and Paragraph Hide-When. Use these tabs to place the outline on the page and to hide it when necessary.

Imagemaps

An imagemap is a graphic (usually a single graphic) that you embed in a page or a form. You place hotspots on the imagemap to perform an action or to link users to another location. You can use the imagemap as a navigation tool in your applications. Similar to an outline, you have to place an imagemap on a page or form in order to use it in the database. To create the imagemap, insert or paste a graphic onto a page or form.

Designer provides a variety of methods that you can use to add graphics to your pages or forms. First, you can copy and paste graphics from other applications. Next, you can use the File . . . Import tool to import graphics in supported formats. Supported formats include .BMP, .JPG/.JPEG, .GIF, .PCX, and .TIFF 5.0. Similarly, use the Create . . . Picture menu choices to import graphics in the same formats (plus .CGM and .PIC formats). Lastly, you can use the shared image resources that were described previously to store graphics with the database and to insert them wherever necessary without adding to the size of the database. To insert shared image resources, choose Create . . . Image Resource.

To make a graphic into an imagemap, add hotspots to the image. You can right-click the image and choose *Add Hotspot Rectangle, Circle,* or *Polygon.* You can also click one of the three Add Hotspot buttons on the Picture Info tab of the Picture properties InfoBox to create polygon-shaped, circular, or rectangular hotspots on the graphic. After clicking a button, use the mouse to draw a hotspot over a portion of the graphic. After creating the hotspot, add an action or link to the hotspot by using the Hotspot properties InfoBox, as shown in Figure 29-14. You can add a URL link, a link to other databases, views, or documents, or a link to a named element (such as another page, a form, a view, or a frame set).

One benefit to using an imagemap is that you can switch the picture in the imagemap without redoing the hotspots. To replace the graphic, click the graphic to select it, and then choose Picture . . . Replace Picture from the menus. If you switch the picture, do not forget to change the caption and alternate text.

Figure 29-14
Hotspot properties

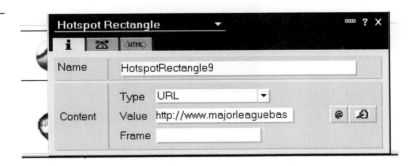

Navigators

If you want to use multiple images as your navigation tool (rather than a single, precreated graphic), you might want to create a navigator instead of an imagemap. A navigator is similar to a graphical table of contents for a database. Unlike outlines and imagemaps, you can use a navigator as an independent design element. Figure 29-15 shows an example of a graphical navigator that enables users to choose views, forms, and actions. The navigator also enables users to open views, forms, and documents without having to use the menus or lists of views and forms. A navigator uses links to move the user to various areas of the application. Notes can display the navigator in the Navigator pane on the right side of the screen or in its own window.

To create a navigator, choose Create . . . Design . . . Navigator from the menus. This action opens an empty Design pane and blank navigator. Right-click the upper pane to choose Navigator properties. Use the Navigator properties InfoBox, which is shown in Figure 29-16, to give the navigator a name, a background color, and a default initial view.

Figure 29-15
Sample graphical navigator

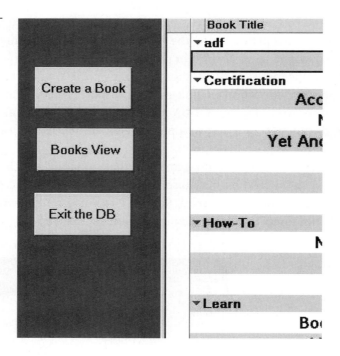

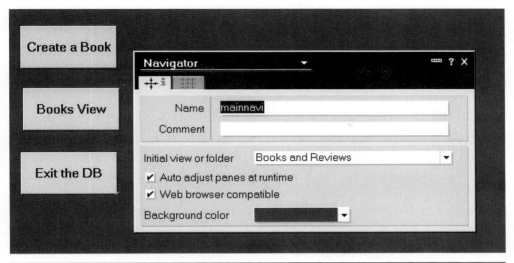

Figure 29-16 Navigator properties InfoBox

Give the navigator a unique name, using any characters you like. As usual, only the first 32 characters appear on menus. The Initial View or Folder option enables a default view or folder to be displayed when the navigator is displayed. This feature is especially useful if the navigator is being automatically launched by using options on the Database properties InfoBox. To automatically resize the panes to accommodate the graphical items in the navigator, enable the Auto Adjust panes at runtime option.

You can add a colored background to the navigator by using the drop-down list on this InfoBox. Additionally, you can add other graphic elements such as graphic buttons and hotspots to the navigator. Copy graphics from other programs and paste them into the navigator by using Paste, or choose Create . . . Graphic Button from the menus. To create a hotspot, select Create . . . Hotspot Rectangle from the menus. To add an action to the button or hotspot, use the Design pane to add a simple function, @Function formula, @Command formula, or LotusScript formula.

To display the navigator, either choose View . . . Show . . . and the name of the navigator, or use the Database properties InfoBox to launch the navigator automatically. You can also launch the navigator by using an action in a view or form. An example of an action to open a navigator would be as follows:

```
@Command ([OpenNavigator]; "MainNavigator"; 1)
```

This command opens the navigator called Main Navigator in its own window. The parameter 1 indicates opening the navigator in its own window; a parameter of 0 would open the navigator in the left-hand Navigator pane.

Summary

Databases need navigation tools (besides views) to make it easy for users to access information. Outlines, imagemaps, and navigators are three useful tools for adding this navigation. The steps to making a usable outline include creating the outline, adding outline entries, embedding the outline on a page or form, and formatting the embedded outline. Web clients can access outlines as HTML or by using a Java applet. Use the Java applet to make accessing the outline more flexible. Remember to place the outline on a page, form, or document in order to make it accessible. Imagemaps are single graphic images that have hotspots placed on them. The hotspots can be links or actions that move the user through the application. A navigator is a set of graphics, also with hotspots, that Notes can display in its own window or in the Navigation pane of an application.

Practice

Next, if you created the R5 Orders and Reviews database with the appropriate elements in Chapter 28, you can open that database to get started.

First, create a new outline to help users navigate the database. Use the *Generate Default Outline* action button to create a starting point. Add outline entries to add a new book to the database, and place the view for retrieving deleted documents one level down in the hierarchy. Note that there are some additional views in the database, which are added for practice. Note that you can obtain a design synopsis for outlines. The details of the design synopsis for this outline are shown in Table 29-1.

After creating the outline, click the *Use Outline* button to embed the outline in a new page. Use the tree style with twisties for the embedded outline. Fit both the height and width to the content of the outline. Use the Java applet for access via the Web. Name the page with the embedded outline OutlinePage. Later, you will want to add this page to a frame set so that the page is part of the main application.

Table 29-1   Outline design synopsis

Name:	MainOutline
Available to public access users:	No
Entry:	**Add a Book**
Alias:	[Not Assigned]
Indentation Level: Type:	0 Action
Formula:	`@Command([Compose]; "Book");`
Target Frame:	[Not Assigned]
Image Resource:	`hp_alpha.gif`
Never use an image:	No
Refuse Selection:	No
Entry:	**Books Only**
Alias:	[Not Assigned]
Indentation Level:	0
Type:	Named Element (View)
Name:	Books Only
Target Frame:	[Not Assigned]
Never use an image:	No
Refuse Selection:	No
Entry:	**Books and Reviews**
Alias:	[Not Assigned]
Indentation Level:	0
Type:	Named Element (View)
Name:	Books and Reviews
Target Frame:	[Not Assigned]
Never use an image:	No
Refuse Selection:	No

continued

Table 29-1 Outline design synopsis *(continued)*

Entry:	By Book Type
Alias:	[Not Assigned]
Indentation Level:	0
Type:	Named Element (View)
Name:	BKType
Target Frame:	[Not Assigned]
Never use an image:	No
Refuse Selection:	No
Entry:	**By Document Author**
Alias:	[Not Assigned]
Indentation Level:	0
Type:	Named Element (View)
Name:	Author
Target Frame:	[Not Assigned]
Never use an image:	No
Refuse Selection:	No
Entry:	**My Reviews**
Alias:	[Not Assigned]
Indentation Level:	0
Type:	Named Element (Folder)
Name:	My Reviews
Target Frame:	[Not Assigned]
Never use an image:	No
Refuse Selection:	No
Entry:	**Special Views**
Alias:	[Not Assigned]
Indentation Level:	0
Type:	(None)

continued

Target Frame:	[Not Assigned]

Table 29-1 Outline design synopsis *(continued)*

Never use an image:	No
Refuse Selection:	No
Entry:	**Retrieve Deleted Documents**
Alias:	[Not Assigned]
Indentation Level:	1
Type:	Named Element (View)
Name:	Retrieve Deleted Documents
Target Frame:	[Not Assigned]
Never use an image:	No
Refuse Selection:	No

Review Questions

1. Julie created an outline and wants to display it as the first item that users see when they open the database. Which of the following steps should she try?
   a. Only navigators can be launched automatically when users open the database.
   b. Use the Database Launch properties to launch the outline automatically when users open the database.
   c. Embed the outline in a form. Use the Database Launch properties to launch the form automatically when users open the database.
   d. Embed the outline in a page. Use the Database Launch properties to launch the page automatically when users open the database.

2. Which of the following steps are required to use an outline?
   a. Create the outline.
   b. Create outline entries.
   c. Enable the Outline applet.
   d. Embed the outline in a page.

3. True or false: An outline can be available to public-access users.
   a. True
   b. False

4. If you enable Designer to generate the default outline, which of the following are included?
   a. All of the shared views in the database
   b. All of the private views in the database
   c. Action to create the default form in the database
   d. Placeholders for shared and private folders

5. Which of the following can be an outline entry?
   a. URL
   b. Another outline
   c. Action
   d. Frame set

6. True or false: If a named element that you want to include in an outline entry does not yet exist, you cannot add it to the outline.
   a. True
   b. False

7. How can Alison use twisties with her hierarchical outline entries?
   a. In the Outline properties, enable the *Show Twisties* property.
   b. Use the tree style.
   c. In the Embedded Outline properties, enable the *Show Twisties* property.
   d. In the Outline Entry properties, enable the *Show Twisties* property.

8. Mike wants to create a hierarchical outline. He only wants users to access one of the hierarchies. How can he accomplish this goal?
   a. He cannot. Once he makes the outline available, users can see all the parts of the outline.
   b. He can use a tree-style outline with a root entry option and the hide title style.
   c. He can use a flat-style outline with a root entry option and the hide title style.
   d. He can use a tree-style outline with a root entry option and the simple title style.

9. Which of the following elements can be displayed independently in the database?
   a. Outline
   b. Imagemap
   c. Navigator
   d. Page

10. Which of the following actions would open the navigator called MainNavi in its own window?
    a. @Command ([OpenNavigator]; "MainNavi"; 1)
    b. @Command ([OpenNavigator]; "MainNavi"; 0)
    c. @Command ([Folder]:Navigator; "MainNavi"; 1)
    d. @Command ([OpenNavigator]; "MainNavi"; "Window")

Review Answers

1. **D is correct.** While you can embed the outline in a form, you cannot launch a form when the database is opened.

2. **A, B,** and **D are correct.** All three are required steps. You do not have to use the Outline applet.

3. **A is correct.** Use the outline properties to make the outline available to public-access users.

4. **A, C,** and **D are correct.** The default outline does not have any actions.

5. **A, C,** and **D are correct.** An outline could only be an outline entry if it had been embedded in a page or form.

6. **B is correct.** To add an element that you have not yet created, just type the name that you intend to give the element. In this manner, you can use the outline for planning your application.

7. **B** and **C are correct.** Twisties are only available with the tree-style outline, and the use of twisties must be enabled on the Embedded Outline properties.

8. **B** or **C is correct.** An outline in either the flat or tree style that has a root entry and a hidden title will initially display only the elements below the selected root entry—with no link to move back in the outline.

9. **C** or **D is correct.** Outlines and imagemaps must be placed on pages or forms in order to be displayed in the database. A page or navigator can be launched independently.

10. **A is correct.** The 0 argument indicates that the navigator should be opened in the Navigator (or Folders) pane.

Creating Framesets

You should be able to answer questions based on the following objective after reading this chapter:

- Create, modify, troubleshoot framesets

Framesets are a new feature to R5 of Notes and Domino that enables you to present a multi-paned interface to both Notes and Web users. Each of the panes is a frame. Each pane, or frame, contains information that can be linked to the information in other frames but is independently scrollable. A frameset enables you to leave one page or other element displayed to users while other content changes. To create a frameset as part of the structure for your application, first create the frameset and then add content to each of the frames.

Create the Frameset

To create a new frameset for the application, go to the Framesets Design view. Click the *New Frameset* action button or choose Create . . . Design . . . Frameset from the menus. Designer displays the Create New Frameset dialog box, as shown in Figure 30-1.

Use this dialog box to choose the layout and initial number of frames for the frameset. The alignment options vary according the number of frames you include in the frameset. You can include between two and four frames, initially; however, you can add or remove frames later. When you click OK, Designer displays the empty frameset in the Work area, as shown in Figure 30-2.

To configure the frameset, open the Frameset properties InfoBox, shown in Figure 30-3. Use the Basics tab to give the frameset a name, alias, and comment. Use this tab also to determine if the frameset should be available to public access users. Use the *Title* field to create a title for the frameset, using either static text or a formula. The title

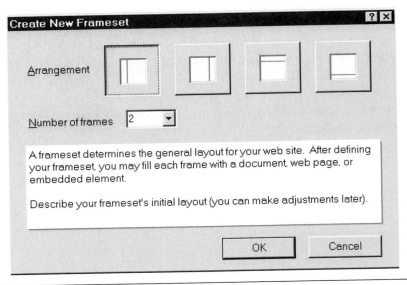

Figure 30-1   Create new frameset

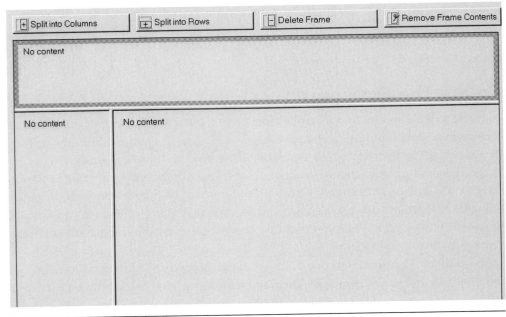

Figure 30-2   New frameset

Figure 30-3
Frameset properties
basics

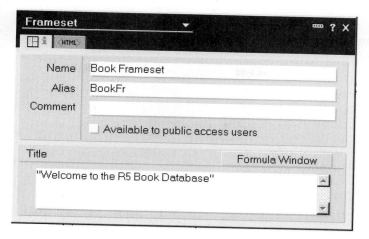

for the frameset appears in the title bar or the Window menu when the frameset is active. Note that since this is a formula window, if you decide to use static text, you must enclose it in quotation marks (""").

Add Content to the Frames

Next, you must give each frame some content. The frames can contain any of the following elements:

- Form
- Folder
- Document
- View
- Navigator
- Page
- Frameset
- URL

To add content to a frame, open the Frame properties InfoBox, shown in Figure 30-4. First, create a unique name for the frame. You will be using the frames as destinations for formulas or other content, so you should make your frame names unique.

Figure 30-4
Frame properties
InfoBox

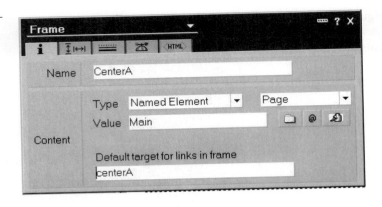

After giving the frame a unique name, choose a type of content for the frame. The *Type* drop-down list contains the following options:

- Link
- Named Element
- URL

To insert a link, go to the view or document you want to link to and choose Edit . . . Copy as Link. Then click the *Paste* button next to the *Value* field to insert the link. Framesets do not support database links.

To insert a named element, select *Named Element* from the *Type* drop-down list. Then select a type of named element, including a page, form, frameset, view, folder, or navigator. To select a named element to insert, type in the name of the element, paste in the name of the element, or click the *Browse* button. You can select an element from the current database or another database on the server. You can also choose an element programmatically by clicking the *Formula* button. Use a formula that evaluates to the name of a specific element. If you select to insert a view or folder as the type of named element, an additional check box is available to choose *Simple Appearance*. This presents the view without an action bar, if the view contains one. Views and folders work best in framesets when you embed them on a page or form. Remember that if you plan to use the frameset for Web clients, you might want to use the view applet.

To insert a URL, type the full URL into the *Value* field, including the protocol, such as **http://www.lotus.com**. Click the *Formula* button to choose a URL programmatically.

Figure 30-5
Specify a target
frame for a form.

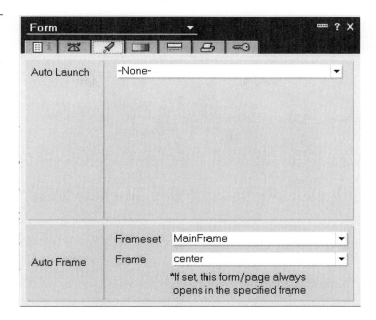

To determine where links in the current frame will open, specify the name of a frame
in the *Default target for links in frame* field. If you do not specify a target frame, the links
in a frame will open in the same frame. If an element, such as a form, has a target frame
set in its properties (see Figure 30-5), that option takes precedence over the target frame
configured here. You can specify a target frame for a page or form on the Page or Form
properties InfoBoxes.

You can also specify a target frame with certain formulas, using @SetTargetFrame.
This function specifies a target frame in which to open a view, page, or frameset. It can
also be used when composing or editing a document. Use @SetTargetFrame in actions
and hotspot formulas that use any of the following @Commands:

- @Command([OpenFrameset])
- @Command([OpenPage])
- @Command([OpenView])
- @Command([Compose])
- @Command([EditDocument])

To use @SetTargetFrame, create a formula such as

```
@SetTargetFrame("Main Frame");
@Command([Compose]; "Main Form")
```

or

```
@SetTargetFrame("Main Frame");
@Command([OpenView]; "Main View")
```

If you have a frameset nested inside a frame, use list syntax to set a target frame. Use the outer frameset's frame as the first element in the list. If a frameset with a frame called "Second Frame" is inside a frame called "Main Frame," use the following formula to set "Second Frame" as the target for the form:

```
@SetTargetFrame("Main Frame": "Second Frame");
@Command([Compose]; "Main Form")
```

To insert other content into the frames, first place the content on a page, form, or navigator. Then launch that element in the frame. If you want to display a company logo from a shared image resource, for example, insert the shared image resource onto a page. Then make that page the content for one of the frames. Similarly, you might want to display an outline in one frame of a frameset. Embed the outline on a page or form and display the page or form in the frameset.

Other Frame Properties

Use the other tabs in the Frame properties InfoBox to determine how the frames will appear and perform. On the Frame Size tab, shown in Figure 30-6, choose the width and height of the frame. These measurements can be relative, a percentage, or pixels. A relative size is based on the other frames in the frameset. You can enable or disable scrolling within the frame. If you choose the default, *Auto*, Notes will display a scroll bar if it is needed. Enable the *Allow Resizing* option if you want users to be able to drag the borders of frames to change their size. This option works on both Notes and the Web.

Use the Frame Border tab, in Figure 30-7, to set a border style. The *3-D Border* option applies to the current frame only by default, although you can apply your choice to all frames in the frameset by clicking the *Apply to all frames* button. The *Border Width* and *Border color* options apply to all frames in a frameset by default. The default border width is seven pixels. You can use the system default color by clicking the button that looks like a monitor at the top of the color drop-down chart.

Use the Advanced tab, shown in Figure 30-8, to configure some additional Web appearance settings. The *Frame Spacing* option determines the amount of space

Figure 30-6
Frame Size tab

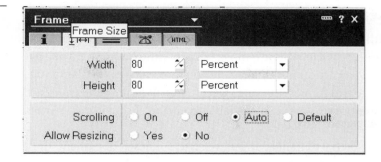

Figure 30-7
Frame Border tab

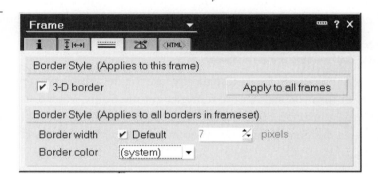

Figure 30-8
Advanced tab

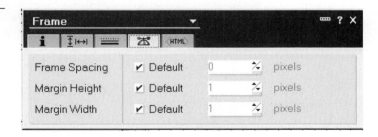

between frames when viewed by Web clients. The default is zero pixels. Use the *Margin Height* and *Margin Width* options to configure the amount of space between the borders and content when frames are viewed in Web clients. The default for each of these is 1 pixel.

Other Frame Options

Although you can only set a maximum of four frames when you initially create the frame, you can add or remove frames while designing. The *Split into Columns* and *Split into Rows* action buttons enable you to break a particular frame into smaller frames. To merge two frames into one larger frame, use the *Delete Frame* action button. All three of those options are also available from the shortcut menu when you right-click in the frame or from the Frame menu.

If you have changed the view, page, frameset, document, or other element in a frame while designing, you can force the frame to display the updated content by choosing *Refresh Frame Content* from the shortcut menu or the Frame menu. If you want to remove the content of the frame without adding new content immediately, you can choose the *Remove Frame Contents* action button, or select that option from the menus.

Launch the Frameset

To launch the frameset automatically, use the default launch options for the database, page, or form. To launch the frameset automatically when a user opens the database, use the Launch tab of the Database properties InfoBox, shown in Figure 30-9. You can launch a designated frameset automatically for either a Notes client or a Web client.

Figure 30-9
Database launch
properties

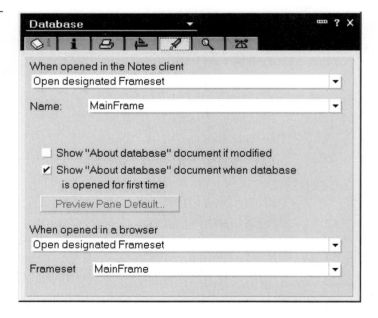

Figure 30-10
Auto Frame options
for a page

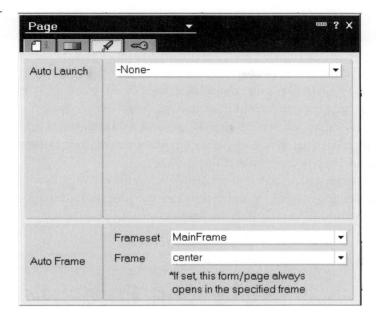

You can also set the launch properties for a page or form. Figure 30-10 shows the *Auto Frame* option for a page. If you set a frame and frameset on this tab, Notes and Domino display the page in this frame. The *Auto Frame* properties for forms are similar; Notes displays the form and all documents created with it in the designated form.

Summary

Use framesets to present a multi-pane display to either Notes or Web users. To use a frameset, first create the frameset. You can create up to four frames initially, although you can add additional frames to this later. After creating the frameset, add content to the frames and set properties for the frames and frameset. Use @SetTargetFrame and *Auto Frame* options to launch design elements automatically in a particular frame.

Practice

Next, if you created the R5 Orders and Reviews database with the appropriate elements in Chapter 29, you can open that database to get started.

First, create a new frameset to use to display a paned interface to users. Use three panes when creating the frameset. For the top frame of the frameset, I created a new page with a company name; you might also add a logo to this page. I called this frame Top. In the left pane of the frameset, called Left, place the navigator you created in Chapter 30. In the Center frame, place the original page from Chapter 27. Now that you have more experience with hotspots, you will want to make the icons on the page into hotspots that perform the appropriate actions. Don't forget to use @SetTargetFrame to ensure that the top and left panes remain constant while the center frame changes. Figure 30-11 shows a sample of the frameset.

You can obtain a design synopsis for a frameset, as shown in Table 30-1. Note that the design synopsis for framesets does not include information about the content of the frames. To see this data, include design synopses for the frame content separately.

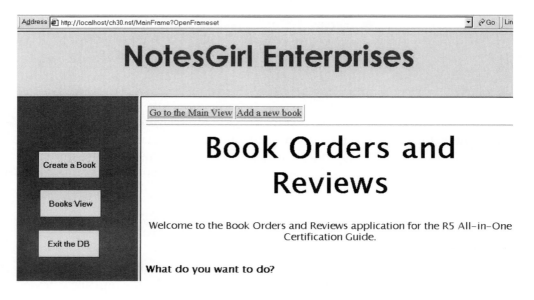

Figure 30-11 Sample Frameset

Table 30-1   Frameset Design Synopsis

Name:	MainFrame
Last Modification:	10/27/99 08:59:38 PM
Comment:	[Not Assigned]
Available to public access users:	No
Window Title Formula:	"Main Frameset"
HTML Code:	

```
<frameset frameborder="1" rows="17%,58%" cols="*">
<frame name="top" frameborder="0" scrolling="yes" noresize>
<frameset rows="*" cols="26%,74%">
<frame name="left" noresize>
<frame name="center">
</frameset>
</frameset>
```

PART IV

Review Questions

1. When Basil creates a new frameset, what is the maximum number of frames he can add initially?
   a. 2
   b. 3
   c. 4
   d. 5

2. Which of the following elements can Missy place directly in a frame?
   a. Shared Image Resource
   b. Page
   c. Form
   d. Frameset

3. When Julieana creates a form, she sets the *Auto Frame* property to launch the form in the "MainFrame" frameset, in the "Left" frame. When she creates the "Left" frame, she sets the target for links in that frame to be the "Center" frame. In which frame does the form launch?

   a. Left

   b. Center

4. Gus wants his company logo to be visible in the HR application at all times. Which of the following will accomplish this?

   a. Create the logo as an image resource. Place the image resource into one frame of the HR application's frameset.

   b. Create the logo as an image resource. Place the image resource on a page and place it into one of the frames in the HR application's frameset.

   c. Create the logo as an image resource. In the properties for the image resource, use the @SetTargetFrame function to place the image in one frame of the HR application's frameset.

   d. Use @SetTargetFrame ("MainFrame": "Left"; 1) to set the image resource in the "Left" frame of the "MainFrame" frameset. The 1 argument means the frame will be locked.

5. True or false: Pamela wants to display a page from the HR application database in the left frame. She wants to display a view from the Company Directory application in the right frame. She can do this.

   a. False, you can only have elements from the current database in the frameset.

   b. True.

6. Alexis created an action button to compose a new document with the "Book" form. She wants the form to be composed in the "Left" frame of the frameset. Which formula did she use in the action button?

   a. @SetTargetFrame ("Left"); @Command([Compose]; "Book")

   b. @Command([Compose]; "Book"; @SetTargetFrame("Left"))

   c. @Command([OpenFrame]; "Left");@Command([Compose]; "Book")

   d. @Command([SetTargetFrame]; "Left"); @Command([Compose]; "Book")

Review Answers

1. **C is correct.**   You can create four frames when you initially create the frameset, although you can add to this number later.

2. **B, C,** and **D** are correct.   You can place pages, forms, and other framesets directly into a frame. To use an image resource, place it on a page or form.

3. **A is correct.**   The *Auto Frame* property takes precedence over the property set in the frame.

4. **B is correct.**   To use an image resource in a frame, place in on a page or form (or navigator) first.

5. **B is correct.**   You can use elements from multiple databases in a frameset.

6. **A** is correct.   Use the @SetTargetFrame with the name of the frame before @Commands to open views, pages, and create forms.

Review Answers

PART V

Application Security and Workflow

The second exam in the Application Development track is the Application Security and Workflow exam (190-511). Passing this exam is the next step in gaining your Certified Lotus Professional (CLP) designation for Application Development, although it does not give you a certification by itself. The audience for this exam is developers with a basic knowledge of the Domino Designer client and the capability to create multiple Notes databases for any of the available clients. You should already have passed the Domino Designer Fundamentals exam and have familiarity with programming with functions and formulas in Domino. The exam has 40 scored questions and 5 unscored questions, and requires a minimum score of 74 percent. The competencies for this exam cover six basic areas:

- Creating workflow applications
- Monitoring, maintaining, and troubleshooting workflow applications
- Planning and designing workflow applications
- Security: monitoring, maintaining, and troubleshooting problems
- Security: planning and design
- Security: setting up, configuring, implementing, and enabling

These general areas of competency are broken down further into specific tasks that you should be able to perform. To see a complete list, refer to the *Lotus Domino R5 CLP Certification Exam Guide*, available for download from **www.lotus.com/ education**. Each chapter in this section lists the specific competency areas that it covers.

Planning and Designing Workflow Applications

You should be able to answer questions based on the following objectives after reading this chapter:

- Planning and designing workflow applications
  - Distribution through routing
  - Parallel/serial distribution
  - Planning for multiple languages
  - Planning for multiple mail systems
  - Tracking through mail-in databases
  - Tracking through replication
- Creating workflow applications
  - Creating/setting up workflow roles (external to Notes)
  - Creating/setting up workflow roles (within Notes)
  - Creating/setting up workflow routing rules (addressing) using multiple mail systems
  - Setup for multiple languages

In this chapter, you will learn how to plan and design a workflow application. You will be able to define workflow and list examples of business processes that can be transformed into workflow applications. We discuss individual elements that make up workflow, such as the object that Notes is routing, the route that the object takes, and the roles that are involved in the process. We define several different distribution methods and list the advantages and disadvantages of each method. Due to the popularity of Notes around the world, our planning includes the possibility of a multiple-language application. We also discuss how to include users of non-Notes mail applications in our workflow process.

The best way to discuss the concept of workflow is to use a real-world example. This chapter includes an example of a company that is currently using a paper-based method to process employee travel expense account reimbursements. We discuss the process currently in place, and then see how to transform the process into an electronic workflow application.

Introduction to Workflow

When planning and designing a workflow application, you must first understand the process that you are automating from beginning to end. Lotus defines a business process as the tasks or steps that are taken to reach a specific business goal. These tasks or steps often involve routing a piece of paper from person to person for modification or approval. The activities (work) and interactions (flow) that are required to reach a business goal are known as workflow. Domino designers automate these activities and interactions by building a workflow application. Workflow applications reduce overhead and errors, speed up the business process overall, make people accountable for tasks assigned to them, and track the status of the document or object that is being passed between people. Examples of processes that can be incorporated into workflow applications are as follows:

- Customer order processing
- Travel expense report reimbursement
- Writing and approving a contract
- Changes to employee records
- Loan approval

NOTE Domino Designer provides a template called Document Library—Notes & Web (doclbw50.ntf) that you can use to quickly create a workflow application. Domino Server comes with a template called Team Room (teamrm50.ntf), which is a discussion/document-management template that contains various workflow features.

Designing an advanced application such as a workflow application requires the designer to understand the processes that are currently in place in an organization. In other words, you must interview potential users. Interviewing users not only ensures that the application will meet the users' needs, but it also forces the company to examine its current business process with a more critical eye. There might be tasks or steps that you can either modify or eliminate from the process. Discussing the application design with potential users benefits everyone involved.

Sample Business Scenario

Let's look at an example of the current travel expense account reimbursement process in place at a fictitious company. ABC Corporation has asked you (the designer) to develop an application that will replace its current paper-based reimbursement system and that will drag the company kicking and screaming into the electronic age. After interviewing a few potential users, you decide that it is hopeless and walk away (just kidding). Employees at ABC Corporation have been using Notes as their e-mail platform for about a year. The company recently heard that Notes is more than just an e-mail package. ABC Corporation is interested in tapping into the power of Domino as an application development tool and has decided that its paper-based reimbursement system should be the first of many business processes that it converts into a Domino application.

From interviewing potential users, you find out that ABC Corporation's travel expense account reimbursement process begins with an employee filling out an expense report form. The employee then walks to his or her manager's office and places the expense report in the manager's In basket. When the manager finds the time to approve the expense report (or finds the expense report at all in his or her In box), the manager sends the approved report to the payroll department. If the total amount of the reimbursement is more than $1,000, the expense report requires a second approval signature from a second-line manager. At any time during this process, any of the approvers or human resources people can reject the expense report and send it back to the employee.

When the payroll department receives the approved expense report, it produces a check for the employee's reimbursement. Once the check is printed, the payroll department stamps the original expense report with a stamp showing the date that the check was cut. The expense report is then filed in a filing cabinet containing previously reimbursed expense reports, and an e-mail is sent to the manager informing him or her that the employee's check is ready to be picked up. The current reimbursement process from beginning to end takes 1 to 2 weeks.

Planning the Application

As a designer, you know that ABC Corporation's travel expense reimbursement process is a workflow application waiting to happen. Do not rush into the design phase until you fully understand and can define ABC's current business process. This understanding is the base upon which you will develop the entire application. Once you fully understand the business process, you can begin planning and designing your workflow application.

Workflow Elements

The first step in planning a workflow application is to determine the various pieces involved in your workflow puzzle. Organize these pieces or elements into the following categories:

- Documents or forms involved in the current process that need to be automated
- Roles involved in the process
- Path upon which the documents or forms travel as they pass through the process
- Jobs or tasks that need to be done by the specific roles

Objects   An object is a document or form that flows through the business process. There can be multiple objects that are routed in a workflow application, but ABC Corporation's ordering process consists of only one object: the employee travel expense reimbursement form. Look at the current hard copy expense reimbursement form and some forms that have already been completed and approved. Make note of information that must be included in the flow, and weed out information that might no longer be useful in the electronic version of the form. Is there additional information that might be needed or can be generated in the electronic version?

Because this form involves the approval of a monetary transaction, you need to keep in mind how you are going to incorporate security into your workflow application. Should you allow the form to be modified once the manager approves the travel expenses? What access level should you assign to the different people who are involved in the reimbursement process?

Roles   As part of the planning process, determine the roles involved in the routing of the object(s) (i.e., who can initiate an action and who or what receives the result of that action). Looking back at the notes gathered from interviewing potential users, you determine that the following roles are involved in the current reimbursement process:

- Employee

- Manager (could be up to two levels of managers)

- Payroll

As you can see from the example, a role can be either a single person or a department. Some roles can participate more than once in the workflow process. For example, the employee's manager will initiate an action by approving the reimbursement report and will be the recipient of an action when payroll notifies him or her that the employee's reimbursement check has been processed.

Routes   The interactions or flow in a workflow define the route. When planning a workflow application, you need to determine the beginning point and ending point in the workflow process and the points of interaction along the way. For example, ABC Corporation's travel expense report begins with the employee and ends with the employee's manager. Along the way, multiple people interact with the report: the employee's manager, possibly a second-line manager, and the payroll department.

Rules   As the workflow object passes between two people or roles, a corresponding action or task takes place. Workflow applications force people to be responsible for a specific task or action by notifying them that a workflow object awaits action. Developers can also incorporate alarms and reminders into the application to remind people that a task is due. Once the user completes the action, workflow notifies the roles that are responsible for the next task or action and sends them the information that they need to complete their part of the workflow process. Rules in a workflow process determine the action that enables the object to proceed down the workflow path, as well as how to handle an exception to that action in your application. If more than one workflow object is involved, know where to route the different objects.

During the planning process, break the workflow into smaller, more manageable workflows and analyze them separately. As an example, break ABC Corporation's travel expense reimbursement process into the mini-workflows shown in Table 31-1. A specific task and corresponding exception is listed each time the object passes from one role to the next.

The Workflow Diagram

Once you create a table that breaks the overall workflow process into smaller workflows, sketch a workflow diagram that depicts the flow of the object in the reimbursement process. Displaying the flow graphically gives you a better idea of the flow and

Table 31-1   Routes and Rules

Route	Rule	Exception
Employee to manager	Completed travel expense reimbursement form is sent to employee's manager.	None
Manager to payroll	Manager forwards approved form to payroll.	Manager rejects form and notifies employee, or if the reimbursement is more than $1,000, the manager forwards the form to a second-line manager.
Payroll to manager	Payroll notifies employee's manager that reimbursement check has been printed.	Payroll rejects form and notifies manager.

ensures that you address all steps of the process. A sample workflow diagram for ABC Corporation is shown in Figure 31-1.

Make sure that your potential users agree with your workflow diagram and that the flows are accurate and correct. Listen to them and take their input seriously, because they are the ultimate users of the system (not you).

Distribution Models

Now that you have created a workflow diagram, you can begin to concentrate on the details of how to implement the workflow. Automating the flow of data through a business process is a major benefit to developing a workflow application. Notes can perform many basic tasks, such as notifying users that a document awaits their attention electronically—with little or no user intervention. No more will you hear excuses such as "I lost it" or "I never received it" from the users who are involved in the process.

By automating ABC Corporation's travel expense reimbursement process, users who are involved in specific tasks or actions related to their role in the reimbursement process are held accountable for their timely involvement. Notification to participants in the workflow process is usually accomplished either through the automatic routing of documents or through mail messages containing links to documents awaiting approval. For the exam, understand the methods of notification as well as the advantages and disadvantages of each.

Distribution Through Routing   Distribution through routing involves sending the approval document directly to each user's mail file for their review. This method is

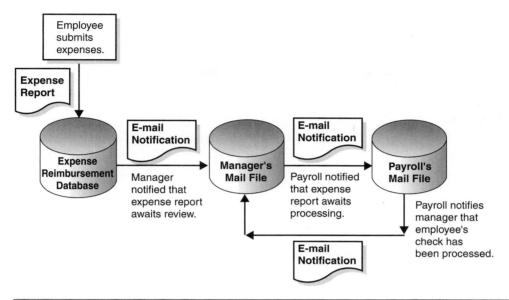

Figure 31-1   Workflow diagram

good for remote users who work and are disconnected from the network. They are able to modify and approve the document directly from their local mail file. There are several disadvantages to the distribution through routing method, however. Table 31-2 shows advantages and disadvantages for using this type of workflow routing method.

Parallel/Serial Distribution   Parallel and serial distribution stores the workflow object in a central, shared database. Domino notifies users that a document awaits their approval through an e-mail message that links them back to the centrally located document. This method works well for most workflow applications. Keep in mind that remote users have to dial into the server in order for their document link to locate the database that contains the document. There are several design methods we can use to alleviate this problem. These methods are discussed in further detail in Chapter 32, "Creating a Workflow Application." The advantages and disadvantages of parallel/serial distribution are listed in Table 31-3.

As we mentioned previously, both parallel and serial distribution stores the approval document in a central, shared database. The difference between parallel and serial distribution is based on when Domino notifies the reviewers of the need to review documents. With parallel distribution, Domino sends an e-mail notification to all reviewers at the same time. The document being reviewed is available to every reviewer, and

PART V

Table 31-2 Distribution Through Routing

Method	Advantages	Disadvantages
Send workflow object from one user to another through their individual mail files.	Easier for remote users because they can locally access their mail instead of having to access a remote database.	The workflow process might take longer, because the tasks are performed sequentially. It requires more disk space than a central, shared database method, because forms must be stored with documents. Replication times might increase because of document size.

Table 31-3 Parallel/Serial Distribution

Method	Advantages	Disadvantages
The workflow object is stored in a central, shared database. Users are sent e-mail notifications that link to the object.	Places the least burden on network resources and conserves server disk space. Users can see comments from other reviewers.	Requires network or remote access in order to view the linked document.

reviews happen simultaneously or in any order. For serial distribution, reviewers receive an e-mail notification at different times. When the first reviewer completes his or her review, the next reviewer gets a request to review the document. If a time limit is set for each review and a reviewer has not yet approved the document within the specified time limit, Domino can send a reminder to that reviewer. Expect to see a question or two on the exam asking about the difference between parallel and serial distribution.

In the case of ABC Corporation, you decide that the best way to implement workflow distribution is through serial distribution. Once the employee fills out the travel expense reimbursement form, the employee's manager is notified that the expense document awaits his or her approval. After the manager reviews and approves the document, the payroll department receives a notification to approve the document and process the reimbursement check. Finally, the employee's manager is notified when the check is ready to be picked up.

Plan for Multiple Languages

If you create a workflow application for use around the world, keep in mind the need for different language versions of your application. If you are using parallel or serial distribution, set the database property of your central, shared database to enable multiple languages. Select Multilingual Database on the Design tab of the Database Properties InfoBox (refer to Figure 31-2). Once you have enabled the database property, select the default language, region, and sort order. The language and region properties are available for individual design elements as well. These properties work in conjunction with the language preference set in the user's Notes client or browser. They ensure that the correct language version of a design element is presented to an international user. Expect to see a question regarding multiple language databases on the exam.

Plan for Multiple Mail Systems

As we discussed previously in this chapter, an essential part of workflow is to notify users when a document is awaiting their action. Whether we use the distribution through routing method or the parallel/serial method, a user's mail file is always one of the points along the workflow path. With this factor in mind, plan and design your workflow application so that non-Notes mail users can participate in the process.

If there are cc:Mail users participating in the workflow application, place a computed MailFormat field on a form to enable cc:Mail users to view Notes documents created by

PART V

Figure 31-2
Multilingual
Database property

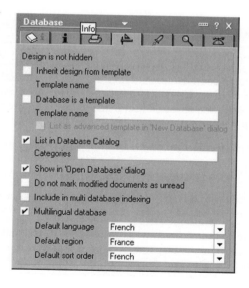

the form. The MailFormat field is a type of reserved field. Reserved fields are discussed in more detail in Chapter 32, "Creating a Workflow Application." Table 31-4 lists the possible values of the MailFormat field and explains each of the values.

If some of your users are Web users with mail databases on a Domino server, use Form or View actions to enable them to participate in the workflow process. Remember that menus displayed in the Notes client are not available to Web users. Create an Approve Document action, for example, so that Web users can route documents using a browser.

Another way to enhance a workflow application for Web users is to ensure that a recipient's Internet address is in the correct format. If you are routing a document or mail message to a user with an Internet address, the address must be in either RFC 822 or RFC 821 format to be valid. You can use the following function in a validation formula to verify the correct format:

```
@ValidateInternetAddress([KEYWORD];Address)
```

- The two choices for the KEYWORD parameter are [Address821] and [Address822]. The differences in address format are listed as follows:
  - [Address821]—smahon@schwarz.com
  - [Address822]—"Mahon, Susan" <smahon@schwarz.com>
- The Address parameter is the address string that is being validated.

Table 31-4 MailFormat Field Values

Value	Description
E (Encapsulated)	The document is encapsulated in a database and is attached to a cc:Mail memo. Notes client must be installed in order to read the document. Use only if information will be lost in conversion to text or memo format. You must store the form in the document.
T (Text)	The document is rendered as text and is pasted into the body of the cc:Mail memo. A recipient using cc:Mail can read the document without using Notes client. You do not need to store the form in the document.
B (Both)	The document is both rendered as text and encapsulated in a database. This ensures that cc:Mail users can read the document without using Notes client.
M (Mail)	The body field of the document is rendered as text and is pasted into the cc:Mail memo. Use only with documents that were created by using a form with a field called Body. You do not need to store the form in the document.

If validation is successful, the return value is NULL. Here is an example:

```
va := @ValidateInternetAddress([Address821];ReviewerAddress);
@If(va = NULL;@Success;@Failure(va))
```

If the contents of the ReviewerAddress field are

```
smahon@schwarz.com
```

then the validation formula returns NULL—indicating a successful validation. If the contents of the ReviewerAddress field are

```
"Susan Mahon" <smahon@schwarz.com>
```

then the validation field returns the following error message:

```
"Invalid RFC821 syntax, no Phrase required."
```

Workflow Tracking

One of the greatest advantages of electronic workflow applications over a paper-based process is the capability to track the object as it moves through the process. In a paper-based business process, the object can get lost when shuffled between people or departments. The object might even get lost for days on someone's desk and be buried under mounds of paper. If you are the employee who just submitted your travel expenses, you expect to be reimbursed in a timely, accurate fashion. If you are the manager, you want to make sure that you are paying your employees promptly and that your employees are not abusing the reimbursement process. By incorporating tracking into your workflow application, the users always know the status of a workflow object and the object's status in the workflow process. You can track the status of a workflow object at each point in the process by performing the following actions:

- Creating a field on a form to store the status of the particular workflow object
- Creating a view listing outstanding items
- Creating a view to show the stage in which certain workflow objects exist

As designated reviewers mark documents as Reviewed, the documents can be mailed to a mail-in database for tracking purposes. Once the documents are in the mail-in database, you can create a Review Status view that categorizes the documents according to where they are in the workflow process. Base the categorized view on the contents of a form field that stores the document status and is updated as each action is performed on the documents.

If you choose to track through replication, you need to be aware of a potential problem. If a Readers field containing usernames is in a document, the field must also include the names of all replicating servers. If not, the document will not replicate to other servers because the servers will not have the capability to see the document to replicate it. This scenario is a potential exam question.

Security Considerations

Another advantage that an electronic workflow application has over a paper-based process is security. Security enables you to secure data in your application and control who can create, read, and edit documents. For example, once the manager has approved the expense reimbursement document, the employee should not be allowed to edit any part of that document. Otherwise, the employee could change a reimbursement amount in the document to make the document look like the manager approved the change. Domino provides a number of ways to control access to parts of your workflow application. You can control access by using the following security tools:

- Database ACL
- Form read access list
- Controlled access section
- Document Reader field
- Encryption

These security features are discussed in depth in Chapter 34, "Domino Security Architecture." Focus on how these different security features are used in workflow applications. You will see questions on the exam regarding security and workflow.

Summary

This chapter has covered the basics of workflow planning and design. You have learned the definition of workflow and how it relates to a business process, and you have seen examples of processes that can be transformed into workflow applications. We looked at a fictitious company and defined the objects, routes, roles, and rules that are involved in the company's travel expense reimbursement process. From this information, we built a workflow diagram to illustrate the workflow process. After designing the diagram, we mentioned how important it is to review the design with potential users. The design review gives them a chance to make design changes and mention additional requests.

We talked about how to implement a workflow process using two distribution methods: routing and parallel/serial. The advantages and disadvantages of each method were defined. We also looked at the difference between parallel distribution and serial distribution.

Because of the popularity of Notes around the world and the influence of the Web, we discussed how to make your workflow application available to a variety of users: multi-national, Web, and non-Notes mail users. We also talked about tracking the status of a document in a workflow application and the importance of security.

Workflow applications are powerful tools that reduce overhead and errors, that make people accountable for their tasks, and that speed up the overall business process. The more workflow applications you design, the more business processes that you will notice are workflow applications waiting to happen.

Practice

Although we have not yet learned how to create forms that route documents, we can see how the @ValidateInternetAddress function behaves. We create a new database containing a form with a ReviewerAddress field. We then add an Input Validation formula containing the @ValidateInternetAddress function. When we test the document in Notes, we enter an invalid name in the field, press F9 to refresh, and receive an error message. Let's perform this task.

1. Open Domino Designer.

2. Choose File . . . Database . . . New to create a new database.

3. Leave Server as Local.

4. Name the database "My Chapter 31 Practice" and use the filename MYCH31-NSF.

5. Base the design on the -Blank- template and click OK.

6. Create a new form called Validate.

7. Add a centered title, such as "Internet Address Field," to the top of the form.

8. Two lines below the title, add a left-aligned field called ReviewerAddress with a field label such as Reviewer.

9. Enter the following formula in the Input Validation event of the ReviewerAddress field (refer to Figure 31-3):

```
@ValidateInternetAddress([Address821];ReviewerAddress);
@If(va = NULL;@Success;@Failure(va))
```

PART V

10. Choose Design . . . Preview in Notes, and save the form.

11. Type the following Internet address in the field, and press F9 to refresh:

```
"Mahon, Susan" <smahon@schwarz.com>
```

Figure 31-4 displays the resulting error message. The user immediately sees why the address did not pass the validation formula. To conform to RFC 821 Address Format Syntax, modify the address by typing the following line:

```
smahon@schwarz.com
```

The Internet address passes the validation formula, enabling you to save the document.

Figure 31-3
Input Validation
formula

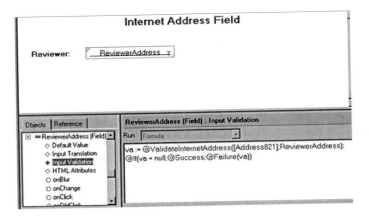

Figure 31-4
Internet address
error message

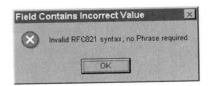

Review Questions

1. Diane is designing a workflow application for her customer. She determines that the forms used in the current business process need to be included in her design. In a workflow process, what are these forms known as?
   a. Items
   b. Objects
   c. Rules
   d. Roles

2. Duane talked with potential users of his workflow application and documented the actions that need to take place at certain points along the workflow path. These actions are determined by the following item:
   a. Objects
   b. Rules
   c. Roles
   d. Routes

3. Darla is drawing a workflow diagram that shows the path that a document travels as it passes from one reviewer to the next. The name for this path is the
   a. Role
   b. Object
   c. Route
   d. Rule

4. Doug is designing a workflow application and knows that many users are currently using cc:Mail for their mail. In order to include them in the workflow process and to enable them to view Notes documents, he places the following field on the form:
   a. MailFormat
   b. MailOptions
   c. SendMail
   d. MailSend

5. In order for the contents of a central, shared database in a workflow application to be viewed by users worldwide in their native language, David sets which database property?
   a. Multiple Language Database
   b. Multi-Language Database
   c. Multinational Database
   d. Multilingual Database

6. Linda is building a workflow application and wants all documents awaiting review to be stored in a central, shared database. She wants only one reviewer at a time to be notified that documents await their attention. Which type of distribution method should she use?
   a. Parallel distribution
   b. Routing distribution
   c. Serial distribution
   d. E-mail distribution

7. Tamara needs to distribute documents to reviewers in her workflow application. She knows that the majority of the reviewers are remote users. Which type of distribution should she use?
   a. Parallel distribution
   b. Routing distribution
   c. Serial distribution
   d. E-mail distribution

8. Rodney wants to implement workflow in his company without burdening network resources or using a large amount of server disk space. He wants all reviewers to be able to review documents at the same time. Which type of distribution should he use?
   a. Parallel distribution
   b. Routing distribution
   c. Serial distribution
   d. E-mail distribution

9. Ralph is creating a form to use in a workflow application. He wants to route documents created with the form to users who have Internet addresses. His company requires Internet addresses to be in the format **smahon@schwarz.com**. Ralph should use which formula in the ReviewerAddress field?
   a. `@ValidateInternetAddress([Address821];ReviewerAddress)`
   b. `@ValidateInternetAddress([Address823];ReviewerAddress)`
   c. `@ValidateInternetAddress([Address822];ReviewerAddress)`
   d. Users who have Internet addresses cannot participate in workflow.

10. Sally wants to track workflow documents through replication. Mobile users have complained that they are not seeing their replicated documents on the server. What is the problem?

   a. The server has Editor access.
   b. There is a Readers field on the form that does not contain any entries.
   c. There is a Readers field on the form that includes usernames but not server names.
   d. The purge interval is set too low.

Review Answers

1. **B** is correct.   The documents that flow along a workflow path are known as objects.

2. **B** is correct.   The rules determine the action that enables the object to proceed down the workflow path.

3. **C** is correct.   The route is the path that the object takes in a workflow process.

4. **A** is correct.   The MailFormat field is the correct name for the field that enables cc:Mail users to view Notes documents.

5. **D** is correct.   The Multi-Lingual Database property must be set to enable the database to support multiple languages.

6. **C** is correct.   Serial distribution stores documents in a central, shared database but only notifies one reviewer at a time.

7. **B** is correct.   Routing distribution delivers the document directly to the reviewer's mail file. Remote users can work locally instead of having to access a remote database.

8. **A** is correct.   Parallel distribution is more efficient and uses the least amount of network resources, compared to routing distribution. Parallel distribution also enables more than one reviewer to review the document at the same time.

9. **A** is correct.   RFC 822 includes the phrase portion of the Internet address, which the company does not want to use.

10. **C** is correct.   If a Readers field is in a document and it contains usernames, the field must also contain the names of replicating servers. If not, the servers cannot see the document, so it will not be replicated.

CHAPTER 32

Creating a Workflow Application

You should be able to answer questions based on the following objectives after reading this chapter:

- Creating workflow applications
- Creating mail-enabled forms
- Creating workflow-related fields: conditional/unconditional fields
- Creating workflow-related fields: document encryption
- Creating workflow-related fields: hide-when fields
- Creating workflow-related fields: keyword fields
- Creating workflow-related fields: reserved word fields
- Creating workflow-related fields: signing
- Creating workflow-related fields: workflow-related field attributes
- Creating workflow-related forms: mail-enabled forms
- Creating workflow-related forms: setting workflow-related form attributes
- Creating workflow-related sections
- Creating/setting up workflow routing rules (addressing) using formulas: booleans
- Creating/setting up workflow routing rules (addressing) using formulas: conditional/ unconditional
- Creating/setting up workflow routing rules (addressing) using formulas: constants
- Creating/setting up workflow routing rules (addressing) using formulas: variables
- Creating/setting up workflow routing rules (addressing) using formulas: @Commands
- Creating/setting up workflow routing rules (addressing) using formulas: @Functions
- Mail encryption
- Setting up events
- Setting workflow-related form attributes

In the previous chapter, we discussed how to plan and design a workflow application. This chapter builds upon your knowledge of workflow as we discuss how to implement a workflow application. We discuss several ways to design a form so that the router knows to route documents created by the form. We also talk about the role of fields in a workflow application and how to use certain fields to route documents automatically or to enable the user to specify whether he or she wants the document routed. We explore encryption and signing as they apply to workflow applications. Finally, we discuss setting up workflow routing rules using several types of formulas consisting of @Functions, @Commands, constants, and variables.

Creating the Workflow Forms

The greatest benefit of transforming a business process into a workflow application is the automatic routing of documents to user mail files and/or central, shared databases. Using the mail functions of Domino, we can route documents based on either a manual or scheduled trigger. A manual trigger can consist of a user clicking a button or action, or entering a specific value in a field and saving the document. A scheduled or automated trigger can result from conditions being met, such as a document being saved or edited, the value of a particular field, or a certain day or time. In order for routing to be successful, the application must meet three requirements:

1. The form that is being used to route documents must be mail enabled. In the next section, we examine ways that a designer and user can mail-enable a form.

2. The document being routed must include a proper address. Addressing is usually accomplished by the parameters of an @MailSend formula or by a SendTo field, both of which are described later in this chapter.

3. A route to the destination database must exist. When the destination is a user's mail file, the router uses the recipient's Person document in the Domino Directory to determine the location of the mail file. In the case of a mail-in database, a mail-in database document located in the Domino Directory supplies the routing information. We discuss mail-in databases in more detail in Chapter 33, "Creating a Mail-In Database."

Mail-Enabled Forms

Our first step in implementing workflow is mail-enabling our forms. We mail-enable a form so that the router knows to route documents created with the form. There are three ways you can mail-enable a form. You can set the *On Close: Present mail send dialog* form property; you can add a MailOptions reserved field to the form; or you can use an @MailSend function to mail the document. You should understand the different mail-enable options for the exam.

When designing a mail-enabled form, you must provide a way for users to read documents created by the form once the documents reach the destination database. To display a document with the form used to create the document, the form must be available in the destination database. There are two options to make the form available. First, you can copy the form to the destination database. The other option is to store the form in the document.

Workflow-Related Form Attributes

In this section, we examine how to mail-enable a form by using the form property method and how to store a form in a document. If mailing is optional, you can use the *On Close: Present mail send dialog* form property. Set the property on the Defaults tab of the Form Properties InfoBox (refer to Figure 32-1). When a user closes the document, Notes prompts him or her to mail, save, cancel, sign, and encrypt the document. The Mail Send dialog box that displays when the document is closed is shown in Figure 32-2. In order to use this method, the form must have a SendTo field that identifies the document's destination—either a mail-in database or a user's mail file. If the router cannot find a SendTo field in the document or if the destination in the SendTo field is not valid, Domino displays an error message (as shown in Figure 32-3) and does not mail the document.

Figure 32-1
Mail Send Dialog
form option

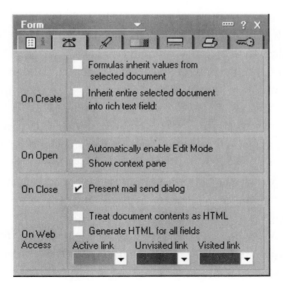

Figure 32-2
Mail Send dialog box

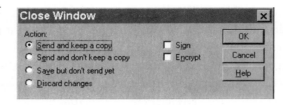

Figure 32-3
Mail Error dialog
box

In order to store a form in a document, you must enable both a database property and a form property. The database property *Allow use of stored forms in this database* must be set for the database receiving the documents with forms stored in them. Set this property on the Database Basics tab of the Database properties InfoBox. This property is already set by default for most databases.

To store the form with the document, enable the *Store form in document* property on the Form Info tab of the Form properties InfoBox (as in Figure 32-4). Notes adds an internal field called $Title to all documents that are created with the form. This field contains the name of the form stored with the document. When the user opens a document created from a form with this property set, Notes uses the form design that is saved with the document to display the document contents.

Keep in mind that storing forms in documents significantly increases the size of the database that contains the documents. This option might not be the best for a mobile user for that reason. Copying the form into the database might be a better idea. Another factor is that the form is not automatically updated to reflect design changes that are made to the original form in the source database. Store a form in a document only if the destination database does not contain a copy of the original form. Stored forms are supported on the Web in Read mode, but do not use the stored form option for documents that are created or edited on the Web. Pay attention to the disadvantages of storing forms in documents, because you might see this type of question on the exam.

Figure 32-4
Store Form in
Document form
property

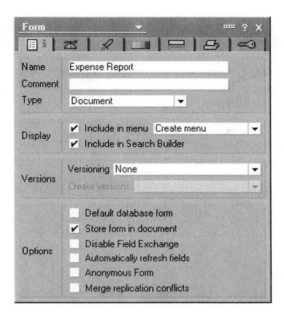

NOTE   To remove a form that is stored in a document, create an agent that
deletes the fields $Title, $Info, $WindowTitle, and $Body from the document.
Add the field Form to the document, with a value of the name of the form that
you wish to use to display the document.

Creating the Workflow

Now that the form is mail enabled, we need to determine where to route the document
and how to trigger the routing. We also need to add a layer of security to our workflow
by using signatures and mail and document encryption.

Workflow-Related Fields

We use fields and field attributes in many ways in our workflow applications. The
router looks at a field to determine the recipient of a routed document. Designers use
fields to route documents based on certain conditions. We also use fields to encrypt
and sign documents. We place sign-enabled fields in multiple controlled-access sections to attach multiple signatures to a document.

In this section, we discuss the many uses of fields in workflow applications. Pay special attention to reserved fields, sign-enabled fields, keyword fields, and encryption.

Document Encryption   Document encryption is listed here under the Workflow Related Fields section, because encryption is really accomplished at the field level. In order to encrypt a document, the designer must first enable fields on a form for encryption. To apply this field property, open the Field properties InfoBox and click the Advanced tab. Open the drop-down list under the heading Security Options and choose *Enable encryption for this field* (as in Figure 32-5). The field is not immediately encrypted; rather, it only has the capability to be encrypted. To encrypt the field, apply an encryption key to the document. Distribute the key used to encrypt the document to users who will need access to the encrypted information. If a user does not have the required encryption key, the encrypted fields in the document appear blank. This type of encryption is not supported on the Web. Chapter 34, "Domino Security Architecture," talks about different methods of creating, applying, and distributing encryption keys.

In a workflow application, documents routed to mail-in databases use the document encryption method. Apply the encryption key to the newly created document. The designer or creator of the document applies the key and then distributes the key to the reviewers. If more than one encryption key is applied to a document, the user sees all encrypted fields if he or she holds just one of the specified keys. Encrypt a document with international encryption keys if both North American and international license users will access the document. A user who has an international license cannot merge a North American encryption key into his or her User ID. Expect to see questions about this scenario on the exam. International versus North American encryption is discussed in more detail in Chapter 35, "Mail and Workstation Security."

Figure 32-5
Enable Encryption
field property

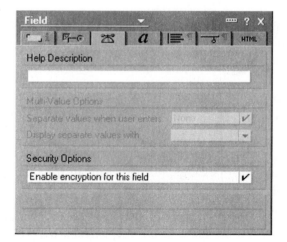

Reserved Word Fields A reserved field has a predefined name and purpose within Notes and can only be used to perform a specific function. Reserved fields can be used to add functionality to a form that you would otherwise have to program yourself. Most fields are limited in the type of information that they can contain. Table 32-1 lists and describes reserved fields that can be used in workflow routing.

A majority of the reserved fields listed in the table are covered in this chapter, because they apply to workflow applications and mailing documents. An additional reserved field not listed in the table, SecretEncryptionKeys, is discussed in the Keyword fields section in this chapter—and in more detail in Chapter 34, "Domino Security Architecture"—in the Encryption section. Pay close attention to the different reserved fields, how they are used, and the values that are permitted in the fields. You will see questions on the exam regarding reserved word fields.

Hide-When Fields Hide-when options and formulas enable the designer to hide fields based on a formula or document event. The Paragraph Hide When tab of the Field Properties infobox (as shown in Figure 32-6) shows how the designer can enable hide-when. The options for hiding fields based on a document event include *Previewed for reading, Previewed for editing, Opened for reading, Opened for editing, Printed*, and *Copied to the clipboard*. Notice that you also have the option to hide a field from Web browsers and from Notes 4.6 or later.

NOTE Hiding fields is not a true security feature. Users can still see the value of hidden fields on the Fields tab of the Document properties InfoBox. To prevent users from seeing data in fields, encrypt the fields.

Designers hide fields that store information that users do not need to see. For example, a designer creates a form with a MailOptions field set to 1 to mail the document when the user saves the document. In this case, the designer hides the MailOptions field using all hide-when options, because the user does not need to see the value. Remembering that a form with a MailOptions field also needs a SendTo field, the designer can hide the SendTo field as well.

NOTE Hide-when is paragraph-level formatting. In other words, if you use hide-when on a field, everything on the same line as the field you hide will use hide-when. Place elements that should have different hide-when settings in different paragraphs by pressing Enter to move to the next line.

Table 32-1   Reserved Fields for Mailing Documents

Field	Use and Value
MailOptions	This field forces Notes to mail the document when a user saves the document. If the MailOptions field value is set to 1, Notes mails the document automatically. If the MailOptions field value is set to 0, Notes does not mail the document. This field takes precedence over the action that the user selects in the Mail Send dialog box.
Sign	This field forces Notes to sign the document when mailing the document. If the Sign field value is set to 1, Notes signs the document automatically when mailing the document. If the Sign field value is set to 0, Notes does not sign the document. This field takes precedence over the action that the user selects in the Mail Send dialog box.
Encrypt	This field forces Notes to encrypt the document with the recipient's public key when the document is mailed. If the Encrypt field value is set to 1, Notes encrypts the document automatically when mailing the document. If the Encrypt field value is set to 0, the document will not be encrypted. This field takes precedence over the action that the user selects in the Mail Send dialog box.
SendTo	When a document is mailed, the Router looks at the entries in the SendTo field and routes the document to the recipients listed in the field. The field must contain valid person, group, or mail-in database names. If the form is mail-enabled, this field is required.
CopyTo	The Router reads the entries in the CopyTo field and sends a copy of the document to each recipient listed.
BlindCopyTo	The Router reads the entries in the BlindCopyTo field and sends a blind copy of the document to each recipient listed.
DeliveryPriority	This field specifies the delivery priority of the document. The priority can be set to High, Normal, or Low and defines how quickly the message will be routed to other mail servers.
ReturnReceipt	This field gives the designer the capability to specify whether Domino will notify the sender when the recipient opens the document.
DeliveryReport	This field specifies when Domino will return a delivery report to the sender. The default choice, *Only On Failure*, sends a delivery report only if the router fails to deliver the message. The other choices include *Confirm Delivery*, *Trace Entire Path*, and *None*.
SaveOptions	This field forces Notes to save the document when the document is mailed. If the SaveOptions field value is set to 1, Notes saves the document automatically when mailing the document. If the SaveOptions field value is set to 0, Notes does not save the document. This field takes precedence over the action that the user selects in the Mail Send dialog box.

Secret Encryption keys .

Figure 32-6
Hide-when options

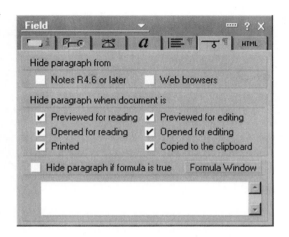

Keyword Fields   As you know, keyword fields provide the user with a list of choices from which he or she can select an item to populate the field. Designers sometimes use reserved fields as keyword fields, enabling the user to determine whether he or she wants to sign, encrypt, or mail a document. For example, you can offer users the choice of mailing a document by making MailOptions an editable dialog list, radio button, listbox, or combobox field type. By using the Enter choices (one per line) on the Field Info tab of the Field properties InfoBox, you can enable the user to choose which mail option he or she prefers (refer to Figure 32-7). Notice that the choices in the list use synonyms that correspond to the appropriate MailOptions field values.

Another example of using keyword fields in workflow applications pertains to document encryption. If a designer wants to enable the document author to choose whether or not to encrypt the document, the designer can place the reserved field SecretEncryptionKeys on the form as an editable dialog list, radio button, listbox, or combobox field. Figure 32-7 shows an example of forcing encryption with a particular key—in this case, an encryption key called SecretKey—if the user chooses to encrypt the document, or not applying an encryption key if the user chooses not to encrypt. If the SecretEncryptionKeys field is empty or null, Notes does not encrypt the document.

Users must have a copy of the encryption key merged into their User ID file so that they can save the document. The designer or database manager (which is sometimes the same person) distributes secret encryption keys to users who need them. Depending on the application design, the designer can choose to present a list of multiple-encryption keys and to enable the user to choose a specific encryption key with which to encrypt the document.

Figure 32-7
SecretEncryption-Keys keyword choices

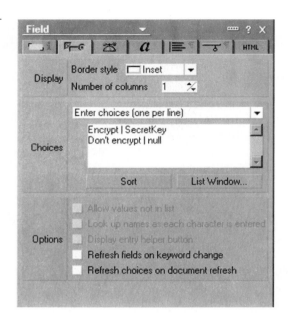

Signing Signing is a process that verifies that the signer was the last person to modify the document. The signature is created with the user's private key in combination with the data in a sign-enabled field. Signing adds a verification stamp to mail messages and fields or sections of a document. When a user accesses the signed document, Notes attempts to decrypt the signature by using the public key that corresponds to the private key used to sign the data. If decryption of the signature is successful, Notes indicates who signed the data. If decryption is unsuccessful, Notes notifies the user that it cannot verify the signature. Unsuccessful decryption of the signature indicates that either the data has been tampered with or that the reader does not have a certificate that is capable of verifying the sender. Signing is not supported on the Web.

In a workflow application, a designer might choose to sign e-mail notifications when manual or automatic actions trigger them. To sign mail messages, use the Sign flag in the last parameter of an @MailSend formula. When Notes evaluates the @MailSend function and generates the e-mail notification, the sender's signature is attached to the message.

To sign documents routed to a mail file, place a Sign reserved field with a computed value of 1 on the form. To enable users to choose whether or not to sign the document, set the *On Close: Present mail send dialog* form property. When a user closes the document, he or she is prompted to mail, save, cancel, sign, and encrypt the document.

We discuss signing mail messages in more detail in Chapter 35, "Mail and Workstation Security." Refer to Chapter 34, "Domino Security Architecture," for more information about signing documents. Signing sections is discussed later in this chapter.

Workflow-Related Field Attributes   Placing a sign-enabled field on a form that has been mail-enabled is another method that a designer can use to place a signature on a document. This method generates a document signature during mailing. To sign-enable a field, assign the field property *Sign if mailed or saved in section* on the Advanced tab of the Field Properties infobox (refer to Figure 32-8).

There can only be one signature associated with a document at any time. If a user modifies a field in the document, Domino replaces the existing signature with the signature of the editor when mailing the document. If there are multiple sign-enabled fields in a document, Domino uses data from each sign-enabled field to generate one signature. After mailing, a modification to any field causes signature verification to fail when the recipient opens the document. To generate multiple signatures for a document, a designer places at least one sign-enabled field in each controlled-access section. Controlled-access sections are discussed later in this chapter.

Workflow-Related Sections

Use controlled-access sections on your workflow-related forms to control who can edit certain fields on a document and to apply signatures to verify the ID of the person who last modified those fields. A section is a group of paragraphs that can collapse into a single line. The section can then be expanded or collapsed, based on user input or designer choice. A controlled-access section functions similarly to a standard section in that it organizes the text and other elements on a form and limits the length of the form. The section has the additional function, however, of limiting who can edit fields in the section. The section also provides a means of attaching multiple signatures to a document. You can have multiple controlled-access sections on a form, but you can have only one signature per section.

Figure 32-8
Signing a field

PART V

For example, let's use the business scenario from Chapter 31, "Planning and Designing Workflow Applications." Remember that ABC Corporation has a paper-based employee expense account reimbursement process. We talked with users of the current system and determined that we need to design an expense report form. The expense report is reviewed by the employee's manager and is either approved for payment or rejected and is sent back to the employee. If the total amount of the reimbursement is more than $1,000, the expense report requires a second approval signature from a second-line manager.

Keeping this business scenario in mind, we need to design our form with two approval fields: one for the employee's immediate manager, and one for the second-line manager (if required). We need to limit Editor access to the two fields. We also want to place signatures on each field to ensure that the managers actually edited the approval fields.

To generate a signature for a section, we must make sure that the section contains at least one sign-enabled field. Once we have a sign-enabled field on the form, we can collapse the field into a controlled-access section. To create a controlled-access section, highlight the field and text to include in the section and choose Create . . . Section . . . Controlled Access. The Formula tab of the Controlled Access Section Properties InfoBox is displayed in Figure 32-9. The Formula tab defines which users can edit the section. The formula can be *Editable*, *Computed for Display*, or *Computed when Composed* and must resolve to a name or list of names. Keep in mind that you are defining editors for fields in the section, not hiding the fields. If you want to make a section truly secure, encrypt the fields in the section. You should note that Section Edit access does not override the database ACL. A user who has Author access or lower cannot edit fields in a section—even if he or she is listed as an editor for the section. You might see a question such as this one on the exam.

Let's review the differences between a sign-enabled field on a form and a sign-enabled field that is included in a controlled-access section. If a field is in a controlled-

Figure 32-9
Controlled Access
Section InfoBox

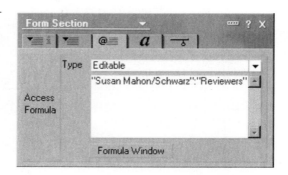

access section, the signature applies only to the section and is generated when the document is saved. A form can have multiple controlled-access sections with a different signature associated with each section. A designer can place a controlled-access section on a subform, which can then be used in multiple forms. If a field is not in a controlled-access section, Domino generates the document's signature when the document is mailed. The signature that is generated applies to the entire document. Pay attention to these differences, because you might see a related question on the exam.

Setting up Workflow Routing Using Formulas

Now, we come to the heart of workflow: routing. There are several methods that we can use to route documents in a workflow application. In this section, we learn about workflow-specific @Functions, @Commands, boolean formulas, and events. Expect several exam questions related to @Functions, @Commands, and simple actions that route documents in workflow applications.

Boolean   Boolean formulas return a value of 1 if the formula evaluates to True and 0 if the result of the formula is False. Two boolean functions that designers use in workflow applications are listed as follows:

- @IsDocBeingSaved
- @IsDocBeingMailed

Use the @IsDocBeingSaved function to check the current state of the document. If the document is being saved, the return value is 1 (True); otherwise, the return value is 0 (False). In a workflow application, use this function in a field formula to prevent document mailing when a user refreshes the document. For example, a computed field called SendToReviewer contains an @MailSend function. This function, discussed later in the chapter, mails the current document to the recipient. Keep in mind that computed field formulas are evaluated on save and refresh. We do not want the document routed every time a user presses F9 to refresh the document. We can use the @IsDocBeingSaved function in a field formula as follows:

```
@If(@IsDocBeingSaved;@MailSend;null)
```

The @IsDocBeingMailed function checks the current state of the document and returns a 1 (True) if the document is being mailed and a 0 (False) if the document is not being mailed. Use this function to track the number of document mailings. For example, you can also use the following function:

```
@If(@IsUnavailable(NumberOfMailings);0;NumberOfMailings +
@IsDocBeingMailed)
```

You can also use this function with an @If statement to control when Domino writes a value to a field. For example, you might have a WorkflowStatus field on a form that indicates where the document is in the routing process. You want the words `Mailed to Reviewer` written to the field only when Domino mails the document. Otherwise, leave the contents of the WorkflowStatus field to the value that is already in the field. The formula would look something like the following:

```
@If(@IsDocBeingMailed;@SetField("WorkflowStatus";"Mailed to
Reviewer");WorkflowStatus)
```

Conditional/Unconditional   In a workflow application, you can control where and when the document is routed. To route documents based on a condition, we use the @If function in our formulas. Designers create conditional formulas and base them on the value of another field. We can also base conditional formulas on an action taken by the user or on the document state, which we discussed in the Boolean Formula section.

Let's go back to the employee expense report reimbursement scenario for ABC Corporation. Once the employee fills out the expense report and saves the document, Domino sends an e-mail notification to the employee's manager. Remember what happens if the expense total is more than $1,000? A second-line manager must approve the expense report. At this point, you can use a conditional formula. There is a field on the expense form called GrandTotal, which contains the total amount reimbursed by the company. We can create a formula that checks the value in the GrandTotal field and routes the document to the second-line manager if the amount is more than $1,000. The formula might look something like the following:

```
@If(GrandTotal > 1000;
@MailSend(SecondLineManager;null;null; "Expense Report
Approval";"An expense report awaits your approval"; null;[Include-
DocLink]);
@MailSend(Payroll;null;null;"Expense Report Approval";"Please
approve this expense report and issue a check to the employee for
the full amount.";null;[IncludeDocLink]))
```

The formula sends an e-mail notification to the second-line manager for approval if the amount in the GrandTotal field is more than $1,000. If the amount is less than or equal to $1,000, Domino sends an e-mail notification to the payroll department, asking it to approve the expense report and issue a check.

Unconditional formulas route documents regardless of field contents. We can use an example from ABC Corporation's expense reimbursement process. When an employee completes the expense report and saves the document, the expense report is mailed to his or her immediate manager. We do not want the document to travel any other route; therefore, no conditions are included in our formula. We could place the following formula in a button:

```
@MailSend(EmployeeManager;null;null; "Expense Report Approval";"An
expense report awaits your approval"; null;[IncludeDocLink])
```

Constants A constant is a value that does not change. Notes recognizes three types of constants, and Table 32-2 lists and describes each of the three types.

In a workflow application, a designer can use the name of a mail-in database (a constant) as the formula for a SendTo field. For example, if we want the router to send all completed expense reports to an archive database, we can place the formula *Expense Report Archive* in a SendTo field on the form. A mail-in database document must exist in the Domino Directory so that the Router knows where to send the document. We discuss mail-in databases in more detail in Chapter 33, "Creating a Mail-In Database."

Designers want to make sure that tasks are completed on time in a workflow application. We can use formulas in workflow to notify reviewers. The formulas contain time-date values that compare the due date of a task with the current date. Formulas send reminders to reviewers if the due date is near, and they also generate alarms if tasks are overdue. In our ABC Corporation example, we can create an agent that generates a reminder and sends the reminder to the employee's manager three days after the employee submits the expense form.

Variables One way to use variables or fields in workflow routing is to place a MailOptions reserved field on a form. We discussed reserved fields in an earlier section and pointed out that a MailOptions field is another way to mail-enable a form. The MailOptions reserved field specifies whether Notes mails a document automatically when saving the document. The MailOptions field is usually a computed, hidden field on the form with a value of either 1 or 0. If the value is 1, Notes mails the document automatically when saving the document. If the value is 0, Notes does not mail the document when saved. No matter which value you choose, enclose the value in quotation marks to indicate a text string. You can also enable users to control whether or not to mail the document by making the MailOptions field an editable keyword field. Use the synonyms 1 and 0 to correspond to the choices in the keyword list.

Table 32-2 Types of Constants

Type of Constant	Description
Text	Any set of characters, including spaces, numbers, and special characters, that are enclosed in quotation marks
Number	Numeric data in the form of integers, decimals, negative numbers, and scientific notation
Time-Date	A time and/or date enclosed in square brackets

If you use either a MailOptions field or the *On Close: Present mail send dialog* form property, you must include a SendTo reserved field on the form. The SendTo field can be an editable or hidden, computed field, but its value must be a text string. The contents of a SendTo field can be the name of a person, group, or mail-in database and can contain multiple values. Notes displays an error message if the router cannot find a SendTo field with a valid address on the document. You can place the CopyTo and BlindCopyTo reserved fields on a form, as well. Their values must also resolve to valid addresses.

@Functions Another option for mail-enabling a form is adding an @MailSend function to the form. The @MailSend function can be used to route documents automatically to recipients who are listed in the document's SendTo field. The document that contains the @MailSend function must have a SendTo field with a valid address, or formula execution will generate an error. An @MailSend function can be used in agents, fields, form and view actions, buttons, and smart icons. This function cannot be included in column formulas, view-selection formulas, hide-when formulas, and window-title formulas.

If the @MailSend function is used with parameters, a new mail memo is created based on the information supplied in the parameters and is delivered to the recipients. The syntax for the @MailSend function with parameters is listed as follows (the parameters are described in Table 32-3).

```
@MailSend(sendTo;copyTo;blindCopyTo;subject;remark;bodyFields;[fla
gs])
```

When you use the parameters of the @MailSend function, be sure to leave null strings for any values that you do not define. For example, in order to compose and send a message to Susan Mahon, copy Libby Schwarz, display Project Meeting Reminder as the Subject, remind the recipients about the project meeting on Thursday, and include the contents of the Tasks field, create the following @MailSend formula:

```
@MailSend("Susan Mahon";"Libby Schwarz";null;"Project Meeting
Reminder";"The next project meeting is scheduled for 2:00 pm
Thursday.  Please complete the following tasks: ";Tasks)
```

In addition to the parameters described in the previous table, optional flags are available as the final parameter of the @MailSend function. These flags correspond to several mail delivery options that are available with a new memo, such as signing, encryption, delivery priority, return receipt, and delivery report. The flags are described in Table 32-4. Note that the flags are optional parameters and are not necessary for

Domino to evaluate the @MailSend function correctly. In addition, you only need to include the flags that you want to use. Null values are not required within the flags.

The next example builds on the previous formula but includes some of the optional flags:

```
@MailSend("Susan Mahon";"Libby Schwarz";null;"Project Meeting
Reminder";"The next project meeting is scheduled for 2:00 pm
Thursday.  Please complete the following tasks: ";null; [Include-
DocLink];[Sign]:[PriorityHigh]:[ReturnReceipt])
```

This formula composes a mail memo and sends it to Susan Mahon, with a copy to Libby Schwarz. The subject of the memo is *Project Meeting Reminder* with the body of the memo displaying the remark and a doclink to the current document. The message

Table 32-3   @MailSend Parameters

Parameter	Description
SendTo	The message will be sent to the users who are listed in this parameter. The parameter value must result in text or a text list.
CopyTo (optional)	The message will be copied to the users who are listed in this parameter. The parameter value must result in text or a text list.
BlindCopyTo (optional)	The message will be blind-copied to the users who are listed in this parameter. The parameter value must result in text or a text list.
Subject	This parameter completes the subject field of the memo.
Remark (optional)	This parameter adds text to the beginning of the body field of the memo.
BodyFields (optional)	This parameter defines the fields in the current document that will be sent in the mail memo. The fields listed in this parameter can be of any data type. To add multiple fields, use the Notes list concatenation format of list items, enclosed in quotation marks and separated by colons (for example, "Tasks" :"Assignee" :"DueDate"). When you include multiple fields, they are listed on the mail memo in the order stipulated. If you do not stipulate any fields in this parameter, use the IncludeDocLink flag to attach a doclink to the current document.
[flags] (optional)	The optional flags are described later in this chapter. You can include multiple flags in the @MailSend function by separating each flag with a colon (for example, `[Sign]: [Encrypt]: [IncludeDocLink]`).

Table 32-4 @MailSend Flags

Flag	Description
[Sign]	This flag appends the user's electronically produced signature to the mail memo.
[Encrypt]	This flag encrypts the document using the recipient's public key, which is found in the Domino Directory. The recipient's private key, which is found in the user's ID file, must be available to decrypt and read the document.
[PriorityHigh], [PriorityNormal], or [PriorityLow]	This flag defines the priority of the mail message. Without a priority flag, Notes uses the default Normal priority to send the message. The priority flag determines how the mail message is sent when the recipient's mail file is on a different server. This flag determines how quickly the message is routed among servers.
[ReturnReceipt]	This flag forces Domino to send a message to the sender when the recipient opens the document.
[DeliveryReportConfirmed]	This flag forces Domino to notify the sender when the document is delivered to the recipient's mail file.
[IncludeDocLink]	This flag includes a doclink in the mail memo that points to the document that was open or selected at the time the @MailSend function was evaluated. Use this flag if you choose not to specify any fields in the BodyFields parameter.

is sent as signed and high priority—and a return receipt is mailed to the creator of the memo when Susan and Libby open the message. Note that when you use multiple flags in the last @MailSend parameter, you should separate each flag with a colon. The colon concatenates the flags into a list format.

@Commands

@Commands are a special type of function that automates the standard Notes menu choices, as well as some special Notes commands. Use them in buttons, actions, and agents. There are several @Commands used in workflow routing. Understand the different types of @Commands and how they are used. Two @Commands that deal with routing in a workflow application are as follows:

- @Command([MailForward])
- @Command([MailSend])

The @Command([MailForward]) function enables a user to mail a document to a recipient when the document does not have a SendTo field. The current document's contents are placed into a mail message. The user can then address the message and send the message just like any other mail message. You can use this method to send a copy of an entire document to mobile users for their review.

The @Command([MailSend]) function works in conjunction with a SendTo field to route documents to either a mail-in database or a user's mail file. When a user edits and closes a document, this function displays the Mail Send dialog box, which prompts the user to mail, save, cancel, sign, and encrypt the document. If the Router cannot find a SendTo field in the document—or if the destination in the SendTo field is not valid—then Domino displays an error message and does not mail the document. You might see an exam question regarding how to use these @Commands in workflow applications.

Setting up Workflow Routing Using Events

In a workflow application, you can add automatic routing to a database through the use of agents. There are several mail-related, simple actions that we can use to create agents. These are predefined actions that enable you to create actions and agents without any programming knowledge. Workflow routing using simple actions is one of the subjects that is stressed on the exam. Keep in mind, however, that actions and agents that are written using the simple-action programming interface are not supported on the Web.

without parameters.

- **Send Document**   This simple action is similar to the @MailSend function. The Send Document simple action routes the current document to recipients who are listed in the document's SendTo field. The Router can send the document to a person, group, or mail-in database. If there is no SendTo field on the document, the Router sends the document to users who are listed in the internal field $UpdatedBy. By default, the document is sent with normal priority and with no delivery report or return receipt—unless the corresponding reserved fields are included in the document.

- **Send Mail Message**   This simple action generates a mail message that contains a copy of the current document and/or a link to the current document. These options correspond to the @Command([MailForward]) function and to the @MailSend function using the [IncludeDocLink] flag. Specify recipients in the To: field, or click the More . . . button for additional addresses using formulas or text in the To:, cc:, bcc:, and Subject: fields. Figure 32-10 shows the Send Mail Message Simple Action dialog box.

Figure 32-10
Send Mail Message
Simple Action dialog
box

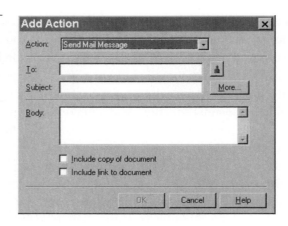

- **Send Newsletter Summary** This simple action enables you to send mail messages that contain doclinks and summaries of the linked documents, which is similar to an @MailSend function on steroids. Notes searches the database for documents that match the options specified in the Agent Design window under *Which document(s) should it act on*. The doclinks to these documents are included in the mail message. You can specify the database view that you want Notes to use when displaying the document summary. If you deselect the option *Include summary for each document using*, only doclinks are sent. Specify a number in the *Gather at least* option to generate mail messages only when a certain number of documents are found that match the search criteria. Specify recipients the same way as the Send Mail Message simple action. Figure 32-11 shows the Send Newsletter Summary Simple Action dialog box.

Mail Encryption

In a workflow application, a designer might choose to encrypt e-mail notifications when manual or automatic actions trigger them. To encrypt mail messages, use the Encrypt flag in the last parameter of an @MailSend formula. When the @MailSend function is evaluated and generates the e-mail notification, the message is encrypted as it travels to the destination mail file.

To encrypt documents as they route to a mail file, place an Encrypt reserved field with a computed value of 1 on the form. To enable users to choose whether or not to encrypt the document, set the *On Close: Present mail send dialog* form property. When a user closes the document, he or she is prompted to mail, save, cancel, sign, and encrypt the

Figure 32-11
Send Newsletter
Summary Simple
Action dialog box

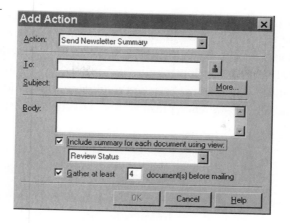

document. Keep in mind that encryption of a document is possible only when the designer enables encryption for some of the fields on a document's form.

Should a designer use mail encryption or document encryption? The answer depends upon where the document is being routed. If a document is routed to an individual's mail file, use mail encryption. The recipient's public key is used to encrypt the message, and the corresponding private key is used to decrypt the message. If a document is routed to a mail-in database, use document encryption. The document is encrypted and decrypted with the same encryption key. We discuss mail encryption in more detail in Chapter 35, "Mail and Workstation Security." Refer to Chapter 34, "Domino Security Architecture," for more information about document encryption.

EXAM TIP This great exam tip applies to many questions asked on the exam. As you know, a Notes user ID cannot be used to access Domino applications from the Web. What does this statement mean? Domino security options, such as encryption, signing, and public/private keys, are not supported on the Web. Why are they not supported? Because they rely on information stored in the Notes user ID in order to work successfully.

Summary

This chapter built upon your knowledge of planning and designing workflow and gave you a more in-depth look at creating a workflow application. We covered several ways of mail-enabling a form by using form properties, reserved fields, and @Functions. We discussed the many uses of fields in workflow applications—as keywords, reserved words, to sign documents and sections, and to encrypt documents. You can develop formulas using @Functions, @Commands, and simple actions to route documents in workflow applications. Finally, we discussed mail encryption and answered the question of when to use document encryption versus mail encryption.

Practice

In this practice, we use the Expense Report-Starting form in the Chapter 32 Practice database to apply several of the techniques learned in this chapter. The base of our workflow design is ABC Corporation's employee travel expense reimbursement process. We sign-enable two fields and collapse them into two separate controlled-access sections. We apply hide-when to one of the sections, based on the results of a field formula. Using @MailSend, we create two button formulas: one conditional, and the other unconditional. If you need some help along the way, take a peek at the Expense Report-Final form. Ready? Here we go.

1. From Domino Designer, open the Chapter 32 Practice database (CH32.NSF).

2. Open the Expense Report-Starting form.

3. Click the field FirstApproval, and open the Field Properties InfoBox.

4. Go to the Advanced tab and select *Sign if mailed or saved in section* under Security Options. We want to make sure that the employee's manager is the one who edited the FirstApproval field, so we generate a signature.

5. Repeat the process for the field SecondApproval.

6. Highlight the text *First Line Manager Approval*, the FirstApproval field, and the text next to the field, then select Create . . . Section . . . Controlled Access.

7. Repeat the process for the text *Second Line Manager Approval* and the field SecondApproval.

8. We want to hide the Second Line Manager Approval section if the GrandTotal field is less than or equal to $1,000. For the section you just created, go to the Section Hide When tab and enter the following formula in the *Hide paragraph if formula is true* pane (refer to Figure 32-13):

```
GrandTotal <= 1000
```

Figure 32-12
Hide Paragraph
formula

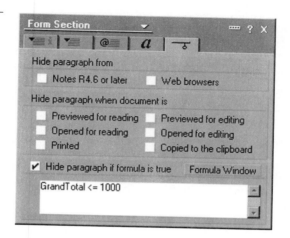

9. Next, we need to notify the employee's manager that the completed expense report is ready for approval. We also want to track the progress of the report through the workflow process, so we update the Status field. Click the Submit Expense Report button and enter the following unconditional @MailSend formula in the Script pane:

```
FIELD Status := "Sent to Manager for Approval";
@Command([FileSave]);
@MailSend(EmployeeManager;null;null; "Expense Report
Approval";"An expense report awaits your approval";
null;[IncludeDoclink]);
@PostedCommand([FileSave]);
@Command([FileCloseWindow])
```

10. Copy the formula to the second Submit Expense Report button. There are two buttons, because we hide one paragraph in Read mode and the other paragraph in Edit mode.

11. Next, we create a conditional formula that notifies the second-line manager if GrandTotal is greater than $1,000 or that notifies the payroll department if GrandTotal is less than or equal to $1,000. We also update the Status field. Click the Submit to Next Approver button, and enter the following @MailSend formula in the Script pane:

```
FIELD Status := "Approved by Employee's Manager";
@Command([FileSave]);
@If(GrandTotal > 1000;
```

```
@MailSend(SecondLineManager;null;null; "Expense Report
Approval";"An expense report awaits your approval";
null;[IncludeDoclink]);
@MailSend(Payroll;null;null;"Expense Report Approval";"Please
approve this expense report and issue a check to the employee
for the full amount.";null;[IncludeDoclink]));
@PostedCommand([FileSave]);
@Command([FileCloseWindow])
```

12. Copy the formula to the second Submit to Next Approver button.

Voila. We are finished. Right now, test the form and view the documents from either the Reports by Division view or the Reports by Manager view.

Review Questions

1. In creating her first workflow application, Julie chooses to mail-enable the forms by selecting the option *On Close: Present mail send dialog* from the Form Properties infobox. Her users complain that they receive an error every time they try to save and send the documents. What did Julie forget to do to the form?
   a. Create a MailOptions field
   b. Create a SaveOptions field
   c. Create a SendTo field
   d. Create a CopyTo field

2. Besides a Mail-In database, what other type of database can receive routed documents?
   a. A workflow-enabled database
   b. A user's mail database
   c. Domino Directory
   d. A personal name and address book

3. How can you deny access to data at the field level?
   a. Sign the field.
   b. Encrypt the field.
   c. Hide the field.
   d. Use the Field property *Deny Access* option.

4. What is the name of the reserved field that a designer uses to enable a user to optionally encrypt a document with an encryption key?

   a. Encrypt

   b. SecretKeys

   c. EncryptionKeys

   d. SecretEncryptionKeys

5. To place the current document's contents into a mail message and route the message to recipients who are listed in the SendTo field, Lauren uses which formula?

   a. @Command([MailForward])

   b. @Command([@MailSend])

   c. @Command([MailSend])

   d. @Command([MailComposeMemo])

6. To enable multiple users to sign a document, Polly needs to

   a. create multiple fields that are sign enabled and place them in separate controlled-access sections

   b. create multiple fields that are sign enabled and place them in one controlled-access section

   c. create multiple fields on a form that are sign enabled

   d. create multiple fields that are sign enabled and place them in a layout region

7. Elizabeth wants to create an agent for Web users that sends a copy of the current document in a mail message to a recipient's mail file. Which simple action does she use?

   a. Send Mail Message simple action

   b. Send Document simple action

   c. Send Newsletter Summary simple action

   d. Simple actions are not supported on the Web.

8. Patricia creates a form that she mail-enables by choosing the form option *On Close: Present mail send dialog*. She also creates a field called MailOptions, sets the value to 1, and creates an editable field called SendTo. What happens when the document is saved?

   a. The Mail Send dialog is presented. The document is mailed or saved, depending on the choices in the Mail Send dialog.

   b. The Mail Send dialog is not presented. The document is mailed.

   c. The Mail Send dialog is not presented. The document is not mailed.

   d. The Mail Send dialog is presented. The document is mailed automatically.

PART V

9. Anthony has Reader access to a database. His name is listed as one of the editors of a controlled-access section. What can he do?

   a. Edit the contents of the fields in the section.
   b. Modify the list of editors for the section.
   c. Read the contents of the fields in the section.
   d. He cannot read the contents of the fields, because they are hidden.

10. Donny creates a sign-enabled field and places it in a controlled-access section. At what point is the signature actually placed on the document?

    a. Immediately
    b. When the document is mailed
    c. When the document is saved
    d. When the document is closed

Review Answers

1. **C is correct.** The *On Close: Present mail send dialog* form property requires a SendTo field that contains a valid person, group, or mail-in database name.

2. **B is correct** Documents only route to a mail-in database or to a user's mail file.

3. **B is correct.** Encryption only enables users who have the correct encryption key to view data in a field. Hiding a field is not true security. Users can always see the contents of hidden fields from the Fields tab in the Document Properties InfoBox.

4. **D is correct.** The reserved field that enables users to choose whether or not to encrypt a document with an encryption key is called SecretEncryptionKeys. Users must have the encryption key in their User ID in order to save the document. The reserved field Encrypt uses the recipient's public key to encrypt the document and uses the corresponding private key to decrypt the document.

5. **A is correct.** The @Command([MailForward]) formula forwards the current document by placing its contents into a mail message, which the user then addresses.

6. **A is correct.** To generate multiple signatures in a document, you must have multiple controlled-access sections on the form. At least one field in each section must be sign-enabled.

7. **D is correct.** Simple actions are not supported on the Web.

8. **B** is correct.   The Mail Send dialog is only presented on close, not save. That is how the form option gets its name. The document is mailed on save because the MailOptions field is set to 1, and the Mail Send dialog is not presented.

9. **C** is correct.   Anthony cannot edit fields in the section, although he is listed as an editor of the controlled-access section. He only has Reader access to the database. A controlled-access section cannot override a user's access level to the database.

10. **C** is correct.   Because the sign-enabled field is placed in a section, the signature is created on save. If a sign-enabled field is not in a controlled-access section, the signature is generated when the document is mailed.

CHAPTER 3

Creating a Mail–In Database

You should be able to answer questions based on the following objectives after reading this chapter:

- Creating workflow applications
- Creating mail-in databases
- Creating/distributing workflow-tracking databases
- Monitoring/maintaining/troubleshooting workflow applications
- Mail-in database problems

Throughout our discussion of workflow applications in the previous chapters, we referred to a distribution method that routes documents to a central, shared database. This type of database is a mail-in database, and this chapter focuses entirely on mail-in databases. We learn when to use mail-in databases and how to create a Mail-In Database document in the Domino Directory. We learn that you can use mail-in databases to track objects in a workflow application. Finally, we look at items that can go wrong with mail-in databases and focus on troubleshooting mail-in database problems.

Mail-In Databases and Workflow

A mail-in database is a database that the Domino Router knows and can find—and that can accept routed or mailed documents. Workflow applications, however, are not the only place to find this type of database. A Domino administrator can choose to route server statistics to a mail-in database so that all statistic documents are stored in a central place. You would not want hundreds of server statistics documents routed to your mail file if you were an administrator.

From the standpoint of workflow, a mail-in database centralizes documents that reviewers must modify and approve. For example, a mobile user can compose an expense report document in his or her mail file, then route the document to a central, shared database that acts as a repository for all expense reports. Other examples of business processes that can take advantage of workflow and mail-in databases in particular are employee or customer surveys, customer sales orders, inquiries about a company's health benefits, and inquiries about employment opportunities.

Think about how Domino delivers mail messages to a mail file. The Router identifies a message awaiting delivery and looks for the name of the recipient. The Router then searches the Domino Directory for the recipient's name, the location of the recipient's mail file, and the route to the destination server. Finally, the Router deposits the mail message in the recipient's mail file.

Mail-in databases operate just like a user's mail file, except that mail-in databases can be any type of database, not just a mail file. In the same way that the Router knows to locate a mail file, the Router must know a mail-in database. We perform this task by creating a Mail-In Database document in the Domino Directory (refer to Figures 33-1 and 33-2). A Mail-In Database document identifies a database by name, just like a Person

Figure 33-1
Basics tab of a
Mail-In Database
document

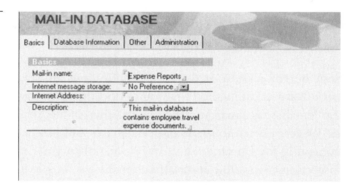

Figure 33-2
Database
Information tab of
a Mail-In Database
document

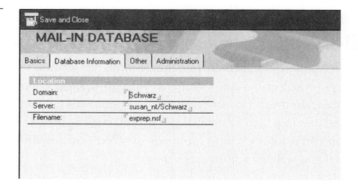

document, so the Router can deliver documents to the database. This document must exist in the Domino Directory of every server that stores a replica of the mail-in database. You might see a question on the exam regarding Mail-In Database documents.

> **NOTE**   Most often, the system administrator will have to create the Mail-In Database documents for you. In most companies, other users, including designers, do not have the necessary access rights to create these documents in the Domino Directory. To create Mail-In Database documents, you need at least Author access to the Domino Directory with the Create Documents privilege.

To create a Mail-In Database document, open the Domino Directory and choose Create . . . Server . . . Mail-In Database. Table 33-1 lists the main Mail-In Database form fields and their corresponding descriptions.

The name entered in the Mail-in name field is the one that you refer to in the SendTo fields. Once you create the Mail-In Database document, Domino displays the database in the Mail-In Databases and Resources view in the Domino Directory (refer to Figure 33-3).

Mail-In Databases and Tracking

We can use mail-in databases in workflow not only to store documents awaiting approval, but also to keep track of the workflow process. This situation is especially true

Table 33-1   Mail-In Database Form Fields

Field	Description
Mail-in name	The name that is used when addressing documents to the mail-in database. Although the mail-in name does not need to be the same as the database title, it must be a unique name in the Domino Directory. If it is not unique, the Router will be unable to deliver mail to the mail-in database.
Description	A brief description of the mail-in database, including its purpose. This field is optional.
Domain	The domain name of which the server storing the mail-in database is a member.
Server	The name of the server on which the mail-in database is located.
File name	The filename of the mail-in database. We assume that the file is in the default Domino Data directory. Include the path below the Data directory if the file is located elsewhere.

PART V

Figure 33-3
Mail-In Databases
and Resources
view in Domino
Directory

for complex workflow applications that require several different roles to perform multiple actions on more than one object. We find it hard to keep track of workflow objects. Each object has a unique character and must be tracked individually. Users who are involved in the workflow application want to know at a glance where the object is in the process. We can keep track of individual objects in the workflow process by designing special views in our mail-in databases. This method of view-specific workflow is a great benefit to users of the application.

Let's go back to our example at ABC Corporation. Employees fill out an expense form and submit the completed form to their manager for approval. In addition to, or in lieu of, generating an e-mail notification alerting the manager to the expense report that is awaiting approval, the manager can view the pending expense report document in a mail-in database using a Pending Approval view. The view might look something like Figure 33-4.

At a glance, managers can see pending expense reports. We can even design the view so that Notes only displays documents submitted by the particular manager's employees in the Pending Approval view. We could accomplish this task by using the following view-selection formula:

```
SELECT EmployeeManager = @Username
```

We also need to think about security in our workflow application. Not every ABC Corporation employee should have the capability to see everyone else's travel expense reports. We could place the newly created expense report form in the mail template and refresh the design of all employees' mail files. The user completes the expense report in his or her mail file and submits the form to his or her manager. The expense report routes to a mail-in database called Expense Reports. This database could have a default access level of No Access and Author or Editor access for employee managers, second-line managers, and the payroll department. All users who are involved in the approval process can now use the Pending Approval view to approve employee travel expense reports.

Figure 33-4

Pending Approval view

	Week Ending	Total Amount	Hotel	Airfare
Chapter 35 Expense R Pending Approval				
▼ Approved by Employee's Manager				
▼ Susan Mahon				
	10/16/99	$1045.00	$250.00	$600.00
▼ Awaiting Manager Approval				
▼ Susan Mahon				
	10/23/99	$1002.00	$252.00	$450.00
▼ Sent to Payroll for Approval				
▼ Susan Mahon				
	10/09/99	$417.00	$92.00	$245.00

Troubleshooting Mail-In Databases

Many factors can go wrong with mail-in databases, and it can be frustrating as you attempt to discover and then (hopefully) solve the problem. Incorrect information in the Mail-In Database document causes most of the problems. The Access Control List of the mail-in database is another culprit.

Listed as follows is a troubleshooting checklist of items that might possibly be incorrect in the Mail-In Database document. Be aware of these potential problems when taking the exam:

- The mail-in name of the database is invalid or is misspelled.
- There are two different Mail-In Database documents pointing to two different filenames, but they both have the same mail-in name.
- The domain name is invalid or is misspelled.
- The server name is invalid or is misspelled.
- The mail-in database was moved from one directory to another, and the change is not reflected in the Mail-In Database document.
- The mail-in database was moved from one server to another, and the change is not reflected in the Mail-In Database document.

Another potential problem is that users who need access to the mail-in database are either not listed in the database's Access Control List or they do not have sufficient access to perform the required task. For example, a reviewer needs at least Author access to the mail-in database—provided that their name is in an Authors field on the document(s)—to approve a document or to modify a field in the document.

Finally, remember that replicas of mail-in databases might be stored on servers across a company. If there is no problem with documents routing to the mail-in database, but there is a problem with the documents replicating to replicas of the mail-in database on other servers, the problem might be replication. One possible reason is that there are

Readers fields in the documents that do not contain the replicating servers' names. This situation would not affect routing to the mail-in database, but it would affect replication. If the server cannot see the document, it cannot replicate the document.

Summary

In this chapter, we discussed how to make a mail-in database known to the Router. You saw several examples of business processes that can benefit from using mail-in databases and learned some of the fields on the Mail-In Database form and the type of information that is needed in each field. Any workflow application can benefit from a tracking database—especially large, complex processes. View design is particularly important in tracking databases. Decide what information is most important for your approvers, and include this data in your tracking views.

Finally, you have seen that many elements can go wrong with mail-in databases, and you have learned how to fix the problems—including how access to a mail-in database and realizing that replication can cause big problems in your workflow application.

Practice

We need to create a mail-in database for ABC Corporation's expense reports and a mail-in database document in the Domino Directory. We also need to modify our expense report form so that documents route to our new mail-in database. The employee's manager will no longer receive an e-mail notification that documents await his or her approval. First-line managers now open the Expense Reports database and check the Pending Approval view to see whether they need to approve an expense report.

The finished mail-in database is called Chapter 33 Expense Reports (CH33EXP.NSF). The modified expense report form is in the database called Chapter 33 Practice (CH33.NSF). Let's begin by creating the mail-in database:

1. Open Domino Designer client.

2. Select File . . . Database . . . New.

3. Choose your server name from the Server field drop-down list. You could choose Local and move the database to the server when you are ready to test the application.

4. The Title is *Expense Reports*.

5. The File Name is EXPREP.NSF (refer to Figure 33-5).

Figure 33-5
Expense Reports
database

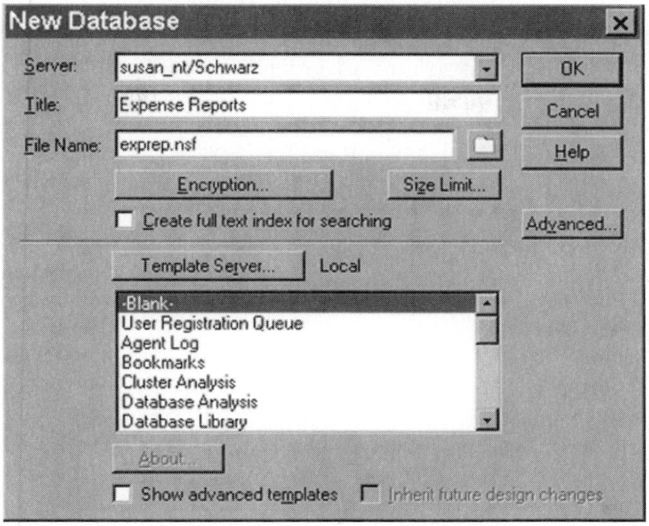

6. You will be creating the database from scratch, so you can leave the Template field blank.

7. Open the Chapter 33 Practice database (CH33.NSF) and copy the Pending Approval view and paste it into the view design list in the Expense Reports database that you just created. If you prefer, make the Pending Approval view the default view, and delete the Untitled view.

Now, we can create the Mail-In Database document in the Domino Directory. You can perform these next steps from either the Notes Client or from Domino Administrator:

8. Select File . . . Database . . . Open.

9. Choose your server name from the Server field drop-down list, and open the Domino Directory.

10. Select Create . . . Server . . . Mail-In Database.

11. The mail-in name is Expense Reports.

12. Place your appropriate domain and server name in the corresponding fields.

13. Assuming that you created your mail-in database in the Data directory, use the filename EXPREP.NSF.

14. Save and close the document.

Now that we have made the mail-in database known to the Router, we need to update the buttons in our expense report form to route documents to the new mail-in database. We also need to add a hidden SendTo field that contains the name of the mail-in database.

1. From Domino Designer, open the Chapter 33 Practice database (CH33.NSF).

2. Open the Expense Report form.

3. Click the first *Submit Expense Report* button, and replace the current formula with the following code:

```
FIELD Status := "Awaiting Manager Approval";
@Command([FileSave]);
@MailSend;
@PostedCommand([FileSave]);
@Command([FileCloseWindow])
```

4. Replace the second *Submit Expense Report* button formula with the following code:

```
@Command([EditDocument];"1");
FIELD Status := "Awaiting Manager Approval";
@Command([FileSave]);
@MailSend;
@PostedCommand([FileSave]);
@Command([FileCloseWindow])
```

5. At the bottom of the form, place a hidden, computed field called SendTo with the formula *Expense Reports*. Now, our @MailSend function will route the document to the mail-in database listed in the SendTo field.

There is one final step left in our workflow application. Think about the mail-in database to which we are routing expense reports. We created the database from scratch and copied a view from another database. When the user opens a document in the Pending Approval view, which form will Notes use to display the document? If there is not a form stored in the document, the default database form is next in line. There are not any forms in our new database. The last step is copying and pasting the form called *Expense Report* from the Chapter 33 Practice database (CH33.NSF) into the mail-in database you just created, called Expense Reports (EXPREP.NSF).

Review Questions

1. Joseph is creating a workflow application that involves routing documents to a mail-in database. What does he do so that the Router recognizes the database as a valid address in SendTo fields?

   a. Create a Mail-In Database document in the personal name and address book

   b. Choose *Enable for Mail* in the Database Properties InfoBox

   c. Create a Mail-In Database document in the Domino Directory

   d. Create a Mail-In Database document in the database to which you want to route documents

2. Sally opens her mail file and clicks a doclink in a mail message. She sees the error message: *You are not authorized to access this database*. What is the problem?

   a. Sally does not have proper access to the mail-in database containing the document that is linked in her mail message.

   b. Sally does not have proper access to the server containing the mail-in database.

   c. Sally does not have proper access in her mail file to view doclinks.

   d. Sally does not have proper access to the Mail-In Database document in the Domino Directory.

3. Janet created a mail-in database for a workflow application involving internal job postings. The company recently upgraded its servers, and the mail-in database was moved to a new server. Users are complaining that documents no longer route to the job postings database. What is the problem?

   a. The Mail-In Database document's Domain field was not modified to reflect the new domain name.

   b. The Mail-In Database document's Server field was not modified to reflect the new server name.

   c. The Mail-In Database document's Filename field was not modified to reflect the new filename.

   d. The Mail-In Database document's Mail-in name field was not modified to reflect the new mail-in database name.

4. Paul created a mail-in database for a workflow application. The documents route to the database, but users say that the error message *Form not found* appears when they try to open a document. What can Paul do to fix the problem?
   a. Set the database property Store form in document.
   b. Copy the form that was used to create the documents into the mail-in database.
   c. Give users Author access to the mail-in database.
   d. Give users the Create documents capability in the mail-in database.

5. Mary uses a mail-in database in her workflow application. Her users are complaining that documents appear in the actual mail-in database, but not in the replicas on other servers. What could be the problem?
   a. The replicas do not have their own Mail-In Database documents in the Domino Directory.
   b. There is a Readers field on the documents that does not contain the names of replicating servers.
   c. The other servers' Server documents are not enabled for mail-in databases.
   d. There is a blank Authors field on the documents.

6. Beth created several manual LotusScript agents in a mail-in database. The mail-in database is moved to another server. Users can no longer run the agents in the database. Why not?
   a. The Mail-In Database document's Server field was not modified to reflect the new server name.
   b. Users are not listed in the Run restricted LotusScript/Java agents field in the old server's Server document.
   c. Users do not have the Create LotusScript/Java agents capability in the mail-in database's ACL.
   d. Users are not listed in the Run restricted LotusScript/Java agents field in the new server's Server document.

Review Answers

1. **C is correct.** A Mail-In Database document in the Domino Directory enables a database to receive routed documents.

2. **A is correct.** Sally does not have access to the mail-in database. If she did not have access to the server containing the mail-in database, she would see a different error message.

3. **B** is correct.   When a mail-in database is moved, you must update the Server field in the Mail-In Database document to reflect the new server name.

4. **B** is correct.   Paul also could have chosen to store the form in the document, but notice that choice A says, "Set the database property *Store form in document.*" Sneaky! The option is actually set through Form properties.

5. **B** is correct.   If there is a Readers field on the routed documents that does not contain replicating server names, the documents cannot be replicated to replicas of the mail-in database because the servers cannot see the documents. It does not matter if the server names are not listed in an Authors field. The Authors field only applies to users or servers that have Author access to a database. We assume that replicating servers have Designer or Manager access to each other.

6. **D** is correct.   Users were able to run manual LotusScript/Java agents on the old server, so the new server's Server document needs to be updated to enable users to run restricted LotusScript/Java agents.

PART V

Domino Security Architecture

You should be able to answer questions based on the following objectives after reading this chapter:

- Security: maintaining/monitoring/troubleshooting problems
  - Database access: ACL changes
  - Database access: roles
  - Field access: authors
  - Field access: readers
  - Form access
  - Section access
  - View access: encryption
- Security: planning/design
  - Determining Notes security levels: database level
  - Determining Notes security levels: document level
  - Determining Notes security levels: field level
  - Determining Notes security levels: form level
  - Determining Notes security levels: network security (firewalls)
  - Determining Notes security levels: server level
  - Determining Notes security levels: view level
  - Determining password security
  - Determining people, roles, and group security
- Security: setting up/configuring/implementing/enabling
  - Databases: ACL
  - Databases: groups
  - Databases: roles
  - Field access: authors
  - Field access: encryption
  - Field access: groups
  - Field access: readers
  - Field access: signing
  - Form access: groups
  - Section access: groups
  - View access: groups

Domino provides a wide range of security options in order to protect your servers and applications. These security options begin at the network level and continue down to the field level. Some of the chapters that you have already read touched on several security features, such as signing, encryption, *Access Control Lists* (ACLs), and controlled-access sections. How can you talk about Domino, though, and not talk about security? This chapter covers a variety of security features that are geared toward the application designer. An application designer and system administrator should work together, however, to develop a security plan for a company. With this idea in mind, we cover topics such as network and server security in this chapter, as well as password security.

Network Security Issues

Securing your Domino infrastructure starts at the network level—limiting access throughout your LAN and WAN and to and from the Internet. Once you place your servers on the Internet in order to route mail or to host a company's Web site, the servers are vulnerable to passive and active attacks from Internet users. By opening your servers to the Internet, make sure that you are not exposing your internal network to abuse.

You can protect your company's network from Internet attacks by installing and configuring a firewall. A *firewall* is a system (or group of systems) that is designed to control access between a company's private network and the public Internet. A firewall can perform the following functions:

- Limit access from the Internet to only those applications that you choose to provide to Internet users

- Limit access to Internet services from within a company's private network

- Act as a gateway for applications that store and forward data, such as e-mail

- Provide encryption for data that is passing between the Internet and an internal network

Chapter 36, "Web Security," goes into more detail about protecting your servers from Internet attacks. We touch on several types of firewalls and talk about the different TCP ports and why you might want to enable users to connect to your Domino server by using these specific ports. For now, understand that configuring a firewall basically comes down to what type of traffic you want flowing in and out of your network and what type of traffic you might want to block.

Server Security Issues

As you already know, *authentication* is the process that takes place between a user and a server, or between two servers, in order to verify each other's identity. Once the user or server passes the authentication process, Domino checks its authorization to access the server. Access to the server is specified in the *Access server* field on the Server document in Domino Directory (see Figure 34-1). If a user attempts to access a server and his or her name is not listed in this field—or if his name is in the *Not access server* field—he or she will see a message stating that he or she is not authorized to access the server.

TIP   Use group names in the Access server and Not access server **fields to avoid having to restart the server in order for Server document changes to take effect. Grant and deny user access to servers by moving users in and out of groups, instead of updating individual entries in the fields and restarting the server.**

A designer should be aware of server-access settings for servers in the organization. When rolling out an application, make sure that users not only have access to the database, but that they also have access to the server on which the database resides. This access includes workflow databases that users might access only through doclinks in mail messages. Take into account mobile users who are involved in the workflow process, and make sure that they have access to the server, as well.

Database Security Issues

Once a user or server has authenticated with and has gained access to a server, the user or server must pass the security test at the database level. Before we discuss the ACL, let's

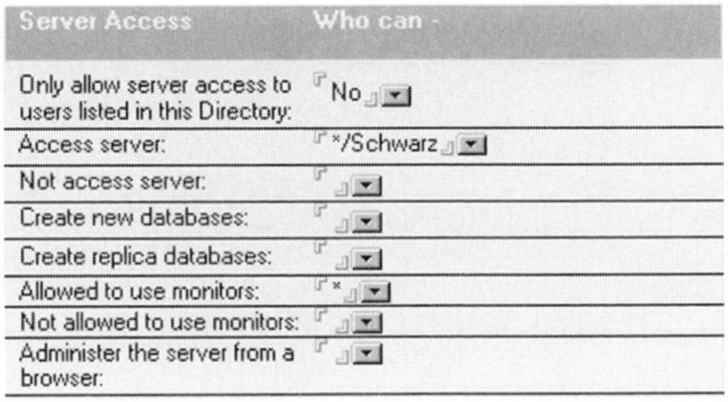

Figure 34-1
Server access fields in the Server document

Server Access	Who can -
Only allow server access to users listed in this Directory:	No
Access server:	*/Schwarz
Not access server:	
Create new databases:	
Create replica databases:	
Allowed to use monitors:	*
Not allowed to use monitors:	
Administer the server from a browser:	

db everyone applies to the local db

look at database encryption. *Database encryption* prevents unauthorized access to a local database. You can choose three different strengths of encryption: strong, medium, and simple (see Figure 34-2). The levels of encryption reflect the strength of the encryption algorithm. You can apply encryption to a new database or to an existing database through the Database properties InfoBox.

Encrypting a database adds an extra layer of security, because the ACL does not protect local databases. Database encryption prevents someone from using another user ID to access a local database. If a user attempts to access a locally encrypted database with another user ID, he or she will see the error message in Figure 34-3. Databases that are copied through the operating system retain their encryption. In addition, someone who is using another user ID will not be able to create new replicas or new copies of local databases by using the Notes client.

Every database has an ACL that defines who can access the database and which tasks they can perform in the database. When a user opens a database, the name in the ID file is compared against names in the ACL to determine that user's access. The user might be listed individually or as a member of one or more groups. Chapter 24, "Understanding and Implementing Basic Security," covers the ACL in more detail. In this chapter, we cover the ACL in terms of determining the security that already exists and modifying that security.

Figure 34-2
Database
Encryption dialog
box

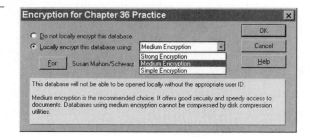

Figure 34-3
Database
Encryption error
message

What Is the Current Security Level?

To determine the current security level for a database, open the database's Groups and Roles dialog box (see Figure 34-4). You can access this dialog box by clicking the key icon in the lower-right corner of the screen on the status bar. When the database is opened, the key changes into an icon that corresponds to the current user's access level in the ACL. The Groups and Roles dialog box lists the groups of which the current user is a member, as well as the roles that are assigned to the user for the current database. To use this feature on local databases, enable the property *Enforce a consistent Access Control List across all replicas of this database*. Otherwise, the Groups and Roles dialog box will be blank.

The possibility exists of assigning conflicting access levels to users or servers. For example, a user is listed individually and is a member of a group that is listed in the ACL. Table 34-1 lists the access conflicts and the way that Domino resolves the conflicts. Pay close attention to how Domino resolves ACL conflicts.

Figure 34-4
Groups and Roles
dialog box

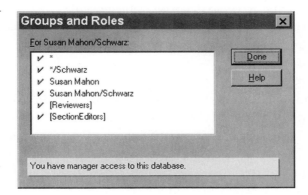

Table 34-1   Resolving ACL conflicts

Conflict	Resolution
A name is listed individually in an ACL and as a member of a group.	The access level that is assigned to the individual name takes precedence over the access level that is assigned to the group. This statement is true even if the individual access level is lower than the group's access level.
A name is found in two or more groups in an ACL.	The name receives the higher access level of the two groups.

Changing Database Security

We can further refine user or server access to a database by using several methods. These methods include refining ACL privileges, assigning roles, and creating database and directory links. Expect to see exam questions involving these methods of changing database security.

ACL

Refining ACL privileges is covered in Chapter 24, "Understanding and Implementing Basic Security." They are listed again in this chapter (see Table 34-2) because they are also covered on this exam. That way, you do not have to flip back and forth between chapters. Remember that some privileges are automatically available at different access levels.

Roles

Roles give the designer the capability to define special groups of users for a database and to further refine access to database elements. Roles are covered in more detail in Chapter 24, "Understanding and Implementing Basic Security." A role can be used anywhere that a group or username can be used, such as in hide-when formulas, view and form access lists, and sections—but a role is stored only in the database, not in the Domino Directory. Who can create roles in a database? The answer might surprise you: only users who are listed with Manager access in the ACL can create roles in a database.

Let's look at how roles and the ACL work together. Do you think that access that is assigned to a user through a role overrides the user's access in the database's ACL? The answer is no. Using ABC Company as an example, we automated its employee travel-expense reimbursement process by designing a workflow application. We created a form called Expense Report that employees fill out and send to their managers for approval. For security purposes, we collapsed the FirstApproval field into a controlled-access section and listed all managers as approved editors of the section. For more information about how to create controlled-access sections, see Chapter 32, "Creating a Workflow Application."

Now that we know a little about roles, we could create a [SectionEditors] role and assign the role to users who are authorized to approve the expense reports. We then modify the list of permitted editors in the controlled-access section to include only users who have been assigned the [SectionEditors] role (see Figure 34-5).

What happens when a user's access level in the ACL conflicts with the access that is given through a role? Let's look at two examples:

Table 34-2 Database ACL privileges

Privilege	Purpose	Assigned by default to
Create documents	Enables authors to create documents.	Managers, designers, editors, and depositors
Delete documents	Enables managers, designers, editors, and authors to delete documents. Authors can only delete documents that they create.	No one
Create personal agents	Enables editors, authors, and readers to create personal agents in a database on a server.	Managers and designers
Create personal folders/views	Enables editors, authors, and readers to create personal folders and views in a database on a server.	Managers and designers
Create shared folders/views	Enables editors to create shared folders and views.	Managers and designers
Create LotusScript/Java agent	Enables designers, editors, authors, and readers to create LotusScript or Java agents in a database on a server.	Managers
Read public documents	Enables Depositor and No Access levels in order to see documents that are created from forms that have the property *Available to public access users* set.	Readers and higher
Write public documents	Enables Depositor and No Access levels in order to create documents from forms that have the property *Available to public access users* set.	Editors and higher

PART V

Figure 34-5
Roles listed in the
Access Formula for
Controlled-Access
section

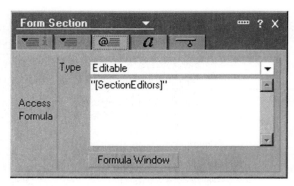

Would need editor access

1. A manager is listed with Author access in the ACL and is assigned the [SectionEditors] role. What access does she have? When she opens the document, she cannot put the document in Edit mode. Therefore, she cannot edit fields in the controlled-access section. One exception exists, however. If her name is listed in an Authors data type field in the document, she can edit the document and fields in the controlled-access section. We discuss Authors fields later in this chapter.

2. A manager is listed with Reader access in the ACL and is assigned the [SectionEditors] role. What access does he have? When he opens the document, he can put the document in Edit mode. He can even edit fields in the controlled-access section. When he attempts to save the document, however, he sees the error message in Figure 34-6.

Domino Administrator can be used to add, rename, and remove roles from a database. Select the name of the database for which you want to manage roles. From the Files tab, open the Tools pane and choose Database . . . Manage ACL (see Figure 34-7). You cannot use Domino Administrator, however, to display names that are assigned to roles, to assign a name to a role, or to remove a name from a role.

Database and Directory Links

You can store a single database or multiple databases in a directory outside the Domino data directory in order to increase database security. Domino enables you to create a link in the Domino data directory that points to either the database or to the directory in which you placed your databases. You then specify ACL access for users or groups for the link itself. The database ACL is still in effect once users access the link and open the database. Pay close attention to database and directory links, because you might see them referred to in an exam question.

Figure 34-6
Not Authorized
error message

Figure 34-7
Managing roles by
using Domino
Administrator

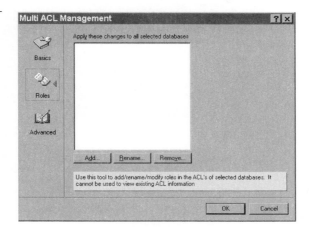

Create a link by using Domino Administrator. Select the name of the server on which to create the link. From the Files tab, open the Tools pane and choose Folder . . . New Link. The Create New Link dialog box opens, as shown in Figure 34-8. In the *Link name* box, enter a name for the link as you want it to appear to the user. Domino automatically appends the extension .dir to directory links and the .nsf extension to database links. Next to *Link to a*, choose Folder or Database. In the *Path and filename to that folder or database* box, enter the full path name to the directory or database to which the link points. For example, enter d:\private for a directory link and d:\private\private.nsf for a database link. Optionally, in the *Who should be able to access this link* box, enter the names of users and/or groups that you want to have access to this link. Do not forget to move the databases to the directory that is specified in the Create New Link dialog box.

Figure 34-8
Create New Link
dialog box

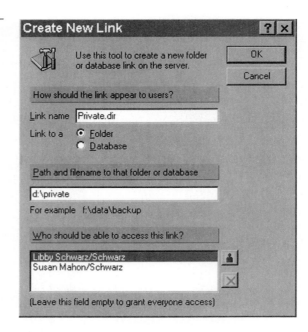

Document Security Issues

Documents are protected in a database beginning with the database's ACL. As you know, the ACL controls can read, create, and edit documents in a database. Beyond the ACL, we can restrict access to documents by using several methods:

- Form Read access list
- Form Create access list
- Readers field
- Authors field

These methods are not mutually exclusive. We can apply all four methods if we prefer, depending on the application. Authors and Readers fields are included in this section rather than "Field security issues," because they pertain to securing a document as opposed to securing an individual field. We discuss each method in detail later in this chapter.

What Is the Current Security Level?

There are several ways to determine the current security level for a document. First, we can determine authorized readers of a document. If a document is created from a form with a Form Read access list, a $Readers field is added to the document. The value of the $Readers field is the form's Read access list. In other words, only users, groups, and servers that are contained in a document's $Readers field can read the document or see the document in the database. We can see the contents of a $Readers field from the Fields tab of the Document properties InfoBox (see Figure 34-9).

$Readers

We can also see a list of authorized readers of a document by looking at the Security tab of the Document properties InfoBox (see Figure 34-10). Later in the chapter, we will learn how to use the InfoBox to modify the list of readers for a particular document.

Figure 34-9
$Readers field in the Document properties InfoBox

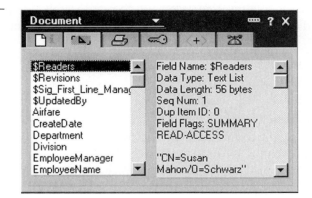

PART V

Figure 34-10
Document security options in the Document properties InfoBox

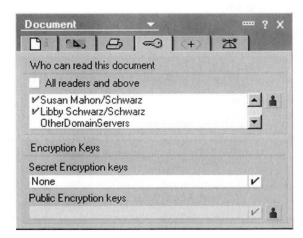

We can also see actual editors of a document (as opposed to permitted editors) if the document contains an Authors field. The $UpdatedBy field on a document automatically stores the names of users who have edited the document. View the contents of the $UpdatedBy field from the Fields tab of the Document properties InfoBox (see Figure 34-11). If the document contains an Authors field, users can hold their mouse pointer over the Authors field to view a text pop-up that displays the contents of the $UpdatedBy field.

Changing Document Security

Now that we know how to check the security of a document, let's find out how to modify the security. In the next few sections, we will discuss each of the four methods of controlling document access mentioned previously. Almost all of these security methods refine the ACL, rather than override it. For example, including someone with Depositor access in a Form Read access list does not enable that person to view documents in the database. Keep this simple fact in mind for the exam.

Form Read Access

By default, anyone who has at least Reader access can read documents in a database. The Form Read access list determines which users (or group of users) can read documents that are created by a specific form. This method applies to every document that is created by using the form. A user who is not on the list, regardless of ACL level, will not be able to see these documents in the database. Remember to include your replicating servers in the list. Otherwise, the documents will not be replicated because the servers cannot "see" them.

Figure 34-11
$UpdatedBy field in
the Document
properties InfoBox

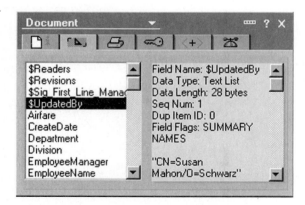

Figure 34-12
Form Read
access list

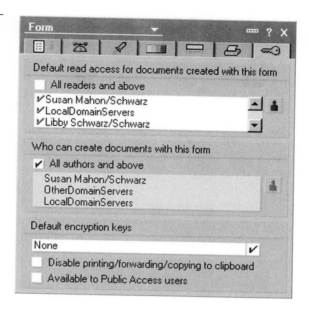

To modify the Form Read access list, click the Security tab in the Form properties InfoBox (see Figure 34-12). Remove the check mark from the *All readers and above* option below *Default read access for documents created with this form*. Click the *Add read access* icon to select each user, group, server, and role that you want to include in the Read access list. As mentioned previously, all documents that are created with this form will contain a $Readers field that contains a list of permitted readers.

We should point out that the author or editors of a document can also determine who can read the document. On the Security tab of the Document properties InfoBox, Read access to a document can be modified with the *Who can read this document* option. This option is similar to the form property in that you can select users, groups, servers, and roles to which you want to give document read capabilities.

Form Create Access

By default, anyone who has at least Author access can create documents in a database. The Form Create Access list determines which users (or group of users) can create documents by using a specific form. A user who is not in the list, regardless of ACL level, will not be able to see the form from the Create menu. A database that is designed with an action button that creates a document by using the restricted form will display an error message to a user who is not listed in the Form Create access list (see Figure 34-13) when he or she clicks the action. Remember that the Form Create access list only refines the ACL; it does not override it. In other words, a user who has

Figure 34-13
Form Create Access
error message

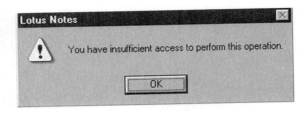

Reader access in the ACL and is included in the Form Create access list will not be able to create a document with the form.

To modify the Form Create Access list, click the Security tab in the Form properties InfoBox (see Figure 34-14). Remove the check mark from the *All authors and above* option below *Who can create documents with this form*. Click the *Add create access* icon to select each user, group, server, and role that you want to include in the Form Create access list.

Readers Field

We have seen how to control document access through ACL settings and form properties. A designer can further limit access to documents through the use of Readers and Authors fields. These fields can be either editable or computed and must resolve to valid user, group, and/or server names. As in Form Create and Read access lists, Readers and Authors fields refine the ACL; they do not override the ACL. Let's begin with Readers fields.

A Readers field in a document restricts who can see the document in a database. To create a Readers field in a document, we create a field of the Readers data type on a form (see Figure 34-15). If the field is editable, the author or editors of the document can specify the users who will have access to the document.

 NOTE When you make the Readers field editable, you might want to add an additional hidden, computed Readers field that includes the names of replicating servers and administrator or database manager names. Without it, if the document author leaves your name out of the editable Readers field, you cannot see the document—regardless of your access to the database.

When using Readers fields, you should recognize that they interact with other security features of a database. Assuming that a user has at least Reader access to a database, the following rules determine who can and cannot read documents:

Figure 34-14
Form Create
access list

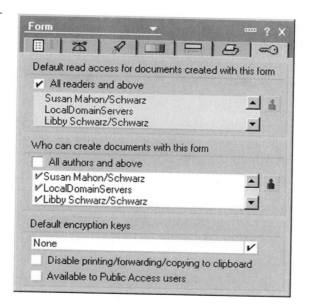

Figure 34-15
Readers Field
properties InfoBox

PART V

- If a document contains a blank Readers field, all users who have Reader access or higher in the ACL can read the document.

- If a document contains multiple Readers fields, all users who are listed in all Readers fields can read the document.

- If a document uses a Form Read access list (described in an earlier section), all users who are listed in the Form Read access list and in any of the Readers fields can read the document.

- If a document contains a Readers field and an Authors field, users who are in the Authors field can read the document—even if they are not listed in the Readers field. Authors fields are discussed in the next section.

Readers fields, as well as Form Read access lists, contribute to a problem with categorized views. If a view is designed with the view property *Unread marks: Standard (compute in hierarchy)* enabled, users see unread marks next to categories that have been updated with newly created documents. Users who are unable to read some of the documents in the view might still see unread marks next to categories that contain no documents when expanded. Be aware of this potential problem when taking the exam.

Authors Field

An Authors field in a document is used to limit the users who can edit the document. This field can give users who have Author access the capability to edit documents, regardless of whether they created the documents. Essentially, this type of field gives Editor access to a document without giving Editor access to the database. Keep in mind that an Authors field does not override a database's ACL, and it only affects users who have Author access to a database.

To create an Authors field in a document, we create a field of the Authors data type on a form (see Figure 34-16). If the field is editable, the author or editors of the document can specify the users who can edit the document.

When using Authors fields, similar to Readers fields, you should recognize that they interact with other security aspects of a database. The following rules determine who can edit documents when the documents contain Authors fields:

- An Authors field does not pertain to users who have Reader access or lower in the database ACL. They *will not* be able to edit documents in the database.

- An Authors field does not affect users who have Editor access and higher in the database ACL. They *will* be able to edit documents in the database. To keep users who have Editor access from editing a document, do not include them in the document's Readers field. They will be unable to see the document in the database (and therefore will not be able to edit the document).

Figure 34-16
Authors Field
properties InfoBox

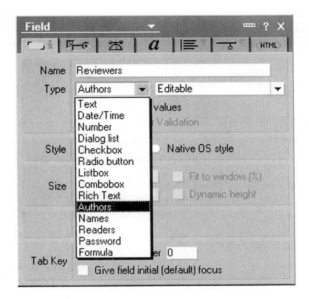

- In a document that has multiple Authors fields, a user who is listed in any one of the fields can edit the document.

- In a document that has an Authors field, if the field is blank, only users who have Editor access or higher in the database ACL will be able to edit the document. If a user has Author access to a database and wants to edit a document that he or she created, the user's name *must* be in an Authors field in the document. To ensure that the creator of a document can edit the documents that he or she created, place a computed-when-composed field on the form with the formula @UserName.

View Security Issues

Once a user has access to a database through the ACL, the user then has to gain access to the database views in order to see the documents. The designer controls access to views through View Read access lists. Users who are not included in a View Read access list will not see the view listed with other views in the database. A View Read access list is not a true security measure, however. Users who have at least Reader access to the database can create private views that display documents that are shown in the restricted view. For more security, use a Form Read access list.

PART V

> **NOTE** Do not create a View Read access list for the default view of a database. Users who are not listed in the View Read access list will be unable to open the database.

Changing View Security

To modify a View Read access list in a database, open the View properties InfoBox and click the Security tab (see Figure 34-17). All users who have Reader access and higher are given access to views by default. If you want to create a view that only certain users can access, remove the check mark from the *All readers and above* option. You then have the option of adding check marks next to users, groups, and servers that should have the capability to see the view. Remember to include all replicating servers in the View Read access list.

   View Read access lists, like all security measures mentioned previously, do not override the ACL. If a user is included in a View Read access list and has Depositor access to the database, he or she will still be unable to see documents in the view.

Field Security Issues

Once a user gains access to the server, database, view, and document, he or she can still be denied access to data at the field level. We apply security at the field level by using

Figure 34-17
View Read
access list

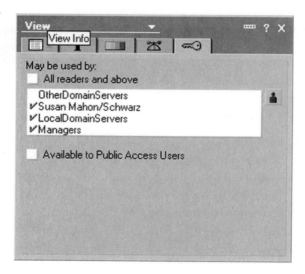

encryption, which means taking data that is stored in a field and encoding it so that only a user who has the correct key can decode and read the data. Another type of security option, called *signing*, is also available at the field level. Signing is a process that places a verification stamp on the document, and this stamp assures the reader that the signer was the last person to modify the document or section. For the exam, you should know the difference between encryption and signing.

Encryption (Non-Mail)

Field-level encryption enables a document's author or editor to apply one or more encryption keys to a document. When the encryption key(s) is applied, any data in encryption-enabled fields in the document is secured through encryption. To use document encryption in a database, you must complete the following four steps:

1. Enable the fields on the form for encryption.

2. Create the secret encryption key(s).

3. Apply the key(s) in one of three ways.

4. Distribute the key(s) to users who will need access to the encrypted information.

Enabling Fields for Encryption

Before encryption can encode field data in documents that you create, the field must be encryption-enabled. To apply this property to fields on the forms that you have created, go to the Advanced tab on the Field properties InfoBox (see Figure 34-18) for a

Figure 34-18
Enable Encryption for this field option on the Field properties InfoBox

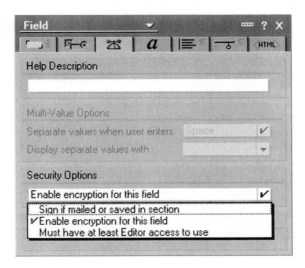

particular field. Click the drop-down list under *Security Options*, and select *Enable encryption for this field*. The field now has the *capability* to be encrypted. We still need to apply an encryption key.

Creating the Keys

The second step on our list is to create the encryption key. Encryption keys are stored in the User ID file. To create an encryption key or to view keys that are currently stored in your User ID file, choose File . . . Tools . . . User ID from the menu. When the User ID dialog box opens, click the Encryption icon to see the Encryption panel (see Figure 34-19). From this panel, you can create, delete, import, export, and mail encryption keys. To create a new key, click the *New* . . . button. The New Encryption Key dialog box, shown in Figure 34-20, enables you to perform the following actions:

- Naming the encryption key

- Deciding whether the key will be used in North America only (Canada and the United States) or internationally

- Commenting on the encryption key, in order to ensure that you (and your users) remember its purpose. This action helps prevent users from accidentally deleting encryption keys.

Applying the Keys

After you have created an encryption key, you have three options for applying that key to a form or to a document in the database:

Figure 34-19
User ID file
Encryption panel

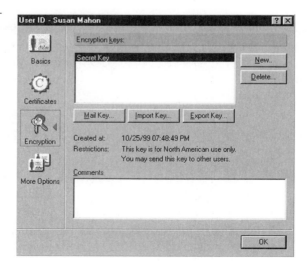

Figure 34-20
New Encryption
Key dialog box

- *Forced encryption* enables the designer to apply the encryption key. To apply encryption keys in this manner, open the Form properties InfoBox to the Security tab, as shown in Figure 34-21. Choose a key or keys from the Default Encryption Keys drop-down list. The key(s) you select is applied by default to the form. Any fields that are set as encryption-enabled will be encrypted by this key(s). Users who need to create documents by using the form must have at least one of the encryption keys that you selected from the list. Users who need to read the encrypted fields must also have at least one of the encryption keys that you selected.

- *Optional encryption*, which is enabled by the designer, enables authors and editors to choose whether or not to encrypt the document. The user can choose encryption through a keyword field, or the option can be determined by using a formula. To apply optional encryption to a form, create a field that has the reserved name SecretEncryptionKeys. This field should be either a keyword field or a text field. The field can be editable or computed but must resolve to the name of a secret encryption key.

- To use a keyword type of field, make the synonyms of the keyword choices the names of the encryption keys. Figure 34-22 shows three keyword choices. If a user chooses the keyword *Secret*, the encryption key called Key1 is applied. If a user chooses the keyword *Confidential*, the encryption key called Key2 is applied. If a user chooses *Do not encrypt*, no encryption is applied to the document.

Figure 34-21
Form properties
InfoBox, Forced
Encryption

Figure 34-22
Keyword encryption

- To use a text field, create the reserved field SecretEncryptionKeys and include a formula that resolves to the name of a secret encryption key. For example, if we base the encryption on the status of a document, we might write the following formula:

```
@If(Status = "Approved" ; "Key1" ; Status = "Pending" ; "Key2" ;
"")
```

This formula checks the field's status and applies Key1, Key2, or no encryption key based on the value of the field.

- *Manual encryption* enables authors and editors to choose whether or not to encrypt the document. When the user creates or edits the document, he or she can open the Document properties InfoBox to the Security tab, as shown in Figure 34-23. The user can then select an encryption key from the Encryption keys drop-down list. The list is generated from encryption keys that are stored in the current User ID file.

Distributing the Keys

Distribute encryption keys once you apply them to a document. Without encryption keys stored in their User ID files, users will not be able to access the data in encrypted fields. To distribute the encryption keys, you can use one of the following methods:

- *Use Notes mail to distribute the encryption keys*. After creating the encryption key, you can distribute the key by using Notes mail. From the Encryption panel of the User

Figure 34-23
Manual encryption, using the Document properties InfoBox

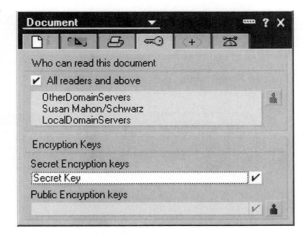

PART V

ID dialog box, select the key that you want to distribute and click the *Mail Key . . .* button. The Mail Address Encryption Key dialog box, as shown in Figure 34-24, opens. The encryption key is distributed to any users who are listed in the To: or CC: fields. You can use the *Address . . .* button to choose names from the Domino Directory if necessary. The Subject: field describes the key and tells the recipient how to accept the key. Notes will prompt you before sending the key to decide whether the recipient should have the right to distribute this key to other users. If you choose Yes, this action can severely limit the security effectiveness of encryption.

- *Use a file to distribute the encryption keys.* You also have the option of distributing the key by exporting it to a file and giving the file to other users. To export the key to a file, select the *Export Key . . .* button in the User ID dialog box. The Export Encryption Key dialog, shown in Figure 34-25, is displayed. You are prompted to secure the encryption key with a password. If you choose not to secure the file, click the No Password button.

You can restrict the use of the encryption key to one user and choose whether the encryption key that is stored in the file can be forwarded to other users by clicking the *Restrict Use . . .* button, as shown in Figure 34-26.

Figure 34-24
Mailing the
encryption key

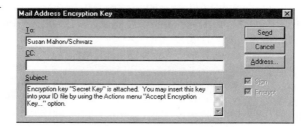

Figure 34-25
Export Encryption
Key dialog box

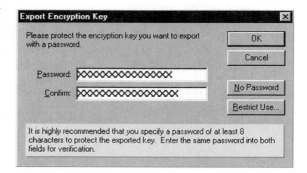

Figure 34-26
Encryption Key
Restrictions dialog
box

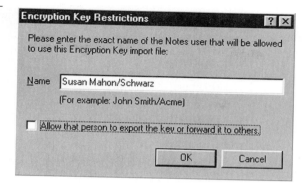

- *Finally, you must give the encryption key file a name and choose the storage location.* The file will have a .KEY extension. You can then distribute the file to other users.

Accepting the Keys

When users receive encryption keys—either through Notes mail or in a file—they must add those keys to their User ID files. To accept a key that has been mailed, the user chooses Actions . . . Accept Encryption Key from the menu while he or she is in the mail message with the encryption key. The Accept Encryption Key dialog box, shown in Figure 34-27, is displayed to the user. The user then clicks the *Accept* button, and the encryption key is stored in the user's User ID file.

If the encryption key is distributed through a .KEY file, the user must import the file into his or her User ID file. To do so, open the User ID file dialog box and click the *Import Key* . . . button. The Accept Encryption Key dialog box is displayed, and the user can click *Accept* to import the file into his or her User ID file.

Signing (Non-Mail)

Signing places a verification stamp on a document, which confirms the identity of the last person who edited the document or section. Signing also guarantees that no one has tampered with the data in the document. A digital signature is created by using the private key in a User ID file in combination with the data in a sign-enabled field.

Signatures can be attached either to sections or to fields within the document. When a user accesses the signed document, Notes attempts to decrypt the signature by using the public key that corresponds to the private key that is used to sign the data. If

Figure 34-27
Accept Encryption
Key dialog box

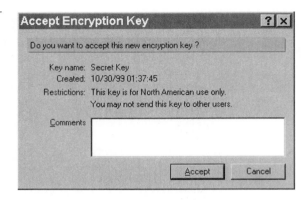

decryption of the signature is successful, Notes indicates who signed the data. If decryption is unsuccessful, Notes notifies the user that it cannot verify the signature. Unsuccessful decryption of the signature indicates that either the data has been tampered with or that the reader does not have a certificate that is capable of verifying the sender. Signing is not supported on the Web. Chapter 32, "Creating a Workflow Application," provides more detail about signing and creating sign-enabled fields.

Password Security Issues

Passwords in Notes are assigned to certifier, server, and user IDs during registration and are used to protect the ID file. When we password-protect an ID, Notes generates a key from the password and uses the key to encrypt the information on the ID. The password itself is not stored in the ID. A user is prompted to enter a password when he or she attempts to access a server-based or locally encrypted database (or when he or she opens the ID file by using File . . . Tools . . . User ID). In this chapter, we discuss the password quality-security feature as it applies to protecting User ID files.

Password Quality

When an administrator registered or recertified a user ID in previous releases of Notes and Domino, he or she could require a minimum number of characters for the password. Domino R5 enables the administrator to place even tighter security on a password by requiring a specific quality level for user ID passwords (see Figure 34-28). This system is known as *password quality-checking*.

Figure 34-28

Setting the
password-quality
scale during
registration

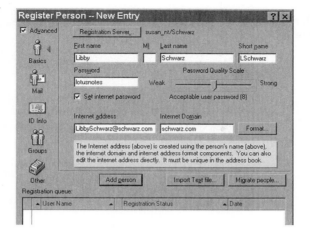

The password-quality scale ranges from 0 to 16. The higher the level, the more complex the password; therefore, the more difficult the password is for unauthorized users to guess. Lotus recommends a password level of at least 8. When choosing a password, keep in mind that an alphanumeric password that includes upper-case and lower-case letters, numbers, and punctuation (for example, Lo6!T2*u#S) would be harder to guess than a word that can be found in the Notes spellcheck dictionary. This type of password would be ideal but difficult to remember and might need to be written down, which defeats the purpose of a secure password. Another option might be to use an entire phrase or passphrase (for example, It was a Dark and Stormy Night), rather than to use a single word. A passphrase is easy to remember and more difficult for an unauthorized user to guess.

The password quality-checking level that is assigned by the administrator takes effect immediately when he or she enters a password for a new ID or when users change the password for an existing ID. The administrator must recertify an existing ID in order to change a password quality-checking level. To recertify an ID and to change the password quality-checking level, go to the Configuration tab in Domino Administrator. From the Tools pane, choose Certification . . . Certify. Once you choose the user ID to recertify, the Certify ID dialog box opens (see Figure 34-29)—enabling you to change the password quality.

When a user changes his or her password, the password must meet the quality level that is set by the administrator. In the Set Password dialog box, Notes displays information about the quality-checking level that is required for the ID file (see Figure 34-30). Users must enter a password that meets the quality level, or they will receive an error message (see Figure 34-31) and will not be able to change the password.

PART V

Figure 34-29
Certify ID dialog
box

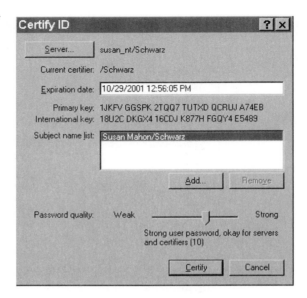

Figure 34-30
Set Password
dialog box

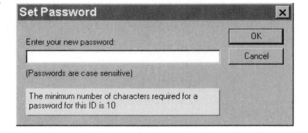

Figure 34-31
Password Quality
error message

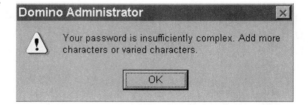

Summary

This chapter discussed Domino security from the network level all the way down to the field level. We know the definition of firewalls and understand how important they are once we expose our servers to the Internet. After gaining access to our network, we can control access to individual servers through the use of the Access server and Not access server fields in a Server document in Domino Directory. Once a user or server accesses a server in our network, we know how to control access to our databases through the use of the ACL. The ACL enables us to determine which users or servers can access our database and what they can do once they are in our database. We also learned how we can move a database out of the Domino data directory and into a non-Domino Directory—controlling access to that directory.

Within a Notes database, there are many levels of security. These levels of security help refine a database's ACL, but they never override it. We looked at how the View Read access list controls who can see a particular view in a database, but we learned that this method is not a true security measure. At the document level, we talked about Form Create access lists, Form Read access lists, Authors fields, and Readers fields. Several examples were given describing how these document-level security features work with each other in order to determine access to documents.

At the field security level, we talked in great detail about encryption. We know how to enable encryption for a field, how to create, apply, and distribute encryption keys, and how to view our own encryption keys in our User ID file. We talked about signing fields and sections and learned that signing does not encrypt information; rather, it only verifies that no one has tampered with the data.

Finally, we talked about password security issues and learned about a new security feature in R5 called password quality-checking. The administrator can set a password-quality level at registration or when he or she recertifies an ID.

Practice

ABC Company wants to begin adding security features to its workflow application. The company would like for you to encrypt the Expense Report database. Next, we will create two roles in the database and use the role names as authorized editors of the controlled-access sections and as authorized readers in a Readers field. Finally, we will create a View Read access list that enables access to one of these roles.

1. From Domino Designer, create a practice database.

2. Right-click the title of the practice database in the pane on the left, and choose Database . . . properties from the popup menu.

3. Click the Encryption Settings button on the Database Basics tab of the Database properties InfoBox, as shown in Figure 34-32.

4. Choose to locally encrypt the database by using the Medium Encryption option, and click OK (see Figure 34-33).

5. Close the Database properties InfoBox.

Now that we have locally encrypted the database, we need to create a Reviewers role and a SectionEditors role.

1. From Domino Designer, right-click the title of the practice database in the pane on the left and choose Database . . . Access Control.

2. Click the Roles icon to display the Roles panel.

3. Click the Add . . . button and create two roles called Reviewers and SectionEditors (see Figure 34-34).

Figure 34-32
Encryption settings in the Database properties InfoBox

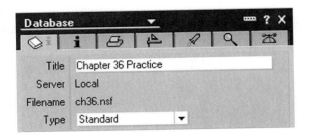

Figure 34-33
Encryption dialog box

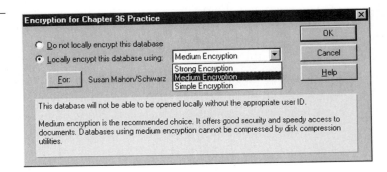

Figure 34-34
Adding roles to the
database

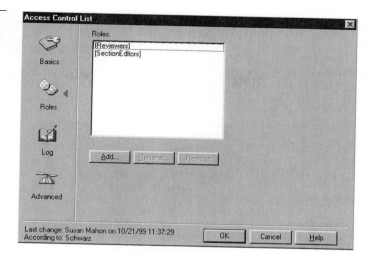

4. Click the Basics icon to display the Basics panel, and add your name to both roles by clicking each role, which places a check mark next to the role. Click OK to save changes in the Access Control List dialog box.

Our next few tasks include adding the SectionEditors role as a permitted editor in the controlled-access sections on the Expense Report form and placing the Reviewers role in a Readers field on the form. We also need to create a View Read access list for the Pending Approval view. Copy forms and views from previously created practice databases, or re-use Chapter 33's practice database.

1. Open the Expense Report form and click the First Line Manager Approval section.

2. From the menu, choose Section . . . Section properties.

3. Click the Formula tab in the Form Section properties InfoBox and type "[SectionEditors]" in the Access Formula box, as shown in Figure 34-35.

4. Repeat the process of adding the role as permitted editors to the Second Line Manager Approval section. Close the InfoBox.

5. Add a hidden, computed Readers type field called Reviewers at the bottom of the form, as shown in Figure 34-36.

6. Place the following formula in the field:

"[Reviewers]":"LocalDomainServers"

7. Save and close the form.

Figure 34-35
Roles in the controlled-access section access formula

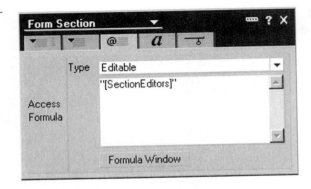

Figure 34-36
Creating the Readers field

8. Open the Pending Approval view, and open the View properties InfoBox.

9. Click the Security tab, and remove the check mark next to All readers and above.

10. Click the LocalDomainServers, "[Reviewers]", and "[SectionEditors]" entries (see Figure 34-37) to include them in the View Read access list for the Pending Approval view.

11. Close the View properties InfoBox and save and close the Pending Approval view.

Congratulations. We have implemented the security features that are required by our customer, ABC Company.

Figure 34-37
Pending Approval
View Read access
list

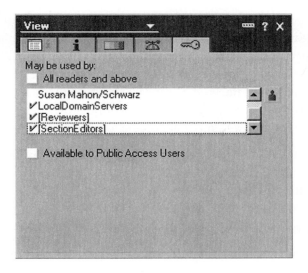

Review Questions

1. Jeff sets the View Read access list for the Status view in order to enable Frank, a user who has Depositor access to the database, to read documents in that view. How does Jeff perform this task?
   a. He puts Frank's name in the View Read access list.
   b. He puts a group that contains Frank's name in the View Read access list.
   c. He puts the user role Depositor into the View Read access list.
   d. He cannot perform this action. The View Read access list cannot override the ACL for the database.

2. Jackie has Editor access to the database, but he cannot see the Managers Only view. Why not?
   a. The view is hidden.
   b. His name is excluded from the View Read access list.
   c. His name is not in the Viewers field.
   d. His name is not in the Readers field.

3. Tracy has Author access in a database ACL and is a member of the Project Leaders group, which has Editor access. What access level does Tracy have to the database?
   a. Editor
   b. Author
   c. Reader
   d. Manager

4. Sharla has Author access to the database, but her name does not appear in the Form Read Access list for the Expense Report form. She can read documents that are created with this form, however. How?

   a. She is listed in the View Read access list as a Reader.

   b. She is listed in the Form Create access list for the Expense Report form.

   c. She is listed in a Readers field on the form.

   d. She is listed in a Names field on the form.

5. Neil wants to deny access to data at the field level. How can he reach this goal?

   a. Use Field View access lists.

   b. Use the Field property, Deny Access option.

   c. Sign the field.

   d. Encrypt the field.

6. Robert wants to view the encryption keys that are currently stored in his User ID file. How can he perform this action?

   a. Choose File . . . Tools . . . Encryption Keys.

   b. Choose Create . . . Design . . . Encryption Keys.

   c. Choose File . . . Tools . . . User ID.

   d. Choose File . . . Database . . . Encryption Keys.

7. Tiffany is a member of both the Project Leaders group and the Project Team group. The Project Leaders group is listed with Editor access in the database ACL. The Project Team group has Author access. What access does Tiffany have to the database?

   a. Editor

   b. Designer

   c. Author

   d. Reader

8. Shaneka, a designer, wants to force the Salary field in the Employee Profile form to be encrypted when users create documents with the form. How can she perform this task?

   a. She can choose a Default encryption key for the form. All encrypt-enabled fields will automatically be encrypted.

   b. She can choose a Default encryption key for the database. All encrypt-enabled fields will automatically be encrypted.

   c. She can choose a Default encryption key for the fields. The fields will automatically be encrypted.

   d. She cannot perform this task. Encryption is always a user option and cannot be enforced by the designer.

9. Bobby creates a form with both a Readers field and an Authors field. He puts Crystal in the Authors field, but he forgets to put her in the Readers field. Crystal has Author access to the database. What access does she have to the documents that are created with the form?

a. She can read the documents that are created with the form, but she cannot edit them.

b. She cannot read or edit documents that are created with the form.

c. She can create but not read or edit documents that are created with the form.

d. She can create, read, and edit documents that are created with the form.

10. Alice wants to give members of the group Project Team the capability to edit the documents that she creates. The group is currently listed with Author access in the ACL. The database manager does not want to give the Project Team group Editor access to the database. How can she enable Project Team members to edit her documents?

a. Project Team members cannot edit her documents without having Editor access to the database.

b. She adds the Project Team group name to the Authors field in the documents that she creates.

c. She adds individual members of the Project Team group to the Authors field in the documents that she creates, because group names are not enabled in Authors fields.

d. She enables the group property *Edit all documents* for the Project Team group in the Domino directory.

Review Answers

1. **D is correct.** He cannot perform this task. A View Read access list cannot override the database ACL.

2. **B is correct.** Jackie is excluded from the View Read access list. The View Read access list limits who can access a view for users who have at least Reader access to the database.

3. **B is correct.** When ACL levels conflict between an individual and between the groups of which the individual is a member, the access level that is assigned to the individual name takes precedence over the access level that is assigned to the group. This statement is true even if individual access is less than group access.

4. **C** is correct. She is in a Readers field on the form. Remember that authorized readers of a document are the combination of a Readers field and the Form Read access list.

5. **D** is correct. Encrypt a field in order to deny access to the field contents. Remember that signing a field does not encrypt the contents of the field; rather, it only ensures that someone has not tampered with the data.

6. **C** is correct. Encryption keys are stored in the User ID file and can be viewed from the User ID dialog box.

7. **A** is correct. When a name is found in two or more groups in a database ACL, the name receives the higher access level of the groups.

8. **A** is correct. Designers can force encryption by applying a Default encryption key to a form. Users who need to create documents with the form must have the encryption key in their User ID file.

9. **D** is correct. Notes assumes that if a user is specifically listed in an Authors field as an authorized editor for the document, he or she can read the document and therefore does not need to be included in a Readers field.

10. **B** is correct. Members of groups that are listed in an Authors type field in a document can edit the document if they have Author access in the ACL. Remember, the Authors field only affects users who have Author access.

Mail and Workstation Security

You should be able to answer questions based on the following objectives after reading this chapter:

- Security: maintaining, monitoring, and troubleshooting problems
  - Agent access
  - Calendaring and scheduling
  - Field access: encryption
  - Field access: signing
  - Workstation (ECL)
- Security: planning and design
  - Determining Notes security levels: workstation level (ECL)
- Security: setting up, configuring, implementing, and enabling
  - Agent access
  - Web: challenging
  - Workstations (ECL)

In the previous chapter, we looked at Domino security from the database level down to the field level as it applies to developers. This chapter begins by describing security that is available to users at their workstations and how they can prohibit certain types of actions from executing on their system. We also look at how security plays a role in agent access to databases and documents from both the Notes client and from a Web browser. We discuss agent-troubleshooting tips in terms of signatures and access. Finally, we cover security issues such as signing and encrypting mail, as well as enabling/prohibiting access to a user's calendar.

Workstation ECL

The purpose of the workstation *Execution Control List* (ECL) is to enable a Notes user to control the effects that a Notes application might have on his or her document, database, or system. The ECL limits the actions of another user's formulas or LotusScript programs when they are run on a workstation. The ECL settings specify what level of access these formulas or scripts have to the user's system. A workstation ECL, for example, can prevent code that would print, modify, or erase data from running on a system. Refer to Table 35-1 for the levels of access.

Before Notes executes the code, the workstation ECL looks for the signature on the database or template that contains the code. The ECL then checks this signature against

Table 35-1 Workstation ECL Access Options

Access Option	Enables Formulas and Code to:
Access to the file system	Attach, detach, read to, and write from workstation files with formulas such as @Command([EditDetach]) and @Command(([FileExport]).
Access to current database	Read and modify the current database using @DeleteDocument and @Command([AddToFolder]).
Access to environment variables	Access to the NOTES.INI file on a workstation using the @SetEnvironment and @Environment functions.
Access to non-Notes databases	Access to databases when the functions @DBLookup, @DBColumn, and @DBCommand specify a non-Notes database driver.
Access to external code	Run LotusScript classes and DLLs unknown to Notes.
Access to external programs	Access other applications, including activating any OLE object.
Capability to send mail	Use functions such as @MailSend to send mail.
Capability to read other databases	Read information in databases other than the current database.
Capability to modify other databases	Modify information in databases other than the current database.
Capability to export data	Print, copy to the clipboard, import, and export data using @Command([FileExport]).
Access to Workstation Security ECL	Modify the ECL with the @EditECL and @RefreshECL functions.

the workstation ECL settings on the user's workstation. Whether or not the code can execute depends on the access enabled by that particular signature. By default, the workstation ECL contains the signature types described in Table 35-2.

NOTE Default and No Signature entries in the ECL settings box are initially set to enable all access options. Use these entries to protect your system and to limit the action that code from unknown sources can perform on your workstation.

Signing Templates and Databases

Every template shipped with Notes contains a signature from Lotus Notes Template Development/Lotus Notes. Every template or database that your company creates should contain the signature of either the application developer or the system administrator. To sign a template or database, open the Domino Administrator, click the Files tab, and then select the template or database that you want to sign. From the Tools pane, choose the Database . . . Sign tool to sign the template or database with a specific ID. The signature should then be entered in the workstation ECL and should be given proper access. To access the workstation ECL, choose File . . . Preferences . . . Notes Preferences, then click the Security Options button at the bottom of the User Preferences dialog box. Notes displays the Workstation ECL Settings dialog box, as shown in Figure 35-1. At this point, you can add specific usernames and grant them the capability to perform the desired actions on your system.

Table 35-2 Workstation ECL Default Entries

Signature	Applies to
-Default-	Formulas and code that contain a signature, but the signature does not match any entry on the ECL
-No Signature-	Formulas and code that do not contain a signature
Domino administrator's name, such as Susan Mahon/Schwarz	Formulas and code signed by the administrator
Lotus Notes Template Development/Lotus Notes	Formulas and code signed by Lotus Development

Figure 35-1
Workstation
Security: Execution
Control List
dialog box

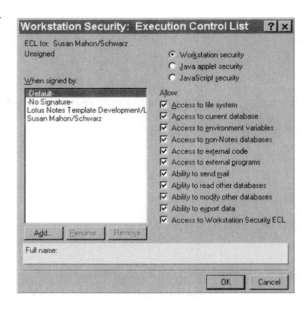

Updating a Workstation ECL
with an Administration ECL

When a user configures a workstation, the setup program copies the administration ECL from the Domino Directory on the user's home server to the workstation, and the administration ECL becomes the default workstation ECL. If you change the administration ECL after users' workstations have been set up, you might want to send updates to multiple users instead of updating workstation ECLs manually. To edit the administration ECL, open the Domino Directory and choose Actions . . . Edit Administration ECL from the menu. From this dialog box, you can change the administration ECL, and you can choose not to enable a user to update the ECL on his or her workstation. Once you have updated the administration ECL, you must distribute the new settings to existing users. The function @RefreshECL copies the administration ECL from a Domino Directory that you specify to a workstation ECL. The syntax of the @RefreshECL function is as follows:

```
@RefreshECL(server:database;name)
```

Here is an example:

```
@RefreshECL("susan_nt":"names.nsf"; " ")
```

- The server parameter is the name of the server and is enclosed in quotes. Specify "" (null) if you do not want to select a specific server from which to copy the ECL changes. The changes will be copied from the user's home server.

- The database parameter is the filename of the Domino Directory, enclosed in quotes, which contains the modified administration ECL.

- If a name for the administration ECL exists, enclose it in quotes after specifying the server and database name. If the ECL is unnamed, specify "" (null).

To distribute the updated administration ECL, address a memo to users whose workstation ECLs you want to update. In the memo, add a button that executes the @RefreshECL formula you created. Describe the purpose of the memo, and instruct users to click the button. Keep it simple. Remember, you are dealing with novice as well as experienced-end users. Before you send the memo, remember to sign it so that the ECL recognizes the memo and enables it to run. When a user clicks the button, Notes merges the administration ECL into the user's existing workstation ECL, as long as the user's ECL lists your signature with access to the user's workstation ECL. Notes adds any new entries in the administration ECL to the user's ECL, but any entries that the user has customized remain.

[handwritten notes: ① To refresh — ⓐ You must have access to ECL — ⓑ new entries are added but customized by user will remain]

Execution Security Alert

When an action from a formula or LotusScript program does not fit within a user's security profile, Notes presents the user with an Execution Security Alert warning message. The message is shown in Figure 35-2. Expect to see a question or two on the exam regarding workstation ECLs and the Execution Security Alert warning message (what causes the message to appear on your screen and what actions are available to you from the warning message dialog box).

Figure 35-2
Execution Security Alert

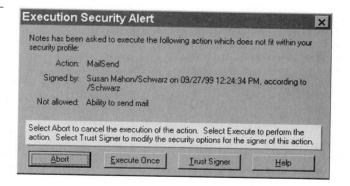

Let's consider the following example of a workstation Execution Control List in action. Fred receives a memo that contains a button. Fred, being a typical, trusting user, does not check the code behind the button before clicking. The button contains an @MailSend function that sends a memo from Fred to his manager, calling his manager a meathead. Luckily, Fred's workstation ECL is set to prevent the sending of mail by using another user's formula for the particular signature on the memo that Fred received. Notes displays the Execution Security Alert warning message on Fred's screen. The options listed on the warning message are shown in Table 35-3. The warning message displays the formula or LotusScript program attempted and the access option associated with the code. The signature on the document (if there is one and if Domino can verify it) is also displayed in the warning message. Otherwise, the words *No Signature* appear as the signer. At this point, Fred chooses to abort the action and never trust the signer again.

NOTE Do you know how to see the code behind a button? Place the document in Edit mode, right-click the button, and then choose Edit Button from the shortcut menu.

Agent Access

As you know from reading Chapter 28, "Actions, Agents, and Hotspots," agents enable you to automate many repetitive tasks. Agents can be private (created by and used only by a user who has at least Reader access to a database), or shared (created by the designer and used by anyone who has sufficient access to the application). In this chapter, we talk about signing an agent, troubleshooting an agent, and determining an

Table 35-3   Execution Security Alert Options

Options	Action
Abort	Action will not be performed.
Execute Once	Perform the action once. The Execution Security Alert warning message will appear the next time a document from the same signer attempts to perform the same action.
Trust Signer	Modify the workstation ECL to accept this action from this signer in the future. The Execution Security Alert warning message will no longer appear when this signer attempts to perform this type of action.

agent's access to an application. We also look at running an agent in an application from a Web client.

When a designer or user creates an agent, Notes places his or her signature on the agent. If the agent is a scheduled or event-triggered agent, the agent runs under the access level of the creator. If the agent has been modified and saved, the signature of the creator is replaced with the signature of the person who last saved the agent. On the other hand, if the agent is triggered manually, the agent takes on the access level of the person who is running the agent. The capability to run agents is also controlled by the Agent Manager and by the refinements of a database's ACL. For more information about the Agent Manager and database ACLs, see Chapter 10, "Configuring Domino Security," or see the section "Troubleshooting an Agent" later in this chapter.

Determining the Signature on an Agent

One element that the exam stresses is how a signature on an agent affects the agent's access to a database. To determine the signature that currently exists on the agent, select the agent in the Agent list from Domino Designer and choose Agent . . . Agent Properties. Click the Fields tab to see a list of internal fields that are associated with the agent. Figure 35-3 shows the Agent properties InfoBox with the Fields tab selected. The presence of a $Signature field indicates that a signature exists for the agent. Choose the internal field $UpdatedBy, and check the username(s) in the pane on the right. Designer displays the hierarchical name of the creator. If Designer lists multiple names, the first name listed is the creator of the agent, and the name at the bottom of the list is the last person who edited and saved the agent. The signature of the last person is the one that currently exists for the agent. Any event-triggered or scheduled agents would run with the security enabled for that person. Manual or user-triggered agents run with the security enabled for the user who is logged in and is running the agent.

Figure 35-3
Agent properties
InfoBox (Fields tab)

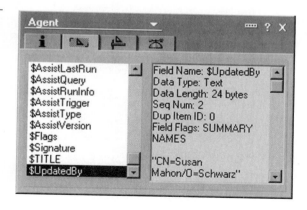

Signing an Agent

Before you can actually sign an agent, you must first determine the Note ID of the agent in the database. (You should know that Notes assigns a specific Note ID to every design element and every document, which is how Notes got its name.) To determine the Note ID of the agent, you must look at the properties of the agent. Select the agent in the Agent list from Domino Designer and choose Agent . . . Agent Properties to bring up the Agent properties InfoBox. Click the Document IDs tab, and locate the Note ID (see Figure 35-4). The Note ID appears on the last line, beginning with the letters NT—for example, NT000019E. You can ignore the zeros between the letters NT and the actual ID number. When referring to the Note ID in the example, refer to it as NT19E.

Now that you know the Note ID of the agent, you are ready to sign the agent with your ID. Signing the agent is done using the Domino Administrator. From the Files tab, select the server and the specific database or template that contains the agent that you want to sign. From the Tools pane, choose the Database . . . Sign tool. The Sign Database tool is shown in Figure 35-5. The tool gives you the option of specifying which design element to sign. The choices are as follows:

Figure 35-4
Agent properties
InfoBox (Document
IDs tab)

Figure 35-5
Sign Database tool

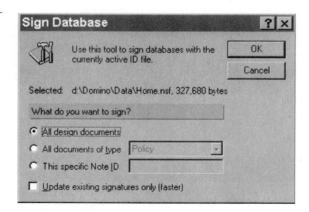

- **All design documents**   Choose this option to sign every design element in the template(s) or database(s) that is currently selected in the list of files.

- **All documents of type**   Select the specific type of design element that you want to sign for the template(s) or database(s) currently selected in the list of files.

- **This specific Note ID**   Type the Note ID of the specific design element that you want to sign.

Because you are only signing the agent and not all design elements in the database, click the radio button next to *This specific Note ID* and enter the Note ID of the agent. The selection *Update existing signatures only (faster)* enables you to update only design elements that have been previously signed. Use this option to change the signature on existing design elements that currently have a signature. When you click OK, a dialog box displays the number of databases processed and the number of errors, if any, that occurred.

[handwritten: update existing signatures — what had previously been signed]

If an error occurred during processing, check the Notes Log for a detailed explanation of the error. You can then use the Find Note tool in the Domino Administrator to display the properties for the design element (the agent, in this case) to help you troubleshoot the problem reported in the Notes Log.

To access the Find Note tool, select the correct server and the specific database or template on the Files tab that contains the design element that failed the signing process. From the Tools pane, choose the Database . . . Find Note tool, as shown in Figure 35-6. Notes can only run the Find Note tool on one database or template at a time. The tool gives you the option of searching for the note as follows:

- By Note ID

- By Universal ID

When you enter the Note ID (the ID number without the NT prefix) and click Find, Domino returns a list of fields, their corresponding values, and properties of the design note. You can use this information to help troubleshoot the processing error.

Troubleshooting an Agent

After creating an agent, you need to test the agent before copying it to the database on the production server. There are two ways to test an agent. You can quickly test an agent by simulating a run without actually affecting the documents in the database. The test run will describe how many documents would be processed and what action would be taken if the agent were actually run. Another way to test an agent is to make a copy of the database and run the agent live. This way, you can see how the agent affected the

Figure 35-6
Find Note tool

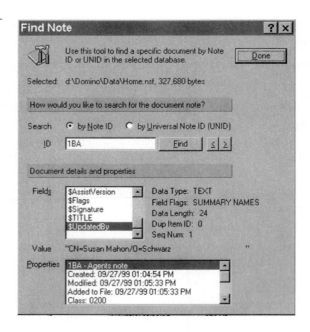

documents in the copy. These two options are covered in more detail in Chapter 28, "Creating Actions, Agents, and Hotspots." Do not run an untested agent on a database currently in production, because it might produce unexpected results.

If the tested agent generated an error or did not produce the results you expected, check the Agent Log (see Figure 35-7). Every time an agent runs, it creates an entry in the Agent Log that includes information about when the agent ran, how many documents it processed, and what actions were taken on those documents. Each new run of the agent overwrites the previous entry. To view the Agent Log, select the agent whose log you want to check from the Agent list in Domino Designer and choose Agents . . . Log from the menu.

There are two possible reasons why the agent might not run as expected:

- Problems with access
- Problems with Agent Manager

Remember that the actions of an agent are dependent upon the access level of the signature on the agent if it is an event-triggered or scheduled agent. The actions that a manual agent can perform are limited to the access of the current user who is running the agent. A user with Reader access to a database, for example, might be trying to run

Figure 35-7
Agent Log

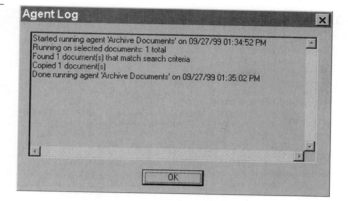

a manual agent that edits a particular field in a document. Because Notes compares the ID of the current user against the database ACL, the user who has Reader access is unable to edit documents (as is the agent).

The Agent Manager is a server task that runs event-driven and scheduled agents, also known as background agents, according to settings in the Agent Manager section of the server document in the Domino Directory. If a background agent is not running correctly or is not running at all, ask your environment's administrator to investigate the settings in the Agent Manager section. The creator of the agent might not have rights to run agents on a particular server, or the action being performed by the agent might be exceeding the maximum execution time setting in the Agent Manager section.

NOTE You should also check the database properties when background agents are not running correctly. Do not forget the Disable Background Agents for this database property.

Using Agents on the Web

When a Web user runs an agent, the agent runs using the signature of the creator or of the person who last modified and saved the agent. This situation is similar to running the agent from a Notes client. You can, however, modify the agent so that Domino checks the rights of the person running the agent instead. This property is set using the Agent properties InfoBox. Select the agent in the Agent list in Domino Designer, and choose Agent . . . Agent Properties to bring up the Agent properties InfoBox. On the Design tab, choose the property Run Agent as Web user (see Figure 35-8). Domino prompts the Web user for

Figure 35-8
Agent Properties
InfoBox (Design tab)

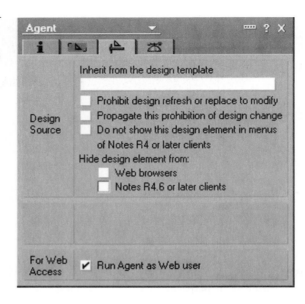

a name and password when she attempts to run the agent. At this point, Domino compares the user's login name against the database ACL to determine whether the user has the necessary rights to perform the action invoked by the agent.

TIP Access to a database from the Web is limited to the access level of the Maximum Internet name & password setting on the Access Control List (ACL) dialog box. This setting overrides the user's assigned access level in the database ACL. You might see exam questions regarding this setting and how it affects the ACL.

Mail Security Issues

Mail security is another type of security that a developer needs to be aware of when designing applications. We will discuss several mail-security issues, such as signing and encrypting a mail memo, the difference between public and private keys and how they are used in mail encryption, international versus North American encryption, and security for calendaring and scheduling.

Public Versus Private Keys

Lotus defines a key as a set of numbers that enables access to data, using methods coded into Domino. A key is used to encrypt data, and then a key (either the same key or a different key) is used to decrypt data. If the same key used to encrypt the data is used to decrypt the data, it is known as single-key encryption. A dual-key system uses two different keys for encryption and decryption. The type of key system we talk about in this chapter regarding mail security is the dual-key system. Pay close attention to the descriptions of public and private keys and know their differences for the exam. Also know the differences between a North American encryption key and an international encryption key in terms of which key can and cannot decrypt the other.

In a dual-key system, the two keys are known as the public key and the private key. Public and private keys are mathematically linked and are used to uniquely identify a user. Each user receives two keys: one public and one private key. Domino generates the public- and private-key pair when registering the user and stores the keys in the user's ID file. In addition, Domino also stores the public key in the user's Person document in the Domino Directory and makes the key available to all users. The private key is kept secret and is available only to the owner of the key.

To create public and private keys, Domino uses the RSA Cryptosystem technology. The strength of the key algorithm (how easily the encryption code can be broken) is different based on the type of Notes license a user has installed. A North American license uses a stronger encryption algorithm for public/private keys and document encryption keys than an international license does. Because of U.S. government restrictions on exporting encryption technology, North American encryption keys should only be used in the United States and Canada. A user who has a North American encryption key can decrypt data that is encrypted with an international-encryption key. A user who has an international license, however, cannot decrypt data that is encrypted with a North American encryption key—because the user cannot add a North American encryption key to his or her international IDs. Is this information confusing? Let's try again. If you are using a North American license and want users outside the United States or Canada to be able to read your encrypted documents, encrypt your data with an international encryption key.

NOTE   Ron Rivest, Adi Shamir, and Leonard Adleman developed RSA Cryptosystem in 1977. RSA stands for the first letter in each of its inventors' last names. For more information, see `http://www.rsasecurity.com/rsalabs/faq/questions.html`.

Signing

Signing a memo ensures that the message was actually sent by the person whose name appears in the Sender field. Signing also ensures that no one has tampered with the memo since the memo was created. Signing a memo does not hide any of the information in the message; rather, it just verifies authenticity. A user can choose to sign outgoing mail, or a designer might add a Sign Reserved field (discussed in Chapter 34, "Domino Security Architecture") to a form, which automatically signs all documents that are created with that form.

A digital signature is created by using the sender's private key. When a signed memo is mailed, the private key is encrypted and is attached to the message, along with the sender's public key and certificates. When the recipient accesses the signed memo, Domino verifies that the sender/signer has a certificate in common with the recipient. If so, Domino uses the sender's public key in the Domino Directory to decrypt the signature. If decryption is successful, the recipient sees a message on the Notes client status bar indicating who signed the message. If decryption is not successful, Domino indicates that it could not verify the signature, although the recipient can still read the memo. This situation could mean that either the message has been tampered with, or the sender does not have a certificate in common with the recipient. Jill, for example, who works for Hill Water Department, receives a signed memo from Jack, who works for Pail Industries. When Jill opens the memo, the message on the status bar indicates that Notes could not verify the signature. Jill is not alarmed, because she knows that there are no cross-certificates in her address book issued to Pail Industries to verify Jack's signature. Besides, she trusts him—they went up the hill together, right?

Encryption

Mail encryption prevents an unauthorized user from viewing the encrypted message body of a mail message. Encryption does not hide the header information—the To, From, and Subject fields—just the contents of the Body field. A user can choose to encrypt incoming mail, outgoing mail, and/or saved mail. A designer can force Notes to encrypt all messages when they are mailed by placing an Encrypt Reserved field (discussed in Chapter 34, "Domino Security Architecture") on the form. The Encrypt Reserved field forces all messages created with the form to be encrypted when they are mailed.

To encrypt a mail message, Domino uses the recipient's public key, which is stored in the recipient's Person document in the Domino Directory. When an encrypted memo is mailed, a random encryption key is generated and is used to encrypt the message. The random encryption key is encrypted with the recipient's public key and is appended to the message. If a message is sent to multiple recipients, the message is encrypted with the random encryption key, which is then encrypted with the public key of each recipient. When the recipient opens the encrypted message, Notes decrypts the random key with the recipient's private key (found in the user ID). If decryption of the random key is successful, Notes then uses the key to decrypt the message so the recipient can read the message. If decryption is unsuccessful, the recipient will not be able to see the contents of the encrypted field in the message.

Calendaring and Scheduling

The calendaring and scheduling feature of Domino enables users to check other people's free time (by using the calendars located in their mail files and the BUSYTIME.NSF database), to schedule meetings with them, and to reserve rooms and resources (such as an overhead projector). Security plays an important role in calendaring and scheduling because of the access that other users must have to your mail file in order to read your calendar, to determine your availability, and to add meetings to your calendar. The ACL associated with a mail file typically lists the following entries and access levels:

- **Default**   No Access
- **Mail File Owner's Home Server**   Manager
- **LocalDomainServers**   Manager
- **OtherDomainServers**   No Access
- **Mail File Owner**   Manager

How does another user gain access to your mail file when they are listed in the ACL with No Access? You can give access to your calendar through the Calendar Delegation profile in your mail file. You can let people create, read, and edit calendar entries without giving them access to other documents in your mail file. To fill out the Calendar Delegation profile, open your mail file and choose Actions . . . Tools . . . Preferences from the menu. Click the Delegation tab, followed by the Calendar Delegation tab. This action displays the Calendar Delegation profile in the Preferences dialog box (see Figure 35-9).

The mail file owner also has the capability to specify individuals or groups who should be permitted to access the owner's free time information in order to check his or her availability. To limit who can view your free time, open your mail file and choose

Figure 35-9
Calendar Delegation profile

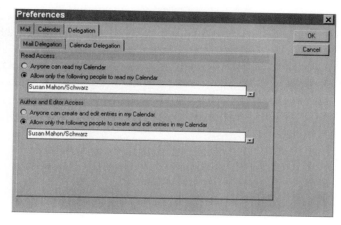

Actions . . . Tools . . . Preferences from the menu. Click the Calendar tab, followed by the Free Time tab. This action displays the Free Time profile in the Preferences dialog box (see Figure 35-10).

When the Delegation information is saved, an agent adds individuals or groups listed in the calendar access fields to the mail file's ACL. If you give a user the ability to read your calendar, that user's name is added to the ACL, is given the access level No Access, and is given the option to Read public documents. A person who has the ability to manage your calendar is added to the ACL, is given the access level No Access, and is given the option to Write public documents. Figure 35-11 displays these ACL options. The options enable you to give users who have No Access or Depositor access the ability to read from or write to your calendar, without giving them Reader or Editor access to your mail file. Expect to see questions on the exam regarding calendaring and scheduling and giving Public Access users read/write access to your mail file. Also, you should understand how a mail file owner can use the calendar delegation profile to control access to his or her calendar.

To enable users to create public documents, you must first create a public-access form. Open the Form properties InfoBox to the Security tab, as shown in Figure 35-12, and select the option *Available to Public Access users*. In addition, you must add a hidden field called $PublicAccess to the form. The field should be a text, computed-when-composed field with a value of 1. These steps have already been completed for all forms that are involved in calendaring and scheduling.

After creating a public-access form, you must create a public folder or view to display the documents that are created with the form. Open the View properties InfoBox to the Security tab, as shown in Figure 35-13, and select the view option *Available to Public Access users*. This option enables users who have No Access and Depositor access to view

Figure 35-10
Free Time profile

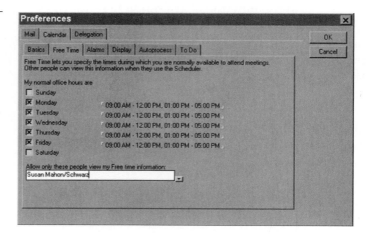

Figure 35-11
Options that are
available with
No Access or
Depositor access
to a database

Figure 35-12
Available to Public
Access Users form
option

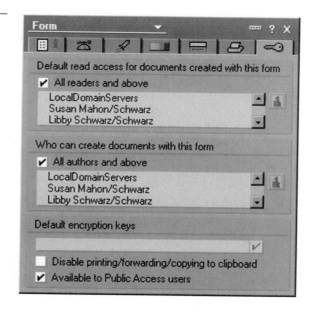

documents created with public forms. The property is already set for the Calendar view
in the mail database.

The exam might have a question regarding Public Access users and agents. Creating
agents for public access gives users with No Access and Depositor the capability to view
and use any agents that are triggered manually.

Figure 35-13
Available to Public
Access Users view
option

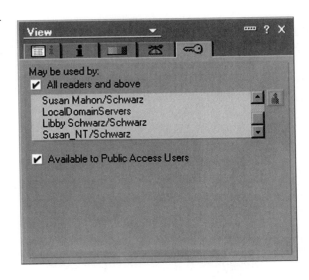

Summary

This chapter has covered security issues in terms of a user's workstation, agents, and calendaring and scheduling. You have learned about the workstation ECL and the role it plays in protecting your documents, databases, and system. You can edit an ECL and should know the access options and some of the corresponding @Commands and/or @Functions. Controlling formula access to your workstation is ultimately up to you. Use the Execution Security Alert message box wisely, and be careful whom you trust.

You learned how to sign an agent, how to verify the signature on an existing agent, and how the signature affects agent access. You were also given some tips that might help you troubleshoot agents if they do not produce the expected results (or if they do not run when you expect them to run).

We discussed the differences between public and private keys, where they are stored, and when you would use them. The differences between North American and international encryption keys and the strength of their encryption algorithm were also mentioned. By law, users outside the United States and Canada should use international licenses and encryption keys. Pay attention to the difference between signing and encryption. Signing does not hide anything; rather, it only verifies the signer and ensures that the message has not been tampered with along the way.

Finally, we looked at the security issues surrounding calendaring and scheduling and how a mail file owner can control access to a user's calendar by using Calendar Delegation profiles and Free Time profiles. The profiles control the access of users who have No Access and Depositor access—also known as Public Access users. Remember that when you design a Public Access form, you need to set the *Available to Public Access users form* property and create a $PublicAccess field with a value of 1. You also need to make sure to create a view that has the view property *Available to Public Access users* set to enable users who have No Access and Depositor access to view documents created with Public Access forms.

Practice

This practice section gives you the opportunity to see the workstation ECL in action. After modifying your workstation ECL, you will run another user's formula on your workstation from a database that is included on the CD-ROM. Because of your ECL settings, the Execution Security Alert warning message will appear on your screen enabling you to abort the action, run the formula once, or trust the signer. You will also be asked to sign an agent that currently exists in the database.

Let's start with setting your workstation ECL. The steps are listed as follows, and the resulting ECL is shown in Figure 35-14.

Figure 35-14
Setting your
workstation ECL

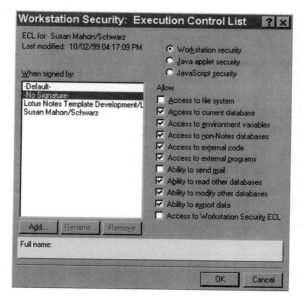

1. Open the Notes Client.

2. Select File . . . Preferences . . . User Preferences.

3. Click the Security Options button near the bottom of the User Preferences dialog box.

4. Click the -No Signature- entry in the When signed by: list.

5. Remove the check marks from the following access options:

   - Access to file system

   - Ability to send mail

   - Access to Workstation Security ECL

6. Click OK to save your changes, and close the Workstation Security: Execution Control List dialog box.

7. Click OK to close the User Preferences dialog box.

Now that your workstation ECL is set to restrict the capability to send mail and not to enable access to your file system or to your workstation security ECL, let's run a few formulas on your workstation that do not fit your security profile.

1. From the Notes Client, open the Chapter 35 Practice database (CH35-NSF).

2. Open the document *Workstation ECL* from the All Documents view.

3. Click the button labeled *Detach Files*. Because the action does not fit your security profile, the Execution Security Alert warning message (see Figure 35-15) appears on the screen.

4. Do you trust the signer? Sure. Click the Trust Signer button. You are then asked where you want to place the detached file. Detach the file to your default-data directory.

5. Click the button labeled *Send Mail Message*. The Execution Security Alert (see Figure 35-16) warns you that this action does not fit your security profile.

6. Click the Execute Once button. A mail message is sent to your mail file.

7. Click the *Update ECL* button in the document. The Execution Security Alert message box appears (see Figure 35-17).

8. Click the Abort button.

Now that you have selected each of the three options in the Execution Security Alert message box, close the document and see how your choices affected your workstation

Figure 35-15
Workstation ECL
after clicking the
Detach Files button

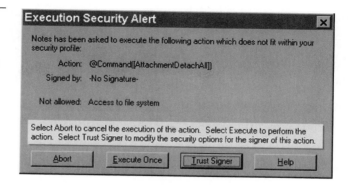

Figure 35-16
Workstation ECL
after clicking the
Send Mail Message
button

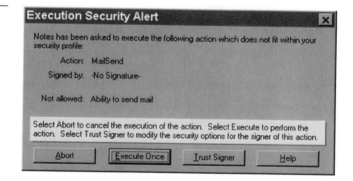

Figure 35-17
Workstation ECL
after clicking the
Update ECL button

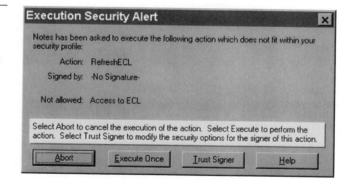

ECL. The only access option that changed is the *Access to file system option for the -No Sig-nature- entry.* You should see a check mark in the box next to this option.

The next activity is to sign an agent in the Chapter 35 Practice database. Before we sign the agent, we need to know its Note ID.

1. From Domino Designer, open the Chapter 35 Practice database (CH35-NSF).

2. Click the Agents view, and right-click the agent titled "Mark/Unmark Documents As Expired."

3. Choose Agent Properties to bring up the Agent Properties InfoBox.

4. Click the Document IDs tab, and record the Note ID.

5. Open Domino Administrator, click the Files tab, and select the Chapter 35 Practice database (CH35-NSF) from the list of databases.

6. From the Tools menu on the right side of the screen, choose Database . . . Sign. The Sign Database tool should appear on your screen (see Figure 35-18).

7. Click *This specific Note ID* radio button, and enter the Note ID of the agent.

8. Click OK. If the agent was signed correctly, you will receive a message stating that one database was processed with zero errors.

9. Close Domino Administrator and return to Domino Designer.

10. Bring up the Agent Properties InfoBox for the agent that you just signed. Click the Fields tab, and scroll down to find the $UpdatedBy field. Your name will appear as the last entry in the list.

Figure 35-18
Sign Database tool

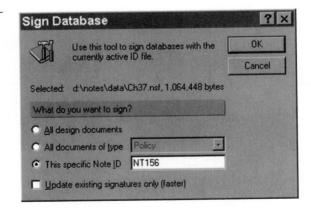

Review Questions

1. David sends Sherri an encrypted mail message. When Sherri opens the message, she can read the contents of all fields in the message. Which keys were used to encrypt and decrypt the message?

    a. Sherri's public key was used to encrypt the message, and her private key was used to decrypt the message.

    b. Sherri's private key was used to encrypt the message, and her public key was used to decrypt the message.

    c. David's public key was used to encrypt the message, and Sherri's private key was used to decrypt the message.

    d. David's encryption key was used to both encrypt and decrypt the message.

2. What security feature displays an Execution Security Alert warning message when an action does not fit within a user's security profile?

    a. Workstation ACL

    b. Workstation ECL

    c. ACL

    d. Encryption

3. The option *Read public documents* becomes available for selection when which of the following access levels are selected in a database ACL?

    a. Reader and Author

    b. Depositor and Reader

    c. No Access and Depositor

    d. No Access and Reader

4. Mary has chosen to send a mail message to Ted by using the Sign option. When Ted receives the mail message and opens it, what happens?

    a. Ted can read the message body, but other users cannot because the message is encrypted.

    b. The message is decrypted using Mary's public key.

    c. The signature is verified using Mary's private key.

    d. The signature is verified using Mary's public key.

5. Kerry creates and signs a shared agent that is triggered manually by the user. The agent modifies a field in selected documents. The database containing the agent lists Kerry as having Designer access in the ACL. Sarah attempts to run the agent, but Notes does not permit her to modify the fields. Why?
   a. Sarah does not have rights to run shared agents on the server.
   b. Because Kerry signed the agent, she is the only one who can run the agent.
   c. Sarah only has Reader access to the database.
   d. The signature on the agent is found to be invalid.

6. A mail file owner can give other users the capability to create and edit calendar entries in his or her mail file without giving them access to other documents by
   a. Giving users Editor access in the database ACL
   b. Setting the view property *Available to Public Access Users*
   c. Giving users access through the Mail Delegation profile
   d. Giving users access through the Calendar Delegation profile

7. Holly wants to run an agent from the Web that modifies a field in a document. Her name is listed individually in the database ACL as Author, she is a member of the group Modifiers that has Editor access, and the *Maximum Internet name & password* for the database is set to Reader. What access does Holly have to the database?
   a. Reader
   b. Editor
   c. Author
   d. Manager

8. The current signature on an agent can be viewed in which field?
   a. $UpdatedBy
   b. $ModifiedBy
   c. $Signature
   d. $Modified

9. Erika is in Canada and creates a document that is encrypted with a North American encryption key. Alfredo is in Mexico and cannot decrypt the document. Why?
   a. Erika has not mailed him the North American encryption key.
   b. Alfredo has an international ID and cannot add a North American key.
   c. Erika does not have access to Alfredo's public key.
   d. Alfredo does not have access to Erika's public key.

10. Randy sends an encrypted message to multiple users by including the name of a Mail only group in the To: field. At what point is the key appended to the message?
    a. When the message is saved
    b. When the message is delivered
    c. When the message is created
    d. When the message is mailed

Review Answers

1. **A is correct.** Remember that mail encryption, unlike document encryption, uses a dual-key system. The recipient's public key, which is available to anyone and is located in the Domino Directory, is used to encrypt the message. The recipient's private key, which is only available to the owner, is used to decrypt the message.

2. **B is correct.** The workstation ECL displays the Execution Security Alert warning message when another user's formula attempts to perform an action that is not permitted by the ECL.

3. **C is correct.** The *Read public documents* option becomes available for selection when either No Access or Depositor access is selected as the access level in a database ACL.

4. **D is correct.** A digital signature is created using the sender's private key. When the recipient opens the signed memo, Domino verifies the signature by using the sender's public key. Remember that the public key is available to everyone, and the private key is only available to the owner. In addition, signing a message does not encrypt any portion of the message.

5. **C is correct.** When a user runs a manually triggered agent, the agent's access is based on the access of the user triggering the agent, not the signer of the agent.

6. **D is correct.** Although there is a Mail Delegation profile, users are given the capability to create and update calendar entries through the Calendar Delegation profile.

7. **A is correct.** Access to a database from the Web is limited to the access level of the Maximum Internet name & password setting on the Access Control List (ACL) dialog box. This setting overrides the user's assigned access level in the database ACL.

8. **A** is correct. The $UpdatedBy field contains all signatures of those who have signed the agent. The $Signature field only indicates that the agent has been signed.

9. **B** is correct. Due to legal restrictions, you cannot mail a North American key outside the United States and Canada. Alfredo's license is international; therefore, he cannot add a North American encryption key to an international ID.

10. **D** is correct. The recipients' public keys were appended to the mail message when the message was mailed.

CHAPTER 36

Web Security

You should be able to answer questions based on the following objectives after reading this chapter:

- Security: maintaining/monitoring/troubleshooting problems
  - Web
- Security: planning/design
  - Determine SSL security
  - Determine Web security levels: database level
  - Determine Web security levels: document level
  - Determine Web security levels: field level
  - Determine Web security levels: form level
  - Determine Web security levels: server level (sockets)
  - Determine Web security levels: view level
  - Determine Web security levels: workstation level
  - Determine Web security: network level (firewalls)
- Security: setting up/configuring/implementing/enabling
  - Web: anonymous groups
  - Web: challenging
  - Web: SSL

In Chapter 34, "Domino Security Architecture," we discussed the security features of Domino from the network level to the field level. This chapter describes many of the same features, but we also cover the features as they apply to users who are accessing our site from a browser. We have to take extra precautions in order to protect our internal network and applications that are connected to the Internet once we open them to Web users.

We begin with a more in-depth discussion of firewalls, where we talk about different types of firewalls and how they protect your system. Security at the database level, as it applies to Web users, is next on our list of features. How do we authenticate users who access our Domino server from the Internet if they do not have a user ID? How can we control their access to individual databases? We continue our discussion of the different levels of Domino security and end with securing data at the field level. The last section of the chapter contains an in-depth discussion of the Secure Sockets Layer (SSL). We define SSL and talk about how we can use it to secure our Domino environment.

Network Level

In Chapter 34, we defined a *firewall* as a system or group of systems that is designed to control access between a company's private network and the public Internet. We normally want information to flow between the private network and the public Internet, but we do not want to give unauthorized Internet users access to our entire private network. In this chapter, we look at firewalls in more depth and learn how we can use them to protect our Domino system.

If you already have a firewall in place, all you need to do is configure Domino and Notes to work with the firewall server. The connection to the firewall server is transparent to the user. If you do not already have a firewall set up, it is important to put one in place before you enable Internet access to your Domino servers and applications. Three different categories of firewalls exist:

- Packet filters
- Circuit-level proxies
- Application-level proxies

Packet filter

A packet filter analyzes a *network packet*, which is a piece of information that is transmitted over a network. The packet filter then enables the information to either pass through or block the information based on specified filter rules, such as the following:

- The source and destination IP addresses
- The origin of the packet (Internet or private network)
- The client and server port numbers
- The session-level protocol that is carried by the packet

Packet filtering is usually implemented through the network router. In our case, we need to make sure that the router is configured to enable inbound and/or outbound Notes and Domino traffic to pass through the firewall. We want the correct ports to be available in order for Notes users to send information to the Internet and in order for Web clients to be able to access Domino applications. Table 36-1 lists the services and associated ports that you need to enable if your clients connect to your Domino server via any of these specific services. For example, if your Domino server hosts POP3 mail files, Web clients must be able to enter through port 110 in order to access their mail.

We can block traffic from entering the default ports and still enable Web clients to access a service. We simply assign the service a new port number and tell our Web clients to access the service on the new port. For example, if we assign the HTTP port the new port number 8080, Web clients must append the port number to the Web site's URL in order to access the site. The URL might be as follows:

http://www.abc.com:8080

Circuit-Level Proxy

Before we talk about the circuit-level proxy, let's define the word proxy. A *proxy* is a system that intercepts requests from one side of the firewall to a server on the other side, communicates to the target server on behalf of the requester, and communicates information back to the requester. To the server on the inside of the firewall, the proxy server is the client. A proxy also logs activity and caches information that users can access.

Table 36-1   Domino Services and Port Numbers

Service	Port Number without SSL	Port Number Using SSL
Note and Domino Remote Procedure Call (RPC)	1352	Not applicable
HTTP	80	443
IMAP	143	993
LDAP	389	636
POP3	110	995
NNTP	119	563
SMTP	25	465

A circuit-level proxy enables clients to pass through a central service, such as SOCKS, and to connect to the TCP/IP port that is specified. SOCKS servers act as the proxy, enabling the client to connect in this case—but they can block unauthorized clients once the source address of the connection requests is authenticated. A circuit-level proxy does not understand the application data that is stored in the network packet.

NOTE For more information about SOCKS, visit the Web site www.socks.nec.com.

Application-Level Proxy

Application-level proxies provide greater security than circuit-level proxies, because they have the capability to understand the information that is contained in the packet. Similar to other proxies, application-level proxies act as intermediaries that communicate on behalf of the requester. In our Domino environment, we can use three types of application-level proxies:

- Domino passthru server
- HTTP proxy
- SMTP router and SMTP listener

In this chapter, we limit our discussion to using Domino passthru server as a type of application proxy. We must first connect our Domino passthru server to the Internet. We then set up Notes workstations and Domino servers in order to use the passthru server when accessing services outside the network. We then set up workstations by specifying the passthru server in the workstation's Location document. Then, we set up servers in order to use passthru in the workstation's Server document.

Database Level

We learned in previous chapters that the Access Control List (ACL) is the security method used by database managers in order to restrict access to a database. The ACL specifies who can access a database and what changes an individual can make to the database once the database is accessed. We can control access to databases for both Notes clients and Web clients by using the ACL.

Anonymous Groups/Users

When a Notes client opens a Domino database, the username on the ID file is compared against names in the ACL in order to determine what type of access the client has. This method does not work for Web clients, however, because they do not have Notes IDs. To enable Web clients to access databases, we can set up Anonymous access to the database. Anonymous access enables Web clients to open a database without identifying themselves.

TIP Any application that will be deployed on the Web should have an Anonymous entry in the ACL of all databases that are used in the application.

When setting up Web clients for Anonymous access, we must ensure that the server the clients will access can support Anonymous access. From Domino Administrator, click the Configuration tab and open the Server document. Click the Ports . . . Internet Ports tab, which displays five additional tabs: Web, Directory, News, Mail, and IIOP. Click the tab for the protocol that you want to use for Anonymous access (see Figure 36-1). To enable Anonymous access for clients who are connecting via TCP/IP, select *Yes* in the Anonymous field in the TCP/IP section. To enable Anonymous access when clients connect via SSL, select *Yes* in the Anonymous field in the SSL section. We will discuss SSL later in this chapter.

Once the server upon which the databases reside is set up to enable Anonymous access, we need to set up Anonymous access to the databases themselves. In the ACL of each database on the server, create an entry called Anonymous and assign an appropriate access level (see Figure 36-2). Base the level of access on how the database is used

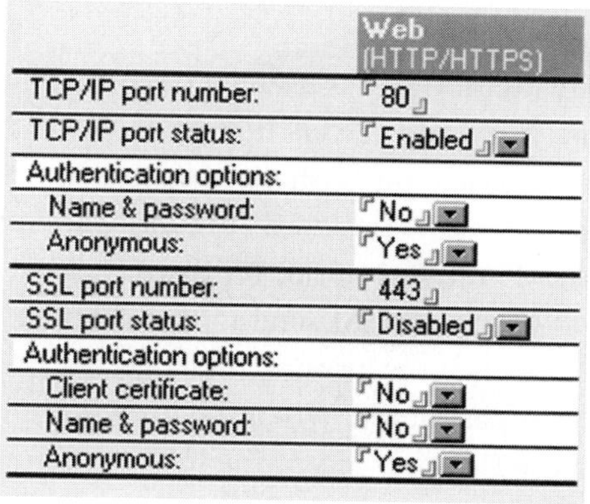

Figure 36-1
Setting Anonymous access in the Server document

	Web (HTTP/HTTPS)
TCP/IP port number:	80
TCP/IP port status:	Enabled
Authentication options:	
Name & password:	No
Anonymous:	Yes
SSL port number:	443
SSL port status:	Disabled
Authentication options:	
Client certificate:	No
Name & password:	No
Anonymous:	Yes

Figure 36-2
Anonymous entry in
the database ACL

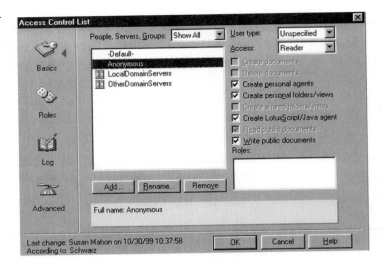

and on the confidentiality of the data that is contained in the database. For most data-bases, assign Reader access at most to the Anonymous entry. If there is no Anonymous entry in the ACL, anonymous users are granted the access that is assigned to the -Default- entry. This access might be a higher level than you want for anonymous Web users.

NOTE If the database ACL does not contain an Anonymous entry, all anonymous users receive the access level that is assigned to -Default-.

Authentication

Authentication is the security method that is used by Domino in order to verify the identity of users and/or servers. Users and servers that have a valid Notes ID can authenticate with a Domino server based on a shared, trusted certificate. To authenticate browser users, Domino uses SSL—the standard authentication protocol for Web clients —and/or name-and-password authentication. We discuss name-and-password authentication in this section, and we discuss SSL later in this chapter.

Name-and-password authentication uses a challenge/response method in order to ask users for their names and passwords. When the browser sends the name and password information back to the Domino server, the information is checked against passwords that are stored in Person documents in the Domino Directory. After Domino identifies the Web client, the client's name is compared against a database's ACL in order to determine the Web client's level of access to the database. Clients who do not have Person documents in the Domino Directory are considered Anonymous and receive the access level that is assigned to that entry in the ACL.

Set up name-and-password authentication in the Server document in the same way that we set up Anonymous access. The only difference is that you choose *Yes* in the Name & password field in the TCP/IP section of the protocol for which you want to set up this type of authentication (see Figure 36-3). In addition, you must create a Person document for Web clients who authenticate via the name-and-password method. You can perform this task manually from the Domino Directory, or you can use a registration database. If you register Web clients manually, the only fields that are required for authentication in the Person document are the User Name and Internet Password fields.

When are Web clients prompted for a name and a password? If a Server document is set to require name-and-password authentication and does not enable Anonymous access for a certain protocol, the client is prompted when he or she accesses the server. If a Server document enables both name-and-password authentication and Anonymous access, a client is prompted for a name and password when he or she attempts to perform an action in a database that goes beyond the access that is granted to Anonymous users in the ACL.

For example, Sally Jones accesses a Domino database from a Web browser. The Anonymous entry in the database's ACL has Reader access assigned to it. Sally clicks a Create Document action from a view that will enable her to create a document in the database. At that point, Domino prompts Sally for her name and password. If she is listed in the ACL individually or is a member of a group that has Author access or higher and the capability to create documents, she will be able to perform that action. Otherwise, an error message appears on her browser.

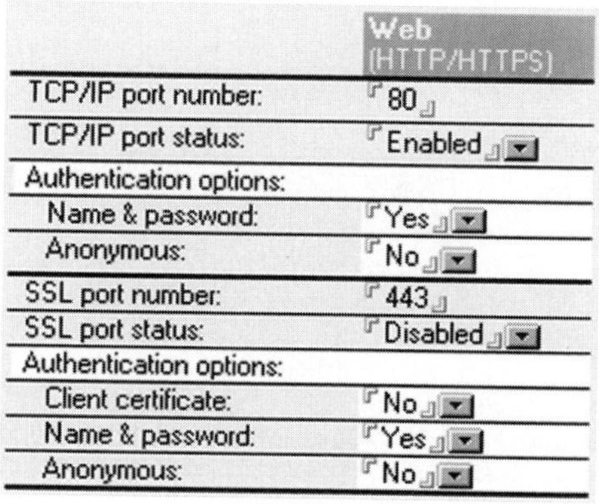

Figure 36-3
Setting name-and-password authentication in the Server document

Web (HTTP/HTTPS)	
TCP/IP port number:	80
TCP/IP port status:	Enabled
Authentication options:	
Name & password:	Yes
Anonymous:	No
SSL port number:	443
SSL port status:	Disabled
Authentication options:	
Client certificate:	No
Name & password:	Yes
Anonymous:	No

The actions that a Web client can perform in a database are also controlled by the *Maximum Internet name & password* setting for the database (see Figure 36-4). This setting enables you to control the maximum level of access that Internet users have to a database from a browser. Web clients never have an access level that is higher than what is specified by the *Maximum Internet name & password* option. This setting overrides the access level that a user might have been given in the database ACL.

(handwritten note: Max intnl pw & name overrides ACL)

(handwritten note: Not for SSL)

Directory/Database Links

In Chapter 34, we discussed database and directory linking as another way to secure databases on a server. We can also use linking to organize databases that are located outside the Domino data directory in order to take advantage of disk space that is available on other servers. If we use a directory link on a Web server to point Web clients to a directory that is outside the Domino data directory, we need to remember to give the clients access to the directory link. For example, include an Anonymous entry in the *Who should be able to access this link* box when you create the link. If there are users who need access that includes name-and-password or SSL-client authentication, remember to include their names in the access list. If we use a database link, add an Anonymous entry and entries for Web clients to the ACL of the database for which you are creating the link.

TIP   Know the difference between an Anonymous entry and the -Default- entry in the ACL. In terms of Web users, Anonymous is a Web user who has not yet authenticated with the Domino server. -Default- indicates any user or server that is not specified in the ACL.

Figure 36-4
Maximum Internet
name and password
option

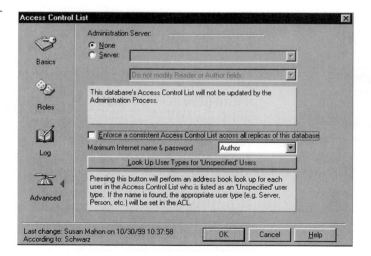

Remapping/Redirection

Occasionally, you might need to reorganize your Web site and move your Domino databases to a different directory or to a new, more powerful server. You want this change to be transparent to your Web clients. In order for users to access the new directory or server by using the old URL, you must create a URL Redirection document. Redirecting a URL displays the page in the new location and returns the new URL to the browser. The Web client is automatically redirected to the new directory or server.

new URL displayed

To create a URL Redirection document, click the Configuration tab in the Domino Administrator. Choose Server in the left pane, and open the Server document for the server on which you want to redirect a URL. Click the Web action button and choose Create URL Mapping/Redirection (see Figure 36-5). On the Basics tab, choose to create a URL→Redirection URL document. On the Mapping tab, type the incoming URL path that you want to map to another URL in the First URL path field. In the Second URL path field, type the full URL path name to which you want to redirect the incoming URL. For example, Figure 36-6 transfers incoming requests for Activities to the Future Activities page at ABC Company's Web site. After saving the document, restart the Domino server in order for the settings to take effect.

Redirecting a URL is the only method for mapping an incoming URL to a Domino-specific URL. Remapping URLs and directories are intended for use with HTML

Figure 36-5
Create URL
Mapping/Redirection
action

Figure 36-6
URL redirection
example

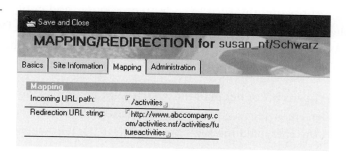

documents, CGI scripts, and other resources (such as .GIF files). Knowing which method enables you to map a URL to a Domino-specific URL is important.

Document Level

We can secure a document from unauthorized Web users with Form Read access lists, Readers fields, or Authors fields. Remember from Chapter 34 that a user who is not included in a Form Read access list or Readers field cannot see documents that are created with that form. Anonymous Web users are blocked from seeing restricted documents until they authenticate with the Domino server. Once they authenticate, users whose names are listed in a Form Read access list or Readers field can read that document. Remember that if an authenticated user's name is not in an Authors field and the user has Author access to a database, the user cannot edit a document (including a document that he or she created).

Field Level

In Chapter 34, we discussed encryption as a way to secure documents and to prevent Notes users from viewing data in specific fields. Remember that encryption enables a designer or a document's author or editor to apply one or more encryption keys to a document. When the encryption key(s) is applied, any data that exists in encryption-enabled fields in the document is secured through encryption. We include encryption in this section, because encrypting a document really means encrypting the encrypt-enabled fields within a document.

Let's begin our discussion of field-level security by stating up front that encryption does not work on the Web. Why? Keep in mind that document encryption is based on a secret encryption key that is stored in a User ID file and that is applied to a document. Domino security options, such as encryption, signing, and public/private keys, are not supported on the Web because user IDs cannot be used to access Domino applications from a Web browser. Expect to see exam questions regarding how Domino security options function from a Web browser. Let's look at a few examples:

- A user opens his or her mail file, which is located on a Domino server from a Web browser. He or she receives a mail message that has been encrypted. When the user opens the encrypted message, he or she sees the following text in the body of the message:

"The body of this message is encrypted and cannot be displayed
by a browser client. Please reopen this message with a Notes
Client or ask the sender for a copy that is not encrypted."

- A user opens an encrypted document in the Expense Report database by using a Web browser. The Approval field is encryption-enabled on the Expense Report form. The document creator has applied a secret encryption key to the Expense Report document. Although the Web client does not have the correct encryption key in his or her user ID, he or she can still see the contents of the encrypted Approval field.

In addition to Form Read access lists and Readers fields, which we can use to hide an entire document from a Web user, we can use the field property *Hide paragraph from Web browsers* (see Figure 36-7) in order to hide specific fields in a document. We know that this method is not a true security measure for Notes users, because they can see the contents of a hidden field from the Document properties InfoBox. Because a Web user cannot access a document's Properties InfoBox, by hiding a field, we are hiding data in the field from a Web browser. Unfortunately, this property affects Web users who need access to the field in order to read or modify data that is contained in the field.

Form Level

A Web browser does not have a Create menu like a Notes client does. You must provide a way for Web clients to create and edit documents. For example, you might create a

Figure 36-7
Hide Paragraph
from Web Browsers
field property

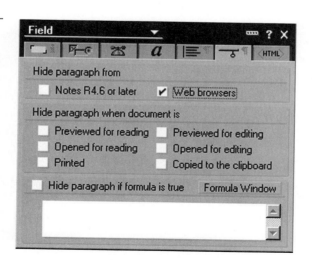

form action to enable users to edit a document and a view action to enable Web users to create documents from a browser. You can use an @Command([Compose]) formula in a form or view action, as well as a button or hotspot on a form or page in order to display a form in a browser. To enable Web clients to edit a document, create a button on a form by using an @Command([EditDocument]) formula. Simple actions and system-supplied actions, such as Edit Document, Forward, and Move to Folder, are not supported on the Web. Be aware of these limitations when you take the exam.

If you want to keep Web users from creating documents with a specific form, do not include their names in the Form Create access list. If you are using a form or view action in order for Notes clients to create documents (but you do not want Web users to see the action), hide the action from Web users through the Action Properties InfoBox (see Figure 36-8).

We can also hide a form from Web users by choosing the *Hide design element from Web clients* option on the Design tab of the Form Design Properties InfoBox (see Figure 36-9). To access the option, click *Forms* from the database's design toolbox, choose the form that you want to hide in the pane on the right, and choose Design . . . Design Properties. Hiding a form from Web clients is useful when you design a form that is for use by Notes clients only.

View Level

We learned in Chapter 34 that we can keep users from seeing certain views by omitting their names from the View Read access list. This technique also works for users who are

Figure 36-8
Hide Action from
Web Browsers
action property

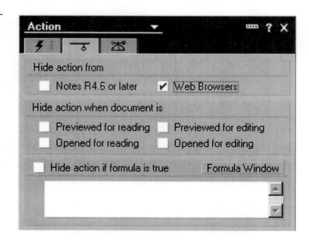

Figure 36-9
Hide Design
Element from Web
Browsers form
property

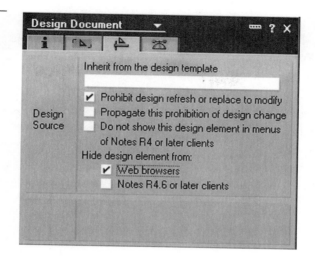

accessing databases from a browser. When designers specify which users, groups, or servers can see a particular view, a Web client will not be able to access that view unless he or she authenticates with the Domino server and is listed in the View Read access list.

We can also hide a view from Web users by choosing the *Hide design element from Web clients* option in the View Design properties InfoBox (see Figure 36-10). In order to access the option, click *Views* from the database's design toolbox, choose the view that you want to hide in the pane on the right, and choose Design . . . Design Properties. Hiding the view from Web clients removes the view from the Folders pane.

You can provide a Web client with access to a view through a form or view action, as well as through a button or hotspot. If you are using a form or view action for Notes clients to access particular views but do not want Web users to see the action, hide the action from Web users through the Action properties InfoBox. Buttons and hotspots can be hidden from Web users by choosing the *Hide paragraph from Web browsers* option in the Button or Hotspot properties InfoBox (see Figure 36-11).

Remember that hiding a view from a Notes client is not a true security measure, because anyone who has Reader access or higher in the database ACL can create a personal view and can see all of the documents in a database. Because there is no Create menu on the browser and personal views are not supported in Web applications, however, hiding a view through either a View Read access list or a hide-when property can act as a security feature for Web clients.

A way around the limitation of Web support for personal views is a new R5 feature called Single Category embedded views. They enable the designer to create customized

Figure 36-10
Hide Design
Element from Web
Browsers view
property

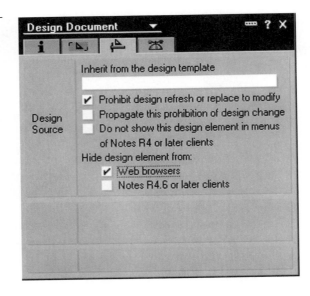

Figure 36-11
Hide Paragraph
from Web Browsers
button property

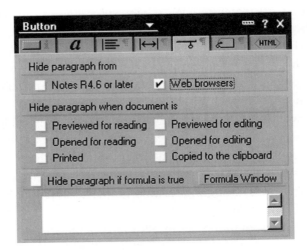

views that are similar to shared, private on first use views. You begin with a categorized view based on data that distinguishes one user from another, such as the username, and use the category to determine which documents display in the Single Category embedded view. Based on this example, a user will only see documents that pertain to him or her. Because designers can use this new feature to limit the documents that are displayed in a view, Single Category views are a way to restrict Web client access to documents in a database. Single Category views are discussed in detail in Chapter 27, "Creating Views, Columns, and Folders."

Workstation Level

At the workstation level, Notes offers protection from attack by Internet users through the use of the workstation Execution Control List (ECL). Chapter 35, "Mail and Workstation Security," covers the workstation ECL in more detail. The ECL protects individual workstations by enabling you to determine which actions can be performed at your workstation by code in documents that were created by other users. You control how much of your system that a script or formula can access. If you receive an unknown mail message or retrieve a document from the Internet, you might want to withhold your trust and not enable certain actions from those documents to be executed at your workstation.

The workstation ECL also enables you to limit access to your system from Java applets and JavaScript applications. Figure 36-12 displays a list of access options that you can enable or restrict for Java applets. Java applets run within your Web browser

PART V

Figure 36-12
Java applet security
ECL

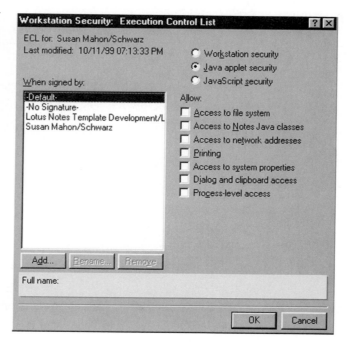

and should not be given access to your file system or to Notes Java classes. Notice that both -Default- and -No Signature- do not permit any access to your workstation (by default). Enable Java applet options only for trusted users or groups. Figure 36-13 displays the list of options for JavaScript applications. The JavaScript ECL controls read-and-write access to your workstation, as well as access to open a URL.

Secure Sockets Layer (SSL)

Secure Sockets Layer (SSL) is a security protocol that provides communications privacy and authentication over the Internet. There are three advantages to using SSL on your Domino server:

- Information that passes between the Domino server and a user or server from the Internet is encrypted.

- The Domino server can authenticate Internet servers and clients that use digitally signed X.509 certificates.

Figure 36-13
JavaScript security
ECL

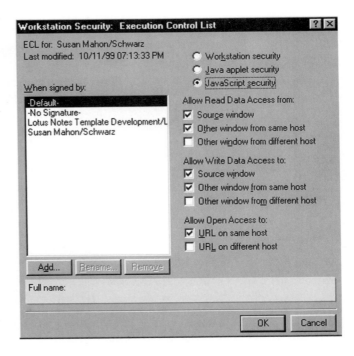

- Messages that are sent between the Domino server and a user or server from the Internet are signed with a digital signature, which ensures that no one has tampered with the data.

NOTE **For more information about SSL, visit** `www.netscape.com/security/techbriefs/ssl.html`.

SSL encryption uses the RSA public/private-key cryptosystem method in order to encrypt data, which is covered in more detail in Chapter 35. The SSL encryption system is similar to the Notes certification process. The server must hold a mathematically-related key pair in order to initiate SSL-encrypted transactions. These keys are stored in a key-ring file along with a server certificate and one or more *trusted root certificates*. The key-ring file can be thought of as a Notes ID, and the trusted root certificates are similar to the certificates that are issued by a Notes certifier. A trusted third party called a Certificate Authority (CA) signs the server certificate and adds its certificate to the server's key-ring file. The CA is the link that enables servers and clients to communicate across a secure SSL connection. The validity of the keys is guaranteed by the fact that a trusted third party signed the server certificate. The CA vouches for the identity of the server. A client can also hold a signed-client certificate in its browser that contains a public/private-key pair and one or more trusted root certificates.

To request a secure channel, the client specifies HTTPS in the URL of the site to which they wish to connect. Domino provides the capability to force an SSL connection, even if the client specifies HTTP. We discuss the method of forcing SSL later in this chapter. When a client connects to a Web site via SSL, the client connects through port 443 instead of port 80. The server then prompts the client for a list of certificates. If the browser client has a trusted root certificate in common with the server, the Domino server opens the SSL connection. If there are no certificates in common, the server asks the Web client if he or she wishes to trust the new certificate. If the user trusts the certificate, Domino opens the connection. After the client and server authenticate, a secret key is generated that is used to encrypt information that is passing between the two.

To enable SSL on your Domino server, you must modify the Server document in the Domino directory. From Domino Administrator, click the Configuration tab, open the Server document, and click the Ports . . . Internet Ports tab. Modify the SSL settings (see Figure 36-14) to specify your key-ring file name, to denote which version of SSL

Figure 36-14
SSL settings in the
Server document

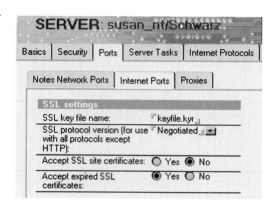

protocol that you use, to indicate whether you want to accept SSL site certificates, and to determine whether you will accept or decline expired SSL certificates.

Once you determine the server's SSL settings, you can enable SSL for some or all of the Internet ports by clicking the tab that is associated with the specific port. For each protocol that you want to enable for SSL, change the SSL port status field to Enabled. You can also specify an authentication option for each SSL-enabled protocol (see Figure 36-15). You can choose Yes or No when you encounter the following three authentication options:

- Client certificate

- Name and password

- Anonymous

You can also require users to access a database via a secure SSL connection. This option is good for Web databases that require monetary transactions. If you choose this option, you must have SSL configured and enabled on your Domino server. To require an SSL connection to a database, you must have Manager access in the database ACL. Select the Database icon from the Bookmarks page and choose File . . . Database . . . Properties. From the Database Basics tab in the Database Properties InfoBox, click Web access: Require SSL connection (see Figure 36-16). A Web user must have an X.509 client certificate in his or her browser in order to open databases that have the SSL connection property enabled.

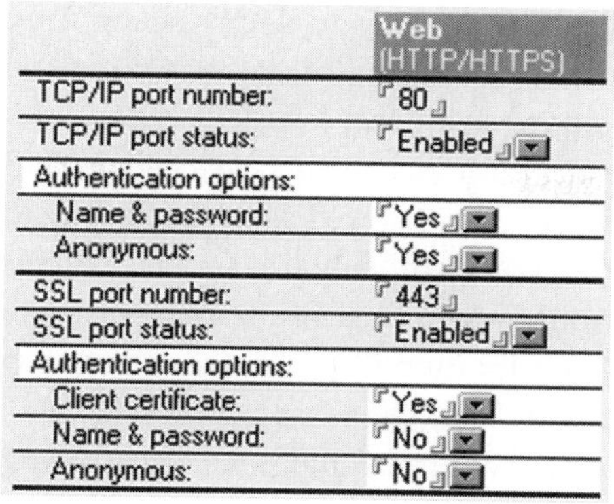

Figure 36-15
SSL authentication
options

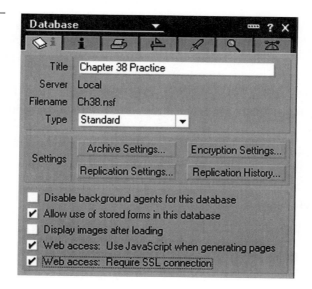

Figure 36-16
Require SSL
Connection
database property

Summary

In this chapter, we discussed the various levels of Domino security from the perspective
of securing Web applications. We introduced the term *firewall* and discussed three different categories of firewalls. From network-level security, we moved down to database-
level security. We mentioned the three different ways in which a Web client can access
our Domino server: anonymously, via name-and-password authentication, or by using
a client certificate. We compared and contrasted remapping and redirection after a dis-

cussion of how to give Web clients access to database and directory links. A brief discussion of securing documents from unauthorized Web users followed the database security section, which led us to field-level security.

When designing applications for Web clients, we need to make sure that clients have a way to create and edit documents—as well as the capability to switch between views in a database. We found one way to provide this functionality by using form and view actions. We also talked about how to hide forms and views from Internet users. Next, we discussed the use of the workstation ECL in order to limit actions that Web users can perform on our workstation, as well as controlling access to your system from JavaScript applications and Java applets. Finally, we discussed in detail the security protocol SSL, the advantages of using SSL, how to enable SSL on a Domino server, and how to enable SSL for some (or all) of your server's Internet ports.

Practice

ABC Company wants to modify the Expense Report database so that its Web clients can access the database, create new expense report documents, and edit existing documents. The company does not, however, want Web clients to create and edit documents unless they authenticate with the Domino server. Authenticated Web clients are members of a group called Web Users in ABC Company's Domino Directory. Once Web clients authenticate, they will receive the access level that is assigned to the Web Users group. Let's get started with the Chapter 36 Practice database (CH36.NSF).

1. From Domino Designer, open the Chapter 36 Practice database (CH36.NSF).

2. Right-click the title of the practice database in the pane on the left, and choose Database . . . Access Control from the popup menu.

3. Add your name to the ACL, and give yourself Manager access.

4. Add an Anonymous entry and assign it Reader access. Add a Web Users group and assign it Author access.

5. Modify the access level that is assigned to -Default- and give it Author access.

6. Go to the Advanced panel and change Maximum Internet name & password to Author access (see Figure 36-17).

We have completed the steps to give our Web clients access to the Expense Report database. Now, we need to give them the capability to create documents and edit documents from the browser. We will create two actions: an Edit Document action on the

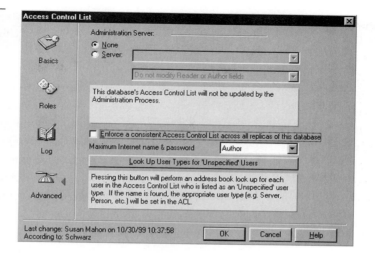

Figure 36-17
Maximum Internet
name & password
option

Expense Report form, and a Create Expense Report action in the Expense Reports by Week view.

1. Open the Expense Report form and click Create . . . Action.

2. Call the action *Edit Document*.

3. Move the action to Position 1 on the action bar, and choose a Notes graphic to display on the action (see Figure 36-18).

4. Click the Action Hide When tab and hide the action when the document is Previewed for editing and Opened for editing.

5. Type the following formula for the Edit Document action:

```
@Command([EditDocument];"1")
```

6. Save and close the form.

7. Open the Expense Reports by Week view.

8. Create an action and call it Create Expense Report.

9. Move the action to Position 1 on the action bar and choose a Notes graphic to display on the action (see Figure 36-19).

10. Type the following formula for the Create Expense Report action:

```
@Command([Compose];"Expense Report")
```

11. Save and close the view.

PART V

Figure 36-18
Edit Document
form action

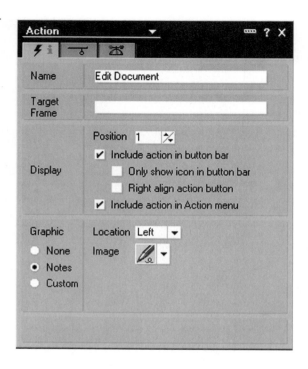

Figure 36-19
Create Expense
Report view action

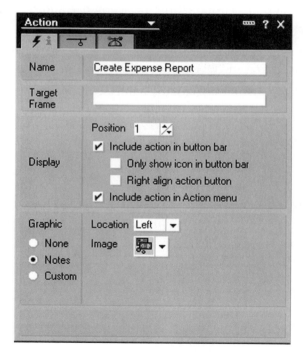

Review Questions

1. Stan designed a database that Web clients use to purchase products. He wants to force an SSL connection when clients access his database. How can Stan perform this task?

   a. He enables the SSL port in the Server document.

   b. He enables the Web access: Require SSL connection property in the Server document.

   c. He enables the Web access: Require SSL connection property in the database.

   d. He enables SSL for the HTTP port (port 80).

2. Now that Stan knows how to force an SSL connection when clients access his database, what type of authentication is required for the Web client to access his SSL-protected database?

   a. Authentication is not required. Clients can access the database anonymously.

   b. Name and password authentication.

   c. Both name and password and client authentication.

   d. Client authentication.

3. Robert wants to enable SSL connections for the HTTP protocol. In the Server document, which port does he enable to allow secure HTTP connections?

   a. Port 443

   b. Port 433

   c. Port 80

   d. Port 8080

4. Patricia developed a workflow application that generates e-mail notifications to reviewers' mail files. Both Notes clients and POP3 clients need access to the mail files. Which ports need to be enabled on the Domino server to enable access for both types of clients?

   a. Ports 110 and 1352

   b. Ports 80 and 443

   c. Ports 80 and 1352

   d. Ports 443 and 1352

5. Jeffrey created a discussion database that he wants to make available to Web clients. He does not want them contributing to the database unless they authenticate with the server by using name-and-password authentication. How can he force name-and-password authentication just for this particular database?

   a. Set the -Default- entry in the ACL to Author.

   b. Set the Anonymous entry in the ACL to Author.

   c. Set the Anonymous entry in the ACL to Reader.

   d. Allow only name-and-password authentication for the HTTP port.

6. Jacob creates a database and wants to give both Notes clients and Web clients access to the database. The database currently has an ACL entry for -Default-, LocalDomainServers, Administrators, Designers, and Managers. The access for -Default- is currently Author. Jacob wants Web clients to be able to read documents but not create documents until they authenticate. He wants Notes clients to be able to create documents in the database. How can he accomplish this task?

   a. Add an Anonymous entry with Author access.

   b. Add an Anonymous entry with Reader access.

   c. Change the -Default- access to Reader.

   d. Do not modify the existing ACL; it already does what Jacob wants.

7. Taffi wants to hide the contents of the Salary field in a document from Web clients. How can she perform this action?

   a. Encrypt the field with a public key.

   b. Encrypt the field with a secret key.

   c. Hide the field from Web browsers.

   d. There is no way to hide field data from Web clients.

8. Stephanie wants to move several databases that are being accessed by Notes clients to a different drive. They currently reside in the Data directory on drive C:\, and she wants to place them on drive D:\ in the Private directory. How can she perform this move and still enable access to her Notes clients?

   a. She cannot. The databases must be in the Data directory or a subdirectory of the Data directory in order for Notes clients to access them.

   b. She creates a database link from the Data directory.

   c. She creates a Redirection document.

   d. She creates a directory link from the Data directory.

9. Leyah created a discussion database that she wants to make available to Web clients. Because a browser does not have a Create menu, what can she do to enable Web clients to create documents in the database?

   a. Create a view button with an @Command([Create]) formula.

   b. Create a view action with an @Command([Create]) formula.

   c. Create a view action with an @Command([Compose]) formula.

   d. She cannot do anything, because Web clients do not have the capability to create documents from a browser.

10. Sue's company recently acquired a more powerful server and wants to move its existing Web site (consisting of Domino databases) to the new server. Sue wants users who type the old URL in the browser to point to the new Domino-specific URL. What does she need to do?

    a. Map the URL to a different directory.

    b. Redirect the URL to a different URL.

    c. Map the URL to a different URL.

    d. Redirect the URL to a different directory.

Review Answers

1. **C is correct.**   He enables the database property *Web access: Require SSL connection*.

2. **D is correct.**   To open SSL-protected databases, Web users must have an X.509 client certificate in their browsers for authentication with the server.

3. **A is correct.**   Domino listens for HTTP over SSL requests on Port 443.

4. **A is correct.**   Notes clients access their mail files on Port 1352, and POP3 clients access their mail files by using Port 110.

5. **C is correct.**   A Web client is not prompted for a name and password until he or she attempts to perform an action that goes beyond his or her level of access in the ACL. Because Jeffrey only wants to require name-and-password authentication for this database, he does not want to enable it in the Server document—because this setting would require name-and-password authentication for every database on the server.

6. **B is correct.** If there is no Anonymous entry in the ACL, anonymous Web clients get the access level that is assigned to -Default-. Therefore, add Anonymous to the ACL and grant it Reader access. Domino prompts Web clients for their name and password when they attempt to create a document, because they are performing an action that goes beyond the rights that are granted to them by their access level.

7. **C is correct.** Encryption does not work on the Web.

8. **D is correct.** She creates a directory link to the Private directory on drive D:\. She must make sure that she includes the names of her Notes clients who need access in the *Who should be able to access this link* box.

9. **C is correct.** Leyah must create an action by using the formula @Command ([Compose]), so that Web clients can access the form in the browser.

10. **B is correct.** The only way to map a URL to a Domino-specific URL is by using a Redirection→URL document.

Troubleshooting Workflow Applications

You should be able to answer questions based on the following objectives after reading this chapter:

- Monitoring/maintaining/troubleshooting workflow applications
  - Mail-enabled field problems: field attributes
  - Mail-enabled form problems: workflow related
  - Workflow distribution problems: replication
  - Workflow distribution problems: roles
  - Workflow distribution problems: routing
  - Workflow distribution problems: rules
- Security: planning/design
  - Determining workflow control

In this chapter, you will learn how to troubleshoot workflow applications. We will redefine how roles, routes, and rules play a part in workflow. We will also discuss replication as it applies to the workflow process. After defining these elements of workflow, we will learn how to troubleshoot each element. Some potential problems that we have already discussed in earlier chapters are included here as a centrally located reference. We will introduce a few new problems that you might encounter when troubleshooting roles, routes, rules, and replication in a workflow application.

Replication Issues

In Chapter 34, "Domino Security Architecture," we discussed several methods of securing documents in a database from unauthorized readers. Creating a Form Read access list and adding a Readers field to a form are two methods that enable us to limit who can read documents in a database. These two methods can potentially cause replication problems in your workflow applications. If workflow participants are complaining that doclinks are not locating the linked documents, check the Readers fields and Form Read access lists to make sure that the names of replicating servers are included. If not, the servers will be unable to replicate the documents because they cannot see them. Place replicating server names in either a Readers field or in a Form Read access list if you are using both document-security methods.

Another potential problem concerning doclinks and replication is due to a replication schedule-timing issue. For example, the Router delivers a mail message to a user's mail file that includes a doclink. If the database in which the linked document resides has not yet replicated, the user clicks the link and cannot open the document.

Enabling multiple reviewers to access documents simultaneously can generate replication and/or save conflicts. Two or more users who are editing the same document in different replicas of a database and are then replicating the database cause a *replication conflict*. The following rules determine which document is declared the winner, or the Main document, and which documents are saved as responses:

- The document that has been edited and saved the most times becomes the Main document. The other documents become Response documents and are given the title "[Replication or Save Conflict]" (see Figure 37-1).

- If all documents are edited and saved the same number of times, the most recently saved document becomes the Main document, and the other documents become Response documents with the title "[Replication or Save Conflict]."

Figure 37-1
Replication or save
conflict in a view

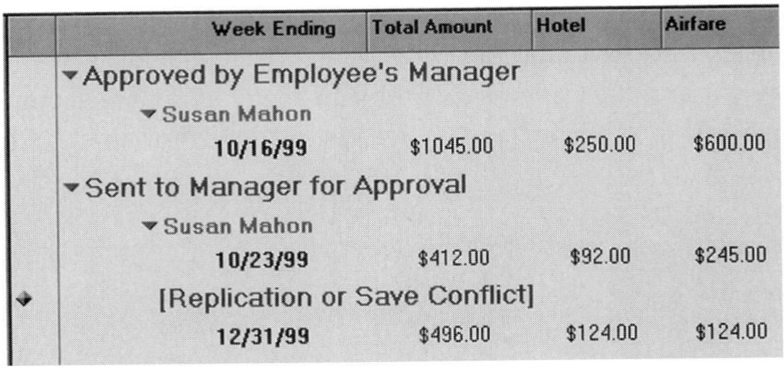

	Week Ending	Total Amount	Hotel	Airfare
▼Approved by Employee's Manager				
▼ Susan Mahon				
	10/16/99	$1045.00	$250.00	$600.00
▼ Sent to Manager for Approval				
▼ Susan Mahon				
	10/23/99	$412.00	$92.00	$245.00
[Replication or Save Conflict]				
	12/31/99	$496.00	$124.00	$124.00

- If a document is edited in one replica but is deleted in another, the deletion takes precedence. If the edited document has been edited more than once—or if the editing occurred after the deletion—the edited document takes precedence and is not deleted.

A *save conflict* occurs when two or more users edit the same document in a database on the same server at the same time. The document that is saved first becomes the Main document. As subsequent users save their documents, Domino displays an error message warning them that they are about to save a conflict document (see Figure 37-2). At that point, they can continue to save or discard the changes that they made to the document and avoid a conflict. If they choose to save the changes, the document is listed as a Response document below the Main document and is given the title "[Replication or Save Conflict]." For the exam, you should understand the difference between a replication conflict and a save conflict.

As a designer, you can reduce the number of replication conflicts in a workflow application. Setting the form property *Merge replication conflicts* (see Figure 37-3) merges conflicts into a single document—provided that all of the edits occurred in different fields. If multiple users edit the same fields, a conflict is still declared. This form property applies to replication conflicts only and does not affect save conflicts. The *Merge replication conflicts* property is not supported on the Web.

Roles/Security Issues

In Chapter 31, "Planning and Designing Workflow Applications," we determined that roles in a workflow application are those people or departments that are involved in the routing of the object(s). Roles enable a designer to define who can initiate an action and who or what receives the result of that action. We need to make sure that

Figure 37-2
Save Conflict error
message

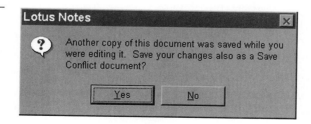

Figure 37-3
Merge Replication
Conflicts form
property

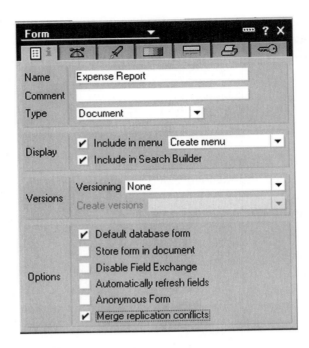

participants in our workflow application are able to carry out tasks that are required by their specific role. In other words, roles need proper access to servers, databases, views, documents, and fields. In this section, we will explore troubleshooting as it applies to workflow application security.

Chapter 36, "Web Security," talked about securing an application from unauthorized Internet users. One method that we discussed was securing your internal network with packet-filtering (implemented through the network router). The router is configured to enable inbound and/or outbound Notes and Domino traffic to pass through the firewall. In terms of troubleshooting, make sure that the correct ports are available for Notes users to send information to the Internet and for Web clients to be able to access Domino applications. If a mail-enabled database sends POP3 mail, for example, make sure that port 110 is open.

At the server level, make sure that users can access servers that host workflow applications. If certain roles in your workflow process access the application through a browser, you must enable server access to those Web clients. Remember that the *Maximum Internet name & password* setting overrides the database ACL for users who are accessing Domino databases from a Web browser. Make sure that this setting is at a high enough access level in order to enable Web clients to perform their assigned work-flow tasks. You might see this subject as an exam question.

At the database level, we must keep in mind the level of access that is granted by the ACL when troubleshooting a workflow application. Users who are attempting to access a doclinked document from a mail message must have at least Reader access to the database that stores the document. A user must also have a connection to the server that is hosting the database that contains the linked document. If the database that contains the document cannot be found, Domino displays the error message shown in Figure 37-4. If users need to approve or modify the doclinked document, they must either have Author access with their names in an Authors field or have Editor access or higher.

Another problem that you might encounter in terms of database access involves mail-in databases. Let's say that you move a mail-in database to a new server. If documents no longer route to the relocated database, check to make sure that the Mail-In Database document was updated to reflect the new server name (see Figure 37-5). If users are unable to run workflow agents on the new server that they were able to run on the old server, make sure that they are authorized to run agents in the new server's Server document (see Figure 37-6).

At the document level, make sure that the users who have roles that require document approval and a signature have the correct access to the document itself. For example, documents in a workflow application pass through an approval process that

Figure 37-4
Doclink error message

Figure 37-5
Mail-in Database document

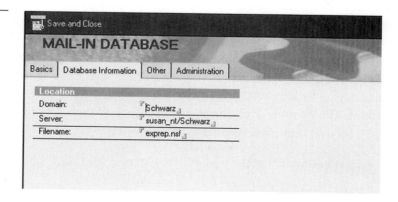

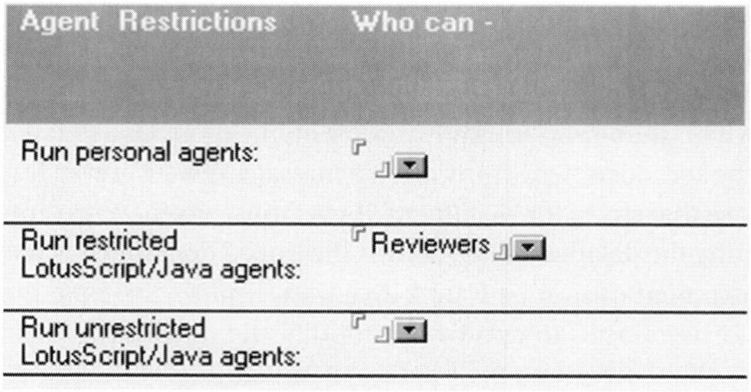

Figure 37-6
Agent restrictions in
the Server
document

Figure 37-6
Agent restrictions in
the Server
document

involves several users. Signatures of all approvers are attached to the documents by using multiple fields that are sign-enabled and that are placed in separate controlled-access sections. Approvers must be able to edit fields in the controlled-access section. Therefore, approvers must be listed with Editor access or higher in the database ACL, or they must be listed with Author access and must be included in an Authors field in the document. Their names must also be in the controlled-access section's list of permitted editors. A controlled-access section cannot override a user's access level to the database.

Finally, at the field level, there are several things to look for when troubleshooting workflow applications. Keep in mind when developing applications for Internet users that field encryption is not supported on the Web. Although a field is encrypted in Notes, a Web client can still see the contents of the encrypted field.

In Chapter 34, we defined forced encryption as an encryption design method that enables the designer to apply the encryption key. If a designer uses the forced encryption method to design a form, users must have at least one of the encryption keys in order to create and save a document with the form. If not, Domino displays the error message shown in Figure 37-7. Users who need to read the encrypted fields must also have at least one of the encryption keys that were used to encrypt the document. If not, the field appears blank, and the user cannot read the data in the encrypted field.

Domino provides several tools to help you troubleshoot problems with workflow applications. In particular, the Domino Web server log (DOMLOG.NSF) and the Domino server log (LOG.NSF) are available to assist you with troubleshooting applications. The Domino Web Server database logs all Web-server information and tracks HTTP request information, such as the following:

- Date and time that the request was made
- Web client's IP address

Figure 37-7
Forced Encryption
error message

- Web client's name, if he or she authenticated

- Type of data that is accessed by the client

- Type of browser that is used by the client

- URL that was visited before accessing your site

Domino logs information regarding the Web server in the Domino Web Server log and/or text files. Logging to a text file is better for large, frequently accessed Web sites. You can create an agent in the Web server database to notify you by mail about specific events in the log, such as when a user cannot authenticate with a Domino server. The Domino server log reports all non-Web server information, such as server activity, database usage, and users who are accessing the server. For the exam, know the difference between the Domino Web Server log and the Domino log.

Routing Issues

We defined a route in Chapter 31, "Planning and Designing Workflow Applications," as the interaction or flow of an object or document in a workflow process. You can experience problems with routing in a workflow application due to several design errors, such as a lack of a SendTo field on mail-enabled forms, syntax errors when using the @MailSend function, and placing incorrect values in reserved fields. In this section, we focus on issues that might cause document routing failure in your workflow application.

The Router is the server task that is responsible for routing or delivering documents to a destination database. In order for the Router to know that it should route a document, we must mail-enable the form that is used to create the document. If we provide a destination address but fail to mail-enable the form, the Router does not know to route the document. The following list describes several methods that we can use to mail-enable a form:

PART V

- Use @MailSend without parameters.

- Use @MailSend with parameters.

- Enable the On Close: Present mail send dialog form property.

- Add a MailOptions field to the form.

With the exception of the @MailSend with parameters method, all of the methods in this list must have a SendTo field on the form. The user sees an error message when mailing a document without a SendTo field (see Figure 37-8). In addition, the SendTo field must contain a valid person, group, or mail-in database address. The SendTo field can contain multiple entries, but each entry must be a unique name. If you are using a formula in order to determine the value of the SendTo field, as opposed to enabling users to enter values, place a computed SendTo field at the bottom of the form, and hide this field from the users.

You should watch out for several syntax errors in the @MailSend with parameters method of document routing. The syntax for the @MailSend function with parameters is listed as follows:

```
@MailSend(sendTo;copyTo;blindCopyTo;subject;remark;bodyFields;
[flags])
```

Chapter 32, "Creating a Workflow Application," gives a detailed explanation of each @MailSend parameter and lists several examples of how to use the function. Two common syntax errors regarding the @MailSend function are using colons instead of semicolons to separate each argument in the @Function and using semicolons instead of colons to separate multiple flags. An @MailSend with an [IncludeDocLink] flag requires network or remote access in order to view the linked document. If there are multiple recipients in the SendTo, CopyTo, and/or BlindCopyTo parameters, make sure that a colon separates each name in the list. On the other hand, be sure to leave null strings for any parameters that you do not define. An @MailSend function can be used

Figure 37-8
Mail Error dialog
box

in agents, fields, form and view actions, buttons, and smarticons; owever, cannot be included in column formulas, view selection formulas, hide-when formulas, and window-title formulas.

Chapter 31 mentioned several other methods of enabling document routing, such as reserved fields and simple actions. When using reserved fields, such as MailOptions, SaveOptions, Sign, and Encrypt, make sure that the values that are stored in these fields are the allowable values for that particular field. For example, the values 1 and 0 are the only values that are permitted in a MailOptions field. Also, keep in mind that the Web does not support actions and agents that are written by using the simple action programming interface.

When designing a mail-enabled form, you must provide a way for users to read documents that are created by the form once the documents reach the destination database. To display a document with the form that was used to create it, the form must be available in the destination database. There are several methods that we can use to make the form available, including the following:

- Store the form in the document.

- Copy the form into the target database.

- Create a form formula in a view that specifies a form with which to display documents from that particular view.

- Create an agent that changes the contents of the document's Form field.

To store a form in a document, remember that you must enable both a database property and a form property. The database property *Allow use of stored forms in this database* must be set for the database that is receiving the documents with forms stored in them. The form property *Store form in document* must be enabled for forms that you wish to store with their corresponding documents. There are several issues that arise when you choose to store a form in a document. First, storing forms in documents significantly increases the size of the database that contains the documents and increases database replication time. Another issue is that the form is not automatically updated to reflect design changes that are made to the original form in the source database. Finally, the Web supports stored forms for documents in Read-mode, but does not support documents that were created or edited by using a stored form.

When creating a form formula in a view that specifies a form with which to display documents, you should ensure that the formula results in a valid form name. If you choose to enable users to read the routed document by changing the document's Form field by using an agent, make sure that the modified name in the Form field results in a valid form name.

NOTE When you change the contents of a document's Form field, it is possible that the document will disappear from some of your views. Check your view selection formulas and make sure that they include the updated form name.

Rules Issues

In Chapter 31, we defined a rule as the corresponding action or task that takes place as the workflow object passes between two people or roles. Once the action has been completed, workflow ensures that the roles that are responsible for the next task or action are notified and that they receive the information they need to complete their part of the workflow process. Rules in a workflow process determine the action that enables the object to proceed down the workflow path and determines how an exception to that action is handled in your application.

Many times, actions, buttons, and agents trigger the flow of objects in a workflow application. For example, we can place a button in ABC Company's Expense Report form that the employee's manager clicks in order to approve the document. The button can automatically modify an approval field and route the document to the next approver.

When troubleshooting this type of design, we need to make sure that the formula behind the action or button is correct and that the action or button only appears at the correct time. Once the employee's manager approves the document, hide the Approve action or button. We can design a tracking field that Domino sets to Yes once the document is approved by the employee's manager. Based on the resulting value in the tracking field, we can hide the action or button from the users. We use this example later in this chapter in the Practice section.

Summary

In this chapter, we began by discussing replication and how mistakes in the design of our workflow application can affect document replication: for example, omitting the names of replicating servers from Readers fields and/or from Form Read access lists. We also mentioned that enabling multiple reviewers to modify documents at the same time might cause replication or save conflicts. One way to prevent conflicts is to enable the *Merge replication conflicts* form property.

Following the replication section, we talked about roles in workflow applications and how we must make sure that users have the proper access from the network level down to the field level, in order for them to carry out their assigned tasks. We also mentioned a possible breach in security when using encryption in a Web-based workflow application, because encryption is not supported on the Web.

We then moved on to routing documents in a workflow application and mentioned several design errors, such as the lack of a SendTo field on mail-enabled forms, syntax errors when using the @MailSend function, and placing incorrect values in reserved fields. The issue of incorrect formulas was also mentioned in our discussion of rules as they apply to actions that are taken on a workflow object.

Practice

In this practice, we use ABC Company's Expense Report form to apply several of the techniques that we learned in this chapter. We create a hidden field used for tracking purposes, then we apply a hide-when formula to the Submit to Next Approver button. Finally, we modify the formula that is currently used in the button to write data to the hidden field, which hides the button (if the first-line manager has already reviewed the document). Use the Expense Report-Final form to check your work.

1. From Domino Designer, open the Chapter 37 Practice database (CH37.NSF).

2. Open the Expense Report form.

3. Create a hidden field called FirstLineApprove at the bottom of the form. You can leave it as an editable text field, because users will not see the field.

4. Click the first Submit to Next Approver form button, and open the Button properties InfoBox.

5. Go to the Paragraph Hide When tab, click the *Hide paragraph if formula is true* box, and type the following formula (see Figure 37-9):

```
FirstLineApprove = "Yes"
```

6. Repeat the process for the second Submit to Next Approver form button.

7. Add the following code to the first Submit to Next Approver button formula as part of the @Do function that is currently found in the formula. The code should be placed immediately following the @SetField that sets the field value for the

Figure 37-9
Hide Paragraph
formula for Submit
to Next Approver
button

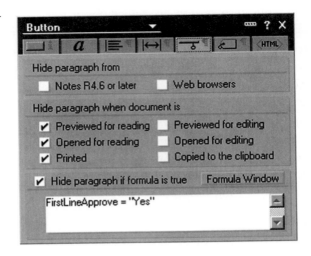

Status field. Remember to place the formula in both @Do functions (see Figure 37-10).

```
@SetField("FirstLineApprove";"Yes")
```

8. Repeat the process for the second Submit to Next Approver form button.

Test the form by creating and approving a new Expense Report document by using the modified Submit to Next Approver button. Once you have saved and closed the document, open it again. The Submit to Next Approver button is not displayed.

Figure 37-10
Submit to Next
Approver button
formula

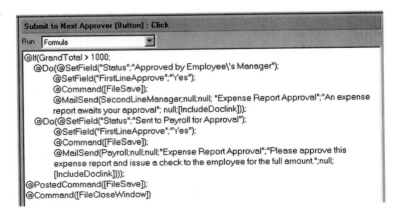

Review Questions

1. Ralph creates a form and sets the form property *Merge replication conflicts*. When he looks at the views in the database, he notices replication or save conflicts. He checks the document fields and determines that users are editing different fields. What is the problem?

   a. Multiple users are editing documents in the same database on the same server.

   b. Multiple users are editing documents in the same database on different servers.

   c. Ralph forgot to enable the field property *Merge replication conflicts*.

   d. Ralph mistakenly gave all users Author access in the database ACL.

2. Users are complaining that their doclinks are not finding the linked document in replica databases. Tina researches the problem and finds that the linked documents are not being replicated. Why not?

   a. The Authors field does not include the names of the replicating servers.

   b. The Readers field does not include the names of the replicating servers.

   c. The Form Create access list does not include the names of the replicating servers.

   d. The Authors field does not include usernames.

3. Sally creates a form for a Web application and sets the form property *Merge replication conflicts*. When she looks at the views in the database, she notices replication or save conflicts. She checks the document fields and determines that users are editing different fields. What is the problem?

   a. Multiple users are editing documents in the same database on the same server.

   b. Multiple users are editing documents in the same database on different servers.

   c. The Merge Replication Conflicts field property is not supported on the Web.

   d. The Merge Replication Conflicts form property is not supported on the Web.

4. George creates a workflow application that routes documents to a central database. Users are complaining that they receive the error message Form not found when they attempt to open a document in the destination database. What is causing the problem?

   a. The designer misspelled the field name Form on the form that was used to create the routed documents.

   b. Domino cannot find the form name in the document.

   c. Domino cannot find the form in the target database that was used to create the routed documents.

   d. The designer forgot to create a field called Form on the form that was used to create the routed documents.

5. Rich fixes the problem in the mail-in database by creating an agent that changes a routed document's Form field to the database's default form name. Users are complaining that they no longer see the documents in several database views. What is causing the problem?

   a. View selection formulas do not include documents that are created with the default form.

   b. The form that was used to create the documents was deleted from the mail-in database.

   c. The view property Display all documents is not enabled.

   d. The form property Display in a view is not enabled.

6. Suzanne creates a database that is part of a workflow application that is accessed by both Notes and Web clients. Document reviewers are listed in the database's ACL with Editor access. Web clients are complaining that they are not allowed to edit the document. What is the possible reason?

   a. They are not listed as permitted editors of the document.

   b. The Maximum Internet name & password database property is set to Author.

   c. There is no Anonymous entry in the database ACL.

   d. The form property Hide design from Web browsers is enabled.

7. Elise creates a form that has several encryptable fields. She designs the form so that when a user saves a document that is created with the form, the document is encrypted with the key called SecretEncryptionKey. She found out that Web clients are still able to see the contents of the encrypted fields. Why?

   a. Because the key was saved with the form, Web clients have access to the key and can view the contents of the encrypted fields.

   b. Because the key was saved with the document, Web clients have access to the key and can view the contents of the encrypted fields.

   c. Encryption is not supported on the Web.

   d. When Web clients create documents with the form, the SecretEncryptionKey is not applied.

8. Mark wants to know whether Web clients are using his workflow application. Specifically, he wants to know when the HTTP request was made, what data the Web clients accessed, and which browser they used to access the data. Which log should he check?

   a. Domino server log (LOG.NSF)

   b. Domino Web server log (DOMLOG.NSF)

   c. Domino Configuration database (DOMCFG.NSF)

   d. Domino does not have a log that records Web information.

9. Michelle placed a SendTo field on a form in a workflow database. Documents that are created with the form are not being routed to the mail-in database name in the SendTo field. What could be causing the problem?

   a. She forgot to mail-enable the form.

   b. She made the SendTo field a multi-value field.

   c. She forgot to enable the form property *Store in mail-in database*.

   d. She forgot to make the SendTo field a computed field.

10. Francie placed the formula listed as follows in a form action. When she clicks the action, she receives an error message. What is wrong with the formula?

```
@MailSend("Susan Mahon";"Libby Schwarz";"";"Meeting";"Don't for-
get the meeting Friday at 10:00";""; [Sign];[IncludeDoclink])
```

   a. She cannot use a null string as an argument in an @MailSend function.

   b. She left out several parameters.

   c. The [Sign] and [IncludeDoclink] flags should be separated by a colon.

   d. All @MailSend parameters should be separated by a colon.

Review Answers

1. **A is correct.** When multiple users edit documents in the same database on the same server, a save conflict is generated. The *Merge replication conflicts* form property only applies to replication conflicts.

2. **B is correct.** The Readers field does not include the names of the replicating servers. We assume that replicating servers are listed in the database ACL with Manager access.

3. **D is correct.** The Web does not support the *Merge replication conflicts* form property.

4. **C is correct.** Domino looks to the document's Form field for the name of the form to use in order to display the document. In this case, the form that is used to create the documents is not found in the target database.

5. **A is correct.** The document's Form field is replaced by a form name that is not included in some view selection formulas. Therefore, documents are not displayed in those particular views.

6. **B is correct.** A database ACL cannot override the Maximum Internet name and password setting for a user who is accessing a database from the Internet.

7. **C is correct.** Web clients see data in encrypted fields because encryption is not supported on the Web.

8. **B is correct.** The Domino Web server log (DOMLOG.NSF) records all Web server information and tracks HTTP request information.

9. **A is correct.** In order for the Router to route documents, forms need a SendTo field—and they must be mail-enabled.

10. **C is correct.** The flags in an @MailSend function must be separated by colons, not semicolons. The arguments in an @function are separated by semicolons.

Domino R5 Application Architecture

The third exam in the Application Development track is the Domino R5 Application Architecture exam (190-512). Passing this exam is the next (perhaps final, if you've taken the exams in order) step in gaining your Certified Lotus Professional (CLP) designation for Application Development, although it does not give you a certification by itself. The audience for this exam is Domino developers with knowledge of designing multi-database applications for different platforms. Additionally, you should have some knowledge of Domino security and administration processes. You should already have passed at least the

Domino Designer Fundamentals exam. The exam has 40 scored questions and five unscored questions, and requires a minimum score of 74 percent. The competencies for this exam cover three basic areas:

- Designing
- Implementing and maintaining
- Planning

These general areas of competency are broken down further into specific tasks that you should be able to perform. All tasks in this exam are geared toward being able to plan and implement a Domino application that may need to interact with multiple areas of the Domino environment. To see a complete list, refer to the *Lotus Domino R5 CLP Certification Exam Guide*, available for download from **www.lotus.com/education**. Each chapter in this section lists the specific competency areas that it covers.

Before taking this exam, you should also read Part III, which covers the Deploying Domino Applications exam. The two exams have competencies that are tightly integrated and by reading the chapters in both sections, you will be more fully prepared for the exams. You may notice that some competencies are not covered a second time in the chapters in Part VI if they were covered sufficiently in the chapters in Part III.

The level of detail and depth covered by both this exam and the Deploying Domino Applications exam may require additional resources. One resource in particular that can be useful is the database available at Notes.net called "Inside Notes: The Architecture of Notes and the Domino Server." This database can be found at **http://notes.net/notesua.nsf/0b345eb9d127270b8525665d006bc355/ec73cbf1c639 2ba385256856005bd224?OpenDocument**. Two additional resources that I highly recommend include the following Redbooks: *Performance Considerations for Domino Applications* and *Lotus Domino R5.0 Enterprise Integration: Architecture and Products*. These and other Redbooks that relate to Lotus technologies can be found at **http://www. lotus.com/redbooks**.

Designing and Planning for Alternative Coding

You should be able to answer questions based on the following objectives after reading this chapter:

- Creating/utilizing Formula Language
- Creating/utilizing LotusScript
- Creating/utilizing HTML
- Creating/utilizing JavaScript
- Creating/utilizing Java

With the wide variety of programming languages available to developers in the Domino Designer, it is difficult to know which to use in every situation. If an application is being developed for the Notes client, Web browser, or both, which languages are available to use in the Domino design elements and what is the best solution? This chapter outlines the main programming languages available to developers with Domino Designer and when is it best to use each one.

Overview

This section will give a brief description of the different types of languages available to developers within the Domino Designer. Even though other languages can be integrated into Notes and Domino applications, the languages outlined are the most widely used and supported within Domino Designer. More detailed descriptions of where to use these languages within the Domino design elements as well as examples of each will be provided later in this chapter.

Formula Language

Formula language is the primary programming language within Domino Designer. Formula language can be in the form of @Functions or @Command formulas. Formulas are best used within the object that the user is currently processing, for example, computing the value of a field within a document or computing the selection formula for a view. Formula language can be used in both Notes and Web-based applications.

LotusScript

LotusScript is a full object-oriented programming language, which is similar in structure to Visual Basic. LotusScript uses pre-defined classes to interface with almost all Domino elements. Domino oversees the compilation and loading of user codes and automatically includes the Domino-class definitions. LotusScript is best used for accessing existing objects, for example, to change a value in one document based on values in another document or for processing multiple documents within a collection. LotusScript is particularly useful when writing background agents for importing information, ODBC, or scheduled events. Even though LotusScript can perform many of the same functions as formula language, it is best to use formula language whenever possible. Like formula language, LotusScript can be used in both Notes and Domino Web-based applications.

HTML

HyperText Markup Language (HTML) is a markup language designed primarily for Web applications. HTML is used in defining the structure of a Web document and improving the presentation to the user. HTML can be used in a variety of Domino design elements such as forms, pages, and views.

JavaScript

JavaScript is a cross-platform, object-oriented scripting language that is executed in the client as opposed to on the server. JavaScript has been integrated into Domino Designer and design elements with the release of R5. JavaScript is best used in Web applications, or when a single application will be used in the Notes client as well as through a Web browser.

Java

Java is a full object-oriented programming language that interfaces to Domino through predefined classes. Java can perform many of the same functions as LotusScript when used in agent, but cannot be used within the Domino UI. Java code can be written natively or imported.

Programmable Objects in Domino: SmartIcons

SmartIcon buttons are associated with an individual user's workspace and are not associated in any way with databases. SmartIcons are part of the user preferences and are not shared among users. Domino comes with over 100 predefined SmartIcon buttons, which perform most of the menu commands. A SmartIcon button executes a formula when clicked and the user has the ability to create over 12 of their own SmartIcons using formula language.

1. Choose . . . File . . . Preferences, SmartIcon Settings. This will open the SmartIcon Settings dialog box which looks like the following:

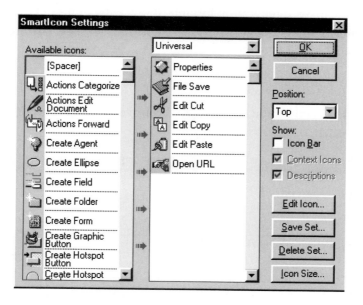

2. Select Edit Icon. This will bring up the Edit SmartIcon dialog box with the SmartIcon that can be programmed.

3. Select a SmartIcon and add a description in the description field.

4. Select the Formula button to associate a formula with the SmartIcon. For this example, our SmartIcon will open the sales.nsf database on the corp_domino01 server to the monthly view.

```
@Command([FileOpenDatabase];
"corp_domino01";"sales.nsf";"monthly")
```

5. Select OK.

Database

Databases contain a variety of objects. Many of these, including Agents, Actions, and Replication formulas may have programming associated with them.

Replication Formula

The replication formula runs on the server or the workstation for which it has been created. The replication formula identifies which documents are to be updated or added to the current database. A replication formula always ends with a SELECT statement. If the last statement in the replication formula is a logical expression, domino inserts the SELECT statement to the expression.

1. From the Notes Workspace, select the icon of the database for which the replication formula will be created.

2. Select File . . . Replication . . . Settings. This will open the Replication Settings dialog box which looks like the following:

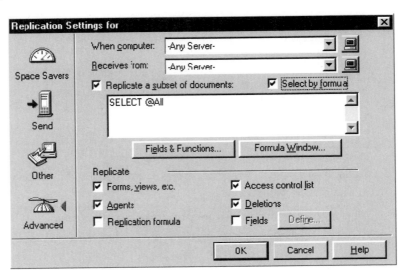

3. Choose the Advanced panel.

4. Check Replicate a subset of documents and Select by formula, this will open the formula window to create the replication formula.

5. For this example we will enter a formula to replicate all documents created with the Sales form that have a status of "Approved:"

```
SELECT Form="Sales" & Status="Approved"
```

6. Click OK.

Agent

An agent is a user-defined procedure that can be initiated in a number of ways. An agent can be triggered on the following:

- **Workstation**   Manually, if a document has been modified, or if documents have been pasted

- **Server or Workstation**   If new mail has arrived or on a schedule

Agents can be written using formula language, LotusScript, Java, or Domino-supplied actions. Formula-based agents run on the documents. SELECT statements can be used to create a subset of documents for which the agent will run on. LotusScript and Java agents run once using the search criteria defined in the particular language.

Example: LotusScript Agent

The following LotusScript agent will loop through all the documents within a database and categorize the document based on the value of the TotalSales field.

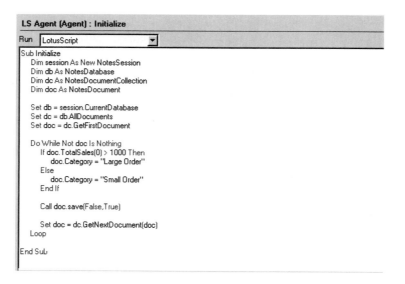

```
LS Agent (Agent) : Initialize

Run  LotusScript

Sub Initialize
    Dim session As New NotesSession
    Dim db As NotesDatabase
    Dim dc As NotesDocumentCollection
    Dim doc As NotesDocument

    Set db = session.CurrentDatabase
    Set dc = db.AllDocuments
    Set doc = dc.GetFirstDocument

    Do While Not doc Is Nothing
        If doc.TotalSales(0) > 1000 Then
            doc.Category = "Large Order"
        Else
            doc.Category = "Small Order"
        End If

        Call doc.save(False,True)

        Set doc = dc.GetNextDocument(doc)
    Loop

End Sub
```

Java Agent

The following Java agent will perform the same calculations as the previous example.

```
Java Agent (Agent) : Action

Run  Java

- JavaAgent.java
import lotus.domino.*;

public class JavaAgent extends AgentBase {

    public void NotesMain() {

        try {
            Session session = getSession();
            AgentContext agentContext = session.getAgentContext();

            // [Your code goes here]
            Database db = agentContext.getCurrentDatabase();
            DocumentCollection dc = db.getAllDocuments();
            Document doc = dc.getFirstDocument();

            while (doc != null){
                double TotalSales = doc.getItemValueDouble("TotalSales");
                doc=dc.getNextDocument();

                if (TotalSales > 1000)
                    doc.replaceItemValue("Category","Large Order");
                else
                    doc.replaceItemValue("Category","Small Order");
                    doc.save(true,false);

                doc=dc.getNextDocument();
            }
        }catch (Exception e){
            e.printStackTrace();
        }
    }
}
```

Formula Language Agent

The following Formula language agent will perform the same calculations as the previous examples using the necessary SELECT statement.

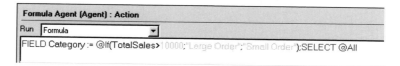

Actions

An action is a custom procedure that can be initiated from a view or a document. Actions can be available to only certain users by creating a *Hide action if formula is true* formula.

LotusScript Action

The following LotusScript action will set the value of the Status field to "Approved:"

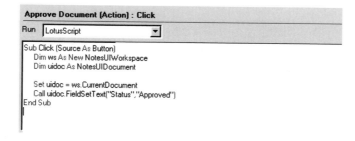

Formula Language

The following Formula Language action performs the same function as the previous LotusScript action, with considerably less coding.

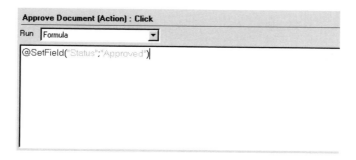

Hotspots

Hotspots can be created in forms, pages, navigators, and layout regions, as well as rich text fields. A hotspot formula is performed when a user selects it and can be of several types:

- **Link Hotspot**   Links to another object
- **Text pop-up**   Displays text
- **Button**   Performs an action and can be a simple action, a formula, LotusScript, or JavaScript code
- **Formula pop-up**   Displays text based on a formula
- **Action hotspot**   Performs an action and can be a simple action, a formula, LotusScript or JavaScript code

JavaScript

The following JavaScript example prompts the user to enter their first and last name and sets the full name value on the document when activated by the onClick event of a button or hotspot. In this example, the text "Click Here" has been highlighted and a hotspot has been created.

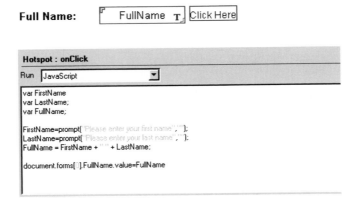

LotusScript

The following LotusScript example can be used in a button or as an action hotspot. When the button or hotspot is mailed to users, the recipient will be prompted for an RSVP when they click the button/hotspot.

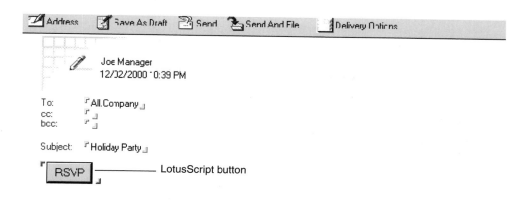

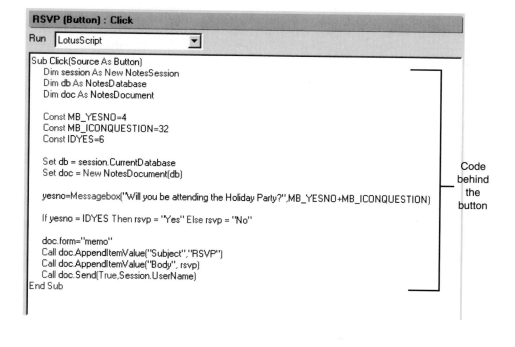

Formula Language

The following formula language button code performs the same function as the previous LotusScript hotspot/button.

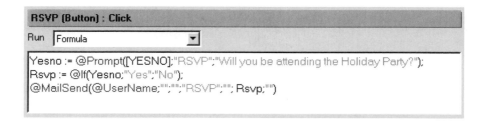

Formula Language (Navigator)

The following formula language action hotspot is part of a navigator. The formula prompts the user for to select a day of the week and then opens that particular view.

Form, Selection, and Column Formulas

When designing a view, you can specify form, selection, and column formulas. These formulas are written using Notes formula language. For Web applications, the column formula can be used to generate HTML code by selecting the View Property, *Treat view contents as HTML*.

Form Formula

A form formula determines which forms are used in different situations. When used in a view, the form formula computes to the name of the form that all documents in the view should be opened with. When used in a form, the form formula determines which form is used when a document is being edited or simply being displayed.

This example will use the Admin form if the current user has been assigned the Admin Role. If the user does not have the Admin role, the User form is used:

All Documents (View) : Form Formula

Run Formula ▼

```
@If(@IsMember(@UserRoles;"[Admin]");"Admin Form";"User Form")
```

Selection Formula

When used in a view, a selection formula determines which documents a view will contain. A selection formula must end with a SELECT statement.

This example will display all documents that have been created with the Order form and have a Total greater than 1000:

All Documents (View) : View Selection

Run Formula ▼

```
SELECT Form="Order" & Total>1000
```

Column Formula

A column formula computes what will be displayed in a column of a view. The column formula must evaluate to a text string. As previously stated, a column formula can be evaluated to HTML code and the view can be set to display the results as HTML code.

This example uses an @If statement to generate a desired text value:

Run Formula ▼

```
@If(Total=0;"No Total";@Text(Total))
```

This example generates HTML code that can be used to display the view in an HTML table:

Window Title, Section Access, Insert Subform, and Section Title Formulas

When creating a form you can compute the window title, section access, and insert subform formulas by using formula language. These formulas are run on the user's workstations when a document is opened for reading or editing.

Window Title Formula

A window title formula computes the value that appears in the title bar of documents using that particular form. The formula must evaluate to a text or numeric value. You may use fields to obtain values. Similar to view-column formulas, rich-text fields cannot be used in window-title formulas.

This example computes the window title depending if the document is new or has been previously created:

Section Access Formula

A section-access formula computes the names of users that have the ability to edit fields within an access-controlled section. If a user's name is not specified in the section-access formula, they will only have read access to the information. However, the section-access formula does not override the user's security specified in the access-control list for the database.

This example computes to multiple names as well as a certain role that can edit the contents of a section:

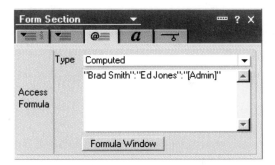

This example computes to all the values of the first column of the People view. All users which names are identified in the view can edit the contents of the section:

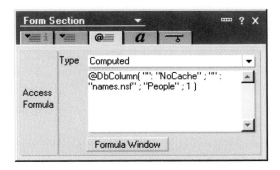

Insert Subform Formulas

An insert subform formula specifies the name of a subform that should be inserted into a form. Similar to a form formula, the subform formula must evaluate to a name of a subform, which is always a text value.

First, insert a new subform by selecting Create . . . Insert Subform. Be sure to have *Insert Subform based on formula* checked. Once the subform has been inserted, define the formula for the name of the subform:

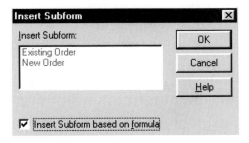

This example inserts the New Order subform if the document is in the process of being created. If the document has previously been created, the Existing Order subform is inserted:

This example inserts the Web Subform if the document is being opened through a Web browser. If the document is being opened in the Notes client, the Notes Subform is inserted:

Section Title Formula

A section-title formula computes the value that appears in the title bar of a collapsible section. The same rules apply to section-title formulas as to window-title formulas, the formula must evaluate to a text or numeric value.

This example computes the section title, placing the value of the name field into the title with static text:

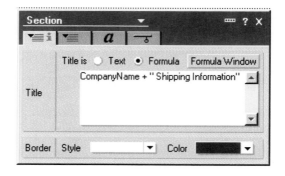

Field Design Formulas

When designing a form that contains fields, formulas can be used to manipulate the information within a field. Field formulas can be used for the following:

- Default value formula
- Input translation formula
- Input validation formula
- Value formula for a computed field
- Keyword field formula

Default Value Formula

The default value of a field is the initial value with the field when the document is first created, or when the document is saved, in the case of uneditable rich-text fields. The user has the ability to change the default value for editable fields, but cannot change the value of uneditable rich-text fields. The default value must compute to the corresponding field type, so if the field is defined as a number, the default value must compute to a number.

This example computes to the date when the document is created. This formula can only be used for a field specified as time/date:

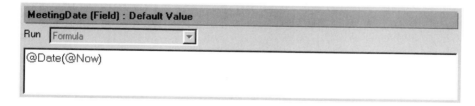

This example computes to the user's surname in uppercase letters:

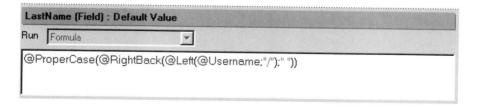

Input Translation Formula

An input translation formula converts the information entered into a field to make modifications to the data or to change the data type to correspond to the particular field. The input translation formula executes when the document is being saved or refreshed. Similar to the default value, the input translation formula must compute to the corresponding field type, so if the field is defined as text, the translation formula must compute to a text value.

This example trims any blank spaces from the data entered in the CatalogNumber field. The @Trim formula is particularly useful for eliminating any unnecessary spaces that could cause lookups to fail.

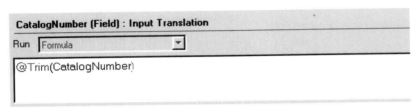

Input Validation Formula

An input validation formula validates the data entered in the field against criteria that has been programmed into the field. The input validation executes after the input translation and computes to either @Success or @Failure.

This formula validates that the date entered into the Order Date field is not greater than today's date:

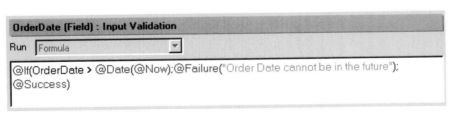

This formula validates that the Name field contains a value and is not left blank:

Value Formula for a Computed Field

If a field has been identified as computed, computed for display, or computed when composed, a formula must be written for the field. Similar to the previous field-related formulas, the value formula must correspond to the correct data type. If the formula does not match the type of field it has been written for, the field will result in an error.

This example computes to the date and time when the document was created. The @Created formula should be used in a computed when composed field since the value will never change regardless to how many times the document is modified.

Keyword Field Formula

A keyword field gives the user a list of options to choose from when selecting the value of a field. The keyword list can be generated using a formula or text list. The options within a keyword list must correspond to the data type of the field that they are available for.

This example performs a lookup to the countries view and returns the values within the second column.

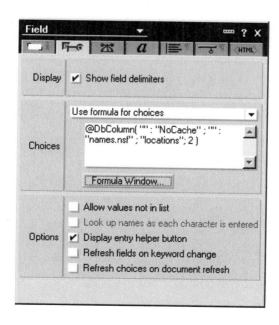

HTML in Form, Pages, or Views

As described earlier in this chapter, HTML is a markup language designed primarily for Web applications. HTML is used in defining the structure of a Web document and improving the presentation to the user. HTML code can be inserted directly into the following design elements:

- Forms
- Pages
- Views

HTML in Forms and Pages

There are a number of ways HTML can be used on a form or page. First, HTML can be imported onto a form or page from an HTML file that has been created using a different authoring tool. When you import HTML, Designer renders it on the form or page already translated from HTML. Secondly, you can simply copy and paste HTML code into the form or page. Once the code has been pasted, you must select the code and specify it as pass-thru HTML. This can be accomplished by selecting the text and a choosing Text—Pass-Thru HTML. Finally, HTML can be entered in the HTML Head Content tab of a form or page or within a field named HTML on a form. Domino will automatically treat the contents of these fields as pass-thru HTML.

HTML Tab

Many design elements contain the HTML tab from within the Properties InfoBox. The HTML properties allow the developer to access core HTML attributes such as ID, class, style, title, or other to format the element for Web applications. The HTML tab is displayed here. Domino incorporates the values of the HTML tag attributes at runtime.

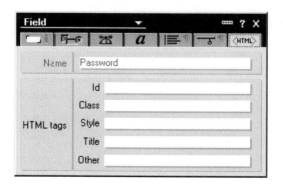

HTML in Views

You can specify the default row and column settings for a view as HTML. In Notes, the view still displays as a standard view, but on the Web, the view uses the HTML formatting attributes you specify in the column formula.

To use HTML in a view, do the following:

1. Open the view in Designer and choose Design . . . View Properties.

2. Click the Advanced tab and select *For Web Access: Treat view contents as HTML*.

3. In the Programmer's pane, write the HTML code in the script area of the Formula box. The HTML must define all formatting and document linking for the view.

Events

Scripts can be written that will be executed at different times during the processing of certain design elements. From the Programmer's pane, you can access objects and events through the Objects tab in the Info List. Databases, views, forms, and fields contain events that run on the user's workstation. A variety of programming languages can be used in response to these events including formulas, LotusScript, JavaScript, or Java. These scripts will be similar in structure to the code examples outlined in the agent section of this chapter. The following tables outline the different events that take place within the objects as well as the languages that can be used.

Database

Event	Language Available	Timing
Postopen	LotusScript Formula	After a database is opened
Postdocumentdelete	LotusScript Formula	After a document is deleted
Queryclose	LotusScript Formula	When a database is being closed
Querydocumentdelete	LotusScript Formula	Before a document is marked for deletion
Querydocumentundelete	LotusScript Formula	Before a document is unmarked for deletion
Querydragdrop	LotusScript Formula	Before a drag-and-drop operation in a view

continued

Event	Language Available	Timing *(continued)*
Postdragdrop	LotusScript Formula	After a drag-and-drop operation in a view
Initialize	LotusScript	When a database is being loaded
Terminate	LotusScript	When a database is being closed

View/Folder

Event	Language Available	Timing
Queryopen	LotusScript Formula	Before a view or folder is opened
Postopen	LotusScript Formula	After a view or folder is opened
Regiondoubleclick	LotusScript Formula	When a region in a calendar view is double-clicked
Queryopendocument	LotusScript Formula	Before a document is loaded
Queryrecalc	LotusScript Formula	Before a view or folder is refreshed
Queryaddtofolder	LotusScript Formula	Before a document is added to a folder
Querypaste	LotusScript Formula	Before a document is pasted
Postpaste	LotusScript Formula	After a document is pasted
Querydragdrop	LotusScript Formula	Before a drag-and-drop operation in a calendar view
Postdragdrop	LotusScript Formula	After a drag-and-drop operation in a calendar view
Queryclose	LotusScript Formula	When a view or folder is being closed
Initialize	LotusScript	When a view or folder is loaded
Terminate	LotusScript	When a view or folder is being closed

Form/Subform/Page

Event	Language Available	Timing
WebQueryopen (form only)	Formula	Before a Web document displays
WebQuerySave (form only)	Formula	Before a Web document is saved

continued

Event	Language Available	Timing *(continued)*
OnHelpRequest	Formula	When help is selected
JS Header	JavaScript	When a document is being loaded
OnBlur	JavaScript	When an object is deselected
On Click	JavaScript	When an object is selected
OnDblClick	JavaScript	When an object is selected with a double-click
OnFocus	JavaScript	When an editable field is selected
OnHelp	JavaScript	When help is selected
OnKeyDown	JavaScript	When a key is pressed down
OnKeyPress	JavaScript	When a key is pressed
OnKeyUp	JavaScript	When a key is released
OnLoad	JavaScript	After a document is opened
OnMouseDown	JavaScript	When a mouse button is pressed down
OnMouseMove	JavaScript	When the mouse is moved
OnMouseOut	JavaScript	When the mouse is moved out of an object
OnMouseover	JavaScript	When the mouse is moved over an object
OnMouseUp	JavaScript	When a mouse button is released
OnReset (form only)	JavaScript	When a document is reset
OnSubmit (form only)	JavaScript	Before a document is submitted
OnUnload	JavaScript	When a document is closed
Queryopen	LotusScript Formula	Before a document is opened
PostOpen	LotusScript Formula	After a document is opened
Querymodechange	LotusScript Formula	Before a document is changed to read or edit mode
Postmodechange	LotusScript Formula	After a document is changed to read or edit mode
Postrecalc	LotusScript Formula	After a document is refreshed
Querysave	LotusScript Formula	Before a document is saved

continued

PART VI

Event	Language Available	Timing *(continued)*
Postsave	LotusScript Formula	After a document is saved
Queryclose	LotusScript Formula	Before a document is closed
Initialize	LotusScript	When a document is being loaded
Terminate	LotusScript	After the document is closed
Click (form only)	LotusScript	When an object is selected

Field

Event	Language Available	Timing
OnClick	JavaScript	When an object is selected
OnChange	JavaScript	When an object is changed
OnBlur	JavaScript	When an editable field is deselected
OnFocus	JavaScript	When an editable field is selected
Entering	LotusScript	When an editable field is selected
Exiting	LotusScript	When an editable field is deselected
Initialize	LotusScript	When a document is being loaded
Terminate	LotusScript	When a document is being closed

Action

Event	Language Available	Timing
OnBlur	JavaScript	When an object is deselected

Button

Event	Language Available	Timing
OnClick	JavaScript	When an object is selected

Hotspot

Event	Language Available	Timing
OnDblClick	JavaScript	When an object is selected with a double-click
OnFocus	JavaScript	When an editable field is selected
OnHelp	JavaScript	When help is selected
OnKeyDown	JavaScript	When a key is pressed down
OnKeyUp	JavaScript	When a key is released
OnMouseDown	JavaScript	When a mouse button is pressed down
OnMouseMove	JavaScript	When the mouse is moved
OnMouseOut	JavaScript	When the mouse is moved out of an object
OnMouseover	JavaScript	When the mouse is moved over an object
OnMouseUp	JavaScript	When a mouse button is released
Click	LotusScript Formula	When an object is selected
Objectexecute	LotusScript	OLE2 server that is FX/NotesFlow enabled
Initialize	LotusScript	When an object is being loaded
Terminate	LotusScript	After an object is closed

Agent

Event	Language Available	Timing
Action	Formula	When an agent is run
Java Agent	Java	When an agent is run
Initialize	LotusScript	When an agent is being loaded
Terminate	LotusScript	When an agent is being closed

Summary

Formula language is the primary programming language within Domino Designer. Formula language can be in the form of @Functions or @Command formulas. Formulas are best used within the object that the user is currently processing, for example, computing the value of a field within a document or computing the selection formula for a view. Formula language can be used in both Notes and Web-based applications. LotusScript is a full object-oriented programming language, which is similar in structure to Visual Basic. LotusScript uses pre-defined classes to interface with almost all Domino elements. Domino oversees the compilation and loading of user codes and automatically includes the Domino-class definitions. LotusScript is best used for accessing existing objects, for example, to change a value in one document based on values in another document or for processing multiple documents within a collection. LotusScript is particularly useful when writing background agents for importing information, ODBC, or scheduled events. Even though LotusScript can perform many of the same functions as formula language, it is best to use formula language whenever possible. Like formula language, LotusScript can be used in both Notes and Web-based applications. HTML is a markup language designed primarily for Web applications. HTML is used in defining the structure of a Web document and improving the presentation to the user. HTML can be used in a variety of Domino design elements such as forms, pages, and views. JavaScript is a cross-platform, object-oriented scripting language that is executed in the client as opposed to on the server. JavaScript has been integrated into Domino Designer and design elements with the release of R5. JavaScript is best used in Web applications, or when a single application will be used in the Notes client as well as through a Web browser. Java is a full object-oriented programming language that interfaces to Domino through predefined classes. Java can perform many of the same functions as LotusScript when used in agent, but cannot be used within the Domino UI. Java code can be written natively or imported. All these design languages can be used in different situations in almost every design element available within Domino Designer as outlined in the examples in this chapter.

Review Questions

1. Notes formula language can be in the form of which type of formulas?
   a. @Formulas
   b. @Commands
   c. All of the above
   d. None of the above

2. True or False: LotusScript, JavaScript and Java are full object-oriented programming languages.
    a. True
    b. False

3. True or False: HTML is a markup language designed primarily for Notes applications.
    a. True
    b. False

4. True or False: Java can be used to create which of the following?
    a. Views
    b. Hotspots
    c. Agents
    d. Forms

5. True or False: LotusScript can be used to compute a Form formula
    a. True
    b. False

6. True or False: Default formulas can compute to any data type, regardless of the data type of the field they are within.
    a. True
    b. False

7. Which of the following are events of form or page?
    a. Queryopen
    b. Entering
    c. Objectexecute
    d. Queryopendocument

8. Which form event occurs last in this list?
    a. Postopen
    b. Postrecalc
    c. Queryclose
    d. Queryopen

9. True or False: The contents of the HTML Head are automatically treated as pass-thru HTML.
    a. True
    b. False

10. A section access formula can be computed as which of the following?
    a. Username
    b. Roles
    c. Groups
    d. All of the above

Review Answers

1. **C is correct.** Standard Notes formula language can be in the form of @Formulas or @Commands.

2. **A is correct.** LotusScript, JavaScript, and Java are all full object-oriented programming languages.

3. **B is correct.** HTML is a markup language primarily used in Web applications.

4. **C is correct.** Java can be used in much of the same ways LotusScript is used in agents.

5. **B is correct.** A form formula is computed using @Formulas, not LotusScript.

6. **B is correct.** In all field formulas, the formula must compute to the same data type as the corresponding field.

7. **A is correct.** Queryopen is the event that takes place right before a form or page is opened.

8. **C is correct.** Queryclose is the event that takes place last in the given events.

9. **A is correct.** The contents of the HTML Head Content are rendered as pass-thru HTML.

10. **D is correct.** A section access formula can be computed to a username, role, or group.

CHAPTER 39

Planning and Designing for Replication and Routing

You should be able to answer questions based on the following objectives after reading this chapter:

- Design applications for replication
- Plan applications based upon impact of replication on Access Control Lists
- Plan applications based upon impact of replication on agent security
- Plan applications based upon impact of replication on document distribution
- Plan applications based upon impact of replication upon hops
- Plan applications based upon impact of replication on how background agents run
- Plan applications based upon impact of replication on HTML
- Plan applications based upon impact of replication on server involvement
- Plan applications based upon impact of replication on the NOTE ID
- Plan applications based upon impact of replication on the UNID
- Plan applications based upon impact of routing on databases
- Plan applications based upon impact of routing on different client types
- Plan applications based upon impact of routing on how messages are sent
- Plan applications based upon impact of routing on remote users
- Set up Authors fields for replication
- Set up groups for replication
- Set up Readers fields for replication
- Set up Roles for replication
- Set up ACLs for replication
- Set up Web users for replication

Each Domino database file (.nsf) has a Replica ID, which is a 16-character hexadecimal number displayed on the Info tab of the database properties as shown in Figure 39-1. This Replica ID is guaranteed to be unique within a Domino Domain. Database files that share the same replica ID are considered replicas. Although they normally maintain the same file and path structure as a matter of convention, this is not necessary in order to retain the same replica ID. Replication is what keeps replica databases synchronized across or within organizations. Chapters 5, 12, 17, and 37 all deal with issues surrounding replication—from configuration to troubleshooting. This chapter assumes you understand what replication is and how it works. Our focus in this chapter is not to review that information but extend that understanding to several practical situations.

In organizations it may be necessary to maintain multiple replicas of a single Domino database. The replicas could exist on multiple Domino servers or as local replicas on user's workstations. These replicas are created from the original database and are very similar to a duplicate copy of the data contained in that database. Based upon the needs of the users accessing individual replicas, it may or may not be necessary to keep all the documents in every replica. This chapter will discuss reasons why it may be a good idea to maintain replicas of entire databases or replicas containing subsets of documents, and how this can be achieved.

Servers connect to each other based on schedules set up in Connection documents. This connection can be left to a schedule or initiated at the server's console. Exactly how the database changes are passed between replicas on different servers is maintained within the individual replica. Although much can be said about designing and configuring a Domino infrastructure by using Domino Domains, each domain having its

Figure 39-1
Info tab

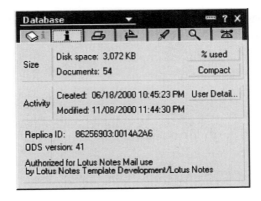

own Domino Directory to drive its architecture, and Domino Named Networks, containing servers sharing a common protocol and constant connectivity within a Domain, our focus will be from an applications perspective. We'll cover how these decisions may or may not influence the planning and design of an application.

Planning a Distributed Application

Domino applications are easily distributed because of replication. The replication process can be customized by configuring the many settings available and by controlling the timing and security of it. Before diving into those tools, a good database designer will learn the business rules that are driving the need for the Domino application. Then, based on the underlying needs, they would apply the configuration settings and make the replication happen.

Let's look at a practical situation to help better understand the following sections. Our company, ABC Inc., has three regional offices, and one home office. Each office has a Domino server and a set of users. ABC currently uses a paper form to request new business cards. This form is completed and sent in to the home office, where it is keyed into a spreadsheet that is sent to the print shop weekly. When the order is sent in, a confirmation is returned to the person who ordered the business cards.

This is a very simple workflow process that is found in nearly all companies and that we can automate using a distributed Domino application. Immediately we have to start making a few decisions when planning the design of this application. The first decision is to create multiple replicas at each regional office or not. In our example, the regional offices do not have sufficient connectivity to support users accessing an application at the home office. The response time is just not fast enough, so there is a need to maintain multiple replicas. The second decision relates to the data. In this case, the home office needs to see all the data, but the remote offices do not have any need to share each other's business card requests. There is simply no need to route that information around.

It appears that this application will need a simple hub and spoke replication topology that pulls data to the home office, or pushes it from the regional sites, but there is a need for two-way replication since a confirmation should be sent back when the order is sent to the printer. As a result, we now know that the regional offices will need a more advanced replication configuration than a simple pull, push, or even pull-push. It's just those considerations that the replication settings allow to be configured.

Replication Design

As we know, replication can be push, pull, or both. Beyond that, there are a couple of ways to control exactly what data can be passed from replica to replica through the process of replication. The two ways are: to use Readers and Authors fields to prevent data from being passed to or updated by the incorrect server or user or by using a database's replication settings.

Certainly an argument could be made for both architectures, so let's look at the merits of each. Placing security on all documents contained in a database is always a good idea when those documents contain sensitive data. First, as a practice, you should allow your servers individually, or the group "LocalDomainServers," the capability to read all documents. This in turn gives each server the capability to receive each document during replication. Second, when setting up security for database replicas, the master replica should have the advanced Access Control List option, *Enforce a consistent ACL across all replicas*, set before the other replicas are created to avoid the security being compromised in a replica. Again, this will be discussed in more detail later, but setting the ACL option will make the application easier to support in the long run; and, while using Readers or Authors fields may appear to serve the purpose, they may not be the solution in this case. If the regional servers can still replicate all documents, then each time their replication occurs, there are too many documents passed between the servers for each regional office as each office does not need to clutter their own business card request documents with another offices' requests. Even if users cannot see the documents, the inefficient replication process is a poor use of the valuable connectivity resource back to the home office, and thus a sub-optimal design.

The database replication settings can better address this need. By using the replication settings correctly, the regional offices will only send and receive their own documents. This too can be done in a number of ways. Because there are so many options to setting up individual replicas replication settings, it is worth spending the time to review these options in light of how they can be used to maintain multiple replicas.

A database's replication settings are accessed by selecting File…Replication…Settings from the menus while in a database, or choosing Replication…Settings from the shortcut menu when you right-click a bookmark or database icon. The first tab that appears is the Space Savers panel. This panel is displayed in Figure 39-2. The *Remove documents not modified in the last XX days* option is useful when disk space is at a premium, but it is the second set of options that will more directly meet our needs. If the *Replicate a subset of documents* option is selected, you can simply choose views and folders from the list displayed in the dialog box, and you are done. In the figure, there are three views that

Figure 39-2
Space savers tab of the replication settings

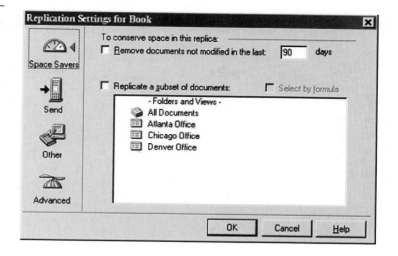

have been created for each regional office. This may seem like a good design, and it is easy to set up, but it is not very scalable. If three more regional offices are added, then three more views need to be created, and three more view indexes maintained for the database. It would be easier to create one view called "Regional Offices" that categorizes the documents by regional office. Then each office would not have the clutter of the extra views for other offices that would always be empty in their replica.

Selecting this option would require a more precise replication setting though. This can be setup by checking the *Select by formula* option, which is available after the *Replicate a subset of documents* option is selected. Creating replication formulas is very similar to view selection formulas discussed in Chapter 27. In our example, we may use something like: SELECT Region = "Atlanta." By using this approach, minimal design will be needed if new offices are added, and each office replicates their own documents back and forth, receiving updates when the requests are processed at the home office, and sending in new requests efficiently.

The Send panel of the replication settings in Figure 39-3 contains three options. These settings would more likely be enabled for local replicas rather than server replicas. The bottom option is checked by default, and is used to disable passing a locally encrypted database back to the server replica, and effectively locking other users out of it. Sometimes different database titles help uses to distinguish between multiple replicas, so this property sometimes doesn't need to pass between replicas.

Not sending deletions to other replicas can be useful locally or on a server-based replica. Quotas on a server replica may necessitate keeping more data locally, and thus keeping documents that have been deleted from the server.

PART VI

Figure 39-3
Send tab of the
replication settings

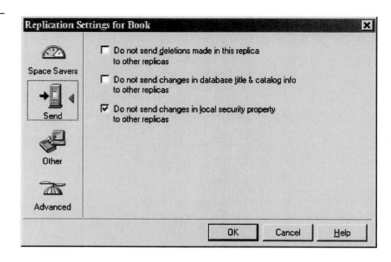

The Other tab of the Replication settings dialog box, shown in Figure 39-4, lets you temporarily disable replication, among other settings. Temporarily disabling replication is not needed under normal circumstances. You might choose to use it when troubleshooting a design problem, however. The CD-ROM publishing date option is helpful for distributing new replicas across slow connections. A replica can be sent via CD-ROM to a remote site that may only have a dial-up connection. If a replica is even over 20 MB, the dial-up connection is liable to time out or fail at some point when creating a replica. By setting a date, the first replication can "catch up" faster by working off a pre-established replication history and therefore further minimizing the time needed to complete the initial replication.

The replication priority is definitely an important setting for server-to-server replication as it can impact the performance of replication across the entire organization. When servers replicate using their Connection documents (if individual databases are not specified), then all databases that share common replicas are replicated. This can take a long time for large organizations that have many databases. Using this option gives the Domino administration team a way to balance the load and still keep those high priority databases up to date (see Figure 39-4).

The server's Connection documents can be set up to replicate *Low & Medium & High*, *Medium & High*, and just *High* priority databases in the Replication/Routing tab. This section of the Server Connection document is included in Figure 39-5. Adjusting the priority settings, using replication types, setting the individual files, and specifying a time limit can all help balance the replication schedule. Keeping this in mind when setting up a new database into an existing schedule will help better manage the traffic.

Figure 39-4
Other tab of the
replication settings

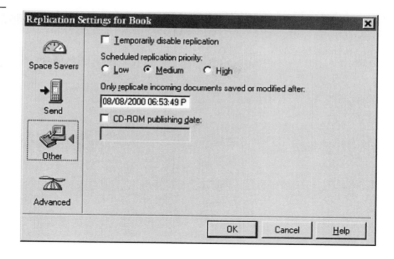

Figure 39-5
Replication/Routing
tab of a Server
Connection
document

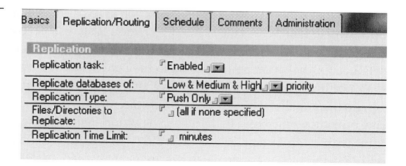

The Advanced panel of the replication settings contains some settings that we have seen, but it enables replication of individual design elements, ACLs, Agents, Deletions, Fields, and Replication formulas to be configured. This is nice, but the real feature of this panel is that it enables you to administer these settings centrally from one replica. You can modify the settings for server-to-server replication by adjusting the *When computer* and *Receives from* fields to specify the desired combinations. Of course if you want to make sure that the replication formula and other options under the replicate section do replicate around, be sure to check the *Replication formula* checkbox shown in Figure 39-6.

Adjusting these settings can make an impact on server replications, and some settings apply to local replications too as mentioned, but there are a couple more settings that specifically address the needs of remote users that maintain local replicas of databases.

Figure 39-6
Advanced tab of the
replication settings

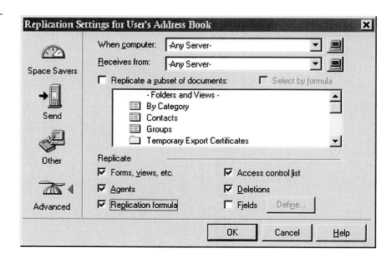

The Replicator page on the Notes client is a familiar tool to both local and remote users and can be a real time saver too. A portion of it is displayed in Figure 39-7. The first-time saver to point out is the capability to select local databases as high priority. When this property is set, by right-clicking on the Replicator page entry to display the setting, a small, red exclamation point appears to the right of the checkbox helper. This in itself does not help replication, but it is very similar to the replication setting above used for server replication. Flagging databases as high priority give the user the option to replicate only those databases by selection the action item *Replicate High Priority Databases* from the Replicator page if they manually initiate the replication, or by specifying a schedule for high priority databases to be replicated in the appropriate Location document.

Figure 39-7
Replicator page

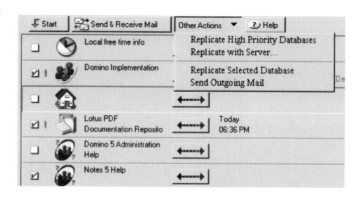

Another helpful tool can be accessed by clicking on the directional arrows that indicate which way replication has been defined to occur. Figure 39-8 displays the replication options prompt that allows you to control whether documents are sent to the server and/or received from the server. Additionally, if documents are received from the server, you may specify to receive full documents, the summary fields and the first 40 KB of rich text, or receive only summary fields.

These settings can conserve disk space in addition to speeding up replication times. Knowing that these are options are available to allow your user community to take advantage of will be appreciated. Designing your application with this in mind will assure its success.

Figure 39-8

Replication options

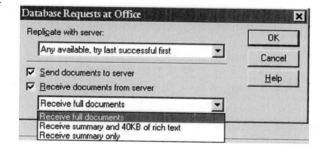

Routing Design Issues

Like replication, routing has been described multiple places in this book (Chapters 4, 11, 17, and throughout Part V). We assume you understand routing and concepts. In this chapter, we extend routing topics to helping you plan your applications based on how routing affects them.

Within the same Domino Named Network (DNN), servers have constant connectivity to each other and mail can be routed immediately as long as the servers can find each other using a shortname in DNS. Connection documents, while not required for servers in the same DNN, can be used to help servers find each other (by giving the IP address) or to create dial-up or other connections for servers in different DNNs. When mail must be routed across dial-up connections, there can be considerable delays. Depending on the priority of the message, it may not be transferred until after midnight.

The actual configuration of your mail routing topology is normally up to the administration team too, much like the replication topology. When developing an application that sends out messages, there are only a few considerations, one of them we just mentioned. Check to make sure you know when low-priority mail routes across your organization. This setting can be found in the Server Configuration document. Each server can have its own, or configurations can be shared across servers. Figure 39-9 shows the section of the Configuration document that relates to low-priority mail routing.

If the default settings are still set, low-priority mail won't be routed until after midnight. As an application developer, in order to assure that your users are satisfied, you'll want to make sure outbound mail is sent with normal or high priority. Setting the reserved field *DeliveryPriority* to "N" or "H" can do this.

In addtion, mail routing usually occurs more often than scheduled replication. To be sure that the documents exist when sending a message containing a document link back a document sent for review on the reviewers' home replica, the distribution of the link may need to be scheduled via an agent. By using an agent, a newsletter could also be sent in order to minimize the number of messages sent. This may even be perceived as a feature to users.

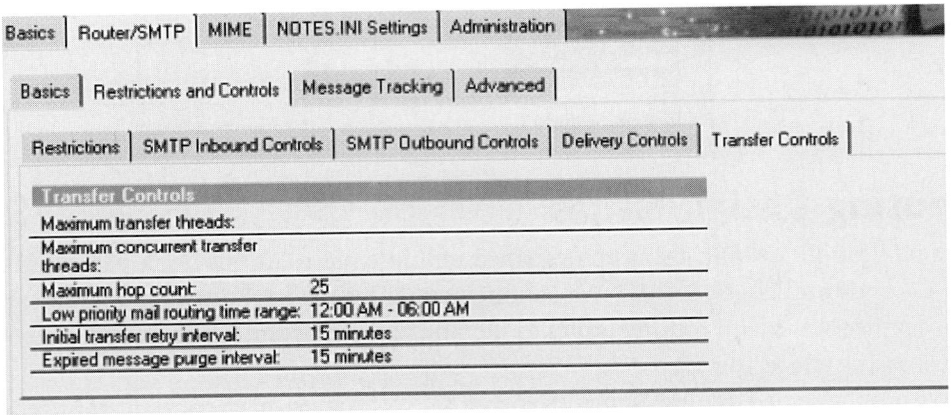

Figure 39-9   Replication options

Summary

Planning for the types of replication and routing conditions that exist or may soon exist in your Domino Domain can help position your applications better within that structure. Based upon the needs of individual users, local replicas may be necessary. For applications, enforcing security locally is more important to preserving the functionality of the way that application was designed. Locally as well as on other servers, it may be a good idea to maintain different types and quantities of documents. These settings can be adjusted by using the replication settings options, or the replicator page among other tools we have discussed here.

Review Questions

1. True or False: The database Replica ID is an 8-digit long hexadecimal number.
   a. True
   b. False

2. True or False: It's never a good idea to create multiple replicas of the same database across an organization.
   a. True
   b. False

3. Which of these is NOT a type of replication?
   a. Pull
   b. Push
   c. Pull-Push
   d. Push-Pull

4. True or False: Replicating a subset of documents can only be set through the use of a replication formula.
   a. True
   b. False

5. What are the types of scheduled replication priorities?
   a. Low, Normal, High
   b. Low, High
   c. Low, Medium, High
   d. Normal, High

6. Server-to-server replication is configured in what documents?
   a. Configuration documents
   b. Server documents
   c. Location documents
   d. Connection documents

7. A client-to-server replication is configured in what documents?
   a. Configuration documents
   b. Server documents
   c. Location documents
   d. Connection documents

8. Using the Replication options dialog to customize the amount of data received from the server, what is NOT an option?
   a. Receive full documents
   b. Receive summary fields and 40 KB of rich text
   c. Receive summary fields only
   d. Receive summary fields and 60 KB of rich text

9. Which of the following must be set in order to assure that the other settings correctly replicate another replica?
   a. Agents
   b. Deletions
   c. Access control list
   d. Replication formula

10. The time interval for low-priority mail routing is set in what documents?
    a. Configuration documents
    b. Server documents
    c. Location documents
    d. Connection documents

Review Answers

1. **B is correct.**   The Replica ID of a database is a 16-character hexadecimal number.

2. **B is correct.**   There may be more than one good reason to maintain multiple replicas of the same databases in an organization.

3. **D is correct.**   Push-Pull is not an option available for server-to-server replication.

4. **B is correct.**   Using a replication formula is only one option; subsets may be chosen by selecting views manually through the space savers or advanced panel.

5. **C is correct.** Low, Medium, and High are the three settings available for scheduled replication priority.

6. **D is correct.** Servers use Connection documents to set the connection schedule.

7. **C is correct.** Notes clients use Location documents to schedule connections to servers.

8. **D is correct.** The amount of rich text received from the server is not customizable and is 40 KB when set.

9. **D is correct.** Replication formula. In order to be sure that all other non-document related replication settings correctly replicate, this option must be checked.

10. **A is correct.** Configuration documents contain the settings for low-priority mail routing.

CHAPTER 40

Distributing Updates

You should be able to answer questions based on the following objectives after reading this chapter:

- Update design by Design Task
- Manually refresh design using a template
- Manually replace design using a template
- Update design by Replication
- Design an update distribution mechanism using Design
- Design an update distribution mechanism using replication
- Design an update distribution mechanism
- Design an update distribution mechanism based on impact on ACLs
- Plan for Design distribution based on ACL impact
- Plan for Design distribution based on repliction
- Plan for Design distribution based on templates

The design of a database is rarely ever finalized. With changes in business processes and increased use of a database, updates to the original design frequently have to be made. Whether it is a design flaw that was discovered or an additional view that has been requested by a user, these changes have to be propagated to the production databases. This chapter outlines the different ways design changes can be distributed to databases. You may want to refer to Chapter 21 for additional discussion.

Design Updates by Designer Task

To ensure consistent design elements across multiple copies of a database, a master template can be created to accomplish this. A master template contains the design elements that will be inherited into any database that is associated with it. Developers can manually synchronize databases with a master template, but more often they rely on the server and the Designer task to do this. When changes have been made to the design of a master template, the Designer task updates all databases that inherit their design from the master template. The Designer task runs on the server on a daily schedule, by default at 1 AM. After the Designer task runs, the server runs the Updall task, which updates the view indexes of any changes made by the Designer task.

Running the Designer task using the Task…Start tool is done as follows:

1. From the Domino Administrator, select the server you wish to run Designer on.

2. Click the Server…Status tab.

3. In the Task panel, which is located on the right side of the dialog, click Task…Start.

4. Select Designer and then click Start Task.

Running the Designer Task using a console command is done as follows:

1. From the Domino Administrator, select the server you wish to run Designer on.

2. Click the Server…Status tab.

3. Click Console.

4. Type **Load designer** in the command line and press ENTER.

Refreshing/Replacing the Design of a Database

Developers can manually refresh/replace the design of a database whose design is linked to a master template. This process is particularly valuable when the Designer task is not running on a server, the design of a database needs to be updated from a master template immediately and cannot wait until the Designer task runs, or the design of a single database needs to be refreshed/replaced instead of every database on a server.

Manually Refreshing a Design

To refresh the design of a particular database from a Master template, follow these steps:

1. Select the database to be updated, and choose File...Database...Refresh Design.

2. Select the Notes server that stores the master template(s) or select Local if the master templates are on your workstation, and then click OK.

3. Click Yes.

The following components are not modified when the design is refreshed:

- Database icon
- Database title and category
- Property *List as advanced template in New Database*
- Database ACL and encrypt database settings
- Using This Database and About This Database documents
- Individual elements whose design is protected from updates

The following components are modified when the design is refreshed:

- Forms, fields, form actions, and event scripts
- Views, folders, and view actions
- Agents
- Navigators
- Shared fields
- File...Database Properties selections, except the *advanced template* option

Refer to Chapters 21 for additional details.

Replacing the Design of a Database

The Replace Design command makes a database identical to a template and is the only way to distribute design changes if the database doesn't inherit its changes from a master template. If you have at least Designer access in the database ACL, you can replace the design of a database with the design from a template.

To replace the design of a particular database from a master template, follow these steps:

1. Select the database on the server and choose File...Database...Replace Design:

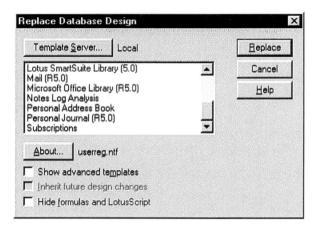

2. Select the template.
3. Click Replace and Yes to confirm.

The following components are not modified when the design is replaced:

- Database icon
- Database title and category
- Property *List as advanced template in New Database*
- Database ACL and encrypt database settings
- Using This Database and About This Database documents
- Individual elements whose design is protected from updates

The following components are modified when the design is replaced:

- Forms, fields, form actions, and event scripts
- Views, folders, and view actions
- Agents

- Navigators
- Shared fields
- File, Database Properties selections, except the *advanced template* option

Inherit Future Design Changes

This option lets you inherit future design changes from a master template automatically and not have to use the replace design command. This will tell the Designer task what template to look to for changes to the database.

Hide Formulas and LotusScript

This option prevents users from making any design change to a particular database. Hiding the design permanently disables all design operations and hides all formulas and scripts. Even users who have Designer or Manager access to the database can't make design changes. This feature is useful for hiding the design of ready-to-use databases that are based on a template you own. When design changes are required, you redesign the template, whose design is not hidden, and then refresh the design of the linked databases.

When you hide a database design, users cannot

- View the settings for design elements
- Modify, add, or delete fields, forms, navigators, pages, or subforms
- Modify or delete existing views
- View, delete, or modify existing agents or add shared agents
- View or change formulas, LotusScript programs, or formulas associated with simple actions
- Change the Database Open properties
- Display a synopsis of the design
- Reveal the design of the database by making a copy or replica of it

To unhide a hidden database desgin, you must replace the design again, using the appropriate template. Just uncheck the *Hide formulas and LotusScript* option.

Design Updates by Replication

If a developer decides not to distribute design changes using design templates, modifications can be distributed using database replication. Replication allows the database developer to properly test changes made to a design in a similar environment. When changes have been made and properly tested in one replica of a database, the developer can rely on Notes replication to distribute the changes to other replicas of the database. The developer can force replication once changes have been made or the Replicator task on the server will initiate replication of changes. Replication is particularly useful for distributing changes to multiple databases that are on different servers.

To ensure a replica of a database has been set up to distribute design changes, follow these steps:

1. Select the database and choose File...Replication Settings.

2. Select the Advanced icon from the left side of the Replication Settings dialog box as shown below.

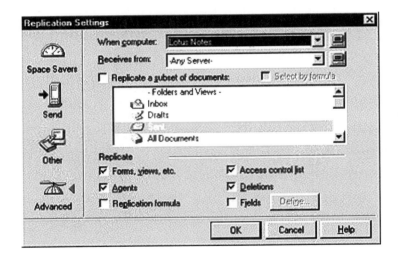

3. Make sure the proper elements have been checked under the Replicate section.

4. Click OK to save any changes.

To receive design changes from a source server, the database replica on the destination server must give the source server at least Designer access and the source server must give the destination server at least Reader access in the ACL. Giving the destination server at least Reader access to the database will allow the server to access the database during replication. Giving the source server at least Designer access to the database will allow the server to make the necessary design updates during replication.

Summary

To ensure consistent design elements across multiple copies of a database, create a master template. A master template contains the design elements that will be inherited into any database that is associated with it. Developers can manually synchronize databases with a master template, but more often they rely on the server and the Designer task to do this. When changes have been made to the design of a master template, the Designer task updates all databases that inherit their design from the master template. Developers can manually refresh/replace the design of a database whose design is linked to a master template. This process is particularly valuable when the Designer task is not running on a server, the design of a database needs to be updated from a Master template immediately and cannot wait until the Designer task runs, or the design of a single database needs to be refreshed/replaced instead of every database on a server. The Replace Design command makes a database identical to a template and is the only way to distribute design changes if the database doesn't inherit its changes from a master template. If you have at least Designer access in the database ACL, you can replace the design of a database with the design from a template. Replication allows the database developer to properly test changes made to design in a similar environment. When changes have been made and properly tested in one replica of a database, the developer can rely on Notes replication to distribute the changes to other replicas of the database. The developer can force replication once changes have been made or the Replicator task on the server will initiate replication of changes. Replication is particularly useful for distributing changes to multiple databases that are on different servers. To receive design changes from a source server, the database replica on the destination server must give the source server at least Designer access and the source server must give the destination server at least Reader access in the ACL.

Review Questions

1. True or False: The Designer task runs on a single database.
   a. True
   b. False

2. The correct command to run the Designer task is
   a. Update design
   b. Load designer
   c. Tell designer start
   d. Replicate

3. True or False: The ACL of a database is updated when design is manually refreshed/replaced.
   a. True
   b. False

4. What access level is required for a source server within a database for the replication of design changes to occur?
   a. Reader
   b. Depositor
   c. Editor
   d. Designer

5. True or False: The template of a database can be set to replicate to other servers.
   a. True
   b. False

6. Which of the following is not modified when replacing the design using the design task?
   a. Views
   b. Documents
   c. Forms
   d. Agents

7. What method cannot be used to update the design of a database?
   a. Updating design by Designer Task
   b. Manually refreshing design using a template
   c. Manually replace the design using a template
   d. Typing **tell designer replace** at the server console

8. True or False: You can protect an individual design element from being modified when replacing design.
   a. True
   b. False

9. When you hide the design of a database, user cannot
   a. View the settings for design elements
   b. Modify or delete existing views
   c. Display the Design Synopsis of the database
   d. View any documents that use hidden forms

10. True or False: If the database has a hidden design, you can't update its design.
    a. True
    b. False

Review Answers

1. **B is correct.** The Designer task runs on all databases on a server, not just a single database.

2. **B is correct.** **Load designer** is the correct command to enter in the console to initiate the Designer task.

3. **B is correct.** The ACL of a database is not updated when design is refreshed/ replaced from a template.

4. **D is correct.** The source server must have at least Designer access to a database for the replication of design changes to occur properly.

5. **A is correct.** You can replicate the template to any server, just like any regular database.

6. **B is correct.** Documents are not affected when modifying design.

7. **D is correct.** The designer task does not accept tell commands.

8. **A is correct.** You can, by selecting *Prohibit design refresh or replace to modify* in the Design documents properties.

9. **A, B,** and **C** are correct. Users can still view documents, even if their design is hidden.

10. **B is correct.** You can still update the design of a database that has a hidden

CHAPTER 41

Designing and Planning for Secure Applications

You should be able to answer questions based on the following objectives after reading this chapter:

- Design a secure application
- Design applications for consistent ACL enforcement
- Design applications to restrict author access to documents
- Design applications to restrict reader access to documents
- Design applications which control document access through Authors fields
- Design applications which control document access through Readers fields
- Design applications which control document access
- Design applications with read only view security
- Design applications with section security
- Design applications with view security
- Design applications with "convenient" security
- Set up ACLs for application security
- Set up Authors fields for application security
- Set up groups for application security
- Set up Readers fields for application security
- Set up Roles for application security
- Set up Web users for application security
- Plan application security based on Notes authentication
- Plan application security based on Password encryption
- Plan application security based on the Domino Directory
- Plan application security based on User IDs
- Plan application security based on Web authentication
- Plan application security based on number of users
- Plan applications based on authentication characteristics
- Plan applications based on Notes ID authentication characteristics
- Plan applications based on Web authentication characteristics

In planning Domino application security, there are many considerations. The main focus is to allow access to selected users, while preventing anyone else from viewing this data. Domino systems are set up to share knowledge. Security surrounding who, when, and how this knowledge is shared is often more complicated than configuring the underlying security. Many chapters in this book describe various security elements (Chapters 3, 5, 10, 18, 24, 34, 35, and 36). You should review all of that material before planning for your secure applications. This chapter will discuss elements of security that specifically relate to the designing and planning for secure applications, but the background and some details are contained in the listed chapters.

Design Secure Applications

In Chapters 6–10, we discussed Domino server configuration. This server configuration broadly defines what groups of users are able to access a Domino server and how users are able to access that server. Beyond those broadly defined policies that are usually defined when a new server is setup, Domino application security is used to accommodate the individual needs of the user groups depending on the knowledge stored in each application and it provides the flexibility to do so in an efficient way. Each company may have very different needs when thinking about the data stored in each Domino application. To accommodate this need, in large organizations, application level security management is often delegated to those individuals that are more familiar with the individuals in their workgroup. The Domino security model accommodates this need quite naturally and has the capability to scale as those needs grow.

As a Lotus product, Domino is fully documented. In addition to the help databases that can be a valuable reference, there are hundreds of published Redbooks, help databases, White papers, and articles. These resources address security issues with more granularity than discussed in this chapter. This chapter focuses on how to bring all of those techniques together in a practical manner.

Domino application security is first controlled through each application's Access Control List (ACL). To access a database application on a particular server, a user must have both the appropriate level of access to the database as well as the appropriate access in the Server Access section of the Server document. Beyond accessing the application, security can be placed on and within individual design elements, such as forms or views. All of these are addressed in detail over the following pages through the use of practical examples, but first let's take a look at what it means to an application that you have gained access to on the Domino server.

Authentication

The process of authentication was described in Chapter 10. As a result of the authentication process, each user is identified. This defines not only the user, but the groups and roles that the user possesses and which of those apply to the application a user accesses. A user's groups and roles are then stored during each session. One of these roles identifies if the user is accessing the application through a Web browser. The Domino security model makes a clear distinction between Web users and Notes client users. Security for these two classes of users should be addressed separately. This will become more apparent and described in more detail later in this chapter.

Notes

Although recent advances have given Web users the same offline abilities that Notes client users have enjoyed since the client software was developed, Notes client users have one distinct advantage over Web browser users: the user ID file. In addition to storing the user's private key, the user's ID file can store private encryption keys. These keys can be used in many ways, as we will soon see.

While accessing data on a Domino server, Notes client users also have the option of encrypting the data as it travels through your network. This setting can be modified by viewing the ports section of your User Preferences.

Lotus Notes client users are able to easily display what groups and roles apply to them at any time (as shown in Figure 41-1) by clicking on the icon just to the left your location indicator. This icon changes depending on the level of access the user has. These levels will be looked at along with the entire ACL shortly. While accessing applications on the Domino server, the Groups and Roles dialog will always display correct information. When accessing local databases, only those applications that *Enforce a consistent ACL across all replicas* will display user information. Otherwise, each user has Manager access to those local applications. This too will be revisited in the ACL section.

Web

Web browsers give users additional flexibility and mobility. Opening up your application to a Web browser users is often as simple as loading the HTTP server task. Loading this service requires that each application be more carefully defined, as the users may

Figure 41-1
User Access dialog

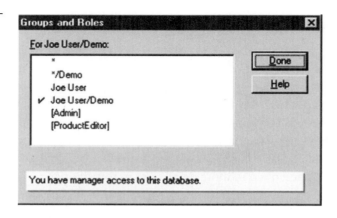

not necessarily be forced to authenticate and could gain access to applications anonymously. Unless a special Anonymous entry is added to each ACL, unauthenticated Web users access an application with the same privileges as the Default user. It is good practice to not allow anonymous access to your Domino server unless you want everyone to be able to access a certain database with the same access level.

Browser authentication relies on a user's name and HTTP password, which are stored in the Domino Directory. Browser users do not require User ID files. This means that they cannot participate in standard Domino signing or encryption. You can provide for X.509 certificates to let browser users have encrypted communications, however.

For browser clients, providing X.509 certificates from a trusted authority like Verisign can let you configure encryption security. This certificate authority will then sign each request made to or sent from the server. Domino has the capability to issue this request with some minor configuration. This would enable SSL connections to the Domino systems. When configured, normal HTTP requests can be automatically redirected to HTTPS.

Application Security

Application security is defined for each Domino database (.nsf) file. A Domino application does not need to be contained in one single file, but it can share data across many. It may have many different business users that have completely different needs. To illustrate this point, the rest of this chapter will use the fictitious needs of ABC, Inc., a small company that has applied Notes in their environment to accommodate the needs of their field sales staff.

Two topics apply to all applications, independent of their design and security configuration that can make a significant impact on the overall security of an application. These are hiding the design and database encryption.

Hiding the design forces design changes to be properly escalated through ABC's design process. When a design is hidden in a database, modifications to it can only be propagated by the Designer task, whether on schedule or initiated by a user. This allows Domino administrators to force application changes to be thoroughly tested and approved. Replacing the design of a database from a template and checking the *Hide formulas and LotusScript* option, as displayed in Figure 41-2, can hide the design of a database.

Once a database's design is hidden, there are advantages and disadvantages. One advantage is that additional control is gained on who can modify a design. More importantly, however, is that the properties of documents can no longer be viewed through the Document properties dialog. You'll see that displaying the properties of a document displays nothing at all, not even the system fields, which display the edit history on a document. Of course, these properties are not available to Web-browser users, so there is no significant impact on them.

There are disadvantages to this form of security too. By hiding the design of formulas and scripts, the application's performance suffers. In order to execute any formula or script, the code must first be decrypted before executing. This may not be obvious to a user, but for large scripts, it can be noticeable. It should also be noted that a clever user could work around this technique by copying documents into a database whose design is not hidden.

Figure 41-2
Replace Design
dialog

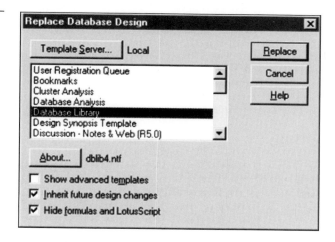

Database encryption is a technique that can be used to assure security for local database replicas. For ABC, the field sales staff can use encryption to lock down their local replicas of sensitive sales contact information. Database encryption is designed to prevent unauthorized local access and is not intended as a replacement for field-level encryption.

You can choose among three levels of encryption: simple, medium, and strong. Three factors must be considered when choosing a database encryption level: the level of security provided, the resulting database access speed, and the need to use a compression utility to compress the encrypted database. Normally, medium encryption is adequate. Strong encryption causes a delay when trying to open documents, while simple encryption offers additional security yet still enables disk compression utilities to compress the file.

Encryption can be set when a new copy or replica is created. To do this, click the Encryption button from the respective dialog, which brings up the dialog that appears in Figure 41-3. Since workstations are not locked up in a server room, local encryption provides that additional layer of security needed. A local replica is encrypted with the user's ID file, so if the file is removed, the same ID file is needed to open the database. Even if the ID file is also taken, the user's password must be cracked in order to compromise the application's access. Even with sophisticated password-cracking tools, ID files are not easy to crack. Thanks to the time-delay and anti-spoofing mechanisms built into the Notes client, it is very difficult to capture or crack Notes ID file passwords.

Figure 41-3
Encryption dialog

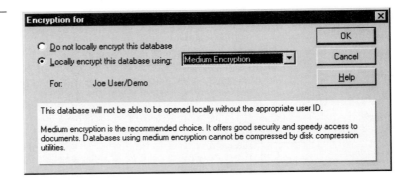

ACLs

The Access Control List has already been mentioned numerous times. It is for good reason since this one feature is arguably the single most important component in a Domino application. It acts as the gatekeeper for applications, allowing those who should be interacting with the data in, and keeping those who shouldn't out. Access levels assigned to users in a database ACL control which tasks users can perform in the database. Access-level privileges enhance or restrict the access level assigned to each name in the ACL. Table 41-1 describes each level of access, as described by Lotus.

These access levels are controlled through the interface illustrated in Figure 41-4. This robust control panel enables a very precise definition of application access. In our example, we have four groups of users: Sales Staff, Sales Support, Production Managers, and Administrators. Each of these groups has been included in the Basics tab of the ACL by using a public group added to the Domino Directory. Spaces aren't used as a convention, although they are perfectly acceptable, but by eliminating the spaces, we accommodate Internet mail addressing.

The group selected in Figure 41-4 is the SalesSupport. This group is defined as a group of people in the user type and has Editor access. The options that are not grayed out are configurable based on need. There is also an entry for *Anonymous*. This user has No Access to the database. This restricts Web browser users to only those with the ability to authenticate. This is one of the first steps to securing your application from unknown users.

Table 41-1 ACL Access Table

Access Level	Privileges
Manager	Can modify ACL settings, encrypt a database for local security, modify replication settings, and delete a database, tasks permitted by no other access level. Managers can also perform all tasks allowed by other access levels.
Designer	Can modify all database design elements (fields, forms, views, public agents, the database icon, Using This Database document and About This Database document), can modify replication formulas, and can create a full-text index. Designers can also perform all tasks allowed by lower access levels.
Editor	Can create documents and edit all documents, including those created by others.
Author	Can create documents and edit documents they create.
Reader	Can read documents in a database but cannot create or edit documents.
Depositor	Can create documents but can't see any documents in the database views, even the documents they create.
No access	Cannot access the database.

PART VI

Figure 41-4
ACL interface

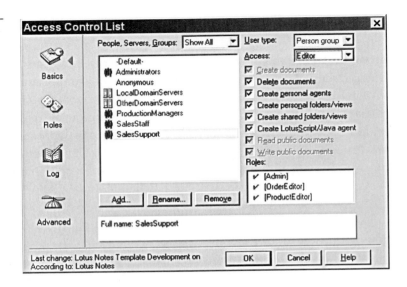

The ACL in Figure 41-4 looks very clean since it is not cluttered with many individual name entries. This is the second key to securing your application. By using groups rather than individuals, you can design the application security once, test and verify that all necessary restrictions are in place, and then roll out your application. This structure gives the application security the capability to scale beyond expectations and still maintain low administrative overhead.

The default access of your application is normally driven by company policy. For ABC, they have set the -Default- access to Author. For most applications, this is a sufficient since additional security can be placed on documents, or removed from them, depending on what the status or sensitivity is of the data in the document.

The Roles panel of the ACL control panel enables you to add, remove, and rename roles. When adding and renaming roles, there is no need to use brackets around your entries as you key them. In fact, the [and] characters are not allowed in role names, so just let Notes add the brackets as your entries are committed. Using roles enables you to better control the security, which we will see shortly. Since you use Roles to help the application security, you should be very careful when removing them or renaming them from applications that have existing documents in them, as you may lose access to key documents. In order to assign roles to users and groups, you must use the Basics tab and place a checkmark by each role you would like to assign to each entry.

The Log panel maintains a history of all modifications to the ACL. Any individual cannot remove this history, so an ACL audit can be done at any time. Selecting individual line items from the log will display the detail of the associated change.

The Advanced section of the ACL control panel provides the capability to control some powerful aspects of the application's security. These options are shown in Figure 41-5. Setting an administration server may be used as a way to propagate name changes throughout a Domino Domain. When an Administration server is set, and a person requests a name change, the Administration process, AdminP, will modify ACL entries for those names. For ABC company, there is no advantage to just using that option, since all ACL entries are group names. However, by setting the Modify Readers and Authors fields option, AdminP can ensure that no secured documents are "lost" as a result of a rename. We will discuss the use of Readers and Authors fields shortly.

Figure 41-5
ACL advanced
options

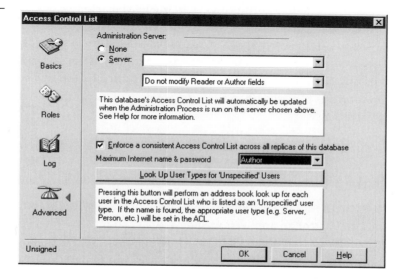

Database security is also driven by enforcement of the ACL. If the ACL is not enforced across all replicas of a database, local replicas can still be compromised. If this option is not set, then users have manager access to all local documents. Users will not be able to replicate the changes they have made in the local replica to the server's replica, based on the server's replica's ACL. Read access restriction on documents is not affected by enforcement of a consistent ACL on local replicas since users cannot replicate documents that they cannot see. This setting should only be turned on by extremely careful administrators because once enabled and replicated across an organization, there may be no way to recover or modify an ACL if all managers are accidentally removed.

Another very important advanced security setting is the *Maximum Internet name & password*. This setting defaults to Editor access but could also be set to *No Access* in order to restrict access to Notes client users only. A good practice is to at least restrict this setting to Author access. This assures that only documents that have been created by or assigned ownership to Web users would ever be modified by a Web user.

The *Look Up User Types for Unspecified Users* option is a nice tool for cleaning up ACLs that may have been modified or setup by a scripted agent or action item. Specifying user types is a good practice, especially for the group LocalDomainServers. Many companies use this as a backdoor into ACLs just in case the primary administration group is removed. If LocalDomainServers is unspecified, then an Administrator could add themselves into this group and regain Manager access to a database that does not name LocalDomainServers as a Server group user type.

The Domino server security flexibility is what makes an ideal enterprise solution. The Domino system may be designed to enable HTTP access to one set of servers while rejecting HTTP traffic on others. This is controlled by the services that are run on each Domino server. Based upon the load, number of users, and server topology, the services offered may vary.

Roles

Roles are a way to customize the security of an application centrally. By adding roles into the ACL of an application, a developer can preserve a security design, yet add and remove groups easily. Looking back at Figure 41-4, the SalesSupport user group has three different roles: Admin, ProductEditor, and OrderEditor. Since there is no "super user" account that automatically can be used to access and update secured documents, using and incorporating an Admin role into your database security model assures you documents will not get "lost" from removing all valid readers in a Readers field. Using descriptive names also helps each application's security model be easily understandable.

Adding roles into the application ACL does very little to the overall security of an application, but when used with form and view security settings, they can be very powerful. They are also very helpful in hide-when formulas for workflow applications to display data conveniently for those when needed to edit and approve documents and when only certain fields on a document contain sensitive data.

Agents

Agents, like macros, are great tools that can help processing and distributing data contained in Notes applications. Since LotusScirpt and Java agents can easily modify thousands of documents through the use of Backend Domino Object Model (DOM) classes, only a limited number of users should be allowed to run them. These are generally much more complex and powerful than simple agents that can be created as personal agents. The capability to run agents can be set for users with Author access or higher, but only Designers and higher can create shared agents. Only Managers always have the ability to run any of these kinds of scripts.

The capability to run an agent must also be correctly configured in the Agent Restrictions section of the Server document. Here you can restrict agents to a limited number of people in an organization. Normally allowing all users to run Personal agents is a safe setting. But you should limit the use of Restricted and Unrestricted LotusScript/Java agents to advanced Notes users such as developers and administrators. You might choose to let only a specific user run these types of agents. If you use this technique, all databases and agents should be signed by this user. Including the LocalDomainServers group is good practice too, so scheduled agents can function properly.

Agents still must conform to the ACL settings of the user that is executing an agent or the signer of a scheduled agent. So, running an agent to modify fields on a document will only update those documents that the user has edit privileges for through an Author field or Editor access in the ACL.

Document Level

Document-level security is the only true way to guarantee Domino security is maintained. Because of the many ways around application-level security, Domino enables the use of Readers, Authors, and signed fields to determine who can view and edit documents. These fields hold true through a Web browser as well as a Lotus Notes client.

By using Readers and Authors data type fields, document-level security can be set to assure that read and edit access is restricted to named parties. Readers fields can be created on a form to allow read access restrictions to documents. A Readers field consists of a list of names to be allowed read access to the document. Authors fields can be created on a form to give users with author access edit abilities to a document. Designing the use of these types of fields can be done in a few ways. For beginner and intermediate developers, the safest way to control document security is by setting it in the Form properties. In our example of ABC, Inc., they have used the Form properties to control which users can read documents created with the form (see Figures 41-6 and 41-7). Documents created with this form have two additional fields added to them. The $Readers field is a Readers data type field that lists all the groups and roles that were specified in the Form properties.

Selecting the *Disable printing/forwarding/coping to clipboard* option, a $KeepPrivate system field has been added with a value of 1. This field assures that data is referenced in the application so that only the most current information is viewable. If documents can be forwarded through email, they will lose the security that the application in which they were created has imposed on them.

Signed fields can also be created on a form to allow a digital signature to be attached when a document is saved or mailed. Digital signatures verify that authors are who they say they are and guarantee that the data in the document has not been tampered with.

Document security can be changed through the Document properties too. Opening the Security tab of the Document properties InfoBox (see Figure 41-8) gives users an easy way to restrict that can read a document. The major disadvantage of this technique is that a user can easily lock out security to only them, so that not even the server can see the document. Servers should always be able to see all documents as a practice in order to allow replication to occur.

Creating new fields that are Readers or Authors data types can also control document access. This method of controlling security is definitely for advanced developers and should contain hidden user groups and servers when applied. Creating a computed

Figures 41-6 and Figure 41-7 Form and Document properties

Figure 41-8
Security for
documents

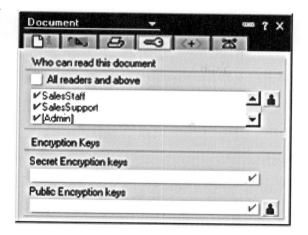

readers field that resolves to a formula based on the contents of another editable names-type field can do this. For example, if ABC, Inc. wanted to control readers of sensitive documents on a convenient as-needed basis, they could simply add a name to the Readers field. The hidden field is really controlling the read access and also adds a group and role. This technique enables good document security while giving the user community a way to easily limit read access. Additionally, access can be controlled to sections of a document. These sections operate on very similar principles as described earlier.

Section Level

Section-level access can be used to control edit access to only part of a document. ABC used a Controlled Access Section to enable who could approve or deny order requests. This control was set up using a simple technique that computes the approver when each document is created. Figure 41-9 shows how a *Computed when composed* setting on the Controlled Access Section forces a Names dialog to open as new order requests are created.

This is a simple example, but a controlled access section has other options too. It could be used to simply enable an editable list of document editors. Selecting the section and choosing Edit List from the Section Properties menu list would then modify this list. Otherwise, the Edit control could be a computed formula that enables only documents that haven't already been approved or denied to be edited.

PART VI

Figure 41-9
Controlled-access
section formula

Field Level

Within a document, another option can be used to secure data. Database designers can design fields that can be encrypted with an encryption key. To decrypt and read the document, users must have the same key. Fields may also be protected during form design from updates by authors after the initial document is created. Field property security options include an option specifying that a user must have at least editor access to use the field.

Field-level encryption is achieved by setting the Field property to enable encryption for this field and by setting the Form property to use a specific encryption key by choosing it from the list of available keys. Using the User ID dialog and choosing the Encryption section can create encryption keys. New keys may be created and existing keys may be mailed to other users. Note that only users with an ID file (no Web users) can participate in encryption.

View Level

Database views can also be used to control database security. These settings are normally used to hide administration views or maybe to only display views that are relevant to a set of users. Limiting the amount of views that are available to all users can help make an application easier to use, not to mention more secure. In our example of ABC, Inc., they could use views to display order requests that do not have a status in a special view that is only available to the SalesSupport and SalesStaff so they can approve or deny order requests, while the rest of the company can see all order requests that have either been approved or denied. Figure 41-10 displays the View properties InfoBox.

Figure 41-10
View Security

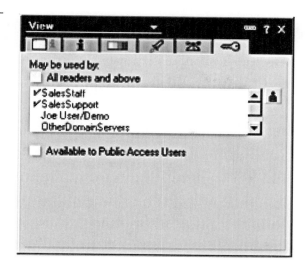

Summary

It should be clear by now that the Domino server is a robust application offering messaging, collaboration, and security. Domino can securely deliver the functionality that meets a company's current requirements and extend that functionality as their requirements change in the future.

To assure the Domino system in place today meets all a company's needs and requirements, a formal Domino security policy should be established to assure both end-user and administrators are aware of the level of security that should be applied to individual applications. This policy should be rigorously reviewed in light of the Domino security levels described earlier and the Domino network infrastructure accurately documented. These tasks will guarantee a secure Domino system at ABC, Inc. and your company for years to come.

Before taking the Domino Application Architecture exam, you should be able to plan and design applications to take all levels of Domino security into account. Use this chapter in combination with the other chapters throughout the book to gain a complete understanding of Domino security.

Review Questions

1. True or False: A central administration team must create encryption keys.
   a. True
   b. False

2. True or False: A user's groups and roles can be listed at any time using the Notes client software.
   a. True
   b. False

3. The ACL of a database must have which entry set greater than *No Access* in order to enter an application through a Web browser without authenticating?
   a. LocalDomainServers
   b. Anonymous
   c. WebUser
   d. WebAccess

4. True or False: It is good practice to list out names of individuals in the database ACL.
   a. True
   b. False

5. What is the minimum access required to edit all documents in a database?
   a. Manager
   b. Designer
   c. Editor
   d. Author

6. What property are you looking at when you are viewing a list of existing fields in a document?
   a. View properties
   b. Form properties
   c. Document properties
   d. Field properties

7. Which two places need to be configured in order to encrypt certain fields for every document created with a certain form?
   a. Field properties and Section properties
   b. Field properties and Form properties
   c. Form properties and Section properties
   d. View properties and Section properties

8. Which section of the ACL is where the *Enforce a Consistent ACL across all Replicas* property is set?
   a. Basics
   b. Roles
   c. Log
   d. Advanced

9. Rich looks at the ACL for the Domino Directory and sees that he has Editor access. Can Rich edit a document he can see?
   a. No.
   b. Yes.
   c. Yes, but there may be documents in the database with Readers fields that Rich cannot see.
   d. Yes, but Rich may only edit these documents on a local replica that does not enforce a consistent ACL.

10. Why should the server group LocalDomainServers always be able to have Reader access to all documents in a database?
   a. This gives Notes Administrators a back-door around Notes security.
   b. Then the server can replicate these documents to other servers.
   c. This gives the server editor rights to each document.
   d. The server can then run unrestricted agents on the documents.

Review Answers

1. **B is correct.**   Any user can create an encryption key by using the Encryption Keys section of the User ID dialog.

2. **A is correct.**   A user can check the groups and roles that apply to the application that they are in at any time. This dialog also checks which groups and roles apply to the access that is displayed.

3. **B is correct.**   If *Anonymous* is included in the ACL and set to *No Access*, a Web user is forced to authenticate when entering it if they have not yet authenticated.

4. **B is correct.**   Individual names should only be used in an ACL when there is only one person who needs the specified level of access. A good example of this is a user's mail file. Otherwise, groups should be the only entries in an ACL.

5. **C is correct.**   Author access only enables edit capabilities to documents created by that user. Both Designer and Manager access enable edits of all documents, but Editor access is the minimum.

6. **C is correct.**   The Document properties can be used to display a list of the fields on a document unless a database's design has been hidden.

7. **B is correct.**   Both of these properties must be used because the field must have the *Enable Encryption for this field* option selected and at least one default encryption key must be specified in the Security tab of the Form properties.

8. **D is correct.**   The Advanced section contains this and other more complicated settings.

9. **C is correct.**   There may, however, be documents in the database with Readers fields that Rich cannot see. Rich can edit all documents in the database, but if documents contain Readers fields that Rich is not listed in by group membership or explicitly, then Rich would not be able to see the documents to be able to edit them.

10. **B is correct.**   The server can replicate these documents to other servers. Although the group LocalDomainServers could possibly be used as a security back-door by listing the groups as unspecified in the ACL, the primary reason to include this group in all Readers fields is for Replication. If a server cannot see a document, then it cannot replicate it to another server.

CHAPTER 42

Design Applications That Integrate with Host Data

You should be able to answer questions based on the following objectives after reading this chapter:

- Overview of Lotus Enterprise Integrator (LEI) and its components
- Overview of Open Database Connectivity (ODBC)
- Utilize Structured Query Language (SQL)
- Maintain Data Integrity
- Design applications based on Data Integrity issues
- Design applications based for data percolation
- Design applications to integrate data from heterogeneous sources
- Design applications to integrate with host data in batches
- Design applications to integrate with host data in both directions
- Design applications to integrate with host data using ODBC
- Design applications to integrate with host data using SQL
- Design applications to integrate with host data via live connections
- Design applications to limit document size

Notes has always been known for its powerful workflow capabilities, but its capability to integrate back-end data into business applications gives developers and users the best of both worlds. This chapter describes how to use data integration tools and services to incorporate traditionally hard to reach data into you business applications. For additional information, including a description of Domino Enterprise Connection Services (DECS), refer to Chapter 19.

Lotus Enterprise Integrator (LEI)

Lotus Enterprise Integrator (LEI) is an enterprise integration tool that moves high volumes of data quickly between data sources and Notes applications. LEI is a multi-tasking server with an administrative application that is designed to support large scale data integration and transfer volume. LEI uses Domino Connectors, which are native connections between Domino and a variety of enterprise systems, to transfer the desired information. These connections allow Domino applications to connect, and authenticate and translate data with relational databases, ERP applications, TP systems, host-based systems and other external data sources. LEI is comprised of three main components:

- Lotus Enterprise Integrator Server
- Lotus Enterprise Integrator Development Client
- Lotus Enterprise Integrator Administrator

LEI Processing

Figure 42-1 outlines the components of the LEI architecture and the flow of data. Connections, MetaConnections, and Activities are created in the LEI Administrator. The LEI Server uses these definitions as instructions for what to execute. When the server finds an Activity that is scheduled to run, it executes that Activity. Activities define the actions that the LEI Server will perform.

Figure 42-1 shows how LEI is used to connect two different data sources, connection A being a Sybase database, and connection B being an Oracle database.

LEI Server

The LEI Server is the main component of the data integration process. The LEI Server polls the LEI Administrator database for instructions to execute, which are LEI Activities. LEI Activities can be either declared or scripted.

- **Declarative Activities**   These activities are form-based activities defined using the LEI Administrator.

- **Scripted Activities**   These activities are written in LotusScript, using Domino Connector LSX with the LEI LotusScript Extensions.

Once an activity is created, it can be run from the Administrator or from the operating system command line. The LEI Server performs the work in transferring data between data sources and destinations.

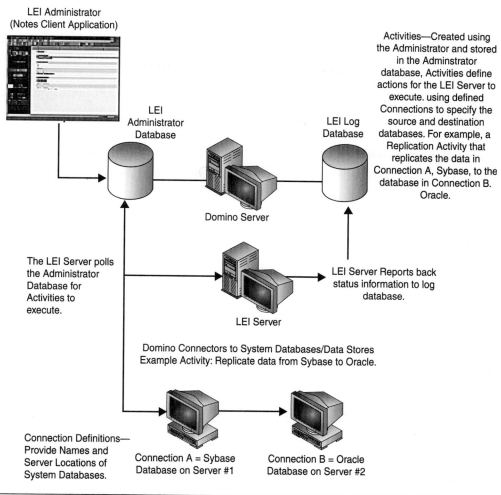

LEI Administrator
(Notes Client Application)

LEI
Administrator
Database

Domino Server

LEI Log
Database

Activities—Created using the Administrator and stored in the Adminstrator database, Activities define actions for the LEI Server to execute. using defined Connections to specify the source and destination databases. For example, a Replication Activity that replicates the data in Connection A, Sybase, to the database in Connection B. Oracle.

The LEI Server polls the Administrator Database for Activities to execute.

LEI Server Reports back status information to log database.

LEI Server

Domino Connectors to System Databases/Data Stores
Example Activity: Replicate data from Sybase to Oracle.

Connection Definitions— Provide Names and Server Locations of System Databases.

Connection A = Sybase Database on Server #1

Connection B = Oracle Database on Server #2

Figure 42-1   LEI data flow

LEI Development Client

The LEI Development Client is an extension to the LEI Administrator that provides development and testing of Scripted Activities without a full LEI Server installation. It allows for initial system setup and testing before they are added to the LEI Administrator database. Action buttons are available in the LEI Development Client for interactive browsing and field mapping of data.

LEI Administrator

The LEI Administrator is a Notes database, which allows developers and administrators to create and configure Connections and Activities to the desired host data source. The LEI Administrator is comprised of four Notes databases, which contain all the instructions for the environment. These instructions can be in the form of LEI Configurations, Connections, Metaconnections, or Activities.

LEI Connections

LEI Connections provide connectivity to the system databases. Connections contain the names and network locations of the source and target data repositories. LEI Connections can be created for the following data sources:

- IBM DB2
- IBI EDA/SQL
- File System
- Lightweight Directory Access Protocol (LDAP)
- Lotus Notes
- Notes Public Name and Address Book (NAB), a.k.a. the Domino Directory
- Open Database Connectivity (ODBC)
- Oracle Server
- Sybase SQL Server
- Text

Before Connections can be created, you need to establish connectivity to the Source database using the communications software that is specific to the data source.

LEI Metaconnections

A Metaconnection is a type of LEI Connection that provides additional functionality to enhance data processing, which regular Connections do not contain. A Metaconnection 'wraps' around the Activity, appearing to the Activity like the original Connection, and appearing to the Connection like an Activity. The different types of Metaconnectors are outlined here.

- **Order Metaconnector**   The Order Metaconnector is used to retrieve a consistent ordering of results from another Connection or Metaconnection. The Order Meta-connection wraps another Connection and orders the result set based on specific criteria.

- **Collapse/Expand Metaconnector**   The Collapse/Expand Metaconnector collapses multiple records using a common key value into a single record with multi-value fields, and expands multi-value fields into multiple records. You can think of the Collapse/Expand Metaconnector as performing an @Explode or @Implode. This Metaconnector collapses records on the fetch operations, and expands them on the write operations according to specific criteria.

- **Metering Metaconnector**   The Metering Metaconnector measures data access rates/volumes and provides other useful statistical usage information.

- **Connection Broker Metaconnector**   The Connection Broker Metaconnetion enables transfer of data between multiple data sources and destinations.

LEI Activities

Activities are the foundation of the LEI environment. A LEI Activity contains the instructions of what to do and when to do it. As previously mentioned, Activities can be created and tested in the Development Client to ensure proper functionality, or in the LEI Administrator once they are ready to be integrated into the LEI environment. Specific types of LEI Activities are

- **Admin-Backup Activity**   Allows a user to schedule and execute backups of the LEI Administrator databases.

- **Admin-Purge Logs Activity**   Allows a user to schedule and execute the purging of LEI logs.

- **Archive Activity**   Allows a user to schedule and execute regular archiving of your databases.

- **Command Activity**   Allows for the execution of operating system and database commands.

- **Direct Transfer Activity**   Allows a user to transfer data between a source and tar-get database by specifying a formula, usually using SQL, Notes formulas, or other data source-specific commands.

- **DPROPR Activity**   Allows you to migrate IBM DPROPR data to other LEI-supported databases.

- **Java Activity** Allows you to schedule LEI server data exchange for Java applications.

- **Polling Activity** Allows you to monitor data sources for specified conditions. When a specified condition is met, LEI executes the specified Activities.

- **RealTime Notes Activity** Enables a Notes database form for direct access to back end source data.

- **Replication Activity** Enables data synchronization between dissimilar databases.

- **Scripted Activity** Allows developers to create their own advanced scripted activities using LEI LotusScript Extensions.

LEI Logs

LEI tracks the system performance of the environment in a system log database. Like other log databases, these databases can be used to assess the performance of the activities of the LEI Server and troubleshoot any problems that may arise. LEI maintains three types of system logs:

- **Activity Logs** These logs track the individual Activities and provide their performance statistics.

- **Operation Logs** These logs track the errors that may occur when Activities are executed.

- **Server Logs** These logs track the operation and performance of the LEI servers.

Open Database Connectivity (ODBC)

Unlike LEI, a knowledge of certain scripts or formulas are required to access back-end data using Open Database Connectivity (ODBC). ODBC can be used to access relational databases such as DB2, Oracle, or Microsoft Access. Using formulas or scripts that are embedded in Domino objects, data can be integrated into Domino applications from many external sources. There are some additional steps that must be followed before ODBC can be used.

Files Required to Use ODBC

When you install Domino Designer, the necessary ODBC modules that support external data access are installed automatically. In addition to the Domino ODBC modules, you will need an ODBC library and a driver for each type of database you want to access. For example, if you are running the Windows 95 operating system, you will need the following modules on your computer:

- **The ODBC 2.0 interface** The ODBC interface defines the library of ODBC functions that perform the connection, query, and data-retrieval processes. The ODBC interface is available from Microsoft.

- **The Driver Manager** The Driver Manager loads the necessary drivers used to access the data and is the interface between Domino and the drivers. The Driver Manager is available from Microsoft.

- **The ODBC Drivers** The ODBC Drivers handle communications between the Driver Manger and the specified databases. Each driver affects the specific capabilities of your application and comes with it's own installation, configuration, and Help documentation. These drivers are available from third-party vendors or through the Lotus Web site.

Registering Data Sources for ODBC

The first step in using ODBC to connect to external data sources is to register the necessary data source. This tells the ODBC driver manager where to find the data source you want to access. Registering a data source creates a connection from a particular ODBC driver with the data to be accessed. The registration information includes the data you want to access, the data's associated server or directory, the back-end DBMS, and the network platform. To register a data source, use the Windows Control Panel, Windows ODBC Administrator Utility, or a script or formula. The most common method for creating data sources is to use the Windows Control Panel. Follow these steps to create a new data source using the Windows Control Panel:

1. Choose Start...Settings...Control Panel.

2. Click the ODBC icon. This will open the main ODBC control panel.

3. Click Add to create a new data source or select a data source from the list and select Configure to update an existing data source.

4. Select the necessary driver and click OK or Finish. This will bring up a dialog box to enter the properties for your new data source.

5. Enter the data source name, description, and requested information.

6. Click Select to find the directory and database file that this data source will connect to.

7. Once all the necessary information has been entered, click OK to create the data source.

Writing Formulas and Scripts to Access Relational Databases

Relational databases can be accessed by ODBC by using formula language or LotusScript. The following @Functions can be used to external databases to return a value or a list of values:

- **@DBColumn**   This formula returns all the values in one column of a table, or all the distinct values.

- **@DBLookup**   This formula returns selected values in one column of a table by matching keys.

- **@DBCommand**   This formula passes a command to an external DBMS and returns the result.

@DBColumn

Syntax:
@DBColumn("ODBC":"NoCache";data_source;user_ID1:user_ID2;password1:password2;table;column:null_handling;"Distinct":sort)

Parameters:
- **"ODBC"**   Keyword. Indicates that you are accessing an ODBC data source.

- **"NoCache"**   Keyword. Optional. If you want to ensure Notes retrieves that latest information for every lookup, specify this option. Omit "NoCache" if you want the results to be cached.

- **Data_source**   Text. The name of the external data source being accessed.

- **User_ID1: user_ID2**   Text list. The user Ids needed to connect to the external database.

- **Password1: password2**   Text list. The passwords required by the user Ids.

- **Table**: The name of the database table being accessed.

- **Column**   Text. The name of the column from which data is being retrieved.

- **Null_handling** Text. Specifies how null values are treated when the data is retrieved.

- **"Distinct"** Keyword. Optional. Removes duplicate values from the list before returning data.

- **Sort** Keyword. Specify "Ascending" to sort the list of values into ascending order. Specify "Descending" to sort the list in descending order.

Example

@DBColumn("ODBC";"NAMES";"";"";"FEMALE";"First_Name")

First_Name	Middle_Name	Last_Name
Debra	Anne	Smith
Kathy	Marie	Jones
Patricia	Lynn	Conner

This example will return a list of First Names ("Debra":"Kathy":"Patricia") from with the Female table using the NAMES database.

@DBLookup

Syntax:

@DBLookup("ODBC":"NoCache";data_source;user_ID1:user_ID2;password1:password2;table;column:null_handling;"key_column;"key";"Distinct":sort)

Parameters:

- **"ODBC"** Keyword. Indicates that you are accessing an ODBC data source.

- **"NoCache"** Keyword. Optional. If you want to ensure Notes retrieves that latest information for every lookup, specify this option. Omit "NoCache" if you want the results to be cached.

- **Data_source** Text. The name of the external data source being accessed.

- **User_ID1: user_ID2** Text list. The user Ids needed to connect to the external database.

- **Password1: password2** Text list. The passwords required by the user Ids.

- **Table** The name of the database table being accessed.

- **Column** Text. The name of the column from which data is being retrieved.

- **Null_handling**   Text. Specifies how null values are treated when the data is retrieved.

- **Key_Column**   Text. The name of the column used for key matching.

- **Key**   Text, number, date-time, or a list. The value to be looked up in the key_column.

- **"Distinct"**   Keyword. Optional. Removes duplicate values from the list before returning data.

- **Sort**   Keyword. Specify "Ascending" to sort the list of values into ascending order. Specify "Descending" to sort the list in descending order.

Example

@DBLookup("ODBC";"NAMES";"";"";"FEMALE";"AGE";"First_Name";"Debra": "Patricia")

First_Name	Middle_Name	Last_Name	Age
Debra	Anne	Smith	25
Kathy	Marie	Jones	18
Patricia	Lynn	Conner	42

This example will return the corresponding Ages (25:42) of the requested First_Name ("Debra":"Patricia").

@DBCommand

Syntax:
@DBLookup("ODBC":"NoCache";data_source;user_ID1:user_ID2;password1:password2;command_string;null_handling)

Parameters:
- **"ODBC"**   Keyword. Indicates that you are accessing an ODBC data source.

- **"NoCache"**   Keyword. Optional. If you want to ensure Notes retrieves that latest information for every lookup, specify this option. Omit "NoCache" if you want the results to be cached.

- **Data_source**   Text. The name of the external data source being accessed.

- **User_ID1: user_ID2**   Text list. The user Ids needed to connect to the external database.

- **Password1: password2**   Text list. The passwords required by the user Ids.

- **Command_string**   Text. An SQL statement, command statement, or name of a procedure to be executed.

- **Null_handling**   Text. Specifies how null values are treated when the data is retrieved.

Example

@DBCommand("ODBC";"NAMES";"";"";"SELECT Name FROM FEMALE WHERE Age=18")

First_Name	Middle_Name	Last_Name	Age
Debra	Anne	Smith	25
Kathy	Marie	Jones	18
Patricia	Lynn	Conner	42

   This example builds an SQL statement that searches the FEMALE table for any records with an Age=18 and returns the Name. In the table above, Kathy would be the only record in the result set. The key to returning the correct information is the SQL, which will be described later in this chapter.

The LotusScript Data Object (LS:DO)

The LotusScript Data Object is a LSX-compliant module that allows you to use LotusScript to write applications that use data from external non-Notes data sources. LS:DO is a set of three LotusScript classes that contain many properties and methods:

- ODBCConnection
- ODBCQuery
- ODBCResultSet

   Using LS:DO, you can write a LotusScript function to perform the following operations:

- Look up or retrieve data stored in external databases.

- Validate information in a Notes database with data stored in an external database.

- Update data stored in an external database.

Unlike LEI, LS:DO is best used for small volumes of data and could have decreased performance when processing large amounts of data.

Creating an ODBCConnection

The following ODBCConnection Properties and Methods are taken from Domino 5 Designer Help. Please refer to this database for additional documentation.

Properties:

- **AutoCommit**   Read-Write. Indicates if auto-commit mode is in effect.

- **CommitOnDisconnect**   Read-Write. Indicates whether pending transactions are committed or rolled back on disconnect.

- **DataSourceName**   Read-only. The ODBC name of the connected data source.

- **GetLSDOMasterRevision**   Read-only. The revision level of the ODBC LSX.

- **SilentMode**   Read-write. Prevents display of a User ID and Password dialog box during program execution.

Methods:

- **CommitTransactions**   Commits changes when transaction mode is in effect. This applies to all transactions pending through the connection, and takes no arguments.

- **ConnectTo**   Connects to a data source.

- **Disconnec**   Disconnects from the data source.

- **GetError**   Returns the latest error code for an ODBC object.

- **GetErrorMessage**   Returns the short error message text associated with an error code.

- **GetExtendedErrorMessage**   Returns the long, descriptive error message text associated with an error code.

- **IsConnected**   Indicates whether the connection object still exists.

- **IsSupported**   Indicates whether an option is supported by the data source.

- **ListDataSources**   Lists all registered data sources as an array.

- **ListFields**   Returns an array of field (column) names in a table.

- **ListProcedures**   Lists the executable procedures at the connected data source.

- **ListTables**   Lists the available tables in a connected data source.

- **RollbackTransactions**   Rolls back changes when transaction mode is in effect. This applies to all uncommitted transactions pending through the connection, and takes no arguments.

ODBCConnection Example

Add the following line to the agent Declarations or wherever the script is being used. Uselsx "*LSXODBC"

```
Sub Initialize
   Dim con as New ODBCConnection
   Con.ConnectTo("DataSourceName")
   While Not con.IsConnected
        Messagebox("Connection to External Database Failed.")
        Exit Sub
   Wend
   Messagebox("Connected to " & con.DataSourceName)
   Con.Disconnect
End Sub
```

The example above declares a new ODBCConnection (con) and uses the data source "DataSourceName" to connect to the corresponding host database. If the connection was a success, a message will appear saying "Connected to DataSource Name," if the connection fails, a message will appear letting the user know the connection has failed.

Creating an ODBCQuery and ODBCResultSet

After the ODBCConnection has been made, the ODBCQuery is created using SQL to obtain the ODBCResultSet. The ODBCQuery defines which records to return from the data source; the result is the ODBCResultSet. The following ODBCQuery and ODBCResultSet Properties and Methods are taken from Domino 5 Designer Help. Please refer to this database for additional documentation.

ODBCQuery

Properties:
- **Connection**   Write-only. Relates a connection object with a query.

- **QueryExecuteTimeOut**   Read-write. Specifies a time-out value in seconds for query execution.

- **SQL**   Read-write. Any SQL statement.

- **UseRowID**   Specifies whether data in the back-end database will be accessed by row ID.

Methods:

- **GetError**   Returns the latest error code for an ODBC object.

- **GetErrorMessage**   Returns the short error message text associated with an error code.

- **GetExtendedErrorMessage**   Returns the long, descriptive error message text associated with an error code.

ODBCResultSet

Properties:

- **CacheLimit**   Read-write. The maximum number of rows to be cached in memory.

- **CurrentRow**   Read-write. The number of the current row in a result set, starting from row 1.

- **FetchBatchSize**   Read-write. Specifies the number of records that will be fetched at any one time. The default is 1 (get just the requested record).

- **MaxRows**   Read-write. Specifies the number of records that will be fetched at any one time. The default is 1 (get just the requested record).

- **Query**   Write-only. Relates an ODBCQuery object with a result set.

- **ReadOnly**   Read-write. Indicates if a result set is read-only. Can be set to True to prevent updates.

Methods:

- **AddRow**   Adds a workspace for a new row.

- **Close**   Closes a result set.

- **DeleteRow**   Deletes the record represented by the current row of the result set from the specified table in the external database.

- **ExecProcedure**   Executes a stored SQL procedure.

- **Execute**   Executes an SQL statement.

- **FieldExpectedDataType**   Gets or sets the data type for a column.

- **FieldID**   Returns the field ID of a field as an integer value, given the field name.

- **FieldInfo**   Returns an array of field information.

- **FieldName**   Returns the field name for a specified column, given its ID (column number).

- **FieldNativeDataType**   Returns the native data type for that column given a specific column.

- **FieldSize**   Returns the maximum size of data for a field.

- **FirstRow**   Sets the current row to the first row in a result set. Equivalent to setting CurrentRow to 1.

- **GetError**   Returns the latest error code for an ODBC object.

- **GetErrorMessage**   Returns the short error message text associated with an error code.

- **GetExtendedErrorMessage**   Returns the long, descriptive error message text associated with an error code.

- **GetParameter**   Returns the last value set for the specified parameter.

- **GetParameterName**   Retrieves a parameter name.

- **GetRowStatus**   Returns the alteration status of the current row.

- **GetValue**   Retrieves the value of the column referenced by **column_id%**, and copies the results to the **variable** field.

- **HasRowChanged**   Indicates if values in the current row have changed in the data source; that is, indicates if values differ from what was fetched into the result set.

- **IsBeginOfData**   indicates whether the cursor position is at the beginning of the result set.

- **IsEndOfData**   Indicates if the cursor position is at the end of the result set.

- **IsResultSetAvailable**   Indicates if the execution of a query yielded any data.

- **IsValueAltered**   Indicates whether a column value was altered by SetValue.

- **IsValueNull**   Indicates whether a column value is a null data value.

- **LastRow**   Sets the current row position to the last row in the result set.

- **LocateRow**   Identifies records that match a specified field value.

- **NextRow**   Sets the current row position to the next row in a result set.

- **NumColumns**   Is the number of columns in a result set.

- **NumParameters**   Returns the number of parameters in an SQL statement.

- **NumRows**   Is the number of rows in a result set.

- **PrevRow**   Positions the current row pointer at the previous row.

- **SetParameter**   Sets the replacement value for the specified parameter.
- **SetValue**   Sets a new value to a column.
- **UpdateRow**   Updates the current row, if changed, to the database.

The following example creates a query that retrieves all the rows in the EMPLOYEE table of the COMPANY data source.

Add the following line to the agent Declarations or wherever the script is being used.
Uselsx "*LSXODBC"

```
Sub Initialize
  Dim Con as New ODBCConnection
  Dim Qry as New ODBCQuery
  Dim Result as New ODBCResultSet
  Dim fName as String
  Dim lName as String
  Dim msg as String
  Set qry.Connection 5 con
  Set result.Query 5 qry
  Con.ConnectTo("COMPANY")
  Qry.SQL 5 "SELECT * FROM EMPLOYEE"
  Result.Execute
  Msg 5 "Employee names:" & Chr(10)
  If result.IsResultSetAvailable then
  Do
       Result.NextRow
       FName 5 result.GetValue("FName",FName)
       LName 5 result.GetValue("LName",LName)
       Msg 5 Msg & Chr(10) & Fname & " " & Lname
  Loop Until result.IsEndOfData
  Messagebox msg,,"Employee Names"
  Result.Close(DB_CLOSE)
  Else
  Mesagebox "Cannot get result set for EMPLOYEES"
  Exit Sub
  End If
Con.Disconnect
End Sub
```

In this example, a ODBCConnection is established using a data source called "Data-SourceName." Once the connection is made, an SQL statement is used to determine the result set, "SELECT * FROM EMPLOYEE." After the ODBCResultSet is created, the script loops through every record in the result set and builds the Msg string with information from each record. When the script reaches the end of the result set, the final Msg string is displayed; in this example, it will be a list of employee names. If the result set could not be established using the given SQL statement, a message is displayed, "Cannot get result set for EMPLOYEES."

Example

In this example, we will import information from a Microsoft Access Database that contains employee information for a given company. The ODBC script is contained within a LotusScript agent, which should be run manually from a Notes database. So the first step is to create ODBC connection to the Access Database. Following the steps previously outlined, we create a new ODBC data source from the Windows Control Panel. The MS Access Database is highlighted (because we are connecting to an Access Database), and we click *Add*. After clicking *Add*, the ODBC Microsoft Access Setup dialog box will appear. We must give the data source a name; for our example, the data source name will be "Employee." After the unique name has been added, the location of the database must be defined; this is done by clicking *Select* and mapping to the corresponding directory of the database. Once the database has been located, the dialog box should look like the following:

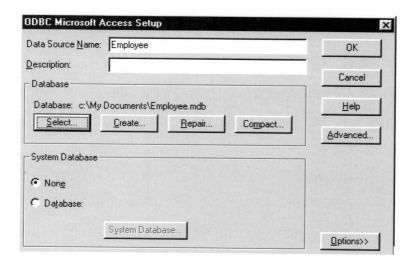

Once all the information in the ODBC Microsoft Access Setup dialog box is correct, click *OK* to complete the setup of the Data Source connection. Now it is time to create the LotusScript agent, which will connect to the Access Database. Open up the existing Notes database, which the Employee information will be imported into, and create a new Agent. The agent should be a LotusScript agent, which will run manually from the Actions menu on all documents in the database. The Agent setup should look like the following:

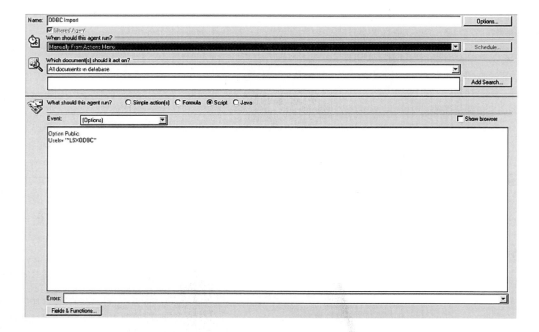

Since this agent will be using the LotusScript Data Object, "Uselsx "*LSXODBC"" had been added to the Options event of the agent. Now that the agent is created, it is time to create the script to connect to the data source, which is done within the Initialize event of the script.

```
Sub Initialize
    Dim Session As New NotesSession
    Dim db As NotesDatabase
    Dim NewEmployee As NotesDocument
    Dim con As New ODBCConnection
    Dim rs As New ODBCResultSet
    Dim query As New ODBCQuery
    Dim sql As String
```

The elements that will be used in the agent are declared in the first eight lines of the agent. For each record of the Access database, a corresponding NewEmployee document will be created in the Notes database. Once the elements have been declared, the next lines will set values to these elements.

```
Set db = Session.CurrentDatabase

'Set up the ODBC connection to the Access Database
Call con.ConnectTo("Employee")
sql = "SELECT * from Employee"

If Not con.IsConnected Then
    Msgbox "Unable to connect to the Access Database"
    Exit Sub
End If

Set query.connection = con
query.sql = sql

Set rs.Query = query
```

The second line in the code above connects to the data source we created in the Control Panel, "Employee." The next line creates the SQL statement which will be used to define our result set, in this example we will be selecting all records within the Employee table of the Access database. After the connection and SQL has been established, it is time to perform the main function of the agent.

```
RS.Execute

Do
    rs.NextRow

    'Create a new Employee document for each record in the Access Database.
    Set NewEmployee = db.createdocument
    NewEmployee.form = "Employee"
    NewEmployee.SSN= rs.GetValue("SSN")
    NewEmployee.Name = rs.GetValue("FullName")
    NewEmployee.Manager = rs.GetValue("ManagerName")
    NewEmployee.Title = rs.GetValue("Title")
    NewEmployee.Salary = rs.GetValue("Salary")
    NewEmployee.Location = rs.GetValue("Location")

    Call NewEmployee.save(True,True)

Loop Until RS.IsEndOfData

con.disconnect
Exit Sub

End Sub
```

PART VI

The main function of the agent loops through all the records of the Access database, and for each record, creates a new Employee Notes document and populates the necessary fields from the Relational database. Once the end of the result set is reached, the connection to the Access database is closed and the agent is exited. Now we have a Notes database that contains the same information as the Access database.

Using Structured Query Language (SQL)

The most common use of Structured Query Language (SQL) when accessing back-end data sources is to limit search, or the result set of information. The host data source may contain thousands of records which would cause a decrease in performance if a Notes application had to process all of these records just to find a smaller subset of documents. There are a number of supported SQL statements that work in ODBC, but the commands most widely used are WHERE, ORDER BY, GROUP BY, and HAVING. These clauses are used to modify the SELECT statement to create the SQL query:

- **WHERE**   The WHERE clause specifies criteria that records must match in order to be retrieved by the query.

  Example: `SELECT * FROM STUDENTS WHERE Name=Darrell`

  This example will return all records that have Name=Darrell from the STUDENTS table.

- **ORDER BY**   The ORDER BY clause specifies which field the retrieved records should be sorted by, in either ascending or descending order.

  Example: `SELECT Total FROM SALES ORDER BY Month`

  This example will return all the Totals from the SALES table and order the results by Month.

- **GROUP BY**   The GROUP BY clause defines a summary query.

  Example: `SELECT Total FROM SALES GROUP BY Employee`

  This example will return a summary of Sum from the SALES table and will group the results by Employee.

only used with   group by

- **HAVING**   The HAVING clause is used only with the GROUP BY clause, and it specifies a condition for the GROUP BY clause.

  Example: `SELECT Total FROM SALES GROUP BY Employee HAVING Name=Mike`

  Building on the previous example, HAVING will further limit the results by adding an additional condition to the GROUP BY statement. This example will return a summary of Sum from the SALES table and will group the results by Employees having Name=Mike.

In previous examples in this chapter, SQL statements were used in almost every type of ODBC formula. SQL statements were used to pass commands using @Formulas, more specify the @Command statement. When using LS:DO to connect to host data, the SQL statement is the most important part of the script to ensure that the correct records are retrieved in the result set.

Example

Building on the example from the last section, let's say we wanted to import information from multiple tables of the Access database, and only for one location. This can be accomplished by modifying the SQL statement within the script. For our example, we want to store employee's personal information in the Notes database, which is stored in the Personal table of the Access database. The primary key that links the two tables is the employee's SSN. To accomplish this, the SQL statement would look like this:

```
'Set up the ODBC connection to the Access Database
Call con.ConnectTo("Employee")
sql = "SELECT * FROM ((Personal INNER JOIN SSN ON Personal.SSN = Employee.SSN)" &_
"WHERE Employee.Location=Chicago) Order By Personal.SSN"
```

The SQL statement joins the Personal table with the Employee table using the primary key: SSN. We only want a single location, so the WHERE statement is used to define our result set. Now that our result set contains information from the two tables, and only contains information for employees with a location of Chicago, we can loop through the result set and create Notes documents.

```
Do
    rs.NextRow

    'Create a new Employee document for each record in the Access Database.
    Set NewEmployee = db.createdocument
    NewEmployee.form = "Employee"
    NewEmployee.SSN= rs.GetValue("SSN")
    NewEmployee.Name = rs.GetValue("FullName")
    NewEmployee.Manager = rs.GetValue("ManagerName")
    NewEmployee.Title = rs.GetValue("Title")
    NewEmployee.Salary = rs.GetValue("Salary")
    NewEmployee.Location = rs.GetValue("Location")

    'Add Personal information from the Personal table.
    NewEmployee.HomeAddress= rs.GetValue("HomeAddress")
    NewEmployee.HomePhone= rs.GetValue("HomePhone")
    NewEmployee.HomeFax= rs.GetValue("HomeFax")
    NewEmployee.HomeEmail= rs.GetValue("HomeEmail")

    Call NewEmployee.save(True,True)

Loop Until RS.IsEndOfData
```

In addition to importing the information from the Employee table, we are also pulling information from the Personal table and storing the information in the Notes database.

Maintaining Data Integrity

Data integrity is always an issue when information is being used in multiple locations. The Notes server uses the replication task to align data in multiple locations to ensure that a user will always see the correct data, but it is not that easy when using ODBC or LEI to access back-end data. This chapter has outlined a few different ways to connect to back-end databases, but when should you use formula languages versus LS:DO or LEI, and how can you assume the data you retrieve is the correct data? These are common questions that users and developers should ask themselves. The first sections described how to access data using LEI. The majority of LEI activities run on schedules, which means data may not always be updated when a user accesses the information in the Notes application. The advantage to using LEI as opposed to ODBC or formula language is that it can transfer large volumes of data in shorter amounts of time, and it does not involve any programming to do so. The main difference between using formula language as opposed to LS:DO is that you cannot write data back to the back-end data source when using formula language. The primary use of formula language and ODBC would be to display information or report generation for users. Formula language can display information at any given time, but if the application involves making calculations and then writing the results back to the back-end data source, formula language may not be the best choice. If the Notes application involved calculations and writing the results back to the host database immediately, LS:DO would be the best choice. It is up to the users of the database and the database designers to weigh what is more important when designing the Notes application.

Example

[handwritten: Complicated calculations : Formula Language not au gotten.]

Using the agent created in the first example, we can make changes to our script that will ensure data integrity with the back-end Access database. First, we must declare additional elements to accomplish our new task.

```
Sub Initialize
    Dim Session As New NotesSession
    Dim db As  NotesDatabase
    Dim EmployeeView As NotesView
    Dim EmployeeDoc As NotesDocument
    Dim NewEmployee As NotesDocument
    Dim con As New ODBCConnection
    Dim rs As New ODBCResultSet
    Dim query As New ODBCQuery
    Dim sql As String
    Dim key As Variant
```

In this example, we have added EmployeeDoc, EmployeeView, and key, which will be used to check for an existing Employee document. Next, values are set to the elements that have been declared.

```
Set db = Session.CurrentDatabase
Set EmployeeView = db.GetView("EmployeeBySSN")

'Set up the ODBC connection to the Access Database
Call con.ConnectTo("Employee")
sql = "SELECT * from Employee"

If Not con.IsConnected Then
    Msgbox "Unable to connect to the Access Database"
    Exit Sub
End If

Set query.connection = con
query.sql = sql

Set rs.Query = query
```

The new EmployeeView is a view within the Notes database that contains existing Employee documents and is sorted by the SSN field.

```
RS.Execute

Do
    rs.NextRow
    'The key to the search is the Employee Social Security Number
    key = rs.getvalue("SSN")

    'Search the Notes Database for an existing empoyee using the SSN
    Set EmployeeDoc = EmployeeView.GetDocumentByKey(key)
```

Similar to previous examples, our script will loop through all the records in the Access database, but this time we will search the view for an existing Employee document using a unique key; in this case it is SSN.

```
    'If the search by SSN returns no document, it must be a new employee so create a new Employee document.
    If EmployeeDoc Is Nothing Then
        Set NewEmployee = db.createdocument
        doc.form = "Employee"
        NewEmployee.SSN= rs.GetValue("SSN")
        NewEmployee.Name = rs.GetValue("FullName")
        NewEmployee.Manager = rs.GetValue("ManagerName")
        NewEmployee.Title = rs.GetValue("Title")
        NewEmployee.Salary = rs.GetValue("Salary")
        NewEmployee.Location = rs.GetValue("Location")

        Call NewEmployee.save(True,True)
    Else
        EmployeeDoc.SSN= rs.GetValue("SSN")
        EmployeeDoc.Name = rs.GetValue("FullName")
        EmployeeDoc.Manager = rs.GetValue("ManagerName")
        EmployeeDoc.Title = rs.GetValue("Title")
        EmployeeDoc.Salary = rs.GetValue("Salary")
        EmployeeDoc.Location = rs.GetValue("Location")

        Call EmployeeDoc.save(True,True)

    End If

Loop Until RS.IsEndOfData

con.disconnect
Exit Sub
```

If the search of the view returns an existing Employee document, a new document is not created and the information in the Notes database is updated with the information from the Access database. If the search returns no documents, this represents a new employee, and a new Employee document is created in the Notes database with the necessary information. This agent will not only import new documents into the Notes database, but it will maintain data integrity with existing documents and the Access database.

Summary

Lotus Enterprise Integrator (LEI) is an enterprise integration tool that moves high volumes of data quickly between data sources and Notes applications. LEI is a multi-tasking server with an administrative application that is designed to support large-scale data integration and transfer volume. LEI uses Domino Connectors, which are native connections between Domino and a variety of enterprise systems, to transfer the desired information. These connections allow Domino applications to connect, authenticate, and translate data with relational databases, ERP applications, TP systems, host-based systems, and other external data sources. LEI is comprised of three main components: Lotus Enterprise Integrator Server, Lotus Enterprise Integrator Development Client, and the Lotus Enterprise Integrator Administrator. The LEI Server polls the LEI Administrator database for instructions or Activities to execute. The LEI Development Client is an extension to the LEI Administrator that provides development and testing of Scripted Activities without being in the LEI environment. The LEI Administrator is a Notes database, which allows developers and administrators to create and configure Connections and Activities to the desired host data source. The instructions within the LEI Administrator can be in the form of LEI Configurations, Connections, Metaconnections, or Activities. Connections contain the names and network locations of the source and target-data repositories. A Metaconnection is a type of LEI Connection that provides additional functionality to enhance data processing. An Activity contains the instructions of what to do and when to do it. ODBC can also be used to access back-end data by writing formulas or scripts that are embedded in Domino objects. @Formulas can be used to only read data as opposed to LS:DO, which can be used to read and write to back-end data sources. There are three ODBC @Formulas: @DBColumn, @DBLookup, and @Command. The LotusScript Data Object is a LSX-compliant module that allows you to use LotusScript to write applications that use data from external non-Notes data sources. LS:DO is a set of three LotusScript classes: ODBCConnection, ODBCQuery, and ODBCResultSet. The ODBCConnection uses a predefined data source within the ODBC Control Panel and connects to the respective database. Once the ODBCConnection has been made, the ODBCQuery is created using SQL to obtain the ODBCResultSet. The ODBCQuery defines which records to return from the data source; the result is the ODBCResultSet. The most common use of Structured Query Language (SQL) when accessing back-end data sources is to limit search or the result set of information. Use this chapter in combination with Chaper 19 to prepare for questions on date integrity and integration with host data.

Review Questions

1. True or False: Lotus Enterprise Integrator is designed for small volume data transfers.
   a. True
   b. False

2. Which of the following are components of the Lotus Enterprise Integrator environment?
   a. Lotus Integrator Server
   b. Lotus Integrator Development Client
   c. Lotus Integrator Administrator
   d. All of the above

3. True or False: The instructions created in the Lotus Integrator Administrator can be Connections, MetaConnections, or Activities.
   a. True
   b. False

4. True or False: The LEI Operations Log tracks individual Activities and provides the performance statistics.
   a. True
   b. False

5. Which formula returns selected values in one column of a table by matching keys?
   a. @DBColumn
   b. @DBLookup
   c. @DBCommand
   d. None of the above

6. True or False: The ODBCConnection uses a pre-defined data source from the Windows Control Panel to connect to a back-end database.
   a. True
   b. False

7. Which of the following elements is used to define which records are returned into a ODBCResultSet?
   a. Activities
   b. ODBCConnection
   c. ODBCQuery
   d. None of the above

8. Which is not a valid SQL statement?
   a. SELECT * FROM EMPLOYEE
   b. SELECT Name FROM EMPLOYEE WHERE Age=25
   c. SELECT Total FROM SALES GROUP BY Employee
   d. All of the above
   e. None of the above

Review Answers

1. **B** is correct.   Lotus Enterprise Integrator is designed to transfer large volumes of data in a short amount of time.

2. **D** is correct.   Lotus Integrator Server, Lotus Integrator Development Client and Lotus Integrator Administrator are all components of the LEI environment.

3. **A** is correct.   The instructions created in the Lotus Integrator Administrator can be Connections, MetaConnections or Activities.

4. **B** is correct.   The LEI Activity Log tracks individual Activities and provides the performance statistics.

5. **B** is correct.   @DBLookup returns selected values in one column of a table by matching keys?

6. A is correct. The ODBCConnection uses a pre-defined data source from the Windows Control Panel to connect to a back-end database.

7. C is correct. The ODBCQuery is a SQL statement that defines which records are returned into a ODBCResultSet.

8. E is correct. All the SQL statements are valid.

CHAPTER 43

Planning for Modes of Usage

You should be able to answer questions based on the following objectives after reading this chapter:

- Plan applications integrated with the Web
- Plan for access mode
- Plan for connected usage
- Plan for constantly connected usage
- Plan for remote access mode
- Plan for usage
- Plan for disconnected usage

Domino applications can be very flexible. When it comes to planning how your application will be made available to your user community, you should carefully decide what restrictions should be placed on it and how your application can be accessed. With the Internet more popular than ever, many companies are now scrambling to make their Notes applications accessible through Web browsers. Although there may be some good reasons to do this, Notes applications may not always need to be made available through a Web browser. Additionally, as today's users are more and more mobile, another decision needs to be made about making an application available to offline users as well as the traditional "connected" users.

Most companies have a vision and a direction about what modes of usage are to be made available to users of Domino-based applications. After the Domino administration team configures the underlying infrastructure to provide the core services that are needed, it is normally left to the developer to make the rest happen. So developers should make it their responsibility as early on in the development cycle as possible to determine what modes of usage are necessary and focus on meeting those needs. That isn't to say that developers should discourage the use of multiple modes of use. Developers should just make sure to accommodate the varying needs, and allow for any extra development time that may be required when setting timelines and delivery dates ,as we will soon see.

In addition to the material contained in this chapter, you should refer to the material in Part III to prepare for the Domino Application Architecture exam. Pay special attention to Chapter 43.

Web Versus Notes

Applications that are designed for both Web browser users and for Notes client users can easily become very complex. Fortunately, most Domino implementations are rolled out within organizations, so the Web browser users can at least be controlled to some extent. Writing Domino applications for the Internet can require a great deal more testing, and often requires the use of duplicate forms to handle Netscape versus Explorer users. To simplify our discussion here, let's focus on the needs of a corporate intranet.

Our example company, ABC Inc., wants to make the application designed to help their field sales staff available through their Web browser. The first thing that should be done when a company first moves to Web-enabling any application is to make a complete audit of those applications that are on the server that will now serve the Notes applications as Web pages. As we mentioned back in Chapter 41 when discussing security, server browsing should be disabled for any production server, and the *Maximum Internet name & password* access should be set to *No Access* for all applications that are not designed to be accessed via a Web browser.

A couple of database properties make a big difference when designing Web applications too. The first is the Web access checkboxes on the Info tab of the Database properties, as shown in Figure 43-1. By checking the *Web Access: Use JavaScript when generating pages* option, you gain more flexibility over the way your custom forms can be used. These extend beyond the performance gains that are made when JavaScript is used to generate pages by evaluating formulas, actions, and hotspots only when they are clicked rather than all at once when the page is displayed. The most obvious difference is that Domino doesn't create a submit button when displaying forms. Without this option enabled, the first button on a form automatically becomes a submit button

Figure 43-1
Info tab of the
Database properties

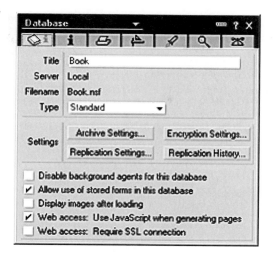

and all other buttons are not displayed. Enabling the option also gives you the flexibility of using hotspots as submit buttons, so you can use images to enhance the presentation of your submit button. And if you want to use more than one button, go ahead. If you are migrating old applications from a release 4.5 environment or don't have it checked on an existing Web application, be careful though as enabling this option can create unexpected side effects.

The *Web access: Require SSL connection* is a good security checkpoint. Requiring Web users to access data in your application with Secure Sockets Layer (SSL) connections forces an additional layer of protection onto the data stored in the application by encrypting the data that is requested and posted from the browser. This setting can also be enforced at the server level where it must first be configured; however, this property is good for servers that don't enforce SSL connections.

Another nice Web option that can make a big difference when developing an application what will be used by both Web users and client users is to modify the launch options on the launch tab of the database properties. This is shown in Figure 43-2. It is often necessary to control the open of a database to a browser by using framesets or pages. In a client, it may be helpful to just load the database as last viewed by the user.

Now that the basics are out of the way, let's take a look at the differences in how Web applications need to be designed to provide similar functionality as in the Notes client. Since Web browsers are "stateless," it can sometimes take a lot of design effort to make a simple Notes client feature even work. To illustrate these differences, we'll take a look at three situations and discuss how they can be handled in each environment. We'll look at field validations, refreshing documents, and dialog boxes. Each of these can be

PART VI

Figure 43-2
Launch tab of the
Database properties

achieved in several ways and can be discussed at great length. Our objective here is only to make sure that you are aware of the obstacles to overcome, rather than describe how to handle specific cases.

Field Validations

In the old days of Notes programming for client-only applications, field validations were straightforward. Developers used to just use input validation formulas for each field with a simple if statement and an @Success and @Failure catch. Today the release 5 Domino Designer Integrated Development Environment (IDE) has evolved to integrate JavaScript directly into field and form events. These additional events are distinguished in the IDE by using small circles, as shown in Figure 43-3. This helps browser users break away from the stateless nature of the browser. JavaScript can be used in field onBlur events to validate field values much like the LotusScript Exiting event could be used for the Notes client to validate complicated relationships. In release 5 JavaScript can also be used to validate fields in the Notes client too. So, when validating fields, you can get the same behavior from both environments.

JavaScript can be used to validate fields more efficiently than the old formula language techniques would by evaluating all required fields at the same time by calling a single function in the onSubmit form event. It's a good practice to include the function in the JS Header form event, and then call the function with the onSubmit, or through your Submit button, but using the onSubmit will still execute in the client. Otherwise

Figure 43-3
JavaScript in JS
Header

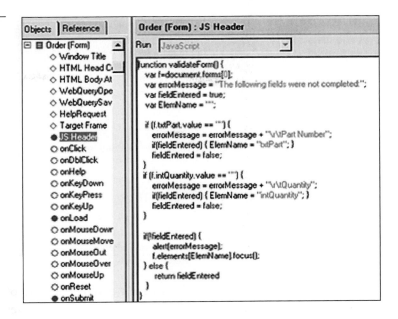

you would probably want to duplicate the JavaScript you used in the Submit button in an Action bar item.

The main thing to remember about field validations on the Web is that you will want to minimize the number of times you remind a user to enter required data and you will want to minimize the number of times a page needs to be reposted from the server. Using one single validation function once just before a page is submitted gives the Web user the choice of what order they would like to complete required fields, instead of being annoyed to the point that they leave your site. The second point is very important when it comes to high-volume sites. By using JavaScript to validate pages before they are ever submitted to the server, the server doesn't need to expend as many resources to process the contents and is therefore more available to process other requests.

Refreshing Documents

The Notes client allows you to use many different types of refreshes in order to get the desired result. This isn't so true on the Web. When programming for client users, you can set the form property on the Info tab to *Automatically refresh fields,* as displayed in Figure 43-4. Even Lotus recommends against using the form option for refreshing documents unless you are testing a form. It is more efficient to set up the field as one of the

Figure 43-4
Form and field
refresh options

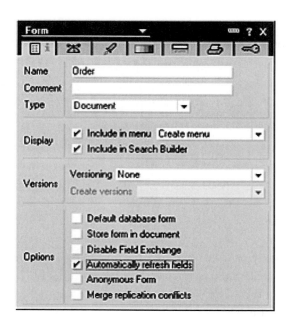

keyword types and use the field option *Refresh fields on keyword change*. This will evaluate the hide when formulas and refresh the choices available when the field option *Refresh choices on document refresh* is enabled.

This control over refreshing a document doesn't help much at all when it comes to Web browser users. It is actually quite complicated to get a Web browser to display similar refreshes without reloading the document, so most developers will just reload the document when it is necessary to refresh a document based upon the selection of a keyword value.

One of the simplest methods of refreshing a document based upon the selection of a keyword choice is to have the user manually refresh the form by using an action button that contains the formulas @Command([ViewRefreshFields]). Make sure you have the database property checked to *Use JavaScipt when generating pages* for this one to work and make sure you have motivated users that like to click buttons. Even though this is Lotus' recommendation in the Designer help, this just isn't very practical.

One of the quickest ways to get a document to refresh automatically based upon the onChange event of a keyword does require reloading the page, but then again so does the @Command above. This is shown below in Figure 43-5. The clever little function does the trick every time. If you design your page so that it isn't loaded with graphics, users may barely notice the reload.

Figure 43-5
Keyword refresh on change

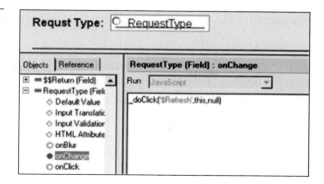

Of course, for the advanced developer there is a way to load a document, and, based upon the choices in one keyword selection, change the choices available in another keyword list. Basically, you can load all your choices into some hidden arrays and run a function in the onChange to swap out the values in the displayed keyword fields. Its actually not so hard if you use some computed text and lookup views to help make the code dynamic, but it is beyond our focus here.

Trying to display fields that may be hidden until a selection is made is not even conceivable since the fields are not even present in the HTML until the document gets reloaded. Although it is worth mentioning that if you want to generate source HTML for hidden fields on a form, you can select the *Generate HTML for all fields* option on the Defaults tab of the Form properties, as shown in Figure 43-6.

Figure 43-6
Form properties
Defaults

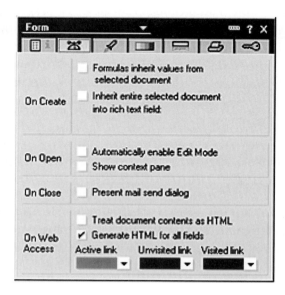

Dialog Boxes

We will cover just one example about dialog boxes to demonstrate the difference between a Web environment and a client one in using dialog boxes for user input. Using dialog boxes interactively is more than throwing up a simple alert JavaScript message, although they can now be coded once and run in both environments with release 5. It concerns using a second popup window to help manage the entry of data into the underlying documents by passing the data between the windows. Its not so complicated to pass data between two browser windows with JavaScript, but it is far more complex than what is needed in the Notes client.

The perfect example of this is the "Address . . . " action item in the release 5 mail file. For the Notes environment, it's one line, @Command([MailAddress]). For the Web browser, JavaScript is used to first determine how large the current window is and then, depending on the browser type, it opens the form "wAddress" into its own window. When you look at this form in Designer, hundreds of lines of JavaScript are revealed. All this can be done in one line for a Notes client environment. I know that there are probably hundreds of lines of compiled code behind the client dialog, but I hope you appreciate the point here: the client-only development time is almost nothing and is very easy to support.

These three situations are just a few of the considerations that must be made when creating an application that will be used in either a Web browser or a Notes client or both. We haven't even mentioned some of the standard techniques that Web developers use like using a hidden $$Return field to display confirmation messages when saving documents. This topic is deep enough to write a 500-page book on alone, and I've read a couple. In general, Web browser-enabling applications does take longer, but there are distinct advantages for the user community. Users can easily access important documents without the need to be tied down to one workstation. Remote users can also dial in and quickly reference documents as Web pages rather than opening full Notes documents from server-based replicas. This brings us to the next topic that specifically addresses the needs of remote users.

Connected Versus Disconnected

Being connected to a Domino server is not always possible. Users are taking their work on the road with them more and more. Fortunately, Lotus Notes has been accommodating to this need since its design. The Notes client is essentially a thin server, providing the object store and messaging features within a secure environment. Before going into more detain about designing applications for the occasionally connected remote user, it is important to review a couple of topics.

In Chapter 41 we discussed database replicas and replication. Maintaining local replicas is much the same as maintaining replicas across servers. Replication between the client and the server uses Connection documents in a slightly different manner.

The Connection documents stored in a Personal Address Book are used to describe how Domino servers are to be accessed, from what locations, and for what users. Today, most companies don't even need Connection documents anymore since most servers use the TCP/IP "port" that can rely on Domain Name Service (DNS) to resolve server names into the corresponding IP address.

Location is everything they say. With the Lotus Notes client, it's quite true. The Location document drives much of the way the Notes client works. In Chapter 9, we walked through the Location document. When it comes to working with remote users that may or may not be connected, location is important for two reasons: replication and mail routing.

The Location documents for those connected locations should schedule the replication of all necessary databases. This helps keep data in synch with local replicas, so that if an update is needed, the process is as fast as possible.

Mail routing is also an important consideration. If names in outbound messages cannot be resolved because the mail file specified is not configured properly, or the mail is specified as "on server" when no server connection is available, then delivery will fail. Also, messages stored in the outbound MAIL.BOX need to be transferred based upon connecting to the Domino server, not based upon how many messages are pending.

So, what are the advantages of working locally versus being connected? The Lotus help database does an excellent job of pointing out the main advantages:

Advantages to working connected	Advantages to working locally
Without local replicas, you save disk space on your workstation.	With local replicas, telephone calls are shorter and cost less.
Mail is routed immediately. If mail is addressed incorrectly, you will be notified right away.	Working locally, performance is faster and you occupy the server's modem for shorter periods of time.
Working directly on the server, you get provided the most current data.	You can send all of your mail to the server at once. You don't have to wait for a memo to be sent before you can write the next one.
You don't have to worry about being disconnected because your telephone connection is idle too long.	You can work when the server is down.

PART VI

In order to effectively use applications in a connected and disconnected mode, there are a few database settings that should be configured. The advanced ACL setting mentioned in Chapter 41 to *Enforce a consistent ACL across all replicas* should always be set for any database so that users maintain local replicas. This is not so much to enforce security locally, but to make sure that user groups and roles work properly. In order to make sure that adequate security is maintained, local replicas should be encrypted as deemed necessary. Additionally, Readers fields can be used in order to make sure that only relevant data is replicated locally. Since replication initiated by a user on schedule or manually doesn't replicate documents that the user was not able to see, only those documents that the user was able to see on the server are stored locally.

The only other thing to know about maintaining and operating Notes client applications locally is to make sure that any external lookup is based upon a replica ID. The database replica ID uniquely identifies a database within a Notes Domain. This 16-digit hexadecimal number can be referenced on the Info tab of the Database properties, as shown in Figure 43-7.

Figure 43-7
Info Database
properties

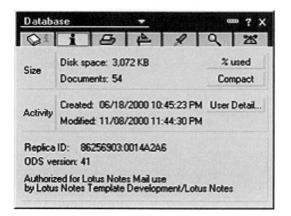

When external database lookups are based upon this replica ID, they will resolve independently of the connection as long as a local replica exists and if a lookup is performed while in a disconnected state. This technique also makes the lookup independent of any file path structure that may exist on the server, so the necessary databases can be stored anywhere in the local data directory. Figure 43-8 shows how to use a replica ID when coding a lookup for keyword choices.

Figure 43-8
Control tab of Field
properties

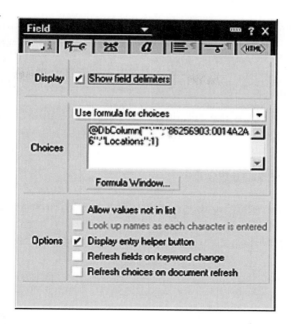

The replica ID-based lookup first looks to the workspace to find a replica icon and uses the first one. If multiple replicas are found, the top one is used when icons are stacked. Otherwise, the one from your home server or the first one added is used. If no icons are found, the current server is searched, and then local one. All this is done in fractions of a second the first time an icon is added, and in subsequent lookups, it's even faster.

When designing applications to be used by remote users, it may be easier to send mail messages and use the *Store Form In Document* form property for applications that remote users do not maintain a local replica for or have little need to access.

A good example of this would be an annual corporate survey. Remote users would be much more likely to complete a survey that was distributed to their inbox and then routed back to the database after successful completion rather than sending out a database link or directions on how to navigate to the survey database. Modem connection speeds can make it downright painful to open up some databases, so if you must load documents over slow connections, minimize the graphics and the use of sections and your users will be much happier.

PART VI

Summary

The Domino server and the Notes client are very powerful tools that can efficiently and effectively help to manage the diverse needs of a corporation's user community. Identifying and planning for those modes of usage early in the development cycle can launch successful applications every time.

Review Questions

1. True or False: Selecting the option *Web access: Require SSL connection* is a good security practice.
   a. True
   b. False

2. True or False: The Notes client and the Web browsers must use the same settings when opening a database.
   a. True
   b. False

3. Where should the option *Web Access: Use JavaScript when generating pages* be selected?
   a. Form Properties
   b. Field Properties
   c. Database Properties
   d. View Properties

4. True or False: @Failure is a JavaScript function to speed up field validations.
   a. True
   b. False

5. When using a single JavaScript function to validate all fields, it's a good idea to put it where?
   a. onSubmit
   b. onLoad
   c. JS Header
   d. onChange

6. When is the best time to validate fields for correct values?

   a. After each field is completed

   b. After each field is exited

   c. Just before a page is submitted

   d. Just after a page is submitted

7. The option *Refresh fields on keyword change* is set in what property and should not be used if at all possible?

   a. Form Properties

   b. Field Properties

   c. Database Properties

   d. View Properties

8. In what property is the option *Generate HTML for all fields* set?

   a. Form Properties

   b. Field Properties

   c. Database Properties

   d. View Properties

9. What is an easy @Command that can be used to refresh a document?

   a. @Command([ViewFieldsRefresh])

   b. @Command([RefreshViewFields])

   c. @Command([FieldsViewRefresh])

   d. @Command([ViewRefreshFields])

10. Where can the replica ID of a database be found?

   a. Form Properties

   b. Field Properties

   c. Database Properties

   d. View Properties

Review Answers

1. **A is correct.**   Forcing all data that enters and exits a database to be encrypted adds another layer of security to the data stored in the application.

2. **B is correct.**   The Launch tab of the Database properties allows for Notes client and Web browser launch settings to be set independently of each other.

3. **C is correct.** The *Web Access: Use JavaScript when generating pages* option is set on the basics tab of the Database properties.

4. **B is correct.** @Failure("Message") is formula language that is normally the false part of a field validation formula and would display a prompt with a message in it on failure.

5. **C is correct.** Putting your JavaScript functions in the JS Header placeholder makes them more easily accessible to other events on the page.

6. **C is correct.** It is best to validate fields just before a page is submitted. This minimizes the annoyance to the user and the taxing of the server's resources.

7. **A is correct.** This option causes all fields to be refreshed when any field is changed.

8. **A is correct.** This option causes HTML to be generated for hidden fields as well as visible ones.

9. **D is correct.** @Command([ViewRefreshFields]) will refresh a document manually when used in a button or hotspot.

10. **C is correct.** The 16-digit hexadecimal replica ID is located on the Info tab of the Database properties.

Planning for Capacity

You should be able to answer questions based on the following objectives after reading this chapter:

- Plan for capacity based on bandwidth
- Plan for capacity based on categorizing needs
- Plan for capacity based on database size
- Plan for capacity based on indexing
- Plan for capacity based on performance
- Plan for capacity based on server size
- Plan for capacity based on sorting needs
- Plan for capacity based on views
- Plan for capacity based on backwards compatability

In today's budget-conscious IT environment, accurate capacity planning is more important than ever. Forecast too little usage, and you will immediately hear the wails and screams of unhappy users. Forecast too much, and IT management wonders where they will recoup all the money they spent on that Quad PIII server to support 10 users in a remote branch. Either way, the costs are heavy.

It would be great if we could perform extended testing using a detailed test environment and advanced tools. In reality, most of the time you will not have that luxury.

Capacity planning is a great deal like weather forecasting. There is no perfect method for determining what is going to happen. The problem is that you are going to be held to a higher standard than your local weatherman. This chapter therefore will focus on giving you an outline of how to approach this phase of your project and general considerations for performance, rather than attempting to give you a magic formula.

So with that said, let's get started with looking at some of the major enhancements that Lotus made in the latest version of Domino. You can see additional capacity planning details in Part III, especially Chapter 20.

Key Performance and Scaling Enhancements

- **On Disk Structure**: Lotus has changed the format of Domino databases themselves in order to make I/O more efficient. Because of this new design, writes to the disk are performed significantly less frequently. Since Domino places a great deal of stress on the I/O subsystem, this is especially significant. In existing organizations, you should see an impact from this immediately—especially on mail and groupware application servers.

- **Transaction Logging**   Initially, you might think that adding transaction logging to Domino would have the effect of slowing performance. You would be wrong. Transaction logging reduces I/O by allowing the server not to have to stop and write each transaction directly to the database. Lotus recommends that the transaction log be on a separate physical disk for best performance. Even if you are using hardware RAID, it may still be a good choice to separate the transaction log to a different disk for sizing reasons.

- **Server Mailboxes**   In previous versions, each server only had one mailbox, which meant all messages lined up in one process. Among other things, that means that if you had one message being sent on a bad connection, it would delay all messages in your mailbox. Now you can create multiple mailboxes on any mail server. This allows a Domino server to make much more efficient use of the hardware, and it therefore speeds message processing.

- **Unlimited Database Size**   According to Lotus, there is no real upper limit to the size of a single database. If you are using an application with a requirement for large databases, this may apply to you.

- **Thread Pooling** R5 allows one thread to handle multiple end user sessions. Fewer threads equals less memory overhead, and that means improved performance.

- **Memory Management**   Domino now can dynamically allocate the buffer pool. It also makes better use of large memory areas. These enhancements mean that the RAM in your server will be utilized in a much more efficient manner than it was in R4.x.

- **Directory Scaling**   The Directory can now scale to handle even the largest enterprises. This greatly simplifies your infrastructure plan. In existing environments, this means that if you want to bring all servers and users into one directory, it will work. If you are planning an Enterprise rollout, it means that you will be able to avoid the overhead and unnecessary complexity of multiple domains.

These major enhancements, along with others, dramatically increase the performance of Domino. Lotus claims that in some cases, hardware that once could support 200 users can now support up to 2,000. For new environments, the bottom line is that Domino 5 does more with the hardware than ever before. For existing environments, you should factor the performance enhancements into your decision on when you upgrade. For instance, if you have a complex application that uses large databases and places a stress on your disk subsystem, you may want to move up your R5 deployment plans or at least consider upgrading that particular server sooner than the rest.

General Considerations

There are a few things you should keep in mind before you start the formal process of deciding how to scale your hardware plan. Going back to our weatherman analogy, understand that no one is going to be able to give you a magic formula that will tell you exactly what you are going to need today and what you are going to need five years from now. You are going to have to gather as much information as you can and then make your best judgment based on the information you have available to you.

Also, always remember that you are not just planning for capacity based on your current expectations. You should do your best to find out what the expected growth is in terms of user base for the next three to five years. This means two things. First, you should plan for expanding in place if possible. That is, if you can, size the environment so that you will not have to add additional hardware or do any major reconfigurations in the foreseeable future. Secondly, you should account for what will happen if your growth happens at a faster rate than you expect. When the load on a server gets to a threshold, you are going to have to have a plan in place to deal with the expansion. You can build extra expansion into your existing servers, or you can plan on adding additional servers as necessary. Either way, you have to account for expansion before you make any kind of purchase.

Platform Choices

The first step to any deployment is deciding which platform to use. Domino supports a large array of operating systems, including Linux, Unix, Windows NT and 2000, and AS/400. This array of choices gives you the ability to make your decision based on what is best for your particular situation. If you can evaluate all the operating systems, and choose which one is best technically for your situation, that is great. But in many cases, that decision will be made for reasons other than what operating system is best technically. Different organizations have different levels of comfort with various operating systems. The beauty of Domino is that Lotus is allowing you a wide array of choices so that it is you making the choice for what is best for you, not Lotus.

When making these choices, however, consider the roles of the servers and their importance in the overall structure of your Domino deployment. What is the risk level associated with this server? What are the consequences should this server go down?

If you have a large enterprise, and a hub server goes down, that could create significant problems potentially for the entire enterprise. If a mail server goes down, only those users are affected. You should take that into consideration when deciding which platforms are in use. Since the AS/400 is more stable than NT, you may find that you want to use AS/400 on Hub servers and NT on Mail servers.

Since Linux is a fairly new player in the operating system scene, here is a little primer on how it may fit into your plans. Linux has been through a bit of a roller coaster ride, as the industry tries to decide where it is appropriate. Linux's advantages are that it is cheap, stable, and works better on less hardware than some of its competitors. Unfortunately, until the new kernel is released for Linux, it does not scale well. If you have people that are familiar with Linux, there is a good use for it though. If you have a remote office with few users and very little technical experience on site, you may want to use Linux. It will allow you to get the most out of a low-end server. It also is good for remote administration, so you can perform those tasks from your desk instead of relying on end users on site.

Performance Considerations

As you go through your process of planning to roll out Domino, you should be gathering as much information about expected usage patterns as you can. Before you sit down to make recommendations, you need to know some basic information. Depending on what the server's specific use is, you will need different information.

Applications:

If you are rolling out an application, you need to talk to the developers. When you talk to the programmers, try to get a good understanding of how the application's architecture is structured. Here is a list of the things you should know:

- Number of views

- Complexity of views

- Does it use agents?

- Expected size of databases

- Will the application archive old data?

- Number of users

- User concurrency rate

- Number of users in three years

- Will the app be available through a Web browser?

- Percentage of use from browsers

The two items that will have the greatest affect on server performance are the re-indexing of views and the use of agents. Once you have all this information gathered, you should have a very good idea of how much of a load the server will be expected to carry. Groupware applications tend to place a great deal of stress on the CPU itself. So if you are going to be re-indexing complex views, or are using a large number of agents, be sure to spend your money on the processor.

If you are going to be using the application over a WAN, then the speed of the connection is going to become an issue quickly. There are only a couple things you can do to improve performance in this area. You can improve the bandwidth of the line itself. This may or may not be an option depending on how complex your network is. If the application is going to be used in several different sites, it becomes much more expensive to upgrade your WAN lines. You can also monitor the line to see what types of protocols are crossing the wire. If at all possible, use only TCP/IP as it is the most efficient protocol for WANs.

If your Domino server has to serve the application through the HTTP service, it is going to cost in additional overhead. Serving to a Web browser puts a greater demand on the CPU.

Mail Servers

Mail servers place different demands on servers. When you talk to the people who know the users' patterns, you should get the following basic information:

- Number of users
- Client mix (percentage of Notes client, of POP3, of Web)
- Geographic distribution of users
- Usage patterns (Heavy, Medium, Light)
- Will mail be archived?
- Expected concurrence

The first thing you should look at is the hard drive configuration. Mail servers place a great stress on the disk system, so you want to make sure you configure them correctly. The first step is estimating how big your mailboxes are going to be. You can enforce a maximum size, but that is almost a political decision rather than a technical one. Also consider archiving. If users will be archiving their mail, you have to know how often, and where the archives are going to be.

In my experience, mailboxes tend to be bigger as users get more and more accustomed to Domino/Notes. So when sizing, base your estimate on the upper limit of mailbox size. For testing, you can migrate one of your power user's mailboxes from your current mail platform to a test Domino server. Multiply the size of the database times the number of users, and that will give you capacity for your current user base.

Then you should factor in the estimated growth for the user base that will be housed on this mail server. So if you expect 20 percent growth, multiply your capacity times 1.2. At this point you are ready to determine the hard drive configuration. The major things to keep in mind on the hard drive configuration are hard drive speed and the number of spindles.

Without question, always get the fastest hard drives available. The other major factor is that the more hard drives you have, the better performance will be. For example, let's say after you figure out current capacity requirements and expected growth, you decide you need 36 Gb of space. You can accomplish this task by using three- to 18-Gb drives in a RAID5 configuration. However, it would be faster is you used five- to nine-Gb drives.

Keep in mind that you have to plan on expansion as well. If your server only holds five drives, and you buy five drives, that server is maxed out. It may be wise for you to buy a model with more drive bays so you can cleanly add more space when it is needed.

The next thing to consider is memory. Depending on the reports you read, you should estimate between 500k/user to 1 Mb/user. I would suggest, if you can afford it, to use the 1 Mb/user rule. If you have a high number of POP3 users, you can lower that figure. Conversely, if you have a large number of Web users, you should increase the RAM.

The last major item to consider is the processor itself. Again, depending on your budget, you should get the most current processor available. But since Mail servers place a lower load on the processor, you can save yourself some money by stepping down a notch or two.

Clustering

Finally, you should consider Domino clustering. Before you make a decision on clustering, you should thoroughly research how it will affect your particular needs, especially if you are rolling out an application. Clustering may or may not work well for your application depending on how you structure it, so make sure you understand exactly how it works before you make a recommendation.

Clustering can provide many benefits. It can do load-balancing between servers, and provides a high degree of availability as well. The scenario you might use would be to get two servers instead of one and split the users between them. So instead of one huge server, you could use two medium servers. Because you have the users split, you can micro-manage performance if necessary by moving users between them. Also, you can add more servers into the mix as your expansion needs dictate. The only drawback is that the disk space requirement is greater than using a single server. If you need 20 Gb of total capacity for your user base, you will need two 20-Gb servers in a clustered environment.

You can also consider clustering in NT and 2000. The main problem is that it is much more expensive than Domino clustering. Most NT clusters will require a high-speed external disk subsystem (like EMC, for example). These subsystems are very expensive.

PART VI

Post-Deployment

Capacity planning does not end after your boss signs off on your hardware order. It is an ongoing process. The only way to accomplish this is by regularly monitoring each server's performance. While this is not the fun part of technology, it is crucial. Specifically, consistent monitoring is the surest way to prove a point.

The first thing you should do is set a baseline for performance. As soon as your server is in production and is fully utilized (meaning all users are working on it), you should start to monitor basic performance statistics relating to the disk subsystem, processor, and memory. Poll these counters once every 60 seconds or so for a week. This sets the baseline. Save the statistics to a spreadsheet or chart.

After the initial week, you should monitor the performance in less frequent intervals. Once a month or so, you can compare the current results to the baseline. Should you see a trend developing, you have the hard evidence you need to get the hardware you need. Providing these reports to your management is a good way to keep yourself disciplined. Besides, management always seems to love graphs of any kind, so it is sure to earn you some brownie points!

Review Questions

1. True or False: Using transaction logging will decrease performance on a Domino server.
   a. True
   b. False

2. A mail server places the greatest degree of stress on the following:
   a. Memory
   b. Processor
   c. Disk Subsystem
   d. Network Infrastructure

3. You should monitor the processor, memory and disk subsystem after your server is in production for what purpose:
   a. To have information in case you need to troubleshoot errors
   b. To be able to compare them to your baseline
   c. To create a baseline

4. You have 200 users, and expect the larger mail files to be 150 Mb. You expect 20 percent growth over the next 3 years. How much disk space should you ask for?
   a. 30 Gb
   b. 36 Gb
   c. 48 Gb
   d. 16 Gb

5. Which of the following configurations will give the best performance in RAID5 with at least 36-Gb capacity?
   a. Three- to 18-Gb drives
   b. Five- to nine-Gb drives
   c. Six- to 18-Gb drives
   d. 10- to nine-Gb drives

6. Which benefit does clustering NOT provide?
   a. High degree of availability
   b. Load-balancing
   c. Reduced hard drive requirements
   d. Flexibility in managing users

7. True or False: The best use of Linux in a Domino environment is as a mail server for more than 1,000 users.
   a. True
   b. False

8. When planning for mail server capacity, you should consider the following:
   a. Current user base
   b. Client mix
   c. Expected growth in user base
   d. User profiles
   e. All of the above

9. If you need 20 Gb of drive space for users in a Domino server, how much total space will you need for those same users on a Domino cluster of two servers?
   a. 10 Gb
   b. 20 Gb
   c. 30 Gb
   d. 40 Gb

10. Domino R5 is not available for the following platform:
    a. Windows NT
    b. Linux
    c. Unix
    d. Novell Netware
    e. AS/400

Review Answers

1. **B is correct.** Transaction logging increases performance by reducing I/O levels.

2. **C is correct.** Users reading mail tend to cause the mail server to access the disk subsystem more than an application server would.

3. **C is correct.** It is important that you monitor performance once the server is in production so that you can have a baseline to compare future performance results to.

4. **B is correct.** Current capacity = 30 Gb (150 Mb * 200). Future growth is 20 percent, so capacity should be 1.2 * 30 Gb = 36 Gb.

5. **D is correct.** 18-Gb drives add capacity, but not performance. The best performance is achieved by using the most number of hard drives.

6. **C is correct.** Clustering requires that you store databases in multiple places, thus requiring extra disk space.

7. **B is correct.** Linux does not scale well in a Domino environment up to R5.0.3. Therefore, it should be used in places where there are less than 150 users.

8. **E is correct.** All of these things should be considered when you size a server.

9. **D is correct.** 40 Gb will be needed: 20 Gb on each server.

10. **D is correct.** Domino R5 is not available for Novell Netware.

INDEX

Symbols

A

INTERNATIONAL CONTACT INFORMATION

AUSTRALIA
McGraw-Hill Book Company Australia Pty. Ltd.
TEL +61-2-9417-9899
FAX +61-2-9417-5687
http://www.mcgraw-hill.com.au
books-it_sydney@mcgraw-hill.com

CANADA
McGraw-Hill Ryerson Ltd.
TEL +905-430-5000
FAX +905-430-5020
http://www.mcgrawhill.ca

**GREECE, MIDDLE EAST,
NORTHERN AFRICA**
McGraw-Hill Hellas
TEL +30-1-656-0990-3-4
FAX +30-1-654-5525

MEXICO (Also serving Latin America)
McGraw-Hill Interamericana Editores S.A. de C.V.
TEL +525-117-1583
FAX +525-117-1589
http://www.mcgraw-hill.com.mx
fernando_castellanos@mcgraw-hill.com

SINGAPORE (Serving Asia)
McGraw-Hill Book Company
TEL +65-863-1580
FAX +65-862-3354
http://www.mcgraw-hill.com.sg
mghasia@mcgraw-hill.com

SOUTH AFRICA
McGraw-Hill South Africa
TEL +27-11-622-7512
FAX +27-11-622-9045
robyn_swanepoel@mcgraw-hill.com

**UNITED KINGDOM & EUROPE
(Excluding Southern Europe)**
McGraw-Hill Publishing Company
TEL +44-1-628-502500
FAX +44-1-628-770224
http://www.mcgraw-hill.co.uk
computing_neurope@mcgraw-hill.com

ALL OTHER INQUIRIES Contact:
Osborne/McGraw-Hill
TEL +1-510-549-6600
FAX +1-510-883-7600
http://www.osborne.com
omg_international@mcgraw-hill.com